Short Story Criticism

Guide to Gale Literary Criticism Series

For criticism on	Consult these Gale series
Authors now living or who died after December 31, 1999	*CONTEMPORARY LITERARY CRITICISM (CLC)*
Authors who died between 1900 and 1999	*TWENTIETH-CENTURY LITERARY CRITICISM (TCLC)*
Authors who died between 1800 and 1899	*NINETEENTH-CENTURY LITERATURE CRITICISM (NCLC)*
Authors who died between 1400 and 1799	*LITERATURE CRITICISM FROM 1400 TO 1800 (LC)* *SHAKESPEAREAN CRITICISM (SC)*
Authors who died before 1400	*CLASSICAL AND MEDIEVAL LITERATURE CRITICISM (CMLC)*
Authors of books for children and young adults	*CHILDREN'S LITERATURE REVIEW (CLR)*
Dramatists	*DRAMA CRITICISM (DC)*
Poets	*POETRY CRITICISM (PC)*
Short story writers	*SHORT STORY CRITICISM (SSC)*
Literary topics and movements	*HARLEM RENAISSANCE: A GALE CRITICAL COMPANION (HR)* *THE BEAT GENERATION: A GALE CRITICAL COMPANION (BG)*
Asian American writers of the last two hundred years	*ASIAN AMERICAN LITERATURE (AAL)*
Black writers of the past two hundred years	*BLACK LITERATURE CRITICISM (BLC)* *BLACK LITERATURE CRITICISM SUPPLEMENT (BLCS)*
Hispanic writers of the late nineteenth and twentieth centuries	*HISPANIC LITERATURE CRITICISM (HLC)* *HISPANIC LITERATURE CRITICISM SUPPLEMENT (HLCS)*
Native North American writers and orators of the eighteenth, nineteenth, and twentieth centuries	*NATIVE NORTH AMERICAN LITERATURE (NNAL)*
Major authors from the Renaissance to the present	*WORLD LITERATURE CRITICISM, 1500 TO THE PRESENT (WLC)* *WORLD LITERATURE CRITICISM SUPPLEMENT (WLCS)*

ISSN 0895-9439

Volume 87

Short Story Criticism

Criticism of the
Works of Short Fiction Writers

Rachelle Mucha
Thomas J. Schoenberg
Lawrence J. Trudeau
Project Editors

THOMSON

GALE

Detroit • New York • San Francisco • San Diego • New Haven, Conn. • Waterville, Maine • London • Munich

Short Story Criticism, Vol. 87

Project Editors
Thomas J. Schoenberg, Lawrence J. Trudeau and Rachelle Mucha

Editorial
Jessica Bomarito, Kathy D. Darrow, Jeffrey W. Hunter, Jelena O. Krstović, Michelle Lee, Russel Whitaker

Data Capture
Francis Monroe, Gwen Tucker

Indexing Services
Factiva®, a Dow Jones and Reuters Company

Rights and Acquisitions
Margaret Abendroth, Jessica L. Schultz, Timothy Sisler

Imaging and Multimedia
Dean Dauphinais, Leitha Etheridge-Sims, Lezlie Light, Mike Logusz, Dan Newell, Christine O'Bryan, Kelly A. Quin, Denay Wilding, Robyn Young

Composition and Electronic Capture
Amy Darga

Manufacturing
Rhonda Dover

Associate Product Manager
Marc Cormier

LIBRARY OF CONGRESS CATALOG CARD NUMBER 88-641014

ISBN 0-7876-8884-3
ISSN 0895-9439

Printed in the United States of America
10 9 8 7 6 5 4 3 2 1

Contents

Preface vii

Acknowledgments xi

Literary Criticism Series Advisory Board xiii

v

Preface

Short Story Criticism (*SSC*) presents significant criticism of the world's greatest short-story writers and provides supplementary biographical and bibliographical materials to guide the interested reader to a greater understanding of the authors of short fiction. This series was developed in response to suggestions from librarians serving high school, college, and public library patrons, who had noted a considerable number of requests for critical material on short-story writers. Although major short-story writers are covered in such Thomson Gale series as *Contemporary Literary Criticism* (*CLC*), *Twentieth-Century Literary Criticism* (*TCLC*), *Nineteenth-Century Literature Criticism* (*NCLC*), and *Literature Criticism from 1400 to 1800* (*LC*), librarians perceived the need for a series devoted solely to writers of the short-story genre.

Scope of the Series

SSC is designed to serve as an introduction to major short-story writers of all eras and nationalities. Since these authors have inspired a great deal of relevant critical material, *SSC* is necessarily selective, and the editors have chosen the most important published criticism to aid readers and students in their research.

Approximately eight to ten authors are included in each volume, and each entry presents a historical survey of the critical response to that author's work. The length of an entry is intended to reflect the amount of critical attention the author has received from critics writing in English and from foreign critics in translation. Every attempt has been made to identify and include the most significant essays on each author's work. In order to provide these important critical pieces, the editors sometimes reprint essays that have appeared elsewhere in Thomson Gale's Literary Criticism Series. Such duplication, however, never exceeds twenty percent of an *SSC* volume.

Organization of the Book

An *SSC* entry consists of the following elements:

- The **Author Heading** cites the name under which the author most commonly wrote, followed by birth and death dates. Also located here are any name variations under which an author wrote, including transliterated forms for authors whose native languages use nonroman alphabets. If the author wrote consistently under a pseudonym, the pseudonym will be listed in the author heading and the author's actual name given in parentheses on the first line of the biographical and critical introduction. Uncertain birth or death dates are indicated by question marks. Single-work entries are preceded by the title of the work and its date of publication.

- The **Introduction** contains background information that introduces the reader to the author and the critical debates surrounding his or her work.

- A **Portrait of the Author** is included when available.

- The list of **Principal Works** is ordered chronologically by date of first publication and lists the most important works by the author. The first section comprises short-story collections, novellas, and novella collections. The second section gives information on other major works by the author. For foreign authors, the editors have provided original foreign-language publication information and have selected what are considered the best and most complete English-language editions of their works.

- Reprinted **Criticism** is arranged chronologically in each entry to provide a useful perspective on changes in critical evaluation over time. All short-story, novella, and collection titles by the author featured in the entry are printed in boldface type. The critic's name and the date of composition or publication of the critical work are given at the beginning of each piece of criticism. Unsigned criticism is preceded by the title of the source in which it appeared. Footnotes are reprinted at the end of each essay or excerpt. In the case of excerpted criticism, only those footnotes that pertain to the excerpted texts are included.

■ Critical essays are prefaced by brief **Annotations** explicating each piece.

■ A complete **Bibliographical Citation** of the original essay or book precedes each piece of criticism. Source citations in the Literary Criticism Series follow University of Chicago Press style, as outlined in *The Chicago Manual of Style,* 14th ed. (Chicago: The University of Chicago Press, 1993).

■ An annotated bibliography of **Further Reading** appears at the end of each entry and suggests resources for additional study. In some cases, significant essays for which the editors could not obtain reprint rights are included here. Boxed material following the further reading list provides references to other biographical and critical sources on the author in series published by Thomson Gale.

Indexes

A **Cumulative Author Index** lists all of the authors that appear in a wide variety of reference sources published by Thomson Gale, including *SSC.* A complete list of these sources is found facing the first page of the Author Index. The index also includes birth and death dates and cross references between pseudonyms and actual names.

A **Cumulative Nationality Index** lists all authors featured in *SSC* by nationality, followed by the number of the *SSC* volume in which their entry appears.

An alphabetical **Title Index** lists all short-story, novella, and collection titles contained in the *SSC* series. Titles of short-story collections, separately published novellas, and novella collections are printed in italics, while titles of individual short stories are printed in roman type with quotation marks. Each title is followed by the author's last name and corresponding volume and page numbers where commentary on the work is located. English-language translations of original foreign-language titles are cross-referenced to the foreign titles so that all references to discussion of a work are combined in one listing.

In response to numerous suggestions from librarians, Thomson Gale also produces an annual paperbound edition of the SSC cumulative title index. This annual cumulation, which alphabetically lists all titles reviewed in the series, is available to all customers. Additional copies of this index are available upon request. Librarians and patrons will welcome this separate index; it saves shelf space, is easy to use, and is recyclable upon receipt of the next edition.

Citing *Short Story Criticism*

When citing criticism reprinted in the Literary Criticism Series, students should provide complete bibliographic information so that the cited essay can be located in the original print or electronic source. Students who quote directly from reprinted criticism may use any accepted bibliographic format, such as University of Chicago Press style or Modern Language Association (MLA) style. Both the MLA and the University of Chicago formats are acceptable and recognized as being the current standards for citations. It is important, however, to choose one format for all citations; do not mix the two formats within a list of citations.

The examples below follow recommendations for preparing a bibliography set forth in *The Chicago Manual of Style,* 14th ed. (Chicago: The University of Chicago Press, 1993); the first example pertains to material drawn from periodicals, the second to material reprinted from books:

Morrison, Jago. "Narration and Unease in Ian McEwan's Later Fiction." *Critique* 42, no. 3 (spring 2001): 253-68. Reprinted in *Short Story Criticism.* Vol. 57, edited by Janet Witalec, 212-20. Detroit: Gale, 2003.

Brossard, Nicole. "Poetic Politics." In *The Politics of Poetic Form: Poetry and Public Policy,* edited by Charles Bernstein, 73-82. New York: Roof Books, 1990. Reprinted in *Short Story Criticism.* Vol. 57, edited by Janet Witalec, 3-8. Detroit: Gale, 2003.

The examples below follow recommendations for preparing a works cited list set forth in the *MLA Handbook for Writers of Research Papers,* 5th ed. (New York: The Modern Language Association of America, 1999); the first example pertains to material drawn from periodicals, the second to material reprinted from books:

Morrison, Jago. "Narration and Unease in Ian McEwan's Later Fiction." *Critique* 42.3 (spring 2001): 253-68. Reprinted in *Short Story Criticism.* Ed. Janet Witalec. Vol. 57. Detroit: Gale, 2003. 212-20.

Brossard, Nicole. "Poetic Politics." *The Politics of Poetic Form: Poetry and Public Policy.* Ed. Charles Bernstein. New York: Roof Books, 1990. 73-82. Reprinted in *Short Story Criticism.* Ed. Janet Witalec. Vol. 57. Detroit: Gale, 2003. 3-8.

Suggestions are Welcome

Readers who wish to suggest new features, topics, or authors to appear in future volumes, or who have other suggestions or comments are cordially invited to call, write, or fax the Associate Product Manager:

Associate Product Manager, Literary Criticism Series
Thomson Gale
27500 Drake Road
Farmington Hills, MI 48331-3535
1-800-347-4253 (GALE)
Fax: 248-699-8054

Acknowledgments

The editors wish to thank the copyright holders of the excerpted criticism included in this volume and the permissions managers of many book and magazine publishing companies for assisting us in securing reproduction rights. Following is a list of the copyright holders who have granted us permission to reproduce material in this volume of *SSC*. Every effort has been made to trace copyright, but if omissions have been made, please let us know.

COPYRIGHTED MATERIAL IN *SSC*, VOLUME 87, WAS REPRODUCED FROM THE FOLLOWING PERIODICALS:

Arizona Quarterly, v. 41, 1985 for "'Circumstance' and the Creative Woman: Harriet Prescott Spofford" by Anne Dalke. Copyright © 1985 by Arizona Board of Regents. Reproduced by permission of the publisher and the author.—*Chaucer Review,* v. 37, 2003; v. 39, 2004. Copyright © 2003, 2004 by The Pennsylvania State University. Both reproduced by permission of The Pennsylvania State University Press.—*College Literature,* v. 24, June, 1997. Copyright © 1997 by West Chester University. Reproduced by permission.—*Comparative Literature,* v. 55, summer, 2003 for "Sexual Poetics and the Politics of Translation in the Tale of Griselda" by Emma Campbell. Copyright © 2003 by University of Oregon. Reproduced by permission of the author.—*Comparative Literature Studies,* v. 37, 2000. Copyright © 2000 by The Pennsylvania State University. Reproduced by permission of the publisher.—*Essays in Arts and Sciences,* v. 27, October, 1998. Copyright © 1998 by the University of New Haven. Reproduced by permission.—*Explicator,* v. 53, fall, 1994; v. 53, summer, 1995; v. 58, winter, 2000; v. 62, fall, 2003. Copyright © 1994, 1995, 2000, 2003 by Helen Dwight Reid Educational Foundation. All reproduced with permission of the Helen Dwight Reid Educational Foundation, published by Heldref Publications, 1319 18th Street, NW, Washington, DC 20036-1802.—*Forum Italicum,* v. 33, spring, 1999; v. 35, fall, 2001; v. 37, spring, 2003. Copyright © 1999, 2001, 2003 by *Forum Italicum.* All reproduced by permission.—*Italian Americana,* v. 21, summer, 2003. Copyright © 2003 by Carol Bonomo Albright and Bruno Arcudi. Reproduced by permission of *Italian Americana,* University of Rhode Island, College of Continuing Education, 80 Washington Street, Providence, RI, 02908.—*Italica,* v. 73, autumn, 1996. Copyright © 1996 by The American Association of Teachers of Italian. Reproduced by permission.—*Legacy,* v. 18, January, 2001; v. 18, October, 2001; v. 19, January, 2002; v. 21, January, 2004. Copyright © 2001, 2002, 2004 by the University of Nebraska Press. All rights reserved. All reproduced by permission of the University of Nebraska Press.—*MLN,* v. 116, January, 2001; v. 117, January, 2002; v. 118, January, 2003; v. 119 Supplement, January, 2004. Copyright © 2001, 2002, 2003, 2004 The Johns Hopkins University Press. All reproduced by permission.—*New Criterion,* v. 22, May, 2004 for "Giovanni Verga's Verismo" by Martin Greenberg. Copyright © 2004 by Foundation for Cultural Review. Reproduced by permission of the author.—*New Republic,* v. 228, March, 2003. Copyright © 2003 by The New Republic, Inc. Reproduced by permission of *The New Republic.*—*Notes and Queries,* v. 40, December, 1993 for "'The Great Landslide Case': A Mark Twain Debt to a 'Musty Old Book'?," by Earl F. Briden. Copyright © 1993 Oxford University Press. Reproduced by permission of the publisher and the author.—*Philological Quarterly,* v. 77, winter, 1998. Copyright © 1998. Reproduced by permission.—*Quaderni d'italianistica,* v. 14, autumn, 1993. Reproduced by permission.—*Romanic Review,* v. 86, November, 1995. Copyright © 1995 by the Trustees of Columbia University in the City of New York. Reproduced by permission.—*Studies in Short Fiction,* v. 30, fall, 1993; v. 31, fall, 1994; v. 35, summer, 1998. Copyright © 1993, 1994, 1998 by *Studies in Short Fiction.* All reproduced by permission.—*Western American Literature,* v. 24, winter, 1990. Copyright © 1990 by The Western Literature Association. Reproduced by permission.—*Zeitschrift für Anglistik und Amerikanistik,* v. 45, 1997. Copyright © 1997 Stauffenburg Verlag Brigitte Narr Gmbh. Reproduced by permission.

COPYRIGHTED MATERIAL IN *SSC*, VOLUME 87, WAS REPRODUCED FROM THE FOLLOWING BOOKS:

Blount, Roy, Jr. From a forward to *A Murder, a Mystery, and a Marriage,* by Mark Twain. W. W. Norton & Company, Inc., 2001. Forward and Afterward Copyright © 2001 by Roy Blount Jr. Used by permission of W. W. Norton & Company, Inc.—Logan, Lisa. From "'There is no home there'": Re(his)tor(iciz)ing Captivity and the Other in Spofford's "'Circumstance,'" in *Creating Safe Space: Violence and Women's Writing.* Edited by Tomoko Kuribayashi and Julie Tharp. State University of New York Press, 1998. Copyright © 1998 State University of New York. Reproduced by permission of the State University of New York Press.—Nissen, Christopher. From *Ethics of Retribution in the* Decameron *and the Late Medieval Italian Novella: Beyond the Circle.* Mellen University Press, 1993. Copyright © 1993 Christopher Nissen. All

Thomson Gale Literature Product Advisory Board

The members of the Thomson Gale Literature Product Advisory Board—reference librarians from public and academic library systems—represent a cross-section of our customer base and offer a variety of informed perspectives on both the presentation and content of our literature products. Advisory board members assess and define such quality issues as the relevance, currency, and usefulness of the author coverage, critical content, and literary topics included in our series; evaluate the layout, presentation, and general quality of our printed volumes; provide feedback on the criteria used for selecting authors and topics covered in our series; provide suggestions for potential enhancements to our series; identify any gaps in our coverage of authors or literary topics, recommending authors or topics for inclusion; analyze the appropriateness of our content and presentation for various user audiences, such as high school students, undergraduates, graduate students, librarians, and educators; and offer feedback on any proposed changes/enhancements to our series. We wish to thank the following advisors for their advice throughout the year.

Decameron

Giovanni Boccaccio

The following entry presents criticism of Boccaccio's collection of tales, the *Decameron* (1348-53). For additional information on Boccaccio's life and short fiction career, see *SSC,* Volume 10.

INTRODUCTION

Regarded as a masterpiece of Western literature and a seminal work of the short story genre, Boccaccio's *Decameron* is a collection of one hundred tales composed between 1348 and 1353. The tales are told by a *brigata* of city-dwellers who retreat from plague-ridden Florence, Italy, to nearby villas in the countryside, where they pass time with storytelling. The narrators draw upon many of the world's literary traditions, both classical and medieval, and relate stories in various styles ranging from comic to tragic, bawdy to courtly, and satiric to serious. Written in vernacular Italian instead of customary Latin, the *Decameron* presents the earthiness, ambiguity, paradox, and subtlety of human experience, reflecting the bad as well as the good with sensitivity and liberality. Departing from the transcendental idealism of such contemporaries as Dante Alighieri and Francesco Petrarch, Boccaccio meticulously describes ordinary people who speak their own idiom and are dressed in distinctive clothing, while engaging in believable human conflicts amid settings based on recognizable locales. Thus, the *Decameron* is one of the first works of the Middle Ages to concentrate on secular matters rather than theological ones. Above all, the morals of most of the stories resist straightforward interpretation, forcing readers to draw their own conclusions. Many critics have regarded the *Decameron* as a transitional work signaling a cultural change away from a unified, God-centered worldview, toward a diverse, human-centered one, encompassing varying, and sometimes conflicting, perspectives.

PLOT AND MAJOR CHARACTERS

The *Decameron* is organized around an elaborate structure of frame stories, a common literary device during the Middle Ages. The work opens with the "Proem," which declares Boccaccio's purpose for writing: to offer help to the lovesick—particularly ladies—as others had

previously helped him. It then proceeds with the "Introduction," which realistically describes the effects of the plague in Italy. The principal frame story of the *Decameron* introduces seven women and three men who meet by chance in the church of Santa Maria Novella in Florence at the height of the Black Death in 1348. When the oldest woman in the group persuades the others to flee to their villas in the hills of Fiesole above the city, all agree to divide their stay among their respective estates. Once there, the group decides to spend the afternoons telling stories with the stipulations that each member tells one story every day and that a different member proposes a different theme each day, thereby providing the minor frame stories of the work. In addition, each day's storytelling session ends with a *canzone,* or a song, some of which critics have ranked among Boccaccio's best poetry.

The daily *novelle,* or stories, assume a host of forms, including anecdotes, fabliaux, folk and fairy tales, and classical fables, and they focus on a range of themes and characters taken from literary traditions around the globe. The stories each day collectively resemble sets of exempla on such virtues as compassion, wisdom, prudence, gratitude, or generosity. In the "First Day," Pampinea, the oldest member, directs the group to tell stories about human vices, in which wit or ingenuity prevails over the forces of fate. Filomena requests stories in which fate trumps human desires in the "Second Day." For example, in the seventh story that day, the beautiful Alatiel is welcomed into her husband's bed as a virgin, despite her history of numerous love affairs. In the "Third Day" the tales concern the fortunes of those who have worked diligently, while the melancholic Filostrato chooses stories about love that ends badly in the "Fourth Day." Continuing with the theme of love in the "Fifth Day," Fiammetta calls for stories of love that begins badly but ends happily.

The "Sixth Day" signals a shift in narrative tone and content as the group turns its attention toward stories about the fleshly pleasures of life. For the next few days the style is relaxed and playful, the content is sexually explicit, and many characters survive catastrophes by their quick wits or practical jokes. Thus, the stories told in the "Sixth Day" involve incidents in which fast thinking saves someone from danger or ridicule, while in the "Seventh Day," the licentious Dioneo asks for stories involving the wiles of women foisted upon unsuspecting men. For example, in the seventh story that day, a cunning wife manipulates her gullible husband to hire a young squire so that she can more easily seduce the youth. In the "Eighth Day" the tales center on pranksters and the games people play in their relationships; but in the "Ninth Day" the topic is left open, which results in the lewdest stories of the collection, with most of them involving love triangles and unfaithful spouses.

The bawdiness abruptly ends in the "Tenth Day" when Panfilo instructs the storytellers to relate tales about magnanimous deeds and heroic actions. In the fourth story that day, a lovelorn knight yearns for a married, pregnant woman who suddenly dies. After he secretly kisses her apparently lifeless lips, she revives and delivers her child, both of whom the unselfish knight restores to a grateful husband and father. The best-known tale of the entire *Decameron* is the tenth story of the "Tenth Day," commonly known as the story of Griselda, which Geoffrey Chaucer later adapted as "The Clerk's Tale" in his *Canterbury Tales*. The story concerns the marriage of the peasant Griselda to the noble Gualtieri, who subjects his new wife to a series of cruel lies, among them that their child is dead and that he loves another woman. After proving her fidelity and obedience to her husband despite the costs to her own happiness, she learns that he was only testing her love for him.

After the last tale in the "Tenth Day," Panfilio suggests that the *brigata* return to Florence, "lest, by protracting our stay, we should cause evil tongues to start wagging." Thus, the ten-person retreat yields the one hundred stories told in ten days from which Boccaccio derived the title *Decameron*, a variation on the Greek word for "ten." The book closes with an epilogue, which comprises a courteous defense against potential negative criticism of the work's style and contents.

MAJOR THEMES

While its individual novellas represent diverse circumstances and various perspectives, the *Decameron* as a whole possesses a distinct thematic pattern, owing in part to Boccaccio's masterful use of framing devices. The minor frames promote stylistic and thematic unity in a work that otherwise might appear disjointed and fragmented. The principal frame story also shares an essential theme with medieval romance, namely the idealistic retreat from the ugly realities of a harsh world to an idyllic, pastoral setting. Self-preservation in the eternal conflict between life and death informs the collection on several levels, from the decision to flee Florence to the numerous stories illustrating the value of a quick wit for survival. While the *brigata* briefly escapes the lethal reality of the plague, their will to tell each other lively tales of humor, romance, and ingenuity affirms life's value amid despair. Along these lines, the *Decameron* incorporates a popular medieval symbol for fate or fortune—the spinning wheel. Also known as "Fortune's Wheel," the rotating symbol not only charts a logical, tightly structured progression of the work's themes, examining the virtues, the vices, and then back again, but it also reflects the seemingly random vagaries of human existence, which contemporaries widely believed were controlled by fortune. The *Decameron*, however, departs from this medieval belief in dozens of stories about people who overcome and even exploit fortune with their cunning or quick wit. At the same time, the handling of theme, situation, and character in the stories rarely approaches didacticism and deliberately leaves their morals open to interpretation. Although most of the stories deal with various degrees of moral and social corruption, the narrators typically let the guilty characters' actions speak for themselves instead of explicitly commenting on them. In addition, Boccaccio's use of vernacular Italian elevates the language of the burgeoning middle class to classical importance, while his realistic depiction of fourteenth-century Florentine society and the activities of everyday life documents various bourgeois values and concerns of mercantile culture, which was at the time spreading across Europe. For this reason, some critics have referred to the *Decameron* as "the mercantile epic."

CRITICAL RECEPTION

Following its first appearance in manuscript form in 1370, the *Decameron* became enormously popular among literate middle-class people, but the aristocracy, the clergy, and other authors were largely indifferent to the work, as was Boccaccio himself. For centuries, most critics viewed the *Decameron* as "immoral" literature, but in the late nineteenth century critical estimations of the work began to rise after Francesco De Sanctis described it as the "Human Comedy," implicitly comparing it to Dante's *Divine Comedy*. Since the middle of the twentieth century, criticism on the literary significance and style of the *Decameron* has been voluminous. Scholars have interpreted its structure, allegory, and irony and explicated the metaphors, symbols, and many allusions in the individual tales, notably references to classical Greek mythology and Roman literature. Indeed, many critics have acknowledged the *Decameron* as a transitional work encompassing the literary legacies of the Middle Ages while anticipating various humanist concerns of the Renaissance, particularly its transformation of medieval exempla into narrative prototypes of the short story form.

Modern commentators have also traced the influence of the *Decameron*'s tone, style, and themes upon numerous writers of different eras, traditions, and genres. Critics have examined the text for correlations between the physical devastation wrought by the plague and the moral malaise of late medieval society. Some have studied the linguistic connections between the work's descriptions of the epidemic and desire, while others have used astrological explanations for the plague to explain the *brigata*'s ethics. Similarly, some commentators have scrutinized the depiction of morality in the *Decameron*, including its exploration of sexually aggressive material in cultural and legal contexts.

Another major area of critical inquiry concerns the *Decameron*'s literary influence on the works of Petrarch and Chaucer, focusing on the last tale of the *Decameron* in relation to both Chaucer's "Clerk's Tale" and Petrarch's translation of it. In addition, philological scholarship has challenged widely held views concerning the source materials of many stories in the collection, surprisingly tracing some origins beyond continental Europe. Feminist critics have alternately praised and condemned the treatment of female characters in the *Decameron*. On one hand, several commentators have observed the women's relative freedom from gendered social conventions in some stories; on the other hand, many critics have examined the role of gender difference in various contexts, including medieval medical practices and power relations, and found mixed messages in the text concerning the status of medieval women. Finally, cultural historians have perceived a critique of medieval European society in many of the stories, particularly in its representations of numerous non-Christian people and places as the sites of the cultural "other." Regardless of its critical context, the *Decameron* has continued to attract readers as living literature confronting fundamental, eternal questions about human nature.

PRINCIPAL WORKS

Short Fiction

Decameron 1348-53

Other Major Works

Caccia di Diana (poetry) 1334
Filostrato (poetry) 1335
Filocolo (prose) 1336-38
Teseida (poetry) 1339-41
L'amorosa visione (poetry) 1342
Elegia di Madonna Fiammetta (poetry) 1343-44
Genealogie deorum gentilium (history) 1350-74
Corbaccio (satire) 1354-55
De casibus virorum illustrium (history) 1355-74
De claris mulieribus (biographies) 1360-74
Trattatello in laude di Dante (biography) 1361

CRITICISM

Christopher Nissen (essay date 1993)

SOURCE: Nissen, Christopher. "Acquisition, Renunciation and Retribution in the *Decameron*." In *Ethics of Retribution in the* Decameron *and the Late Medieval Italian Novella: Beyond the Circle*, pp. 7-29. Lewiston, N.Y.: Mellen University Press, 1993.

[In the following essay, Nissen describes three "ethical modes" structuring the Decameron, *demonstrating the role of ethics in the text itself and its wider impact on the history of the novella genre.]*

The prevailing interest in the novella as a vehicle for the literary portrayal of society has naturally been directed primarily at the **Decameron,** the collection which has received the most attention. **Decameron** studies reveal, in the main, a considerable tendency toward sociological analysis in their approach to the work.¹ It is not difficult to see why: even to the casual glance, Boccaccio appears in his book to be principally concerned with the depiction of society and social values; it is in this depiction that most critics in the past century have sought clues to explain the *Decameron*'s overall meaning. This accent on sociology derives in part from Boccaccio's sustained interest in describing societal relationships, but also to a great extent from the *Decameron*'s clear evidence of kinship with older medieval traditions of exemplary and sententious literature. The text is pervaded with ethical language which appears to suggest that the reader is expected to appreciate the work for its didactic content.² Inevitably, the various sociological studies have frequently centered on the problem of determining precisely how the *Decameron* is to be read ethically, and this problem has given rise to much controversy. A substantial critical school, inspired by Francesco de Sanctis' assertion over a century ago that Boccaccio was ideologically more dedicated to art than to morality, has found little didactic purpose in the *Decameron*; greatly impressed by Boccaccio's frequent assertions that his work is meant to give delight, these critics frequently portray him as an "anti-Dante," dedicated to art and entertainment for their own sakes.³ This trend has more recently been refuted by scholars who have sought instead to emphasize the *Decameron*'s morality, and to clarify the work's meaning through the identification of ethical or didactic notions within the text.⁴ *Decameron* critics have long been inclined toward somewhat polemical refutations of preceding notions in their search for *sovrasenso*, a single concept summing up the work's overall meaning. The *Decameron* has been assigned a dizzying array of concise "labels" over the years; few other works of medieval literature have inspired so much controversy.

Although it is by now traditional to begin a new study of the *Decameron* with a capsule history of earlier *Decameron* criticism, listing its distinguished canon of theorists, this will not be necessary here. My study will concern itself with ethics, and thus with literary manifestations of sociology, but it is not my intention to declare yet another formula for *sovrasenso*, to reveal some heretofore undiscovered totalization of meaning in the book. I propose rather to describe what I see as certain primary structures giving us a key to understanding Boccaccio's awareness of the role of ethics in the novellas he creates. The *Decameron* is generally seen to put forth a grand view of the human experience, a picture made large of man and society. If this is so, then is there a key to help us grasp a unified scheme for the ethics of Boccaccio's novellas? What moral system do they set forth and how does the reader, now or at any other time in history, "read" them ethically? Given the

great influence Boccaccio had on subsequent generations of *novellieri*, how can we trace the wider impact of Boccaccio's ethical notions on the history of the novella genre?

Analysis of ethics necessitates analysis of culture: culture is the matrix within which ethical systems are formulated, and cultural considerations, as manifested in the text, must lie at the root of any examination of *Decameron* ethics. The hundred tales present a particularly intricate picture in this regard, for within the forest of individual narratives two different cultural worlds can clearly be distinguished, representing two contrasting sets of values.

The critical studies which first emphasized the *Decameron*'s relationship to Trecento culture and society in the 1950's and 1960's frequently stressed the idea that Boccaccio constructed his book around a commingling of aristocratic and bourgeois values.⁵ This approach produced a pair of studies, by Vittore Branca and Mario Baratto, which have provided much of the basis for my own analysis of ethics in terms of the *Decameron*'s cultural dichotomy. In his article "Registri narrativi e stilistici nel *Decameron*" Branca delineates the two social worlds of the work as they relate to Boccaccio's use of literary style: the real, corresponding to bourgeois values, and the ideal, corresponding to the aristocratic; that is to say the world as it is and the art of living well according to an ideal of virtue.⁶ In Branca's view, Boccaccio epitomizes the division between these stylistic and social realms in his portrayal of two iconic novella characters, Ciappelletto in the first tale and Griselda in the last: Ciappelletto lives according to "ragion di virtù," akin to the "arte di ben vivere" which infuses the *Decameron*'s general moral message (44) Stylistically the first is comic and "low," the last is tragic and sublime, with all the tone of hagiographic narrative. These two stories are the "gothic pilasters" of Boccaccio's great building, and stand as points of reference for all that goes on between them. The two worlds are fluid, not rigidly delineated: they may share a single *topos* in many novellas, for example that of mistaken amorous encounters in the dark, and yet remain intact and distinct in terms of style. This *topos* appears in numerous tales as different as those of Frate Alberto ("**4.2**") and Tito and Gisippo ("**10.8**"); stylistically the tone of the stories varies from the low to the lofty yet the *topos* remains the same. Style is the key: word choice, portrayal of sentiments, use of *cursus* tell us which world, ideal or real, is being presented. Implicit in the ideal/real dichotomy is a sense of variability of ethical worlds, for the social values between the two are so at odds as to create opposing ethical systems. Branca does not, however, explore this idea systematically or at any great length. Overall Branca's view of the *Decameron* reveals a progression from vice to virtue, from "low" to "high," from Ciappelletto to Griselda: what Branca does not seek to describe are the ethical subcategories we may be able to identify in conjunction with his stylistic *registri*.

Style is also the subject of Mario Baratto's study *Realtà e stile nel Decameron,* and like Branca he searches for a breakdown into categories, a description of divisions into discrete stylistic tendencies, based primarily on considerations of genre type. Baratto's intent is to isolate and describe the stylistic patrimony that Boccaccio passes on to succeeding generations, and he acknowledges that Branca in his "Registri narrativi e stilistici" does much the same thing, although we are told Branca's biform structure does not fit exactly into Baratto's more complicated scheme (12, note 3). Baratto sees Branca's division between comic and tragic overcome and even nullified by a more complex internal dialectic between various narrative modes. Nonetheless he finds a place for Branca's biform scheme in his discussion of the *Decameron's* moral content. Throughout the *Decameron,* says Baratto, mercantile ethics predominate but co-exist uneasily with aristocratic ethics, as they are most plainly set forth in the Tenth Day; this we may regard as a manifestation of the crisis of the new bourgeoisie which required recourse to other ethical systems in its illustration of examples of high virtue (62-65). Mercantile morality is the overriding norm of the *Decameron,* but it is jarred by the intrusion of aristocratic ideals of magnanimity and self-sacrifice. Baratto resolves this confusion by calling Boccaccio's world view open-minded and intuitive, and his moral vision by necessity provisional, capable of shifting according to the situation confronting novella characters (59-62). There can be no totalizing morality, such as can be found in Dante's *Commedia.* Baratto regards the ethics of novella texts as separate from the moralizing commentary which appears in the *cornice*; for him such observations are marginal to the ethical world view revealed within the novellas themselves (52). The novella texts do not set out to display established truths according to a programmatic, inviolate system: they only show us "situazioni da verificare" (53). Man is judged by man, not by God or any other higher truth. According to Baratto, Boccaccio forges his sense of ethics out of the choices characters must make when confronted by the dominant forces of the *Decameron's* world: nature, fortune and society. In terms of social structures Boccaccio's provisional sense of novella ethics manifests itself along the lines of the confrontation between bourgeois and aristocratic values: the resulting scheme for ethics resembles that which Branca would like to impose upon the *Decameron's* stylistic diversity.

For all his dismissal of Branca's biform analysis of Boccaccio's style as too simplistic, Baratto cannot resist noting a similar tendency toward duality and polariza-

tion in his own discussion of the clash between different social realities in the *Decameron.* Boccaccio, the merchant's son who spent his young manhood in the Angevin court, could not help but aid in portraying the moral crisis of his age when he set out to write a book that he felt should be built of discrete cultural elements. Baratto recognizes the split between the ethical consciousness of the merchant class and that of the aristocracy as Boccaccio sets it forth, and indeed he must, for without such recognition the *Decameron's* moral structure becomes very difficult to comprehend. Deprived of this awareness we would be baffled not only by the startling co-existence of novella characters such as Ciappelletto, Guglielmo Borsiere, Frate Cippolla and Griselda within a single work, but also by the differing moralistic observations that the tale-tellers themselves make concerning their novellas. To a great extent Branca's ideal/real scheme is of primary importance not only for understanding Boccaccio's use of style, but also for understanding his moral consciousness and how he applies it to his text. Different values are evoked according to the different worlds portrayed, and it is only in the unifying light of the *cornice*, which links the disparate parts and infuses them with wider meaning, that we are able to recognize the *Decameron* as an integral text and, indeed, a monument of world literature.

Branca, searching for the medieval elements in the work, finds patterns and thematic subdivisions in its structure and even has recourse, as we have already noted, to medieval architectonic metaphor when he calls the tales of Ciappelletto and Griselda "gothic pilasters" holding all the novellas together and giving them meaning within a scheme of linear progress toward a quasi transcendent goal. Branca's view of Boccaccio's "human comedy" reveals a world dominated by the three primary forces of *Fortuna, Amore* and *Ingegno,* which receive final summation in the apotheosis of *Virtù* in the **"Tenth Day."**[7] For Branca, a correct reading of the *Decameron* requires awareness not only of the stylistic and cultural dichotomy which distinguishes between real and ideal worlds, but also awareness of the schematic subdivisions that tell of different realms of human experience. In this study I intend to demonstrate further the *Decameron's* susceptibility to such a paradigmatic approach by postulating a system of three ethical modes for Boccaccio's novellas. I do not set this system forth in order to refute Branca's reading or indeed to reduce *Decameron* exegesis to yet another facile definition of *sovrasenso,* but rather to provide a key, as yet undescribed by others, to help us comprehend patterns of textual ethics as they are manifested within the work. I shall now proceed to an explanation of what I mean by ethical modes, beginning with an exposition of some of the general features of the ethical structures of the *Decameron* novellas.

Boccaccio's purpose in writing the ***Decameron*** is stated plainly enough in his **"Proemio"**—he means to provide delight and entertainment for women (7-8, 10). The *brigata*'s purpose in recounting novellas, as Boccaccio has his character Pampinea inform us, is to find the most pleasant way to pass the hot hours of the afternoon during a self-imposed exile from a scene of iniquity, dissolution and death (47, 111). Such emphasis on delight and entertainment should not, however, lull us into forgetting that the 101 stories contained within the ***Decameron*** (100 tales recounted by the *brigata,* and one tale told by the author himself in the introduction to the **"Fourth Day"**) are derived from literary traditions substantially endowed with exemplaristic or didactic characteristics. Boccaccio calls his stories "novelle, o favole, o parabole, o istorie"; in explaining these terms Branca reminds us that we may identify several literary traditions standing behind the ***Decameron*** stories, among them *exempla*, parables, *fabliaux* and tales of historical figures.[8] In the mind of the medieval reader some of these traditions were primarily moralistic and indeed all of them had at least some didactic purpose. Even the *fabliau,* which differs ideologically from the *exemplum,* often explicitly claims in its concluding verses that the reader may derive an edifying lesson from the humorous story it has set forth.[9] In any case the medieval reader would have had ample cause to expect moralistic content in any collection of tales because so many previous collections, such as the well known *Libro dei sette savi, Gesta romanorum, Disciplina clericalis,* etc. were primarily and explicitly exemplary.[10] Indeed the ***Decameron*** provides, in the form of commentary on the novellas contained within it, constant references to the didactic potential of the tales. Each novella seeks to illustrate a certain human truth, and the tale teller often sets out in the opening commentary (or *cappello*) to explain what the novella reveals and what the hearer may learn from it. Let this example, drawn from the *cappello* to **"3.3,"** be regarded as characteristic of a tendency which pervades the whole work:

> La quale (beffa), o piacevole donne, io racconterò non solamente per seguire l'ordine imposto, ma ancora per farvi accorte che eziandio che i religiosi, a' quali noi oltre modo credule troppa fede prestiamo, possono essere e sono alcuna volta, non che dagli uomini, ma da alcune di noi cautamente beffati.

(347: **"3.3,"** 4)

Leaving aside the irreverent irony implicit in the lesson, as the tricking of priests is certainly not usually a feature of the *exemplum,* we can still note that Filomena's purpose here is to "farvi accorte," to instruct through an example. In numerous other *cappelli* a preferred term is "dimostrare,"or "mostrare": the terminology of didactic literature.[11]

It would nonetheless be a mistake to conclude from these observations that the ***Decameron*** is collection of

exempla in the same fashion as the *Disciplina clericalis* or the *Libro dei sette savi.* It clearly is not. The true *exemplum* is an aphorism expanded into narrative, ultimately a tool of the sermon wherein it aids the illustration of universal truths, external to the tale itself, which become crystallized in the form of a *sentenza.* Lucia Battaglia Ricci calls the *exemplum* "la verifica narrativa di una tesi precedentemente enunciata," distinguishing it from the novella as created by Boccaccio in that it does not employ "mimetic" narration based on the actual experiences of life.[12] Unlike the *exemplum,* the novella may advocate a clear-cut behavioral norm and at the same time consciously seek to entertain its audience without appearing to contradict itself. The primary purpose of the ***Decameron*** is not to educate its readers in the same way *exempla* collections do: we may note that the truths illustrated in the ***Decameron*** are not always oriented toward teaching correct behavior, toward helping the reader distinguish between right and wrong actions. We see this characteristic in the stories of the **"Second Day,"** which present by and large ethically neutral messages meant to reveal the effects of fortune on human affairs. These novellas show human truths without seeking to establish a norm for correct behavior or correct choices made by individuals.[13] Nonetheless the ***Decameron*** novella frequently employs homiletic structures that ultimately derive from both the *exemplum* and the *fabliaux*: it does "demonstrate" truths rendered explicit by statements in the *cornice* structure (external to the narrative world of the novella itself, and thus akin to the *sentenza* of more specifically exemplaristic tale types), truths which give the story some additional purpose beyond mere entertainment. The medieval reader, accustomed to expect homiletic structures and content in most kinds of short tales and tale collections, would hardly be surprised to find them substantially present in the ***Decameron.***[14]

These homiletic structures, pertaining to individual novellas, are set within the wider context of the *cornice's* own value system, which in turn is enclosed by the **"Proemio"**'s stated purpose, to undertake the kind and compassionate task of entertaining confined females. The *brigata* demonstrates proper conduct through words and behavior without resorting to blatant didacticism or indeed bothering to go far in analyzing the apparent ethical contradictions between the various novellas. Baratto notes that the central stated exigency of the text, that of the need to seek recreation through delight, tends to overcome any tendencies of the *brigata* characters to make moralizing comments.[15] The *brigata* derives its sense of manners and propriety from the nexus between two seemingly contradictory social needs, those of discretion and delight, of "onestà" and "diletto": together they provide for a sort of ambiguity which precludes an overtly moralistic tone. The linking factor in the presentation of so many ethically varied novellas, so heterogenous in values, is the essential law of "diletto." Indeed it seems a law, set out for us repeatedly by the *brigata* and so pointedly that it attains something of a didactic tone:

> Amorose donne, se io ho bene la 'intenzione di tutte compresa, noi siamo qui per dovere a noi medesimi novellando piacere; e per ciò solamente che contro a questo non si faccia, estimo a ciascuno dovere essere licito (e cosí ne disse la nostra reina, poco avanti, che fosse) quella novella dire che piú crede che possa dilettare . . .

(83: "**1.4**," 3)

This didacticism is provisional, a characteristic of the exigencies of this particular group ("se io ho bene la 'ntenzione di tutte compresa"); these people have made a point all along of spending this brief interlude in their lives according to a provisional moral code, since plague-stricken Florence has been temporarily deprived of morals. When Dioneo repeats these sentiments later on in the *cappello* to "**5.10**," "diletto" is again a prime factor in justifying the choice of action of the *brigata*:

> E per ciò che la fatica, la quale altra volta ho impresa e ora son per pigliare, a niuno altro fine riguarda se non a dovervi torre malinconia, e riso e allegrezza porgervi, quantunque la materia della mia seguente novella,innamorate giovani, sia in parte men che onesta, però che diletto può porgere, ve la pur dirò.

(693: "**5.10**," 4)

Diletto and *onestà* here clash head on, and *diletto* has the better part of the encounter. Ethically the *brigata* tends more to distance itself from the novellas than to live according to their systems, all the while providing judgments in the *cappelli* which point up valuable lessons to be derived from each novella. After paring away the *Decameron*'s various textual layers, from the "**Proemio**" to the *cornice,* we arrive at the novellas and their own peculiar moral world, infused with didactic content by their *cappelli* which most properly belong to the textual world of the *cornice*. This brings us to the basic question which has long been asked: what is the prevailing sense of ethics in the *Decameron* novellas? How can we identify a moral system which predominates in the exemplary actions of their characters? The simple answer is that there is no single system. The dichotomy of values and cultural settings in the *Decameron,* the clear distinction between "mondo aristocratico" and "mondo comunale," provide us with a pair of differing systems. As Branca speaks of "registri stilistici," he might well have distinguished between corresponding "registri etici." Ethics in its most fundamental sense constitutes the potential for an individual to make correct choices of action in a social context. In the majority of *Decameron* novellas one or more characters are presented as making clear choices for right action; these are the protagonists with whom the reader is expected to identify, whose moral choices are defen-

sible according to a moral system fully understood and accessible in terms of reader expectations. The peculiarity of the *Decameron* is that it has more than one such system; previous tale collections typically do not present so much variety in this regard. The *Decameron* is a document of the urban Italian Trecento, representing a society in a state of flux and social change, with a concomitant shifting of values.

With the *Decameron* it becomes necessary to talk of opposing ethical systems, opposing modes of ethical discourse which, on the level of the text, embrace a wide variety of factors: elements of style mingle with presentation of character type and sociological references to create an overall tone of "propriety" for a given novella. Recognition of the ethical mode which predominates in a novella involves awareness of the most fundamental goals of the character whom the text presents as morally defensible, a sense of which basic choices result in the presentation of the moral good, of how a just end is achieved. To some extent this can be determined through the didactic statements of the frame characters in the *cappelli,* but the central element for establishing a tale's ethical content must lie in choices, the choices that characters are shown to make as the story unfolds. Boccaccio is the first European tale teller to pay careful attention to this point; the characters he creates are imbued with a moral individuality which allows them to break out of the flat iconic molds of the *exemplum* tradition.[16] The notion that action is the principal narrative element of the *Decameron* novella has been made much of by formalist and structuralist students of Boccaccio, and the observations of such critics as Tzvetan Todorov and Marga Cottino-Jones in this regard show a certain awareness of the ethical implications inherent in characters' choices of action.[17] I hope now to demonstrate how these choices, embodying the basic ethical substance of the *Decameron* novella, can be reduced to three fundamental patterns of behavior, patterns which we may conveniently term ethical modes.

The ethical mode which is perhaps most fundamental to the *Decameron* is the one in which characters may be seen to gain materially or hedonistically while remaining praiseworthy; the example they set is one upholding the propriety of gain. This mode is most readily associated with Giorgio Padoan's "mondo comunale," with Branca's "mondo reale" or "mondo comico": for the purposes of this study I would like to call it Ethics of Acquisition. Opposite it, naturally enough, stands a contrary mode in which material or hedonistic gains are foregone according to another system of values: this is the mode corresponding to the "mondo ideale," to be associated with adherence to aristocratic or feudal values of magnanimity, charity or largesse. This mode I will call Ethics of Renunciation. Ethics of Acquisition and Ethics of Renunciation are the opposing moral poles of the novella characters; their correct choices in society frequently reflect clear identification with one or the other of these modes. Yet these two are not sufficient in themselves to describe all motivation for right behavior in Boccaccio's characters, and indeed one more mode remains to be described. This is Ethics of Retribution wherein "right" characters deliberately (or at times, instead, almost unwittingly), set out to correct or punish the behavior of "wrong" ones who are often clearly labelled as such.

I must stress that these modes may go beyond considerations of novella type or stylistic mood. Ethical modes do not always correspond exactly or uniformly to the social status of characters or to the different narrative styles, "high" and "low," to be found in the *Decameron,* despite the clear tendency or Renunciation to be a characteristic of the ideal world and Acquisition to be a characteristic of the real, as we have noted. These modes reflect, in the most direct way, the primary goals and choices of action of ethically correct characters. Seen in these terms, such characters are either acquiring, relinquishing or punishing: in their actions lies the essence of whatever moral message the reader may extract from the tale. Reading the tales in terms of ethical modes allows for some blurring of the lines between various stylistic tale types, for Acquisition is not solely a motivation of lower class characters in the more comic situations of adultery and *beffa,* and Renunciation is not solely the domain of aristocratic or solemnly tragic figures, despite the fact that such modes derive ultimately from the spirit and mood of different, even opposing, social worlds. Ghismonda ("**4.1**"), an aristocrat, chooses a moral good in the name of personal gain while Cisti ("**6.2**"), a baker, chooses to do right in the name of virtuous renunciation. The values according to which Cisti lives his life derive ultimately from the *cortesia* of the feudal aristocracy and are therefore to be associated with the "mondo aristocratico"; the fact that here a baker lives by them merely reflects the intricate state of social consciousness in Trecento Florence, the confluence of societal norms as Boccaccio sees them. In his stylistic analysis Baratto recognizes distinct variations of story type in the *Decameron* which he identifies according to a variety of criteria, so that ultimately he can identify in each tale categories he calls *racconto, romanzo, novella, contrasto,* etc.[18] We may be inclined to recognize the validity of this approach and yet not feel we must reject the validity of a scheme of ethical modes, for the two systems can co-exist and even overlap without contradiction. The *Decameron,* as I have said, is highly susceptible to paradigmatic analysis, to division into categories reflecting variations in narrative type. On different planes different subdivisions, which are not necessarily mutually exclusive, suggest themselves. On one plane, the stylistic, we may follow Baratto's lead and identify tale types which, we may then find, cannot correspond to wholly different subdivisions

on another plane, the ethical. We have noted how Branca recognizes the stylistic variability of certain *Decameron topoi,* such as confusion of identity in darkened beds: a *topos* is fluid, interchangeable, not fixed by a certain stylistic category. In a similar way an ethical mode may prevail to some extent in differing stylistic categories: the solemn, tragic tone of Ghismonda's tale does not preclude acquisition, so often to be associated with comic characters, as a factor in this particular character's choice of goals. Simple acquisition does not go far enough in describing the motivations of a protagonist as richly complex as Ghismonda, who in the end becomes a tragic heroine relinquishing her very life, but it is certainly a feature of her initial motivations in carefully choosing a lover to satisfy the longings of her body. This story can stand as an example of contamination of modes: acquisition is here glorified by an act of sublime renunciation, renunciation of life itself in the name of love. Boccaccio's ethical modes relate to his differing novella types in the same way his *topoi* do; they are capable of shifting somewhat between stylistic categories.

Through examination of various structural features in and around a given novella we may form a kind of ethical "portrait" of it, a portrait which leads us to conclusive identification of the ethical mode which predominates in it. The two novellas I have chosen as introductory models for analysis show us traits of acquisition (Agilulf and the groom, "**3.2**") and renunciation (Federigo degli Alberighi and the falcon, "**5.9**").

The novella of Agilulf provides us with some intriguing moral material because its presentation of didactic content is not simplistic or linear: the king and his groom each present different, parallel moral lessons. It is a novella about which a great deal can be said with regard to the subject of ethics.

The first line of approach in determining the ethical content of this novella (or indeed that of any *Decameron* novella) is to take note of certain external factors belonging more properly to the *cornice* than to the text of the novella itself, but which provide the initial orientation for the study of novella ethics. Of primary importance is awareness of the day in which the novella is recounted: here we are in the "**Third Day,**" wherein we read of novella protagonists who gain things they want or regain lost things through their own cleverness, through human intelligence which can defeat the machinations of Fortune. Given this awareness, we can readily identify the protagonist of this tale and recognize in him those qualities of wit which, in the context of this day's theme, are set forth for our admiration. He is the *pallafreniere,* or groom, and the choices of action he makes are those which are ethically correct for this particular narrative moment in the **Decameron.** We are clearly expected to find him praiseworthy, for he gains something he has long desired, and gains it through cleverness.

Still within the realm of the *cornice* lies the next element we must consider, i.e. the *cappello,* placed in this case in the mouth of Pampinea:

> Sono alcuni sí poco discreti nel voler pur mostrare di conoscere e di sentire quello che per loro non fa di sapere, che alcuna volta per questo, riprendendo i disaveduti difetti, in altrui, si credono la lor vergogna scemare là dove essi l'acrescono in infinito: e che ciò sia vero nel suo contrario, mostrandovi l'astuzia d'un forse di minor valore tenuto che Masetto, nel senno d'un valoroso re, vaghe donne, intendo che per me vi sia dimostrato.

> (338-39: "**3.2**," 3)

There is a sort of contradiction here, which makes this story so interesting. Boccaccio means the protagonist to be the groom but a major part of the story's moral lesson will derive from the right actions of the king, his antagonist. The first will be acclaimed for his *astuzia* while the second will appear to be no less admired for his *senno.* Boccaccio stresses the king's discretion and wisdom in the *cappello,* and as it turns out, these will be characteristics which will apply as well to the groom, who is so careful to hide his love. Boccaccio's language tells us about his characters' motivations—they act in their own best interests, for personal gain. The two main characters stand in conflict, but each has a reward of sorts. The groom outwits the king but the king makes the best of things by displaying a discretion uncommon to men in his position: his *senno* provides a contrast for the groom's *astuzia.* In the wider context of the **Decameron,** wit and discretion emerge as essential components of Ethics of Acquisition—they recur constantly when characters are to be praised for gain. Traditional "high" virtue, as it appears in Boccaccio's world, is exemplified best by acts of renunciation and liberality, and can frequently be a public act designed to attract attention and general praise. On the other hand acquisition, for all that it may be a good thing and an ethically correct goal, is best sought away from the public eye, in the margins of social awareness. In this novella all is done in secret: the king discovers something it behooves men in his position never to know ("che per loro non fa di sapere"). Having discovered it he shows great wisdom in staying discreet and maintaining appearances, gaining thereby the avoidance of shame and tarnished honor. Likewise the groom acts secretly and to his consistent advantage, first in assuaging his love desire, second in employing his *astuzia* to outwit the king.

Curiously, Pampinea mentions "i disaveduti difetti" with reference to acts like those of the groom. Branca's footnote calls these "le colpe non conosciute, non evi-

denti, nascoste."[19] This term "difetti" reminds us that Boccaccio's Ethics of Acquisition treads a narrow line between sin and virtue (unlike Ethics of Renunciation, the type of traditional, aristocratic "high" virtue which is closer to Christian ethics) and that acquisition for personal gain, even in the context of a didactic lesson, still occurs at someone else's expense. Boccaccio was very aware of how controversial his tendency to uphold Ethics of Acquisition would become, as we realize in reading those passages in the **Decameron** which defend the work against critical reproach for moral content.[20] Throughout the **Decameron,** what may seem a "difetto" to one person may become another's ethical right, the right to acquire what he or she wants, the more so since it is "disaveduto," i.e. done discreetly.

The creation of the ethical portrait continues in the presentation of the natures and deeds of the characters. About Agilulf we read standardized, positive things: he is a good king, whose *vertù* and *senno* make his kingdom prosper (339, 5). Similar terminology may be found in exemplary portraits of good potentates throughout medieval literature, in the historical tales of the *Novellino* and the *Fiori e vita dei filosafi* to cite examples near in time and tone to the **Decameron.** Agilulf's "goodness" as a positive character is given great emphasis in his initial description and this becomes a basic premise of the tale.[21] The portrait of the groom reflects instead certain ideals of the medieval love lyric. He is proud to love far beyond his station ("pur seco si gloriava che in alta parte avesse allogati i suoi pensieri") and in any case his "vilissima condizione" does not preclude greatness of soul capable of the highest and most worthy passions (399, 5-7). In the fashion of the love ideal of the *dolce stil novo,* we are reminded here that social rank has nothing to do with ability to feel such stirrings and to dedicate oneself to faithful service in love. Boccaccio takes pains to sanctify the *pallafreniere's* bizarre passion, to ennoble it, by describing him in such terms. His love is rendered proper, even solemn, by these reference to codes of amorous behavior; there are echoes here of certain doctrinal pronouncements of Andreas Cappellanus.[22] In his own humble way the groom provides the requisite courtly service to his lady, becoming her most loyal attendant. He associates himself all the more to the culture of the high love ethic when he contemplates suicide, the ultimate sacrifice of the desperate courtly lover (340). Boccaccio feeds the reader a steady stream of such specific references designed to arouse feelings of sympathy for the groom's state and admiration for his behavior, yet we can detect elements here of Boccaccio's typical merging of social and ethical currents, in keeping with his recognition of the peculiar state of Trecento culture. The groom's sexual conquest of a completely unaware love object by means of a clever trick is not typical of the more exalted love traditions, and is certainly far from the ideals of *fin' amors.* It is, in fact, the *amor* *naturale* which is so often manifested in Boccaccio's tales of middle class sexual adventures, reworked with the trappings of that *amor cortese* which pervades the **Decameron,** even in untraditional contexts. The groom may be moved by the highest feelings of love, and he may be inclined to conceive of that love in highflown terms, but the fact remains that he can never reveal even the slightest hint of his desire to his lady nor to anyone else, because of the stark social realities which are the essence of this tale. His love is not so much un-requited as completely unknown to anyone. The groom, faced with the choice between lyric anguish in the face of utter deprivation and cunning action in the name of acquisition, chooses the latter, rendering his lady an ab-solutely passive object to be gained by skill, instead of a lofty *domna* whose mercy must be sought through heartfelt pleas.

Thus we see that the groom reflects not only ideals of service and sacrifice, but also the shrewdness of the re-alist, as befits a protagonist of the **"Third Day."** He is intelligent enough to know that revelation of his desire will gain him nothing, so he says nothing and makes no gesture that might betray him (339, 6). He comes to his choice of action through rational reflection and assess-ment of his condition: "E pensando seco del modo, prese per partito di volere questa morte per la quale ap-parisse lui morire per l'amore che alla reina aveva por-tato e portava: e questa cosa propose di voler che tal fosse, che egli in essa tentasse la sua fortuna in potere o tutto o parte aver del suo desidero" (340, 10). His situ-ation is so hopeless that death must be his prime course of action, and yet it is a kind of rational death, oriented towards a challenge of fortune that might give him all or part of his desire and thereby infuse his act with pur-pose and significance. He commits this deed in the name of acquisition, an acquisition which we are clearly to perceive as righteous. After he takes his brief posses-sion of the queen's body he resolves not to lose the bliss he has acquired ("pur temendo non la troppo stanza gli fosse cagione di volgere l'avuto diletto in tristizia" 342, 16), so he discreetly withdraws and preserves his life. Against all odds, through intelligence, he achieves his goal.

The most overtly didactic message of the tale arises from the example of the king's discretion, as indicated by the *cappello* and borne out by repeated assertions made in the narrator's own voice. But the tale resolves itself in a battle of wits between the groom and the king, with repeated references to the intelligence of both. Each makes the best of a bad situation and is con-tent with the outcome. The king acts not only to pre-serve his own honor but also that of his queen, whose innocence he is shrewd enough (and merciful enough) to recognize (342, 18). The portraits of the deeds and natures of these men stress both their intelligence and competence in acting in their own best interests. The

groom gained as much as fortune would ever concede him, and as he is wise enough to recognize this fact, he never again will so tempt fate ("né piú la sua vita in sí fatto atto commise alla fortuna" 345, 31). Ethics of Ac-quisition is the ethics of rational choice, of the intellect and the process of intellection, of the wise recognition of the scope and limits of the gifts of fortune. All of these characteristics are well reflected in this novella, and recur frequently in many others throughout the **Decameron.**

The novella of Federigo, which we shall use as a model for the mode of Renunciation, is told in the **"Fifth Day,"** wherein love stories have happy endings. For most of the tales of this day the predominant mode tends to be Acquisition, so Federigo's stands as something of an exception. And indeed, Fiammetta's *cappello* gives no clear indication of which mode will come to the fore, since she only alludes in passing to Federigo's great sacrifice by telling the ladies that this story will show how deep an influence they have on men of noble hearts (". . . quanto la vostra vaghezza possa ne' cuor gen-tili . . ." 682, 3). Fiammetta leaves the question of characters' choices of action out of her preamble, con-centrating instead on a didactic message for the discern-ing reader: the tale should inspire ladies to bestow their amorous gifts as they themselves choose, not as For-tune, the fickle arbiter, would decide. We must therefore establish the dominant ethical mode of this tale through the presentation of characters within the novella text it-self, through the portrayal of their choices and deeds, most notably Federigo's.

Of Federigo we hear that he is a nobleman distinguished in arms and *cortesia* (682-683, 5). The word *cortesia* immediately channels us into a moral atmosphere that differs significantly from that of the tale of Agilulf, de-spite Agilulf's regality and kingly virtue. Specific men-tion of *cortesia* evokes an ideal, in which desire for gain is submerged by the need for magnanimity and self-sacrifice; avarice has no place in the *corte d'amore,* the poetic realm of the courtly lover.[23] We have shifted ethical worlds and expectations. Various *topoi* conso-nant with the world of *cortesia* and the feudal aristoc-racy now begin to present themselves: for example, we see now a *topos* not uncommon in the novella tradition, that of the lovesick knight who jousts to win his love and is left impoverished.[24] Despite his ultimate motiva-tion, which is that of desire to possess a woman, his acts are those of feudal service, which take the form of sacrifice and adherence to a sense of duty. Left poor, we hear that he endures his lot with patience, as befits a man who has dedicated himself to chivalric ideals of dignity in the face of defeat. Throughout this novella Boccaccio sounds the note of *cortesia* with the kinds of characters he presents, their activities (jousting, falconry), their humble and decorous ways of address-ing one another, etc. In tales of this sort, Boccaccio tempers his characters' naked desire for gain with the solemnity of aristocratic ritual (as we see in Federigo's dedication to knightly service for love) or with the stylized and quasi-surreal *topoi* of the romance tradition (as in the case of the boy who falls grievously ill and can only be cured by gaining the object of his desire.)[25] Humility, honorable deeds and self-sacrifice predominate over the gross motivations of acquisition. Boccaccio balances his portrait of the gentle nobleman Federigo with those of the other characters who, nonetheless, belong to the class of the *borghesia*. Giovanna has the principal qualities of faithful devotion to her husband and tender love for her son, while the husband himself is honorable and generous.

Boccaccio employs elements of *cortesia* in constructing his tale and characters, but allows these elements to mingle with certain traits more typical of the middle class: for example, Federigo's love has no regard for those tenets of aristocratic love doctrine which demand a man choose for a love object a woman higher born than himself. Moreover, when Giovanna finds herself dealing with her brothers' objections in her choice of a new husband, we must recognize a motif more typical of the world of the *borghesia,* one which would naturally appear out of place in the *cortesia* ambience. But all this hardly puts the novella on a different track. A melancholy tone of lofty renunciation has been sustained throughout the tale, and this tone is not substantially jarred by the addition of the brothers' concerns. Boccaccio wants to resolve his tale in terms of the **"Fifth Day"**'s overall theme of love tales with happy endings, and the device of marriage allows him to do this even though it runs counter to the tale's primary narrative focus. The brothers' role and the marriage stand as a sort of detached element in the novella, added to help us recognize the benefits the *borghese* Giovanna has derived from her lesson in aristocratic virtues. By her appreciation of Federigo's gesture, Giovanna can be "promoted" into the ranks of the aristocracy—we can regard her as an *exemplum* of manners for her class. Marriage is the social mechanism which, in effect, creates this "promotion."

Boccaccio builds his tale around a central act of pathetically ironic renunciation: the confused Federigo, challenged to commit a great act of self-sacrifice in the name of hospitality and courtly largesse, unwittingly eliminates his chance to earn his lady's favor through bestowing the falcon to her alive—in effect, one act of renunciation precludes the other, leaving him profoundly distressed ("m'è sí gran duolo che servire non ve ne posso, che mai pace non me ne credo dare" 689, 36). This tragic sense of irony is heightened by the lady's grief at what she has brought about and by the eventual death of the boy. But sacrifice, for the faithful knight no less than for the pious Christian, has its reward in final acquisition, and Federigo gains both the woman and

material wealth at the tale's conclusion. This resolution in marriage and material gain shows how completely Boccaccio allows his tale to be pervaded by elements of the *borghese-comunale* world, and yet we must still note that Federigo is motivated not so much by *borghese* intelligence as by dogged adherence, in the face of all rejection and adversity, to the ideals of *cortesia*. His moral lesson is one of the value of renunciation.

In both of these novellas, the prime substance of plot lies in the protagonist's central choice of action. The groom chooses his secret conquest of the queen, and Federigo chooses to sacrifice his falcon. Each choice reflects a completely separate moral ideal. Character choice combines with lesser factors such as style, character type, *topoi,* etc. to produce varying moral moods, which is to say (in terms of the present study) varying ethical modes. These moods reflect patterns of character behavior and plot which in time become familiar to the reader of the *Decameron* novellas, resolving themselves into predictable and recurring conclusions for the different tales. Exposition of the system of ethical modes helps us analyze and systematize the varying moral atmospheres that infuse different novellas in turn, allowing us to understand characteristics which otherwise can appear vague and even contradictory.

Although all *Decameron* novellas tend toward a certain specific and readily identifiable cultural orientation, some of them may still resist easy categorization according to ethical modes: these are for the most part the stories in which human choice of action is not an important factor. This is especially true of the tales of the **"Second Day"**; here the driving force shaping human affairs is not so much free will as the machinations of *fortuna,* or adverse circumstance. Nevertheless this day can be said to play an indirect role in the presentation of ethical modes, for the illustration of the effects of *fortuna,* as introduced here, attains its true culmination in the eventual triumph of Ethics of Acquisition in the **"Third Day,"** wherein characters achieve their desires and defeat *fortuna* through their own intelligence. Thus the tales of the **"Second Day"** ultimately make a contribution to Boccaccio's general apotheosis of the power of human intelligence and the capacity of individuals to control the world around them.

The figure of Ciappelletto is also quite problematic, not because he makes no choice, but because the choice he makes defies easy interpretation in terms of ethics. This tale of a profoundly evil man who becomes a saint through a false deathbed confession appears as a tissue of ironies, ironies no less apparent in the tale-teller's commentary than in the story itself. The narrator Panfilo presents the novella as an illustration of the notion that God, through his infinite mercy, will grant sincere prayers even if they are mistakenly directed at false saints. But the reader finds this tone of exemplary righteousness attenuated by the comic portrayals of both the overly naive confessor and the simple-minded Burgundians who are all too quick to venerate the supposed saint. Even though the topic is serious, and Panfilo's pronouncements are quite solemn, the story comes across as something of an amusing parody of that most solemn of genres, the saint's life.[26]

Nor does the text make completely clear Ciappelletto's motivations for choosing to make his outrageous confession. His hosts, expatriate Italian businessmen, are afraid their affairs will suffer if Ciappelletto dies without confession in their house, and yet they imagine that any true confession of his iniquities will surely lead to an equally detrimental denial of absolution (56-57, 23-26). Ciappelletto reassures them that he will arrange things to their advantage if they will but fetch a confessor. He says he has done so much to offend God that one more sin could make no difference, but we are left wondering about his real motivations for this uncharacteristic altruism. Boccaccio allows him to speak, but does not reveal his innermost thoughts, nor permit us to follow the interior deliberations which lead to his act of perverse generosity.[27] We see him choose, but we are not made to understand his choice.

If we examine Ciappelletto in terms of ethical modes, we can almost trace a hint of Ethics of Renunciation in his willingness to sacrifice his chances for salvation, however remote, for the good of his compatriots, while the wily trick he plays on the monk shows some parallels with the actions of Boccaccio's many heroes of ethically correct acquisition. But we cannot acribe the overall tone of this novella to either of these modes. No matter how much some of his deeds may resemble those of Boccaccio's many morally justified characters, it is well not to forget what a monster he has deliberately been made out to be. He cannot play the role of the ethically correct protagonist, for this story is not meant to have such a protagonist.[28] Like Frate Alberto ("4.2"), Ciappelletto as a central character amuses us, but does not gain our admiration. The ethical substance of this story is not transmitted through the characters' actions within the narrative, but rather through the external "application," which appears as the narrator's final commentary. This is not Boccaccio's usual pattern; he rarely has the *brigata* pronounce anything more than the sketchiest of concluding comments at the end of a novella. We are close here, in a certain sense, to the world of the traditional *exemplum*, wherein characters' choices are not especially relevant, and the story in and of itself is neither moral nor immoral—what matters ultimately is the extra-textual final statement, which serves to define the story's *a priori* ethical message.[29] Having read the events of this tale, we are at a loss as to how to appreciate them ethically until Panfilo speaks up and gives us an exemplary interpretation:

. . . grandissima si può la benignità di Dio cognoscere verso noi, la quale non al nostro errore ma alla purità della fé riguardando, cosí faccendo noi nostro mezzano un suo nemico, amico credendolo, ci essaudisce, come se a uno veramente santo per mezzano della sua grazia ricorressimo.

(70, 90)

There has been controversy about the degree to which we are to accept this application at face value, and indeed there is far more irony implicit in the relationship between this conclusion and the tone of the tale itself than we should ever expect to find in the traditional *exemplum*.[30] Nonetheless Boccaccio's conclusion is the only aid he provides, in the absence of clear adherence to any ethical mode, to help us resolve the moral vacuum which the tale creates.

Modes of Acquisition and Renunciation ought not to be difficult for a reader to grasp as concepts, since *Decameron* criticism has long been accustomed to the idea of a socio-stylistic dichotomy between real and ideal worlds; recognition of these two modes springs ultimately from continued awareness of at least the bare outlines of this dichotomy. Retribution, which will be the major emphasis of this study, is another matter: it seems less likely to suggest itself as a cohesive unit in the scheme of the *Decameron's* ethical structure, even if it is so frequently a central element of plot. This is due in part to the fact that it does not fall neatly into one or the other of the two categories of the dichotomy, as we shall see. But it must also be acknowledged that there has been little critical attention paid to Boccaccio's treatment of morally sanctioned punishment, even though it is a phenomenon pervading a great many of his novellas.

It must continually be remembered that Boccaccio allows so much of the burden of his novella ethics to fall on the shoulders of his free-thinking characters: Ciappelletto aside, the ability of these characters to choose correct courses of action is consistently held up for our admiration in the vast majority of *Decameron* stories. If retribution is so frequently an element of plot, a type of "transformational action" (in Cottino-Jones' terms)[31] which carries the narrative to its proper conclusion, it is because characters are repeatedly shown to be choosing it as the best means to bring that proper conclusion about. Character choice, oriented toward acquisition, renunciation or retribution, remains a central dynamic in the ethical system of the *Decameron* novella.

Notes

1. See Petronio, "I volti del *Decameron*" for an outline of critical works relevant to this topic.

2. For an indication of the difficulties some critics have had in accepting the presence of ethical language in the *Decameron* see Marcus, *An Allegory*

of Form 24. Marcus notes that Boccaccio avoids passing any moral judgment on the content of his tales; in effect he strives for ethical objectivity by letting the audience created for each story interpret that narrative's specific moral content.

3. For examples of this viewpoint see De Sanctis 1: 327-330, Singleton, and Almansi's *The Writer as Liar* 1-7. Hastings too claims prevalence for the role of art, but in more cautious terms (3-7).

4. See for example Ferrante, Cottino-Jones' "The City/Country Conflict," Marino and Potter.

5. This idea came to prominence in Branca's *Boccaccio medievale,* a book which appeared in its first edition in 1956. The approach received further attention in Petronio's "La posizione del *Decameron*" and in Padoan's "Mondo aristocratico e mondo comunale."

6. This article has also been adapted for the 1975 edition of Branca's *Boccaccio medievale,* in the chapter entitled "Registri strutturali e stilistici," 86-133.

7. For a summary of this scheme see Branca, *Boccaccio medievale* 16-17.

8. Boccaccio 9. Branca's note 1 gives us his explanation of the terminology. For a further discussion of these terms see Borlenghi, *La struttura e il carattere della novella italiana* 25-28, and also Stewart.

9. Concerning these sententious passages, and the ironic relationship between them and the *fabliaux* plots, see Nykrog 100-103 and Muscatine 101-104. For examples of sententiousness in certain *fabliaux* see the conclusions of "Les tresces" (6: 258: 427-434) and "Brunain, la vache au prestre" (5: 47-48: 64-72) in Noomen and van den Boogaard.

10. See Ricci 13-48 for "Il libro dei sette savi." The tales of the Italian novella collections which immediately precede the *Decameron,* such as the *Novellino* and the stories in codex II. III. 343 of the Biblioteca Nazionale and the ms. Panciatichiano 32 (see Lo Nigro for all of these), tend to be exemplary even if they rarely have explicit *sententiae,* deprived as they are of *cornici* or authors' pronouncements on individual novellas.

11. Some examples: 71:"1.2" (dimostrare); 90:"1.5" (mostrare); 113:"1.9" (dimostrare); 535:"4.6" (dimostrare).

12. Ricci xxxi. For further discussions of the relationship between *exemplum* and novella see the chapter entitled "L'esempio" of Borlenghi in *La struttura e il carattere della novella italiana,* especially

22-24, Battaglia's essays "L'esempio medievale" and "Dall'esempio alla novella" in *La coscienza letteraria del medioevo,* and Delcorno 405.

13. On this topic see Bardi 30, 35-37. Despite the general incapacity of the characters of this day to control the course of events in their lives, she notes the transition in several characters from helpless passivity to a defiant ability to make wise choices: here too, *ingegno* has a role.

14. Joy Potter has noted that 55 *Decameron* novellas have some sort of sententious commentary (34); she also lists the 45 which do not (174-175). She remarks that some of these morals are ironic, as Muscatine does for the *fabliaux* (see note 9).

15. "Il diletto del racconto non solo sposta su un nuovo piano la tensione stilistica del Boccaccio, ma annuncia una concezione della forma artistica che va oltre i canoni tradizionali. Si pensi, ad esempio, al modo con cui il Boccaccio giustifica l'audacia contenutistica di certe novelle: opponendo una difesa di ordine edonistico a un'accusa di ordine moralistico" (76). Baratto goes on to cite several examples of Dioneo's justifications for story content, noting that ". . . la preoccupazione moralistica è esplicitamente subordinata all'intento edonistico" (77).

16. See Neuschäfer's first chapter for a fine analysis of the development of Boccaccio's characters away from the relatively simple dimensionality of the earlier narrative traditions towards an ethically more ambivalent "bipolarity" (*Doppelpoligkeit*). In this regard see also Baratto 15-16.

17. See Todorov 34-41. Todorov breaks the action of the *Decameron* novellas into three basic categories: *a* (action with the aim of modifying a situation), *b* (action to break laws or commit wrongs), and *c* (action directed toward punishment). My study, although ultimately quite different in purpose and method and concentrated entirely on the ethical implications of narrative action, owes a debt to Todorov's approach. See also Cottino-Jones, "Observations on the Structure of the *Decameron* novella." However, for a description of the all too real drawbacks inherent in the application of structuralist methods to the *Decameron* see Fido 73-78. For a useful distinction between novellas controlled by action and those controlled by external events ("adventures") see Scaglione, "The Narrative Vocation." For another study of ethical modes, from which this chapter is in part adapted, see Nissen, "Ethical Modes in Boccaccio's *Decameron*."

18. See Baratto's chapter "Storicità e invenzione nel *Decameron*" (23-48) for a summary of this tendency toward narrative multiplicity in Boccaccio's work.

19. Boccaccio 338, note 6.

20. See the "Introduction" to the "Fourth Day" (459-470), and the "Conclusione dell'autore" (1255-1261).

21. For an identification of Agilulf as the central character of the tale, endowed with an "exemplary" tendency toward silence, see Grimaldi.

22. See especially Cappellanus 1.12, which includes a dialogue between a man of lower rank and a noble woman on the subject of love.

23. Andreas Cappellanus himself specifically condemns avarice in his list of rules of love at the end of Book II of the *De amore*: "Amor semper consuevit ab avaritiae domiciliis exsulare" (282), and also among his commandments to lovers, wherein he is even more forceful: "Avaritiam sicut nocivam pestem effugias et eius contrarium amplectaris" (94).

24. See *Decameron* "5.8" (673), and Sabadino *Porretane* 34. See also motif T 75.2 in Rotunda, 186.

25. See motif T24.1 in Rotunda, 184.

26. Concerning the parallels between Ciappelletto's story and hagiographic style see Shklovskij, Branca's *Boccaccio medievale* 95, Mazzotta's *World at Play* 61-62, and Baldissone 17-18. See De' Negri for a general treatment of hagiographic style in the *Decameron*. For a very complete summary of the critical controversy surrounding this tale see Fido 45-52.

27. For a study of Ciappelletto's hidden motives, and Boccaccio's depiction of the interiority of this character see Seung 195-196.

28. Fontes-Baratto sees the ethical ambiguity of Ciappelletto, the first *beffatore* of the *Decameron,* as projecting itself to some extent over every subsequent *beffatore* who appears in the book (36-38).

29. Concerning the moral ambivalence of the *exemplum* plot see Battaglia, "L'esempio medievale" (*La coscienza letteraria* 470). The *Gesta romanorum* tales can stand as a case in point; they are morally almost meaningless without the allegorical overlay of the final *sententia*.

30. For a point of view which underscores the tale's ironic aspect see Marcus *An Allegory of Form* 17-19. For Croce, the moral essence of the novella could only be summed up in terms of total ambivalence: "La novella . . . niente afferma e niente nega" (89).

31. Cottino-Jones, "Observations" 382-385. For Cottino-Jones, characters' choice of action is a central element of novella structure: "The main characters are described inasmuch as their specific characteristics are functionally involved in the actions they will be performing in the narrative process" (386).

Works Cited

[Almansi, Guido]. *The Writer as Liar: Narrative Technique in the Decameron*. London and Boston: Routledge and Kegan Paul, 1975.

Baldissone, Giusi. "Il piacere di narrare a piacere." *Prospettive sul Decameron*. Ed. G. Barberi Squarotti. Torino: Tirrenia, 1989. 9-23.

Baratto, Mario. *Realtà e stile nel Decameron*. Roma: Riuniti, 1984.

Bardi, Monica. "Il volto enigmatico della fortuna." *Prospettive sul Decameron*. Ed. G. Barberi Squarotti. Torino: Tirrenia, 1989. 25-38.

Battaglia, Salvatore. *La coscienza letteraria del medioevo*. Napoli: Liguori, 1965.

Boccaccio, Giovanni. *Decameron*. Ed. Vittore Branca. Torino: Einaudi, 1980.

[Borlenghi, Aldo]. *La struttura e il carattere della novella italiana dei primi secoli*. Milano: Cislaghi, 1958.

Branca, Vittore. *Boccaccio medievale*. Firenze: Sansoni, 1975.

Cappellanus, Andreas (Cappellano, Andrea). *De amore*. Ed. Graziano Ruffini. Milano: Guanda, 1980.

Cottino-Jones, Marga. "The City/Country Conflict in the *Decameron*." *Studi sul Boccaccio* 8 (1974): 152-157.

———. "Observations on the Structure of the *Decameron* Novella." *Romance Notes* 15 (1974): 378-387.

Croce, Benedetto. *Poesia popolare e poesia d'arte*. Bari: Laterza, 1967.

Delcorno, Carlo. "L'*exemplum* nella predicazione medievale in volgare." *Concetto, storia, miti e immagini del medio evo*. Ed. Vittore Branca. Firenze: Sansoni, 1973. 393-408.

De Sanctis, Francesco. *Storia della letteratura italiana*. Torino: Einaudi, 1975. 2 vols.

Ferrante, Joan. "The Frame Characters of the *Decameron*: A Progression of Virtues." *Romance Philology* 19 (1965): 212-226.

Fido, Franco. *Il regime delle simmetrie imperfette: Studi sul Decameron."* Milano: Franco Angeli, 1988.

Fontes-Baratto, Anna. "Le thème de la *beffa* dans le *Décaméron*." *Formes et significations de la "beffa" dans la littérature italienne de la Renaissance*. Vol. 1. Paris: Université de la Sorbonne Nouvelle, 1972. 2 vols.

Grimaldi, Emma. "Il silenzio di Agilulf." *Misure critiche* 42 (1982): 5-22.

Lo Nigro, Sebastiano, ed. *Novellino e conti del 200.* Torino: UTET, 1963.

Marcus, Millicent. *An Allegory of Form: Literary Self-Consciousness in the Decameron.* Saratoga: Anma Libri, 1979.

Marino, Lucia. *The Decameron "cornice": Allusion, Allegory and Iconology.* Longo: Ravenna, 1979.

[Mazzotta, Giuseppe]. *The World at Play in Boccaccio's Decameron.* Princeton: Princeton University Press, 1986.

Muscatine, Charles. *The Old French Fabliaux.* New Haven and London: Yale University Press, 1986.

Neuschäfer, Hans-Jörg. *Boccaccio und der Beginn der Novelle.* München: Wilhelm Fink Verlag, 1969.

Nissen, Christopher. "Ethical Modes in Boccaccio's *Decameron.*" *Romance Languages Annual* 1 (1989): 191-196.

Noomen, Willem and Nico van den Boogaard, eds. *Nouveau recueil complet des fabliaux.* Assen: van Gorcum, 1983-. 6 vols.

Nykrog, Per. *Les fabliaux: Étude d'histoire littéraire et de stylistique médiévale.* Genève: Droz, 1973.

Padoan, Giorgio. "Mondo aristocratico e mondo comunale nell'ideologia e nell'arte di Giovanni Boccaccio." *Studi sul Boccaccio* 2 (1964): 81-216.

Petronio, Giuseppe. *Il Decameron: saggio.* By Giovanni Boccaccio. Bari: Laterza, 1935.

————. "La posizione del *Decameron.*" *Rassegna della letteratura italiana* 61, 2 (1957): 189-207.

————. "I volti del *Decameron.*" *Boccaccio: Secoli di vita. Atti del Congresso Internazionale: Boccaccio 1975.* Eds. Marga Cottino-Jones and Edward F. Tuttle. Ravenna: Longo, 1977. 107-124.

Potter, Joy Hambuechen. *Five Frames for the Decameron: Communication and Social Systems in the Cornice.* Princeton: Princeton University Press, 1982.

Ricci, Lucia Battaglia, ed. *Novelle italiane: Il Duecento, il Trecento.* Milano: Garzanti, 1982.

Rotunda, D.P. *Motif-Index of the Italian Novella in Prose.* Bloomington: Indiana University, 1942.

Sabadino degli Arienti, Giovanni. *Le Porretane.* Ed. Bruno Basile. Roma: Salerno, 1981.

Scaglione, Aldo. "Giovanni Boccaccio, or the Narrative Vocation." *Boccaccio: Secoli di vita. Atti del Congresso Internazionale: Boccaccio 1975.* Eds. Marga Cottino-Jones and Edward F. Tuttle. Ravenna: Longo, 1977. 81-104.

Seung, T.K. *Cultural Thematics: The Formation of the Faustian Ethos.* New Haven and London: Yale University Press, 1976.

Shklovskij, Victor. "Some Reflections on the *Decameron.*" *Critical Perspectives on the Decameron.* Ed. Robert S. Dombroski. London: Hodder and Stoughton, 1976.

Singleton, Charles. "On Meaning in the *Decameron.*" *Italica* 21 (1944): 117-124.

Stewart, Pamela. "Boccaccio e la tradizione retorica: La definizione della novella come genere letterario." *Stanford Italian Review* 1 (1979): 67-74.

Todorov, Tzvetan. *Grammaire du Decameron.* The Hague-Paris: Mouton, 1969.

Reginalde Hyatte (essay date fall 1994)

SOURCE: Hyatte, Reginalde. "Boccaccio's *Decameron* and de Ferrières's *Songe de pestilence.*" *Explicator* 53, no. 1 (fall 1994): 3-5.

[*In the following essay, Hyatte investigates the late-medieval astrological explanation for the plague to demonstrate thematic unity in the* Decameron.]

The opening section of Boccaccio's **Decameron** poses a problem of unity. The introduction to the first day, which established the frame story serving to unify the one hundred novellas, describes at length and in detail the 1348 plague in Florence and its effects upon the *brigata* of storytellers that forms there. Why, then, is the plague absent from the subsequent narrative? Aldo S. Bernardo has argued that the introduction's description of the plague and the *brigata*'s reaction to the epidemic guide "the alert reader" to a unified interpretation of the tales that follow: hedonism, "moral and spiritual truancy," complete unconcern about the misfortune of others, false goodness and self-centeredness (which "is the exact opposite of Christian doctrine and life"), and "the laughter of fools" are some of the dominant characteristics that such a reader might note in the general reaction to the plague by the forming *brigata,* and these same traits are prominent in very many of the tales, which the brigata recounts later.[1] Bernardo's argument that the *brigata*'s reaction would appear contemptible in the eyes of an alert contemporary reader[2] poses another problem: such a reading is in direct conflict with the fictive storytellers' most favorable evaluation of their own conduct, as evidenced, for example, in their high self-praise in the tenth day's conclusion for what Bernardo sees as signs of their morally, socially, and spiritually reprehensible attitudes and behavior. Further, Bernardo contends that in the introduction, the plague "is clearly associated with divine wrath rather than planetary influences since it arrived from the East and assumed different symptoms in the West."[3]

It seems unnecessary, however, and strained to argue the unity of **The Decameron** on grounds of failings among the gay, amorous storytellers that only a reader whom Boccaccio might have qualified as hypercritical or even prudish, rather than alert, could detect. We propose here that Boccaccio's reference to planetary influence as the source of pestilence in the introduction provides a major thematic "key" to the subsequent tales, from which pestilence as physical illness is absent. The introduction's reference to malign planetary influences might have suggested to a mid-fourteenth-century reader an epidemic of several specific vices and social and spiritual corruption that late-medieval writers commonly included in their astrological explanation for pestilence. A case in point is Henri de Ferrières's mid-fourteenth-century *Le songe de pestilence*: there the plague is associated with the prevalence of many sorts of wickedness, perversity, and oppression and with the corruption of Church and state, all of which result from the same malignant celestial influence as pestilence and which, also, appear as leitmotifs in **The Decameron**'s tales.

In *Le songe de pestilence*, a French dream allegory from around 1374-1377 that is appended to *Les livres du roy Modus et de la royne Ratio,* Henri de Ferrières explains that the malign influence that brings about pestilence has other, widespread moral, social, and spiritual effects. First, God's wrath and malign planetary aspects are related as cause and effect. In chapter 240, *Ci Devise de la pestilence et de la cause pourquoi elle avendra,* the narrator prophesies (in retrospect!) concerning the conjunction of three planets in 1345 along with a solar eclipse and the appearance of a comet: so as to punish people for their great sins, the Holy Spirit will order the malign celestial influence, which will engender pestiferous vapors.[4] He cites the authority of Aristotle,[5] Masha' Allah's *Des interprétations,* and Ptolemy's *Tetrabiblos* in noting that in addition to the Apocalypse's pestilence, famine, war, and death, "we see very many evils which will come about through the said influences, and through people full of vices, by which there will be much conspiracy, treachery, and deceit in the world. And there will be little faith among the people, and they will love neither God nor the Holy Church, and there will be nothing at all of truth, charity, or humility, and the great will devour the middling, and the middling will devour the small, whereby the aforesaid pestilences are granted to occur throughout the world."[6] The epidemic moral and spiritual evils associated with plague deriving from malign influences listed here all figure prominently in many of **The Decameron**'s tales: lying, deceit, treachery, disrespect for the Church, and lack of Christian faith, charity, and humility. The social disorder in class oppression that

Henri de Ferrières prognosticates in hindsight is another thematic element found, for example, in the social injustice and cruelty to inferiors in novellas **"4.5"** about Lisabetta and **"10.10"** about Griselda as well as in numerous tales that recount the clergy's abuse, especially for sexual gratification or financial gain, of those, often the poor, for whose spiritual welfare it is responsible. His observations about prevalent lawlessness and faithlessness parallel Boccaccio's claim in **The Decameron**'s introduction that "all respect for the laws of God and man had virtually broken down and been extinguished in our city."[7]

Le songe de pestilence's retrospective prophecy based on astrological interpretation aims to account in particular for mid-fourteenth-century France's moral, spiritual, and social disorder in the early period of the Hundred Years' War. Chapter 241, *Les causes des maus qui sont a venir u roialme de France plus que ailleurs,* attributes to the malign celestial influence and the resultant corrupt vapors a number of other vices that figure prominently in **The Decameron**'s tales: unchastity, godlessness, hypocrisy, flattery, vanity, covetousness, and lust.[8] In regard to the three estates, the corruption of the clergy mentioned in the prophecy is a central theme in many of **The Decameron**'s novellas.

We can conclude that the mid-fourteenth-century literary idea of the plague extends beyond the epidemic disease itself[9] to include, along with war, death, and famine, a cluster of associations comprising specific vices, social disorder, injustice, and lawlessness, and the perversion of the Christian faith and Church. Therefore, in respect to **The Decameron,** it is not advisable to argue against the text in alleging "moral and spiritual truancy" among the members of the *brigata* in the introduction and frame story in order to demonstrate the collection's overall unity. The late-medieval astrological explanation for pestilence assumes that its causes—divine wrath and planetary influences—also cause the epidemic vices, deceit, lawlessness, disorder, and un-Christian behavior that are thematic constants in **The Decameron**'s tales. In contrast to these vices that it flees, the fictive *brigata* offers a courtly example of moderation, prudence, justice, and constancy.

Notes

1. "The Plague as Key to Meaning in Boccaccio's *Decameron*," in *The Black Death: The Impact of the Fourteenth-Century Plague,* ed. Daniel William, Medieval and Renaissance Texts and Studies, 13 (Binghamton: Center for Medieval and Early Renaissance Studies, 1982) 39-64. The citations are from pp. 39, 52, 49, and 48 respectively.

2. Bernardo 44-45.

3. Bernardo 42.

4. *Le songe de pestilence,* vol. 2 of *Les livres du roy Modus et de la royne Ratio,* ed. Gunnar Tilander, 2 vols. (Paris: Société des Anciens Textes Français, 1932) 199-201.

5. The pseudo-Aristotelian *De causis proprietatum elementorum,* an anonymous Arabic work dating, perhaps, from the tenth century. G. Tilander published excerpts from contemporary sources for this passage and parallel texts in vol. 2, 239-41.

6. *Le songe* 200-01.

7. *The Decameron,* trans. G. H. McWilliam (Harmondsworth: Penguin, 1972), 52-53.

8. *Le songe* 202.

9. As Janet Levarie Smarr notes, the connection between the symptoms of lovesickness, a recurring motif in *The Decameron's* tales, and of plague is a common literary topos that Boccaccio develops in other fictional works—*Boccaccio and Fiammetta: The Narrator as Lover* (Urbana and Chicago: U of Illinois P) 266.

Nelson Moe (essay date November 1995)

SOURCE: Moe, Nelson. "Not a Love Story: Sexual Aggression, Law and Order in *Decameron* X 4."[1] *Romanic Review* 86, no. 4 (November 1995): 623-38.

[*In the following essay, Moe focuses on the socio-ethical significance of the sexually aggressive subject matter of the fourth novella of the "Tenth Day," discussing the cultural implications of the narrator's extensive use of legal discourse.*]

In the fourth novella of the **"Tenth Day"** of the **Decameron,** Boccaccio reworks a tale which had originally formed part of the thirteenth "Question of Love" in his *Filocolo.*[2] This essay focuses on Boccaccio's reformulation of the socio-ethical significance of the act of sexual aggression which, in different ways, is the focal point of both versions of the tale.[3] In particular I investigate a crucial aspect of the **Decameron** revision that has gone unobserved in the scholarship to date: its transformation of a tale of passion into a tale of property; a tale of one man's love for a woman into a tale of his exchange of her with another man so as to impose his order and consolidate his power in the community of men. In the context of this transformation I discuss the extensive use of legal discourse in the **Decameron** revision which serves as the prism through which an illicit act of passion is simultaneously elided and legitimated.

Let me begin by offering a brief summary of the tale, at least insofar as the two versions of it correspond to one another. A beautiful, young lady married to a rich, noble man is loved by a knight. She, however, has no interest in requiting the knight's love, and he goes off in despair to a nearby city to serve as *podestà,* or chief magistrate. During his tenure there news reaches him of the lady's death who, it happens, was pregnant at the time. In a brief interior monologue the knight resolves to go to the tomb where she is buried and have that kiss that was denied him while she was alive. He does just that, but gets carried away and begins to fondle her as well. In the process he detects signs of life and takes her away to his home, where, with the help of his mother she is revived. At the knight's request she remains at his home, soon giving birth to a son. Immediately thereafter the knight invites the lady's husband and many others to a sumptuous banquet where he gallantly presents the lady and child to her husband.

This then is the basic plot of the tale, remarkably similar in both versions.[4] The differences between them, which are great, involve instead such aspects as characterization, discursive style, ideological content, and the narrative context in which the tale is told. As is well known, the episode of the Questions of Love in the *Filocolo* occupies an important place in the textual prehistory of the **Decameron,** not only because of the link formed by the two versions of the tale under consideration here, but because the narrative frame—or *cornice*—of these questions anticipates that of the later work.[5] Like the *lieta brigata* in the **Decameron,** the young men and women in the *Filocolo* decide to pass the hottest hours of the day in a cool, shady garden, telling each other stories. There is however an essential difference between these two settings. Whereas the *Filocolo* episode is inspired by the rhetoricolegal form of the *quaestio,* each tale being a pretext for the *disputatio* between one member of the group and the queen, in the **Decameron** this disputational frame is replaced by a thematic one: except for the first and ninth days, and except for Dioneo who is allowed to recount ad libitum, the tales must address a specific theme—fortune, human ingenuity, tragic and happy loves, etc.

Thus in the *Filocolo* the tale serves as pretext for this question posed by the narrator, Messallino: "Per che si dubita qual fosse maggiore, o la lealtà del cavaliere o l'allegrezza del marito, che la donna e 'l figliuolo, i quali perduti riputava sì come morti, si trovò racquistati, priegovi che quello che di ciò giudicherete ne diciate" ("IV" 67, 23).[6] Within the context of the Questions' overarching theme of love, the two sub-themes of the knight's loyalty and the husband's joy are applied in retrospect to the tale.

In the **Decameron** the overarching theme of the day is not love but "those who have performed liberal or munificent deeds, be it in the cause of love or otherwise." Love is the sub-theme here, and in the three novelle preceding our tale it has in fact been absent. Lauretta, the tale's narrator, explains her introduction of it as a kind of narrative expedient, to be understood within the particularly competitive context of the **"Tenth Day"** in which each narrator tries to surpass the other with his or her tale of munificence:

> —Giovani donne, magnifice cose e belle sono state le raccontate, né mi pare che alcuna cosa restata sia a noi che abbiamo a dire, per la equal novellando vagar possiamo . . . se noi ne' fatti d'amore già non mettessimo mano, li quali a ogni materia prestano abondantissima copia di ragionare.
>
> ("X 4," 3)[7]

Love provides the occasion for the act of munificence to be narrated. But as Lauretta observes in her conclusion to the tale, it also enables her to outdo her fellow storytellers. Because love is involved, the knight's act of generosity exceeds those narrated in the preceding three tales, for the knight "non solo temperò onestamente il suo fuoco, ma liberalmente quello che egli soleva con tutto il pensier disiderare e cercare di rubare, avendolo, restituí. Per certo niuna delle già dette a questa mi par simigliante" (48).

The two versions of the tale are therefore framed differently in their respective narrative contexts, the first a Question of Love concerning the knight's "loyalty" and husband's "joy," the second a tale of the knight's munificence in a matter of love. But it is within the text of the tale itself that we really begin to see the significant differences between them, and to appreciate the new type of writing Boccaccio is engaged in in his **Decameron** revision. A comparison of the first sentences of each tells us a good deal about the new directions in which Boccaccio takes the story in the **Decameron.** The *Filocolo* novelletta begins with these lines:

> Io udii già dire che nella nostra città un gentile uomo ricco molto avea per sua sposa una bellissima e giovane donna, la quale egli sopra tutte le cose del mondo amava. Era questa donna da un cavaliere della detta città per amore intimamente amata, ma ella né lui amava né di suo amore curava: per la qual cosa il cavaliere mai da lei né parola né buon sembiante avea potuto avere. E così sconsolato di tale amore vivendo, avvenne che al reggimento d'una città, assai alla nostra vicina, fu chiamato, ove egli andò, . . .
>
> ("IV" 67, 2-3)

The **Decameron** novella commences thus:

> Fu adunqe in Bologna, nobilissima città di Lombardia, un cavaliere per virtú e per nobiltà di sangue raguardevole assai, il qual fu chiamato messer Gentil Carisendi, il qual giovane d'una gentil donna chiamata madonna Catalina, moglie d'un Niccoluccio Caccianemico, s'innamorò; e perché male dello amor della donna era, quasi disperatosene, podestà chiamato di Modona, v'andò.
>
> (5-6)

No doubt one of the first things that strikes the eye here is the increased geographical and historical specificity of the *Decameron* version. The *Filocolo* tale is set in "our city" which, pronounced by the narrator Messallino, refers to his native Grenada, but which in its vagueness functions as a kind of every-city. The time is unspecified. The husband is a rich nobleman; the woman a "most lovely young lady;" the knight a generic knight.

In the **Decameron** each of these narrative details is inscribed in a specific geographical and social context. The city is Bologna, "that most noble city in Lombardy." The knight, "distinguished for his valor and noble blood," is named messer Gentil Carisendi, the lady is named madonna Catalina and the husband Niccoluccio Caccianemico. Though not specified, the time must—due to the presence of these two famous Bolognese families—be in the recent past where, it is worth recalling, approximately nine tenths of the **Decameron** novelle are set.[8]

The geographical and socio-historical specificity of these lines is no doubt a prime example of what Branca terms the "new narrative dimensions" of the **Decameron.**[9] As we will see in our novella, these proper names are not cosmetic additions slapped onto otherwise unaltered units of plot and characterization but part of a more thorough-going transformation of the tale's narrative style and concerns.[10]

The choice of Bologna as setting for the tale exemplifies the significance a geographical location can have in the logic of a Decameronian narrative. Typically, Boccaccio attributes moral and cultural characteristics to certain cities which in turn play a role in the overall problematic of the tale. In the second novella of the **"Fourth Day,"** set in Venice, Boccaccio represents Frate Alberto's conniving as an organic part of the city's corruption as a whole; the Venetians in some sense deserve him ("IV 2," 8). Though scarcely a hundred miles distant, our somber tale set in Bologna is at the moral antipodes of that Venetian tragi-comedy. Bologna and its citizens are generally represented in a favorable light in the **Decameron,** as noble, courteous and amorous. Here the nobility of Bologna is one with the nobility of messer Gentil Carisendi: "Fu adunqe in Bologna, nobilissima città di Lombardia, un cavaliere per virtú e per nobiltà di sangue raguardevole assai, il qual fu chiamato messer Gentil Carisendi."[11]

Lauretta's mention of Bologna in the first lines of her tale thus evokes an elevated moral ambience for the novella that will be sustained throughout, one consonant with the day's lofty theme of munificence. But if Bologna is a moral landscape it is at the same time a city with a determinate intellectual and institutional significance. For Boccaccio, as for the Italian and European intelligentsia of his day, Bologna was synonymous with the study of law and, secondarily, of medicine and clerical studies. He sums up this image of Bologna at the beginning of another novella with this typical stroke of social contextualization: "Sí come noi veggiamo tutto il dí, i nostri cittadini da Bologna ci tornano qual giudice e qual medico e qual notaio . . ." (**"VIII 9,"** 4).[12]

Bologna is then an exemplary, legal city in an exemplary Day—an appropriate setting for a tale of law and order. The first lines of the **Decameron** novella do more, however, than just situate the tale in Bologna. They also rearrange the characters' order of appearance, in this way too recasting the tale's concerns. In the *Filocolo* novelletta the knight is introduced after the husband and lady, in the second sentence of the tale and there only as a predicate of the lady: "Era questa donna da un cavaliere della detta città per amore intimamente amata." In the course of the tale he emerges as its main character, but he still shares the stage with the husband and lady. There is a kind of plurality of focus, reemphasized at the end by the Question which addresses both the loyalty of the knight and the happiness of the husband.

The **Decameron** version begins instead with the knight, messer Gentil Carisendi, who, as Dennis Dutschke notes, is the subject of all the verbs in the tale's opening sentence, "from the opening *fu* to the closing verb, *v'andò*."[13] He and his socio-ethical project—to be discussed below—are the tale's new unifying element; the increased clarity of focus in the novella is in fact in direct proportion to the increased definition of this character and his actions. And though the putative subtheme of the novella is chivalry and courtesy, one is immediately struck by the matter-of-fact style and callous logic of Carisendi's first utterance in comparison with the highly rhetorical and chivalric manner of the *Filocolo* knight. Upon hearing of the lady's death in the *Filocolo,* the knight says to himself:

> "Ahi, villana morte, maladetta sia la tua potenza! Tu m'hai privato di colei cui io più ch'altra cosa amava, e cui io più disiderava di servire, ben che verso di me la conoscessi crudele. Ma poi che così è avvenuto, quello che amore nella vita di lei non mi volle concedere, ora ch'ella è morta nol mi potrà negare: ché certo, s'io dovessi morire, la faccia, che io tanto viva amai, ora morta converrà che io baci."
>
> ("IV" 67, 4-6)

In comparison, Messer Gentile says this:

> "Ecco, madonna Catalina, tu se' morta: io, mentre che vivesti, mai un solo sguardo da te aver non potei: per che, ora che difender non ti potrai, convien per certo che, cosí morta come tu se', io alcun bascio ti tolga."
>
> (8)[14]

The narrator would have us believe that Carisendi's love for Catalina is noble, capable of inspiring an act of "munificence;" but it is the calculating, even predatory nature of Carisendi's thoughts towards her that stands out. The gist of this brief internal monologue may be similar in both cases, to kiss her now that she is dead and cannot resist, but the **Decameron** strips down the rhetorical embellishment of the *Filocolo* to the bare terms of the sexual aggression: "ora che difender non ti potrai, convien per certo che . . . io alcun bascio ti tolga."[15]

Everything about Carisendi's behavior from this point on in the novella is highly calculated in comparison to the rather haphazard actions of the *Filocolo* knight. In the sentence immediately following the lines just quoted, a verb appears that is symptomatic of this new decisiveness, one that will be repeated a number of times later in the tale: "E questo detto, essendo già notte, *dato ordine* come la sua andata occulta fosse. . . ." One of Carisendi's defining characteristics is that he gives orders and, more generally, that he imposes *his* order upon his surroundings. The significance of this will become clearer as we consider the second part of the novella, but let us now turn to the tomb scene itself.

Having stated his aim to steal a kiss from Catalina, Carisendi rides to the place where she is buried. In the *Filocolo* this passage reads as follows:

> . . . sopra la sepoltura dove sepellita era la donna se n'andò, e quella aperse, e confortando il compagno che 'l dovesse sanza alcuna paura attendere, entrò in quella e con pietoso pianto dolendosi cominciò a baciare la donna e a recarlasi in braccio. E dopo alquanto, non potendosi di baciare costei saziare, la cominciò a toccare e a mettere le mani nel gelato seno fra le fredde menne, e poi le segrete parti del corpo con quelle, divenuto ardito oltre al dovere, cominiciò a cercare sotto i ricchi vestimenti: le quali andando tutte con timida mano tentando sopra lo stomaco la distese, e quivi con debole movimento sentì li deboli polsi muoversi alquanto.
>
> (6-8)

In the **Decameron** the scene reads thus:

> e aperta la sepoltura in quella diligentemente entrò, e postolesi a giacere allato il suo viso a quello della donna accostò, e piú volte con molte lagrime piangendo il basciò. Ma sí come noi veggiamo l'appetito degl'uomini a niun termine star contento ma sempre piú avanti desiderare, e spezialmente quello degli amanti, avendo costui seco deliberato di piú non starvi, disse: "Deh! perché non le tocco io, poi che io son qui, un poco il petto? Io non la debbo mai piú toccare né mai piú la toccai."
>
> Vinto adunque da questo appetito le mise la mano in seno: e per alquanto spazio tenutalavi gli parve sentire alcuna cosa battere il cuore a costei. . . .
>
> (9-12)

This scene has been rewritten in a number of significant ways. It is first of all striking that the **Decameron** considerably tones down the description of the knight's apparent necrophilia. Such details from the *Filocolo* as "chilled bosom," "cold breasts," and "the secret parts of her body," are reduced in the *Decameron* to a much more general and innocuous level of description. The *Filocolo* also more forcefully communicates the insatiability of the knight's desire, along with his desperation and loss of control, by constructing the scene as an uninterrupted erotic crescendo, from kissing the lady to fondling her breasts to feeling "her secret parts" to the ultimate discovery of the faint signs of life. The *Decameron* breaks up this erotic concatenation and inserts between Carisendi's more discrete kissing her face and putting his hand upon her breast two notable new elements: a clause of communal or choral censure, and Carisendi's brief, second monologue.

In the *Filocolo* the phrase "ardito oltre al dovere" provides a minimal note of censure of the knight's behavior; he acts in excess of, "oltre," a rather vaguely expressed ideal, "il dovere." The *Decameron* reformulates and expands the ethical terms of this censure, describing the act in terms of the knight's insatiable "appetite" and "desire." But even more significant is the presence of what we might call a communal or choral voice that expresses this reproach, the first-person plural that recurs throughout *Decameron* in the formula "come noi veggiamo . . .": "Ma sí come noi veggiamo l'appetito degl'uomini a niun termine star contento ma sempre piú avanti desiderare. . . ." Phrases like this, encountered above in the sentence referring to the common sight of men returning from Bologna as judges, doctors, and clerks, are used in the *Decameron* to express the familiarity of a phenomenon.[16] Carisendi's behavior here is no doubt excessive, if not aberrant, but the text suggests that, as a lover is involved, this comes as no great surprise. The phrase thus domesticates the alien, morbid quality of the *Filocolo* passage; Carisendi's behavior may be reprehensible, but it is somehow human, a part of "our" experience. The violence of the act has been notably socialized and attenuated.

The second new element in the *Decameron* version of the scene is Carisendi's brief utterance following the censuring comment just discussed: "Deh! perché non le tocco io, poi che io son qui, un poco il petto? Io non la debbo mai piú toccare né mai piú la toccai." In effect, Carisendi shrugs his shoulders at the chorus's mild reproach, warding off its half-hearted slap on the hand with a coy remark that tends to preclude the possibility of morally condemning his behavior. As with his decision to steal a kiss from Catalina, his criteria of judgement are restricted to the pragmatics of the situation, all based on the self-serving logic of: I want this; there's nothing stopping me from taking it; I'll take it.

As we have seen, Boccaccio substantially revises the tomb scene in the *Decameron,* eliminating some of the *Filocolo*'s more morbid details and diffusing some of

its original erotic power. All in all, the *Decameron* offers a more decorous rendition of the knight's aggression against the lady, one more consonant with the lofty atmosphere of the **"Tenth Day."** At the same time Boccaccio reworks the knight's character, making him sound more like a savvy merchant than gallant knight. We saw too that the newly inserted clause of choral censure and Carisendi's additional utterance hinted at a subtle shift in the moral framework of the scene, away from the abstract idealism of the *Filocolo,* summed up by the concept of "il dovere," towards a type of ethical pragmatism.

In the second half of the novella the precise nature and social significance of this pragmatism is made manifest in the banquet scene at Carisendi's home. There, through a legalistic representation of his encounter with Catalina, he succeeds in transforming what has thus far been a narrative of excess desire into one of law and social order. Between the two halves of the novella—the tomb and the banquet—there is a brief intermediate scene in which this thematic shift is set in motion.

Having resuscitated madonna Catalina with his passionate proddings, Carisendi takes her to his home in Bologna. There, upon waking and hearing the story of how she got there, madonna Catalina asks to be taken home to her husband, appealing to the knight's courtliness and love for her: ". . . il pregò, per quello amore il quale egli l'aveva già portato e per cortesia di lui, che . . . alla sua propia casa la lasciasse tornare" (16). Carisendi immediately responds: "Madonna, chente che il mio disiderio si sia stato ne' tempi passati, io non intendo al presente né mai per innanzi . . . di trattarvi né qui né altrove se non come cara sorella" (17). Like every other action of Carisendi's, this one involves no hesitation, reflection or soul-searching. Except for a moment of tergiversation in the tomb, Carisendi simply announces his decisions and acts upon them. He decided to kiss the lady and kissed her; now he announces that he will treat her like a sister, and so it will be. But no sooner has he announced this noble change-of-heart than he adds this condition: I will treat you like a "dear sister," he tells her, "ma questo mio benificio operato in voi questa notte merita alcun guiderdone."

The term "guiderdone" employed here, "guerdon," is taken from the stylistic register of courtly love that is an important element of this novella. Its presence in the Italian poetic tradition dates back at least as far as Giacomo da Lentini, who uses it to ask his lady to reward him for his faithful service, as in these opening lines of one canzone: "Guiderdone aspetto avere / da voi, donna, cui servire / non m'è noia."[17] Dante, however, staunchly opposed the approach to love that "guiderdone" evokes. Beginning with his "poetics of praise" in *Vita Nuova* XVIII and culminating in the *Commedia,* Dante rebels against the mundane, quid pro quo concept of reward implied by "guiderdone." The love poet should not write with the aim of receiving recompense from his lady, he argues, but simply of praising her.

A latter-day "guiderdone" mentality returns at this point in the **Decameron,** however, with a vengeance, in the guise of Carisendi's request. His statement here inaugurates the out-and-out reformulation of the terms of the tale that will take place in the second half of the novella. As we just saw, Catalina's prayer, ". . . il pregò, per quello amore . . . ," held out the possibility that this was in fact a love story, one in which sexual passion is converted into an honest, "sisterly" love. This indeed is an essential part of the moral that Lauretta draws from it at the end of the novella when she stresses that the knight "temperò onestamente il suo fuoco." But the turn away from desire announced by Carisendi is not so much a conversion as a transvaluation of the very terms of *amor* and *caritas* which, at least initially, had appeared to be the moral framework for the tale. The precise nature of Carisendi's guerdon makes it clear that the focus of the tale from this point forward will not be his love for Catalina but his intervention in the social order represented by her husband and the town's leading citizens: ". . . io intendo di voi, in presenzia de' migliori cittadini di questa terra, fare un caro e uno solenne dono al vostro marito" (20). With this Catalina's status in the economy of the tale shifts from an object of desire to an object of exchange. In both cases she is an object, lacking in subjectivity and literally reified—first as a corpse, then as a gift—but it is only in the second instance that she is actually turned into an instrument to be used in Carisendi's endeavor to increase his social status and power.[18]

Her reification is further underscored in the banquet scene at Carisendi's home where, describing to his guests the "Persian" custom which is the strategem he employs to give Catalina back to her husband, he places her in a chain of equivalences governed by the term "thing:" ". . . gli mostra quella *cosa,* o moglie o amica o figliuola o che che si sia, la quale egli ha piú cara. . . ." (24). It is this "thingness," this lack of agency, that renders her such an effective object of exchange between Carisendi and Catalina's husband, a condition which at the end of the banquet scene is described in terms of her *silence*: "La donna, sentendosi al suo marito domandare, con fatica di risponder si tenne; ma pur per servare l'ordine posto tacque" (33).[19] The end result of this exchange, we will see, is the binding together of the two clans of Carisendi and Caccianemico, an axis of power from which she herself disappears once she has performed the function of bringing them together: "e messer Gentile sempre amico visse di Niccoluccio e di' suoi parenti e di quei della donna" (46). The silent servant of the male order, her function in the tale's economy of social relations is eloquently summed up by Claude Lévi-Strauss: "[the ex-

change of women] provides the means of binding men together, and of superimposing upon the natural links of kinship the henceforth artificial links . . . of alliance governed by rule."[20]

From the scene of Carisendi's request for guerdon forward, the novella thus makes a decisive departure from the *Filocolo*'s abstract thematics of love and honor, articulating instead the new problematic of woman's role as object of exchange in the negotiation of social order between men. This new concern with order, which we just now considered from the point of view of Catalina's transformation into a "gift" and "thing," is highly evident in the first three paragraphs leading into the final banquet scene, where the verb *ordinare,* first encountered as Carisendi set off for the tomb (9), rings out three times: "*ordinò* che le cose oportune tutte vi fossero;" "*ordinò,* quella mattina . . . un grande e bel convito a casa sua;" "avendo . . . con lei *ordinato* il modo che dovesse tenere . . ." (22-24). What remains for us to consider is precisely how Carisendi succeeds in imposing *his* order upon Catalina's husband and the "town's leading citizens," which, we will now see, he does by representing his relationship to Caterina through the legal prism of property rights.

It is worth recalling that as podestà—or chief magistrate—Carisendi occupies what was traditionally the highest position of legal authority in the thirteenth- and fourteenth-century Italian commune.[21] As in the novelle of Gabriotto and Andreuola (**"IV 6"**) and of Madonna Filippa (**"VI 7"**), the podestà exercises an extensive range of juridical duties, hearing cases, deciding guilt and innocence, determining punishment. This might be no more than general sociological background to the novella if a legal framework and discourse did not play such a significant role in the reorientation of the tale along the lines of social order that I have been describing and, specifically, if Carisendi did not make such explict use of legal terms, concepts and formulas in the final banquet scene. As we will now see, the law proves integral both to the structure of the novella and to Boccaccio's revision of the *Filocolo* tale as a whole.[22]

In the banquet scene Carisendi presents his guests with a legal test case, prefaced by the mention of the Persian custom referred to above whereby the host invites his friend to his home, "e quivi gli mostra quella cosa, o moglie o amica o figliuola o che che si sia, la quale egli ha piú cara" (24). He asks whether a man who throws his faithful servant out onto the street when he takes sick has any right to ask for him back when, upon being taken in by someone else, he regains his health:

> "Vorrei io ora sapere se, tenendolsi e usando i suoi servigi, il suo signore si può a buona equità dolere o ramaricare del secondo, se egli raddomandandolo rendere nol volesse."

(27)

His jury of guests deliberates the case, producing, of course, the desired *sententia*—that the man has no claim upon the servant:

> I gentili uomini, fra sé avuti varii ragionamenti e tutti in una sentenzia concorrendo, a Niccoluccio Caccianemico, per ciò che bello e ornato favellatore era, commisero la risposta. Costui . . . disse sé con gli altri insieme essere in questa opinione, che il primo signore niuna ragione avesse piú nel suo servidore, poi che in sí fatto caso non solamente abandonato ma gittato l'avea, e che per li benifici del secondo usati giustamente parea di lui il servidore divenuto, per che, tenendolo, niun noia, niuna forza, niuna ingiuria faceva al primiero. . . .

> (28-9)

Finally, he shows "the thing he loves most," madonna Catalina. She, they must agree, is like the faithful servant and therefore belongs to Carisendi:

> ". . . se mutata non avete sentenzia da poco in qua . . . questa donna meritamente è mia, né alcuno giusto titolo me la può radomandare."

> (40)

By way of a careful and legally precise argument, Carisendi persuades his guests of his "just entitlement" to Catalina, rewriting the text of his sexual aggression against her by renarrating it in terms of property rights. His diversion of attention away from the sexual aspect of the story is thus achieved not simply by an elision of that scene of violence but by a radical redirection of the narrative away from a problematic of passion to one of property.[23] In effecting this shift, Carisendi's argument is in accordance with the medieval legal category of *raptus,* where it is not the specifically sexual component of the offence but the proprietary one that is the determining factor. As James Brundage observes:

> Both medieval and modern notions of rape emerged from the *raptus*—literally carrying off by force—of the Roman law. Thus in ancient Roman law *raptus* consisted in the abduction of a woman against the will of the person under whose authority she lived. Sexual intercourse was not a necessary element of *raptus.* The specific malice of the offense consisted not in the sexual ravishment of the woman, but in stealing her away from her parents, guardian, or husband. *Raptus* might also be used to describe theft of property as well as of a person, so long as violence was employed in the act.[24]

Carisendi's sexual aggression is of course not a case of *raptus,* and yet the legal framework of *raptus* informs his argument, albeit in an inverted manner. To wit, instead of standing trial for the seizure of Niccoluccio Caccianemico's property (Catalina), Carisendi in a sense puts Niccoluccio on trial for committing what amounts to the opposite of *raptus*: the unjustified *disposal* of his own property ("non solamente abandonato ma *gittato* l'avea"). In both cases what is at issue is the legal guide-

lines for the possession and taking-possession of woman, guidelines of which Carisendi—and his audience of "leading citizens"—is perfectly aware and which he manipulates with complete mastery.

By now it should be clear that Carisendi is no mere *motteggiatore,* one of the classic Decameronian characters who makes the most out of a bad situation, or perhaps even momentarily calls into question the social hierarchy, through a clever turn of phrase. He is rather engaged in an out-and-out reordering of his social world. The end of the banquest scene tale provides one last indication of the thoroughly discursive nature of this operation. Here Carisendi shows that his power lies not only in his ability to lay down the law, but also, as a result of his legal upper-hand, in his ability to reposition others advantageously in relation to himself by *renaming* them. In the new version of reality that he institutes things are not, and are not called, what they used to be but assume the positions and names stipulated by him: "Leva sú, compare; io non ti rendo tua mogliere, la quale i tuoi e suoi parenti gittarono via, ma io ti voglio donare questa donna mia comare con questo suo figlioletto, il qual son certo che fu da te generato e il quale io a battesimo tenni e nomina'lo Gentile" (42-42). Carisendi has transformed, by fiat, Niccoluccio into his *compare,* a kind of godbrother; Catalina into his *comare,* and the boy-child into his godson, named after himself. Through the *comparatico* Carisendi thus establishes a place for himself in the Caccianemico clan as the son's spiritual father while also ensuring his new "sisterly" ties to Catalina.[25]

To conclude, Boccaccio's revision of the *Filocolo* novelletta in **Decameron "X 4"** contains a series of significant changes comprising various aspects of the tale's linguistic style and mode of narrative presentation, as well as its social and ethical vision. The **Decameron** novella achieves a consistency and clarity of focus, closely related to the consistent character of the knight who, in the guise of messer Gentil Carisendi, is promoted to protagonist of the tale.

With Carisendi at its center, Boccaccio provides the thematically diffuse *Filocolo* novelletta with a single thrust: the transformation of a tale of love and passion into a tale of law and order through the exchange of woman as property. To this end he down-plays the erotic dimension of the tomb scene, both minimizing its original morbidity and rendering it familiar. Then in a brief scene between the tomb and banquet, the text manages the transition from the tale's initial framework of chivalry and courtly love to the new, pragmatic world of exchange that Carisendi embodies and espouses. Finally, in the banquet scene in his home, Carisendi deftly represents his relationship to Catalina in the legal terms of a property relationship, simultaneously eliding the sexual aggression by which he came to possess her and consolidating his power in the community through his subsequent gesture of "munificence." By the end of the tale madonna Catalina has not only been silenced but has in fact dropped out of the picture altogether, leaving messer Gentile united with "Niccoluccio and his relatives and those of the woman" in eternal friendship. With her body and her silence—first as a corpse and then as a gift—Catalina is thus relegated to providing "the means of binding men together, and of superimposing upon the natural links of kinship the henceforth artificial links . . . of alliance governed by rule."[26]

Notes

1. An earlier version of this essay was delivered as a lecture at the University of Michigan on March 15, 1991. I wish to thank Teodolinda Barolini, Renzo Bragantini, Claude Cazalé-Bérard, Ross Chambers, Franco Fido, Pier Massimo Forni, Eugenio Giusti, Kathryn Gravdal, Julia Hairston, Robert Hollander, Victoria Kirkham, Gregory L. Lucente, Millicent Marcus, Giuseppe Mazzotta, Jeffrey Schnapp, Karen Van Dyck, and David Wallace for their helpful comments on an earlier draft.

2. The other well-known case of such revision in the *Decameron* is the following novella in the "Tenth Day," which consists of the reelaboration of the fourth "Question of Love" in the *Filocolo*. The *Filocolo* was written in Naples c. 1334-1336, some fifteen years before the *Decameron*. For a brief discussion of the relationship between *Decameron* "X 4" and "X 5," see fn. 19 below.

3. I employ the deliberately imprecise term "sexual aggression" to describe the act in the tale which, while by no means a case of rape, is evidently (for both Boccaccio and ourselves) beyond the pale of morally acceptable behavior. My intention in describing it from the outset in this fashion is to avoid applying legally precise modern terms such as "sexual assault" or "sexual violence" which might confuse the issue of how the text itself grapples with the morality and legality of the act.

4. It would, for example, be nearly impossible to differentiate them through the type of structural narrative analysis employed by Tzvetan Todorov in his *Grammaire du Décaméron* (The Hague—Paris: Mouton, 1969). "X, 4" is in fact one of the novellas about which Todorov has least to say in his "Grammar." His comments are limited to this: "Enfin, il est possible de modifier la situation en instaurant un certain système d'échange: en payant, ou en donnant gratuitement. Dans "IV, 3," un des couples arrive à se sauver en achetant la garde; Madeleine sauve sa soeur en s'offrant au duc. Dans la dixième journée, c'est le don généreux qui modifie la situation: ainsi Messire Gentil rend

à Niccoluccio sa femme, alors qu'il aurait aimé la garder pour lui ("X, 4"), etc." (37-8).

5. On the *Filocolo* Questions of Love, see Pio Rajna, "L'episodio delle Questioni D'Amore nel *Filocolo* del Boccaccio," *Romania* 31.2 (1902) 28-81; Victoria Kirkham, "Reckoning with Boccaccio's Questioni D'Amore," *MLN* 89.1 (1974) 47-59; Paolo Cherchi, "Sulle 'quistioni d'amore' nel *Filocolo*," in *Andrea Capellano, i trovatori e altri temi romanzi* (Rome: Bulzoni, 1979) 210-17; Luigi Surdich, "Il *Filocolo*: le 'questioni d'amore' e la 'quête' di Florio," in *La cornice di amore* (Pisa: ETS, 1987) 13-75.

6. *Filocolo*, Antonio Enzo Quaglio, ed., in *Tutte le opere di Giovanni Boccaccio*, Vittore Branca, ed. (Milan: Mondadori, 1967), vol. 1. All quotations from the *Filocolo* are taken from this edition.

7. *Decameron*, Vittore Branca, ed. (Turin: Einaudi, 1987). All quotations from the *Decameron* are taken from this edition.

8. See Branca's introduction, "Una chiave di lettura per il *Decameron*. Contemporaneizzazione narrativa ed espressionismo linguistico," in *Decameron* viii.

9. See the chapter titled "Le nuove dimensioni narrative e il linguaggio storicamente allusivo," in Vittore Branca, *Boccaccio medievale e nuovi studi sul Decameron* (Florence: Sansoni, 1986) 165-87, particularly 176 with reference to the novella under consideration.

10. See, for example, Giovanni Getto, *Vita di forme e forme di vita nel Decameron* (Turin: G. B. Petrini, 1958) 4: "I particolari storici e geografici, in effetti, non nascono da un'esteriore ricerca di inquadramento, dal proposito di creare un addentellato storico . . . essi sono al contrario qualcosa di più radicale, in quanto emanazione spontanea di quel piacevole ricordare, che di essi si nutre e in essi si colloca come in una naturale prospettiva, nello spazio e nel tempo propri dei fatti evocati."

11. See Mario Baratto, *Realtà e stile nel Decameron* (Rome: Riuniti, 1984) 145-6: "L'azione è situata a Bologna: una città che non è più il soggetto della novella, una dimensione avventurosa o drammatica di per sé, ma è ora oggetto di un ordinamento civile, dimensione scenica che l'individuo riconosce come il proprio campo d'azione, se appartiene alla classe che domina per ricchezza, per prestigio sociale, per ricercatezza culturale. E infatti Gentile Carisendi è tutt'uno con l'ambiente che lo circonda; nella sua figura i miti amorosi e cortesi si trasformano nei riti sociali di una *élite* cittadina."

12. Bologna may have a more intimate connotation for Boccaccio as well, regarding the city's place

in the biographies of the major Italian poets before him. The lion's share of major Italian writers before Boccaccio studied or taught law there: Guido Guinizzelli, Dante, Petrarch, Cino da Pistoia. With regard to Cino, a professional jurist, there is evidence that Boccaccio followed his lessons in canon law at the University of Naples between 1330 and 1331 (see Vittore Branca, "Notizie e e documenti per la biografia del Boccaccio: L'incontro napoletano con Cino da Pistoia," *Studi sul Boccaccio* 5 [1969] 1-12, as well as his *Giovanni Boccaccio. Profilo biografico* [Florence: Sansoni, 1977] 30-32). Thus while Boccaccio could not add the University of Bologna to the ideal, poetic curriculum vitae that he so carefully constructed, he could place himself in the company of his beloved Dante and Petrarch as a poet who in his youth had studied law in the Bolognese tradition.

13. Dennis Dutschke, "Boccaccio: a Question of Love (A Comparative Study of *Filocolo IV, 13* and *Decameron "X, 4"*)," *The Humanities Association Review* 6 (1975) 306.

14. Pier Massimo Forni has suggested that this address—in both the *Filocolo* and *Decameron*—bears the traces of Apollo's address to Daphne in Ovid's *Metamorphoses* (lecture, The Johns Hopkins University, Baltimore, 25 Sept. 1990). In the *Metamorphoses* the scene is of course also one of sexual aggression: "at, quoniam coniunx mea non potes esse, arbor eris certe" (I, 557-559). Another likely precedent for this address is the "Elegia di Costanza" attributed to Boccaccio, in which a similar love-in-the-tomb scene appears: "utinam te mortuam darent, / ut videre possem, et quos michi vita negavit / mors daret amplexus" (vv. 94-96) (in Vittore Branca, *Tradizione delle opere di Giovanni Boccaccio* [Rome: Edizioni di Storia e Letteratura, 1958] 206).

15. Branca glosses the phrase thus: "Senza cioè il consenso della donna" (1139).

16. For a partial listing of this formula's appearances in the *Decameron,* considered as an example of Boccaccio's "adherence to daily reality," see Giorgio Padoan, *Il Boccaccio. Le muse il Parnaso e l'Arno* (Florence: Olschki, 1978) 20-21. Pier Massimo Forni provides a more extensive analysis of the rhetoric of familiarity in the *Decameron* in "Retorica del reale nel *Decameron*," *Studi sul Boccaccio* 17 (1988) 183-202; "Forme innocue nel *Decameron*," *MLN* 103 (1989) 39-47; "Come cominciano le novelle del *Decameron*," in *La novella italiana* (Rome: Salerno, 1989), vol. 1, 689-700.

17. *Poeti del duecento*, Gianfranco Contini, ed. (Milan-Naples: Ricciardi, 1960), vol. 1, 58.

18. It is worth noting that this is done with her "consent," but in a situation in which she is "obliged" to agree to Carisendi's request. The formula with which Carisendi requests his guiderdone does not allow for her refusal: "voglio che voi non mi neghiate una grazia la quale io vi domanderò."

19. In his analysis of the tale of Alatiel, Cesare Segre cites Niccoluccio's reaction to Catalina's silence ("Messere, bella cosa è questa vostra, ma ella ne par mutola") as further evidence of the intimate relation between "mutism" and reification in the *Decameron* (see *Le strutture e il tempo* [Turin: Einaudi, 1974] 153).

20. *The Elementary Structures of Kinship* (Boston: Beacon Press, 1974) 480. The thematization of the exchange of woman between men also prompts us to consider the following story in the *Decameron* in a new light—the novella of madonna Dianora ("X 5"), which shares the preceding novella's pedigree as the only *Decameron* offspring of the *Filocolo* Questions of Love. Approaching the novella from this perspective allows us to see something that has been missed in the previous scholarship: that their placement in a sequence appears to be motivated precisely by this theme of women exchanged among men. Indeed the presence of the theme in both novelle suggests that their reelaboration occurred in serial fashion. For whereas the novella of messer Gentil Carisendi reworks and expands two key elements that were present in the thirteenth Question of Love—the conversion of his passion into brotherly affection and the binding together of the two men in perpetual friendship—these same elements reappear in the novella of madonna Dianora *though they are absent from the fourth Question of Love on which it was based.* In other words, Boccaccio's expansion of the themes of tempered passion and the exchange of women between men in the fourth novella evidently spills over into the fifth, structuring it and shaping its concerns. Thus the juxtaposition of the two novelle not only helps us to clarify the importance of these themes but allows us to construct a provisional theory with respect to their genesis.

21. Cf. O. F. Robinson, T. D. Fergus and W. M. Gordon, *An Introduction to European Legal History* (Abingdon: Professional Books, 1985) 183-186; Robert Davidsohn, *Storia di Firenze* (Florence: Sansoni, 1962), vol. 5, especially the chapter "L'ordinamento giudiziario," 569-576; and Daniel Waley, *The Italian City-Republics* (London: Longman, 1988) 40-45.

22. The legal dimension of this novella has received little attention from scholars, evidently because Carisendi is off-duty and the institutional location of the tale not official but private. One brief but

notable exception is Victoria Kirkham's discussion in *The Sign of Reason in Boccaccio's Fiction* (Florence: Olschki, 1993) 160. For a relevant consideration of the legal subtext of Madonna Filippa's defense before the podestà of Prato, see Kenneth Pennington, "A Note to *Decameron* 6.7: the Wit of Madonna Filippa," *Speculum* 52.4 (1977). Giuseppe Mazzotta examines the significance of law in the *Decameron* more generally in the chapter titled "The Law and its Transgressions" in *The World at Play in Boccaccio's* Decameron (Princeton: Princeton University Press, 1986) 213-240. And, for a brief consideration of the language of judges in the book, see Branca's "Una chiave di lettura per il *Decameron*" (xxvii-xxx).

23. In their introduction to the collection *Rape and Representation* (New York: Columbia University Press, 1991), editors Lynn A. Higgins and Brenda R. Silver highlight the recurrence of the "elision," "erasure" and "displacement" of the scene of sexual violence in texts by male authors as part of the "legitimation" and "naturalization" of that violence (1-11). For a study of rape and representation in medieval France, see Kathryn Gravdal, *Ravishing Maidens. Writing Rape in Medieval French Literature and Law* (Philadelphia: University of Pennsylvania Press, 1991).

24. James A. Brundage, "Rape and Seduction in the Medieval Canon Law," *Sexual Practices and the Medieval Church,* eds. Vern L. Bullough and James Brundage (Buffalo: Prometheus, 1982) 141. For a brief consideration of rape statutes and prosecution in mid-fourteenth century Florence, see Umberto Dorini, *Il diritto penale e la delinquenza in Firenze nel sec. XIV* (Lucca: Domenico Corsi, 1916) 66-76. For a more detailed and analytical discussion of the problem in mid-fourteenth century Venice, see the chapter titled "Violence and Sexuality: Rape" in Guido Ruggiero's *The Boundaries of Eros. Sex Crime and Sexuality in Renaissance Venice* (Oxford: Oxford University Press, 1985) 89-108.

25. In his recent comparison of the *Filocolo* novelletta and *Decameron* "X 4," Steven Grossvogel describes Carisendi's action here as a "palinode" to *Decameron* "VII 3," in which frate Rinaldo becomes a godfather and *compare* for the very purpose of making love to the child's mother (*Ambiguity and Allusion in Boccaccio's* Filocolo [Florence: Olschki, 1992] 241). On the parodic representation of the *comparatico* in Decameron "VII 3," see Rosario Ferreri, "Rito battesimale e comparatico nelle novelle senesi della VII giornata," *Studi sul Boccaccio* 16 (1987) 307-14. The *instrumental* nature of the institution of *comparatico* has been highlighted by anthropologists (see,

for example, Maurice Bloch and Scott Guggenheim, "Compadrazgo, Baptism and the Symbolism of a Second Birth," *Man* 16.3 [1981] 377).

26. Lévi-Strauss 480.

Jessica Levenstein (essay date autumn 1996)

SOURCE: Levenstein, Jessica. "Out of Bounds: Passion and the Plague in Boccaccio's *Decameron*." *Italica* 73, no. 3 (autumn 1996): 313-35.

[*In the following essay, Levenstein explores the connections between descriptions of the plague and desire in the* Decameron, *examining the thematic and linguistic links between the Introduction and the* novelle *of the "Fourth Day."*]

The plague that Boccaccio describes in the introduction to the **Decameron** cannot be controlled by any human act. Municipal ordinances regulating the transport of refuse from the city and limiting the movements of the afflicted do not prevent the spread of the disease; devout prayer brings no improvement to the suffering city. The responses of the Florentines to the threat of the epidemic, including seclusion, flight, herbal remedies, and continual carousing, neither guarantee health nor accelerate illness: regardless of their behavior, all Florentines are equally susceptible to the disease—in the narrator's words, "in quella non valendo alcuno senno né umano provedimento" ("I, intro.," 9).[1] Similarly, the erotic love depicted in the stories of the Fourth Day can in no way be governed by human will. The parents, brothers, and husbands who attempt to control the passions of their children, sisters, and wives find themselves frustrated by the overwhelming force of burning desire and confronted by the tragic consequences of their intervention. As Neifile pronounces at the beginning of the tale of Girolamo and Silvestra, "alcuni . . . non solamente a' consigli degli uomini ma ancora contra la natura delle cose presummono d'opporre il senno loro; della quale presunzione già grandissimi mali sono avvenuti e alcun bene non se ne vide giammai" ("**IV, 8,**" 3). Nor is Neifile alone in recognizing the fundamental tension of Filostrato's day; in the course of "**Day Four,**" several other *novellieri,* the narrator of the day's introduction, and various characters within the *novelle* also explicitly spell out the impossibility of a triumph of human *senno* over passionate desire. The insistent opposition of *senno* and *la natura delle cose* and the inevitability of nature's victory over human wisdom, then, unarguably link the eros depicted in the "**Fourth Day**" to the plague portrayed in the introduction. Both pestilence and desire invariably overpower human *ingegno* and in so doing they both consistently subvert legal codes and disrupt traditional familial bonds. Moreover,

Boccaccio connects the plague and passionate love through a nexus of thematic and linguistic similarities involving the imagery and language of excess, containment, and escape. The emphatic association between the plague and desire potentially endows both afflictions with a deep implicit significance, and prompts a series of vexing questions. For instance, given that the plague's connection to eros suggests the indomitable nature of passion, would it not be possible to conceive of an internalized epidemic, impossible to elude? Does the *brigata*'s return to a still-plagued city signal a failure to flee the plague within them? While I am neither willing to reduce the plague to a metaphor for erotic passion,[2] nor determined to posit a one-to-one correspondence between the two,[3] I do believe that exploring the connections between the plague and desire will considerably amplify any reading of the actions of the *brigata,* and of the *Decameron* as a whole. To examine these connections, and to attempt to answer the questions provoked by them, I will offer a reading of the introduction and several of the **"Fourth Day"**'s *novelle* that takes particular account of the thematic and linguistic links between Boccaccio's description of plague-ridden Florence and the extended consideration of passionate love that comprises the introduction to and the stories of Filostrato's reign. I will then attempt to investigate the consequences of these links for the entire *Decameron,* and I will conclude by briefly reflecting on the significance of the *brigata*'s return to the city.

Before looking at the *Decameron*'s introduction it will be useful to recall several basic elements of the **"Pro-emio"** that anticipate some of the central concerns of the introduction and the **"Fourth Day."**[4] The narrator, who describes himself as once inflamed by love "beyond measure" ("oltre modo"), offers one hundred stories to the *vaghe donne,* claiming that the restrictions placed on their liberty by their parents, brothers, and husbands make them particularly vulnerable to lovesickness. The narrator explains: "ristrette da' voleri, da' piaceri, da' comandamenti de' padri, delle madri, de' fratelli e de' mariti, il piú del tempo nel piccolo circuito delle loro camere racchiuse dimorano e quasi oziose sedendosi . . ." (**"Proemio 10"**). The enclosure of the women forces them to hide their passions and, once hidden, the flames of love afflicting the women gain strength. The freedom granted to men, on the other hand, allows them access to various means of alleviating their pain, such as hunting, fishing, and gambling, and they are consequently less prone to the sorrow of lovesickness. Because of Fortune's inequitable treatment of women the narrator decides to present them with his tales as a succor and refuge. The brief **"Pro-emio"** closes with the narrator's hopeful claim that his stories will provide both pleasure ("diletto") and useful advice ("utile consiglio") to the ladies who read them.[5]

In the introduction that follows the **"Proemio"** the narrator describes the nature of the plague of 1348 and its disastrous effects on the moral fabric of the city of Florence.[6] Explaining that human ingenuity is unavailing in the face of the plague's assault, the narrator goes on to describe the physical symptoms of the epidemic:

> . . . nascevano nel cominciamento d'essa a' maschi e alle femine parimente o nella anguinaia o sotto le ditella certe enfiature . . . e da questo appresso s'incominciò la qualità della predetta infermità a permutare in macchie nere o livide, le quali nelle braccia e per le cosce e in ciascuna altra parte del corpo apparivano. . . .

> (**"I, intro.,"** 10-11)

While the word for swellings, "enfiature," is a hapax in the *Decameron,* Janet Smarr points out that "[the description of] the plague symptoms of swellings on the body matches Boccaccio's own earlier descriptions of the effects of love as a poison which swells the body."[7] Smarr cites two examples, *Teseida* III, 33 and *Elegia di Madonna Fiammetta* I. The example from the *Teseida,* a passage describing Palemone's and Arcita's love for Emilia, likens love to a snake bite that induces immediate swelling. The citation from the *Elegia* also uses the imagery of a snake bite to represent lovesickness; the night before she falls in love with Panfilo, Fiammetta dreams that the poison from a snake wound causes her body to swell: "Ma la piaga, la quale infino a quella ora per la sola morsura m'avea stimulata, piena rimasa di veleno vipereo, non valendovi medicina, quasi tutto il corpo con *enfiatura* sozzissima parea che occupasse."[8] Again, in this earlier work, Boccaccio associates swelling, which in the *Decameron* is firmly linked to plague symptoms, with *aegritudo amoris*. In this example, however, the use of the very word that Boccaccio uses to describe the early effects of the plague, *enfiatura,* provides a clear verbal connection between the *Elegia*'s lovesickness and the *Decameron*'s plague. Moreover, just as Fiammetta points out the ineffectiveness of medicine in the face of her dream's illness, the narrator of the *Decameron*'s introduction moves from his description of the swelling to an assertion of the plague's resistance to the efforts of physicians: "a cura delle quali infermità né consiglio di medico né virtú di medicina alcuna pareva che valesse o facesse profitto" (**"I, intro.,"** 13). The *Decameron*'s portrayal of the plague-stricken Florentines who suffer from a disease that causes *enfiature* and remains unresponsive to medical attention clearly recalls the *Elegia*'s metaphorical depiction of Fiammetta's lovesickness.

While Boccaccio uses *enfiatura* to characterize lovesickness outside of the *Decameron,* he uses the adjectival form of the noun, *enfiato,* three times, in the *Decameron*'s story of Simona and Pasquino, to describe the effects of a poisonous sage leaf. I will consider this tale and examine the ways in which the adjective connects the tragic **"IV, 7"** to the introduction's portrayal of the plague when I turn to the **"Fourth Day,"** but I will first return to the introduction itself.

After he explains that the efforts of the medical establishment are unavailing, the narrator describes the speed of the illness: "non altramenti che faccia il fuoco alle cose secche o unte quando molto gli sono avvicinate" (**"I, intro.,"** 14). If we look again to Boccaccio's minor works, this simile also provides a convincing link between the effects of the disease and the effects of love. As Branca's notes point out, the metaphor of fire on an oily surface also occurs in the *proemio* of Boccaccio's *Filostrato*. The narrator, Filostrato, misses his absent beloved, Filomena:

> Quindi ogni aura o soave vento che viene, così nel viso ricevo quasi come il vostro sanza niuna fallo abbia tocco. Né è perciò troppo lungo questo mitigamento, ma quale sopra le cose unte veggiamo fiamme talvolta discorrere, tale sopra l'afflitto cuore questa soavità discorre, fuggendo subita per lo sopravvegnente pensiero che mi mostra non potervi vedere, essendo già di ciò sanza misura acceso il mio disio.[9]

The narrator of the *Filostrato*'s poem uses the oil on fire metaphor to describe how he is affected by a breeze blowing from the direction of Sannio, where his love is visiting. The flame on an oily surface functions here as an image of frustrated desire for an absent lover. In the *Decameron,* the same image of a flame running over "le cose . . . unte" serves as a figure for the pestilence racing through the healthy Florentines who cross its path. Again, Boccaccio has employed the same imagery to describe the effects of lovesickness and the consequences of the plague.

The language of excess ("sanza misura") employed in this passage from the *Filostrato* is also evident in the *Decameron*'s introduction. The narrator describes varying reactions to the plague. Some attempt to avoid the disease through moderation; they avoid "superfluità," and seal themselves off from the diseased city ("in quelle case ricogliendosi e racchiudendosi" [**"I, intro.,"** 20]).[10] Others follow the dictates of their appetites "senza modo e senza misura" and spend their days in perpetual debauchery (**"I, intro.,"** 21). The opposition between the Florentines who wander through the plague-stricken city without regard for "misura" and the Florentines who close themselves off from the plague by literally shutting their doors to the outside world recalls the **"Proemio"**'s implicit contrast of the narrator's experience of passion "oltre modo" (**"Proemio 3"**) to the oppressive enclosure of the *vaghe donne* within the confines of their rooms. The dichotomy will be reprised in the persistent polarity of the **"Fourth Day"**: the immoderate behavior of the lovelorn is juxtaposed against their adversaries' deliberate strategies and predilection for enclosure. As we will see, the language of containment and excess provides another important connection between the plague of the introduction and the passion of Filostrato's reign.

As the description of the depraved Florentines would indicate, the plague leads to a breakdown of legal codes. Not only are civic decrees ignored, but the fundamental rules governing familial behavior are also disregarded. The very structure of the family is disassembled by the pernicious presence of the plague: "l'un fratello l'altro abbandonava e il zio il nepote e la sorella il fratello e spesse volte la donna il suo marito; e, che maggior cosa è e quasi non credibile, li padri e le madri i figliuoli, quasi loro non fossero, di visitare e di servire schifavano" (**"I, intro.,"** 27). Examining the results of this disintegration of family bonds, the narrator focuses on female modesty. While a well-bred woman in pre-plague Florence would have objected to the attendance of a male servant, the collapse of the family and the consequent desertion of the sick creates a desperate situation in which female victims of the plague freely expose their bodies to male attendants: ". . . a lui senza alcuna vergogna ogni parte del corpo aprire . . . solo che la necessità della sua infermità il richiedesse; il che in quelle che ne guerirono fu forse di minore onestà, nel tempo che succedette, cagione" (**"I, intro.,"** 29). The direct result of the plague, then, is the collapse of the family, which, in turn, leads to the impurity of women. Confronted by the circumstances surrounding the epidemic, they come to value their "onestà" less and less. As we consider Pampinea's speech to the *brigata* assembled at Santa Maria Novella, to which we will now turn, we will continue to observe an increasingly firm association between the plague and *disonestà*.

Pampinea begins her speech to the young ladies gathered in the church by acknowledging their shared anxiety. They all have reason to fear for their lives. She asserts, "io comprendo . . . ciascuna di noi di se medesima dubitare" (**"I, intro.,"** 55), a statement that seems ambiguous enough to leave some room for interpretation. On the one hand, we might read Pampinea's words as "I understand . . . that each of us is doubtful on her own account." After all, the women are indeed quite vulnerable; their families are all dead or absent and the plague shows no signs of abating.[11] On the other hand, it might also be possible to understand Pampinea's words as an expression of self-doubt, as in "I realize that each of us has doubts about herself." Perhaps Pampinea is fearful that the conditions of the plague will force her and her friends to risk their virtue, just as the women described by the narrator diminish their modesty by exposing themselves to male servants. Pampinea's statement seems to allow for both renderings. Is Boccaccio therefore attempting to obscure the precise location of the object of the *brigata*'s anxiety? Are they fearful *for* themselves in the face of some external danger, or are they afraid of something situated *within* themselves?

As Pampinea's speech proceeds from a discussion of the general moral decay of the Florentines to a denunciation of the more specifically sexual sinfulness of her countrymen, the indication of an internal threat grows stronger. At first Pampinea laments the disregard for proper burial practices and the defiance of city law. She then indignantly represents the riotous behavior of the stopgap sextons in terms that suggest sexual misconduct: she describes "la feccia della nostra città, del nostro sangue riscaldata, chiamarsi becchini e in istrazio di noi andar cavalcando e discorrendo per tutto, con disoneste canzoni" (**"I, intro.,"** 57). "Cavalcare" is occasionally an equivocal verb in the *Decameron,* used as a metaphor for sexual intercourse, and its proximity to the adjective "disoneste" in this sentence further emphasizes its possible double meaning.[12] Moreover, while "disoneste" can mean "immoral" in a general sense, in this context "disoneste canzoni" clearly refers to obscene songs, such as the ones that Dioneo happily lists in the conclusion to the **"Fifth Day."**[13] Pampinea deplores the impropriety of the "becchini," but it is their lechery that prompts her virulent outburst. Finally, Pampinea's condemnation of monastic malfeasance exposes the essence of her grievance. Lamenting the failure of the average lay person to draw the distinction between the "cose oneste" and "quelle che oneste non sono" (again making use of this central opposition), Pampinea bewails,

> e non che le solute persone, ma ancora le racchiuse ne' monisteri, faccendosi a credere che quello a lor si convenga e non si disdica che all'altre, rotte della obedienza le leggi,[14] datesi a' diletti carnali, in tal guisa avvisando scampare, son divenute lascive e dissolute.
>
> (**"I, intro.,"** 62)

It is the specifically sexual indulgences of the monks that prompt Pampinea's ire. They do not merely fulfill their appetites, they fulfill their carnal appetites, and it is on this point that Pampinea lingers, designating the behavior of the monks with distinctly sexual adjectives. Pampinea's language, however, indicates that it is not the monks' carnality alone that signals the utter dissolution of the city; it is their attempt to "scampare," to escape, their enclosure. She exclaims that even monks shut up in monasteries ("racchiuse ne' monisteri") have indulged in carnal pleasures, "in tal guisa avvisando scampare." The monks' escape from their confinement seems as disturbing to Pampinea as their sexual activity. We may recall that the women in the **"Proemio"** are, like the monks, *racchiuse.* Does Pampinea's indignation at the monks' "escape" express a fear that even confinement fails to guarantee chastity? As a woman herself, accustomed to passing her time "racchiusa," and here in Santa Maria Novella appearing in a structure also associated with enclosure, the *hortus conclusus,*[15] Pampinea may fear the fate of the monks. Although also enclosed, she may, like them, attempt to "escape" and succumb to carnal pleasures. Does she not trust her own ability to stay *racchiusa*? After all, unlike the women of the **"Proemio,"** the women of the *brigata* have no family members to enforce their confinement. Their "escape" would be unopposed.[16] Moreover, as the narrator of the introduction indicates, even bedridden women who are literally *racchiuse* in their own homes, are at risk of jeopardizing their virtue. Noblewomen, confronted by the devastating effects of the epidemic, are forced to imperil their *onestà* by exposing their bodies to the male servants who wait on them.

As Pampinea's address proceeds, she continues to make use of the enclosed/free binary opposition (which we might also conceive of as closed/open, or inside/outside). The connotations of such an opposition, however, begin to mutate. She announces, in a period that is worth quoting at length:

> E per ciò, acciò che noi per ischifaltà o per traccutaggine non cadessimo in quello di che noi per avventura per alcuna maniera volendo potremmo *scampare*, . . . : io giudicherei ottimamente fatto che noi, sí come noi siamo, sí come molti innanzi a noi hanno fatto e fanno, di questa terra *uscissimo,* e *fuggendo* come la morte i *disonesti* essempli degli altri *onestamente* a' nostri luoghi in contado, . . . ce ne andassimo a stare, e quivi quella festa, quella allegrezza, quello piacere che noi potessimo, senza trapassare in alcuno atto il segno della ragione, prendessimo.
>
> (**"I, intro.,"** 65; my emphasis)

Pampinea's proposal seems to suggest that remaining in the city might allow the ladies to succumb to an unnamed sin; they might fall ("cadessimo"). Clearly Pampinea's verb choice here evokes the biblical *caduta,* and alludes to the sin she fails to name: if the women do not succeed in escaping from Florence ("scampare," "uscissimo," "fuggendo") they not only risk death, but risk *disonestà* ("disonesti essempli") as well. Escape no longer suggests transgression, but implies salvation, and enclosure no longer signifies virtue, but denotes sin. In the wake of the plague, the terms of the binary have been reversed.

Pampinea maintains the Edenic association begun in her "cadessimo" with her use of the phrase "senza trapassare in alcuno atto il segno della ragione." The locution undoubtedly makes reference to Adam's account of the Fall in Eden in *Paradiso* XXVI, 115-17: ". . . non il gustar del legno / fu per sé la cagion di tanto essilio, / ma solamente il trapassar del segno." By alluding to Adam's address to the pilgrim, Pampinea again underscores the nature of the proposed flight; she urges her friends to flee the site of possible sexual transgression and to avoid replicating the Fall of Adam and Eve.[17] As Pampinea's final words to the assembled ladies reiterate, to flee is to preserve their chastity, while to stay is to relinquish it.[18]

In addition to evoking Dante's Adam, Pampinea's coda stresses the central role of reason for the *brigata*. Pampinea proposes a pleasure trip to the country, using language that suggests carefree amusement ("festa," "allegrezza," "piacere"), yet she urges the *brigata* to keep their diversions within the bounds of reason. Again, Boccaccio employs the imagery of confinement and transgression while continually inverting the two categories. Pampinea first condemns the monks who wish to escape their confinement, endowing confinement with a positive value and escape with a negative one; then, urging her friends to avoid the monks' fate, she advocates an escape from the city, reversing her terms and endorsing flight; finally, she imposes a boundary around the pleasure garden of the *brigata*'s future, in the form of the "segno della ragione," again valorizing confinement and discouraging trespass. Several critics read Pampinea's call for reason as evidence of the *brigata*'s symbolic significance. Smarr, for example, writes, "with the assembling of the ladies, reason begins to reassert its dominance" and she sees the *brigata*'s withdrawal from the city as an "ascent, both physical and moral, from the animal or appetite-driven to the human or rationally good."[19] As we will see, however, the *brigata*'s relationship to reason, and to boundaries generally, is considerably more complex than these critics hold, and the certainty of their "ascent" is difficult to maintain in the wake of the content of their stories and their premature return to the plague-ridden city.[20] What I will argue for, and what we have already witnessed in Pampinea's slippery hold on the opposition of freedom and enclosure, is Boccaccio's depiction of a struggle, rather than an ascent. Rather than communicating a victory, the *brigata*'s words and actions enact a conflict.

Before we look at the *novelle* of the **"Fourth Day,"** it will be fruitful to examine the setting of Filostrato's tragic reign, a garden that, in the terms set up by Pampinea's speech, might be construed as a prelapsarian Eden.[21] As we survey the garden we see that it is represented simultaneously as a lush pleasance and a model of horticultural organization. It is characterized by beautiful order ("bello ordine" [**"III, intro.,"** 11]): its gorgeous flora are meticulously arranged; and its plants are neatly set out ("ordinate poste" [**"III, intro.,"** 7]). Although redolent with flourishing plant life, including grape vines, promising an abundant yield, and citrus trees, heavy with fruit, the garden is nothing if not controlled; the language of enclosure is employed throughout its description. The paths, for example, are hemmed in by plants ("le latora delle quali vie tutte di rosa' bianchi e vermigli e di gelsomini erano quasi *chiuse*"

[**"III, intro.,"** 6]) and the grass is surrounded by fruit trees ("un prato . . . *chiuso* dintorno di verdissimi e vivi aranci e di cedri, li quali, avendo i vecchi frutti e' nuovi" [**"III, intro.,"** 8; my emphasis]). Moreover, the garden itself is completely walled ("tutto era da torno *murato*" [**"III, intro.,"** 5; my emphasis]), circumscribed by a man-made device. The confinement of the flora recalls the *vaghe donne* of the **"Proemio,"** and the monks of the introduction, *racchiuse* within their rooms and cells. The tension, however, between the aromatic, fruitful plants and the order imposed on their growth more aptly recalls the situation of the *brigata*. Just as the young men and women aim for pleasure within the bounds of reason, so does the garden present fertile flowering, regulated by an unseen hand. Moreover, as in the **"Proemio"**'s statement of purpose, the garden provides both *diletto* and *utilità*: its fountain powers two working mills, which bring substantial profits to their owner. As we see, then, the second locale of the *brigata*'s retreat, and the setting for the tragic love stories of the **"Fourth Day,"** metaphorically responds to both the *brigata* and the work that tells their story. Furthermore, the description of the garden maintains the *Decameron*'s unstable binary of liberty and enclosure, thereby linking it to the imagery surrounding the plague and making it an appropriate setting for the **"Fourth Day"**'s tales of passionate desire.[22]

As the *brigata* approaches the **"Fourth Day"** the sexual impulses of both the men and women present are reconfirmed. While the women have laughed heartily at the tale of Alibech and Rustico, arguably the most obscene tale in the collection, and have frankly expressed their own wishes for sexual fulfillment several times,[23] the men, represented by Filostrato, express their sexual frustration through the metaphor of the wolves and the sheep (**"III, concl.,"** 1-3).[24] Moreover, Filostrato commences his reign by addressing the women as "amorose donne" (**"III, concl.,"** 5). Yet the *brigata* remains unwilling to act on its desires. If we understand the circumscribed structure of the lush second garden to be a figure for the *brigata*'s own contained passion, we will note with interest that, left to their own devices, the men and women choose not to wander from the garden's borders. We read, "era sí bello il giardino e sí dilettevole, che alcuno non vi fu che eleggesse di quello uscire per piú piacere altrove dover sentire" (**"III, concl.,"** 7). In other words, the members of the *brigata* settle for the possibility of less pleasure by staying within the garden's confines. By pursuing *piacere* only up to a certain point, their actions reflect their adherence to Pampinea's dictates, yet, at the same time, the *brigata*'s obedience prompts us to ask whether they trust themselves beyond the garden walls. After all, they move from a situation in Florence where their physical movements are no longer restricted by family members, and where chaos reigns, to a situation in the country where they gladly sojourn in an enclosed space and establish an elaborate code of behavior by which to govern their actions. Their reluctance to stray beyond the bounds of the garden further suggests their own need for restraint and again points to their true motive for fleeing the city: they could not rely on themselves to maintain their *onestà* in an atmosphere of utter freedom.

Many of the stories of the **"Fourth Day"** reassert the *brigata*'s dilemma, using many of the same terms established by the introduction's description of the plague. The **"Fourth Day"**'s introduction, a device signaling the singularity of the day, uses the *exemplum* of Filippo Balducci and his son to defend the narrator's work against its critics. The tale establishes the fundamental tension of the day, that of the struggle between *ingegno* and *natura,* by illustrating the unconquerable power of desire. The narrator tells how, despite Filippo's significant effort to prevent his son from experiencing worldly things, which includes secluding the boy on a deserted mountaintop for eighteen years, and despite Filippo's valiant, if comical, attempt to discourage his son's interest in the "brigata di belle giovani donne e ornate" by misidentifying the ladies as "papere," the father must admit his defeat: the boy's nature proves too strong for the father's cunning. The narrator writes, "sentí incontanente piú aver di forza la natura che il suo ingegno" (**"IV, intro.,"** 29). As in the introduction's description of the plague, in which human *senno* has no power over the raging epidemic, here human *ingegno* proves to be no match for *natura.*

The narrator articulates Filippo's lesson once more as he concludes his defense: "alle cui leggi, cioè della natura, voler contrastare troppo gran forze bisognano, e spesse volte non solamente invano ma con grandissimo danno del faticante s'adorperano" (**"IV, intro.,"** 41). The laws of nature are too strong to oppose; resisting them can cause serious harm. The **"Fourth Day"**'s introduction, then, with its *exemplum* of Filippo Balducci, and its vigorous defense of the content of the *novelle,* recalls the introduction's description of the plague and anticipates the day's central tension.[25]

The first story of the day perfectly illustrates this tension and exemplarily demonstrates the **"Fourth Day"**'s insistent connections to the concerns of both the introduction and the *brigata*. As the storytellers gather around the beautiful fountain in the middle of the garden,[26] Fiammetta narrates the tragic tale of Tancredi and Ghismonda. Tancredi, the Prince of Salerno, is distraught to discover an affair between his unmarried daughter, Ghismonda, and a palace servant, Guiscardo. He has the man killed and serves his daughter her lover's heart in a golden cup. Pouring poisonous liquid into the cup, she drinks its contents, and dies.[27] From the beginning of the tragic tale, the Prince is associated

with *ingegno*: Fiammetta describes Tancredi as "signore assai umano e di benigno ingegno" (**"IV, 1,"** 3). His daughter, on the other hand, adheres to the dictates of nature, seeking out a means to satisfy her sexual appetite. As she herself explains to her father, after he has confronted her with his knowledge of her affair, she is not made of stone; she has no choice but to obey the promptings of the flesh. Indeed, Ghismonda's constant repetition of the word *carne* both emphatically identifies her with her physical self, and underscores her carnal cravings.[28] The standard opposition between *ingegno* and *natura* is embodied in the conflict between Tancredi and Ghismonda.

The tension between the two categories, however, becomes significantly more complicated once we recognize Tancredi's incestuous passion for his daughter.[29] As Fiammetta points out, the prince's special love for his daughter prevents him from marrying her off until she is several years older than is customary, and once she has been widowed her father maintains his reluctance to part with her. She is still a young woman, and as she later puts it, "piena di concupiscibile disidero" (**"IV, 1,"** 34). Instead of satisfying her longings, however, she is waiting in her father's palace for a wedding that may never occur, recalling the figure of the *vecchi frutti* hanging from the branches of the citrus trees in the second garden (**"III, intro.,"** 8). Ghismonda's erotic needs are utterly disregarded by her father, and her delayed naming indicates a neglect for her independent existence altogether.[30] Rather than remind her father to find her a spouse, which, according to Ghismonda, would not be an "onesta cosa" (**"IV, 1,"** 5),[31] Ghismonda finds a lover, instructing him to enter her room through an abandoned cave that leads to it.

The physiognomy of the cave itself is of enormous interest. Leaving aside the obvious symbolism of the brambly cave and the leather-suited lover who enters it,[32] we might note the untended plantlife of the grotto; Fiammetta's description reads, ". . . la grotta, quasi da pruni e da erbe di sopra natevi era riturato" (**"IV, 1,"** 9). The thorns and weeds are left to spread where they will; no human hand restricts their growth, or arranges their placement. The cave is a picture of nature left to its own devices. It is utterly out of control and completely disordered. In other words, it is the very antithesis to the garden in which the storytellers are assembled, and, as such, it easily stands as a figure for unrestrained natural impulses.[33] Indeed, it furnishes an apt entry to the bedroom where Ghismonda unleashes her desires, and it provides a fitting backdrop for Tancredi's discovery of her passion.[34]

According to Fiammetta, Tancredi visits Ghismonda's room one morning after breakfast and, seeing that she is walking in the garden, decides to wait for her on a low stool by her bed rather than pull her away from her pleasure ("non volendo lei torre dal suo diletto" ["**IV, 1,**" 17]). Finding all of the room's windows closed ("trovando le finestre della camera chiuse" ["**IV, 1,**" 17]), the prince pulls the bed-curtain around him, as if purposely attempting to conceal himself ("quasi come se studiosamente si fosse nascoso" ["**IV, 1,**" 17]), and promptly falls asleep. While he naps Ghismonda returns, opens the secret door for Guiscardo ("aperto l'uscio a Guiscardo" ["**IV, 1,**" 18]), and proceeds to have sex with her lover inches away from the prince. Waking, Tancredi is dismayed beyond belief ("dolente . . . oltre modo" ["**IV, 1,**" 19]), but, remaining cautiously hidden, does not cry out. When the lovers depart, Guiscardo returning to the *grotta,* and Ghismonda exiting the room ("s'uscí della camera" ["**IV, 1,**" 20]), Tancredi drops down to the garden through the bedroom window, despite his advanced age ("ancora che vecchio fosse, da una finestra di quella si calò nel giardino" ["**IV, 1,**" 21]). As Guido Almansi points out, the plot provides no explanation for Tancredi's fenestral exit. Rather, the prince's unconventional withdrawal speaks to a change in his emotional state.[35] Earlier in the scene the prince is entirely associated with enclosure. He lies asleep, wrapped in a bed-curtain, in a room with no open windows. His eyes are closed; the curtain is closed; the windows are closed. His passionate daughter, on the other hand, returns from a garden, where she has been enjoying her *diletto,* and *opens* a door for her lover. When she has satisfied her considerable sexual appetite, she *exits* the room, and her lover returns to a grotto whose significance we have already explored. The opposition of outside and inside, or opened and closed, is clearly employed here to signal the conflict between Ghismonda and her father.[36] As Tancredi literally opens his eyes to his daughter's sex life, he crosses from one side of the binary opposition to the other. He feels an excessive emotion ("dolente oltre modo") and not only does he leave the room, but he leaves via the window, into the garden. He and his passion have been awakened at the same moment and the shifting opposition of freedom and confinement has communicated his awakening to the reader.[37]

The symbolic significance of the window is easy to understand: it provides a means of access between the inside and the outside. As such, windows frequently play crucial roles in the many stories in the **Decameron,** which involve illicit sexual activity.[38] Tancredi's use of the window, then, gestures toward his movement from the physical confinement that represents his repression to the opening that suggests the presence of his forbidden passion.

The excess symbolized by the open window also characterizes the prince's reaction to his discovery. The violence of this excess expresses itself in Guiscardo's mur-

der. Before he dies, however, Guiscardo utters the single line allotted to him: "Amor può troppo piú che né voi né io possiamo" ("**IV, 1,**" 23).[39] With admirable concision Guiscardo articulates the central theme of the day: love, as part of nature, cannot be stopped by human will.

Ghismonda's actions speak as loudly as Guiscardo's words; her suicide signals her autonomy from the rule of her father. She has utter command over herself. She demonstrates her self-control in her final confrontation with her father, in which we observe an odd reversal of Tancredi's and Ghismonda's traditional roles. During their meeting, in which Ghismonda learns of her lover's capture, she does not shed a single tear: "ma pur questa viltà vincendo il suo animo altiero, il viso suo con maravigliosa forza fermò" ("**IV, 1,**" 30). Tancredi, on the other hand, weeps like a child who has been spanked: "come farebbe un fanciul ben battuto" ("**IV, 1,**" 29). The simile clearly recalls the miserable lover of the *Vita nuova* (XII, 2). In likening Tancredi to the Dantean protagonist, Boccaccio draws attention to the origin of the prince's tears: his frustrated erotic passion for his daughter.[40] The prince's tears also serve to draw attention to his daughter's contrasting, tearless response. Where Tancredi is out of control, his daughter adeptly conquers her *viltà.*[41] As Giuseppe Mazzotta points out, "Tancredi is a tyrant, who cannot rule over others any more than he can rule over himself, or, simply, he cannot rule over others *because* he cannot rule over himself."[42] As the *novella* closes, Tancredi's change is complete. No longer restrained or controlled, Tancredi's passionate tears reveal the truth of Guiscardo's statement. The prince was neither able to control his daughter's desires by confining her to his palace, nor successful in checking his own incestuous passions. Like the plague in the introduction, the forces of love are too strong to master.

The tragic tale of Tancredi and Ghismonda affects the women in the *brigata* so strongly that, like Tancredi, they start to cry. Their tears may reflect their identification with Ghismonda, given that their story shares many of the same elements as Ghismonda's story. For example, Ghismonda's mother is never mentioned. Her family structure appears incomplete. As we know, the families of the *brigata* have also been disrupted. Like Ghismonda, the women in the *brigata,* although as old as twenty-eight, are unmarried. Also, the *diletto* that Tancredi assumes Ghismonda to derive from her stroll in her garden recalls the *piacere* that impels the company to remain in their garden. Finally, the insistent opposition of confinement and freedom recalls the language of Pampinea's speech, and firmly links the subject of "**IV, 1,**" passion, to the subject of the introduction, plague. I would, however, suggest that the tears of the *brigata* may represent their identification with Tancredi as much as their identification with his daughter: confronted by the depiction of the prince's failure to contain his passion, the *brigata* may be on the verge of recognizing the inevitability of their own downfall.[43]

Several of the remaining stories of the **"Fourth Day"** reiterate the points made in **"IV, 1"** and amplify our understanding of both the **"Fourth Day"**'s connection to the introduction and the motivation behind the *brigata*'s retreat. The second, fourth, and fifth *novelle*, like the tale of Ghismonda and Tancredi, all tell of an opposition between sexual desire and familial rule. In the second story, Frate Alberto leaps into the Grand Canal to escape from Monna Lisetta's angry and quickly approaching brothers-in-law to great comic effect. The fourth story, on the other hand, narrates a tragic opposition between family and desire: Gerbino's love for the daughter of the King of Tunis impels him to violate the pledge of the grandfather who raised him, which in turn prompts his grandfather to put his own grandson to death, to keep his word to the Tunisians. The well-known tale of Lisabetta and the pot of basil, **"IV, 5,"** also depicts a lover whose family members oppose her affair. A sister to Ghismonda, Lisabetta has not yet been married and when her brothers discover her love for Lorenzo they kill their sister's lover for fear of staining the family's reputation. Like the *brigata*, and again like Ghismonda, Lisabetta derives pleasure from a garden, although in Lisabetta's story, her garden, a basil pot concealing her lover's severed head, is of pitifully reduced proportions.[44]

Moving to the sixth and seventh stories of the day we observe that the settings of the amorous liaisons of these *novelle* are, like the *brigata*'s location on the **"Fourth Day,"** gardens. In fact, the garden of the sixth story is described as a "bel giardino" (**"IV, 6,"** 9), thus recalling the "bel giardino" of **"IV, intro.,"** 44. The ill-fated lovers of Panfilo's tale, the unmarried Andreuola and the humbly born Gabriotto, frolic at the base of a beautiful fountain ("a piè d'una bellissima fontana" [**"IV, 6,"** 12]), just as the *brigata* gathers around their own lovely font ("vicini alla bella fonte" [**"IV, intro.,"** 45]). The seventh story's lovers, Simona and Pasquino, also dally in a garden, with tragic consequences.[45] The physical similarities between the location of the storytellers and the setting for the fatal liaisons of the sixth and seventh tales suggest several compelling conclusions. The shared garden setting seems to mark the activity of the *brigata*, storytelling, as an analogue for the activities of Andreuola, Gabriotto, Simona, and Pasquino: sex. Yet, at the same time, the tragic outcome of the lovers' Edenic sojourn again implies the inevitability of the *brigata*'s own fall. Finally, the events of the sixth and seventh stories remind us that, as in Jonathan

Usher's phrase (276), the garden is an essentially ambivalent symbol, one that simultaneously denotes innocence and transgression.

Before we glance at the final stories of the **"Fourth Day,"** we may recall the verbal echo of the plague's symptoms in the story of Simona and Pasquino. As already noted, the seventh story is the only place in the *Decameron* where we find the adjective *enfiato*. When Pasquino rubs his teeth with a poisonous sage leaf he dies immediately, completely swollen, with dark spots covering his entire body ("tutto enfiato e pieno d'oscure macchie per lo viso e per lo corpo divenuto" [**"IV, 7,"** 14]).[46] The word "enfiato," and the presence of the "oscure macchie," remind us immediately of the "certe enfiature" and the "macchie nere o livide" of the plague victims (**"I, intro.,"** 10-11). Pasquino's death could easily be attributed to the same disease that prompts the *brigata* to flee the city. The verbal echoes of the plague in the description of Pasquino again associates the epidemic with love. By attributing his friend's death to his liaison with Simona, lo Stramba's accusation, charging Simona with poisoning her lover (**"IV, 7,"** 14), reinforces the connection between desire and plague. Moreover, the link between the afflicted Florentines and the lover in the garden implies that no place is safe from disease, least of all a garden. The ramifications for the assembled storytellers are clear: their retreat does not guarantee their immunity from the plague.

The eighth story of the **"Fourth Day,"** the tale of Girolamo and Salvestra, sustains the connection between the plague and desire, both by illustrating and rearticulating the impossibility of a triumph of *senno* over *natura* (**"IV, 8,"** 3), and by employing the language of excess associated with the plague in the introduction ("oltre misura" [**"IV, 8,"** 14]; "oltre modo" [**"IV, 8,"** 25]). Moreover, as, Branca's notes point out (*Decameron* I, 561n5), Neifile's exclamation at the close of the story recalls a similar locution in the introduction. Neifile declares, "Maravigliosa cosa è a pensare quanto sieno difficili a investigare le forze d'amore!" (**"IV, 8,"** 32). Similarly, as he begins to describe the qualities of the plague, the introduction's narrator proclaims, "Maravigliosa cosa è a udire quello che io debbo dire" (**"I, intro.,"** 16).[47] The shared "maravigliosa cosa" connects "le forze d'amore" with the "qualità della pestilenzia" (**"I, intro.,"** 17), again placing the two phenomena in Mazzotta's metonymic contiguity with one another (30).

Passion and the plague are once more equated in the ninth story, in much the same way as in Fiammetta's tale of Tancredi and Ghismonda. The fervent desire of Guiglielmo Rossiglione's wife for his friend and *doppelgänger*, Guiglielmo Guardastango, prompts Rossiglione to kill Guardastango and force his wife to eat the dead man's heart.[48] Like Ghismonda, when confronted with Guiscardo's heart, Rossiglione's wife takes her own life; she jumps out of a window. Just as her love for Guardastango is "fuor di misura" (**"IV, 9,"** 6), so too does her death take her *fuori*. Her passion for her lover is characterized by her excess, by her passing beyond a certain limit. Her love passes beyond *misura*, and, at her death, her body passes beyond the *finestra*. Unlike the members of the *brigata*, the wife of Rossiglione and lover of Guardastango is not reluctant to "trapassar il segno." The immoderate desire of the ninth story's heroine, like the plague that occasions the bucolic sojourn of the storytellers, acknowledges no obstacles and knows no bounds.

As we come to the end of the **"Fourth Day,"** the bounds that hold the *brigata*'s movements in check seem to begin to give way. When Dioneo finishes his tale and Filostrato crowns Fiammetta the next day's queen, the company disperses to wander around the garden. The text reads:

> Costoro adunque, parte per lo giardino, la cui bellezza non era da dover troppo tosto rincrescere, e parte verso la mulina che fuor di quel macinavano, e chi qua e chi là, a prender secondo i diversi appetiti diversi diletti si diedono infino all'ora della cena.
>
> (**"IV, concl.,"** 7)

The members of the *brigata* have finally left the garden's borders. No longer confined by boundaries, they appear free to move about wherever they wish, and some of them choose to move outside the garden of "bello ordine." The *brigata*'s departure from the garden walls here stands in explicit contrast to their willingness to remain within the confines of the garden at the close of the **"Third Day."** In the course of a day the company has grown more venturesome, more experimental, and, it would appear, more intent on satisfying their appetites. The ten stories of the day have effected a change in their behavior.

While we consider the *brigata*'s striking gesture of transgression, however, we might wish to bear in mind the destination of the company's bold journey; their excursion only takes them as far as the two windmills. The purpose of the mills is manifestly utilitarian: they harness the energy of the fountain's waters and channel it for a tidy profit. The *brigata*'s interest in the mills, then, like their appreciation of the controlled, but lush, garden, might stem from a metaphorical identification of the mill's operation and the organization of their retreat. Just as the *canaletti . . . belli e artificiosamente fatti* (**"III, intro.,"** 10) direct the water from the *bella fonte* to the useful mills, the thematically predetermined and carefully arranged stories of the *brigata* conceal any potential erotic impulses of the storytellers and direct their desires toward a common goal. As the garden settings of the sixth and seventh stories of the day make clear, the *brigata*'s tales can be seen as a means of sub-

limating their own carnal desires. Like the mill, the *brigata* puts pleasure to use, conducting their erotic impulses toward narration instead of sex and depicting others fulfilling the passions that they themselves resist. Nevertheless, given the company's previous reluctance to stray beyond the garden walls, I would argue that their adventurous actions at the end of the **"Fourth Day"** point to a new willingness to overstep the bounds that confine them.

The effects of the **"Fourth Day"** are far-reaching. Not only do the ten *novelle* alter the *brigata*'s sense of boundaries, but they prompt a remarkably uniform response. The *brigata* collectively objects to the theme imposed on them by Filostrato. At the beginning of her story, Pampinea decides to deviate from the mood established by the previous tale (**"IV, 2,"** 4); as Dioneo begins, he voices complaints about the topic foisted on his friends (**"IV, 10,"** 3); accepting her crown, Fiammetta admonishes Filostrato with the words "acciò che meglio t'aveggi di quel che fatto hai . . ." (**"IV, concl.,"** 5). The *brigata* continues to grumble throughout the following day (e.g., **"V, 2,"** 3), apparently still aching from the previous day's sorrow. The storytellers' obvious discomfort with telling and hearing the *novelle* of Filostrato's day, and the change in their movements induced by them, attest to the presence of something powerful within the stories. It would appear that the *novelle* communicate something to the *brigata* that the *brigata* does not want to hear: the stories, with their insistent correspondence between passion and plague, suggest that the disease that the storytellers flee cannot be eluded. The force of law cannot stop it; the authority of familial bonds cannot check it; even the erection of physical barriers cannot prevent the course of passion. As Tancredi's painful awakening makes clear, bolted doors and locked windows cannot block the path of desire. As the *brigata* wanders past the confines of their garden we might imagine that they are coming to grips with the truth: what they flee is inside them and cannot be contained.

Nevertheless, although the company returns to Florence considerably earlier than they had originally planned, the *brigata* does not return defeated. As Panfilo tells us at the close of his reign, the young men and women have all behaved "onestamente" throughout their sojourn in the country (**"X, concl.,"** 4), returning to avoid the threat posed by new members to their company. The ten Florentines have not yet relinquished their contest with the disease within them. Rather, they return to the city as they left it: engaged in an ongoing battle with the conflicts that plague them. They may come home wiser, perhaps less optimistic about their ability to conquer the forces within them, but they do not come home losers. The ***Decameron*** is not a depiction of the failure of the storytellers to maintain their *onestà*, any more than it is a representation of the triumph of the company over the destructive forces represented by the plague.[49] Rather it is a portrait of a struggle, taking place within the breasts of seven women and three men, during two weeks in the hills above Florence.

Notes

1. For all citations from the *Decameron,* and for all references to Vittore Branca's notes, I will be using Giovanni Boccaccio, *Decameron,* ed. Vittore Branca, 2 vols. (Turin: Einaudi, 1980).

2. I assent to Vittore Branca's exhortation to preserve the historical reality of the plague (". . . nello stesso tempo, piano e quadro dovevano superare sensi allegorici e metaforici e allusivi per ancorare saldamente alla realtà, alla 'storia,' quelle rappresentazioni esemplari" [*Boccaccio medievale e nuovi studi sul "Decameron,"* 6th ed. (Florence: Sansoni, 1986) 34]). I do not, however, consider it reductive to examine the plague in light of affinities to lovesickness that are clearly present within the text. Nor do I believe that it deprives the plague of its historical and literal reality to develop an understanding of the meaning of the epidemic within the *Decameron* that might transcend physical disease.

3. Perhaps Giuseppe Mazzotta's phrase for the relationship between lovesickness and the plague strikes the proper balance between exact correspondence and nebulous link. He asserts that *aegritudo amoris* "stands in a metonymic contiguity to the plague" (*The World at Play in Boccaccio's* Decameron [Princeton: Princeton UP, 1986] 30). On lovesickness in the *Decameron,* see Aldo D. Scaglione, *Nature and Love in the Late Middle Ages* (Berkeley: U of California P, 1963) 60-65; and Massimo Ciavolella, "La tradizione dell' 'aegritudo amoris' nel *Decameron,*" *Giornale storico della letteratura italiana* 147 (1970): 498-517.

4. For a reading of the *proemio* that draws attention to the proem's explicit connection between sexuality and pestilence, see Robert Hollander, "The Proem of the *Decameron*: Boccaccio between Ovid and Dante," *Miscellanea di studi danteschi: in memoria di Silvio Pasquazi,* eds. Alfonso Paolella, Vincenzo Piacella, Giovanni Turco (Naples: Federico & Ardia, 1993) 430.

5. For more on this binome, see Robert Hollander, "*Utilità* in Boccaccio's *Decameron,*" *Studi sul Boccaccio* 15 (1985-86): 215-33.

6. For a representation of the plague that differs from Boccaccio's, see Gene A. Brucker, "Florence and the Black Death" in *Boccaccio: secoli di vita,* eds. Marga Cottino-Jones and Edward Tuttle (Ravenna: Longo, 1977) 30.

7. Janet Levarie Smarr, *Boccaccio and Fiammetta: The Narrator as Lover* (Urbana: U of Illinois P, 1986) 266 n2.

8. Giovanni Boccaccio, *Elegia di Madonna Fiammetta,* eds. Carlo Salinari and Natalino Sapegno (1952; Turin: Einaudi, 1976) my emphasis.

9. Giovanni Boccaccio, *Filostrato,* in *Tutte le opere di Giovanni Boccaccio,* ed. Vittore Branca (Verona: Mondadori, 1964) vol. 2, *proemio* 14.

10. For the tradition of Florentine asceticism and the culture of penitence, see Lucia Battaglia Ricci, *Ragionare nel giardino: Boccaccio e i cicli pittorici del "Trionfo della morte"* (Rome: Salerno, 1987) 45-96.

11. I, intro. 69: "per ciò che i nostri, o morendo o da morte fuggendo, quasi non fossimo loro, sole in tanta afflizione n'hanno lasciate." The *brigata*'s missing families also link them to the characters of the stories of the "Fourth Day," many of whom lack one or both parents.

12. The "Third Day" provides several examples of Boccaccio's equivocal use of "cavalcare." See the story of Masetto's exhausting sojourn at a Tuscan nunnery ("III, 1.32" and "III, 1.34") and the bawdy tale of Don Felice and Isabetta, the wife of Puccio de' Rinieri ("III, 4.25"). See also "VIII, 4.32," for a later example of this verb's sexual connotations. It is true that Pampinea is ostensibly and plausibly describing church officials riding horseback, yet, at the same time, it does not seem infeasible, given the additional meaning of "cavalcare" within the *Decameron* and given Pampinea's subsequent description of the misconduct of other individuals associated with the church, that she is also condemning behavior of a sexual nature.

13. Branca points to the central importance of the words "onestà," "onesto," and "onestamente" for the *brigata,* calling them the "parole-emblema della vita di questi giovani" (*Boccaccio medievale* 39). It seems fair to attribute the same centrality to the antonyms of these "parole-emblema." As we will see, the *brigata*'s preoccupation with the *onestà-disonestà* dyad continues throughout the introduction and surfaces with regularity in the stories of the "Fourth Day." See Branca's extensive list of the uses of *onestà* and its variants in the *Decameron,* also in *Boccaccio medievale* 39.

14. The phrasing of this statement distinctly recalls Cato's indignant question to Dante and Virgil when he sees that their path to the shores of Purgatory has taken them through Inferno. He asks, "Son le *leggi* d'abisso così *rotte*? / o è mutato in ciel novo consiglio, / che dannati, venite a le mie

grotte?" (*Purg.* I, 46; my emphasis). I am using Petrocchi's edition of the *Commedia,* 4 vols. (Milan: Mondadori, 1966-67). While Pampinea seems entirely ignorant of the long tradition of clerical misbehavior, she expresses her outrage at the upheaval of monastic convention and the monks' disobedience of their holy vows in the same language as Cato, as if suggesting that, for her, a monastic vow ought to carry the same weight as Cato's divine law. For more on Boccaccio's relationship to Dante, see Robert Hollander's extensive work on the subject, for example: "Boccaccio's Dante: Imitative Distance (*Decameron* "I 1" and "VI 10")," *Studi sul Boccaccio* 13 (1981-82): 169-98; "*Decameron*: the Sun Rises in Dante," *Studi sul Boccaccio* 14 (1983-84): 241-55; and "Boccaccio's Dante," *Italica* 63 (1986): 278-89.

15. See Mazzotta, *The World at Play* 53.

16. Teodolinda Barolini's article, "'Le parole son feminine e i fatti sono maschi': Toward a Sexual Politics of the *Decameron* (*Decameron* II 10)," *Studi sul Boccaccio* 21 (1993): 175-97, addresses the issues of female enclosure and the effects of escape. See, especially, 181-82 and 194-95. In looking at "II, 9," Barolini examines the freedom that accompanies Zinevra's assumed male identity, writing: "Zinevra takes on male mobility in order to return to female immobility; she transforms herself into a man in order to be able to go back to being a woman, the loyal wife of the foolish and disloyal Bernabò" (182). The use of escape in order to restore a condition of confinement will prove central to my discussion of the *brigata*'s ambivalence toward the garden setting of the "Third" and "Fourth Days," and their precipitous return to Florence after the "Tenth Day." Although we employ many of the same terms, Barolini's investigation of Boccaccio's use of the confinement/transgression dyad differs greatly from mine. The *Decameron,* however, consistently proves elastic enough to accommodate easily many divergent, and equally persuasive, critical opinions; multiplicity is arguably the core attribute of Boccaccio's work.

17. Pampinea's exhortation, however, will lead them into a garden, rather than away from one, and, as we examine the setting of the "Fourth Day," it will profit us to remember the Edenic backdrop of their retreat. Mazzotta, who also notes the Dantean suggestion of Pampinea's language, reads Pampinea's line as an example of Boccaccio's irony (42).

18. "ricordivi che egli non si disdice piú a noi l'onestamente andare, che faccia a gran parte dell'altre lo star disonestamente" ("I, intro. 72").

19. Smarr, *Boccaccio and Fiammetta* 167. Giorgio Bárberi Squarotti similarly asserts that the *brigata*'s pursuit of reason differentiates them from the pleasure-seeking citizens of Florence, and redeems their flight from the crisis stricken city. He writes that reason is figured "come crisma che consacra la validità, ora, della scelta del modo d'agire di Pampinea, delle altre sei donne, di tutti coloro che abbandonano la città, in quanto li distingue nel privilegio di obbedienze a una legge superiore . . ." ("La 'cornice' del 'Decameron' o il mito di Robinson," *Il potere della parola: studi sul "Decameron"* [Naples: Federico & Ardia, 1989] 23). Edith Kern also reads the *Decameron* as "an illustration of Boccaccio's belief . . . in the powers of Love and Nature tempered by Reason" ("The Gardens in the *Decameron* Cornice," *PMLA* 66 [1951]: 523). Mirko Bevilacqua, while also examining the *brigata*'s investment in the bounds of reason, frames the issue in terms of a discussion of class and the carnivalesque. See "Il 'giardino' come struttura idelogico-formale del *Decameron*," *L'ideologia letteraria del* Decameron (Rome: Bulzoni, 1978) 73-74. Branca, arguing, like Kern, for the triumph of the *brigata*'s virtue, writes: "attraverso la prova eccezionale voluta dalla Provvidenza . . . attraverso l'oscura e spietata procella della peste, essi avevano serbata intatta, anzi avevano rafforzata e accresciuta la loro gentilezza e la loro generosità" (*Boccaccio medievale* 37). Aldo S. Bernardo also tends toward a moral reading of the *Decameron.* His understanding of the *brigata,* however, seems to contradict Branca's hopeful interpretation. Bernardo calls the *brigata* the "exemplification of the false good whose self-centeredness is the exact opposite of Christian doctrine and life" and he sees the plague's function as a reminder of the fragility of the human condition ("The Plague as Key to Meaning in Boccaccio's *Decameron*," *The Black Death: The Impact of the Fourteenth-Century Plague,* ed. Daniel William [Binghamton: Center for Medieval and Early Renaissance Studies, 1982] 49).

20. It is important to keep in mind Pampinea's proposal to remain in the country until the plague has passed ("I, intro. 71"). The *brigata*'s return two weeks later to an unchanged city must therefore be considered premature.

21. For a far-reaching examination of the implications of the *brigata*'s geographical shift, see Marga Cottino-Jones, "The City/Country Conflict in the *Decameron*," *Studi sul Boccaccio* 8 (1974): 147-84.

22. Discussion of the second garden generally acknowledges the friction between its fertility and its confinement, but, more often than not, attempts

to look for the conflict's solution rather than observe its operation. For example, Kern forcefully argues for the garden's representation of the triumph of reason over nature. She writes, "it should be pointed out quite clearly that Nature and Love in the *Decameron* are not wild, romantic forces. The Venus of Boccaccio is also the goddess of 'beautiful order' . . . and therefore Nature's strength is tempered by reason" (520). Lucia Marino, on the other hand, fails even to recognize the tension between the two forces in the second garden, calling it an "other worldly paradise, somehow abstracted from historical time," in apparent oblivion of the presence of the profit-making mills (*The* Decameron *"Cornice": Allusion, Allegory, and Iconology* [Ravenna: Longo, 1979] 87). Jonathan Usher, however, does not attempt to place the garden within the realm of reason or outside the realm of time. Rather, he remarks, "the garden remains essentially ambivalent as a symbol" ("Frame and Novella Gardens in the *Decameron*," *Medium Aevum* 58 [1989]: 276). It is the garden's ambivalence which forms the essence of Boccaccio's description and which so compellingly links it to depictions of the plague, lovesickness, and the *brigata* itself. For a cogent discussion of the second garden's artificiality and its consequent reflection of the order established by the *brigata,* see Bárberi Squarotti 38-42, especially 39-40.

23. Female members of the *brigata* exclaim "Idio faccia noi goder del nostro [amore]" in "III, 6.50" and "III, 7.101" and employ a similar expression in "III, 3.55."

24. See Marina Scordilis Brownlee, "Wolves and Sheep: Symmetrical Undermining in Day III," *Romance Notes* 24 (1984): 262-66.

25. This partial *novella* also establishes a central paradigm for the day, that of love, coercion, and transgression. See Roberto Fedi, "Il 'regno' di Filostrato: natura e struttura della Giornata IV del *Decameron*," *MLN* 102 (1987): 48.

26. The *bella fonte* ("IV, intro. 45") provides the perfect setting for the *brigata*'s activities. Like the fountain, which serves both an ornamental and a functional purpose, the *brigata* is concerned both with *piacere* and *ordine.*

27. Among the more interesting critical readings of this much discussed *novella* are Giovanni Getto, *Vita di forme e forme di vita nel* Decameron (Turin: Petrini, 1958 [rpt. 1986]) 95-138; Carlo Muscetta, *Giovanni Boccaccio* (Bari: Laterza, 1972) 221-25; Giuseppe Mazzotta 131-58; Guido Almansi, "Lettura della novella di Tancredi e Ghismonda," *Il Verri* 27 (1968): 20-35 (trans. into

English as chapter five of *The Writer as Liar: Narrative Technique in the "Decameron"* [London: Routledge and Kegan Paul, 1975] 133-57); Millicent Marcus, *An Allegory of Form: Literary Self-Consciousness in the* Decameron (Saratoga, CA: Anma Libri, 1979) 44-63; and Marga Cottino-Jones, *Order from Chaos: Social and Aesthetic Harmonies in Boccaccio's* Decameron (Washington: UP of America, 1982) 66-79.

28. In fact, Ghismonda uses the word *carne* a total of five times in the space of two pages of Branca's edition. See "IV, 1.33" (twice); "IV, 1.34"; "IV, 1.39" (twice).

29. The initial discussion of Tancredi's incestuous desire can be found in Alberto Moravia's 1953 essay, "Boccaccio," *Il Trecento* (Florence: Sansoni, 1953) 141 (rpt. in *L'uomo come fine e altri saggi* [Milan: Bompiani, 1963] 65-87). Muscetta takes up this reading in *Giovanni Boccaccio* (221), and Guido Almansi develops it at length in "Lettura della novella di Tancredi e Ghismonda" (22). I will not rehearse the specific details of these critics' reasoning; I will only note that I find the argument convincing. David Wallace also notes the incestuous overtones of Tancredi's affection for his daughter, but he reads them as a personal extension of the king's political power, writing, "the hints of incestuous motivation that run through this *novella* . . . issue from the collapsing of the political into the personal that obtains in despotic realms: Tancredi cannot bear to see another man share his daughter's affections because she is his only heir; a man who shared his daughter would threaten to share the power of the princedom that Tancredi, at present, uniquely embodies . . ." (*Giovanni Boccaccio*: Decameron [Cambridge: Cambridge UP, 1991] 54).

30. She is not named until "IV, 1.17."

31. Ghismonda's concern for *onestà* naturally links her to the young women hearing her story, whose own preoccupation with *oneste cose* has already been established. For the conflict between Ghismonda and the social conventions that constrain her to conceal her lover, see Cottino-Jones, *Order from Chaos* 68-70.

32. Almansi provides a thorough examination of this point in "Lettura della novella di Tancredi e Ghismonda" (27).

33. Cottino-Jones also notes the conflict between the neglected *grotta* and the formal gardens depicted elsewhere in Boccaccio's work. In her reading of *loci naturali* in the "Fourth Day," the *giardino* of the first *novella* becomes a symbol of restrained courtly society and Guiscardo's overgrown *grotta*

stands as an emblem for unbridled love (*Order from Chaos* 70). Cottino-Jones examines these gardens, grottos, and woods within the larger context of social conflict, and she presents a convincing reading of the "Fourth Day"'s gardens as contested areas of love, escape, and violent retribution ("The City/Country Conflict" 166-68; *Order from Chaos* 70-79), concluding that, in the *novelle* of this day, the *loco naturale* functions as an essentially ambiguous symbol.

34. Wallace observes that "the boudoir, with its two entrances, now becomes a contested, intermediate realm: one door leads to the public domain of court society, and the other opens out to the wild side, a subterranean world of illicit desire" (55). In this reading, Ghismonda's bedroom functions as the geographical mediator between controlled conformity and unrestrained passion. As such, it is an ideal location for the revelation of both Ghismonda's and Tancredi's concealed desires.

35. Almansi 29.

36. For an alternate reading of the bedroom setting of this scene, which construes my inside/outside dyad as inside/non-existent, see Vittorio Russo's 1965 essay, "Il senso del tragico nel Decameron," *'Con le muse in Parnaso.' Tre studi sul Boccaccio* (Naples: Bibliopolis, 1983) 66-67. Russo suggests that, despite the action that takes place outside of the bedroom, the only scenes enacted for this *novella*'s reader are staged in Ghismonda's bedroom, thereby heightening the theatrical tragedy of the tale.

37. In Almansi's words: "Il salto della finestra non è quindi una necessità dell'azione, ma una rappresentazione indiretta in termini esterni e comportamentistici dell'eccitazione fisica e del turbamento sensuale del personaggio" (29).

38. The window can function as a sign for the possibility of sex, as in "III, 5," where two towels hanging from a window become a signal from one lover to another, or as in "VII, 8" where the towels are replaced by a piece of string; it can provide a means of access between two lovers, as in "III, 3," where a young man steals into a young woman's bedroom at her bidding; and it can furnish a means of escape if the illicit sex is threatened with discovery, as in "IV, 2," where Frate Alberto dives out of Monna Lisetta's window.

39. Getto argues that Guiscardo's sentence draws attention to the subjectivity of love: as the first word and the subject of the verb, "amor" literally dominates the sentence (108). John Charles Nelson also focuses on Guiscardo's parting words, claiming that they articulate Boccaccio's naturalist ethic.

See John Charles Nelson, "Love and Sex in the *Decameron*," *Philosophy and Humanism: Renaissance Essays in Honor of Paul Oskar Kristeller,* ed. Edward P. Mahoney (New York: Columbia UP, 1976) 138.

40. Branca (*Decameron* I, 478 n1) also notes the Dantean parallel, as does Mazzotta in *The World at Play* (145).

41. For more on the connotations of a woman who is *ferma* rather than *mobile,* see Barolini's discussion of Zinevra's unwavering loyalty in "'Le parole son feminine e i fatti sono maschi': Toward a Sexual Politics of the *Decameron*" (181-82). According to Mario Baratto, Ghismonda's self-restraint is a characteristic typical of a Boccaccian woman. Mario Baratto, *Realtà e stile nel Decameron* (Rome: Editori Riuniti, 1984) 191.

42. Mazzotta, *The World at Play* 141-42. The concept of self-dominion is an important one for Boccaccio. See Guido di Monforte's counsel to Carlo: "grandissima gloria v'è aver vinto Manfredi, ma molto maggiore è se medesimo vincere . . . vincete voi medesimo e questo appetito raffrenate" ("X, 6.32"). Florio's father, Felice, uses much the same language in the *Filocolo,* when he advises: "e non pensi quanta sia la viltà, la quale ha il tuo animo occupato in disporti ad amare così fatta femina, come tu ami . . . hai lasciato vincere il tuo virile animo . . . (*Filocolo*, in *Tutte le opere*, ed. Antonio Enzo Quaglio, vol. 1, II, 14.3). Felice's use of gender in relation to love and self-control is particularly interesting in light of Boccaccio's depiction of a feminized Tancredi at the end of "IV, 1." Ghismonda herself makes the connection between disordered passion and women when she disdainfully commands, "Or via, va con le femine a spander le lagrime" ("IV, 1.45").

43. Almansi, writing of Tancredi, uses terms that we might easily instead apply to the *brigata*: Tancredi's madness ". . . è la follia di un uomo diviso da se stesso, che non riesce più a comprendersi e che tenta disparatamente di razionalizzare i suoi istinti e le sue azioni" (32).

44. For more on Lisabetta's miniature, and macabre, garden, see Usher 280, and for a reading of Filomena's story that takes account of its folkloric origins, see Millicent Marcus, "Cross-Fertilizations: Folklore and Literature in *Decameron* 4, 5" *Italica* 66 (1989): 383-98.

45. For more on the garden setting of "IV, 7," see Cottino-Jones, *Order from Chaos* 74-75.

46. For the medical tradition surrounding the poisonous sage leaf, see Manlio Pastore Stocchi, "La salvia avvelenata (*Decameron* IV 7)," *Studi sul Boccaccio* 7 (1973): 192-96.

47. Branca also cites the appearance of this phrase in "IV, intro. 24," "Maravigliosa cosa a udire!" where, in the context of the tale of Filippo Balducci and the *papere,* it again refers to the indomitable force of desire. Mario Petrini discusses the repetition of this exclamation as an intervention of the narrator's voice in *Nel giardino di Boccaccio* (Udine: Del Bianco, 1986) 58, as does Luigi Russo, who remarks on the proliferation of the word "maravigliosa" in the introduction; for him, however, the narrator's wonder and amazement indicates a certain detachment from the fear and sorrow he might be expected to express. Russo argues that the narrator's response to the horror of the plague, namely, astonishment, rather than terror, and stupor, rather than dolor, indicates Boccaccio's interest in recounting an entertaining story rather than narrating a personal history (*Letture critiche del* Decameron [1956; Bari: Laterza, 1986] 43).

48. Rossiglione's wife is never named, thus recalling, and taking to an extreme, Ghismonda's delayed naming.

49. For this popular interpretation of the *Decameron* see, among others, the works cited of Vittore Branca and Janet Smarr, and, particularly, Thomas Greene, "Forms of Accommodation in the *Decameron,*" *Italica* 45 (1968): 297-313. Many readers of the *Decameron* point to the *brigata*'s return to Florence as evidence of their victory over the plague and its attendant crises. See, for example, Raffaello Ramat, "Indicazioni per una lettura del *Decameron,*" *Miscellanea storica della Valdelsa* 69 (1963): 119 (rpt. in *Saggi sul Rinascimento* [Florence: La Nuova Italia, 1969] 117-29); Cottino-Jones, "The City/Country Conflict" 183-84; and Bárberi Squarotti 58. Ramat suggests that the *brigata* flees Florence to affirm essential moral values; the reappearance of the ten men and women in the city stands as evidence of the selfless purpose motivating their initial decision to abandon it. Cottino-Jones asserts that the *brigata*'s homecoming "suggests that they consider this experience of the natural world essential, in as much as it has provided them with the necessary means to face the city again and to potentially shape there a perfected form of social existence" (183). Similarly, Bárberi Squarotti argues that the *brigata* comes back to the city because "la funzione è compiuta, il gruppo ha attuato il suo compito di istituire di nuovo leggi, ordini, modelli, regole di vita. . . ."

Esther Zago (essay date 1997)

SOURCE: Zago, Esther. "Women, Medicine, and the Law in Boccaccio's *Decameron.*" In *Women Healers and Physicians: Climbing a Long Hill,* edited by Lilian R. Furst, pp. 64-78. Lexington: University Press of Kentucky, 1997.

[*In the following essay, Zago examines medieval medical practices concerning the treatment of melancholia within the social and scientific contexts represented in the* Decameron, *focusing on the role of gender difference.*]

In her recent study, *Lovesickness in the Middle Ages,* Mary Frances Wack notes that, whereas women as desiring subjects as well as desired objects can be found at any place and at any time in literary texts, women as clinical subjects were absent from medical academic literature until the late fourteenth century. Wack aptly surmises that "the relative silence of the physicians concerning women follows from, in the first instance, their preoccupation with analyzing *amor hereos* from a masculine perspective. . . . Moreover, men's lovesickness needed explanation and cure because it made them 'other.' Its signs and symptoms feminized them, separated them from normal masculine ways of behaving."[1]

Boccaccio's **Decameron** is a salient example of a literary text in which lovesickness in both men and women is sympathetically described. To define this condition, Boccaccio uses the medical term *malinconia* [melancholy] in the preface and on several other occasions; in certain instances the term is used to identify sexual frustration. However, Boccaccio makes a clear distinction between those women who allow themselves to be overcome by their sexuality, and those who acknowledge it and respect it. My inquiry will focus on this second group.

The purpose of this essay is therefore twofold. First, I hope to show that in analogous situations in which men and women fall victims of the melancholy condition caused by lovesickness, the therapy available privileges men, thus excluding women from taking advantage of it. Second, I will argue that precisely because women are not allowed the freedom, the diversions, and the justifications available to men, they are more likely to "listen" to their bodies as well as to their minds; they can also speak in self-defense, thus challenging male authority both in the private space of the home and in the public space of the court of law.

Before examining the tales in question, it may be appropriate to situate the **Decameron** within its social and scientific context.

The importance of this collection of one hundred stories within the western tradition does not need to be emphasized here; it will suffice to remember that it generated the paradigm for a new genre, the short story. Most of the tales are set on the stage of the merchant's world of fourteenth-century Europe, focusing on Italy, with occasional excursions into the larger Mediterranean area. The case of the *Decameron* is of special interest also because it was composed sometime after 1348 and before 1354,[2] at the time of the Black Death. As Glending Olson[3] has pointed out, several plague tracts circulated in Europe. The critic cites in particular what is considered to be "the most influential treatise of its time, the *Compendium de epidimia* of the Faculty of Medicine at the University of Paris, written in 1348 at the request of the King of France." Olson quotes from this tract: "[S]ince bodily infirmity is sometimes related to the accidents of the soul, one should avoid anger, excessive sadness, and anxiety. Be of good hope and resolute mind; make peace with God, for death will be less fearsome as a result. *Live in joy and gladness as much as possible, for although joy may sometimes moisten the body, it nevertheless comforts both spirit and body.*" (emphasis added).

Boccaccio gives similar advice in his preface to the *Decameron,* and in the introduction to the first day. In addition, he dedicates his work to women who love and who need the comfort of literature. More specifically, Boccaccio has in mind women—paraphrasing Dante's address in the famous *canzone* of his *Vita Nuova,* "Donne ch' avete intelletto d'amore"—who have an "understanding of love"; he dismisses all others for whom the solace of needles, reels and spindles provides sufficient diversion. Note that Boccaccio is not here making a distinction of social class, but rather of intelligence, knowledge and sensitivity. The concept of the aristocracy of the mind is never very far from the mercantile world.

The decades that followed the plague epidemic coincided with the first appearance, especially in northern Italy, of health books. The physical condition of the body, the question of nutrition, and norms of hygiene acquired much greater importance than they had had in the past, a phenomenon which points to a decidedly more secular attitude towards the body. The space for such views may have been cleared in literary texts by the absence of the papacy from Rome throughout most of the fourteenth century.[4]

According to medieval medical treatises, based on Greek texts and Arab commentaries, the body's health depended on the equilibrium of each of the four humors, and of the corresponding four temperaments. Any form of imbalance could have pernicious effects on both the body and the mind. Boccaccio's interest in the interdependency of body and mind is apparent at the very onset of the *Decameron* in two famous passages: the preface, and the introduction to the first day. The latter shows the extent to which, in the macrocosm of an epidemic disease such as the plague, men's mental faculties are impaired to the point of subverting moral and social values. The former addresses the complementary phenomenon in the microcosm of lovesickness, where a mental affliction prevents the body from accomplishing its normal functions.

Recognized as disease in all medical treatises from antiquity to the Middle Ages, lovesickness was classified as a malady caused by the overproduction of black bile, which upset the equilibrium of body and mind.[5] As mentioned earlier, medical treatises of the medieval period indicate a certain interest in the *aegritudo amoris*[6] in men, but do not pay much attention to lovesickness in women. Boccaccio makes up for such neglect by dedicating his one hundred tales precisely to women affected by that condition. The passage in question is from the preface:

> E se . . . alcuna *malinconia,* mossa da focoso desio sopraviene nelle lor menti, in quelle conviene che con grave noia si dimori, se da nuovi ragionamenti non è rimossa: senza che elle sono men forti che gli uomini a sostenere. [emphasis added].[7] [And if, in the course of their meditations, their minds should be invaded by *melancholy* arising out of the flames of longing, it will inevitably take root there and make them suffer greatly, unless it be dislodged by new interests. Besides which, their powers of endurance are considerably weaker than those that men possess.][8]

It is clear that Boccaccio is not alluding here only to cases of melancholy brought about by a precise object of desire; he addresses also the larger question of sexuality, and of those erotic impulses which, according to a widespread belief, were stronger in women than in men.[9] Boccaccio neither confirms nor denies this assumption, but he perceptively suggests that there may also be a psychological reason for the high frequency of melancholy and sexual frustration among women. In his often quoted preface, he notes that most men, if they choose to do so, can divert their minds from melancholy thoughts by seeking out public spaces, where they can occupy themselves with conventionally masculine activities, such as sports and business. Women, instead, being confined to the private space of the home, have no alternative but to give in to their amorous dreams, hopes, and frustrations. The "new interests," namely the therapy which Boccaccio has in mind, is the solace of literature: the author "prescribes" his own literary corpus as a medical treatment for the mind, which, in turn, may help heal the body. In fact, it would not be too farfetched to suggest an association between literary intercourse and sexual intercourse. Furthermore, we shall see that the remedy for the corresponding condition in men as prescribed by the medical profession as well as by health books was in fact sexual intercourse.

The number of cases of lovesickness and/or melancholy in the *Decameron* is relatively small, but nonetheless sufficient to mirror medical and social attitudes about that illness, which are clearly gender-determined. Several stories in the collection allude also to the historical reality of gender discrimination within the legal system in medieval Italy. For example, in cases of flagrant adultery, men were generally acquitted, whereas women had to pay a fine; in ecclesiastical law, women, but not men, could be condemned to separation from the family, and charged with financial losses.[10]

I will discuss some specific examples of practices, both medical and legal, which are gender-determined. I will then focus on the cases of three women who appropriate therapeutic and legal measures which are denied to them by male authority.

As stated earlier, such cases are few in number, and, in the complex world of the *Decameron,* they represent the exception rather than the rule; nonetheless, they underscore women's ability to diagnose the symptoms of lovesickness in themselves and in others, and to actively seek a healing solution, even though it may be socially dangerous, and even fatal. In other words, their behavior appears to counter some of Boccaccio's own statements regarding the character of women. For example, in the preface he says that women's "powers of endurance are considerably weaker than those that men possess" (46). And in the introduction to the first day, he has Filomena, one of the ten storytellers, declare that women are "fickle, quarrelsome, suspicious, cowardly, and easily frightened" (62). However, such statements can be interpreted as public posturing for the sake of prudence: Boccaccio was keenly aware of the misogynist backlash which his work incited.[11] I will argue that several women in the *Decameron* are far more perceptive and steadfast than men; they also have a clear understanding of erotic impulses as psycho-physiological phenomena which can and must be treated before they degenerate into illness, thus causing irreparable damage to body and mind.

Boccaccio's knowledge of the medical literature on the subject of lovesickness has been the object of much speculation in recent years, and Massimo Ciavolella[12] has convincingly showed that the representation of *aegritudo amoris* in Boccaccio's *Decameron* is firmly grounded not only in literary and medical traditions going back to antiquity, but specifically in two late thirteenth-century texts, the *Lilium medicinae* and the commentary to Cavalcanti's famous *canzone,* "Donna me prega," by Dino del Garbo. The first text is of particular relevance to my assumptions, and my discussion in this section is greatly indebted to Ciavolella's article.

The *Lilium medicinae* was a medical encyclopedia written (circa 1285) by Bernard of Gordon (Bernardus Gordonius), one of the most esteemed physicians of the Montpellier school. Therein he defines *aegritudo amoris* as follows: "morbus qui hereos dicitur est sollicitudo melancholica propter mulieris amorem" [The disease, which is called hereos, is a melancholy fixation on the love for a woman].[13] The author goes on to state that men afflicted by the disease, may, if not adequately treated, fall into a manic state or even die. It appears that one of the most appropriate treatments consists in convincing the subject "ad diligendam multas, ut distrahatur amor unius propter amorem alterius" [to make love to many women so that the love for one woman may be diverted in favor of the love for another] (511).

Dino del Garbo, in his commentary on "Donna me prega" by Guido Cavalcanti,[14] follows exactly Bernard of Gordon's discussion of the *aegritudo amoris,* stating unequivocally that love is considered a sickness by the experts of medical science.[15] Boccaccio knew this text, referred to it in the *Teseida* and even recopied it in his own hand. The *Lilium medicinae* is not the only text in which sexual intercourse is indicated as therapy for men afflicted with lovesickness. As Wack (66-67) points out, the remedy is recommended in several medical treatises all through the Middle Ages.

It is a known fact that medical science in antiquity and throughout the Middle Ages considered women's sexuality with contempt, but the *Decameron* provides a privileged locus for showing that male and female desires are equal, and that women are justified in appropriating a therapy which the medical profession prescribed to women only in cases of hysteria. The cases I propose to study are precisely those of women who have no access to medical treatment and who have to invent their own cure: women who heal themselves.[16]

Let us now turn to the *Decameron* and examine first two cases, one involving a man and the other a woman, both struck by lovesickness, and the way in which the remedy of sexual intercourse is problematized by gender.

Giachetto's love for Giannetta is a story within the story of the vicissitudes suffered by the count of Anguersa (**"Day II, 8"**). Forced to abandon his two children, the count does not know that one of them, the daughter, is living as a maid in the household of a wealthy and noble couple. The couple's son, Giachetto, falls in love with the girl, but dares not reveal his feelings to his parents because he is under the impression that the object of his desire is socially inferior to him. He falls seriously ill, several doctors are called, but no remedy is found. It so happens that a young doctor is at Giachetto's bedside, feeling his pulse, when Giannetta comes into the room. The young doctor notices that the pulse rhythm accelerates; when Giannetta leaves the room the pulse rhythm becomes normal. Resorting to a pretext, the doctor calls the girl back: once again the patient's pulse accelerates.[17] The doctor is then sure of his diagnosis, which he communicates to the worried parents:

La sanità del vostro figliolo non è nell'aiuto de' medici ma nelle mani della Giannetta dimora, la quale si come io ho manifestamente per certi segni conosciuto, il giovane focosamente ama, come che ella non se ne accorge per quello che io vegga. Sapete omai che a fare v'avete, se la sua vita v'è cara.

[270-71]

[Your son's health cannot be restored by any doctor, for it rests in the hands of Giannetta. As I have discovered through certain unmistakable symptoms, the young man is ardently in love with her, though as far as I can tell, she herself is unaware of the fact. But you will know now what measures to apply if you want him to recover.

(198-99)]

The young doctor is somewhat allusive in prescribing the therapy, but quite clear about the outcome if the "cure" is not administered. The mother—not the father—understands perfectly what the doctor is talking about. She sends for Giannetta and tells her that it is time for her, young and beautiful as she is, to have a lover. But the girl refuses: her only richness is her honor, she will take a husband, never a lover. The parents have to consent to the marriage, even though they consider it a mésalliance.

This story is interesting for several reasons. First, Giachetto manifests all the symptoms of lovesickness described in the medical treatises: his humoral imbalance causes him to suffer from an acute case of melancholy, and his mind is deeply troubled by feelings of shame and fear. It is also interesting to note that Boccaccio uses for Giachetto's condition exactly the same vocabulary which he uses for women in the preface to the *Decameron*.[18] What we have here is classic case of the "feminization" mentioned by Wack, which so intrigued medieval doctors.

Boccaccio's scientific knowledge concerning *aegritudo amoris* is further evidenced by the behavior of Giachetto's mother. The promptness with which she reacts to the doctor's speech clearly indicates that he is suggesting a therapy which is familiar to her. She doesn't stop for a moment to question its morality, and she immediately tries to arrange, more or less tactfully, for her son to "take his pleasure" with Giannetta.

A similar situation, this time with a young girl as protagonist, occurs in the seventh novella of the tenth day. Lisa, an apothecary's daughter, falls in love with Peter of Aragon, king of Sicily. Painfully aware of her impossible love—not only is the object of her desire a king, but he already has a wife—the girl falls seriously ill. When the king hears of Lisa's story, he is deeply moved; he arranges to visit her and comforts her with such kind words that Lisa immediately begins to get better. When she fully recovers her health, the king visits her again and, right there and then, presents her with the gift of a bridegroom. Ciavolella (499) notes the similarity between the stories of Lisa and Giachetto, but sees the *topos* of lovesickness only as it relates to the theme of the king's nobility and magnanimity. Without denying the validity of this interpretation, I believe it is important to call attention to the fact that, when Lisa is struck by *aegritudo amoris*, neither the doctors nor the parents envisage sexual intercourse as therapy for her. It is the king himself who prescribes it, euphemistically, in the form of marriage. Given the fact that Lisa cannot have the king in her bed, she will have to settle for a husband chosen by the king: some other lover of her own choice would have been totally out of the question. Within the topos of the *aegritudo amoris*, the stories of Giachetto and Lisa show the extent to which sex as therapy is available only in a man's world, regardless of whether he is the beneficiary or the prescriber of the benefice.

In the preface to the *Decameron* Boccaccio argues that women, subject as they are to male tutelage, have to keep their "amorous flames," their "burning desires," their melancholy spells, well hidden. Let us consider now two of the most famous heroines of the *Decameron* from a social and medical perspective. Ghismonda (**"Day IV, 1"**) and Lisabetta (**"Day IV, 5"**) represent a polarity in the social scale. Ghismonda is the daughter of Tancredi, prince of Salerno; Lisabetta, an orphan, lives with her merchant brothers in Messina. They do, however, share a similar fate. Ghismonda is a childless young widow who, conforming to the customs of her rank, has returned to live at her father's court. Because of his love—so possessive as to border on incest—the prince neglects to find a new husband for his daughter. Lisabetta is still unmarried because her brothers have not taken the time and care to find a suitable match for her, thus denying her sexuality. Both women lead secluded lives, be it in a princely court or a merchant's house. Both women become aware of their sexual impulses; they sense that unfulfilled desires lead to frustration and melancholy. They cannot, as men do, leave their households and seek diversion elsewhere. But they know their minds and respect their bodies. They reject the simple solution of finding an occasional lover with the complicity of a mercenary servant, as happens in many of the *Decameron* stories (which have given such a bad reputation to their author). Both seek out a young man, worthy of their love, although inferior to their station in life. They take the initiative of making their desires manifest to the men. Both women know that transgressing both male authority and social barriers, with all the dangers inherent in that act, is preferable to suppressing one's own nature. Both men are killed; both women end up paying with their own lives for their transgression, Ghismonda by her own hand, Lisabetta, more fragile, by letting herself die of grief.

Most traditional criticism of the parallel stories of Ghismonda and Lisabetta focused on the way in which Boccaccio shows that Lisabetta, who comes from the lower merchant class, is capable of love just as noble and tragic as that of Ghismonda, a prince's daughter.[19] The tendency of modern criticism, on the other hand, would be to make of Ghismonda the fearless advocate of equality between the sexes in terms of sexual desire. But in the context, and for the purpose of this essay, it is important to analyze the structure of Ghismonda's speech to her father when he discovers her double transgression. She has to articulate her defense on two grounds, and in terms that her father could not possibly refute. Addressing first the question of her sexuality, she reminds him of his own nature and youthful impulses:

> Esser ti dové, Tancredi, manifesto essendo tu di *carne,* aver *generato* figliola di *carne* e non di pietra o di ferro. . . . Sono adunque, sí come da te *generata,* di *carne,* e sí poco vivuta, che ancor son giovane, e per l'una cosa e per l'altra piena di concupiscibile desiderio, al quale maravigliosissime forze hanno date l'aver già per essere stato maritata, conosciuto.

> [479, emphasis added]

> [You are made of *flesh and blood,* Tancredi, and it should have been obvious to you that the daughter you *fathered* was also made of *flesh and blood,* and not of stone or iron. . . . Since you were the person who *fathered* me, I am made of *flesh and blood* like yourself. Moreover, I am still a young woman. And for both of these reasons, I am full of amorous longings, intensified beyond belief by my marriage, which enabled me to discover the marvellous joy that comes from their fulfillment.

> (337, emphasis added)]

The most striking feature of this first part of Ghismonda's speech rests on the emotional charge with which the words *carne* (flesh) and *generato/a* (fathered) are invested. From a rhetorical standpoint the effect is powerful because it unmasks the father's refusal to face the issue of his daughter's sexuality; from a scientific perspective it establishes the truth of an undeniable natural and physiological process. The medical justification for Ghismonda's desire can be found in an eleventh-century work on women's diseases signed by a woman, Trotula. According to the author, who in turns relies on Galen, women produce a secretion similar to that of the male: "Especially does this happen to those who have no husbands, widows in particular and those who previously have been accustomed to make use of carnal intercourse. It also happens in virgins who have come to marriageable years and have not yet husbands."[20] Trotula goes on to explain that, if such secretion accumulates, it produces hysteria; intercourse and pregnancy can be recommended as therapy. It is safe to assume that the remedy could be administered only in a situation legitimized by marriage. Ghismonda makes it clear to her father that she does not consider her sexuality demeaning in any way; on the contrary, she would appear to be exalting her sexuality by appropriating the vocabulary of the medical treatises.

Ghismonda goes on to remind her father of his own sexuality in his youthful years. In the second part of her speech she addresses the question of her having chosen a lover socially inferior to her. Here again she places the emphasis on the word *carne*:

> [R]iguarda alquanto a' princípi delle cose: tu verdrai noi d'una massa di *carne* tutti la *carne* avere e da un medesimo Creatore tutte l'anime con uguali forze, con iguali potenze con iguali virtù create.

> [480; emphasis added]

> [Consider for a moment the principles of things, and you will see that we are all of one *flesh* and that our souls were created by a single Maker, who gave the same capacities and powers and faculties to each.

> (338, emphasis added)]

Once more, she hinges her argument first on biological factors, and she uses all her oratorical skills to restate the theory of the nobility of the soul as superior to that of an acquired title.[21]

From a medical perspective, Ghismonda's speech is less revolutionary than it appears at first, since it looks at sexual desire as a natural process that implicates both the mind and the body. As mentioned earlier, its most striking characteristic is the high frequency of the word *carne,* which is endowed with positive connotations. Boccaccio astutely presents Ghismonda as a "virile" personality. When her father confronts her with her "guilt," she understands that her lover's fate is signed, and yet she does not cry as most women would have done in similar circumstances. It is actually her father who bursts into tears. Ghismonda, determined to follow her lover in death, announces her intention to take her own life with "un-feminine" resolution and pride. She even tells him to go off and shed his tears among women. The "masculinization" of Ghismonda stands in opposition to the "feminization" of her father. It is Tancredi who suffers from an acute case of lovesickness and an incestuous one at that. By switching their roles in this manner, Boccaccio reveals the hypocrisy of Tancredi's feelings towards his daughter, and of society towards women. Furthermore, it is significant that Boccaccio should have entrusted Ghismonda, a prince's daughter, with the task of defending women's sexuality: it certainly gives more credibility to the cause. Lisabetta, more feminine and less eloquent, would have been incapable of constructing her self-defense with equal rhetorical ability.

In spite of its rigid structure—ten days, ten stories each day, told by ten different people—the *Decameron* has its own asymmetries, and involves a play of mirrors which, across the boundaries of days and themes, calls attention to the possibility of looking at the same problem from different perspectives. The stories of Ghismonda and Lisabetta are told on the fourth day, which focuses on unhappy or tragic love, so their stories too have the prescribed outcome. But Boccaccio does not neglect the possibility that women's initiative to appropriate for themselves what is typically prescribed for men only may also have a happy outcome.

The narratives of the sixth day focus on the cases of men and women who succeed in escaping from danger by virtue of their intelligence and wit. The seventh story presents the case of a woman from Prato by the name of Madonna Filippa. The location is important: in the thirteenth and fourteenth centuries Prato was one of the busiest centers in Tuscany for cloth manufacture and trade. We can therefore assume that Fillippa's social environment is that of the merchant class. The lady is not too happily married, and she has a relationship with a young and handsome man. Her husband discovers her adultery. Had he killed his wife and her lover on the spot, he would have been acquitted; being too cowardly, he turns her over to the courts, knowing full well that she—not her lover—will be sentenced to death. Pennington[22] reminds us that such harsh law was no longer enforced in the fourteenth century. We might say that Boccaccio makes *fabula* out of history, but we might also notice that Filippa's lover is not summoned to trial, nor is he mentioned again in the rest of the story. In court, Filippa states her case with logical and rhetorical skills worthy of Ghismonda, and according to strict argumentative procedure. She acknowledges the truth of her adultery, but she argues that on that matter, laws which concern women are made by men and favor men. Filippa makes her husband admit that he, her husband, took from her what he needed and wanted. But what about her own needs and desires?

> [I]o che doveva fare di quel che gli avanza? debbolo io gittare a' cani? non è egli molto meglio servirne un gentile uomo che più che sè m'ama, che lasciarlo perdere e guastare?
>
> [748]

> [What am I to do with the surplus? Throw it to the dogs? Is it not far better that I should present it to a gentleman who loves me more dearly than himself, rather than allow it to turn bad and go to waste?
>
> (500)]

Filippa astutely transforms the moral issue of adultery into the economic issue of waste, an argument which was bound to convince the mercantile mentality of Prato's judges and citizens. Filippa obtains the predictable result: she is acquitted, amid the laughter and joking of the public, and she even obtains that the law be changed.

The question of women appropriating a measure available to men only is thus transferred from the medical to the legal field, but the essence of the argument is the same.

The import of this extraordinary story is in a sense confirmed by that of another, more conventional, one. It is the second story of the second day. The situation is far less serious than that in the other cases so far examined, but it has its own contribution to offer. It deals with a man and a woman whose paths cross by chance, and who share a few hours of happiness. The woman is a widow, and the mistress of the local lord. Obviously marriage is out of the question, but the relationship is honorable. One evening the woman is expecting her lord to spend the night with her; she prepares a warm bath and delicious food for him, only to learn that he has been detained by a sudden engagement and will not be able to join her for the night. Greatly disappointed, she hears a noise coming from outside and discovers a wounded man by her house. With the help of a servant she brings him in, gives him a bath, her deceased husband's clothes, the dinner she had prepared for her lord, and finally an invitation to share her bed. On one level, this is the delightful story of a charming and elegant "one night stand without strings attached." On a deeper level, it shows a woman's understanding of her sexuality, and the extent to which she values it. In a sense, it relates to Filippa's argument on waste. Why not make a gift of a surplus which otherwise would be lost? She does more than provide the man with food, clothes and sex: she restores his self-confidence and the trust in human nature, which he had lost when he was attacked. More important, she appropriates sex as therapy to cure her own disappointment and loneliness. What the text is implying here is that a fleeting sexual encounter can be as valid a therapy as a long-term relationship, if it is the result of a conscious, rational, and "generous" (read *noble*) choice. Healthy sexuality and secular morality seem to share some common ground. It is, of course, a secular morality which closely follows the development of an increasingly secular attitude towards the human body.

Unfortunately, these views could only prosper in the greenhouse of literary imagination. Criticism of Boccaccio's sympathy for women developed early on, and the scriptor deemed it necessary to justify and restate his position in the introduction to the fourth day. Ironically enough, only a few years after completing the **Decameron,** Boccaccio yielded to his own religious scruples and anxieties (too modern a term?) over his corpus of short stories. In the *Corbaccio,* he launched an attack against women worthy of any of the countless misogynist texts of the Middle Ages.

Medical literature was not even remotely touched by Boccaccio's "defense of good women" in the **Decameron.** Yet by the end of the fourteenth century, a more urgent reality probably impelled physicians to recommend sexual intercourse to women suffering from erotic frustration, lovesickness and melancholy, since it had the desirable effect of making women pregnant: in the aftermath of the black plague and with the high index of infant mortality, there was everything to be gained by encouraging women to produce children as often as possible. As a result, medical attention focused more on the uterus and less on the brain. Mary Frances Wack makes an interesting observation about lovesickness in men and women:

> In the Middle Ages a number of academic physicians viewed *amor hereos* as a disease located in the brain rather than in the testicles, and primarily as an affliction of noblemen. . . . The disease gradually shifted "downward" to become, in the estimation of some later writers, an illness of the sexual organs of women. . . . Such a gradual "decline" in the localization of *amor hereos* may help to account for its transformation from a "heroic" malady to a "hysteric affliction."
>
> (123)

Wack calls her remark "an admittedly metaphorical description of the change" which occurred in the fifteenth and sixteenth centuries, but it has a ring of truth about it. It also echoes the old medieval prejudice that women's sexual appetites were insatiable by placing a negative psychological connotation on female sexuality. Towards the end of the sixteenth century, the word "hystérique" made its entrance in the French vocabulary to describe "un accès d'érotisme morbide féminin" [an attack of morbid feminine eroticism].[23] Even more than in the Middle Ages, Renaissance women could heal neither themselves nor others: in the next three centuries of scientific progress and intellectual revolution, until the birth of modern medicine in the nineteenth century, they remained marginalized at best or entirely excluded.

Notes

1. Mary Frances Wack, *Lovesickness in the Middle Ages: The "Viaticum" and Its Commentaries* (Philadelphia: Univ. of Pennsylvania Press, 1990), 175.

2. The precise date of composition of the *Decameron* is the subject of scholarly dispute. There is agreement, however, that the work must postdate 1348, because it opens with a graphic description of the plague that struck Florence that year, which provides the frame for the narration.

3. Glending Olson, *Literature as Recreation in the Later Middle Ages,* (Ithaca: Cornell Univ. Press, 1982), 168-69.

4. The seat of the papacy was transferred to Avignon, France, in 1309, where it remained until 1376.

5. The best study on melancholy remains *Saturn and Melancholy,* by Raymond Klibansky, Erwin Panofsky, and Fritz Saxl (London: Nelson & Son, 1967). Other relevant studies with emphasis on medieval literature include: Giorgio Agamben, *Stanze* (Torino: Einaudi, 1979); and Jacques Roubaud, *La fleur inverse* (Paris: Ramsay, 1986). For the use of the term "melancholy" in the *Decameron,* see Esther Zago, "Gender and Melancholy in Boccaccio's *Decameron," Lingua e Stile* 27.2 (1992): 235-49.

6. Lovesickness was called either *aegritudo amoris* or *amor hereos.* Whereas the first term does not present any problem, the genesis of the second is very complex. See J.L. Lowes, "The Loveres Maladye of Hereos," *Modern Philology* 2 (1914): 491-546.

7. Giovanni Boccaccio, *Decameron,* ed. Vittore Branca (Torino: Einaudi, 1987), 6. All subsequent references in Italian are to this edition.

8. Giovanni Boccaccio, *The Decameron,* trans. G.H. McWilliam (Harmondsworth, England: Penguin Books, 1972), 46. All subsequent references in English are to this translation.

9. On Medieval views of women's sexuality, see Vern L. Bullough, "Medieval and Scientific Views of Women," *Viator* 4 (1973): 485-501.

10. See Kenneth Pennington, "A Note to *Decameron* VII, 6. The Case of Madonna Filippa," *Speculum* 52 (1977): 902-5.

11. See, for example, the following passage from the introduction to the fourth day: "Sono adunque, discrete donne, stati alcuni che, queste novellette leggendo, hanno detto che voi me piacete troppo e che onesta cosa non è che io tanto diletto prenda di piacervi e di consolarvi e, alcuni han detto peggio, di commendarvi, come io fo" (460-61) [Judicious ladies, there are those who have said, after reading these tales, that I am altogether too fond of you, that it is unseemly for me to take so much delight in entertaining and consoling you, and, what is apparently worse, in singing your praises as I do (325)]. The most plausible explanation for this comment on public reaction to the *Decameron* within the text itself is that some of the stories must have circulated separately, prior to the completion of the work.

12. Massimo Ciavolella, "La Tradizione della *Aegritudo Amoris* nel *Decameron," Giornale Storico della Letteratura Italiana* 147, 460 (1970): 496-517. For Boccaccio's interest in science, see also Marga Cottino-Jones, "Boccaccio e la Scienza," in *Letteratura e Scienza nella Cultura Italiana* (Palermo: Manfredi, 1979), 356-70.

13. Quoted by Ciavolella, 511. All subsequent references in Latin are to this article, and all translations are mine.

14. Guido Cavalcanti (1260?-1300) was Dante's "first friend." His celebrated poem, "Donna me priega," is a dark song in which love is described in scientific and astrological terms.

15. Ciavolella, 512.

16. The traditional role of woman as healer is represented in the *Decameron* by Gilette de Narbonne ("Day III, 9"), the source for Shakespeare's play *All's Well That Ends Well*.

17. For the sources of this case of lovesickness, see Ciavolella, 508-9.

18. Compare the preface, p. 7: "Esse dentro a' dilicati petti, *temendo* e *vergognando*, tengono l'*amorose fiamme nascose* . . ." [For the ladies, out of *fear* or *shame*, conceal the *flames* of *passion* within their fragile breasts . . . (46)]; and in the story under discussion, p. 269: "egli . . . *temendo* non fosse ripreso che bassamente si fosse a amar messo, quanto poteva il suo *amore teneva nascoso*" [since he was *afraid* of being reproached with falling in love with a commoner, he did all he could to keep his *love* a *secret* (198)]. Giachetto's mother urges him to get rid of "la *vergogna* e la *paura*" (172) [the *sadness* and *anxiety* (199)]. Emphasis added in the original text and in the translation.

19. It was a widespread belief in medical literature that only noblemen suffered from lovesickness. In literary texts, women were included, but only in the "noble" genres, such as epic poetry and tragedy, not in comedy or farce.

20. Quoted by Bullough, 495.

21. The concept is certainly not new on the European literary scene, and it has well known antecedents in Boethius, Andreas Cappellanus, Jean de Meung, the Stilnovists, to name a few.

22. Pennington, 902.

23. *Dictionnaire Etymologique Larousse*.

Marilyn Migiel (essay date winter 1998)

SOURCE: Migiel, Marilyn. "Encrypted Messages: Men, Women, and Figurative Language in *Decameron* 5.4." *Philological Quarterly* 77, no. 1 (winter 1998): 1-13.

[*In the following essay, Migiel explicates the power relations implicit in each gender's use of figurative language in the fourth* novella *of the "Fifth Day," demonstrating the tale's pro-woman message on one hand and its affirmation of male supremacy on the other.*]

In an expert and thought-provoking reading of tragic and comic stories in the *Decameron,* Millicent Marcus proposes that several of the most brutal tragedies are the result of the literalization of metaphor, and that Filostrato's tale of Ricciardo Manardi and Caterina da Valbona (*Decameron* "5.4") rewrites those tragic stories in order to show the beneficial consequences of embracing figurative exchanges.[1] Filostrato's tale is, in Marcus's words, an "an adventure in circumlocution," where the young lovers succeed, first of all, because from the very beginning they share a figurative language ("dying" for love, suffering "heat," "hearing the nightingale sing") that will allow them to circumvent protective parents and fulfill their desires.[2] Further helping to tip the scales away from death is Caterina's father, Messer Lizio, who rather than take offense, is open to accept and even himself to deploy the metaphors that the young lovers have offered. In the novella's most comic transposition of figures, Messer Lizio takes a veiled metaphor for sex ("making the nightingale sing") and extends and reshapes it so that it becomes, as Marcus notes, a "conceit for marriage":[3] "converrà che primieramente la sposi, sì che egli si troverà aver messo l'usignuolo nella gabbia sua e non nell'altrui" ("he will have to marry her first; thus he shall have put his nightingale into his own cage and not into anybody else's!" ["5.4," 38; p. 339]).[4] Acceptance of figurative language shields Caterina, Ricciardo, and Messer Lizio from the tragedy that had befallen Ghismonda, Guiscardo, and Tancredi in *Decameron* "4.1."

A reading like Marcus's, which emphasizes the enormous difference that language can make, does much to explain why Filostrato's story is so striking and compelling.[5] No doubt, we are moved and reassured by the idea that the production and the manipulation of language is salutary. The tale further reinforces this by rendering the characters' dialogue very prominently, first as Caterina seeks to persuade her mother to let her sleep on the balcony (where she hopes to meet Ricciardo); then as Caterina's mother intercedes with her father; and finally, after the lovers are discovered *in delicto flagrante,* when Ricciardo pleas with Caterina's father to spare his life. One senses that the energy of life is conveyed in the possibility of continued expression. It is when silence falls that one suspects the worst.

Although I affirm the validity of Marcus' reading, which is most certainly supported by the novella, I believe that another reading of men, women, and figurative language in *Decameron* "5.4"—a reading in tension with Marcus's affirmation of the young lovers' active choice and expression—remains nestled here. If we read Filostrato's story with attention to the power relations formed around the use of figurative language, we see that the story isn't really very reassuring to readers—or at least not to readers of a feminist persuasion. As in several of his other stories, Filostrato keeps the control of social codes and of language in the hands of men, especially elder men. He presents a conflicted view of women: empowered on one hand to express their sexuality (at least initially, and within certain bounds), but ultimately dispossessed of language.

The novella shows us that the creative use of language will make not a whit of difference in social relations if the status quo is significantly threatened. Ricciardo can fall in love with Caterina, even fiercely (*fieramente* ["5.4," 6]), and is not necessarily destined for a tragic end because the social configuration of the characters is different from those we saw both in the tragic stories of *Decameron* "4" and to French and Provençal sources and analogues.[6] Caterina is unmarried (unlike the wives in the *vida* of Guilhem de Cabestanh, in *Decameron* "4.9," and in Marie de France's "Laüstic"), so her relationship with Ricciardo is potentially licit. Her parents are anxious to find a good match for her (as Tancredi was not in *Decameron* "4.1" and Lisabetta's brothers were not in "4.5"). A male's overbearing feelings toward the young woman in his charge are avoided at least partly because a mother is present (as she was not in *Decameron* "4.1" or "4.5").[7] Finally, Guiscardo of *Decameron* "4.1" and Guilhem de Cabestanh of the Provençal narrative, though worthy and loving, do not have the wealth and nobility that make Ricciardo of a social standing at least equal to—if not better than—that of Caterina's family.

If we keep these social power relations in mind, we will be more likely to see that the free agency of the young lovers is a myth. Sexuality is hardly the arena where they (or we, for that matter) enjoy the greatest degree of choice. Their "success," if one wishes to call it that, is the result of the compatibility of the expression of their desires with that of the dominant ideology of their immediate family and community.

Encouraged to empathize with the young lovers seeking happiness in **"Day 5"** of the *Decameron,* we may not want to see this inevitable fact. As long as we place ourselves as desiring subjects, we will interpret the events first through the eyes of Ricciardo (because the story begins with him, his desire for Caterina, and his plan for satisfying his desire), and then from the perspective of Caterina (because she seeks to persuade her mother that she needs to be on the balcony). These identifications will tend to remain steady as long as the novella keeps the reader focused on the tension-filled moments when the lovers might fail in their quest for love and life. Ricciardo suggests, with the unwittingness of a young lover accepting the dominant language of love, that he could die of his passion ("Caterina, io ti prego che tu non mi facci morire amando" ["5.4," 8]). He could die as he makes the dangerous ascent to the balcony in order to spend the night with Caterina. His near encounter with death is exposed in its full horror

when Filostrato describes, with language certain to remind us of the throbbing excised hearts of earlier tragic tales, the moment of discovery and recognition: "Quando Ricciardo il vide [messer Lizio], parve che gli fosse il cuore del corpo strappato" ("When Ricciardo saw him [Messer Lizio], he felt as if his heart were being ripped from his body" ["5.4," 42; p. 340]). Moments like these intensify our bond of empathetic identification with Caterina and Ricciardo, encouraging us to focus on their ability to overcome obstacles, and making us fear for them when they seem doomed.

The lovers avoid a tragic end, but not necessarily because they control figurative language. We cannot be entirely certain that we know what Caterina means when she says that she is hot at night and would be comforted by the song of the nightingale. Is she referring to the heat of her passion? Perhaps. Is she equating the nightingale with Ricciardo, rather than with a more general notion of amorous desire and fulfillment? This already seems less certain, especially since the situation of "listening to the nightingale," common in medieval love poetry from the twelfth century on, was "identified with that long, or endless period when the lover is aware of his love, but still knows himself unable to reach it".[8] Since Caterina's actual design is never revealed, we know solely what *we* think her language means. Only a few readers—and in my assessment, only those predisposed to spy erotic imagery at the least provocation— assume that Caterina is talking about her own burning passion when she complains of the heat; even readers aware that the nightingale is traditionally a poetic emblem of amorous desire are unlikely to think that the nightingale could be Ricciardo himself.[9] On margin, readers tend at this early point in the novella to see Caterina's statements as her mother does, i.e., as exclamations of delight in the offerings of nature. Even when Ricciardo and Caterina meet on her father's balcony, and Filostrato states that "they took their pleasure in each other, making the nightingale sing many times" ("piacer presono l'un dell'altro, molte volte faccendo cantar l'usignuolo" ["they took delight and pleasure in one another, and as they did, they made the nightingale sing time and time again" ("5.4," 29; p. 339)]), it is not yet a given that the reader will take the nightingale to mean, as it clearly does after Messer Lizio arrives on the scene, Ricciardo's male member. In the context of a novella that has not yet turned bawdy, it seems more likely that "they made the nightingale sing" would be the equivalent of phrases like "there were fireworks" or "the earth shook," stand-ins for the more explicit "they had sex." Although we piece the puzzle together as the novella progresses, and see the full significance of early figurative language only retrospectively, we like to believe that we have always been fully aware of what Caterina's language meant; many readers tend even to affirm her control of her language because it is unsettling to think that a speaker could wield figurative language without judging its full range and impact.

We ought to be reminded of the opaqueness of Caterina's language by the presence of several other phrases that are likely to stump us. Interceding for her daughter, Madonna Giacomina argues that Caterina should be allowed to sleep on the balcony because "I giovani son vaghi delle cose simiglianti a loro" ("Young people like things that are like themselves" ["**5.4**," 25; p. 338]). To what is she comparing the young people? The nightingale? The cool nights? The phrase seems so peculiar that Guido Waldman, in translating it, twists it so that it makes more sense, rendering it as "Those are the sorts of things that give pleasure to youngsters."[10] Likewise, when Messer Lizio responds to his wife's request by saying, "Che rusignuolo è questo a che ella vuol dormire? Io la farò ancora adormentare al canto delle cicale" ("What is this nonsense about being serenaded to sleep by a nightingale? I'll make her sleep to the tune of the crickets [lit., cicadas] in broad daylight!" ["**5.4**," 23; p. 338]), what does he mean to say? The sense of his statement is something like, "She'll sleep when and how *I* want her to sleep!", with perhaps, I would argue, a veiled threat (something like "I could be truly unpleasant about this if I wanted to be!" or "I'll make her see stars in broad daylight!"). The point is not to decide on an exact translation of Messer Lizio's grousing, but rather to remember that his figurative language permits multiple translations. Between metaphorical language and its referent, there is room for maneuvering, and for misunderstanding. Not always are we in control.

The figurative language of the novella resists us, but we resist thinking that might be the case. Why? To the extent that they focus on meaning as an end term rather than on the process by which meaning is constructed in a text, readers tend to forget about initial interpretive difficulties they may have encountered. In the case of *Decameron* "**5.4**," they genuinely do not ever remember the time when they were not fully aware of the way that words like "heat" and "nightingale" could become sexually charged.

The novella privileges the moment of discovery, especially as it returns insistently to the image of Messer Lizio drawing back the curtain. When Messer Lizio first enters the balcony, he wishes to see how the nightingale allowed Caterina to sleep: "E andato oltre pianamente *levò alto la sargia* della quale il letto era fasciato, e Ricciardo e lei vide ignudi e iscoperti dormire abbracciati . . ." ("and walking out onto the balcony *he lifted up the curtain* around the bed and saw Ricciardo and Caterina sleeping completely naked in each other's arms . . ." ["**5.4**," 32; p. 339; emphasis mine]). This language of lifting the curtain, easily a metaphor itself for

arriving at the meaning of a metaphor, is repeated when Lizio brings his wife Giacomina to see the scene for herself: "giunti amenduni al letto e *levata la sargia*, potè manifestamente vedere madonna Giacomina come la figliuola avesse preso e tenesse l'usignuolo . . ." ("when they both reached the bed and *lifted the curtain*, Madonna Giacomina saw for herself exactly how her daughter had managed to catch and hold on to the nightingale" ["**5.4**," 36; p. 339; emphasis mine]). The moment of lifting the curtain is so important that it is repeated yet a third time, when the lovers awaken, even though we are never given any indication that Caterina's parents would have let it down; so when Ricciardo wakes, realizes it is day, and calls out in distress to Caterina, Messer Lizio, "[having] raised the curtain" ("levata la sargia" ["**5.4**," 41; p. 340]), appears before them.

Since none of us really wants to believe that we could be duped (at least not for long) by someone else's crafty use of metaphoric language, we are likely to elect to be in the position of Messer Lizio, bourgeois mentality and all. (The novella even plays on our fears that we could be misled by our unconscious desires, and it offers us some encouragement to believe that Messer Lizio is cognizant of what both the lovers and he are doing even from the beginning. Why else should he lock the door to the balcony, for example? He cannot possibly fear that someone will enter the balcony from the inside.) As the novella steers the reader to shift subject position, it reinforces the idea that sexual activity is permissible only if it remains within the bounds of institutional authority.

Power, manifesting itself as control of discourse and of choice, moves into the hands of Messer Lizio. In a story where dialogue among the characters plays a very significant part, Messer Lizio is the last person to pronounce a long speech, threatening Ricciardo with death but giving him the option of contracting a marriage. Since Ricciardo is given no choice but to comply with Messer Lizio's will, it would seem that *his* ability to act, *his* power, is limited. But in fact, he shares in the elder man's power. His elegant and courteous speech puts him on par at least with the authoritative father, who, although he is a "cavaliere" ("knight" ["**5.4**," 4; p. 336]) and is certainly capable of solemn pronouncements (as in "**5.4**," 43), has previously been heard to speak with less refined vocabulary and rhythms, most especially when he addresses his wife: "Via, faccialevisi un letto tale quale egli vi cape . . ." (["**5.4**," 26]) and "Sù tosto, donna, lievati e vieni a vedere" (["**5.4**," 33]).[11] Tipping the balance in favor of Ricciardo, of course, is the *Decameron*'s ironic commentary on the *Divine Comedy*'s presentation of Messer Lizio as a figure exemplary of a lost Golden Age of courtliness and disinterested benefaction. In the Terrace of Envy, Guido del Duca, lamenting the loss of that golden era, exclaims: "Ov'è 'l buon Lizio e Arrigo Mainardi? / Pier Traversaro e Guido di Carpigna? / Oh Romagnuoli tornati in bastardi!" ("Where is the good Lizio and Arrigo Mainardi, Pier Traversaro and Guido di Carpigna? O men of Romagna turned to bastards!" [*Purgatorio* 14.97-99]).[12] The Lizio da Valbona of *Decameron* "5.4," however, would have some difficulty holding his own against the virtues of the historical personage acclaimed in the *Purgatorio* 14; he sometimes seems as if he emerged from the fabliau tradition instead. As for Ricciardo, his situation is different. While the narrator/Author of the *Decameron* has evidently been inspired by the name "Arrigo Mainardi" in *Purgatorio* 14.97, his claim to higher ideals is unsullied by a negative comparison to character in Dante's poem. There is no historical record of a *Ricciardo* Manardi, and the Ricciardo of *Decameron* "5.4" appears to adhere to Guido del Duca's ideals in *Purgatorio* 14 (including, one gathers, the anxiety about bastardization of family lines).

The characters who recede as the men consolidate their institutional and discursive power are the women, who stand as mere witnesses to the men's agreement. Caterina, who may never have been especially conscious of the levels of figurative language that she manipulates, exercises ever diminishing control of language. By the end of the story, it seems that she has just stumbled unwittingly upon the language that has ultimately functioned in her favor. When her father confronts her and Ricciardo, she lets go of the nightingale and of the possibility of speaking about it; she is reduced to tears and pleas. What she says is marked as less important than what the men say because it is reported in indirect discourse. She becomes ever less visible to us.

Meanwhile, Caterina's mother, Madonna Giacomina, falls short of the task of reading and speaking. Caterina's statements sail over her head, and she is never given the opportunity to play an active role in discovering the "real meaning" of Caterina's language. In accord with medieval misogynist views of women as mobile, she is presented as unable to stay with any given opinion for very long. She changes her mind when a new (even if opposing) point of view is advanced. She docs not respond at first to Caterina's request, but does so after Caterina complains insistently about the heat; later, she is quick to be angry with Ricciardo, but is silent after she sees her husband's reaction. Furthermore, although she was originally presented as a figure who could mediate between the young and the old, it is she who threatens to become the critical and punitive judge when she finds herself betrayed by Ricciardo: "tenendosi forte di Ricciardo ingannata, volle gridare e dirgli villania" ("Feeling that she had been treacherously deceived by Ricciardo, the lady wanted to scream at him and to insult him" ["5.4," 37; p. 339]). This is, I think, a bid to make Messer Lizio to look even more kind, compromising, merciful by comparison. Responsibility

for any threat of unhappiness is shifted onto a woman (though we should note that screaming at Ricciardo and insulting him would be a far cry from tearing out his heart).

The novella strains at the end to make it look as if power is shared equally even if it is not. Consider the moment when the parents exit, leaving the young lovers alone: "messer Lizio e la donna partendosi dissono: 'Riposatevi oramai, chè forse maggior bisogno n'avete che di levarvi'" ("Messer Lizio and his wife left them, saying: 'Now go back to sleep, for you probably need sleep more than you do getting up'" ["5.4," 47; p. 340]). What can it possibly mean that "Messer Lizio and his wife" say this sentence? That they pronounce it in unison? The prospect seems quite absurd. More likely, the reader imagines Messer Lizio—who, after all, has been doing most of the talking since Madonna Giacomina fell silent—pronouncing the statement with Madonna Giacomina willing to go along with his views.[13]

Filostrato and Messer Lizio play with figurative language in the presence of women. They flaunt it. They dare the women to understand. Their goal is to control figurative language, to make it a matter of male rather than female prerogative. Filostrato makes figurative language about sexuality a point of contention as he describes the sleeping lovers, and tells his listeners that Caterina had hold of "quella cosa che voi tra gli uomini più vi vergognate di nominare" ("that thing which you ladies are ashamed to name in the company of gentlemen" ["5.4," 30; p. 339]). It might appear that Filostrato acknowledges the ladies' sense of decorum when he refuses to name that thing upon which Caterina's hand rests. He is honorable, they are honorable, and indeed, what could the problem with this be? But there is a problem because Filostrato's editorial comment is not as accomodating and gracious as that. In effect, rather than recognizing the integrity of the ladies, he is obliquely accusing them of engaging in duplicitous behavior—of having one standard of conduct and speech in public, another in private. He is cornering them, so that their only legitimate option is denial of conspiracy and renunciation of figurative language as furtive. The unstated consequence of such a renunciation is male control of figurative language, male awareness of secrecy.

It seems that Filostrato has changed his tune since "**Day 4**," so after he finishes his story on "**Day 5**," the women of the group laugh. But even if they accept the humor, they might wish to be more discerning. The fact that his story of Guiglielmo Rossiglione and Guiglielmo Guardastagno (*Decameron* "**4.9**") and his story of the nightingale (*Decameron* "**5.4**") have different outcomes—tragic on one hand, "comic" on the other—is of little relevance to the deep structure of the tales. Filostrato has continued to narrate the same story about alliances among men, male power, male mastery.

The Author's rubric to *Decameron* "**5.4**" highlights relations among men. It reads: "Ricciardo Manardi è trovato da messer Lizio da Valbona con la figliuola, la quale egli sposa e col padre di lei rimane in buona pace" ("Ricciardo Manardi is found by Messer Lizio da Valbona with his daughter, whom he marries, and he remains on good terms with her father" ["**5.4**," 1; p. 336]).[14] The translator Guido Waldman, finding the Author's rubrics unappealing to modern audiences, often takes the liberty of rewriting them.[15] His substitute rubric for this tale reads, "Lizio's daughter Caterina sleeps out on the balcony in the fresh air and listens to the nightingale; how she catches one and what results."[16] It is true that Guido Waldman captures the story that *we might very much wish to see*. He draws us into the tale with an enigmatic statement of the sort that modern readers very much like. He emphasizes Caterina's agency; he makes the novella a story about an enterprising young woman who gets her man—alive. But Waldman's rubric is, as should be clear from my argument above, a misrepresentation of what is really at issue in the story. It is the Author's rubric that is on the mark, encouraging us to see that the novella is ultimately not about a woman's agency, but about the consolidation of power relations among men.

By the time Filostrato tells this tale, he has played enough of his cards for readers to be able to see beyond surface messages (apparent philogyny) to the deeper message (concerns about male power, especially among rivals). Awareness of this allows us to reevaluate the "philogyny" of other of Filostrato's novellas in which sexuality is at issue: Rinaldo d'Asti ("**2.2**"), Masetto da Lamporecchio ("**3.1**"), Madonna Filippa ("**6.7**"), Peronella ("**7.2**"). In almost all these novellas, the sexual encounters are presented as victories for the male rival: Rinaldo d'Asti returns home unscathed after an encounter with robbers and, more important, a one-night stand with a woman who took him in after her lover failed to appear that evening; Masetto da Lamporecchio successfully cuckolds Christ, and avoids having to shoulder the financial and emotional responsibilities of parenthood; and Peronella's lover Giannello achieves sexual satisfaction as he possesses her (but no attention is given to her sexual feelings).

On one hand, a pro-woman message, on the other, a message about the supremacy of male relations. Filostrato, the sole narrator of the *Decameron* who speaks of his identity (at the end of "**Day 3**"), tells us that he is "overcome by love," just as the name imposed upon him would reveal. Telling us that he is masked, he dares the listener/reader to see who he really is.[17] But what Filostrato tells us is not only that he is "overcome by love." To think so is to have missed the main point, which is that he is the bearer of an encrypted message.

So we should not be surprised that in his novellas, we find a "cryptonomy" similar in structure to the one that Nicolas Abraham and Maria Torok identified for Freud's Wolf Man.[18]

For Freud, the Wolf Man's neurosis could be drawn back to a single decisive event in the Wolf Man's past: the primal scene or primal fantasy in which the Wolf Man had witnessed his parents engage in *coitus a tergo*.[19] Abraham and Torok, on the other hand, privilege "words" over "events"; they read the dreams and the symptoms of the Wolf Man (material articulated in splintered fashion across Russian, German, and English) as a tongue-tied dialogue about the real or the fictional status of an event. According to Abraham and Torok, the Wolf Man found himself forced to state whether the event he witnessed was real or imagined, and could not in all good faith do so.[20]

Like Freud's Wolf Man, Filostrato "is himself only when he creates himself as enigma."[21] Of central importance in his cryptonomy is the nightingale. This bird (the *usignuolo* or *rusignuolo* of *Decameron* "**5.4**") stands in for the lover Ricciardo and his male member. Transposed into Italian as "Rossiglione," from the French *Roussillon* or *Rossillon* which is related to the Old French word for "nightingale" (rossignol), it stands in also for the (by law) "legitimate" husband in Filostrato's tale of Guglielmo Rossiglione and Guglielmo Guardastagno (*Decameron* "**4.9**"). Finally, as the transposition takes place on classical Latin terrain, the nightingale (Philomela) stands for Filomena, the woman of the group with whom Filostrato is presumed to be enamoured.[22] Thus, the "nightingale," the name assigned to "quella cosa che voi tra gli uomini più vi vergognate di nominare" ("that thing which you ladies are ashamed to name in the company of gentlemen" ["**5.4**," 30; p. 339]), also masks *that thing which Filostrato is incapable of speaking*. This is not, as some might be tempted to think, because "nightingale" signifies the "penis" as a name under censure. Rather, it is because the nightingale signifies a censored knot of subject positions: the puissance of the legitimate husband/father; the virility of the male rival who threatens the husband/father; and the woman who is the object of their desires.[23]

Listening to the nightingale is a form of listening to the crypt. The crypt displaces and fragments identity; so does the nightingale, the bearer of the silenced and encrypted message. The nightingale stands not only as the symbol of elusive amorous desire, but also of the identity (and ideology) that eludes us. Listening to the nightingale therefore reminds us, no matter how heartening the story about the pleasures of capturing that nightingale, that the reassurance about the identity of what we have caught is likely to be only temporary.

Notes

1. Millicent Marcus, "Tragedy as Trespass: The Tale of Tancredi and Ghismonda ("IV, 1"),￼" chap. 3 of *An Allegory of Form: Literary Self-Consciousness in the* "Decameron"(Saratoga, CA: Anma Libri, 1979), 44-63.

2. Ibid., 56.

3. Ibid., 58.

4. Here and afterwards, for the Italian text, see Giovanni Boccaccio, *Decameron,* ed. Vittore Branca (Milan: Mondadori, 1985); the English translation is taken from Giovanni Boccaccio, *The Decameron,* trans. Mark Musa and Peter Bondanella (New York: Penguin Books, 1982).

5. As Mario Baratto notes, "La V. 4 resta singolare, si potrebbe dire unica, nel *Decameron,* per il tema che la occupa interamente e ne guida lo stile narrativo" (*Realtà e stile nel* "Decameron," 2nd ed. [Rome: Editori Riuniti, 1993], 257).

6. See the *Vida* of Guilhem de Cabestanh, the *Roman du Chatelain de Couci,* and Marie de France's "Laüstic."

7. Comparing *Decameron* "5.4" with "4.1," Marcus notes, "Though Caterina is also an only child born in her father's dotage, the active presence of the mother in the story defuses the incestuous possibilities which govern Ghismonda's fate" (*An Allegory of Form,* 56).

8. See Thomas Alan Shippey, "Listening to the Nightingale," *Comparative Literature* 22.1 (1970): 51.

9. Indeed, as Shippey has argued, the effectiveness of *Decameron* "5.4" depends on the reader noticing that Caterina's use of the courtly phrase "listening to the nightingale" (a traditional representation of the longing of the frustrated lover) is incongruent with her situation as a lover who achieves sexual fulfillment ("Listening to the Nightingale," 52n).

   Louise O. Vasvari, in *"L'usignuolo in gabbia*: Popular Tradition and Pornographic Parody in the *Decameron,*" *Forum Italicum* 28:2 (Fall 1994): 224-51, argues, on the basis of what she calls "pornithology," that the reader should equate the nightingale with the male genitalia because birds are in general an eroticized metaphor in Italian and Latin. But it seems revealing that Vasvari can cite no instances aside from *Decameron* "5.4" in which the nightingale per se (as opposed to the cock, the blackbird, or the sparrow, for example) is used as a metaphor for the penis.

10. Giovanni Boccaccio, *Decameron,* trans. Guido Waldman (Oxford U. Press, 1993), 342.

11. Vittore Branca points out in the notes to his edition of the *Decameron* that Ricciardo's earlier plea to Caterina is articulated as a sequence of four hendecasvllables; see also *Boccaccio medievale e nuovi studi sul "Decameron,"* 7th ed. (Florence: Sansoni: 1990), 70.

12. Italian text and English translation are taken from Dante Alighieri, *The Divine Comedy,* translated, with a commentary, by Charles S. Singleton, 6 vols. (Princeton U. Press, 1977).

13. It is also possible that since the command to "rest" is a coded invitation to engage in further sexual activity, putting this sentence in the mouth of "both parents" shields us from the shock value that the statement would have if it were put into the mouth of a woman.

14. In the opening section of his novella, Filostrato even leads his listener to believe that perhaps the main source of interest (even erotic interest) might be between the men. Introducing Ricciardo. Filostrato says, "Ora usava molto nella casa di messer Lizio e molto con lui si riteneva" ("5.4.6"), only later to reveal that the subject of this sentence, "un giovane bello e fresco della persona" ("5.4.6") is a match for the beautiful and attractive daughter of Messer Lizio.

15. Waldman explains, "Readers today, whatever their susceptibilities, usually take it amiss if a publisher or reviewer gives away the tale's ending before they have started reading it. I have therefore in certain cases rewritten the story's *heading* to preserve the element of surprise . . ." (Boccaccio, *Decameron,* trans. Waldman, xxxiii).

16. Ibid., 340.

17. See Roberto Fedi, "Il 'regno' di Filostrato: Natura e struttura della Giornata IV del *Decameron,*" *MLN* 102 (1987): 43: "La dichiarazione è per molti versi eccezionale. E' infatti la prima volta che un personaggio della cornice mostra, per così dire, la sua carta d'identità al lettore, riferendosi apertamente a sé ad alla sua origine ed al suo ipotizzabile futuro di personaggio (ne seguirà l'esempio solo un altro narratore, anch'egli veramente singolare: Dioneo, ma nel suo consueto modo svagato e scherzoso, e senza fare cenno alle sue origini)."

18. Nicolas Abraham and Maria Torok, *The Wolf Man's Magic Word: A Cryptonomy,* trans. Nicholas Rand, foreword by Jacques Derrida (U. of Minnesota Press, 1986).

19. Sigmund Freud, "From the History of an Infantile Neurosis (1918 [1914])," in vol. 17 of *The Standard Edition of the Complete Psychological Works,* trans. James Strachey (The Hogarth Press, 1955).

20. See Rand, "Translator's Introduction" to *The Wolf Man's Magic Word*, lviii. In general, Rand identifies the difference between the two readings of the Wolf Man as follows: Freud's theory of the primal scene or fantasy allowed for a coherently organized narrative that does not fully grasp the incredibility and the "unreadability" of the Wolf Man; Abraham and Torok's theory provides insight into the Wolf Man's "life poem" because they are able to see that the Wolf Man's dreams and symptoms are organized around mutually exclusive assertions.

21. Ibid., lix.

22. See Ovid, *Metamorphoses* 6.668, where however, we are never told what birds Procne and Philomela are turned into. By extension, however, Procne and Philomela come to refer to the swallow (*hirundo*) and the nightingale (*luscinia, lusciniola*) respectively.

23. Only on "Days IV-V" do we see how important the nightingale, as a figure with an encrypted message, has become; but in retrospect, one suspects that as early as "Day 2," Filostrato may have anticipated the importance he will ascribe to names on "Day 4" (especially *Guiglielmo Rossiglione* and *Guiglielmo* Guardastagno [emphasis mine], when he notes that the encounter between the lady and Rinaldo d'Asti takes place at *Castel Guiglielmo* ("2.2.1," 13, 14, 15).

Janet Levarie Smarr (essay date 2000)

SOURCE: Smarr, Janet Levarie. "Non-Christian People and Spaces in the *Decameron*." In *Approaches to Teaching Boccaccio's* Decameron, edited by James H. McGregor, pp. 31-8. New York: Modern Language Association of America, 2000.

[*In the following essay, Smarr explains how non-Christian people and places are represented in the* Decameron, *showing their relationship to Christian European culture and their various functions as the site of the "other" in the text.*]

Although most of the *Decameron*'s adventures take place in Europe and among Christians, some of the tales occur in Asia or Africa or concern people of other races and religions. How are non-Christian people and places represented in this work? How do they relate to the people and places of Europe that are, of course, predominant? And what are the functions served by introducing these "other" spaces? Other peoples interact with Europeans in three types of cases: that of non-Christians in Europe, that of non-Christians in Africa or Asia, and that of Christians traveling to the non-Christian world.

Students can be asked to think about the representations in each of these cases as a part of their mapping of the *Decameron*'s world, the values it offers, and the strategies by which it engages these values. In courses where the *Decameron* is taught along with Dante's *Commedia*, as in our Masterpieces of Western Literature survey, the differences between the two works' representations of non-Christians and of the possibilities for relationships across cultures can also be fruitfully explored, and students can be asked to speculate on what might make for divergences even among Florentines of the same half-century. They can also be asked to suggest what other categories, such as genre, might be relevant to this analysis and to consider the connection with questions of gender.

There are, of course, important differences between Jews and Muslims: for one thing, the Jews lacked a geographical area of their own and were not political military foes as were the Muslims; for another, because Boccaccio had deep connections with the business world, he was more likely to have actually known Jews in Italy than to have met real Muslims. The first difference means that the Muslim world offered not only a separate race and faith but also a separate space that appears in Boccaccio's narratives. The second difference is reflected in the fact that while Boccaccio can tell a story about a Jewish merchant living in France, his Muslim characters are either women in clearly fantastic tales or else the legendary Saladin, but not ordinary Muslim businessmen. Notwithstanding these important differences, Jews and Muslims were frequently linked in late medieval thought as simply non-Christians, especially in law (Daniel, *Islam* 116; Camille 164), and both were often dehumanized in popular texts. Thus it makes some sense to treat Jew and Muslim together under the rubric of the cultural other.

NON-CHRISTIANS IN EUROPE

As early as the second tale the *Decameron* introduces a Jew who lives in Paris on friendly terms with a French businessman. Abraam is described initially as "diritto e leale" (48) ("honest and upright" [33]), the almost identical terms that in the same sentence describe Giannotto: "lealissimo e diritto." Giannotto sees Abraam as "valente e savio e buono" (49) ("valiant, wise, and good" [33]) and as marred solely by his lack of Christian faith. Although Abraam is content with his religion, Giannotto never ceases to press the issue.

In contrast to the character of this Jew is that of the papal court, the very center of Catholicism, which has supposedly the right faith but is marred by every imaginable sin. The virtues of Christianity reside more often among honest merchants—even Jewish ones—than among the leaders of the church. Nonetheless, the very wickedness of the curia persuades Abraam that God must be favoring the Christian religion since it grows despite its priests.

Ultimately, Abraam is baptized with a version of his friend's name, "Giovanni." The two friends have become totally indistinguishable. Thus we are reminded that the two men were always almost entirely the same, except for their religion. The period of their observance of different faiths does not seem to create any meaningful differences in their ways of life, nor does the conversion lead to any other specified changes in Abraam. He is the same good man he was, and the same friend, but now a Christian. That difference, however, is important in itself.

Perhaps as a structural mirror to the second tale, the penultimate ("10.9") also offers a non-Christian in Europe and a friendship that traverses faiths. As the setting involves Saladin's coming to spy on European preparations for a religious war in the Middle East, the context is one of hostile relations. Nonetheless, the tale presents an exchange of loving generosities. The sultan and his companions "apertamente conobber messer Torello niuna parte di cortesia voler lasciare a far loro" (927) ("they clearly saw that Messer Torello meant to omit no aspect of courtesy in their regard [660]). Messer Torello's behavior is closer to the aristocratic emphasis on liberality (the very word *cortesia* names its social context) than to the merchant ethic of calculation and profit. Yet Messer Torello senses that his guests are nobler than they appear, and his courtesy wins the sultan's love.

Part 2 of the tale takes place in Alexandria where Messer Torello has been taken as a prisoner of war. Just as Abraam was called "the Jew" in Christian Europe, so Torello in Muslim Alexandria is called "the Christian" until the sultan happens to recognize him. Saladin's opportunity to return the extravagant courtesies he had received enables the two men to become equal; the sultan even expresses his improbable invitation that they rule together "equally lords": "Sarebbemi stato carissimo [. . .] che quel tempo, che voi e io viver dobbiamo, nel governo del regno che io tengo parimente signori vivuti fossimo insieme" (934) ("I should have liked nothing more than for the two of us to spend the rest of our lives here together, ruling as equals over the kingdom I possess" [666]). Thus class distinctions have been overcome along with distinctions of race and religion. The two men continue to correspond and remain fast friends, this time without any anxiety about the Muslim's salvation. Given Saladin's popular reputation for extreme wealth and generosity, the tale seeks to show how a gentleman of Pavia can equal him in spirit if not in material wealth. The Muslim, his religion seemingly forgotten, has become a model worthy of emulation.

In both these tales, two cultural worlds are compared. In one, the Christian world is found to be clearly inferior in its behavior to the other but nonetheless truer in its belief. In the tale of Messer Torello, religious issues are left aside. The other world far surpasses in wealth and power, even magical power, the world of Italy; yet the Italian is seen as nonetheless equal in personal qualities. In both tales, a strong bond of affection connects good men across the divisions of religion and race.

The case is different in two tales in which the Muslim visitor is female. One is the story of Alatiel ("2.7"), a Saracen with an Arabic-sounding name: The men through whose hands she passes in a series of misadventures are all foreign to her and do not speak her language; they are Christians. The first, knowing the Muslim is unaccustomed to wine, intentionally gets her drunk to satisfy his lust; most of the subsequent lovers are quickly willing to commit murder to obtain her, "lasciando ogni ragione e ogni giustizia dall'una delle parti" (169) ("put[ting] aside all reason and justice" [116]). Not the bonds of brothers or of host and guest or of friends can restrain these acts of violence and betrayal. The foreign woman is an object, but a desirable object. Men do not perceive the danger she brings, for it is not the danger of an external enemy but the peril of their own inner sinfulness, aroused by her exotic beauty.

At last she comes into the hands of men who can speak her language, one, in the service of the king of the Turks, who takes her to Rhodes and later his friend who takes her to Cyprus. There she encounters the old merchant who can return her to her father's court. Once she is among people speaking her language, men not only treat her more kindly but also treat each other more considerately. The acts of violence end, and the men even ask her what she wishes to do. At her return home she will have a proper wedding, a rite none of the men in the West cared to honor. Civilized behavior lies in the land of the other, while Christians are full of treachery, murder, lust, and disregard for the institutions of the church. Yet the narrator's warning seems to be addressed not to the men but to the woman: one should not wish for beauty because it is a cause of harm. Although this tale does not explicitly contrast Muslim and Christian behavior, it does take the measure of Western mores (somewhat like the stories of Abraam and Saladin) by stringing together from the two cultures a continuous series of men who take possession of Alatiel.

Very similar is the case in tale "3.10," in which Alibech, a woman who has an Arabic-sounding name, comes from Tunis into the desert to learn how to serve God. Like Abraam, she has heard the Christian faith frequently recommended by its adherents; as in the tale of Abraam, Christian behavior does not live up to its tenets. The Christian hermit Rustico who takes her in first sins with pride, thinking he can use her to test his willpower, then sins with lust, and is finally ridiculed by his inability either to maintain his vows or to fulfill her desires. He is revealed to be lacking in both spiritual and physical potency. Dioneo's tale is more humorous and less grim in its depiction of Christian failings than the story of Alatiel, but again the allure of the Arab woman unleashes the worst in the Christian male. Rustico's metaphor about the devil raising its head is only too true. Alibech and Alatiel may represent the perceived sexual laxity of Islamic law, which was accused of seducing Christians and others who encountered it (Daniel, *Islam* 98-102, 137-50, esp. 137, and *Arabs* 42-43, 235; Southern 68-69; Polo 58). The Eastern female comes as an unexpected test, and the Christian man fails it miserably. The men who desired these two women are left either dead or, at best, exhausted and humiliated. Whereas the visiting male, Jew or sultan, openly criticizes or praises the West, the female does not comment on the behavior of the men she encounters. Either ignorant or helpless, or simply unable to communicate, she accepts whatever men do. It is we who are left to comment and judge.

NON-CHRISTIANS IN AFRICA OR ASIA

If Christians at home are not always on their best behavior, a remarkably positive presentation is given to non-Christians on their own turf. We have noted already the dazzling splendor and generosity of Saladin in tale **"10.9"** and his willingness to befriend a foreigner—even an enemy—whose personal qualities are worthy. On the same day, on which the topic is magnanimity, tale **"10.3"** gives another example of a foreigner's supreme generosity. It is worthy of note that this last day, which explicitly offers positive examples to "correct" the follies and vices of the previous nine, presents two exemplary figures from beyond the Christian West. Positive examples on that day also come from ancient Greece (**"10.8"**), from a female of the lowest class (**"10.10"**), and from both Guelph and Ghibelline parties (**"10.6"** and **"10.7"**). There seems to be an intent here to demonstrate that admirable behavior can be found anywhere. The implication, of course, is that virtue is universal and not culturally bound in any way by history, gender, class, or faith.

The shift to a non-Western site follows a tale in which it is proclaimed almost a "miracle" that a clergyman would demonstrate gratitude, compassion, and generosity. The third tale on **"Day 10,"** though actually originating from Persian and Arabic sources (it appears in Saadi's *Bustan* about the ruler of Yemen and an Arab chieftan), is set, unusually, in China. This tale claims to follow the reports of Genovese merchants to that distant land, though it continues to use names belonging more to the Middle East than to the Far East.[1] Being on a trade route and eager to make himself known in some good way, the Chinese ruler Natan builds a magnificent palace in which he plays splendid host to all who come.

His neighbor Mitridanes, equally wealthy, envies his reputation and tries to imitate his behavior. So far the Chinese rulers appear similar to the sultans as possessors of fabulous wealth and an abundance of beautiful goods. Travel accounts such as Marco Polo's or the romances of Alexander and the widely circulating letter supposedly from Prester John all described the East as a place of fabulous wealth and splendor. Mitridanes's increasingly envious desire to get rid of Natan only allows Natan the opportunity to demonstrate the ultimate generosity in his willingness to give away his life. Shamed, Mitridanes becomes his friend and the tale ends with their exchange of courteous sentiments.

Within their final conversation lies the critical comparison to unspecified other emperors and kings who seek to augment their fame not by acting generously but by killing innumerable people, burning villages, and destroying cities. This behavior is clearly associated with the "perverse desire" (614) of which Mitridanes totally repents. Moreover, the story's audience within the **Decameron** comments that Natan's liberality with his own blood surpasses the day's previous examples of Spanish king and French clergyman. Once more, the foreigner serves as a vantage point from which to assess and criticize behavior in the West.

There is no attempt at a realistic presentation of either Saladin's or Natan's court; each is an extreme or ideal against which the West is to be measured. Fabulous wealth is required to sustain the initial liberality; the ultimate gift of one's own life, however, lies within anyone's reach. Nonetheless, only in faraway places can such total generosity be imagined to exist until the very last tale of the **Decameron,** when an Italian peasant girl caps all other examples.

A more puzzling tale, different from any discussed so far, is the famous story of the three rings (**"1.3"**). The Saladin of this tale, in need of money for his wars, looks for an excuse to confiscate the wealth of a Jew in Alexandria. This story follows the tale about the Jewish and Christian merchants whose friendship leads to the Jew's conversion; and it seems to comment on this conversion, but the implications of the comment are far from clear. Like Abraam and Giannotto, Saladin and Melchisedech are two of a kind, not in justice and reliability but in avarice and shrewdness. Their fast friendship, across religious lines, results from their recognition of this similarity; there is no suggestion of a change of faith but rather a shared complicity in the refusal to acknowledge Christianity's truth.

The issue of faith is raised by the snare Saladin sets, by asking the Jew which of the three religions, Islam, Judaism, or Christianity, is best. He anticipates one of two possible answers: Islam, to flatter the sultan, or Judaism, in loyalty to the Jew's own faith; Christianity is never a serious option here. The Jew's response makes all three religions equal in both sincerity and uncertainty: each thinks his own faith is true, but no one knows which is right. Indeed, the father in the Jew's story makes two more rings because he indeed loves all three sons and wants to "satisfy" them all. It would be easy to take this tale as a cautious exhortation of tolerance.

However, another message may equally be implied. In the tale of three rings which Melchisedech tells as an analogy, the father who had two copies made of the ring "appena conosceva qual si fosse il vero" (56) ("could hardly tell which was the real one" [38]); his sons "qual fosse il vero non si sapeva conoscere" (56) ("could not recognize the true one" [38]). Thus the three religions are not in fact indistinguishable. Filomena might expect her totally Christian audience to enjoy a sense of superiority in being able to know how to recognize that their own faith is the true one. She might expect them to find amusing the mutual assurances of two infidels that no one can know the real truth. Perhaps Abraam's disinterested acknowledgment in tale "2" of the superiority of the Christian faith prepares the ground for the Jew's self-serving disclaimer in tale "3." In the latter case, the first tale to be set in non-Christian lands specifically emphasizes the Muslim and Jew's religious difference and the ignorance or self-interest that prevents their recognition of the true faith. Any smugness of a Christian reader, however, quickly comes up against the criticisms of Christian behavior discussed above.

CHRISTIANS IN THE NON-CHRISTIAN WORLD

Two tales, "2.9" and "5.2," present the travels of a Christian into the lands of the East. The European protagonists, one male and two females, are driven eastward by troubles at home that their sojourn abroad allows them to resolve. The Orient becomes that generic "other" space—like the pastoral realm or the forest—where a healthy inversion of the home situation makes possible its ultimate amelioration. As in the stories of generosity, it is an idealizing fantasy rather than a realistic representation.

Tale "2.9" is actually a double border crossing: Zinevra becomes a man as well as an Arab. The racial other and sexual other are equated; and both transformations work with perfect ease. Bernabò had praised his wife's abilities to ride, hawk, read, write, and keep accounts as well as any man. All she needs to do, when her husband sends orders to have her killed, is to don male clothes, and no one can tell that she is female. Having left the dangers of Italy for Alexandria and mastered the Arabic language, she becomes the sultan's captain of the guard, in charge of a market where both Christians and Muslims do business together. As her abilities have made sexual difference irrelevant, so commerce has apparently rendered racial or religious differences negligible. It is through this market and its circulation of goods from all over the world that Zinevra is able to find the clues and explanation for what had caused her husband's mysterious fury. Moreover, if in Italy she was at the mercy of men (her husband, Ambrogiuolo, and the pitying servant ordered to kill her), in Alexandria she is in a position of official power that can summon both Ambrogiuolo and her husband to justice before the sultan. The East provides a justice denied in the West.

The wealth of the East reappears in the gold, silver, and jewels that the sultan showers on her; however, the real value to Zinevra of the East lies in its escape from the structures of home. Just as the merchants and goods of the world circulate here out of their original contexts, so her own position in life is free to change—from female to male, from servant to captain, from victim to winner, from tricked to tricker ("l'ingannatore rimane a' piè dello'ngannato" [204, 218] is the repeated proverb that frames the tale: "the deceiver lay at the mercy of the deceived" [141, 152]). Interestingly, amid this total flux, it is her *constanzia* ("constancy") that is especially praised. But it is the swirl of goods and people that enables her to find once again her lost goods, her deceiver, and her husband and to recover her original social position.

As Zinevra was praised for constancy, so the woman of tale "5.2" is even named Gostanza, a name she deserves for her constancy in love. Her beloved Martuccio, rejected as too poor a suitor by her upper-class father, goes off to make his fortune. His own excessive greed leads to his capture by Saracen pirates, who leave him in a prison in Tunisia. Thinking him dead, Gostanza commits herself to sea in a small boat, only to end up also in North Africa. There Gostanza, like Zinevra, learns Arabic and takes up a new life in a Muslim household.

War not commerce provides the opportunity in this tale for Martuccio, who, by giving a bit of clever advice, brings himself to the attention and favor of the king. Now the roles have been reversed, for he is wealthy and of high status while Gostanza has become a modest artisan working in silk and leather. This reversal is underscored when, seeking to meet him again, she has herself announced (albeit with double meanings) as his servant from their old country. Enriched by the usual splendid gifts of the Tunisian king, they are able to go home and marry, that is, to obtain the situation they had sought in the first place.

Just as in tale "2.9," the Muslim world is, on the one hand, similar enough to their own culture to allow them to adapt and flourish; on the other hand, it is an other space in which their previous differences in status and wealth can be completely reversed. Thus their temporary displacement into the Muslim world enables them to overcome their own world's social obstacles to their marriage.

Boccaccio had access to a wide range of attitudes toward Jews and Muslims through the ecclesiastical writings, chronicles, romances, and tales that he might have encountered. Excerpts from some of these texts may be introduced to students in a seminar. He shares many of these attitudes, and if he seems to be situated in a fairly tolerant end of the spectrum, it is not through any noticeably deeper knowledge of the other culture. When considering Islamic religion in his scholarly writings, such as the *De Casibus* and *Esposizioni*, Boccaccio joined the clerical tradition in dismissing Islam with contempt. So, too, he clearly considers it a good ending that the Jew of tale **"1.2"** becomes Christian. But when considering the secular side of Muslim society in his novelle, he presents it not only as an outside place from which Europe can be criticized or its hierarchies reversed but also as a place of justice, liberality, and honor, readily open to friendships that cross the cultural divide.

Note

1. This tale is also translated in Hitti 155-56 and in Crane 199-201.

Works Cited

[Boccaccio, Giovanni]. *Decameron.* Ed. Vittore Branca. Milan: Mondadori, 1976. Florence: Einaudi, 1980. Milan: Mondadori, 1985. Boccaccio, *Tutte le opere,* vol 4.

Camille, Michael. *The Gothic Idol: Idology and Image-Making in Medieval Art.* Cambridge: Cambridge UP, 1991.

Crane, T. F. "The Sources of Boccaccio's Novella of Mitridanes and Natan (*Dec.* X, 3)." *Romanic Review* 12 (1921): 193-215.

Daniel, Norman. *The Arabs and Medieval Europe.* London: Longman, 1975.

———. *Islam and the West: The Making of an Image.* Edinburgh: Edinburgh UP, 1966.

Dante Alighieri. *La commedia secondo l'antica vulgata.* 2. Inferno. Ed. Giorgio Petrocchi. Florence: Le Lettere, 1994.

Hitti, Philip K. *Islam and the West: A Historical Cultural Survey.* New York: Van Nostrand, 1962.

Polo, Marco. *The Travels of Marco Polo.* Trans. Ronald Latham. New York: Penguin, 1982.

Saadi. The Bustan *of Sadi.* Trans. A. Hart Edwards. Lahore: Sh. Muhammad Ashraf, n.d.

Southern, R. W. *Western Views of Islam.* Cambridge: Harvard UP, 1978.

N. S. Thompson (essay date 2000)

SOURCE: Thompson, N. S. "Local Histories: Characteristic Worlds in the *Decameron* and the *Canterbury Tales.*" In *The* Decameron *and the* Canterbury Tales: *New Essays on an Old Question,* edited by Leonard Michael Koff and Brenda Deen Schildgen, pp. 85-101. Madison, N.J.: Fairleigh Dickinson University Press, 2000.

[*In the following essay, Thompson examines the narrative style of Geoffrey Chaucer's* Canterbury Tales *in connection with Boccaccio's transformation of classical* exempla *into the* novelle *of the* Decameron, *demonstrating multiple parallels between the narrative details of the two works.*]

If, in its broad range of short, spare narratives, *Il Novellino*[1] (ca. 1300) reflects the concerns and some of the dealings of the new town dwellers of thirteenth-century Italy, it is the later collection of Boccaccio's **Decameron** (ca. 1351) that actually portrays that life in all its detail. If *Il Novellino* is a collection of serious *exempla,* the **Decameron** is exemplary only in that its narratives are purportedly taken from real life. Whether they are to be read for good or ill, or to be taken seriously or not, is ostensibly left up to the reader.[2] This is the lesson that Chaucer learned from Boccaccio and that he put to good use in his *Canterbury Tales.* Not only did Chaucer learn to illustrate the life around him in telling detail, but he did so by using a mixture and mixing of genres that in his antecedents is found only in Boccaccio.[3] Only in the **Decameron** do we find discussion of the usefulness of literature mingled with popular narrative which, as in Chaucer, paradoxically becomes a vehicle for serious literature.

In this essay, I wish to look at elements of the narrative style of the *Canterbury Tales* in the specific context of Boccaccio's transformation of exemplary narratives into *novelle*[4] and also to show some of the wealth of narrative detail paralleled by the *Canterbury Tales.*

AUTHENTICATING FICTION

In the *Winter's Tale* act IV, Mopsa is trying to sell his songs to the Clown:

> Pray now buy some. I love a ballet in print, a-life,
> for then we are sure they are true.
>
> (IV. iv. 260)

His statement measures the distance that truth indices had traveled from the Middle Ages to the Renaissance. If we take his observation as an existential statement based on phenomenological grounds, his statement is true; but what, we might ask, is a "true ballad"? One that simply fulfills the requisites of form and/or genre, or one that we feel possesses a "poetic truth"?

In the Middle Ages, although script had its authority, the popular index of narrative "truth," in Mopsa's most basic sense of "here is a good song, so buy it," was, of course, the asseveration that it had been heard, that it was, like Mopsa's ballads, on the market and, more-over, had been tested there and "purchased," at least by the present narrator. If it had found one buyer, then it had to have something in it. It was in effect a form of *captatio benevolentiae*. The narrator of *Sir Gawain and the Green Knight* says that he will relate his narrative exactly as he had heard it:

> I schal telle hit as-tit, as I in toun herde
>
> (I. 31)[5]

which is a curious admission for someone to make about where they had heard a courtly romance, but is, I suspect, part of the many ironies and the overall critique of chivalric values that the poem encompasses. It is also a manifest untruth, a throwaway touch of bravado after that magnificent opening fanfare, which catalogs the narrative's genealogical history and which the narrator is very unlikely to have heard "in toun."

If this kind of authenticating strategy had become common in literature for the narrative voice—and one only has to think of Dante's supreme authenticating fiction that the events of the *Commedia* actually happened to him—then in the *Decameron* and the *Canterbury Tales* we not only see the procedure used in the narrator's ex-position of the framework, but in dramatic form inside it—in what the narrators have to say about their tales. Perhaps Chaucer-the-pilgrim is closer to Dante-the-pilgrim than he is to Boccaccio in that he has most definitely heard the narratives related and will do his ut-most to reproduce them as they were told. We are never quite sure how Boccaccio has achieved knowledge of his particular collection of tales.

It is to Boccaccio that we owe the use of an authenti-cating fiction that a narrative is true not only because it was once told but, moreover, because it actually hap-pened in a known locality (near or far) to a known or named person or persons. A study of Boccaccio's sources reveals that he presents a narrative in the same popular guise, whether it genuinely appears to derive from local anecdote (given the lack of any other ante-cedent or analogue), whether it is the reworking of a common or literary *exemplum,* or even a reworking of his own earlier work, such as the *Teseida* (in **"Day 7.10"**) or the *Filocolo* (in **"Day 10.5"**).[6] All are given a new substantiation from lived local experience. In **"Day 4.2,"** an archetypal narrative whose versions go back to

ancient Greece in the story of Cupid and Psyche, Boc-caccio creates a Venetian setting for his narrative of Frate Alberto and actually extends his realism to in-clude local Venetian custom and dialect. Similarly, many other narrative transformations are given an exact loca-tion in a precise Italian town or village.[7]

The *Decameron* frame, too, is a highly precise one: we know the plague occurred in Florence in 1348, we know of the people's reaction to it in contemporary chroni-clers but are not, of course, given the exact location of the villa retreats chosen by the *brigata*. Their retreat seems to suggest a reflective or meditative stance on life. They escape Florence and its plague in order to contemplate human actions and, therefore, will relate them as they have happened or have been observed. Where readers are charmed by the *brigata*'s elegant re-straint and measure, they might be amused by their self-control in the face of the examples of behavior they relate in their realistic *novelle*. Their symbolic names derived from Greek[8] also distance the *brigata* from the local Tuscan setting and language. Nevertheless, **"Day 1"** begins with a series of "cases" of folly or overbear-ing behavior from a whole series of recognizably real historical figures in realistic locations. There is, there-fore, a linking movement from the realism of the frame to the realism of the historical perspective, which in turn persuades the reader to believe the narrator's asser-tion that a local history was "true."[9]

In the opening *novella,* Ser Cepparello is portrayed as the unscrupulous agent of a Florentine merchant operat-ing in France and is based on an actual agent from Prato (whose account book for the years 1288-1290 still exists),[10] although there is no record of his evil ways. The Florentine merchant for whom he works, Musciatto Franzesi, achieved great wealth in his dealings in France and is noted by both Villani and Compagni in their *Cronache* as an extremely unpleasant individual who actually managed to become an advisor to Philip the Fair, a position he used exclusively to his own advan-tage. The ruthless business dealings of Florentine mer-chants and their agents are a general target here, but Boccaccio makes it so much more in that Ser Ceparello manages to break all Ten Commandments and, at the opening of Boccaccio's "comedy," could well be seen fictively as an entrance to hell, except that he becomes unwittingly sanctified by the pious people of France.

In the very next tale of the conversion of Abraam the Jew, which had been often used as an *exemplum* by preachers, Boccaccio takes a well-known narrative and sets it specifically in Paris to continue his French con-nection. The narratives continue with figures great and small, from Saladin (*Decameron* **"1.3"**) and Philip II of France (*Decameron* **"1.5"**) to Guglielmo Borsiere (*Decameron* **"1.8"**) and Guy of Lusignan, the King of Cyprus (*Decameron* **"1.9"**). all of whom are specifically related to events in their times and are not simply convenient historical markers.

If there is a very precise feeling for history in the *Decameron,* with the vitality of life in and around the Mediterranean correctly and minutely identified, it serves as authentification itself for the special role Florence has to play in the scope of the collection. If, in many *novelle,* we are caught up in the great historical sweep of events at any time in the preceding two centuries, the city on the Arno has become not the vital nucleus of Dante, a symbolic center for man's extravagance and evil, as well as his past good, but a small-time town full of petty cheats and buffoons where the odd noble character pursues or espouses virtue without any hope that this will generate a wider reaction in the tranquil mediocrity around him.

This is a curious picture to develop in that it is in direct contrast to the portrait of the city turned upside down by the plague seen in the **"Proemio"** and privileges the everyday world of the streets rather than the great enterprises on which Florence was engaged. Which, Boccaccio is asking, represents the greater reversal of values? Naturally enough, it is Florence that is used to give credibility to an ancient tale and for Boccaccio's defense in the author's **"Introduzione to Day 4."**

CREATING LOCAL HISTORY

We can see precisely what Boccaccio is doing in creating a "local history" if we look at his "own" narrative told at an important juncture in the **"Introduzione to Day 4."** First recorded in the Middle East in the work of John of Damascus, the tale has many analogues, all of which echo the ultimate origin in Buddhist or Hindu sources, in that they treat of a privileged youth shut away from the world and his subsequent reaction to the sight of women when he first encounters them in puberty. It is found in Jacques de Vitry's *Exempla* and Etienne de Besancon's *Alphabetum narrationum,*[11] among other collections, but perhaps the best example, certainly the shortest, is given in *Il Novellino,* where it preserves its function of *exemplum* rather than becoming a *novella.* A brief examination will say much about Boccaccio's creation of a local world and give substance to what his technique of *amplificatio* generally was with regard to his short fiction sources.

> A uno Re nacque un figliuolo. I savi strologi providero che, s'elli [non] stesse anni dieci che non vedesse il sole, [che perderebbe lo vedere]. Allora il fece notricare e guardare in tenebrose spelonche. Dopo il tempo detto, lo fece trarre fuori ed innanzi a lui fece mettere molte belle gioie e di molte belle donzelle, tutte cose nominando per nome, e dèttoli le donzelle essere domòni. E poi li domandaro, quale d'esse li fosse più graziosa. Rispose:—I domòni.—Allora lo Re ciò si meravigliò molto, dicendo:—Che cosa è tirannia e bellore di donna!
>
> (XIV)

[A son was born to a king. The wise astrologers foresaw that, unless he did not see the sun for ten years, he would lose his sight. So the king had him brought up and watched over in shadowy caves. After the said time, he had him brought out and placed before him many beautiful jewels and many beautiful damsels, giving each object a name and calling the girls demons. then he asked which were the more beautiful. The son replied: The demons. Then the King was greatly astonished by this, saying: What tyranny the beauty of women is!]

In Boccaccio's version, the narrative becomes that of a named citizen of Florence, Filippo Balducci, a man of humble condition, who, on the death of his wife, decides to take his young son and live a life of retreat on Monte Asinaio (a deformation of the known retreat for hermits on Monte Senario), dedicating himself to God. However, every so often he is forced to go to the city for necessities, and when the boy is eighteen, Filippo eventually decides to take him along and is forced to name all the boy sees:

> Quivi il giovane veggendo i palagi, le case, le chiese e tutte l'altre cose delle quali tutta la città piena si vede, sì come colui che mai può per ricordanza vedute no' n'avea, si comminciò forte a maravigliare e di molte domandava il padre che fossero e come si chiamassero.
>
> (**"4 Introduzione,"** 19)
>
> [Seeing the mansions, the houses, the churches and all the other things of which all the city was seen to be full, and as one who had no recollection of ever seeing such things, the young man began to marvel greatly and asked his father what many of these things were and what they were called.]

His father tells him the truth about everything in sight, but when a company of beautiful young women passes, returning dressed up from a marriage feast, he replies to his son's query that they are an "evil thing" (mala cosa) and nothing other than "geese" (papere). The son says he should like one to feed, to which the father adds he does not know where they bite. Filippo then regrets having taken his son to the city ("e pentessi d'averlo menato a Firenze").

In a purely literary sense, there is no absolute imperative for Boccaccio to have transformed this timeless *exemplum* with its wry double vision of women into a "local history" where, as a humorous tale of folly, it takes its place among the narratives of doting old judges (*Decameron* **"2.10"**), pious simpletons (*Decameron* **"3.4"**), and the cruel farces of Bruno and Buffalmacco but with its hint at the verbal smartness, which many Florentines in **"Day 6"** are able to use with greater success.

If we may then summarize Boccaccio's treatment of such narratives, we see first that he gives a name to his characters and places them in a particular geographical setting. More importantly in terms of literary realism, however, that "name" is married to a particular individual whose character is finely drawn, with specific character traits and speech. The action is contemporary and familiar to the fourteenth-century audience (and, where historical, comes within their range of knowledge) and portrays a social framework that is verifiably real as, in this case, where Monte Senario is a well-known retreat for hermits. Finally, and most important of all, especially for comparison with Chaucer, the action and social framework are set in a continuum of time where there is a "before" and an "after" that has to be accounted for. After the events of the narrative, there is a real world to which the characters must return, in which and to which the characters must be responsible for their actions. Filippo Balducci knows there can now be no undoing of what he has done; his son cannot escape the reality of the world by the simple expediency of a censuring label. Indeed, it is his own responsibility as to what response he does make in the future with regard to the world and its lovely "geese."

This is a technique of open-endedness that is often thought of as exclusively modern, whereas it is fundamental to the local history of both Boccaccio and Chaucer. What, they ask, will be the consequences of the action for the world and specifically for the reader who makes up that world? As in the **"Introduzione to Day 4,"** many *novelle* have an "unfinished" aspect that leads us to wonder on the true outcome of the action, even where that may only be to wonder how the characters will manage to continue the precarious course of behavior they have embarked on. Often this consideration will be primed because there is no just distribution of praise or blame in the *novella,* or even of justice itself, which is seen in the bawdier *novelle* and tales, such as the endings of **Decameron "9.6"** and the *Reeve's Tale,* among others.

CHAUCERIAN LOCAL HISTORY

I have established a separate case elsewhere for regarding some of Chaucer's popular narratives not as *fabliaux* but, because of their context, characterization, mixture of styles, play of genres, and morality, as more akin to the *novelle* of the **Decameron.**[12] The tales of the Miller, Reeve, and Shipman all exhibit a density of textual weaving and an ambiguous play on response that make the term *fabliau* at best unsatisfactory, where it is not simply innaccurate. A similar kind of elaborate play over genre can be seen with the tales of the Merchant, Clerk, and Franklin, whose tales have been variously seen to have analogues in Boccaccio's collection. My final section will concentrate on a further range of detailed comparisons, but first I wish to show how the general atmosphere of Boccaccio's transformations pervades the *Canterbury Tales.*

I have noted previously the ironic contrast between frame and content in the **Decameron,** where the great sweep of time, history, and human affairs contrasts with the petty goings-on in and around Florence. Although Chaucer the pilgrim says he will relate the tales he has heard as faithfully as possible, being "true" to the "fictions" he has heard (see page 92), the realistic frame of the pilgrimage provides an irony of a different kind, but reflects the use Boccaccio makes of the contrast between the larger world and the local. As is well known, the pilgrimage that should have been a religious retreat from everyday life becomes instead a carnivalesque parade. Chaucer, however, is able to remind his readers of the journey that all must take in life and from this life to the life beyond. As the great enterprise of communal Florence (which Dante saw inheriting the values of Republican Rome[13]) becomes forgotten in petty squabbling and cheating, so the great Christian enterprise of salvation—to say nothing of the storytelling competition—becomes lost as the pilgrims indulge themselves in their own petty squabbles and, for most of them, their local, and even personal, histories. If Boccaccio persuades by the realism of frame, history, and locality, then Chaucer adds the greater reality behind the pilgrimage as a grimly ironic reminder of where certain of his pilgrims, if not most, might be going. It is, however, the contrast between the local and the greater world that is important.

Moreover, what is striking about all of Chaucer's popular narratives is that they exhibit the same kind of amplification of text and response that Boccaccio creates. What could simply have been the narration of a plot—even an elaborate or farcical one—is transformed by Boccaccio via the portrayal of realistic, named characters into a real-life, cultural context of time and place where we feel the characters could walk off the page and into life. This is not the case with *fabliaux,* where characters are not usually named—they are simply a "maiden," "wife," "priest," or "peasant," and are there to serve the plot and moral, such as they may be. If a town or character is named, then we learn no further details, nor does location or character underpin the action in any way. Furthermore, the action is contained solely in and by the narrative. This is also true of the narratives of *Il Novellino,* whereas in the **Decameron,** not only does the reader feel the weight of the real world pressing down on the action, but also in the consequences of the action and its aftermath, where we are left to ponder on what those might be.

In the *Canterbury Tales,* this is seen nowhere more clearly than in the wake of the events of the *Miller*'s and the *Reeve's Tales,* where we can only feel sympathy for the ongoing plight of the two young women who are trapped in unenviably narrow lives and guarded by jealous menfolk. We are left to wonder what the real-life consequences of the events in the action would be or would have been. Similarly, in the *Clerk's Tale,* we are forced to consider the possibility of the narrative as a realistic tale and its consequences, if only because Harry Bailly does.[14] The Clerk himself, although he says his narrative is allegorical (IV. 1142-48), anticipates the reading of it as an exemplary tale for womanhood in his references to the Wife of Bath. Not only this, but the detailed geographical placing of the *Clerk's Tale,* which Chaucer takes from Petrarch, indeed stresses its features of "local history":

> A prohemye, in the which discryveth he
> Pemond and of Saluces the contree,
> And speketh of Apennyn, the hilles hye,
> That been the boundes of West Lumbardye,
> And of Mount Vesulus in special,
> Where as the Poo out of a welle smal
> Taketh his first sprynging and his sours,
> That estward ay encreseth in his cours
> To Emele-ward, to Ferrare, and Venyse,
> The which a long thyng were to devyse.
>
>   (IV. 43-52)[15]

If the narrative were simply an allegorical *exemplum,* this description would indeed already be a "long thyng . . . to devyse," but unless we read the tale as a horrifically realistic action, then its higher meaning is lost. We have to feel Griselda's various renunciations in realistic terms; otherwise, the greater meaning is diminished.

The fact of using Petrarch as an authority and source points again to the example of the **Decameron.** I have noted previously the asseverations of the *brigata,* who assure the reader of the truth of what they are saying, and the vital conceit of the author, who is relating the *novelle* as faithfully as possible. It is something that Chaucer the pilgrim is also keen to emphasize with the following reasoning:

> Whoso shal telle a tale after a man,
> He moot reherce as ny as evere he kan
> Everich a word, if it be in his charge,
> Al speke he never so rudeliche and large,
> Or ellis he moot telle his tale untrewe,
> Or feyne thyng, or fynde wordes newe.
>
>   (I. 731-36)

In general, the Canterbury pilgrims do not actually say where their narratives come from or from whom they come, nor do they specifically say that their narratives come from real life. What happens is that Chaucer dramatizes the narration and shows the pilgrims (some or all) responding to the narratives as if they were true. Where the Florentine *brigata* simply assert that what they are telling is the truth, Chaucer shows the pilgrims assuming this to be the case in the responses he depicts, notoriously in the Reeve's taking the *Miller's Tale* as a "true" slander on carpenters (and himself), while the Friar and the Summoner receive the same response to their respective callings.

There are important adumbrations of this. The Canon's Yeoman relates the truth about his master's wiles and continues with a further narrative about another "chanoun of religion" and alchemist "amonges us" (VIII. 973) whose narrative is given all the features of local history. What is more, the Yeoman first introduces the canon as known to him personally, although refuting the assumption that it is his "own" canon of whom he will speak, before he begins the tale formally with "In London . . ." (VIII. 1012).

Curiously enough, for a narrative distant in time and setting to the narrator, the *Prioress's Tale* is told as if it were an eyewitness report of a local happening. How could she possibily have such detailed local knowledge as to know that the main street was "free and open at eyther ende" or that the "litel scole of Christen folk" stood "Doun at the ferther ende"? And why should it matter? The Prioress is so taken up with emotional identification with the plight of the "litel clergeon" that she actually pictures him "As he sat in the scole at his prymer" (VII. 517); indeed, the mother's desolation at her loss is also graphically portrayed as if in reportage. In fact, so caught up is the Prioress that she misses the unchristian and fanciful elements of her tale, which are far from edifying.

However, it is instructive to see in general terms just how far Chaucer, like Boccaccio, has traveled from the kind of narrative seen in *Il Novellino* and why it is important to see his narrative technique in terms of the kind of elaboration and contextual play seen in the **Decameron.**

If there is one person on the pilgrimage who is desperate to be believed, it is the Pardoner. He makes his living by it. His graphic account of the adventures of three young Flemings at the time of the plague has all the trappings of that particular setting, familiar and horrific to almost everyone at the time, if only by secondhand account. However, the origin of the tale is an Oriental *exemplum* taken from Buddhistic tradition and, again, found in *Il Novellino,*[16] where it is given as an event in the life of Christ:

> Andando un giorno Cristo co' discepoli suoi, per un foresto luogo, nel quale i discepoli, che veniano dietro, videro lucere da una parte piastre d'oro fine. Onde essi, chiamando Cristo, maravigliandosi perchè non era ristato ad esso, sì dissero:—Signore, prendiamo quello oro, che ci consolerà di molte bisogne.—E Cristo si volse, e ripreseli e disse:—Voi volete quelle cose, che togliono al regno nostro la maggior parte dell'anime. E che ciò sia vero, alla tornata n'udirete l'assempro.—E passaro oltre. Poco stante, due cari compagni lo trovaro; onde furo molto lieti, ed in concordia andaro [l'uno] alla più presso villa per menare uno mulo, e l'altro rimase a guardia. Ma udite opere ree, che ne seguiro poscia, de' pensieri rei che 'i nemico diè loro! Quelli tornò col mulo e disse al compagno:—Io ho

mangiato alla villa e tu dèi aver fame: mangia questi duo pani così belli, e poi caricheremo.—Quelli rispose:—Io non ho gran talento di mangiare, ora, e però carichiamo prima.—Allora presero a caricare. E quando ebbero presso che caricato, quelli ch'andò per lo mulo, si chinò per legar la soma, e l'altro li corse di dietro a tradimento, con uno appuntato coltello, ed ucciselo. Poscia prese l'uno di que' pani e diello al mulo, e l'altro mangiò elli. Il pane era attoscato: cadde morto elli e'l mulo, innanzi che movessero di quel luogo, e l'oro rimase libero, come di prima. Il nostro Signore passò indi co' suoi discepoli, nel detto giorno, e mostrò loro l'assempro che detto avea.

(LXXXIII)

[One day Christ and his disciples were walking through wooded country when the disciples, who were walking behind him, saw the glitter of fine gold piasters to one side. Calling to Christ, marveling that he had not stopped at them, they said:—Lord, let us take this gold which will satisfy many needs.—And Christ turned and came up to them and said:—You wish for that which takes the greater number of souls from our kingdom. And you will hear the truth of this by example when we return.—And they went away. Shortly after, two close friends found the gold, at which they were delighted and, by agreement, one went to the nearest village to bring a mule, and the other remained on guard. Now hear the evil deeds which then followed from the evil thoughts which the Enemy [Devil] gave them! The man returned with the mule and said to his friend:—I have eaten in the village and you must be hungry: eat these two small loaves which are so good and then we'll load up.—The other replied:—I've no wish to eat right now, let's load up first.—Then they began loading. When they had almost finished, the one who fetched the mule bent down to secure the load and the other ran treacherously behind him with a sharp knife and killed him. Then he took one of the loaves and gave it to the mule and ate the other himself. The bread was poisoned: both man and mule fell down dead before they could leave the place and the gold was left abandoned, as before. Then, on the same day, our Lord passed by with his disciples and showed them the example as he had said.]

If he came by it in such a form, the major transformation of this narrative in Chaucer's hands is the addition of the framework of death and the heretical desire to negate it by the "thre rioters," who thus deny Christ's promise of everlasting life. Equally, it is only by adding a local setting and the reality of the plague that the audience is reminded of the ever-present threat of the Grim Reaper and that they had better avail themselves of the opportunity to make their peace with God because of the very uncertainty of life. Thus, by this very "moral" tale, wrapped up as a sermon, the Pardoner is able to achieve his "vicious" ends, opening up his auditors to the ministrations of a quick-and-easy pardon. The moral thrust of the narrative moves away from the general truth espoused by the original (which is still governed by the Pardoner's use of "Radix malorum est cupiditas" [VI. 334]) to the creation of an individual response where the reader/hearer's own conscience is stimulated to examine itself. As with the more "popular" narratives, there is a careful inscription of a response which not only turns from literature to life, but involves the individual's personal beliefs and puts them under scrutiny.

It would be masking a complex reality to assume the previous *exemplum* or something like it was the only direct source for Chaucer, yet it could well have been, as the only other analogues all show a hermit or similar figure who "demonstrates" the example. Nevertheless, it does show that Chaucer belongs to a literary tradition where his narrative art can be seen in continuum from, as the Italian scholars have it, *l'esempio alla novella*.

SOME PARTICULAR EXAMPLES

In my final section, I wish to consider in greater detail how the combination of literary elements in the **Decameron** is similar to the kinds of transformations Chaucer achieves in the *Canterbury Tales*. There are many elements in Chaucer's practice that have parallels in the earlier collection, apart from those often mentioned[17] and the separate arguments advanced in my longer study. Above all, we find in Chaucer the same kind of detail that Boccaccio used to make local history. Before I look at the detail in the *Miller's* and the *Reeve's Tales,* each set specifically in a university town,[18] it is worth mentioning the general variety of local settings among all of the tales. Obviously, the *Cook's Tale* is set firmly in Cheapside and has all the flavor of a **Decameron** novella in the making, where the Cook's mention of "oure citee" mirrors the *brigata*'s familiar use of "nostra città" for Florence. The Friar's use of "my countree" (III. 1301) is perhaps more general, but the Summoner's rejoinder opens specifically with:

Lordynges, there is in Yorkshire, as I gesse
A mersshy contree called Holdernesse

(III. 1709-10)

which is similar to the openings of the Miller's and the Reeve's tales in Oxford and Cambridge (Trumpington). Abroad, one can note the precise locations and the important associations of St. Denis in the *Shipman's Tale,* Pavia in the *Merchant's Tale,* and Saluzzo in the *Clerk's Tale.* This kind of reference is important in building up a credible literary portrait, however fanciful the plot, and is an important connection with Boccaccio's practice.

In the first article to attempt a serious overall consideration of the influence of the **Decameron** on the *Canterbury Tales,* Donald McGrady mentions Boccaccio's *novella* "**2.10.**"[19] As I have already mentioned, this connection is not without interest for a reading of the *Miller's Tale,* especially if one is willing to consider reviving R. K. Root's idea of Chaucer's "memorial borrowing" of Boccaccio,[20] as McGrady does. In the same article, he notes the first mention of *Decameron* "**3.4**" as an obvious analogue for the *Miller's Tale* in an unpublished dissertation by Richard S. Guerin (1966).[21] This *novella* is not given in Bryan and Dempster's *Sources and Analogues,* nor is it discussed in an unpublished Oxford B. Litt. thesis by Moira F. Bovill.[22]

The *novella* of a clerkly scholar who invents a bogus scheme of salvation for an extremely pious old man in order to enjoy the physical pleasures of the old man's wife is obviously of interest for the *Miller's Tale.* What links the two narratives is the motif of a secret knowledge of salvation that the scholar imparts (in Boccaccio, the attainment of paradise and in Chaucer, salvation from the Flood) as the basis of a scheme for getting the husband apart so that the two lovers may enjoy each other intimately almost under the husband's nose. Both schemes of salvation are tightly woven into the narrative. Paradise is used for its potential bawdy wordplay, while the Flood is fundamental to the climax after the branding. In *Decameron* "**3.4**," there is no prophecy of the Flood, no "misdirected kiss," nor the branding revenge, even though the last two were common narrative motifs, known in Italy if only in Masuccio Salernitano's version.[23] What both narratives have in common is the gulling of a husband who is credulous in matters of religion and who thinks that a special divine knowledge has been made available to him. In the religious climate of the fourteenth century, this was a notable failing:[24] both husbands think they are privy to divine knowledge and are deceived on the earthly plane as well as the spiritual.

McGrady thinks that the inside and outside lover motif was taken by Chaucer from *Decameron* "**8.7**" and the discountenancing of the husband from *Decameron* "**7.4**," although it has to be admitted that these were common motifs for any potential writer. What is interesting, though, is that, like Guerin, McGrady admits the possibility of Boccaccio's influence and implies that Chaucer's knowledge of the *Decameron* was so great that he could pick and choose from its huge variety of episodes, characters, and motifs:

> In the *Miller's Tale,* his most elaborate and finely wrought *fabliau* (*novella* is perhaps a more appropriate term), Chaucer reverses, then, the approach observed in his other *Decameron* imitations, for its principal episodes are Boccaccian, and the accessory incidents are taken from different sources. At the same time, the *Miller's Tale* carries a step further a practice used consistently by Chaucer in his *fabliaux,* which is to combine two narrative sources for his main action; the story of the Miller intertwines elements from at least three *Decameron* tales, wedding them to the additional motifs of the Flood and the branding.[25]

With regard to *Decameron* "**7.4**," it should be remembered that the husband is an extremely jealous drunk

and that the woman is in love ("Amore" helps her "ingegno"[26]), so that our sympathies are most definitely with her and not with the husband.

Furthermore, there are several details from other *novelle,* not just *Decameron* "**3.4**," which parallel Chaucer's narrative. First of all, there is the same credulous, God-fearing old man, who has "una donna e un fante" serving him, just as John the Carpenter has his "knave" and his "wenche." The *senex* theme (a large one in the *Decameron*) is certainly a preoccupation of the Reeve, I. 3867. Furthermore, one can see the motif of Riccardo's astrology and the monk's invention of stargazing for Fra Puccio coalesced in the astrology-prophecy motif of Nicholas's scheme.

In *Decameron* "**3.4**," the monk is a young scholar newly returned from Paris, in close proximity to the family ("stretta dimesticchezza"; cf., the friar's closeness to Thomas's family in the *Summoner's Tale*), who is "assai giovane e bello della persona e d'aguto ingegno e di profonda scienza" [quite young and handsome in his appearance, of sharp intellect (or wit), and of deep learning ("**3.4**," 7)]. Like the friar, Nicholas is young, attractive, and learned: his "fantasye" could even be an echo of the monk's "ingegno."

Isabetta is described in the same visual and tactile way as Alison, if much more briefly. She is "fresca e bella e ritondetta che pareva una mela casolana" [fresh and beautiful and round as a red apple ("**3.4**," 7)] and elsewhere "fresca e ritondetta" [fresh and round ("**3.4**," 9)]. Alison is described in similar detail:

> Hir mouth was sweete as bragot or the meeth,
> Or hoord of apples leyd in hey or heeth
>
> (I. 3261-62)

What is more, Isabetta has a quick tongue ("mottegevole") and has a humorous exchange with her husband on the other side of the bedroom wall, which parallels Alison's ready repartee with Absolon.

Absolon himself may parallel something of a character from the very next *novella, Decameron* "**3.5**." Zima is so named because he is "l'azzimato" (the dressed-up one) and fastidious about his appearance: "sì ornato e sì pulito della persona andava" [he went about so dressed up and clean in his appearance ("**3.5**," 5)], but—unlike Absolon—although of humble origins ("picciola nazione"), he is a serious courtly lover: "aveva lungo tempo amata e vagheggiata infelicemente la donna di messer Francesco" [for a long time he had loved and unhappily longed for Messer Francesco's lady ("**3.5**," 5)]. Furthermore, he gives a very eloquent speech in courtly style, decorated with many expressions from *stilnovismo.* The clownish, parodic figure of a lover has a potential model in the character of Calandrino in

Decameron "**9.5**," who is musical, uses poetic language, and desires an ardent kiss; nor should we forget the ardent priest of Varlungo (*Decameron* "**8.2**"), who exhibits similar characteristics.

If Chaucer was inspired to draw upon narrative motifs from the *Decameron* in order to recombine them for his own ends, then, as I hope I have shown, there was no shortage of ways or material for him to have done so. One might also note, for example, that the *novella* after *Decameron* "**9.5**" happens to be precisely the analogue for the *Reeve's Tale*.

The Reeve gives a sentence for which his tale is an *exemplum*: "a gylour shal hymself bigyled be" (I. 4321), which is a common theme in the *novelle*, openly stated in *Decameron* "**2.9**":

> suolsi tra' volgari spesse volte dire un cotal proverbio: che lo 'ngannatore rimane a piè dello 'ngannato
>
> ("**2.9**," 3)
>
> [Among the common people, such a proverb is often said: that the deceiver will find himself at the mercy (lit. "feet of") the deceived]

and used to end the *novella* as well ("**2.9**," 75). It is a theme found in *Decameron* "**2.1**," "**2.9**," "**3.5**," "**5.10**," "**8.8**," and "**8.10**."

Following the work of Guerin, McGrady[27] notes additional circumstances in the *Reeve's Tale* that coincide with *Decameron* "**9.6**," namely:

1. The male characters drink heavily;

2. The guests pay for their lodging;

3. The daughter sleeps in a bed rather than a bin;

4. The wife remarks that she almost made the mistake of going to the guests' bed;

5. The husband never realizes that his wife, as well as his daughter, has fallen into his guests' hands.

There is more. In Boccaccio, the two young men go out of town to a specific location (a pass in the Mugello) for a specific purpose, embodying an opposition between town and country upon which Chaucer builds. There is an antecedent situation in the love between Pinuccio and Niccolosa, who at first takes great pride in being loved by the young gentleman ("forte si gloriava"); she leads him on a little, but after a time reciprocates his love, and a potentially difficult situation arises where society's (and presumably the family's) censure is involved. Boccaccio also emphasizes the fact that the girl, at fifteen or sixteen, still has no husband. In Chaucer, pride and censure are located specifically in the young girl's family and are the direct cause of her

remaining single at the "ripe" age of twenty. An antecedent relationship is suggested in Chaucer, by Aleyn's remark to Symkyn: "How fare thy faire doghter and thy wyf?" (I. 4023), a greeting not found in any of the other analogues.

Boccaccio mentions the young men's horses and their horseback journey. Chaucer uses the horse as an emblem of sexuality. Symkyn unties the clerks' horses in order to deceive them, unleashing not only their wild canter to the mares, but also his own deception in the riot of sexuality during the night. A detail becomes moulded into the overall pattern of the "gyler bigyled." If there is no criticism of the Church in *Decameron* "**9.6**," it pervades the *Decameron* as a whole (and was, of course, common to the age).

In both narratives, the wives save the day, but in different ways. In *Decameron* "**9.6**," the wife restores harmony, and neither she nor her husband are any the wiser; in the *Reeve's Tale,* the wife's response to the altercation between her husband and the clerk is physical intervention, where she unexpectedly deals out rough justice on Symkyn and allows John and Aleyn to make good their escape. Of course, it is not the harmonious situation left in *Decameron* "**9.6**": Chaucer prefers to leave us with an unresolved episode, perhaps to stimulate a more incisive satiric reception. There can be no harmony in such a world (cf., ending to the *Miller's Tale*).

The *Reeve's Tale,* therefore, can be seen to have elements from the *Decameron* where no other source is posited. As with the *Miller's Tale,* it leaves the reader with a sense of further chaos (the aftermath of explanations, recriminations, and excuses), while at the same time allowing some protagonists success in their deception. In Boccaccio, the *fabliaux*-style *novelle* end on notes of continuing harmonious "transgression": the lovers are able to pursue their affairs beyond the ends of the narratives. In Chaucer, justice enters in a rough guise: there is graphic description of almost slapstick violence, on which a "churl" might be expected to dwell, but, as with Boccaccio, Youth and Nature are seen to triumph over Age and Hypocrisy, even though the victory is neither as subtle nor as complete.

Another general feature may now be noted. If Chaucer is having fun at the expense of the two university towns (as intellectual rivals to London, perhaps), giving a particular setting to a narrative and group of plots that occur elsewhere, this is mirrored in Boccaccio's similar use of place in the *Decameron.* He sets traditional narratives in specific locations and often strikes out against Florence's rivals, such as Siena or Venice, by representing their inhabitants in an unfavorable light, and using dialects as part of the caricature. Both *Decameron* "**4.2**" and "**6.4**" have fun at the expense of Venice and its dialect; Siena is the butt of humor in *Decameron* **"7.10,"** **"8.8,"** and **"9.4,"** and Riccardo di Chinzica's Pisan dialect is used to make him appear mean and provincial (as opposed to Paganino's swashbuckling panache). Perhaps Boccaccio is at his most devastating in the portrait of the vain, credulous Lisetta in the Venetian *novella* of Frate Alberto (*Decameron* **"4.2"**), where her dialect emphasizes her foolishness. Dialect in Boccaccio, then, is used to indicate provincialism, meanness, or foolishness (and sometimes all three). Although not the place to examine it in detail here, this is done with consummate skill and exactness of vocabulary and ear; the language gives just enough of the significant characteristics for a more general "reading" to be implied in the reader's mind.

As Tolkien pointed out many years ago,[28] Chaucer shows a similar skill in the northern dialect of the two clerks, Aleyn and John. Although the northern "hicks" finally get the better of the East Anglian "hick," are we not meant to see them as potential gulls at the beginning of the narrative so that the turnaround in their fortunes is more of a surprise?

Boccaccio adopts a particular adaptation of rustic speech in one of the analogues to the *Shipman's Tale,* giving it a special quality of vitality and paradoxically showing us two rural wits. One can also note Boccaccio's use of malapropisms and metaplasms in this *novella* and elsewhere (e.g., *Decameron* **"8.2,"** 27, and Chaucer's use of the same e.g., III. 1189).[29] I hope the previous discussion has shown that there is enough parallel detail to support a case for the similarity of narrative technique in the *novelle* and the *Canterbury Tales.* This creation of detailed local characters in local settings underpins the creation by both authors of narrators whose popular narratives wish to be seen as illustrative material drawn from a [Illegible Text] of personal knowledge and experience. If Boccaccio and Chaucer both wished to free fiction from the old hermeneutical models, they could have thought of no more "human"—and realistic—way of doing so. They sought to show fiction as the refreshingly spontaneous reflection of individuals responding to life—allowing narrative an interpretative space which, if all too often abused, certainly mirrors the freedom of creation. Of course, the fact that this whole strategy was built upon a wealth of prior fiction shows just how effective was their common guise of a "local history" already heard "in toun."

Notes

1. *Il Novellino,* introduction by Giorgio Manganelli (Milan: Rizzoli, 1975). All quotations are from this edition with author's translations.

2. See *Decameron, Conclusione dell'autore.* Author's translations. 11-19.

3. For the generic argument, see my study, *Chaucer, Boccaccio and the Debate of Love* (Oxford: Clarendon Press, 1996).

4. This is an area well studied by Italian scholars, beginning with Salvatore Battaglia, *Giovanni Boccaccio e la riforma della narrativa* (Naples: Liguori, 1969). Vittore Branca also addresses the topic in "Studi sugli *exempla* e il *Decameron,*" *Studi sul Boccaccio* 14 (1983-84): 178-98; Chiara Degani, "Riflessi quasi sconosciuti di *exempla* nel *Decameron,*" *Studi sul Boccaccio* 14 (1983-84): 189-207; Carlo Delcorno, "Studi sugli *exempla* e il *Decameron* II," *Studi sul Boccaccio* 15 (1985-86): 189-214; Alberto Limentani, "Boccaccio e le sue fonti," *Cultura e scuola* 2.8: 15-19; Hans-Jorg Neuschäfer, *Boccaccio und der Beginn der Novelle* (Munich: Fink, 1969). Most recently, Francesco Bruni discusses it in the comprehensive study *Boccaccio: L'invenzione della letteratura mezzana* (Bologna: Mulino, 1990). A stimulating discussion of aspects of the topic can also be found in *La Nouvelle: Actes du Colloque Internationale de Montréal,* edited by M. Piconi, G. Di Stefano, and P. D. Stewart, McGill University, 1982 (Montréal: Plato Academic Press, 1983).

5. *Sir Gawain and the Green Knight,* edited by J. R. R. Tolkien and E. V. Gordon, rev. N. Davis, 2d edition (Oxford: Clarendon Press, 1967).

6. See notes to Branca's edition; A. C. Lee, *The Decameron: Its Sources and Analogues* (London: Nutt, 1909).

7. For example, Arezzo ("7.4"), Bologna ("7.7"), Certaldo ("6.10"), Milan ("8.1"), Naples ("2.5"; "3.6"), Palermo ("8.10"), Perugia ("5.10"), Pisa ("2.10"), Pistoia ("3.5"), Prato ("6.7"), Rimini ("7.5"), Saluzzo ("10.10"), Siena ("7.10"), Treviso ("2.1"), Venice ("4.2").

8. See notes to Branca, *Decameron* (1980), 31; also Joan M. Ferrante, "The Frame Characters of the *Decameron*: A Progression of Virtues," *Romance Philology* 19 (1965): 212-26; J. Markulin, "Emilia and the Case for Openness in the *Decameron,*" *Stanford Italian Review* 3 (1983): 183-99; Victoria Kirkham, "An Allegorically Tempered *Decameron,*" *Italica* 42 (1985): 1-23.

9. For example, Filomena ("3.3," 3), "Io intendo di raccontarvi una beffa che fu *da dovero* fatta da una bella donna e uno solenne religioso . . ." My italics; cf. "3.4," 4; "3.8," 3.

10. Branca, *Decameron* 49.

11. Ibid., 462.

12. See chapter V in my *Chaucer, Boccaccio and the Debate of Love.*

13. See Charles T. Davis, *Dante's Italy and Other Essays* (Philadelphia: University of Pennsylvania Press, 1984).

14. In many manuscripts the Host wishes he had a wife as deferential as he sees Griselda (IV. 1212).

15. See Petrarch, *Epistolae seniles* XVII. 3 (to Boccaccio), known as *De insigni obedientia et fide uxoria,* in *Sources and Analogues of Chaucer's Canterbury Tales* edited by W. F. Bryan and G. Dempster (London: Routledge, 1958).

16. Another version of this narrative, similarly reduced to the "bare minimum," has been found in a British collection of Latin *exempla* dating originally to the 1350s. See S. Wenzel, "Another Analogue to *The Pardoner's Tale,*" *Notes and Queries* NS 42.2 (1996): 134-36. Although slim evidence, it adds support to the idea that Chaucer perhaps knew the narrative in its reduced form.

17. See, for example, L. Morsbach, "Chaucers Plan der *Canterbury Tales* und Boccaccios *Decamerone,*" *Englische Studien* 42 (1910): 43-52; R. K. Root, "Chaucer and the *Decameron,*" *Englische Studien* 44 (1911): 1-7. The parallels cited are (1) narrators form an assembled company; (2) company has a common purpose; (3) stories connected by links; (4) a member of the company acts as director/arbiter of the storytelling (Root, 1).

18. J. A. W. Bennett, *Chaucer at Oxford and Cambridge* (Oxford: Clarendon Press, 1974).

19. D. McGrady, "Chaucer and the *Decameron* Reconsidered," *ChauR* 12 (1977): 1-26, where *Decameron* "2.10" is mentioned in connection with Peter G. Beidler's article on *Decameron* "8.9" and the *Merchant's Tale,* "Chaucer's *Merchant's Tale* and the *Decameron,*" *Italica* 50 (1973): 266-84.

20. R. K. Root, "Chaucer and the *Decameron.*"

21. McGrady, "Chaucer and the *Decameron* Reconsidered," 17.

22. Moira F. Bovill, "The *Decameron* and the *Canterbury Tales*: A Comparative Study" (B. Litt. thesis, Oxford University, 1966).

23. Bryan and Dempster, *Sources and Analogues,* 107.

24. Heiko A. Oberman, "Fourteenth Century Religious Thought: A Premature Profile," *Speculum* 53 (1978): 80-93, esp. 92-93.

25. McGrady, "Chaucer and the *Decameron* Reconsidered," 14.

26. Branca says that the three great themes of the *Decameron* are *Amore, Fortuna, Ingegno*; see V. Branca, *Boccaccio medievale e nuovi studi sul Decameron* (Firenze: Sansoni, 1981), 135.

27. McGrady, "Chaucer and the *Decameron* Reconsidered," 9.

28. J. R. R. Tolkien, "Chaucer as Philologist," *Transactions of the Philological Society* (1934): 1-70.

29. Cf., *Riverside Chaucer,* 863.

Bibliography

PRIMARY SOURCES

[Boccaccio, Giovanni]. *Decameron.* Translated by Mark Musa and Peter Bondanella. New York: New American Library, 1982.

Sir Gawain and the Green Knight. Edited by J. R. R. Tolkien and E. V. Gordon. Revised by N. Davis. 2nd ed. Oxford: Clarendon Press, 1967.

SECONDARY SOURCES

[Battaglia, Salvatore]. *Giovanni Boccaccio e la riforma della narrativa.* Naples: Liguori, 1969.

Beidler, Peter G. "Chaucer's *Merchant's Tale* and the *Decameron.*" *Italica* 50 (1973): 266-84.

[Bennett, J. A. W.]. *Chaucer at Oxford and Cambridge.* Oxford: Clarendon, 1974.

Bovill, Moira F. "The *Decameron* and the *Canterbury Tales*: A Comparative Study." B.Litt. thesis, Oxford University, 1966.

[Branca, Vittore]. "Studi sugli *exempla* e il *Decameron.*" *Studi sul Boccaccio* 14 (1983): 178-98.

Bruni, Francesco. *Boccaccio: L'invenzione della letteratura mezzana.* Bologna: Mulino, 1990.

Bryan, W. F., and Germaine Dempster, eds. *Sources and Analogues of Chaucer's "Canterbury Tales."* Chicago: University of Chicago Press, 1941. Reprinted, New York: Humanities Press, 1958.

Davis, Charles T. *Dante's Italy and Other Essays.* Philadelphia: University of Pennsylvania Press, 1984.

Degani, Chiara. "Riflessi quasi sconosciuti di *exempla* nel *Decameron.*" *Studi sul Boccaccio* 14 (1983-84): 189-207.

Delcorno, Carlo. "Studi sugli *exempla* e il *Decameron* II." *Studi sul Boccaccio* 15 (1985-86): 189-214.

[Ferrante, Joan M.]. "The Frame Characters of the *Decameron*: A Progression of Virtues." *Romance Philology* 19 (1965): 212-26.

[Kirkham, Victoria E.]. "An Allegorically Tempered *Decameron.*" *Italica* 42 (1985): 1-23.

Lee, A. C. *The Decameron: Its Sources and Analogues.* London: Nutt, 1909.

Limentani, Alberto. "Boccaccio e le sue fonti." *Cultura e scuola* (1962) 2.8: 15-19.

McGrady, Donald. "Chaucer and the *Decameron* Reconsidered." *ChauR* 12 (1977): 1-26.

Morsbach, Lorenz. "Chaucers Plan der *Canterbury Tales* und Boccaccios *Decamerone*." *Englische Studien* 42 (1910): 43-52.

Neuschäfer, Hans-Jorg. *Boccaccio und der Beginn der Novelle.* Munich: Fink, 1969.

[Oberman, Heiko A.]. "Fourteenth Century Religious Thought: A Premature Profile." *Speculum* 53 (1978): 80-93.

Root, Robert K. "Chaucer and the *Decameron*." *Englische Studien* 44 (1911): 1-7.

Thompson, N. S. *Chaucer, Boccaccio, and the Debate of Love: A Comparative Study of the Decameron and the Canterbury Tales.* Oxford: Clarendon, 1996.

Tolkien, J. R. R. "Chaucer as a Philologist." *Transactions of the Philological Society* (1934): 1-70.

[Wenzel, Siegfried]. "Another Analogue to *The Pardoner's Tale*." *Notes and Queries* 42.2 (1996): 134-36.

Simone Marchesi (essay date January 2001)

SOURCE: Marchesi, Simone. "'Sic me formabat puerum': Horace's *Satire* I,4 and Boccaccio's Defense of the *Decameron*." *MLN* 116, no. 1 (January 2001): 1-29.

[*In the following essay, Marchesi explains the significance of the allusion to Horace's* Satire *I, 4, in the closing line of the Introduction to the "Fourth Day" with respect to Boccaccio's defense of the* Decameron, *illuminating the intertextual relationship between the works.*]

The few lines which close Boccaccio's preemptive defense of the *Decameron* summarize, in what amounts to a final blow at his detractors, the strategy of contrasting his opponents' criticism with Nature, the same that the Author deploys throughout the **"Introduction to Day IV."** Addressing his female audience, he writes:

> E se mai con tutta la mia forza a dovervi in cosa alcuna compiacere mi disposi, ora più che mai mi vi disporrò, per ciò che io conosco che altra cosa dir non potrà alcuno con ragione, se non che gli altri e io, che v'amiamo, naturalmente operiamo [. . .] Per che tacciansi i morditori, e se essi riscaldar non si possono, assiderati si vivano.

> (*Decameron* "IV, Introduzione," 41)[1]

If the nature of those who attack him, Boccaccio implies, is such that they cannot be warmed by passion, his own nature predisposes him precisely to love. Fol-

lowing its lead, he will continue in the work of pleasing, consoling and even praising women (*Decameron* **"IV, Introduzione,"** 5: "piacervi, consolarvi e . . . commendarvi"). When it is read in the light of the defensive line the text has chosen from its beginning, nothing of what Boccaccio states in the paragraph quoted above is unexpected. What precedes in the **"Introduction"** has prepared the reader for a conclusion of this sort. After all, Boccaccio had phrased the accusations leveled against his work in such a way as to contrast Nature and morals, and it is only proper that the closing argument of the defense insist now on those terms, reasserting the overwhelming force of natural instincts and denouncing as unnatural the moralistic attacks on the work. From the very beginning of the **"Introduction to Day IV,"** the reader is invited to acknowledge that the censorious remarks on the work are fundamentally the sign of a natural shortcoming on the part of those who move them.

Something for which, on the contrary, the reader is not prepared is the last line, the seal of Boccaccio's whole argument: "e ne' lor diletti, anzi appetiti corrotti, standosi, me nel mio, questa brieve vita che posta n'è, lascino stare" (42).[2] If it is clear that the pleasure, which the author wants to prolong, coincides with his traditional, Ovidian *servitium amoris* (his "duty of pleasing" his female audience), what are the pleasures—that Boccaccio immediately qualifies as "corrupted appetites"—in which the detractors of the *Decameron* are immersed? The text of the **"Introduction to Day IV"** has provided the reader with no hint as to what they might be. Though a subtle Dantean echo of the *priamel* at *Paradiso* XI, 8-9 ("chi nel diletto della carne involto / s'affaticava")[3] can perhaps be perceived in the background and could help decipher the allusion to the corrupted appetites, one cannot find any clear statement of what these sinful pleasures are. The attacks on the *Decameron* may have been harsh, or disingenuous, or even a bit hypocritical (insofar as they were motivated by repressive idealism or misogynous humanistic poetics),[4] but they certainly did not seem to be the consequence of a vice.[5] Boccaccio's final puzzling remark, with which, to my knowledge, no scholar has dealt extensively, is possibly the first and foremost signal that the text relies on some assumptions and, I would add, an intertext, which the reader is called to detect and reconstruct. What I intend to do in the following pages is, thus, to bring to the attention a text by Horace, namely *Satire* I,4, with which there is no doubt Boccaccio was familiar and whose role as an intertext for his defense of the work has been so far underestimated.[6] When it is read alongside the **"Introduction to Day IV,"** Horace's *Satire* I,4 does not only provide the reader with a set of characters for which Boccaccio's label is well suited, it also gradually reveals other subtler points of contact with the **Decameron**'s self-defense. It puts perhaps in a clearer light the assumptions underlying the rhetorical project of the hundred tales as well.

Let us begin with a closer look at what I propose are the main common elements between the two texts. A brief summary of the 143-line *Satire* might be useful, since it will isolate some of the features which Boccaccio imports, with a certain degree of modification, into his own text. Following a method not at all alien to a medieval mind, one can start by dividing the *Satire* into its main parts. Three distinct sections are recognizable. Lines 1-38 contain, intermingled, the first charge leveled against the poet (the insinuation that his attacks are randomly hostile), a first "genealogical" argument in defense of the text (the tradition of Old Attic Comedy and Lucilius himself both included harsher poetry than Horace's), and finally a hint to the fact that the accusers are motivated by their vices and by the fear of the satirist's reproach. Lines 39-105 contain the strict defense of poetry that Horace develops in two ways. First, he downplays the role of satire in the system of literary genres (it is *sermo,* he claims, not high poetry, and hence arguably no poetry at all). Then he stresses the mild nature of his own work (the acrimonious conversation of the parasites and the angry attacks of forensic orators, in particular of prosecutors, both surpass the satirist's poems in bitterness). Lines 106-143 host the final defensive argument: satire is an educational tool, the same Horace's father used to shape him into a honest man when he was a child. The same method, we are meant to understand, Horace will continue to exercise upon himself and his fellow-citizens, by noting what consequences vice has in his neighbor's lives. The close of the *Satire* suggests, finally, that Horace's writing can also function as a substitute for his father's teachings, since it works as the lighthearted expression of the poet's externalized, reified, and incessant self-scrutiny.

The brief (and, perhaps, slightly tendentious) summary of the *Satire*'s line of argumentation offered here already shows some of the elements that Boccaccio might have found appealing when embarking on his defense of the **Decameron.** The Horatian move of linking the genre of satire with that of comedy, the consequent downplaying of the text's stylistic engagement, the characterization of the attackers, even the recourse to a compact apologue about teaching moral virtues, in which a father-son relationship is involved, are all elements which appear to correspond to analogous gestures in Boccaccio's text. The impression is reinforced, one may add, by another factor, which at first may seem purely coincidental: the position of the two apologetic pieces in their collections. I will discuss this point briefly, before coming back to other, arguably less casual relationships.

Horace's and Boccaccio's apology share their relative position with respect to the macro-texts that contain

them and for which they function as "midway proem."[7] Both the first book of Horace's *Satires* and the **Decameron** are made up of ten elements, ten poems and ten "giornate," and in both of them the defense of the whole work occupies the fourth slot.[8] This curious coincidence is reinforced by the presence of parallel apologetic texts in the tenth slot of both systems; *Satire* I,10 is again a "defense of poetry," similarly defensive is also the *Conclusione dell'Autore* with which the **Decameron** comes to a close. It is perhaps worth noticing that all the classical intertexts which have recently been indicated as antecedents for the **"Introduction to Day IV"** (for the most part, and rightly so, Ovidian) are either proemial and programmatic texts, or at any rate do not occupy the "midway" position in their collections.[9] In addition to Ovidian antecedents, Pier Massimo Forni proposes to look also at *Vita nuova* XXV as a possible model for the decision that Boccaccio took of interrupting the narrative flow of his work inserting a "polemic-argumentative parenthesis" in his text.[10] The parallel is certainly suggestive. But even in this case, in spite of all the proximity of the two macro-texts' structure, the Dantean model is providing Boccaccio with a defense of the work contained in its second half. The parallel with Horace's positioning of his self-defense, *before* the middle point of the work has been reached by the narrative, stands out for its uniqueness.[11]

But there is more. Horace's *Satire* I,4 and Boccaccio's apology of the **Decameron** seem also to respond to the same literary strategy of importing a fictional diachronic perspective into the "a-chronic" system of the book. In Horace the phenomenon is easier to detect, since the poet reacts against critics whose voices he incorporates into his apologetic text and to whose charges he answers by quoting from previous texts in the collection. Just as their attacks converge on the poems which precede *Satire* I,4 in the collection, so does Horace's defense. As C.A. Van Rooy notes, I,1 deals with *avaritia* and I,2 with *adulteri,* the vices specific to the human types described in I,4 as *dignos culpari.*[12] Lines 91-93 contain a verse lifted up from I,2 (line 27), moved into the new context, and introduced by a clear signal of temporal discrepancy: "ego si *risi,* quod ineptus / *pastillos Rufillus olet, Gargonius hircum,* /invidus et mordax *videor* tibi?"[13] The three verbs link, and at the same time force to collide, the fictional past of the book's beginning section on the one hand with the intra-textual present-tense of the quoted statement, and on the other hand with the extra-textual present-tense of the attackers. This is a play not at all alien to Boccaccio's "frame-shifts" as described by Joy Hambuechen Potter.[14] Other elements of *Satire* I,4 refer to its antecedents in the book. The poet Crispinus in line 14 is the same unrefined poet whom *Satire* I,1 took as an example of rugged prolixity; the vulgar Tigellius of line 72 is probably the same Tigellius, the singer, with whom Horace has dealt at I,2.3 and I,3.4 (such, at least, he is considered by the scholiast, in spite of his being presented as dead in I,2 and as potentially alive here). Style, moral attitudes, hence, and characters are all features of the text of *Satire* I,4 which direct the reader's attention back to previous elements of the collection, the present poem being the recapitulation of the preceding ones.[15]

Now, both the harking back of the apologetic piece and the insistence on its being a reaction to attacks which originate from the foregoing texts are features that Boccaccio includes into the **"Introduction to Day IV."** He first insists on the timeliness of his defense, on the necessity of having it now, after only one-third of the work has gone by:

> Per ciò che, se già, non essendo io ancora al terzo della mia fatica venuto, essi son molti e molto presummono, io avviso che avanti che io pervenissi alla fine essi potrebbono in guisa esser multiplicati, non avendo prima avuta alcuna repulsa, che con ogni piccola lor fatica mi metterebbono in fondo.

> **(*Decameron* "IV, Introduzione," 10)**[16]

In these lines, which the reader is only partially allowed to take at face value, the author appears to imply that the reading of his first thirty *novelle* prompted his detractors' critiques. The impression is stronger when one notes how Boccaccio incorporates in the justification of the work some allusions to material already presented in the first part of the book. Three elements stand out in this category: first, the *motto* in paragraph 33: "perché il porro abbia il capo bianco, che la coda sia verde," which recalls **"I,10,"**17: "e come che nel porro niuna cosa sia buona, pur men reo e più piacevole alla bocca è il capo di quello, il quale voi generalmente, da torto appetito tirate, il capo vi tenete in mano e manicate le frondi."[17] The second recovered element is the sententious statement we find in paragraph 38: "a nessun caglia più di me che a me," which echoes a passage in Bartolomea Gualandi's tirade in **"II,10,"**37: "Del mio onore non intendo io che persona, ora che non si può, sia più di me tenera."[18] Finally, the third case of interference between the text of the **"Introduction"** and previously developed material is constructed by the parallel "servizio di Dio" to which are devoted both the young hermit Rustico of **"III,10,"** and the similarly young (but not at all similarly "inspired" hermit) Balducci in the apologue of the goslings. Both living in seclusion, the first is completely given to "pensier santi, orazioni e discipline" (**"III,10,"**10), until Alibech comes by, just as the second "in digiuni e in orazioni vivendo" listens to his father's teachings, who "della gloria di vita etterna e di Dio e de' santi gli ragionava, nulla altro che sante orazioni insegnandogli" (**"IV, Introduzione,"** 15),[19] until he descends to Florence and comes across a "brigata di belle giovani" (**"IV, Introduzione,"** 20).[20]

When we do not treat as a pure coincidence the fact that both Horace and Boccaccio recur to analogous strategies when defending their works and allow *Satire* I,4 to function as an antecedent for the **"Introduction to Day IV,"** we can readdress also the question of the existence of an early dissemination of the *novelle,* of that "redazione extravagante" which has been postulated by some scholars but of which no philological evidence, surprisingly enough, has surfaced yet. Although Branca and Padoan insist, in fact, that the words we read in the **"Introduction to Day IV"** should be taken as a decisive proof of an early Florentine circulation of the first three *giornate,* the profoundly literary nature of Boccaccio's gesture—the central argument of this paper—should make us reconsider the degree to which the author's claims may reflect an actual, historical situation.[21] As a consequence of seeing Horace's model looming large beneath the ***Decameron's*** surface, we should carefully weigh Boccaccio's statements. We should be particularly careful when we attempt to extend their significance from the strictly literary realm of textual interpretation to the reconstruction of an "extra-textual," historical, and philological truth.[22]

Let us come back to the analysis of some other elements that the two texts share. Other common features, as I have suggested, are the defensive nature of both texts and the presence in them of a similar topical gesture; *i.e.,* the claim of humility. If we compare what Boccaccio says in his **"Introduction"** with what Horace claims for his collection of satires, we cannot help noticing, beyond some similarities in the language, the marked parallelism of their rhetorical attitudes:

> Agedum, pauca accipe contra.
> Primum ego me illorum, dederim cui esse poetas,
> Excerpam numero: neque enim concludere versum
> dixeris esse satis; *neque, si qui scribat uti nos
> sermoni propiora, putes hunc esse poetam.*

> (*Satire* I, 4.39-43)

> Per ciò che [. . .] non solamente pe' piani ma ancora per le profondissime valli mi sono ingegnato d'andare; il che assai manifesto può apparire a chi le presenti novellette riguarda, le quali non solamente *in fiorentin volgare e in prosa scritte* per me sono e senza titolo, ma ancora *in istilo umilissimo e rimesso quanto il più si possono.*

> **(*Decameron* "IV, Introduzione,"** 3)

In the background of Boccaccio's semi-serious auto-definition of the ***Decameron*** as a work composed by "little tales . . . written in the vulgar tongue and in prose . . . lack*ing* even a title, . . . and couched in as humble, unassuming style as could be" generic references to a variety of texts have been detected, from the *Novellino* or the collections of *exempla* of eastern origin to Ovid's *Amores* to Dante's *Commedia* via Epistle XIII, and all have been thoroughly illustrated.[23] It still needs to be noted, however, that in alluding to Dante's *Commedia,* which, according to the Epistle to Cangrande, was composed "remisse et humiliter" (X,30 and 31),[24] Boccaccio is paralleling in matter and in form Horace's genealogical reference to his comic, and thus humbly non-poetic, models:

> Idcirco quidam Comoedia necne poema
> esset quaesivere, quod acer spiritus ac vis
> nec verbis nec rebus inest, nisi quod pede certo
> differt *sermoni, sermo merus.*

(45-48)

One more text may be signaled as pertinent: the pseudo-Acronian gloss to Horace's syntagm "sermoni propiora." The gloss reads: "Vicinia fabulis aut orationi; *sermoni* cottidiano."[25] Pseudo-Acron continues, glossing lines 46-48: "In comoedia neque verba elata sunt neque sensus, sed solo metro differt comoedia a prosa oratione."[26] The *Satire*'s and the **Decameron**'s style, both composed "in stilo umilissimo e rimesso," approach the genre of comedy; the first programmatically links its stance to the Old Attic Comedy, while the second invokes as a precedent Dante's comic work. Both occupy the lowest step in the ladder of the styles, the one closest to conversation and prose.[27]

To be sure, in both cases we have to take the author's words with extreme care. Boccaccio and Horace are well aware that what they declare about their present literary enterprise is basically an elaborate and witty play with the canon and the audience, and the main thrust of their ironic argument is to be found precisely in their (and the reader's) awareness of this play. It is not necessary to recall how the author of the **Decameron** will soon answer to its poetic detractors that "queste cose tessendo" (and he is still talking about the most humble *novelle* of his), "né dal monte Parnaso né dalle Muse non mi allontano quanto molti per avventura s'avvisano" (36).[28] Horace's defensive gesture had the same twist: if it is true that the satirical author must be excluded from the number of those whom one may call "poets," it is also true that the texts he produces are as carefully crafted as those by any other poet. Or rather, they are definitely better. The basic tenet of the Alexandrian poetic code, to which Horace programmatically adheres, opposed precisely a refined, carefully constructed, and "tenuis" poetry (the "recte" of New Poets' writings) to the "multum" of the unkempt, overproductive writers (as Horace puts the matter in lines 12-13 of the present *Satire*). This post-neoteric mood, which will surface again in *Satire* I,10, controls the carefully constructed set of stylistic oppositions between Horace's poetry (the work of a poet "tersus atque elegans, decens et ridens," as reads Porphyrion's gloss to line 8) and that of both his antecedent (the "muddy" Lucilius) or his contemporary challengers (the "casual" Crispinus). The irony underlying Horace's (and

Boccaccio's) statement is evident, thus, from the very beginning of their texts. A clear disavowal of what *prima facie* appeared as a serious declaration of poetic modesty comes very soon to deconstruct that claim, to show its rhetorical ancillary nature.[29]

A third feature of Horace's *Satire* should not be passed over in silence. It may have also shaped Boccaccio's sense of his work's purpose and form: the theme of "invidia" on which a good deal of the Latin satirist's defense relies. The "lectura Horatii," as Villa pointedly defined the multiform wealth of continuous commentaries and lemmatized glosses to the Horatian *corpus,* stresses that the text of *Satire* I,4 is opposing the tone of its author to the one peculiar to his detractors, to those "biting" and envious characters who would spare no friend or enemy in their attacks. It is perhaps not a product of mere chance that together with Ovidian subtexts (particularly those from *Tristia* appropriately signaled by Forni) and Dantean reminiscences (the echoes of *Paradiso* XVII, 132-135 signaled by Branca, which are equally evident and essential) Boccaccio's text refers also to Horace's. Thematically, the opposition between the "biting" criticism of his attackers and his own "lighter" response (the same we sense in Boccaccio's statement in paragraph 9: "Le quali cose io con piacevole animo, sallo Idio, ascolto e intendo")[30] recalls the distance which Horace feels is setting him apart from his detractors and the other practitioners of vulgar, violent satire. The pseudo-Acronian and Porphyrian glosses are again useful in this case. They let us appreciate how in the "sucus nigrae lolliginis" and the "aerugo mera" of the ill-willed satirists which Horace depicts in lines 100-101, one should see the products of envy, a vice from which the poet declares he is immune: "quod vitium procul afore chartis / atque animo prius, ut si quid promittere de me / possum aliud vere, promitto" (101-103).[31] Porphyrion writes: "Ex lolliginis suco livorem mentis vult intellegi, ex aerugine venenum." His gloss resounds also in Pseudo-Acron's comments to these lines: "*Sucus* virus, id est, *livor* mentis, noxia malignitas." The theme was anticipated in lines 93-94, whose gloss reads: "*Ego si risi . . . lividus et mordax videor tibi? Ego si aliquem merito vituperavero, reprehendis? Lividus: Invidus,* malus." Horace does not enjoy damaging others (line 78), he does not attack to "bite" as a rabid dog would do; he is neither "acer" (as Caprius, a negative example in line 65) nor does he bite ("rodit" in line 81) those whose vices he reprimands. The "invidus, malus" satirist, the "mordax" Juvenal-like spirit is kept out of the text. Now, if we read back into Horace's text the terminology by which Boccaccio will define and categorize the two kinds of "motti" which make up the topic of the Day in **"VI,3,"**3-4, we realize that *Satire* I,4 is fashioning the same distinction between those who bite "as dogs" (the work's detractors) and those who bite "as sheep" (the poet), a distinction that Boccaccio will appropriate in Lauretta's meta-narrative commentary.[32]

Although those who censure the author of the *Decameron* are, like the satirist of the vilest kind, both motivated by "invidia" and accused of distributing lacerating "morsi," the text of the **"Introduction to Day IV"** does not seem to "bite back" at his attackers. Or rather, it does not bite back in the same violent and harsh way. The way in which Horace dealt out his criticisms is consistently characterized by his text as "light-hearted" (lines 90, in *antiphrasis,* and 103-104, probably also 139) and the *scholia* insist on the *mira urbanitas* with which Horace was able to deliver his blows, his *amaritudines.*[33] In the same way one may characterize the irony with which the *Decameron* answers its detractors. In the end, the author is right to describe his *animo* as *piacevole;* in his defense no personal attacks are perceivable, no ruthless spite in the response to his critics. The *Decameron* does not gratuitously attack, *gaudens laedere,* anyone.

But what about the fact that the *Decameron* does stigmatize its critics as being under the sway of "appetiti corrotti"? Is not the paragraph from which my discussion started, liable to being described as harsh and gratuitously biting, inspired by a "will to harm"? In my view there is no contradiction between the characterization of the author's serene spirit and the text of his defense. There is, in fact, a reason behind the isolated virulence of his last remark. Boccaccio's attack is justified by the necessity, to which any satirical piece is bound, to identify, expose and attempt to correct the moral shortcomings of both its audience and its "human" subject-matter.[34] It is again from Horace's text that I would argue one is allowed to recover the rationale for Boccaccio's gesture. The context of the accusations leveled against Horace's *Satire* in lines 22-25 makes clear that those who attacked his work did so because they felt threatened by it. A close consideration of that portion of the text will clarify the matter.

Horace acknowledged that almost no one read his works and he himself was afraid to read them in public, since the greatest part of the audience hated the literary genre of Satire ("quod sunt quos genus hoc minime iuvat," line 24). This happened because they knew that they deserved to be blamed for their lack of morals ("utpote pluris / culpari dignos," lines 24-25). In truth, continued Horace, almost everyone seems to labor under some passion, almost everyone seems to be affected by some vice, and it comes as no surprise that they fear poetry and hate poets ("omnes hi metuunt versus, odere poetas," line 33). Now, since the duty of the satirist is exactly, as Pseudo-Acron glossing line 70 defines it, "mordere vitiosos," the audience of Horace ends up fearing, and therefore hating and finally attacking his work. If

Boccaccio thought he could import this typology of the public into his own text, the lines from which my analysis has started are no longer enigmatic: they reproduce, in epitomized form, the longer syllogistic reasoning of Horace. If the detractors of the *Decameron* attack it, they must be doing so because they feel threatened by whatever criticism of their vices it may contain; they must have, therefore, some vice. Their pleasures must be, in other words, vices, and their appetites "corrupted." The text of the **"Introduction to Day IV"** allows only the last element of the reasoning to come to the surface, and its sudden appearance calls for interpretation, unless, as I argue here, its suddenness is only due to our having failed to detect and exploit the previous intertextual signals in the text, which all pointed to Horace's *Satire* as a necessary antecedent. If, in sum, one reads Boccaccio's seemingly gratuitous assault with Horace's *Satire* in mind, it soon ceases to appear either surprising or gratuitous.

If Boccaccio's text, in fact, does not provide clues about the moral faults that its detractors have in addition to their natural shortcoming (their being "cold"), Horace's *Satire* goes into this matter at some length. Lines 25-32 provide the reader with a thorough review of misdirected appetites ranging from "avaritia" to "ambitio," from adulterous love to corruption of young boys, from veneration of wealth to self-destructive exercise of commerce:

> Quemvis elige turba:
> aut ob avaritiam aut misera ambitione laborat.
> hic nuptarum insanit amoribus, hic puerorum;
> hunc capit argenti splendor; stupet Albius aere;
> hic mutat merces surgente a sole ad eum quo
> vespertina tepet regio . . .
>
> (25-30)[35]

To be sure, Horace's catalogue is not enough to account for the five detailed objections the critics of the *Decameron* are moving against its author. One should not, however, underestimate the coincidence that the vice over which Horace lingers the longest (4 lines, half of his tirade) may be read also into Boccaccio's text, in his presentation of the social subject which is responsible for the fourth objection:

> Hic mutat merces surgente a sole ad eum, quo
> vespertina tepet regio; quin per mala praeceps
> fertur, uti pulvis collectus turbine, nequid
> summa deperdat metuens aut ampliet ut rem.
>
> (30-33)[36]

It is exactly to this mercantile type of man that the fourth objection to the *Decameron* and the author's response are perfectly suited. Now, one is not in any way diminishing Vittore Branca's insight about the value of the *Decameron* as "the epic of the merchant class" if one notes how this "merchant" epic has in many cases an anti-mercantile twist. Or better, it presents the reader with a detailed set of advisable limitations to the dangerous activities of its "heroes."[37] It is hard to resist the temptation of seeing behind the parable of Landolfo Rufolo—to name only one merchant in the **Decameron**'s world, who would undergo any trial so that he may, in Horace's words, add to his wealth—the same frantic, incessant and senseless activism of Horace's merchant. Even if it is only the Landolfo of the beginning of **Decameron "II,5"** that we see in Horace's text, a character who has not yet been converted by the inconstancy of Fortune to real-estate investment, we cannot deny that he decidedly shares the frame of mind and the social and political milieu of Boccaccio's fourth censor. As Landolfo and the two anonymous merchants in Horace and Boccaccio come from the same class and share the same entrepreneurial ethics, they are also united as fictional "misopoetists" beneath the *stilus* of the satirist.

It is not, again, a matter of chance that, in the description of the stormy voyages of Horace's merchant, the text of *Satire* I,4 comes into contact again with the letter of the **"Introduction to Day IV."** In Horace, the merchant's continuous and senseless movement through the dangers of travel is paired, in a tight ironic simile, with that of the dust being taken up by a whirlwind. In a different context, but with identity in the terms of comparison (human being and dust), Boccaccio uses the same image. The parallel is in the same closing section in which we find also the puzzling reference to the detractor's vices, and this makes the connection perhaps even stronger: "per ciò che io non veggo che di me altro possa avvenire che quello che dela minuta polvere avviene, la quale, *spirante turbo,* o egli di terra non la muove, o se la muove la porta in alto" (**"IV, Introduzione,"** 40).[38] One can always say that a different text could be offered as the target of Boccaccio's allusive technique here, namely Dante's line "come la rena *quando turbo spira*" from *Inferno* III, 60.[39] But there, in spite of the closer formula, the synaesthetic reference to a sound whirling in the murky atmosphere of hell as sand moves in a windstorm is joining together elements which are farther away from those in Boccaccio's text than are the deluded human being and the dust in Horace's *Satire.* We are confronted, I would argue, with a second—and by no means last—instance in Boccaccio's text of a double allusion, which is on a first plane Dantean and only secondarily Horatian. As it was the case for the nature of the "diletti" of the **Decameron**'s critics, when to be noticing the echo from *Paradiso* XI, 8 was not enough to fully appreciate the richness of Boccaccio's multi-layered allusive web, also for the "whirling dust" of this passage the chain of references extends beyond Boccaccio's first vernacular *auctor* and reaches the Latin writer of satires. In both cases the

reader is invited twice to open up the surface of the text, to reveal a first source, and then perhaps a more pertinent and more subtle one.[40]

The impression gathered so far in comparing the argumentation of Boccaccio's defense to the one of Horace's *Satire* I,4 is that the latter may be part of the intertextual grid Boccaccio invites his audience to recognize when reading his text. The moral determinations of the critics of both the **Decameron** and of the first book of *Satires* are similar, just as similar are the tactics deployed by the two authors; analogous are the structures of the books and parallel the position occupied by the defensive pieces in both of them. Now, if it is true that singular, episodic coincidences, along with possible isolated verbal echoes, are not enough to justify postulating a pattern of allusions between two texts, it is hard to deny that "episodic" coincidences change their nature—and their critical "weight" increases—when they present themselves in clusters and are supported by the presence of similar rhetorical attitudes connecting the primary and the "target" text. This is particularly true in the highly self-conscious contexts of metaliterary discourses, such as are both *Satire* I,4 and the **"Introduction to Day IV."**

Now, if it is true that some elements of "how" Boccaccio's allusive technique works here begin to become apparent, the reason behind the very presence of Horace's text at such a critical point in the **Decameron** still needs to be addressed. Assuming that the pattern of allusions needs to have a purpose, that it cannot be either self-sufficient or merely decorative, I will argue in the following pages that Boccaccio's strategic allusions throughout the **"Introduction to Day IV"** do in fact have a specific goal. They are functional to the author's definition of the core of his answer to the **Decameron**'s (imagined) critics, but they might also help to shape our sense of the work as a whole. On that account, I turn now to a short analysis of the apologue of the "goslings," which I would like to read, in a Horatian light, more as defending Boccaccio's stylistic and poetic practice than as advancing any "new" moral perspective.

The traditional readings of the "incomplete novella," championed by scholars like Baratto, Fedi and Scaglione, have always considered it as some sort of "Naturalist Manifesto" which Boccaccio would underwrite and include at the heart of his work, and whose principle, namely that sexual desire is impossible to curb and hence should be let free, should guide our interpretation of the **Decameron** as a liberating, anti-medieval text.[41] This interpretation, suggestive as it may be, is not I believe exhaustive. It does not account, for example, for the possibility of providing as well an opposite reading of the apologue based on the presence, in all but one of the *novelle* of Days **"IV"** and **"V,"** of the destructive consequences of unbridled desire. The

Decameron's insistence on the intrinsic dangers that lie in adopting an unconditionally hedonistic ethics (and a literalistic poetics) can cast some doubt on Boccaccio's adherence to the principle he allegedly proposes here.[42] It is possible that the difficulty we experience trying to establish the moral determinations of characters and plot in Filippo Balducci's story issue not only from the text's very openness, but also from our overlooking the possibility that it may deal also with a different set of problems. When one looks at the *novelletta* in the frame of a strictly ethical debate, one actually runs the risk of disregarding a fundamental factor: the apologue is an integral part of a literary as well as ethical polemic and it occupies a middle ground between morality and style. To understand the text fully, one cannot separate it from the web of allusions to which the surrounding argument continually refers. The first layer of this web is, again, Dante and the second, I maintain, is Horace. It is on the basis of Boccaccio's implied traditions that the story of Filippo Balducci and his son is in the end more concerned with commenting on different teaching strategies than with the subject matter of instruction *per se*. The point of the text is not to advance a new morality, but to comment on methods of instruction, not so much *what* should be taught, but rather *how* one should teach it.

Focusing on some usually underconsidered details of the story I will attempt to support the claim made above. It is hard to deny that, from the very givens of the apologue, the text of the *Decameron* insists on considering the way in which Filippo Balducci brings up his only child, once he has moved away from the city. The description of the only course offered in the program of instruction of the young man is based—the text details an overloaded, parodic catalogue—on negation and consequent abstraction:

> Per che, data ogni sua cosa per Dio, senza indugio se n'andò sopra Monte Asinaio, e quivi in una piccola celletta se mise col suo figliuolo, col quale di limosine in digiuni e in orazioni vivendo, sommamente si guardava di non ragionare, là dove egli fosse, d'alcuna temporal cosa né di lasciarnegli alcuna vedere, acciò che esse da così fatto servigio nol traessero, ma sempre della gloria di vita eterna e di Dio e de' santi gli ragionava, nulla altro che sante orazioni insegnandogli. E in questa vita molti anni il tenne, mai della cella non lasciandolo uscire né alcuna altra cosa che sé dimostrandogli.

("**IV, Introduzione**," 15)[43]

It is true that part of the negative structure of the educational program devised by the old Balducci is filtering into Boccaccio's text from its most direct sources, *i.e.*, the exemplary tradition, in which the core of the story was the sudden exposure of a young man, who had been sheltered from the world since his childhood, to the temptations of real life ("temporal cos*e*"). This does not suffice, however, to dismiss as purely derivative

Boccaccio's playful insistence on detailing the young Balducci's education. Negative expressions recur eight times to describe the father's program of instruction, and they give the narrative point an almost overstated rhetorical emphasis. The father *never* talks about *any* temporal matter and *never* allows the son to see *any*, fearing he may *not* be strong enough to continue on the ascetic path he had prepared for him. Also the little bit of "positive" instruction (the discourse about the glory of Life Eternal and God and the Saints) that the old Balducci gives his son—in turn totally removed from direct experience, which is in his curriculum systematically deferred—is counterbalanced by a negative statement: "teaching him *nothing but* holy prayers." In the sixteen years of his "training" on Monte Senario, the young Balducci "has *never* been allowed to leave the cell and has been shown *nothing* but his own father." He has been educated only through the action of an authoritative discourse, embodied and hammered home by the father.[44]

The insistence on the negative teaching *techniques* around which the young Balducci's education revolves is not at all gratuitous. Also the close of the apologue, which depicts the father finally realizing how Nature can overpower his "ingegno," is contrasting directly the father's program and method of education (in the nexus "*suo* ingegno" the stress falls, I would argue, on the possessive adjective) with the force of the instructional method proper to Nature. More than being the epigraph of the first chapter in the history of the contrast between the principles of Nature and of Civilization, the close of the apologue is, I believe, a methodological commentary.[45] At the end of the unfinished novella it is the old man's teaching philosophy that fails in front of a more powerful and more effective one, the one Boccaccio labels "Natura." The father's "ingegno" is first the whole program of instruction followed in the "Thebaid" of Monte Senario and then the faint attempt to export it also into the realm of the city.[46] In the world of urban life, the strategy of negation ("do not talk about, do not show") is resisted and opposed by a new reality, which also contains potentially a new method. The overwhelming "presence" of the objects, against whose immediate evidence the discourse of the father can exercise only its nominative power, is irreconcilable with the former pattern of instruction. Realizing the danger of a direct exposure to the world, the old Balducci has to devise—and quickly, if he does not want to lose the fruit of his former teachings—a new strategy. Faced with the combined action of the irreducible reality of social life and the son's "natural" curiosity, the father chooses to exercise his power in a definite direction, which—it must be noted—is not at all the only possible one. He turns the act of naming the objects for his son into an agent of abstraction. The technique he adopts, and adapts, from his former teaching philosophy seems at first actually to be working. The son responds at first with the prescribed ascetic attitude, registering the no-menclature and moving on: "Il padre gliele diceva; e egli, avendolo udito, rimaneva contento e domandava d'un'altra" (20).[47] The father's teaching method comes to an impasse only when, facing the last object, the women, he clumsily tries to turn them into "goslings." When he is finally confronted with the task of removing the object, which he had decided not only never to show, but also never to name, he witnesses the collapse of his own educational system. Here, leaving his *novella* incomplete, Boccaccio leaves off. It may be true that at this point the Narrator of the **Decameron** may have proven his *moral* point (that Nature shapes human beings in such a way as they cannot but yield to the power of love). But it is equally true that he has been able also to prove a subtler, and in no way less important, *methodological* point: that a teaching based only on removal and repression is sooner or later destined to fail.

When it is read from the point of view of the instructional methodology, the story of Filippo Balducci is recounting the failure of his *ingegno,* of his whole project of education. But what does it tell us about the other pole of the final opposition, *Natura*? Can it be qualified better? How does Nature form the young Balducci? And, more precisely, if Filippo Balducci's methodology is flawed, how can one learn to teach according to Nature? It is here that Dante's *Comedy* and Horace's *Satires* come back into play, both presenting an instructional method, which radically opposes the one chosen by Filippo Balducci. The opposition resides not primarily in the content of the instruction imparted in the three texts, but in the method used to impart it.[48]

Dante is the first intertext, which can provide a commentary on a teaching model that better exploits the "natural" tendency of the human soul. If we re-read the passage in *Paradiso* XVII that Boccaccio used when constructing the double metaphor of "the fierce wind and the bitings of envy," we realize that it can hardly be understood when it is taken out of context. Cacciaguida, answering the question of his great-grandson, instructs him to "let all that *he has* seen be manifest" because, he says:

> Questo tuo grido farà come vento,
> che le più alte cime più percuote;
> e ciò non fa d'onor poco argomento.
>
> (*Paradiso* XVII, 133-35)[49]

He immediately continues with an explanation of the rationale behind Dante's whole *visione,* his experience of the three realms, evaluating its aptness as a means of instruction "a pro del mondo che mal vive":

> Però ti son *mostrate* in queste rote,
> nel monte e nella valle dolorosa

> pur l'anime che son di fama note
> *ché l'animo di quel ch'ode, non posa*
> né ferma fede per essempro ch'aia
> *la sua radice incognita e ascosa.*
>
> (136-42)[50]

Cacciaguida, whose figure stands out as the one of the "true" father, one authorized by lineage and more importantly by his carrying out of God's instructional plan with Dante, teaches the Pilgrim-Poet how to teach through his work.[51] It is not surprising, perhaps, that at the core of his methodological comments we find a strong statement advocating the exemplary mode of instruction. What Dante has seen, sees and will see, remarks Cacciaguida, is shown to him ("però ti son *mostrate . . .* pur l'anime") so that it may be turned into an example, a discourse which derives its authority from its origin in (and its adherence to) immediately present reality. The lapidary rationale Cacciaguida provides for God's way of teaching is that the soul does neither rest nor trust unless what is proposed, its reality and its roots, are "known and shown." It is not hard to see, at this point, how Filippo Balducci functions as the foil for Cacciaguida, insisting on *not showing* what his program of education should in truth be all about. It is precisely by refusing the exemplary mode of instruction and relying solely upon an abstract, authority-based system of precepts, that the Florentine solitary condemns his own "unnatural" teaching ultimately to failure. To be sure, the parallel between the *Commedia* and the **Decameron** does not extend also to the subject matters. While the first insists on considering reality representable (in Auerbach's terms) only after it has been freed from the contingencies of time and space, the latter programmatically limits its scope and field of rhetorical action to *this* world. Both texts are, however, undeniably interested in discussing (and surely also proposing) what is the right way to teach.[52]

Dante's *Commedia* is not, I would argue, the only text in which Boccaccio could find the exemplary mode of instruction he so strongly advocates in his defense of the **Decameron.** It is again in Horace's *Satire* I,4 that he found an antecedent. The Latin poet provided in that text a positive *exemplum* of a reality-based teaching method, which succeeded both in shaping its subject into a decent human being and in holding up when confronted with the shock-effect of the direct exposure to, and experience of reality. The last section of the poem recounts how the education Horace received from his father—notably the same he is passing along by way of his book of satires—was based explicitly on the refusal of any authoritative and abstract discourse about morality. To the abstract teaching of the philosopher (portrayed in an ironic language alluding to the Stoic figure of the Sage: "sapiens") Horace's father substituted the practice of adding a moral commentary to the review of concrete examples of virtues and vices. This,

Horace implies, made his father's teaching more effective, and—more to the point—taught him how to teach. Addressing his critics and asking to be at the same time granted the right to write satires and be forgiven for his texts, he indicates the example of his father: "Insuevit pater optimus hoc me, / ut fugerem exemplis vitiorum quaeque notando" (lines 105-106).[53] He reiterates the concept when he comes to the positive side of his instruction: "Sic me / formabat puerum dictis et, sive iubebat / ut facerem quid: 'habes auctorem, quo facias hoc,' / unum ex iudicibus selectis obiciebat" (lines 120-123).[54]

If we read in mutual perspective the texts of Horace, Dante and Boccaccio, we see how the teachings of Horace's father come to coincide exactly first with what Cacciaguida defends as the appropriate teaching technique, and then with what Filippo Balducci does *not* choose to do, when he leaves his hermitage to come to terms with the city. The father of Horace's *Satire,* just as Cacciaguida does, pointed his young son in the direction of reality, not away from it, choosing to confront the examples (however negative they may be) of people worthy of blame, from the squanderer to the sex-addicted adulterer.[55] He refuses as ineffective, at that stage of his son's moral development, the authority-based method of the philosopher who, moving from abstract principles ("what is good, what is bad") pretends effectively to teach about what is to be sought after and what is to be avoided:

> Aiebat: "Sapiens, vitatu quidque petitu
> sit melius, causas reddet tibi; mi satis est si
> traditum ab antiquis morem servare tuamque,
> dum custodis eges, vitam famamque tueri
> incolumem possum . . ."
>
> (*Satire*, I, 4.115-19)[56]

But why should the **Decameron** recur to these texts and insist on the teaching techniques of literary characters like Cacciaguida or Horace's mainly fictional father in order to defend itself from the attacks of its critics? In the five-point critique of the **Decameron** no item was dedicated to criticize this aspect of the work. The reason Boccaccio adopted the strategy he did in the **"Introduction to Day IV"** is to be found, I believe, in his perceiving his own work as satirical in nature and modeling this aspect of the **Decameron** on Horace's book. Just as Horace's *Satire* I,4, Boccaccio's self-defense fosters the notion that the book is a teacher of morality, one which can form better human beings. Both the Latin poet and the vernacular writer of *novelle* aim at defending not only the subject matter of their works, but primarily their function as surrogate teachers. By following the model of Horace's father and rejecting the one embodied by Filippo Balducci—that is by choosing to represent reality and draw a difficult (but more solid) moral from it—the **Decameron** also launches into a

teaching of morality through an exemplary mode, which is reminiscent (and, at the same time, subversive) of the medieval exemplary tradition.[57] Its mode of instruction is here profoundly satirical, Horatian in nature.[58] The method, one may add, is even endorsed outside the authorial discourse by no less a character than Dioneo. In his meta-narrative commentary in the close of **Decameron "VII,10"** Dioneo compares and contrasts his own exemplary novella on *l'au-delà* with the abstract and casuistic arguments on the *gradus consanguinitatum* Frate Rinaldo advances in **"VIII,3."** Dioneo, reinforcing the author's position, concludes that an exemplary rhetoric, the one embodied by Tingoccio's momentary return from Purgatory, is a much more effective tool than the abstract reasoning of the friar in Elissa's story: "Le quali cose se frate Rinaldo avesse sapute, non gli sarebbe stato bisogno d'andar silogizzando quando convertì a' suoi piaceri la sua buona comare" (30).[59]

Like the examples of vices and virtues in the program sketched out by Horace's father for his son-poet, the *novelle* of the **Decameron** appear to be offering themselves as an aid to build a sense of morality, first in the *brigata* and then in the outermost frame, in which the work locates its final, historical audience. The human beings molded by the old Horatian (and new Boccaccian) curriculum of study will perhaps not be better ones than those instructed by a philosopher through the use of pure authoritative arguments. Their morals will, however, have a better chance at withstanding the impact of reality when they face it. To be sure, the new and open exemplary mode defended by Boccaccio is neither the perfect teaching tool, nor is it the only one possible. There is a time (and a place in the literary system) in which it will not be needed, any more than grown-ups need the flotation devices named by Horace's father in his epiphonema: "simul ac duraverit aetas / membra animumque tuum, nabis sine *cortice*" (119-120).[60] But now, at this stage of life and in the present literary mode, both Horace's public and Boccaccio's need them. The role of satire, of an instruction that works through the exemplary force of fables, is the same that cork plays for someone learning to swim: fables need now to be there, but they will not be needed forever. It is only appropriate, then, that the author who will defend in his later and more passionate apology for poetry the assumption that truth lies under the "bark" (*sub cortice*) of the poets' fables,[61] may allude here to his own "fables or histories or parables," in a final witty intertextual play, as "bark" themselves.[62]

Notes

1. [And if ever I went out of my way to satisfy you ladies in anything, I'm all the readier to do so now, aware as I am that all anyone is entitled to say is that I and others who love you are acting in

accordance with Nature [. . .] Silence, therefore, my critics! If you're insensitive to warmth, very well—stay chilled . . .] I quote the text from Giovanni Boccaccio, *Tutte le opere,* Vittore Branca ed., vol. IV (Milano: Mondadori, 1976). Translations are from Giovanni Boccaccio, *The Decameron,* Guido Waldman trans. (Oxford-New York: Oxford University Press, 1993).

2. [You're welcome to your pleasures, your perverse appetites, but leave me to such joy as this brief life affords.]

3. [One labored tangled in delights of flesh.] I quote Dante's texts from Dante Alighieri, *La Divina Commedia,* Giorgio Petrocchi ed. (Torino: Einaudi, 1975). The translation is Allen Mandelbaum's, as published in *The Divine Comedy of Dante Alighieri* (Toronto: Bantam Books, 1984).

4. Two hypotheses have been advanced regarding the social and cultural composition of the groups to which the *Decameron*'s detractors belong. See the typology sketched by Marga Cottino-Jones, *Order from Chaos: Social and aesthetic harmonies in Boccaccio's "Decameron"* (Washington, DC: University Press of America, 1982), who sees Boccaccio defending his work from "the extreme moralist, [. . .] the middle-aged 'wise men,' [. . .] the would-be *litterateurs,* [. . .] the materialist, [. . .] and finally the realist" (6-7). On a cultural determination of the accusations leveled against the *Decameron* insists, on the contrary, Gregory B. Stone, *The Ethics of Nature in the Middle Ages: On Boccaccio's Poetaphysics* (New York: St. Martin's Press, 1998), who notes: "These detractors, incidentally, are clearly recognizable as proto-humanists, those who dictate that the writer should compose in the paternal rather than the maternal tongue, in Latin rather than in Italian" (67). Both scholars are, in my view, only partially right. They do not consider that their sociopolitical and cultural determinations cannot account for Boccaccio's closing remarks about his detractors' morality. On the dialogue between the author and his detractors, see also Michelangelo Picone, *Autore/narratori,* in *Lessico critico decameroniano,* Renzo Bragantini and Pier Massimo Forni eds. (Torino: Bollati Boringhieri, 1995 [hence *LCD*]), 34-59, in particular 42-47.

5. More deeply unsubstantiated, and hardly sensitive to the context of Boccaccio's defense appears the interpretation of Aldo Scaglione, *Nature and Love in the Late Middle Ages* (Berkeley-Los Angeles: University of California Press, 1963), 107, who sees homosexuality as the target of Boccaccio's remarks. A more vague, though safer characterization of the work's critics can be found also in Raffaello Ramat, *L'introduzione alla "Quarta Giornata,"* in *Saggi sul Rinascimento* (Firenze: La Nuova Italia, 1969), 50-69.

6. For the familiarity Boccaccio had with the texts of Horace, see at least the following contributions: Claudia Villa, "La tradizione medioevale di Orazio," in *Atti del Convegno di Venosa: 8-15 novembre 1992* (Venosa: Osanna, 1993), 193-202; Robert Hollander, *Boccaccio's Dante: the Shaping Force of Satire* (Ann Arbor: The University of Michigan Press, 1997), 159-163 and *passim.* For the problem of what manuscript of Horace Boccaccio was reading, see Oskar Hecker, *Boccaccio Funde* (Braunschweig: Georg Westermann, 1902), 79-80; Enrico Rostagno, *L'Orazio Laurenziano già di Francesco Petrarca* (Roma: La Libreria dello Stato, 1933); Antonia Mazza, "L'Inventario della 'parva libraria' di Santo Spirito e la biblioteca del Boccaccio," *Italia Medievale e Umanistica* IX (1966), 20 and 62. See also the description of the codex Laurenziano XXXIV.5 in *Sesto Centenario della morte di Giovanni Boccaccio: Mostra di manoscritti, documenti e edizioni,* 2 vols. (Certaldo: A cura del Comitato Promotore, 1975), 1:147. Many of the conclusions reached by Claudia Villa in her "Dante lettore di Orazio," in *Dante e la "Bella Scola" della poesia* (Ravenna: Longo, 1993), 87-106, are exportable also to the context of Boccaccio's reception of the Latin poet. For an impressive *recensio* of the whole Horatian manuscript tradition, see Claudia Villa, "I Manoscritti di Orazio I e II," *Aevum* XLVI-XLVII (1992-93), 95-135 and 3-103.

7. For a detailed treatment of the Latin tradition of having "proemi al mezzo" in collections of poetry, see Gian Biagio Conte, "Proems in the Middle," *Yale Classical Studies* XXIX (1992), 147-160 and Stephen Hinds, "*Proemi al mezzo*: Allusion and the limits of interpretability," *Materiali e discussioni per l'analisi dei testi classici* XXXIX (1997), 113-122. Quintilian recognizes the topos of the midway invocation to the Muses in the proem to Book IV of his *Institutiones oratoriae,* in a language of which Boccaccio might have been reminiscent: "Perfecto, Marcelle Vittori, operis tibi dicati tertio libro *et iam quarta fere laboris parte transacta, nova insuper mihi diligentiae causa et altior sollicitudo, quale iudicium hominum emererer, accessit.*" [I have now, my dear Marcellus Victorius, completed the third book of the work which I have dedicated to you, and have nearly finshed a quarter of my task, and am confronted with a motive for renewed diligence and increased anxiety as to the judgment it may be found to deserve.] I quote Quintilian's text from M. Fabi Quintiliani *Institutionis oratoriae libri XII,* L. Radermacher ed. (Leipzig: Teubner, 1907); the translation is from *The Institutio Oratoria of Quintil-*

ian, H.E. Butler trans. (Cambridge, MA-London: Harvard University Press-Heinemann, 1960). For Boccaccio's parallel phrasing see below, note 15. About a possible rhetorical background for the project of the hundred tales, see Wesley Trimpi, *Muses of one mind: The literary analysis of experience and its continuity* (Princeton: Princeton University Press, 1983), 342-344.

8. It cannot be passed over in silence the fact that Boccaccio's own manuscript of Horace, the Laurenziano XXXIV.5, follows a tradition in dividing the poems which makes Satire I,4 the fifth text in the collection.

9. See the full review of the proposals in Pier Massimo Forni, *Forme complesse nel "Decameron"* (Firenze: Olschki, 1992), 57-65, who summarizes, adding new material, the traditional views and insists on *Amores* 361-398. See also Luciano Rossi, "Presenze Ovidiane nel *Decameron,*" *Studi sul Boccaccio* XXI (1993), 125-137. For the representation of an "autobiographical scheme" drawn from Ovid's *Tristia* in the apologue of the "goslings," see Federico Sanguineti, "La novelletta delle papere nel *Decameron,*" *Belfagor* XXXVII (1982), 137-146; on the same line, with the advantage of linking the fourth day's to the tenth day's defense, moves also Janet Levarie Smarr, "Ovid and Boccaccio: a Note on Self-defense," *Mediaevalia* XIII (1987), 247-255, esp. 250.

10. Forni's comment reads: "Nella *Vita nuova* il Boccaccio trovava un esempio di inserimento di una parentesi ragionativo-polemica all'interno del flusso narrativo" (67).

11. The parallel situation of the apologetic texts is reinforced, as I have suggested, by the presence of a second, final defense of the works at the very end: the *Conclusione dell'Autore,* which is still part of "Day X," is in fact echoing Horace's last *Satire* of the first Book (I,10) both for its position, and for its being concerned primarily with matters of style, while I,4 (just as *Decameron* "IV, *Introduzione*") was mixing moral questions and comments on poetics. For a through review of the connections between *Satire* I,4 and I,10, see C.A. Van Rooy, "Arrangement and Structure of Satires in Horace, *Sermones,* Book I: Satires 1 and 10," *Acta Classica* XIII (1970), 7-27, esp. 9 and 19-20.

12. A fully developed argument can be found in C.A. Van Rooy, "Arrangement and Structure of Satires in Horace *Sermones,* Book I, with more special reference to Satire I,4," *Acta Classica* XI (1968), 38-72, esp. 56-62 and 65-68.

13. [As for me, if I have had my laugh because silly "Rufillus smells like a scent-box, Gargonius like a goat," do you think I am a spiteful, snappish cur?]

I quote the text and the translation of the *Satire* from the Loeb edition of Horace, *Satires, Epistles and Ars Poetica,* H. Rushton Fairclough trans. (Cambridge, MA-London: Harvard University Press-Heinemann, 1929^2).

14. For the theme of "frame-shifting" and "frame-breaking" in the *Decameron,* see Joy Hambuechen Potter, *Five Frames for the "Decameron": Communication and Social Systems in the "cornice"* (Princeton: Princeton University Press, 1982), 83-96 and 123-135.

15. My treatment of Horace's *Satire* is indebted particularly to the results reached by J.E.G. Zetzel, "Horace's Liber Sermonum: The Structure of Ambiguity," *Arethusa* XIII (1980), 59-77, esp. 64-65 and Kirk Freudenbergh, *The Walking Muse: Horace on the Theory of Satire* (Princeton: Princeton University Press, 1993), 92-128. The discussion of Horace's literary stance by Niall Rudd, *The Satires of Horace* (Berkeley: University of California Press, 1966), 86-131, still proves very useful.

16. [For if before I've completed even one-third of my labour they're already such a swarm and lay such claims upon me, I suspect that before I reach the end, if they're not stopped in their tracks, they will have increased and multiplied to a point where they could trample on me without the smallest effort—and there is nothing you ladies would be able to do about it, for all your considerable powers.]

17. [Whereas the leek may have a white head, it keeps its tail green. . . . While the leek is totally inedible, its head is less noxious and somewhat more savoury than the rest. You ladies, however, generally get it all wrong: you hold the leek by the head and eat the leaves.]

18. [So let no one be more concerned about my welfare than I am. . . . I am not going to have anyone show greater concern for my honour than I do, now that it's too late.]

19. [All pious thoughts and devotions and holy disciplines. . . . Living of prayer and fasting . . . All he ever spoke to him about was the glory of life eternal, the glory of God and His saints, and all he ever taught him were holy prayers.]

20. On another element of continuity between "Day III" (particularly 10) and "Day IV" insists Roberto Fedi, "Il regno di Filostrato: Natura e struttura della Giornata IV del *Decameron,*" *Modern Language Notes* CII (1987), 39-54, esp. 41-43, who compares Filostrato's intervention at "III, *Conclusione,*" 1 to a *cobla capfinida* between the two *giornate.* If he is probably right on this matter, his

argument on the ensuing special status of the first male narrator (as revealing explicitly to the reader his "total literariness") is in my view untenable. FiÄµstrato's epiphonema in "III, *Conclusione*," 6 "né per altro il nome, per lo quale voi mi chiamate, da tale che seppe ben che si dire mi fu imposto" [and whoever it was who gave me the wretched lovesick name by which you all call me knew exactly what he was doing] is not referring to the extradiegetic author, but to the character's intradiegetic narrators. If Boccaccio's text can be ambiguous in the present passage, a simple juxtaposition of paragraphs 51 and 79 in the "*Introduzione* to Day I" can clarify the matter. While the narrator of the *Decameron* admits that *he* is nicknaming the women of the *brigata*: "per nomi alle qualità di ciascuna convenienti o in tutto o in parte *intendo di nominarle*" [I will provide them with names that to a greater or lesser degree reflect each one's character], each component of the male triad does already bear his nickname when he enters the narrative: "De' quali l'uno *era chiamato* Panfilo e Filostrato il secondo e l'ultimo Dioneo" [The first was called Pamphilo, the second Philostrato, and the last Dioneo]. At the beginning of his reign, hence, Filostrato does not meta-narratively refer to "Boccaccio." He simply echoes (and reverses) the paradigmatic passage in *Vita Nuova* II,1, in which Beatrice's name—which was given her by those "who did not know what they were thus calling"—is glossed and made finally clear by the author of the framing narrative. More than referring to the "author" of the *Decameron* the character attempts perhaps to fashion himself as authoritative.

21. The most detailed defense of this thesis can be found in Vittore Branca, *Tradizione delle opere di Giovanni Boccaccio,* 2 vols. (Roma: Edizioni di Storia e Letteratura, 1991), 2:147-162, which elaborates on older contributions. Shorter notes are in Guido di Pino, *Il "proemio" e l'introduzione alla quarta "giornata,"* in *La Polemica del Boccaccio* (Firenze: Vallecchi, 1953), 209-220. Giorgio Padoan argues the same point as Branca in a long article "Sulla genesi e la pubblicazione del *Decameròn*," in *Boccaccio, le Muse, il Parnaso e l'Arno* (Firenze: Olschki, 1978), 93-121, in particular 97-102. See also, on a different point but accepting the same framework, Maria Picchio Simonelli, *Prima diffusione e tradizione manoscritta del "Decameron,"* in *Boccaccio: Secoli di vita,* Marga Cottino-Jones and Edward F. Tuttle eds. (Ravenna: Longo, 1977), 125-142, esp. 132-133. For the opposite view, see Charles S. Singleton, "On meaning in the *Decameron*," *Italica* XXI (1944), 117-124, in particular 121. See also Giorgio Billanovich, *Restauri boccacceschi* (Roma:

Edizioni di Storia e Letteratura, 1947²), 153. More recently Fedi, "Il regno di Filostrato," 45 insists on the rhetorical nature (*ordo artificiosus*) of Boccaccio's choice of postponing his defensive remarks.

22. I am inclined to consider compelling the arguments about the absence of any "extravagant" philological tradition advanced by Singleton and Billanovich, though the ones proposed by Branca are in themselves powerful. The peculiar (possibly allegorical?) nature of the first three *canzoni* with respect to the others; the correspondence between the proem's declaration that only women will sing and the fact that this happens only in the first part of the work; the correspondence between the implicit theme of "Day I" with the one of "Day VI" ("motti"); the contradiction between what is stated in the "*Introduction* to Day IV" about the *sine titulo* status of the work and the presence of the title in the *incipit* and in front of each novella (see Simonelli, "Prima diffusione," 133), are all features of the text which may force the readers to take "alla lettera" Boccaccio's statements. Still, the possibility of seeing, behind the defense of the work, precisely that "rhetorical motivation" which Branca considered absent, allows one to at least question these arguments.

23. See Smarr, *Ovid and Boccaccio,* 252; Potter, *Five Frames,* 83-84; Forni, *Forme complesse,* 60-66; and Villa, *Dante lettore,* 95-97. See also Carlo Delcorno, *Ironia/Parodia,* in *LCD,* 162-191, esp. 172-174. On the peculiar situation of Dante's Epistle to Cangrande, known to Boccaccio probably as non-Dantean but still connected to the *Commedia* as part of the proemial material, see Robert Hollander, *Dante's Epistle to Cangrande* (Ann Arbor: University of Michigan Press, 1993), 26. For the antecedents of Dante's *formula,* see L. Jenaro-McLennan, "Remissus est modus et humilis (Epistle to Cangrande, § 10)," *Lettere Italiane* XXXI.3 (1979), 406-418.

24. The text of Dante's *Epistle* XIII is quoted from Dante Alighieri, *Epistola a Cangrande,* Enzo Cecchini ed. (Firenze: Giunti, 1995).

25. This is a topical formula, very close to one which can be read, in a section devoted to the tone of voice to be kept in the *actio,* at *Rhetorica ad Herennium* III,23: "Sermo est oratio remissa et finitima cottidianae locutioni."

26. I quote the texts of Horace's *scholia* from *Acronis et Porphyrionis Scholia in Quintum Horatium Flaccum,* Friedrich Hauthal ed., 2 vols. (Berlin: Springer, 1866), 1:73-94. For the questions concerning the transmissions of these texts and of another corpus of glosses (the tradition of the so-

called λφψ), see the appendix "Ancient Scholia" in the article "Horace" by Richard Tarrant, in *Text and Transmission: a Survey of the Latin Classics,* L.D. Reynolds ed. (Oxford: Clarendon Press, 1983), 182-186, esp. 186. See also R.G.M. Nisbet and M. Hubbard, "The ancient commentators" in *A Commentary on Horace: Odes I* (Oxford: Clarendon Press, 1970), xlvii-li. On the more general question of the commentary tradition to classical texts, see J. Zetzel, "On the History of Latin Scholia," *Harvard Studies in Classical Philology* LXXIX (1975), 335-354. Another possible source for the proximity of the literary genres can be found in Isidore's *Etymologiae,* VIII, vii, 7: "Duos sunt autem genera comicorum, id est veteres et novi. Veteres, qui et ioco ridiculares extiterunt, ut Plautus, Accius, Terentius. Novi, qui et Satirici, a quibus generaliter vitia carpuntur, ut Flaccus, Persius, Iuvenalis vel alii" (quoted in Zygmunt Barański, *"Sole Nuovo, Luce Nuova"* (Torino: Scriptorium, 1996), 144.

27. For the literary status of comedy in Dante's works, see Villa, "Dante lettore," 97, who stresses the cogency of the role played by the "lectura Horatii" in shaping his definition of *comedia* and in assigning it the lowest level in the ladder of styles. See also the comments by Cecchini, *Epistola a Cangrande,* 41-43. Boccaccio could have been encouraged also by Horace's "genealogical" defense-argument in *Satire* I,4 to place the genre of Satire on the same level as Comedy.

28. [So as I work at this loom I'm not straying from Parnassus or the Muses nearly as much as many people may think.] The best definition of Boccaccio's attitude is in Branca, *Tradizione,* who rightly qualifies as "sempre sorridente" the author's insistence "sull'umiltà e la popolarità delle sue doti di scrittore negli interventi diretti del *Decameron*" (160).

29. Van Rooy, "Arrangement and Structure" (1968), 67-68 stresses the play between the statement in I,4.39 (I am not among those you may call poets) and I,4.143, where Horace suggests that he precisely is part of the *manus poetarum,* the ranks of the poets.

30. [And if I listen to them, God knows I shrug them of lightly enough.]

31. [Here is the very ink of the cuttlefish; here is venom unadulterated. That such malice shall be far from my pages, and first of all from my heart, I pledge myself, if there is aught that I can pledge with truth.]

32. For this connection, see Hollander, *Boccaccio's Dante,* 161.

33. See at least how Porphyry glosses 52 and 105 and how Pseudo-Acron reiterates his formula for line 110. The latter acknowledges also the "iucunditas" in Horace's words, glossing line 56 with the words "jucunde de comico."

34. As Hollander (*Boccaccio's Dante,* 159-160) underlines, Boccaccio appropriates Pseudo-Acron's definition of Satire twice in his *Esposizioni* (to *Inferno* I,73 and to *Inferno* IV,90), labeling Horace "ac[c]errimo riprenditore de' vizi" [Most acrimonious reproacher of vice].

35. [Choose anyone from amid a crowd: he is suffering either from avarice or some wretched ambition. One is mad with love for somebody's wife, another for boys. Here is one whose fancy the sheen of silver catches; Albius dotes on bronzes; another trades from the rising sun to regions warmed by his evening rays . . .]

36. [Another trades from the rising sun to regions warmed by his evening rays; nay, through perils he rushes headlong, like dust gathered up by a whirlwind, fearful lest he lose aught of his total, or fail to add to his wealth.]

37. On the topic, see the seminal works by Vittore Branca, "L'epopea mercantile," in *Boccaccio medievale* (Firenze: Sansoni, 1956), 71-99 and Giorgio Padoan, "Mondo aristocratico e mondo comunale nell'ideologia e nell'arte di Giovanni Boccaccio," *Studi sul Boccaccio* II (1964), 81-216.

38. [For I can't see myself faring any worse than a handful of dust: when the wind blows, either the dust remains undisturbed or else it's caught up into the air.]

39. [Like sands that eddies when a whirlwind swirls.] In addition to this line Branca (*Decameron,* 1202) recalls also Boccaccio's own gloss to Dante's line, in which the disorderly circular movement of the wind is underlined.

40. A last Horatian *tessera,* though a more dubious one, can be added to the mosaic of references which cluster around the answer to the fourth attack. In paragraph 38 Boccaccio writes: "e assai già, dietro alle loro favole andando, fecero la loro età fiorire, dove in contrario molti nel cercar d'aver più pane, che bisogno non era loro, perirono acerbi" [And many are the poets who, by attending their poetry, quickened the age in which they lived, whereas all too many of those who amassed bread beyond their proper needs came to an untimely end]. Two sources have traditionally been assigned to this passage: on the one hand *Paradiso* XIX, 48, "Per non attender lume, cadde acerbo" [fell—/ unripe because he did not wait for

light], by Branca, *Decameron,* 1202, and Potter, *Five Frames,* 86; and on the other hand Seneca, *Epistulae* CXIII,10, by Giuseppe Velli, *Petrarca e Boccaccio: Tradizione, Memoria, Scrittura* (Padova: Antenore, 1995²), 216-217, in an argument he takes up again in *Memoria,* in *LCD,* 222-248, esp. 239-243. To these intertexts I would like to add the possible resonance of lines 126-129 of *Satire* I,4: "*avidos* vicinum funus ut aegros / examinat mortisque metu sibi parcere cogit, / sic teneros animos aliena opprobria saepe / absterrent vitiis" [As a neighbor's funeral scares *gluttons* when sick, and makes them, through fear of death careful of themselves, so the tender mind is oft deterred from vice by another's shame]. Notably similar in the two passages is the ambiguity, obscured by the modern translation of "avidos" with "gluttons," which exists between the "gluttons" and the "avaricious." It is enough to go back to Horace's *scholia* to see it fully signaled: "Avidos et aegros *dupliciter possumus accipere*; nam et de *avaro* utrumque recte dicitur et de *aegrotante* et de *languido.* Si avarum accipis, sibi parcere persequitur, i. e. largius vivere admonetur, quia avarus est morti vicinus. Quemadmodum, [inquit,] aegrotantem vicinum funus absterret a cibi aviditate, ita saepe amicos teneros a vitiis infamia revocat aliena" (Pseudo-Acron, *ad loc.*).

41. Mario Baratto, *Realtà e stile nel "Decameron"* (Roma: Editori Riuniti, 1984), 56; Fedi, "Il regno di Filostrato," 48; Scaglione, *Nature and Love,* 104. For an incisive critical review of some of the most significant "pronunciamenti" on this matter see Stone, *The Ethics,* 62.

42. This is the perspective adopted and defended by Giuseppe Mazzotta, *The World at play in Boccaccio's "Decameron"* (Princeton: Princeton University Press, 1986), 131-158. On the moral ambiguity of love's force, see now Jessica Levenstein, "Out of Bounds: Passion and the Plague in Boccaccio's *Decameron,*" *Italica* LXXIII (1996), 313-335. For similar conclusions on the problematical "openness" of the *novelletta*'s text see also Victoria Kirkham, "Love Labors Rewarded and Paradise Lost (*Decameron* III, 10)," *Romanic Review* LXXII (1981), 79-93, who argues that the "alternative missing conclusions" of the text are provided by the following two *giornate.* The untold outcome of the potential love-story between the young Balducci and the women is, in her view, either an "unhappy" outcome or a "happy" one, depending on the negotiation of the power-balance between the old and the new generation and the "marital status" of the stories' protagonists. A more sophisticated point, but insisting on the same narratological openness of the *novelletta,* can be found in Albert Russell Ascoli, "Boccaccio's Auer-

bach: Holding the Mirror up to *Mimesis,*" *Studi sul Boccaccio* XX (1990), 377-397, esp. 385. Armand Francillon ("Quelques observations sur la Quatrième Journée du *Décameron,*" *Études de Lettres* I [1978], 19-30) considers, on the contrary, the text as a playful anticipation of the "matière grave" of the following day. A similar reading, but with an emphasis on the failed dialogue "between the Narrator and his misinformed critics," is in Cottino-Jones, *Order,* 67.

43. [So he distributed all that he possessed among God's poor and left at once for Mount Asinaio, where he established himself with his son in a small cell. They lived a life of prayer and fasting, supported by alms, and he took elaborate care to avoid ever discussing any temporal matter in his son's presence or giving him sight of any temporal objects, lest these might tempt him away from the service of the Lord; all he ever spoke to him about was the glory of life eternal, the glory of God and His saints, and all he ever taught him were holy prayers. He held his child to this life for many a year, never letting him out of the cell, never permitting him the sight of any but himself.]

44. I find myself, on this particular point, in agreement with Stone, *The Ethics,* who comments on the passage: "Prohibiting his son from 'seeing things' [. . .], Balducci attempts to preempt his son's empirical experience of nature by overloading him with authoritative doctrine" (68). I lose track, however, of the Lacanian argument he develops throughout the rest of his chapter, especially since he claims that the first *Non(m) du père* is contained in Balducci's re-naming of the women as "*pa'-père.*" I see the father's imposition of a law as being already in full swing during Balducci's training on Mount Senario.

45. The semantic field covered by the word "ingegno" in vernacular is extremely wide, but it cannot coincide simply with the one of "cultura." "Ingegno" can be rendered with a number of English equivalents; while "intelligence" is the most respectful of its Latin etymology, "craftiness" or even "resourcefulness" can be other acceptable translations, which tend to overlap the value of the term with the Latin "industria" (a famous juxtaposition in Cicero, *De inventione* I.xxxiv.35). In spite of the variety of the semantic values of the word, it is hard to see how Nature could be contrasted directly against any of them. As human faculty, *ingegno* is not on the same logical (or ontological) level as Natura; when, on the contrary, it is so, the result is a confusion since in that case *ingenium* and *natura* are etymologically indiscernible (among Boccaccio's favorite texts, see Horace,

Ars poetica 408-410, and Ovid, *Amores* I, 15.14). The terms come in contact and can be contrasted only when a precise field of application is given to both of them, when one is considering an object that can be produced "natura aut arte." It is only when both are not taken in themselves, but are seen as guiding an action, *i.e.* when they appear as two "methods," that they may be juxtaposed. In the story of Filippo Balducci, what at first appeared as the clash of two ontological principles is, in truth, a conflict between two teaching techniques, clearly to the disadvantage of the one practiced by the father.

46. On the marked opposition between a "worldly" and an "unworldly" Thebaid-like style of life in the culture of Boccaccio's Florence, see Lucia Battaglia Ricci, *Ragionare nel giardino. Boccaccio e i cicli pittorici del "Trionfo della morte"* (Roma: Salerno Editrice, 1987).

47. [And as his father told him, he would be satisfied and question him about the next sight.] On the relevance of the *novelletta* for the understanding of the *Decameron's* semantic strategies, and its treatment of "the pathology of the sign," see Giovanni Sinicropi, "Il segno linguistico del *Decameron*," *Studi sul Boccaccio* IX (1975), 169.

48. In addition to the intertext I propose here, Hollander, *Boccaccio's Dante,* 75 argues for the presence of *Purgatorio* XXVI, 67-70 behind the *novelletta's* plot.

49. [As does the wind, / so shall your outcry do—the wind that sends / its roughest blows against the highest peaks; / that is no little cause for claiming honor.]

50. [Therefore, within these spheres, upon the mountain, / and in the dismal valley, you were shown / only those souls that unto fame are known—/ because the mind of one who hears will not / put doubt to rest, put trust in you, if given / examples with their roots unknown and hidden, / or arguments too dim, too unapparent.]

51. Other arguably false or, at least, provisional "father-figures" have been met by Dante in other critical spots of his itinerary through the three realms, all characterized by their double (?) role of "teachers-parents," the first and foremost examples of this category being Virgil and Brunetto Latini. For the latter, see Peter Armour, "Dante's Brunetto: The Paternal Paterine," *Italian Studies* XXXVIII (1983), 1-38. On the theme, see in general Mario De Rosa, *Dante e il Padre Ideale* (Napoli: Federico & Ardia, 1990), esp. 101-119.

52. On this issue, see the recent contribution by Lucia Battaglia Ricci, *'Una novella per esempio': Novellistica, Omiletica e Trattatistica nel Primo Tre-*

cento, in *Favole Parabole Istorie: Le forme della scrittura novellistica dal Medioevo al Rinascimento,* G. Albanese, L. Battaglia-Ricci, and R. Bessi eds. (Roma: Salerno, 2000), 31-53.

53. ['Tis a habit the best of fathers taught me, for, to enable me to steer clear of follies, he would brand them, one by one, by his examples.] It is noteworthy that Horace consistently conflates matters of style and of morality in his defense, not very differently from what we witness also in the *Introduction* to "Day IV."

54. [With words like these would he mould my boyhood; and whether he were advising me to do something, "You have an example for so doing," he would say, and point to one of the special judges.]

55. It should be noted that the verb Horace uses here to describe his father's technique of instruction, "notando" in line 106, covers a wide field, its meaning ranging from a physical practice to a literary one. "Notare" means, in fact, at the same time "to point the finger at" (what the father used to do), "to pay attention to" (what the young Horace did) and "to write down" something (what both Horace-the-poet is doing and his co-practitioners of Satire—especially Lucilius, who followed the example of Eupolis, Cratinus and Aristophanes—once did). For the peculiarity of this pattern of education to Roman life, see Stanley F. Bonner, *Education in ancient Rome: From the Older Cato to the Younger Pliny* (Berkeley and Los Angeles: University of California Press, 1977), 17-19.

56. [Your philosopher will give you theories for shunning or seeking this or that: enough for me, if I can uphold the rule our fathers have handed down, and if, so long as you need a guardian, I can keep your health and name from harm.] The nexus "vitatu quidque petitu / sit melius" is not foreign to Boccaccio's intertextual technique. It may also be proposed as a good intertext for *Decameron,* **"Proemio,"** 14: "In quanto potranno conoscere [*scil.* le donne] quello che sia da fuggire e che sia similmente da seguitare," in addition to another Ovidian reference that Hollander (*Boccaccio's Dante,* 367-368) proposes to see in the sentence, namely *Remedia Amoris,* 790: "Quos fugias quosque sequare, dabo" [I will show what food is to be avoided and what sought after], which is in turn a parody of a formulaic structure repeated at least twice in *Aeneid* III, 367-368 and 459: "Quae prima pericula vito? / Quidve sequens tantos possim superare labores?" and "Et quo quemque modo fugiasque ferasque laborem" [What dangers shall I avoid first? What should I do to overcome such great toils? . . . And in what way you will either

avoid or endure the test]. The presence, however, of a similar conceptual nexus among the topical examples of speculative discussions in the Latin rhetorical tradition discourages from assigning a singular "source" to Boccaccio's phrase. (See, for example, Cicero, *De oratore* III.xxix.116; *Topica* xxii.85 and xxxiii.89, but the theme is ubiquitous.)

57. The young Balducci is able to defeat, in one of the shortest *quaestiones disputatae* ever held, the arguments of his father just by turning his teaching method upside-down; Boccaccio deals similarly with the exemplary tradition he exploits in this very "unfinished novella." The young Balducci is able to reach his conclusion that women cannot be a bad thing, what his father claimed they were, simply by working inside the father's horizon. His debate with the father can be summarized as follows: 1) these creatures which appear here now are more beautiful than the painted angels that you have shown me many times; 2) if those angels were beautiful and (one can almost hear, retorted against the father, an implied "hence") good, these creatures cannot *a fortiori* be worse, they must be better. On the oblique relationship between Boccaccio's unfinished novella and the exemplary tradition which preceded him, see Giancarlo Mazzacurati, *Il sistema del "Decameron"* (Napoli: Liguori, 1979), 68-94; Salvatore Battaglia, *La coscienza letteraria del Medioevo* (Napoli: Liguori, 1965), 447-547; Hans-Jörg Neuschäfer, *Boccaccio und der Beginn der Novelle* (München: Wilhelm Finkl Verlag, 1969), 56-58; Sanguineti, "La Novelletta," 142-144; Millicent Marcus, *An Allegory of Form: Literary Self-Consciousness in the "Decameron"* (Saratoga, CA: Anma Libri, 1979), 12; Potter, *Five Frames,* 37-39; and Giancarlo Mazzacurati, *Rappresentazione,* in *LCD,* 269-299, in part. 293-299. For a different tradition, the medieval Elegiac Comedy, see Francesco Bruni, *Boccaccio: l'invenzione della letteratura mezzana* (Bologna: Il Mulino, 1990), 321-323.

58. Among the Horatian active relics in the *Decameron* Hollander (*Boccaccio's Dante,* 70n) points out that the first word of Boccaccio's work, "umana," coincides with the opening of Horace's satire "De arte poetica." If he is right, the Horatian program of the *Decameron* extends to the whole authorial, metaliterary frame.

59. [And had Brother Rinaldo known about it, he wouldn't have needed to go splitting hairs when he talked *his* godson's mother into submission.] On Dioneo's story in "Day VII," see the note by Rosario Ferreri, "Rito battesimale e comparatico nelle novelle senesi della VII Giornata," *Studi sul Boccaccio* XVI (1987), 307-314. See also Alessan-

dro Duranti, *Le novelle di Dioneo,* in *Studi di Filologia e Critica offerti dagli allievi a Lanfranco Caretti,* 2 vols. (Roma: Salerno Editrice, 1985), 1:1-38, esp. 27-28. Relevant to the discussion are also Emma Grimaldi, *Il privilegio di Dioneo* (Napoli-Roma: ESI, 1985), 257-258 and more recently Albert Russel Ascoli, "Pyrrhus Rules: Playing with Power from Boccaccio to Machiavelli," *Modern Language Notes* CXIV (1999), 14-57, in part. 14-18 and 37-48. Contributions seem in general to downplay the role of Dioneo's dialogue from a distance with Elissa, and the possibility that it may hint at a developing relationship between the two characters in the "cornice." One can, I believe, temptatively trace a pattern of courteous exchanges (the crown moves from her to him, he selects her to sing at the end of his kingship's Day, just as she will choose him) and of allusive responses in the ballate Dioneo and Elissa sing (to each other?) at the end of each day. In this subtly alluded narrative Dioneo's final remarks may fit, together with the "good humour" (buona tempera) of the King in *Decameron* "VI, Conclusione," 48, which may suggest that he has interpreted Elissa's song as a declaration of love for him.

60. ["When years have brought strength to body and mind, you will swim without the cork."]

61. See the *Genealogie Deorum gentilium* XIV,1,2: "et forsan legens *latentes nuper sub rudi cortice sensus* nunc productos in lucem, non aliter quam si ex igneo globo recentes scaturire latices videas, etc." [Perhaps as you read, you will wonder to see the meaning that was lately hidden under a rough shell brought forth into the light—as if one were to see fresh water gushing from a globe of fire—etc.] I quote the text from Giovanni Boccaccio, *Tutte le opere,* Vittore Branca ed., vol. VIII.2 (Milano: Mondadori, 1998), 1359. The translation is quoted from Charles G. Osgood, *Boccaccio on Poetry* (Princeton: Princeton University Press, 1930), 16. For the tradition of the *cortex* image, see the commentary by Brigitte Hege, *Boccaccio's Apologie der heidnischen Dichtung in den "Genealogie deorum gentilium"* (Tübingen: Stauffenburg Verlag, 1995), 160-161. Ramat, who discusses the similar situation in the two works, has the advantage of seeing that Boccaccio's literary polemical target does not shift from the time of the *Decameron* to that of the *Genealogie* (52). On the same line, see the more recent observations of Fedi, "Il regno di Filostrato," 45-46. The opposite thesis of a strong discontinuity in themes and style between the "young" Boccaccio of the *Decameron* and the "old" one of the *Genealogie* is advanced

by Bruni, *Boccaccio,* 53-95. For an autobiographical reading of both texts, see Sanguineti, "La Novelletta," 141.

62. For their criticism of an earlier version of this paper, and their gentle guidance during my research
I should like to thank R. Hollander and A. Bar-
chiesi. Of them I might truly say, with Horace,
that "sic me formaba*nt* puerum."

Donald McGrady (essay date January 2001)

SOURCE: McGrady, Donald. "Boccaccio Repeats Himself: *Decameron* II, 6 and V, 7." *MLN* 116, no. 1
(January 2001): 193-97.

[*In the following essay, McGrady observes similarities
in the subplots of the sixth* novella *of the "Second Day"
and the seventh* novella *of the "Fifth Day."*]

Commentators of the **Decameron** do not seem to have
perceived that Boccaccio tells the same story twice,
once as part of a longer story, and once as an independent tale. The initial appearance is within the body of
the sixth *novella* of **"Day II,"** which recounts the misfortunes of Arrighetto Capece and his wife Beritola
Caracciola:

> Arrighetto is imprisoned when there is a change of re-
> gime in Sicily, and Beritola flees to Lipari with her son
> of eight years, Giuffredi; there she gives birth to an-
> other son, Scacciato. Continuing toward Naples with
> her sons and a nurse, Beritola's ship is forced to stop at
> an island, where pirates carry off her family; Beritola
> remains on the island, nursing two baby goats. Eventu-
> ally another ship arrives, and a gentleman named Cur-
> rado de' Malespini and his wife take Beritola and the
> goats home to Lunigiana, where Beritola serves the
> lady as a maid. Meanwhile, the pirates go to Genoa,
> where they sell Beritola's sons and nurse to Guaspar-
> rino d'Oria as servants. At the age of sixteen Giuffredi,
> now known as Giannotto, leaves Guasparrino and un-
> dertakes a series of adventures (which constitute the
> story-within-a-story), ending up serving in the home of
> Currado, where his mother is (although they seldom
> see one another, and do not realize who the other is).
> After another revolution reverses the family's political
> misfortunes, Giannotto reveals his identity to Currado,
> who reunites him with his mother and proposes that he
> marry his daughter. They contact Guasparrino in Genoa,
> who, learning Scacciato's identity, marries him to a
> daughter before sending him to Lunigiana. The family
> is finally reunited with Arrighetto, who has been re-
> stored to political favor and has recovered his confis-
> cated property.

It is usually stated that no direct sources are known for
this larger story, although it bears "some resemblance to
the legend of St. Eustache or the knight Placidus, whose
wife is carried off by the master of a vessel, and whose

two sons are also carried away by a wolf and a lion, the
family after many adventures being finally brought together again. (The story is found narrated in the 'Golden
Legend,' the 'Gesta Romanorum,' No. 110, the various
Lives of the Saints . . .)" (Lee, 34; see also Branca,
200, n. 2). However, it would appear that the legend of
Placidus (which shows a general similarity to the story
of the Biblical Job) is close enough to Boccaccio's tale
that one or more versions of it can safely be considered
its sources of inspiration. Much less evident is the origin of that part of **"II, 6"** which recounts the misadventures of Giuffredi-Giannotto:

> As seen earlier, Giannotto leaves Guasparrino's house-
> hold at age sixteen; he wanders for several years, and
> then enters the service of Currado. Soon he and Spina,
> Currado's daughter, fall desperately in love and enter
> upon physical relations. Becoming emboldened by their
> success at hiding their passion, they grow careless, and
> one day make love in a forest while on a walk with
> others; Currado discovers them and has his servants
> imprison them in a castle, intending to execute them;
> however, Spina's mother prevails upon her husband not
> to kill the lovers. A year passes, and Giannotto learns
> of the political upheaval that will restore his father to
> favor; he reveals his identity to Currado, who proposes
> the restoration of his honor by marriage to Spina; this
> solution is welcomed by the lovers, who marry soon
> thereafter.

The story of Giuffredi-Giannotto obviously has only a
tenuous relation to the rest of the story of madama
Beritola: originally designed as one more of the family's misfortunes, it takes on a life of its own, growing
disproportionately to the rest of the narrative: the various adventures of this elder son occupy 173 of the 498
lines of text (23 of the 83 sections in the Branca
edition), slightly over a third of the total. This same
disproportion is reflected in the summary of the *novella*
attached by Boccaccio to his tale:

> Madama Beritola, con due cavriuoli sopra una isola
> trovata, avendo due figliuoli perduti, ne va in Lunigi-
> ana; quivi l'un de' figliuoli col signore si pone e con la
> figliuola di lui giace e è messo in prigione: Cicilia ri-
> bellata al re Carlo e il figliuolo riconosciuto dalla ma-
> dre, sposa la figliuola del suo signore e il suo fratel
> ritrova e in grande stato ritornano.

In view of the importance accorded by Boccaccio to
this part of his narrative, it is surprising that some scholars have ignored it when dealing with the plot: neither
Lee nor his predecessors allude to this subplot, although
Rotunda (and Thompson, who follows him) does include it in his identification of the different narrative
motifs present in **Decameron "II, 6"** (which he twice
lumps together with **"II, 8"**):

> N251. *Man pursued by misfortune.* (Placidus,
> Eustacius). His goods are destroyed, his wife carried
> off by a ship's captain (pirates) and his children by ani-
> mals. He finally recovers them all. **Decameron, "II, 6"**
> and **"8"** (Lee, 34, 39).

N730. Accidental reunion of families. *Decameron,* "II, 6" and "8" (Lee, 34, 39).

T31.1. *Lovers' meetings: hero in service of lady's father. Decameron,* "II, 6."[1]

After subordinating the narrative of Giannotto's amorous adventures to the larger story of a family's misfortunes, Boccaccio decided to make it an independent tale in "**Day V, 7,**" where the plot goes as follows:

> Amerigo Abate purchases several children from Genoese corsairs, believing them all to be Turkish. One of them, Teodoro, is more intelligent than the others, and Amerigo esteems him highly; he has him baptized, calling him Pietro, and eventually makes him his majordomo. Violante, Amerigo's daughter, falls head over heels in love with Teodoro-Pietro, and he with her; they consummate their passion while on a walk with others, during a storm, and continue their relations until she becomes pregnant. Amerigo finds out about the affair after she has given birth, and denounces Teodoro-Pietro for rape; the youth is condemned to be hanged; on the way to the gallows, he is stripped to the waist and flogged. Fineo, an Armenian gentleman, notices that Teodoro-Pietro has an unusual birthmark on his shoulder, just as did a son of his who was carried off by pirates when a child; he calls out to him in Armenian, and Teodoro replies in the same language, thus establishing that he is indeed Fineo's lost son. The execution is stopped, and the respective fathers offer their children the chance to marry, which they are delighted to accept; Teodoro and Violante go with Fineo to live in Armenia.

It is obvious that the core of the subplot of *novella* "**II, 6**" is identical to that of "**V, 7**": a male child of noble family is carried off by pirates and sold into slavery; his merits are recognized by his owner, who gives him a position of responsibility; some years later, the youth and his owner's daughter become enamored and have physical relations, which go undiscovered for some time; upon learning of his daughter's dishonor, the father has the lovers imprisoned, intending to have them executed (since the social inferiority of the outsider precludes a marriage that would restore the family honor); a fortunate event allows the youth's identity and noble lineage to become known, and the disgraced girl's parents welcome her union with her lover.

Although the nucleus of "**V, 7**" is an exact replica of "**II, 6**," Boccaccio has changed the surrounding circumstances of the former to such an extent that commentators have not observed that it is indeed the same story. Thus the names and nationalities of the protagonists are different, the setting is changed from Lunigiana to Trapani, and most of the attendant circumstances are utterly dissimilar: thus, while the main plot in "**II, 6**" treats the various misfortunes of Giuffredi's family, nothing at all is known about Teodoro's in "**V, 7**" (except that they are Armenian), until his father, who is a member of the nobility, appears toward the end. But

the largest difference between the two stories is that "**V, 7**" incorporates the time-worn motif of the recognition by a distinctive birthmark (a favorite in the Greek novel), whereas in "**II, 6**" the protagonist's identity is clear all along, but is kept secret for reasons of security; indeed, it is Giuffredi-Giannotto himself who chooses to make his background known, once the political circumstances are propitious. Structurally, this accessory agnition corresponds to the relation of the various other disasters that befall the Capece family, if we consider for a moment that the central part of the story is that of the youth of apparently inferior class who seduces his owner's daughter, but whose true gentle origin is then discovered, and who ends up marrying his sweetheart.

Nonetheless, there are certain common details between "**II, 6**" and "**V, 7**": in both the corsairs who carry off the boy are Genoese, in both the masculine protagonists undergo a change of name (Giuffredi-Giannotto and Teodoro-Pietro), and in both the young lovers have amorous relations while on a walk with the household (in "**II, 6**" Giannotto and Spina first consummate their passion "in un luogo dilettevole e pien d'erbe e di fiori e d'alberi," § 37, while in "**V, 7**" a storm overtakes the company, and Teodoro and Violante take refuge in a "chiesetta antica," reminiscent of the cave where Aeneas and Dido initially tasted the fruits of forbidden love, § 13).[2] One similarity of detail is particularly striking, because it reveals how the two stories were associated in Boccaccio's mind: in "**II, 6**" the father of the female protagonist is Currado Malaspina (§ 33), while in "**V, 7**" Currado is the name of the judge who at the injured father's behest condemns Teodoro to die (§ 28).

Neither "**II, 6**" nor "**V, 7**" are among the *Decameron* tales that inspired the most imitations by subsequent writers (among the best-known descendants of these two stories are treatments by Giraldi Cintio, respectively in *Gli ecatommiti* V, 8 and II, 3; see Lee, 35-36 and 165-66). Nonetheless, it has been known for over a century that "**V, 7**" strongly influenced Ariosto's delicious comedy of *I suppositi* (see Marpillero, 299-300), and it has recently been discovered that it also is the main source of Lope de Vega's finest comedy, *El perro del hortelano* (see McGrady). Interestingly enough, the detail that most distinguishes "**II, 6**" from "**V, 7**"—the recognition scene at the end of "**V, 7**"—, has been fundamentally modified in both of these works: in *I suppositi* the agnition does not concern the hero (Erostrato), but his servant (Dulippo), and in *El perro* the device is turned on its head, since the recognition is fraudulent (Count Ludovico is duped into believing that Teodoro—the name comes from Boccaccio—, a *hijo de la tierra* ['bastard'] is his son). Like Boccaccio, for whom the agnition is merely an accessory episode added to the main story, Ariosto and Lope also find the recognition scene to be expendable.

Notes

1. Branca (200) omits motif T31.1, and mistakenly includes B580. Animal helps man to wealth and greatness and B590. Miscellaneous services of helpful animals. It will become obvious that "V, 7" should likewise be included under motif T31.1. Branca registers no folkloric parallels for the latter *novella,* for which Rotunda gives only H51.1. *Recognition by birthmark (mole).*

2. Branca notes that Boccaccio "si compiace spesso di circondare gli amori giovanili di una natura lussureggiante e fiabesca," and that the seduction scene in "II, 6" "ha poi stretta somiglianza con quella centrale della V 7" (211, n. 8). Note, however, that the similarity lies not in the setting, but in the circumstance of occurring while on a family outing.

Works Cited

Boccaccio, Giovanni. *Decameron.* Vittore Branca ed., 6th ed., Turin: Einaudi, 1991.

Branca, Vittore: see Giovanni Boccaccio.

Giraldi Cintio, Giovanni Battista. *Gli ecatommiti.* Florence: Borghi, 1834.

Lee, A. C. *The Decameron: Its Sources and Analogues.* London: Nutt, 1909; reprint, New York: Haskell House, 1972.

Marpillero, Guido. "*I Suppositi* di Lodovico Ariosto," *Giornale Storico della Letteratura Italiana,* 31 (1898): 291-310.

McGrady, Donald. "Fuentes, fecha y sentido de *El perro del hortelano*" (in press).

Rotunda, D. P. *Motif-Index of the Italian «Novella» in Prose.* Bloomington: Indiana University, 1942.

Thompson, Stith. *Motif-Index of Folk-Literature.* 2nd ed. Bloomington: Indiana University, 1955-1958. 6 vols.

Vega, Lope de. *El perro del hortelano.* Victor Dixon ed. London: Tamesis, 1981.

Mark Taylor (essay date fall 2001)

SOURCE: Taylor, Mark. "The Fortunes of Alatiel: A Reading of *Decameron* 2, 7." *Forum Italicum* 35, no. 2 (fall 2001): 318-31.

[*In the following essay, Taylor contrasts the points of view in the opening and closing sections of the seventh* novella *of the "Second Day," focusing on the narrative significance of the heroine's relative freedom from gendered social conventions at the center of the tale.*]

Panfilo's story of Alatiel, the seventh *novella* of the **"Second Day"** in the *Decameron,* tells of the daughter of the Sultan of Babylon, who is sent to marry the King of Algarve; her ship sails off course and is wrecked, delaying her marriage for four years; during this period Alatiel enjoys the attentions of many men, who make "love to her on thousands of different occasions" (147) before finally she returns home and is then dispatched again to Algarve, who delightedly accepts her as a virgin.[1] The whole tale, as even this brief summary shows, is a kind of triptych in which panels of an Alatiel subjected to the will of her father (and to some extent her future husband) are divided by the account of her adventures with other men, adventures that are never revealed to her father and Algarve, who would of course find her ruined by them if they knew. Alatiel's four years of sexual adventures represent an interruption of the normal forms of her world, forms that are in place precisely to prevent such an interruption, a kind of timeout, a manifestation of forbidden, repressed material bracketed within ordinary, everyday life. To some extent this plot imitates the familiar sequence of much Renaissance pastoral in which, for example, as in Shakespeare's *A Midsummer Night's Dream,* lovers escape a world of patriarchal suffocation into a green world where they can find themselves before returning whence they have come. Alatiel escapes from a world of order, contract (i.e., an arranged marriage), and predictability and enters into one of violence, lawlessness, and uncertainty, and much later returns to the world of order. "[W]hen [a green world] has fulfilled its moral, esthetic, social, cognitive, or experimental function," Harry Berger writes, "it becomes inadequate and its creator turns us out."[2] If it is tempting to list freedom as a condition of her green world, however, one should note that Alatiel is never free from the compulsions and desires of males, even if those of her lovers please her, and those of her father might not. Nevertheless, the long central part of Alatiel's story, her four years of absence from father and betrothed, demands to be understood by continual reference to what comes before and after; the contents of the story—matters of valuing and worth, sexuality and virginity, even the significance of beauty—look one way in the outer panels, another way in the center. It is the primary purpose of this paper to chart the difference in these perspectives.

The story of Alatiel imitates the plot of the *Decameron* itself. Beminedab, her father, and Algarve, and occasionally Alatiel herself, inhabit a frame, or *cornice,* within which, unknown to Beminedab and Algarve, her episodic adventures occur. In similar fashion the frame of plague-ridden Florence encloses the adventures the young aristocrats of the *brigata* undergo, like the visit to the Valley of the Ladies at the end of the **"Sixth Day,"** and the hundred tales they tell. All of this is unknown in Florence. And just as the story of Florence is enclosed within another *cornice,* the audience of women in love for whom Boccaccio desires "to provide succour and diversion" (3), so is the story of Beminedab and Algarve, and the story inside it, attended to by the ladies of the *brigata*. It is true, of course, that all ten men and women listen to all the tales in the ***Decameron,*** but the ways in which the ladies may be imaginatively involved in the fortunes of Alatiel are unusual in their emphasis.[3] In his preamble Panfilo reproves them for "sin[ning] above all in one particular way, which is in your desiring to be beautiful" (126); then he tells the story of Alatiel, as if to show what can happen if one is indescribably beautiful; then, preceding the eighth tale of **"Day 2,"** Boccaccio tells us how much the ladies "were sighing" over what they had heard, perhaps "not so much because they felt sorry for Alatiel, but because they longed to be married no less often than she was" (148). Seeing the adventures of Alatiel and the two *cornici* that surround them as a microcosm for the ***Decameron*** is highly suggestive; on the one hand, it shows us the limitations of the merely literary adventures of the *brigata,* small things next to what Alatiel has done; on the other, we can the more appreciate the security of Algarve, however illusory its foundation, by measuring it next to the reality of Florence. Moreover, Alatiel's sexual adventures emphasize by contrast the extraordinarily proper behavior of the *brigata*.

The tales of the **"Second Day,"** under the rule of Filomena, center at her command upon "those who after suffering a series of misfortunes are brought to a state of unexpected happiness" (68), a description to which Panfilo's tale bears a somewhat problematic relationship. There is no doubt that many of Alatiel's adventures are fairly called "misfortunes"—as her travails approach their end, Panfilo tells us, "For a long time now, the fair lady had been a plaything in the hands of Fortune [*trastullo della fortuna*]" (142), and he describes some of her alliances with such phrases as "a more terrible friendship" (130-31) and "another calamity" (131-32); however, from early on these adventures also gratify her even as they are occurring. With one of her lovers, we are told, Alatiel continues "to derive pleasure from the fate to which Fortune had consigned her" (139). There is no evidence, as a matter of fact, that any of the thousands of different occasions of lovemaking gives Alatiel anything but pleasure; Boccaccio's translator, G. H. McWilliam, even suggests that her name is an anagram of *La Lieta,* "The Contented Lady" (xcvi)—contented because sexually satisfied. Her adventures are, for her, unpredictable and often dismaying but never disagreeable for longer than a moment. After killing Pericone, for instance, "Marato . . . began consoling her to such good effect that she soon returned his affection and forgot all about Pericone" (131). Furthermore, as we shall see, it is to be questioned that what Alatiel returns to four years after she left it, her father's palace and intentions and then finally marriage to the King of Algarve, a man she has never met, will produce

exactly a state of unexpected happiness. So notwithstanding Filomena's directive, one might describe the tale of Alatiel in abstract terms as regression from a period of sexual happiness to the confines of an arranged marriage.

A consideration of how, and how well, individual *novelle* conform to the subjects of their days, as I have cursorily done with this one tale, can be a useful critical instrument for understanding the variety and focus of the ***Decameron.*** So can a consideration of how a tale would look in the environment of another day's subject. The story of Alatiel would fit seamlessly into the **"Seventh Day,"** during the rule of Dioneo, who at the end of **"Day 6"** had proclaimed as the next day's subject, "the tricks [*delle beffe*] which, either in the cause of love or for motives of self-preservation, women have played upon their husbands, irrespective of whether or not they were found out" (478). At the end of the tale of Alatiel we learn that "despite the fact that eight separate men had made love to her on thousands of occasions, she entered [the King of Algarve's] bed as a virgin and convinced him that it was really so" (147). It would be hard to imagine a more definitive *trick* than this one—by and large the tales of **"Day 7"** involve a wife cuckolding her husband with a single lover, often by a single sexual act—and if it can be objected that *technically* Algarve is not yet actually Alatiel's husband during her lengthy Club Med holiday, his assumption of entitlement to her celibacy during that period is not therefore, as we shall see, any the less. The tale denies Algarve a narrative: he never gets to tell us what he wants and expects, but the tacit premises of the tale suggest that he believes he deserves a virgin wife, that any alternative would never enter his head. Consequently, to restate the achievement of **"2,7"** in terms of the subject of a day to which it was not assigned is not promiscuously to juggle the contents of the ***Decameron*** but rather to view this tale from an unusual perspective that may prove highly illuminating.

Panfilo tells the tale of Alatiel on the **"Second Day,"** not the seventh, but it will be instructive to consider a major detail of the story he does tell on the **"Seventh Day,"** the ninth *novella,* the story of Lydia, her "elderly husband" Nicostratos (534), and his servant and eventually her lover Pyrrhus. Lydia falls in love with Pyrrhus and enlists her maid Lusca as go-between. Pyrrhus promises Lusca that he will yield to Lydia's desires—but only if Lydia "will do three things . . . : first, she must kill Nicostratos' favourite sparrowhawk before his very eyes; second, she must send me a tuft of Nicostratos' beard; and lastly, she must send me one of the best teeth he has left in his jaw" (536). She must, in other words, do three things that it seems she cannot or will not do, but of course she accomplishes them all. That Lydia is able to perform the impossible, and then also, as she has promised, "to make love to Pyrrhus under the old man's nose, and then persuade Nicostratos that he was suffering from hallucinations" (537), simply underscores the magnitude of her capability. Lydia, although a very desirable woman, nevertheless parodies in her actions the accomplishments of the *male* hero of folklore, who typically, to win the maiden, must perform three tasks, like clearing, sowing, and harvesting a field, perhaps in a single day. No one can do this, one would think, but the hero does. In comically imitating these accomplishments, Lydia is doing the kind of thing that only a man, a superman at that, can do. Panfilo, or Boccaccio, is casting a female in a role usually assigned to a man.

This role reversal, which challenges categories of gender, is perhaps the most salient fact about Panfilo's story on **"Day 7,"** and though perhaps less obvious it is of fundamental importance also to his story on **"Day 2."** If Alatiel were a man, tomcatting abroad for a few years before settling down, the story about her behavior, now his behavior, would be unremarkable. That it is a woman who has sex thousands of times with eight partners of the opposite sex and then acts and is accepted as if nothing out of the ordinary has occurred—that is what makes the tale. This detail invites a comparison of the sexual statistics Alatiel compiles and other features of her travels with those of her ultimate model, earlier than the countless heroes of late Greek and Medieval romances, the Odysseus of Homer. Odysseus, it is true, takes ten years to travel from Troy back to Ithaca, whereas Alatiel's "odyssey" (as almost all commentators call it) lasts only four, but whereas the lands real and imaginary that he visits are probably all very close to Greece, mainly in or bordering on the Aegean and Ionian Seas, Alatiel travels from Babylon and Alexandria as far west as Majorca, then eastward to Corinth in the Peloponnese, to the suburbs of Athens, to the Aegean islands of Aegina and Chios, to Smyrna on the mainland of Asia Minor, then to Cyprus, and finally back to Alexandria and Babylon. Women, of course, never travel, never move from home at all in the *Odyssey,* perhaps because the one woman given to wanderlust, Helen, had caused so much trouble; Alatiel travels thousands of miles upon the sea, much farther than not only Odysseus but also her various mates, who accompany her for only small segments of her voyage. Although the *Odyssey* is sometimes criticized these days for the world of male privilege it presents, including the right to travel, in fact the sexual dimensions of this privilege are severely circumscribed. Not only does Odysseus behave himself at home, he enjoys the favors of only two females, both goddesses, Circe and Calypso, during his travels, with the second of whom he settles in for seven long years of monogamy.[4] Although Alatiel's sexual liaisons are serial rather than simultaneous, "monogamous" would be an odd word to characterize them. And whereas Odysseus enjoys comfortable beds in his goddesses' palaces, two of Alatiel's

passionate couplings (with Marato, lover number two, and with the Cypriot merchant, lover number eight) take place on board ship. It is obviously true that Odysseus is a man of action, who repeatedly takes the initiative and makes his own luck, whereas Alatiel is a woman of stunning passivity (except at one moment, to be considered below), who is powerless to resist the initiatives (directed toward her) of the men she encounters.[5] At the same time, however, the scope of her travels is far greater than his, and next to hers, his sexual activities are very minor matters.

The plot of the literary mode of romance involves the hero's separation from his home, his initiation into a world of experience where he will prove supreme, and his return home. Thus the *Odyssey* is a romance, and thus the odyssey of Alatiel is also. But although the world of experience of Odysseus encompasses many dimensions, that of Alatiel has only one: sex. There, of course, she is supreme; her lovers may regard her as the fuel that feeds their passions, but she outlasts them all even if they do not all die. In Dioneo's tenth *novella* of **"Day 5,"** the "old bawd" tells the wife of Pietro di Vinciolo that "one woman could exhaust many men, whereas many men can't exhaust one woman" (434-35). The story of Alatiel gives uncommon force to this sentiment. As Penelope waits for many years for the return of a man she is not certain still lives, so does the King of Algarve wait, though a shorter time, for his intended, from all vicarious experience of whose adventures he will be entirely, and happily, excluded.

Alatiel does not seek her lovers, but she finds them and enjoys them, and after four years of sexual escapades, she is, so far as her father and husband are concerned, as she was in the beginning, perfectly preserved in the convent of *san Cresci in Valcava.* (It is interesting that Alatiel's father does not get the point of "Saint Stiffen-in-the-Hollows.") What is the context of Alatiel's all-important virginity? For her father and husband, it is the emblem, even the precise equivalence, of her value or worth, as in modern Turkey (near to Alatiel's part of the world), where girls who fail virginity tests can be expelled from school and are driven not uncommonly to suicide.[6] It bestows upon her whatever value they agree she owns. It is a physiological detail by which she is transformed into a commodity. Possessing virginity, she is worthy of the King of Algarve; deprived of it, she obviously would not be. Vittore Branca calls the **Decameron** the "Mercantile Epic," and although the seventh story of **"Day 2"** is not especially concerned with merchants and commerce, both are implicit parts of its environment. The Genoese brothers with whom Alatiel and Marato leave Majorca have "a full cargo for Corinth in the Peloponnese" (131), and when these brothers conspire to murder Marato and take his mistress, they "agreed to make the lady's conquest a mutual affair, as though love were capable of being shared out like merchandise or profits" (132). Alatiel is thus another part of their goods. Branca himself points out that Sardinia, which Alatiel's ship passes before crashing on Majorca, was a center of the Bardi company's grain trade and that because of this economic prominence it was "an obligatory point of navigation in the western Mediterranean, between Africa and the ports of Provence and Catalonia."[7] Hence, on her way ostensibly to Algarve, "aboard a well-armed and well-appointed ship with a retinue of noblemen and noblewomen and a large quantity of elegant and precious accoutrements" (126), a ship, it could go without saying, that she does not herself pilot, Alatiel is just another noblewoman—or just another precious accoutrement, or just another cargo being moved from place to place in the Mediterranean. And so she will be again, four years later, when she starts off once more for Algarve. But whereas grain, the foundation of the Bardi fortune, has intrinsic value in its ability to keep people alive, Alatiel has value because her father and fiancé say she does, and they say this because she is a virgin, or so they think. And so they are tricked. On the other hand, the strength of their conviction reifies the abstraction that virginity mainly is; and for practical purposes, like marriage, their belief restores Alatiel's virginity to her. When Shakespeare's Othello says, "I had been happy if the general camp, / Pioners and all, had tasted [Desdemona's] sweet body, / So I had nothing known,"[8] he is describing the conditions sufficient for the happiness of another Moor, too, the King of Algarve. Virginity can be a fact less of a woman's body than of a man's imagination.

In the European romance tradition, Northrop Frye once wrote, "virginity is to a woman what honor is to a man, the symbol of the fact that she is not a slave."[9] But virginity is such a symbol only when it is a projection of the woman's own will. Preserving her virginity in the face of all the men who would take it, the woman asserts one kind of freedom. But when virginity is a condition imposed upon the woman by men, and indeed the only condition for which they value her, then it becomes a perfect disregard of her will or her freedom. Such a woman is imprisoned in her virginity, not emancipated by it, and such a woman would Beminedab and Algarve have Alatiel be.

The value of Alatiel for her father and husband, again, consists in her virginity. Ironically, it is in her sexual availability, which presumes the absence or at least insignificance of virginity, that her value for the other men in the *novella* consists. Not speaking Alatiel's language, Pericone, her first lover, cannot know before they have slept together that he is her first, but he is untroubled one way or the other by her sexual experience or lack thereof (unlike Algarve, who presumably will be hugely gratified to have her "[enter] his bed as a virgin"). What does trouble him is her rejections. "As

the days passed, and Pericone came into closer proximity with the object of his desires, his advances were more firmly rejected, and the flames of his passion raged correspondingly fiercer. Realizing that his flattery was getting him nowhere, he decided to fall back on ingenuity and subterfuge, holding brute strength in reserve as a last resort" (129-30). In the event, this last resort is unnecessary since on "a great festive occasion" Pericone has Alatiel "supplied with a succession of different wines." Since alcohol "is prohibited by her religion, she was unaccustomed to drinking, and by using this in the service of Venus, he thought it possible that she would yield to him." All works out according to this plan, with Alatiel actually taking the initiative when they go to her chamber, and she "undressed in Pericone's presence as though he were one of her maidservants, and got into bed. Pericone lost no time in following her example . . . and without meeting any resistance on her part, he began making amorous sport with her." Alatiel enjoys the sport so much that "she could not see why she had waited for an invitation before spending her nights so agreeably" (130), a degree of pleasure, unmixed with regret or recriminations, that surely must qualify any suspicions of date rape. Thereafter, all her subsequent lovers are aware of at least some part of her earlier sexual experience, and although there is no suggestion that this experience makes her more desirable to them—that they want her because she has been wanted, that other men have validated her sexual acceptability, in the way of René Girard's mimetic desire—it certainly does not make her less desirable.[10] It is true that until Alatiel meets Antioco, lover number seven, who "was familiar with her language," a circumstance that "pleased her immensely because for several years she had been more or less forced to lead the life of a deaf-mute as she could neither understand what anybody was saying nor make herself understood," a man with whom she "became good friends" as well as "lovers" (140)—until Alatiel meets him, her lovers seek no more in her than their sexual gratification. But her own sexual gratification is never less than theirs, and it is certainly not the point of view of the tale that this gratification is less worthy as the end of a male-female association than the woman-as-commodity-owned-by-a-man association she will know with Algarve.

Men desire Alatiel because she is beautiful, and the narrative of Alatiel's beauty deserves some attention. She "was the most beautiful woman to be found anywhere on earth," Panfilo asserts, simply, at the beginning of his tale (126). Pericone "found that she was even more beautiful than he had ever thought possible" (129). The Genoese traders desire Alatiel because she "had the body of an angel and a temperament to match" (132), and the Prince of Morea, "on discovering her to be more beautiful than she had been reported . . . immediately fell so ardently in love with her that he could think of nothing else." With him "her beauty flourished to such a degree that the whole of the eastern empire seemed to talk of nothing else" (133), and gazing upon her, men like the Duke of Athens "could scarcely believe that she was a creature of this earth" (134). Antioco, though able to respond to more intellectual virtues, was "so overwhelmed by her beauty" that "he had fallen in love with her" (140). Antigono, not a lover but the man who will engineer Alatiel's return to her father, becomes interested in her when by chance "he happened to catch sight of the lady at one of the windows" of the house where she is staying in Paphos, and saw that "she was very beautiful" (142). Of the men in Alatiel's life, only her father and the King of Algarve do not take special notice of her beauty, a circumstance that suggests, interestingly, that her beauty is primarily a characteristic of the four years away from them.

Alatiel's beauty fires the sexual desire of almost all the men who see her. It makes them attentive, then single-minded, obsessed, then duplicitous, and finally, if there is no other way, murderous. For the critic Guido Almansi her beauty is so much more than human that Alatiel is not merely "'a beautiful woman.' She is a superhuman figure; mythic, or at least closely related to myth."[11] Therefore, male knowledge of her is mythic, too, as well as fatal. "The uniqueness and superlativeness of the whole experience can only be sealed by [her lovers'] death. If a single lover survived, it would trivialize the adventure and reduce Alatiel to the role of *femme fatale,* or *belle dame sans merci,* or just a vulgar consumer of men. Alatiel's lovers die, and as they die they enshrine the loved woman, who becomes a priestess of Eros, not a nymphomaniac."[12] That love for Alatiel, of whom no one tires, who makes hungry where most she satisfies, is somehow outside normal, quotidian experience is obvious enough, but Almansi's formulation is insufficiently attentive to the facts of Alatiel's story. Not all of her lovers die. After Costanzo, lover number 5, takes her away from the city of Athens and the Duke of Athens, lover number 4, we hear nothing more of the Duke. When Uzbek, the next lover, captures her and Costanzo in Chios and takes them with him to Smyrna, we may assume that he kills Costanzo, that such would be the logical thing to do in this violent world, but we are not told so. And the last lover, the Cypriot merchant, is "away on a trading mission in Armenia" (142), when Antigono meets Alatiel, and he is never heard from again. According to Giuseppe Mazzotta, "Alatiel's beauty is that strangeness which, though part of the world's desire and provisional enjoyment, can never be assimilated into the structure of exchange."[13] It differs thus from her real or imagined virginity, which even in its absence remains a feature of economic exchange.

As often as Alatiel's beauty is asserted, it is curious that we know absolutely nothing about what she looks like unless, because she "had the body of an angel," we know what an angel looks like. It is true that in the *Decameron* Boccaccio is not much given to physical descriptions. With the apparent minor exceptions of Filomena (who looks "most shapely and attractive" on the day she presides [70]) and Neifile (whose eyes at one point "glittered and shone like the morning star" [186]) and the apparent major exception of Fiammetta ("who had long, golden curls that cascaded down over delicate, pure, white shoulders, a softly rounded face that glowed with the authentic hues of white lilies and crimson roses, a pair of eyes in her head that gleamed like a falcon's, and a sweet little mouth with lips like rubies" [363])—*apparent,* because all these details are highly conventional—we do not know, for instance, what the females in the *brigata* look like other than that they are "fair to look upon, graceful in bearing, and charmingly unaffected" (13); we learn even less about their male compan- ions. With one interesting exception the men in the seventh *novella* of **"Day 2"** are described only with a few stock phrases suggestive of sexual potency: Pericone is "a very powerful, vigorous-looking fellow" (129), the Duke of Athens is "a handsome, powerfully proportioned youth" (133), and so forth. The exception is Marato, who, we are told, is "fair and fresh as a garden rose" (131), *bello e fresco come una rosa.* What is interesting about these words is not that they tell us much about Marato's appearance, because they do not, but that they are part of the conventionalized vocabulary for representing a woman's beauty, a vocabulary we often call Petrarchan though, of course, it is much older than Petrarch. The application of these words to Marato is another sign, a minor one, of the tale's tendency to reverse the traditional roles of male and female, but it is more important as a suggestion that the rhetorical figure of *energia,* whereby persons are described with such power that they appear present, has otherwise been suppressed in the tale. This suppression in turn implies that Panfilo's narrative is both specialized and selective, that details not given could have supplemented those we have, or been substituted for them altogether.

Novella 7 of **"Day 2"** contains at least three separate narratives of Alatiel's adventures: the first, the longest, the one we think of as Panfilo's story, extends from Alatiel's leaving Babylon for Algarve right after we have met her (126) to her leaving for Algarve again, four years later (147). Just before the end of this narrative, Alatiel incorporates into it the story she tells her father (145-46), which was invented by Antigono, at the center of which is her lengthy incarceration in the convent in Aiguesmortes. Just before this moment, reference is made to a third narrative, which we do not get to hear: "And so saying, never ceasing to weep, she told [Antigono] *everything that had happened* to her since the day on which she was shipwrecked off Majorca . . ." (143-44; my italics). This narrative is not identical with Panfilo's, though at first it might seem so. "Everything that had happened to" Alatiel implies her knowledge of what happened and her understanding of the way it happened; the words imply, in short, her point of view. But, for example, the degree of Pericone's frustration with her initial rejection of him, described above, is something she could not know; nor could she know of the way the Duke of Athens and his henchman murder and then defenestrate the Prince of Morea and his servant Ciuriaci; nor of the fate of Uzbek, killed fighting the King of Cappadocia; nor of countless other details in Panfilo's narrative of moments bearing on her life when she was not present. We, the tale's readers, know these things, but beyond her basic responses to sexual encounters ("Great indeed was their mutual delight" [130], "they had a very happy time of it together" [140], "they were each consumed with an almost equally intense longing" [142]), where her response is often, as in these examples, not differentiated from her lover's, we know little of Alatiel's feelings and thoughts. That these thoughts are framed in a language not her lovers', not our own, and even Panfilo's only because of a rare degree of authorial intrusion, makes them the more mysterious. Alatiel's sexual pleasure may be as great as that of her lovers, but of her anticipation, of her desire before the fact, if it exists, we learn nothing. In his narrative Panfilo always displays the ardency of *their* desire, which drives the plot of the *novella*: Alatiel waits, receives, responds, remains as mysterious to us as to them, and survives.

Alatiel's single initiative in her tale, interestingly, is her decision to abandon her adventures and satisfy, finally, the purposes of her father. "When she espied Antigono" in Cyprus, ". . . being suddenly filled with the hope that there might be some possibility of returning once more to her regal status with the help of this man's advice, [Alatiel] sent for him at her earliest opportunity" (142), requests his cooperation, and is assured by Antigono that "'I shall have no difficulty in restoring you to a higher place than ever in your father's affection, and you will then go to marry the King of Algarve, as originally arranged'" (144). All this, of course, comes to pass. Her request, however, is the only indication that Alatiel's "regal status" much interests her, and it is tempting to suppose that her sudden hope is motivated less by the desire to get on with her life than by Boccaccio's own desire to give a kind of closure to his fiction. Here, too, the tale appears a microcosm of the *Decameron*. Panfilo's sensible-seeming proposal, at the end of **"Day 10,"** that the *brigata* "should return whence we came . . . lest aught conducive to tedium should arise from a custom too long established, and lest, by protracting our stay, we should cause evil

tongues to start wagging" (796), cannot alter the fact that the plague in Florence rages no less fiercely than a fortnight earlier. Return would place the *brigata* in extreme peril, were they real people, but Boccaccio sees that it is time for his long book to end.

Alatiel goes, finally, to the King of Algarve, where—I quote this ironical formula for the last time—"despite the fact that eight separate men had made love to her on thousands of different occasions, she entered his bed as a virgin and convinced him that it was really so" (147). What does that mean? Or, rather, does the **Decameron** provide any context within which we are invited to make a conjecture about the sexual relations of Alatiel and Algarve? At the end, Aldo Scaglione writes, Alatiel has "gained a lot of not unpleasant experience, all to the good of her future husband."[14] In other words, Scaglione implies, Algarve will be the beneficiary, however unknowingly, of the sexual wisdom she has acquired; not for ever will she act the virgin. Well, good for Algarve, if so, but I am less certain that Boccaccio's many tales of passionate women, of feckless or inadequate husbands, and the constraints of conventional marriages point in this direction. Bette Talvacchia has recently called attention to the "extreme distrust of physical pleasure [that] has always informed one current within the Catholic church's teaching on sexual matters, which would define sexual desire under any circumstances as a manifestation of lust, one of the seven deadly sins."[15] In the **Decameron,** the avoidance of any arousal of precisely this desire characterizes many marriages. In the sixth *novella* of **"Day 3,"** for instance, Catella Sighinolfo keeps her assignation with Ricciardo Minutolo, believing that she is meeting her own husband, who believes, so she thinks, that *he* is meeting Ricciardo's wife. In the darkness of the bagnio, their trysting place, Catella is amazed that Filippello Sighinolfo, as she believes him to be, shows passion as a lover that he never showed as a husband. "'Alas! who have I been loving devotedly for all these years?'" she asks him. "'A faithless cur, who thinks he has a strange woman in his arms, and lavishes more caresses and amorous attention upon me in the brief time I have spent with him here than in the whole of the rest of our married life. . . . I must say you have given a splendid display of manly vigour here today, in contrast with the feeble, worn-out, lack-lustre manner that you always adopt in your own house'" (233-34). Two centuries later Torquato Tasso would use this tale to illustrate a general principle: "A husband should strive to preserve his wife's sense of shame not only in all the other acts and occupations of life but also when embracing her: husbands do not embrace their wives as lovers. No wonder, then, that her lover's kisses seemed sweeter than her husband's to [Catella]. . . ."[16] So perhaps marital propriety will prevent Algarve's ever getting to know his wife very well. And if that is so, then Alatiel, the contented lady, will have to content herself with the memory of four good years.

Notes

1. Giovanni Boccaccio, *The Decameron,* tr. G. H. McWilliam, 2nd edition (London and New York: Penguin Books, 1995). All English quotations from the *Decameron* are from this edition with page numbers given parenthetically in my text. The several phrases quoted in Italian are from Boccaccio, *Decameron, Introduzione, commenti e note a cura di* Antonio Enzo Quaglio (Rome: Garanzi, 1974).

2. Harry Berger, Jr., "The Renaissance Imagination: Second World and Green World" in *Second World and Green World: Studies in Renaissance Fiction-Making* (Berkeley and London: U of California P, 1988), 36.

3. On the *cornici* of the *Decameron,* and the *cornici* within them, see Joy Hambuechen Potter, *Five Frames for the "Decameron": Communication and Social Systems in the Cornice* (Princeton: Princeton UP, 1982).

4. See, for instance, Sharon Uemura Ronholt's letter complaining about Odysseus's "unacceptable" "sexual politics" in *The New York Times Book Review* of January 19, 1997, p. 4, and my letter in defense of Odysseus (and Homer) in the same publication, February 16, 1997, p. 4.

5. There is not much that even a less passive woman could do in Alatiel's circumstances, or perhaps one should say that these circumstances would render almost any woman passive. It is worth noting, however, that after the shipwreck on Majorca, Alatiel "implored . . . the three surviving members of her female retinue . . . to preserve their chastity, declaring her own determination to submit to no man's pleasure except her husband's. . . ." The three women, who quite unaccountably are about to disappear from Alatiel's life and story, promise to "do their utmost to follow her instructions" (129). Is there a suggestion here, however faint, that death at one's own hand is preferable to dishonor? If so, it is not an alternative that elsewhere occurs to Alatiel.

In "Seduction by Silence: A Gloss on the Tales of Masetto (*Decameron* III, 1) and Alatiel (*Decameron* II, 7)" (*Philological Quarterly,* 58 [1979], 1-15), [Illegible Text] Marcus posits Alatiel's failure to speak her lovers' languages as the condition of her passivity: "Alatiel's speechlessness accounts not only for her promiscuity but for her passivity as well. Without language she is unable to formulate the dictates of her own will, let alone assert these in her relations with others. She thus becomes the [Illegible Text] and impersonal object of Everyman's desires, forfeiting her individuality in the process" (7).

6. See Stephen Kinzer, "Turks Clash Over Defense of Virginity Tests," *The New York Times,* January 8, 1998, A3.

7. Vittore Branca, *Boccaccio: The Man and His Works,* tr. Richard Monges (New York: New York UP, 1976), 283. Book II of this volume is devoted to the *Decameron,* and its third chapter (276-307) is titled "The Mercantile Epic."

8. William Shakespeare, *Othello,* ed. Norman Sanders (Cambridge: Cambridge UP [The New Cambridge Shakespeare], 1984), 3.3.346-48.

9. Northrop Frye, *The Secular Scripture: A Study of the Structure of Romance* (Cambridge, MA: Harvard UP, 1976), 73.

10. René Girard, *A Theatre of Envy* (New York: Oxford UP, 1991), 9-15 and *passim.*

11. Guido Almansi, *The Writer as Liar: Narrative Technique in the "Decameron"* (London: Routledge, 1975), 124.

12. Almansi, 125.

13. Giuseppe Mazzotta, *The World at Play in Boccaccio's "Decameron"* (Princeton: Princeton UP, 1986), 103.

14. Aldo Scaglione, *Nature and Love in the Late Middle Ages* (Berkeley: U of California P, 1963), 90.

15. Bette Talvacchia, *Taking Positions: On the Erotic in Renaissance Culture* (Princeton: Princeton UP, 1999), 117.

16. "The Father of the Family" (*Il padre di famiglia,* 1580) in *Tasso's Dialogues: A Selection with the Discourse on the Art of the Dialogue,* tr. Carnes Lord and Dain A. Trafton (Berkeley: U of California P, 1982), 91. Robert Herrick would make much the same point in his epigram "Kissing and Bussing": "Kissing and bussing differ both [i.e., from each other] in this; / We busse our Wantons, but our Wives we kisse." *The Poems of Robert Herrick* (London and Oxford: World's Classics, 1933), 200.

Franco Masciandaro (essay date January 2003)

SOURCE: Masciandaro, Franco. "Madonna Isabella's Play and the Play of the Text (*Decameron* VII.6)." *MLN* 118, no. 1 (January 2003): 245-56.

[*In the following essay, Masciandaro studies the thematic and textual significance of "play" in the sixth no-*

vella *of the "Seventh Day," assessing reader-response to narrative "play" in terms of the conflict between the text's world and reader expectations of that world.*]

> "The text game brings to the fore what has been obscured by the representative character of the various positions, and what emerges will in turn have retroactive effect on representation. Play becomes a mode of discovery but is also itself changed by what it has set in motion; as a result, in the text game the play-forms themselves switch kaleidoscopically between what they are and what is eclipsed by their being."
>
> Wolfgang Iser, *The Fictive and the Imaginary*[1]

The principal aim of my paper is to shed new light on the creative power of play that informs the tale of Madonna Isabella [**"VII.6"**] by viewing it primarily not from the perspective of the players but from the changing perspectives arising from the play itself.[2] As Gadamer has shown in his *Truth and Method,* play (like the work of art) has its own essence, independently from the conscience and intention of those who play[3]; and as Umberto Eco has observed, "il soggetto innesca il processo ('alea iacta est') ma non sa cosa succederà: il gioco si articola da solo."[4] Thus, in examining the ludic action set in motion by Madonna Isabella, I shall focus on the ways in which it develops and is modified by unforeseen events. These, while provoking in her a kind of vertigo, will in fact bring out new ludic resources in the form of improvised mimicry and staging that raise the game to a higher level of theatrical complexity whereby the real and make-believe, instrumental and free play perfectly blend into one seamless performance. I shall also examine the play of the text itself, showing how it mimics the key features of Isabella's play and acts as a force that, as it emphasizes the ludic inventiveness of the protagonist, not only sets limits to her exuberant sexual desires but engenders a beneficent outcome, for her and for all the players in the *novella,* that far exceeds her intention to escape the death that she fears her wronged husband will bring upon her. Moreover, I shall assess the reader's response to the play of the text, and therefore how he or she is being "played" by it, and, specifically, how the textual world clashes with the reader's expectations, especially as they are shaped at the beginning of the tale. Hence my reading *sub specie ludi* will reaffirm the inexhaustible creativity of the hermeneutic project of discovering in Boccaccio's text the ever-present and yet elusive "principle of complexity"[5] whereby in the very moment of such discovery we experience the "vertigo" produced by the unexpected reversal of perspectives, or the transition, as it has been aptly characterized, "from the *notum* to the *novum*: from flows of continuity to their fraction, from the well-known to the new, and from the ordinary to the extraordinary."[6]

As I identify the constitutive elements of play in the tale of Madonna Isabella, I shall adopt the four terms, *agon, mimicry, alea,* and *ilinx* that Wolfgang Iser has borrowed from Roger Caillois,[7] applying them to literary text play. I shall pay special attention to the creative relationship between the fictive and the imaginary out of which, in the words of Iser, "play arises,"[8] emphasizing the distinction between *game* and *play*—a distinction that, as Umberto Eco has noted, Huizinga neglected to consider in his *Homo Ludens,* and that in Italian corresponds to the distinction between *gioco giocante* and *gioco giocato,* and which of course must be viewed also as a relationship, such as the one between *langue* and *parole.*[9] As I have done in another study,[10] I shall also examine the interrelation of violence and play, showing how the former may be neutralized by the latter, that is, by the very force that at any moment could provoke violence.

Boccaccio sets up the game to be played out in the tale of Madonna Isabella by defining it as a variation on the theme of the *beffa,* chosen for the **"Seventh Day,"** particularly as exemplified by the preceding tale of the jealous husband-turned-confessor who was tricked by his wife:

> Maravigliosamente era piaciuta a tutti la novella della Fiammetta, affermando ciascuno ottimamente la donna aver fatto e quel che si convenia al bestiale uomo. Ma poi che finita fu, il re a Pampinea impose che seguitasse; la quale incominciò a dire:
>
> —Molti sono li quali semplicemente parlando, dicono che Amore trae altrui del senno e quasi chi ama fa divenire smemorato. Sciocca oppinione mi pare: e assai le già dette cose l'hanno mostrato, e io ancora intendo di dimostrarlo.
>
> (**"VII.6,"** 2-3)[11]

Along with the *brigata,* with whom we share in some measure the wonderment and delight that is generally associated with play but also their judgement of the appropriateness or "poetic justice" of the *beffa* played on the "bestiale uomo" by his wife, we may at first expect the next tale to be another example of the cleverness of women vs. the foolishness of their husbands in the realm of eros. Yet we soon experience a dramatic shift of perspective as we observe that the tale which Pampinea is about to narrate is part of a larger game that is characterized by an *agon* between those who naïvely speak of Love that takes away one's presence of mind and those who hold the contrary view that Love increases lovers' ingenuity. Especially significant, as it will become increasingly clear as the story unfolds, is that Pampinea intends to win the game she has just announced (which echoes the Provençal *joc parti*) by opposing to the many who speak foolishly of Love's power a superabundance of proofs of the true nature of such power by adding yet another tale to those that have already been narrated and have amply proved Love's might. This superabundance is also reflected in the profusion displayed by the text itself as it is fashioned by Boccaccio, the *magister ludi*. At the textual level we in fact observe, in the space of the brief exordium, a number of words that signal abundance and variety—"molti," "assai", "ancora," "mostrato," and "dimostrarlo"—, to which we should add the very name of the narrator, quite appropriately Pampinea, that is, "the luxuriant."

The theme of abundance and variety announced in the exordium is then further elaborated, constituting a veritable *leitmotiv*:

> Nella nostra città, copiosa di tutti i beni, fu una giovane donna e gentile e assai bella, la qual fu moglie d'un cavaliere assai valoroso e da bene. E come spesso avviene che sempre non può l'uomo usare un cibo ma talvolta disidera di variare, non soddisfacendo a questa donna molto il suo marito, s'innamorò d'un giovane il quale Leonetto era chiamato, assai piacevole e costumato, come che di gran nazion non fosse, e egli similmente s'innamorò di lei: e come voi sapete che rade volte è senza effetto quello che vuole ciascuna delle parti a dare al loro amor compimento molto tempo non si interpose.
>
> (4-5)

The words defining the setting of Pampinea's tale—the *brigata*'s city, Florence—resonate with special meaning as they create the illusion that this city not only was once upon a time but still is the place where all the good things in life are to be found in great abundance. This is not the Florence that the *brigata* has recently and temporarily left behind, which is being devastated by the plague, and where physical and moral decay abound. The hyperbole "copiosa di tutti i beni" obviously speaks of an ideal city, as ideal in fact as the *Valle delle Donne,* where the *brigata* has moved at the end of the **"Sixth Day,"** and which now must be brought to mind as a particularly appropriate scene of Pampinea's narration of Madonna Isabella's story. Here Boccaccio has represented a perfectly ordered *locus amoenus,* which, shaped like an amphitheater, constitutes an ideal synthesis of the garden and the city, which is now echoed in the ideal Florence that frames Pampinea's story. Significantly, the *Valle delle Donne* is characterized by superabundance. At the center of the valley, surrounded by a luxuriant meadow and a great variety of trees, there is a "piccol laghetto, quale talvolta per modo di vivaio fanno ne' lor giardini i cittadini che di ciò hanno destro . . .", whose water "alla sua capacità *soprabondava* . . ." (26-28). We may recall that this scene of abundance is enhanced by the beautiful naked bodies of the seven women of the *brigata* who swim in this fish-pond, playing at pursuing fish—a *festa,* Boccaccio tells us, that ends with their catching some of them. We may see this as an allu-

sively erotic "sport" that frames and foreshadows the "fishing" practiced by women in the *novelle* of the **"Seventh Day."**[12]

To the plenitude represented by the scene of Pampinea's story corresponds a certain plenitude in the qualities that define each of the characters introduced. In fact, they all have in common the adverb *assai*. Madonna Isabella is portrayed as "una giovane donna e gentile e assai bella." And noting that her husband is not, as one might have expected, a foolish man or "bestiale uomo," but a "cavaliere assai valoroso e da bene," we must count him as one more good possessed by Madonna Isabella. In light of such richness we as readers do not foresee that these two characters will somehow become antagonists, and that Isabella's husband will be the object of her *beffa*. And when these expectations are modified by the new element that Boccaccio introduces in the game he is staging, namely, Isabella's desire for variety in the sphere of eros, we note that the opposition or *agon* between Isabella and her husband is tenuous, since the reason given for her infidelity is not that he is incapable of also being a valorous knight in bed, but that he cannot be at once himself and someone else, or, as the desire for variety ultimately demands, one and many. Similarly, as we turn our attention to Leonetto, we observe that the *agon* defining his relation to Isabella's husband is also tenuous, mildly reflecting the conventional opposition, in terms of social status, of the worthy young man of humble origin to the noble knight. Significantly, what gives Leonetto the edge in this *agon,* at least as it is defined at the outset of the game which is yet to be played out, is his being at once "costumato'—and therefore somewhat like his antagonist, who is "da bene"—and "assai piacevole," possessing therefore a quality which, unlike that of the knight who is "assai valoroso," belongs more to the aesthetic than to the ethical sphere. This quality is commensurate with Isabella's great beauty and equally great desire to catch new, and hence more pleasing "fish" than she has already caught. If the presence of *agon* here is tenuous and diffused, indirectly involving the good knight, it is however the dominant, characterizing element of the game of Isabella's love triangle. Yet, it does imply the presence of *alea* or chance, *mimicry* or deception, and *ilinx* or the vertigo of subversion, of the carnivalesque, which may interact with *agon* with the unforeseeable effect of either neutralizing the violence generally associated with it or exacerbating it. Thus, as we "play along" with the narrator, sharing her expectations of Isabella's fruition of the plenitude she longs for and that she intends to find in Leonetto, we also secretly sense that this game may perhaps be unexpectedly disrupted, through *alea* and/or *ilinx,* transforming the noble knight into a wrathful wronged husband, and therefore into a very dangerous opponent.

As Pampinea utters these words about the consummation of the love that binds Isabella and Leonetto, "a dare al loro amor compimento molto tempo non s'interpose," she is seemingly completing her definition and introduction of a game that will be successfully played out. Yet, we soon discover that this game is drastically altered by the unexpected intrusion of a Messer Lambertuccio, who has fallen desperately in love with Isabella. Although she finds him a "spiacevole uomo e sazievole," when he threatens to bring shame on her if she does not yield she agrees to do his bidding (6). We now witness an interesting twist in the motif of abundance and variety that so far has characterized Isabella and her game: what began as one love triangle has now proliferated into three. Ironically, Isabella, whose desire is not satisfied by her husband ("non sodisfacendo a questa donna *molto* il suo marito"), rejects Ser Lambertuccio's numerous entreaties ("costui con ambasciate sollicitandola *molto* . . ."), finding him "sazievole" (i.e., literally "satiating" or "filling" and therefore "tiresome"). The textual play reveals to the eyes of the privileged reader the paradoxical relationship between desire and satiety, since the latter is both the goal and, once attained, the death of the former. Hence the fulfilment promised by variety proves to be a mirage, for desire is rekindled and is steered toward a new object whenever the attained object is not satisfying. This is obviously hidden from the eyes of our protagonist, for, unaware of the "lesson" implicit in her finding Messer Lambertuccio "sazievole," and therefore of what the mechanism of desire demands—that she will eventually find Leonetto, like her husband, unable to satisfy her—she continues to pursue her "game."

As we turn our attention to the way in which the game is played by Isabella and the other three characters, I will briefly enumerate the scenes that, in rapid succession, lead to Isabella's singular performance as both actress and stage director of her play-within-a-play (7-14). The setting is no longer Florence, but Isabella's beautiful country villa. Her husband is expected to be away for a few days. She sends for Leonetto, who, "lietissimo incontanente v'andò." No sooner has Leonetto joined Isabella in her bedroom than Messer Lambertuccio, "sentendo il marito della donna essere andato altrove, tutto solo montato a cavallo a lei se n'andò e picchiò alla porta." The maid, "incontanente," informs her lady that "messer Lambertuccio è quaggiù tutto solo." The iteration of the phrase *tutto solo* obviously resonates with irony, for he, contrary to his desire to be alone with Isabella and, implicitly, to be her uncontested lover, is, at least temporarily, *de trop*. Moment of *ilinx* for Isabella, whom we suddenly see transformed from "la donna" to "la più dolente femina del mondo." In fear, she asks Leonetto to hide behind the curtains of her bed until Messer Lambertuccio's departure. The equally fearful Leonetto—despite what one might at first expect (*nomen numen*), or perhaps we should say

because of it, as suggested by the diminuitive ending of his name—does not confront his rival, concealing himself as the lady requested. Messer Lambertuccio enters Isabella's bedroom and proceeds to gratify his desire. Now it is Leonetto who is and must feel *de trop*. Meanwhile, just as he interrupted Leonetto so is Messer Lambertuccio soon interrupted by the unforseen return of Isabella's husband. Again, we witness the swiftness of the sequence of scenes: As the maid sees him approach the villa, "subitamente corse alla camera della donna e disse: Madonna, ecco messer che torna: io credo che egli sia già giú nella corte." *Alea* and *ilinx*, which have been predominant as the play developed, are now intensified and almost overwhelm Isabella, to the point that she considers herself dead ("si tenne morta"), for she fears her husband's wrath and violence, as we had envisaged earlier. This is the moment when she is more played upon than playing. The rapid succession of scenes of the arrival of three men, which is punctuated by the adverbs *incontanente, subitamente, già giú*—whose comic effect, produced by what Bergson has termed *du mécanique plaqué sur du vivant*,[13] is not lost on the reader—and is obviously governed by the narrative technique of *variatio*, at once mimics and exposes the mechanism of her desire for abundance and variety, parodying the much longed-for *immediate* fruition of the object of such desire. Yet, with equal swiftness ("subitamente") she is inspired, and instead of being crushed by *agon, alea,* and *ilinx,* she neutralizes their force, incorporating them in *mimicry,* as she invents and directs a new play (15-16):

> La donna, udendo questo e sentendosi aver due uomini in casa (e conosceva che il cavaliere non si poteva nascondere per lo suo pallafreno che nella corte era), si tenne morta; nondimeno subitamente gittatasi del letto in terra prese partito e disse a messer Lambertuccio: "Messere, se voi mi volete punto di bene e voletemi da morte campare, farete quello che io vi dirò. Voi vi recherete in mano il vostro coltello ignudo e con mal viso e tutto turbato ve n'andrete giù per le scale e andrete dicendo: 'Io fo boto a Dio che il coglierò altrove'; e se mio marito vi volesse ritenere o di niente vi domandasse, non dite altro che quello che detto v'ho, e montato a cavallo per niuna cagione seco restate."

The violence inflicted on Isabella by the villain of the story is now exorcized through play. Beginning with her leaping out of bed, Madonna Isabella is acting out her original desire to reject Messer Lambertuccio's forceful advances, correcting her adversary's less than courteous behavior. Significantly, as she enjoins him to brandish his "coltello ignudo"—an image whose sexual overtones cannot be overlooked—she dramatically represents and unmasks the violence she has suffered while also projecting on the screen of the imaginary her feared violence at the hands of her husband. "Vi recherete in mano il vostro coltello *ignudo*" clearly expresses at once instrumental and free play, unlike the merely instrumental function represented later by the image of the dagger when she tells her husband "Qua entro si fuggì un giovane . . . , che messer Lambertuccio *col coltello in man* seguitava . . . ," and which is then iterated in Leonetto's account of being chased by Messer Lambertuccio: "come poco lontano da questo palagio nella strada mi vide, cosí *mise mano al coltello*. . . ." Equally significant is the fact that Isabella now succeeds in attracting Messer Lambertuccio into the ethical sphere of the good, when, upon asking him, "Messere se voi mi volete punto di bene . . . farete quello che io vi dirò," he complies. An important component of this good is his flawless performance, which is achieved by the fortuitous confluence of the real and make-believe, the fictive and the imaginary, and of instrumental and free play expressed, for example, by his own *variatio* of the words prompted to him by Isabella:

> "Messer Lambertuccio disse che volentieri; e tirato fuori il coltello, tutto infocato nel viso tra per la fatica durata e per l'ira avuta della tornata del cavaliere, come la donna gl'impose cosí fece. . . . Messo il piè nella staffa e montato sú, non disse altro se non: 'Al corpo di Dio, io il giugnerò altrove' e andò via."

> (17-18)

Astonished by the sudden appearance (and disappearance) of messer Lambertuccio and puzzled by his demeanor and words, Isabella's husband, on mounting the stairs, and finding his wife at the top "tutta sgomentata e piena di paura," in answer to his question about Messer Lambertuccio's strange behavior is given this plausible explanation (20-21):

> "Messere, io non ebbi mai simil paura a questa. Qua entro si fuggí un giovane, il quale io non conosco e che messer Lambertuccio col coltello in man seguitava, e trovò per ventura questa camera aperta e tutto tremante disse 'Madonna, per Dio aiutatemi, ché io non sia nelle braccia vostre morto'. Io mi levai diritta, e come il voleva domandare chi fosse e che avesse, e ecco messer Lambertuccio venir sú dicendo: 'Dove se', traditore?' Io mi parai in su l'uscio della camera: e volendo egli entrar dentro, il ritenni, e egli in tanto fu cortese, che, come vide che non mi piaceva che egli qua entro entrasse, dette molte parole, se ne venne giú come voi vedeste."

We now marvel at and delight in the creativity of play, as we see Isabella's feared violence and death transformed and transcended through the interrelation of the real and make-believe, of the fictive and the imaginary. More specifically, as suggested earlier, it is *mimicry* that finally absorbs into itself all the other categories of play, *agon, alea,* and *ilinx,* which are in some measure connected with the exacerbation of difference that could provoke strife and violence. Significantly, through *mimicry* Isabella now introduces the ethical dimension that had been suppressed in the first game she and Leonetto had set out to play, as well as in the new game that the unexpected appearance of Messer Lambertuccio had

forced her and her lover to play. As she invents and recounts the scene of Messer Lambertuccio's unexplained pursuit of Leonetto "col coltello in man," uttering the words "Dove se', traditore?", she is projecting unto this imaginary scene the reality of her infidelity and of Leonetto's, and Lambertuccio's betrayal of the good knight. Indeed, had the truth been revealed to her husband, we can easily imagine a scene in which *he,* as Isabella had feared, seeking revenge for the dishonor suffered, would be the one brandishing his dagger and uttering similar words as he pursued her and her two lovers. We may also note that while portraying Messer Lambertuccio as a violent intruder she also points out that he was "in tanto cortese" that he, in order not to displease her, did not enter her bedroom. Thus, as she once again projects unto a fictional scene her original desire that Messer Lambertuccio not enter her room against her will, she restores the chivalric ethos that he had betrayed, creating in the realm of the imaginary (and hence in the eyes of both her noble husband and the reader) the figure of one who is not a knight in name only—"un cavalier chiamato messer Lambertuccio," as he has been introduced in the story—but of one who is more like her own husband, who has been defined "un cavaliere assai valoroso e da bene."

Another creative moment of Isabella's improvised mimicry, to be ascribed more to free than to instrumental play, marks her depiction of the fictional scene of Leonetto's pleading with her with these words: "Madonna, per Dio aiutatemi, ché io non sia nelle braccia vostre morto." As an expression of instrumental play, these words are intended to relate to Isabella's husband Leonetto's narrowly escaped death at the hands of Messer Lambertuccio. As an expression of free play, by alluding to the old amatory metaphor of the lover who dies (or wishes to die) in his lady's arms, they reveal Isabella's last attempt to recapture through fiction and the imaginary that which the real, with the unexpected arrival first of messer Lambertuccio and then of her husband, has denied her.

In response to Isabella's fictional representation of Messer Lambertuccio as both a violent intruder and a courteous knight and of herself as a resolute and prudent lady, the noble knight says to her: "Donna, ben facesti: troppo ne sarebbe stato gran biasimo se persona fosse stata qua entro uccisa; e messer Lambertuccio fece gran villania a seguitar persona che qua entro fuggita fosse" (23). Thus, the one who at the outset of Isabella's game had been given the role of an antagonist, as the husband who could not satisfy her exuberant sexual desire and hence in her eyes (and in the eyes of Pampinea and her audience, including of course that other audience constituted by us the readers) as one who deserves her *beffa,* after being momentarily perceived as one who might bring her death, is the one who recognizes the goodness of her actions, for having deflected Messer Lambertuccio's violence. Hence, in the eyes of the reader, the difference between these two characters appears to have been erased, for she can now be seen as a "donna" who is beautiful and cunning but also, like her husband, "da bene." Most notably, this "goodness" is commensurate with the goodness affirmed by her husband, as he, participating unwittingly in her game, actualizes through fiction and, correspondingly, the imaginary, the noble qualities that had characterized him at the outset. Paradoxically, it is in the realm of make-believe, that he proves to *be* "da bene."[14] And as Isabella's story is then confirmed by Leonetto's own story that, unexplainably pursued by Messer Labertuccio, he had found refuge in the lady's bedroom (27), the good knight, true to his character, plays the role of the noble host and peacemaker (28-29):

> Disse allora il cavaliere: "Or via, non aver paura alcuna; io ti porrò a casa tua sano e salvo, e tu poi sappi far cercar quello che con lui hai a fare. E, come cenato ebbero, fattol montare a cavallo a Firenze il ne menò e lasciollo a casa sua; il quale, secondo l'ammaestramento della donna avuto, quella sera medesima parlò con messer Lambertuccio occultamente e sí con lui ordinò, che, quantunque molte parole ne fossero, mai per ciò il cavaliere non s'accorse della beffa fattagli dalla moglie.

Pampinea's tale thus comes to a close, once again bringing into sharp focus the motif of abundance, although not in the sphere of desire, as we witnessed at the beginning of the *novella,* but in the sphere of the good engendered by play and ultimately by its driving force—*words.* It is the abundance of words ("quantunque poi *molte parole* ne fossero . . .")[15], that now, as earlier in Isabella's improvised mimicry, is clearly affirmed as a powerful antidote to her inordinate desire and to the violence that it may have provoked. Contrary to Isabella's (and the reader's) expectations, her play-within-a-play not only has succeeded in neutralizing first Messer Lambertuccio's violence (had he discovered Leonetto in her bedroom) and then her husband's violence, which (had he known the truth) would have been directed at her as well as her two lovers, but has also set in motion a series of good deeds whereby all the antagonists in this play are transformed into creative actors, each contributing to a new-found equilibrium of forces. This transformation has been brought about by the fruitful interaction of the fictive and the imaginary, and of instrumental and free play. Hence we must ascribe to the realm of the imaginary and free play the transformation of Leonetto from a handsome lad of humble origin into the noble knight's equal, as he not only has had supper with Isabella and her husband but has also (temporarily) "cut the figure" of a knight as he, mounting a horse, is accompanied by Isabella's noble husband to his home in Florence. Thus free play has far exceeded the instrumental play as devised by Madonna Isabella.[16] More importantly, the play of the text, while celebrating Isabella's presence of mind and inventiveness as stage di-

rector and performer in her play-within-a-play, has also brought to light the fact that, contrary to Pampinea's enthusiastic defense of Love's power announced at the beginning of our *novella,* it was not Love but fear (of death) that heightened Isabella's presence of mind, and finally, that her play helped to educate her desire. A significant sign of the salutary effect of this implicit lesson is the absence, at the close of the tale, of the conventional "happy ending" often encountered throughout the *Decameron,* which, as we find at the end of the preceding story, tells of how "la savia donna, quasi licenziata a' suoi piaceri . . . , discretamente operando poi piú volte con lui [her lover] buon tempo e lieta vita si diede" (**"VII.5,"** 59).

If play—Isabella's and the play of the text—is a creative, irenic force that is incommensurable with the power principle[17], as manifested in Isabella's unbridled eros, which prompted her to "catch more fish," and in Messer Lambertuccio's naked use of force, which reflects the archaic, aristocratic mentality of "might makes right," it is also, as Boccaccio reminds us again and again in his work, a marginal, fragile force, as marginal and fragile as the delight and laughter that it engenders.[18]

Notes

1. Iser, xviii.

2. On the ludic dimension of the *Decameron* see Giovanni Getto, *Vita di forme e forme di vita nel "Decameron,"* Mario Baratto, *Realtà e stile nel "Decameron,"* Joy H. Potter, *Five Frames of the "Decameron,"* Giuseppe Mazzotta, *The World at Play in Boccaccio's "Decameron,"* Michelangelo Picone, "Gioco e/o letteratura. Per una lettura ludica del *Decameron*", in *Passare il tempo. La letteratura del gioco e dell'intrattenimento dal XII al XVI secolo,* vol. I.

This is an expanded version of a paper I presented at the AAIS Conference, New York, April 13-15, 2000.

3. Gadamer, 103: "The players are not the subjects of play; instead play merely reaches presentation (Darstellung) through the players."

4. Umberto Eco, *"Homo ludens* oggi." Intr. to Italian translation of Johan Huizinga's *Homo ludens,* xx.

5. Forni, *Forme complesse nel "Decameron",* a critical study that is guided by this principle, and, in the words of the author (8-9), "si colloca . . . sotto questo segno, è anche un invito a pensare testo e significazione in termini di complicazione e complessità."

6. Forni, *Adventures in Speech,* 44.

7. Iser, 261-263; Caillois, 14-23.

8. Wolfgang Iser, *The Fictive and the Imaginary*, xvii: "By opening up spaces of play, the fictive compels the imaginary to take on a form at the same time that it acts as a medium for its manifestation. What the fictive targets is as yet empty and thus requires filling; and what is characteristic of the imaginary is its featurelessness, which thus requires form for its unfolding. Consequently, play arises out of the co-existence of the fictive and the imaginary."

9. Eco, xvii-xviii.

10. Masciandaro, "La violenza e il giuoco nella novella di Martellino (*Decameron* II. 1): La problematica dell'improvvisazione," 39-52, now in Masciandaro, *La conoscenza viva. Letture fenomenologiche da Dante a Machiavelli*, 89-98.

11. Quotations are from Vittore Branca's edition of the *Decameron* (Torino: Einaudi, 1987). All emphasis is added.

12. Foster Gittes, "Boccaccio's 'Valley of Women': Fetishized Foreplay in *Decameron* VI," 147-74.

13. Bergson, *Le rire: Essai sur la signification du comique*, 29.

14. Cf. Segre, "Funzioni, opposizioni e simmetrie nella giornata VII del *Decameron*," in *Le strutture e il tempo*, 131: "L'arroganza con cui il potente Lambertuccio s'è imposto alla donna e la natura pavida del modesto Leonetto diventano finzione che giustifica la presenza dei due in casa e che, risvegliando la generosità signorile del marito, crea una momentanea alleanza DM [donna-marito] in difesa di A1 [amante1=Leonetto] . . ."

15. They echo, again as a *variatio,* the "many words" spoken to Isabella by Messer Lambertuccio in her fictional account given to her husband: "dette *molte parole,* se ne venne giú come voi vedeste" (21), in contrast to the few words actually spoken by him ("Messer Lambertuccio *non disse altro se non*: 'Al corpo di Dio, io il giugnerò altrove'"), following Isabella's instructions.

16. Cf. Iser, 261: "Free play triumphs over instrumental play, but no matter how drastically the former rejects the latter, instrumental play will still be a necessary foil in order to prepare for the unexpected, as the pragmatically oriented movements begin to break down."

17. Cf. Mihai I. Spariosu, *The Wreath of Wild Olive. Play, Liminality, and the Study of Literature,* 303: "By an 'irenic' mentality, I mean a mode of thought, behavior, and pathos grounded in the principle of peace (the adjective 'irenic' comes from the Greek noun *eirene,* peace), understood not as antinomic to war, but incommensurable with and therefore inaccessible to the power principle."

18. Cf. Mazzotta, 212: "The *Decameron* constantly moves between the dream or utopia and the pleasure of the representation: laughter is the precarious point where these polarities intersect and at the same time pull apart. This constant movement discloses laughter as the domain of the imaginary which seeks pretexts and occasions to become 'real' and is always a put-on." See also his essay "Liminalità e utopia della letteratura," 363-378.

Bibliography

Baratto, Mario. *Realtà e stile nel "Decameron."* Vicenza, 1970.

Bergson, Henri. *Le rire: Essai sur la signification du comique.* Paris, 1940.

Boccaccio, Giovanni. *Decameron.* Vittore Branca ed. Torino, 1987.

Caillois, Roger. *Man, Play, and Games.* Trans. Meyer Barash. Glencoe, Ill., 1958.

Eco, Umberto. "*Homo ludens* oggi." Intr. to Italian translation of Johan Huizinga's *Homo ludens.* Torino, 1973.

Forni, Pier Massimo. *Forme complesse nel Decameron.* Firenze, 1992.

———. *Adventures in Speech.* Philadelphia, 1996.

Foster Gittes, Tobias. "Boccaccio's 'Valley of Women': Fetishized Foreplay in *Decameron* VI." *Italica* 76. 2 (1999): 147-74.

Gadamer, Hans-Georg. *Truth and Method,* 2nd, revised ed. Trans. Joel Weinsheimer and Donald G. Marshall. New York, 1989.

Getto, Giovanni. *Vita di forme e forme di vita nel "Decameron."* Torino, 1958.

Huizinga, Johan. *Homo Ludens: A Study of the Play Element in Culture.* Trans. R.F.C. Hull. New York, 1950.

Iser, Wolfgang. *The Fictive and the Imaginary: Charting Literary Anthropology.* Baltimore, 1993.

Masciandaro, Franco. "La violenza e il giuoco nella novella di Martellino (*Decameron* II. 1): La problematica dell'improvvisazione." *Italian Culture* VIII (1990): 39-52, now in *La conoscenza viva. Letture fenomenologiche da Dante a Machiavelli.* Ravenna, 1998.

Mazzotta, Giuseppe. *The World at Play in Boccaccio's "Decameron."* Princeton, NJ, 1986.

———. "Liminalità e utopia della letteratura," in *Intersezioni* XIX (December 1999): 363-378.

Picone, Michelangelo. "Gioco e/o letteratura. Per una lettura ludica del *Decameron*." In *Passare il tempo. La letteratura del gioco e dell'intrattenimento dal XII al XVI secolo,* vol. I, 105-127. Roma, 1993.

Potter, Joy H. *Five Frames of the "Decameron."* Princeton, N. J., 1982.

Segre, Cesare. *Le strutture e il tempo.* Torino, 1974.

Spariosu, Mihai I. *The Wreath of Wild Olive: Play, Liminality, and the Study of Literature.* Albany, NY, 1997.

Franco Masciandaro (essay date spring 2003)

SOURCE: Masciandaro, Franco. "Melchisedech's *Novelletta* of the Three Rings as Irenic Play (*Decameron* I.3)." *Forum Italicum* 37, no. 1 (spring 2003): 20-39.

[*In the following essay, Masciandaro investigates the cultural significance of "play" informing the third novella of the "First Day" from various perspectives arising from the tale's narrative "game," focusing on the role of Melchisedech's subtext in starting, developing, and ending "play."*]

As is generally known, the ludic dimension of the **Decameron** has been the object of several important studies, most notably, Giuseppe Mazzotta's *The World at Play in Boccaccio's "Decameron"* and, more recently, Michelangelo Picone's essay "Gioco e/o letteratura. Per una lettura ludica del *Decameron*."[1] The principal aim of my paper is to shed new light on the creativity of play informing the third story of the **Decameron** by viewing play primarily not from the perspective of the players but from the changing, unpredictable perspectives arising from play itself. As Gadamer has shown in *Truth and Method,* play (like the work of art) has its own essence, independently from the conscience and intention of those who play: "The players are not the subjects of play; instead play merely reaches presentation (Darstellung) through the players"[2]; and as Umberto Eco has observed, "il soggetto innesca il processo ('alea iacta est') ma non sa cosa succederà: il gioco si articola da solo."[3] Thus, in examining the ludic action set in motion by Saladino—the riddle of the three laws, which masks his violence directed at Melchisedech—I shall focus on the ways in which it develops and is brought to an unforeseen end by the tale of the wise Jew. I shall also examine the interrelation of violence and play, showing how the latter, by virtue of its marginal or liminal nature, may neutralize and transcend the former. My analysis is supported by the concept of liminality developed by contemporary literary theory, especially as we find it creatively formulated and practiced as a hermeneutical device in the work of Giuseppe Mazzotta. In the cited book on play in the **Decameron,** Mazzotta characterizes the *brigata*'s temporary escape from the city devastated by the plague into the utopia of the literary experience as "an antiworld, disengaged from history only in order to reflect from this marginal state both on itself and on the chaos of the world, and ultimately to return to the world with a vitally renewed apprehension of its structures."[4] Thus the "marginal state" of literature or, more precisely, of literature-as-play, can also be described as a creative liminal space. Elaborating Mazzotta's probings into the liminal nature of literature as well as Wolfgang Iser's theory of play, Mihai Spariosu writes: "The fictive in literature becomes a 'transitional object,' a ludic borderline phenomenon, 'always hovering between the real and the imaginary, linking the two together.'"[5]

As I identify the constitutive elements of play in our *novella,* I shall adopt the four terms, *agon, mimicry, alea,* and *ilinx* (or vertigo), that Wolfgang Iser has borrowed from Roger Caillois, applying them to literary text play.[6] Moreover, I shall use the term "irenic" as defined by Spariosu: "By an 'irenic' mentality, I mean a mode of thought, behavior, and pathos grounded in the principle of peace (the adjective 'irenic' comes from the Greek noun εἰρήνη, peace), understood not as antinomic to war, but as incommensurable with and therefore inaccessible to the power principle."[7] Especially useful in my interpretation of Melchisedech's tale *sub specie ludi* is the contrast between the irenic (or "median") mentality and the archaic mentality of "might makes right" discussed by Spariosu:

> A cursory look at the history of the Western world shows that over the centuries our mentality has invariably remained divided between two basic sets of values: an archaic one, which rests on the principle of "might makes right" and is particularly present in traditional communities; and a modern or a "median" one, which prevails mostly in large-scale, democratic societies and which attempts, with various degrees of success, to separate might from right, often enlisting the help of religion to this purpose. These two valuation sets can be traced back to certain social groups, such as a warrior aristocracy, whose viewpoint largely determines cultural values, say, in archaic Greece or early medieval Europe, and various median groups (priests, rich farmers, merchants, craftsmen, artists, and so forth) whose viewpoint gains considerable influence, say, in classical Greece or modern Europe.[8]

In light of the overarching considerations sketched above, an important concern of my essay is to explore the implications of irenic play within the economy of the **Decameron** as a whole—aware of the significant placing of the tale of Saladino and Melchisedech at the threshold or *limen* of the "secular" stories—as well as within the larger economy discussed by Mazzotta, Iser, and Spariosu.

The liminality of our tale is also determined by its relation to the two stories that immediately precede it. Filomena, in fact, introduces her story-within-the-story as a new point of departure for the **Decameron** in opposition to the tales of ser Ciappelletto and of Abraam Giudeo ("**I.3,**" 3-4):

La novella da Neifile detta mi ritorna a memoria il dubbioso caso già avvenuto a un giudeo. Per ciò che già e di Dio e della verità della nostra fede è assai bene stato detto, il discendere oggimai agli avvenimenti e agli atti degli uomini non si dovrà disdire: a narrarvi quella verrò, la quale udita, forse più caute diverrete nelle risposte alle quistioni che fatte vi fossero.[9]

In her insightful article dedicated to our tale Millicent Marcus has observed: "What distinguishes the tale of Melchisedech from those which precede it, according to Filomena, is subject matter: theirs sacred, hers profane. But here the narrator draws too clear a distinction, for the earlier tales also speak to the human condition, while her own tale is by no means indifferent to the question of faith. To what, then, does Filomena refer when she announces the secularization of her storytelling mode?" The critic answers this question noting that "the distinction which Filomena here draws is one of genre: her tale does not pretend to be an 'exemplum' of divine truths, but unabashed fiction, with no promise of theological teachings . . . The tale denies any continuity between divine and human utterance by making man's failure to discern final truths its salient theme."[10] I find this reading to be accurate only insofar as it identifies the distinction between Filomena's own assessment of her tale and her predecessors' stated views of their respective tales, namely, that the prayers addressed to God through a mediator such as the false saint Ciappelletto are answered, and that the Vatican's iniquity becomes in the eyes of Abraam Giudeo the paradoxical proof of the truth of the Christian faith. In other words, such distinction is significant only as it pertains to how each narrator sets up a *game* that is yet to be played out. Here I am thinking of the usefulness of the distinction between *game* and *play* (which does not exist in the Romance languages and in German)—a distinction that, as Umberto Eco has noted, Huizinga neglected to consider in his *Homo Ludens,* and which of course must be viewed also as a relationship, such as the one between *langue* and *parole.*[11]

What motivates Filomena to draw such a sharp distinction between her storytelling and that of her predecessors, and therefore to ignore the presence in their tales of the unexpected creativity, to use Iser's phrase, of the "fictive and the imaginary out of which play arises"[12]? A few examples, taken for brevity's sake only from the tale of Ciappelletto, will suffice to illuminate Filomena's (contrived?) radical departure from both Panfilo and Neifile. The very discontinuity between "divine and human utterance" claimed by Filomena as the distinguishing trait of her tale, is temporarily affirmed in the first tale when, towards the end, the narrator envisages the possibility that ser Cepparello may have truly repented at the point of death and that he may be saved ("**I.1,**" 89). This imagined "happy ending" is soon not so much displaced as left suspended by these remarks: "ma per ciò che questo n'è occulto, secondo quello che

ne può apparire ragiono, e dico costui più tosto dover essere nelle mani del diavolo in perdizione che in Paradiso" (89-90). Concerning the creativity of play, everyone will recall that, from the beginning of the tale, ser Cepparello is characterized by an extraordinary wickedness that is inseparable from an equally extraordinary sense of play, as manifested, for example, in his delight in giving false testimony, whether asked for it or not, and in drawing up, free of charge, as many false documents as were requested of him. Nor can we forget the creativity of his deception, when free and instrumental play are closely interwoven as he, with his confession, saves not only the property and the lives of the two Florentine usurers, but transforms, at least temporarily, the wicked Burgundians into a pious community.[13] And, finally, there is something unexplainable from the perspective of the *game,* for which ser Cepparello has been chosen by Musciatto Franzesi as the player whose wickedness can best counter the wickedness of the Burgundians, and yet quite understandable from the perspective of *play* whereby he unexpectedly appears to be more played-upon than playing, when a transfiguring light is suddenly cast on him, as we read that, entering the new theatrical space in Burgundy, "dove quasi niuno il conoscea [. . .], quivi *fuori di sua natura benignamente e mansuetamente* cominciò a voler riscuotere e fare quello per che andato v'era" (19). Against all our expectations, ser Cepparello now appears transformed into a new character or player, who is well on his way to becoming saint Ciappelletto (with or without quotation marks), that is, a character who, as described at the end of the tale, can be viewed from two opposing perspectives, as a false or a true saint, or at least as a great sinner who, at the eleventh hour, may have truly repented, addressing his confession to God.[14] Significantly, the textual play suggests such turning to God as it tells of ser Ciappelletto's "confession" to the two Florentine usurers: "Io ho, vivendo, tante ingiurie fatte a Domenedio, che, per farnegli io una ora in su la mia morte, né più né meno ne farà . . ." (28-29). A similar suggestion of an ambivalent intertwining of a false and true confession can be found in these words: "vi priego, padre mio buono, che così puntualmente d'ogni cosa mi domandiate *come se mai confessato non mi fossi . . .*" (34-35). Thus, the liminal space of fiction (of "as if") introduced here by Ciappelletto opens the text to shifting interpretations: we are in fact "played" by the text, in such a way that we are led to view Ciappelletto now as a liar (when he tells the friar that he usually goes to confession at least once a week, 32) and now—paradoxically, through fiction—as one who speaks the truth about never having confessed his sins.

Equally remarkable is the fact that by acting, contrary to his nature, *benignamente e mansuetamente,* ser Cepparello transforms Musciatto Franzesi's game from one marked by *agon* between wicked opponents—ser Cepparello and the Burgundians—to one defined by irenic play, namely, the *mimicry* of ser Cepparello's acting as a benign and saintly person and the *ilinx* produced by his disruption of the conventional game of combating violence with violence. Thus, not only are the wicked Burgundians transformed by these two creative dimensions of play, but so is, apparently or perhaps actually, Cepparello himself, by seeming to become or by indeed becoming, if not one with his mask of the saint, at least, as suggested earlier, a sinner who is predisposed to repentance and a true confession. As for the reader—not to mention Boccaccio's *brigata*—, whose final judgement of ser Cepparello's play is suspended as it oscillates between condemnation and absolution, he or she may appreciate the creative, irenic play enacted in the first tale of the **Decameron** while experiencing the delight provoked by the unexpected shifts of perspective of the textual play, especially when it neutralizes and transcends *agon* and hence, as noted earlier, is incommensurable with the principle of power.

In light of these remarks we can see more clearly that Filomena's motivation for narrating the tale of Melchisedech is marked by *agon,* and therefore, in competition with her predecessors, by the desire to win the game of narrating the more delightful and instructive tale. Correspondingly, we can also better understand why her success as narrator, in perfect consonance, of course, with the success of Boccaccio, the *magister ludi,* is necessarily dependent on the element of surprise, and therefore on keeping the cards close to the vest, as the *game* is set up as a competition or *agon* between the wisdom of Melchisedech and the veiled violence of Saladino, a game that, as is played out, calls forth unforeseen resources of play, especially in the form of *mimicry* and *ilinx,* which will help bring about an equally unforeseen conclusion.

As Filomena identifies the main players or antagonists of her "novelletta," she begins to bring to the fore what has been obscured by her initial characterization of the opposition between Saladino's power and violence and Melchisedech's wisdom:

> Il Saladino, il valore del quale fu tanto, che non solamente di piccolo uomo il fé di Babilonia soldano ma ancora molte vittorie sopra li re saraceni e cristiani gli fece avere, avendo in diverse guerre e in grandissime sue magnificenze speso tutto il suo tesoro e per alcuno accidente sopravenutogli bisognandogli una buona quantità di denari, né veggendo donde cosí prestamente come gli bisognavano avergli potesse, gli venne a memoria un ricco giudeo, il cui nome era Melchisedech, il quale prestava a usura in Alessandria. E pensossi costui avere da poterlo servire, quando volesse, ma sí era avaro che di sua volontà non l'avrebbe mai fatto, e forza non gli voleva fare; per che, strignendolo il bisogno, rivoltosi tutto a dover trovar modo come il giudeo il servisse, s'avisò di fargli una forza da alcuna ragion colorata.

(6-7)

Saladino now appears at once as powerful and weak, for the very exercise of his power manifested in the many wars he has waged, as well as the display or rhetoric of power represented by his extraordinary acts of munificence, have diminished his power. Equally significant is the fact that to some degree this has also been caused by what lies beyond Saladino's control, that is, by "alcuno accidente," and therefore, in ludic terms, by *alea.* Thus, we experience a kind of double vision as we see Saladino occupy center stage while at the same time he is forced to move to the margins, the very place on the scene of this life that he once occupied, when he was a *piccolo uomo.* Similarly, Melchisedech, appears at once as a marginal figure, being the sultan's subject and a Jew, and a central, powerful figure, being a rich man who does not willingly lend his money, and therefore as the sultan's worthy antagonist. It cannot go unnoticed that Saladino's temporary marginality, due to his pressing need of money, makes him a very dangerous antagonist, feeling constrained ("strignendolo il bisogno") to use force. His decision not to use naked force, but rather "una forza da alcuna ragion colorata," clearly reflects the archaic, aristocratic mentality of "might makes right," whose refinement, as it masks violence with the pretext of "reason" or just cause, is in reality a more pernicious exercise of power, for its aim is at once to legitimize violence and to exact from the innocent victim an admission of guilt and therefore of deserving the violence inflicted upon him.

Having summoned Melchisedech, welcoming him in a friendly manner and having him sit beside him, Saladino addresses him with these words:

> "Valente uomo, io ho da piú persone inteso che tu se' savissimo e nelle cose di Dio senti molto avanti; e per ciò io saprei volentieri da te quale delle tre leggi tu reputi la verace, o la giudaica o la saracina o la cristiana."

(8)

Saladino's riddle bears traces of the archaic function of the riddle as a ritualized contest or play, whereby knowledge of the origin of things and of the order of the world could be attained, but also as an instrument of violence. As Huizinga has observed,

> The riddle is a sacred thing full of secret power, hence a dangerous thing. In its mythological or ritual context it is nearly always what German philologists know as the *Halsrätsel* or 'capital riddle', which you either solve or forfeit your head. The player's life is at stake. A corollary of this is that it is accounted the highest wisdom to put a riddle nobody can answer. [. . .] Gradual transitions lead from the sacred riddle-contest concerning the origin of things to the catch-question contest, with honor, possessions, or dear life at stake, and finally to the philosophical and theological disputation.[15]

We should also note that Saladino, true to tradition, as he receives Melchisedech *familiarmente* and invites him to sit beside him (8), knows that "the game of question and answer must be played on an equal footing."[16] Equally traditional, is the suddenness with which the solution comes to Melchisedech's mind ("aguzzato lo 'ngegno, gli venne *prestamente* avanti quello che dir dovesse . . . ," 9-10). As Huizinga again remarks, "The answer to an enigmatic question is not found by reflection or logical reasoning. It comes quite literally as a sudden solution—a loosening of the tie by which the questioner holds you bound."[17] At the level of the text play *prestamente*—as *venne . . . avanti* recalls *venne a memoria*—mimics the suddenness of Saladino's solution to his monetary problems ("bisognandogli una buona quantità di denari, né veggendo donde cosí *prestamente* come gli bisognavano avergli potesse, gli venne a memoria un ricco giudeo . . . ," 6), with the fundamental difference that, unlike Saladino's, Melchisedech's flash of insight belongs not to the material but the poetic or ludic sphere, which is incommensurable with the former as "being" is incommensurable with "having."

As we see Saladino act as the proverbial cat who plays with the mouse, we discover that, paradoxically, it is this very play which, while it is intended to conceal violence, temporarily suspends it, opening a narrow, liminal space within which Melchisedech finds a way to transform his adversary's power play into irenic play. Filomena prepares us to better discern the significance of this transformation by unmasking Saladino's fictionalization of Melchisedech as wise (the strawman that he can easily defeat) with these words: "Il giudeo, il quale *veramente* era savio uomo, s'avisò troppo bene che il Saladino guardava di pigliarlo nelle parole per dovergli muovere alcuna quistione" (9). Melchisedech's authentic wisdom is demonstrated not only by his accurate reading of the sultan's insidious words, whose aim is not to inquire about the true faith but to elicit a response which will inevitably lead to his entrapment, but, more importantly, by his creative use of words, which at once mimic and transfigure the words with which Saladino has devised his game. Thus the *quistione* as "argument" or "quarrel" that Saladino intends to pick with him, is transformed by Melchisedech into a *beautiful question*: "Signor mio, la quistione la qual voi mi fate è bella, e a volervene dire ciò che io ne sento mi vi convien dire una novelletta . . ." (10-11). The sultan's dangerous verbal disguise is deflected by Melchisedech's introduction of an aesthetic value that is incommensurable with agonistic play, and as such prepares the ground upon which the fictive as a creative force can take shape, engendering, together with the imaginary to which it is inextricably joined, free, irenic play.

I will now enumerate the most striking elements of Melchisedech's parable that illustrate the creativity of play, especially in the form of *mimicry*. His opening words, "Se io non erro, io mi ricordo aver molte volte

udito dire" clearly echo Saladino's "io ho da piú persone inteso che tu se' savissimo." Similarly, as he introduces the figure of "un grande uomo e ricco . . . , il quale, intra l'altre gioie piú care che nel suo tesoro avesse, era uno anello bellissimo e prezioso; al quale per lo suo valore e per la sua bellezza volendo fare onore e in perpetuo lasciarlo ne' suoi discendenti, ordinò che colui de' suoi figliuoli appo il quale . . . fosse questo anello trovato, che colui s'intendesse essere il suo erede" (11-12), he projects on the screen of the imaginary the figure of one who, being "un grande uomo e ricco," mimics Saladino as a man of great worth ("il valore del quale fu tanto") and rich—as he was formerly and as he again wishes to be—while it also mimics the worth of the narrator himself as a wise and rich man. Significantly, by introducing once again the aesthetic dimension, as he mentions not only the worth but the extraordinary beauty of the ring, Melchisedech signals the creative presence of something that is incommensurable with the worth and power associated with character and wealth. As we read of the ring being handed down from generation to generation until it came into the possession of a man who had three equally virtuous and obedient sons, we find that they, like the ring and like the "quistione" as characterized by Melchisedech, are said to be "belli" (12). Like Melchisedech, the father who loves all three sons equally is a "valente uomo." And like Melchisedech, his worth is exemplified by his creative use of fiction, of *mimicry,* as he, unable to choose to which of the three he would leave the ring, and wishing to avoid contentiousness among them, he had a good jeweler secretly make two identical copies of the ring. These resembled the first one so closely that he himself who had them made could hardly tell which was the original. Thus, upon the father's death, each son believed to be the possessor of the true ring and the rightful heir. Melchisedech offers this important gloss to his *novelletta*:

> "E cosí vi dico, signor mio, delle tre leggi alli tre popoli date da Dio padre, delle quali la quistion proponeste: ciascun la sua eredità, la sua vera legge e i suoi comandamenti dirittamente si crede avere e fare, ma chi se l'abbia, come degli anelli, ancora ne pende la quistione."

> (16)

While affirming the creativity of fiction, as that which suspends judgement, and consequently difference as a cause for dissension and violence, Melchisedech also affirms as fact, or truth, that the three laws were given by God the Father to the three peoples. Hence God Himself must be viewed as the highest *magister ludi,* who has set up the game to be played out by his children. As it has been aptly observed, "Other forms of playfulness mask ultimate despair; true playfulness can exist only where, in the strictest theological sense, both

God and Man are really at play."[18] Significantly, this play need not be marked by *agon,* that is, by the stark opposition between the fictive as false and the real as true, for, as Melchisedech's parable clearly illustrates, this opposition is indeed neutralized and transcended by the affirmation of the creative dimension of fiction—of fiction which, as the Latin verb *fingere* from which it is derived, means not only to feign or deceive but also to form or to conceive.

The most striking proof of the creativity of fiction is in the radical transformation of the two antagonists, Saladino and Melchisedech: the sultan abandons deception and force as expressions of his power, making his needs known to the moneylender, and, more importantly, confessing to him that he would have incurred dire consequences had he not so wisely avoided the trap set before him; and Melchisedech is now liberal with his money, willingly giving Saladino as much as he desires. Still more significant is that the two antagonists have in the end become life-long friends:

> Il giudeo liberamente d'ogni quantità che il Saladino il richiese il serví, e il Saladino poi interamente il sodisfece; e oltre a ciò gli donò grandissimi doni e sempre per suo amico l'ebbe e in grande e onorevole stato appresso di sé il mantenne.
>
> (18)

This friendship, like the beauty which joins together the *quistione* about the three laws, the three sons and the three rings, and hence the real and the imaginary, including perhaps our own play of interpretation, is incommensurable with the archaic mentality of "might makes right," as well as with the utilitarian merchant ethos, which here—if we were to share Dioneo's viewpoint—may seem to be celebrated.[19] The beauty of this friendship, analogous to the beauty of our *novelletta* as irenic play, is a palpable, accessible measure of the transcendent truth that is shared by the three faiths, and of course by both Melchisedech and Saladino, who clearly resemble the virtuous and beautiful three sons—all equally loved by the Father. This is no "unabashed fiction."[20] Nor is it to be identified with what Jean-Luc Marion has termed the *idol,* that is, "an epistemologically local name or image of divinity" which "refuses distance, and instead tries to appropriate and stabilize transcendence and sacrality."[21] Rather, I see fiction, and hence the irenic play of Melchisedech's *novelletta,* to correspond to the *icon,* which according to Marion, "tries to capture neither the human signifier, nor the divine signified but merely the relationship between the one and the other."[22]

The friendship, unexpectedly born of fiction, which joins together as equals Saladino the Moslem and Melchisedech the Jew, brings to mind the friendship between Giannotto and Abraam, who are described as being equally upright and honest men: "In Parigi fu un gran mercatante e buono uomo il quale fu chiamato Giannotto di Civigní, *lealissimo e diritto . . .* : e avea singulare amistà con uno ricchissimo uomo giudeo chiamato Abraam, il quale similmente mercatante era e *diritto e leale* uomo assai" (4). However, in the eyes of Giannotto, despite the goodness and wisdom of his friend, he fears that Abraam's soul will go to its perdition if he does not convert to the Christian faith (5-6). From the vantage point of the tale of Saladino and Melchisedech, as we consider the unexpected, paradoxical transformation of Abraam from one who, concerning which was the true faith, "niuna ne credeva né santa né buona fuor che la giudaica, e che egli in quella era nato e in quella intendeva e vivere e morire, né cosa sarebbe che mai da ciò il facesse rimuovere" (7-8), to one who became a Christian after witnessing the moral and spiritual decay of the very center of Christendom, we gain a deeper insight into the ludic character of that transformation. We can no longer view Abraam's conversion (as we might have done before reading Melchisedech's solution to the riddle of the three faiths) from a pious, conventional perspective shared by Giannotto, Filomena, and the whole *brigata* concerning the "verità della nostra fede." Nor can we firmly hold a skeptical view. In light of the at once concealed and revealed truth "shared" by the three faiths in the ludic space of Melchisedech's *novelletta,* we may now be delighted by the interplay of the fictive and the imaginary informing the story of Abraam's conversion. As we read the tale's closing words,

> Giannotto il levó del sacro fonte e nominollo Giovanni, e appresso a gran valenti uomini il fece compiutamente ammaestrare nella nostra fede, la quale egli prestamente apprese: e fu poi buono e valente uomo e di santa vita,
>
> ("I.2," 29)

we note that the textual play reveals no substantial change in Abraam. Beginning with his baptismal name, rather than marking a difference it reaffirms his being like his Christian friend, whose name, Giannotto, is a variant of Giovanni, and who has been described, as noted earlier, as a "buono uomo . . . , lealissimo e diritto." We also observe that Abraam/Giovanni, like those who instruct him in the new faith, and are characterized as *valenti uomini,* is said to have become—as "e fu poi" suggests—"buono e *valente uomo*"; however, contrary to this suggestion that Abraam's transformation into a "buono e valente uomo" occurred *after* (and because of) his conversion and ensuing teachings imparted to him, the text had already defined him as a "valente e savio e buono uomo" (5-6) *before* his conversion. Similarly, as we note that the word "ammaestrare" harks back to the words describing Abraam's great learning in Jewish doctrine, "e come che il giudeo fosse nella giudaica legge un *gran maestro . . .*" (9), we see Abraam as having been all along, implicitly, the "Giovanni" that he has now "become." Moreover, the word *prestamente* marking his learning about his new faith, underscores the narrowness of the gap separating him from his Christian friend and teachers. And even as we read that he led a "*santa* vita" as a result of his conversion, we realize that this marks not a departure from Abraam's former life, when he had firmly adhered to the Jewish faith, which he believed to be the only one that was "*santa* e buona" ("Il giudeo rispondeva che niuna ne credeva né santa né buona fuor che la giudaica," 7). Thus, the text play at once dramatizes the immense distance or *difference* (and corresponding spiritual danger, in the eyes of the pious Giannotto and of all those who may share his viewpoint, including, of course some readers) separating the two equally good friends and the narrow, liminal space that presents them as nearly identical, and in a sense interchangeable, as these words pronounced by Giannotto, *tacitamente,* invite us to envisage:

> "Perduta ho la fatica la quale ottimamente mi pareva avere impiegata, credendomi costui aver convertito: per ciò che, se egli va in corte di Roma e vede la vita scellerata e lorda de' cherici, non che egli di giudeo si faccia cristiano, ma *se egli fosse cristian fatto senza fallo giudeo si ritornerebbe.*"

("**I.2**" 12)

How, then, are we to interpret Abraam's conversion, or, to put it another way, how does Boccaccio wish us to view it, especially in light of Melchisedech's *novelletta* of the three rings? At first we may be inclined to consider it as a mere accident, or "unabashed fiction." Hence, as nominalists, we would dissociate words from reality, and, correspondingly, would judge Boccaccio's literary fiction as being intentionally divorced from truth; and Abraam would appear to be similar (though under the positive sign) to those corrupt prelates in the Vatican whom he had pointedly condemned for having used words as false masks of their sinful deeds:

> Avendo alla manifesta simonia 'procureria' posto nome e alla gulosità 'substentazioni', quasi Idio, lasciamo stare il significato di vocaboli, ma la 'ntenzione de' pessimi animi non conoscesse e a guisa degli uomini a' nomi delle cose si debba lasciare ingannare.

(21-22)

Abraam's condemnation expresses his deep belief in an authentic relationship between words and actions—a belief that, significantly, is grounded in God's perfect knowledge of both the meaning of words and of men's hidden evil intentions, and which Abraam shares with Boccaccio, who pointedly, though in a lighter vein, affirms it in his unfinished story of Filippo Balducci, which he narrates in the **"Introduction to the Fourth Day"** ("Il padre . . . non le volle nominare per lo proprio nome, cioè femine, ma disse: 'Elle si chiamano

papere'", 23). This clearly suggests that Abraam could not consider his conversion to the Christian faith to be true in name only. But does this "truth" invalidate the "truth" of his original belief in the Jewish doctrine, especially if we view it in light of the paradoxical yet authentic "equality in difference" we found in Melchisedech's story? The play of the text, as I have so far attempted to define, invites us to apprehend not so much the relativization of truth, or the *agon* between (as Marion would put it) two epistemologically local names or images of truth, which inevitably provoke contentiousness and violence, but rather its expansion and revitalization by the *relationship* linking one to the other and ultimately by their *mimicry* of a projected or imagined absolute truth. Thus, if considered *sub specie ludi,* as he is "played-upon" by Giannotto's entreaties and especially by the infernal scenes of the depravity of the Christian clergy he witnesses in Rome, Abraam's unexpected conversion reveals a newly-found ability to step out of a form that he once considered fixed ("né cosa sarebbe che mai da ciò il facesse rimuovere," 7-8). By exchanging his original "ring" with one that resembles or *mimics* it to the point of seeming indistinguishable (as nearly indistinguishable as "Giovanni" is from "Abraam")—to (playfully) "read" his conversion from the perspective opened to us by Melchisedech's *novelletta*—Abraam overcomes the danger of transforming his true belief in an equally true religion into an *idol*—which, as noted earlier, "refuses distance, and instead tries to appropriate and stabilize transcendence and sacrality"—and learns *to play* (with all the seriousness of play, as Huizinga would say),[23] joining God as Playmaker. In fact, the text speaks of the possible presence of the Holy Spirit, first in Giannotto's simple words, which may have begun to persuade Abraam to follow his friend's advice (9), and finally, and more crucially, as the very foundation of the Christian religion that, in stark contrast to those who in the Vatican are bent on destroying it, Abraam seems to discern:

> E per ciò che io veggio non quello avvenire che essi procacciano, ma continuamente la vostra religione aumentarsi e piú lucida e piú chiara divenire, meritamente *mi par discerner lo Spirito Santo esser d'essa, sí come di vera e di santa piú che alcuna altra, fondamento e sostegno.*

(26-27)

The phrase "mi par discerner" manifestly speaks of the ludic, liminal space of which Abraam is, together with the play of circumstances, or the *alea* of the Holy Spirit, a co-creator. In this space he at once reaffirms and transcends his former belief and his former identity, going beyond the religious experience as *idol* by rediscovering it as *icon,* and thus, as cited earlier, as that which "tries to capture neither the human signifier, nor the divine signified but merely the relationship between the one and the other."

Are we very far from a theological truth, or a truth manifested by a *theologia ludens,* of which Mazzotta has written at the end of his book on the **Decameron**? Here, commenting on the contradictions, which, as we have observed in Abraam, "are present within each figure" in the **Decameron,** so that "each figure is always on the point of becoming other than itself,"[24] and speaking of Boccaccio's "elusiveness," Mazzotta notes:

> The elusiveness is Boccaccio's irony, the perspective which gives a dark edge to his humor and which brings with it the disclosure that simulations, jests, the turns of the imagination, are not mere interludes in the business of life but the shadow of the play of the world.

> This insight into play, as the ludic and the elusive, departs from the containment of play in Aristotle and St. Thomas but recalls, I would like to suggest, Dante's figuration. Dante [. . .] elaborates in *Paradiso* [. . .] a *theologia ludens* as he envisions the song of the blessed, the "triunfi," the dance of the heavens, and the spectacle of the stars wooing each other in God's vast theater. In the **Decameron** the theology is absent or it is present as the object of laughter, but play is the category through which Boccaccio enjoins us to look at the world and at its suspected but also elusive secrets.[25]

In *Paradiso* XIX we find a striking example of a *theologia ludens* that resembles the one we have seen adumbrated in Melchisedech's tale and in the story of Abraam and Giannotto, with the obvious difference that in Dante it is staged in Heaven while in Boccaccio it is staged in the here and now of our world (but let us not forget that Dante is also, as Auerbach has demonstrated, *poet of the secular world*). In this canto is inscribed the startling answer, by the blessed souls of the just who comprise the figure of the Eagle, to Dante's troubling question about the salvation of those who, though virtuous, know not Christ and die unbaptized and without faith. These "lucenti incendi / de lo Spirito Santo" say in a single voice:

> "A questo regno
> non salì mai chi non credette 'n Cristo,
> né pria né poi ch'el si chiavasse al legno.
> Ma vedi: molti gridan 'Cristo, Cristo!'
> che saranno in giudicio assa men *prope*
> a lui, che tal che non conosce Cristo;
> e tai Cristian dannerà l'Etïòpe,
> quando si partiranno i due collegi,
> l'uno in etterno ricco e l'altro inòpe.

(103-111)

In light of this performance of Dante's *theologia ludens*—not to mention the one that unveils God's unfathomable justice in saving Ripheus (*Par.* XX.67-69), the Trojan hero briefly mentioned in the *Aeneid* (II.339, 394, 426-427)[26]—Melchisedech's *novelletta,* as well as the tale of Abraam Giudeo (*and* of Ciappelletto), acquires greater resonance as we catch glimpses, through the very laughter directed if only obliquely at theology,

of suddenly unconcealed theological truths. However, the moment we fix our gaze upon such revelation Boccaccio's text play invites us to shift focus, so that we may experience once again, and with equal suddenness, the ambivalence and elusiveness woven into the fabric of the world he fashions before our very eyes—the same ambivalence and elusiveness that first drew us in, turning us into players for whom the hermeneutical game is never fully played out and whose outcome is always uncertain.[27]

I will now close with a few notes on the theme of friendship, whose significance in the tale of Saladino and Melchisedech (and to a lesser degree, in the story of Giannotto and Abraam)[28] I have already discussed, but whose deeper resonance within the larger economy of Boccaccio's storytelling project as a whole needs to be explored more extensively than this space allows. Like free play, in contrast to instrumental play, friendship is characterized by disinterestedness and by being incommensurable with power (and its play). Moreover, as it binds two people as equals—despite their difference in social status or religious belief—it constitutes the foundation or nucleus of an ideal *communitas* where harmony reigns.[29] Such friendship and harmony are manifestly embodied in the *brigata.* Together with the figures whose irenic play we have been probing, including Ciappelletto (for having introduced a bit of harmony in the midst of the iniquitous Burgundians), this little community may be seen as a utopian alternative to the social disintegration provoked in the city by the plague. But this utopia, as we enter the multifarious world of the ninety seven stories that follow, proves to be almost as rare as the few, isolated instances of acts of selflessness described by Boccaccio in the Introduction.[30] The following passage stands out as especially pertinent to our present concern:

> Era con sí fatto spavento questa tribulazione entrata ne' petti degli uomini e delle donne, che l'un fratello l'altro abbandonava e il zio il nepote e la sorella il fratello e spesse volte la donna il suo marito; e, che maggior cosa è e quasi non credibile, li padri e le madri i figliuoli, quasi loro non fossero, di visitare e di servire schifavano. Per la qual cosa a coloro, de'quali era la moltitudine inestimabile, e maschi e femine, che infermavano, *niuno altro subsidio rimase che o la carità degli amici (e di questi fur pochi)* o l'avarizia de' serventi.

(27-28)

Significantly, here the rare love of friendship is represented as being stronger than the natural love that binds family members. Equally striking is that Boccaccio at once contrasts friendship with avarice and, paradoxically, joins them together as he tells us that they provided the only available care to those who fell ill. Thus, in the "frame" of the **Decameron** Boccaccio gives intimations of what the reader will encounter in the world of the narratives: both the conflict between good and evil and their being inextricably (and often creatively) intertwined.

Melchisedech's and Saladino's friendship, which marks the victory over the avarice of the former and the violence of the latter, while it echoes the rare friendship mentioned in the **"Introduction"** it also points to the celebration of friendship represented by the stories of the **"Tenth Day."** Here we find the following passage where friendship is at once extolled and lamented as an ideal that is rarely actualized:

> Santissima cosa adunque è l'amistà, e non solamente di singular reverenzia degna ma d'essere con perpetua laude commendata, sí come discretissima madre di magnificenzia e d'onestà, sorella di gratitudine e di carità, e d'odio e d'avarizia nemica, sempre, senza priego aspettar, pronta a quello in altrui virtuosamente operare che in sé vorrebbe che fosse operato; li cui sacratissimi effetti oggi radissime volte si veggiono in due, colpa e vergogna della misera cupidigia de' mortali, la qual solo alla propria utilità riguardando ha costei fuor degli estremi termini della terra in esilio perpetuo rilegata.

> ("**X.8**," 111-13)

Once again, we are invited to glimpse the evanescent presence of friendship, which is emphatically linked to the sacred (as it is named *santissima,* and whose effects are said to be *sacratissimi*), and which is as evanescent as the beautiful words that sing its praise with such pathos. Secretly wedded to words and hence to the fictive and the imaginary that engender play, friendship lives at the margins of the world and its power, indeed is "in essilio perpetuo rilegata." Yet, this marginality may be transformed into a creative liminality where as "exiles"—like the members of the *brigata,* and like the author of the **Decameron,** along with many of his figures, such as Saladino and Melchisedech, Giannotto and Abraam, and even Ciappelletto—may constitute, though fleetingly, a *communitas* that is disinterestedly engaged in the play of conversation, temporarily creating order (without, however, making an *idol* of it) out of chaos. I am reminded of the words of Socrates, the great conversationalist and friend (*Gorgias* 508b):

> Wise men, Callicles, say that the heavens and the earth, gods and men, are bound together by fellowship and friendship, and order and temperance and justice, and for this reason they call the sum of things the 'ordered' universe, my friend, not the world of disorder or riot.[30]

Notes

1. Giuseppe Mazzotta, *The World at Play in Boccaccio's "Decameron"* (Princeton, NJ: Princeton UP, 1986), and his essay, "Liminalità e utopia della letteratura," in *Intersezioni*, XIX, 3 (December 1999): 363-378; Michelangelo Picone, "Gioco e/o letteratura. Per una lettura ludica del Decameron,"

in *Passare il tempo,* vol. I (Roma: Salerno Editrice, 1993), pp. 105-127. See also Giovanni Getto, *Vita di forme e forme di vita nel "Decameron"* (Torino: Petrini, 1958), pp. 164-1887; Mario Baratto, *Realtà e stile nel "Decameron"* (Vicenza: Pozza, 1970), pp. 238-269; Joy Potter, *Five Frames of the "Decameron"* (Princeton, NJ: Princeton UP, 1982), pp. 120-151; and Franco Masciandaro, "La violenza e il giuoco nella novella di Martellino (*Decameron* "II.1"): La problematica dell'improvvisazione," *Italian Culture* VIII (1990): 39-52, now in *La conoscenza viva: Letture fenomenologiche da Dante a Machiavelli* (Ravenna: Longo, 1998), pp. 89-98.

A shorter version of this paper was presented at the AATI Conference, Washington D.C., November 16-17, 2001. I am grateful for the comments and suggestions by the two anonymous readers of the first draft submitted to this journal.

2. Hans-Georg Gadamer, *Truth and Method,* 2nd, rev. ed., trans. Joel Weinsheimer and Donald G. Marshall (New York: Crossroad, 1989), p. 103.

3. Umberto Eco, *"Homo ludens" oggi,* Intr. to Italian translation of Johan Huizinga's *Homo ludens* (Torino: Einaudi, 1973), p. xx.

4. Giuseppe Mazzotta, *The World at Play in the "Decameron,"* 55.

5. Mihai I. Spariosu, *The Wreath of Wild Olive: Play, Liminality, and the Study of Literature* (Albany, NY: SUNY Press, 1997), p. 51.

6. Wolfgang Iser, *The Fictive and the Imaginary* (Baltimore and London: The Johns Hopkins UP, 1993), pp. 261-263; Roger Caillois, *Man, Play, and Games,* tr. Meyer Barash (New York: Free Press of Glencoe, 1961), pp. 14-23.

7. Spariosu, 303.

8. *Ibid.,* 6.

9. Quotations are from Vittore Branca's edition of the *Decameron* (Torino: Einaudi, 1987). All emphasis is added.

10. Millicent Marcus, "Faith's Fiction: A Gloss on the Tale of Melchisedech (*Decameron* I, 3)," *Canadian Journal of Italian Studies,* vol. 2 (1978-1979): 40, 44.

11. Eco, xvii-xviii. *"Game,"* comments Picone (p. 116), "è il gioco astratto, dotato di sue regole specifiche; è il 'gioco giocante': lo stato di *langue* che racchiude una complessa e completa *competence* ludica; è la 'matrice combinatorial di mosse possibili'. *Play,* dal canto suo, indica le infinite realizzazioni del *game* stesso; è il 'gioco giocato': lo stato di *parole* che comprende tutte le singole *performances* di un determinato gioco."

12. Iser, xvii.

13. Cf. Picone, 126-127: "L'interpretazione istrionica di Ciappelletto, da strumentale che era all'inizio (togliere dall'imbarazzo i due usurai fiorentini), diventa nel corso del suo svolgimento gratuita, fine a se stessa, insomma gioco purissimo. In effetti, Ciappelletto non si presenta nelle vesti di un santo qualsiasi, bensí in quelle del santo per eccellenza, del santo piú virtuoso che abbia mai attraversato le vie del mondo. Bastava un'esibizione assai piú limitata della propria virtú per ottenere il risultato voluto."

14. The text does in fact speak of a narrow space between his confession to the friar and the moment of his death during which he might have truly repented: "Ser Ciappelletto poco appresso si comunicò: e peggiorando senza modo ebbe l'ultima unzione e poco passato vespro, quel dí stesso che la buona confessione fatta avea, si morì" ("I.1.81"). Moreover, the textual play, while depicting, as it does here, a parody of a "buona confessione," does also suggest that, as I am attempting to show, even *before* (with his startling metamorphosis into a gentle and amiable fellow) and *during* his confession to the holy friar ser Ciappelletto may be seen as undergoing an authentic conversion.

15. Johan Huizinga, *Homo Ludens: A Study of the Play Element in Culture* (Boston: Beacon Press, 1955), pp. 108-109, 113.

16. *Ibid.,* 115.

17. *Ibid.,* 110.

18. Robert Royal, "The Literary Value of Hope," in *Play, Literature, Religion: Essays in Cultural Intertextuality,* ed., Virgil Nemoianu and Robert Royal (Albany, NY: SUNY Press, 1992) 175.

19. This is Dioneo's (not Boccaccio's) perspective ("I.4.3"): "avendo udito che per li buoni consigli di Giannotto di Civigní Abraam aver l'anima salvata e Melchisedech per lo suo senno *le sue ricchezze* dagli augati del Saladino difese. . . ." We should note, in passing, that here Dioneo also misses the mark concerning the real cause of Abraam's conversion to the Christian faith, which, as the text play clearly points out, was his witnessing, *against* Giannotto's "buoni consigli" not to go to Rome, the corruption of the Vatican that compelled Abraam to become a Christian ("I.2.18-27").

20. Nor do we find here any evidence that, as Giorgio Padoan has observed in his "Mondo aristocratico e mondo comunale nell'ideologia e nell'arte di Giovanni Boccaccio," *Studi sul Boccaccio,* II (1964): 166, "La novella delle tre anella dimostra questo disinteresse del Boccaccio per ogni ponderata discussione del fatto religioso [. . .], l'affermazione dell'uguaglianza delle tre grandi religioni lo lascia alquanto indifferente." We find a similar viewpoint in Getto 36-37. Carlo Muscetta, however, offers an interpretation that is closer to mine in his *Giovanni Boccaccio* (Bari: Laterza, 1972) 182: "È Boccaccio che vuol . . . evitare di impegnarsi apertamente e direttamente, e ricorre alla parabola che esprime oggettivamente un'audace posizione di vera e propria tolleranza religiosa."

21. Jean-Luc Marion, *L'idole et la distance* (Paris: Grasset, 1977), pp. 24-25, as paraphrased by Virgil Nemoianu in "Literary Play," in *Play, Literature, Religion,* 8.

22. Jean-Luc Marion, 25-27, paraphrased by Nemoianu, 8.

23. Huizinga, 45: "The significance of 'play' . . . is by no means defined or exhausted by calling it 'non-earnest', or 'not serious'. Play is a thing by itself. The play-concept as such is of a higher order than is seriousness. For seriousness seeks to exclude play, whereas play can very well include seriousness."

24. Mazzotta, *The World at Play,* 268.

25. *Ibid.,* 268-269. For an elaborate discussion of *theologia ludens* in Dante's *Paradiso* see Mazzotta's *Dante's Vision and the Circle of Knowledge* (Princeton, NJ: Princeton UP, 1993), chapter 11, "Theologia ludens," pp. 219-241.

26. On the possibility of salvation for virtuous pagans see St. Thomas, *Summa Theologiae* II-II, q. 2, a. 7, ad 3.

27. On the creativity of ambivalence in the *Decameron* see the fine study by Roberta Bruno Pagnamenta, *Il "Decameron". L'ambiguità come strategia narrativa* (Ravenna: Longo, 1999).

28. Surprisingly, though in a less pure form, even Cepparello appears to be capable of friendship (like the proverbial "honor among thieves," some might say) as he, disinterestedly offers to help the two Florentine usurers, who fear the violence of the wicked Burgundians.

29. Cf. Simone Weil, *The Simone Weil Reader,* ed. George A. Panichas (New York: McKay, 1977), p. 369: "'Friendship is an equality made of harmony,' said the Pythagoreans. There is harmony because there is a supernatural union between two opposites, that is to say, necessity and liberty, the two opposites God combined when he created the world and men. There is equality because each wishes to preserve the faculty of free consent both in himself and in the other."

30. Plato, *The Collected Dialogues,* edited by Edith Hamilton and Huntington Cairns, Bollingen Series LXXI (Princeton, NJ: Princeton UP, 1989), p. 290.

Emma Campbell (essay date summer 2003)

SOURCE: Campbell, Emma. "Sexual Poetics and the Politics of Translation in the Tale of Griselda."[1] *Comparative Literature* 55, no. 3 (summer 2003): 191-216.

[*In the following essay, Campbell discusses the relationship between gender and translation with the contexts of Boccaccio's, Francesco Petrarch's, and Geoffrey Chaucer's stories of Griselda, demonstrating how gender politics and the politics of translation influence each other.*]

> Historiam tuam meis verbis explicui, imo alicubi aut paucis in ipsa narratione mutatis verbis aut additis, quod te non ferente modo sed favente fieri credidi. [. . .] Quam quidem an mutata veste deformaverim an fortassis ornaverim, tu iudica.

> I have told your story in my own words, or rather changing or adding a few words at some points in the narrative because I believed that you would not only allow it to be done, but would support it. [. . .] Whether, in changing its garment, I have deformed it or, perhaps, beautified it, you be the judge.
>
> Petrarch, *Epistolae Seniles* 17, 3[2]

The above comments, written by Petrarch to Boccaccio, invite a complex reading of the structures of power and authority implicit in medieval translation. The story as Petrarch describes it is a feminized object passed between men,[3] an object whose surfaces yield, firstly, to the vestimentary alterations performed by its male author and, secondly, to the judgment of the male reader. Yet Petrarch's description of the costume change that Boccaccio's story ["10.10"] undergoes also suggests that the "body" of the text somehow eludes authorial control, that it confounds the authority that appropriates it. Its first author—Boccaccio—ostensibly has a claim to the narrative that makes it "his": the story is, as Petrarch suggests, *historiam tuam* ("your story"). But the tale to which Petrarch refers also belongs to him: he is the one who has taken possession of it and changed its garment, and it is this newly adorned narrative that he submits to Boccaccio for consideration. However, this is not the end of the matter. For, dressed in its brand new clothing, this text has to undergo one further appropriation: the passage before the reader's gaze that will determine whether it is a monster or an angel, a deformation or an improvement. Indeed, it seems in this context somehow appropriate that the story is resubmitted to its previous author in a different form, leaving it unclear as to whether the tale is *historiam tuam* as a result of its relationship to him as an author or as the outcome of his new engagement with it as its reader.

Petrarch's description to Boccaccio of his translation of the story of Griselda thus invites a number of questions concerning the relationships that medieval authors forge between readers, authors, and texts. This article will attempt both to respond to and to develop some of these questions within the context of modern theories of translation and textuality.

I

The story of Griselda is, in the words of Carolyn Dinshaw, "a story of translation" (132), that is, a story both of the physical translation of its heroine from hovel to mansion and of the processes of *translatio* that underwrite the text's literary genealogy. For Dinshaw, the text—like its heroine—is a body passed between men: just as Griselda is claimed by her new husband through a ritual that has her dressed in new garments, so the text she inhabits is dressed and undressed by the translations to which it is subjected by successive male authors. However, Dinshaw goes on to suggest that the rendering of the story of Griselda in Chaucer's *Clerk's Tale* not only reproduces the structure of (male) clerical *translatio,* but also exposes and undermines that structure as it does so. The *Clerk's Tale* thereby reveals the paradox at the heart of all such acts of translation and, Dinshaw argues, simultaneously aligns itself with the position of Griselda herself insofar as she represents the translated, feminine body of the text.

Dinshaw's account of the Griselda story draws together many issues relating to gender and translation that have concerned both the tale's medieval translators and the modern critics who have since commented upon their work. A number of scholars have remarked upon the fact that both Petrarch and Chaucer, in their respective versions of the tale, seem more than aware of the possible analogy between their appropriation of storymatter and the manner in which Griselda is appropriated and transformed by her husband. Indeed, this view would seem to be supported by a medieval concept of textuality in which bodies of textual matter frequently characterized as feminine are alternately clothed or uncovered by masculine acts of reading or writing.[4]

As far as modern interpretations of the tale are concerned, feminist and non-feminist scholars alike have remarked upon the possible significance of Griselda's behavior vis-à-vis her husband, suggesting that the tale might be thought of in terms of relationships of power between individual and state, tyranny and republicanism, writer and text, or man and woman (see Morse, "Critical Approaches"). Moreover, at least some of this criticism focuses on the role of translation in the negotiation of these relationships. Considering Chaucer's text in relation to its Latin and French sources, Wendy Harding reads the metaphor of clothing in the text in relation to Chaucer's concept of literary activity and argues that this metaphor does not quite fit either the transformed Chaucerian narrative or the heroine it frames (194-210). In a similar vein—although one not explicitly concerned with issues of gender politics—David Wallace demonstrates how successive translations of Boccaccio's tale are used to displace, establish, or undermine certain kinds of political and textual authority, and suggests how these textual processes might be linked to broader political ideologies contemporary with the texts themselves (156-215).

The paradoxical structure that Dinshaw associates with translation in Chaucer's tale also seems to be a more general feature of the story's medieval (and post-medieval) evolution. Lesley Johnson's article on Griselda, although contesting Dinshaw's reading, draws attention to how interpretation of the story—especially in relation to the figure of Griselda herself—is often troubled by what Johnson refers to as the heroine's various "textual incarnations." Although Griselda's literary longevity suggests that her story represents "a model of femininity that transcends time and cultural specificity," that model is not an unchanging, universal category but the product of the heroine's association with a range of constantly shifting feminine roles. Indeed, Charlotte Morse's article on Griselda's exemplarity almost involuntarily makes a similar point. While arguing that medieval writers and audiences would have viewed Griselda as an exemplary figure, Morse offers examples that reveal an almost total lack of consensus concerning what exactly Griselda exemplifies, in what sense she is to be emulated, and who is intended to follow such a seemingly extreme example.[5] Translation thus seems repeatedly to re-affirm Griselda's status as a paragon (if not as an easily emulated paragon), while simultaneously displacing and undermining that status.

As both Johnson's and Morse's work suggests, the tale of Griselda does not, however, unproblematically submit itself either to translation or to interpretation. Hermeneutic difficulties concerning Griselda's status as a wife and quasi-saint trouble some of the earliest translations of the story, both as a text to be read and also as a text to be written and re-written. The various ways in which the tale's medieval authors engage with these difficulties can be discerned most clearly in the different emphases they give to Griselda's roles as a woman, as a wife, and as a moral example within that context. This, I would suggest, is because medieval versions of the story often come dangerously close to challenging the naturalness of contemporary notions of gender hierarchy while, at the same time, seeming to confirm and reinforce those hierarchies.[6] The logical development of the story requires Griselda's complete and unfailing submission to the will of her husband and feudal lord, Gualtieri (or Walter), yet, in testing the reliability of his wife's obedience, Gualtieri behaves in an extreme—not to mention irrational—manner, pushing Griselda to the limits of human endurance in a gratuitous exercise of the power he already has over her. By attempting to ascertain the limits of his wife's pliability, Gualtieri's behavior towards Griselda thus seems to communicate something fundamentally unnecessary and absurd about the subordination of female to male in both feudal and conjugal relations. More to the point, while implementing a prerogative that reaffirms the "correct" relationship of male to female, Gualtieri's actions challenge his own, supposedly natural, superiority by associating his superior status as a man and husband with those qualities of wilfulness and irrationality more usually associated with women and wives.[7]

These tensions are registered in some of the French translations of Petrarch's text, which often address the example Griselda provides for women.[8] In treating the central paradox of the story, these translations suggest that Griselda's example applies particularly to women and wives, while simultaneously asserting that this example should not be taken too literally by the story's female readers. This assertion leads some of these texts to attempt to combine what seem to be incompatible readings of the story. Griselda is presented as both a model of virtue for married women and as a martyr aided by God in her resistance to tyranny, as a speculum for contemporary wives seeking to improve their conduct towards their husbands and as an example of unsurpassable Christian virtue. Indeed, some of the hermeneutic difficulties encountered by the text's medieval readers and translators are illustrated by the compiler of the *Ménagier de Paris*. Addressing the story to his young wife, the compiler underlines its value as an example of wifely obedience and Christian virtue, while nonetheless insisting that he does not intend to visit Walter's excessive (and improbable) cruelty upon her. In other words, the tale is a model for the good wife, yet it is not to be read as a comment on the behavior of men within marriage; wifely virtue is thus both framed within the gender hierarchies supported by marital relationships and distanced from those hierarchies at the point where they begin to look unfair and absurd.

In giving the story new form, translators of the tale of Griselda are thus compelled to engage with the significance of gender within the structure of the narrative they appropriate and to consider Griselda's problematic role as a woman and as a wife within that context. Morse and Johnson similarly point out the difficulties of the tale as an example of ideal feminine conduct for modern readers and authors, who struggle to reconcile the ambiguous message of the text with interpretations and re-writings informed by modern approaches sensitive to the issues raised by feminist discourse. The problems that both medieval and modern authors and readers encounter in finding meaning in the story thus most frequently concern Griselda herself and how her "example"—if indeed it is to be construed as such—relates to the tale's readers and audiences. More to the point, Griselda's problematic exemplarity is closely related to her status as a model of *female* virtue, a status that clearly affects how the message of the story is taken to apply to readers in the world outside the text.

It is this interface between translation and gender politics in the tale of Griselda that I wish to consider in this article. Although a substantial amount of work has been published on questions regarding this interface, it seems to me that arguments such as those I have cited stop short of considering how gender politics and what might be termed a politics of translation impact upon one another. That is to say, how do processes of translation influence both the representation of gendered identities and the wider significance of that representation? This is perhaps especially the case in considerations of Chaucer's text, which has typically been interpreted as a restoration of "gender, the here and now, and a consideration of woman's point of view" (Dinshaw 153), a critique of certain forms of oppression (which are not necessarily related to the oppression of women by men), or an ironic masterpiece in which meaning is impossible to locate. What I would like to consider here is the *precise sense* in which different translations of the story of Griselda—particularly those of Petrarch and Chaucer—are "about" the relationship between gender and translation and, moreover, what this says about how we might interpret medieval narrative from a political perspective sensitive to gender issues. By doing so I hope not only to challenge certain assumptions about medieval textual processes, but also to ask questions concerning the subversive potential of representational forms when considered in relation to those processes.

II

Judith Butler's theory of "gender trouble" has been widely used in literary criticism (among other disciplines) for some time now, and has a certain currency among medievalists working in a variety of fields.[9] In her work on the subversive potential of performance as a representational form, Butler suggests that it is possible to destabilize gender roles and the hierarchies that these roles conventionally establish by performing those roles in ways that challenge the system from which they emerge (*Gender Trouble*). Gender identity is, claims Butler, an effect of repeated performances; thus, by producing performances of gender that fail to confirm its credibility as a stable identity—performances that, in other words, reveal the repetitive nature of its constitution—gender and the social norms it supports may be unsettled and transformed.

Although Butler's notion of performance has sometimes been characterized as constructivist by those who have used and critiqued her work, this characterization often obscures what is arguably the most significant aspect of

her theory of performativity. Performance in the sense that Butler gives it is not simply a matter of acting out the gender role that one chooses, of performatively inscribing a "cultural" identity onto a "biological" body; performance is a form of citation that inscribes the body within symbolic systems, thereby rendering it intelligible.[10] Thus, as Butler indicates elsewhere in her work on gender and sexuality, her notion of gender performativity can only be thought of in relation to the reiterative practice of regulatory sexual regimes and the forms of identity that those regimes make possible (*Bodies that Matter* 15). The point of performance is thus not to step outside the symbolic systems that establish primary and stable identity; the point is, rather, to expose—from a situation within symbolic regimes—both identity and the stability with which it is associated as effects of continuous citation. Thus, what is troubling about performance is its demystifying potential. By exposing identity as accreted rather than fixed, performance does not parodically deform an original identity: what is parodied is the notion of an original identity *per se* (*Gender Trouble* 171-80).

Recently, Butler has applied a similar notion of performance—this time in a postcolonial context—to what she describes as "cultural translation" (see "Restaging the Universal"). Put simply, this theory asserts that claims to the universal that help to support oppressive colonialist regimes can be subverted by an exploitation of their reliance on linguistic representation. Butler argues that the universal can only be claimed through its expression within a certain cultural and linguistic context; the authority of the universal claim thus derives not from its anterior status as universal but rather from its acceptance as universal in all of the cultural and linguistic contexts in which it appears. Cultural translation can therefore be used to expose the limits of the dominant language by bringing into relief the nonconvergence of discourses and so exposing the universal as a space filled out by specific contexts. In other words, translation can demonstrate the contingency of the universal claim by pointing out all that it excludes or suppresses in being established, thereby destabilizing the authority of that claim and opening up the possibility of resistance to it.

For the purposes of this article, what interests me about Butler's theory is not its account of universality but its description of the subversive potential of translation. Indeed, her description of what she terms "restaging the universal" seems to provide a much more general account of how acts of translation—as either oral or written reiterations of established discourse—work to destabilize the prior authority attached to that discourse:

> The established discourse remains established only by being perpetually re-established, so it risks itself in the very repetition it requires. Moreover, the former dis-

course is reiterated precisely through a speech act that shows something it may not say: that the discourse "works" through its effective moment in the present, and is fundamentally dependent for its maintenance on that contemporary instance. The reiterative speech act thus offers the possibility—though not the necessity—of depriving the past of the established discourse of its exclusive control over defining the perameters of the universal within politics. This form of political performativity does not retroactively absolutize its own claim, but recites and restages a set of cultural norms that displace legitimacy from a presumed authority to the mechanism of its renewal.

("Restaging the Universal" 41)

This account of the politics of translation as a "restaging" of an historical set of cultural norms in a manner that is at once traditional and disruptive shares a number of similarities with descriptions of the cultural dynamics of vernacular translation in the Middle Ages. Rita Copeland's study of the disciplinary evolution of translation from late antiquity to the fourteenth century argues that, largely as a result of its contested status in the disciplinary competition between rhetoric and grammar that begins in Roman culture, medieval translation is a "hermeneutical performance": that is, it negotiates between hermeneutics and rhetoric, *modus interpretandi* and *modus inveniendi,* exegesis and representation. Partly as a result of this, vernacular translation is able to assert its "service" to an authoritative source, even as it "displaces the originary force of its models" (4). This displacement is, moreover, an integral part of the late medieval valorization of vernacular literature vis-à-vis Latin literary culture, particularly in the case of those translations that stress their independent status as literary texts (what Copeland terms "secondary translation"). Translation as a type of medieval academic discourse in the vernacular is thus situated somewhat ambivalently in relation to traditional disciplinary and linguistic hierarchies. On the one hand, vernacular translation appropriates and reinforces the value systems implicit in a textual tradition centered on Latin models, both offering access to an older, more arcane Latin culture and reproducing the systems that sustain an academic tradition based upon that culture. On the other hand, it is the vernacular (rather than Latin) which is thereby inscribed as the language of cultural authority, upsetting the linguistic hegemony that traditionally invests Latin with greater cultural value than vernacular discourse.

Although Copeland's notion of performance and its relationship to translation is not framed in precisely the same way as is Butler's, her work nonetheless suggests that the dynamics of translation described by Butler have historical correlatives in the shifts taking place in medieval academic traditions contemporary with the work of Boccaccio, Petrarch, and Chaucer. For Copeland, as for Butler, translation can both claim and subvert dominant cultural authority through the citational

representation of an established discourse. Copeland's work complements Butler's theory in that it allows the historical content of such a move to be introduced into the latter's theoretical setting, thereby suggesting that this citational dynamic has a particular historical significance for the valorization of vernacular discourse taking place in medieval Western Europe. By contrast, recourse to Butler's theory enables a closer examination of the interface between medieval textual processes and gender politics. For, when seen in relation to her earlier work on gender, Butler's description of translation affords a means of considering the relationship between gender and textuality in medieval literature in terms of the ideological norms that different versions of texts both reinscribe and potentially disrupt. What Butler's arguments suggest is that mimesis—or re-presentation—has the potential to diminish any claim to primary or authentic meaning by separating the term from its putative authority: what precedes representation is not anterior to that representation but rather one of its effects.[11] One of the contentions of this article is that this dislocation not only bears upon the linguistic hierarchies implicit in medieval cultural representation but also affects the gender norms inscribed by such cultural representations.

My use of Butler's argument in relation to the story of Griselda thus returns to points made by Dinshaw and Johnson concerning both the conservative and the destabilizing effects of translation, yet it also offers a means of developing the arguments made by these scholars with regard to Griselda herself. What Butler's theory suggests is that different translations of the tale of Griselda do not constitute appropriations of a feminine textual body. Rather, they (at least potentially) expose the discursive limits of the appropriated story in such a way as to reveal the feminine bodies of both Griselda and the text she inhabits as absences concealed behind the rhetorical garments that different authors weave around them. What this means is that the "bodies" of Griselda and her story are only revealed through their textual reclothing; the gender of these bodies and its ideological deployment in the narrative are thus effects of textual performances that can either confirm or disrupt the identities of those bodies in anterior versions of the tale.

How this applies to the texts I will be considering will, I hope, become clearer in the course of my argument. I will suggest, firstly, that Boccaccio's story—although perhaps less explicitly concerned with translation than the two later versions of Petrarch and Chaucer—nonetheless highlights the problematic status of the female body as it is framed by various possible interpretations of the narrative. Secondly, looking at Petrarch's appropriation of Boccaccio's tale, I will explore how the text's feminine status is construed in relation to the materiality of Griselda as a woman, considering how the meanings that accrue to her femininity might be problematically related to the translation in which she appears. Finally, examining the Chaucerian translation, I will consider how the depiction of Griselda as an exemplary and inimitable wife, along with the rather tongue-in-cheek glosses to which the story is subject in this version, might illustrate (and be used to critique) Butler's concept of translation as a subversive political strategy.

III

Boccaccio's rendering of the Griselda story in the *Decameron* is the first example of the tale in its written form.[12] The narrative setting of the tale of Griselda, which appears in the *Decameron* as the last tale of the final day, provides an important frame for the reading of the story. The tenth day sees a movement towards moral tales and the promise of order and resolution, yet the moral substance of the tales told on the final day is often ambiguous, and the story of Griselda, rather than resolving these ambiguities, instead serves to complicate them further. As Guiseppe Mazzotta has suggested, the *Decameron*'s treatment of ethics relies upon such tensions and ambiguities (*World at Play* 105-30). The reflection on ethics that Boccaccio's text seems to encourage reorients the traditional focus on *meditatio mortis* and *contemptus mundi* found in contemporary philosophical discourse in order to concentrate instead upon the problematics of living in an imperfect world. Moreover, this ethical reflection not only reworks the goals of philosophical thought in this respect, but also challenges its mode of articulation by privileging the notion of play as the appropriate idiom through which to explore socio-ethical questions. Boccaccio's use of irony, his subversion of literary register, and his problematization of questions of meaning and interpretation can thus be seen to invite ethical reflection. Seen in this light, Dioneo's tale of Griselda, along with the problems it presents, can be read in terms of some of the poetic and philosophical preoccupations that run throughout the *Decameron* and that similarly inform other works by Boccaccio.[13] However, as I will argue, these epistemological and literary preoccupations are here also closely linked to the dynamics of a gendered literary practice: "sexual poetics" implicitly underwrite hermeneutic disruption and the ethical questioning that this disruption invites.

The presentation of the tale of Griselda in Boccaccio's text suggests that the questions of order, authority, and interpretation that have informed the *brigata*'s narrative entertainments on previous days are similarly at issue in the story to be told by Dioneo. The fact that the tale is narrated by the one member of the *brigata* who enjoys greater artistic freedom than the others in matters of storytelling indicates that the story may require a more complex reading than the nine other tales told on the

last day. Indeed, Dioneo's preamble makes it clear that his narrative fulfils none of the criteria mentioned by Panfilo in his request for exemplary tales of those who have performed liberal or munificent deeds (*di chi liberalmente ovvero magnificamente [. . .] operasse*) (*Dec* [*Decameron*] "9." "Conc," 4-5).[14] Dioneo freely admits that his tale deals with a marquis whose actions are brutal rather than munificent, and that his audience would be well advised not to follow the example of such a man.[15] In his opening remarks Dioneo thus suggests that the moral scheme outlined by Panfilo—in which good or valorous deeds are to be praised, rewarded, and used as examples—somehow fails to apply to his own narrative. Dioneo's comments inform his audience that they are not to approach this tale in the same manner as they have the other stories, that instead of expecting a lesson in good conduct, they should anticipate a tale that requires them to judge the narrative in negative relation to the exemplary model from which it takes its cue.

Although Griselda is not mentioned in these opening remarks, Dioneo's subsequent telling of the story filters questions of judgment, interpretation, and exemplarity almost exclusively through the various actions to which her body is subjected. Modes of reading, as well as the use of images of dressing and undressing, are crucial in this respect. Gualtieri's initial reading of Griselda's beauty is seen by him as evidence of her suitability as a wife (*Dec* "10. 10," 9) and results in her accession to a role that her husband prepares for her through the fashioning of new garments that represent her status as a noble wife ("10. 10," 14). Having been stripped in full public view and dressed in these new clothes. Griselda acquires a new, publicly legible nobility that not only complements her dress but also presumably reflects her husband's wisdom and discernment in choosing her as a wife. In demonstrating that she is worthy of the clothing she now wears, Griselda is living proof of her husband's abilities as a perceptive judge of character, a judgment that ostensibly relies upon his talent for reading female bodies:

> per ciò che niun altro che egli avrebbe mai potuto conoscere l'alta virtù di costei nascosa sotto i poveri panni e sotto l'abito villesco.
>
> ("10. 10," 24-26)

> for no one apart from Gualtieri could ever have perceived the noble qualities that lay concealed beneath her ragged and rustic attire.

Thus, although Gualtieri's subjects had initially criticized his choice, they now regard him as the most discerning man on earth. This shift in public opinion is the result of reading Griselda's qualities in relation to her new dress, as opposed to the rags she has left behind, of learning to see that which Gualtieri both perceived and rendered visible through his appropriation of the pretty young pauper he has married and re-clothed. Indeed, the description of Griselda after her marriage suggests that Gualtieri is not only a judicious *reader* of the excellent wife he now possesses, but also the *author* of her newly acquired nobility in so far as the social and vestimentary status that Gualtieri confers upon Griselda both reflects her innate qualities and also works to produce and display these qualities to a wider public.[16]

The consonance of virtue and attire that Griselda's marriage reveals is interrupted when she is forced to return to her father's hovel after her supposed divorce and to assume once again the clothing she had left behind when she married. Her divorce once again emphasizes the significance of Griselda's clothing as a symbol of the noble status that Gualtieri has conferred upon her through marriage. Having been repudiated by her husband, Griselda is asked to leave the court with only the dowry with which she came, which, as she herself points out, means leaving the court with nothing on, since Gualtieri took her to wife naked as on the day she was born.[17] However, Griselda's request that, in exchange for her lost virginity, the body in which she has borne Gualtieri's children should be covered with a shift before she leaves the court renegotiates the relationship between clothing and the nobility it displays. Griselda's clothing (or lack of it) symbolizes her rightful status as Gualtieri's wife and as mother of his children and also serves as a potent reminder of the virtuous qualities for which she was originally recognized and married by her husband. The flimsy attire in which Griselda leaves the court thus displays her nobility in a way similar to, yet crucially different from, the expensive clothing that she leaves behind. Her virtue is no longer read in the context of her noble attire; rather, it appears as an innate quality materialized in the inadequate dress in which she leaves her marital home. Thus, by emphasizing the dissonance between her former status as a pauper and what is now perceived to be her innate nobility, Griselda's humiliating return to her former circumstances—and to the clothing that goes with them—confirms the noble nature for which she has become known among Gualtieri's subjects. Moreover, in providing further proof of her obedience as a wife, Griselda's re-clothing serves to reinforce the validity of Gualtieri's original judgment of her as suitable marriage material even as he supposedly revises that judgment by casting her off.

This contrast is further exploited when, dressed as a pauper, Griselda prepares the wedding festivities for Gualtieri and the woman whom he leads her (and his people) to believe will be his new wife. It is significant that the last test of Griselda's wifehood comes in the form of an act of reading performed on another female body. Having prepared a splendid feast for her young replacement, Griselda is asked by Gualtieri to give her opinion of the girl that he has chosen to take her place.

The girl to whom Gualtieri refers is in fact their daughter, yet this is only revealed to Griselda after she has responded to his question; Griselda's pronouncement on their daughter therefore interprets her as a replacement for Griselda herself and as a prospective wife to Gualtieri. In response to her husband's question, Griselda replies:

> "a me ne par molto bene; e se così è savia come ella è bella, che 'l credo, io non dubito punto che voi non dobbiate con lei vivere il più consolato signore del mondo; ma quanto posso vi priego che quelle punture, le quali all'altra, che vostra fu, già deste, non diate a questa, ché appena che io creda che ella le potesse sostenere, sì perché più giovane è, e sì ancora perché in dilicatezze è allevata, ove colei in continue fatiche da piccolina era stata."

("10. 10," 59)

> "I think very well of her. And if, as I believe, her wisdom matches her beauty, I have no doubt whatever that your life with her will bring you greater happiness than any gentleman on earth has ever known. But with all my heart I beg you not to inflict those same wounds upon her that you imposed upon her predecessor, for I doubt whether she could withstand them, not only because she is younger, but also because she has had a refined upbringing, whereas the other had to face continual hardship from her infancy."

Griselda's response provides another instance of the alignment of her own opinion with that of Gualtieri, yet it is also a comment on his judicious reading of her before their marriage and a repetition of the reading process that accompanied it. Griselda, like Gualtieri, considers the beauty of the prospective wife in terms of her inner qualities (here interpreted as her knowledge or wisdom), and thus as a mark of her suitability for marriage. Gualtieri's original judgment of Griselda is not, however, unproblematically endorsed by her own pronouncement: if his judgment were clearly correct in the first place there would be no need to marry someone else. Moreover, were he to marry the girl that Griselda considers suitable, Gualtieri would be contracting himself to the daughter he has sired by the woman to whom he is still legally married, thereby making him guilty of both incest and bigamy.

Perhaps more importantly, Griselda's comments present the action that has resulted from Gualtieri's judgment of her as doubly problematic. Her plea that her successor be spared the punishments that Griselda herself has had to endure in marriage suggests that the proof of a good wife should be measured in relation to the happiness of her husband rather than her endurance of the torments he inflicts upon her. Furthermore, Griselda's description of these wounds suggests that she is somewhat exceptional in being able to bear this suffering: as Griselda points out, the girl who is supposedly to replace her would be unlikely to endure such trials on account of her age and upbringing. Thus, although Griselda implies that another woman can adopt the role that she has been forced to leave behind and fulfil—as did she—all the basic criteria, Griselda also points out that this is all another wife should be asked to do. The precedent that Griselda has set [Illegible Text] to translate to the woman who will supplant her; it fails to apply precisely because Griselda's example is entirely unique.

Griselda's reading of her daughter, which is also in a sense a re-reading of herself as originally seen by Gualtieri, thus implicitly endorses his original criteria for spotting a good wife, while nonetheless critiquing his methods of testing the wife he chooses. Furthermore, Griselda's pronouncement makes any subsequent reading of her example as a model for other wives rather difficult and in fact introduces a series of readings of the story which attempt to deal (usually inadequately) with this crucial problem.

When seen in this context, Gualtieri's subsequent claim that his cruelty towards Griselda was designed to have an educational value both for Griselda and for his people seems almost wilfully absurd. Gualtieri explains his actions in the following terms:

> "ciò che io faceva, ad anteveduto fine operava, vogliendo a te insegnar d'esser moglie e a loro di saperla torre e tenere, e a me partorire perpetua quiete mentre teco a vivere avessi [. . .]"
>
> ("**10. 10,**" 61)
>
> "whatever I have done was done for a set purpose, for I wished to show you how to be a wife, to teach these people how to choose and keep a wife, and to guarantee my own peace and quiet for as long as we were living beneath the same roof."

The instructional value that Gualtieri claims for his conduct towards his wife further complicates the possibility of reading the tale as an *exemplum*. In Gualtieri's speech it is not Griselda who is singled out as exemplary, but rather his own process of choosing, maintaining, and educating a wife, a process that—as Griselda herself has suggested—is inapplicable to other women. Furthermore, Gualtieri's motivations are not validated by the events of the story itself: since Griselda is the perfect wife *before* her trials, what could Gualtieri possibly hope to teach her by testing the limits of her patience? Given the fact that his behavior has fragmented his family and upset himself, his wife, and his subjects, how have his actions guaranteed him a quiet domestic life? More to the point, how do his actions demonstrate how to choose and keep a wife? Nor does the response of Gualtieri's people clarify matters: Griselda is thought to be wise (*savissima*), as is her husband (*savissimo*), but Gualtieri's actions are denounced as cruel and unnecessary ("**10. 10,**" 66).[18] How either of them is to be emulated in practical terms remains unclear.

The hermeneutic difficulties that the comments of both Griselda and Gualtieri raise are by no means resolved in the conclusion to the story, which once again focuses attention upon the interpretation of Griselda and the translatability of the role that she inhabits. In keeping with his preface to the story, Dioneo's summing up seems deliberately to discourage any reading of the story as an *exemplum,* much less as a model for relationships between men and women. The initial comments he makes in his conclusion suggest that the tale is not about marital relations at all but rather about the insoluble paradoxes of social hierarchy:

> Che si potrà dir qui, se non che anche nelle povere case piovono dal cielo de' divini spiriti, come nelle reali di quegli che sarien più degni di guardar porci che d'avere sopra uomini signoria?
>
> ("**10. 10,**" 68)
>
> What more needs to be said, except that celestial spirits may sometimes descend even into the houses of the poor, whilst there are those in royal palaces who would be better employed as swineherds than as rulers of men?

Considered alongside the story he has just told, Dioneo's gloss thus implicitly dismisses Gualtieri as an unfit ruler and elevates Griselda to the position of a divine spirit, a narrative move that would polarize them in such a way as to efface the exemplary value both of their conduct and of their relationship to one another as man and wife.

Dioneo's comment on the tale nonetheless returns to the problem of how the outward signs of identity and social position might match, or fail to match, the bodies that they envelop. Significantly, Griselda's body is presented as especially elusive in this respect. Unlike her husband, who Dioneo suggests is a *vilain* disguised as a marquis, Griselda is not simply a noblewoman in a pauper's clothing; she is, following the logic of the same gloss, a *divino spirito*. Thus, Griselda's body—which has been the focus of so much stripping and re-clothing in the tale—would be elided by her redefinition as a spiritual as opposed to a corporeal being: as a celestial spirit, Griselda would transcend both her poor dress and the dress to which she returns as a rich and noble wife and mother.

However, the suggestion of Griselda's dematerialization in Dioneo's conclusion results in yet another fantasy of bodily substitution, this time involving not her daughter but another anonymous, and considerably less virtuous, wife. As a conclusion to his brief epilogue to the tale, Dioneo remarks

> Al quale [Gualtieri] non sarebbe forse stato male investito d'essersi abbattuto a una, che quando fuor di casa l'avesse in camiscia cacciata, s'avesse sì ad un altro fatto scuotere il pelliccione, che riuscita ne fosse una bella roba.
>
> (*Dec* "**10. 10,**" 69)

It would have served him [Gualtieri] right if he had chanced upon a wife, who, being driven from the house in her shift, had found some other man to shake her coat for her, earning a fine new dress in the process.

Dioneo's comment thus reintroduces a reading that sees the tale in terms of marital and sexual relations, presenting his audience with an alternative female body to be dressed and undressed. In fantasizing another woman in Griselda's place, Dioneo offers his audience a possible counter-narrative to the one he has just told,[19] opening up the space that Griselda occupies in the tale to other bodies, writings, and readings. This alternative Griselda seems to confirm the impossibility of translating Griselda's example onto other female bodies (at least those bodies that have a less than celestial constitution), yet she also exposes the illusion that lies behind that example. This new Griselda's nakedness is not covered by a virginal shift; rather, it is flaunted as another layer of clothing. The *pelliccione* or coat that she offers for shaking and re-dressing is not a naked body but a female surface to be appropriated and re-clothed, a surface that invokes the absence rather than the presence of the female bodies which the text has woven itself around.[20] As the subject of a narrative of her own in which the absent, fictionalized sexual body is submitted to another man in return for a fine new dress, this alternative Griselda seems to embody the principle of translation itself, a principle that exposes the fissures in the narrative it parodies by introducing new bodies and contexts to disrupt the coherence of the established text.

IV

What Dioneo's final interpretation demonstrates is the problem of reading Griselda's virtue in connection with her status as a woman and a wife, and the relationship that this bears to translation as both a narrative mechanism and a function of exemplarity. It is precisely these difficulties that Petrarch attempts to resolve in his own translation of the tale, which, although using Boccaccio's vernacular text as its source, alters the language and narrative tone of the Italian original to produce a more serious, moral tale written in Latin.

Petrarch's rewriting of the story and the unity that he thereby attempts to impose upon his source frames a response to Boccaccio in more ways than one. Petrarch's translation appears in the final book of an epistolary exchange with Boccaccio which continued for more than twenty years, an exchange that centers on the nature and function of literature. When considered both in this context and in relation to Petrarch's oeuvre more generally, his translation of the tale of Griselda—which self-consciously attempts to refine the moral meaning of the tale—clearly reflects Petrarch's humanist belief in literature's influence on the formation of the morally re-

sponsible subject (see Mazzotta, *Worlds of Petrarch*, esp. 80-101). On a more local level, however, the tale also implicitly addresses issues raised in one of Boccaccio's previous letters to Petrarch. In the letter that directly precedes the epistle containing his translation, Petrarch presents a series of arguments contradicting Boccaccio's request that he take literary retirement on account of his old age. As Warren Ginsberg has recently indicated, the translation of Boccaccio's tale contained in the letter that follows both rearticulates these arguments in literary form and provides proof of the poet laureate's continuing poetic activity (240-68).

The epistemological issues that Petrarch's tale of Griselda raises are thus intimately related to the poet's sense of his own vocation, as well as to his artistic and moral sensibilities. However, Petrarch's translation also returns to questions concerning the sexual politics that implicitly inform his literary practice and the humanist ideology with which it is infused. In the preface to his translation Petrarch explains to Boccaccio that by rendering the story in Latin he intends to bring it to an international readership; the other changes he makes to the narrative similarly condition it for the audience of learned male readers that this choice of language implies.[21] Petrarch characterizes the development of this project of rewriting as a love affair between author and text that tellingly recalls Gualtieri's courtship of Griselda, for Petrarch describes the process of altering the language and style of Boccaccio's story, the beauty of which had struck him on reading the **Decameron,** as a means of "changing its garment" (*mutata veste*) (cf. Wallace 191-94). Moreover, these substantial alterations to the text's "garment" are clearly designed to transform what Petrarch implicitly regards as the original story's rather poor Boccaccian clothing, thereby reaffirming his superior status as both a learned literary authority and as master of Boccaccio's text.

What remains most striking about this new version of the tale is the change Petrarch effects in his representation of Griselda. Petrarch's revisions have the effect of shifting attention from the brutality of Gualtieri's (Valterius's) behavior to the virtue that his behavior elicits from his wife. Griselda's moral value is consistently presented as the primary thematic focus of the tale, which emphasizes her Christian and ostensibly human qualities of patience and humility. In Petrarch's tale the courtly dimension of Boccaccio's Griselda disappears altogether: it is not Griselda's manners and beauty that are initially remarked upon by Valterius but her exceptional virtue (*virtutem eximiam*), and attention is deliberately diverted from her physical attractiveness in order to foreground the inner beauty that others have hitherto failed to recognize (*Sen* 17. 2, 14-18). Petrarch's representation of Griselda in fact bears a remarkable resemblance to hagiographical representations of some of the virgin martyrs, where the young saint's physical attractiveness is mentioned only to draw attention towards a more profound spiritual beauty. Indeed, Petrarch possibly goes even further than typical hagiographical representations in his emphasis on the non-corporeal attractions of his heroine, since her physical body is not subjected to the same level of scrutiny as are the naked and brutally tortured bodies of many female martyrs.[22]

This concentration on Griselda's spiritual characteristics is echoed elsewhere in the narrative. Indeed, at the moment of her supposed divorce, when she is asked to return to her father's house with nothing but the dowry she came with, Griselda declares before God that she has always remained a maid at heart, drawing attention away from the physical reality of her relationship with her husband and her two children to focus instead upon the continuing integrity of her spiritual being. As will be clear from my earlier discussion of this incident in the *Decameron,* in which Griselda refers explicitly to her lost integrity as Gualtieri's wife, Petrarch's rewriting deliberately downplays the material emphasis of the Boccaccian source. The words Griselda uses in Petrarch's text are in this sense significant. In claiming that she has always remained a maid in spirit (*animo semper ancilla permansi*) (17.5, 12-15), Griselda emphasizes her role as a servant and embodiment of Christian virtue rather than as a wife, associating herself with that other (rather more famous) handmaid of the Lord, the Virgin Mary. In the late Middle Ages virginity was, of course, thought of as a moral and spiritual state as well as a physical condition, and in this sense Griselda's claims are not particularly unusual—nor do they necessarily contradict her social and physical status as a married woman (see Millett and Wogan-Browne 37-43; and Salih 16-40). It is, however, worth noting that her claim to spiritual maidenhood counterbalances a very public discussion of the physical and sexual aspects of her body. Griselda's exile from the court with nothing to cover her naked womb is a very real possibility at this point in the text, and Griselda's assertion thus re-emphasizes her spiritual wholeness at a time when those aspects of her body associated with her sexual and maternal function are more "visible" than ever.

The conflicting images of Griselda as wife, mother, and inviolate maid found in the above passage seem to articulate a more fundamental problem of representation in Petrarch's translation, a problem that is clearly related to the humanist morality that this version of the story of Griselda is supposed to exemplify. Petrarch's attempt to make Griselda a moral heroine often means that the "reality" of her status as a wife and mother become problematic, a difficulty that emerges quite clearly in Petrarch's conclusion, where he seeks to reinforce this reading of the tale. In his closing remarks, Petrarch underlines those aspects of Griselda's temperament that he has sought to accentuate throughout the story in his

careful modifications to Boccaccio's text. Griselda's constancy is praised as a quality that all readers of the tale should endeavor to reproduce in their obedience towards God, and her suffering at the hands of Valterius is suggested as a model for the good Christian enduring the trials sent by his own, divine Lord and Master (*Sen* 17. 6, 69-81).[23]

In addition to offering his readers a key to reading the tale in terms of the soul's relationship to God, however, Petrarch's conclusion also points to what he intends to exclude from his translation. Petrarch highlights the fact that his tale is not supposed to be an example to contemporary married women (*matronas nostri temporis*), as Griselda's patience seems hardly imitable when considered in relation to wives of the current age (17. 6, 69-73). Indeed, Petrarch openly admits that his choice of Latin as the appropriate idiom for the tale's composition is intended to encourage an altogether different kind of reading, a reading that necessarily dissociates Griselda's virtue from her gender and implicitly excludes the female reader from the moral lessons that the text contains (cf. Wallace 160-65).

While Petrarch's final comments clearly identify Griselda with the human soul rather than the female body,[24] his insistence on the way the tale should *not* be approached calls attention to some of the difficulties of the reading that he proposes. While literary precedents for women exemplifying virtues that could transcend sex and gender boundaries were by no means lacking by the fourteenth century, these women usually renounced their worldly identity in some fundamental way.[25] By contrast, what remains problematic about Griselda's qualities is that they can never be entirely detached from the physical and social functions she performs as a woman. Not only is Griselda's obedience a part of her marriage vow, but her reward for her continuing loyalty to Valterius is her reinstatement as a mother and a wife, a reinstatement that marks a return to her worldly, female status rather than a movement away from it. Although Petrarch's gloss re-emphasizes the reading of the tale that he would privilege as its translator, it fails to account for some of the fundamental ambiguities in this interpretation and, in its attempt to redirect the text's meaning, possibly even draws attention to those elements he wishes to suppress.

I do not mean to suggest by this that Petrarch was unaware of the questions that his translation posed with regard to the literal and metaphorical meanings that might accrue to his female protagonist. On the contrary, his final gloss would seem to suggest that he was more than conscious of the possible misreadings of the text that the latent tension between these meanings might cause. As I have argued, Petrarch's text attempts to address many of the difficulties raised by Boccaccio's rendering of the story as an exemplary narrative, yet ultimately fails to close down the disruptive alternative readings that challenge that exemplarity. On the one hand, Petrarch's translation seems actively to engage with a dilemma implicit in Boccaccio's tale, admitting that the example Griselda sets can only problematically be applied to other wives. It is thus Dioneo's *divino spirito* that takes center stage in Petrarch's narrative, not Dioneo's noble and inimitable wife or the less scrupulous female counterpart for Griselda that Dioneo introduces at the end of his tale. Petrarch's text openly asserts this shift from literal to allegorical representation as a mechanism that enables the translation of Griselda's example into a metatextual environment, an environment in which the feminine spirit can act as a supposedly universal model for the genderless souls of educated men.

On the other hand, however, Petrarch exposes the mechanisms of gendered authorship that inform his comments to Boccaccio precisely through his attempts to erase the material connotations of Griselda's femininity. Like his patient female protagonist, the text that Petrarch appropriates is given a significantly more elaborate dress and transported to a different social milieu; yet what lies behind its clothing is a rhetorical feminine form that emerges in the gap between textual and actual femininity. This form is not so much a submissive feminine *surface* as it is a space designated as female onto which different meanings can be imposed. What is problematic about this empty body, however, essentially concerns the associations that its designation as female potentially produces, associations that threaten to return the text to the literal reading that Petrarch has tried to eschew. Thus, Petrarch's final attempt to restrict the meaning of his Latin text once again draws attention to possible alternative readings of the story he has presented and, in so doing, suggests that his authority as the story's translator is based not on the "truth" of a textual body but on the exclusions that occur through processes of rhetorical clothing performed by male authors and readers.

V

Chaucer's rendering of the Griselda story, by contrast, does not so much change its garment as attempt to unravel the one that Petrarch has given it. The story as it is told in the *Canterbury Tales* has Petrarch's revised 1374 text as at least one of its primary sources, and makes a point of citing Petrarch's tale as the inspiration for the Clerk's own narrative.[26] The reference to the eminent Italian author in the *Clerk's Prologue* is by no means a straightforward acknowledgement of the tale's origins, however, for while the Clerk dutifully gives an account of the illustrious poet's literary merits, he begins his tale by reciting, then discarding, a large section of poetic material from Petrarch's text which he deems to be irrelevant to his own narrative (39-55).[27] Thus, be-

fore the story even begins, the Clerk alerts his audience to the fact that what is being presented to them is no simple imitation of an eminent *auctor* but a critical translation of Petrarch's tale, a translation both situated in a respected tradition of clerical authority and prepared to challenge the text upon which it is based.

The Clerk's demonstration of his editorial skills is, of course, related to the Host's demands that his story, which is to be told in plain English, "that we may understonde what ye seye" (12-20), neither preach to nor bore its common listeners. By setting aside the "heigh stile" used in Petrarch's proem, the Clerk thus indicates that, while he still intends to tell a clerical tale, he is also prepared to adapt his material for his lay audience (see Scanlon 179-81). The style and language of the tale will henceforth no longer adapt it to a Latin-literate élite, but will reincorporate the popular listener that Petrarch's text excludes. The Clerk thus makes use of the literary process of translation to redefine both the text and the type of authorship that he represents. In this respect, the tale told by Chaucer's Clerk corresponds to Copeland's notion of "secondary translation": the literary source of the story is cited as the basis both for the appropriation of its authority and the reassertion of that authority in an alternative, vernacular form. Furthermore, this movement away from the authoritative Latin register of the Petrarchan text towards the English vernacular in which the *Clerk's Tale* is narrated marks at least two other significant shifts. First, the Clerk's story is—within the microcosmic framework of the *Canterbury Tales*—an oral rather than a literary "text" and is delivered to a mixed audience of both literate and unlettered pilgrims. Second, the Clerk's prefatory remarks also trace a geographical shift from Italy to England and thus from Italian humanism, with its foundations in the Italian city-states, to the clericalism of the English university. The framing of the Clerk's narrative thus reestablishes the boundaries of cultural authority in both geographical and ideological terms, implicitly claiming the English university (and the cleric who represents it) as the site upon which scholarly and worldly discourses might meet (see Ginsberg 261-68). This redefinition of textual authority has implications for a gendered notion of literary activity that I will come to in a moment. One of its more immediate consequences for the narrative itself is that it begins a process that not only remodels the tale for a lay public, but also works against the interpretation of the story encouraged in Petrarch's conclusion, an interpretation that excludes contemporary married women from the example that the text is supposed to set.

Unlike Petrarch, the Clerk actively encourages the listener to respond to the text as a story about wives, and repeatedly suggests the social and political interactions of men and women as a means of identifying with and interpreting the story.[28] In the first half of the tale, the

Clerk introduces this theme only twice: interrupting his narrative first to criticize the cruel treatment of wives endorsed by some men (456-62) and later to lament the immoderate cruelty of married men when they "fynde a pacient creature" on whom to experiment (622-23). The final sections of the tale, however, expand upon these tentative encouragements to see the tale as a comment on the interaction of married men and women by placing increased emphasis on the importance of gender as a filter for the story's meaning, thereby drawing out the complexity of the story when read in terms of a married audience. While Walter is pondering the extraordinary patience of his wife after the abduction of her children, for example, the Clerk invites his female listeners to respond directly to the marquis's treatment of her, asking them "if thise assayes myghte nat suffise?" and demanding to know what more a husband could do to prove Griselda's wifehood (*wyfhod*) and steadfastness (696-700). While repeatedly condemning Walter's cruelty, the Clerk also calls attention to the fact that Griselda's behavior is entirely as it should be, for "a wyf, as of hirself, nothing ne sholde/wille in effect, but as hir housbonde wolde" (715-21). The complex reading of the tale that the Clerk invites from his audience thus encourages them to evaluate the actions of the two protagonists by reference to their own concept of behavior within marriage and the expectations that they would usually apply to men and women inside that institution.[29] Not only is the listener thus encouraged to frame the text's literal meaning in terms of gender politics, he (or, in this case, she) is also asked to respond to male and female behavior in the text in terms of his (or her) own gender, giving the tale's meaning a dynamic relationship to gender difference in the fictional and nonfictional worlds outside it.

This reading strategy is reinforced in the representation of Griselda. As the above citations suggest, Griselda's status as a wife acquires a more literal significance in Chaucer's text than it is given in either Boccaccio's or Petrarch's narrative. Some of the ways in which this representational shift is achieved are illustrated in Chaucer's treatment of Griselda's rejection by her husband and her exile from the court, when a number of additions to Petrarch's text seamlessly transform her from maid into "trewe wyf." Petrarch's attempt to offset the attention paid to Griselda's sexual and maternal body with her claim to spiritual maidenhood in this scene is entirely erased from the *Clerk's Tale*. The Chaucerian Griselda fails to mention her spiritual virginity and, moreover, alludes no fewer than three times to the physical "maydenhede" that she has given to Walter in their marriage. Whereas Petrarch's only reference to Griselda's virginity in this episode is related to her request for a shift to cover her body as she leaves the court, in Chaucer's version, Griselda's maidenhood is traded in for a smock.[30] Furthermore, Griselda's virginity is also emphasized as one of the three things (along

with "feith and nakednesse") that she originally brings to her marriage (865-66)[31] and as evidence of her continuing legitimacy as Walter's "trewe wyf" (837-38).[32]

The counter-reading of the Petrarchan Griselda that the Clerk's narration encourages is taken a stage further in his closing remarks. Although he translates Petrarch's conclusion almost word for word, the Clerk distances himself from Petrarch's gloss by pointing out that this reading of the story pertains to the text of his predecessor. The humanist interpretation endorsed by Petrarch, which would erase the exemplary value of Griselda's humility for married women, is prefaced in the Clerk's conclusion by a demand that his audience "herkneth to what *this auctour* seith" (1141, emphasis added) and followed by a reminder that "therefore Petrak writeth/ this storie, which with heigh stile he enditeth" (1147-48). The Clerk's presentation of Petrarch's gloss thus establishes a distance between the Clerk's narrative and the meaning associated with its literary source that allows, and ostensibly invites, a critical comparison of the revised, vernacular narrative with the authorial meaning that Petrarch gives his Latin tale. Having bound Griselda's virtue to her status as a wife in his telling of the story, the Clerk's translation of Petrarch's reading (which, as mentioned before, attempts to separate Griselda's spiritual qualities from her mundane, female roles) inevitably amplifies the problems inherent in the conclusion of his source. Indeed, the awkwardness of applying Petrarch's reading to the Clerk's Griselda is made even more apparent by its obvious contravention of the Host's request for a narrative that neither preaches to nor confuses its audience with its use of "heigh stile." Petrarch's gloss not only sits uncomfortably with the Clerk's representation of Griselda, it also clashes with the formal and stylistic criteria that the Clerk's story is supposed to meet in the context of the storytelling competition.

The comments the Clerk makes after citing Petrarch's conclusion substantially revise Petrarch's meaning. Like Petrarch, the Clerk confirms the impossibility of applying Griselda's example to contemporary women, but he uses this not as a means of marginalizing his female audience but as a step towards offering them an alternative example to follow. Far from condemning those women who fail to live up to the standard of patient endurance set by his female protagonist, Chaucer's Clerk seems positively to endorse their rejection of masculine authority. Griselda's example is set aside as an unrealistic aspiration for contemporary married women, and the ideal that she represents is superseded by an altogether different paradigm of female behavior, a paradigm inspired by the Wife of Bath and her "secte" of domineering women (1170-72).

The Clerk thus adapts his source text in a way that challenges the gender-exclusive meaning suggested by Petrarch and, as if to underline this tension, encourages his audience towards a response to the story that ultimately makes wives the central focus of the text's example. This new model of female behavior is celebrated in a song to the Wife of Bath and women like her in the very last section of the *Clerk's Tale*: the "envoy de Chaucer." The envoy begins by killing off Petrarch's heroine once and for all by announcing that "Grisilde is deed, and eek is hir pacience" (1177)—both apparently now buried in Italy. Griselda's death directly precedes an incitement to all female listeners to react against the example that she sets, telling "archewyves" never to give clerks occasion to write any more such tales of patient married women (1185-87). This invitation to resist masculine repression in both its political and its literary forms is immediately followed by a catalogue of pieces of advice instructing women to antagonize, dominate, and verbally abuse their menfolk.[33]

The model of female behavior that replaces Griselda's patience and humility quite obviously derives much of its inspiration from the images of garrulous and domineering women described in the writings of clerical misogyny. But it would be a mistake to view this as merely the replacement of an unattainable passive femininity with a misogynist counter-representation of female behavior. While the envoy certainly makes ironic allusion to this kind of clerical stereotyping, what is being represented here is in fact more complex than a simple transition between definitions of the feminine. What is being parodied is not only feminine identity as it is variously constructed through texts but also the process of translation that makes that construction possible in both its literary and non-literary forms, a process at the very heart of the antifeminist trope.

What is particularly significant about the model of female behavior with which the envoy confronts us is that it both addresses itself explicitly to a female audience and also invites their participation in the creation of the text's meaning as a comic *exemplum*. In inviting his female listeners to "emprenteth wel" in their minds the behavioral paradigm that he represents in his envoy (1193), Chaucer underlines the fact that it is only in shaping the activity of women outside the text that the model he proposes can be effective as an example of feminine conduct. Moreover, this participation is invited on the understanding that women submit themselves to a textual model that confirms certain negative stereotypes of them, a submission that, while supposedly contesting male authority, in fact serves to reinforce it. In undermining Petrarch's text through translation, the Clerk (and Chaucer) thus establish another form of male, clerical authority that includes women in the text by insisting that they both acknowledge the negative representations of themselves by male authors and reproduce those stereotypes through their own behavior. What is created in the *Clerk's Tale* is a textual model that would justify and confirm (in a less problematic way than would the example of Griselda) the assertion of masculine control over both the feminine surfaces of texts and the female bodies ostensibly located within and outside them.

VI

By way of my own envoy, I would like to return to Butler's concept of cultural translation as a discursive strategy with subversive political potential. As I have argued, in the different versions of the Griselda story by Boccaccio, Petrarch, and Chaucer the representation of the feminine and the various ways it is defined and interpreted as body and as text is consistently presented as being somehow at issue. What all of the translations I have considered suggest—in more or less explicit and self-conscious ways—is that gender, or more specifically the gendered identities of bodies as they are produced through texts, is, as Butler suggests, a matter of repeated performance. The gender of the text, and of the bodies interpellated by the text, is, in all of these narratives, established, disrupted, and re-established as it is constantly rearticulated through processes of translation.[34] Moreover, these processes often expose the constructed, repetitious nature of the gendered textual identities that they appropriate through their different re-presentations of those identities.

As will perhaps already be clear from my reading of Chaucer, it is in the *Clerk's Tale* that the translation process comes closest to reproducing Butler's concept of a form of performative re-presentation that can parody and thereby expose the discourse it appropriates. Yet, as I have suggested, Chaucer's re-writing of Petrarch's text only disrupts *certain kinds* of authority; it ultimately fails to stage a serious critique of the gender politics implicit in authorship itself and in fact reproduces the clerical authority it undermines in a different—albeit parodic—form. I am not of course suggesting that Chaucer should be expected to produce such a critique, nor do I wish to imply that Chaucer was a fourteenth-century feminist manqué. What Chaucer's text does manage to achieve is to illustrate more explicitly and more self-consciously than either Boccaccio's or Petrarch's versions the exclusion of what might be termed "real" politics—especially gender politics—from the text.[35] In addition to the fact that the Chaucerian text presents us with a model for female conduct that combines numerous negative stereotypes of female behavior, the "real" woman who ultimately provides the focus for the text's example is Chaucer's own fictional creation: the Wife of Bath.

This is of course part of Butler's point: translation *can* but does not *have to* disrupt the authority it cites. Indeed, more often than not, it merely appropriates and re-establishes that authority in an alternative form.[36] This raises many questions concerning the possible difficulties of using this concept of translation as the foundation for a philosophy of political resistance. On a more local level, however, it also cautions against making certain kinds of claims about the disruptive potential of medieval texts. This is not a criticism levelled at anachronism; rather, it concerns the nature of critical terminology. As much work on the carnivalesque has shown, readings of medieval texts as "subversive" cannot afford to overlook the precise sense in which this term is meant, nor the extent to which it forms part of a broader rearticulation of authority.[37] Indeed, this is something to bear in mind not only when approaching medieval texts, but also when considering the role of critical discourse in interpreting those texts. For, in the sense that these critical readings produce their own versions of medieval narratives, they too participate in an ongoing translation process with its own investment in interpreting, authorizing, and re-authorizing these texts.

Notes

1. I am immensely grateful to all those who have read and commented on this article in its various forms, including the anonymous reader for *Comparative Literature*. Special thanks go to Catherine Batt, Janet Cowen, Simon Gaunt, and Bob Mills. I would also like to thank Catherine Keen, whose comments on the *Decameron* and help with the Old Italian were invaluable.

2. Quoted from the edition of the Latin text in Severs 290-92. Translations are taken from *Francis Petrarch: Letters of Old Age* 2:655-71.

3. My reasons for assuming that the tale is characterized as a feminine object by Petrarch will become clearer in the course of this article. It is nonetheless worth pointing out at this stage that the gender of *historia*—or story—in Latin would mean that it would be thought of, at least in grammatical (and allegorical) terms, as feminine.

4. In late medieval descriptions of literary activity it is often the case that reading and writing are described as gendered, and even as sexually charged, experiences. In the thirteenth-century *Roman de la Rose,* for example, Genius encourages men to propagate the species by using their styluses to write on the tablets that Nature has prepared for them. Richard of Bury's *Philobiblion* (circa 1345) similarly describes the textual encounter in sexualized terms, using metaphors of unveiling to convey the experience of textual exegesis and to warn against the dangerous seductions of the text. This presentation of exegetical experience as a process of uncovering with sinful erotic potential points to a conception of the text that is echoed widely elsewhere in medieval literature, where the use of clothing metaphors to describe the process of representation has a long history. Authors such as

Macrobius depict Nature clothing herself in mysterious representations in order that she may only have to reveal herself to prudent, learned individuals. In less learned traditions, texts ranging from the romances of Chrétien de Troyes to the fabliaux often draw upon similarities between language and clothing, both of which are thought to cover—often inadequately—what is conceived to be the naked body of Nature or Truth. See Genius's speech (ll. 19509-19692) in Jean de Meun's and Guillaume de Lorris's *Le Roman de la Rose.* For discussions of medieval concepts of textuality in connection with the themes of gender and/or undressing see R. Howard Bloch's discussion of clothing metaphors in the fabliaux in *The Scandal of the Fabliaux* (Chicago: University of Chicago Press, 1986. 22-58); and the introduction to Dinshaw's *Chaucer's Sexual Poetics* (esp. 18-25).

5. I disagree with Morse's suggestion that modern readers find Griselda's exemplary status problematic in a way that is not reflected in medieval readings of the tale; indeed, I believe that Morse unintentionally gives ample evidence for my disagreement in her own article. See "The Exemplary Griselda" 51-86.

6. I would not therefore agree with readings that assert a single medieval mentality (as opposed to a modern deconstructionist one) that viewed the depiction of Griselda's relationship to power as unproblematic. Many of these readings rely heavily on religious or moral analogues for Griselda, thereby overlooking some of the more troubling implications of this reading in the work of different authors. I have already mentioned Morse's article on "The Exemplary Griselda" in this context. See also Victoria Kirkham's reading of Boccaccio's—and, implicitly, Petrarch's—version of the story.

7. Gail Ashton suggests that this paradox has subversive potential in Chaucer's version of the story: Griselda's perfect mimicry of idealized femininity produces, claims Ashton, a transgressive model of female behavior. Elaine Tuttle Hansen has also suggested that Griselda is a figure of resistance through her passive subversion of masculine oppression. As will be clear from my own argument, I agree with these readings only up to a point, yet they nonetheless emphasize what I consider to be the central paradox of the story. See Ashton and Hansen.

8. Philippe de Mézières and the compiler of the *Ménagier de Paris* address the story to women. The tale also appears in the *Livre du chevalier de la Tour Landry pour l'enseignement de ses filles,*

another text that gives the story an implicit educational value for women. See Morse's discussion of these translations in "The Exemplary Griselda," 74-83.

9. An exhaustive survey of this literature would be impossible. However, Butler's influence on critical thinking about medieval gender is evident in a number of recent interdisciplinary essay collections: *Constructing Medieval Sexuality,* ed. Karma Lochrie, Peggy McCracken, and James A. Schulz; *Becoming Male in the Middle Ages,* ed. Jeffrey Jerome Cohen and Bonnie Wheeler; *Premodern Sexualities,* ed. Louise Fradenburg and Carla Freccero; *Medieval Masculinities: Regarding Men in the Middle Ages,* ed. Clare A. Lees.

10. Butler's later book, *Bodies that Matter,* engages with and responds to misreadings of *Gender Trouble* in some detail. Both her preface and introduction to this later work explicitly address her disagreement with traditional feminist accounts of constructivism. See esp. ix-xii and 1-23.

11. Butler's argument might be compared to Derrida's critique of logocentrism. Derrida's point would be that the immediated presence to consciousness of being which logocentrism represents is not originary; what *is* originary is alienation from presence (an alienation that Derrida associates with *différance*). See Christina Howells's discussion of these points (esp. 43-95).

12. No literary source has been found for Dioneo's tale. Petrarch, however, implies that Boccaccio's story drew upon Italian popular tradition, and the tale has been found to have analogies with the Cupid-Psyche motif elaborated in Apuleius's *Golden Ass.* See the detailed footnote of Vittore Branca in his edition of the *Decameron,* note 5, 643-44. See also Lee 348-56.

13. See Stone, *The Ethics of Nature in the Middle Ages: On Boccaccio's Poetaphysics.* Some of the conclusions presented in the final chapter of this book are, however, problematic.

14. All quotations of Boccaccio's text are from Branca's edition of the *Decameron.* Translations of quotations have been taken (with some modifications) from *The Decameron,* ed. and trans. G.H. McWilliam.

15. Dioneo's definition of Gualtieri's behavior as "matta bestialitade" associates Gualtieri's conduct with an important Aristotlean/Dantean category of vice. See Haines 233-40; and Mazzotta, *The World at Play* 126-28.

16. We are told that Griselda seems a different woman after her marriage—both in customs and in spirit—and that this is concomitant with her change of attire: "la giovane sposa parve che co' vestimenti insieme l'animo e i costumi mutasse" ("10. 10, 24").

17. "Comandatemi che io quella dote me ne porti che io ci recai: alla qual cosa fare né a voi pagator né a me borsa bisognerà né somiere, per ciò che di mente uscito non m'è che ignuda m'aveste" ("10. 10, 45") ("As to your ordering me to take away the dowry that I brought, you will require no accountant, nor will I need a purse or a pack-horse for this to be done. For it has not escaped my memory that you took me naked as on the day I was born"). This speech echoes the words of Job (Job 1, 21).

18. This may be further complicated by the fact that Gualtieri is also declared a wise man (*molto savio*) at the very beginning of the tale, where the remark refers to the marquis's indifference towards marriage ("10. 10, 4").

19. As Guiseppe Mazzotta has indicated, the use of the phrase "scuotere il pelliccione" echoes an earlier reference to "il pilliccion ti scotesse" in the comic tale that Dioneo tells on day four, where the wife of a physician and her maidservant successfully collaborate to conceal an affair involving the wife and her lover. Dioneo's comment thus implicitly alludes to a female character in a story with an altogether different, less virtuous outcome (*The World at Play* 129-30).

20. In Old Italian, *pelliccione* is a fur-trimmed cloak or gown (the modern Italian word for fur-coat is *pellicia*).

21. References to Petrarch's version of the story are taken from Severs's edition of the Latin text.

22. For examples of this kind of literature see the Lives of St. Agnes and St. Margaret in Denomy and Hahn.

23. As Ginsburg suggests, the emphasis of the imitability of Griselda's constancy (as opposed to her patience, which is inimitable) is deliberate: Griselda's patience relies upon a vow to her husband that implicitly removes her subsequent freedom of choice, whereas her constancy represents a repeated affirmation of her vow over time. Petrarch's emphasis on constancy—as the continual affirmation of moral choice and exercise of individual will—would seem more in keeping with humanist values. Ginsberg nonetheless downplays the fact that Petrarch's statement concerning the inimitability of patience is directed particularly at contemporary wives (256-57).

24. The identification of Griselda with the soul would not necessarily have involved suppressing her gender altogether, as the soul was sometimes thought

of as female in the later Middle Ages. (Though this view is being increasingly challenged by medievalists.) Indeed, my point here is not that Petrarch denies Griselda's femininity but rather that he suppresses the physical aspects of her gender by reconceptualizing it in terms of the spirit. See Bynum 165-70. For a reading that challenges this view see Mills.

25. The corpus of female saints' lives has recently been the subject of a great deal of attention from scholars working on medieval concepts of the body and on women's history. Recent examples of work of this kind on Middle English and/or Anglo-Norman material include Wogan-Browne, "The Virgin's Tale" and *Saints' Lives*; Salih; Winstead; Schulenburg; and Delany.

26. Chaucer's translation was most probably also based upon at least one of the French translations of Petrarch's version. See Severs, and also Farrell and Goodwin.

27. References to the *Clerk's Prologue* and the *Clerk's Tale* have been taken from *The Riverside Chaucer.* Line numbers are cited as they appear in this edition.

28. Elizabeth Salter, on the other hand, argues that the *Clerk's Tale* creates a more pathetic, spiritualized heroine than Petrarch's (37-65). Salter also claims that, through its ironic emphasis of the exemplarity of women like Chaucer's Wife, the envoy succeeds in making the supposedly unattainable perfection of Griselda seem "a more acceptable, less preposterous creation than the Wife of Bath and 'archewyves' of her kind" (65). Although I would agree that Chaucer's version retains, and even augments, many of the spiritual aspects of Petrarch's heroine, this must, I think, be seen alongside the emphasis on her qualities as a wife.

29. This is an approach to narrative interpretation often associated with the Host, who repeatedly brings the figurative to bear on his own married circumstances. See, for example, the Host's words after Chaucer's tale of Melibee (*Riverside Chaucer* 240-41).

30. It is also worth noting that, in Petrarch's tale, this reference to Griselda's virginity marks an exchange that effectively severs her physical and psychological ties to her husband, one that results in her description of herself to Valterius as "your former (*quondam*) wife" (17. 5, 35).

31. Petrarch only mentions faith and nakedness (*fides et nuditas*) in his reference to Griselda's "dowry" (17. 5, 22-26).

32. This re-introduces some of the spirit of the Boccaccian original; however, Chaucer (the Clerk) is even more emphatic than Boccaccio (Dioneo) in stressing the physicality of Griselda's virginity and its relationship to her marriage. Although it is unclear whether Chaucer was in possession of the Boccaccian text as he was writing the *Canterbury Tales,* the similarities are nonetheless striking.

33. A possible intertext here is Ovid's *Amores,* which makes similar use of misogynist stereotyping. Those episodes in which a young female character receives a series of pieces of advice from her old nurse instructing her how to exploit her lovers and generally abuse men seem especially pertinent. This Ovidian material also influenced the depiction of La Viclle in the *Roman de la Rose.*

34. My use of the notion of interpellation is based upon Althusser's concept of the term, a concept that has been taken up elsewhere in Butler's work. Althusser's theory is based upon the idea that the subject, as it is constituted by language, is called into being when it recognizes itself in the discourse that represents it (a form of recognition that is also therefore a misrecognition). Interpellation itself is the call to being to which the subject responds; it is the representation of the subject that invites that subject to constitute itself within language. My point is therefore that the texts I have discussed perform similar maneuvers in constructing and reconstructing bodies that enable the Althusserian call to be articulated in different ways (a call that is arguably a part of the didactic/exemplary function itself). See Althusser 67-126. See also Butler's explanation (and critique) of this theory in *The Psychic Life of Power* 106-31.

35. Although my reading of the *Clerk's Tale* differs from that of Dinshaw, she similarly points out that the subversive qualities of Chaucer's narrative should be considered in textual rather than political terms. However, some other readings have been less clear in this respect. See, for example, Ashton and Tuttle Hansen.

36. This is also a point that Butler makes in relation to her theory of gender performance: "Parody by itself is not subversive, and there must be a way to understand what makes certain kinds of parodic repetitions effectively disruptive, truly troubling, and which repetitions become domesticated and rearticulated as instruments of cultural hegemony" (*Gender Trouble* 176-77). See also Copeland, esp. 221-29.

37. The ambivalence of the carnivalesque as a force that has no specific oppositional function is emphasized by Mikhail Bakhtin in his canonical work on carnival in the work of Rabelais; see *Rabelais and His World.*

Works Cited

Althusser, Louis. "Idéologie et appareils idéologiques d'état." *Positions.* Paris: Éditions Sociales, 1976. 67-126.

Ashton, Gayle. "Patient Mimesis: Griselda and the *Clerk's Tale.*" *The Chaucer Review* 32 (1998): 232-38.

Bakhtin, Mikhail. *Rabelais and His World.* Trans. Hélène Iswolsky. Bloomington: Indiana University Press, 1984.

Bloch, R. Howard. *The Scandal of the Fabliaux.* Chicago: University of Chicago Press, 1986.

Boccaccio, Giovanni. *Decameron.* Ed. Vittore Branca. 2 vols. Florence: Felice le Monnier, 1960.

———. *The Decameron.* Ed. and trans. G.H. McWilliam. 2nd ed. Harmondsworth: Penguin Books, 1995.

Butler, Judith. *Bodies that Matter: On the Discursive Limits of 'Sex.'* New York: Routledge, 1993.

———. *Gender Trouble: Feminism and the Subversion of Identity.* New York: Routledge, 1990.

———. *The Psychic Life of Power: Theories in Subjection.* Stanford: Stanford University Press, 1997.

———. "Restaging the Universal: Hegemony and the Limits of Formalism." Judith Butler, Ernesto Laclau, and Slavoj Žižek. *Contingency, Hegemony, Universality: Contemporary Dialogues on the Left.* London: Verso, 2000. 11-43.

Bynum, Caroline Walker. *Fragmentation and Redemption: Essays on Gender and the Human Body in Medieval Religion.* New York: Zone Books, 1992.

Chaucer, Geoffrey. *The Riverside Chaucer.* Ed. L.D. Benson. Oxford: Oxford University Press, 1988.

Cohen, Jeffrey Jerome, and Bonnie Wheeler, eds. *Becoming Male in the Middle Ages.* London: Garland Publishing, 1997.

Copeland, Rita. *Rhetoric, Hermeneutics, and Translation in the Middle Ages: Academic Traditions and Vernacular Texts.* Cambridge: Cambridge University Press, 1991.

Delany, Sheila. *Impolitic Bodies: Poetry, Saints, and Society in Fifteenth-Century England, the Work of Osbern Bokenham.* New York: Oxford University Press, 1998.

Denomy, A. Joseph, ed. *The Old French Lives of Saint Agnes and Other Vernacular Versions of the Middle Ages.* Cambridge, MA: Harvard University Press, 1938.

Dinshaw, Carolyn. *Chaucer's Sexual Poetics.* Wisconsin: University of Wisconsin Press, 1989.

Farrell, Thomas J., and Amy W. Goodwin. "The 'Clerk's Tale.'" *Sources and Analogues of the "Canterbury Tales."* Cambridge: D.S. Brewer, 2002. 101-53.

Fradenburg, Louise, and Carla Freccero, eds. *Premodern Sexualities.* London: Routledge, 1996.

Ginsberg, Warren. *Chaucer's Italian Tradition.* Ann Arbor: University of Michigan Press, 2002.

Hahn, Cynthia, ed. *Passio Kiliani, Ps. Theotimus, Passio Margaretae, Orationes.* Graz, Aus.: Akademische Druck-U. Verlangsanstalt, 1988.

Haines, Charles. "Patient Griselda and Matta Bestialitade." *Quaderni d'Italianistica: Official Journal of the Canadian Society for Italian Studies* 6 (1985): 233-40.

Hansen, Elaine Tuttle. *Chaucer and the Fictions of Gender.* Berkeley: University of California Press, 1992.

Harding, Wendy. "Griselda's 'Translation' in the *Clerk's Tale.*" *The Medieval Translator, Traduire au Moyen Age.* Vol. 6. Ed. Roger Ellis, René Tixier, and Bernd Weitmeier. Turnhout: Brepols, 1998. 194-210.

Howells, Christina. *Derrida: Deconstruction from Phenomenology to Ethics.* Cambridge: Polity Press, 1998.

Johnson, Lesley. "Reincarnations of Griselda: Contexts for the *Clerk's Tale?*" *Feminist Readings in Middle English Literature: The Wife of Bath and All Her Sect.* Ed. Ruth Evans and Lesley Johnson. London: Routledge, 1994. 195-220.

Kirkham, Victoria. "The Last Tale in the *Decameron.*" *Mediaevalia* 12 (1989 for 1986): 205-38.

Lee, A.C. *The "Decameron": Its Sources and Analogues.* London: David Nutt, 1909.

Lees, Clare A., ed. *Medieval Masculinities: Regarding Men in the Middle Ages.* Minneapolis: University of Minnesota Press, 1994.

Lochrie, Karma, Peggy McCracken, and James A. Schulz, eds. *Constructing Medieval Sexuality. Medieval Cultures Series* 11. Minneapolis: University of Minnesota Press, 1997.

Mazzotta, Guiseppe. *The World at Play in Boccaccio's "Decameron."* Princeton: Princeton University Press, 1986.

———. *The Worlds of Petrarch.* Durham, NC: Duke University Press, 1993.

de Meun, Jean, and Guillaume de Lorris. *Le Roman de la Rose.* Ed. Armand Strubel. Paris: Livre de Poche, 1992.

Millett, Bella, and Jocelyn Wogan-Browne, eds. *Medieval English Prose for Women: Selections from the Katherine Group and "Ancrene Wisse."* Oxford: Clarendon Press, 1990.

Mills, Robert. "Ecce Homo." *Gender and Holiness: Men, Women, and Saints in Late Medieval Europe.* Ed. Samantha J. Riches and Sarah Salih. London: Routledge, 2002. 152-73.

Morse, Charlotte. "The Exemplary Griselda." *Studies in the Age of Chaucer* 7 (1985): 51-86.

———. "Critical Approaches to the *Clerk's Tale.*" *Chaucer's Religious Tales.* Ed. C. David Benson and Elizabeth Robertson. Cambridge: D.S. Brewer, 1990. 72-83.

Petrarch, Francis. *Francis Petrarch: Letters of Old Age: Rerum senilium libri, I-XVII.* Vol 2. Trans. A.S. Bernardo, S. Levin, and R.A. Bernardo. Baltimore: The Johns Hopkins University Press, 1992.

Salih, Sarah. *Versions of Virginity in Late Medieval England.* Cambridge: D.S. Brewer, 2001.

Salter, Elizabeth. *Chaucer: The "Knight's Tale" and the "Clerk's Tale."* London: Edward Arnold, 1962.

Scanlon, Larry. *Narrative, Authority, and Power: The Medieval Exemplum and the Chaucerian Tradition.* Cambridge: Cambridge University Press, 1994.

Schulenburg, Jane Tibbetts. *Forgetful of Their Sex: Female Sanctity and Society ca. 500-1100.* Chicago: University of Chicago Press, 1998.

Severs, J. Burke. *The Literary Relationships of Chaucer's "Clerkes Tale."* New Haven: Yale University Press, 1942.

Stone, Gregory B. *The Ethics of Nature in the Middle Ages: On Boccaccio's Poetaphysics.* Basingstoke: Macmillan Press, 1998.

Wallace, David. "'Whan She Translated Was': A Chaucerian Critique of the Petrarchan Academy." *Literary Practice and Social Change in Britain, 1380-1530.* Ed. Lee Patterson. Berkeley: University of California Press, 1990. 156-215.

Winstead, Karen A. *Virgin Martyrs: Legends of Sainthood in Late Medieval England.* Ithaca: Cornell University Press, 1997.

Wogan-Browne, Jocelyn. *Saints' Lives and Women's Literary Culture c.1150-1300: Virginity and its Authorisations.* Oxford: Oxford University Press, 2001.

———. "The Virgin's Tale." *Feminist Readings in Middle English Literature: The Wife of Bath and All Her Sect.* Ed. Ruth Evans and Lesley Johnson. London: Routledge, 1994. 165-94.

Thomas J. Farrell (essay date 2003)

SOURCE: Farrell, Thomas J. "Source or Hard Analogue? *Decameron* X, 10 and the *Clerk's Tale.*" *Chaucer Review* 37, no. 4 (2003): 346-64.

[*In the following essay, Farrell demonstrates the extent to which the final* novella *of the* Decameron *influenced Geoffrey Chaucer's* Clerk's Tale, *clarifying a number of possible philological relationships.*]

In the absence of authoritative external definitions of the word *source* as it is used by literary scholars, Chaucerians have largely had to create their own. Surprisingly, the *Oxford English Dictionary* contains no specifically literary sense of the word. Even the definition that comes closest to being useful for philological study—'A work, etc., supplying information or evidence (esp. of an original or primary character) as to some fact, event, or series of these'—cites people as sources more often than texts, and so diminishes its value in any text-based study.[1] The situation is only somewhat better in other traditional reference works. *A Handbook to Literature* is perhaps the most helpful: its initial, *OED*-like 'The person, manuscript, or book from which something is derived' is elaborated by a later distinction between a Primary source and a Secondary source: the former 'represents a direct and immediate acquaintance with the information' contained in the source, and the latter an 'indirect acquaintance.'[2] Such sources could still be people, but the distinction between primary and secondary sources seems promising in its ability to distinguish various degrees and perhaps kinds of importance that a text might have to a composing author. But the imprecision of words like *represents* and *acquaintance* still leaves obvious shortcomings for those interested in source study: not every work with which an author is acquainted is meaningful as a source.[3] In more recent reference works, the concept of a source in that sense is likely to disappear entirely: the term *source* does not make the cut for inclusion in *Critical Terms for Literary Study,* implicitly being replaced by Louis A. Renza's essentially Bloomian essay on "Influence."[4]

W. F. Bryan and Germaine Dempster's original *Sources and Analogues of Chaucer's Canterbury Tales,* published in 1941, did not entirely resolve these uncertainties. In the introduction to that volume, Bryan specified that only written texts available to Chaucer should be sought as sources:

> The purpose is to present in so far as possible the sources of the *Canterbury Tales* as Chaucer knew these sources or, where direct sources are not now known, to present the closest known analogues in the form in which Chaucer presumably may have been acquainted with them.[5]

Some form of 'direct acquaintance' is confirmed in this definition of a source, but imprecision remains. Bryan does not clarify under what conditions we might presume that Chaucer was acquainted with an analogue, and most of his contributors reserve the term *analogue* for works that Chaucer did not know.[6]

More progress is evident in the work done by the contributors to the first volume of the current *Sources and Analogues of the Canterbury Tales,* edited by Robert M. Correale and Mary Hamel, whose labor evinces a consistent, viable, and rigorous—albeit everywhere implicit—definition of *source*.[7] Even before its publication, moreover, one contributor articulated explicitly and formally a set of definitions that expresses the consensus achieved by those working on *Sources and Analogues*. My first goal in this essay is therefore to substantiate and confirm that consensus definition of *source*. Using it, I will then have a firm basis for turning to the recently revisited question of whether Boccaccio's **Decameron "X, 10"** provided a source for the *Clerk's Tale*.

The introductions to the individual chapters in *Sources and Analogues* build on its predecessor's conviction that a source will tell us something about the text Chaucer worked from. Robert R. Edwards suggests that if Chaucer "did not have a copy of the text at hand," it would "not [be] a direct source" (*SA* [*Sources and Analogues of the Canterbury Tales*], 214) of the *Franklin's Tale*: for him, a direct source requires a "direct and immediate acquaintance" with the text under consideration, and the simplest way to imagine such an acquaintance is in the form of a manuscript in front of Chaucer as he wrote. In discussing the possible sources of the *Pardoner's Prologue*, Mary Hamel uses similar language: "the most appropriate text to demonstrate Chaucer's source may well be that of the C-fragment of the Middle English *Romaunt of the Rose*, which exemplifies the kind of text Chaucer most likely had access to" (*SA*, 269).

When John Finlayson recently proposed that **Decameron "X, 10"** is a source for the *Clerk's Tale*, he also apparently used the word in the same sense.[8] Finlayson begins his argument with the claim that Chaucer, having learned about Boccaccio's *novella* from the opening "Librum tuum" section of Petrarch's *Epistolae Seniles* XVII.3, would surely have sought out a copy of the Italian text.[9] He would therefore have had a copy of **Decameron "X, 10"** alongside his Petrarch and his French *Livre Griseldis*. Finlayson is probably right that Chaucer knew the "Librum tuum" section of Petrarch's letter—it is printed in *Sources and Analogues* from Cambridge, Peterhouse MS 81 because the vast majority of manuscripts do include it—but his claim that "All the fourteenth- and fifteenth-century manuscripts of Petrarch's tale have this preface" is simply and importantly wrong.[10] In the separate study that substantiated the conclusions first published in Bryan and Dempster, J. Burke Severs lists five such manuscripts that lack the "Librum tuum," and two others that have radically abbreviated it.[11] Among the manuscripts lacking the "Librum tuum" is Corpus Christi College (Cambridge) MS 275, whose variant readings connect it more closely than any other manuscript thus far collated to the glosses from Chaucer's manuscript copied in the margins of Hengwrt and Ellesmere.[12] None of these facts, however, diminishes the evidence that, whether Chau-

cer read the "Librum tuum" or not, he is likely to have known of the **Decameron**.[13]

In constructing his theory of how Chaucer came to write the *Clerk's Tale*, Finlayson also (but clearly inadvertently) raises another possible criterion in the definition of a source. To support his belief in Chaucer's familiarity with the **Decameron**, he cites several other scholars with similar views. Specifically, N. S. Thompson has argued that we may assume "stronger connections than have previously been thought" between the **Decameron** and the *Canterbury Tales*.[14] Finlayson finds this a tepid conclusion: "What exactly a stronger connection that is *not* an acceptance of Chaucer's knowledge and use of the **Decameron** might be is not clear."[15] But there are possible connections short of "knowledge and use." In the same "Librum tuum" section of *Seniles* XVII.3 that Finlayson used to argue for Chaucerian knowledge of the Boccaccian text, Petrarch himself suggests that, although he knew about the **Decameron**, his knowledge was in many ways superficial:

> [Excucurri] eum, et festini viatoris in morem, hinc atque hinc circumspiciens, nec subsistens. . . . Inter multa sane iocosa et levia, quedam pia et gravia deprehendi, de quibus tamen diffinitive quid iudicem non habeo, ut qui nusquam totus inheserim. At [quod] fere accidit eo more currentibus, curiosius aliquanto quam cetera libri principium finemque perspexi.

> I skimmed through the book like a hurried tourist, glancing here and there, but not stopping. . . . Among many stories which are, to be sure, amusing and slight, a few more pious and serious ones caught my attention. But even about those I have no definitive opinion, for nowhere did I read carefully all the way through. Like most such skimmers, I considered the beginning and end of the book more closely than the rest.[16]

This kind of knowledge of a text could hardly be the basis for a poet's use of it. Before he begins to retell the Griselda story, however, Petrarch demonstrates a much deeper familiarity with, even study of, that narrative:

> In altero autem historiam ultimam et multis [precedencium] longe dissimilem posuisti, que ita michi placuit meque detinuit ut, inter tot curas pene mei ipsius que immemorem me [fecere], illam memorie mandare voluerim, ut et ipse eam animo quociens vellem non sine voluptate repeterem, et amicis ut fit [confabulantibus] renarrarem.

> But at the other end you have placed last—and in great contrast to much of what precedes it—a story that so pleased and engaged me that, amid enough duties to make me almost forget myself, I wanted to memorize it, so that I might recall its pleasures as often as I wished and retell it in conversation with my friends, as the opportunity might arise.

(*SA*, 108-11)

Similarly, many of the contributors to *Sources and Analogues* assert a distinction between the memory of a text read, perhaps years before—in Finlayson's terms a text Chaucer *knew*—and a written text in front of him as he wrote—a text Chaucer *used*. Often, that distinction is the criterion for establishing whether a given work is a source. When Edwards argues that a text that Chaucer did not have at hand as he wrote the *Franklin's Tale* could therefore not be a direct source, he is arguing that the **Decameron** cannot be a direct source. While not discounting Chaucer's knowledge of the **Decameron,** Edwards prefers as a source the version of the same story in the *Filocolo* because its plot regularly tracks the *Franklin's Tale* more exactly, because it includes plot elements contained in Chaucer's tale but omitted from **Decameron "X, 5,"** and because it provides a closer parallel to the conclusion of the *Franklin's Tale (SA,* 214). In the same way, Sherry L. Reames, drawing on her own scholarship, lists as the two principle sources of the *Second Nun's Tale* two separate abridgments of the Latin *Passio S. Ceceliae,* the first of which "Chaucer closely followed for the etymology of Cecilia's name and approximately the first half of the narrative," and the second "from which Chaucer derived almost everything from line 349 to the end of the tale" *(SA,* 494). Again, Edward Wheatley cites the arguments that Robert Pratt made about the debt of the *Nun's Priest's Tale* to the *Roman de Renart* and *Renart le Contrefait* by "listing the verbal parallels between the Old French and Middle English texts" *(SA,* 450-51). In all of these cases, we can cite the precise translations that demonstrate Chaucer's use of a specific source.[17]

There are, however, several cases where no substantial verbal parallels like those in the *Second Nun's Tale* identify the text or texts that Chaucer used as a source. In those cases, and even in the absence of such verbal echoes, the scholars working on *Sources and Analogues* have found it possible to think of a remembered Boccaccian text as a source. Thus Helen Cooper thinks of the *General Prologue* as Chaucer's "elaboration of a model he recalled from the **Decameron**" (SA, 13) and Peter G. Beidler argues that we can best understand the particulars of the *Reeve's Tale* by imagining multiple influences: "Perhaps after having read or heard a number of these many versions of the cradle-trick story over the years, Chaucer drew upon his memory of several of them to fashion his own wonderful story" *(SA,* 26). Beidler argues that **Decameron "IX, 6"** is one of those versions and therefore "a source for certain features in [Chaucer's] cradle-trick tale that he could not have found in the French or Flemish analogues" *(SA,* 26). Cooper avoids the word *source,* but her thesis is that Chaucer was following the structure of the **Decameron** in a manner evidenced by "the kind of creative reinvention that would more plausibly come from thinking about Boccaccian ideas than from reworking his precise words" *(SA,* 9).[18]

Working inductively from these statements toward a definition, we may conclude that a source is necessarily a written text known by Chaucer, but that such knowledge is not sufficient to make a work a source. Clear verbal echoes are the best evidence that Chaucer used a copy of the text in his own process of composition. In the absence of such verbal echoes, influence on other verbal structures, like the plot similarities in the *Reeve's Tale* or the design similarities in the Canterbury frame, may be evidence of a source relationship.[19] In such cases, the number of incidents of possible influence is clearly crucial. Beidler calls Boccaccio a likely source for "certain features" of the *Reeve's Tale* largely because he can cite twelve plot elements shared by it only with the **Decameron,** but still considers the **Decameron** a source for those features rather than for the tale itself. In a similar vein, Peter Nicholson notes that "None of the three surviving examples is sufficiently like the *Friar's Tale* to have served as Chaucer's 'source,' nor can any be presumed to have been known to him directly" *(SA,* 92).[20] Consequently, Beidler prefers a different word for the whole structure: "none of the analogues—at least not in the forms that survive—can be said to represent 'the source' of Chaucer's tale" *(SA,* 23).

As I noted in my introduction, a clear and useful taxonomy of these textual relationships already exists. In "Just Say Yes, Chaucer Knew the *Decameron,*" Beidler proposes the following terminology for scholarly source study:

> *Source*: a work that we are sure that Chaucer knew, either because of external evidence or because of the closeness of narrative or verbal parallels. . . .
>
> *Hard analogue*: a work that would have been available to Chaucer and that bears certain striking resemblances, usually more narrative than verbal, to the Chaucerian work in question. A hard analogue can be said to have "near-source status" if it is old enough for Chaucer to have known it and if it gives closer parallels in plot or character than are available in other works Chaucer could have known, even if there are no or few specific language parallels. . . .
>
> *Soft analogue*: a work that, either because of its date or because of the remoteness of its specific parallels with the Chaucerian narrative in question, Chaucer could scarcely have known.[21]

Beidler develops these definitions in his argument about the antecedents of the *Shipman's Tale,* but their value extends beyond that context. The definition of a *source* articulates the criterion of verbal similarity that, in my argument, is evidence that Chaucer *used* a particular text. His novel category of *hard analogue* is distinguished by the criterion (whose value to scholars Finlayson's argument has also demonstrated) of Chaucerian *knowledge* of a text even where evidence of his *use* of that text is lacking. In brief, Beidler's terms provide both a cogent statement of Chaucer's possible relationships to other texts and a useful summary of the way that source scholars already use the words under discussion: a *source* is a text available to Chaucer as he wrote, a *hard analogue* is a text that Chaucer evidently knew but seems not to have used, and a *soft analogue* is a text that Chaucer did not know. Beidler has given us good definitions of useful terms, and we should all be adopting this usage, as I shall in the rest of this essay.

* * *

As I will demonstrate below, the resemblances between *Decameron* **"X, 10"** and the *Clerk's Tale* are both fewer and less substantial than those demonstrated by Beidler or Cooper to their texts. My conclusion is that, just as it was for the *Shipman's Tale,* the **Decameron** is thus appropriately classified as a hard analogue of the *Clerk's Tale.* But I do not mean that classification as a dismissal of either the Boccaccian text or the category of analogue, whose importance I will discuss in my conclusion.

Finlayson identifies "awkward similarities" between Boccaccio and Chaucer that lead him to conclude that many moments in the *Clerk's Tale* "can be seen to have a strong, often detailed relationship to Petrarch's own source, Boccaccio" and that Chaucer's text reveals what he calls "a return to elements of Boccaccio's version."[22] As evidence, he discusses four aspects of the Griselda fable: 1) the characterization of cruelty in the sergeant who acts as Walter's surrogate in the removal of the children; 2) the characterization of Walter himself; 3) the suffering endured by Griselda; and 4) the narrator's response to the story in each text.[23] Although Finlayson's evidence is new, this is not an entirely new approach to the question. Severs had listed six different correspondences between Boccaccio's and Chaucer's texts, cited from an old article by W. E. Farnham. Severs, believing that Chaucer did not know the **Decameron,** judged these correspondences, both individually and as a group, insufficiently pointed to overturn that belief. Finlayson, who already accepts Chaucerian knowledge of the **Decameron,** believes that his four correspondences prove that Chaucer was using the Boccaccian text. I agree with Finlayson that Chaucer knew the **Decameron,** but I want to modify his argument: the absence of verbal parallels in his correspondences will indicate that Chaucer did not *use* Boccaccio's text, and his knowledge without use makes that text a hard analogue rather than a source. I will consider each of the correspondences in turn.

Finlayson's argument about Chaucer's delineation of cruelty in the sergeant barely discusses Boccaccio for the simple reason that the *famigliare* who is the **Decameron**'s equivalent character shows no signs of cruelty and is rather obviously unrelated to the character that Chaucer has created:

Poco tempo appresso, avendo con parole generali detto alla moglie che i subiti non potevan patir quella fanciulla di lei nata, informato un suo famigliare, il mandò a lei, il quale con assai dolente viso le disse: «Madonna, se io non voglio morire, a me convien far quello che il mio signor mi comanda. Egli m'ha comandato che io prenda questa vostra figliuola e ch'io . . . » e non disse più.

A little while later, having told his wife in general terms that his subjects could not abide the daughter she had borne him, he gave certain instructions to one of his attendants, whom he sent to Griselda. The man looked very sorrowful, and said:

'My lady, if I do not wish to die, I must do as my lord commands me. He has ordered me to take this daughter of yours, and to . . .' And his voice trailed off into silence.[24]

On the occasion of the removal of the second child, the man is not even mentioned:

Dopo non molti dì Gualtieri, in quella medesima maniera che mandato aveva per la figliuola, mandò per lo figliuolo: e similmente dimostrato d'averlo fatto uccidere . . .

Before many days had elapsed, Gualtieri sent for his son in the same way that he had sent for his daughter, and having likewise pretended to have had the child put to death. . . .[25]

Finlayson himself demonstrates clearly enough how the notion of cruel actions introduced by Petrarch is elaborated in the anonymous French translation and in Chaucer into a character who is himself cruel, or at least perceived to be so. But it is quite clear that Chaucer was not using a text of Boccaccio in any of that development.[26]

When Finlayson turns to the development of Walter's character, the primary issue is the invocation of Walter's *pietas,* a significant change that Petrarch had introduced into Boccaccio's tale. In Boccaccio, Gualtieri is simply amazed at Griselda:

Il famigliare, presa la fanciulla e fatto a Gualtier sentire ciò che detto aveva la donna, maravigliandosi egli della sua constanzia, lui con essa ne mandò a Bologna.

The servant took away the little girl and reported Griselda's words to Gualtieri, who, marvelling at her constancy, sent him with the child to . . . Bologna.[27]

The workings of Gualtieri's own mind are not an issue here. Petrarch, in distinction, pauses over the moment, and his syntax focuses our attention on Walterus and the narrator's exploration of his character:

Reversus ad dominum, cum quid dictum quidve responsum esset exposuisset et ei filiam obtulisset, vehementer paterna animum pietas movit; susceptum tamen rigorem [propositi non] inflexit.

He returned to the marquis, explaining what he had said and what reply was made, and showed him the child. A father's devotion moved Walter's feelings deeply, but he did not bend from the rigorous course of his intention.

(SA, 120-21)

The *Livre Griseldis* reproduces Petrarch, omitting only the specification that Walter's emotion is paternal: "[il fut] meu de grant pitié" (he was moved to great pity).[28]

Chaucer presents the most complex narrative, and the complexity seems to be generated by his dissatisfaction with the Petrarchan sentiment:

> This sergeant cam unto his lord ageyn,
> And of Grisildis wordes and hire cheere
> He tolde hym point for point, in short and pleyn,
> And hym presenteth with his doghter deere.
> Somwhat this lord hadde routhe in his manere,
> But nathelees his purpos heeld he stille,
> As lordes doon, whan they wol han hir wille.

(IV 575-81)[29]

As I note in *Sources and Analogues*, Chaucer's manuscript of Petrarch may have eliminated the notion of paternal piety here (*SA*, 121n25). In any case, he carries out a fuller reversal of the Petrarchan thrust by making the evocation of that "routhe" a concessive clause leading to the more emphatic assertion of Walter's stubbornness, now characterized as distinctly high-handed, lordly. To that extent, the English poet's delineation of character has changed his Petrarchan source in a direction that is at least roughly Boccaccian: we are allowed to see in Walter, as in Boccaccio's Gualtieri, much less sympathy than Petrarch's Walterus shows. Still, while the ideology of Chaucer's text is more like Boccaccio's than like Petrarch's, there is no verbal evidence that Chaucer arrives at his ideological position *via* Boccaccio's text: no parallels in wording or (beyond what we know he derived from Latin and French sources) plot. There is no marvelling at Grisilde's constancy: the Clerk's word *routhe* (IV 579) is semantically much closer to the French *pitié* and the Latin *pietas* than to Boccaccio's *maravigliandosi*. Throughout this passage, Chaucer follows the plot and the words of Petrarch and the French while dissenting from their take on Walter in words, syntax, and even a rationale that are not derived from any other text. As he does at many points of the story, Chaucer here reads the elaborations introduced by Petrarch, finds them excessive, and so reduces them. In doing so, he typically moves the story's ideological position back closer to the one occupied in Boccaccio; but his words could have been (although I do not claim that they were) written by someone completely unfamiliar with the *Decameron*.

The same situation obtains in the other passages about Walter cited by Finlayson. One of these, Walter's reaction to Grisilde's speech when he announces his intention to remove their son (IV 667-72), has no parallel in Boccaccio. Similarly, the narrative question—"But now of wommen wolde I axen fayn / If thise assayes myghte nat suffise?" (IV 696-97)—that introduces one of the more potent condemnations of Walter's excess, appears in Boccaccio's text in very different form:

> I subditi suoi, credendo che egli uccidere avesse fatti i figliuoli, il biasimavan forte e reputavanlo crudele uomo e alla donna avevan grandissima compassione.

> His subjects, thinking he had caused the children to be murdered, roundly condemned him and judged him a cruel tyrant, whilst his wife became the object of their deepest compassion.[30]

Of the two essential changes between the Italian and the English, one—the move from indirect condemnation of the Marquis through the characters in the story to direct narratorial criticism—has already been made in both Petrarch and the French:

> Poterant rigidissimo coniugi hec benivolencie et fidei coniugalis experimenta sufficere. Sed sunt qui, ubi semel inceperint, non desinant; imo incumbant hereantque proposito.

> These proofs of conjugal good will and faithfulness might have been enough for the most demanding husband; but some people, having begun a course of action, will not desist. No, they press on further, clinging to their plan.

(SA, 122-23)

> Povoient, je vous prie, a ce seigneur ces experimens d'obeïssance et de foy de mariage bien souffire? Mais y sont aucuns que quant il ont aucune chose commancié ou en propos qui continuent tousjours plus.

> Now, I entreat you, couldn't these trials of obedience and marital fidelity quite suffice for this lord? But there are some who when they have begun something or have it in mind persist in it nevertheless.

(SA, 156-57)

The other change is the specification of women in the audience, a distinctive feature at several moments in Chaucer's handling of the tale. While the parallels between Chaucer and his Latin and French sources are obvious, then, it is difficult to imagine the way in which he is supposed to be indebted to Boccaccio in a passage like this.

The closest parallel between Chaucer and Boccaccio in the development of Walter's character comes when, having sent her back to her father's house, he responds to her request for a garment with which to cover the nakedness that was her dowry:

> Gualtieri, che maggior voglia di piagnere aveva che d'altro, stando pur col viso duro, disse: «E tu una camiscia ne porta.»

125

Gualtieri wanted above all else to burst into tears, but maintaining a stern expression he said: 'Very well, you may take a shift.'[31]

> "The smok," quod he, "that thou hast on thy bak,
> Lat it be stille, and bere it forth with thee."
> But wel unnethes thilke word he spak,
> But wente his wey, for routhe and for pitee.

(IV 890-93)

In both of these passages, Gualtieri/Walter avoids the tears that flow in Petrarch and the French: "Habundabant viro lacrime, ut contineri amplius non posset" (Tears welled up in the man; he could no longer be contained) (*SA*, 124-25); "Lors ploura forment de pitié le marquis si que a paine contenir se povoit" (Then the marquis wept so hard from pity that he could hardly contain himself) (*SA*, 160-61). Finlayson believes that, given Chaucerian knowledge of the *Decameron*, this change has an inescapable point of origin:

> [T]he proper conclusion is that Chaucer has recognized the inconsistency generated by Petrarch's presentation of both Walter and the sergeant as deeply, sympathetically moved by what they are doing to poor Griselda, while at the same time, as narrator, directly condemning Walter's actions as unjustifiable. Thus Chaucer may be seen as returning to Boccaccio's simpler presentation of Walter.[32]

In this reading, Chaucer finds the psychology of his Latin and French sources to be at odds and resolves the problem by drawing on the *Decameron*. There is no reason to reject such a reading out of hand; I have no wish to deny that his memories of Boccaccio may have sharpened Chaucer's unwillingness to accept elements of the Petrarchan version. But other conclusions about the passage might also be drawn: for instance, that Chaucer wanted to reduce the sympathy shown by Walterus, a character Chaucer preferred to depict as unsympathetically tyrannical, or that Chaucer wished to minimize emotional aspects of the story that Petrarch had underscored.[33] Like Finlayson's, these readings are plausible *prima facie* explanations of the narrative facts; their differences are derived from different axioms about Chaucerian poetics. The existence of those otherwise similar interpretations, only one of which requires use of the *Decameron* as a source, demonstrates again the value of incontrovertible verbal parallels rather than interpretation to establish Chaucer's use of an antecedent text.

There is a similar case in what Finlayson delineates as "the human suffering of Griselda."[34] Since the parallel is somewhat complex, it may be best to track the different versions against the narrative sequence of the Clerk's Tale:

1. Grisilde believes that Walter has ordered the death of their daughter.

2. Walter tells her that he plans to do with their son what he did with their daughter.

3. Grisilde responds to that news.

4. After the boy is removed, Walter's subjects assume that the children have been murdered.

5. Walter continues his test.

Boccaccio, Petrarch, the French, and Chaucer all record steps 1 and 2 in more or less the same way. But Griselda's response (step 3) is presented rather differently. It begins in Boccaccio as a simple statement of submission:

> «Signor mio, pensa di contentar te e di sodisfare al piacer tuo e di me non avere pensiere alcuno, per ciò che niuna cosa m'è cara se non quanto io la veggo a te piacere.»

> "My lord, look to your own comfort, see that you fulfil your wishes, and spare no thought for me, since nothing brings me pleasure unless it pleases you also."[35]

In Petrarch and the French, the resignation of that response is developed a bit further but in the same vein: she has no independent will in such questions; she has no part in the children except the labor; he is the lord of her and them and should employ them according to his own judgment, not seeking her consent. Chaucer's version, however, introduces a new idea:

> "I have," quod she, "seyd thus, and evere shal:
> I wol no thyng, ne nyl no thyng, certayn,
> But as yow list. Naught greveth me at al,
> Though that my doughter and my sone be slayn—
> At youre comandement, this is to sayn.

(IV 645-49)

She goes on to add the bits about labor, his lordship, using his things, and consent. But the mention at this point of the slaying of her children is unprecedented.

As the tale proceeds, all four versions note (step 4) the rumors among the townsfolk that Walter has had the children killed. Petrarch, the French, and Chaucer move on to discuss his intransigence (step 5), but (as Finlayson notes) Boccaccio has the women of the town bring those rumors to his wife; as for Griselda, "altro non disse se non che quello ne piaceva a lei che a colui che generati gli avea" (all she ever said was that the decision of their father was good enough for her).[36] Thus, while Petrarch and the French always keep the idea of killing inside Griselda's mind, Boccaccio, like Chaucer, creates a moment when Griselda discusses the supposed murder of her children. The Chaucerian comment on slaying is very different: in placement, in specificity, especially in the rhetorical effect of Grisilde confronting Walter, but it remains possible that Chaucer, having read Boccaccio, remembered the narrative value of any direct mention of killing and therefore employed a parallel strategy to his own ends. The differences in placement and voice still argue strongly against use of the *Decameron,* but this case may again show the value of bringing Chaucer's knowledge of the *Decameron* into play.

None of Finlayson's other evidence comes closer to a verbal echo than this, so if we are to think of the *Decameron* as a source it must be on the basis of the "influence on other verbal structures" like plot or design that I mentioned in beginning.[37] Since the plot of the *Clerk's Tale* demonstrably follows Petrarch and the French in opposition to the *Decameron* at a number of obvious points, Finlayson focuses his attention on the structural parallel between the *Envoy* to the *Clerk's Tale* and the concluding comment made by Boccaccio's narrator Dioneo; he argues that both conclusions "reject any possible application of Griselda's behavior to real life" in emphatically un-Petrarchan terms.[38] I have had my say on the *Envoy* already, so I will not argue interpretation here.[39] I agree that Chaucer does not wholly accept Petrarch's conclusion to the tale, and that in moving away from Petrarch, in being not entirely satisfied to understand it only as a compelling moral exemplum, he again necessarily comes a bit closer to Boccaccio.

But what are the signs of Boccaccio's influence on the *Envoy*? Both involve the mention of beasts—Dioneo calls Walter worthy to be a swineherd and the Clerk invokes camels, tigers, and quail in his suggestions to women. And there are vaguely parallel comments about Griselda vis-à-vis other women:

> Chi avrebbe, altri che Griselda, potuto col viso non solamente asciutto ma lieto sofferir le rigide e mai più non udite pruove da Gualtier fatte?

> Who else but Griselda could have endured so cheerfully the cruel and unheard of trials that Gualtieri imposed upon her without shedding a tear?[40]

> But o word, lordynges, herkneth er I go:
> It were ful hard to fynde now-a-dayes
> In al a toun Grisildis thre or two.

> (IV 1163-65)

David Wallace has argued for an ideological similarity—a "conjunction of sex and commerce"—evidenced in the Clerk's invocation of Alys of Bath as the dedicatee of the *Envoy*. Just as Dioneo concludes his tale by hinting that a woman in Griselda's position might do better to prostitute herself than return to Gualtieri (Finlayson argues), the Clerk deflects any serious attention to Grisilde's supposed virtue by invoking the Wife of Bath, who might be thought to have adopted a similar strategy in her first three marriages. Wallace's analysis is a useful supplement to Finlayson's argument,

since the sudden invitation to think about Griselda in the previously unimagined terms of her sexuality is surely the most suggestive parallel in the structure of the two works.[41] In creating the Wife of Bath, Chaucer has himself laid the groundwork for this distinction between her materialism and the abstract virtue of Grisilde, but it is quite possible that memories of Boccaccio have affected Chaucer's thinking at some level.[42] To say so much, however, is still (or again) not to say that the *Decameron* is a source. Because it "bears certain striking resemblances, usually more narrative than verbal, to the Chaucerian work in question," it still fits very comfortably within Beidler's definition and is therefore best understood as a hard analogue.

* * *

What remains then, is a delineation of the significance to critical analysis of the categories of source, hard analogue, and soft analogue, that is, an explanation of why it is valuable to distinguish among them. When we know a source text—in the case of the *Clerk's Tale,* Petrarch's *Historia Griseldis* and the anonymous *Livre Griseldis*—we can recognize with reasonable confidence where Chaucer decided to change the shape of the tale he inherited. We know, for instance, that Chaucer created a parallel between Grisilde's wedding day and the day on which Walter's test ends by specifying in each case that the bridal party arrived at the scene of the action at "undren" (IV 260, 981), a detail that is either absent from or at odds with his sources. However we might wish to explain it, source study tells us simply that Chaucer designed that parallel deliberately. Sources, then, are most instructive when they differ from the later text, since that difference signals a rejection of the form of the story taken in the source.

Two caveats are necessary. While changing the source is a more easily noticed choice, Chaucer also consistently decides to follow the source text, and that can also be an important choice, as it presumably is in the careful iteration of the Petrarchan moral at the end of the *Clerk's Tale*: "This storie is seyd nat for that wyves sholde / Folwen Grisilde . . ." (IV 1142-43). The choice to copy needs to be interpreted no less than the choice to alter, since the claim that "therefore Petrak writeth / This storie" (IV 1147-48) begs the question of why Chaucer writes it. But the decision to follow the source is often not as recognizably significant as in this case. Second, given the vagaries of textual *mouvance* in manuscript culture, only rarely can we be sure that we know the exact text of the manuscript Chaucer was working from. Relying on the Petrarchan text printed by Severs, even recent commentators have suggested that Chaucer substituted "inportable" (IV 1144) for Petrarch's description of Griselda's behavior as "vix imitabilis";[43] but in this case we know that Chaucer's manuscript of Petrarch read "inimitabilis," and Amy W.

Goodwin has suggested that Chaucer may have known the phrase "impossible à porter" in the conclusion of Philippe de Mézières's telling of the Griselda story (*SA*, 134).

Hard analogues like the ***Decameron*** will not sustain such close analysis. Differences between a Chaucerian text and a hard analogue necessarily mean less than such differences from a source: because we have defined a hard analogue as a text Chaucer knew (presumably from a reading some time in the past) rather than a manuscript present for his use, we cannot have any confidence that, in writing his version of the story, Chaucer was reacting specifically to what the hard analogue says. Instead, hard analogues are more likely to be suggestive and valuable when they show parallels to the Chaucerian narrative. Such moments are the best part of Finlayson's analysis: Chaucer's employment of the idea of Grisilde talking about the murders of her children or the structural shift in Dioneo's conclusion and the Clerk's *Envoy*. While the differences between a Chaucerian text and a hard analogue are too easily explicable in other terms, specific parallels indicate the parts of a previously read text most likely to have stuck in the mind and influenced Chaucer's understanding of or attitude towards a textual moment.

Both sources and hard analogues are material for study that is ultimately philological in nature. Both, that is, give us some insight into the way that Chaucer used background materials, and so give us some anagram of authorial intent. Soft analogues necessarily have a different function, since, as Beidler reminds us, "Chaucer could scarcely have known" such texts: neither similarities nor differences are the result of intent. The soft analogue of the *Clerk's Tale* told in Christine de Pizan's *Livre de Cité des Dames* is a case in point. Surprisingly, it contains a closer parallel to Chaucer's tale than either Boccaccio, Petrarch, or the *Livre Griseldis* at the moment when Griselda responds to Walter's warning about their son: she says that "if her son's death was not enough, she was ready to die if he wanted."[44] Although this is noticeably closer to Chaucer's "Though that my doughter and my sone be slayn" (IV 648) than either of the sources or the hard analogue, we know that Chaucer did not decide at any level to imitate Christine's effect, since her book was written in 1405, long after Chaucer was nailed in his own chest.

Instead, we can learn from a soft analogue something about the horizons of discourse in the later Middle Ages, about, that is, the parameters for meaning that the Griselda story could have suggested to another writer who was writing close to Chaucer in time and place. The specter of infanticide, hardly mentioned in earlier versions of the story, is a feature that both Chaucer and Christine decided to emphasize. It is beyond the scope of my argument to ask why they did so, but the presence of that response in more than one version of the story indicates how, at least around 1400 and in Northern Europe, there was a willingness to confront the "monstrosity" of the story more directly than had been done before. Such insights help us to contextualize the story: Anne Middleton may fairly be thought to have begun the current focus on social issues in the *Clerk's Tale* with similar kinds of attention to the social and literary contexts provided by several analogues as well as the sources of the tale.[45] As scholarship has become more interested in social and cultural attitudes than authorial interpretations, soft analogues have become an increasingly important area of inquiry, but their importance is distinct in kind from the importance of sources and hard analogues.

In respect to the *Clerk's Tale,* then—and probably to the other tales of Canterbury with which it has been connected—the ***Decameron*** remains in the position of hard analogue. There is much good evidence that Chaucer had encountered it and read extensively and often carefully in it. By tracing the at least occasional moments of similarity, especially in terms of the ideology of the tale or the narrative attitude toward the plot, between it and the *Clerk's Tale,* Finlayson has made a good case for that relationship. The evidence of verbal similarity that would make ***Decameron*** "X, 10" a source is not present, and so that part of his argument fails, but in the long run the recognition of a hard analogue may be more important than the thesis he advanced.

Notes

1. S.v. *source,* n. 4e, *Oxford English Dictionary Online,* August 27, 2002, http://dictionary.oed.com/entrance.dtl.

2. William Harmon and C. Hugh Holman, *A Handbook to Literature,* 9th edn. (Upper Saddle River, N.J., 2003), 481.

3. This is a small disagreement with Paul Strohm, who argues (drawing on Judith Butler) that "a text has more sources than it can name" ("Chaucer's Lollard Joke: History and the Textual Unconscious," *Studies in the Age of Chaucer* 17 [1995]: 23-42, at 26). While I would agree unequivocally that a text has more influences than it can name, one of my purposes here is to restrict usage of the word *source* to narrower limits.

4. Frank Lentricchia and Thomas McLaughlin, eds., *Critical Terms for Literary Study,* 2nd edn. (Chicago, 1995), 186-202.

5. W. F. Bryan and Germaine Dempster, eds., *Sources and Analogues of Chaucer's Canterbury Tales* (1941; repr. Atlantic Highlands, N.J., 1958), vii.

6. Bryan is partly dealing with the vicissitudes of editing very diverse kinds of contributions. While J. Burke Severs, in his chapter on the *Clerk's Tale,* not only identified its sources but claimed to have produced the textual form in which Chaucer read those sources, other contributors working on less tractable materials employed more flexible definitions. Bryan's phrasing describes well enough the chapter on *Thopas* by Laura Hibbard Loomis; she argues that the poem "has no one source," but that Chaucer possessed the Auchinleck MS that contains many of the romances she cites as (presumably) analogues (*Sources and Analogues,* 486, 489). I have discussed the problem of the analogue Chaucer knew in "Philological Theory in *Sources and Analogues," Medieval Perspectives* 15 (2000): 34-48.

7. *Sources and Analogues of the Canterbury Tales,* ed. Robert M. Correale and Mary Hamel (Cambridge, Eng., 2002); hereafter cited as *Sources and Analogues* or, in textual references, *SA.*

8. John Finlayson, "Petrarch, Boccaccio, and Chaucer's *Clerk's Tale," Studies in Philology* 97 (2000): 255-75. Recently, other scholars have also been interested in the influence of Boccaccio on this tale, albeit less directly than Finlayson: Leonard Michael Koff, "Imagining Absence: Chaucer's Griselda *and* Walter *without* Petrarch," in *The Decameron and the Canterbury Tales: New Essays on an Old Question,* ed. Leonard Michael Koff and Brenda Deen Schildgen (Madison, N.J., 2000), 278-316; and Lynn Staley, "Chaucer and the Powers of Sanctity," in David Aers and Lynn Staley, *The Powers of the Holy* (University Park, Penn., 1996), 179-259.

9. Finlayson, "Petrarch," 258.

10. Finlayson, "Petrarch," 258.

11. J. Burke Severs, *The Literary Relationships of Chaucer's Clerkes Tale* (1942; repr. Hamden, Conn., 1972), 42-58. The five fifteenth-century manuscripts lacking the "Librum tuum" are CC2, Bod, Add, Vesp, and Roy12. The two abbreviated versions, in CC4 and Pal, would at least have made more difficult the identification of the *Decameron* as Petrarch's source. Two of the eight additional manuscripts consulted for *Sources and Analogues* also lack the "Librum tuum": G1 and G4. Charlotte Cook Morse demonstrates that some five-sixths of the manuscripts of the *Historia Griseldis* remain uncollated ("What to Call Petrarch's Griselda," in *The Uses of Manuscripts in Literary Studies: Essays in Memory of Judson Boyce Allen,* ed. Charlotte Cook Morse, Penelope Reed Doob, and Marjorie Curry Woods [Kalamazoo, Mich., 1992], 263-303).

12. On the relationship of CC2 and the glosses, see Germaine Dempster, "Chaucer's Manuscript of Petrarch's Version of the Griselda Story," *Modern Philology* 41 (1943): 6-16. Because it perpetuates misconceptions that have proved hard to eradicate, another philological slip in Finlayson's argument requires correction: he claims that "Petrarch, in a letter to Boccaccio which immediately follows his letter retelling the story, writes about some contemporary reader-response" (273). This is technically correct with respect to the minority of manuscripts (including Pe, the base text in *Sources and Analogues*) that present a complete copy of *Seniles* XVII. However, the second letter mentioned by Finlayson, *Seniles* XVII.4, was composed a year after XVII.3 (Severs 7-11) and is not a part of "the text" of *Historia Griseldis* in most manuscripts. Charlotte C. Morse argues that Chaucer is unlikely to have known *Seniles* XVII.4 ("Exemplary Griselda," *Studies in the Age of Chaucer* 7 [1985]: 64-65).

13. Peter G. Beidler demonstrates that the evidence that Chaucer did not know the *Decameron* was never very strong ("Just Say Yes, Chaucer Knew the *Decameron*: Or, Bringing the *Shipman's Tale* Out of Limbo," in *The Decameron and the Canterbury Tales: New Essays on an Old Question,* ed. Leonard Michael Koff and Brenda Deen Schildgen [Madison, N.J., 2000], 25-46).

14. N. S. Thompson, *Chaucer, Boccaccio, and the Debate of Love* (Oxford, 1996), 313.

15. Finlayson, "Petrarch," 256.

16. All quotations and translations from Petrarch's *Seniles* XVII.3 are taken from my edition in *SA,* 108-29; this passage is on 108-109. It is worth reiterating that this text does not pretend to be a Petrarchan text in the way that Severs's edition did; it was selected because its variants frequently align with what we know about Chaucer's manuscript.

17. Chaucer follows a source text perhaps most closely in the *Tale of Melibee.* William R. Askins is able to point to "the discovery of the manuscript [of Renaud de Louens's *Livre de Mellibee*] which most closely resembled Chaucer's text" (323) and which was, therefore, the base text for both Severs's edition in Bryan and Dempster and Askins's in *SA.* Richard Newhauser differentiates between "illustrative sources" from which the exemplary material of the *Parson's Tale* are drawn, the "contextual sources" that provided its discursive frameworks, and "verbal sources," which "approximate, as nearly as can now be reconstructed, the material which Chaucer drew on more directly for his own presentation of penitential and moral-theological concepts and the verbal formulations

in which the reader finds them in the *Parson's Tale*" (*SA*, 530). The texts he presents are very heavily weighted towards the last category.

18. When she does use the word *source* in other contexts, Cooper also prefers a more rigorous definition: "While Langland's poem may be the *inspiration* for Chaucer's, however, it is clearly not the source in the same sense as the *Teseide* is for the Knight's Tale. I do not imagine that Chaucer composed the General Prologue with a copy of *Piers Plowman* open in front of him, and his work is certainly not Langland's rewritten in riding rhyme" ("Langland's and Chaucer's Prologues," *Yearbook of Langland Studies* 1 [1987]: 71-81, at 77).

19. John Scattergood argues that it may be "pointless to search for sources and analogues for the *Cook's Tale*" (*SA*, 82) among literary narratives; he therefore discusses non-narrative sources like *The Chamberlain's Devout Instructions to Apprentices* because Perkyn Revelour "breaks not only the general spirit of his apprenticeship but also every specific rule" (*SA*, 84). In this case, the "other verbal structures" are the clauses of the typical apprentice's agreement.

20. Similarly, Vincent DiMarco notes that "the fragmentary nature of [the *Squire's Tale*], as well as the strong likelihood of Chaucer's dependence on oral reports and reminiscences of travelers and merchants, renders the possibility of finding a written source for the story unlikely indeed" (*SA*, 169). In many ways the *Monk's Tale* is the epitome of such a model; Thomas H. Bestul notes that, "As many scholars have pointed out, it is often impossible to identify specific sources and fruitless to try, since Chaucer seems to have based many of his stories on several possible literary sources and frequently depended on what is best termed general knowledge" (*SA*, 412).

21. Beidler, "Just Say Yes," 41-42. These exact quotations of Beidler's definitions are incomplete largely in their omissions of his examples for each category; *Decameron* "X, 10" is cited as an example of a hard analogue.

22. Finlayson, "Petrarch," 257, 274, 274.

23. In discussing the different versions of the story, I have attempted to enhance the clarity of my argument by distinguishing the two main characters by the spelling adopted for each in the cited text of the different versions. This works best for the marquis, who is in Boccaccio called Gualtieri, in Petrarch Walterus, in the *Livre Griseldis* Wautier (a form I have no occasion to cite), and in Chaucer Walter. There is less differentiation of his wife's name, but I have distinguished Chaucer's Grisilde from the Griselda named in Boccaccio and Petrarch. When quoting other scholars I have of course used the form of the name employed by those scholars.

24. The Italian text of the *Decameron* is cited from the edition by Vittore Branca (Milano, 1985), 897. The English translation is by G. H. McWilliam (Baltimore, 1972), 817.

25. *Decameron*, ed. Branca, 898; trans. McWilliam, 818.

26. At many points, Finlayson is less interested in arguing for the source status of *Decameron* "X, 10" than against the emphasis on Chaucer's originality in the *Clerk's Tale* as depicted by Severs in *Literary Relationships*. Although he may exaggerate the degree to which contemporary scholarship sees Chaucer as original, I have no fundamental argument with this aspect of his analysis. Presumably the discussion of the sergeant, which focuses on textual development from Latin to French to English, was directed at the originality thesis, since it is clearly counterproductive in the source thesis.

27. *Decameron*, ed. Branca, 897; trans. McWilliam, 818.

28. Text and translation of the Anonymous French are from Amy W. Goodwin's edition in *SA*, 140-67, and will henceforth be cited by page number. This passage is on 152-53.

29. All quotations of Chaucer are from *The Riverside Chaucer*, ed. Larry D. Benson, 3rd edn. (Boston, 1987).

30. *Decameron*, ed. Branca, 898; trans. McWilliam, 819.

31. *Decameron*, ed. Branca, 899-900; trans. McWilliam, 820.

32. Finlayson, "Petrarch," 263.

33. The notion that Chaucer wanted to make Walter more obviously a tyrant and thus not sympathetic is consonant with David Wallace, *Chaucerian Polity: Absolutist Lineages and Associational Forms in England and Italy* (Stanford, 1997), 261-98, which seems to me currently the most influential approach to the tale. I have argued that the *Clerk's Tale* consistently reduces the emotional effects in Petrarch in "The Style of the *Clerk's Tale* and the Functions of Its Glosses," *Studies in Philology* 86 (1989): 286-309.

34. Finlayson, "Petrarch," 264.

35. *Decameron*, ed. Branca, 898; trans. McWilliam, 818.

36. *Decameron,* ed. Branca, 898; trans. McWilliam, 819.

37. Finlayson also argues that Chaucer drew on Boccaccio in deciding that Grisilde should express her consent to marriage with Walter ("Petrarch," 267-68). The argument is complex, and involves, I believe, a misreading of Severs, whose distinction between Griselda's willing obedience (in Petrarch) to Walterus and her willing-ness (in Chaucer) to marry Walter is elided. But the essence of the argument is that Gualtieri's blunt "Griselda, vuoimi tu per tuo marito?" (and her equally laconic reply "Signor mio, sì" [*Decameron,* ed. Branca, 895]) are the source of Walter's "Wol ye assente, or elles yow avyse?" (IV 350) in Chaucer. Once again, however, Chaucer's question occurs in a crucially different place and context: he asks Grisilde his question in private, not in front of all of the people, as in Boccaccio, who emphasizes the embarrassment thus caused to her. At the point where Gualtieri asks Griselda whether she wishes to marry him, Walter announces a *fait accompli* to the crowd: "This is my wyf" (IV 369). The verbal parallels that would indicate use of the *Decameron* are still absent.

38. Finlayson, "Petrarch," 272.

39. See "The Chronotopes of Monology in Chaucer's Clerk's Tale," in *Bakhtin and Medieval Voices,* ed. Thomas J. Farrell (Gainesville, Fla., 1996), 141-57. Howell Chickering believes that the *Envoy* presents "an unresolvable and ironically contradictory perspective" on the tale ("Form and Interpretation in the *Envoy* to the *Clerk's Tale,*" *Chaucer Review* 29 [1995]: 352-72, at 356). Finalyson's belief in the untenability of the tale's viewpoint thus seems hardly inevitable and, more important here, essentially interpretive.

40. *Decameron,* ed. Branca, 903-904; trans. McWilliam, 824.

41. Wallace, *Chaucerian Polity,* 292-93; Finlayson develops his parallel argument on 272-73. Grisilde's asexuality in the tale is well articulated by R. E. Kaske, "Chaucer's Marriage Group," in *Chaucer the Love Poet,* ed. Jerome Mitchell and William Provost (Athens, Ga. 1973): "though [the Clerk's] tale contains no explicit comment on the importance of sexual relations, their role—at least by comparison with the other tales in the group—is muted to the point where one hears of Griselda's children with something like surprise" (54). At this point Finlayson again declines to make an issue of Boccaccio as source: "The invocation of the Wife here, therefore, *whether or not directly inspired by Dineo's fabliau-like remark,* indirectly and dramatically parallels Boccaccio's introduction of a radically different way for women to respond to matrimonial abuse" ("Petrarch," 272; my emphasis).

42. The contrast between Alice and Grisilde has been articulated in many ways. The immediate influence for this articulation is John Alford, "The Wife of Bath Versus the Clerk of Oxford: What Their Rivalry Means," *Chaucer Review* 21 (1986): 108-32.

43. Helen Cooper, *The Oxford Guides to Chaucer: The Canterbury Tales,* 2nd edn. (Oxford, 1996), 190.

44. The text of *Le Livre de la Cité des Dames* is still available only in the unpublished 1975 dissertation of Maureen Curnow (Vanderbilt). The English translation is from *The Book of the City of Ladies,* trans. Earl Jeffrey Richards (New York, 1982), 172. Chaucer was also clearly not a source for Christine, who worked with the translation of Petrarch by Philippe de Mézières and perhaps also with the Petrarchan text (see Richards, 265-66).

45. Anne Middleton, "The Clerk and His Tale: Some Literary Contexts," *Studies in the Age of Chaucer* 2 (1980): 121-50. Wallace also thinks of the Boccaccian text as an analogue, and in these terms: "My argument does not assume that Chaucer knew the Boccaccian Griselde story, although it is quite possible that he did. I am suggesting, however, that the political dimensions of Boccaccio's *novella,* its embeddedness in contemporary ideological debate, do have an important bearing on our reading of the *Clerk's Tale*" (*Chaucerian Polity,* 282). In a paper at the 37th International Congress on Medieval Studies (2002), Amy W. Goodwin argued that Philippe de Mézières's translation of Petrarch also has the characteristics of a hard analogue to the *Clerk's Tale.* Although Middleton does not discuss Christine's exemplum, it was first brought to the attention of Chaucerians by Diane Bornstein, "An Analogue to Chaucer's 'Clerk's Tale,'" *Chaucer Review* 15 (1981): 322-31. The publication of Bornstein's article a year after Middleton's also marks the growing interest in analogues.

Susanna Barsella (essay date January 2004)

SOURCE: Barsella, Susanna. "The Myth of Prometheus in Giovanni Boccaccio's *Decameron.*" *MLN* 119 Supplement, no. 1 (January 2004): 120-41.

[*In the following essay, Barsella delineates the epistemological, theological, and literary implications of the classical Prometheus myth which informs the purpose of the* Decameron, *illuminating the relationship between this work and Boccaccio's* Genealogie deorum gentilium.]

In his article "La *Dignitas hominis* e la letteratura Patristica"—a "too often neglected article," as Charles Trinkaus holds in *In Our Image and Likeness*—Eugenio Garin showed that humanist spirituality took new inspiration from Early Church Fathers such as Nemesius of Emesa, Arnobius, and Lactantius. Before Garin, Renaissance scholars had stressed the spiritual character of Humanism and its focus on the philosophy of man.[1] The humanists' predominant interest in moral philosophy and theological anthropology led them to recover the Patristic tradition, for in this tradition the questioning about the nature of man and his function in the cosmos had been pivotal. The Fathers had cast the Christian idea of the Incarnated God in the Judaic theological anthropology, which was based on the biblical narration of the Creation of man in God's image (*Gen.* 1.27). Their vision, as Garin argues, combined conceit for the frailty of human nature and exaltation for the divine imprint man bears in his soul.[2] Like the early Fathers, the humanists were a product of a civic culture, committed to the social and political lives of their cities and, like them, seeking to reconcile Christian ideals and secular world. In this ideal of Christian civilization, the poet's intellectual and educative role was determinant for the construction of a just and pious society. The humanists' recovery of both Patristics and classical antiquity, including the encyclopedic compilations of mythological repertoires such as Boccaccio's *Genealogie deorum gentilium,* should be considered against this backdrop, where the poet was conceived of as a moral philosopher.

In reaction to the late Scholastics' separation of reason and Revelation, "Aristotle and the Bible"—to use Garin's words—the early Florentine humanists saw in the synthesis of the Fathers' spirituality with a mysticism of Neo-Platonic origins, a way to reconcile classical and Christian traditions. These humanists, says Garin, elaborated on Patristic themes by using religious rather than classical motives, so that Adam and not Prometheus symbolized their idea of Man-God.[3] Only later in the Renaissance the heirs of Giannozzo Manetti, Bartolomeo Facio, Lorenzo Valla, and Giovanni Pico reintroduced and reappropriated classical materials and used the image of Prometheus to "break the religious circle in which Cusano and the Florentine Academy had tried to confine the concept of humanity."[4]

This article makes two points: first, that the research for a unity of what Garin called *docta religio* (the spiritual religion) and *pia philosophia* (the philosophy of man) was already present in an early-humanist author, the most famous of Petrarch's friends, Giovanni Boccaccio.[5] Second, that Boccaccio, before the humanists of the '400, and influencing them, had already tried to reconcile Christian and classical thoughts through the recovery of Patristic theology. Unlike them, however, he did elaborate on classical motives, combining both pagan and Christian materials in a renovated spiritual union of religion and poetry. In Boccaccio, the poets' educative function consisted in encasing the worldly commitment to the construction of a just society within a Christian superstructure.[6] His innovative views eminently emerge in his conception of the poet-philosopher, which appears in all his challenging originality in Boccaccio's reinterpretation of the myth of Prometheus as a myth of civilization. In the Titan who presented men with the divine gift of fire to save them from extinction, the author of the *Decameron* realized a sort of christening of classical mythology. This was, after all, the goal of one of his most compelling works, the *Genealogie deorum gentilium,* where the myth is expounded.[7] This version of the myth, centered on the humanizing power of knowledge, permeates the *Decameron.*

The discovery of an intratextual dialogue between these two major Boccaccio's works is not surprising if we take into account that Boccaccio worked on both in parallel for several years, and continued to revise both of them until the end of his life.[8] The analysis of the genesis of Boccaccio's Prometheus allows us to isolate the nexus between these two works, and evaluate their common educational goal.

The epistemological, theological, and literary implications of the critical passage from a medieval to a humanistic system of thought during the XIVth century are found, more vividly than in any other literary work of this period, in Boccaccio's *Decameron.* Permeated by an intellectual reaction against Scholasticism, this work introduced the theme of the Christian poet-philosopher's commitment to ethical ends, already marking the recovery of Patristic civic theology.

Boccaccio conceived of literature as having a special function in moral philosophy, determined by the very nature of literature as rhetorical art. Accordingly, he structured the *Decameron* as a work of practical moral philosophy, so as to exploit the educative strength of literature. Central to his ideological construction was the figure of Prometheus, which lays behind the "proemial author." In the classical Titan Boccaccio merged the philosophical ideal of the wise man and the Patristic ideal of holiness, and transformed him in a figure of wisdom. This was not an ascetic kind of wisdom, however, but a knowledge intended to civilize men by making them capable to live together according to the ideals of civic virtue.

The overtly declared moral intent of the *Decameron* reveals its poietical and philosophical qualities, and suggests that a Promethean figure plays a role in it. **"Proemio 14"** illustrates the *Decameron* as a collection of stories, *novelle,* tales, fables narrated to soothe young women's love pains, so that they may receive delight and useful advice.[9]

the said ladies [. . .] may equally derive both delight from the entertaining things therein shown, and useful advice, for they will learn what to avoid and likewise what to pursue. Both these things, I believe, cannot be realized without enduring a pain.[10]

Kurt Flasch remarked that this formulation of the book's end ("cognoscere quello che sia da fuggire e che sia similmente da seguitare") was a conventional statement characterizing moral philosophy texts.[11] For its own nature, this type of literature did not deal with abstract notions but rather offered cases, examples, stories on which the reader may apply his own capacity to discern good and evil. The eminently practical moral purpose of the *Decameron* determines its literary profile. Since it must comply with the rules of the moral genre, it must offer a sufficient variety of case-studies. Boccaccio derived the models for this genre from the two pillars of civil life, law and religion.[12]

The much discussed Boccaccian realism should be evaluated in this light, for realism is a typical trait of moral practical literature, to which the *Decameron* belongs. The notion of 'realism' refers here to the increased evaluation of the material aspects of reality that characterized the historical development of the communal civilization, and shaped Western thought after the reintroduction of Aristotelism in the tenth-twelfth centuries. Reality, conceived as form-embedding matter, was seen as encompassing philosophical and theological truths, and deemed worthy of both scientific investigation and artistic representation.[13]

The ethical function of the *Decameron* is visible in the fictional author's motivation to write a collection of stories for an audience of lovesick women. The proemial narrator justifies his act of writing by invoking a principle of fairness. He argues that it is fair to communicate to others, and particularly to those most in need, what one has learned from others' wisdom and from his own experience. The author of the **"Proemio"**'s confesses that he benefited from a friend's advice while besotted with love. Now that he has overcome the disorder of the senses, he feels morally obliged to benefit those held by passion by communicating them what he learned.

This motivation suggests that Boccaccio modeled the fictional narrator of the **"Proemio"** on the ideal of the sage, the emblematic figure of ancient moral philosophy. Both Boccaccio and Petrarch elaborated on the idea of the poet-philosopher, which remained a leitmotiv in their relationship and a constant in Boccaccio's works. The author's most extensive speculation on this theme is contained in his defense of poetry in book XIV of the *Genealogie*.[14] The poet-philosopher, like the wise man, is a figure of practical wisdom, learned in natural and moral philosophy, who offers what he apprehends in contemplation and meditation for the benefit of the community. Analogously, the proemial narrator of the *Decameron* teaches what he learned from doctrine and experience for the benefit of the little community of lovesick women. The figure of the wise man not only shapes the poetic invention of the proemial author, but also the entire structure of the framework (*cornice*), the story of the ten young Florentines which encases the one hundred *novelle*. The decameronian fictional company only temporarily leaves Florence to retreat in abodes nearby the city, to which they do return after a period dedicated to moral and physical edification.

Having established the moral purpose of the book and the presence of the idea of the poet-philosopher in the proemial narrator of the *Decameron,* it is now time to investigate the intellectual components of this idea. Boccaccio derived the philosophical paradigm of the poet-philosopher by combining classic and early Patristic cultures.[15] He elaborated on two models: the myth of Prometheus and its Christian reinterpretations, and the hagiographical tradition of the desert Fathers.[16] He focused on the former in book IV of the *Genealogie*, while an example of the latter is his *Vita sanctissimi Pier Damiani*.

In 1361 Boccaccio, who was then in Ravenna, received Petrarch's request to research San Peter Damiani. Petrarch was in Milan and intended to use this information for his *De vita solitaria*. Boccaccio found Giovanni da Lodi's *Vita*, Peter Damiani's contemporary friar of Fonte Avellana, and rewrote it. He introduced *ex novo* a chapter on the vanity of earthly goods (IV) and one on the benefits of the solitary life (VI) with the overt intention to adapt the Saint's life to the *topoi* of Christian hagiography. In 1362 he sent Petrarch his *Vita sanctissimi Pier Damiani* accompanied by epistle XI.[17] In Boccaccio's rewriting the saint had become a figure in which the *topos* of the ascetical anchorite had merged with the classical model of the sage. The anchorites and the Desert Fathers were symbols of the purity of early Christianity. These figures in many ways overlapped with the classical ideal of the wise man. The hermits were not cast away from their communities. On the contrary, their 'strategic' position at the city's outskirts allowed them to remain uninvolved in the political and institutional life of the Church and to continue their crucial function as the community's spiritual and moral guides. This was a role that the secularized Church of the *comuni* had gradually lost. The physical marginality of hermitage at the city borders was a privileged location which was symbolically reproduced in the geographical disposition of the two abodes of the company (*brigata*) in the *Decameron*.[18]

The *Vita* of Peter Damiani followed a predictable pattern: born as shepherd, he was then educated in the liberal arts, learned in the sacred scripture, devoted to benefit and educate the others, and committed to building new convents and churches. By adapting the historical character to a classical philosophical model, Boccaccio made the saint and the man of wisdom coincide. The same pattern is recognizable in the decameronian narrator and also behind the withdrawing *brigata*. The central feature of the saint's *Life* is once again the public use of a wisdom.

The idea of returning to the secular world after a temporary contemplative retreat denotes also the other component of the Boccaccian poet-philosopher, Prometheus. As the philosopher, so the ancient mythological character symbolically granted men a spark of divine knowledge, allowing them access to spiritual life.[19] Before the poet's extensive treatment of the myth in *Genealogie* IV, Prometheus appeared in two Boccaccio's early writings, the *Filocolo,* composed around 1336, and a narration of difficult interpretation known as *Mythological Allegory,* supposedly composed around 1339.[20] In *Filocolo* I.2 the author dedicates his book to young women in love, who inspire the narrator to teach them about constant and loyal love. Immediately after this sort of invocation to the Muses—in *Decameron* **"IV"** the author explicitly declares that women were his Muses— Boccaccio introduces a prayer to Zeus.[21] This pagan divinity, as the following narration illustrating the origins and the fall of man, are mythological allegorizations of Christian materials. Transposed in medieval syncretic terms, the framework of *Filocolo* I.2 recalls the *incipit* structure of didactic poems such as Hesiod's *Works and Days* and Virgil's *Georgics*. In both these poems, quoted in the *Genealogie,* the invocation to the Muses introduces a prayer to Zeus as God of Justice, and precedes a narration of the origins as progressive decadence from a mythical golden age to the human era. The scheme of invocations of the *Filocolo* points at Boccaccio's early interest in the moral-didactic literature.

In the mythologized transposition of the Biblical Creation of *Filocolo* I.3, Prometheus figures as the first being that Zeus/God created after Pluto/Devil's rebellion.[22] God gave Prometheus/Adam company and placed his creatures in a holy garden ("il santo giardino").[23] Boccaccio modified this part of the Biblical narration of Creation by leaving aside the figure of Eve, whom he substituted with the Creation of the human species. In this version, the Eden corresponded to the pagan mythological golden age.

The *Mythological Allegory* follows a similar pattern. Boccaccio transposed Creation into a pagan imagery where Zeus created the world and, with his own hands, Prometheus. When Prometheus left the Elysium, the golden age began. This narration was based on the Ovidian *Metamorphosis* and its later Christian reinterpretations, which Boccaccio knew through the medieval mythographers.[24]

The most important text for Boccaccio's reinterpretation of the myth of Prometheus is *Genealogie* IV.44. In this text the Titan was no longer the mythological transposition of Adam but became, mediated through classical Latin and Christian authors, a figure of God-Creator.[25] This shift from first man to creator indicates Boccaccio's changed interpretation of the symbolic role of Prometheus as inventor of the arts, that is of the civilized human being. The poet here re-elaborated the figure of the Titan in an original humanist perspective which embedded an analogy between man and God, technique and Creation, which he illustrated in the atemporal form of the myth.

In *Genealogie* IV. 44 the story of Prometheus unfolds in three phases, moving from myth to legend to history. First Boccaccio reported the Latin classical versions of the myth by Ovid, Horace, and Claudian, together with Servius' and Fulgentius' later interpretations. In the ancient Latin versions, Prometheus created the first man from mud and water.[26] Servius and Fulgentius added that Prometheus stole the fire from the gods to animate his creature, whom Prometheus called Pandora. Enraged by Prometheus' trick, the gods fastened him to the Caucasian rocks and sent an eagle to eat his heart.[27]

After this exposition, before proceeding with the explanation of the allegorical meaning of the myth, Boccaccio provides his reader with a narration partly legendary ('people say') and partly based on a 'historical' account of the story derived from a mysterious Theodontius.[28] According to this still unidentified medieval source of the ninth-tenth centuries, the Promethean myth developed from the true story of a historical character, the son of Japeth and the Nimph Asia, who left his family and possessions to move to Assyria (a far away savage province symbolizing withdrawal from the civilized world) where he listened to the Chaldeans' sermons before retreating on the Caucasus.[29] Here, through meditation on experience ("longa meditatione ex experientia") he learned natural philosophy ("astrorum cursu, procuratisque naturis fulminum et rerum plurium causis") and eventually returned to Assyria to teach what he had learned.[30] The Promethean wisdom was not religious but philosophical and scientific, and it was useful so long as it was communicated and benefited humankind. The originality of Boccaccio's interpretation of the two Prometheus, the symbolic creator and the historical civilizator, was striking. Not only it differed from the tradition—although Boccaccio largely drew from it— but it remained an *unicum* also with respect to his contemporaries and successors, who nonetheless knew and used the *Genealogie*.[31]

The key to Boccaccio's allegorical explanation of the myth relies on his conception of practical wisdom. As creator of man, Prometheus was an allegory, and therefore an ancient theological intuition, of the God Creator.[32] As an historical figure, he represented a philosopher who used his wisdom to emancipate humankind from a natural, savage, state. The historical and philosophical necessity of the wise man to restore humankind's superiority over the wild animals, originated from the loss of perfection that followed Adam and Woman's Fall. Since when man lost God's favor he ceased to be His product to became an imperfect product of Nature. Only through a process of continuous effort toward wisdom could human beings improve themselves and become capable of building a Christian community. This vision was not unique to Boccaccio, and it had an authoritative antecedent in Hugh of Saint Victor's *Didascalicon,* a systematic treatise illustrating the crucial role of human science in the partial restoration of Adam's lost paradise.[33]

In this theological framework, the task of Prometheus-philosopher was to educate the 'natural' (animal) man and transform him into a civil man. Only in this way the only form of perfection man can attain could be fully realized:

> Those who are produced by nature are uncouth and ignorant and, unless educated, are base, rude, and beast-like. Over these rises the second Prometheus, that is the learned man, and receiving them as they were of stone, almost creates them anew, teaches and educate them. Through his demonstrations he makes these natural men civil, famous by their customs, science, and virtue so that it is clear that some have been produced by nature and others have been transformed by knowledge.
>
> (*Geneal.* IV.44.11-12)[34]

The Boccaccian exegesis of Prometheus embedded the medieval conception of man that derived from Augustine and Hugh of Saint Victor. Although irretrievably wounded by original sin, man could, nonetheless, cooperate to gaining a state of Grace. In the Victorine vision, where everything pertaining to the human sphere was subordinated to the ultimate goal of restoring a lost human perfection, every art could be used as an instrument to reach this supreme goal. In Boccaccio, however, art was no longer simply instrumental to salvation, nor its intent was to show human beings the path leading to Grace. Though a faithful Catholic, the author did not believe one could proceed along a straight path toward salvation, whose mystery was impenetrable to human mind. As Millard Meiss observed for the figurative arts, after the plague divine matters could no longer be objects of representation.[35] Like Petrarch in the *Secretum,* Boccaccio conceived of man's itinerary to God through the full blooming of his *humanitas*. Being a civil man capable of living in a human community according to reason and virtue—Aristotle and the Fathers' ideals—was a necessary step to become a citizen of the heavenly city. This was the goal men should pursue in their lives.

Like for the humanists later on, in Boccaccio the idea of *humanitas* was not separable from that of *civitas* and the investigation of human nature was justified independently of the ultimate spiritual end of human life. The key word Boccaccio used in the above quoted passage from *Genealogie* IV.44 is "civil" ("hominibus civiles"). The primary function of Prometheus, and symbolically the poet-philosopher of Boccaccio's own times, is to educate men to natural and moral knowledge so that they may live in a secular, political, context according to the principles of justice and piety. This ideal of Christian commitment to the secular society was also the Fathers' ideal, influenced by the Hellenistic philosophy of man, and by Aristotle's book X of the *Ethics to Nichomacus*. In this book, the philosophers do not live isolated from the community but serve it, contributing to enhance civil life through their educative responsibility.

The pedagogical character of Boccaccio's conception of poetry was coherent with the momentum that moral philosophy gained at the turn from the Middle Ages to Humanism. Shaken by the waves of negative events that had shattered Europe during the fourteenth century, late medieval philosophers started to abandon any claim to know what was beyond experience. The progressive dismissal of the assumption of an ontological relation between being and appearance reached its climax with William of Ockham. The resulting new epistemology favored natural and moral sciences over metaphysics, and attributed to poetry a new and more appropriate ethical function.

Boccaccio's claim that poetry was independent of philosophy and theology, later theorized in *Genealogie* XV.8, was already present in the **Decameron**.[36] Poetry, he argued in that text, is "physiology" and "ethology," that is a science investigating nature and human customs:[37]

> *It is called* mythical, from the Greek *mythicon,* a myth, and in this kind, as I have already said, is adapted to the use of the comic stage. But this form of literature is reprobate among better poets on account of its obscenity. Physical theology is, as etymology shows, natural and moral, and being commonly thought a very useful thing, it enjoys much esteem. Civil or political theology, sometimes called the theology of state worship, relates to the commonwealth, but through the foul abominations of its ancient ritual, it was repudiated by them of the true faith and the right worship of God.
>
> (*Geneal.* XV.8,2)[38]

This philosophical vision of literature hinged on the figure of the poet-philosopher.

If the entire cognitive apparatus of medieval thought had failed in indicating the way the human and the divine could be related (for this is what was ultimately at stake); if neither monastic nor Scholastic theologies had been able to provide a valid foundation for the construction of a just Christian community, then moral theology needed to be rethought and brought back to the early teachings of the Apostolic and Early Fathers. The mendicant orders had tried to accomplish this, but in the end had failed. Given the philosophical premises against ontology, Scholastic moral theology had become inadequate, and classical thought could provide a viable model for a renewed Christian morality.

In this setting, not only poetry (religious and secular alike) found a specific moral function independent of philosophy and sacred theology (that is Christian), but it also vindicated the relevance of rhetoric to ethical ends. Beyond the intention to please the reader, the proemial "diletto" lays claim to literary excellence, as evidenced by the rich texture of Boccaccian prose. Having lost the instrumental function of serving hagiography and exemplarity, poetry regained a status of "poiesis" whose value consisted in its technical features.

Boccaccio's reevaluation of the civic role of poetry implied that moral teaching and exemplarity of virtue were not exclusive pertinences of the clergy. Rather, since ethical virtue was a civic value, and therefore the object of human ethology (that is, of poetry), the poet-philosopher was its most suitable teacher.

Central to the above delineated system of thought, was Aristotle's *Ethics to Nicomachus,* which Boccaccio knew and studied.[39] He probably copied it, together with Aquinas' commentary, in the early 1340s when contacts with the Dominican Studium of Santa Maria Novella can be conjectured.[40] A series of annotations from different years, however (judged on the basis of the different periods of Boccaccio's handwriting), suggests that he studied this text until the end of his life. Book X of the *Nicomachean Ethics* was most likely one of the sources of Boccaccio's reinterpretation of the Promethean myth in the *Decameron,* for the model of the wise man behind the fictional author was already sketched in Aristotle's pages.

The Aristotelian philosopher and the holy man of early Christianity combined in the boccaccian Prometheus by maintaining their prominent symbolism of civilizing figures. Neither the exemplary meditative lives of the anchorites nor the ancient sage devoted their knowledge to their own spiritual benefit only. Rather, they were committed to the edification of the perfect (Christian) community. It would be anachronistic, therefore, to see in Boccaccio's vision of the philosopher and the poet the traits of the solitary man withdrawn from civic life in search of an individual equilibrium with nature and God. This would attribute to Boccaccio a sterile version of wisdom, more appropriate to a Romantic rather than to a philological image of the author. For Boccaccio the

function of poetry, its philosophical [UNK]ργον, was the perfectioning of human beings so that they may become good members of the Christian society. In his view the ideals of classical philosophy and civic theology met, giving origin to the "second" Prometheus, whose mission of civilization places the realization of human nature at the core of Renaissance philosophy.[41]

Both mythology and rhetoric played a crucial role in Boccaccio's claim of an autonomous ethical function of poetry, for both provided the classical materials the poets use to cloak their truths under fabulous 'cortecce' (barks).[42] The criterion for the interpretation of mythology that Dante called 'allegory of the poets,' was known in the Middle Ages as *integumentum*.[43] The general principle that poets signify through exemplary "beautiful lies" also animates the Decameronian *novelle*, where a poetic of *verisimile* actualizes the present in a mythological form.

Following these principles, the investigation of the textual meaning of the *Decameron* reveals in the proemial introduction the presence of a Promethean figure, linked to a notion of practical moral knowledge. The fictional "author" has learned to become detached from his passions (in analogy with the earthly goods in Patristic hagiography) and he is now able to communicate his wisdom to the others, helping them to learn virtue, leave their "natural" state of spiritual slavery, and become civilized human beings.[44] The author pursues his goal through a collection of exemplary narratives no longer taken from the *repertoire* of sacred theology but from the ethological materials available to the moral poet— the deeds and facts of human civil life. As Prometheus went back to civilize the uncouth Assyrians, so the author teaches his own meditative experience (a meditation on natural philosophy, not on metaphysics) to an equivalent 'natural' subject (women enslaved to passions) in the urban community. He portrayed this subject in lovesick women, left without any defense or governance by their personal 'disease' (love, that is, the affliction of passion), like the Florentines had been by the ravages of the plague.[45] In Boccaccio's view, they are the weakest victims of the often erring fortune.[46]

Lucia Marino noticed the in the Proemio of the *Genealogie* Boccaccio described the mythographer's work as a 'Promethean' task. Through this reference to the 'second' Prometheus, the author assimilated his own mythographical endeavor to a sage's humanizing task. Indeed, it would be difficult not to project the image of the Promethean philosopher onto the real Boccaccio. Such a projection was implicit in the author's theorization of the 'civic' poet's intellectual commitment. Through his reinterpretation of Prometheus, Boccaccio revindicated to himself the lofty role of 'civilizator' in the troubled, after-plague, Florentine world, not only as a mythographer but above all, as a poet.[47] In so doing, he strengthened and nobilitated the social status of the poet as a 'worker' who participates in the construction of the virtuous, ideal, city. This was, already, a fully humanist vision.

Notes

1. See Garin (1938). The return to the origins of the humanists intermingled many components. Before Garin, scholars like Gentile, Burckhardt, and Burdach had stressed the high spirituality of Humanist thought, its rediscovery of classical antiquity, its continuity with Hellenistic philosophy, and the presence of religious motives inspired by oriental mysticism, in particular the Hermetic tradition. The humanists' criticism of Scholasticism, and their preeminent interest in moral philosophy and anthropology, led them to recover the practical moral philosophy of the Fathers, centered on the problems relative to the conciliation of the Christian and the secular lives. On the Renaissance of Patristic studies see also Charles Stinger (83-166). On the Patristic influence on the humanists' treatises on the human condition see Charles Trinkaus, *In Our Image and Likeness. Humanity and Divinity in Italian Humanist Thought* 1970, (171-321) and, for a comment on Garin's article, (187-89).

2. Since the high Middle Ages, the celebration of human dignity had been accompanied by the despise for the worldly condition of man. Innocent III's highly influential *De contemptu mundi* should have been followed, in Innocent's plans, by a treatise celebrating the worth of human being.

3. Giannozzo Manetti, for example, criticized the Latin poets' interpretation of Prometheus as creator of man in his *De dignitate et excellentia hominis,* III,6. He referred to Ovid's and Horace's interpretations on the one side, and to their Christianization by Fulgentius and the Fathers on the other. Raymond Trousson notices that an attempt to reconcile paganism and Christian religion was hardly thinkable in the early centuries of Christianity. On the contrary, apologetes like Tertullian used an Euhemerist interpretation of pagan mythology to ridicule the ancient gods and prove the supremacy of Revelation. In so doing, however, they also saved pagan culture from oblivion. Starting from Lactantius and Isydore, the Fathers begun to interpret ancient poetry as a sort of 'partial' Revelation God conceded to the ancients through inspired poets. These would therefore become assimilated to prophets, among whom they often figured in the iconography of the Middle Ages. See Trousson (91-121). The tendency to attribute a Christian meaning to the pagan deities combined with the Euhemerist tradition, which interpreted the pagan gods as exceptional men di-

vinized by their contemporaries. Christian apologetes had used Euhemerism to prove the inconsistency of pagan religions, but the Middle Ages gave it a different function. The human origin of the ancient gods strengthened human dignity and became a motive of admiration, especially for those gods that were interpreted as the ancient heroes of civilization, like Prometheus. See [Illegible Text] (23-30).

4. Cassirer 149, quoted in Garin 105.

5. Garin notices that the Humanists sought a spiritual and moral unity: "Unità innanzi tutto religiosa, ove in una ispirazione originaria si superano anche le antitesi confessionali; fusione di questa *docta religio,* religione spirituale, con la *pia filosofia,* filosofia dell'uomo, per rifarsi, oltre le opposizioni delle scuole, a quegli ideali di cui i Padri già si erano compiaciuti, di un logo rivelatosi variamente a tutti gli uomini di buona volontà." Garin 1938 (107).

6. On this point see Trinkaus, *In Our Image and Likeness. Humanity and Divinity in Italian Humanist Thought* 1970 (18-28).

7. Hugh IV, king of Cyprus, requested Boccaccio to compose a vast mythological repertoire. After some esitation, described in the *Proemio* addressed to the king's officer Donnino of Parma, the poet accepted the commissioned task and began working on the first version of the *Genealogie* from around 1350. See also note 8. For detailed information on the composition and the editions of the *Genealogie* see Vittorio Zaccaria's *Nota al testo* (1592-1599) in his edition of the *Genealogie.* For a comment and an interpretation of the text see Branca, *Boccaccio medievale e nuovi studi sul Decameron* 285 ff.

8. Boccaccio presumably started working on the *Decameron* after 1348, the year of the great plague that devastated Europe and Florence. Some scholars, however, suggest this term for the *Introduzione* but not for all the *novelle,* some of which were likely composed before. Most critics consider 1353 the date of completion of the *Decameron,* with the exception of Vittore Branca, who argues in favor of an earlier date, 1351. In any case, Boccaccio never ceased working on his masterpiece, as the manuscript he copied in 1370 shows (Hamiltonian 90, Staatsbibliotheck, Berlin). Around 1350, while he was still working on the *Decameron,* Boccaccio began the composition of the *Genealogie deorum gentilium,* which he copied in a semi-definitive version between 1365 and 1370 (Pluteo LII 9, Laurenziana Library, Florence). Boccaccio continued to emendate this manuscript of the *Genealogie* until after 1372. See

Battaglia Ricci, *Boccaccio* 2000 (122-23) and (219-24) Branca, *Giovanni Boccaccio. Profilo biografico* 1997 Branca and Ricci; Vittore Branca's introduction to his edition of the *Decameron* (1992), and Vittorio Zaccaria's introduction to his edition of the *Genealogie* (1998).

9. In Rhetoric the scope of the deliberative discourse is to indicate what is useful and what is to avoid, what is useful and honorable and their opposites. These principles of ethical relevance were at the basis of Cicero's *De officiis.* See the exposition on the deliberative genre of causes in Cicero's *De oratore,* II, 333-40 and Quintilian, *Istitutio oratoria,* III, IV, 12-16 and III, VIII. See also Ciccro (attr.), *Rhetorica ad C. Herennium,* I,2.

10. "Le già dette donne [. . .] *parimente diletto* delle sollazzevoli cose in quelle mostrate e *utile* consiglio potranno pigliare, in quanto potranno cognoscere quello che sia da fuggire e che sia similmente da seguitare: le quali cose senza passamento di noia non credo che possano intervenire." "Proemio 14." The italics of the Italian quotation are mine, as well as the English translation. The 'passamento di noia' alludes to the effort necessary to learn one's own path to virtue. According to Aristotle, ethical virtue is a state that man must conquer in order to reach the wise man's happiness. 'Noia' means pain and effort, as it is clear from other contextual passages in the *Proemio* (where this term occurs 6 times). In this case 'noia' indicates the 'ἔργον' (trial) involved in the process of acquiring virtue. According to Aristotle, ethical virtue requires both decision and a choice of the mean between two opposite excesses. Unless otherwise indicated, all Italian quotations are from the 1992 edition of Boccaccio's *Decameron* edited by Vittore Branca. English translations are from G. H. McWilliam or from J. M. Rigg. The latter is from the Decameron Web site of Brown University.

11. According to Kurt Flasch, this formulation "indicava per ogni dotto del XIII e XIV secolo un chiaro programma, che egli conosceva almeno dai testi di Cicerone: non si tratta di ciò che giova o danneggia il singolo in senso convenzionale, bensí di ciò che *veramente* e *in sostanza* è utile o dannoso. Anche i filosofi del medio evo utilizzavano questa formula in tal senso. Essa compariva in più scuole di pensiero; la usava tanto Tommaso d'Aquino quanto Guglielmo d'Ockham. E generalmente stava a indicare: qui si tratta dei concetti fondamentali della filosofia morale." Flasch 26. Boccaccio, however, did not pursue this program as a speculative moral philosopher but as a practical moral philosopher, for this is the field most appropriate to morally committed poetry.

The author deals with a particular reality that he represents by imitating real life (the criterion of *vero-verisimile* stated by Fiammetta in the introduction to Calandrino's novella "IX.5,5").

12. This brings attention to the critical issue of coherence between content and form. A literary work of ethics should have a form suitable to its particular genre. For this reason Boccaccio inaugurated a new literary form that drew from the tradition of exemplary literature but renovated it and, through the critical device of parody, submitted to his exigencies. His models came from various sources, all worth deeper investigation. To the traditionally studied subtexts of the Boccaccian *novelle,* such as religious and vernacular literary texts, at least three other sources may be added: the manuals of moral philosophy; the *quaestiones disputatae* studied in Civil and Canon Law; and the manuals for confessors. All of these texts are organized as collection of 'cases.' Fredi Chiappelli first formulated the hypothesis of a possible influence of Boccaccio's juridical studies on the structure of the *Decameron* Chiappelli (105-11).

13. With the developments of the last period of Scholastics, when the so called 'question of universals' evolved toward 'nominalistic' positions with John Duns Scotus and William Ockham, natural philosophy and 'realism' in art further developed. As Pier Massimo Forni observed: "È assai importante, addirittura decisivo, direi, che il realismo boccacciano sia valutato sullo sfondo di quei cruciali mutamenti di pensiero, e anzi di visione del mondo divulgatisi nel corso del Duecento, che portarono a esaurimento la grande stagione ascetico-penitenziale cristiana." Forni 1995 (312-13).

14. Petrarch developed his conception of *theologia poetica* in his *Invective contra medicum,* written between 1351 and 1353, the years in which Boccaccio completed the *Decameron.* The same idea recurs also in Petrarch *Familiare* X.4 to his brother Gherardo. Charles Trinkaus remarks that "the emphasis of the *Invectives* is to assert poetry (aided by rhetoric) as a source of philosophical and theological truth, and to argue the superiority of the psychotherapy of the liberal arts over the physician's bodily medicine" Trinkaus, *Petrarch and the Formation of Renaissance Consciousness* (95). The consonance between Petrarch and Boccaccio's ideas on the poetical value of theology, and vice versa, is remarkable. It seems possible that Boccaccio had already embedded these ideas in the *Decameron* at the time of its composition. See also Curtius (225-27).

15. For Boccaccio's use of ancient and contemporary sources, both pagan and Christian, see Vittorio

Zaccaria's introduction to his edition of Boccaccio's *Genealogie* (13-40).

16. In antiquity the myth of Prometheus was centered on the antagonism between men and Gods, and on men's frustrated desire for immortality. With Hesiod (*Theogonia* 507-616; *Works and Days* 47-105) and Aeschylus (*Prometheus Bound*) the Titan became the initiator of civilization. This function remains also in Plato's version of the myth in the *Protagoras* (319 D-322 D). Beginning from the IVth century B.C., he was seen as the material maker of man from mud and water. This interpretation appeared in the authors Boccaccio quoted, both pagan such as Ovid (*Metamorphosis* I.77-88), Horace (*Carmina* I, 19, 13), and Claudianus, and Christian, such as Servius and Fulgentius. Lucian of Samosata cast Prometheus in the Epicurean evolutionism, in which he became a symbol of the human creation of the gods. In the early centuries of Christianity a Euhemerist interpretation prevailed and the attempt to give a pseudo-historical account of the origin of the gods remained a distinctive trait also of later medieval mythographer, including Boccaccio. Lactantius initiated an allegorical exegesis of the myth, attributing to the poets a divine inspiration which empowered them to reach the truth, although in a un-revealed and confused way. Lactantius concreted the allegorical Prometheus 'maker' of the first human being and transformed him in the inventor of statuary, that is in the first one who created an image of man. Taking from Lactantius, later medieval writers developed the idea of Prometheus as re-creator of man, who transformed uncouth into learned men. He so appeared for example in Vincent of Beauvais *Speculum historiale* (I,CXVI). In the Middle Ages and Renaissance all of mythographers used but differed from Boccaccio's version. The spiritual meaning of this Promethean symbol was linked to the image of Christ's redemptive work only in the late fifteenth century, although with significant exceptions. With Ficino and Pico, the Promethean myth was projected in the idea of man's deification, and in the sixteenth century the image of rebellion and self-affirmation, detached from a religious context, was already present. See Trousson (25-194) and Peroni (451-57). For an elaboration on the parallel between Prometheus-sculptor and the poet in French Renaissance literature, see the treatment of the myth in Maurice Scève's *Délie* in Defaux (261-95).

17. Boccaccio wrote in Epistle XI: "non solamente non trovo che tale scritto sia abbastanza degno dei meriti di quel reverendissimo uomo, ma neppure del tuo ingngno, anzi lo vedo ridondante di tale e tanta abbondanza disordinata di parole superflue che nel leggerlo mi viene a noia" Boccaccio, *Epistole e lettere,* Epistole e lettere (XI.17). For an analysis of Boccaccio's rewriting of Peter Damian's life see Bufano (334-62) and Battaglia Ricci, "Scrittura e riscrittura: Dante e Boccaccio 'agiografi'" 1998 (165-75). Peter Damiani was also a significant figure from another point of view. At the beginning of the eleventh century this monk had strongly opposed the application of classical philosophy to Christian theology and had asserted the existence of a radical antinomy between free will—expressed by philosophy—and divine Grace—expressed by theology. Damiani attacked Boethius' use of Aristotelian Περί ἐρμηνείας to deal with the problems connected to the relation between free will and Grace. He showed that the utilization of Greek philosophical categories to theological problems led to contradictions and aporias. As Salvatore Camporeale remarks, Lorenzo Valla shared Damiani's views and attacked Scholastic theology on the same grounds as Damiani. "Il fatto storico culturale, infatti, della controversia circa la funzionalità o la incompossibilità della filosofia classica in teologia sembra doversi individuare (nell'ambito della prima scolastica) con la reazione anti-filosofica condotta da Peter Damiani, nei primi decenni del secolo XI. Questi assumerà come emblematico [. . .] il tentativo di risolvere l'antinomia libero arbitrio/ predestinazione salvifica mediante l'utilizzazione della logica aristotelica" Camporeale 1976 (67). For a discussion of Damiani's critique to Boethius' application of Aristotle's Περί ἐρμηνείας see Isaac. Perhaps it was not fortuitous that Boccaccio, who was among the early humanist critics of Scholastics and its programmatic submission of philosophy to theology had an interest in this figure beyond the accomplishment of his master's desires.

18. This position of marginality with respect to the city was also characteristic of the mendicant order convents in the Middle Ages. Santa Maria Novella, where the ten narrators meet at the beginning of the *Decameron,* was built in the "newly cultivated" fields (*terrae novellae*) just outside the Florentine Carolingian walls.

19. As Erwin Panofsky noticed, the two versions of the myths of Vulcan and Prometheus in the *Genealogie* are connected. Boccaccio gives a double account of Vulcan (XII. 70) story, as for Prometheus, one mythological and the other historical. According to Panofsky, Vulcan would represent the fire of technological knowledge, which endows men with the arts and is intended to satisfy their basic needs. Prometheus instead, would represent the fire of spiritual knowledge, corresponding to a higher stage of human development

and satisfying the needs related to higher forms of social organization. Boccaccio distinguishes three types of fire, the substance of fire, which we cannot perceive, and the fire which we can experience. This latter is of two species, 'natural' (lightning) and artificial', i.e. created by man. This artificial fire is linked to the arts, which Boccaccio lists before inserting a long quotation from Vitruvius, containing the Epicurean evolutionist account of the origin of human society whose archetype is the Lucretius' book V of *De rerum natura*. This is what an ancient author without Revelation as Vitruvius could imagine about human origins, says Boccaccio. Had he read the *Pentatheucum*, "he would know that Cain not only built houses, but also cities" (XII.70, 10). Civic life is associated with Revelation and Old Testament. Vulcan's fire would therefore be necessary for the life of the natural man, while Prometheus' would enlighten the civilized life of political man. This distinction recalls the one Plato presented in the myth of the origin of the *polis* narrated in *Republic* 367E-370C. It seems unlikely, however, that Boccaccio directly knew this text. For a discussion of the symbolical relation of the myths Vulcan and Prometheus see Panofsky (50-51).

20. The *Mythological Allegory* is one of the texts collected in the *Zibaldone Laurenziano* XXIX.8. Boccaccio copied it (61r-62r) without a title. In his edition of 1928, Francesco A. Massera titled it *Allegoria mitologica*. As Manlio Pastore Stocchi observes, the narrative seems to allude to historical facts covered by a mythological veil. It contrasts old and new interlacing classical and Christian symbologies that show the young Boccaccio's syncretism. See Pastore Stocchi's introduction to the Italian-Latin in Branca's edition of Boccaccio's complete works. See Boccaccio, *Allegoria mitologica* (1093-123), Boccaccio, *Filocolo* I.3. Prometheus appears also in *Rime* XXXVIII, in relation to his supplice at the rock. The sonnet suggests that Zeus' eagle every day ate Prometheus's heart instead of his liver. Another allusion to the titan's cunning theft of the fire (*sagacissimo furto*) is in a letter to Zanobi da Strada, epistle VI, written in 1348.

21. *Introduzione* "Day IV" 36.

22. Cfr. The story of Adam and Eve in Boccaccio, *De casibus virorum illustrium,* De casibus I.

23. According to Trousson the figures of Prometheus and Adam merged relatively late in the Renaissance. Boccaccio's allegorical interpretation, therefore, would be an exception that influenced later mythographers. See Trousson 138.

24. The main classical Boccaccian sources for Prometheus are Ovid, *Metam.* I.76-88 and Horace,

Carmina I.16. Both these texts describe Prometheus as the creator of the first man. He created him from mud and, seeing he was weak, he stole the fire from the gods to give it to men so that they may learn how to survive.

25. See in particular Fulgentius, Mitologiac II.6.

26. The most influential source of this Prometheus-creator is Ovid in *Met.* I.76-88, in which the god makes the first man from a mixture of soil and river water ("quam satus Iapeto mixtam pluvialibus undis / finxit in effigem moderantum cuncta deorum" *Met.* I.82-83).

27. The same pattern is in Boccaccio's sonnet XXXVIII, where the heart replaces the liver of the classical version. In the passage from the *Genealogie* Boccaccio explicitly recalls Aeschylus' *Prometheus Bound.*

28. Maybe a Neapolitan philosopher of the ninth century. For the scarce information available on this author and the relative bibliography see Zaccaria's note 24 to *Geneal.* I. *Pr.* II.10.

29. According to the Biblical genealogy of *Genesis* 10:1-5, Japeth was one of Noah's sons. His offspring populated the Mediterranean islands and coasts. He was, therefore, the progenitor of the Caucasian race.

30. We should remember that Aristotle defined epistemological knowledge as the knowledge of the causes. There is an implicit allusion to Aristotle's *Physics*, although this definition was also present in the *Ethics.*

31. Boccaccio's *Genealogie deorum gentilium* had an extensive success during the Renaissance, and became one of the most authoritative mythological repertoires. According to Wilkins, it had eight editions between 1472 and 1532. Its influence is visible also in Renaissance art. Panofsky shows that Boccaccio's *Genealogie* is a source for the cycles of paintings by Piero di Cosimo representing the early history of man. See Wilkins and Panofsky (33-68).

32. Boccaccio reports medieval authorial opinions on Prometheus by Lactantius, Eusebius, Augustine, Rabanus, Yves of Chartres. All of them allegorically interpreted the mythical Titan as a figure of wisdom. See *Geneal.* IV.44,19-21. In the same passage Boccaccio did not interpret work as a punishment but as a sort of disease (*macilenza*) that exhausted human beings after the Fall. Creative work, however, was not associated here with physical effort.

33. Hugh of Saint Victor, *Didascalicon. De studio legendi.*

34. "Qui a natura producti sunt, rudes et ignari veni-
unt, imo ni instruantur, lutei agrestes et belue.
Circa quos secundus Prometheus insurgit, id est
doctus homo, et eos tamquam lapideos suscipiens
quasi de novo creet, docet et instruit, et demon-
strationibus suis ex naturalibus hominibus civiles
facit, moribus scientia et virtutibus insignes, adeo
ut liquido pateat alios produxisse naturam et alios
reformasse doctrinam." All English translations
from *Genealogie* are by C. Osgood.

35. Meiss, *Painting in Florence and Siena after the
Black Death.*

36. The hypothesis that Boccaccio did not apply the
concept of poetry expressed in *Geneal.* XIV, argued by some critics such as Francesco Bruni,
does not seem to take sufficiently into account the
fact that Boccaccio continued to revise and tran-
scribe the *Decameron* until the end of his life. See
Battaglia Ricci, *Boccaccio* 2000 (122-28). Boccaccio copied his masterpiece around 1370, in the
codex Hamilton 90, as Vittore Branca and Pier
Giorgio Ricci have demonstrated. See Branca, et
al. 1962. Ricci notices that "questo *Decameron*
faticosamente copiato e carezzato in età che si
vuole di pentimento e di ripudio, vuol dire pur
qualcosa per chi sappia intendere" Ricci, "Ho
partecipato alla scoperta del 'Decameron' autografo" 1985 (260). The critic probably alludes to
the letter Boccaccio wrote to Mainardo Cavalcanti
in 1373, in which he apparently rejected his vulgar masterpiece. This letter is an isolated case
and, notwithstanding its clear evidence as a fact,
should be evaluated in the context of the reasons
that moved Boccaccio to express these ideas. See
Billanovich 162.

37. Boccaccio includes among these Hesiod's Ἔργα,
Virgil's *Georgies,* Columella's *De re rustica,* and
Varro's *De re rustica,* all quoted in the *Genealo-
gie.*

38. "*Mythica* autem dicitur *fabulosa* e *mythicon* grece,
quod latine *fabula* sonat, et hec comedis, de quibus supra, et theatris accommoda est, que ob tur-
pia in scenis actitata ab illustribus poetis etiam
improbatur. *Physica* autem, que, ut interpretatione
vocabuli percipitur, *naturalis* est, nec non et mora-
lis, quoniam mundo utilis videatur, laudabilis est.
Civilis vero seu *politica,* que et *sacrificula* dici
potest, ad urbem spectare dicitur, que ob sacrorum
veterum abominabilem turpitudinem a veri Dei
cultu atque rectitudine fidei reprobanda est." [Ital-
ics are in the text]. See also the Proemio to *Geneal.* 16-18 and 45. In this latter passage Boccaccio declares the ancient poets were filled with
"mudana sapientia," that is, with a true knowledge
of the human world hidden under a fabulous veil.

39. See Flasch (29-34).

40. It is the codex Ambrosiano 204 Inf, belonging to
Boccaccio's private library. See Branca, *Giovanni
Boccaccio. Profilo biografico* 1997 (183-85). The
codex does not appear in the inventory of Santo
Spirito's "parva libraria" because it was probably
removed before its compilation in 1451. See
Mazza (69-70). Anna Maria Cesari argues that Aristotle's text, Thomas' commentary and all the
glosses and annotations are by Boccaccio's hand.
Cesari dates the manuscript around 1339/40, by
comparing the codex's handwriting with letters
from the same period, including the *Mavortis miles*
to Petrarch. The editors of the Biblioteca Medicea
Laurenziana catalog listing Boccaccio's manuscripts and documents argue that the author copied Thomas' commentary and annotations but not
the *Ethics,* apparently written by a professional
hand. These editors substantially agree with Cesari on the date of the manuscript but also observe
that some of the annotations present graphic characters typical of Boccaccio's later handwriting.
These observations suggest that Boccaccio's pro-
tracted study of this text begun most likely before
the *Decameron* and continued until he was old,
since he quoted Aristotle's work in his *Esposizioni
sopra la Comedia di Dante.* In his commentary to
canto IV Boccaccio also quoted Albert the Great's
(Aquinas' master in France) commentary to the
Ethics. Boccaccio could have been introduced to
this text in the first years after his return to Florence, when he probably entered in contact with
the Florentine Dominican convent of Santa Maria
Novella, where Remigio dei Girolami—who had
been Thomas' disciple in Paris—had introduced
the teaching of Thomas' works since the beginning
of the century. This would move the date of the
codex to the early 1340s. See Cesari (69-100) Biblioteca Medicea Laurenziana (130-40) Marchesi
(36-37); and Franceschini (234-39). For a study
on Boccaccio's handwriting see Ricci, "Evoluzione nella scrittura del Boccaccio e datazione degli
autograli" (286-96). For Remigio dei Girolami's
chronology see Panella 1990 (145-311).

41. This was again the role of the philosopher in Aristotle's *Ethics.* Boccaccio also defines the work of
the poet in the *Trattatello,* where he wrote: "Li
poeti nelle loro opere, le quali noi chiamiamo
'poesia' quando con finzioni di varii iddii, quando
con transmutazioni di uomini in varie forme e
quando con leggiadre persuasioni, ne mostrano le
cagioni delle cose, gli effetti delle virtù e de' vizii,
e che fuggire dobbiamo e che seguire, acciò che
pervenire possiamo, virtuosamente operando, a
quel fine il quale essi, che il vero Iddio debita-
mente non conosceano, somma salute credevano."
This passage is from *Trattatello* 142, quoted from
Zaccaria's introduction to Boccaccio's *Genealogie*

(31). See also the explicit declaration of writing the book as a 'labor,' where he also indirectly quotes Virgil's verse "labor omnia vicit / improbus" from *Georgics* I.145-146, the crucial verses highlighting Virgil's Epicurean conception of work as the essential instrument of human progress.

42. Garin noticed the novelty of Boccaccio's views on poetry: their independence from philosophy and their intrinsic homology with the theology of the ancient poets described in *Geneal.* XV.8. For the medieval notion of *integumentum* as mythological wrapping of Christian meaning see Chenu 1955. For an application of this concept to Boccaccio's poetics see Zaccaria's introduction to *Genealogie* 23.

43. See Chenu 1955.

44. "Therefore with the doctrine of knowledge he receives from God, the wise man enlivens, that is awakens, the asleep soul of the man of mud, that is of the ignorant man. Only then he may be said alive, when from being a brute he becomes, or has been made, a rational man." [Doctrina igitur sapientic a Deo suscepte prudens homo animat, id est sopitam animam excitat lutei, id est ignari, hominis, qui tunc vivere dicitur, dum ex bruto rationalis efficitur, seu effectus est.] *Geneal.* IV.44,16.

45. "He had found them uncouth, utterly primitive, and living according to the customs of animals, and he left them, almost redone, civilized" [rudes et omnino silvestres et ritu ferarum viventes invenerat, quasi de novo compositos civiles relinqueret homines] *Geneal.* IV.44,9.

46. Boccaccio's conception that Fortune can make mistakes and that one may correct these mistakes was a Humanistic intellectual trait characterizing the *Decameron* since its beginning in the "Proemio." See also Pampinea's introduction to "VI.2." Boccaccio's Humanism is usually seen more in his later Latin and erudite works rather than in the *Decameron*. See for example "Motivi preumanistici" in Branca, *Boccaccio medievale e nuovi studi sul Decameron* 1992 (277-99).

47. Boccaccio, *Genealogie deorum gentilium, Genealogie* I.41. So Lucia Marino concludes her insightful article: "The mythographer as Prometheus serves a social, civic, humanizing function. In so doing, he is as necessary to society as the poets themselves and as the philosopher-teachers who do not speak primarily in symbols or fables." That the poets had a recognized humanizing role was not granted, however, and it can be hardly presupposed. This article has shown that Marino's observations can and should be extended to the case of the poet-philosopher.

Works Cited

Battaglia Ricci, Lucia. *Boccaccio*. Roma: Salerno, 2000.

———. "Scrittura e riscrittura: Dante e Boccaccio 'agiografi'". *Scrivere di santi. Atti del II Convegno di studio dell'Associazione italiana per lo studio della santità, dei culti, dell'agiografia. Napoli, 22-25 ottobre 1997.* Gennaro Luongo. Roma: Viella, 1998. 147-75.

Biblioteca Medicea Laurenziana. *Mostra di manoscritti, documenti e edizioni. I, manoscritti e documenti.* Certaldo: Comitato promotore, 1975.

Billanovich, Giuseppe. *Restauri boccacceschi.* Roma: Edizioni di Storia e Letteratura, 1945.

Boccaccio, Giovanni. *Allegoria mitologica.* Vittore Branca. Tutte le opere di Giovanni Boccaccio. Milano: Mondadori, 1992. 1093-123.

———. *De casibus virorum illustrium.* Vittore Branca. Tutte le opere di Giovanni Boccaccio. Milano: Mondadori, 1983.

———. *Decameron.* Vittore Branca. Torino: Einaudi, 1992.

———. *Epistole e lettere.* Vittore Branca. Tutte le opere di Giovanni Boccaccio. Milano: Mondadori, 1992. 495-878.

———. *Filocolo.* Mario Marti. Opere minori in volgare. Milano: Rizzoli, 1969.

———. *Genealogie deorum gentilium.* Vittore Branca. Tutte le opere di Giovanni Boccaccio. Milano: Mondadori, 1998.

Branca, Vittore and Pier Giorgio Ricci. *Un autografo del 'Decameron'. Codice Hamiltoniano 90.* Padova: Università degli Studi, 1962.

Branca, Vittore. *Boccaccio medievale e nuovi studi sul Decameron.* Firenze: Sansoni, 1992.

———. *Giovanni Boccaccio. Profilo biografico.* Firenze: Sansoni, 1997.

Bufano, A. "Il rifacimento boccacciano della 'Vita Petri Damiani di Giovanni da Lodi'". *Studi sul Boccaccio* XI (1981): 334-62.

Burckhardt, Jacob. *The Civilization of the Renaissance in Italy.* S.G.C. Middlemore. London: Penguin, 1990.

Burdach, Konrad. *Riforma, Rinascimento, Umanesimo.* Delio Cantimori. Firenze: Sansoni, 1935.

Camporcale, Salvatore I. "Lorenzo Valla tra medioevo e rinascimento. Encomio s. Thomae—1457". *Memorie Domenicane. Nuova Serie* VII (1976): 11-194.

Cassirer, Ernst. *The Individual and the Cosmos in Renaissance Philosophy.* Mario Domandi. New York: Dover, 2000.

Cesari, Anna Maria. "L'Etica di Aristotele del Codice Ambrosiano A 204 inf.: un autografo del Boccaccio". *Archivio Storico Lombardo* Serie Nona V-VI (1968): 69-100.

Chenu, Marie-Dominique. "*Involucrum*. Le mythe selon les théologiens médiévaux". Archives d'histoire doctrinale et litteraire du Moyen Âge XXII (1955): 75-79.

Chiappelli, Fredi. "Discorso o progetto per uno studio del *Decameron*." *Studi di Italianistica in onore di Giovanni Cecchetti*. P. Cherchi and M. Picone. Ravenna: Longo, 1988. 105-11.

Cicero, M. Tullius Attributed. *La retorica a Gaio Erennio (Rhetorica ad C. Herennium)*. Milano: Mondadori, 1992.

Cicero, M. Tullius. *De Officiis*. Oxford: Clarendon, 1994.

———. *Dell'oratore (De oratore)*. Milano: BUR, 1994.

Curtius, Ernst R. *European Literature and the Latin Middle Ages*. Princeton: Princeton UP, 1983.

Defaux, Gérard. "L'idole, le poète et le voleur de feu: erreur et impieté dans *Délie*." *French Forum* 18.3 (Sept 1993): 261-95.

Flasch, Kurt. *Poesia dopo la peste. Saggio su Boccaccio*. Bari: Laterza, 1995.

Forni, Pier Massimo. "Realtà/verità". *Lessico critico decameroniano*. Renzo Bragantini and Pier Massimo Forni. Torino: Bollati Boringhieri, 1995. 300-19.

Franceschini, Ezio. "L' "Aristotele latino" nei codici dell'Ambrosiana". *Miscellanea G. Galbiati*. Milano, 1951.

Fulgentius, Fabius Planciades. *Opera*. Helm, Rudolf. Stuttgart: Teubner, 1970.

Garin, Eugenio. "La "Dignitas Hominis" e la letteratura patristica". *La Rinascita* I (1938): 102-46.

Gentile, Giovanni. *Giordano Bruno e il pensiero italiano del Rinascimento*. Firenze: Vallecchi, 1920.

Hugh of Saint Victor. Didascalicon. De studio legendi. Critical, Buttimer, Charles H. Washington D.C.: The Catholic University Press, 1939.

Isaac, Jean. *Le "Peri hermeneias" en Occident de Boèce à saint Thomas. Histoire littéraire d'un traité d'Aristote*. Paris: Vrin, 1953.

Manetti, Giannozzo. *Ianotii Manetti De dignitate et excellentia hominis*. Elizabeth R. Leonard ed. Padova: Antenore, 1975.

Marchesi, Concetto. *L'Etica Nicomachea nella tradizione latina medievale*. Messina: Trimarchi, 1904.

Mazza, Antonia. "L'inventario della "Parva libraria" di Santo Spirito e la biblioteca del Boccaccio". *Italia medievale e umanistica* IX (1966): 1-74.

Meiss, Millard. *Painting in Florence and Siena after the Black Death*. Princeton, New Jersey: Princeton UP, 1951.

Osgood, Charles G. *Boccaccio on Poetry. Being the Preface and the Fourteenth and Fifteenth Books of Boccaccio's Genealogia Deorum Gentilium*. Indianapolis, New York: The Bobbs-Merrill Company, 1956.

Panella, Emilio G. *Nuova cronologia remigiana*. Archivum Fratrum Praedicatorum. Roma: Istituto Storico Domenicano, 1990.

Panofsky, Erwin. *Studies in Iconology. Humanistic Themes in the Art of the Renaissance*. Boulder, Colorado: Westview, 1972.

Peroni, Lucilla. "Il motivo di Prometeo nella filosofia del Rinasciemento". *Rivista Critica di Storia della Filosofia* XIX.IV (Ott.-dic 1964): 451-57.

Quintilian. *La formazione dell'oratore (Institutio oratoria)*. Milano: BUR, 1997.

Ricci, Pier Giorgio. "Evoluzione nella scrittura del Boccaccio e datazione degli autografi". *Studi sulla vita e le opere del Boccaccio*. Pier Giorgio Ricci. Milano-Napoli: Ricciardi, 1985. 286-96.

———. "Ho partecipato alla scoperta del 'Decameron' autografo". *Studi sulla vita e le opere del Boccaccio*. Pier Giorgio Ricci. Milano-Napoli: Ricciardi, 1985. 256-60.

Seznec, Jean. *La survivance des dieux antiques*. Paris: Flammarion, 1993.

Stinger, Charles L. *Humanism and the Church Fathers. Ambrogio Traversari (1386-1439) and Christian Antiquity in the Italian Renaissance*. Albany: State U of New York P, 1977.

Trinkaus, Charles. *In Our Image and Likeness. Humanity and Divinity in Italian Humanist Thought*. Notre Dame, Indiana: U of Notre Dame P, 1995.

———. *Petrarch and the Formation of Renaissance Consciousness*. New Haven and London: Yale University Press, 1979.

Trousson, Raymond. *Le theme de Promethee dans la literature europeenne*. Geneve: Droz, 2001.

Wilkins, E.H. "The Genealogy of the Editions of the *Genealogia deorum*". *Modern Philology* XVIII (1919): 423-38.

Amy W. Goodwin (essay date 2004)

SOURCE: Goodwin, Amy W. "The Griselda Game." *Chaucer Review* 39, no. 1 (2004): 41-69.

[*In the following essay, Goodwin examines the dialogic relationship between the final* novella *of the* Decameron *and Francesco Petrarch's translation of it, focusing on Petrarch's audiences, the framing devices of both versions, and the narrative strategies each author used in his tale.*]

Criticism of Boccaccio's Griselda story, like that of Chaucer's *Clerk's Tale,* is rich with complementary, competing, and contradictory arguments about its author's intentions. By contrast, criticism of Petrarch's Latin Griselda story has suggested near agreement that Petrarch eliminated or suppressed the difficult interpretive issues that Boccaccio, Chaucer, and their modern readers have clearly prized in favor of a straightforward moralized exemplum.[1] Reasons why this view has prevailed are not far to seek. The moral conclusion Petrarch appended to the tale and the use made of his version by fourteenth- and fifteenth-century translators and redactors support it. Yet Petrarch's elaborate epistolary frame—the four letters of *Seniles* XVII that surround the tale—make the work something more than simply a clearly moralized translation of Boccaccio's Griselda story. Presenting with the tale a self-conscious study of translation and narrative art and a complex portrait of Petrarch, the letters suggest that it is multi-intentioned, the quality that has made Boccaccio's Griselda story and Chaucer's *Clerk's Tale* so open to debate.

In her 1980 essay "The Clerk and His Tale: Some Literary Contexts," Anne Middleton offered an innovative interpretation of Petrarch's Griselda story, contesting the prevailing view that Petrarch had rescued the tale from Boccaccio's ironic treatment, which had undercut its moral sentence.[2] Her argument had many strands, all of which anticipated her reading of the *Clerk's Tale.* She broadened the context for understanding Petrarch's Latin translation to include the second, third, and fourth letters of *Seniles* XVII and the reception of his tale in late fourteenth-century France and in the *Canterbury Tales.* Building on Glending Olson's argument that Petrarch saw the **Decameron** as recreational rather than didactic literature, Middleton emphasized the "recreative status the act of composition had for" Petrarch, showing that this status was implied by the way he framed the tale with a critical assessment of the **Decameron** in *Seniles* XVII.3, "a general meditation on the pleasures and value of the life of the writer" in *Seniles* XVII.2, and a discussion of the tale's genre and the responses of Petrarch's two readers in *Seniles* XVII.4.[3] For Middleton, Petrarch's presentation of his translation to Boccaccio "[rcdcfincd] thc pleasures of the text, according to Petrarch's idea of the literate man's 'pley.'"[4] While she argued that the moral sentence was indeed important to Petrarch, she insisted that his real interest lay in the tale's pathos or "affective powers" and in the challenge of adapting Boccaccio's vernacular story for the recreation of elite Latin readers whose more sober values contrast with those of Boccaccio's audience.[5]

Middleton's essay has had a curious afterlife. Her main and compelling argument—that Petrarch took up the translation as a pleasurable activity, and that his attention in *Seniles* XVII to the act of composition and to

his own version's effect on readers indicated that the tale's didactic value was just one aspect of its attractiveness—has not altered in a significant way subsequent approaches to Petrarch's Griselda story. Charlotte Morse's "The Exemplary Griselda" (1985) offered a substantial counterargument. Reasserting the tale's status as a moral exemplum, Morse cited evidence of Petrarch's lifelong commitment to exemplary narratives as illustrated in his letters and his treatises *De viris illustribus* and *De remediis utriusque fortune.*[6] Though both essays are widely cited, often together as if they were complementary rather than contradictory, Morse exposed the weaknesses of Middleton's argument: a focus on Petrarch's stated aims and a failure to compare Boccaccio's and Petrarch's renderings to determine their differences and through them the implied values of their audiences. Many of the changes Petrarch made within the narrative actually augmented the tale's didactic content; thus Middleton's main thesis contradicted Petrarch's painstaking elaboration of political and remedial virtues within the tale. Most critics since Morse have continued to insist, justifiably, on Petrarch's interest in the tale's exemplary values.

Middleton's secondary argument linking Petrarch's Latin adaptation with the culture of Latin readers has had wider influence but has also been challenged. David Wallace has characterized Petrarch's audience as "a small, consciously exclusive, masculine group of initiates dedicated to the pursuit of Latin culture: just such a group, in fact, as Petrarch describes in framing his Griselda story."[7] Like Middleton's, Wallace's insights into Petrarch's rendering of the tale derive in part from an examination of how Chaucer appears to have read it, as indicated by the kinds of changes he made in the *Clerk's Tale.* But the two essays could not be more different. Where Middleton focused on the letters of *Seniles* XVII, for Wallace these letters are relatively unimportant for establishing the context of the Griselda story. Where Middleton defined the "Petrarchan Academy" in terms of its constituents' notion of recreational literature, for Wallace this group of readers, carefully selected by Petrarch, functions to control thc transmission and reception of Petrarchan texts.[8] Wallace's broad aim is to put Petrarch's texts into relation with his life and work.[9] Key for Wallace are Petrarch's service to tyrants in exchange for their patronage, his misogyny, and his "willingness to view certain human beings as nonsubjects."[10] He cites chilling passages from Petrarch's works to give examples of Petrarch's elitism and ruthless exclusivity. With respect to the Griselda story, Wallace's aim is to distinguish Petrarch's ideological commitments from those of Boccaccio and Chaucer. He argues, "The *fyn,* or final effect, of Petrarchan humanism and of Petrarchan poetics . . . is to announce and embellish the will of the state as embodied in the person of a single masculine ruler." Discounting Petrarch's attempt in the moral conclusion to differentiate Walter from God, Wallace contends that the "implied analogy between Walter and God can be taken seriously in Petrarch's text because Walter's tyrannical proclivities are played down or passed over without comment."[11] Though Wallace does not examine Petrarch's treatment of Walter or cite lines from Petrarch's Griselda story, subsequent critics have used the term "Petrarchan Academy" to distinguish what have seemed like Petrarch's conservative aims from those of Chaucer and Boccaccio, who were writing for a mixed audience whose concern over Walter's appalling behavior might overshadow their admiration for Griselda's virtuous example.[12]

Middleton's and Wallace's arguments differ strikingly in part because of the different contexts that they find crucial for understanding Petrarch's Griselda story, and both are persuasive in bringing to bear on the Griselda story important facets of Petrarch's complexity. Yet for both, Chaucer's reading of Petrarch's intentions—though they read the *Clerk's Tale* differently—provides support for their own arguments. This approach, I think, ignores what should be the starting place for understanding Petrarch's Griselda story, that is, the relationship between Boccaccio's narrative and Petrarch's translation. The transmission of Petrarch's Griselda story in fourteenth- and fifteenth-century Europe treated it as a fairly autonomous text, its translators and adapters broadening its audience and moral application. But Petrarch's Griselda story was first of all a response to Boccaccio, and it is the complexity of his tale as a response that this essay will explore. I argue that the letters of *Seniles* XVII not only introduce and comment on Petrarch's translation, but function as an integral part of the translation. Petrarch uses the letters to take up issues Boccaccio raises in his own complex frame for the Griselda story and the *Decameron,* and shapes a self-presentation as Boccaccio's translator. By bringing to bear two perspectives on his Latin Griselda story, as both tale and translation, Petrarch makes reading his Griselda story something of a study or game; the reader has the essential role of conducting a dialogue between Petrarch's and Boccaccio's tales. In the sections below, I take up the issues of Petrarch's audiences, the framing devices surrounding Boccaccio's and Petrarch's narratives, and the narrative strategies each uses within his tale. Examining the ways in which Petrarch restages the interpretive problems that Boccaccio valued in his own tale, I try to show Petrarch's accomplishment on its own terms, providing a reading of Petrarch that may or may not conform to the way in which his Griselda story is represented in Chaucer's *Clerk's Tale.*

PETRARCH'S AUDIENCES

Petrarch's discussion of the Griselda story in *Seniles* XVII.3 and XVII.4 gives it an existence independent of the letters, for he recounts having recited Boccaccio's Italian tale to his friends; claims to have decided to

translate it for readers who do not know Italian; reports that some have admired his Latin translation and requested it; and, in the final letter, relays and comments on the responses of two readers. These different kinds of oral and written performance imply different audiences, although in some cases their memberships may overlap. And these audiences differ from the one Petrarch inscribes within *Seniles* XVII.3, which must know Italian, and has Boccaccio as its chief member. While it is true that Petrarch often wrote his letters for an audience broader than the individual he addresses, his addressee here is extremely important. In dedicating the tale to Boccaccio, Petrarch links the two Griselda stories together, insisting that his own version is accountable only to Boccaccio and urging him and all others to treat the two narratives as companion pieces:

> Whether I have deformed it or, perhaps, beautified it by changing its garment, you be the judge—for it all began there, and it goes back there; it knows the judge, the house, the way—so that you and whoever reads this may be clear on one point: that you, not I, must render an account of your works. Whoever asks me whether it is true, that is, whether I have written a history or just a tale, I shall reply with the words of Crispus, "Let the responsibility fall on the author" . . . namely my Giovanni.[13]

The humor in these lines may fly in different directions. In his conclusion to the *Decameron,* Boccaccio had simultaneously abjured and accepted responsibility for the work's effects on readers, and here Petrarch takes another leaf from Boccaccio's book. Yet in sending Boccaccio and all others to the Griselda story in the *Decameron,* Petrarch suggests that it is the translation as well as the tale itself that he commends to Boccaccio.

Just before the passage above, Petrarch claims to have followed Horace's advice to translators not to follow an exemplar word for word. Translation is a form of imitation, and Horace links them together in his *Art of Poetry.*[14] Petrarch discussed imitation in three earlier letters, *Familiares* I.8, XXII.2, and XXIII.19, the latter two to Boccaccio. For Petrarch the duty of the imitator is not to reproduce the exemplar, but like bees who create honey and wax from nectar, the imitator should transform the original into something new and valuable. In *Familiares* XXIII.19, to explain the relationship between an original and its imitation, he compared it to that between a father and son, who are not exact replicas:

> [T]hey have a certain something our painters call an 'air,' especially noticeable about the face and eyes, that produces a resemblance; seeing the son's face, we are reminded of the father's, although if it came to measurement, the features would all be different, but there is something subtle that creates this effect. We must thus see to it that if there is something similar, there is

also a great deal that is dissimilar, and that the similar
be elusive and unable to be extricated except in silent
meditation, for the resemblance is to be felt rather than
expressed.[15]

His point in using this metaphor differs wholly from
that of the bee simile. The act of perceiving similarities
and differences is itself pleasurable. By offering his
own Griselda story as a translation, Petrarch encourages
readers to study his art of imitation. His juxtaposing the
two tales certainly implies that he did not think that his
own version eliminated the complexity of Boccaccio's:
an imitation that simplified would be no achievement.
Instead, Petrarch's dedication of the tale suggests that
he vaunts his version as a rival. Yet it is very difficult to
detect whether Petrarch thinks that he has one-upped
Boccaccio or, if he does, the kind of one-upmanship
that has occurred; thus Middleton argued that Petrarch's
translation is less of a "rival creation" than "a commentary," and in some respects a "critical 'quiting.'"[16] If Petrarch competes with Boccaccio with his Latin translation, he has chosen a tale he admires tremendously, not
one that he necessarily thinks is defective. Through his
dedication the vernacular tale becomes the subtext of
his own Latin rendering.[17]

Seniles XVII.3 begins with something like a cursory
commentary on the **Decameron,** which Petrarch admits
he has not read completely. He notes the appropriate
match among the style, the idiom, the light-minded audience, and the author's own youth.[18] His own mature
values temper his assessment of the whole **Decameron,**
shaping his interests as a reader and distancing him
from Boccaccio's audience, which Boccaccio identifies
facetiously in the introduction as women unhappy in
love. Although Petrarch deprecates Boccaccio's readers
as the "common herd" (655), where the work's concerns coincide with Petrarch's own—in Boccaccio's description of the plague, his treatment of detractors, and
his Griselda story—his praise is lavish; the distance between Boccaccio's readers and Petrarch's becomes immaterial; and the distinction between Boccaccio's
youthful concerns as an artist and Petrarch's more mature ones vanishes entirely.[19] He writes that the final tale
of Griselda nearly made him forget himself. What Petrarch means is equivocal, but that he felt himself to enter perfectly into Boccaccio's audience for the Griselda
story and that he tried to repeat that experience for his
friends is surely important. And it is especially important that Petrarch's first telling of the Griselda story,
like Boccaccio's own tale, was in Italian.

Petrarch's views with respect to Italian are complicated.
Kenelm Foster argues that Petrarch found Italian to be
an excellent language to express sentiment, but that he
abhorred in the audience of Italian readers those who
were uneducated and unrefined. During the last twenty
years of his life, he was working on his vernacular po-

ems the *Canzoniere* and the *Triumphs.* It is neither Italian nor Italian readers per se that Petrarch objected to
but the broad democratic reach of Italian.[20] His report in
Seniles XVII.4 of two readers of his Latin Griselda
story describes their contrasting responses. Petrarch's
Latin readers are not a homogeneous group although
they are an exclusive one. The audience Petrarch inscribes within the letters of the Griselda story narrows
the reach of Boccaccio's audience to those who know
both Italian and Latin.

NARRATIVE FRAMES

The **Decameron** builds many complex relationships
among tales and tellers, some of which Chaucer will
later use in his *Canterbury Tales.* My focus here is on
Boccaccio's final tale's immediate frame, which Robert
Edwards has divided into three principal parts: the day's
theme of generosity or magnificence, Dioneo's commentary introducing and concluding the tale, and the
debate the tale provokes among the *brigata.*[21] As Millicent Joy Marcus has argued, the frame interferes with
readers' attempts to take from the tale a univocal exemplary meaning by offering perspectives on the tale that
thwart an unthoughtful acceptance either of Griselda's
virtuous example or of Gualtieri's role in demonstrating
her virtue. Boccaccio underscores the tale's open-
endedness with the *brigata*'s final discussion, which describes not one particular view but rather general disagreement about the tale's meaning. The female
members of the *brigata* debate the story at great length,
some criticizing one aspect and some praising another:
They do not resolve the argument or even conclude
their discussion, for Panfilo, noting the setting sun, interrupts the conversation to recall the *brigata* to the
business of returning to Florence. Thus the final word
on Boccaccio's Griselda story seems to be that there is
no final word.[22]

Dioneo's opening and closing commentary broadens the
tale's thematic scope to include, besides the virtue of
magnificence, an inquiry into the nature of virtuous and
blameworthy behavior. Dioneo associates Gualtieri's
behavior with "matta bestialitá" (bestiality, or senseless
brutality) and Griselda's with "divini spiriti" (celestial
spirits).[23] These labels, like the theme of magnificence,
refer us to Aristotle's *Nicomachean Ethics,* but now to
a later section, Book 7, on conditions associated with
virtue and vice.[24] We might see them loosely as two
ends of a spectrum running from the subhuman to the
superhuman: bestiality, vice, incontinence, continence,
virtue, the celestial. Aristotle includes bestiality with
vice and incontinence as three states to be avoided,[25]
distinguishing bestiality as more frightening than either
incontinence or vice, for in acts of bestiality reason is
lacking entirely, whereas with incontinence one's reason has been overcome either by feelings or appetites,
and with vice one's reason has been corrupted (*Ethics*

1150a-1151a25). Both bestial and celestial behaviors are extremely rare (*Ethics* 1145a30), so in the frame, at the very least, Dioneo suggests the rarity of the two main characters.

Modern critics have given Dioneo's labels a negligible role because Dioneo is, in Edwards's words, "a licensed figure of dissonance" and, in Tania Itala Rutter's, "a foil for others' virtues."[26] Rutter finds the labels ambivalent, particularly in Dioneo's concluding comment:

> Che si potrá dir qui, se non che anche nelle povere case piovono dal cielo de' divini spiriti, come nelle reali di quegli che sarien piú degni di guardar porci che d'avere sopra uomini signoria?
>
> (318)

> What more needs to be said, except that celestial spirits may sometimes descend even into the houses of the poor, whilst there are those in royal palaces who would be better employed as swineherds than as rulers of men?
>
> (794-95)

Rutter cautions us that we must not designate Gualtieri as the one more suited to tending swine or Griselda as the one most approaching a celestial spirit, and suggests instead—I think wrongly—that both could fit into either category.[27] For Edwards, Dioneo has "misapplied" the label of bestiality because it designates such a rare human behavior, and Gualtieri's behavior "fails the test of subhuman extremity," but the charge nonetheless serves "to register, by his partial and defective analogy, the alarm that Gualtieri's actions provoke."[28] The main problem with both Edwards's and Rutter's readings is that they effectively do away with Dioneo's comments rather than make use of the allusions to the *Nicomachean Ethics* to deepen our understanding of the tale. If Gualtieri's actions are not bestial, then what are they? The tale does not answer this question definitively because Gualtieri is somewhat inscrutable mimetically and thematically. The difficulty of choosing one interpretation of Gualtieri and/or other aspects of this tale is affirmed by Boccaccio's representation of general debate among the *brigata*.

Although Edwards has some justification for saying that Dioneo has misapplied the term, the error is merely a technical one, and Dioneo offers, perhaps, a correction at the tale's conclusion when he compares Gualtieri not to a beast but to a swineherd, one who tends beasts. Swineherds rule beings lacking reason, and Dioneo's new analogy suggests Gualtieri's unsuitableness as a ruler and a husband. His opening reference, however, is not entirely wrong: Dioneo does use the term to condemn Gualtieri's behavior. Although to suit his purposes Aristotle narrows the meaning of bestiality to the most extreme acts of cruelty, such as cannibalism, he also recognizes the word's broader usages. It is a term

of reproach: "we also call by this evil name those men who go beyond all ordinary standards by reason of vice" (*Ethics* 1145a30). Later he applies the term to a very different condition, "every excessive state" and gives these examples, "the man who is by nature apt to fear everything, even the squeak of a mouse, is cowardly with a brutish cowardice [and] . . . foolish people those who by nature are thoughtless and live by their senses alone are brutish." Certain diseased states and forms of insanity resemble bestiality: "those who are so as a result of disease (e.g. of epilepsy) or of madness are morbid. Of these characteristics it is possible to have some only at times, and not to be mastered by them . . . but it is also possible to be mastered, not merely to have the feelings" (*Ethics* 1149a5-15). While not a cannibal, in his cruelty and his excessive, insatiable testing of Griselda, Gualtieri is bestial according to the other senses Aristotle grants this term. Moreover, the purpose of Aristotle's discussion in Book 7 is less to insist on the most extreme form of bestiality than to establish the nature of the more common condition of incontinence and the role of reason in virtuous and blameworthy actions. What is common to the three conditions of bestiality (in all its forms), vice, and incontinence is the subordinate role reason plays with respect to appetites and feelings. In virtue, reason predominates; by contrast, feelings and appetites dominate these other behaviors. At the end of the tale, once Gualtieri has taken back Griselda and restored her children to her, the people, while decrying his harsh tests, attribute to Gualtieri wisdom, but they attribute to Griselda greater wisdom. Gualtieri's reason has certainly aided him in devising his plots and examining Griselda's responses, but his reason has been in the service of his appetites and feelings; it has not ruled them. Dioneo's comments in the conclusion prompt readers to discriminate between the role reason plays in Griselda's and Gualtieri's behaviors.

In comparing Gualtieri to a swineherd, Dioneo raises the possibility that we should consider Griselda's behavior to have been beastlike. Yet Griselda does not in any way conform to Aristotle's notion of a bestial human being. I think that Dioneo's final comments persuade against this analogy by distinguishing Griselda from another kind of wife who might be guided by her appetites once driven out of the palace by her husband. Dioneo's crude alternative to Griselda's behavior makes pleasure the end another wife might have sought after being rebuffed by Gualtieri:

> Chi avrebbe altri che Griselda potuto col viso non solamente asciutto ma lieto sofferir le rigide e mai piú non udite pruove da Gualtier fatte? Al quale non sarebbe forse stato male investito d'essersi abbattuto ad una che, quando fuor di casa l'avesse in camiscia cacciata, s'avesse sí ad uno altro fatto scuotere il pilliccione, che riuscito ne fosse una bella roba.
>
> (318)

Who else but Griselda could have endured so cheer-
fully the cruel and unheard of trials that Gualtieri imposed upon her without shedding a tear? For perhaps it
would have served him right if he had chanced upon a
wife, who, being driven from the house in her shift,
had found some other man to shake her skin-coat for
her, earning herself a fine new dress in the process.

(795)

Dioneo's final comments about Griselda point out her
rarity and question her efficacy as a model subject for a
tyrant, but they also clarify her virtue. He posits an alternative scarcely imaginable for Griselda because her
behavior has never had honor, riches, or sensual pleasure as its end, but rather the happiness that follows
from virtuous activity, which is, for Aristotle, the highest good. Boccaccio's Griselda story demonstrates the
self-sufficiency of virtuous activity by bestowing riches,
honor, and children on Griselda and then depriving her
of these goods without deterring her from acting virtuously.[29] Dioneo's strategy in the frame is to use irony to
subject the protagonists' actions to further ethical and
political scrutiny, yet not to undercut the tale's treatment of moral virtue.

Even without Dioneo's allusions to Aristotle's *Nichomachean Ethics* in the frame, the tale itself raises questions about how Gualtieri's and Griselda's behaviors
should be understood. Boccaccio's frame does not,
therefore, raise *new* issues about the Griselda story, but
it does provide crucial perspectives for assessing both
Gualtieri and Griselda. Petrarch forgoes using the
Nichomachean Ethics as the tale's ethical framework.
In *On His Own Ignorance and That of Many Others*,
Petrarch has acknowledged Aristotle's "penetrating insight" into the nature of both virtue and vice, but he
nonetheless faults the work:

> by no facts was the promise fulfilled which the phi-
> losopher makes at the beginning of the first book of his
> *Ethics,* namely, that "we learn this part of philosophy
> not with the purpose of gaining knowledge but of be-
> coming better."

For Petrarch, Aristotle's text lacks the power to move
its readers; it increases their knowledge but it does not
affect their will.[30] His choice to drop Boccaccio's framing allusions to Aristotle is strategic and ambitious. He
does not eliminate from his own narrative Dioneo's
thoughtful concerns, but, indeed, as we shall see in the
next section, he includes them within his translation,
the moral conclusion, and the final letter, *Seniles*
XVII.4.

All four letters of *Seniles* XVII frame Petrarch's
Griselda story by raising issues about the translator and
the translation. The letters themselves tell the history of
Petrarch's Griselda story in part because they were not
written in the order in which he directs Boccaccio to
read them. Charles Trinkaus has noted that Petrarch
"contrived" what he sought to present as "spontaneous."[31] It is likely that Petrarch's conception of his
project to translate the Griselda story grew after the
translation of the narrative was completed, probably
some time in early spring of 1373. The letter prefacing
the tale, *Seniles* XVII.3, followed the translation. *Seniles* XVII.2, dated April 27, came next and refers at
the end to the next letter containing the Griselda story.
Seniles XVII.1 is a cover letter explaining the order of
the letters and briefly commenting on how they came to
be composed. *Seniles* XVII.4, dated June 8, 1373, by
Petrarch, was actually written in the following year,
possibly only weeks before his death in July 1374.[32] Although this letter was prompted by Petrarch's learning
that the other three letters had failed to reach Boccaccio
and were probably stolen, it takes up initially a discussion of the translation, including Petrarch's report on
his two readers, and concludes with Petrarch saying
farewell to Boccaccio, friends, and letter writing.

Read together, the letters do not suggest a consistent
view of the Griselda story but rather what may be Petrarch's ambivalence over the value of his translation.
Seniles XVII.3 is full of enthusiasm over his own
Griselda story, but in *Seniles* XVII.1 Petrarch speculates
that Boccaccio might think he was "address[ing] pointless things" had he only sent him the letter containing
the Griselda story (643). At the end of *Seniles* XVII.2
he slights his translation by contrasting it with his other
grander undertakings: "the next letter to you will be a
sign of how far I am from counsels of idleness. For, not
content with the huge projects I have begun, for which
this brief life does not suffice nor would suffice, were it
doubled, I daily hunt for new labors on the outside, so
great is my hatred for sleep and lazy repose" (653-54).
In *Seniles* XVII.4 the confident tone of the preceding
letters is replaced by ill humor. Saying goodbye to Boccaccio and all those with whom he has corresponded,
he denigrates his translation, distinguishing between
"flimsier scribblings" and more "worthwhile study,"
and vowing that in future letters "I shall write so as to
be understood but not to amuse myself" (671). The
Griselda story is no longer a worthy endeavor to stave
off "lazy repose" but rather an idle diversion itself. Petrarch's fluctuating estimate of his translation may suggest his uncertainty about its reception, but it is clear
that he uses these four letters to present a complex self-
portrait. His first three letters are not concerned with
the tale's ethical values but rather with the characters of
the author and translator, Boccaccio and Petrarch, and
with the nature of the Griselda story.

By translating Boccaccio's vernacular tale into Latin,
Petrarch pays high tribute to the author and his tale. In
the order of composition, the translation came first. The
four letters of *Seniles* XVII, full of autobiographical details and pointed artifice, were composed around this

signal act as Petrarch attempted to place his rendering of the Griselda story within the context of his own accomplishments, his age, and his relationship with Boccaccio.[33] As Petrarch relates in *Seniles* XVII.3, responses to his Latin Griselda story were favorable. His task in this letter is not only to link Boccaccio's tale and his translation, but also to present the translation in a clever and gracious way that acknowledges this extraordinary act of literary homage, for although Boccaccio has been Petrarch's disciple and eulogist, with his Griselda story he has inspired Petrarch.[34] Expecting Boccaccio to recognize the irony, Petrarch aggrandizes the exemplary text he will translate and adopts the guise of an aspiring student.[35]

In *Seniles* XVII.3, Petrarch's remarks signal a pedagogical model of translation. He recounts having memorized Boccaccio's Italian tale, recited it to his friends, and translated it into Latin. Crassus, in Cicero's *De Oratore*, reports having used this same procedure in his youth.[36] Citing Cicero, Quintilian also recommends translation, calling it an "exercise."[37] Pliny the Younger emphasizes the critical scrutiny translation provides the student:

> The most useful thing, which is always being suggested, is to translate Greek into Latin and Latin into Greek. This kind of exercise develops in one a precision and richness of vocabulary, a wide range of metaphor and power of exposition, and moreover, imitation of the best models leads to a like aptitude for original composition. At the same time, any point which might have been overlooked by a reader cannot escape the eye of a translator.[38]

But the narrative of his experience of the Griselda story is not the only clue he gives Boccaccio. In *Seniles* XVII.1, Petrarch coaches him:

> When you come to the end, you will be worn out and will say: "Is this my sick friend, that busy old man? Or someone else with the same name, a healthy young man with time to spare?"
>
> (643)

Throughout *Seniles* XVII.2, Petrarch prizes his old age: his lifelong experiences confer invaluable benefits. He contends that old age may be "a disease of the body but the health of the mind" (646). Conscious that death approaches, he resolves "to double my pace, especially now, and hasten to the goal at sunset as though I had lost part of the daylight" (647). In fact, Boccaccio will discover a "healthy young" Petrarch in *Seniles* XVII.3, where he takes up the concerns of Boccaccio when as a young man he wrote the ***Decameron.*** At the beginning of *Seniles* XVII.3, Petrarch names Boccaccio's youth as the efficient cause of the Griselda story.[39]

At the beginning of *Seniles* XVII.4, in what seems like a non sequitur, Petrarch links his age when writing the Griselda story with its genre, both issues he has already raised in the preceding letters:

> My love for you has prompted me, old as I am, to write what I would scarcely have written when I was young. Whether the contents are true or fictitious I know not, since they are no longer histories but just tales.
>
> (669)

Critics have seen his comments about the tale's genre as bearing on the ethical and emotional force of the tale rather than on Petrarch's adopted persona for telling the Griselda story or the relationship between his and Boccaccio's tales.[40] Petrarch's early years as a writer were much different from Boccaccio's. His blurring of genres may suggest that the individual type of narrative is less important than another category to which both history and fable can belong: narrative compositions for students, suitable forms for experimentation. Both Cicero and Quintilian associate the writing of certain kinds of narratives with literary exercises. Cicero singles out "*fabula, historia,* and *argumentum*" as three kinds of narratives whose purpose is "amusement" and "valuable training."[41] Quintilian begins his discussion of the kinds of exercises teachers of rhetoric should give students with the composition of narratives. He leaves the writing of "fictitious" (*fabulam*) and "realistic" narratives (*argumentum*) to teachers of literature and reserves for rhetoricians the "historical" narrative (*historiam*), "whose force is in proportion to its truth." Indeed, Quintilian contends that embellishing a narrative properly will exercise a student's imagination, and even purple prose, while a fault of excess, is less blameworthy than a "poverty of wit."[42] Petrarch's artful pose as translator gives him the leeway to present the translation as something of an exercise, although his self-consciousness suggests otherwise, and to ensure that his readers take full measure of his craft.

If *Seniles* XVII.1, XVII.3, and XVII.4 point with subtle wit to the incongruity of Petrarch translating the Griselda story at his advanced age and suggest that this act of translation was for him something of a flirtation with youth, XVII.2 solemnly recalls Petrarch's many achievements. Although it takes up the question of Petrarch's retirement, this subject, I think, is a pretense; the letter's real function is to provide the next letter containing the Griselda story with a portrait of the multi-talented Petrarch. By implicitly establishing Petrarch's preeminence, *Seniles* XVII.2 serves to correct in advance the stance he will take as Boccaccio's translator and thus highlights the artfulness of this pose. Petrarch covers three topics in this letter: he begins by addressing the disparate material fortunes of the two, not a new topic to either of them, in part offering the philosophical consolation that inasmuch as Boccaccio has lacked material prosperity he has received far more valuable talents.[43] He then turns to Boccaccio's request that he cease his labors to preserve his health, refuting this argument forcefully, stressing the evils of idleness that would actually bring on his death. He concludes with a retrospective on his life in response to Boccaccio's claim that he should be contented with his accomplishments. The letter's emphasis on the close relationship between these friends veils Petrarch's self-promotion. He insists on their mutual love and their one mind in many matters and cites Boccaccio's praise of his achievements, enabling him, then, in his own voice more modestly to discuss them and in some instances denigrate the importance Boccaccio has attributed to them. With Boccaccio as his interlocutor, this letter offers a portrait of Petrarch that rivals his unfinished "Letter to Posterity" (*Seniles* XVIII). His reminders of his age, however, also imply that he will bring to his translation his own mature concerns.

NARRATIVE ART IN THE GRISELDA STORY

There is no straightforward way to tell the Griselda story. Every writer must confront the tale's extreme artificiality. Its overt didacticism must be disguised on the one hand, and sufficiently lucid on the other. Walter's cruelty and Griselda's unnatural submission must be acknowledged but subordinated to the virtuous behavior the tale examines. More than most tales, this one keeps the reader teetering on the verge of disequilibrium between two unproductive reading strategies: falling into the illusion that Walter and Griselda are real people, or rejecting it. The best reader must be of two minds. As we will see below, Petrarch suggests the consequences of either pole in *Seniles* XVII.4 when he recounts the reading experiences of the tearful Paduan and the unmoved Veronese.

We turn first, however, to the ethical frameworks that are used by Boccaccio and Petrarch to gloss the actions in this narrative. Besides Dioneo's comments about bestial and divine behavior, the day's theme—stories of magnificent or liberal deeds intended to inspire the listeners to valorous actions—is a means by which to understand the story of Griselda. But who performs the magnificent deed in this tale? As Edwards has pointed out, for Aristotle the virtue of magnificence is concerned with wealth and involves an appropriate expenditure of large scale (*Ethics* 1122a20).[44] Dioneo attributes to Gualtieri a kind of magnificence in the frame, but by likening it to bestiality and advising his listeners not to follow Gualtieri's example, he leaves unsaid who in the tale is worthy of emulation. Griselda's low birth, her lack of wealth, and her lack of any monetary spending whatsoever make her an unlikely candidate and have led some readers to attribute this virtue to Gualtieri. However, Boccaccio introduces a third means to assess Griselda's behavior by substituting virtues for riches, making Griselda extraordinarily wealthy. These three ethical schemes may not be the only ones organizing the tale, but I think that they dominate it.[45]

Boccaccio's clever exchange of wealth for virtue is systematic. Although Petrarch commends Griselda's constancy, and Chaucer's Clerk will additionally single out her patience as a particularly feminine virtue, Boccaccio attributes to Griselda a full set of related virtues. Virtues, as St. Gregory wrote, "fly in one flock," appearing singly only rarely.[46] Boccaccio had a number of groups to choose from: for example, the cardinal virtues consist of prudence, justice, fortitude, and moderation; the theological virtues consist of faith, hope, and charity.[47] As Victoria Kirkham has argued, Boccaccio draws on the large store of remedial or medicinal virtues that help one to combat the deadly sins and other spiritual maladies.[48] While membership in this group is less fixed than that in the other groups, it can include humility, charity, patience, meekness, mildness, mercy, compassion, fortitude, constancy, magnanimity, obedience, abstinence, and continence.[49] Griselda exhibits all of these virtues, and many of them she pays out like coins to pass Gualtieri's harsh tests.

Throughout the thirteenth-century manual *Summa virtutum de remediis anime* (hereafter *SV*), the interrelatedness of the remedial virtues is stressed through metaphors and explicit discussions suggesting how one virtue engages the aid of others or assists others in their duties. Humility, for example, is first in the "preservation" of the other virtues; charity is "first as their mistress and form" (*SV* 76). Charity achieves its effects through other virtues and is "first said to be 'patient'" (*SV* 160), while Patience safeguards the other virtues like a "chest in which the treasure of virtues is kept" (*SV* 164). Obedience is compared to a gardener who "plants the virtues and guards them after planting" (*SV* 218). Mercy, like compassion, is one of the daughters of charity and "the companion of every good work" (*SV* 258, 262). The general senses of both abstinence, "the restraint of all illicit impulses" (*SV* 266), and continence, which rules "desire" through "judgment" (*SV* 278), indicate how these two virtues enlist the behavior of others mentioned above to check an improper impulse. For his tale to conform to the theme of magnificence, Boccaccio must demonstrate Griselda's magnificent expense of virtues in meeting Gualtieri's harsh demands, and to this end Boccaccio uses vocabulary associated with the remedial virtues throughout the work. Indeed, it is difficult to find a substantial passage that does not examine virtues. Where Boccaccio's Griselda uses the virtues as strategies in the trials she undergoes, Petrarch's Griselda uses them also in her daily comportment. In both versions Griselda alludes to them through her vocabulary, while the narrators and Gualtieri/Walter often refer to them explicitly. The result is that both Gualtieri and Griselda may be seen to operate in something like an economy of virtue.

Both Griselda's and Gualtieri's behaviors conform to the literature on the remedial virtues: Gualtieri's behavior models what is to be withstood, Griselda's what is to be emulated. The various facets of the tests exploit distinctions and intersections among the virtues and probe their natures. Unlike more fully mimetic characters, Gualtieri and Griselda function on one level as exegetes who moralize their actions as the narrative progresses. Their textbook-like exactitude, however, clashes with their other function as mimetic characters in a fiction that is realistic to the extent that the tests are intended to be psychologically unbearable and unreasonable. Gualtieri's cruelty is at odds with his fine moral discrimination. The reader's dismay over Griselda's choice to give up her children to be murdered rather than object and disobey may be complicated by the presence of another discordant response—approval at her successfully passing Gualtieri's tests. The narrative sets up a pattern in which Griselda is to pass her tests in conformity not to life but to the literature on the remedial virtues whose purpose is to aid with the problems of living. Boccaccio conceals this dynamic somewhat in his treatment of the people who respond to Gualtieri and Griselda as real people, modeling for us the same mimetic response. Yet through Dioneo's concluding remarks, as we have seen, Boccaccio both questions Griselda's believability and dodges this issue through allusions to the *Nichomachean Ethics.*

Readers who see Petrarch as rescuing the tale for its moral sentence may be underestimating both Boccaccio's treatment of moral issues and Petrarch's understanding of the tale's difficulties. His admiration for Boccaccio's Griselda story must surely have arisen from his appreciating the issues that Boccaccio's frame and tale have raised. In contrast with Boccaccio's experiment of bringing to bear competing ethical responses onto the same set of actions, Petrarch sets himself the artistic challenge of increasing nearly to the breaking point two opposed kinds of engagement: he overloads the narrative's didactic content as he deepens the reader's emotional response. Petrarch boldly purples the prose, and we should recognize as Petrarch's artistic, experimental choices the surfeit of moral didacticism and the increased emotional involvement of the reader.

All characters in Petrarch's adaptation become at some point sources of moral philosophy or edification. Moral maxims fill their speeches as he supplements Boccaccio's narrative with something like the wisdom his character Reason expounds in *The Remedies of Fortune Fair and Foul.* This technique is clear from the beginning when Walter's people combine an eloquent dynastic argument for marriage with a *memento mori* to persuade Walter of the urgency they feel.[50] When Walter asks Janicola if he will accept him as his son-in-law, Janicola is terrified but reminds himself of his obligations to his lord. Even Walter's servant is a sententious henchman who, on the one hand, hints at the treachery he will do to Griselda's children and, on the other, asserts the obedience due to one's ruler. In Petrarch's rendering, moral sentence is never without some element of

pathos. Much less a purist than Boccaccio, he offers an eclectic mixture of virtues, politically expedient behavior, and generally accepted good qualities. Indeed, it is in part his inclusion of different orders of virtues that led to his version's huge popularity in the succeeding centuries and its occurrence in a wide variety of manuscript collections.

Petrarch makes all aspects of Griselda's upbringing and daily life exemplary, developing her beyond Boccaccio's Griselda, whose Gualtieri merely had noted her "manners" (785) ("costumi" [309]) and found her beautiful. As Emilie Kadish has argued, Petrarch's introduction of Griselda and Janicola seems almost like a new beginning of the story.[51] Structurally, Petrarch draws a parallel between the powerful marquis who seeks an excellent wife and the poor Janicola who has such a daughter. In displaying how Griselda treats her father, Petrarch foregrounds her charity; thus her first acts as well as her final ones have their source in charity, the virtue that informs the others. Dipping into his *Remedies Against Fortune*, Petrarch sketches more fully Griselda's upbringing of poverty, simplicity, and ceaseless toil to establish virtues that will arm her for the adversity to come.[52] Morse has pointed out that Petrarch drew on stoic virtues, which he combined unproblematically with Christian ones.[53] In his treatment of the latter, he makes Griselda conform more fully to the scholastic discussions of the source and order of virtues. Twice he associates her with God's grace, first telling readers that "gratia celestis" (line 114) (heavenly grace [114]) had touched her and then commenting after her marriage that "divine favor" shone upon her (116) (divini favoris affulserat [line 173]).[54] Both references precede an exposition of her virtues.

Augustine, Thomas Aquinas, and the compiler of the *Summa virtutem* grappled with the problem of whether the individual was meritorious in acting virtuously or whether the source of all virtue was God. Aquinas and the *Summa virtutem* adhere to Augustine's definition that "virtue is a good quality of mind by which we live rightly, of which no one can make bad use, which God works in us without us" (*SV* 62-64). But Aquinas shows that virtue is both "acquired and infused," the two means Petrarch represents.[55] In both Boccaccio's and Petrarch's renderings Griselda acquires new virtues after her marriage, but Petrarch's Griselda develops into an ideal ruler whose responsiveness to the affairs of the state contrasts with her husband's more whimsical rule and whose ability to settle disputes associates her with the cardinal virtues of prudence, "right reasoning *about things to be done,*" and justice, "which concerns what is due to another."[56] Indeed, by becoming the marquis's wife, Griselda realizes her great potential, unanticipated by the meager circumstances of her birth.

Petrarch also makes the tale's treatment of the remedial virtues more pronounced in the dialogues and his narrator's commentary on the action. In testing Griselda, Petrarch's Walter, like Boccaccio's Gualtieri, tries to goad her into breaking her vows, but unlike Gualtieri, Walter also tries to prompt her to respond virtuously. He arranges the first test to methodically elicit from Griselda a very considered response, rather than anything spontaneous and emotional, embedding the people's complaint in comments that remind her of both her humble origins and his own high regard. He frames the test in such as way that his part is to respond to the people; Griselda's is to respond to him in conformity with her marriage agreement. After the second test, Walter lessens the distance between the people's view of Griselda and his own by omitting reassurances of his love, thus trying to goad her to anger. One of the best examples of Petrarch's intensification of the vocabulary of the remedial virtues is the passage in which Walter decides whether Griselda is showing true or false patience. Boccaccio has Gualtieri raise merely to dismiss the possibility that perhaps Griselda was glad to be rid of her children (789). By contrast, Petrarch's commentary alludes to a form of false virtue with the phrase "ab animi feritate":

> ut nisi eam nosset amantissimam filiorum, paulominus suspicari posset hoc femineum robur quadam ab [animi] feritate procedere

(lines 268-69)

> Had he not known her to have loved the children greatly, Walter might have suspected this feminine strength to proceed from some kind of savagery of spirit.

(122)

Even more than in Boccaccio's rendering, by his embellishments Petrarch makes his characters conform to the literature on the virtues so that as troubling as Walter and Griselda's deeds are, I think that on some level readers also approve of Griselda's textbook conformity to her vows.

Petrarch does alter our rhetorical engagement with the story by expanding the narrator's commentary on Walter and by greatly diminishing the ethical role of the people, who no longer exemplify the ordinarily human in a sympathetic way. It is not clear to me that Petrarch thematizes them as consistently as Boccaccio does. He cannot completely eliminate their positive ethical role in the narrative. In fact, that the people recognize Griselda's virtues once she is married is one way in which Petrarch elaborates her virtues. But once Walter begins to test Griselda, Petrarch insulates the people from the court so that they no longer have any advisory capacity, which they have in Boccaccio's narrative, and they can have no clear understanding of what is actually happening.[57] They become an audience much farther removed from the events than Petrarch's readers, to whom the logic behind Walter's actions is revealed. Their typical

response is wonder at what appears to be happening. As a narrative device they create some suspense, and Petrarch may be calling Boccaccio's attention to his own manipulation of them in his narrator's comment, when the people believe the forged papal bulls, that "nec operosum sane fuit aggrestibus rudibusque animis quod libet persuadere" (line 289) (it was by no means difficult to persuade the ignorant peasants of any story [122]).

Petrarch denigrates the people less to criticize their ill-formed judgments—as when they condemn Walter as inhumanly cruel—than to show how unsuitable they are to make informed judgments. The people really make only two errors in judgment: first by thinking that a nobly born wife will be the most appropriate one for Walter, and second by concluding that the new wife will be more appropriate than Griselda because she appears to be nobly born. While it is clear that they have forgotten the lesson Griselda's virtuous behavior has taught them, their interest in Walter's wife differs from his own. It is not clear that they have forgotten their political interest in their ruler leaving an heir. It is hard to fault Walter's subjects for believing the information that he has calculatedly circulated. The lesson that virtue can be hidden is one that they and other guests must relearn at the second wedding. If Petrarch does use them thematically, it is as victims of Walter's tyranny.

Petrarch's narrator is no less critical of Walter than Dioneo is of Gualtieri within the narrative, but because Petrarch has radically altered the framing devices Boccaccio uses—eliminating Dioneo's extra-diegetic remarks that view Gualtieri with contempt—his narrator's often oblique condemnations, occurring only within the story, can sometimes be misread as timid. But in both narratives the focus on Walter serves to deepen the reader's understanding of Griselda's virtuous behavior, and whatever else Walter is thematically, he is first and foremost her exegete. Stronger criticism of Walter would obscure Griselda's exemplarity and call it into question. Labeling Gualtieri's behavior was a problem for Dioneo, whose final condemnation revises his initial one. Boccaccio makes the changing perspectives on Gualtieri a functional part of the tale's polyvalence. Petrarch will also follow this strategy in his presentation of Walter.

Petrarch consistently represents Walter as being guided by his desires rather than his reason, but rather than being overcome by his feelings and appetites, as in the case of simple incontinence, here his reason operates in their service. Thus when "Walter was seized by a desire . . . he decided to test further the already proven faithfulness of his dear wife, and to repeat the test again" (118) [Cepit, ut fit, interim Walterum, cum iam ablactata esset infantula, mirabilis quedam quam [laudabilis] doctiores iudicent cupiditas, satis expertam care fidem coniugis experiendi altius et iterum retemptandi (lines

192-94)]. Indeed, Walter is caught in the throes of his own willfulness:

> Poterant rigidissimo coniugi hec benivolencie et fidei coniugalis experimenta sufficere. Sed sunt qui, ubi semel inceperint, non desinant; imo incumbant hereantque proposito.
>
> (lines 272-74)

These proofs of conjugal good will and faithfulness might have been enough for the most demanding husband; but some people, having begun a course of action, will not desist. No, they press on further, clinging to their plan.

> (122)

Aquinas's explanation of the perversion of the appetitive faculty leading to vice or brutishness sheds light on Walter's behavior:

> As a good action is not without practical reason and right desire—we pointed this out in the sixth book (1269)—a perversion of these two faculties can bring about an act to be avoided in moral matters. If then perversity occurs on the part of the appetitive faculty so that the practical reason remains right, there will be incontinence—a condition that is present when a man has correct evaluation of what he ought to do or avoid but draws away to the contrary by reason of the passion of desire. But if the perversity of the appetitive faculty becomes so strong that it dominates reason, reason follows that to which the perverted desire inclines, as a kind of principle, considering it to the ultimate end.[58]

For Aquinas, the disposition to perform an evil action by choice is a vice. Petrarch falls short of condemning Walter's action as evil, but by elaborating his faulty decision-making process, Petrarch establishes in Walter a pattern in which impulses, desires, and feelings are the ends his reason serves. For example, when the servant has returned with Walter's daughter, the narrator comments, "vehementer paterna animum pietas movit; susceptum tamen rigorem [propositi non] inflexit" (lines 226-27) (A father's devotion moved Walter's feelings deeply, but he did not bend from the rigorous course of his intention [120]). Reason is not the arbiter between his desires to show compassion and to test his wife, but rather the slave of the stronger passion.

Petrarch's negative characterization of Walter is cumulative, and the narrator's censure takes different forms. In the first two examples above, the narrator generalizes Walter's behavior. In the last example, the criticism of Walter seems diluted by the suggestion that he does feel compassion. But this mitigating of Walter's cruelty misreads Petrarch's attempt to show the war between Walter's impulses. Throughout the tale, commentary critical of Walter is infused with descriptions of his actions so that it seems more specific than general or categorical. Petrarch's emphasis on Walter's passion for

hunting has not struck all readers as censorious or related to his later testing of Griselda. Yet in his *Remedies* Petrarch has derided hunting as an anti-intellectual, trivial, and slothful pursuit.[59] In the narrative he juxtaposes Walter's devotion to hunting with his neglect of other duties and the future. His impulsiveness is suggested again when his people present him with a reasonable argument for marriage, and Petrarch, departing from Boccaccio, represents Walter as being swayed by the depth of their feeling rather than their argument:

> Moverunt pie preces animum viri. . . . Ceterum subiectorum michi voluntatibus me sponte subicio, et prudencie vestre fisus et fidei. . . . Itaque quando vobis placitum est ita uxorem ducam.
>
> (lines 91, 93-94, 99)

These pious prayers moved the heart of the man. . . . Even so, I submit myself freely to the will of my subjects, confident in your prudence and faith. . . . And therefore, because it pleases you, I will choose a wife.

> (112)

The justness of the people's request seems secondary to the emotional effect their eloquent, deferential petition has on Walter.

The narrator does come close to suggesting that Walter is bestial. This view is associated with that of the people, whose incomplete knowledge of events makes their judgment muddled:

> Ceperat sensim de Waltero decolor fama crebrescere: quod videlicet effera et inhumana duricie, humilis penitencia ac pudore coniugii, filios iussisset interfici. Nam neque pueri comparebant, neque ubinam gencium essent ullus audierat; quo se ille vir alioquin clarus et suis carus multis infamem odiosumque reddiderat. Neque ideo trux animus flectebatur, sed in suscepta severitate [experiendique] sua dura illa libidine procedebat.
>
> (lines 279-84)

Gradually, ugly rumors began to spread about Walter: because of his wild and inhuman harshness, humiliated by remorse and shame of his wife, it was said, he had ordered the children murdered. For the children were nowhere to be seen and no one had heard where they were. In this way a man otherwise beloved and illustrious made himself notorious and hated by many. Yet his harsh spirit was not deflected; he persevered in his established sternness and his cruel desire to test Griselda.

> (122)

The people's assessment is based on the false rumor that Walter has had his children murdered, but their faulty premise undermines their conclusion. The narrator's own more knowledgeable judgment links Walter's methodical testing of Griselda—not the murder of her children—with cruelty.

Like Boccaccio, Petrarch returns to the problem of classifying Walter in his own innovative frames, the moral conclusion and the final letter of *Seniles* XVII. Although

Wallace has found warrants for what has seemed like Petrarch's muted criticism of Walter, I hope to have shown that Petrarch's criticism is not muted but implies that the impulsive Walter is a dangerous kind of ruler whose reason can serve good or bad impulses equally, and that artistic and thematic motives rather than strictly ideological ones explain the forms Petrarch uses to criticize Walter. Even though Boccaccio gives a stronger role to the people in objecting to Gualtieri's behavior, he gives them no power to resist him. Their exemplarity, moreover, points not to their actions but to the ways in which they form judgments—the slippery relation between reason and will—in contrast to those of the two main characters. Their approval or censure has no effect on Gualtieri. Dioneo's final commentary suggesting that he does not belong in a palace offers a way of understanding Gualtieri but not of removing him.

Petrarch's moral conclusion responds to the frame of **"Day 10"** of the *Decameron* in some obvious ways. Although no longer exemplifying magnificence but something closer to great-heartedness, the tale satisfies Panfilo's request for exemplary tales that will inspire valorous actions. For Panfilo, the doer of such deeds will win fame and the kind of afterlife it confers (699). Petrarch, however, is less interested in fame than in the spiritual value of the conduct. His moral conclusion also responds to Dioneo's negative application in his introduction, where he has advised his listeners not to follow Gualtieri's example. Petrarch's phrasing of his moral conclusion recalls Dioneo's: the marquis's actions were remarkable "non cosa magnifica ma una matta bestialitá" (308) (not so much for their munificence as for their senseless brutality [784]). Petrarch, however, explains both who should emulate and what is to be emulated: he writes that he has told the story "non tam ideo, ut matronas nostri temporis ad imitandam huius uxoris pacienciam, que michi vix mutabilis videtur, quam ut legentes ad imitandam saltem femine constanciam excitarem" (lines 396-99) (not so much to urge the matrons of our time to imitate the patience of this wife [which seems to me almost unchanging] as to arouse readers to imitate her womanly constancy" [128]). Middleton sees Petrarch's references to "matrons of our time" and "readers" as marking a distinction between the community of readers of the *Decameron* and that of Petrarch's story.[60] This analogy, is, I think, problematic because it dismissively narrows Boccaccio's audience and removes from it Petrarch himself, and because it skirts the interpretive problems that Petrarch is trying to solve.

John Finlayson argues that Petrarch "differentiates between reading the story as about the human situation of a much tested wife . . . and drawing from it some general *significacio,* as from a parable or exemplum."[61] Yet Petrarch's ending with its precise qualifications seems to undo Boccaccio's carefully wrought open-endedness, which had provided different perspectives without explicitly endorsing any one—not all of which were equally satisfying. Edwards argues that Petrarch responds to Boccaccio's Griselda story and "its interpretive complexity in ways that promise, then forestall debate over meaning," for Petrarch's aim is not "merely to represent a virtue; rather he wants to affect the reader's understanding."[62] I agree in part with Edwards, but Boccaccio has done far more than represent a virtue. Rather than forestalling debate, Petrarch changes the terms of the debate in interesting and valuable ways. In his moral conclusion Petrarch attempts to complete the tale by offering Griselda as a model of feminine Christian constancy and by acknowledging the imperfect analogy between Griselda's obedience to Walter and the Christian's to God. He commends the tale to readers,

> ut quod hec viro suo prestitit, hoc prestare deo nostro audeant, qui licet ut Iacobus ait Apostolus intemptator malorum sit, et ipse neminem temptet: probat tamen.
>
> (lines 399-401)

> that they might dare to undertake for God what she undertook for her husband. God is the appropriate tester of evils, as the Apostle James said; but he tempts no one himself. Nevertheless he tests us.
>
> (128)

By foregoing allusions to the *Nichomachean Ethics* in his frame, Petrarch does eliminate the kind of intellectual play that Boccaccio's tale had provided. But by replacing Aristotle with St. James, Petrarch substitutes Scripture as the measure of the characters' actions. The Epistle of St. James is full of exhortations to practical Christian deeds, stern admonishments against evil ones, and assurances of God's justice—to be tempted is to be drawn into an evil desire, which gives birth to sin and then death. Petrarch's conclusion challenges Boccaccio's use of Aristotle and raises the issue of who will recognize this challenge. Because of Petrarch's earlier identification of two mutually exclusive audiences—those who do not speak Italian (for whom he claims to have written the tale) and those who know both Italian and Latin (whom he addresses in his dedication), Petrarch's moral conclusion can have two very different readings. For those who do not know Boccaccio's tale, the conclusion clarifies and privileges an exemplary reading, while acknowledging the tale's difficulties. For Petrarch's inscribed readers, his translation has been a study of imitation, and these readers may be provoked not just to compare the two renderings but also to debate the very grounds for moral action and moral judgment.

If Petrarch had left the Griselda story alone after his moral conclusion, one might argue that he attempted to trump Boccaccio by replacing Boccaccio's use of Aristotle in his frame with Christian Scripture. But a year later Petrarch was still considering the interpretive problems the tale poses, and, in his final letter, he takes up issues that his moral conclusion had not resolved. Although the loss of the first three letters prompts the writing of *Seniles* XVII.4, Petrarch's intention to imitate Boccaccio's narrative also motivates it. Petrarch opens the letter by reminding Boccaccio that he has translated the tale for him, and, once again, in an allusion to Boccaccio's **"Author's Conclusion,"** he makes Boccaccio the authority for his own translation: "I prefaced that the guarantee would rest with the author, that is, with you" (669). In the final pages of the *Decameron,* Boccaccio had answered objections to his work by comically pointing out the ways in which readers impose on texts their own values and preoccupations, over which an author has no control. Petrarch's own two readers, both of whom he praises for their abilities, illustrate this point in their extreme reactions to his Griselda story. The first reader, the Paduan, is so overcome with weeping that he cannot read the tale and finally hands it over to another to complete. The second reading occurs sometime later, and, in this one, the Veronese reads the tale from start to finish without shedding a tear and then explains why the tale has not moved him. While Petrarch praises the response of the Paduan and repudiates the judgment of the Veronese, neither of these readers responds to the tale in the spirit Petrarch establishes in his moral conclusion.

Petrarch links the responses of both readers to their different characters. He acknowledges how open to interpretation is the Paduan's weeping by his comment, "I interpreted it in the best light and understood the man's heart was very sensitive; for, in truth, there is no more kindly man, at least not that I know" (669). The Paduan's disposition makes him a sympathetic reader but also leads him to a certain kind of meaning. Petrarch glosses the man's tears with lines from Juvenal's Satire XV, a pagan's poem: "Nature admits / She gives the human race the softest hearts; / She gave us tears—the best part of our feelings" (669). While these lines endorse the human capacity for compassion, the satire from which they are taken is about cannibalism, and they refer to the inability of human justice to rectify the atrocities that bestial human beings commit against others. The lines surrounding the passage Petrarch quotes read as follows:

> You could never devise a fitting punishment for this crime, or
> A penalty stiff enough for a people in whose minds
> Hunger and rage are alike, on a moral par. When Nature
> Gave tears to mankind, she proclaimed that tenderness was endemic
> In the human heart: Of all our impulses, this
> Is the highest and best. So we are moved to pity the plight
> Of a friend on the dock—or a ward who's brought his guardian

> To court for embezzlement, and whose adolescent kiss-curls
> Make you wonder whether those tearstained cheeks are a boy's
> or a girl's.[63]

For Petrarch, the Paduan's tears are directed at Walter's extreme cruelty and not at Griselda's virtuous triumph. The Paduan has responded to the tale as "matta bestialitá."

The Veronese reader contrasts his own dry-eyed response to the Paduan's, yet his comments echo in a different register Dioneo's own concluding remarks that have questioned both a real wife's steadfastness and whether such treatment as Walter's would best be served by fidelity. The Veronese comments:

> I too would have wept, for the touching subject and the words fit for the subject prompted weeping, nor am I hard-hearted; but I believed, and still do, that the whole thing was made up. For if it were true, what woman anywhere, whether Roman or of any nation whatever will match this Griselda? Where I ask, is such great conjugal love, equal fidelity, such signal patience and constancy?

> (669-79)

Aristotle's *Nichomachean Ethics,* as I have argued above, is the moral guide we use in Boccaccio's text to evaluate Dioneo's comments. However much the remarks of the Veronese resemble Dioneo's, Petrarch makes his readers bring to bear on them a different understanding. Petrarch reports that to avoid an unpleasant exchange he did not debate the views of the Veronese, but in the letter he rebuts the charge that Griselda is unbelievable with a list of pagan figures whose great deeds model and extend human potential.[64] He locates the deficiency of the Veronese's response in his disposition: "[T]here are some who consider whatever is difficult for them, impossible for everyone, and they so judge everything by their own measure as to put themselves in the first place" (670). This critique recalls Petrarch's even harsher condemnation of Boccaccio's critics in *Seniles* XVII.3: "[T]here is a breed of men who are insolent and lazy, who rebuke in others whatever they themselves either do not want, do not know, or are unable to do" (655). If the Paduan's sensitivity and kindliness made him somewhat unique, the Veronese is presented as belonging to a class of readers who dismiss in texts what does not conform to their own cynical views. Petrarch's accomplishment in this final letter is dazzling. His treatment of his two readers not only extends his imitation of Boccaccio's Griselda story to encompass Boccaccio's **"Author's Conclusion"**; the order and content of these two readers' responses correspond to Dioneo's opening and closing comments on Boccaccio's tale. Moreover, Petrarch's commentary on the Paduan's and the Veronese's responses clarifies his challenge to Boccaccio's use of Aristotle: what Petrarch opposes to Aristotle is not exclusively Christian Scripture, but rather those works that engage one's emotions to revile evil and commend and emulate virtue.

In some ways, *Seniles* XVII.4 revises the self-portrait Petrarch has given in the second letter. With the Veronese reader, Petrarch has failed; his tale has not inspired the man's heart or altered his disposition. The response of the Veronese, perhaps more than that of the Paduan, colors the rest of the letter as it takes up motifs found in the first three: letter writing, the border guards, Petrarch's health and age, and the turmoil in the country. With respect to all of these issues, Petrarch is pessimistic and resigned. One has little control over not just the reception of texts, but much else in life. Petrarch dismisses his project to translate the Griselda story and to link the two versions together as a game, for he vows in future letters to "write so as to be understood but not to amuse myself" (671). These comments reflect no reproach of Boccaccio's tale. The Paduan and the Veronese have responded to Petrarch's own telling of the Griselda story, and their response to his version could not be more different from his own to Boccaccio's tale.

Notes

I am grateful to the Rashkind and Craigie Funds at Randolph-Macon College for support during the research and writing of this essay.

1. For critical histories of Boccaccio's Griselda story, see Millicent Joy Marcus, *An Allegory of Form: Literary Self-Consciousness in the Decameron* (Saratoga, Calif., 1979), 97-99; Robert Hollander with Courtenay Cahill, "Day Ten of The *Decameron*: The Myth of Order," in Robert Hallander, *Boccaccio's Dante and the Shaping Force of Satire* (Ann Arbor, Mich., 1997), 110-12; Jill M. Ricketts, *Visualizing Boccaccio: Studies on Illustrations of The Decameron: From Giotto to Pasolini* (Cambridge, Eng., 1997), 28-29. For twentieth-century criticism of *CIT*, see Charlotte C. Morse, "Critical Approaches to the Clerk's Tale," in *Chaucer's Religious Tales,* ed. C. David Benson and Elizabeth Robertson (Cambridge, Eng., 1990), 71-83. Some recent critics of *CIT* have begun to rethink the relationship between Petrarch's and Chaucer's Griselda stories and have argued for a more complex understanding of Petrarch's thematic and artistic concerns: see Anne Middleton, "The Clerk and His Tale: Some Literary Contexts," *Studies in the Age of Chaucer* 2 (1980): 121-50; Kathryn L. Lynch, "Despoiling Griselda: Chaucer's Walter and the Problem of Knowledge in *The Clerk's Tale*," *Studies in the Age of Chaucer* 10 (1988): 41-70; Michaela Pasche Grudin, "Chaucer's 'Clerk's Tale' as Political Paradox," *Studies in the Age of Chaucer* 11 (1989): 63-92; Rodney Delasanta, "Nominalism and the *Clerk's Tale* Revisited," *Chaucer Review* 31 (1997): 209-31; Warren Ginsberg, "Petrarch, Chaucer, and the Making of the Clerk," in *The Performance of Middle English Culture: Essays on Chaucer and the Drama in Honor of Martin Stevens,* ed. James J. Paxson, Lawrence M. Clopper, and Sylvia Tomasch (Cambridge, Eng., 1998), 125-41; and John Finlayson, "Petrarch, Boccaccio, and Chaucer's 'Clerk's Tale,'" *Studies in Philology* 97 (2000): 255-75.

2. Robert R. Edwards has most recently seen Petrarch's telling of the Griselda story as a "rescue of sorts" in his "'The Sclaundre of Walter': The 'Clerk's Tale' and the Problem of Hermeneutics," in *Mediaevalitas: Reading the Middle Ages,* ed. Piero Boitani and Anna Torti (Cambridge, Eng., 1996), 15-41, at 27. For criticism arguing that Petrarch eliminates Boccaccio's ironic treatment of the tale and elaborates its moral, religious, and/or political themes, see J. Burke Severs, *The Literary Relationships of Chaucer's "Clerkes Tale"* (1942; Hamden, Conn., 1972), 6-20; Robin Kirkpatrick, "The Griselda Story in Boccaccio, Petrarch and Chaucer," in *Chaucer and the Italian Trecento,* ed. Piero Boitani (Cambridge, Eng., 1983), 231-48; Alfred L. Kellogg, *Chaucer, Langland, Arthur: Essays in Middle English Literature* (New Brunswick, N.J., 1972), 276-329; Larry Scanlon, *Narrative, Authority, and Power: The Medieval Exemplum and the Chaucerian Tradition* (Cambridge, Eng., 1994), 175-91. For two different interpretations arguing that Petrarch either rejected or misread the moral meaning of Boccaccio's Griselda story, see N. S. Thompson, *Chaucer, Boccaccio, and the Debate of Love: A Comparative Study of the Decameron and The Canterbury Tales* (Oxford, 1996), 279-312; and David Wallace, *Chaucerian Polity: Absolutist Lineages and Associational Forms in England and Italy* (Stanford, Calif., 1997), 261-98.

3. Middleton, "Clerk and His Tale," 127, 130, 133-35; Glending Olson, "Petrarch's View of the *Decameron*," *Modern Language Notes* 91 (1976): 69-79.

4. Middleton, "Clerk and His Tale," 127.

5. Middleton, "Clerk and His Tale," 134, 126-27.

6. Charlotte C. Morse, "The Exemplary Griselda," *Studies in the Age of Chaucer* 7 (1985): 51-86.

7. Wallace, *Chaucerian Polity,* 264.

8. Wallace, *Chaucerian Polity,* 265-66.

9. Wallace, *Chaucerian Polity,* 268.

10. Wallace, *Chaucerian Polity,* 273.

11. Wallace, *Chaucerian Polity,* 262, 282.

12. For two critics who use the term "Petrarchan Academy" or the notion it represents of idealized, learned male readers to distinguish among the different audiences for the Griselda story, see Edwards, "Sclaundre of Walter," 24, and Scanlon, *Narrative,* 178, 185.

13. Francis Petrarch, *Letters of Old Age: Rerum senilium libri I-XVIII,* trans. Aldo S. Bernardo, Saul Levin, and Reta A. Bernardo, 2 vols. (Baltimore, 1992), 2:656. All future references in English to Petrarch's letters collected in *Seniles* will be from this edition and will be cited by page number. For Petrarch's Griselda story, I use Thomas J. Farrell's edition and translation, which I cite below (note 54).

14. Alex Preminger, Leon Golden, O. B. Hardison, Jr., and Kevin Kerrane, eds., *Classical and Medieval Literary Criticism: Translations and Interpretations* (New York, 1974), 161.

15. Petrarch, *Rerum familiarium libri I-VIII,* trans. Aldo S. Bernardo (Albany, N.Y., 1975), 41; *Letters on Familiar Matters: Rerum familiarium libri XVII-XXIV,* trans. Aldo S. Bernardo (Baltimore, 1985) 301-2. See also Thomas Greene, "Petrarch and the Humanist Hermeneutic," in *Italian Literature: Roots and Branches,* ed. G. Rimanelli and K. J. Atchity (New Haven, 1976), 211-12. Warren Ginsberg finds Petrarch's ideas about imitation to be important for establishing the relationship between the two texts and argues that Petrarch expects Boccaccio to read his translation "poised between recognition of differences and appreciation of a fundamental continuity" ("Petrarch," 134). Our arguments differ, however; Ginsberg's position is that Petrarch invites Boccaccio to "join in a hermeneutical revision which asks nothing less than the active reformation of his [Boccaccio's] authorial self. Thus, for Ginsberg, Petrarch's tale offers a corrective to Boccaccio's by transforming it "into the exemplary rhetorical discourse of moral and religious fervency" (130-31).

16. Middleton, "Clerk and His Tale," 128, 130.

17. In discussing Petrarch's verse and style, Thomas Greene argues that Petrarch wrote "verse that could itself be sub-read and demanded to be sub-read, verse bearing within it the latent presence of an ancient author" (211).

18. Olson, "Petrarch's View," 70-71.

19. For readers of the *Decameron,* see Vittore Branca, *Boccaccio: The Man and His Works,* trans. Richard Monges (New York, 1976), 198-99. Branca argues for an upper middle-class merchant audience for the *Decameron* and notes that no copies of the *Decameron* were found in the prestigious libraries in the fourteenth or early fifteenth centuries.

20. Kenelm Foster, *Petrarch: Poet and Humanist* (Edinburgh, 1984), 25-34.

21. Edwards, "Sclaundre of Walter," 24.

22. See Marcus's discussion of the open-endedness of the Griselda story (*Allegory of Form,* 97, 101-2).

23. Giovanni Boccaccio, *Il Decameron,* ed. Charles S. Singleton, 2 vols. (Bari, 1955), 2:308, 318 (all quotations in Italian are from this edition, cited by page numbers); *Decameron,* trans. G. H. McWilliam, 2nd edn. (New York, 1995), 784, 794 (all English citations of *The Decameron* are from this translation, cited by page numbers).

24. Charles Haines argues that Dioneo's reference to "matta bestialità" alludes to Dante's *Inf.* XI. 79-83. See his "Patient Griselda and *matta bestialitade,*" *Quaderni d'italianistica* 6 (1985): 233-40. See also Giuseppe Mazzotta, *The World at Play in Boccaccio's Decameron* (Princeton, 1986), 125.

25. Aristotle, *Ethica Nicomachea,* trans. W. D. Ross, in *The Basic Works of Aristotle,* ed. Richard McKeon (New York, 1941), 1145a15. All future citations of the *Nicomachean Ethics* will be from this edition, cited by section and line numbers.

26. Edwards, "Sclaundre of Walter," 27; Tania Itala Rutter, "The Function of Dioneo's Perspective in the Griselda Story," *Comitatus* 5 (1974): 35.

27. Rutter, "Function," 38.

28. Edwards, "Sclaundre of Walter," 26.

29. On the subordination of honor, riches, and pleasure to the end of happiness and the self-sufficiency of the final good, see *Nichomachean Ethics,* 1097a30-1097b10. Aristotle defines happiness as "a sort of good life and good action" (1098b20). He believes, however, that without certain "external goods," happiness "is impossible, or not easy." Goods such as wealth, "friends" and "political power" are instruments that assist noble deeds. Low birth, ugliness, lack of children or their death, and solitariness make a person "not very likely to be happy" (1099b1-5).

30. Francis Petrarch, *On His Own Ignorance and That of Many Others,* trans. Hans Nachod, in *The Renaissance Philosophy of Man,* ed. Ernst Cassirer, Paul Oskar Kristeller, and John Herman Randall, Jr. (Chicago, 1956), 103. For Petrarch's view of Aristotle and Aristotelians, see Jerome Taylor, "Franceys Petrak and the Logyk of Chaucer's

Clerk," in *Francis Petrarch, Six Centuries Later,* ed. Aldo Scaglione (Chapel Hill, N.C., 1975), 364-83; and Charles Trinkaus, who claims that Petrarch attacked "the cult of Aristotle," not Aristotle, knew the *Nicomachean Ethics* "fairly well," and used it as one of his sources for *De remediis utriusque fortune* (*The Poet as Philosopher: Petrarch and the Formation of Renaissance Consciousness* [New Haven, 1979], 21, 15, 121).

31. Trinkaus, *Poet as Philosopher,* 91.

32. For the composition of the letters, see Severs, *Literary Relationships,* 7-11; and Nicholas Mann, *Petrarch* (Oxford, 1984), 100.

33. For Petrarch's preoccupation with summing up his life in his last years, see Mann, *Petrarch,* 103.

34. In Boccaccio's *Genealogia Deorum Gentilium* (ed. and trans. Charles G. Osgood, *Boccaccio on Poetry: Being the Preface and the Fourteenth and Fifteenth Books of Boccaccio's Genealogia Deorum Gentilium* [1930; repr. Indianapolis, 1956]), he praises Petrarch effusively, as "that distinguished man Francis Petrarch, at whose feet I have long been a listener" (7), "the greatest poet of our time" (89), and "the present glory of the art of poetry" (92). See also Petrarch's letter to Boccaccio discussing their relative fame, *Seniles* V.2, in *Letters of Old Age,* trans. Bernardo, Levin, and Bernardo, 1:157-66.

35. The act of translation was not neutral but conferred a kind of cultural significance on the source and target languages. See Rita Copeland, *Rhetoric, Hermeneutics, and Translation in the Middle Ages: Academic Traditions and Vernacular Texts* (Cambridge, Eng., 1991), 10-11, 21-36). Translating a vernacular text into Latin and imitating his own disciple probably posed some thorny issues for Petrarch, but the rhetorical stance of translator offered him a range of classical and contemporary models to choose from to represent the author, the work, and himself. Petrarch's solution was to choose a pedagogical model which conceives of translation as "both an exercise and artform" (Copeland, 9). Its purpose was to give the aspiring rhetor insight into the power and form of superior works of oration and poetry, and it combines felicitously the translator's interests as both reader and orator.

36. "For my part, in the daily exercises of youth, I used chiefly to set myself . . . [to read] some poetry, the most impressive to be found, or to read as much of some speech as I could keep in my memory, and then to declaim upon the actual subject-matter of my reading, choosing as far as possible different words. But later I noticed this defect in my method, that those words which best befitted each subject, and were the most elegant and in fact the best, had been already seized upon. . . . Thus I saw that to employ the same expressions profited me nothing, while to employ others was a positive hindrance, in that I was forming the habit of using the less appropriate. Afterwards I resolved,—and this practice I followed when somewhat older,—to translate freely Greek speeches of the most eminent orators. The result of reading these was that, in rendering into Latin what I had read in Greek, I not only found myself using the best words—and yet quite familiar ones—but also coining by analogy certain words such as would be new to our people, provided only they were appropriate" (Cicero, *De Oratore,* ed. and trans. E. W. Sutton and H. Rackham, Loeb Classical Library 1 [Cambridge, Mass., 1988] I.34.154-56.)

37. "Our earlier orators thought highly of translation from Greek into Latin. . . . Cicero himself advocates it again and again, nay, he actually published translations of Xenophon and Plato, which were the result of this form of exercise. . . . The purpose of this form of exercise is obvious. For Greek authors are conspicuous for the variety of their matter, and there is much art in all their eloquence, while, when we translate them, we are at liberty to use the best words available, since all that we use are our very own" (Quintilian, *Institutio Oratoria,* trans. H. E. Butler, Loeb Classical Library 4 [Cambridge, Mass., 1993], X.5.2-4).

38. Pliny the Younger, *Epistulae,* VII.9.1-3 (cited by Copeland, *Rhetoric,* 31).

39. For a description of the "Aristotlian Prologue," see A. J. Minnis, *Medieval Theory of Authorship,* 2nd edn. (Philadelphia, 1988), 28-29. See also Copeland, *Rhetoric,* 112.

40. Middleton, "Clerk and His Tale," 133-35; Morse, "Exemplary Griselda," 61-63; Edwards, "Sclaundre of Walter," 22-23.

41. Cicero, *De Inventione,* I.19.27 (*De Inventione, De Optimo Genere Oratorum, Topica,* trans. H. M. Hubbell, Loeb Classical Library 2 [Cambridge, Mass., 1976]).

42. Quintilian, *Institutio Oratoria,* trans. Butler, II.4.2-4.

43. See *Seniles* I.5 in which Petrarch responds to Boccaccio's complaints of his poverty by inviting him to come live with him (*Letters of Old Age,* trans. Bernardo, Levin, and Bernardo, I:25-26).

44. Edwards writes that magnificence "is concerned only with expenditures; furthermore, it entails connoisseurship, a large outlay done in good taste

(1122a17)" and notes, moreover, that the character of the giver is important, "not the objects of his generosity," for his "disposition, the natural inclination of character, is what measures the ethical qualities of action—whether it is generous, prodigal, or miserly; magnificent, vulgar, or petty" ("Sclaundre of Walter," 25).

45. Giuseppe Mazzotta, for example, sees the tale as a subversive "allegory of order," marriage being the "exemplary metaphor of order and reconciliation" (*World at Play,* 120, 122). The tale also contains the "paradigm" of Job (123). Nigel Thompson identifies many religious allusions in the tale (*Chaucer, Boccaccio, and the Debate of Love,* 287-93), which "link Griselda's patience to that of Job, and her sufferings to those of the Virgin and even of Christ," and he argues that "a pattern of redemption can be seen in the whole novella" (287).

46. Siegfried Wenzel, ed. and trans., *Summa virtutem de remediis anime* (Athens, Ga., 1984), 76. On the tendency of virtues to overlap, see Ralph Hanna III, "Some Commonplaces of Late Medieval Patience Discussions: An Introduction," in *The Triumph of Patience: Medieval and Renaissance Studies,* ed. Gerald J. Schiffhorst (Orlando, Fla., 1978), 65-87; Robert S. Gerke, "Fortitude and Sloth in the *Wife of Bath's Tale* and the *Clerk's Tale,*" *Patristic, Medieval and Renaissance Conference Proceedings* 5 (1980): 119-35.

47. For a discussion of the different orders of virtues, see Wenzel, ed., *Summa virtutum,* 7-8 (hereafter cited in the text by page number).

48. Victoria Kirkham, "The Last Tale in the *Decameron,*" *Mediaevalia* 12 (1989): 205-23.

49. These are the virtues covered in the *Summa virtutum.*

50. Francis Petrarch, *Remedies for Fortune Fair and Foul,* trans. Conrad H. Rawski, 5 vols. (Bloomington, Ind., 1991). Versions of the people's meditation on death occur at 1:308 and 3:115, 194, 197.

51. Emilie Kadish, "The Proem of Petrarch's *Griselda,*" *Mediaevalia* 2 (1976): 189-206, at 190.

52. Griselda's upbringing instills in her the virtues Petrarch prizes in his *Remedies* (trans. Rawski; see n. 50 above). For example, hard work is linked with virtue (1:63, 3:131-32). A spare diet is linked with virtue (3:41-42). Poverty teaches moderation and fights pride (3:34-35). Although adverse fortune may strip one of the trappings of wealth, living well means living "prudently, soberly, and honorably"; virtue "will clothe" whom Fortune

has stripped naked (3:36-37). Virtue is also associated with hardness and inertia with softness (3:131-38).

53. Morse, "Exemplary Griselda," 57.

54. Thomas J. Farrell, ed. and trans. "*Historia Griseldis*: Petrarch's *Epistolae Seniles* XVII.3," in *Sources and Analogues of the Canterbury Tales,* ed. Robert M. Correale and Mary Hamel, 2 vols. (Cambridge, Eng., 2002), 1:108-29. All Latin quotations and English translations of Petrarch's Griselda story will be from this edition. Latin quotations are followed by line numbers; English translations by page numbers.

55. Thomas Aquinas, *Treatise on the Virtues,* trans. John A. Oesterle (1966; repr. Notre Dame, Ind., 1984), 55-56.

56. Aquinas, *Treatise on the Virtues,* trans. Oesterle, 84, 101.

57. Grudin points out "the several instances in which the people counsel Walter" in Boccaccio's tale but also argues that Boccaccio satirizes the people's "gullibility" ("Chaucer's 'Clerk's Tale,'" 72n22, 72).

58. Thomas Aquinas, *Commentary on Aristotle's Nicomachean Ethics,* trans. C. I. Litzinger (Notre Dame, Ind., 1993), sect. 1294.

59. Petrarch, *Remedies,* trans. Rawski, 1:97-100.

60. Middleton, "Clerk and His Tale," 128.

61. Finlayson, "Petrarch," 270.

62. Edwards, "Sclaundre of Walter," 22.

63. Juvenal, *The Sixteen Satires,* trans. Peter Green (Harmondsworth, 1974), 285-86. Boccaccio would recognize this allusion to Juvenal's poetry, for in *Genealogia Deorum Gentilium* he points out that the satires of Juvenal "inveigh against vice and the vicious" and, moreover, puts Petrarch in his company (trans. Osgood, 75, 91).

64. See Morse's discussion of the importance of exemplary narratives for Petrarch and his response to the Veronese ("Exemplary Griselda," 59-62).

FURTHER READING

Criticism

Kircher, Timothy. "The Modality of Moral Communication in the *Decameron*'s First Day, in Contrast to the Mirror of the Exemplum." *Renaissance Quarterly* 54, no. 4 (winter 2001): 1035-73.

Contrasts the methods of moral instruction in the *novelle* of the "First Day" and medieval *mendicant exempla.*

Migiel, Marilyn. "Domestic Violence in the *Decameron.*" In *Domestic Violence in Medieval Texts,* pp. 164-79. Gainesville: University Press of Florida, 2002.

Discusses the thematic significance of domestic violence in the *Decameron.*

———. *A Rhetoric of the Decameron.* Toronto: University of Toronto Press, 2003, 219 p.

Provides an overview of Boccaccio's representation of women in the *Decameron,* focusing on the feminist implications of the text's narrative strategies.

Nissen, Christopher. "The Motif of the Woman in Male Disguise from Boccaccio to Bigolina." In *The Italian Novella: A Book of Essays,* edited by Gloria Allaire, pp. 201-17. New York: Routledge, 2003.

Studies the significance of the disguised woman figure in medieval Italian fiction, including the *Decameron.*

Pearcy, Roy J. "An Anglo-Norman Prose Tale and the Source of the Seventh Novel of the Seventh Day in the *Decameron.*" *Comparative Literature Studies* 37, no. 4 (2000): 384-401.

Traces the source materials of the seventh *novella* of the "Seventh Day" to an Anglo-Norman prose treatise, refuting the widely held view that Boccaccio derived his tale from Continental sources.

Additional coverage of Boccaccio's life and career is contained in the following sources published by Thomson Gale: *Classical and Medieval Literature Criticism,* **Vols. 13, 57;** *European Writers,* **Vol. 2;** *Literature Resource Center;* *Reference Guide to Short Fiction,* **Ed. 2;** *Reference Guide to World Literature,* **Eds. 2, 3;** *Short Story Criticism,* **Vol. 10;** *Twayne's World Authors,* **and** *World Literature and Its Times,* **Ed. 7.**

Harriet Prescott Spofford
1835-1921

(Born Harriet Elizabeth Prescott) American short story writer, novelist, poet, playwright, and essayist.

INTRODUCTION

Spofford is acknowledged as an important figure of both American realism and romanticism. While containing the distinctly lyrical, melodramatic qualities of romanticism, her short fiction also offers a stark depiction of life in turn-of-the-century America, particularly with regard to women's issues. Though her stories were originally published in some of the most prestigious periodicals of her time, her reputation declined amid shifting literary trends. Recent criticism, however, has focused on Spofford's accomplishments as one of America's first female authors to gain popular appeal and earn critical approval.

BIOGRAPHICAL INFORMATION

Spofford was born in the frontier town of Calais, Maine, in 1835 to Joseph Newmarch Prescott and Sarah Jane Bridges Prescott. When Spofford's father left for Oregon in 1850 to earn money for his family, her mother moved with their five children to Newburyport, Massachusetts. After attending the Putnam Free School in Newburyport, Spofford studied at the Pinkerton Academy in Derry, New Hampshire, until 1855. The following year her father returned home from Oregon an invalid, and the Spofford women began running a boarding house to make ends meet.

Spofford also began writing to provide much needed income for the family. She started attracting notice as an author with the publication of "In a Cellar" in the February 1859 issue of the *Atlantic Monthly*. Her first novel, *Sir Rohan's Ghost* (1860), was published shortly afterward. Spofford was soon making acquaintance with such figures of New England's literary elite as John Greenleaf Whittier, Harriet Beecher Stowe, and William Dean Howells. It was around this same time that she met the lawyer Richard S. Spofford, Jr., whom she married in 1865.

Spofford began publishing frequently in *Harper's Bazaar* in 1868, establishing a relationship with the magazine that would last until 1890. She and her husband moved to a house on Deer Island, Massachusetts, in 1874, which prompted Spofford to begin writing pieces on interior design and homemaking. Her grief over the death of her husband in 1888 increased her devotion to her writing. Spofford's final years were spent traveling throughout France and Spain. She died in 1921 at her home on Deer Island and was buried in Newburyport.

MAJOR WORKS OF SHORT FICTION

The Amber Gods, and Other Stories (1863) is Spofford's first collection, and consists primarily of work previously published in magazines. Spofford's mixture of realism and romanticism is evident throughout the book. "Circumstance," her most famous story, won the admiration of the poet Emily Dickinson. The plot concerns the capture of a frontier woman by an animalistic "Indian Devil." The woman soon discovers that she is able to entertain her captor by singing. As the night draws on, she grows worried that the man will become bored with her voice, so she tries to sing a wide variety of musical styles. Eventually the woman resigns herself to singing for her own pleasure, lest her anxiety over pleasing her captor hinder her voice. After her husband arrives and slays the man, they journey back home to find their village destroyed by an Indian attack. Despite its harsh depiction of Native Americans, "Circumstance" represents one of the earliest meditations on the power of the female artist in American literature. Similarly, "The Amber Gods" features Spofford's reversal of the typical nineteenth-century heroine. The female protagonist is an amoral and overly assertive young beauty who vies with her good-natured cousin for the affections of a young artist. Though she marries the man, a hereditary disease leads her to an early grave. Spofford ultimately portrays the young beauty as an artistic muse who drains the life from those around her.

During the 1860s Spofford experimented with the popular genre of detective fiction. "Mr. Furbush," which features the introduction of Spofford's titular detective, was soon followed by Furbush's second and final adventure, "In the Maguerriwock." The latter story is notable for depicting the use of photography, which was relatively new at the time. The stories in her second collection, *A Scarlet Poppy, and Other Stories* (1894), are more humorous in tone, and satirize the ritual of courtship and marriage. "Her Story," from *Old Madame, and Other Tragedies* (1900), demonstrates a darker side of Spofford's marital tales. While imprisoned in an insane asylum, a young wife recounts the details of her husband's infidelity. Though her madness was triggered by the disintegration of their marriage, she still longs for the day her husband will take her home to their children. The interconnected stories in her final two volumes, *Old Washington* (1906) and *The Elder's People* (1920), represent Spofford's interest in the self-contained life of small towns.

CRITICAL RECEPTION

Though famously criticized during her lifetime by Henry James, who found her prose overly romantic, Spofford has since become recognized as one of America's first feminist writers. "Circumstance," in particular, has been cited as one of the finest short stories of nineteenth-century American literature, and reviewers often praise its feminine revision of the traditional captivity narrative. Moreover, "Circumstance" is noted for its allegorical treatment of the conflict between man and nature, though some scholars find its depiction of Native Americans racially insensitive.

Spofford's stories have been analyzed as critiques of imperialism and cultural intolerance as well. Other critics have noted the importance of the visual arts to many of Spofford's tales, and a mythological subtext has been noted in such works as "Her Story," which is used to explain the significance of divisions between men and women. Though Spofford's fame has dwindled over the years, her stories continue to be well regarded for their artistic merit and celebration of womanhood.

PRINCIPAL WORKS

Short Fiction

"In a Cellar" 1859; published in the magazine *Atlantic Monthly*
The Amber Gods, and Other Stories 1863
A Scarlet Poppy, and Other Stories 1894
Old Madame, and Other Tragedies 1900
Old Washington 1906
The Elder's People 1920

Other Major Works

Sir Rohan's Ghost (novel) 1860
Azarian: An Episode (novel) 1864
A Master Spirit (novel) 1896

An Inheritance (play) 1897
In Titian's Garden, and Other Poems (poetry) 1897
The Great Procession, and Other Verses for and about Children (juvenilia) 1902

CRITICISM

Anne Dalke (essay date 1985)

SOURCE: Dalke, Anne. "'Circumstance' and the Creative Woman: Harriet Prescott Spofford." *Arizona Quarterly* 41, no. 1 (1985): 71-85.

[*In the following essay, Dalke argues against Henry James's dismissal of Spofford's writing, citing the depiction of intense, inward experience in Spofford's stories as a breakthrough in feminine literary perspective.*]

It's a little hard to introduce Harriet Prescott Spofford. Her name doesn't sound like that of a writer whom one could take seriously. It's a triple name, with many syllables and many harsh double consonants.[1] An even greater obstacle than those multiple grating sounds is Spofford's critical reputation. She was widely read in her own lifetime, but her place in posterity was fairly well established by Henry James's 1865 review of her novel *Azarian*. James used the review primarily as a forum for trying out his own early theories on realistic fiction. In the process, he demolished "Miss Prescott" for her all-too-"intense" style.[2]

Few scholars since have spoken of or for her,[3] and only this semester, ten years after I first heard her name mentioned, in an undergraduate seminar on American literary realism (and heard that name as summarily dismissed), did I discover that Spofford had defended herself quite ably against James's charges. Her short story **"Circumstance,"** which James knew, and which was published five years before *Azarian*,[4] makes a convincing claim for a form of creation which accords with James's theories on the goal of fiction, but challenges his views on the best means of attaining that goal. That challenge is made from a standpoint that is emphatically female. Spofford suggests in her story that the "realist school," which James commends in his review, is inadequate to encompass the exigencies of female circumstance. The story thus functions not only as a defense but as an early sample of a tradition of American writing by women, a tradition which is concerned with exploring extreme states of consciousness. That tradition includes names as long known as that of Emily Dickinson, and as newly rediscovered as that of Charlotte Perkins Gilman.

James judges Spofford's work against the standard set by a great French realist. Spofford's "descriptive manner" is distinguished from the "realistic system" of Balzac (p. 272), who reproduces objects "with the fidelity of a photograph" (p. 273). Balzac clearly aims at "giving the facts of things," James claims; he does his work "scientifically" (p. 273). James ends his essay with an exhortation to Spofford to do likewise, "to be *real*, to be true to . . . the delicate perception of the actual" (pp. 276-77).

The stylistic distinction James makes is clearly a sexual one as well. The male author he discusses is thoughtful, scientific, while the women he mentions tend to verbal excess and chatter. Spofford's primary fault, for example, is her "intensity" (p. 276). Unlike the realists, who describe things "only insofar as they bear upon the action, and not in the least for themselves," Spofford describes "simply for the sake of describing, and of so gratifying her almost morbid love of the picturesque" (p. 273). Her fault is endemic to her sex. "Miss Prescott uses far too many words, synonymous words and meaningless words. Like the majority of female writers,— Mrs. Browning, George Sand, Gail Hamilton, Mrs. Stowe,—she possesses in excess the fatal gift of fluency" (p. 275). If the fault she possesses is explicitly feminine, the virtue she lacks is as decidedly male: "Miss Prescott adds, tacks on, interpolates, piles up." She never scratches out. But a "true artist should be as sternly just as a Roman father" (p. 275).

Spofford gives too much attention, in sum, to detail external to the action. And she thus offends her readers in her assumption "that the fleshly element carries such weight" (p. 271). But it must be only male readers who are so offended. For James observes that women characters (and presumably, with them, female readers) "can endure twenty times more than men . . . repeated posing, attitudinizing, and changing of costume" (p. 271).

James faults Spofford, finally, not only because her tales are "marvellously void of human nature and false to actual society" (p. 269), but because she creates, in place of a duplication of the world as he saw it, something entirely new and other: she invents "new and unprecedented phases of humanity . . . [and] equally unprecedented nouns and adjectives" (p. 277). She imagines another world altogether, and presents it in new language as well. Her "inordinate fondness for the picturesque" (p. 270) obstructs what should be her prime function: "an author's paramount charge is the cure of souls, to the subjection, and if need be to the exclusion of the picturesque" (p. 270).

Spofford begs to differ. In **"Circumstance"** she concerns herself quite literally with the salvation of her protagonist's soul, a salvation which is accomplished precisely by the means James condemns. Spofford

moves in her story beyond the mere "perception of the actual" to imagine the extreme and urgent requirements of a women's situation. The story posits a very different view of female fluency from that described by James: it is not "pernicious" (p. 277), but salutary, preservative, even redemptive.

James chides Spofford, for example, for her "childish attempts at alliteration" (p. 275). To be sure, Spofford luxuriates in the sounds of words. Her sunrises and sunsets, for example, are assuredly overwritten: "the evening star hung over a tide of failing orange that slowly slipped down the earth's broad side to sadden other hemispheres with sweet regret" (**"Circumstance,"** p. 156). But it is precisely this element in Spofford's style, her tendency to repeat sounds for the sheer pleasure of repetition, which she defends in her story. James dislikes Spofford's tendency to record "not so much the observation of the objects of external nature as the projection of . . . [her] fancy upon them" (p. 269). But fanciful play with words, the placement of familiar terms in new arrangements, saves the heroine of **"Circumstance"** from death. The creation of a "wearisome series of word-pictures" (p. 270), which James denounces in Spofford's fiction, proves, in this one of her stories at least, an act of salvation: a great power to ward off the awful transformations of the world.

"Circumstance" challenges James's views on the creative imagination by showing a creative woman at work. The tale is, in miniature, a Bildungsroman,[5] the story of the education of a realist into the horrors—and the ecstasies—of the fanciful life. The protagonist of Spofford's story learns that the realistic mode of perception is inadequate to deal with the dangers which confront her and discovers simultaneously her own creative power and her power to save her family from harm.

Like Kate Chopin's short story, "Désirée's Baby," Spofford's **"Circumstance"** is a tale about the uncertain margins of existence.[6] The precarious nature of security and the tenuous position their protagonists hold against the threat of change is represented in the work of both authors by the edges of space in which their stories are set. Cynthia Griffin Wolff has discussed at length Chopin's inclination to place her fiction on the boundaries. The bayous and beaches of Louisiana give physical expression to the sense of vulnerability that pervades Chopin's fiction, which posits a world in which the foundations of everyday life are, at best, shaky. Spofford's **"Circumstance"** is placed on another edge: that of the great northern forest in the state of Maine. It is set, as well, at a marginal time: "It was . . . just on the edge of evening that she . . . began to cross the meadowland" (p. 156).

Spofford's protagonist seems quite comfortable in such a setting. She has yet to be educated into the undependable nature of existence, yet to discover the possibility that, even at the most apparently secure moments, circumstances may shift, the equilibrium she so staunchly maintains may be attacked.

Indeed, when her lingering enjoyment of the "companionship of growth . . . the sweet home-feeling of a young . . . wood" is interrupted by a mysterious vision, her response is maddeningly calm, irritatingly cool. This woman, used to dealing with hard fact, sees suddenly before her a winding sheet, waved by "four wan hands," and accompanied by a spectral, melancholy voice (p. 156). The resolutely down-to-earth protagonist simply looks about her, shakes her shoulders, and goes on. She is not frightened, only "a little vexed" at the "hallucination" (p. 157). But her ability to dismiss a fanciful vision with a realistic shake is soon tested again, and tested even more severely: a fabulous flying dragon swoops down and snatches her up into a tree. This seems no real beast, but a decidedly mythical wild animal, brought in to challenge the limits of factual perception.

And yet Spofford assures us that the dangers of the northern woods are not imaginative, "not visionary" (p. 157). The confrontation in which her protagonist engages is less a battle with a forest creature, the "savage and serpentine and subtle and fearless . . . Indian devil" (p. 157), than it is a battle with her self.

Walking on the edge of the woods, at the edge of evening, this young woman slips over the margin and encounters her own worst self in the forest. She fights in the dark woods not something other, but her own lower nature.

In her recent attempt to identify and define a tradition of great fiction by American women, Wolff suggests that writers such as Jewett, Chopin, Wharton, and Cather use a focus that is "intensive, rather than extensive. The plots of their stories do not include adventurous exploits into an American wilderness."[7] But Spofford combines the inner with the outer focus, the exploration of internal with that of external space. No less than Melville in *Moby-Dick* does she use her protagonist's journey as a means of provoking self-examination and reveals thereby not only the dangers of life in the wilds, but the dangers of self-discovery as well.

With acute psychological accuracy, Spofford allows her character to compare the present threat of death with all other possibilities and finds the current danger the worst. Death by water would be gentle, death in battle glorious, death by fire not nearly as horrible as this death: "Fire is not half ourselves . . . is not to be known by the strength of our lower natures let loose, does not drip our blood into our faces from foaming chaps, nor mouth nor slaver above us with vitality. Let us be ended by

fire, and we are ashes . . . let us be ended by wild beasts, and the base, cursed thing howls with us forever through the forest" (p. 162). Death by wild animal is the worst of all possible deaths, because it, like death by disease, is "bred of your own flesh . . . this . . . fiend, this living lump of appetites" (p. 162).

This realist confronts, then, the extreme margins of realism: the naturalistic rendering of the self as no more than animal, as an entirely physical being which eats, which stinks, which drools and slobbers, and which, when it has finished, will assimilate herself—and whatever imagination she may have of a self better than that which he represents—into himself.

The protagonist of Spofford's story succeeds in subduing that lower self, by rising above it. Much is made of the fetid smell of the breath of the beast, but this young woman makes more of her own exhalations. She puts down the base self by developing, suddenly, on penalty of death, the higher one: she becomes imaginative, creative. She begins to sing: "she saw that while the beast listened he would not gnaw. . . . She had heard that music charmed wild beasts . . . and when she opened her lips . . . it was not for shrieking, but for singing" (p. 158). She discovers the power of song and thereby conquers her terror: "If there were yet any tremor in the tone, it was not fear,—she had learned the secret of sound at last" (p. 160).

The first songs recall the happy home life of the protagonist: she begins by singing the cradle songs she used to rock her baby to sleep and the gay fiddle tunes she used to dance to. Her selections become gradually more frantic; she sings national airs, clan cries, war tunes. The desolation of her situation produces "wild, melancholy, forsaken songs" (p. 163): ballads, songs of vagrants and sailors, and ghastly romances. The songs become, in other words, increasingly removed from her own experience, increasingly imaginative. Only such sustained invention can save her from annihilation: she knows, though she finds the thought appalling, "that with her voice ceased her existence!" (p. 163).

This woman has discovered the force of artistic expression, the ability to keep off disaster by the power of poetry. To be sure, she creates no new rhymes, rhythms, or tunes of her own. She only reproduces those of others, but nonetheless demonstrates thereby the great power of the creative process: her singing is a metaphor for all writing, all reading, all renditions of the written word.

Eventually, however, Spofford's protagonist confronts her physical limitations: a dry, hard throat, painful breath, and a burning tongue. Despairing of the strength to sing forever, she undergoes a transformation. She ceases to long for life, but begins instead to celebrate the life after death she is sure awaits her. Her sequence of songs modulates from those of an earthly to those of a religious nature. Even the early hymns of petition, which ask for salvation from death, give way to those of jubilation. She forgets her own recent "strange pity for her own shapeless form that was to be" (p. 166), in her rapturous expectation of the life to come. What Spofford celebrates here as the "sublime faith of our fathers, where utter self-sacrifice alone was true love" might be more accurately described in Charlotte Perkins Gilman's phrase as "the work of our mothers."[8] For although the protagonist gives up all hope of life on this earth, she continues to sing and so assures her earthly salvation at the hands of her husband.

It has taken Spofford's protagonist all night to reach the state of utter reliance on God. When first captured by the beast, "She did not think . . . to call upon God. She called upon her husband" (p. 158). When he fails to answer that call, she feels the betrayal as a loss of religious faith: "she sought eagerly for some reason why her husband was not up and abroad to find her. He failed her,—her one sole hope in life; and without being aware of it, her voice forsook the songs of suffering and sorrow for . . . hymns full of the beauty of holiness, steadfast, relying, sanctified by the salvation they had lent to those in worse extremity than hers" (p. 164). Her religious transformation comes about, in other words, when she finds her husband wanting. She turns to God and the hope of heaven only in the absence of an earthly savior.

This woman rises so far above earthly thoughts, in fact, that she mistakes the first sounds of her husband's belated approach for those of an animal: "A remote crash of brushwood told of some other beast on his depredations" (p. 168). While the protagonist herself has subdued her beastly nature and nearly attained to heaven, through her approaching death, her husband has fallen, in her perception, from savior to beast.

His arrival revives, however, all the woman's longings for life and family happiness: "the fervent vision of God's peace was gone. Just as the grave had lost its sting, she was snatched back again into the arms of earthly hope" (p. 170). The "arms" are implicitly those of her husband, who resumes, with his arrival, a godlike role. His wife prefers the death he brings to that to which she has reconciled herself: "She was quite aware, that, if her husband shot now, the ball must pierce her body before reaching any vital part of the beast,—and yet better that death, by his hand, than the other" (pp. 169-70). With her husband's return, the protagonist finds herself no longer able to imagine an existence separate from that of the beast, freed by it into life eternal. She will die when it does; she is one with the thing she had once risen above.

But a shot from her husband's rifle does free her from the beast after all and does so just as her voice fails. The power of the female artist, Spofford thus seems to suggest, has limits. Although she can stave off destruction with her song, the actual demolishment of evil must come from her husband. And yet the final redemptive act of the story is the woman's deliverance of her family from harm. In the ironic reversal with which **"Circumstance"** ends, the protagonist discovers that the home she had dreamt of as a place of security is desolate. The woman in need of salvation has saved her family in turn: "There is no home there. The log-house, the barns, the neighboring farms, the fences, are all blotted out and mingled in one smoking ruin. Desolation and death were indeed there, and beneficence and life in the forest. Tomahawk and scalping-knife, descending during that night, had left behind them . . . this work of their accomplished hatred" (p. 172).

Spofford ends her story by reiterating the idea with which it began: life, as she portrays it, is lived on the edge, security liable to violation at any moment. Her protagonist experiences only a temporary vision of normalcy before her complacency is challenged again. This woman, who was educated into the limits of a realistic vision of the world and introduced to a sense of her own power of fancy and creativity, is returned to the real world, only to find it illusory. Just when she is feeling most secure, most restored to family and home, the latter is obliterated. The dream of her home, which sustained her through much of her experience of hell and which she gave up only reluctantly for a vision of heaven, proves nonexistent.

And yet such obliteration, such demolishment, allows for the creation of an entirely new self. The pragmatic realist is transformed into a creative, innovative woman by her encounter with the beast; the same creative woman thinks herself "newly made" (p. 171) after her release from that experience. And now, for the third time in eighteen pages, she finds herself once again facing a whole new life. Like Milton's Eve and Adam, Spofford's protagonist and her husband are placed, in the story's final line, with "the world . . . all before them, where to choose" (p. 172).

Unlike Milton's characters, however, those created by Spofford are not cast out from Eden, but preparing to enter into the state of paradise. This husband and wife have not condemned one another to damnation and exile, but rather have proved mutually restorative. He has saved her; she has saved both him and their child; together they face a family life in which both husband and wife possess a new and shared sense of power.

The established nineteenth-century American literary tradition has its beginnings in the work of a man who repeatedly portrays the death of a woman as the necessary prelude to the creation of art. Edgar Allan Poe's Ligeia and Madeline join the dead subject of "The Oval Portrait" as examples of women who must die so that their male relatives may re-create them in artistic form.[9] Spofford is interested no less than Poe in exploring the furthest reaches of awareness. She stands at the head of a female tradition which does the same. But she portrays a very different kind of creative experience from that set forth in Poe's short stories and shows as well its very different effect on family life. The creative woman in Spofford's short story finds the first sources of her poetry in her family experience, is redeemed from danger by the same source and returned to family life again. Her family enables her to survive; she finds within it not only a wellspring of creativity but eventual deliverance as well.[10] Her husband and child are together her muse. But her creation of song does not need to kill off its sources in order to find expression. Spofford's protagonist not only draws on her family to stave off destruction, but actually succeeds in saving them, by her own experience, from the threat of death.

The radical revision Spofford effects in the nineteenth-century male perception of the creative process—the creation, not only of art, but of the self in its relation to the family and community—is perhaps most clearly seen, however, in a comparison of her work not with that of Poe, but with that of Hawthorne. In reworking Milton's fable, Spofford revised as well another story of lost Eden: that of Hawthorne's "Young Goodman Brown." Like the journey of young Brown, the experience of Spofford's protagonist in the forest is a journey into the soul; the devil she encounters in the woods, like the one Brown meets, is her own darker side.[11] Spofford's protagonist leaves behind her godlike husband to engage in battle with her devil; Young Goodman Brown similarly deserts a spouse who represents, if not God, his "Faith" in that deity. Spofford and Hawthorne exploit the same situation, however, to very different ends. The loss of religious faith in the spouse leads in Hawthorne's story to loss of confidence in the self and results in disillusionment and misanthropy. A similar, temporary, loss provokes Spofford's protagonist not to despair but to the discovery of and subsequent development of faith in her own creative power, a faith strong enough to withstand whatever circumstance might bring. She is rewarded with life for her self-reliance.

Spofford reworks Hawthorne's story from a female perspective; she makes a woman the protagonist and a woman the savior as well. But in telling their very different tales, Hawthorne and Spofford use the same mode of presentation: both of their stories are set in the surreal other-world of the forest. Neither story aims to be "literally real" (James, p. 272). In his review, James praises Balzac for his minute description and condemns Spofford for her lack of the same. But Spofford, like

Poe and Hawthorne, is interested in fidelity of another sort. She is attempting to be true, not to external features, but to an inward reality of extreme experience. In her story she refuses the limits and structure of realism for a very different sort of literary endeavor, one which attempts to record not mere changes in fashion but the revision of a soul. She records not what is but what could and should be.

In his review of *Azarian,* James allows such latitude to Hawthorne, but denies it to Spofford. At the end of his essay he introduces an opposition very different from that which structures the center of his piece. James juxtaposes in conclusion not description and realism, but realism and idealism. The female picturesque authors he condemns are thus ranked not only below the male realists, but below a third category of writers who surpass the "vulgar realism" of their day not in their "perception of the actual," but in their "strong grasp of the possible" (pp. 272, 277). James counsels Spofford to school herself in "fidelity to minute social truths" (p. 276); he argues that she should learn to be a better observer. But he suggests as well that there is a form of fiction far superior to that of mere observation: that which attempts to portray the ideal.

This was precisely the kind of fiction Spofford was trying to write. But while James praises Hawthorne's "potent imagination" as a "grand instrument," he denounces Spofford's "unbridled fancy" as "pernicious dependence" (pp. 276-77). He thus gives specific attachment and peculiar sexual import to the distinctions Coleridge develops in his lectures on Shakespeare. Coleridge presents imagination as the superior faculty, the creative force, while inferior Fancy can only select and arrange materials previously created.[12]

Spofford suggests in her story, of course, precisely this function of fancy: the bringing together of previously created material, specifically the songs composed by others. But such an act is for her protagonist a creative one as well. Fancy has in Spofford's story a great power to hold off the awful transformations of the world. Her protagonist cannot change that world, cannot rearrange it, but she can deflect its awful effect from herself and from her family. She develops thereby not only a new creative self but a new family pattern as well.

James anticipates in his review my claim that Spofford cannot be judged by the standards he upholds: "she may meet us with the reply that a correct portraiture of nature and society was not intended. She may claim the poet's license. . . . But woe to the writer who claims the poet's license, without being able to answer the poet's obligations; to the writer of whatever class who subsists upon the immunities, rather than the responsibilities, of his task" (p. 269).

Spofford would say to James, and in her absence I say for her, that it is the responsibility of the poet to have license, to be free. She would agree with James that the goal of fiction is to "save souls," to provoke that radical revision of self which clarity of vision entails. But she would argue as well that a nineteenth-century woman author could only perform that act by her refusal to record life as it is, by her insistence on imagining a world entirely other.

Spofford is excluded by James from both the realistic and idealistic traditions, as he defines them. She has been excluded as well by all recent attempts to define a tradition of American women writers. In her introduction to the Norton edition of *The Country of the Pointed Firs,* for example, Marjorie Pryse suggests that Harriet Beecher Stowe, Mary Wilkins Freeman, and Sarah Orne Jewett will find their eventual places in the literary canon as the "earliest American realists."[13] But writing at the same time as the realists were women such as Gilman, Dickinson, and Spofford who, although capable of minute records of the actual, are most exciting in their exploration of the edges of experience and the depths of psychological distress, and in the intensity of their imagination of alternate worlds. *The Yellow Wallpaper,* for example, shows the descent of a woman into madness,[14] while Gilman's Utopian fictions imagine self-reliant women using their abilities to improve society.[15] As Gilbert and Gubar have shown, Emily Dickinson's poems chronicle not only her actual assumption of the role of madwoman, but her imaginary celebration of the power of creative woman as well.[16] Spofford's **"The Amber Gods"** is spoken by a madwoman from beyond the grave; its bleak vision of the world as it is is counterposed, as we have seen, by **"Circumstance,"** which celebrates, like Emily Dickinson's poetry, the abilities of creative woman.

Emily Dickinson testified to the power of Spofford's imagination. She asked her sister-in-law to keep her supplied with Spofford's work: "You stand nearer the world than I do, Susan. Send me everything she writes." And Dickinson claimed that "Circumstance . . . followed me in the dark."[17] But the poet seems not to have thought of herself and Spofford as writing within the same tradition.[18] Although her poems explore the same circumstances that Spofford exploits, the murderous as well as the saving power of female creativity, Dickinson nonetheless insisted that **"Circumstance"** was "the only thing I ever read in my life that I didn't think I could have imagined myself!"[19]

It has been my argument that several women of that age were imagining the same things, were creating, even though they may not have been aware of it, a tradition of their own in nineteenth-century American literature, a tradition misunderstood then both by themselves and their male reviewers, and still misunderstood today. Dickinson and Gilman each came slowly into recognition in the twentieth century. It is high time that Spofford joined them there.

Notes

1. Spofford objected to her own name on precisely these grounds. Elizabeth K. Halbeisen reports that Spofford "disliked the sound of her name, . . . declaring it was all harsh double consonants, and she was delighted with the negress who in naming a baby chose Genevieve as better expressing Mrs. Spofford!" *Harriet Prescott Spofford: A Romantic Survival* (Philadelphia: University of Pennsylvania Press, 1935), p. 184.

2. James's review of "*Azarian: an Episode.* By Harriet Elizabeth Prescott" was first published in *The North American Review,* 100 (1865), 268-77, to which publication all citation has been made. The review was reprinted in James's collected *Notes and Reviews* (Cambridge, MA: Dunster House, 1921).

3. William Dean Howells did republish "Circumstance" in *The Great Modern American Stories: An Anthology* (New York: Boni and Liveright, 1920), and "A Reminiscent Introduction" recalled "the awful joy of Miss Prescott's (not yet Mrs. Spofford's) tremendous story of Circumstance, still unsurpassed of its kind" (p. vii).

4. "Circumstance" was first published in *The Atlantic Monthly,* May 1860, and reprinted in Spofford's collection, *The Amber Gods and Other Stories* (Boston: Ticknor and Fields, 1863; rpt. Freeport, NY: Books for Libraries Press, 1969). All references to the story are taken from this collection. James compared *The Amber Gods* with *Azarian* and found the former "admirably sober and coherent" (Review of *Azarian,* p. 268).

5. It is emphatically *not* the female version described in Susan J. Rosowski's essay on "The Novel of Awakening," *Genre,* 12 (1979), 313-32. The process of discovery that Rosowski traces involves an inward movement toward greater self-knowledge, a coming to terms with oneself as a woman, and a final awakening to limitations. Spofford's story, in which a woman discovers her creative power, is very different from the novels Rosowski suggests fit her pattern: *Madame Bovary, The Awakening, My Mortal Enemy, Daughter of Earth,* and *Middlemarch.*

6. See Cynthia Griffin Wolff, "Kate Chopin and the Fiction of Limits: 'Désirée's Baby,'" *Southern Literary Journal,* 10, No. 2 (1978), 123-33 for a discussion of the "metaphor of margins" and the "abundant . . . violation" of boundaries in Chopin's fiction.

7. Cynthia Griffin Wolff, Introduction, *Classic American Women Writers* (New York: Octagon Books, 1980), p. 2.

8. See Charlotte Perkins Gilman, *His Religion and Hers: A Study of the Faith of Our Fathers and the Work of Our Mothers* (New York: The Century Co., 1923; rpt. Westport, CT: Hyperion Press, 1976) for an extended examination of the differences between religious thought induced by male experience of death and that induced by the life-giving experience of women.

9. See Daniel Hoffman, *Poe Poe Poe Poe Poe Poe Poe* (Garden City, NY: Doubleday & Company, Inc., 1972), pp. 316-17: "Poe makes the artist a cannibal or vampire whose subject *must die* so that there may be art . . . the death of a beautiful woman, Poe's prescribed them[e] for poetry, makes necessary that the beautiful woman die."

10. Such an argument differs dramatically from that of those contemporary feminists who claim that family attachments do not give force to creative life, but rather hamper it. See, for example, Tillie Olsen, "Silences: When Writers Don't Write," in *Images of Women in Fiction: Feminist Perspectives,* ed. Susan Koppelman Cornillion, rev. ed. (Bowling Green, OH: Bowling Green University Popular Press, 1973), pp. 97-112.

11. Cf. Thomas F. Walsh, Jr., "The Bedeviling of Young Goodman Brown," *Modern Language Quarterly,* 19 (1958), 331-36.

12. See *The Collected Works of Samuel Taylor Coleridge, V: Lectures 1808-1819: On Literature,* with which compare Chapter 13 of "Biographia Literaria," *The Collected Works, VII, 1,* 304-05.

13. Marjorie Pryse, Introduction to the Norton Edition, *The Country of the Pointed Firs and Other Stories,* ed. Mary Ellen Chase (New York: Norton, 1981), p. ix. Pryse claims that Stowe was "the founder of American realistic fiction, decades before William Dean Howells and Henry James would become its self-designated American theoreticians." Her tradition of female realists includes, in addition to Stowe, Freeman, and Jewett, Elizabeth Stuart Phelps, Rose Terry Cooke, Alice Brown, Mary Noailles Murfree, and Kate Chopin.

14. See Elaine R. Hedges, Afterword, *The Yellow Wallpaper* by Charlotte Perkins Gilman (Old Westbury, NY: The Feminist Press, 1973), pp. 37-63.

15. See Ann J. Lane, Introduction, *The Charlotte Perkins Gilman Reader: "The Yellow Wallpaper" and Other Fiction* (New York: Pantheon Books, 1980), p.xxvii.

16. Sandra M. Gilbert and Susan Gubar, *The Madwoman in the Attic: The Woman Writer and the Nineteenth-Century Literary Imagination* (New Haven: Yale University Press, 1979), pp. 581-650.

17. As reported by Thomas Wentworth Higginson, "Emily Dickinson's Letters," *The Atlantic Monthly,* 68 (1891), 446.

18. See, however, Ellen Moers's claim that Dickinson's "passion for women's literature stands out oddly against the background of the rest of her reading . . . she read and reread every Anglo-American woman writer of her time." *Literary Women* (Garden City, NY: Doubleday & Company, Inc., 1976), pp. 60-61.

19. As reported by Halbeisen, p. 80.

Eva Gold and Thomas H. Fick (essay date fall 1993)

SOURCE: Gold, Eva and Fick, Thomas H. "A 'masterpiece' of 'the educated eye': Convention, Gaze, and Gender in Spofford's 'Her Story.'" *Studies in Short Fiction* 30, no. 4 (fall 1993): 511-23.

[*In the following essay, Gold and Fick investigate the reference to the Greek myth of Cupid and Psyche in "Her Story."*]

There have been calls of late for critical attention to the long-neglected works of Harriet Prescott Spofford. Most of these calls have cited **"Circumstance,"** a story concerned with issues of women's voice and characterized by Emily Dickinson as "the only thing . . . that I do not think I could have written myself" (Bendixen x).[1] Spofford's recent editors have also drawn attention to **"Her Story,"** a tale of rivalry between two women, both unnamed, one the wife of a wealthy minister and the other his ward.[2] The wife narrates her story from the madhouse to which she has been committed—"bur[ied] . . . alive" in "this grave" (148) by her husband Spencer. As this brief summary suggests, **"Her Story"** in many ways anticipates the themes and critical interests of Charlotte Perkins Gilman's "The Yellow Wallpaper" (1892). Like "The Yellow Wallpaper," **"Her Story"** offers a critique of the social conventions that define women as dependent and of the prevailing literary conventions complicitous in this agenda.[3] But unlike Gilman's later tale, **"Her Story"** is concerned not so much with the divisions between men and women as with the origins and significance of divisions among women. Specifically, it explores the way the oppositions common to male- and female-authored fictions (blond-passive-chaste; dark-aggressive-sexual) serve to divide women from each other. Further, it interrogates the cultural and psychological grounds of these oppositions, locating them in the desire of patriarchal institutions to divide what is frightening or threatening to them. Spofford's adaptation of the Gothic mode demonstrates how the concept of the "other woman" objectifies the status of woman as "other" in the service of intra-gender warfare. For all their apparent differences, the two rivals are shown to be sisters who are equally subject to male authority, which is maintained by the myths of our culture and by the conventions of looking that situate women as objects of a male gaze.

As both psychologists and literary critics argue, the male fear of female sexuality—of the woman as "other"—may give rise to reductive stereotypes that serve to distance and diminish women. One of the most common of these strategies, as Karen F. Stein explains, is to split the concept of woman "into pairs of stereotyped antitheses: saint/sinner, virgin/whore, . . . angel, witch" (124).[4] These schematically opposed types are familiar from classic male texts and popular women's fiction. Among the male-authored texts, James Fenimore Cooper's Leather-Stocking Tales are probably most notorious for their depiction of pure but childish blonds and experienced but compromised brunettes. Conventional oppositions are not, however, restricted to male-authored texts. Mary Jane Holmes's *Tempest and Sunshine* (1854), for example, follows two sisters—the blond Fanny ("Sunshine") and the dark-haired Julia ("Tempest"), whose nicknames epitomize their characters and plot-functions. Spofford's **"Her Story"** first appears to center on several equally clear oppositions—dominance and dependence, dark and light, sanity and madness, freedom and confinement—each of which is sustained by the enabling thematic opposition of loving wife and predatory other woman. **"Her Story"** evokes one of the contrasts common in Gothic and other nineteenth-century American fictions: the good, pure-hearted, submissive women and the scheming vampire and housebreaker. But more than most other writers of the period, Spofford is concerned with the deadly effect of such stereotyped antitheses even as she uses of them.

Spofford is attentive to such matters partly because she wrote **"Her Story"** during a period of transition and redefinition in women's literature. In the late 1860s and early 1870s, as Nina Baym points out, the once-popular literature she calls "woman's fiction" was rapidly losing its audience. This literature focused on a dependent woman's movement toward independence and self-sufficiency; it chronicles "the 'trials and triumph' . . . of a heroine who, beset with hardships, finds within herself the qualities of intelligence, will, resourcefulness, and courage sufficient to overcome them" (22). By the time **"Her Story"** appeared in *Lippincotts* in 1872, however, woman's fiction had lost its audience to other genres such as the Gothic romance, in which the woman tries to become a powerful male's only dependent—something quite different from the focus on independence in woman's fiction (Baym 30, 296).

Spofford was well aware of these changes; indeed, the rivalry between the two women can be understood as partly a response to the shifting concerns of popular women's fiction. In the destructive triangular relationship at the heart of **"Her Story,"** the two unnamed women vie, each in her own way, to become the husband Spencer's only dependent. The interloper actively solicits Spencer's attention and patronage through the appropriation of male spheres of knowledge and an aggressive coquetry, while the wife exercises the charms of passivity, submission, and domestic duty. The narrator practices the art of submission unaccompanied by self-knowledge; her story inverts the lesson of woman's fiction, in which a heroine deprived of support nevertheless wins her way in the world. Like most such heroines, she is an orphan and dependent; but unlike them she does not develop any sense of her own worth. When she encounters her future husband for the first time she is "singing like one possessed" (151); she soon becomes his wife and attribute.

Indeed, the issue of possession and self-possession is central to the story, as the other woman's career also suggests. If we believe the narrator, the other woman is her diametrical opposite. While the narrator-wife is Protestant, of limited and parochial education, accomplished mainly in music and the domestic arts, and submissive to a fault, the other woman is dark, probably Catholic, European-educated and well traveled, an expert artist, well versed in classical architecture, and, above all, aggressive in pursuit of her man. The narrator's language evokes the military flavor of her rival's campaign: "she brought forward her forces by detachment" (154). And the woman's "forces" seem at times to challenge acceptable female behavior, as when she spends a morning fearlessly breaking in a "fiery" horse (155).

Like many women's texts, then, **"Her Story"** sees dependence as disastrous; the narrator-wife is vanquished by her more independent and aggressive rival. But it also portrays authorized forms of women's aggression as themselves creations of patriarchal culture and therefore of questionable value for women. The other woman's bold assertiveness and the wife's demure acquiescence are polar responses to the same controlling conditions, and Spofford's strategy in **"Her Story"** is to bring us to consciousness of the likeness underlying apparent oppositions.

Our confidence in binary oppositions is challenged by the narrator's remarks first to her childhood friend, Elizabeth, who visits her in the retreat and to whom she relates her story, and later, by remarks to her rival, the other woman. To Elizabeth the narrator asserts: "I am as much myself, I tell you, as you are" (149). This comment may certainly be taken to denote disordered thinking; but it also points to the fact that Elizabeth and the narrator are both women and thus to an intersection of interest and identity that the narrator does not acknowledge. Similarly, although the narrator's rival appears to be her nemesis, in fact the two have much in common, both as women, and, especially, as Spencer's women. The narrator criticizes her rival as "one of those women delightful to men indeed, but whom other women—by virtue of their own kindred instincts, it may be, or by virtue of temptations overcome—see through and know for what they are" (154). This effort at censure and division in fact expresses a profound truth: women have "kindred instincts." There are further suggestions of this kinship. In an act that at first suggests mental instability the narrator reverses her initial description of the rival as "wondrous fair": "Fair, did I say? No: she was dark as an Egyptian" (149). And dark she stays for the rest of the story. But the narrator's slip suggests what becomes increasingly clear: the women's rivalry obscures a fundamental identity of condition and interest, an identity that is obscured by the conventions of light and dark women that the narrator almost reflexively evokes, and that proceed from the categorical oppositions of patriarchal authority.

It becomes increasingly clear, therefore, that the distinction between aggressive other woman and passive narrator is more apparent—or instrumental—than real and natural. Indeed, the categories of opposition and difference give place, suggestively, to intimations of identity. The narrator is an orphan, "quite dependent" (150), and becomes Spencer's wife; the other woman—evidently also an orphan—becomes Spencer's ward; as her guardian, he has been given a proprietary interest in her life. Furthermore, each woman calls the other mad. The narrator early asserts that her rival "was the mad woman, not I" (148) and later says "She will die in a madhouse"(157); the rival, kissing the narrator's children, taunts, "When you are gone to a madhouse, don't think they'll have many such kisses" (162). Both are proven correct: both end up confined in the same "Retreat" (148).

Thus **"Her Story"** goes beyond the exploration and criticism of passive acquiescence in woman's fiction to examine the way culturally sanctioned forms of women's aggression can maintain existing structures of authority. What passes for self-assertion in this tale is often revealed to be the opposite. This is nowhere more apparent than in the other woman's assumption of the role of Spencer's Muse, a role charged with ambiguity and danger.[5] The other woman is a fabulous polymath, versed in painting, music, architecture, sculpture—and she offers her knowledge in service to Spencer's project: a church that shall be a monument to himself. She shows Spencer her portfolios, full of "pencil-sketches from the Rhine and from the Guadalquivir, rich watercolors of Venetian scenes, interiors of old churches, and sheet after sheet covered with details of church architecture" (155). Spencer is suitably impressed: "I see you have mastered the whole thing," he says; "You must instruct me here" (156). And she does, closeting

herself with Spencer (while the narrator tends to her wifely duties) "criticizing, comparing, making drawings, hunting up authorities" (156) and redesigning the church that is to enshrine Spencer's pride.

At first this assumption of cultural authority seems admirable. It is tempting to see learning as the sign of triumphant access to previously forbidden areas, since in 1872 women were much less likely than men to have the sort of education that was a major criterion of intellectual and political leadership. Thus Susan K. Harris argues that in Augusta Evans Wilson's *St. Elmo* (1866) the heroine, Edna Earl, establishes her identity, despite the censure of Wilson and her characters, by seizing written discourse, "a source of cultural hegemony generally forbidden women" (64). Indeed, Wilson's own prose is a Mather-like "cloth of gold" embellished with impressive and sometimes impenetrable allusions:

> To-day peering into the golden Gardens of the Sun at Cuzco; tomorrow clambering over Thibet glaciers, to find the mystic lake of Yamuna; now delighting to recognize in Teoyamiqui (the wife of the Aztec God of War) the unmistakable features of Scandinavian Valkyrias; . . . she spent her days in pilgrimages to mouldering shrines, and midnight often found her groping in the classic dust of extinct systems.
>
> (qtd. in Harris 67)[6]

But the appropriation of written discourse can pose problems; since the terms of cultural discourse are controlled by men, women who appropriate such discourse may be bound by conditions of expression that are not their own. In *St. Elmo,* Edna Earl goes "groping in the classic dust of extinct systems," but we must recall that these are systems that have been predicated largely upon her exclusion. In **"Her Story"** the other woman's apparent mastery likewise entails the evacuation of self. She is, as the narrator comments, a "being of infinite variety—to-day glad, to-morrow sad, freakish, and always exciting you by curiosity as to her next caprice" (154), and she has powers of mimicry the narrator likens to "necromancy" (155). Like that sometime hero of American culture, the confidence man, the other woman is a consummate shape-shifter. But while the confidence man thrives in highly fluid public situations—where appearance and social position have become disassociated—this confidence woman's transformations take place in a highly restrictive situation, in Spencer's home, where she remains a ward.[7]

It is telling, then, that the central symbol of the story refers to a classical myth exploring the proper relation between men and women. When Spencer brings his bride to his home (that is now to be theirs) he points to "a marble Eros" that "held a light up, searching for his Psyche." Spencer offers this interpretation: "Our love has found its soul" (153). But the statue—as well as the myth of Cupid and Psyche—suggests another interpretation, one in which Spencer plays the male Eros, while the narrator—and later her rival—plays the female Psyche.

In the most familiar version of the myth, that by Apuleius, Cupid falls in love with Psyche and sequesters her in a palace, forbidding her to look at him. When her two jealous sisters tell Psyche that Cupid is a monster, however, she takes a lamp and looks upon the sleeping god.[8] A drop of oil from the burning lamp awakens him, exposing the scopic transgression for which Psyche is subsequently abandoned by Cupid. Far from suggesting the union of Spencer and the narrator as Spencer's interpretation of the myth suggests, the myth of Cupid and Psyche teaches a lesson of submission with the threat of punishment and it does so in terms of a controlling gaze. The work of feminist critics has emphasized the gendered character of the gaze as theorized by Jacques Lacan, whereby the (male) one who gazes has power over the (female) object of the gaze (Lacan 67-119).[9] The statue is an iconographic presence that functions as a warning to reinforce this lesson: women are properly objects of the male gaze, and may themselves look upon their gods (or monsters) only at the peril of being abandoned or imprisoned. And it is by further charting the economy of the gaze in **"Her Story"** that we recognize that as objects of the male gaze the two rivals are really "sisters."

The lesson of the statue of Cupid is most directly meant for the narrator. It is quite literally a liminal image: she is a newlywed, entering her home for the first time. And it is especially important that she is shown this statue en route to her music room. Recall that music, and especially singing, has been her sole act of assertion; it is by singing "as though one possessed" (151) that she attracts the gaze of her husband. Now she must pass the lesson of Cupid before entering the room where she can give "voice."[10] But in fact the narrator has little need for the lesson of the statue; from the outset she presents herself as the object of a male gaze. She admits that she treats her husband as a "god" and an "idol" (152) and lucidly defines her place in the specular economy: "I was a pleasant thing to look at myself once on a time. . . . He used to tell me so: those were his very words" (150). Her first sight of Spencer, in church, is especially revealing: "I looked up and saw him at the desk. He was reading the first lesson 'Fear not, for I have redeemed thee, I have called thee by thy name: thou art mine' . . . I said to myself, It is a vision, an angel; and I cast down my eyes. But the voice went on, and when I looked again he was still there" (150). This moment offers a promise of union and equality: "as he rose I saw him searching for the voice unconsciously, and our eyes met" (151). Both the man and the woman look and acknowledge the fact of their looking; both gaze at another and are objects of another's gaze. Each is equally aggressive in assuming the gaze; each is equally vulnerable to the gaze of another.

Such assertiveness on the part of the narrator is short-lived, however, and for good reason: it is dangerous. The admonitory statue of Cupid suggests that with marriage the wife must no longer gaze upon her husband. Only once more does the narrator look so forcefully, and this look is the immediate cause of her incarceration. Consumed by jealousy and a sense of powerlessness and then deprived of sleep while nursing her dangerously ill daughter, one unbearable night she runs to the music room planning "to tell [Spencer] all." There she finds her rival singing and Spencer watching, "white with feeling, with rapture, with forgetfulness"; she herself hesitates, and looks, and finally enters the room unseen. She sees Spencer and her rival embrace: "And suddenly I crashed down both my hands on the keyboard before me, and stood and glared upon them" (164). As she glares upon them the narrator is finally in a position of power and mastery. But this moment is brief. She is punished for usurping the prerogative of the gaze, for violating the lesson of the statue: "And I never knew anything more till I woke up here" (164) in the madhouse, she says.

But what about the narrator's rival? Initially, the other woman seems to occupy a powerful—and male—position in the specular economy: she is an artist who makes accomplished portraits of both the narrator and her husband. Yet, like her actions, her art is not intended to record her own "vision" so much as to attract another's; her art places Spencer at the center and in control. The other woman offers Spencer a flattering mirror of himself with a portrait that exaggerates his "careless grace." And her drawing of the narrator is a gambit in her campaign against the conventional wife. It is designed to exaggerate her "primness" and Spencer, the narrator believes, "saw there the ungraceful trait for the first time" (155). With her art, the other woman thus displaces the narrator as the object of Spencer's gaze. But in so doing the rival displaces herself as well.

This displacement is most clearly evident in the climactic scene, when the other woman makes her most open bid for Spencer's attention and patronage. For most of the story Spencer himself seems unaware of the other woman's campaign. At one point he tells his wife that the rival's beauty "is not the kind . . . I admire," a comment the other woman overhears and seeks to remedy: "Then I must teach you, sir. . . . Now look at me." To this, the wife tells Spencer "Shut your eyes" (157). But Spencer looks, accepting the other woman's instruction, which offers an eroticized version of her cultural sophistication as an alternative to tedious wifely adoration.

> "You mustn't call it vanity," she said. "It is only that it
> is impossible, looking at the picture in the glass, not to
> see it as I see any other picture. But for all that, I know

it is not every fool's beauty; it is no daub for the vulgar gaze, but a masterpiece that it needs the educated eye to find. I could tell you how this nostril is like that in a famous marble, how the curve of this cheek is that of a certain Venus, the line of this forehead like the line in the dreamy Antinous' forehead. Are you taught?"

(157)

Spencer submits to the rival's instruction—an eroticizing of Western European aesthetics that reduces the woman herself to an object of the gaze. To herself and to others the woman becomes what Karen Halttunen calls a "painted woman"; the mirror reflects not the self but a "masterpiece." The other woman is correct when she maintains that vanity plays no part because what the rival sees in the mirror, what she offers to Spencer, is not herself but a composite of male creations.

The dangers of this stance are suggested most strikingly in the conclusion to this powerful scene. In an action that, for nineteenth-century readers, unambiguously suggested sexual invitation, at the beginning of her performance the other woman lets down her hair, "till the great snake-like coils unrolled upon the floor" (157). At the end she twists up and secures it again with her arrow fasteners, turning back to the evening paper with supreme self-control. Not so Spencer: "as he lay back in his lordly way, surveying the vision from crown to toe, I saw him flush—I saw him flush and start and quiver, and then he closed his eyes and pressed his fingers on them, and lay back again and said not a word" (158). Spencer's orgasmic response to the vision, or to the viewing, of the other woman reveals that as an image her purpose is to give him pleasure, a pleasure she does not share. She is then truly a "master piece."

The statue of Cupid is thus not just a warning to the passive narrator: it also addresses the other woman's more aggressive bid for power. So although the rival does succeed in displacing the wife from her home and from her husband's affections, she does not increase her authority but instead assumes the wife's precarious position. For all her apparent differences from the wife, the rival's position has always been precarious; Spencer has always had power. The fundamental powerlessness of the rival has been suggested not only by her dependent status as Spencer's ward, but by her actions: for all their relative assertiveness, her painting, mimicry, and false devotion have been designed to solicit Spencer's gaze. As the narrator comments, she dances "only when Spencer was there to see" (155). The rival's aggressiveness is, at root, only apparent; her posture is one of deference and homage. She may, for instance, look at Spencer, but her look does not empower her; rather, it serves to affirm his power. The wife says of her rival: "She knew how, by a silent flattery, as she shrank away and looked up at him, to admire his haughty stature, and make him feel the strength and glory of his manhood

and the delicacy of her womanhood" (149). As the decorous wife remarks, "I never had the face to praise him; she had" (149). For the rival, as for the wife and Psyche, the possibilities of the gaze are determined by her god and implicitly by her gender.

"Her Story" summarizes the Catch-22 of codes governing women's conduct: damned if you do and damned if you don't. When the other woman looks, she does so to validate Spencer's "manhood"; more characteristically, like the wife, the rival is to be looked at by Spencer. It is not surprising, therefore, that the rival should eventually join the displaced wife in her madhouse: in final pages of **"Her Story"** the early suggestions of kinship between the women are tragically fulfilled. As the wife remarks of her own plight, "just as all roads lead to Rome, all roads led me to this Retreat" (148). This applies as well to the plight of the rival; as Susan Koppelman remarks, "Madness is the most persistent metaphor for the fate of the woman who has given over responsibility for her inner self to a man who proves a deceiver" (xxvii).

Near the end of her narration to Elizabeth, the wife speaks of a "hopeless case" recently confined to the madhouse and of the "new service" that somewhat alleviates her weary life: to make this woman smile.

> She is a little woman, swarthy as a Malay, but her hair, that grows as rapidly as a fungus grows in the night, is whither than leprosy: her eyebrows are so long and white that they veil and blanch her dark dim eyes; and she has no front teeth. A stone from a falling spire struck her from her horse, they say. The blow battered her and beat out reason and beauty. Her mind is dead; she remembers nothing, knows nothing; but she follows me about like a dog; she seems to want to do something for me, to propitiate me. All she ever says is to beg me to do her no harm. She will not go to sleep without my hand in hers. Sometimes, after long effort, I think there is a gleam of intelligence, but the doctor says there was once too much intelligence, and her case is hopeless.
>
> Hopeless, poor thing!—that is an awful word; I could not wish it said for my worst enemy.

(166)

There is so much in this curious description to suggest the rival that the reference to "my worst enemy" only confirms an identification the narrator cannot quite make. Like her rival, the "other" madwoman is dark and has hair "that grows as rapidly as a fungus," recalling the narrator's earlier description of the rival as a "thing of slime and sin, a splendid tropical growth of passionate heat and the slime" (161). Most significantly, she is characterized by the doctor as having once had "too much intelligence." Recall that the other woman displaced the narrator by contributing her vast knowledge of European art and architecture to the design of

Spencer's church, which the narrator herself characterizes as the product of a faith that is less "piety than partisanship" (153). A piece from the phallic steeple thus seems the befitting medium of chastisement for one whose great intelligence can be a threat as well as a convenience.

Clearly, the swarthy Malay is in one sense an image of the narrator's completed revenge: the woman has lost her beauty and her intelligence and now slavishly seeks to propitiate the narrator. At the same time, however, her fate makes her a specular image of the wife; revenge can be found only in a common imprisonment. The other woman's strategies do not so much assert her independence as inscribe her in the typical economies of gender-determined power relations since by presenting herself as a product of classical culture, and by offering herself as spectacle for the male gaze, the other woman prepares the conditions for her incarceration and constant surveillance. And in one of the tale's most trenchant ironies, **"Her Story"** begins and ends as "his-story." The narrator refuses to blame her husband and longs for him to take her back. She tells her story to a woman whom she believes is Spencer's emissary and can take Spencer's place: "I picture to myself how he will send another—some old friend who knew me before my trouble—who will see me and judge, and carry back report that I am all I used to be—some friend who will open the gates of heaven to me, or close the gates of hell upon me—who will hold my life and my fate" (166). At the end the narrator continues to think in the terms that have imprisoned both herself and her rival: she presents herself as one to be seen and therefore possessed *in absentia* by her husband. Since the narrator recognizes Elizabeth only as one who will look for the husband, Spencer remains a "god."

Significantly, the narrator does not detect the potential for another sort of "heaven" implicit in her relationship with Elizabeth.[11] Elizabeth is the only woman with a name in **"Her Story"** and she is furthermore identified as a childhood friend of the narrator's, someone for whom the narrator has an identity apart from her husband. The story's final line therefore evokes a "heaven" the speaker is unable to recognize, one available not in the absent patriarchal audience, but in the immediate female one: "If—oh if it should be you, Elizabeth!" (166). At its close, **"Her Story"** evokes a matriarchal paradise grounded in the real-life experiences of love and friendship among nineteenth-century women and their fictional counterparts.[12] Spofford presents an implicit argument for a fuller kind of "her story" but with a pragmatic sense of the difficulties to be surmounted. Although she does not share the expectation of independence promoted in the once-popular genre of woman's fiction, she does anatomize the conditions of women's dependence in a world dominated by the male gaze. With her female narrator and audience (both Elizabeth within the story and the largely female readership of periodical fiction), Spofford also lays in place the conditions that would permit the telling of what would truly be her story.

Notes

1. Emily Dickinson to Susan Huntington Dickinson, quoted by Bendixen (x). Bendixen's essay is currently the best introduction to Spofford's life and work. For an excellent critical perspective on "Circumstance" see Dalke.

2. Susan Koppelman first reprinted "Her Story" in The Other Woman: Stories of Two Women and a Man (1984), an anthology of stories about women involved with adulterous men. "Her Story" has since been reprinted in Spofford, *"The Amber Gods" and Other Stories*; parenthetical page references are to this edition.

3. In "A Map for Rereading," for example, Annette Kolodny uses "The Yellow Wallpaper" to demonstrate how interpretative strategies are "learned, historically determined, and thereby necessarily gender-inflected" (452). Kolodny argues that the incomprehension and even hostility that greeted Charlotte Perkins Gilman's "The Yellow Wallpaper" can be attributed to gendered interpretative strategies: confronted by a story of captivity and madness, male readers expected to find an exploration of the individual psyche such as one sees in tales such as Poe's "The Pit and the Pendulum." Gilman, however, is interested in exploring cultural and social entrapment, rather than the more egocentric captivity experienced in tales like "The Pit and the Pendulum," which in superficial ways Gilman's tale recalls.

4. Similarly, the opposition between good and evil women in women's fiction may internalize women's ambivalence toward the female, an ambivalence characteristic of the female Gothic, many of whose conventions Spofford appropriates (Fleenor, Introduction 11).

5. Women writers have explicitly and implicitly acknowledged the dangers of playing the Muse, one who can inspire and direct but not create. In "The Prologue," Anne Bradstreet, the first published American poet, defends her literary debut against those who would say she is not the author by evoking the Muses: "Be sure the antick Greeks were far more milde; / Else of our Sex why feigned they those nine, / And Poesy made *Calliope's* own childe?" Yet she must immediately qualify even this mild claim for literary authority: "Let *Greeks* be *Greeks*, and Women what they are; / Men have precedency and still excell" (7). The potential danger of the Muse-figure's precari-

ous status is explored in a much darker vein in Edgar Allan Poe's "Ligeia" (1838).

6. Cotton Mather defends his own densely allusive prose in *Manuductio ad Ministerium* (1726), his handbook for divinity students. He calls his critics' disapproval sour grapes, commenting that the best writer "pretends not unto reading, yet he could not have writ as he does if he had not read very much in his time; and his composures are not only a cloth of gold, but also struck with as many jewels as the gown of a Russian ambassador" (21). But Mather, like Spencer, is a minister whose erudition has a cultural sanction and authority that Edna Earl, or Augusta Evans Wilson for that matter, can claim only precariously.

7. Explorations of the confidence man are legion. Lindberg terms the confidence man "a representative American, perhaps even our covert hero" (3). The title of Halttunen's study of the sentimental ideal of social conduct, *Confidence Men and Painted Women,* suggests some of the differences between men and women in nineteenth-century America. While the confidence man could be a public figure, defined through his actions, the painted woman was primarily a private figure, defined by appearance.

8. Note that the relation between Cupid and Psyche is surrounded by rivalry between women: first Venus, Cupid's mother, wants to punish Psyche for attracting to herself the worship that should be Venus's; later, Psyche's sisters are jealous of Psyche's marriage to a god. We rely on the story of Cupid and Psyche by Apuleius as translated by Robert Graves (Apuleius 1-27).

9. Lacan's concepts have been used (and criticized) by feminist critics of literature and film, who have been concerned with analyzing the gendered character of the gaze in our culture. For a sampling of work that has influenced our reading of "Her Story," see Mulvey and Doane. For extensions of these ideas from film to literature, see Newman.

10. This is particularly significant given the interest in women's voice in "Circumstance." In fact, where "Circumstance" explores the power of woman's voice, "Her Story" examines the limitations placed on woman's vision. On "Circumstance," see Dalke.

11. As Susan Koppelman notes,

> The most significant characteristic in . . . women's stories of the other woman is a wished-for, implied, or sometimes actually achieved bonding between the two women that occurs near the story's end and provides a moment of transcendence, in which the women triumph over the damage to their lives and self-esteem.

(xxi)

"Her Story" presents two such moments of potential bonding for the narrator, although neither is fully achieved—with the other woman herself and with Elizabeth.

12. Carroll Smith-Rosenberg discusses the importance of loving friendships between nineteenth-century women. Rachel Halliday in Harriet Beecher Stowe's *Uncle Tom's Cabin* (Chapter 13) is perhaps the most familiar matriarch of the fictional woman's paradise. But there are also more secular examples such as Celia Barnes in Rose Terry Cooke's "How Celia Changed Her Mind," which ends with a paradise of old maids celebrating the pleasures of their outcast marital condition.

Works Cited

Apuleius. "Cupid and Psyche." Trans. Robert Graves. *Spells of Enchantment: The Wondrous Fairy Tales of Western Culture.* Ed. Jack Zipes. New York: Viking, 1991. 1-27.

Baym, Nina. *Woman's Fiction: A Guide to Novels by and about Women in America, 1820-1870.* Ithaca, NY: Cornell UP, 1978.

Bendixen, Alfred. Introduction. Spofford, *"The Amber Gods"* ix-xxxiii.

Bradstreet, Anne. *Complete Works of Anne Bradstreet.* Ed. Joseph R. McElrath, Jr. and Allan P. Robb. Boston: Twayne, 1981.

Cooke, Rose Terry. "How Celia Changed Her Mind." *How Celia Changed Her Mind & Selected Stories.* Ed. Elizabeth Ammons. New Brunswick, NJ: Rutgers UP, 1986. 131-50.

Dalke, Ann. "'Circumstance' and the Creative Woman: Harriet Prescott Spofford." *Arizona Quarterly* 41 (1985): 71-85.

Fleenor, Juliann E., ed. *The Female Gothic.* Montreal: Eden P, 1983.

———. Introduction. Fleenor, *Female Gothic* 3-28.

Halttunen, Karen. *Confidence Men and Painted Women: A Study of Middle-Class Culture in America, 1830-1870.* New Haven: Yale UP, 1982.

Harris, Susan K. *19th-Century American Women's Novels: Interpretative Strategies.* Cambridge: Cambridge UP, 1990.

Holmes, Mary Jane. *Tempest and Sunshine.* Ed. Donald A Koch. New York: Odyssey P, 1968.

Kolodny, Annette. "A Map for Rereading: Or, Gender and the Interpretation of Literary Texts." *New Literary History* 11 (1980): 451-67.

Koppelman, Susan. *The Other Woman: Stories of Two Women and a Man.* New York: Feminist Press, 1984.

Lacan, Jacques. *Four Fundamental Concepts of Psycho-Analysis.* Ed. Jacques-Alain Miller. Trans. Alan Sheridan. New York: Norton, 1981.

Lindberg, Gary. *The Confidence Man in American Literature.* New York: Oxford UP, 1982.

Mather, Cotton. *Manuductio ad Ministerium. The Native Muse: Theories of American Literature from Bradford to Whitman.* Vol. I. Ed. Richard Ruland. New York: Dutton, 1976. 18-22.

Mulvey, Laura. "Visual Pleasure and Narrative Cinema." *Screen* 16.3 (1975): 6-18.

Newman, Beth. "'The Situation of the Looker-On': Gender, Narration, and Gaze in *Wuthering Heights.*" *PMLA* 105 (1990): 1029-41.

Smith-Rosenberg, Carroll. "The Female World of Love and Ritual: Relations Between Women in Nineteenth-Century America." *Disorderly Conduct: Visions of Gender in Victorian America.* New York: Knopf, 1985. 53-76.

Spofford, Harriet Prescott. *"The Amber Gods" and Other Stories.* Ed. Alfred Bendixen. New Brunswick, NJ: Rutgers UP, 1989.

———. "Her Story." *"The Amber Gods"* 148-66.

Stein, Karen F. "Monsters and Madwomen: Changing Female Gothic." Fleenor, *Female Gothic* 123-37.

Stowe, Harriet Beecher. *Uncle Tom's Cabin, or, Life among the Lowly.* New York: Library of America, 1982.

Susanne Opfermann (essay date 1997)

SOURCE: Opfermann, Susanne. "How Woman Came to Be Somebody, Which Is All Body and No Body: Harriet Prescott Spofford's 'Circumstance.'" *Zeitschrift für Anglistik und Amerikanistik* 45, no. 2 (1997): 119-28.

[*In the following essay, Opfermann discusses the conflict between civilization and natural impulses in "Circumstance" as allegory.*]

Die Grenze ist nicht das, wobei etwas aufhört, sondern [. . .] die Grenze ist jenes, von woher etwas *sein Wesen beginnt.*

(A boundary is not that at which something stops but [. . .] the boundary is that from which *something begins its presencing.*)

(Martin Heidegger, "Bauen Wohnen Denken" 149.)

Narratives by respectable Victorian women writers usually avoid close descriptions of bodies and physical processes. The following excerpt from the story **"Circumstance"** of 1860 may therefore come as a surprise:

She shuddered now in the suspense; all calm forsook her; she was tortured with dissolving heats or frozen with icy blasts; her face contracted, growing small and pinched; her voice was hoarse and sharp [. . .]. One gasp, a convulsive effort, and there was silence.

Is this the description of a climactic moment of terror or of another climax, a sexual one?

The story is by Harriet Prescott Spofford (1835-1921),[1] a member of the New England cultural elite, a prolific writer of tales, novels, non-fiction, and poetry, whose work was highly esteemed and appeared in prestigious journals such as the *Atlantic Monthly,* which also published **"Circumstance."** Spofford was one of those women writers who made their living by the pen, a career choice that had become possible once a national market for literature had been established. Although she sometimes wrote for 15 hours a day (Langford: 1889, 34), whereby she gained what Henry James maliciously called her "fatal gift of fluency" (James: 1865, 275),[2] she clearly distinguished between pieces written quickly to make money and her more ambitious literary work. **"Circumstance,"** written when Spofford was just 24 years old, belongs to the latter group.

The story is set in early winter in the wilderness on the Maine frontier during late colonial times. It tells of a nameless pioneer woman who, after a day spent with a sick neighbor, is on her way home to her husband and child. While she crosses the meadowland she has a vision of a winding-sheet and a ghastly, hollow voice sighs three times, "The Lord have mercy on the people." Far from being frightened by the apparition the woman blames it on her strained and over-excited nerves and without hesitation enters the darkening forest. Suddenly she is seized by "a swift shadow, like the fabulous flying-dragon" (269), a wild animal known as the Indian Devil. The creature carries her up in a tree and is about to devour her when she accidentally discovers that her singing will distract it. As long as she sings ever new songs the animal is calmed. The entire night she sings, moving from lullabies to sailors' songs and patriotic songs, then to church songs and hymns. Toward morning she has conquered her fear of death and given herself up to God. But when she sees her husband, who has been searching for her, she loses "the fervent vision of God's peace" (277) and again wants to live. Her husband discovers her but cannot shoot for fear of hitting his wife. So she has to continue to sing while he waits for his chance to take a shot. Finally her voice fails, but at that moment her husband manages to kill the beast. When they return home they find that their log-house and all the neighboring farms have been destroyed by Indians during a nocturnal raid. "For the rest,—the world was all before them, where to choose" (278)—thus the story ends.

The tale contains not a line of dialogue.[3] Quite openly it makes use of the Scheherazade motif: the protagonist sings for her life just as the narrator of *The Arabian Nights* saves her life only by telling ever new tales. Spofford's contemporary readers would also have recognized the intertextual reference to Milton's *Paradise Lost,* from which the closing sentence of **"Circumstance"** is taken. In its literary conventions the text is situated somewhere between Poe's *Tales of Terror,* which explore the terrors of the soul, and Hawthorne's *romance,* that makes use of the supernatural to penetrate beneath surface reality into deeper truths. The ironic turn at the end increases the story's effect.

The story was very well received; Edmund Clarence Stedman chose it for his famous anthology *Library of American Literature* (1891) and William Dean Howells with enthusiastic praise included the tale in *The Great Modern American Stories* (1920). We know of an interestingly ambivalent reaction from Emily Dickinson who wrote to Thomas Wentworth Higginson[4] in 1862, "I read Miss Prescott's **'Circumstance,'** but it followed me in the Dark—so I avoided her," but commented to her sister-in-law, "it is the only thing I ever read in my life that I didn't think I could have imagined myself" and asked her, "send me everything she writes" (quoted in Fetterley: 1985, 264).[5]

By the 1940s, however, when the canon of American literature had become profoundly masculinized, Spofford along with most other formerly famous American women writers was relegated to critical oblivion from which she was only resurrected by feminist scholarship. Meanwhile the story has become a classic and has been included in the *Heath Anthology of American Literature.*[6] Among recent critics there is much praise for the literary excellence of the story. Surprisingly, Spofford, who clearly descended from the romantic storytelling conventions of the first half of the nineteenth century, has recently been lauded as a realist. Thelma Shinn, in her introduction to **"Circumstance,"** calls it "a fine example of Spofford's realism. Based on a true incident in the Prescott family" (1990, 82). The biographical source referred to is Spofford's great-grandmother who is said to have been held captive by a panther a whole night long and to have saved her life by singing. This has led to an identification of the Indian Devil with a 'panther,' that is, a mountain-lion. Although the first paragraph of the story speaks of the wilderness as "untrodden save by stealthy native or deadly panther tribes" (268), the creature that attacks the woman is never called anything but an Indian Devil. *Webster's Third International Dictionary* identifies this term not with the panther but with an even smaller animal, the wolverine, which is a further strain on the story's credibility. We should assume then, that Spofford chose the term for other reasons—perhaps even racist ones?[7] Judith Fetterley voices some uneasiness about the "racist imagination" that she sees at work in the story (267). I will return to this point.

Fetterley, Anne Dalke, whose 1985 article is still the most extensive interpretation of the story, as well as Alfred Bendixen all read **"Circumstance"** as a symbolic tale "exploring the conflicts and agonies facing the woman artist" (Bendixen: 1989, xxvii). However, such a reading has troubling consequences. To see the protagonist as the representative woman artist leads one to conclude that Spofford believed women to be just performers and not creators of art in their own right. And even if one agrees with Dalke who—at a time when feminist criticism was looking for tales of women's power—argued that the woman saves her family from destruction, there is still the vexing damsel-in-distress motif, the fact that the woman cannot save herself but is only freed by her husband. However, these possibly irritating features of the text make much more sense when the story is placed in a different context. Before I offer my own interpretation I would like to sketch the theoretical basis I will argue from.

The writing of fictional narrative is a specific form of cultural performance. A culture is composed of a great number of code systems charged with symbolic meaning, from dress codes to public rituals, that govern the sociocultural intercourse. These codes are dynamic, i. e. they change over time, though not at the same rate, and they are discursively linked, i. e. their meaning for the members of that culture depends on the more fundamental system of norms and values of this culture, i. e. on that which in this culture is considered as "true," "natural," or "self-evident," in short, on what Foucault calls its "regime of truth." What is held as truth in a culture is also subject to change. Systems of norms and values are based on practices of exclusion because sense (that which is accepted as true) is established by being foreclosed from non-sense. In so far as they make sense, literary texts participate in their culture's regime of truth as well as in its exclusionary practices and thus they make the cultural order visible. Because due to the convention of fictionality they need not portray what has happened they are, however, also particularly apt to articulate contradictions and deficits of their cultural order. Thus they can function as experimental spaces, i. e. the fictional text translates elements of social reality into the imaginary where they can be experienced and transgressed. And because art can convey multiple meanings it can simultaneously present what is seemingly exclusionary. Therefore literary texts reflect their culture in two ways: on the one hand a culture is *reflected* in its literature and can be analyzed through it, while on the other hand literary texts *reflect on* their culture, they are a place where cultural norms are renegotiated time and again. For this reason it is one of the social functions of fictional narrative to outline, reflectively and projectively, structures of identity that are endemic to a cultural order and make possible the cultural and national coherence of its subjects. If it is true that we as individuals acquire our identity by continuously telling our life as a story that makes sense, and by rewriting this story whenever necessary, it follows that we as subjects of our culture acquire our cultural identity through the narratives of our culture, i. e. mostly through stories, films, etc. This obviously applies to the conceptualization of gender relations and gender difference in a given culture. Literary narratives stage, explore, project and perhaps subvert notions of gender just as they outline versions of identity and individuality. In order to function well a culture is dependent on the more or less rigid self-control of its members. Narrative serves to maintain this self-control because it establishes structures of subjectivity while also providing a space in which these structures can be transcended.[8]

We may read Spofford's tale along these lines as a text on the construction of gendered subjectivities and gender difference together with its exclusionary practices according to the notions of gender valid in the nineteenth century. In the most general terms the text reflects on the enabling conditions of nineteenth-century American culture. The story is set in colonial times and thus imaginatively takes place in the pre-history of the nineteenth century but it uses the time of writing as an implicit point of reference. The subjectivities Spofford establishes are historical ones—she describes the ancestors and the preconditions of her own historical moment. That we are dealing with a story of origins is emphasized by the intertextual reference to *Paradise Lost,* Milton's story of Adam and Eve, which is another tale of human beginnings. The representativeness of Spofford's tale is further underlined by the namelessness of the story's characters. Neither the protagonist nor her husband or child are given a name. Equally primal is the place of action, the frontier, where no stable order has as yet been established. The site where culture and wilderness meet is not clearly demarcated, it is shifting and threatened by disintegration. Nothing is fixed, things can change quickly, identities are insecure and still in flux. As argued above, demarcations are essential for the establishment of sense (by means of excluding non-sense). Frontiers exist without and within; symbolically speaking, the frontier is also the place for borderline experiences in the psychological sense. Spofford makes use of this associative field to portray the gendered psychic constituents of American identity.

In the representation of psychic processes Spofford can rely on the romantic tradition and such predecessors as Charles Brockden Brown, Poe and Hawthorne, who, in a similar manner, portrayed the encounter with one's inner self as a journey into the wilderness or into other dark spaces. Spofford's protagonist is not eager for this encounter, she is very much down-to-earth, not given to superstitious fancies or visions, and "happy in her situation" (269). As long as she possibly can, she rationalizes the uncanny, which in psychological terms is the repressed. The vision of the winding-sheet she explains to herself as a stress symptom; the fears that might be provoked on entering the darkening forest, "a region whose dangers were not visionary" (269), she keeps at bay by thinking of her child at home; the strange lingering twilight in the forest she identifies as aurora borealis. But her energetic orientation of her perception towards what is real and reasonable, as a strategy to fend off what is threatening, predictably does not work: the uncanny seizes and overwhelms her. Spofford's use of the personifying term for the animal adds another dimension to the menace: "It was that wild beast—the most savage and serpentine and subtle[9] and fearless of our latitudes—known by hunters as the Indian Devil" (269), she writes. For the symbolic level of the story it is important that what threatens the woman has an animal, human, and superhuman (devilish) quality. A chain of analogy of beast-Indian-Devil is thus established which correctly models a typical chain of analogy in Puritan thinking. At the same time, however, and of greater import is the fact that only by using an anthropomorphic term can "the other" that confronts the woman be made similar to her, an aspect which is essential for a psychological reading. The confrontation of human and inhuman is thus transcribed into an all-human confrontation that is structured by a clear hierarchy of good and bad. Still, by this means the other is no longer totally alien, but rather it is both, alien and similar, other and self, which means that it is a repressed part of the self.[10]

In the characterization of this other his physical, sensual and even sexual qualities are strongly emphasized throughout. By means of the male pronoun it is also clearly connoted as masculine, a point I will return to. "He commenced licking her bare arm with his rasping tongue and pouring over her the wide streams of his hot, foetid breath" (269), "the rough, sharp, and multiplied stings of his tongue retouched her arm" (270), "the long red tongue thrust forth" (270), he lays his "paw across her with heavy satisfaction" (271), "clasping her to his rough, ravenous breast" (272); we read of "savage caresses" (273). The Indian Devil is called a "living lump of appetites" (271) but his "diabolical face" (271) makes him disgustingly human as well. Unmistakeably, then, in Freudian terms this elementary and potentially destructive force that overwhelms the woman and holds her captive is her instinctual nature, her sexual drive.[11] In this context it seems quite appropriate that she calls for her husband when she is captured: "[s]he did not think at this instant to call upon God. She called upon her husband" (270).

This instinctual nature is portrayed as physical, as bodily, a portrayal which should be considered in terms of the relation of corporeality and femininity as the nineteenth century saw it. The paradoxical relationship which in modern civilization constitutes the relation of body and society in general, repeats itself in the nineteenth-century female body in particular; parallel to the repression of the body from the public into the private sphere a revalorization of the body takes place. During the Victorian era this double process of repression and revalorization was specifically inscribed in female bodies. Woman was constructed as a moral being without physical passions and thereby she became bodiless, so to speak, but at the same time she was all body, reduced to her body and its procreative function that was considered its most important office. Inherent in this concept lies a strange split between corporeality and consciousness: although their bodies are all-important women should not be conscious of them. This presupposes an act of repression, the dissociation of physical sensations from consciousness, especially tabooed ones such as sexual desire, and their relegation to the unconscious. Spofford's text stages this psychic drama: the attempt of woman to control and transcend her sexual nature, an attempt that is almost successful.

Spofford translates this drama into a confrontation of natural force and cultural achievement. The speechless power of the wild creature shall be tamed by song, which is a combination of music and language that distinguishes man over and against animals. A considerable portion of the text is taken up by a description of the songs the woman sings; thereby the terrors of the night and the emotional phases she goes through are convincingly portrayed. There is an obvious development from lullabies to dance songs to church songs. Each of these three kinds of song comments on female corporeality as well—the cradle songs point indirectly to the transformed body of motherhood, the dance songs refer to the erotic body and the hymns indicate the transcendence of the body. When the protagonist has oriented her thinking towards God and excluded every other thought, she finally conquers her physical desire by transforming it into a higher love. "'My beloved is mine, and I am his,' she sang over and over again" (274). In this love for God her instinctual nature is repressed and "she could almost have released herself from his [the Indian Devil's] custody" (275-76). But this victory is only temporary, the repressed will return. And so, when she sees her husband, "[a] thrill of joy pierced and shivered through her" (277). "In vain she tried to sing, 'There remaineth a rest for the people of God,'—her eyes trembled on her husband's, and she could only think of him" (277). Her desire is rekindled and takes possession of her. Her physical state drives towards the orgiastic climax described in the passage that I quoted at the beginning of this text:

> She shuddered now in the suspense; all calm forsook her; she was tortured with dissolving heats or frozen with icy blasts; her face contracted, growing small and pinched; her voice was hoarse and sharp,—every tone cut like a knife,—the notes became heavy to life,—withheld by some hostile pressure,—impossible. One

gasp, a convulsive effort, and there was silence,—she had lost her voice.

(277)

At the moment of crisis, when in the struggle between animal force and cultural refinement the instinctual gets the upper hand, the husband kills the wild creature desire. This could be read as an accusation of men who cannot cope with female desire and therefore have to eliminate it. Such a reading is, however, simplistic. A clear casting into male aggressor and female victim would miss the point that through the longest part of the tale it is the woman who, on her own and of her own accord, attempts to subdue the animal force in herself. As I see it, the text at this point stages a much more basic drama, the moment of differentiating gender into two sexes by establishing difference as bodily. Once gender difference becomes physical, the sexes are "naturally" separated into male and female and thus into fundamentally different beings according to the notions of the nineteenth century. This is dramatized in the text by the erasure of desire from one sex, woman. For the text makes quite clear that desire at first is a human property, the animal nature belongs to both sexes. When the woman first hears her husband approach she mistakes him for "some other beast" (276). Only when the female desire is extinguished does woman become an unequivocally cultural being and the animal nature turns into an attribute of masculinity alone, which is in accordance with nineteenth-century convictions. Thus the text establishes a notable difference between the sexes with a bang, as one might say, but at the same time this supposedly natural difference is exposed to be a cultural achievement. The text does not evaluate this separation into difference. Although one could argue that the woman saves husband and child, one could also say that the husband saves himself as well as the child because he goes out to look for his wife. Actually, what happens is that they save each other without knowing it and this is tantamount to saying that they mutually enable each other. Each of them is the necessary condition for the other, neither part of the opposition man-woman can exist by itself.

Of course, Spofford cannot write about gender and gender difference without employing the categories of gender. The terms of gender difference, man and woman, are necessarily present from the beginning. Woman and man already exist because otherwise the text would be unintelligible, and yet Spofford manages to tell how they become man and woman, i. e. how they become "naturally" different. She solves this problem by marking the state of non-differentiation with feminine as well as masculine attributes. Both, man and woman, are placed in situations which are more typical of the other sex, at least according to the nineteenth-century concept of "separate spheres." Thus it is the woman who is out in the wilderness while the man is at home and worries about her, cares for the baby, rocks his cradle and plays the violin for him. When he goes out to search for his wife he carries the baby in one arm and his gun in the other, thus literally bearing the signs of masculinity and femininity. On the woman's side her "masculine" attributes correspond to his "feminine" ones—her desire is connotated as masculine by the use of the male pronoun for the Indian Devil. Among the songs that the woman sings are "a wild sea-song, such as some sailor might be singing" (270), i. e. "a distinctly masculine form of music," as Bendixen rightly notes (1989: xxviii). Even on the level of intertextuality we find such a doubling of feminine and masculine literary motifs, for not only is the woman aligned with Scheherazade but also with Orpheus, the poet-musician whose magic musical powers charmed wild animals.

After the symbolic death of the instinctual nature of woman the family returns home. Now they are referred to as "father" and "mother," terms that emphasize their functions in the family. The mother follows her husband. That she has now reached a different state is brought out by her description: "she seems to herself like some one newly made" (278). The events of the night are already being repressed, she is content with the present, to her "the night was a dream; the present stamped upon her in deep satisfaction" (278). In dreams, however, when the control of the consciousness relaxes, the memory of instinctual nature resurfaces, the repressed leaves its imprint. As imprint of the other it is discovered by the woman. Just before she and her husband exit from the forest, "the wife lingers over a singular foot-print in the snow, stoops and examines it" (278). It is a trace of violent devastation. "Tomahawk and scalping-knife, descending during that night, had left behind them only this work of their accomplished hatred and one subtle foot-print in the snow" (278). The adjective 'subtle' echoes the description of the Indian Devil, made memorable by the alliteration of "savage, serpentine, subtle."[12] Explicitly then, again, these two events are related and mutually comment on each other. The same elemental force has been at work, the same dichotomies are lined up: nature *versus* culture, savage *versus* civilized, Indians *versus* Whites. To read this as racist discourse is beside the point because these seemingly stereotypical oppositions are complicated by their mutually referential relation. The demarcation between Whites and Indians is exposed as a cultural construction, as an exclusion of self, and, by implication, as the forfeiture of paradise. Thus Spofford's tale exemplifies Stuart Hall's argument, brought forth in a different context, that "the kinds of 'closures' which are required to create communities of identification—nation, ethnic group, families, sexualities, etc.—are arbitrary closures" (Hall: 1996, 117). Furthermore, the setting of this boundary is represented as basic for the architecture of (white) culture. The text thus anticipates Freud's dictum that civilization necessitates the sublimation of instincts,

but locates this in woman who has achieved this sublimation, albeit not entirely by herself, and is thus implicitly assigned the greater force in the production of culture, whereas the man's playing of the violin already takes place within a family setting. Because this is indeed a story of woman's power and not, or not only, a tale of destruction and loss, it is appropriate that it ends on a note of restrained cheerfulness. "For the rest,—the world was all before them, where to choose," closes Spofford, where Milton continues,

> Their place of rest, and Providence their guide:
> They hand in hand with wand'ring steps and slow,
> Through Eden took their solitary way.
>
> (Book XII, 649)

Spofford's tale is remarkable for its imaginative reconstruction of gender difference as cultural construction made manifest in physical bodies. **"Circumstance"** furthermore provides a case in point as to how literary texts negotiate cultural norms and beliefs, how an author can by narrative means display as well as deconstruct the discursively formatted knowledge of her era. Thus, even though the text confirms the hegemonic truth about the "nature of the sexes," it also represents this seemingly natural fact as a cultural achievement, when female desire (perhaps out of fear of its elemental force?) is sacrificed in order to establish gender difference. Neither man nor woman alone are responsible for this, they both strive for this goal. With the establishment of gender difference the fundamental ordering structure of the social and symbolic order of the Victorian era has been founded as well. Spofford's text alerts us to the fact that there may be more body to nineteenth-century American women's writing than meets the eye.

Notes

1. To this day the best biographical source on Spofford is Elizabeth Halbeisen's *Harriet Prescott Spofford: A Romantic Survival* (1935).

2. In a scathing critique of Spofford's novel *Azarian* in the renowned *North American Review* (Jan. 1865) James extended this criticism to Elizabeth Barrett Browning, George Sand, Gail Hamilton and Harriet Beecher Stowe as well. At that time James was just 21 years old and had not published a novel himself. Before the beginning of his own fictional career James wrote a whole series of reviews of books by women—all of them negative, most of them devastating. It seems that he systematically took up all the well-known women authors of the 1860s and used them as a negative other to define and develop his own ideas of literature. For an evaluation of the long-term effect of such misogyny on the scholarly discourse of the twentieth century see my *Diskurs, Geschlecht und Literatur,* 36-62.

3. The story is a borderline case of authorial-figural narration. It is mostly told by a third-person narrator but contains two instances when an authorial 'I' intrudes briefly (cf. 276; 278). The beginning of the tale, "She had remained, during all that day, with a sick neighbor" (268), strikes one as an early instance of figural narration with its abrupt start and its use of the referenceless third-person pronoun.

4. Higginson, one of Dickinson's most important correspondents, was also a life-long friend and mentor of Spofford's, who had met him while she went to school in Newburyport, R.I., where Higginson was pastor of the Unitarian parish. He encouraged her writing and later liked to tell how he was called on to guarantee the authenticity of a story that Spofford had submitted to the *Atlantic Monthly*. The editor, James Russell Lowell, first thought it a translation from the French since he could not believe that a young woman of 23 years of age who had never been to Europe could have written so competently of the life in Parisian *salons*, which indicates that Spofford was well versed in American stereotypes of French society. With the publication of this particular story entitled "In A Cellar" in the *Atlantic Monthly* in 1859 Spofford later officially dated the beginning of her literary career, which lasted until her death in 1921. On the relationships of female authors and male mentors in the nineteenth century see Shirley Marchalonis' *Patrons and Protégées* (1988).

5. Maryanne Garbowsky suggests that Dickinson's poem "'Twas like a Maelstrom, with a notch" (No. 414) was inspired by "Circumstance."

6. The story was first reprinted in Judith Fetterley's *Provisions* (1985). It is also included in a recent collection of tales by Spofford, *The Amber Gods and Other Stories,* edited and introduced by Alfred Bendixen. This reprint is not identical with the collection that Spofford published under the same title in 1863.

7. One might argue as well that Spofford critiques a racist practice since she explicitly links the term "Indian Devil" to a male tradition of naming when she writes, "known *by hunters* as the Indian Devil" (269; emphasis added) and later has her protagonist wonder "less his name of Indian Devil were not his true name" (271).

8. For a more detailed discussion of this context see Ulla Haselstein's forthcoming study, *Poetik der Gabe.*

9. In this case the alliteration is functional because it strengthens the linking of semantic potentialities. This may easily be overlooked; Spofford's deliberate use of this stylistic device in *Azarian* was trivialized by Henry James as "childish attempts at alliteration" (275).

10. Dalke and Bendixen see this as well when they speak of the woman's confrontation with her lower or sexual nature but they do not explore this line of reasoning.

11. The woman's confrontation with female sexuality is already hinted at in the beginning when the woods are presented in feminine metaphors, "a fringe on the skirts of the great forests" (268). The woman gets under this skirt, so to speak, when she "lifts the bough of the warder of the woods and enters" (269). I am indebted to Ulla Haselstein for this observation.

12. This may also be read as an intertextual reference to *Paradise Lost,* where the serpent is called "subtlest beast" (Milton: Book IX, 560), as well as, of course, a reference to the Bible which speaks of the serpent as "more subtil than any beast of the field which the Lord God had made" (Genesis 3.1). Spofford's tale obviously reenacts the biblical fall in physical terms, for when the husband shoots the woman falls from the tree where the Indian Devil has held her captive: "in the wide arc of some eternal descent she was falling;—but the beast fell under her" (277). Thus woman is saved but paradise, a metaphor for the experience of sexual fulfilment, is lost in the act.

Works Cited and Consulted

Bendixen, Alfred (1989). Introduction. *'The Amber Gods' and Other Stories.* By Harriet Prescott Spofford. Ed. Alfred Bendixen. American Women Writers Series. New Brunswick, London: Rutgers UP: ix-xxxiv.

Dalke, Anne (1985). "'Circumstance' and the Creative Woman: Harriet Prescott Spofford." *Arizona Quarterly* 41.1: 71-85.

Fetterley, Judith (1985). Introduction to "Circumstance." *Provisions: A Reader from 19th-Century American Women,* ed. Judith Fetterley. Bloomington: Indiana UP: 261-268.

Foucault, Michel (1978). "Wahrheit und Macht." Interview with Michel Foucault by A. Fontana and P. Pasquino. Transl. Elke Wehr. *Dispositive der Macht: Michel Foucault über Sexualität, Wissen und Wahrheit.* Berlin: Merve: 21-54.

Garbowsky, Maryanne M. (1981). "A Maternal Muse for Emily Dickinson." *Dickinson Studies* 41: 12-17.

Halbeisen, Elizabeth K. (1935). *Harriet Prescott Spofford: A Romantic Survival.* Philadelphia: Univ. of Pennsylvania Press.

Hall, Stuart (1996). "Minimal Selves." 1987. *Black British Cultural Studies: A Reader.* Ed. Houston A. Baker, Jr., et al. Chicago, London: Univ. of Chicago Press: 114-119.

Haselstein, Ulla. *Poetik der Gabe: Kulturberührung im literarischen Text.* (forthcoming)

Heidegger, Martin (1985). "Bauen Wohnen Denken." *Vorträge und Aufsätze.* 1954. Pfullingen: Neske: 139-156.

[James, Henry Jr. (1984)] Rev. of *Azarian: An Episode,* by Harriet Elizabeth Prescott [Spofford]. *North American Review* (Jan. 1865): 268-77. Repr. in *Henry James: Literary Criticism: Essays on Literature, American Writers, English Writers.* Ed. Leon Edel. New York: Library of America: 603-13.

Langford, Laura Holloway (1889). *The Woman's Story, as Told by 20 American Women.* New York: J.B. Alden.

Marchalonis, Shirley (1988). *Patrons and Protégées: Gender, Friendship, and Writing in Nineteenth-Century America.* New Brunswick: Rutgers UP.

Milton, John (1968). *Paradise Lost and Paradise Regained.* 1667. Ed. Christopher Ricks. New York: New American Library.

Opfermann, Susanne (1996). *Diskurs, Geschlecht und Literatur: Amerikanische Autorinnen des 19. Jahrhunderts.* Stuttgart: Metzler.

Shinn, Thelma (1990). Introduction to Harriet Prescott Spofford. *The Heath Anthology of American Literature.* Vol. 2. Ed. Paul Lauter et al. Lexington, MA, etc.: D.C. Heath: 81-83.

Spofford, Harriet Prescott (1985). "Circumstance." *Atlantic Monthly* 1860. Repr. in *Provisions: A Reader from 19th-Century American Women.* Ed. Judith Fetterley. Bloomington: Indiana UP: 268-78.

Lisa Logan (essay date 1998)

SOURCE: Logan, Lisa. "'There is no home there': Re(his)tor(iciz)ing Captivity and the Other in Spofford's 'Circumstance.'" In *Creating Safe Space: Violence and Women's Writing,* edited by Tomoko Kuribayashi and Julie Tharp, pp. 117-29. Albany: State University of New York Press, 1998.

[*In the following essay, Logan describes "Circumstance" as a commentary upon the male-dominated tradition of captivity narratives in early American fiction.*]

I.

> Spaces can be real and imagined. Spaces can tell stories and unfold histories. Spaces can be interrupted, appropriated, and transformed through artistic and literary practice.
>
> —bell hooks, *Yearning: Race, Gender, and Cultural Politics*

In *Hard Facts,* Phillip Fisher argues that the nineteenth-century American novel "executes the past" through popular forms. This "retroactive" use of the past—in popular settings and stories that recognize, repeat, and "work through" it—"transform[s] the present" by rationalizing and making acceptable "hard facts," including the killing of Indians, the system of slavery, and industrial capitalism (3-8). The historical novel thus rehistoricizes and naturalizes an American history that is already complete. Fisher's point is that historical fiction imposes on its subject a narrative that suits the ideological present—that the *spaces* of American history, including the wilderness, home, and city, are, to paraphrase bell hooks, subject to appropriation and transformation through literary practice. Fisher's argument illustrates how the uncomfortable facts of American history can be contained and *made safe* through narrative.

This safety is often achieved through the use of racialized discourses. As Toni Morrison's *Playing in the Dark* has shown, a reexamination of the Africanist presence in American literature uncovers the assumptions and ideologies of Anglo American writers. Morrison demonstrates that figures of race are central to narratives of Anglo American selfhood; through these figures, Anglo writers confront their own national and cultural identities. The Africanist presence, Morrison argues, has permitted American writers to contemplate risky subjects in safety (28).

Narratives of cultural identity are closely tied to the ideologically charged spaces of American national and individual histories. As Biddy Martin and Chandra Talpade Mohanty point out, identities are linked to ideologically grounded "homespaces." They argue that the perceived safety of home is founded on unquestioned assumptions about self and Other:

> [Home] refers to the place where one lives within safe, protected boundaries; 'not being home' is a matter of realizing that home was an illusion based on the exclusion of specific histories of oppression and resistance, the repression of differences even within oneself.
>
> (196)

For Martin and Mohanty, "home" becomes a metaphor for identity. "Home" represents a set of positions that we occupy unself-consciously; the ideological underpinnings of these positions are covered over and unacknowledged.

I wish to locate the captivity narrative and Harriet Prescott Spofford's short story **"Circumstance,"** a nineteenth-century revision of this genre, at the interstices of Fisher's, Morrison's, and Martin and Mohanty's theories. To convey and stabilize the cultural meaning of American selfhood, the captivity narrative depends on configurations of the American landscape, such as home and wilderness, in which gendered and racialized ideologies are imbedded. According to Fisher, the captivity narrative "miniaturizes" early national history, casting Anglo Saxon "invaders as prisoners" (43) and legitimizing their campaign of genocide against Native Americans. It typically traces the white victim's capture, imprisonment, rescue, and restoration against the dramatic and binarily opposed settings of home and wilderness. For women writers, this movement between home and wilderness, safety and danger, is further complicated by their disempowered positions in a dominant culture that maps its racialized and gendered ideologies onto their bodies and which struggles to make women's acts and words "safe." In a culture that determines when and how women can be subjects in discourse and that imposes material sanctions on women who do not comply, women who write about captivity tread a tricky path between safety and danger.

Mary Rowlandson's captivity narrative *The Sovereignty and Goodness of God* (1682), for example, explicitly underscores her position of safety within a culture that aggressively contains women's difference and disorder within hegemonic structures. Throughout her narrative, Rowlandson negotiates safe spaces from which to speak, spaces which have been disrupted by her Indian captivity and by Puritan attitudes toward "public" women and their speech. Rowlandson fashions acceptable narrative positions for herself, including that of chaste and pious Christian, Puritan goodwife and deputy husband. She constructs her captors as her polar opposite, the savage and heathen racial Other.[1] Against this fixed and stereotyped notion of the Other, the woman writer negotiates a safe discursive position.

At the same time, however, the very presence of the Other disrupts and brings into question that safety. The captivity experience unsettles the spatial categories of home and wilderness, exposing the ideologies on which they rest as tenuous. The certainty of these spaces is predicated on unexamined assumptions about and uncontested distinctions between self and Other, right and wrong, truth and lies. The captivity experience destabilizes these assumptions and distinctions and challenges the ideological foundations underlying the safety of home. In the captivity narrative, as in Martin and Mohanty's essay on identity politics, home becomes not only a physical space but a metaphor for women's unsettled and unsettling position.

In revisiting the captivity narrative, Harriet Prescott Spofford's short story **"Circumstance"** is similarly concerned with woman's cultural and discursive "place." The story transpires in the wilderness and domestic spaces of America's early national history. In representing the captivity narrative from a nineteenth-century perspective, Spofford's story engages in the politics of

historicization; she "interrupts, appropriates, and transforms" history's spaces. In Spofford's narrative, as in the early American captivity narrative, domestic and wilderness spaces serve as metaphors for hegemonic definitions of safety and danger which are mapped onto "woman" and which threaten to erase female subjectivity. As in nineteenth-century romantic fiction, Spofford invokes cultural configurations of race as she engages questions of American space and woman's "place." Like Rowlandson's narrative, **"Circumstance"** is concerned with woman's negotiation of safe spaces in culture and in discourse. In negotiating woman's position, Spofford's story brings into tension women's literary traditions, American romanticism, and figures and discourses of race. Ultimately, she seems to challenge the stability of these categories and, in doing so, to question the safety of woman's "place" in the national spaces of home and wilderness.

II.

There is no home there. The log-house, the barns, the neighboring farms, the fences, are all blotted out and mingled in one smoking ruin. Desolation and death were indeed there, and beneficence and life in the forest.

—"Circumstance"

Spofford sets her story in the margins, at the edge of the northern forest of Maine and, as Anne Dalke has pointed out, explores the tenuousness of experience. That tenuousness, I argue, stems from the text's collapsing of typical categories of home and wilderness. The heroine has spent the day at the "home" of a sick friend, a home associated with illness, pain, and death. Unlike Rowlandson, who often "can not find her way," she is not afraid to enter the forest alone and perceives "the sweet *home*feeling of a young and tender wintry wood" (84, my emphasis). As this "sincere and earnest woman" "sallie[s] forth" into the evening wilderness, her husband remains at home with the baby. She must traverse three miles of woods to get home, described as "one of a dozen log-houses . . . with their half-cleared demesnes separating them . . . from a wilderness untrodden save by stealthy native or deadly panther tribes" (84). The ominous proximity of the "stealthy native" and "deadly panther tribes" undercuts the security and safety of home. Home is situated at the edge of a "great forest," in "half-cleared demesnes"; while Spofford's language is apparently oppositional, it also suggests the mutually dependent natures of home and wilderness— one is made possible only by the "clearing away" of the other. This language undercuts and problematizes the opposition of home to wilderness and recalls Martin and Mohanty's observation that home is "an illusion of coherence and safety based on . . . exclusion . . . [and] repression" (196). While nineteenth-century culture represses what lies outside home as "Other," Spofford's story seems to forward home's uncertain and illusory qualities. Home is never quite "cleared" of the wilderness; the forest compromises its "domain"—questions the rights and privileges which it assumes.

The heroine's "captivity" aloft in a tree in the "arms" of an "Indian Devil" panther reenacts the captivity narrative's concern with home and wilderness, and the relationships between these categories and women's subjectivity. Like Rowlandson, who negotiates safe speaking positions before an audience wary of women's public speech, Spofford's heroine's voice—her singing—meets the demands of her captor, satisfies her instinct, and represents conscious choices and strategies. Her song at once complies with and questions essentialist definitions of women's words: "Again her lips opened by instinct but the sound that issued thence came by reason. She had heard that music charmed wild beasts . . ."(86). Her singing is a choice, a substitution of song for scream. What she sings is inadvertent and unconscious: "[A] little thread of melody stole out, a rill of tremulous motion; it was the cradle-song with which she rocked her baby . . ."(86). Although she sings an expected song, one seemly for a woman and a mother, the circumstances of her singing disrupt the "safety" of cultural images of "woman." The picture of a mother singing her child to sleep before the hearth, which a lullaby invokes, alters to a woman rocking and singing in the arms of a dark and savage panther. By shifting the circumstances of the heroine's singing from home to wilderness, Spofford suggests that a woman's voice might be heard in other spaces than the home.

"Circumstance" questions safe categories of home and wilderness in other ways as well. One of the first images to cross the heroine's mind following her capture is of her child "sleeping rosily" and "the father cleaning his gun, with one foot on the green wooden rundle" (86). The home, traditionally the domain of the wife, is here secured by the father; the wife, typically safe at home, confronts the wilderness alone. The images of her husband's well-oiled gun and his foot that rocks the cradle bring into view exactly who "keeps" the home and at what cost. Distinctions between home and wilderness are blurred and uncertain. As the heroine endures her torture, she dreams of home:

> She fancied the light pouring through the chink and then shut in again, with all the safety and comfort and joy, her husband taking down the fiddle and playing lightly with his head inclined, playing while she sang, while she sang for her life to an Indian Devil. Then she knew he was fumbling for and finding some shining fragment and scoring it down the yellowing hair. . . .
>
> (88)

Here Spofford juxtaposes the heroine's night peril with the idyllic "safety and comfort and joy" of the lit cabin. The heroine's singing to her husband's fiddle seems to

merge with her wilderness singing. She imagines her husband "playing while she sang, while she sang for her life to an Indian Devil." Her husband's safety and comfort is almost at the expense of her danger. His "fumbling for and finding some shining fragment" parallels the fumbling of her captor's claws in her clothing, his "scoring it down the yellowing hair" recalls the beast's "scoring" of her white flesh. In this passage, distinctions between the safety of home and the danger of the wilderness are made murky as the figure of the husband blurs into that of the beast.[2]

Perhaps most ambivalent and uncertain is the story's attitude toward rescue. In Rowlandson's narrative, restoration constitutes reassimilation into her former home and position. Yet her text questions this restoration through its depiction of her sleepless nights and constant worry over the uncertainty of her physical and spiritual safety. "Circumstance," too, insistently challenges notions of rescue and the promise of safety held out by husband and home. With her husband's appearance, the heroine forgets her "fervent vision of God's peace" and imagines only her log home:

> Cheerful home sound then, how full of safety and all comfort and rest it seemed! what sweet morning incidents of sparkling fire and sunshine, of gay household bustle, shining dresser, and cooing baby, of steaming cattle in the yard, and brimming milk-pails at the door! what pleasant voices! what laughter! what security!
>
> (95)

The heroine may recover this idyll only through the loss of her spiritual vision, her voice, and, of course, through more danger. Since the panther's body covers her own, her husband's bullet must "pierce her body" before "reaching any vital part of the beast" (94). Domestic bliss is possible only at the expense—indeed the annihilation—of her voice and self. Her vision of her happy home is followed by her discovery that "her voice was hoarse and sharp,—every tone cut like a knife,—the notes became heavy to lift,—withheld by some hostile pressure,—impossible. One gasp, a convulsive effort, and there was silence . . ."(95). Home and safety, the passage seems to imply, are exclusive of woman's voice. Her silence is effected by some "hostile pressure," which is at once the physical strain of singing all night and, perhaps, the presence of cultural forces militated against women's expression.

Ironically, it is the beast—the Indian Devil, the violent Other—who saves her. The panther, spying her husband, springs up and seizes her, and her husband fires. The Indian Devil's body breaks his captive's fall and rescues her from her husband's gunfire. "Circumstance" seems to ask who the Other really is, who has the power to rescue, and what that rescue implies.

But Spofford has still more questions about home and safety. Returning to their log-house, the family discovers "no home there" (96). Their settlement has burned to the ground in an apparent Indian attack. As the two look on, the husband's gun falls away from him, reinforcing his inability to "rescue." They are faced with a curious truth: "Desolation and death were indeed there, and beneficence and life in the forest" (96). "Circumstance" questions the boundaries between safety and danger and inverts the assumptions beneath early America's opposing definitions of home and wilderness.

III.

> Fire is not half ourselves; as it devours, arouses neither hatred nor disgust; is not to be known by the strength of our lower natures let loose; does not drip our blood into our faces from foaming chops, nor mouth nor slaver above us with vitality. Let us be ended by fire, and we are ashes, for the winds to bear, the leaves to cover; let us be ended by wild beasts, and the base, cursed thing howls with us forever through the forest.
>
> —"Circumstance"

In *Playing in the Dark*, Toni Morrison links the Africanist presence in American literature to nineteenth-century American romanticism. The romantic tradition, she observes, offered Anglo American writers a strategy for dealing with their "New World" fears and for exploring Americans' boundless capacity for uncertainty; the African American served as a metaphor for the limitless terror Anglo Americans faced and which they termed the "power of blackness." These romantic fears are, of course, cast in a different light for women, whose marginalized positions in nineteenth-century culture necessarily complicate Morrison's characterization of the romantic "terror of human freedom." Throughout "Circumstance,"[3] Spofford's use of race exists in tension with her more explicit critique of dominant cultural narratives about woman's "place." I suggest that we read this tension as a cultural politics. We might ask, how do figures of race and racialized discourses allow Spofford to contemplate dangerous subject matter safely?

The captivity narrative relies on figures of race to negotiate American history and cultural identity. The threat of national and cultural disorder is expressed in the unsettled wilderness and mapped onto an inexplicably "savage" racial Other. Spofford's nineteenth-century captivity narrative negotiates the spaces of American history from a woman's perspective, exploring home and wilderness as positions from which women might speak. Spofford's story challenges categories of home and wilderness, a challenge which depends on the story's use of the racial Other, onto whom ideas about violence, power, and sexuality are displaced. I wish to consider how this displacement at once questions and conserves racialized categories of self and Other. Specifically, the figure of the Indian Devil affords Spofford a site for exploring in safety culturally disruptive notions about woman's "place."

Judith Fetterley has argued that Spofford's Indian Devil is a metaphor for "unrestrained male sexuality . . . often let loose on the bodies of women" (226). The Indian Devil "lick[s] her bare arm with his rasping tongue and pour[s] over her the wide stream of his hot foetid breath" (86). She "saw instinctively the fierce plunge" of his claws, and feels them tear her with "agony" and "quivery disgust" (86). Caught in his "great lithe embrace," she sees with horror white and red—his white tusks, red glaring eyes, and long red tongue, her own white flesh and crimson blood. As Fetterley notes, the passage can be read as "an experience of 'rape,' a nightmare as likely to occur in the home as in the woods" (266). This violence, I argue, at once historicizes and sexualizes nineteenth-century relationships between Native American men and Anglo American women. In this way, the "Indian Devil's" death is made "safe."

The image of the husband with his gun seems consistently and closely linked to sexual violation. When her captor first seizes her, she calls not upon God but on her husband. Her singing is punctuated by images of her husband safe at home, rocking the baby, cleaning his gun, rosining his bow. At one point, his fingerwork at the fiddle blurs into the Indian Devil's clawing at her body. Her husband's approach is heralded by "[a] remote crash of brushwood [that] told of some other beast on his depredations" (93). His intrusion marks yet another violation—her loss of voice and vision. It may be, as Fetterley contends, that Spofford's Indian Devil encodes the violence men promise for women at home, an encoding that Spofford anticipates her women readers will understand. The racialized "beast," then, offers a safe space for Spofford to articulate such a revolutionary notion.

But I suggest that this reading needs to be complicated for a number of reasons. First, I suggest that we consider the violence the heroine endures from her sexualized and racialized captor within other paradigms. Fetterley asks us to view the story in terms of the "violation and vulnerability" women faced when they entered into art. Invoking Hawthorne's remarks that literature should "exhibit women's bodies, naked, without restraint of decency," Fetterley argues that the violence in "Circumstance" represents women's sense of "shame and loathing at such enforced and public exposure" (265). I contend, however, that dominant cultural constructions of "true womanhood" are equally violent in that they threaten to erase women's subjectivity. Essentialist definitions of "woman" and her "place" violate women by demanding that they enact their lives and works according to hegemonic definitions. The panther promises punishment if the singing fails to please. Similarly, nineteenth-century American culture's expectations for women's acts and words promise the withdrawal of those privileges extended to feminine "virtue" if women fail to live up to those expectations. The promise of privilege to the virtuous implies that certain women may *deserve* a whole range of violent and punitive remunerations, which could include bad reviews, failure to find work, abandonment, and rape. Violence, therefore, is linked not only to women's vulnerability or wish to remain private. Rather, one's biological circumstance, being born a woman, invites exposure, scrutiny, and, possibly, violation. The heroine's vocal response to her capture and violation places in tension woman's voice and her violation. The juxtaposition of these terms recalls that captivity has historically been a pretext for women's writing as well as a place where the meaning of women's subjectivity has been struggled over. The captivity narrative, produced in an era that punished women's public speech with excommunication and banishment, concerns women's negotiation of discursive space. Spofford substitutes the Indian Devil of her maternal grandmother's legend for Rowlandson's "heathens," and the heroine's singing replaces Rowlandson's "true story."[4]

As Anne K. Mellor argues, romanticism "requires the construction of an Other, which is seen as a threat to the originating subject . . ."(3). The romantic artist constructs *his* beloved as Other, who must be possessed, consumed, effaced, and destroyed if he is to achieve his goal. According to Mellor, consummation "can only be achieved through the literal annihilation of the consciousness of the division between the lover and his beloved" (26). Mellor's comments recall the famous American romantic heroines, Ligeia, Madeline Usher, Beatrice Rappaccini, all victims of violent male artist figures. Spofford, whose style and subject matter place her within traditions of American romanticism,[5] writes from a discursive moment that mythologized the male artist and predicated his aesthetic transcendence on the possession and destruction of the female Other. In returning to the captivity narrative to imagine her female artist (the singing heroine), Spofford returns to a genre in which the *racialized* Other enables the subject's spiritual vision and conversion. The racialized Indian Devil provides both a safe *and* dangerous site for exploring the woman artist's position and voice.

But the panther does not merely represent the Other. As in Rowlandson's captivity narrative, in which the wilderness experience destabilizes categories of self and Other, and as in romantic fiction, in which, as Morrison writes, the "subject of the dream is the dreamer" (17), Spofford's text conflates categories of self and Other. The narrator observes that, unlike fire, beasts such as the Indian Devil are "half ourselves" when "the strength of our lower natures [are] let loose" (89). I find it significant that the beast's consonance is with "our" natures, implying that boundaries such as human/beast, white/Indian, Christian/heathen, and male/female are indistinct. This indistinctness is perhaps most visible when the husband shoots the panther out of the tree, and there

follows "a terrible yell of desperation . . . that filled her ears with savage echoes" (95). Here Spofford removes the agency from this "terrible yell." Whether these "savage echoes" issue from the panther, the husband, or the woman herself is left—deliberately, I think—ambiguous. The question of agency here foregrounds the collapsing of categories that Spofford effects and hints quietly that woman's voice *might* articulate the unseemly. The panther—the racialized figure, the easy stereotype—affords Spofford a strategy through which to explore this possibility obliquely and in safety.

IV.

> Oh, was there no remedy? Was there nothing to counteract it, nothing to dissipate that black drop, to make it colorless, powerless, harmless, a thing of air? Were there no sweet, good people among all those dead and gone women? . . . What gifts were these grandmothers going to give the child then? she asked.
>
> —Spofford, **"The Godmothers"**

"Circumstance," a revision of the early American captivity narrative, "interrupts, appropriates, and transforms" the spaces of American history as they map dominant ideologies onto women's bodies. The story is concerned with "place," which I have tried to define as at once the physical settings of home and wilderness and the ideological categories of self/Other, man/woman imbedded in them. **"Circumstance"** struggles with the meanings and uses of the past from the nineteenth-century present Spofford occupied. In considering what those meanings and uses might be, I turn to Spofford's short story **"The Godmothers"** (1896).

Like **"Circumstance," "The Godmothers"** focuses on the collision of two worlds. The heroine, Rosomond, has left her American home for marriage to a L'Aiglenoir and has just given birth to an heir in her husband's "ancestral stronghold." As the heroine lies "faint and weak" in a "dim vast chamber," the L'Aiglenoir grandmothers "step from [the] frames" of their sea-gallery portraits (207), reminding the heroine of their history of scandal, forgery, counterfeit, adultery, opium, poison, cruelty, the guillotine, and the madhouse—a history of "black blood" (214). Rosomond responds to these visitors with terror, crying "What gifts were these grandmothers going to give the child then?" (215).

Like **"Circumstance,"** this story is concerned with a history of "blood," only the politics of possession and empire are displaced onto the French aristocracy. Its concern with national "color" is displaced onto the "purples and scarlets" of the European grandmothers versus Rosomond's own wan and pallid American ancestors. Rosomond's question—what shall be passed on to her child?—is, according to Phillip Fisher, the question of all American writers: What is the relationship of history to the national identity of the present? I suggest that **"The Godmothers"** speaks intertextually to the American romantic fiction and women's captivity traditions which Spofford worked within by engaging this question. Spofford attempts to work out a safe and "usable past" from which to speak and which to pass on.

The story seems expressly concerned with woman-centered traditions. Rosomond's husband is "away on the water, or in the hunt, or at the races" (208). The L'Aiglenoir stronghold has historically been kept by its women, who, to bring the family its lands and titles, traded themselves and their integrity. Rosomond at first discounts them as "all only tradition," saying that their lives "would have been dreadful if [the stories] were true" (209). Her husband reminds her, however, that "happiness has no history," "virtue has few adventures," and that "the big wills, the big passions" are "memorable . . . and drown out the others" (209-10). His words seem to address directly Spofford's own position within women's and canonical literary traditions. What is her "place" to be? What is her relationship to her literary descendants and ancestors? What will be remembered and how?

"The Godmothers" centers its treatment of American history and literary traditions, as in **"Circumstance,"** on color. Rosomond contrasts the "pallor of her colonial and nineteenth-century New England grandmothers with the "purples and scarlets of [European] women of great passions, of scope, of daring and deed and electric force" (214). Rosomond views Anglo American women's histories and traditions as wan and disempowered. She imagines her New England ancestors:

> Far off, by the curtain of the doorway, huddled together like a flock of frightened doves—gentle ladies, quiet, timid, humble before heaven, ladies of placid lives, no opportunities, small emotions, narrow routine, praying by form, acting by precedent, without individuality, whose goodness was negative, whose doings were paltry, their drab beings swamped, and drowned, and extinguished. . . .
>
> (214)

Rosomond's grandmothers are colorless as drab doves, adhering to the outward forms of religion and culture in dull lives that fail to question the "narrow routine" of woman's "place." In leaving America for Europe, Rosomond rejects her American grandmothers' "passive virtues" of self-effacement, self-sacrifice, and quiet acceptance for "great drama" and a "larger nature." Her choice seems to suggest a failure to locate within American culture a place from which to counter its "pallid" narratives of femininity.

"The Godmothers" represents Spofford's engagement with divergent narratives of American history and literary tradition. The L'Aiglenoirs recall the uncomfortable

truths about America's past that **"Circumstance"** invokes: colonial expansion and the genocide of Native Americans. The L'Aiglenoir family was borne of rape, after a "sea-rover had scaled the heights" of a lady's castle and "taken her, loathing and hating him, to wife" (212). This family history speaks to both the disturbing history of American expansionism *and* the impact of patriarchal culture on racialized and gendered Others. Out of these tensions emerged a tradition of Anglo women's writing based on the domestic and wilderness captivity of women's lives, a tradition which, like dominant cultural narratives and canonical literary traditions, often relied on figures of race and color.

"The Godmothers" seems to respond to troublesome American histories and traditions by reimagining a whitewashed and safe space from which the young child, the L'Aiglenoir of the twentieth century, like the woman writer, might emerge. Such a space is figured forth in the beautiful and "original savage," "swift and supple . . . with free and fearless foot, large-limbed and lofty as Thusnelda, clad in her white wolfskin, with the cloud of her yellow hair fallen about her, carrying her green bough, strong, calm, sure" (216). In Spofford's "original savage" a romanticized Native American woman blurs into a curiously Nordic goddess. Her values are ". . . scorn for the ignoble, trust in thy fellow, dependence on thine own lust sinew and unconquerable will,—familiar friend of hardship and content, spare, and pure, and strong,—joy in the earth, the sun, the wind, faith in the unseen" (216). This noble savage, her blonde whiteness a product of nineteenth-century aesthetics of feminine beauty, represents "the unpolluted, strong, wild strain in [her son's] blood, the vital savage" (216).

"The Godmothers" attempts to rewrite American history onto an Anglo woman's body, to construct a history and tradition that is safe to pass on. The story evinces an incredible amount of anxiety about nation, Anglo American women, and American history and literary traditions. Spofford maintains the integrity of "blood" by positing the pre-colonial, pre-slavery, and insistently white body of a European ancestral godmother. In this way, she makes the spaces of history and tradition "safe." Rosomond's husband tells her that "pictures are no more certified than the traditions" (210). **"Circumstance"** and **"The Godmothers"** attempt to reimagine and transform American history and traditions. Her fiction presents its own gallery of pictures that revises the spaces in which history and tradition have mapped discursive and cultural meanings onto women's bodies. In trying to make these spaces "safe," her fiction is no more or less "certified" than those histories it appropriates and transforms. Spofford's is a whitewashed "picture" in the gallery, illustrating what is at stake in making American spaces safe.

Notes

1. For a more detailed discussion of Rowlandson's negotiation of discursive space, see my "Mary Rowlandson and the 'Place' of the Woman Subject."

2. Judith Fetterley writes about the sexual overtones of the panther's attack, arguing that it represents the displaced and menacing sexual power of men "who cannot be the woman's husband," that is, Native Americans. Fetterley argues that, although the text hints that "home is where the beasts are," it "stops short" of identifying the husband with the panther (267). Fetterley concludes that Spofford's story exemplifies the pervasive racist imagination of nineteenth-century white writers. My reading, however, suggests that Spofford's boundaries are less explicit than Fetterley implies. I wish to explore the relationship of Spofford's use of race to American literary and historical spaces.

3. Spofford's other works, such as "The Amber Gods," "The Black Bess," "The Moonstone Mass," and "The Godmothers," operate this way as well.

4. Halbeisen describes the story's inception in Prescott family legend. Spofford's links to Rowlandson are even more coincidental than her use of captivity conveys: the Prescott family settled in Lancaster, Massachusetts and was probably living there at the time that Rowlandson was taken captive.

5. Bendixen makes this point in more detail, xxii.

Works Cited

Bendixen, Alfred. "Introduction" to *'The Amber Gods' and Other Stories* by Harriet Prescott. Spofford. Ed. Alfred Bendixen. New Brunswick: Rutgers University Press, 1989.

Dalke, Anne. "'Circumstance' and the Creative Woman: Harriet Prescott Spofford." *Arizona Quarterly* 41.1 (Spring 1985): 71-85.

Fetterley, Judith, ed. *Provisions: A Reader from Nineteenth-Century American Women.* Bloomington: Indiana University Press, 1985.

Fisher, Phillip. *Hard Facts: Setting and Form in the American Novel.* New York: Oxford University Press, 1985.

Halbeisen, Elizabeth K. *Harriet Prescott Spofford: A Romantic Survival.* Philadelphia: University of Pennsylvania Press, 1985.

hooks, bell. *Yearning: Race, Gender, and Cultural Politics.* Boston: South End Press, 1990.

Logan, Lisa. "Mary Rowlandson and the 'Place' of the Woman Subject." *Early American Literature* 28:3 (Winter 1993): 255-77.

Martin, Biddy and Chandra Talpade Mohanty. "Feminist Politics: What's Home Got to Do With It?" *Feminist Studies/Critical Studies.* Ed. Teresa de Lauretis. Bloomington: Indiana University Press, 1986.

Mellor, Anne K. *Romanticism and Gender.* New York: Routledge, 1993.

Morrison, Toni. *Playing in the Dark: Whiteness and the Literary Imagination.* New York: Vintage, 1992.

Spofford, Harriet Prescott. *'The Amber Gods' and Other Stories.* Ed. Alfred Bendixen. New Brunswick: Rutgers University Press, 1989.

Lisa M. Logan (essay date January 2001)

SOURCE: Logan, Lisa M. "Race, Romanticism, and the Politics of Feminist Literary Study: Harriet Prescott Spofford's 'The Amber Gods.'" *Legacy* 18, no. 1 (January 2001): 35-51.

[*In the following essay, Logan traces themes of imperialism, artistic creation, and the objectification of foreign cultures in "The Amber Gods."*]

> Far off, by the curtain of the doorway, huddled together like a flock of frightened doves—gentle ladies, quiet, timid, humble before heaven, ladies of placid lives, no opportunities, small emotions, narrow routine, praying by form, acting by precedent, without individuality, whose goodness was negative, whose doings were paltry, their drab beings swamped, and drowned, and extinguished. . . .
>
> Harriet Prescott Spofford (**"The Godmothers"** 214)

In the above passage, Rosomond, an American expatriate who has just given birth, imagines the wan, disempowered, or absent histories of her New England foremothers. In this timid "flock of frightened doves," she recognizes not individuality but merely obedience to culture's outward forms. Their daily living fails to question the "narrow routine" of woman's position; their lives are not merely "paltry" but oppressed, "swamped, and drowned, and extinguished." Much of Harriet Prescott Spofford's writing, like the postpartum vision of this protagonist, exhibits similar anxiety. Her stories seem to ask, what foremothers' (hi)stories and traditions of expression might women draw on? How, in life and in literature, might women identify a usable past of their own? And with what language might they speak of it?[1]

Appropriately or ironically, Spofford's concern with women's history and literary traditions seems to be what is at stake in contemporary Americanist and feminist scholars' reluctance to embrace this author as one of our own foremothers. In December 1996 (seven years after Rutgers University Press published *"The Amber Gods" and Other Stories,* the first collection of Spofford's fiction to appear in print for nearly a century), the Modern Language Association included its first session on this nineteenth-century writer, "New Perspectives on Harriet Prescott Spofford."[2] Following the panelists' presentations, a member of the audience asked a question that seems central to this writer's fate in American literary studies: how might scholars and teachers assess Spofford's race politics? In this essay, I maintain that the problem of Spofford's race politics offers a significant critical entry into this enigmatic author's fiction; specifically, an analysis of Spofford's race politics in **"The Amber Gods"** (1860) enables our scrutiny of gender- and race-bound theories that underpin not only Spofford's fiction but American literary romanticism. I use an approach informed by feminist and postcolonial theories to consider how the story advances the perspective of its marginalized nineteenth-century white, upper-middle-class heroine/narrator, Giorgione, with—indeed, perhaps even at the expense of—the troubling characterization of a woman of color, known merely as "little Asian." Through the juxtaposition of these women, the story resists and revises patriarchal and hegemonic romantic scripts even as it complies with their racist agendas. **"The Amber Gods,"** I argue, makes visible those narratives that American literary romanticism and, until recently, its study, have buried: agendas of colonization and expansionist imperialism mounted against racialized and gendered Others.[3]

Evidence of troubling race politics abounds in Spofford's fiction: **"Circumstance"** (1860), her most widely anthologized piece, concerns the captivity and metaphorical rape of a white woman by a wild animal known as the "Indian Devil." In **"The Black Bess"** (1868), the white male protagonist, a train conductor, experiences nightmares in which his engine (Black Bess) is the instrument of his betrothed's death. The white American protagonist in **"The Godmothers"** (1896) fantasizes about a Nordic, feminine American ancestor, an "original savage," who erases U.S. colonial and expansionist history. Feminist critics, in the process of recovering Spofford's work, have prefaced their remarks with disclaimers about her race politics. In her groundbreaking anthology *Provisions,* Judith Fetterley introduces **"Circumstance"** with the recognition that Spofford's fiction "exemplifies the insidiousness and pervasiveness of the racist imagination" (267). Fetterley's comments are certainly on target, but I want to deliberate further Spofford's treatment of race in the context of American literary romanticism and nineteenth-century U.S. policies of gender and race imperialism. In so doing, I will advance the ways that Spofford at once resists and participates in American romanticism's imperialist agenda; moreover, I will show how the study of Spofford—

despite and perhaps even because of our ambivalence about her race politics—is central to any consideration of these issues.[4]

"TERROR OF DARKNESS"

In *Playing in the Dark: Whiteness and the American Literary Imagination,* Toni Morrison challenges the project and accepted definitions of canonical American romanticism by demonstrating white writers' use of the racialized Other—American Africanism—to represent the fears of the dominant culture:[5]

> Romance, an exploration of anxiety imported from the shadows of European culture, made possible the sometimes safe and other times risky embrace of quite specific, understandably human, fears: Americans' fear of being outcast, of failing, of powerlessness; their fear of boundarylessness, of Nature unbridled and crouched for attack; their fear of the absence of so-called civilization; their fear of loneliness, of aggression both external and internal. In short, the terror of human freedom. . . . It offered platforms for moralizing and fabulation, and for the imaginative entertainment of violence, sublime incredibility, and terror—and terror's most significant, overweening ingredient: darkness, with all the connotative value it awakened.
>
> (36-7)

In "Romancing the Shadow," the chapter from which I take the above quotation, Morrison emphasizes romanticism's ability to "embrace" Anglo-Americans' fears, frequently manifested as "terror of darkness." For example, she demonstrates that *The Narrative of Arthur Gordon Pym* uses the American Africanist presence as a metaphor for Anglo-American insecurities about New World freedom. This strategy, known in pre-Morrison critical parlance as "the power of blackness," might be viewed as a hallmark of American literary romanticism, exemplified by Melville's Queequeg, Tashtego, Pip, and Babo. While critics have surely noticed these characters, Morrison notes, they have failed to acknowledge the capacity for the "Africanist presence" to convey information about the writer and, more broadly, the white literary imagination. A primary function of Morrison's paradigm, then, is that it makes visible what critics in the past have ignored: the ways that Anglo-American romantic writers used the racialized Other as a kind of "cultural shorthand" to talk about the American self.[6]

Many contemporary critics contend that Spofford wrote in an American romantic tradition.[7] Between 1860 and 1900, she published dozens of short stories that used romantic styles, conventions, and plots, including tales of detection, the supernatural, psychological horror, and arctic exploration. However, unlike the romantic fiction that Morrison discusses, much of Spofford's work concerns a woman protagonist. The heroine of **"The Amber Gods,"** Giorgione Willoughby, experiences nineteenth-century womanhood as a state of restriction rather than the unlimited freedom of her fictional male counterparts. Hardly faced with the "terrors of human freedom," she complains instead of being "boxed up with proprieties and civilities from year's end to year's end" (46). The story takes as its site of terror not limitless *human* freedom but the cultural limitations of one nineteenth-century white woman, and eerily collapses two days—the day she is married and the day she dies—so that she almost seems to prepare herself for both at once. While Giorgione's gendered relationship to freedom differs markedly from that of the Anglo-American individual in Morrison's argument, **"The Amber Gods"** does share in Anglo-American romantic fiction's obsession with race. Moreover, just as Morrison's reading of canonical American romanticism makes visible the absent presence of the racialized Other, so Spofford's story makes palpable (in admittedly troubling ways) that which romantic discourse usually silences: the figure of the gendered and racialized Other.[8]

"The Amber Gods" unfolds the story of its narrator, the beautiful, self-absorbed, twenty-two-year-old Giorgione, who, with feminine wiles and a string of ostensibly cursed amber beads, foils her cousin Louise's relationship with artist Vaughan Rose and marries him herself. Rose soon tires of his artist model/wife, who promptly wastes away, seemingly from his inattentiveness. At story's end she realizes by the position of the hands on the clock that she must, in fact, have already died.

From the amber beads of great-grandfather Willoughby's "little Asian" slave to the golden beauty of the narrator Giorgione to her artist-lover Vaughan Rose's palette, the text's clear subject is color. Using the racialized figure of the "little Asian," Spofford's story invites readers to focus on the implications of the following question: what does it mean—in a racist, imperialist, and patriarchal culture—to be "yellow"? Giorgione narrates a range of culturally specific definitions of "yellow," definitions which, because they remain unexamined in the text, render impossible the discovery of exactly which ethnicity and cultural history the word "Asian" might reference.[9] Certainly, "Asian" is an inadequate category for study; but perhaps, for twenty-first-century critics, at least, that is precisely the point. The conflation of all things "yellow" as "Asian" enables us to consider more closely certain unspoken nineteenth-century assumptions about gender, race, and American romantic art underpinning this story.

In keeping with American romantic fiction's use of racialized Others, the body of the unnamed female Asian slave enables the textual presentation of an outlandish white heroine that challenges nineteenth-century ideologies of gender and their capacity to limit women's possibilities. Throughout her accounts of Willoughby family legend, Giorgione narrates the Asian slave as Other.

Whether an ill-behaved child of six defying great-grandmother Willoughby's orders, or a wrinkled, ninety-year-old dwarf interfering in Mr. Willoughby's advances toward her Italian mistress (who will marry young Willoughby and become Giorgione's mother), the slave's small, non-white body is consistently associated with the natural and the primitive. As Other, her body and its performances transgress nineteenth-century norms of femininity:

> She spoke no word of English, and was full of short shouts and screeches, like a thing of the woods . . . she turned the house topsy-turvy, cut the noses out of the old portraits, and chewed the jewels out of the settings, killed the little home animals, spoiled the dinners, pranced in the garden with Madam Willoughby's farthingale, and royal stiff brocades rustling yards behind,—this atom of a shrimp,—or balanced herself with her heels in the air over the curb of the well, scraped up the dead leaves under one corner of the house and fired them,—a favorite occupation,—and if you left her stirring a mess in the kitchen, you met her, perhaps, perched in the china-closet and mumbling all manner of demoniacal prayers, twisting, writhing, and screaming over a string of amber gods that she had brought with her and always wore.
>
> (43-4)

The slave girl's linguistic and bodily disobedience signals her refusal to accept a domestic social order that dictates who shall wear which clothes, perform which household chores, and utter which prayers—in short, an order that reads her body as justification for her enslavement. She will not be domesticated; in a culture that associates domesticity with femininity, that is to say, she will not be a "woman." The "little Asian" slave affords Giorgione what Morrison calls "economy of stereotype" (67), invoking widespread and hegemonic assumptions about the non-white female body as primitive, wild, and exotic. Most significant, it is through the implicit alliance of this non-European and therefore racially Other servant and the half-Italian Giorgione that the text registers its heroine's physical, social, and intellectual transgressions of true womanhood.

Alfred Bendixen has noted that Giorgione's first-person narrative "give[s] voice to a woman that her own culture would have labeled 'unspeakable'" (xxiv). My focus, however, is on what is at stake in the clear textual links among this "unspeakable" heroine, the slave woman, and Otherness. Signaled by her skin color and her inheritance of the slave's rosary beads (the amber gods), Giorgione's Otherness is the trope that enables this transgressive woman's voice. The deployment of the Other serves as a narrative methodology through which the narrator can believably and safely transgress the limitations that hamper white women characters in nineteenth-century American fiction.

The textual associations among Giorgione, the Asian slave, and constructions of the Other operate on several levels, all of which threaten to destabilize or deconstruct middle-class ideologies of gender even as they comply in troubling ways with nineteenth-century ideas about race. As Bendixen notes, the historical Giorgione, for whom the heroine is named, was a Venetian painter who died an early death from "a plague he contracted from his lover" (xxvi). His importance to art history lies in what Giorgio Vasari describes as his capacity to "infuse his figures with spirit and to counterfeit the freshness of living flesh" (cited in Bendixen xxvi), and his shift from "static" medieval art to Renaissance "liberation through color" (Bendixen xxvi). With this allusion, Bendixen mounts an argument for viewing Vaughan Rose, rather than Giorgione, as the story's protagonist. Examined through the lens of postcolonial theory, however, color functions as a defining characteristic in this liberation narrative of aesthetic "progress," just as eighteenth- and nineteenth-century pseudo-scientific "progress" relied on skin color to generate racialized and gendered taxonomies of human beings.[10] In the nineteenth century, the United States deployed these taxonomies in its global and domestic policies, including policies on immigration, abolition, and westward and hemispheric expansion.[11]

The painter Giorgione's reputed fusion of flesh with spirit, moreover, reinforces yet another discursive strategy of Othering achieved through references to Catholicism. Carved of amber into "hideous, tiny, heathen gods," the rosary of the story's title elicits in its characters typical antebellum fears of and fascination with what Jenny Franchot terms "Romanism," a "series of proliferating traits" that disrupted white middle-class gender ideologies in the nineteenth century (83). Like the racialized Other, Romanism, which destabilized dearly held Protestant categories of public/private and flesh/spirit, served as a metaphor for the "contaminated," the "exotic," and the "fearful" (Franchot xx).[12] Spofford's narrator Giorgione clearly shares her culture's fascination with Romanism, saying that the beads are "too foreign" for her more traditional cousin Louise.[13] Like "Asian" and "yellow," Catholicism, the religion of Giorgione's mother and her "Asian servant," produces an Othering effect—an unspecific cloud of connotations suggestive of the foreign, the exotic, and the sexually transgressive.

If the story consistently links the domestic and linguistic transgressions of both Giorgione and her family's legendary slave to the color yellow, these emphatically racialized links are nonetheless peculiarly ambiguous about specific ethnic categories. Although of Italian descent, Giorgione repeatedly describes herself as "yellow," deeper in color than other New England women. For Giorgione, her epidermis warrants permission to talk and behave with an exoticized sensuality that exceeds cultural norms. In order to reap the benefits of such Othering, the text effects some rather curious con-

tortions. For example, the narrator's "yellow" color is linked to Italy and the tropics, especially the West Indies, rather than Asia. She relates that "when I reached the islands my sight was as clear as my skin; all that tropical luxuriance snatched me to itself at once, recognized me for kith and kin" (46). Perhaps the safety of an insistently Italian heritage and ethnicity enables the otherwise dangerous use of "skin" and "kin" to suggest Giorgione's affinity with West Indian natives. Her skin color denotes a visible consonance with the tropical climate's native inhabitants and their presumed luxurious exoticism, an Otherness based in racial essentialism; at the same time, this Otherness is offset—made safe, if you will—by her clearly European ancestry. The linkage of "skin" and "kin" is consistent with late-eighteenth- and nineteenth-century scientific theories about race. According to Robyn Wiegman, "As late as the 1840s and 1850s, in fact, the preeminent authority on race in the states was still Samuel Stanhope Smith," who in 1787 wrote a "theoretical treatise on the origin of race, which he posited as climate and custom" (34). Stanhope's theory advances "race" as a scientific fact rooted at once in the observer's reading of behavior (culture) and skin (climate). Selectively appropriated by the narrator, these theories about race offer her a culturally acceptable device for asserting a privileged difference from white women *and* women of color.

Sander Gilman observes that "one of the black servant's central functions in the visual arts of the eighteenth and nineteenth centuries was to sexualize the society in which he or she is found" (228). Operating in similar structural fashion, the alliance of the beautiful Giorgione with the Willoughby slave's ambiguous ethnicity accomplishes several ends. First, the exoticization of Giorgione through the presence of a racialized Other may address the problem faced by Anglo-American nineteenth-century authors of portraying a sympathetic black body.[14] Perhaps a light-skinned Other was more palatable to readers. Next, the sensuality of what Amy Ling calls the "exotic, inscrutable, mysterious oriental" is displaced onto the Anglo-Italian American body of the heroine (143).[15] By contrast, the body of "little Asian" is emphatically asexual; described as malformed, ugly, and insane, she is by turns too young or too old to invoke such associations in Spofford's readers. The ambiguity of ethnic associations—Giorgione's skin color is associated with Asia, Italy, and the West Indian planter *as well as* slave classes—seems to invoke vaguely even as it directly avoids specific arguments about African American slavery and the growing presence of Asian immigrants that were dividing the United States.[16] Even so, the Asian slave and those sexually transgressive qualities she may have conjured in nineteenth-century readers' minds are mapped onto the body of Giorgione, shifting and making more appealing to a culture of white middle-class readers the racialized connotations of "yellow." Unlike the brown-skinned

Willoughby slave or pale and boring cousin Louise and similar Victorian "wax dolls," Giorgione is shockingly, vibrantly, and sensually alive. To be yellow is to have "delicious curves," "perfect roundings, flexible mouldings" and melting lips (38). She is like "wild honey," a "West Indian magnolia" and Cleopatra (39, 48). Amber suits her because it is "not dyed, but created" (38); in other words, like the sensuality of Giorgione herself and the racialized Other who confers it, amber is "natural." Her expressive sensuality reflects what Edward Said has described as Orientalism in Western cultural assumptions about the carnal nature and sexual availability of women of color.[17] Indolent, luxurious, tropical, Romanized, and undomestic, the protagonist is a fascinatingly "great creature without a soul" (56).

Giorgione's assertions of excessive and transgressive physicality and her insistence on the clear relationship of her tropical appearance to her essence results in her exemption from domestic servitude (rather curiously, given nineteenth-century arguments about the "suitability" of the bodies of women of color for slavery[18]). In the absence of a female head of household, the economically disadvantaged cousin Louise manages the Willoughby home, nurses sick children, plays the piano, sings, sews, and is even dispatched to care for a dying aunt. Meanwhile, Giorgione reaps the benefits of Louise's servitude, lying on the couch, expressing her own expansive and self-satisfied sensuality, disdaining sympathy for the ill, and inheriting the wealth of the aunt whom she refused to nurse. Her behavior refutes nineteenth-century beliefs that woman's "natural" state is domesticity; however, her defiance of these beliefs is tempered by the fact that she is not as pale as the normative domestic woman, and, therefore, perhaps her behavior is to be expected. It is important to note, however, that Giorgione's insistently nondomestic and transgressive physicality and language are protected by the wealth, class, and privilege of the Willoughby name and fortune—that neither poor white women such as Louise nor women of color should expect the same indulgence from patriarchy that Giorgione elicits from her father.

Her privileged appropriation of the position of Other buys her leisure even as it ignores the ways that the institution of slavery relies on taxonomies of skin color to categorize human difference. The Willoughbys' slave's transgressions are not met with similar rewards. Instead, according to Giorgione, she is "packed off" to another slave port but escapes from a shipwreck to Italy, where "she chose to remain . . . a mysterious tame servant" (44). That she "chose" to be at once "tame" and "servant" demonstrates how Giorgione's privilege has produced a limited understanding of agency and enslavement. Moreover, Giorgione endorses a class hierarchy based on skin color when she effuses,

"What a blessing it is that the blacks have been imported [to the West Indies]—their swarthiness is in such consonance!" (53). Again, from her privileged position as a white woman of the leisure class, Giorgione disregards the brutal history of West Indian slavery and revolution, viewing African slaves as landscape ornaments placed there for her benefit. Additionally, her patrician bearing, her sensual decadence, and her Italian and New England ancestry effectively intertwine "Old World" aristocracy with the "New World" mercantile and planter classes. Ultimately, Giorgione's politics and personal history mark her as complicit in the trafficking of African slaves to the Caribbean and the consumption of slave labor's products.[19]

As I have argued, however, her self-presentation also relies on the imagery of a colonized racial Other to convey her difference from her New England sisters and cousins.[20] Using racial stereotypes and racist assumptions, the text conducts a displaced discussion of women's roles in nineteenth-century American culture. To Giorgione, these stereotypes and assumptions offer a strategy through which she performs and justifies her disdain for the confines of femininity. Their use in the narrative highlights the ways that women's access to domesticity depends on privilege. As Giorgione admits, "There, now! you're perfectly shocked to hear me go on so about myself; but you oughtn't to be. It isn't lawful for anyone else . . ." (39). Because she is the last daughter of an old New England family built on the slave trade, her "splendid selfishness" is "authorized" (39); she is trained to be aristocratic and decorative and to "worship beauty" (40).

In cooperating with dominant cultural constructions of the racialized woman as exotic, sexualized Other, Spofford's story seems in accord with the race politics of nineteenth-century American romanticism as described by Morrison, a politics that silences, colonizes, erases, and/or destroys the racialized Other. But the fact that Giorgione herself is complicit in and wills this objectification of her body merits our attention. Characters in the story (and, no doubt, readers of the *Atlantic,* where the story was first published) accept her self-construction as Other, and that acceptance is based on assumptions that skin color points to less visible but no less essential aspects of human nature. Giorgione's insistence that her skin, hair, and eye color are signs of her essential character makes any consideration of **"The Amber Gods"** also a consideration of the related operations of race and gender politics.

"His Blaze is My Ashes"

In a complicated and even tortured convergence of metaphors, **"The Amber Gods"** relies on one form of essentialism to challenge another. Although Spofford's story critiques the limits placed on women's expression outside the domestic sphere, it does so while preserving racist ideologies. Giorgione's death contains the transgressive Other, reifying cultural scripts about true womanhood: the bad girl does not get the guy, or, if she does, she dies. Because the heroine occupies at once a privileged class status and a marginalized gender identity (the latter, as I have argued, achieved through racially charged language), the story offers readers more than another Pym-like example of romanticism's use of the Other. Rather, Spofford's Other serves as a vehicle through which to explore transgression and its consequences. A forum for portraying an unimaginable white woman, the text also considers the implications of existing as Other in the imperialist culture that condoned gender and race oppression and produced romantic artistic expression. **"The Amber Gods"** treats the death of a beautiful woman, which Poe named "unquestionably, the most poetical topic in the world,"[21] from the position of the woman herself. Through this revisionist perspective, and because or perhaps in spite of the heroine's doubled status as privileged and Othered, the text critiques, by calling attention to their presence, the relationships among nineteenth-century romanticism and race- and gender-based U.S. imperialist ideologies and policies.

In her discussion of the gendered dynamics of the British romantic aesthetic, Anne K. Mellor articulates the destructive and imperialist impulses at work in the mythology of the romantic artist. She argues that because this artist views the beloved as an extension of himself and because consummation requires the obliteration of difference, romantic idealism has a very real cost. The individual's desire for transcendence through the artistic expression of passionate love can end only in destruction, objectification, and death. One can apply Mellor's critique to American romanticism as well; the annihilation of the Other is amply illustrated by the fictional fates of Ligeia, Beatrice Rappaccini, Madeline Usher, and, as I will show, Giorgione Willoughby.

"The Amber Gods" demonstrates that art (legend, narrative, poetry, or painting) (re)-presents that to which humans assign value, circulating and maintaining systems of meaning, order, and power. In this story, as in language systems, aesthetic and cultural values are constructed on the basis of difference—between light and dark, master and servant, artist and object, and self and Other. Just as Giorgione's body is the vehicle through which Rose achieves transcendence, her story of the "little Asian" reveals the economy by which the Willoughby family earned the privilege it currently enjoys. Moreover, Giorgione's own Othering narrative of herself reifies those very gender- and race-based oppressions she would resist. At the same time, however, as Judith Butler says of gender, the repetition in narratives

and other art forms of dominant cultural values suggests the tenuousness of those values and the need for their consistent reinforcement, lest we forget them.[22] In this sense, Giorgione's personal narrative, like **"The Amber Gods,"** also offers what Butler would call a site of possibility and transgression.

Reading **"The Amber Gods"** as a "parable about the nature of art and the artist," Bendixen describes Spofford's moral: "[T]he artist must first come to know and then transcend the world of sensuous experience represented by [Giorgi]one" (xxvi). Since Vaughan Rose is the artist and Giorgione merely represents that which must be transcended, Bendixen concludes that Rose is the story's protagonist. Such a reading solves the problem shared by many of my students of identifying with an admittedly selfish, self-absorbed, and possessive heroine, whom critics have labeled a "victim of her own diseased sensibility" (Bendixen xvix), and as Barton Levi St. Armand asserts, a "psychic vampire" (qtd. in Bendixen xxiv).

Viewed from a postcolonial perspective, however, a reading that privileges Rose's importance over Giorgione's tends to replicate nineteenth-century romantic sensibilities and fictions of femininity. It suggests that, because she is more body than spirit and because she is not a "true woman," Giorgione can be neither sympathetic heroine nor artist. Bereft of a subject position, the romantic narrative positions her to be destroyed. A postcolonial critical lens permits us to locate in such readerly distaste for Giorgione the persistence of romantic ideology, which foregrounds art as an independent and aesthetic entity and ignores the material realities of its production. While it is true that Giorgione pursues Rose because she "desire[s] only the unpossessed or unattainable" (49), an admission that seems to approximate the romantic aesthetic, she wins him by becoming a *vehicle* for *his* artistic expression. We must not overlook the problem that Giorgione, a creative self-fashioner herself, fails to generate a language or position outside of domesticity that affords her subjectivity. Instead, she fashions an identity as an aesthetic object, transforming herself into the reluctant Rose's beloved. Posing as his objet d'art, she "schools [him] in the sacredness of color" (72), but she cannot prevent the violent outcome of his artistic "transcendence." Through the possession, consummation, and annihilation of his lover, Rose enacts the lessons of color—that romantic transcendence of the body is a privilege reserved for the Anglo-American male. In **"The Amber Gods,"** women may suppress their bodies by "growing souls," as Louise has, or they may remain merely bodies, like Giorgione and her family's unnamed slave. Women merely represent the binaries of body and soul to the transcending male artist, who, with pleasure and authority, reads these terms onto their persons. In this reading, **"The**

Amber Gods" *is* a fable about art, but not the fable that earlier critics have read. Rather, the story traces the imperialist project of romanticism, which constructs, colonizes, and annihilates the racialized and gendered Other.

Throughout the story, the text offers a critique of romantic ideology, tying it to the language of power. Rose pursues an artistic ideal of mastery, and his language and actions place him within an imperialist paradigm. That Giorgione apprehends aesthetic principles is apparent when she interrupts Rose's conversation with her father as he is confessing that he "cannot make copies." She exclaims, "Oh, how splendid! Because then no other man comes between you and Nature; your ideal hangs before you, and special glimpses open and shut on you, glimpses which copyists never obtain" (50). Rose's corrective and unelaborated response, "I don't think you are right" (50), illustrates his distaste for her unwomanly interruption and reflects the low esteem with which he regards her capacity to understand art at all. As the story unfolds, Rose permits Giorgione to enter his artistic world only when she acquiesces to objectify his unmediated ideal. In other words, as a woman, Giorgione may *represent* nature or the ideal with her body, but she may not *express* these things with brush, pen, or voice.

About the relationships among love, romantic art, and the Other, Mellor writes that "love is the means by which the poet attempts to rise on an almost Platonic ladder to the most transcendent and visionary of human experiences" (25); however, she continues, "consummation . . . can only be achieved through death, through the literal annihilation of the consciousness of division between the lover and his beloved" (26). Rose is at first revolted by Giorgione, this "great creature without a soul" (Spofford 56). However, he reasons that if he can "redeem" her through his art, then he can possess her. On the assumption that he can reform her soullessness, that is, obliterate her difference, he seals their engagement with a quote from Browning's "Pippa Passes":

> Shall to produce form out of unshaped stuff
> Be art,—and, further, to evoke a soul
> From form, be nothing? This new soul is mine!
>
> (74)

With this speech, Rose colonizes his future wife for the purposes of his art and justifies with the language of transcendence his possession and ultimate destruction of her body. He acts as artistic missionary on his own "errand into wilderness" to redeem the heathen body of the beloved/Other, for whom he feels both "derision and desire."[23] In addition to the Christian terms describing this imperialist mission of transcendence, Rose resembles an explorer in the New World, converting raw nature and materials into product. His possessive excla-

mation, "This new soul is mine!" betrays his materialist motives. (One notes that this "soul" he seeks to redeem and possess is fortuitously attached to a voluptuous and desirable female body.[24])

Rose's transformation into romantic lover/artist is described with the language of imperialism as well. Once married, Giorgione writes, "[T]he mist left him . . . he spread his easel . . . he became artist,—ceased to be man" (79-80). The spreading of his easel signals the increasing dominion of the romantic artist/self, a walking, talking transparent eye-ball, whose aesthetic project apprehends and obliterates all in its path. His wife, who, as his object, experiences in material ways the imperial politics of this transformation, boasts that she, "from the *slave* of bald form, [has] enlarged him to the *master* of gorgeous color" (80; emphasis added).[25] An artistic expansionist, Rose ruthlessly pursues his ideal through a project of "mastery," violent colonial acts that capture, ravage, and consume his wife. She writes that he left her "as the empty husk" (80). His aesthetic violence finds its ultimate expression in her completed portrait: "He hung me up beside my ancestors. There I hang . . . his blaze is my ashes" (80). Rose's exploration and discovery yields his dominance; Giorgione, the Other, hangs as a trophy piece on the artist's wall. The new American artist defeats and defines the Old World European; the explorer in the New World enslaves and annihilates the gendered and racialized Other he encounters.

If Rose's art and language express his power and domination, Giorgione's self-fashioning evokes the "natural" and "primitive" constructions by imperial nations of the colonial "native." In addition to the eroticism and exoticism her rhapsodies on color evoke, she adorns herself with "concretions and growths . . . Indian spices and scarlet and white berries, and flowers . . . sandalwood and ebony and pearls, and . . . amber" (41). Giorgione represents herself as an exotic colony, a rich wilderness, raw product to be converted to loot through Rose's civilizing aesthetic productions. Her "yellow" coloring, "not dyed but created" (38), suggests the prehistoric environment in which amber is formed. Her connection through color to the "natural" and to a racialized, essentialized Other, allies her with those women of color whom European explorers met when they "discovered" the Americas. Her fate—to be painted into a frame, a captive of the artistic and colonizing imagination—recalls the colonial subject, the racialized Other, the "little Asian," Arawak, Algonquin, or African, who is enslaved, silenced, and destroyed. This narrative of colonization challenges the ideal of nineteenth-century womanhood even as it raises questions about the practical possibilities for resistance. Although Giorgione struggles to express a feminine subjectivity outside of domesticity, her strategies of expression remain the "master's tools";[26] ultimately, her language defeats neither Rose's aesthetic nor his power.

If the heroine's demise articulates the place of the gendered and racialized Other as death or decoration, her struggle nevertheless asserts resistance and critique. If Rose's position as romantic artist empowers him to colonize Giorgione because she represents the Other, her enthusiastic performance of that role challenges his power over her and his privilege to define art, history, and nation. Like the Asian slave's negations, curses, mumblings, and "short shouts and screeches," Giorgione's monologue resists the customs and commands of the dominant culture and its representatives. She expresses herself in sensual, luxurious, immodest, self-absorbed, and, by nineteenth-century standards, shockingly unfeminine terms. For example, the story opens with Giorgione's self-description, consisting of four lengthy and characteristically vain paragraphs about her beauty and character; she concludes that "the traits being brought out, [the reader will] perceive nothing wanting; the thing [her narrative self-portrait] is perfect, and you've a reason for it" (39). Like the Asian slave, who learned only two words of English and broke the "ancient quiet" with a "Bedlam of outlandish sounds," Giorgione speaks a different kind of "poetry" that defies "every nice old custom" which might confine her (44). This "poetry," because it is uncustomary, nontraditional, and unlawful, challenges dominant discursive practice.

If her style of expression resists those cultural technologies that construct her as object rather than producer of art, she must nevertheless use the language of the dominant culture in order to be understood. Her language reinforces even as it destabilizes structures of power because, as the language of the dominant culture, it relies on assumptions about race to assert her transgressive femininity. Her language is not simply racist. Rather, the systems of thought underlying it empower Giorgione to express herself only as Other, and that Otherness perpetuates her colonization.[27]

Throughout the story, the Asian slave and Giorgione attempt to articulate in language those subject positions that nineteenth-century culture constructed as merely object and Other. Consistently, as when Rose repudiates Giorgione's rights to enter a conversation about art, those invested in dominant discourse and the hierarchies it reproduces respond by diminishing or negating the Other's gestures of subjectivity. The Asian slave is repeatedly referred to with the appellation "little" before the descriptor of her race. Following family legend, Giorgione refers to her as "imp," "dwarf," and "sprite." The slave's escape during a shipwreck, which could be viewed as a powerful act of survival and self-assertion, is instead narrated as a curious combination of comedy, witchcraft, and, most dismissively, as the

retaliation of a "vindicative child," whose "calling and singing and whistling up the winds" produced the "fierce fog and foam" that drowned her captors (44). Similarly, Giorgione is called by her "baby name," "Yone," suggesting that her transgressions are the merely charming acts of a spoiled child.

In addition to these linguistic avenues, those in power also assert their positions by objectifying the slave and Giorgione. Significantly, the metaphor of the frame occurs twice in the text to register the fate of the disorderly Other. In one instance, Giorgione is held captive inside her artist-husband's framed portrait of her; once she achieves the status of wife, he hangs her on the wall. The frame serves to suppress his wife's transgressive tendencies and to freeze her into the image her husband paints; soon after, she takes to her bed, her health declines, and she dies. The portrait suggests the ways in which human constructions of reality and the hierarchies they impose "frame" gendered and racialized Others within authorized discourses at great cost to actual lives. Curiously, when recounting her family's legend of its Asian slave, Giorgione says that her ancestors "*framed* many a wild picture of the Thing" (44; emphasis added). Here Giorgione participates in the privilege afforded to the white narrator-artist, who determines what is civilized or primitive, free or enslaved, self or Other. Yet Giorgione's power to narrate the slave legend proves a weak imitation of the master; her act is finally deconstructed by Rose's "framing" of her. Her form of expression, which she understands as poetry, is unrecognized by and distasteful to her husband. A New World artist and a student of Old World masters, he makes certain that she is merely object and not creator of art.

"What Has Cast Such a Shadow Upon You?" ("Benito Cereno" 314)

Throughout **"The Amber Gods,"** Giorgione raises questions about European and U.S. colonial history that Rose struggles to silence or correct. His arguments reveal his privilege to name what is history and culture—even what is the "world." Many of their conversations focus on the West Indies, a choice tourist destination for wealthy Anglo-Americans in the mid-nineteenth century; the climate was recommended by doctors to patients who, like Giorgione's mother, suffered lung disease.[28] The heroine herself is "at home" in the island climate and landscape, but this identification is complicated by the history of slavery there, in which the Willoughby family is implicated.[29] Her paternal ancestor, the seafaring great-grandfather of New England, "actually did bring home cargoes of slaves" (43). This family money enables Giorgione's leisure and tourism. As a tourist, Giorgione consumes West Indian resources and sights as products and views the islands through "imperial eyes," which romanticize the history of slavery.[30]

In her discussions about the West Indies, Giorgione strives to establish a subject position through a reliance on the racialized Other, while Rose's appropriation of that same hierarchy results in her objectification. From Rose's perspective, Giorgione represents a *facsimile* of a West Indian product; she is a West Indian flower to be plucked or "deflowered" and artificially preserved. Although he devalues West Indian culture, he is not above using its representation, in the person of the exoticized Giorgione, as material for his own cultural productions. He, too, imports and transforms into product the artifacts of colonial culture. His language marks his identification with a Eurocentric imperialist world view that most values the traditions and paradigms of western culture. Significantly, he studies art in Europe, where he imbibes the aesthetic and cultural values of western nations. In keeping with these values, he dismisses West Indian native culture, asserting that "only the first, most trifling, and barbarian movements" of history took place there (53). His comment conveys at once a disapproval of the "barbarian" slave trade and an effacement of New England's complicity in slavery in the West Indies, here minimized as "trifling." Although he seems to oppose the barbarism of slavery, his comments assert a dehumanizing view of non-European civilization that, in the eighteenth and nineteenth centuries, made slavery possible.[31]

In keeping with his imperialist emotional, aesthetic, and intellectual politics is Rose's insistence on viewing island culture as primitive: "A mere animal or vegetable life is not much. What was ever done in the tropics?" (53). Such definitions of history, culture, and even people operate as technologies for marginalizing the "native" and, by affiliation, through the story's taxonomy of skin color, Giorgione. "Animal and vegetable life" is physical and not spiritual, the object of art and not artist, spoken of and not speaker. In contrast to Rose, Giorgione desires a history that includes women as subjects. As I have argued, Rose's narratives of art, language, and history objectify the Other and offer no subject position for a woman such as his wife, who struggles to create a new way of speaking. Yet by allying herself with the histories of the Caribbean, Giorgione implicates herself in yet another colonialist narrative, the history of slavery in the Americas that has profited her family. In an attempt to escape this history of colonization and to locate a history from which she can speak, Giorgione reverts to a narrative of a prehistorical, pre-colonial past world.[32] Her amber is synecdoche for an imagined moment of lush, tropical, Edenic prehistory, when beauty was not made by art and culture was not determined by power. In this "pristine world" a "magic tree" "ooze[s] . . . fine solidified sunshine . . . drop[s] its . . . fruits . . . bursting with juice" (55). In Giorgione's imagined world of natural rather than constructed systems and hierarchies, things live in majesty and die only when they spend themselves. Unfortunately, her constructed world, like the one which she means to escape, depends on cultural narratives that polarize light and dark, civilization and nature.

Rose, of course, finds Giorgione's prehistory as disorderly, repellent, and threatening as he initially finds her sensuality. He dubs her vision a "furious epoch where rioted all monsters and poisons,—where death fecundated and life destroyed,—where superabundance demanded such existences, no souls, but fiercest animal fire" (56). In her search for a meaningful history, Giorgione imaginatively reverts to a time before culture; this pre-cultural fantasy threatens those truths and values on which Rose has built his life and art (and on which Giorgione herself has predicated her self-representation). To Rose, a world without western culture and imperialism is a world upside-down; death multiplies, life kills, and the idea of soul, whose redemption justifies the process of colonization and destruction of the Other, is displaced by a very physical "animal fire." While Giorgione's prehistorical past is no more imaginary than Rose's definition of history, his vision has cultural capital. Without a tradition from which to speak or a framework through which to express her subjectivity, Giorgione is an Other painted into Rose's history, a portrait stabilized in his cultural space. Like the Asian slave, she is an "imprisoned thing" (54).

The story's conclusion is no less ambivalent about the relationships among woman's place and nineteenth-century racial, cultural, and aesthetic politics. Since Giorgione's color, like her luxuriant prose and body, is linked throughout the story to her "rank" and "decaying race," her death may seem a logical culmination of this Old World aristocratic family "illness." As I have argued, however, the conclusion also enacts the fates of gendered and racialized Others in a racist and sexist imperial culture. Before her illness, Giorgione remarked that "nothing could have been finer than to have a dwarf in those old [Italian] palaces" (45). With the decline of her physical body and the relegation of its image to a portrait on the wall, Giorgione is herself dwarfed and objectified by the imposing power of the master. In neither case, however, does the Other's story end with silence. The Asian slave declares a curse on the beads from across the Atlantic: "[A]ll their blessing would be changed to banning" (45). Similarly, the heroine's voice uncannily traverses the boundary of death and continues to extend across time to contemporary readers. Perhaps Giorgione's story suggests that women may contemplate their position in nineteenth-century American culture and in romantic mythology only from the future, from death, or from the safe yet troubled (and troubling) spaces of hegemonic race narratives.

If **"The Amber Gods"** critiques and capitulates to nineteenth-century constructions of race and gender, then that is where we must locate Spofford's importance to literary study. With a complexity that challenges the labels we assign it, her work brings into conversation intersecting narratives about American imperialism, romanticism, and gendered and racialized bodies. Using the "master's tools," the very discourse under critique, the text asserts that these narratives are fantasies of power that colonize the material and expressive lives of women and people of color. As scholars and teachers we might handle the complicated and difficult race politics her stories present with the knowledge that such subjects are always risky—but less so than ignoring them would be.

Notes

1. My essay "'There is no home there'" considers the short story "Circumstance" in the context of early American women's traditions of writing.

2. I presented an earlier portion of this essay at that conference. Panelists included Margaret R. Higonnet (moderator), Debra Bernardi, Paula Kot, and Katharine M. Rodier. I am grateful to Paula Kot for organizing and including me in this session and to all participants, including Martha Cutter, Kevin Meehan, and especially Linda Karell, whose helpful comments inform this essay. Additionally, I thank the anonymous readers at *Legacy* for astute suggestions that led me to strengthen my argument.

3. Toni Morrison's *Playing in the Dark* and Dana D. Nelson's *The Word in Black and White* are starting points for linking American romanticism and matters of race. My use of the word "imperialism" refers to the process by which a powerful and seemingly homogenous center (such as the United States and its representatives, in particular, or Western culture, in a more broad sense) oppresses, represses, or marginalizes difference, often in race- and gender-based ways. In this essay I am interested in the ways that structures erected by the processes of U.S. imperialism, both political and cultural, participate in materially restricting the daily lives of those considered Other (e.g., women and people of color) and in the devaluing of their histories, voices, and identities. For my thinking on these theoretical points, I am indebted to Morrison, Nelson, and the following: Kaplan, "Left Alone with America," especially her idea that unfounded assumptions about American exceptionalism have disallowed academic discussions of United States imperialist politics and culture; the essays collected in Gates's edited volume, *"Race," Writing, and Difference,* particularly those by Gilman and Pratt; Hall, "Gender Politics and Imperial Politics"; Spivak, "Can the Subaltern Speak?"; Mohanty, "Under Western Eyes"; Said, *Orientalism*; Ashcroft et al., *The Empire Writes Back.*

4. Despite its somewhat Gothic style and subject matter, Spofford's work has not fully been considered within a tradition of American romantic fiction that includes Poe, Hawthorne, and Melville. Oddly, however, Spofford's fiction was also dismissed by critics from realist traditions, including Henry James, because it was too "romantic." Locating Spofford in women's literary traditions may be complicated by the fact that contemporary readers most appreciate the detective fiction, tales of psychological horror, and polar exploration narrative reprinted in Rutgers University Press's edition of *"The Amber Gods" and Other Stories*; domestic fiction typically excludes these plots. Thus, literary categorization has somewhat disabled discussion of Spofford's work. Bendixen, Dalke, and Fast consider Spofford's place in American literary history; Halbeisen's biography, subtitled "A Romantic Survival," is somewhat dated but still helpful.

5. Several recent discussions of American romanticism contend with the movement's relationship to nineteenth-century U.S. policies of continental and hemispheric expansionism, Indian "removal," and slavery; see, for example, Rogin, Romero, Dimock, Emery, Nelson, and Cheyfitz. Additionally, Phillip Fisher argues that the American novel is rooted in the "hard facts" of slavery, Indian removal, and urbanization.

6. Jane Tompkins uses this term in *Sensational Designs* to describe how nineteenth-century American popular fiction relied on cultural stereotypes.

7. Bendixen argues that Spofford "endowed the symbolic romance with a feminine and sometimes feminist sensibility" and that her fiction is characterized by the "intense individualism, even narcissism of romantic literature, its pre-Freudian psychological investigation, and its stylistic complexity" (xi, xxxiv). Dalke notes that Spofford found "Jamesian realism inadequate to encompass the exigencies of female circumstance" and that the protagonist of "Circumstance" critiques the "realistic mode of perception" (72, 74). Fetterley maintains that Spofford "might be called a romanticist who began to write at a time when the literary establishment was moving in the direction of realism" (263).

8. "The Amber Gods" is perhaps just one example of Spofford's consistent use of racialized Others. In addition to references earlier in this essay to Spofford's troubling race politics, Fast observes that the story "Desert Sands" (1863) "is structured, and limited, by Spofford's examination of the angel and demon stereotypes and by her racial assumptions" (38).

9. Perhaps the term "Asian" plays with Giorgione's Italian ancestry to signal the misnaming by another Italian, Christopher Columbus, of those natives he encountered in the West Indies while searching for the East Indies (Asia). In addition, the narrator refers to her as an "islander" and a "black slave" (43, 45), clues that suggest she may have been of mixed ancestry, perhaps African, Native American, and even European. Her status as a house servant further supports this hypothesis. This ambiguity, with its hints of miscegenation, mirrors Giorgione's dual descent from Old and New Worlds, southern European and Anglo-American. From my admittedly anachronistic twenty-first-century perspective, Spofford's ambiguity about the slave's "race" merely emphasizes the ways in which that difference itself and the Othering it generates in an imperialist and patriarchal culture is most important to this text. Rosalind Beiler helped me to work through these points and also recommended the work of historian Winthrop D. Jordan, who makes important arguments about the stratification of white, black, and mixed race persons in seventeenth- and eighteenth-century Caribbean culture.

10. One such scientist, anthropologist Johann Blumenthal, ranked the *Georgians,* people from Italy and other European regions, highest for their beauty. Perhaps the auditory link between "Giorgione" and "Georgian" is coincidental; yet it bears mention that Georgian women were used from the thirteenth through the fifteenth centuries in the white slave trade. See Schiebinger (130-33).

11. See Dimock, Emery, Rogin, Romero, and Takaki for discussions of the oppressive impact of these policies on women and people of color.

12. Franchot makes the compelling argument that anti-Catholic discourses enabled Protestant Americans to voice their fears about miscegenation, racial and ethnic "mingling," and other threats to "American cultural purity" (xxi-xxv).

13. Giorgione's argument that her father should give the beads to her rather than her cousin parodies the marriage ceremony; she wants them "to have and to hold, for better, for worse" (41). This passage plays into sensational accounts of Catholic priests as "savages in the American wilderness" and "seducers of virgins" (xxv), including Rebecca Reed's *Six Months in a Convent* (1835) and Maria Monk's *Awful Disclosures of the Hotel Dieu Nunnery* (1836). See Franchot 135-61.

14. Sanchez-Eppler describes the challenges white nineteenth-century writers faced of depicting sympathetic black characters in their fiction (see especially 14-49).

15. According to Schiebinger, while racial scientists in the nineteenth century viewed women and people of color as inferior when measured against the European male norm, black women occupied the very bottom of the racial hierarchy with other women of color only slightly higher, according to their skin color. Unlike so-called "true women," paragons of piety and purity, African women were seen as perversely sexual and wanton (158).

16. Hyong-In Kim notes that from the 1830s European slave traders increasingly turned from Africa to Asia. Takaki argues that throughout the 1860s and 1870s, Chinese immigrants were, like Africans and African Americans, considered "heathen, morally inferior, savage, and childlike" (216).

17. Fast traces a similar use of Orientalism in "Desert Sands," which features an exoticized, sexualized woman from India.

18. Many scholars have treated Western myths about the physical and biological suitability of women of color for slavery and servitude. See Brown and White, for example.

19. Historical studies that inform my discussion of the history of the slave trade in the Caribbean include Bush, *Slave Women in Caribbean Society, 1650-1838*; Dunn, *Sugar and Slaves*; Curtin, *The African Slave Trade*.

20. Wiegman contends that such imagery derives from pseudo-scientific treatises on "the visible taxonomy of skin" (33).

21. See Poe's "Philosophy of Composition" (1576).

22. I admit to quite a bit of license in using this metaphor. However, I believe that Giorgione's consistent decision to *perform* in language rather than merely to occupy her feminine identity suggests exactly those ideas that Butler uses in *Gender Trouble.*

23. Hall observes that these responses to the colonized object are, according to Homi Bhabha, typical of the colonizer (50).

24. Perhaps Rose's linkage of sexuality with spirituality was viewed with less irony by nineteenth-century readers. As Fast has shown, historical evidence suggests the presence of nineteenth-century "arguments for sexuality's enhancement of spirituality" (39).

25. Giorgione's pride in her "master" suggests a colonial mentality similar to that which Frederick Douglass attributes to his fellow slaves, who argued over whose master was wealthier. See *The Narrative of the Life of Frederick Douglass* (266).

26. I am, of course, using Audre Lorde's famous phrase.

27. Spivak articulates the difficulties for the colonized subject of constructing subjectivity from within imperialism and patriarchy.

28. In 1859 the *Atlantic Monthly,* which published "The Amber Gods" (January and February 1860), serialized Julia Ward Howe's travel narrative, *A Trip to Cuba.* In addition to the health benefits of southern climates, travel afforded women access to behaviors that they could not engage in at home. According to Leo Hamalian, "For most women, immobilized as they were by the iron hoops of convention, the term 'abroad' had a dreamlike, talismanic quality. It conjured up a vision composed of a whole cluster of myths, half-myths, and truths—of sunlight, of liberty, of innocence, of sexual freedom, of the fantastic and the healing, of the unknown and the mysterious—all those concepts that stood in direct confrontation to domesticity" (qtd. in Schriber xviii).

29. Despite her advocacy of women's issues, Howe's *A Trip to Cuba* accepts slavery in the Caribbean without question or critique except when conditions for slaves seem unusually cruel. Spofford may have relied on the myth that West African slaves were "seasoned" in the West Indies when, in fact, Newport, Rhode Island, regularly supplied slaves to these islands. See Coughtry, *The Notorious Triangle,* and Rawley, *The Transatlantic Slave Trade.*

30. "Imperial eyes" comes from Pratt's groundbreaking essay on imperialism and travel.

31. For a fuller discussion of early Western theories about race, see Wiegman, particularly 21-42.

32. Giorgione's longing for a white matriarchal prehistory anticipates the theme of "The Godmothers" (1896).

Works Cited

Ashcroft, Bill, Gareth Griffiths, and Helen Tiffin. *The Empire Writes Back: Theory and Practice in Postcolonial Literatures.* New York: Routledge, 1989.

Bendixen, Alfred. Introduction. *"The Amber Gods" and Other Stories.* By Harriet Prescott Spofford. Ed. Alfred Bendixen. New Brunswick: Rutgers UP, 1989. ix-xxxiv.

Brown, Gillian. *Domestic Individualism: Imagining Self in Nineteenth-Century America.* Berkeley: U of California P, 1990.

Bush, Barbara. *Slave Women in Caribbean Society, 1650-1838.* Bloomington: Indiana UP, 1990.

Butler, Judith. *Gender Trouble: Feminism and the Subversion of Identity.* New York: Routledge, 1993.

Cheyfitz, Eric. *The Poetics of Imperialism: Translation and Colonization from The Tempest to Tarzan.* New York: Oxford UP, 1991.

Coughtry, Jay. *The Notorious Triangle: Rhode Island and the African Slave Trade, 1700-1807.* Philadelphia: Temple UP, 1981.

Curtin, Philip D. *The African Slave Trade: A Census.* Madison: U of Wisconsin P, 1969.

Dalke, Anne. "'Circumstance' and the Creative Woman: Harriet Prescott Spofford." *Arizona Quarterly* 41 (1985): 71-85.

Dimock, Wai-Chee. *Empire for Liberty: Melville and the Poetics of Individualism.* Princeton: Princeton UP, 1989.

Douglass, Frederick. *A Narrative of the Life of Frederick Douglass, an American Slave. The Classic Slave Narratives.* Ed. Henry Louis Gates, Jr. New York: Mentor, 1987. 243-331.

Dunn, Richard. *Sugar and Slaves: The Rise of the Planter Class in the English West Indies, 1624-1713.* Chapel Hill: U of North Carolina P, 1972.

Emery, Allan Moore. "'Benito Cereno' and Manifest Destiny." *Nineteenth-Century Fiction* 39 (1984): 48-68.

Fast, Robin Riley. "Killing the Angel in Spofford's 'Desert Sands' and 'The South Breaker.'" *Legacy* 11 (1994): 37-54.

Fetterley, Judith, ed. *Provisions: A Reader from 19th-Century American Women.* Bloomington: Indiana UP, 1985.

Fisher, Phillip. *Hard Facts: Setting and Form in the American Novel.* New York: Oxford UP, 1985.

Franchot, Jenny. *Roads to Rome: The Antebellum Protestant Encounter with Catholicism.* Berkeley: U of California P, 1994.

Gates, Henry Louis, Jr., ed. *"Race," Writing, and Difference.* Chicago: U of Chicago P, 1985.

Gilman, Sander. "Black Bodies, White Bodies: Toward an Iconography of Female Sexuality in Late Nineteenth-Century Art, Medicine, and Literature." Gates 223-61.

Halbeisen, Elizabeth K. *Harriet Prescott Spofford: A Romantic Survival.* Philadelphia: U of Pennsylvania P, 1935.

Hall, Catherine. "Gender Politics and Imperial Politics: Rethinking Histories of Empire." *Engendering History: Caribbean Women in Historical Perspective.* Ed. Verene Shepherd, Bridget Bereton, and Barbara Bailey. New York: St. Martin's, 1995. 48-59.

Howe, Julia Ward. *A Trip to Cuba.* Atlantic Monthly 3 (1859): 601-08, 686-92; 4 (1859): 184-93, 323-27, 455-60, 602-14. Boston: Ticknor and Fields, 1860.

Jordan, Winthrop D. "American Chiaroscuro: The Status and Definition of Mulattoes in the British Colonies." *William and Mary Quarterly* 19 (1962): 183-200.

Kaplan, Amy. "Left Alone with America: The Absence of Empire in the Study of American Culture." *Cultures of United States Imperialism.* Ed. Amy Kaplan and Donald E. Pease. Durham: Duke UP, 1993. 3-21.

Kim, Hyong-In. "Asian Americans." *The Historical Encyclopedia of World Slavery.* Ed. Junius P. Rodriguez. Vol. 1. Santa Barbara: ABC-Clio, 1997. 240-41.

Ling, Amy. "Maxine Hong Kingston and the Dialogic Dilemma of Asian American Women Writers." *Ideas of Home: Literature of Asian Migration.* Ed. Geoffrey Cain. East Lansing: Michigan State UP, 1997. 141-56.

Logan, Lisa. "'There is no home there': Re(hi)stor(iciz)ing Captivity in Harriet Prescott Spofford's 'Circumstance.'" *Safe Space: Violence and Women's Writing.* Ed. Tomoko Kuribayashi and Julie Tharp. Albany: State U of New York P, 1997. 117-30.

Lorde, Audre. *Sister/Outsider: Essays and Speeches by Audre Lorde.* Trumansburg: Crossing, 1984.

Melville, Herman. "Benito Cereno." *Great Short Works of Herman Melville.* Ed. Warner Berthoff. New York: Harper and Row, 1969. 238-315.

Mellor, Anne K. *Romanticism and Gender.* New York: Routledge, 1993.

Mohanty, Chandra Talpade. "Under Western Eyes: Feminist Scholarship and Colonial Discourses." *Feminist Review* 30 (1998): 65-88.

Morrison, Toni. *Playing in the Dark: Whiteness and the Literary Imagination.* New York: Vintage, 1992.

Nelson, Dana D. *The Word in Black and White: Reading "Race" in American Literature 1638-1867.* New York: Oxford UP, 1993.

Poe, Edgar Allan. "The Philosophy of Composition." *The Norton Anthology of American Literature.* Vol. 1. Ed. Nina Baym et al. New York: Norton, 1998. 2 vols. 1572-80.

Pratt, Mary Louise. "Scratches on the Face of the Country; OR, What Mr. Barrow Saw in the Land of the Bushmen." Gates 138-62.

Rawley, James A. *The Transatlantic Slave Trade.* New York: Norton, 1981.

Rogin, Michael Paul. *Fathers and Children: Andrew Jackson and the Subjugation of the American Indian.* New York: Knopf, 1975.

Romero, Lora. "Vanishing Americans: Gender, Empire, and New Historicism." *The Culture of Sentiment: Race, Gender, and Sentimentality in 19th-Century America.* Ed. Shirley Samuels. New York: Oxford UP, 1992. 115-27.

Said, Edward W. *Orientalism.* New York: Random, 1978.

Sanchez-Eppler, Karen. *Touching Liberty: Abolition, Feminism, and the Politics of the Body.* Berkeley: U of California P, 1993.

Schiebinger, Londa. *Nature's Body: Gender in the Making of Modern Science.* Boston: Beacon, 1993.

Schriber, Mary Suzanne. *Telling Travels: Selected Writings by Nineteenth-Century American Women Abroad.* DeKalb: Northern Illinois UP, 1995.

Spivak, Gayatri Chakravorty. "Can the Subaltern Speak?" *Marxism and the Interpretation of Culture.* Ed. Cary Nelson and Lawrence Grossberg. Chicago: U of Chicago P, 1988. 271-313.

Spofford, Harriet Prescott. "The Amber Gods." 1860. *"The Amber Gods" and Other Stories.* Ed. Alfred Bendixen. New Brunswick: Rutgers UP, 1989. 37-83.

——. "The Godmothers." 1896. *"The Amber Gods" and Other Stories.* Ed. Alfred Bendixen. New Brunswick: Rutgers UP, 1989. 206-16.

Takaki, Ronald. *Iron Cages: Race and Culture in Nineteenth-Century America.* New York: Knopf, 1979.

Tompkins, Jane. *Sensational Designs: The Cultural Work of American Fiction, 1790-1860.* New York: Oxford UP, 1985.

White, Deborah Gray. *Ar'n't I a Woman: Female Slaves in the Plantation South.* New York: Norton, 1985.

Wiegman, Robyn. *American Anatomies: Theorizing Race and Gender.* Durham: Duke UP, 1995.

Carol Holly (essay date October 2001)

SOURCE: Holly, Carol. "'Grand and Sweet Methodist Hymns': Spiritual Transformation and Imperialistic Vision in Harriet Prescott Spofford's 'Circumstance.'" *Legacy* 18, no. 2 (October 2001): 153-66.

[In the following essay, Holly highlights the significance of Methodist beliefs to the spiritual journey of the female protagonist in "Circumstance," and explores the story's racist undercurrents.]

A frontier woman in early Maine journeys home after tending a sick friend. Setting out at dusk, she is surprised by the ghostly vision of a "winding-sheet" and the sound of a "spectral and melancholy voice." Three times the voice cries, "The Lord have mercy on the people!" Hurrying on, the woman refuses to let herself be unsettled by such "fancies and chimeras." But as she enters the woods, she is attacked by an animal called the "Indian Devil" and is swept as its prey into a tree.

Through the long night, the heroine prolongs her life by singing to the beast. At dawn she is rescued by her husband. Just as the husband has rescued his wife, however, so has the wife saved her husband and child. In their absence, their small settlement has been attacked by the Indians and, like Adam and Eve at the end of *Paradise Lost,* the members of this small family find themselves standing alone, facing an unknown future. "The world was all before them, where to choose" (Spofford, **"Circumstance"** 85, 96).[1]

This, briefly summarized, is the plot of Harriet Prescott Spofford's remarkable story, **"Circumstance."** First published in 1860 in the *Atlantic Monthly,* the story was based on an event in the life of Spofford's maternal great-grandmother, Mrs. Josiah Hitchings. Only the bare outlines of Mrs. Hitchings's experience appear to have been preserved by family legend.[2] But Spofford had no difficulty re-creating the experience with the kind of lavish poetic detail that had become the trademark of her early fiction. She not only describes the harrowing circumstances that beset the heroine throughout her night in the forest, but also dramatizes the inner workings of the heroine's consciousness as she moves from her fear of a horrific death by mutilation to a transforming experience of evangelical Christian renewal. Spofford specifically grounds the heroine's religious experience in the singing of Methodist hymns, based largely on scripture, and in the memory of her first communion.[3] She also reveals that the ecstatic spiritual experience that results from the singing of hymns has prepared her heroine for a future that, as the passage from Milton suggests, is as limitless as the uncharted wilderness.

Although **"Circumstance"** depicts the liberating potential of Christian revelation for a white woman on the frontier, the heroine's self-renewal nonetheless is deeply compromised. Her spiritually reconstituted identity and the promise of her family's future depend upon the demonizing of native American people and the rhetoric, however indirect or subdued, of manifest destiny. The end of the story, in fact, expresses an imperialistic vision of the land stretched out "all before" the young family and a confidence in the extension of empire that, in the American nationalist project, was constructed in part upon the Christian ideology of the new nation.

"GRAND AND SWEET METHODIST HYMNS"

No sooner has the heroine of **"Circumstance"** been attacked by the "Indian Devil" (or panther) than she begins to experience an ordeal both physical and mental. Held in the clutches of a wild animal, facing death by mutilation, she remains highly conscious of her fate: "Let us be ended by fire," she thinks, "and we are ashes, for the winds to bear, the leaves to cover; let us be ended by wild beasts, and the base, cursed thing howls

with us forever through the forest" (89). In part, the woman feels a disgust for the "strength of our lower natures let loose" or the animalistic dimension of human nature of which the beast reminds her (89). But she does not struggle explicitly with her own "lower nature," as Anne Dalke suggests (76). She is overtaken instead by a fear similar to that faced by many American women who made journeys into the wilderness—the fear of turning savage and becoming wild themselves. The capacity to go "wild," it was thought, existed just below the surface of civilized existence; it would not take much for a civilized, Christian woman to descend to the level of an animal or a savage. "When applied to women," writes Annette Kolodny, "such fears became even more virulent in their expression, suggesting a culture that felt itself more profoundly threatened by the specter of the white woman—as opposed to the white man—gone savage" (56).

The fear of becoming wild in **"Circumstance"** is of a somewhat different order, however, than that described by Kolodny. For the woman of **"Circumstance,"** wildness will not result from living a life in the wild, apart from civilizing influences, but from being literally incorporated into the body of a beast. That "living lump of appetites," that "base, cursed thing" with its "rasping tongue" and "foetid breath," its claws dripping with blood and its eyes flashing with the thrill of the hunt—it is the fear of becoming one with this animal, of its howling with her "forever through the forest," that is the greater threat (86, 89). As such, the woman is faced with the possibility of being physically incorporated into the savagery of the wilderness that stretches beyond the settlement. The death she would experience there would be not only physical but also spiritual, and with that death her darkness would be complete. The fact that the victim is a white woman whose body and soul, according to nineteenth-century white culture, must remain pure and undefiled makes the imagined violation all the more horrifying.[4]

Fortunately, the morbidity of the heroine's thoughts move her to a state of mind and a series of songs that prepare the way for her salvation: "[W]ithout being aware of it, her voice forsook the songs of suffering and sorrow for old Covenanting hymns,—hymns with which her mother had lulled her, which the class-leader pitched in the chimney-corners,—grand and sweet Methodist hymns, brimming with melody and with all fantastic involutions of tune to suit that ecstatic worship" (90). Spofford is quite explicit about the context in which the heroine renews her faith in God through song.[5] She was raised in a home in which Methodist meetings were held—the "class-leader" was often present—and hymns celebrating the promise of God's covenant of salvation to His people were sung.[6] The woman remembers that her mother had "lulled her" with these Methodist hymns, overflowing with rich "melody" and complex variations in "tune." When she is at the point of despair, facing physical and spiritual death alike, these hymns and their promise of salvation come to the woman "without her being aware of it" (90).

There are two ways of thinking about how the memory of these hymns and the assurance their lyrics contains comes unbidden to the woman at the point of her greatest despair. Working from a Christian framework, we could say that they either come directly from God, as in Paul's conversion on the road to Damascus, or from ways of knowing that God has planted in the believer, as in the reading of scripture.[7] Because the hymns that well up from her memories of childhood are based upon scripture, the Psalms in particular, we know that the woman's knowledge of God comes from the Bible. What is more, this scriptural knowledge has been planted in her not only by the class-leader who would visit her home to minister to the family but also, and more frequently, by her mother who sang the hymns to her child. By recalling these hymns in her time of trouble, the heroine renews her own faith in God and draws on the memory of her mother's faith as well. She draws on the strength that her mother drew from her faith, and she shares with such nineteenth-century heroines as Rachel Halliday in *Uncle Tom's Cabin,* Mara Kittridge in *The Pearl of Orr's Island,* and Ellen Montgomery in *The Wide, Wide World* a form of Christian belief that is rooted in women's experiences and ways of knowing.

Of additional importance to the nature of the woman's religious experience is the fact that it springs from the *Methodist* class meetings and hymns of her childhood. Some background on the history of Methodism will illustrate my point.[8] Unlike the adherents of the more orthodox, Calvinist denominations with their belief in an arbitrary, wrathful, and punitive God, the Methodists insisted that God was accessible to everyone. His love was unconditional and His grace freely bestowed upon people from all walks of life. Methodists privileged "the sanctity and authenticity of personal experience and emotion over formal knowledge" and, like other evangelical Protestants, they defined the personal experience of conversion as the pivotal and defining moment in the life of the Christian (Tiro 662). Donald Mathews explains that for the Methodists it was "'not what but *how* the Christian ought to believe'" that mattered. Conversion was a matter not of "spiritual authenticity" or "affirmation of correct doctrine," but rather of "the interior self's sensation of spirit" (93). The founder of Methodism insisted that "the power and assurance of Divine Love could enter the believer's heart at any moment in such fullness that the responsive love to God and man simply replaced all sinful actions, thoughts, and tempers" (Bucke 302).

Essential to the personal relationship with God that was forged during the conversion experience, Susan Juster

writes, is the relinquishment of "all claims of independent agency," as in **"Circumstance,"** and the "individual's complete submission to the will of God." Following the loss of the pre-conversion self is "its reconstitution under the divine power of the Spirit" and the eventual recovery for men and women alike "of moral agency and spiritual potency" (37). Juster also notes that for nineteenth-century evangelical Christians the "model of regeneration . . . ultimately echoes the Biblical affirmation that in Christ there is neither Jew nor Greek, slave nor free, male nor female. Though evangelical men and women reach the pinnacle of grace through different paths, the final destination is the same for both sexes: a mature union with God" (36-37). The singing of hymns was one of Methodism's most important methods of teaching the people about the covenant of God, that grace and salvation is bestowed freely to all. As Leslie Church explains, it was the singing of hymns that helped stabilize Methodism as a movement: "The hymns of John Wesley taught the people the fundamental truths on which Christianity was founded, helped them to understand their new spiritual experience, and challenged them to transform their vision of Christ into Christian service. He offered them Christ as directly in his hymns as did any of the evangelists in their sermons, and the very metres he chose helped them to remember the offer, and to ponder over and over again the fullness of its meaning" (228). Hymns, it was thought, sang the promise, the covenant of Christ, "into mind and heart. Doctrine was no longer contained in abstract and prosy definitions, unintelligible to the great majority; it lived, for evermore, in simple, inspired phrases so unforgettable that the singers became, in their own way, thinkers who presently made truth their own" (Church 230). Hymns thus became "a liturgy engraven on the hearts of the poor," and singing "a spiritual exercise" (Church 229, 233).

In **"Circumstance,"** it is in part the "liturgy engraven" on the heroine's heart in childhood that allows her as an adult to move quickly to the point where, in the midst of her frightening ordeal, she can surrender to God her sense of personal agency and well-being: "'Though He slay me, yet will I trust in him,'" she sings, drawing on the book of Job (91; Job 13:15).[9] What is more, Spofford's imagery suggests that this trust is a matter not of grudging necessity but of rare and wonderful beauty. The "hope" that springs from "despair" as she begins her hymn singing is compared to "some snowy spray of flower bells" that grows "from blackest mould." The "sublime faith of our fathers," and the "utter self-sacrifice" and love that inspired them, she claims, is "the fragrance" of "unrequired subjection," sweeter and more pleasant than the aroma "of golden censers swung in purple-vapored chancels." She even draws on a Psalm (105: 7) that begins by summoning the people of Israel to sing praises to the Lord, as the woman herself is now doing, and goes on to demonstrate God's faithfulness to the covenant He made with His people: "'He is the Lord our God; his judgments are in all the earth'" (91). In turn, the heroine lavishly celebrates the self-sacrifice of the "fathers"—ancient Hebrews like Job—whose "sublime faith" she is now drawing on for wisdom, fortitude, and strength.

It is not only the language of the hymns but also their music that moves the heroine to her exalted state and ultimately to a newly constituted, strengthened self. In sharp contrast to the "more sedate, orderly" hymns of the orthodox New England households, "those of the Methodists were fast in cadence, high in volume, and demanded the participation of all present" (Tiro 658). Similarly, the heroine's hymns brim with "melody and with all fantastic involutions of tune." They possess a "potent sway of sound" that enables her voice to soar "into the glorified chants of the churches" (90-91). Spofford's point is to show that in itself the fervent singing of such music has the power spiritually to transport the heroine beyond her worldly state, her state of danger, into an other-worldly realm. What is more, like many evangelical hymns of the nineteenth century, the melodies she sings cannot help but powerfully engage the affections and cultivate a sense of intimacy with the Divine.[10] Clearly, then, the singing of Methodist hymns from childhood as a means of keeping the "Indian Devil" at bay will enable the heroine of **"Circumstance"** to undergo a religious revelation every bit as personal, emotional, and intense as were the fears of savagery and mutilation she experienced previously, and it will enable her not only to survive the attack but also, by virtue of her capacity to survive, to grow inwardly in strength, maturity, and power.

"THE HOLY JERUSALEM DESCENDING OUT OF HEAVEN"

The heroine takes the next step in her spiritual journey when she recovers her memory of her first communion: "Never ceasing in the rhythm of her thoughts, articulated in music as they thronged, the memory of her first communion flashed over her." It is important to her spiritual growth that the woman has already renounced her reliance on earthly means of salvation, including her own unaided powers. But it is important to her spiritual transformation that the strength she is now experiencing develops within herself, from the remembered words and rhythms of sacred music and from the memory of the foundational spiritual experience the music evokes. "Again she was in that distant place on that sweet spring morning"; again she experiences the rapture of her first communion, "as the cup approached and passed, how the sense of delicious perfume stole in and heightened the transport of her prayer, and she had seemed, looking up through the windows where the sky soared blue in constant freshness, to feel all heaven's balms dripping from the portals, and to scent the lilies of eternal peace" (91).

The imagery in this passage—the "perfume" of the cup, the fresh "blue" of the sky—gives a sense of physical immediacy to the woman's experience in the past, and her ecstatic response to this experience of the physical becomes a measure of her spiritual bliss. Not only are these things of the world experienced as fresh and invigorating in themselves, but the intangible things they point to (the presence of heaven and the promise of eternal peace) are then compared to material things (fragrant lilies and dripping balm) that themselves are soothing and sweet. The woman now sees that she experienced her first communion with such intensity because her spiritual need was particularly acute: "Perhaps another would not have felt so much ecstasy as satisfaction on that occasion; but it is a true, if a later disciple, who has said, 'The Lord bestoweth his blessings there, where he findeth the vessels empty'" (91). The youthful memory of spiritual emptiness being filled to overflowing thus prepares the woman for the blessing she will receive in the present. As it was in the past, so will physical sensation now be translated into spiritual bliss, and the promise of God's salvation be experienced in terms of earthly delights. So will the remembered promise of the covenant of Christ, symbolized by the elements of the Eucharist, begin to fill the emptiness of her present despair with the promise of God's saving grace.

But just how does this process work? According to Methodist theology, the sacrament of communion fills a spiritual void in the individual soul because it offers a "direct encounter with the gracious promise of the gospel." It offers the "immediate remembrance of the sacrificial love of God in Christ" through the eating and drinking of the bread and the wine. Put another way, the Eucharist provides the symbolic occasion in which the people of God could feast on Christ "'in their souls, by faith'" (Bucke 313). By this account, the woman's harrowing fear of physical and spiritual desecration is transformed by her memory of communion into an experience of grace. The memory of the sacrament in which the heroine first feasted symbolically on the body and blood of Christ has replaced her earlier fear not only of being feasted upon by the "Indian Devil," but also of being incorporated forever into the body of a beast and the spirit of an unredeemed wilderness.

Having renewed the memory of her first communion, the woman is now able to interpret her wilderness experience in an entirely new spirit. First she redefines inherited notions of the space and time in which relationship with God is possible: "'And does it need the walls of a church to renew my communion?'" she asks herself; "'Does not every moment stand a temple foursquare to God?'" (91). Then she draws on the erotically charged language of the "Song of Solomon" to affirm the ectastic sense of intimacy with God that results from her experience of the Eucharist: "'My beloved is mine, and I am his,' she sang over and over again" (91; Song of Solomon 2:16). In this passage, the act of physical consumption of God's body that is symbolized in the ritual of communion is replaced by the image of sexual union with God. The experience of spiritual intimacy and ecstasy expressed in this erotically charged image seems to have nullified the threat of sexual violation in the "Indian Devil's" rapacious attentions to the heroine.[11]

The heroine's powerful experience of intimacy with God in turn inspires a vision of union with the natural world that was celebrated by other nineteenth-century Romantics: "[H]ow at one with Nature had she become! how all the night and the silence and the forest seemed to hold its breath, and to send its soul up to God in her singing!" (92). The heroine's ecstatic revelation of intimacy with God and God's natural world moves the heroine to an important stage in her spiritual development. Her singing now "was no longer despondency." Neither was it "prayer" nor "petition." She has relinquished the need to be spared "'the sleep of death'" (Psalm 6:5); she has ceased to fear the separation from God that would come with her death. She has moved from the despairing cry of Psalm 6:5, "'in death there is no remembrance of thee,'" to the comfort and consolation of Psalm 23: "'Yea, though I walk through the valley of the shadow of death, I will fear no evil.'" Not only have prayers of supplication been replaced by songs of consolation, not only have her fears of death been replaced by a belief that in death "no evil" can touch her, but the woman has also moved from her fear of separation from God to the assurance and acceptance of eternal life with God after death. The text suggests, in fact, that she embraces this assurance with a good deal of enthusiasm: She *lingered, and repeated, and sang again,* 'I shall be satisfied, when I awake, with thy likeness'" (92; Psalm 17: 15; emphasis added).

So great is the woman's elation over the promise of eternal life that her songs continue to celebrate God's victory over death and the "'fulness of joy'" she will experience in God's presence: "'at thy right hand there are pleasures forevermore,'" she sings (Psalm 16: 11). She even moves to an acceptance of the fact that God makes provision for all living things, panthers included: "Not once now did she say, 'Lord, how long wilt thou look on; rescue my soul from their destructions, my darling from the lions,'—for she knew that the young lions roar after their prey and seek their meat from God" (Psalm 35: 17). Instead she sings, "'O Lord, thou preservest man and beast!'" (Psalm 36: 6). At this point in the story, the woman's visionary experience is not static but active, not simple but complex. It grows in power, certitude, and complexity as she continues to sing God's praises and begins to envision "the Great Deliverance" (92). It appears that her vision of and union with God's creation has even come to include the

beast that holds her in his grasp, threatening her with death. Momentarily at least, the opposition established early in the story between civilization and the wilderness, between the woman and the "Indian Devil," has been dissolved.

Up to this point, most of the passages the woman sings are taken directly from the Psalms, and, both individually and together, the psalms reflect directly on the woman's deliverance from physical and spiritual harm. Now, as the night begins to wane and the dawn to illuminate the woods, the heroine's "vision" climbs to that "higher picture" of God's kingdom—"the holy Jerusalem descending out of heaven from God"—that is depicted in Revelation as the fulfillment of the Lord's covenant in both the Hebrew Scriptures and the New Testament. The light of the sun's early rays reminds her of the great, bejewelled Holy City that is to come—"its great white throne, and the rainbow round about it, in sight like unto an emerald." The light also reminds her of the Light of God's continual presence in the world that will eradicate the darkness once and for all: "'And there shall be no night there [Rev. 21: 25],—for the Lord giveth them light'" (93).

The woman has ceased to dream of escaping from the panther who, with the coming of dawn, appears to have relaxed his hold on her. In "her divine rapture" she experiences "how mystically true it is that 'he that dwelleth in the secret place of the Most High shall abide under the shadow of the Almighty'" (Psalm 91: 1). The Psalm's reference to the "secret place of the Most High," known by the woman as "mystically true," suggests that something particularly intimate and rare is promised to God's faithful—eternal knowledge of and relationship with the very "Heart of the World," the very soul of the Divine (93, 91).

"Like Some One Newly Made"

We are told at the end of the 1863 version of **"Circumstance"** that, after her husband rescues her from the panther, the woman "seems to herself like some one newly made" (96).[12] Spofford does not detail the nature of the woman's transformation at the end of the story. But the experience that precedes her rebirth holds the key to the woman's new sense of herself. Of particular importance is the fact that, as the panther held her in his grasp, she drew all night on the power of her voice to confront and surmount the threat of a horrible death. In doing so, she also drew on the memory of her spiritual resources (and on those of her mother) and, by singing hymns based largely on the Psalms, she came to renew her relationship with God. In undergoing this powerful experience, the woman ecstatically embraced God's promise of everlasting life in the New Jerusalem. The lavish poetic rendering of the heroine's spiritual rapture not only characterizes the workings of God in her life, by this account, but also speaks to the transforming power at work beneath the woman's apparent victimization by the panther. That she feels reborn at the end of the story attests to the fact that, having given herself (and her *self*) up to God, and having become one with God and the natural world, she has partaken of God's life-giving power. She has been reconstituted as a person of unusual assurance and grace.

Dalke writes that Spofford has portrayed "the extreme and urgent requirements of a women's [sic] situation" and "a view of female fluency" as "salutary, preservative, even redemptive" (73). But Juster's research on the conversion experiences of nineteenth-century evangelical American women suggests that this fluency specifically depends upon the heroine's newly restored relationship with God. According to Juster, women had to relinquish dependency on others as preparation for conversion, and the "experience of grace" then "implicitly strengthened women's sense of personal autonomy and moral agency" (53). The empowering effect of this experience for women was clearly manifested in their new-found ability to express themselves. "It is precisely this process of recovering a distinctive voice that is at the core of women's experience of grace," argues Juster, and "the metaphor of the loosed [or "liberated"] tongue recurs throughout the female accounts of conversion" (57).

The very end of the story, taken from the final line of *Paradise Lost,* also supports this view of the woman's rebirth and the effect of the rebirth on the family's future: "The world was all before them, where to choose." With this line Spofford has woven into **"Circumstance"** what Kolodny calls the "vocabulary" and "symbolic system evocative of Eden" used by countless white Americans to interpret their experience in a new land (176). In **"Circumstance,"** this language suggests that the woman has fallen from the innocent happiness she enjoyed before her panther captivity into the world of knowledge and experience. As Ian Marshall puts it, "the Milton allusion suggests the fortunate side of humanity's fall. The world beyond the homestead, that of the wilderness, is a world of possibility, and Spofford's view of that world incorporates the knowledge of experience" (55). The heroine has strengthened her inner resources and renewed her faith in God's promise of salvation; at the end of the story, she and her husband are like Eve and Adam, about to embark on a new life together.[13] Husband and wife are connected to the future not only by the vast possibilities from which they must "choose" but also by the presence of their infant child who will travel into the future and partake of these choices with them. Their child will, in fact, inherit their legacy.

Contributing to this reading is the text of Psalm 91, the initial verses of which were central to the woman's experience of religious renewal: "'[H]e that dwelleth in

the secret place of the Most High shall abide under the shadow of the Almighty'" (93). A reading of the entire psalm shows that it iterates the dangers that can befall a person—"the snare of the fowler," the "noisome pestilence," "the terror by night," "the arrow that flyeth by day." It then promises that, while "the wicked" are destroyed, the subject of the Psalm will be rescued from all danger, *including the threat of lions,* and restored to a long life: "Thou shalt tread upon the lion and adder: the young lion and the dragon shalt thou trample under feet. / Because he hath set his love upon me, therefore will I deliver him. . . . With long life will I satisfy him, and shew him my salvation." By this account, the woman's rescue by her husband is providential, as is their salvation from the Indians, and her future holds the promise of a long and fruitful life. Her spiritual rebirth also suggests that, as the person who has been touched and strengthened by God, she will lead the way to the future that lies before the family at the end of the story. Spiritually strengthened and charged, hers is the voice that the future will hear.

"THE WORLD WAS ALL BEFORE THEM"

"Circumstance" provides an astonishingly positive account of female transformation and agency. It can be likened to the conversion narratives written by nineteenth-century Protestant women who found a sense of voice and agency as a result of their union with a power that superseded and transcended patriarchally defined limits on women's lives.[14] The story also shares much in common with colonial Indian captivity narratives—Mary Rowlandson's and Hannah Swarton's narratives are but two examples—in which white women were strengthened in their faith and their sense of personal resourcefulness by their captivity experiences. But like those captivity narratives, **"Circumstance"** is compromised by an imperialistic ideology, deeply racist, that the heroine's unifying Christian vision fails to contain and transform.

At the beginning of the story, the "stealthy native" people who inhabit the wilderness are indistinguishable from the "deadly panther tribes" who live there as well (84). The term that describes the panther who holds the woman captive, "Indian Devil," conflates the beast's predatory designs with those of native people and associates the people themselves with the devil. We learn at the end of the story, Judith Fetterley writes, that "this 'Indian Devil' is less deadly than the actual Indians whose 'tomahawk and scalping-knife, descending during the night, had left behind them only this work of their accomplished hatred.'" By the end of the story, the meaning of the ghostly warning at the beginning also becomes clear: "'The Lord have mercy on the people.'" "For 'people,'" Fetterley notes, "we read 'whites.'" (We also read the "chosen people" of God.) "[F]or 'mercy,'" Fetterley adds, "we read protection against the Indians who are not people but devils, capable of every atrocity." From beginning to end, Fetterley concludes, the story "exemplifies the insidiousness and pervasiveness of the racist imagination in white American literature" (267). The story's Gothicism only serves to strengthen the potency of this racist image.

But there is more to the story's racism than racist language and image. Toni Morrison claims that "rawness and savagery" in much American literature provides "the staging ground and arena for the elaboration of the quintessential American identity. . . . [T]he imaginative and historical terrain upon which early American writers journeyed is in large measure shaped by the presence of the racial other" (44, 46). The texts to which Morrison refers generally feature the white American hero, and the darkness against which the white man's identity is realized is the presence of the African American as "other." But Morrison's observations apply equally well to the image of the Native American in **"Circumstance."** Here the heroine's rebirth is defined in opposition to the presence of the savage beast, the "Indian Devil," and the savage dark-skinned men with whom the beast is associated. It is made possible by the experience of grace that grows out of her encounter with the "Indian Devil's" threat of physical and spiritual desecration. I have argued that the climax of the heroine's spiritual vision momentarily dissolves the binary oppositions between beast and heroine, evil and good. But the narrative reasserts and reinforces these oppositions when it portrays the Indians' savage destruction of the heroine's community.

By the time **"Circumstance"** appeared in the *Atlantic Monthly,* the state of Maine was settled country, and the danger in New England of Indian attack was nonexistent. Nonetheless, the fear and hatred of wild, dark-skinned peoples remained intimately entwined in the ethos of a Christian nation that continued to do battle with indigenous peoples in the west. Readers of the *Atlantic Monthly* would not only recognize the familiar association of the beast with the heathen and the heathen with the devil, they would also recognize as implicit in the heroine's spiritual victory the necessary demise of savage beast and beastly heathen. "Taught from infancy to see the Indian as gothic monster," Teresa Goddu notes, "Americans were predisposed to accept Indian extermination as justified" (57).

The imperialistic design of the story is particularly pronounced in the sense of territorial entitlement that the narrator confers on the heroine and her family at the end of the story: "[T]he world was all before them, where to choose." Quoting Milton, the narrator posits a vision of the American wilderness associated with the ideology of manifest destiny, the belief that, as John O'Sullivan put it in 1845, it was the "manifest destiny" of the United States "to overspread the continent allot-

ted by Providence for the free development of our yearly multiplying millions" (28). Deeply interwoven into this imperialist ideology was an equation between the chosen people of Israel—the people of the Hebrew Scriptures to which the heroine so fervently appeals—and the God-given destiny of Christian, Anglo-Saxon peoples in the North American continent. By this account, the heroine's vision of the New Jerusalem portrayed in the apocalyptic book of Revelation not only intersects with the imperialistic language at the end of the story, but also hints at the heroine's potential involvement in the establishment of God's earthly kingdom in the new land.[15]

Charles Sanford notes that the "seeds" of American imperialism can be discerned in such early Puritan texts as John Cotton's *God's Promise to His Plantations* (1630), a biblically based text which "hardly conceals a chosen people's grand design to dispossess the Indians from their lands" (15). In the eighteenth and nineteenth centuries, evangelical movements like Methodism shared much in common with the ideology of expansion and conquest that shaped the development of early America. The leaders of the Methodist movement in North America believed that, as one preacher put it, "'God's design in raising up the Preachers called *Methodists'*" was "'[t]o reform the Continent, and to spread scriptural Holiness over these Lands'" (qtd. in Schmidt 75). Yet another preacher predicted that "'by the goodness of God such a [religious] flame will soon be kindled as would never stop until it reached the great South Sea' [i.e. the Pacific]" (qtd. in Bucke 288). Historians of Methodism observe that Methodism played a central role in "'helping to save the ever advancing American frontier from barbarism'" (qtd. in Bucke 492). They claim that "Methodism was on the march to conquer the land. Its preachers possessed a divine compulsion to enlarge their borders" (Bucke 367). Methodism, it appears, not only flourished in the climate of territorial expansion in the nineteenth century, as histories of Methodism reveal,[16] but fueled by a belief in its own brand of "manifest destiny,"—Methodism, it was thought, "'will take the world,'"—the Methodist movement inevitably contributed to this climate of expansion as well (qtd. in Bucke 492).

The relationship between the Methodist movement and the situation of Native Americans during the Christian European colonization of America is, of course, more complicated than this brief history—and the racist dynamic of **"Circumstance"**—suggests. Karim Tiro claims that Methodism enabled Pequot preacher William Apess to develop a positive conception of himself as a Pequot and to "articulate to a broad audience a critique of the dominant culture and a vindication of the indigenous one" (654). Mathews features the capacity of Methodism to subvert the dominant social order in white America and "to establish a new order" for traditionally marginalized peoples (96). But in **"Circumstance,"** the heroine's spiritual transformation and its promise of unlimited possibilities for the young white family depends upon a vision, both religious and nationalistic, of unfettered imperialistic conquest and expansion—the sort of expansion and conquest that occurred throughout the North American continent in the nineteenth century. The wilderness or Indian land, by this account, is a "Utopian site which projects the fantasies and needs" of Christian colonizers (Pfaelzer 124). It should come as no surprise that, at the end of the story, the "Indian Devil" is dead, and the only trace of the Indians who burned the settlement of "the people" is a single, soon-to-vanish footprint in the snow.

Lora Romero's work on the "vanishing" American Indian is helpful in considering the significance of this footprint. She describes as a "virtual 'cult of the Vanishing American'" in antebellum America the belief that "the rapid decrease in the native population noted by many Jacksonian-era observers was both spontaneous and ineluctable" (35). As James Fenimore Cooper wrote in the introduction to the 1831 edition of *The Last of the Mohicans,* it was "the seemingly inevitable fate of all these [native] people . . . [to] disappear before the advances, or it might be termed the inroads of civilisation, as the verdure of their native forests falls before the nipping frost" (6-7). Romero notes that the "elegiac mode here performs the historical sleight of hand crucial to the topos of the doomed aboriginal: it represents the disappearance of the native not just as natural but as having already happened" (35). The "historical sleight of hand" performed by Cooper is repeated at the end of **"Circumstance"** both in the image of the single footprint in the snow, an imprint that will vanish with the next snowfall, and in the promise of westward expansion for the white, Christian family. It is repeated several years later when Spofford comments on the fate of a native American who appears in Joaquin Miller's poem, "The Last Taschastas": "[This is] an individual, be it said, who, having stalked through our literature since the days of Fenimore Cooper, here fires a poisoned arrow, and sails away into the Western sea, so that we may reasonably indulge the hope that we have really had the last of him'" ("Joaquin Miller's Poems" 372).

In the early nineteenth century, territorial expansion and racialized genocide were essential to the realization of American imperialistic ambitions, and many white American literary texts "provided a discourse that justified" the expansion of the new nation (Goddu 56). But white America had its literature of imperialistic justification later in the century as well. Jean Pfaelzer argues that by the 1870s, a decade after the publication of **"Circumstance,"** "pressures toward an ideology of nationhood prompted elegiac and wishful representations of American unity in such forms as plantation novels,

regionalist fiction, domestic novels, pastoral utopias, idealized tales of colonial revival, and stories about the inevitable eradication of Native American Indians." She then features Rebecca Harding Davis's "A Faded Leaf of History" (1873) as a text that "hints at the link between the narrative of the feminization of power and racial genocide, the geopolitics of the conflation of the body and the state" (112-13, 119). Like "A Faded Leaf," **"Circumstance"** constitutes a narrative of the "feminization of power." It offers a powerful vision of the capacity of spiritual revelation to empower a white Christian woman on the frontier. But it achieves this vision at the expense of the "vanishing" American Indian and, in doing so, joins the ranks of other nineteenth-century texts by white Americans that justify racial genocide and the on-going expansion of empire in the American west.

Notes

1. The version of "Circumstance" used in this essay is taken from Alfred Bendixen's recent edition of Spofford's short stories, *"The Amber Gods" and Other Stories.* Bendixen's text is based on the first edition of *The Amber Gods* (Boston: Ticknor and Fields, 1863). A slightly different version of "Circumstance" appeared on the first occasion of the story's publication in the May 1860 issue of the *Atlantic Monthly.* For discussion of a slight, but significant, change between the 1860 and 1863 versions, see note 12.

2. Of this event, Spofford's biographer, Elizabeth Halbeisen, says only that the experience of Mrs. Josiah Hitchings "gave her great-granddaughter the inspiration for one of her finest stories. . . . Mrs. Hitchings was said to have sung all night in the grasp of a panther, as does the heroine of 'Circumstance' in the grasp of the 'Indian Devil'" (12).

3. Critics who acknowledge the centrality of the heroine's religious experience in "Circumstance"—Alfred Bendixen and Judith Fetterley—do not develop a reading of that experience in any detail. Ian Marshall's more recent essay is a possible exception to this rule. But Marshall reads the woman's experience in terms of what he sees as the story's eco-feminist celebration of the heroine's relationship with nature. Ann Dalke reads the story primarily as the story of a woman who discovers "the force of artistic expression, the ability to keep off disaster by the power of poetry" (77). This tendency to ignore the particulars of the heroine's religious experience is typical of writing on American women writers. Jenny Franchot observes that Americanists in general have "produced very little work of interest on religion and American writing" (834), and, following Fr-

anchot, Karen Kilcup notes that "[s]pirituality in literature by women other than African Americans remains a relatively unexplored area" ("Introduction" 11). It is to explore a small portion of this unmapped terrain that I have built on the more general insights of previous Spofford critics and undertaken a detailed examination of the heroine's spiritual transformation in "Circumstance."

For a brief discussion of "Circumstance" in the context of other nineteenth-century American literary expressions of religious experience, see MacFarlane. For insight into the absence of critical work on American literature and religion, see also Bush and Warren.

4. In *Women, Ethnics, and Exotics,* Kristin Herzog notes that nineteenth-century American culture believed that "the demonic was constantly lurking" both "in the primitive native, as in woman" (xiii).

5. There is no evidence to suggest that "Circumstance" was written during a period in which religion played a prominent role in Spofford's life. We know, in fact, "relatively little about Spofford's life during the 1860s," the decade in which the story was written (Bendixen xvi). What *is* known is that Spofford was deeply conversant with the Bible. Bendixen notes that Spofford's "first exposure to poetic language seems to have come from hearing the Bible read to her each evening by one of her aunts" (xiii). Halbeisen claims that Harriet's mother read to her daughter "the old stories" of the "Holy Land" and that, at a very young age, "Harriet showed signs that the familiarity with the Bible, so evident in Prescott letters, was having its effect upon her" (20).

According to Bendixen, "Spofford's life was marked by an increased interest in religious principles and a deepening faith in Christianity" after her husband's death in 1888. In a passage that echoes the heroine's experience in "Circumstance," she wrote to John Greenleaf Whittier in 1889 of "the comfort she tried to derive from 'the uplifting and rarefying power of *faith,*—faith the *evidence* of things unseen.'" Bendixen notes that Spofford's "increased belief in religious faith" is often reflected in the "poems, essays, and fiction she wrote in the last three decades of her long life" (xxi).

6. According to Karim Tiro,

> Methodist "class meetings" were gatherings of local faithful for the purpose of prayer and discussion of the spiritual status of its members. . . . [C]lass leaders were defined as 'virtually subpastors' . . . [who] were chosen ostensibly on the basis of their "deep personal piety, mature ex-

perience, and ability to give religious counsel and advice wisely and affectionately, and to influence the younger members to systematic attention to all their Christian duties."

(676)

7. I am grateful to my colleague Mark Granquist for providing me with this information.

8. Published sources reveal no direct link between Spofford's life and the Methodist movement. But historians describe Methodism as a religious and cultural presence of which few Americans could have been unaware. Methodism got its start in eighteenth-century America as an itinerant evangelical religious movement. Becoming an official denomination in 1784, the Methodists surpassed the Baptists in church membership by 1820 and became the largest religious denomination in America (Wentz 166). As one authority puts it, "the [Methodist] church expanded in geographical area and in membership until it became a major influence in both the religious and social aspects of the new nation" (Bucke 361). By 1850 Methodism numbered over one million adherents. "If the colonial period of our history was the age of Calvin," writes Richard Wentz, "the nineteenth century was the Wesleyan [or Methodist] era" (152).

It appears, then, that a mid-nineteenth-century writer could count on reader recognition when using Methodism as the source of a character's spirituality or religious practices. In the best-known novel of the period, *Uncle Tom's Cabin,* Harriet Beecher Stowe drew on Methodism in creating the character of Uncle Tom, the pious slave who sings Methodist hymns as a way of fortifying his faith. Methodism, by contrast, comes under indictment in *The Narrative of the Life of Frederick Douglass* when it is identified as the denomination of choice of several particularly cruel, Christian slaveholders.

9. All of the biblical passages in Spofford's text are taken from the King James Version of the Bible. It does not appear that Spofford drew so much on actual Methodist hymns—though all Methodist hymns were required to be based on scripture—as much as on her own knowledge of the Bible, with a special emphasis on the Hebrew Scriptures, the Psalms in particular.

10. For a discussion of the purposes of evangelical or "gospel" hymns in the nineteenth century, see Sizer.

11. Spofford writes that the beast licks the heroine's "bare arm with his rasping tongue," that he pours "over her the wide streams of his hot, foetid

breath," that he holds her "in his great lithe embrace" and clasps "her with invincible pressure to his rough, ravenous breast" (86, 89). Fetterley explains that in "the context of mid-nineteenth-century America, this language constitutes a familiar code for referring to unrestrained male sexuality, that lower nature often let loose on the bodies of women" (266).

12. The version of "Circumstance" that appeared in the 1860 issue of the *Atlantic Monthly* was altered slightly by Spofford when she published the story in 1863 in *The Amber Gods and Other Stories*. The original version concludes the tale without commenting on the heroine's condition. The revised version adds the lines,

> It is not time for reaction,—the tension not yet relaxed, the nerves still vibrant, she seems to herself like someone newly made; the night was a dream; the present stamped upon her in deep satisfaction, neither weighed nor compared with the past; if she has the careful tricks of former habit, it is as an automaton . . . .
>
> (96)

The addition of a line that distinctly comments on the condition of the heroine following her religious experience suggests that Spofford herself came to see her heroine as having experienced a re-birth. Indeed, although there is no evidence to link Spofford specifically to the Methodist movement, the language of her revision is not unlike the language of the "New Birth" used by Methodists to describe the condition of the soul following a conversion experience. As Mathews puts it, a "compelling, inner sense of transformation" or "New Birth" attended the Methodist experience of personal conversion (93).

13. Dalke's reading of the ending is very similar to mine: "Unlike Milton's characters . . . those created by Spofford are not cast out from Eden, but preparing to enter into the state of paradise. This husband and wife have not condemned one another to damnation and exile, but rather have proved mutually restorative" (80).

14. For studies on nineteenth-century conversion narratives by women, see Brereton and Juster.

15. The idea that the uncharted wilderness of the New World represented a millenial paradise—a location for the eventual establishment of God's Kingdom on earth—runs throughout the early history of the United States. For an overview of the history of this idea, see Wojcik 21-36.

16. For a discussion of the growth of Methodism throughout the United States, see Bucke, chapters 6-10, in the section entitled "A New Church in a New Nation."

Works Cited

Bendixen, Alfred. Introduction. *"The Amber Gods" and Other Stories.* By Harriet Prescott Spofford. Ed. Bendixen. New Brunswick: Rutgers UP, 1989. ix-xxxiv.

Brereton, Virginia Lieson. *From Sin to Salvation: Stories of Women's Conversions, 1800 to the Present.* Bloomington: Indiana UP, 1991.

Bucke, Emory, et al., eds. *The History of American Methodism.* Vol. 1. New York: Abingdon, 1964. 3 vols.

Bush, Harold K., Jr. "'Invisible Domains' and the Theological Turn in Recent American Literary Studies." *Christianity and Literature* 49 (1999): 91-109.

Church, Leslie. *More About the Early Methodist People.* London: Epworth, 1949.

Cooper, James Fenimore. Introduction. 1831. *The Last of the Mohicans: A Narrative of 1757.* 1826. Ed. James Franklin Beard. Albany: State U of New York P, 1983. 5-8.

Dalke, Anne. "'Circumstance' and the Creative Woman: Harriet Prescott Spofford." *Arizona Quarterly* 41 (1985): 71-85.

Fetterley, Judith, ed. Introduction. *Provisions: A Reader From 19th-Century American Women.* Bloomington: Indiana UP, 1985. 1-40.

Franchot, Jenny. "Invisible Domains: Religion and American Literary Studies." *American Literature* 67 (1995): 833-42.

Goddu, Teresa A. *Gothic America: Narrative, History, Nation.* New York: Columbia UP, 1997.

Halbeisen, Elizabeth. *Harriet Prescott Spofford: A Romantic Survival.* Philadelphia: U of Pennsylvania P, 1935.

Herzog, Kristin. *Women, Ethnics, and Exotics: Images of Power in Mid-Nineteenth-Century American Fiction.* Knoxville: U of Tennessee P, 1983.

Juster, Susan. "'In a Different Voice': Male and Female Narratives of Religious Conversion in Post-Revolutionary America." *American Quarterly* 41 (1989): 34-62.

Kilcup, Karen. "Introduction: A Conversation on Nineteenth-Century American Women's Writing." Kilcup, *Nineteenth-Century American Women Writers* 1-14.

———, ed. *Nineteenth-Century American Women Writers: A Critical Reader.* Malden: Blackwell, 1998.

Kolodny, Annette. *The Land Before Her: Fantasy and Experience on the American Frontiers, 1630-1860.* Chapel Hill: U of North Carolina P, 1984.

MacFarlane, Lisa. "Introduction: The Spiritual Landscape of New England." *This World is Not Conclusion: Faith in Nineteenth-Century New England Fiction.* Ed. MacFarlane. Hanover: UP of New England, 1998. 1-25.

Marshall, Ian. "Literal and Metaphoric Harmony with Nature: Ecofeminism and Harriet Prescott Spofford's 'Circumstance.'" *Modern Language Studies* 23 (1993): 48-58.

Mathews, Donald. "Evangelical America—The Methodist Ideology." Richey and Rowe 91-99.

Morrison, Toni. *Playing in the Dark: Whiteness and the Literary Imagination.* New York: Vintage, 1993.

Pfaelzer, Jean. "Nature, Nurture, and Nationalism: 'A Faded Leaf of History.'" Kilcup 112-27.

O'Sullivan, John. "Manifest Destiny." Sanford, *Manifest Destiny* 26-32.

Richey, Russell, and Kenneth Rowe, eds. *Rethinking Methodist History: A Bicentennial Historical Consultation.* Nashville: Kingswood, 1985. 91-99.

Romero, Lora. *Homefronts: Domesticity and Its Critics in the Antebellum United States.* Durham: Duke UP, 1997.

Sanford, Charles. "Introduction: 'God's Promise to New England.'" Sanford, *Manifest Destiny* 15.

———, ed. *Manifest Destiny and the Imperialism Question.* New York: Wiley, 1974.

Schmidt, Jean Miller. "Reexamining the Public/Private Split: Reforming the Continent and Spreading Scriptural Holiness." Richey and Rowe 75-88.

Sizer, Sandra. *Gospel Hymns and Social Religion.* Philadelphia: Temple UP, 1978.

Spofford, Harriet Prescott. "Circumstance." 1860. *"The Amber Gods" and Other Stories.* Ed. Alfred Bendixen. New Brunswick: Rutgers UP, 1989. 84-96.

———. "Joaquin Miller's Poems." Rev. of *Songs of the Sierras*, by Joaquin Miller. *Old and New* (1871): 371-76.

Tiro, Karim. "Denominated 'Savage': Methodism, Writing, and Identity in the Works of William Apess, A Pequot." *American Quarterly* 48 (1996): 653-79.

Warren, Joyce W. "Introduction: Canons and Canon Fodder." *The (Other) American Traditions: Nineteenth-Century Women Writers.* Ed. Warren. New Brunswick: Rutgers UP, 1993. 1-25.

Wentz, Richard. *Religion in the New World: The Shaping of Religious Traditions in the United States.* Minneapolis: Fortress, 1990.

Wojcik, Daniel. *The End of the World as We Know It: Faith, Fatalism, and Apocalypse in America.* New York: New York UP, 1997.

Theresa Strouth Gaul (essay date January 2002)

SOURCE: Gaul, Theresa Strouth. "Captivity, Childbirth, and the Civil War in Harriet Prescott Spofford's 'Circumstance.'" *Legacy* 19, no. 1 (January 2002): 35-43.

[*In the following essay, Gaul explores Spofford's portrayal of motherhood, underscoring the role of birth imagery in "Circumstance."*]

Harriet Prescott Spofford's short story **"Circumstance"** narrates the experiences of a colonial woman walking home through the Maine countryside. She is seized by a panther, borne into the boughs of a tree, and held by the panther through the whole of one long wintry night. First published in May 1860 in the *Atlantic Monthly* and later reprinted in a collection entitled ***The Amber Gods and Other Stories*** (1863), the story confirmed Spofford's status as a rising young literary talent. From Emily Dickinson to William Dean Howells, many of her contemporaries commented on the fascination the story provoked in its readers (Bendixen x). Today, the story is widely anthologized and thus likely to meet with new generations of readers, but it has not yet received the sustained critical attention its complexity warrants.[1]

Perhaps most striking to a modern reader is the imagery of sexual violation that pervades the story. The panther seems quite obviously to be a predator of the sexual variety familiar to late twentieth- and early twenty-first-century parlance.[2] While remaining attuned to the imagery of sexual violation, I will argue in this essay that interpreting the encounter between woman and panther as primarily a sexual one obscures the recognition of another significant set of images within the story, those suggesting that the woman figuratively gives birth while in the tree. By uncovering the childbirth imagery in **"Circumstance,"** I explore how Spofford complicates feminist understandings of the ways the history of motherhood—and more particularly, childbirth—has been suppressed in the literature of preceding centuries. Patricia Yaegar, for example, notes that "the invisibility of gestation and parturition" is "one of our most persistent cultural myths" (263). She calls for feminist scholars "to make these repressed stories visible" by conducting "an investigation into the literary tropes and principles that preside over the presentation, deformation, or concealment of the story of reproduction in literary and cultural texts," resulting in an increased attentiveness to what she calls "a poetics of birth" (263, 264, 269). Critics who have focused on the rape imagery in **"Circumstance"** to the exclusion of the birth imagery have perhaps unwittingly participated in what Yaeger has identified as a "copulative politics" beyond which she believes critics must move (263).

By turning my attention to images of childbirth in **"Circumstance,"** I do not intend to diminish the importance of the rape reading. The goal of this essay is instead to bring together these two seemingly disparate interpretations by exploring how a scene of rape might *simultaneously* function as a scene of childbirth. To this end, I will explore the cultural and historical contexts—including Indian-white relations as depicted in captivity narratives, images of panthers attacking women in American literature, and mothers' roles as prescribed in conduct literature—which granted that duality its resonance in the mid-nineteenth century.

After tending a sick neighbor, the unnamed protagonist of Spofford's story traverses the wilderness back to her home.[3] Of a practical nature, she is unshaken by a vision of a winding sheet in the air and a ghostly voice chanting, "The Lord have mercy on the people" and continues on her way, only to be seized by a panther and lifted into the tree (85).[4] As she is mauled by the panther, she screams, discovering inadvertently that the echo of her shrieks seems to quiet the animal. Remembering the adage that "music charmed wild beasts" (86), she begins to sing, a tactic she continues throughout the long night as a method of staving off his attack. Her songs range from lullabies to reels to war songs, and as she sings, she contemplates her own death. Her mind flashes back to scenes of childhood and to the husband and child who are even then awaiting her return in their frontier cabin. Eventually, her songs turn to religious topics, and she finally achieves a transcendent sense of calm about her impending death.

Meanwhile, her husband has become concerned over the woman's absence. Convinced he has heard her voice rise over the sound of the wind, he packs up the baby and his gun and leaves the cabin to search for her. After following her voice, he discovers her "circumstance" in the tree. When the protagonist glimpses her husband and child, she loses her sense of tranquility and her voice at the same time: her singing quavers to a halt. The beast, enraged by the cessation of song, begins to attack. Her husband, though fearing that to shoot the beast would also endanger his wife, eventually fires and kills the panther. The family is reunited, and together they walk back to their cabin, only to discover that their home has been burned by Native Americans while they were in the forest.

At a crucial moment early in the story, immediately after the protagonist has been seized but before she has hit upon a method to stave off the attack of the panther, the animal rends her arm with its claws. Spofford's language, read carefully, serves to frame the encounter as a scene of conception and childbirth. She imagines "the fierce plunge of those weapons" (the impregnation), "the long strips of living flesh torn from her bones" (the birth), and "the agony" (the pains of labor) (86). A loud shriek "tore through her lips" followed by a flow of blood that leaves her body "once white, now crimson"

(86). This scene of figurative childbirth is brought to culmination when the beast then "looked up alertly" at her, much like a newborn child affixing its eyes on its mother for the first time after birth (86). The woman's response to the sight of her newborn is, significantly, to sing it a lullaby. The first song to issue from her lips is "the cradle-song with which she rocked her baby," the child that was even at that moment "sleeping rosily on the long settee before the fire" tended by its father (86). "How could she sing that?" she questions herself (86). The answer to her frantic query seems clear given the symbolism of the preceding scene: the very songs used to soothe her human baby have the same effect on her wilderness offspring.

This panther-baby's demands upon her throughout the night are unceasing, much like a newborn's. He thrusts out his tongue, follows her every movement with his eyes, frets his nails upon her arms and in her clothing, behaviors characteristic of infants. Indeed, the woman's issuance of a steady stream of song that calms and soothes him establishes the scene as a metaphoric breastfeeding act.[5] Like a child that has nursed until it is full, the panther displays "heavy satisfaction" and begins to grow drowsy, as he "half closed his eyes, and sleepily reopened and shut them again" (88, 89). As he sleeps, reclining on her, "a half-whine of enjoyment escaped him," and he moves his head contentedly and lovingly against her (90).

Reading the woman's encounter with the panther, which I have earlier described as suggestive of sexual violation, as a scene of childbirth requires that the panther must be simultaneously read as a rapist and a newborn baby. Many observers of nursing mother/child pairs have noted the links between sexuality and breastfeeding, ranging from Sigmund Freud, who wrote, "No one who has seen a baby sinking back satiated from the breast and falling asleep with flushed cheeks and a blissful smile can escape the reflection that this picture persists as a prototype of the expression of sexual satisfaction in later life" (qtd. in Smith, "Suckers" 176), to late twentieth-century how-to books on breastfeeding which describe the feelings of sexual stimulation sometimes aroused by nursing (Eiger 193-96). Stephanie Smith adds associations of violence to those of breast-feeding and sexuality in her exploration of the term "sucker" when she emphasizes the double-valence of that word in the image of the innocent breastfeeding baby and the sexualized vampire ("Suckers" 176). As Smith writes, "The bloodsucker, as a figure of common violence, is, like the suckling child, a violence-marked legible body, endlessly readable despite persistent and sometimes well-meaning attempts to forestall the multiplicity of interpretation" ("Suckers" 197). Smith illustrates how the unstable signifier—infant or vampire in her formulation, satisfied baby or sexual partner in Freud's, nursing infant or rapist in Spofford's—becomes indelibly linked with violence. The multiple subject positions occupied by the panther, then, become the mechanism by which Spofford links sexual violence to the institution of motherhood.

Moreover, Spofford gives this violent encounter a racialized component with her imagery associating the panther with the figure of an American Indian.[6] The text foregrounds the relationship between animal and human quite insistently. Spofford represents panthers and American Indians as similar in their tribal affiliations and as the sole inhabitants of the wilderness the woman enters when she writes that the "wilderness [was] untrodden save by stealthy native or deadly panther tribes" (84). Later, the panther is described as "that wild beast—the most savage and serpentine and subtle and fearless of our latitudes—known by our hunters as the Indian Devil" (85). American writers applied similar strings of adjectives to Native Americans during the period, and the familiar nickname of the cat highlights its associations with American Indians. One writer in the *North American Review* displays the common tendency to equate Native Americans with animals in his comment that American Indians "were as wild, fierce, irreclaimable, as the animals, their co-tenants of the forest" ("Policy" 391).

In addition to overt textual associations between the panther and Native Americans, the behavior of the cat also brings to mind stereotypes of American Indians' behavior as captors of white women and, especially, as sexual aggressors.[7] If white men's sexual violations of women remained nearly unspoken in the culture of the time, American Indians' purported violations of white women—who were also often mothers—had received articulation within the captivity narrative genre. Indeed, captivity narratives brought together sexuality and maternity in a way similar to **"Circumstance."** Substantial numbers of women taken captive during the colonial period had recently given birth and/or were breastfeeding their infants. The perceived—if not always actual—sexual threats faced by captive women had to be negotiated in relation to the demands of caring for their nursing babies or older children. Captivity narratives are filled with white women who are simultaneously mothers and (potential or actual) rape victims, as is Spofford's protagonist.

Sexuality, violence, and motherhood also converge in a tradition of literary depictions of violent encounters between women and panthers, the exploration of which provides a fuller context for examining Spofford's story. For example, James Fenimore Cooper depicts a panther captivity in *The Pioneers* (1823). Cooper's heroine, Elizabeth, is terrorized by a crazed panther at the summit of a mountain. Elizabeth is lured into danger by the cry of a panther cub, which she mistakes for the call of a human child. Guided by her maternal impulses to save the "sufferer," whom she imagines to be "a little one" who has "strayed from its parents" (309), Elizabeth pursues the sounds through the forest until she eventually encounters the mother panther. The encounter is shaped, as in Spofford's story, to resemble an American Indian's attack on a white woman. Upon realizing the seeming inevitability of her death, Elizabeth's "hands were clasped in the attitude of prayer . . . her cheeks were blanched to the whiteness of marble, and her lips were slightly separated with horror. . . . [T]he moment seemed now to have arrived for the fatal termination, and the beautiful figure of Elizabeth was bowing meekly to the stroke" (312). Emphasizing her Christian resignation and whiteness, Cooper's stylized language here is more suggestive of death by scalping than by panther attack. This description of Elizabeth is similar to Cooper's descriptions of Alice Munro as she is menaced by Magua in *The Last of the Mohicans* (125). Furthermore, Elizabeth's dangerous situation allows for the exercise of male heroism, a trope common within the captivity narrative as well,[8] as she is defended nobly first by a male mastiff and later by Natty Bumppo.

In addition, in Cooper's telling as in Spofford's, the panther attack is infused with complicated sexual dynamics. After the experience, Elizabeth has lingering dreams of the event: "[T]he sweetness of her midnight sleep would be disturbed, as her active fancy conjured, in dreams, the most trifling movements of savage fury, that the beast had exhibited in its moment of power" (*The Pioneers* 313). The description here of the panther as savage, a term also used by Spofford, and Natty Bumppo's subsequent scalping of the dead panther in order to gain the bounty serve also to link Cooper's panther with Native Americans. Bounties were also placed on American Indians' scalps during the colonial period, a fact captive Hannah Duston exploited when she killed and scalped ten of her Indian captors in an infamous case in 1697. Duston received a bounty from the Massachusetts Bay Colony for the scalps (Derounian-Stodola 55-56). Given, then, the associations Cooper makes between the panther and American Indians, and given Elizabeth's attractions to the mysterious Oliver, who at this point in the novel is widely believed to be of American Indian descent, it seems likely that Elizabeth's recurring dreams of the savage beast's "power" suggest a suppressed sexual fascination with Oliver.

If Cooper's rendering of a panther attack highlighted issues of race and sexuality, William Gilmore Simms's 1869 serialized novel, *The Cub of the Panther; A Mountain Legend,* elucidates the trope's connection to motherhood. Simms portrays a panther stalking a pregnant woman on a deserted mountain through a raging blizzard, describing her terror in a way reminiscent of descriptions of Indian attacks:

[S]he hears the shrill but soft cry of her fierce pursuer in the distance; as she hears his stealthy foot approaching on the snow; as she feels his hot breath borne to her on the wind; as she beholds him crouching, in a very ball of muscle, and preparing to make his final leap upon his prey, while his small red eyes flash out with demoniac appetite.

(155)

Simms records the origin of this scene in his 1847 journal of his travels through the mountain regions of North Carolina. He jots down references to having heard a folk legend about the panther: "Green's wife story of the male panther—The appetite of the beast for women in pregnancy & c—Horrid story of his eating one in this situation & of the discovery of her remains by her husband" (qtd. in Simms 273). The appetite of the savage panther for pregnant women echoes Mary Rowlandson's description of the slaying of the pregnant Goodwife Joslin, who is described by Rowlandson as having been stripped naked and tortured until death by the Algonquins holding her captive (20).

While captivity narratives, the folklore surrounding panthers, and other literary renditions of panther attacks from important cultural frameworks for Spofford's story, another significant context exists in discourses of motherhood. Nineteenth-century beliefs regarding pregnancy held that there was a direct correspondence between a mother's emotional state and her offspring's physical and emotional nature:

[I]t was a common conviction that sudden frights, strong passions, or ungratified longings for peculiar things would disfigure the child. The theory that a mother can impress her child is an ancient explanation for hereditary deformities and character traits. . . . The "passions and surfeits" of the mother made strange impressions on the infant, even affecting its soul.

(Scholten 20)

Women's desires, then, could be written on the child; the exterior of the offspring could reveal the woman's inmost longings.

The influence of the mother's emotions continued into her child's infancy. Lydia Maria Child emphasizes in *The Mother's Book* (1831) how the mother's emotions might mark not only the exterior but also the interior of the child:

[T]he mother should keep her own spirit in tranquility and purity; for it is beyond all doubt that the state of a mother affects her child. . . . Children have died in convulsions, in consequence of nursing a mother, while under the influence of violent passion or emotion; and who can tell how much of *moral* evil may be traced to the states of mind indulged by a mother, while tending the precious little being, who receives everything from her? Therefore the first rule, and the most important of all, in education, is, that a mother govern her own feelings, and keep her heart and conscience pure.

(3-4)

If "the child was the mother reborn" as, according to Jan Lewis, one author of a conduct book has maintained (216), then Spofford's protagonist's newborn must represent all of those passions and emotions that the protagonist had learned to repress within herself in order to be a proper mother as prescribed by Child. The woman's offspring, significantly, takes the shape of a panther, one of the most dreaded predators of the eastern seaboard, associated with the terrors of the wilderness by the early colonists, and hunted nearly to extinction by the time Spofford was writing. This was an animal whose agility and power had given it special status with American Indians, and whose ritual killing was a symbol of status and masculinity for white American men of the period. As portrayed in the story, it is a snarling, spitting, violent beast, uncontrolled and irreclaimably wild. The protagonist has left behind the domestic realm, husband, and child, to enter the wilderness and give birth to another self, a self that is unrestrained, passionate, and undomesticated. This self is animal and native, and has, in turn, taken the proper wife and mother captive.

The protagonist's task, then, is to subdue and constrain the panther-self in order to preserve herself from utter destruction: the release of such emotion and passion spells the potential death of the woman. Her singing of various songs throughout the night becomes a self-preserving act and a means of subduing the emotions represented by the panther. Art is thus employed in the service of patriarchy. Anne Dahlke has argued that the woman functions as a feminist heroine through her discovery and celebration of her artistic voice (74-81). This reading is enticing because of the apparent power the woman finds in the exercise of her voice, especially given the ways in which western culture has tended to sunder creativity from procreativity. Smith has explored how the "maternal (reproductive) body signified the opposite of artistic production" in the nineteenth century, creating a "disjunction between cerebral and corporeal conception" (*Conceived by Liberty* 2, 7). Susan Stanford Friedman has demonstrated how even the language of childbirth has enforced such a disjunction: "*Creation* is the act of the mind that brings something new into existence. *Procreation* is the act of the body that reproduces the species" (373). It is tempting, then, to articulate a reading that posits that the dual experiences of sexuality and childbirth in the tree have enabled this heroine to join her procreative with her creative functions in a celebration of the possibilities for female artistry, thus resisting the cultural bifurcation of the two.

It is important to remember, however, that Spofford's protagonist is a double-victim in this story: a rape victim and the victim of a reproductive process that seems forced upon her. She seems to exhibit what Richard Henry Dana described of his wife's labor in 1842: "All self control is gone & the woman lies a mere passive instrument in the hands of an irresistible power" (qtd. in Hoffert 76). She does not want to give birth to this other self that is represented by the panther, and she does not willingly mother it; rather, she maintains it only to preserve her life. Indeed, in the medical diagnoses of the period, the protagonist might be viewed as exhibiting symptoms of puerperal insanity. Doctors believed that women were especially susceptible to this condition because of "the shock of giving birth, and by the exhaustion induced by nursing the baby" (Hoffert 114), the figurative situation of the protagonist in this story. Doctors identified in women thus afflicted an inability "to fulfill their role as mothers" and "an aversion to the newborn" (Hoffert 114-15). The woman's singing, then, is not a creative act bringing self-fulfillment and satisfaction, but a desperate one that carries with it a physical and emotional toll.

Any reading celebrating the protagonist as an artist figure also obscures the fact that the protagonist's singing serves to reconcile her to her death and to God, the ultimate patriarch. She loses her voice upon the appearance of her husband and child not because the domestic suppresses her artistic creativity but because her singing was only a stand-in for the constraining authority of her husband; it is no longer necessary as he reassumes his place of authority, gun in hand. The panther, representing suppressed emotion, has been kept subdued all night by the woman and is eventually killed by the husband, an act that returns the protagonist to her roles as wife and mother and sends her back to the domestic sphere. The irony of the end of the story, when they discover that their home has been destroyed by Native Americans, is that just when the woman thinks she has regained security in her family and in her home, she experiences the falseness of that illusion. The scripted narrative she has been enacting through her singing and her return to her proper roles is violently destroyed with the burning of her home. She and her husband must now create a new narrative, hence the significance of the last line: "[T]he world was all before them, where to choose" (96).

In this essay, I have traced the relationships between captivity narratives, panther imagery, and conduct literature as they come together in Spofford's story in a provocative meditation on the violence motherhood does to women, especially in a culture that consistently associates women with procreation rather than creation. The suggestiveness of the title, **"Circumstance,"** further highlights the junctures between Spofford's story and other cultural discourses. As defined by Webster in 1847, "circumstance" has a literal meaning of "that which stands around or near" and a related meaning of "something attending, appendant, or relative to a fact, or case: a particular thing, which though not essential to an action, in some way affects it" (207). Interestingly, none of the contexts I have examined hit directly upon

the meanings cited above: surely the captivity motif, the panther images, and the status of the woman as a mother are all directly and essentially relevant to the story, however interpreted. Indeed, it is necessary to look elsewhere for the circumstance "stand[ing] around" the text yet nowhere directly referred to in it.

The publication of the story during the period immediately preceding the Civil War raises the possibility that Spofford's invocation of the captivity narrative genre represents a displacement of her meditations on the heightening conflict between the North and South onto the similarly violence-marked period of colonial Indian-white warfare. To be sure, the story seems upon first glance to have little to do with the conflict that would soon consume the nation. However, the stark representation of violence within the story—including the aggressive assault of the panther on the woman and images of bloody wounds and possible dismemberment—indicates an oblique connection. The woman's vision of the winding sheet and auditory hallucination of the voice repeating "The Lord have mercy on the people" sound an almost prophetic tone when considered in relation to the impending conflict (85).

Without question, the story explores the issues of rebellion and division that Elizabeth Young has described as characteristic of women's Civil War writing (20). Indeed, it is possible to chart a Civil War analogy in the predicament of this mother of two children. One of the children has "fringed-gentian eyes," "chubby fists," and "fine breezy hair" (87), while the other has eyes "like balls of red fire," "gnashing" "white tusks," and "hot, foetid breath" (86-87). Perhaps the firstborn, human child symbolizes the north, slumbering under the watchful eye of the father (i.e., president), while the dangerous and angry panther represents the rebellious south.[9] The woman, according to this reading, becomes a figure of a United States that has birthed two radically different siblings.[10] To paraphrase Young, Spofford here gives a mother to the "story of national self-division" (1). The protagonist's salvation lies with the human child and its father; her destruction is threatened by the panther. Ironically, the ending of the story shows the home destroyed regardless of the outcome of the conflict. Perhaps that is Spofford's most prescient comment on the effects of wars within and without.

Notes

1. The few critics who have considered the story have generated a plethora of possible interpretations, indicating the richness of its symbolic structure. "Circumstance" has been variously interpreted within a Christian framework as a spiritual test (Bendixen xxvii; Dahlke 73; Fetterley 267), within a feminist framework as the story of the development of the woman artist (Bendixen xxvi;

Dahlke 74; Fetterley 264), as a reworking of the male initiation story epitomized by Nathaniel Hawthorne's "Young Goodman Brown" (Bendixen xvii; Dahlke 81-82), within a literary-historical framework as a commentary on the inadequacies of realism (Dahlke 74), and as a meditation on the relationship between author and reading public in the mid-nineteenth century (Bendixen xxvi-xxvii).

2. In the nineteenth century, as Judith Fetterley has explained, the language Spofford uses to describe the attack of the panther on the woman "constitutes a familiar code for referring to unrestrained male sexuality. . . . The woman's experience can be read, then, as an experience of 'rape'" (266). Bendixen also reads this story as one depicting sexual violence (xxvii).

3. Shirley Samuels has suggested that it is possible to infer that the protagonist is returning home from attending another woman's labor and delivery (Response). The story refers to "a sick neighbor" and the fact that the woman has been exhausted by the exercise of "care and sympathy" (84).

4. Tawny in color, the eastern panther is an animal that has been variously known by the names of mountain lion, cougar, "painter," catamount, puma, and American lion. See Parker for a discussion of the panther's history and cultural significance.

5. I owe thanks to Bonnie Blackwell for first suggesting this resemblance to me.

6. Fetterley is the only commentator on the story to have remarked upon its racial dynamics. She concludes that "'Circumstance' exemplifies the insidiousness and pervasiveness of the racist imagination in white American literature" (267).

7. Although captivities taking place in New England during the colonial period (the setting of Spofford's story) did not typically involve rape, nineteenth-century captivities occurring in the west often did, a fact exploited in the increasingly fictionalized and sensationalized captivity narratives of the nineteenth century (Derounian-Stodola and Levernier 3-4). Spofford, writing in the mid-nineteenth century, explores the threat of sexual violation contained within contemporary captivity narratives in her story despite the fact that she is writing about an earlier period and situating her story in New England.

8. As June Namias writes, "[N]ineteenth-century cultural frontier history thus juxtaposes the ascendancy of white male supremacy from the mountain to the prairie, while simultaneously depicting a weak, infantilized female needing male protection against the evil of Indian wildness" (70).

9. Spofford's abolitionist tendencies are described by Bendixen (xvii).

10. Smith mentions that Columbia was often imbued with maternal imagery during the post-revolutionary period (*Conceived by Liberty* 11), but Young argues that "the literature of the Civil War regularly underscores and capitalizes on the generative power of masculinity," enabling a "fantasy of self-fathering" (1).

Works Cited

Bendixen, Alfred. Introduction. *The Amber Gods and Other Stories.* New Brunswick: Rutgers UP, 1989. ix-xxxiv.

Cooper, James Fenimore. *The Last of the Mohicans.* 1826. New York: Oxford UP, 1998.

———. *The Pioneers.* 1823. *Cooper: The Leatherstocking Tales.* Vol. 1. New York: Library of America, 1994. 1-465.

Child, Lydia Maria. *The Mother's Book.* 1831. New York: Arno, 1972.

Dahlke, Anne. "'Circumstance' and the Creative Woman: Harriet Prescott Spofford." *Arizona Quarterly* 41.1 (1985): 71-85.

Derounian-Stodola, Kathryn Zabelle, ed. *Women's Indian Captivity Narratives.* New York: Penguin, 1998.

Derounian-Stodola, Kathryn Zabelle, and James Levernier. *The Indian Captivity Narrative* 1550-1900. New York: Twain, 1993.

Eiger, Marvin S., and Sally Wendkos Olds. *The Complete Book of Breastfeeding.* New York: Workman, 1987.

Fetterley, Judith. Commentary. *Provisions: A Reader from Nineteenth-Century Women.* Bloomington: Indiana UP, 1985. 261-68.

Friedman, Susan Stanford. "Creativity and the Childbirth Metaphor: Gender Difference in Literary Discourse." *Feminisms: An Anthology of Literary Theory and Criticism.* Ed. Robyn R. Warhol and Diane Price Herndl. New Brunswick: Rutgers UP, 1991. 371-96.

Hoffert, Sylvia D. *Private Matters: American Attitudes Toward Childbearing and Infant Nurture in the Urban North,* 1800-1860. Urbana: U of Illinois P, 1989.

Lewis, Jan. "'Mother's Love': The Construction of an Emotion in Nineteenth-Century America." *Social History and Issues in Human Consciousness: Some Interdisciplinary Connections.* Ed. Andrew E. Barnes and Peter N. Stearns. New York: New York UP, 1989. 209-29.

Namias, June. *White Captives: Gender and Ethnicity on the American Frontier.* Chapel Hill: U of North Carolina P, 1993.

Panther, Abraham. "Panther Captivity." 1787. Derounian-Stodola 81-90.

Parker, Gerry. *The Eastern Panther: Mystery Cat of the Appalachians.* Halifax, NS: Nimbus, 1998.

"Policy and Practice of the United States and Great Britain in the Treatment of Indians." *North American Review* 24 (1827): 365-443.

Rowlandson, Mary. *A True History of the Captivity and Restoration of Mrs. Mary Rowlandson.* 1682. Derounian-Stodola 1-51.

Samuels, Shirley. Response to "Violence in Nineteenth-Century American Women's Writing" panel. Society for the Study of American Women Writers: First International Conference. St. Anthony's Hotel, San Antonio. 16 Feb. 2001.

Scholten, Catherine. *Childbearing in American Society, 1650-1850.* New York: New York UP, 1985.

Simms, William Gilmore. *The Cub of the Panther; A Hunter Legend of the "Old North State".* 1869. Ed. Miriam Jones Shillingsburg. Fayetteville: U of Arkansas P, 1997.

Smith, Stephanie A. *Conceived by Liberty: Maternal Figures and Nineteenth-Century American Literature.* Ithaca: Cornell UP, 1994.

——. "Suckers." *Differences: A Journal of Feminist Cultural Studies* 10 (1998): 175-208.

Spofford, Harriet Prescott. "Circumstance." 1860. *The Amber Gods and Other Stories.* Ed. Alfred Bendixen. New Brunswick: Rutgers UP, 1989. 84-96.

Webster, Noah. *An American Dictionary of the English Language.* 1847. Chicago: 1890.

Yaeger, Patricia. "The Poetics of Birth." *Discourses of Sexuality: From Aristotle to AIDS.* Ed. Domna C. Stanton. Ann Arbor: U of Michigan P, 1992. 262-96.

Young, Elizabeth. *Disarming the Nation: Women's Writing and the American Civil War.* Chicago: U of Chicago P, 1999.

Birgit Spengler (essay date January 2004)

SOURCE: Spengler, Birgit. "Gendered Vision(s) in the Short Fiction of Harriet Prescott Spofford." *Legacy* 21, no. 1 (January 2004): 68-73.

[*In the following essay, Spengler assesses the function of the visual arts in "The Amber Gods," "Desert Sands," and "Mr. Furbush."*]

In *Techniques of the Observer,* Jonathan Crary describes important changes in visual technology and visual culture that predate both the advent of impressionism and Wharton's or James's obsession with observers and beautiful objects. Crary has located a break with the hitherto dominant perspectivalist scopic regime in the early nineteenth century. I will argue that this break is reflected in the fiction of Harriet Prescott Spofford (1835-1921), a central but as yet underestimated writer in the American literary tradition, especially with regard to issues of vision. My general thesis is that a strong interest in questions of vision goes further back than the rise of impressionism and that there is a tradition in American women's writing that is concerned with vision and visual structures from the middle of the nineteenth century to the present. Spofford's concern with vision places her in this tradition and renders her a significant example of the inextricable links between vision and gender.

In the following, I will investigate Spofford's interest in vision in three areas: visual technological innovations, questions of artistic representation in the fine arts, and the implications of social regimes of vision with regard to gender. I will argue that Spofford's depiction of visual practices and her ambivalence about the changes she describes indicate a crisis in seeing that is closely linked to her examination of gender relations. But before I concentrate on Spofford, I briefly want to come back to the break Crary has described, to explain why and how questions of "looking" had already become increasingly important during the early and mid-nineteenth century.

At the beginning of the nineteenth century, the camera obscura, relying on the principles of Cartesian perspectivalism, had served as an example for both the functioning of perception and epistemological insight for at least two hundred years. According to this model, vision is primarily in the service of a nonsensory faculty of understanding, knowledge is founded on a supposedly objective view of the world. The light falling through the hole in the camera obscura corresponds to the light of reason in the inner space of the mind that alone facilitates knowledge of the world. The camera obscura decorporealizes vision and performs a process of individuation. It relies on the assumption of a profound distinction between interior observer and exterior world, and it presupposes a quasi-immaterial and monocular observer.

Physical research, physiological discoveries, and philosophical inquiries into the possibilities of human understanding from the early 1800s onward undermine the camera obscura model of vision in various ways and render the relation between observer and world more ambivalent. New scientific findings emphasize the binocularity of human sight, acknowledge its temporality, locate vision in the materiality of the body, and thus endow the observer with "a new perceptual autonomy and productivity" (Crary, "Modernizing" 35). Vision is considered subjective, temporal, and nonveridical. On the other hand, the merging of the domain of optics with new knowledge about the functioning of the body in the human sciences is part of the reorganization of knowledge and the increasing interest in controlling and utilizing the capacities of the human body as described by Foucault. The looking subject is positioned at this watershed between old and new understandings of vision, between notions of objective truth and subjective insight as well as between autonomy, standardization, and regulation. The boom in the invention of optical devices in the middle decades of the nineteenth century brought publicity to new knowledge about human sight and ruptured the assumptions about human vision of a broad public.

In Spofford's stories, references to optical devices, physical phenomena, and the visual arts give evidence of her knowledge of how such elements reflect changes in understanding the world, their consequences, and, possibly, their epistemological implications. Even though she does not focus on issues of vision exclusively, they form a continuous sublayer and often have a considerable influence on plot and/or characters.

In the detective story **"Mr. Furbush,"** for example, a murderess is hunted down by means of photographic evidence and the relatively new possibility of the almost infinite enlargement of a print. In Spofford's description of this process of revelation, the camera, in conjunction with the sunlight falling through its shutter, functions as a technology of truth: "[T]he sun had made a revelation of that room's interior upon this sheet of sensitized paper, his Ithuriel's spear had touched this shapeless darkness and turned it into form and truth" (624). Milton's angel Ithuriel, whose spear's touch exposes the devil's disguise and makes him appear in his true form, is used as a metaphor for the epistemological possibilities of a new visual technology. Moreover, the camera functions as a means for observation and control. The countless windows of the hotel where the murder has been committed, and the camera eye, accidentally focusing on the window where the deed took place, are reminiscent of Bentham's Panopticon where observation is most effective when the inmate is under the constant threat of surveillance. In **"Mr. Furbush,"** photography renders the possibilities for observation and surveillance both more consistent and more unpredictable.

However, even though the camera figures as a means to reinstate truth and order, its epistemic power is not unreservedly embraced in the story. Significantly, it is the detective, himself a figure of enlightenment, justice, and order, whose qualms suggest a profound ambivalence about the possibilities and consequences of new visual technology that lie at the heart of the story. Several factors emphasize this ambivalence. The camera, even

though it plays a pivotal role in convicting the murderess by recording her deed, can only render a superficial truth without accounting for the "whys" and "hows" of the murder. Finding the murderess and understanding her motives are presented as matters of chance and human intuition and thus question the unlimited power of technological innovations. Furthermore, by occasioning a revelation of the woman's innermost being, the camera helps to bring things to light that might be better left in the dark. Mr. Furbush's unease about his discovery, his sympathetic perceptions of the murderess, and his feeling of guilt after she drops dead in the shock of discovery leave the preying/prying on human beings and the human soul afforded by the camera morally questionable. The end of the story emphasizes Furbush's conflicting impulses: he refrains from using the knowledge provided by the camera and quits his job because he has "sickened of the business" (626), but he yields to his fascination with the possibilities of photography by opening up a photo studio. Finally, the narrative voice also accentuates undecidability and ambivalency by rendering the end of the story in an enigmatic and roundabout way that leaves the reader unsure about how to interpret story-line and Mr. Furbush's principles. Thus, while the possibilities of new visual technologies are in a way celebrated in Spofford's story, she also presents a profound cautioning of its possible consequences and effects on human beings and leaves detective and reader in a state of ambiguity.

On a second level, Spofford's interest in nineteenth-century debates on vision and optics is reflected in her concern with color, light, and perception, issues she focuses on in relation to questions of artistic representation in texts such as **"The Amber Gods"** and **"Desert Sands."** Both stories allude to changes in the fine arts that took place during the first half of the century and that were aligned with the break Crary describes. From at least the 1830s onward, painters like Joseph Mallord William Turner (1775-1851) and Eugène Delacroix (1798-1863) had begun to express "the impact of . . . scientific, technological, and economic developments" in painting (Jay 153). Both artists employed color in an increasingly liberal way, and Turner's rediscovery of Leonardo's *sfumato* challenged "the geometricalized optics of the perspectivalist tradition" (Jay 153-54). Spofford's depiction of art registers these changes and recalls both Delacroix and Turner as well as the Orientalist fashion in painting of her time. Sydney's career as an artist in **"Desert Sands"** evokes Delacroix's biography and Turner's colors, while the artist Vaughan Rose in **"The Amber Gods"** reflects the general trend toward a liberation of color embodied by both artists.[1]

Sydney's journey to Africa, initiated by his fascination for the exotic Vespasia, is an attempt to invigorate his art with new impressions. His working process and the impact on his art of new visual experiences recall Delacroix's journey to North Africa in 1832. Like Delacroix, Sydney unremittingly fills his sketchbooks with sketches and scenes that he transforms into paintings after his return home. Furthermore, the African experience triggers his use of increasingly strong and brilliant colors. Africa is a "feast of lustre" and a "debauch of light" that makes him realize that *chiaro-oscuro* is a technique of the past (212, 203). After his return home, Sydney describes the world in colors reminiscent of Turner's great paintings: "[G]old has reddened and deepened and vanished in purple, . . . the air is interfused with a soft voluptuous sense that I feel as I might feel a new tint, be it mauve or fuchsine" (175). He tries the strength of his palette to the utmost and creates his masterpieces (213). However, Sydney's achievement involved both the exploitation of the exotic and the familiar, represented by the two women characters, and is reminiscent of nineteenth-century imperialist practice.[2] Sydney's onsetting blindness at the height of his vision suggests that, metaphorically speaking, his artistic development is a process of darkness rather than enlightenment.

In **"The Amber Gods,"** the male artist Vaughan Rose goes through a similar development toward more color to strengthen his art. He learns "the sacredness of color" through the female narrator, Yone, the story's "Africa" in the sense of the culturally other and provider of the colorful (72). However, once the artist has exploited her attractions and has sufficiently appropriated color, he detaches himself from her and employs his skills to subjugate Yone—i.e., the "other"—in painting.[3] In both stories, changes in the artist characters' understanding of art reflect that common ways of seeing and of rendering visual experience were in the process of being undermined. However, in both cases the negative implications of the gaze as a form of power and appropriation check any too enthusiastic espousal of the achievements so ruthlessly obtained.

With my third point, I want to show that Spofford's interest in issues of vision informs a more thoroughgoing concern with the gender implications of visual practices and the gaze. Her ambivalence toward new visual technologies and toward changes in perceiving the world in the fine arts, both indicative of a "crisis in seeing," inform her sense of what could be described as a "crisis" in gender relations, rendered specifically in terms of the visual relations between the sexes. It is particularly through the gaze that the characters in some of Spofford's best stories negotiate power and gender relations and that typical gender roles are subverted.

The power and gender implications of looking and being looked at are at the center of Spofford's story **"The Amber Gods."** Like her namesake the Renaissance painter Giorgione, Yone Willoughby, the posthumous female narrator of the story, pays homage to the female

body unreservedly and unashamedly dwells in her own beauty. If Giorgione's *Venus* was revolutionary because he made a female body without supplementary surroundings or attributes the sole topic for a large canvas painting, Spofford repeats this revolutionary gesture by making a throughly self-absorbed and unconventional heroine the visual and narratorial focus of her story.

Yone's ambivalent and unconventional role in scopic relations suggests that traditional gender roles have become unstable. She assumes a double status as both subject and object of looks that rejects binary classifications. As befits her role as narrator, Yone asserts her point of view and her right to look by observing and interpreting the other fictional characters. Specifically, it is the artist Vaughan Rose who becomes an object of her desirous gaze. He fills a traditionally female role in scopic relations, while Yone takes on the supposedly male part of the observer. Yone's descriptions of Rose in feminized terms further emphasize their role reversal. Even when Yone deliberately fashions herself as a beautiful sight for Rose or the reader, she does not turn into a passive object of the gaze. She controls and guides the reader's mental eye onto her body by way of her self-approving gaze into the mirror and, in a comparable way, she actively creates visual experiences for Rose. In contrast, the artist remains passive even in the process of perception. Yone's visual presence takes on the form of a dangerous invasion that is beyond Rose's control: she can "fill his gaze without any action from him" (48). Thus, it becomes clear that even when Yone bestows on him the role of the observer, Rose is not the "owner of the gaze" nor is he, per se, in a position of power.

While the first section of **"The Amber Gods"** strongly suggests a role reversal based on the visual relations between the sexes, the second part of the story is more ambivalent about the possibilities of changes in scopic regimes. It becomes clear that even though Yone has appropriated a look of her own, her gaze is of limited power unless she develops a technique or medium to render it in material form. Throughout the story, Yone asserts her subjectivity and rejects the attempts of male characters to impose their perspective—to speak for or about her—but she cannot voice her point of view without reverting to "other folks' words" (51), that is without referring to a male cultural tradition that has provided no specific outlet for female self-expression. This absence turns out to be crucial in the second part of the story and changes both scopic relations and relations of power between the two characters. Whereas before the wedding Rose tries in vain to enforce his vision and to capture Yone on canvas, after the marriage his attempts to subsume Yone as an object of his gaze finally succeed. He fixes her into a formula, hangs her up, "revealed and bare" beside her ancestors, and leaves the real Yone an "empty husk" (80). And yet, despite the fact that Yone's death at the end of the story seems to privilege Rose's vision of her as an object of the past, she contests his point of view even from beyond the grave. In telling her own story in a "posthumous reverie" (St. Armand 99), Yone demonstrates that she will *not* be silenced and will *not* let her gaze be ursuped. Yone's tale, the "posthumous reverie," can be interpreted as her discovery of a form of self-expression and self-assertion. Despite the fact that within the narrative this self-expression is ambivalent as it takes on the immaterial form of a ghost speaking, Spofford's story, rendered in the material and public form of printed pages in one of the most prestigious nineteenth-century magazines, demonstrates a woman's succesful appropriation of a voice of her own.

In her exploration of a nineteenth-century discourse on seeing, Spofford is concerned with various aspects of visual practices, whether connected to visual technology, the fine arts, or gender relations. Her ambivalence about the possibilities and consequences of new developments in scopic relations indicates a "crisis in seeing," a rupture between "old" and "new" ways of seeing that Spofford also perceived at the heart of changes in gender relations. She conveys the instability of traditional gender roles as the instability of scopic relations between the sexes and shows the importance of the gaze in determining gender relations. The fact that woman's role in gender relations and her social position are repeatedly negotiated visually in Spofford's stories expresses her sense that the far-reaching consequences of the "crisis in seeing" would not leave gender relations untouched.

Notes

I am grateful to the participants of the American Studies colloquium at Goethe University, Frankfurt am Main, for their stimulating comments on an earlier version of this paper.

1. Turner's paintings *The Burning of the Houses of Lords and Commons* (1834) and *Slave Ship (Slavers Throwing Overboard the Dead and Dying, Thyphon Coming On)* (1840) seem to be fitting examples that demonstrate the dissolving of form resulting from Turner's *sfumato* technique, his fascination with light, and his liberation of color. Delacroix's painting *Löwenjagd* (*Lion Chase*) (c. 1860), on view in the Kunsthalle, Bremen, Germany, clearly participates in the Orientalist fashion of the time in terms of subject matter. Furthermore, the scene—depicted mostly in yellow, white, and light shades of red and blue—is so intensely infused with light that the forms and outlines of the objects in the painting begin to dissolve.

2. Turner's *Slave Ship* combines the liberation of color described by Spofford with her critique of

the implications and consequences of imperialist practice. Schueller has provided a more detailed analysis of Spofford's critique of imperialist appropriation and the concomitant subordination of women. Fast has emphasized the interdependence of racial and sexual stereotypes in "Desert Sands."

3. In contrast to Bendixen, I do not read Yone as a representation of sensuous experience that needs to be overcome by the artist. My reading of this aspect of the relationship between the two characters agrees with that of Logan, who sees the story as a critique of Rose's colonization, appropriation, and destruction of Yone's body.

Works Cited

Bendixen, Alfred. Introduction. *"The Amber Gods" and Other Stories.* By Harriet Prescott Spofford. Ed. Alfred Bendixen. New Brunswick: Rutgers UP, 1989. ix-xxxiv.

Crary, Jonathan. *Techniques of the Observer: On Vision and Modernity in the Nineteenth Century.* Cambridge: MIT P, 1990.

———. "Modernizing Vision." *Vision and Visuality.* Ed. Hal Foster. New York: New, 1988. 29-44.

Fast, Robin Riley. "Killing the Angel in Spofford's 'Desert Sands' and 'The South Breaker.'" *Legacy* 11 (1994): 37-54.

Foucault, Michel. *Discipline and Punish: The Birth of the Prison.* 1976. Trans. Alan Sheridan. New York: Pantheon, 1979.

Jay, Martin. *Downcast Eyes: The Denigration of Vision in Twentieth-Century French Thought.* Berkeley: U of California P, 1993.

Logan, Lisa M. "Race, Romanticism, and the Politics of Feminist Literary Study: Harriet Prescott Spofford's 'The Amber Gods.'" *Legacy* 18 (2001): 35-51.

Schueller, Malini Johar. *U.S. Orientalisms: Race, Nation, and Gender in Literature, 1790-1890.* Ann Arbor: U of Michigan P, 1998.

Spofford, Harriet Prescott. "The Amber Gods." *"The Amber Gods" and Other Stories.* Ed. Alfred Bendixen. New Brunswick: Rutgers UP, 1989. 37-83.

———. "Desert Sands." *The Amber Gods and Other Stories.* Boston: Ticknor and Fields, 1863. 175-215.

———. "Mr. Furbush." *Harper's New Monthly Magazine* 30 (1865): 623-26.

St. Armand, Barton Levi. "'I Must Have Died at Ten Minutes Past One': Posthumous Reverie in Harriet Prescott Spofford's 'The Amber Gods.'" *The Haunted Dusk: American Supernatural Fiction, 1820-1920.* Ed. Howard Kerr, John W. Crowley, and Charles L. Crow. Athens: U of Georgia P, 1983. 99-119.

218

FURTHER READING

Criticism

Bendixen, Alfred. "Harriet Prescott Spofford (1835-1921)." In *Nineteenth-Century American Women Writers: A Bio-Bibliographical Critical Sourcebook*, edited by Denise D. Knight and Emmanuel S. Nelson, pp. 377-85. Westport, Conn.: Greenwood Press, 1997.

> Discusses Spofford's life and works in the context of American literature.

St. Armand, Barton Levi. "'I Must Have Died at Ten Minutes Past One': Posthumous Reverie in Harriet Prescott Spofford's 'The Amber Gods.'" In *The Haunted Dusk: American Supernatural Fiction, 1820-1920*, edited by Howard Kerr, John W. Crowley, and Charles L. Crow pp. 101-19. Athens: University of Georgia Press, 1983.

> Explores Spofford's narrative technique and the supernatural elements in "The Amber Gods."

Shinn, Thelma J. "Harriet Prescott Spofford: A Reconsideration." *Turn-of-the-Century Women* 1, no. 1 (summer 1984): 36-45.

> Examines the treatment of women in Spofford's fiction.

Sussex, Lucy. "The First American Woman to Write Detective Fiction? Harriet Prescott Spofford." *Mystery Scene*, no. 68 (2000): 44.

> Examines three of Spofford's early detective stories and emphasizes her significance in the history of crime fiction.

Additional coverage of Spofford's life and career is contained in the following sources published by Thomson Gale: *Contemporary Authors*, **Vol. 201;** *Dictionary of Literary Biography*, **Vols. 74, 221; and** *Literature Resource Center.*

Mark Twain
1835-1910

(Pseudonym of Samuel Langhorne Clemens; also wrote under the pseudonyms Thomas Jefferson Snodgrass, Josh, Muggins, Soleather, Grumbler, and Sieur Louis de Conte) American short story writer, novelist, essayist, travel writer, and autobiographer.

The following entry provides an overview of Twain's short fiction. For additional information on his life and short fiction career, see *SSC,* Volume 6; for discussion of the short story collection *The Mysterious Stranger,* see *SSC,* Volume 26; for discussion of the short story "The Celebrated Jumping Frog of Calaveras County," see *SSC,* Volume 34.

INTRODUCTION

Widely regarded as the father of modern American literature, Twain is one of the most famous authors in the English language. Although he is best known for his novels about the iconic Tom Sawyer and Huckleberry Finn, Twain also produced numerous works of short fiction, ranging from "The Celebrated Jumping Frog of Calaveras County" to "The Man That Corrupted Hadleyburg." Firmly rooted in the frontier humorist tradition, Twain's short stories and sketches often blur the boundaries between journalism and fiction, easily moving from factual narrative to humorous exaggeration and burlesque. In addition, his stories accurately duplicate regional idiom and typically express a vital desire for social justice and egalitarian ideals, exemplifying American pragmatism.

BIOGRAPHICAL INFORMATION

Clemens was born the son of a justice of the peace in the frontier town of Florida, Missouri. At the age of four, Clemens moved with his family to the Mississippi River town of Hannibal, Missouri, which would inspire many of the settings and characters of his early fiction. After his father died in 1847, he quit school and was apprenticed full-time to a local printer. When his brother launched the *Hannibal Journal* in 1850, Clemens set type for the newspaper, which published several of his first sketches, but he left Hannibal soon afterwards. During the 1850s Clemens briefly traveled to the East

Coast and then wandered the Midwestern countryside, working first as an itinerant printer and later as a travel correspondent for his brother's newspaper.

In 1857 Twain boarded a Mississippi River steamboat as an apprentice to the pilot, earning his own pilot's license in 1859 and plying the river until the Civil War halted commercial traffic. In 1861 Clemens enlisted in the Confederate militia but shortly joined his brother in the Nevada Territory where he mined silver and began reporting for the *Territorial Enterprise* in Virginia City. There, in 1863, he adopted the pseudonym "Mark Twain," a nautical term signifying the water depth for safe passage of vessels. In 1865 Twain reported an old folktale he heard at a California mining camp, which won him national attention and later became the title story of his first book, *The Celebrated Jumping Frog of Calaveras County* (1867).

After concluding a travel assignment to the Sandwich Islands (present-day Hawaii) in 1866 for the *Sacra-*

mento Union, Twain embarked on a five-month steamship tour of the Mediterranean region for the *Alta California* and *New York Tribune* newspapers, which periodically printed his humorous correspondence detailing the clash between New and Old World cultures. Twain later collected these hugely popular letters in *The Innocents Abroad* (1869) and soon became one of the most sought-after humorists on the American lecture circuit. In 1870 he married Olivia Langdon and settled in Hartford, Connecticut, the following year.

Although he continued to entertain audiences in the United States and abroad with popular lecture tours for several years after his wedding, Twain began to write in earnest. During the next two decades, he published most of his best-known works including *Roughing It* (1872), *The Gilded Age* (1873), *The Adventures of Tom Sawyer* (1876), *The Prince and the Pauper* (1881), *Life on the Mississippi* (1883), *The Adventures of Huckleberry Finn* (1884), and *A Connecticut Yankee in King Arthur's Court* (1889). The unprecedented commercial success of his literary endeavors made Twain one of the richest men in the United States during the 1880s, but large financial investments in the ill-fated Paige typesetting machine and the collapse of his own publishing company forced him to file bankruptcy in 1894. To avoid creditors Twain copyrighted subsequent writings in his wife's name, among them the novel *Pudd'nhead Wilson* (1894), and to regain solvency he traveled the globe on a year-long lecture tour, settling in England to write *Following the Equator* (1897), an essay collection describing the tour. While there, he was notified that his favorite daughter had died from meningitis. Her death so badly shocked him that his later work reflects a philosophical turn toward introspection, pessimism, and polemic. In 1900 Twain returned to the United States and published the short story collection *The Man That Corrupted Hadleyburg.*

During the last decade of his life, Twain continued to write through his bitterness and grief, which further deepened after the deaths of his wife and another daughter in 1904. In 1906 Twain began compiling his memoirs, and he traveled to England to accept a literary degree from Oxford University in 1907. Twain died in 1910 at Stormfield, an Italianate villa in Redding, Connecticut, built with proceeds from serialized excerpts of the autobiography that he published prior to his death.

MAJOR WORKS OF SHORT FICTION

Like his more famous novels, Twain's short stories and sketches use deadpan humor, frontier idiom, and satire to expose the foibles and the folly of humanity. First published in the *Saturday Press* in 1865 as "Jim Smiley and His Jumping Frog," "The Celebrated Jumping Frog of Calaveras County" experiments with the narrative technique, point of view, and language that Twain employed in his subsequent works. The tale is framed by a story about a genteel Easterner who is sidetracked from locating an acquaintance by a frontiersman who spins a colorful yarn about a frog-jumping contest. In his story, a compulsive gambler, who wins money by betting on a pet frog that he trained to jump, is duped by a wily stranger, who takes the gambler's bet and then, while the gambler is distracted, fills the frog's gullet with buckshot, rendering the frog immobile. Another early story, "The Great Landslide Case," demonstrates how Twain exploited the boundary between journalism and fiction. Originally published in 1863 as a newspaper sketch about a mock trial following a Nevada landslide and then completely revised in 1870 to exaggerate its scope and effects, this tale recounts an elaborate prank foisted upon a territorial attorney general, who discovers during the trial that the plaintiff was responsible for the catastrophe.

Other stories introduce themes and techniques that Twain later examined and used in his novels. For instance, "A True Story, Repeated Word for Word as I Heard It," first published in the *Atlantic Monthly* in 1874, represents Twain's treatment of the African American experience, realistically narrated in the idiom of former slaves. In this story, a domestic cook recalls the harsh circumstances of her own life as a slave, including her tireless efforts to reunite with her son. Twain's penchant for satire manifests itself in light-hearted sketches of Victorian domesticity and technological progress. For example, "Experience of the McWilliamses with Membranous Croup" (1875) details the domestic mishaps of Mortimer McWilliams and his wife acting upon their doctor's advice, while "The Loves of Alonzo Fitz Clarence and Rosannah Ethelton" (1877) traces the title couple's courtship and marriage via telephone, and "A Telephonic Conversation" (1879) illustrates the drawbacks of only hearing one side of a dialogue.

Some of Twain's stories are designed to make serious points about subjects ranging from human conscience and morality to the evils of war and materialism. In "The Facts Concerning the Recent Carnival of Crime in Connecticut" (1876), the narrator must kill his conscience—in the figure of a freak-show dwarf—so that he may embark upon a blissful crime spree, while "Edward Mills and George Benton" (1880) implicates the hypocrisy of smug reformers as an unworthy, profligate man consistently reaps life's rewards while his modest, virtuous cousin endures hardship and tragedy. Narrated from the perspective of a deserter, "The Private History of a Campaign That Failed" (1885) traces the adventures of a group of young Confederate militiamen who "play soldier" only when so inclined, until one day they mistakenly kill an unarmed man after heeding rumors about nearby enemy troops.

Framed as an arrogant anthropologist's record of the standards of Eskimo wealth, which resemble similar standards in the United States, "The Esquimau Maiden's Romance" (1893) recounts the tragedy of an Eskimo maiden whose suitor is wrongly suspected of stealing one of her rich father's prized fishhooks and then set adrift on an ice floe to perish. Often compared to the biblical account of the Fall, "The Man That Corrupted Hadleyburg" (1899) is one of the most anthologized works of American short fiction. The story concerns the inhabitants of a small town that prides itself on its wholesome virtue, which is undone after they unwittingly offend a passing stranger who sets in motion a meticulously contrived plan that reveals their greed and hypocrisy.

Twain's body of work also contains a number of posthumously published stories and sketches. "Huck Finn and Tom Sawyer among the Indians" represents Twain's plans to continue the adventures of his famous protagonists, which he ultimately abandoned. This long fragment portrays Native American culture in an unflattering light and also reflects Twain's growing pessimism about humanity. In it, Huck, Tom, and Jim initially set out to disprove the savage stereotype of Native Americans but eventually witness the brutal rape and murder of a pioneer family at the hands of Sioux warriors. In another episode, the sins of the white race are harshly portrayed as a military officer molests several young boys. Published nearly a century after it was written, the experimental "A Murder, a Mystery, and a Marriage" grew out of a literary competition among William Dean Howells, Twain, and other notable American authors. Starting with a basic plot outline, each author was to flesh out a narrative for subsequent publication in the *Atlantic Monthly*. Twain's tale of murder and deception centers on a mysterious Frenchman who courts the town beauty of a rural Missouri community.

CRITICAL RECEPTION

Although Twain published many stories and sketches throughout his career, few have received substantial critical attention. The majority of critics have focused on the short fiction written during the last two decades of his life, when his longing for an idealized past as a haven from a hostile present became pronounced. Indeed, many commentators have observed a subtle division in Twain's outlook on the human condition throughout his career, swinging between exuberant, even irreverent, humor on one hand and an almost misanthropic pessimism on the other. Nevertheless, most

scholars have perceived an authentic desire for social justice and egalitarianism informing all of Twain's writings. Along these lines, feminist critics have explored the cultural implications of Twain's use of transvestism in some stories, demonstrating how his cross-dressing characters and episodes challenged perceptions of gender and race during the late nineteenth century. Cultural historians have likewise investigated the subversive context of Twain's humor as well as his role in contemporaneous debates about Old and New World social values and American and indigenous cultures. Critics have also traced the role of Twain's journalistic habits in the creation of numerous short stories, identifying sources and explaining their significance. Above all, most scholars have credited Twain's idiomatic style with liberating American fiction from the staid influence of European literature.

PRINCIPAL WORKS

Short Fiction

The Celebrated Jumping Frog of Calaveras County and Other Sketches 1867
A True Story and the Recent Carnival of Crime 1877
The Stolen White Elephant 1882
Merry Tales 1892
Tom Sawyer Abroad, Tom Sawyer, Detective, and Other Stories 1896
The Man That Corrupted Hadleyburg and Other Stories and Essays 1900
A Dog's Tale 1904
The $30,000 Bequest and Other Stories 1906
The Mysterious Stranger and Other Stories 1922
The Adventures of Thomas Jefferson Snodgrass 1928
Jim Smiley and His Jumping Frog 1940
A Murder, A Mystery, and a Marriage 1945
The Complete Humorous Sketches and Tales [edited by Charles Neider] 1961
Early Tales and Sketches. 2 vols. [edited by Edgar M. Branch and Robert H. Hirst] 1979-81
Wapping Alice [edited by Hamlin Hill] 1981
Huck Finn and Tom Sawyer among the Indians and Other Unfinished Stories [edited by Dahlia Armon and Walter Blair] 1989

Other Major Works

The Innocents Abroad, or the New Pilgrims' Progress (letters) 1869
Roughing It (travel essay) 1872
The Gilded Age [with Charles Dudley Warner] (novel) 1873

CRITICISM

Wayne R. Kime (essay date winter 1990)

SOURCE: Kime, Wayne R. "Huck among the Indians: Mark Twain and Richard Irving Dodge's *The Plains of the Great West and Their Inhabitants.*" *Western American Literature* 24, no. 4 (winter 1990): 321-33.

[*In the following essay, Kime delineates the plot and character development of "Huck Finn and Tom Sawyer among the Indians," highlighting the characterization of Native Americans and contemplating Twain's reasons for abandoning the project.*]

While *Adventures of Huckleberry Finn* was going through the press during the summer of 1884, Mark Twain decided to write a sequel. His eight years of intermittent work on the novel had endeared the character of Huck Finn to him, and to further showcase his vagabond hero he planned to portray the fulfillment of Tom Sawyer's wish, expressed in the final chapter, that he, Huck, and Jim should "go for howling adventures amongst the Indians, over in the territory, for a couple of weeks or two."[1] Twain busied himself on and off with his new project for several weeks, but after completing nine chapters for a total of approximately 22,000 words he abandoned it, turning his mind to others among his multifarious undertakings. In later years he wrote further of both Huck and Tom, but so far as is known he never resumed work on this particular fragment.

The surviving text, entitled **"Huck Finn and Tom Sawyer among the Indians"** and edited by Walter Blair,[2] reveals that he was developing in his novel a contrast between romantic misconceptions of Indian character, all derived from books, and the less flattering profile enforced by experience of Indians at first hand. The contrast between romance and reality was of course a staple of Twain's comic repertoire, one he had often employed with happy results. Here, appropriately enough, Tom Sawyer serves as spokesman for the exalted ideas about Indians that the narrative reveals to be absurd. Why, then, did Mark Twain set aside this work, which seemed to offer so promising an opportunity to debunk false beliefs? The answer lies in his own beliefs about Indian character and in the specific Indian behavior he was dealing with. What he considered to be the reality about Indians was in its fullness far from comic. In fact, it was so troubling that it led him to set aside his new book as impracticable along the lines he had laid out in the initial chapters.

Twain had written about the Red Man on several occasions before he began **"Huck Finn and Tom Sawyer among the Indians."** He initiated his long campaign against James Fenimore Cooper's unrealistic portrayal of the Mingos and the Delawares as early as 1867, when he affirmed in an article for the San Francisco *Alta California* that the "Cooper Indians . . . died with their creator." In *Roughing It* (1872) he ironically represented himself as a naive "disciple of Cooper and a worshiper of the Red Man," recording his impressions of the Goshoot Indians of Utah, "the other 'Noble Red Men' that we (do not) read about." Shaken by the contrast to his expectations embodied by the wretched Goshoots, the young Twain is led "to examining authorities" in order to learn whether he has been viewing the Indian "through the mellow moonshine of romance." He reports his findings:

> The revelations that came were disenchanting. It is curious to see how quickly the paint and tinsel fell away from him and left him treacherous, filthy and repulsive—and how quickly the evidences accumulated that wherever one finds an Indian tribe he has only found Goshoots more or less modified by circumstances and surroundings—but Goshoots, after all.

Twain's self-portrayal in *Roughing It* and elsewhere suggests that any sentimental believer in the nobility of Indian character will come to his senses once he consults the "authorities" or observes Indians close up.[3]

In **"The Noble Red Man,"** published in *The Galaxy* for September 1870, he carries his indictment of Indians a long step further. Here his tone is not pleasant irony but outrage. Having summarized the conventional literary myth, he draws upon De Benneville Randolph Keim's *With Sheridan's Troopers on the Borders* (1870) to cite examples of Indian treachery, cruelty, and brutality toward frontier settlers and their families. Among the offenses he names are torture, rape, scalping, and the savages' "favorite mutilations," which "cannot be put into print." In light of these barbarities he takes issue with persons in the eastern states who set up a "wail of humanitarian sympathy" whenever they learn that the United States Army has dealt the offending brutes a well merited rebuke. As Twain represents him in this sketch, the Indian is "ignoble—base and treacherous, and hateful in every way."[4]

Mark Twain believed that his own limited contacts with Indians enabled him to speak of them with a certain authority. And so, when he encountered a new book by an acknowledged authority on Indian beliefs and behavior, a man of wide experience whose views tallied with his own, he studied that author with interest and approval. Such an individual was Lieutenant-Colonel Richard Irving Dodge, whose much-praised *The Plains of the Great West and Their Inhabitants* was issued by G. P. Putnam's Sons of New York in January 1877.[5] A career officer in the United States Army, Colonel Dodge had been stationed on the frontier for upwards of twenty years and had come to know various tribes of Indians intimately, both as peaceable acquaintances and as foes. His wideranging book, based almost entirely on his own observations and inferences, was in three parts: "The Plains," describing the geology, topography, weather, and techniques for safe travel in the region; "Game," recounting the habitats, habits, and best methods for bagging indigenous animals; and the longest section, "Indians," a cradle-to-grave account of native customs and beliefs. In this latter section Dodge sought to do justice to the praiseworthy elements of Indian character and also to show concern for the sufferings brought on the Indian population by the United States government and its citizens. But his main purpose was to annihilate with one telling stroke the persistent popular belief in the nobility of Indian character. This false notion, he wrote, was credited by those who took "Cooper's and other similar novels" as gospel or who were influenced by the "sentimental humanitarianism" preached by unscrupulous professed philanthropists (255). Practical experience of Indians resulted in a radically different conception, he claimed. Dodge went on to present a body of material that demonstrated what he considered the essential savagery of plains Indians. But he warned at the outset that cultivated persons might find it difficult to believe his statements. "As well undertake to give to a pure and innocent maiden a realising sense of the depths of degradation to which some of her sex have fallen," he wrote. "The truth is simply too shocking" (256).

Mark Twain read *The Plains of the Great West* with close attention,[6] and on February 22, 1877 he wrote William Dean Howells recommending, no doubt face-

tiously, that the soldier-author be made head of the "Indian Department," or Bureau of Indian Affairs. "*There's a man,*" he continued of Dodge, "who knows all about Indians, & yet has some humanity in him—(knowledge of Indians, & humanity, are seldom found in the same individual.)"[7]

When, more than seven years after his discovery of Colonel Dodge, Twain prepared to write a sequel to *Adventures of Huckleberry Finn,* he did not fail to recall how much he had been impressed by *The Plains of the Great West.* In accordance with his practice of reading up on a particular subject prior to writing of it, he directed his nephew and business associate Charles L. Webster to send "right away" the books he needed, "*personal narratives* of life & adventures out yonder on the plains & in the Mountains . . . especially life *among the Indians.*" He requested only one work specifically, "a book by *Lieut. Col. Dodge, USA*" whose exact title he could not recall. "I think he has written only the one book," he wrote, "& so any librarian can tell you the title of it."[8] But in fact Dodge was by now the author of two books about the plains, and Webster located a copy of the second one, *Our Wild Indians* (1882), an expanded but watered-down version of the section on Indians in *The Plains of the Great West.*[9] Besides what Webster sent him—*Our Wild Indians, The Life and Times of Hon. William F. Cody, Known as Buffalo Bill* (1879), and an unspecified "old frontier book"—Twain dipped into several other works dealing with Indians.[10] In drafting **"Huck Finn and Tom Sawyer among the Indians"** he gleaned details from all these sources, but as Walter Blair points out, the 375 annotations he had entered in his copy of *Our Wild Indians* suggest that Dodge became his premier authority.[11] Actually *The Plains of the Great West* proved even more useful to him than *Our Wild Indians.* By some means he turned up a copy of the earlier work—perhaps the one he had read seven years earlier—and looked through it again. As a result, he was able to appropriate much material from *The Plains of the Great West* that Dodge had not seen fit to include in *Our Wild Indians.*[12]

Twain made such extensive use of secondary sources because he wished to portray scenes and events that were characteristic of the plains but his own memory was insufficient as a resource. Even when at work on *Roughing It,* more than a decade earlier, he had confessed to his brother Orion that he had virtually no recollections of the stage journey from Missouri west to Virginia City they had made together in 1861. For his account of the plains in that book he had relied on hints from his reading and on notes supplied him by Orion.[13] Similarly in the present case, he sought out authentic details by searching through books.

Thus Twain's portrayal of Indian character and the behavior that manifests it derives almost exclusively from information he found in *The Plains of the Great West;*

and this material he wove deep into the fabric of his narrative. Dodge's multifaceted account of plains Indians touches on topics as diverse as religious beliefs, attitudes toward children, amusements, and tactics in war, and the novelist used many of these discussions. But the area of Indian behavior most central to his story line is their bestial cruelty, according to Dodge, toward their female captives. Through the greater part of the fragment Twain keeps this unsavory characteristic before the reader's consciousness yet just out of open view.

At the outset of the story Huck, Tom, and Jim are visiting at a hemp farm in western Missouri. Huck and Jim are content with the lazy life they lead, but Tom is restless and insists that they all "cut for the Injun country and go for adventures" (93). In response to his comrades' concern that Indians are said to be a "powerful ornery" lot (94), Tom refutes them with a 500-word panegyric that carries the day. The three set out, and after five days of travel they encounter a family also on their way west. These are the Millses—parents, three strapping sons, and two daughters, one seventeen and the other seven years of age. Peggy Mills, the elder daughter, is beautiful and kind, and she exerts the same effect upon Huck that Sophia Grangerford and Mary Jane Wilks had done. He admires her unreservedly, allowing that "mornings it warn't ever sun-up to me till she come out" (100). Huck, Tom, and Jim accompany the Mills family for two more weeks until one evening, camping along the Platte River, they meet a group of five Indians.

At this point Huck learns from Peggy that she is awaiting the arrival any day of her beau, Brace Johnson, a young frontiersman whom she is soon to marry and accompany to Oregon. Peggy tells Huck all about Brace, noting with regret that he is a bitter Indian hater. She wishes he were on the scene now, she says, to see how kind and friendly the Indians they have met really are. Laughingly, she pulls from her bosom a small dirk Brace Johnson has given her, explaining with fond incomprehension that he actually has made her promise to kill herself with it should she ever fall into the hands of Indians. Just as Peggy is showing the knife to Huck, one of the five Indians catches sight of it and commences to beg for it. She refuses, but after several more days of persistent entreaties she relents, permitting the Indian to borrow it.

The Indians gradually gain the trust and regard of the entire party, especially Tom Sawyer. However, once they learn that Brace Johnson is expected, and possibly others with him, they act upon a deep-laid plan of treachery. Separating Huck and Tom from the rest of the emigrants on a pretext, they massacre Mr. and Mrs. Mills and their three sons, set fire to the wagon, steal the horses and supplies, and kidnap Peggy, her sister Fl-

axy, and Jim. Huck chances to witness the entire scene, but he can do nothing. The next morning he and Tom reunite amid the ruins, overwhelmed by the experience and the lonely desolation of its aftermath. Huck breaks the silence with a question:

> "Tom, where did you learn about Injuns—how noble they was, and all that?"
>
> He gave me a look that showed me I had hit him hard, very hard, and so I wished I hadn't said the words. He turned away his head, and after about a minute he said "Cooper's novels," and didn't say anything more. . . .
>
> (109)

Twain's Indian theme is almost in full view here, and it is sadly comic at best, for Tom's vaunted friends are guilty of ingratitude, cowardice, thievery, kidnapping, and multiple murder. Yet in the ensuing chapters the author gives reason to believe that still more damning evidence of Indian savagery may well come to light.

Three days after the tragedy Brace Johnson arrives and, being well versed in the ways of Indians, comprehends at once what has happened. Brace assumes that Peggy has perished, but when Huck informs him that she was taken from the camp alive he becomes frantic with anxiety. After a few moments, though, he calms himself with the reflection that she must have used the dirk to take her own life. Huck knows that Peggy may not have had the weapon returned to her by the importunate Indian, but to comfort Brace he lies, assuring him that it was in her possession. Nevertheless he cannot understand why the young plainsman should take satisfaction in his loved one's self-inflicted death. And so, he reports, "I up and asked Brace if he actually hoped Peggy *was* dead; and if he did, *why* he did. He explained it to me, and then it was all clear" (113). But Huck Finn affords the reader no indication of exactly what was "all clear." In a manner that recalls in some respects his reluctance to describe the traumatic scene of young Buck Grangerford's death, he keeps the information to himself. By this means, as by the prominent motif of the dirk, Mark Twain arouses uneasy curiosity about Brace Johnson's concerns for Peggy.

Why, we are tacitly invited to ask ourselves, *should* Brace wish his loved one dead rather than alive and at the mercy of Indians? Colonel Dodge answers this question at some length in a chapter of *The Plains of the Great West* entitled "Captives." He writes:

> Either the character and customs of the Indians have greatly changed, or Cooper and some other novelists knew nothing of Indians when they placed their heroines as captives in the hands of these savages. I believe I am perfectly safe in the assertion that there is not a single wild tribe of Indians in all the wide territory of the United States which does not regard the person of the female captive as the inherent right of the captor,

and I venture to assert further that in the last twenty-five years no woman has been taken prisoner by any plains Indians who did not as soon after as practicable become a victim to the lust of every one of her captors.

The rule is this. When a woman is captured by a party she belongs equally to each and all, so long as that party is out. When it returns to the home encampment, she may be abandoned for a few days to the gratification of any of the tribe who wish her, after which she becomes the exclusive property of the individual who captured her, and henceforward has protection as his wife.

No words can express the horror of the situation of that most unhappy woman who falls into the hands of these savage fiends. The husband or other male protectors killed or dispersed, she is borne off in triumph to where the Indians make their first camp. Here, if she makes no resistance, she is laid upon a buffalo robe, and each in turn violates her person, the others dancing, singing, and yelling around her. If she resists at all, her clothing is torn off from her person, four pegs are driven into the ground, and her arms and legs, stretched to the utmost, are tied fast to them by thongs. Here, with the howling band dancing and singing around her, she is subjected to violation after violation, outrage after outrage, to every abuse and indignity, until not infrequently death releases her from suffering. The Indian woman, knowing this inevitable consequence of capture, makes no resistance, and gets off comparatively easy. The white woman naturally and instinctively resists, is 'staked out,' and subjected to the fury of passions fourfold increased by the fact of her being white and a novelty. Neither the unconsciousness nor even the death of the victim stops this horrible orgie; and it is only when the fury of their passions has been glutted to satiety that she is released if alive, or scalped and mutilated if dead. If she lives, it is to go through the same horrible ordeal in every camp until the party gets back to the home encampment.

(395-96)

In short, Brace hopes Peggy has used her dirk to spare herself a fate he considers worse than death.[14]

Within a few moments of learning from Brace the predicament Peggy may have fallen into, Huck makes a shocking discovery. Helping examine the burnt campsite for evidence of the Indians' identity and further intentions, he glimpses the dirk lying on the ground. He conceals it at once, again wishing not to give pain to his elder companion, and later he makes a place for it in his coat lining. Carrying the dirk with him "was like having a keepsake from Peggy," he remarks with feeling, "and something to remember her by, always as long as I lived" (113).

Brace, Huck, and Tom pursue the fleeing Indians so as to ascertain Peggy's fate and, if possible, to rescue her, the little girl, and Jim. Brace Johnson is confident that these latter two will not have been harmed, but he is no

less certain that the dead body of Peggy will be found where the Indian party has made its first night's camp. Unable to face the task of burying her, he calls upon Huck and Tom to perform that office, and they agree. After a long journey the three reach the Indian campsite. Huck and Tom explore the area thoroughly, but Peggy is not there. Huck thereupon proposes that they lie to Brace, informing him that they have located her body and laid her to rest. And Tom, always a willing party in efforts at mystification and make-believe, is not averse. Even so, he too cannot understand why Brace should wish his fianceé dead and buried rather than alive and awaiting rescue. "So," Huck explains, "it looked like I'd got to tell him why I reckoned it would be better, all around, for Brace to think we found her and buried her, and at last I come out with it, and then Tom was satisfied" (118). But once again Huck does not confide in the reader this secret which he has reluctantly divulged even to his friend Tom. Through his protagonist's continued reticence Twain builds the impression that some unspeakable fate awaits Peggy. The idea of mass rape, ultimate expression of Indian bestiality, lies just below the surface. Meanwhile, Brace Johnson credits the untruth told him by the two boys.

In Chapters Six through Eight of **"Huck Finn and Tom Sawyer among the Indians"** this subject matter is temporarily set aside. The three companions are delayed in their pursuit of the savages by misadventures of a kind often met with by plains travelers. Using Colonel Dodge's account as his factual basis, Twain first portrays the party as becoming separated amidst a dense fog, and subsequently as nearly suffering disaster together in a flash flood produced by a distant "waterspout."[15] In the ninth and final chapter he returns to the primary focus of the action, the search for Peggy and her companions, and reintroduces his original theme of contrast between romantic illusion and harsh reality. Huck notices that in their conversations Tom "was putting the Injuns below the devils, now. You see, he had about got it through his noodle, by this time, that book Injuns and real Injuns is different" (138). But Twain seems determined to press for an even more profound contrast. One evening the three travelers reach an Indian campsite that has been occupied only a day or two before, and by as many as one hundred persons. Searching for signs as usual, Huck happens onto another bit of evidence, "a ragged piece of Peggy's dress as big as a big handkerchief, and it had blood on it" (137). He hides this from Brace, but a moment later he and Tom must hurry to rub out a footprint they recognize as Peggy's. The boys are "most dead with uneasiness" (137), for they fear Brace will discover their secret that the girl is apparently still alive. The grave implications of their most recent discoveries become unmistakable when, during the same scene, Brace discovers four stakes driven into the ground. It will be recalled that, according to Colonel Dodge, "staking out" was a common practice by Indians to punish women captives who resisted them. This is clearly the significance of the otherwise meaningless detail of the four stakes that Twain chooses to introduce here. Having found the stakes, Brace stands silent over them and looks hard into the eyes, first of Huck, then of Tom, "till it got pretty sultry," as Huck observes; but after a moment the young man says, half to himself, "'Well, I believe you'" (137). Evidently he has inferred that a white woman has been taken captive by the Indians, and he is debating whether, notwithstanding what the boys have told him, the victim may be Peggy.

Shortly after this scene Twain's melodramatic tale of kidnap and rescue breaks off. Brace has just dressed himself in outlandish garb, planning to feign insanity so that the superstitious Indians will permit him to enter their camp and reconnoitre. But what further adventures the author may have had in store for the three fellow travelers we can only speculate. Knowing his often haphazard methods of composition as we do, it seems doubtful that he had formulated any detailed long-range scheme. The fate of Peggy remains uncertain, although a strong likelihood has been implied. The dirk she has agreed to carry in her bosom, the whispered explanations between Brace and Huck and subsequently Huck and Tom, the information withheld from the reader about the content of these statements, and finally the bloody scrap of clothing, the footprint, and the four stakes in the ground—all these details point to the conclusion that she has suffered the fate which, according to Dodge, every white woman endures when she is abducted by Indians.

Why, therefore, having developed his narrative to this point with such clear direction, did Twain suddenly abandon it? Several explanations present themselves. Perhaps he had intended for Peggy to be rescued unharmed by the Indians but judged that he had written her into her predicament so firmly that any alternative explanation of the evidence would be implausible and not worth the effort. Or perhaps he chafed at the need to depend upon secondary sources, having become accustomed to tapping private stores of memory as he portrayed Huck and his bygone world. He was not in his own element writing about the plains, any more than Huck—quintessentially a river boy—could be truly at home there. Twain may indeed have sensed inadequacies in the portrayed Huck of this sequel that he was unable to patch over. In general, the narrator of the fragment is only a faint copy of the vivid boy of the novel. A specific shortcoming is that his emotional response to the possibility that Peggy is being debauched by the Indians remains a virtual blank. Except to speak guardedly of her peril, to retain the dirk as a (macabre) keepsake, and to sympathize with the anguish of Brace,

Huck registers no personal reaction to the painful knowledge he bears. When he and Tom discover the bloody scrap of clothing and the telltale footprint they express concern, not about Peggy, but over being "in a scrape" with Brace (137). Twain may have wished to represent Huck as incapable of reacting to the heroine's plight as a mature person would, but this is not the impression given by his narrative. The impression is rather that he was unable or unwilling as an author to address explicitly the subject of rape.

Given his possible impatience at having to rely upon printed "authorities" and his difficulties with Huck, Twain may well have concluded that his entire plot line was flawed. Pointing out the contrast between the Indians of sentimental legend and those of reality is after all a slim foundation on which to build an entire novel. As we have seen, the folly of Tom Sawyer's ideas about Indian character becomes grimly obvious only one-third of the way through the fragmentary tale. After the massacre of the Mills family the focus shifts to Peggy and the accumulating evidence of her condition. But here Twain was entering perilous cultural territory, and at some point it surely became clear to him that a fiction like this, centering on suspected rape, would quite possibly work lasting harm to his reputation. He was pushing his exposé of Indian nature dangerously far.

"Huck Finn and Tom Sawyer among the Indians" was leading the author into so many difficulties and dangers that his ceasing work on it at this point is hardly surprising. The real wonder is that, having designed the piece as he had, he extended it even to the length he did. Perhaps he had formed some general intention for the completed book which he doggedly sought to realize until at last he gave it over as hopeless. For example, the narrative's kidnap and rescue pattern, with the featured victim a spotless maiden and the wrongdoers nefarious Indians, suggests that he was modelling it on the melodramatic formula regularly employed by contributors to the popular Beadle and Adams series of dime novels. Beadle and Adams cautioned their prospective authors that "We prohibit subjects or characters that carry an immoral taint"; and however loosely this proscription may have applied to theft, drunkenness, and murder, it effectively banished explicit reference to sex from dime novel series.[16] Thus when Ina, the "sweet young heroine" of Edward Ellis' *Seth Jones,* falls into the hands of Indians her protector does realize that "a fate from the sensuous captors far worse than death itself, was to be apprehended" (45, 93). Twain is less conventional and less comfortable. He insists that the reader remain aware of Peggy's full danger through several chapters, and by details like the four stakes he strongly suggests that she has indeed met with violence. In this and other respects his fragmentary tale may plausibly be viewed as an aborted experiment at bringing a measure of reality to the convention-ridden escapism that characterized the cheap fiction of his day.

Of course, if Twain believed that such an effort could possibly win popular approval, the chapters he completed must stand as one more evidence of his frequent incapacity to judge the presentability of his own writings. More likely in this case he knew what he was about and recognized almost from the beginning that serious risks were involved. He probably foresaw that, just as the non-sexual "immorality" of *Adventures of Huckleberry Finn* would shock and offend some readers, the taboo subject matter of its sequel would do so as well. The impulses to challenge the adherents of conventional views and to outrage the starched guardians of decorum never lay far from the surface in Mark Twain's character. Clearly a major impetus for his writing **"Huck Finn and Tom Sawyer among the Indians"** was his impatience with those folk whose still-prevalent notions of Indian character he thought ridiculously unfounded. One may imagine the satisfaction he initially took in devising a fiction which demolished the romantic myth of Indian virtue so absolutely as this one did. And yet, by presenting the Indians as brutal rapists he was also portraying Peggy Mills as in all likelihood the victim of rape. Here Twain fronted the problem he found insoluble: that his young heroine—generous, confiding, womanly, yet virginal—was the embodiment of an ideal which he himself worshipped. He shared Huck Finn's tendency to idolize certain women, and the potentially degrading position he had placed Peggy in must have given him distress. However he dissented from certain readers in his estimate of Indian character, in regard to young women portrayed in fiction he shared the squeamish sentimentality that dominated popular taste in his era. The narrative framework he had created to explode false ideas about Indian character was forcing him into a task of authorship he was unwilling to complete.[17]

Thus Twain gave over his plan to portray Huck Finn out west. Throughout the project he had derived information from Colonel Dodge's *The Plains of the Great West,* framing scene after scene on the basis of that work. He heartily assented to Dodge's unflattering portrayal of the Indian, and in years to come he was to renew his bitter attacks on the sentimental conception of the Red Man fostered by James Fenimore Cooper. Even so, for reasons both professional and personal he determined that this particular novel was unworkable, and so he turned his attention elsewhere. Notwithstanding his respect for Dodge as a humane and courageous historical witness, he seems to have resigned himself to the view that, in this situation, historical truth and the representation of that truth in fiction could correspond only up to a point. Huck Finn's adventures on the western frontier had taken Twain so far beyond the frontiers of

civilized behavior that he judged it best to discontinue the expedition and retreat—for a time at least—to the literary settlements.

Notes

1. *Adventures of Huckleberry Finn* in *The Complete Works of Mark Twain* (New York, 1918), IX, 404.

2. Blair, ed., *Mark Twain's Hannibal, Huck and Tom* (Berkeley, 1969), pp. 92-140. Parenthetical page-references to "Huck Finn and Tom Sawyer among the Indians" in the text that follows denote this edition.

3. For the newspaper article see Franklin Walker and G. Ezra Dane, eds., *Mark Twain's Travels with Mr. Brown* (New York, 1940), p. 266; the Goshoot discussion is in Chapter XIX of *Roughing It*—for the quoted passages see *Complete Works,* VI, 132, 134. See also "A Sketch of Niagara," Buffalo *Express,* August 21, 1869, in which Twain declares that "the noble Red Man has always been a friend and darling of mine" and proceeds to recount his unsatisfactory interview with a group of picturesquely apparelled individuals whom he takes to be Indians but who prove to be Irishmen, fresh off the boat. This work was reprinted as "Niagara" in *Sketches New and Old* (1875); for the quoted passage see *Complete Works,* XIX, 62.

4. "The Noble Red Man," *The Galaxy,* September 1870, pp. 428-29.

5. This same work had appeared in England a few weeks earlier as *The Hunting Grounds of the Great West* (London: Chatto & Windus, 1876). Early editions are scarce, but a facsimile edition of *The Plains of the Great West* was issued in 1959 by Archer House of New York. Parenthetical page-references to Dodge's book in the text that follows denote the facsimile. A critical edition of the work has recently been issued, edited by Wayne R. Kime and entitled *The Plains of North America and Their Inhabitants* (Newark: University of Delaware Press, 1989.)

6. The author's annotated copy of *The Plains of the Great West* forms part of the Twain collection at the Redding, Connecticut library. It is not clear whether he annotated the book in 1877 or at a later date.

7. *Mark Twain-Howells Letters. The Correspondence of Samuel L. Clemens and William D. Howells, 1872-1910,* ed. Henry Nash Smith and William M. Gibson (Cambridge, Mass., 1960), I, 172.

8. Twain to Charles L. Webster, n.p., July 6, 1884, in Samuel C. Webster, *Mark Twain, Business Man* (Boston, 1946), pp. 264-65.

9. *Our Wild Indians,* issued by A. D. Worthington of Hartford, Connecticut, was a popular success, selling more than 37,000 copies by 1890. Twain had probably heard of *Our Wild Indians* and confused it with *The Plains of the Great West.* His efforts to conjure up the title of the earlier work ("'25 Years on the Frontier'—or some such title—I don't remember just what. Maybe it is '25 Years Among the Indians,' or maybe '25 Years in the Rocky Mountains.'"—Webster, pp. 264-65) suggest the lengthy subtitle of *Our Wild Indians,* which begins: *Thirty-Three Years' Personal Experience Among the Red Men of the Great West.*

10. These included Washington Irving's *A Tour on the Prairies* (1835), Francis Parkman's *The Oregon Trail* (1849), Keim's *With Sheridan's Troopers on the Borders,* and George A. Custer's *My Life on the Plains* (1874). All but Irving are identified as among Twain's sources in *Mark Twain-Howells Letters,* II, 496, note 2.

11. Blair, ed., *Mark Twain's Hannibal, Huck and Tom,* p. 85.

12. For example, compare Dodge's thorough statement about Indian debauchery quoted below from *The Plains of the Great West* with the shortened and sanitized version in *Our Wild Indians,* pp. 529-30.

13. Franklin R. Rogers, ed., *The Pattern for Mark Twain's* Roughing It: *Letters from Nevada by Samuel and Orion Clemens, 1861-1862.* (Berkeley, 1961), p. 16.

14. The practice of carrying a weapon or saving a rifle shell in order to take one's own life when faced with capture by Indians is discussed in *The Plains of the Great West,* pp. xlix, 417.

15. Compare "Huck Finn and Tom Sawyer among the Indians," pp. 123-25, 133-35 with *The Plains of the Great West,* pp. 47-49, 81-85.

16. "Introduction" to Edward S. Ellis, *Seth Jones* and Edward L. Wheeler, *Deadwood Dick on Deck,* ed. Philip Durham (New York, 1966), p. ix. Parenthetical page-references to *Seth Jones* in the text that follows denote this edition. The most authoritative repository of information about the dime novel series remains Albert Johannsen's *The House of Beadle and Adams and Its Dime and Nickel Novels: The Story of a Vanished Literature,* 2 vols. (Norman, Okla., 1950); for discussion of *Seth Jones* see I, 31-33.

17. In identifying skittishness about sex as the most powerful reason why Twain abandoned this novel I concur with Walter Blair in his comments that accompanied the text when it was first published, in *Life,* 65 (December 20, 1968), 32-50; see p. 50. Other commentators on the sexual subject matter include Albert E. Stone, Jr., *The Innocent Eye: Childhood in Mark Twain's Imagination* (New Haven, 1961; reprinted New York, 1970), pp. 179-80, and Everett Emerson, *The Authentic Mark Twain: A Literary Biography of Samuel L. Clemens* (Philadelphia, 1984), pp. 148-49.

Earl F. Briden (essay date December 1993)

SOURCE: Briden, Earl F. "'The Great Landslide Case': A Mark Twain Debt to a 'Musty Old Book'?" *Notes and Queries* n.s. 40, no. 4 (December 1993): 479-81.

[*In the following essay, Briden identifies Sir Richard Baker's* Chronicle of the Kings of England *as a probable source for the final revision of "The Great Landslide Case," speculating about Twain's discovery of the source.*]

Mark Twain published three versions of **'The Great Landslide Case'.** The first, which appeared in 1863, was a brief newspaper sketch of a mock trial occasioned by a Nevada landslide. The second, published in 1870, was a complete rewriting of the story, one detail of which Twain expanded into a tall-tale episode. The third appeared as chapter 34 of *Roughing It* (1872), and, as Frederick Anderson and Edgar M. Branch point out, was based 'in all respects' upon the decisive 1870 printing.[1] It has not been noted, however, that the inspiration for Twain's 1870 expansion of the story in a tall-tale direction may well have come from a passage in Sir Richard Baker's *Chronicle of the Kings of England,* a book Twain discovered in the fall of 1864.

When the tale appeared in the San Francisco *Morning Call* of 30 August 1863, it offered a single point of narrative interest: the sham trial staged by Nevada wags at the expense of the territorial attorney general. The joke's occasion, a heavy wash of detritus down a mountain slope, was thus presented summarily: 'Two years ago, during the season of avalanches, Tom Rust's ranch slid down from the mountain side and pretty nearly covered up a ranch belonging to Dick Sides'.[2] In the second version, printed in the Buffalo *Express* of 2 April 1870, the landslide itself takes on interest as a tall-tale event. In this account Sides sets the hoax in motion by telling an extravagant lie about an avalanche that brings Tom Morgan's ranch—'fences, cabins, cattle, barns and every thing'—down on top of his ranch 'and exactly covered up every single vestige of his property to a depth of about six feet'; now Morgan refuses to vacate the premises because his 'cabin was standing on the same dirt and same ranch it had always stood on . . .'.[3]

Twain's extraordinary image of a ranch that slides down a mountain and comes to rest, entire and intact, upon another ranch may have had its source in his reading.

As a local reporter for the San Francisco *Call,* Twain covered the Mechanics' Institute Industrial Fair in September 1864. His *Call* article of 16 September describes a Fair exhibit that he found 'by far the most interesting curiosity of all', a 'Chronicle' he examined and quoted, from memory, in his news item. This 'voluminous and very musty old book' was the fourth edition (1665) of Sir Richard Baker's *A Chronicle of the Kings of England . . . with a Continuation to the Year 1660 by E. Phillips,*[4] which includes among its curiosities the following description of an earthquake in Queen Elizabeth's time:

> In her thirteenth year, a prodigious Earthquake happened in the East parts of *Herefordshire,* at a little Town called *Kinnaston.* On the seventeenth of *February,* at six of the clock in the evening, the earth began to open, and a Hill with a Rock under it (making at first a great bellowing noise, which was heard a great way off) lifted it self up a great height, and began to travell, bearing along with it the Trees that grew upon it, the Sheep-folds, and Flocks of Sheep abiding there at the same time. In the place from whence it was first moved, it left a gaping distance forty foot broad, and fourscore Ells long; the whole Field was about twenty Acres. Passing along, it overthrew a Chappell standing in the way, removed an Ewe-Tree planted in the Churchyard, from the West into the East; with the like force it thrust before it High-wayes, Sheep-folds, Hedges and Trees, made tilled ground Pasture, and again turned Pasture into Tillage. Having walked in this sort from *Saturday* in the evening, till *Munday* noon, it then stood still.[5]

All of the main features of the historian's description are distinctly echoed in Twain's. Most importantly, both ranch and farm, each with its land, shelters, and livestock, are carried off whole, and each comes to rest superimposed upon its counterpart, ranch on ranch, and farm on farm (so that tilled ground is now pasture and pasture, tillage). Both occupy elevated spots, and each loudly signals its removal, the ranch with a great 'racket', the farm with a 'great bellowing noise'. In its motion, each drives everything before it: in Twain's narrative, the sliding ranch sends trees, rocks, cattle, and cordwood tumbling into the valley;[6] in the historian's, the moving farm thrusts along roads, sheep-folds, hedges, and trees.

Twain's *Call* article implies that he examined the *Chronicle* with his own family history in mind. He comments on 'the chapter which gives the names of the members of the High Commission before which Charles I. was tried and condemned to death'.[7] In his *Autobiography* he discusses a Clemens tradition that placed High Commission member Gregory Clement among his ancestors. Yet Twain's interest in ancestors might have induced him to look into Baker's account of Elizabeth's reign as well, since family tradition also numbered 'pirates and slavers in Elizabeth's time' among his forebears.[8]

In any case, Twain found in this 'musty old book' items of interest beyond the account of Charles. The *Call* article points out that the book 'contains the genealogy of the reigning monarchs and that of all the nobility of England', and records Twain's appreciation of its 'quaint language, spelling, and typography'.[9] And the striking parallels between his 1870 tall-tale account of an avalanche and Baker's earthquake description suggest the likelihood that he indeed stumbled upon and appropriated the latter, which should thus be numbered among the 'sources' of '**The Great Landslide Case**'.[10]

Notes

1. *The Great Landslide Case by Mark Twain: Three Versions,* ed. Frederick Anderson and Edgar M. Branch (Berkeley, 1972), 37.

2. Mark Twain, *Early Tales & Sketches,* vol. i, ed. Edgar M. Branch and Robert H. Hirst (Berkeley, 1979), 280. The first version of the tale was entitled 'A Rich Decision'.

3. *The Great Landslide Case,* 31-2. Entitled 'The Facts in the Great Landslide Case', the Buffalo *Express* version is reprinted in this volume, 31-5.

4. *Clemens of the 'Call': Mark Twain in San Francisco,* ed. Edgar M. Branch (Berkeley, 1969), 111-12. Branch identifies the 'Chronicle' on the strength of Twain's quotation, evidently from memory and thus inaccurate, of Baker's description of the falling of the head of Charles' staff during the reading of the charge. This description appears in the 4th edn (London, 1665), 619.

5. Baker, 421-2.

6. *The Great Landslide Case: Three Versions,* 32.

7. *Clemens of the 'Call',* 112.

8. *Mark Twain's Own Autobiography: The Chapters from the 'North American Review',* ed. Michael J. Kiskis (Madison, 1990), 4-5 and n. 10, 262-3. Interestingly, Twin mistakenly identified his regicide ancestor as 'Geoffrey Clement'.

9. *Clemens of the 'Call',* 112.

10. Effie Mona Mack contends that the story of the mock trial is 'as old as the very hills of Nevada'; however, she offers no specific folklorist source of Twain's ranch-moving landslide. See *Mark Twain in Nevada* (New York, 1947), 143-8.

Lawrence I. Berkove (essay date fall 1994)

SOURCE: Berkove, Lawrence I. "'A Difficult Case': W. D. Howells's Impression of Mark Twain." *Studies in Short Fiction* 31, no. 4 (fall 1994): 607-15.

[*In the following essay, Berkove examines William Dean Howells's "A Difficult Case" for evidence that Twain's philosophical beliefs and artistic principles influenced the story's protagonist and themes.*]

There is little doubt today about the nature and extent of the influence of William Dean Howells on Mark Twain, but what of the reverse situation? Is it possible that Howells restricted a long and close friendship with Twain to a personal level and that he never assimilated the relationship to the point of expressing it in his art? "A Difficult Case" (1900) is evidence that Twain did leave his mark on both Howells's thought and art, deepening him and inspiring him to write one of his richest, most skillful, and most powerful short stories.

The story, all Howells scholars agree, has been largely overlooked. Yet, paradoxically, most modern commentators on the story praise it as one of Howells's best. Although their interpretations of it vary, the main point of agreement among them is that a main character, Ransom Hilbrook, resembles Mark Twain. The first person to sense this resemblance was Mark Twain himself. Reading the story as it was published in July and August of 1900 in the *Atlantic Monthly,* Twain wrote Howells that "I read the Difficult Situation [sic] night before last, & got a world of evil joy out of it" (Smith et al. 719). What has led scholars to link Twain to Hilbrook is that character's objections to the doctrine of the immortality of the soul. In *My Mark Twain* (1910), Howells described the impact of Twain's belief on Livy Clemens: "After they had both ceased to be formal Christians, she was still grieved by his denial of immortality, so grieved that he resolved upon one of those heroic lies, which for love's sake he held above even the truth, and he went to her, saying that he had been thinking the whole matter over, and now he was convinced that the soul did live after death. It was too late" (32).

Although little has been written about the story, what there is covers a lot of ground. Henry James singled it out for brief praise in a letter to Howells, calling it "beautiful and admirable, ever so true and ever so *done*" (James 198).[1] Edwin Cady called it one of Howells's "most moving stories," finding it an affirmation of love (Cady 201-02). Edward Wagenknecht saw little in it beyond the story level of a minister who "wears out his health and strength in struggling with the doubts of an aged parishioner," and Howells's "most elaborate discussion of the immortality question in fiction" (Wagenknecht 242, 253). Kenneth Eble briefly describes the story as reflecting Howells's weak faith in a personal God and personal immortality, but recognizes in Hilbrook "a central character, suggestive of Mark Twain" (Eble 201-02). In a recent discussion of the story—and, apparently, the only extended one—John Crowley declares it to be "one of Howells's finest short works," and views it as representing both Howells's transition from realism to romance, and his virtual identification with the Rev. Ewbert's affirmation of "a willed belief in the ideal of love and a commitment to life itself, whatever its mysteries and imperfections" (Crowley 138, 144).

The salient features of "A Difficult Case" are easily summarized. The setting of the story is the town of Hilbrook, which changed its name from West Mallow when Josiah Hilbrook, one of its successful sons, endowed it with a university to be named after him. He also separately endowed a church building and a parsonage in the town, and a fund to support the preaching of the doctrines of the Rixonite church, a small sect to which he belonged, whose distinguishing characteristic was its belief in a "patient waiting upon the divine will, with a constant reference of this world's mysteries and problems to the world to come" (149).

Emily Ewbert, the wife of Rev. Clarence Ewbert, the town minister, admires her husband's verbal ability and resents that so few university people attend his sermons. When Rev. Ewbert discovers that Ransom Hilbrook, a cousin of Josiah, though raised a Rixonite, had lost his faith in an afterlife in the Civil War, he "set himself, with all his heart and soul, to dislodge Hilbrook from his deplorable conviction" (165). To Ewbert's surprise, he learns that Hilbrook, whom everyone assumed was only a bachelor farmer, had once had a wife and child—both of whom had died. He also discovers that although Hilbrook speaks in vernacular, he is actually deeply read in the literature of immortality, from Plato to Swedenborg to John Fiske, and that he is "a doubter whose doubt was hopeless through his knowledge" (165).

Ewbert attempts to win Hilbrook back to faith by engaging him in theological discourse. At first Ewbert seems successful, but after Hilbrook thinks over each of Ewbert's arguments he comes back with a rebuttal. What started out as a comfort mission becomes an intellectual contest that increasingly drains Ewbert and leads him to devise ingenious counter-arguments of whose truth he has doubts. Eventually, Hilbrook gives up on Ewbert and starves himself to death in the hope that death is the absolute end, and that there will be no afterlife. Ewbert preaches a funeral sermon for Hilbrook in which he teaches the lesson derived from the old man's death that his hearers should keep "themselves alive through some relation to the undying frame of things, which they could do only by cherishing earthly ties" (219). Many university people come to the sermon and are moved by it, and, in the story's last line, "Mrs. Ewbert augured the best things for her husband's future usefulness from their presence" (220).

It is impossible to do justice to the subtleties of a text by a plot summary, but even in this overview, readers familiar with Twain might be reminded of **"The Man That Corrupted Hadleyburg"** (1899) by the name change from West Mallow to Hilbrook. Another connection to Twain might be made to *What Is Man?,* which, though published in 1906, had its genesis in Twain's 1893 paper, "What Is Happiness?," which he had worked on in Vienna in 1898 (Wagner-Martin 783). In that work, an old man remorselessly assaults the idealism of a young man with a depressing but persuasive pessimism. Howells most probably read **"The Man That Corrupted Hadleyburg"** when it came out in the December 1899 issue of *Harper's Monthly,* and though Twain was overseas from January 1896 until October 1900, Howells had almost certainly learned from Twain the plan of the gestating *What Is Man?*[2]

Whatever external similarities there may be of "A Difficult Case" to one or another of Twain's works, the deepest and most convincing similarities lie within its text. The story is written with superb irony, both subtle and sharp. Attractive though he might seem, it is not at all the Rev. Ewbert who is the story's hero, but Ransom Hilbrook. Hilbrook is a character of austere integrity. He tests every doctrine and argument against the standard of truth, which he determines for himself by both his learning and his experience. There is no guile or pretense to him; he is "perfectly sincere" (177) and speaks his mind directly, plainly, and uncompromisingly. He objects with a simple "it ain't true" to the idea that people mourn all their lives over past sorrows. Calling on his own experience to support this judgment, he says of his grief at losing a sweetheart to Josiah, *"It wore out."* He recalls that he subsequently married and was pleased with his wife, but then "[s]he died when I was away at the war, and the little boy died after I got back. I was sorry to lose her, and I thought losin' *him* would kill me. It didn't. It appeared one while as if I couldn't live without him, and I was always contrivin' how I should meet up with him somewhere else. I couldn't figure it out. . . . Well . . . that wore out too" (173-74).[3]

In contrast to Hilbrook, Rev. Ewbert is not very admirable. For one thing, he appears not to be doctrinally committed.[4] We are early told of him that "the version of his [Rixon's] gospel which his latest apostle gave taught a species of acquiescence which was foreign to the thoughts of the founder." Instead of encouraging his parishioners to take constant spiritual stock of themselves while interrogating "Providence as to its will concerning them," Ewbert preaches that "while they fulfilled all their plain, simple duties toward one another, God would inspire them to act according to his purposes in the more psychological crises and emergencies, if these should ever be part of their experience" (149-50). It is important to keep in mind that Howells is not, in this story, necessarily advocating or rejecting any real theological issue, but is primarily using a theological issue for the story's purposes. The real function in the story of what may seem a technical theological distinction is to provide a key to Ewbert's personality.

How it does this can be seen from several perspectives. First, it underlines the significance not of Ewbert's putting a slightly different emphasis upon Rixon's teachings, but of his teaching a doctrine "foreign" to Rixon's mind. In other words, though a Rixonite in name, he is not a Rixonite in belief or practice. There is quite a difference between Rixon's emphasis upon passively waiting for a sign from God, and Ewbert's position of embarking on a course of action and trusting—or expecting—that God will supply one with an inspiration whenever one needs it. Second, Ewbert is not shown to have any basis in Scripture or experience for his theological change. He is a young man, preaching of things beyond his ken, taking undue liberties with the doctrines of his church, and assuming authority that properly belongs to Rixon, supposedly his spiritual guide.[5] Third, his own theories do not work, or in the words of Hilbrook, "ain't true." Their most conspicuous failure is demonstrated with Hilbrook. Hilbrook has suffered several psychological and spiritual crises beyond anything Ewbert has ever endured: loss of a sweetheart, war, and the deaths of a wife and son, and God has not supplied him with any compensating inspiration. Hilbrook therefore bases his doubts on his own experience and is honest with himself, whereas Ewbert cannot claim any authority outside of his own mind for his theories, and is not honest with himself. The text, in fact, damningly describes his efforts to resuscitate Hilbrook's belief in an afterlife as having been undertaken "upon terms which, until he was himself much older, he could not question as to their beneficence, and in fact it never came to his being quite frank with himself concerning them" (216).

Finally, Hilbrook may be seen as a better disciple of Rixon than Ewbert. Hilbrook has spent his whole life passively waiting for a sign. One has not come, but then Rixon never promised that one would; his teachings were limited to recommending a spiritual discipline. It is Ewbert who commits God to delivering inspiration on demand, a promise that is patently undeliverable. As long as Hilbrook remains merely passive in his unbelief, he continues to live, but he precipitates his own death when he adopts the this-worldly "spin" on Rixonism that Ewbert advocates.

The situation and the language describing it are thoroughly ironic. Howells obviously realized that passivity could be inverted into a kind of action. Hilbrook takes his own life by active passivity; he decides to take no nourishment. The point is made with elegant irony in the scene in which Ewbert discovers Hilbrook in bed. To Ewbert's suggestion that he get up, Hilbrook responds, "I ha'n't got any call to get up" (211). The word "call" has a Rixonite connotation of a summons from God as well as its primary denotation of "reason." When Ewbert tries to entice Hilbrook into survival by asking him if he is hungry, "'Yes, I'm hungry,' the old man assented, 'but I don't want to eat anything'" (213). The sentence clearly puts a great deal of volitional weight on the verbal "don't want" and reinforces the emphasis by the locution "don't want to eat anything" instead of "don't want anything to eat." Hilbrook indifferently "submits" to the help offered by people called in, a farm-wife and a doctor, but says that "he would have no agency" in taking medicine. Instead, he displays "absolute apathy" as to what goes on about him. Hilbrook may be said to have turned Rixonism against itself, but it is Ewbert who starts him. The one thing that Ewbert truly teaches Hilbrook is the means of the logic he uses, which converts passivity into action.

The more Ewbert is frustrated by Hilbrook's refutations of his various arguments, the more his Christian compassion for the old man is shown to be a professional front—and the more he strains not so much to tell the truth as to win.

> Some new thoughts had occurred to him [Ewbert] in corroboration of the notions they had agreed upon in their last meeting. But in response Ewbert found himself beset by a strange temptation—by the wish to take up these notions and expose their fallacy. They were indeed mere toys of their common fancy which they had constructed together in mutual supposition, but Ewbert felt a sacredness in them, while he longed so strangely to break them one by one and cast them in the old man's face.
>
> (196)

The most insidious of these notions is his disingenuous imputation to Hilbrook of a desire to have enough consciousness in an afterlife to enjoy his unconsciousness (179).[6] It tricks the old man at first, but he finally sees through it. "There ain't anything *in* that. I got to thinking it over, when you was gone, and the whole thing went to pieces. That idea don't prove anything at all, and all that we worked out of it had to go with it" (211). When Ewbert offers to put the notion together again, the old man says, dryly: "*You* can, if you want to . . . I got no interest in it any more; 'twa'n't nothing but a metaphysical toy, anyway" (212). The original magazine version of the story uses the much sharper "casuistical" instead of "metaphysical," thereby unmistakably denigrating Ewbert (*Atlantic Monthly* 215). It is the last straw for Hilbrook; after he figures out the fallacy of Ewbert's notion, he decides to die.

To give Ewbert his due, it was not his intention to push Hilbrook to this radical step. On the other hand, he entered into a debate on a tremendous subject with the old man without ever compassionately gauging how much the topic meant to him and without matching him in understanding or commitment, let alone honesty. Ewbert never appears to be quite as un-Christian as his wife does when she rejects Hilbrook, "What did it matter whether such a man believed that there was another world or not?" (217), but his real motivation in carrying on the contest was not so much Christian as it was pride. He either does not realize or care to recognize his

responsibility for the doctrine that he preaches: his last sermon reaffirms the this-worldly activism that contradicts the main tenet of the Rixonism to which he was supposedly dedicated. The final irony is that whatever success he has as a Rixonite minister with the university people who attend the funeral is owing to a non-Rixonite notion, and one whose fatal casuistry has been demonstrated.

It is now possible to link "A Difficult Case" more closely to Twain and his works. The biographical similarities that earlier critics have noticed can be specified. Hilbrook and Twain share a number of important qualities besides their denial of a belief in the soul's immortality and an afterlife: they are both self-taught vernacular philosophers, plain-spoken and direct, experiential rather than theoretical, and "realistic" rather than romantic. They have both known suffering and bereavement. They see life as hard, painful, and probably not worth the candle. And God does not appear to either of them as merciful and benevolent. They also both have a gritty integrity that consists of describing things exactly as they see them and of not being awed by authority or intimidated by sacrosanctity. They both penetrate to the essence of things and stick to their positions.

Of Twain's works, **"The Man That Corrupted Hadleyburg"** offers the richest number of connections to Howells's story. The convenient name change of Hadleyburg to something else is paralleled in "A Difficult Case" not only by the readiness with which West Mallow gives way to Hilbrook but also by the unexamined ease with which Ewbert slips from one religious and philosophical position to another, and by the revelation that his true character is quite different from the superficial pose he maintains. But, like the citizens of Hadleyburg, neither he, nor his wife, nor the townspeople are conscious of the ironic discrepancies between what they affirm and what they are.

It is not that Howells imitated **"Hadleyburg"** or any other Twain story, but rather that he appears to have assimilated Twain more deeply than has hitherto been realized. If Howells had attempted merely to parrot **"Hadleyburg,"** it would have been obvious long before this, and probably not much better than imitations usually are. But 30 years of friendship with someone as intense, forthright, and closely reasoned as Twain had to have left an impression on Howells, at least in terms of some of Twain's values, ideas, and ways of thinking.

"A Difficult Case" is unusual among Howells's stories in that it gives so much respect to a fatalist and pessimist. The tale is not, of course, simply a reflex of Twain's views; Howells loaded it with his own concerns, and his deft use of irony toward Rev. Ewbert's hypocrisy is in line with the realism Howells advocated and practiced. Still, in light of the impact that ideas and attitudes associated with Twain have in the story, a question may remain about how much of Howells, himself, is invested in it.

Eble reports that in "Eighty Years and After" (*Harper's Weekly,* December 1919) Howells related how he in his early life had had a "faith in an afterlife, which gave way to 'the prevailing agnosticism of the eighteen seventies and eighties'" (Eble 216). Howells was too serious and independent a thinker to have drifted into agnosticism on a prevailing fad; like Livy Clemens he must have come up against arguments he could not refute. The issue of immortality was not decided in this story for Howells but continued to vex him for years.[7] Undoubtedly, Howells encountered many agnostics and atheists, but his long-term and close friendship with Twain would have made him a prime influence in Howell's life. "A Difficult Case" may have involved Howells in some painful recollections and deliberations, but if the story is rare Howells it is nevertheless authentic Howells.

In addition to the superb artistry that makes it deserving of more recognition and consideration than it has received, "A Difficult Case" is a remarkable testimony to Howells's friendship with Twain. The position represented by the Twain-like Hilbrook was not one with which Howells wanted to identify. Troubled as he was with the tragic death of a daughter[8] and with his own spiritual doubts, Howells was himself in search of grounds for consolation and security. That he could embark upon such a personally painful topic and endow Hilbrook, under these circumstances, with such integrity is an eloquent compliment to Twain's spiritual depth and honesty and reveals a new aspect of the nature of the powerful bonds between these two friends.

Notes

1. James's letter was written from Lamb House, Rye, on 10 August 1901, and was his response to his receipt of Howells's newly published *A Pair of Patient Lovers,* in which collection "A Difficult Case" was included.

2. Although no direct references to "The Man That Corrupted Hadleyburg" occur in the Twain-Howells correspondence, Howells and Twain regularly exchanged publications as soon as they came out, and Howells in his 14 January 1900 letter to Twain wrote that he hoped to review the volume of short works, in which "Hadleyburg" appeared, that was to come out later that year. As for *What Is Man?,* what Twain called "my Bible," specific allusions to it occur at least as early in their correspondence as Twain's letter of 2 April 1899, and the allusions are in a context that strongly implies Howells's familiarity with its content.

3. In a similar mood, Twain, some years after the 1896 death of his daughter Suzy, reflected: "It is

one of the mysteries of our nature that a man, all unprepared can receive a thunder-stroke like that and live" (qtd. in Kaplan 335).

4. In response to a bereaved mother's pleas for assurance about seeing her child in a hereafter, "[h]e had not the heart to refuse her this consolation, and he had pushed himself, in giving it, beyond the bounds of imagination." When the mother confessed she did not understand his position, he responded by becoming more emphatic (168). On this occasion he experiences an inward collapse. The increasing weariness he feels after his encounters with Hilbrook is related to this, in that in both situations he advocates positions that he does not believe in. Thus, he is attempting to overcome his own intimations of truth as well as honest questioners.

5. In this portrait of a young minister out of his depth and not true to the doctrines of his religion, Howells interestingly parallels Harold Frederic's *The Damnation of Theron Ware* (1896).

6. An eerie antecedent to this idea occurs in a letter from Twain's daughter Suzy, in a letter quoted by Clara Clemens. Supposedly written when she was 18 (1890), she confided some of her religious musings to her Aunt Sue: "While one can have a good sized piece of sky in one's sight, though, one must possess some consciousness of eternity—even if it be an unconscious consciousness" (Clara Clemens 64-65). At this point, one can only speculate how Suzy's phrase might have been brought to the attention of Howells.

7. In 1910 Howells wrote "A Counsel of Consolation" for the purpose of guiding those in bereavement. He made no attempt in this essay to speak with authority, preferring to "trust" rather than believe. Significantly, however, he described himself as one of those who "patiently wait for the fulfillment of the hopes which Christianity has worded from the Greek philosophers rather than from the Hebrew prophets" (5). He spoke of the apparition of "visions of the night, which I would have the sorrower at least passively accept, or not positively refuse" (6), and recommended the authority of a priest of any church or some strongly believing friend; "it is enough if either be sincere" (10). Howells's position more closely resembles Rixon's original doctrine than Ewbert's or post-Ewbert Hilbrook's, and his emphasis upon *sincere* belief again implies a rejection of Ewbert. I wish to thank Professor Don L. Cook of Indiana University for his assistance in locating this work.

8. Crowley suggests that through the story Howells dramatized "a dialogue between his best and worst attitudes" toward the death of his daughter, Winifred, which occurred in 1889 (144).

Works Cited

Cady, Edwin H. *The Realist at War: The Mature Years (1885-1920) of William Dean Howells.* Syracuse, NY: Syracuse UP, 1958.

Clemens, Clara. *My Father Mark Twain.* New York: Harper, 1931.

Crowley, John W. *The Mask of Fiction: Essays on W. D. Howells.* Amherst: U of Massachusetts P, 1989.

Eble, Kenneth E. *Old Clemens and W. D. H.: The Story of a Remarkable Friendship.* Baton Rouge: Louisiana State UP, 1985.

Howells, William Dean. "A Difficult Case." *A Pair of Patient Lovers.* New York: 1901.

————. "A Difficult Case," Part II. Atlantic Monthly 86 (August 1900): 205-17.

————. "A Counsel of Consolation." *In After Days/Thoughts on the Future Life.* New York: Harper, 1910. 3-16.

————. *My Mark Twain.* New York: Harper, 1910.

James, Henry. *Henry James Letters, 1895-1916.* Ed. Leon Edel. Cambridge: Harvard UP, 1984. Vol. 4. of *Henry James Letters.* 4 vols. 1974-84.

Kaplan, Justin. *Mr. Clemens and Mark Twain.* New York: Simon, 1966.

Smith, Henry Nash, William M. Gibson, and Frederick Anderson, eds. *Mark Twain-Howells Letters: The Correspondence of Samuel L. Clemens and William D. Howells.* Cambridge: Harvard UP, 1960. 2 vols.

Wagenknecht, Edward. *William Dean Howells: The Friendly Eye.* New York: Oxford UP, 1969.

Wagner-Martin, Linda. *"What Is Man?" Mark Twain Encyclopedia.* Ed. J. R. LeMaster and James D. Wilson. New York: Garland, 1993.

Craig Frischkorn (essay date summer 1995)

SOURCE: Frischkorn, Craig. "Twain's 'Edward Mills and George Benton: A Tale.'" *Explicator* 53, no. 4 (summer 1995): 214-16.

[*In the following essay, Frischkorn interprets "Edward Mills and George Benton" as a satirical allegory about the consequences of undeserved rewards.*]

Mark Twain's **"Edward Mills and George Benton: A Tale"** was first published in the August 1880 issue of *Atlantic*; it was reprinted in *The $30,000 Bequest* (1906) and *Collected Tales, Sketches, Speeches, and Essays 1852-1890.* The story has received almost no critical evaluation apart from MacDonald, who only comments that the story is "a more complicated joke on the heroes than earlier stories but still undeveloped in plot and character" (244). Plot and character are indeed flat, but I suggest we should read the tale as a satirical allegory on the harmful effects of undeserved rewards. Twain clarifies his stance in the "nature versus nurture" debate, and his ideas well precede Thorndike's research on instrumental conditioning (1895), the scientific community's discovery of Mendel's research on genetics (1900), and Pavlov's discoveries in behaviorism and conditioning (1904). Twain presents an unjust system of punishment and reward, which is applied by society and by the Brants, the set of parents who adopt two orphan cousins, George and Edward.

In the upside-down reward system of this tale, the negative behavior of George receives only positive reinforcement, while the positive behavior of Edward is only ignored and ultimately punished at the expense of rewarding George, who is repeatedly judged to be more "needy." Twain's target for the satire is clear: weak-willed parents and "enabling" moral organizations.

Much of the story revolves around an empty maxim that the Brants blindly repeat: "Be pure, honest, sober, industrious, and considerate of others, and success in life is assured" (747). The parents "were always saying" it, and both children "could repeat it long before the Lord's Prayer." Although both children learned to repeat the saying, George only mouths it while living a life that is the complete opposite. For Edward, however, the maxim is the "unswerving rule" of his life.

The short instructive narrative follows both George and Edward from cradle to grave. Even as a baby, George demands and receives his parents' attention and rewards: "he had to be humored in his desires." Meanwhile, Edward is utterly ignored by the Brants, and later by society, because "he needed no efforts of theirs," and "he was so good, so considerate, and in all ways so perfect" (74).

This pattern continues throughout the boys' lives, and the Brants continue this attitude even after they die: in their will, they leave all their property to George, who "needed" their property, but not to Edward. Their will, moreover, stipulates that the wastrel George must buy out Edward's business partner, so that hard-working Edward will be forced to be George's partner, becoming literally his brother's keeper.

Both Edward and George are allegorical types: Edward is good; George is bad. George—after womanizing, drinking, gambling, and forging—tries to rob the bank where Edward works. Because he kept to the principles of purity and honesty that the Brants had taught him, Edward refuses to cooperate with George by opening the safe. But this sacrificial act results in the masked George's murdering Edward. After George is arrested and sentenced to die, women's charitable and religious organizations make a final attempt to enable him one more time. This time there is no extra chance for George. The very first punishment he receives is also his last: he is hanged for murdering Edward.

Part of the maxim taught by the Brants mysteriously reappears as an inscription on good Edward's tombstone, but only part. The conclusion to the saying, which assured "success" for doing good, is strangely omitted from the stone. In order to draw attention to the irony of the maxim, Twain gives an emphatic short paragraph to declare, "Nobody knows who gave the order to leave it that way, but it was so given" (752). The unfinished epitaph is Twain's comment on the vanity of Edward's pure and noble life. Moreover, after Edward's sacrificial death, the moral organizations neglect his widow and children and instead build a church, in another dose of Twainian irony. These very organizations and churches promulgated the maxim that resulted in Edward's murder. The organizations apparently must continue to enable those who do not live by the moral maxims. This social practice is costly for people who do live by such sayings. Twain has created an early, harsh satire on deceptive religious clichés, enabling parents, and charity organizations in **"Edward Mills and George Benton: A Tale."**[1]

Note

1. B & R Samizdat Express has added *The $30,000 Bequest and Other Stories* (including "Edward Mills") to its collection of electronic versions of the works of Mark Twain (e-mail: samizdat world.std.com).

Works Cited

MacDonald, Ruth. "Edward Mills and George Benton: A Tale." *The Mark Twain Encyclopedia*. Ed. J. R. LeMaster, James D. Wilson, and Christie Graves Hamric. Hamden, Conn.: Garland, 1993. 244.

Twain, Mark. "Edward Mills and George Benton: A Tale." *Collected Tales, Sketches, Speeches & Essays: 1852-1890.* New York: Library of America, 1981. 747-52.

Cynthia Ozick (essay date 1996)

SOURCE: Ozick, Cynthia. "Mark Twain's Vienna." In *Fame & Folly: Essays*, pp. 151-70. New York: Alfred A. Knopf, 1996.

[*In the following essay, Ozick explores the relationship between the prevalent anti-Semitism of 1890s Vienna and Twain's works that were written at the time of his residency there, particularly* The Man That Corrupted Hadleyburg.]

SOME INTRODUCTORY MUSINGS ON THE NATURE OF THE FACSIMILE

In contemplating the difference between a Victorian museum and one of our own era, what is the instantly recognizable contemporary element? Never mind that display cases have evolved from what used to be called "vitrines" (glass boxes on wooden legs); or that pictures are no longer strung from rococo cornices; or that museum visitors, too, have evolved—from isolated passionate starers to dogged mobs in motion, with headsets plugged into their ears. The absolute difference is in the growth of the lobby shop: here nearly every treasure of the galleries overhead appears in facsimile. The past is exactly duplicated in the present: for a few dollars you can own a Canaanite clay oil lamp or a carved Egyptian cat.

Jorge Borges in one of his ingenious *ficciones* imagines the paradox of a man who has written a "modern" *Don Quixote,* identical in every syllable to Cervantes' *Don Quixote.* Yet the difference is extreme: whereas the original work manifested a robust contemporary style of speech appropriate to the seventeenth century, the modern duplicate turns out to be hopelessly archaic. Or consider the plaster casts of those pitifully fleeing figures of Pompeii, whose shapes have already been preserved, two thousand years ago, in cooled volcanic ash: sculpted twice, they are twice removed from the ancient catastrophe they copy.

The idea of the facsimile is, in our time, itself a kind of volcanic eruption: this or that newfangled device can spew out an instantaneous copy of practically anything. All the same, there is a divide between the original and its imitator. The divide is history. When you purchase one of those clay oil lamps from a museum shop, and take it home and put it on a shelf, you may dream over it all you like, summoning up the past with your marveling caress—but the past of what? Its history is a molding machine in Newark, New Jersey. The original of anything carries the force of its own contemporaneity. Polishing my grandmother's brass candlesticks, I feel how *her* hand once did the same, and her spirit accompanies the act. Rare-book collectors know all this: the living touch of an aging binding is instinct with its period, and with the breath of its first owner.

A facsimile edition is something else altogether. Though it suggests a Zeitgeist long evaporated, still it can only *suggest*; so it places on its readers a burden of history-imagining that a genuine first edition will not. A first edition of an old book is an heirloom, a relic, an authentic survival of the past; in its own presence and essence, it *is* the past, a palpable instance of time-travel. But a facsimile edition, because it is the product of machined reproduction, stirs up a quandary: even if we are seduced into pretending so, ancestral eyes and hands did *not* encounter this very volume.

The quandary is this. Mark Twain in any available edition—and there are scores of these—augurs a reader's private exchange with an American classic. But Mark Twain in a facsimile edition is designed to be a wholly dissimilar experience; and yet it is not, and cannot be. Touch a facsimile volume, and what you touch is the refined technology of photocopying—no time-travel in *that*. I am looking now at a facsimile of a Harper & Brothers publication of *The Man That Corrupted Hadleyburg and Other Stories and Essays,* dated 1900. The print is large and clear, the margins generous. There is a frontispiece photograph of Mark Twain, captioned "S. L. Clemens." The copyright, curiously, is not in the name of S. L. Clemens (or of his pseudonym), but in that of Olivia L. Clemens, his wife. (She died in 1904, predeceasing him by six years). The fifteen items in the Table of Contents disclose their sources; of periodicals once renowned (*Harper's Magazine, The Century, The Cosmopolitan, The New York World, The Youth's Companion, The Forum, McClure's,* and *The North American Review*), only *Harper's* recognizably survives. The several illustrations (artist unidentified), with their captions excerpted from the text, are redolent of nineteenth-century charm—the charm of skilled and evocative drawings—and may make us nostalgic for a practice long in disuse: every tale equipped with its visual interpretation. (But it was a practice serious authors grew tired of and finally could no longer endure. Henry James, for instance, banished internal illustrations from his New York Edition and turned to photography for the frontispiece.)

A facsimile volume, then, can offer only this much of "history": a list of forgotten magazines, a handful of old-fashioned drawings, an imitative binding. The rest of it is the job of reading; and a facsimile volume, despite its hope of differentiating itself from an ordinary sort of book, reads, after all, like any other reprint. With this caution. A run-of-the-mill reprint will supply you with a text—fiction or essay—and leave you on your own, so to speak. A facsimile edition, on the other hand, because it deals in reproductive illusion—like that clay oil lamp bought in a museum gift shop—demands what illusion always demands: confirmation (or completion) in solid data. In brief: context or setting.

If I read **"The Man That Corrupted Hadleyburg"** in an indifferent or insipid edition, I read it as a celebrated story by Mark Twain, with all that signifies intrinsically. But if I read that same story in an ambitious and even beautiful facsimile format, the extrinsic urges itself on the text with the inexorability of a compensating force. The facsimile volume advertises a false authenticity—but it can lay no claim to being a historical object, any more than the museum-shop lamp can. Without the testimony of the archaeologists to give it context, the duplicate clay is merely last Tuesday's factory item; and without the surround of 1900, what is the *raison d'être*

of an imitation 1900 edition? The facsimile cries out for an adumbration of the world into which the original was introduced; that is its unique and pressing power, and the secret of its admittedly physical shock on our senses. Reproduction exacts history.

* * *

"The Man That Corrupted Hadleyburg" was written in 1898, in Europe: specifically, Vienna. Mark Twain was still under the shadow of an indelible bereavement; only two years earlier, in 1896, Susy, the oldest and probably the most literarily gifted of the three Clemens daughters, had suddenly been carried off by cerebral meningitis. Restlessness and grief drove Mark Twain and his family—his wife Livy and their two remaining daughters, Clara and Jean—from England to Switzerland to Vienna, where they settled for nearly two years. Clara had come to study piano and voice with distinguished Viennese teachers; Jean was being treated, intermittently and inconclusively, for epilepsy. But Mark Twain was there, willy-nilly, as Mark Twain abroad—which could only mean Mark Twain celebrated and lionized. Vienna was a brilliant magnet for composers and concert artists, for playwrights and satirists, for vivid promoters of liberal and avant-garde ideas. Mark Twain was courted by Hapsburg aristocrats—countesses and duchesses—and by diplomats and journalists and dramatists. He spoke at pacifist rallies and collaborated in the writing of a pair of plays urging women's suffrage (they never reached the stage and the manuscripts have not survived). He obliged this or that charity by giving public readings; one of them, in February 1898, was attended by Dr. Sigmund Freud. Set within resplendent architecture and statuary, the intellectual life of the city dazzled.

But there was another side to fin-de-siècle Vienna: its underside. Vienna was (then and later) notoriously, stingingly, passionately antisemitic. The familiar impulses that jubilantly welcomed Hitler's *Anschluss* in 1938, and defiantly elected Kurt Waldheim, a former Nazi, as president of Austria in 1986, were acted upon with equal vigor (and venom) in 1898, when the demagogue Karl Lueger held office as Vienna's popular mayor; and Lueger was a preparatory template for the Nazi politics that burgeoned in Vienna only two and a half decades on. In Mark Twain's Vienna, the cultural elite included prominent Jewish musicians and writers, among whom he flourished companionably; his daughter Clara married Ossip Gabrilowitsch, a Russian Jewish composer-pianist and fellow music student. These warm Viennese associations did not escape the noisome antisemitic press, which vulgarly denounced Mark Twain either as Jew-lover or as himself a secret Jew.

In 1898, the European press in general—whether in Paris or Brussels or Berlin or Vienna or even Moscow—was inflamed by an international controversy: the fever of the Dreyfus Affair was erupting well beyond France itself, where Captain Alfred Dreyfus, a Jewish army officer, had been falsely incriminated on a charge of treason. Polity after polity was split between Drey-fusards and anti-Dreyfusards; and in Vienna, Mark Twain boldly stood for Dreyfus's innocence. In 1898, Zola published his great *J'Accuse,* and escaped arrest by fleeing to England. It was the year of a vast Euro-pean poisoning, by insidious sloganeering and hideous posters and caricatures; no single country went unsul-lied.

And it was in this atmosphere that Mark Twain sat down to write **"The Man That Corrupted Hadleyburg"**—a story about a town in which moral poisoning widens and widens, until no single person remains unsullied. No one can claim that the Dreyfus Affair, a conspiracy to entrap the innocent, impinged explicitly on Mark Twain's tale of a citizenry brought down by revenge and spreading greed. But the notion of a society—even one in microcosm, like Hadleyburg—sliding deeper and deeper (and individual by individual) into ethical per-version and contamination was not far from a portrait of a Europe undergoing the contagion of its great com-munal lie. The commanding theme of **"The Man That Corrupted Hadleyburg"** *is* contagion; and also the smugness that arises out of self-righteousness, however rooted in lie it may be.

Hadleyburg's lie is its belief in its own honesty; it has, in fact, sheltered itself against the possibility of corrup-tion, teaching "the principles of honest dealing to its babies in the cradle," and insulating its young people from temptation, "so that their honesty could have ev-ery chance to harden and solidify, and become a part of their very bone." Yet the absence of temptation is com-monly no more than the absence of a testing occasion, and when temptation finally does come to Hadleyburg, no citizen, despite stringent prior training, can with-stand it. Dishonest money-lust creeps over the town, first infiltrating a respectable old couple, then moving from household to household of nineteen of the town's most esteemed worthies. An archetypal narrative, it goes without saying: the devil tempting the seemingly pure, who turn out to be as flawed as the ordinary hu-man article usually is. The Faustian bargain trades inno-cence for gold.

A first reading of **"The Man That Corrupted Hadley-burg"**—i.e., a first reading *now,* nearly a century after its composition—is apt to disappoint through overfamil-iarity. It is not that familiarity lessens art; not in the least; more often it intensifies art. The experience of one *Hamlet* augments a second and a third, and this is as true of *Iolanthe* as it is of Shakespeare; but surely we don't go to *Hamlet* or *Iolanthe* for the *plot.* In the last several decades Hadleyburg, as the avatar of a cor-rupted town, has reappeared in short stories by Shirley

Jackson ("The Lottery") and I. B. Singer ("The Gentle-man from Cracow"), and in *The Visit,* a chilling drama by Friedrich Dürrenmatt. And not only through such lit-erary means: in the hundred years since Mark Twain in-vented Hadleyburg, a proliferation of story-appliances (radio, film, television, and video-recorders), spilling out scores of Hadleyburgs, has acquainted us with (and doubtless hardened us against) the stealthy despoliation of an idyllic town by a cunning stranger. Hadleyburg, for us, is largely a cinematic cliché worn down, by now, to a parody of itself; nor do we have any defence against our belatedness (to use a critical term made fa-mous by Harold Bloom).

But all that applies only to a first reading, when what will stand out is, mainly, the lineaments of the narrative itself. Behind the recognizable Faustian frame are two unlikely categories of ingenuity. The first touches on the identity of the tempter. Hadleyburg, we are told, "had the ill luck to offend a passing stranger . . . a bit-ter man and vengeful."

> All through his wanderings during a whole year he kept his injury in mind, and gave all his leisure mo-ments to trying to invent a compensating satisfaction for it. He contrived many plans, and all of them were good, but none of them was quite sweeping enough; the poorest of them would hurt a great many individu-als, but what he wanted was a plan which would com-prehend the entire town, and not let so much as one person escape unhurt. At last he had a fortunate idea, and when it fell into his brain it lit up his whole head with an evil joy.

We know no more than this about the injured stranger and never will know more. (Here the illustrator has supplied a gloating figure in overcoat, top hat, and cra-vat, rubbing his hands together and hooking his feet around the legs of a chair. Ears, nose, and chin are each pointedly pointed, and you almost expect to catch the point of a tail lashing behind.) There is no shred of a hint concerning the nature of the offense, or exactly who committed it. This forcefully suggests the Demi-urge, who hates the human race simply for its indepen-dent existence, especially when that existence is em-broidered by moral striving; the devil requires no motive. And as the powerful sovereign of a great and greatly populated kingdom, he has no need of revenge. The Demiurge's first and last urge is gluttony—the lust to fatten his kingdom with more and more souls. Ven-geance is clearly a human trait, not the devil's; so we may conclude that the "passing stranger" is, in truth, no different in kind from any indigenous citizen of Hadley-burg, and that the vengeful outlander and the honest na-tive are, in potential and surely in outcome, identical.

And, indeed, at the end of the day, when Hadleyburg has been fully corrupted, there is nothing to choose be-tween the "evil joy" of the schemer and the greedy dreams of the townsfolk who scheme to enrich themselves through lies. The contest is not between the devil and man, but between man and man.[1] And it is not so much a contest as a confluence. In other words, we may be induced to imagine that *all* the citizens of Hadleyburg are "passing strangers": strangers to themselves. They have believed that they are one thing—pure hearts burnished and enameled by honesty—and they learn that they are another thing: corruptible, degraded, profoundly exposed.

Then is the corrupter of Hadleyburg *not* the devil? And if he is not, is there, after all, *no* Faustian frame? Is what we have, instead, the textual equivalent of the sort of optical illusion that permits you to perceive, with unqualified clarity, two different pictures, but never at the same instant? Nearly everyone has experienced the elusive vase that suddenly shows itself as a pair of silhouettes, and the maddening human profiles that unaccountably flash out of sight to reveal a vase: is *this* the conceptual design of Mark Twain's narrative? That the outline of the corrupter is inseparable from the outline of the corrupted—that they are one and the same, ineluctably and horribly fused—but that our gaze is barred from absorbing this metaphorical simultaneity? A far more subtle invention than the Faustian scaffold on which this tale has always been said to depend.

On the other hand, Hadleyburg's tempter (whether or not he is intended to be a Mephistophelean emblem) *does* have a palpable identity of another kind—one we can easily grasp; and this is Mark Twain's second category of ingenuity. The stranger is a man who relishes the manipulation of words: certain phrases must be reproduced, and they must be precisely the *right* phrases, every syllable perfected. When a sack is deposited at the house of Mr. and Mrs. Richards, an explanatory note is attached. The note is far from brief; it has a plot, a trajectory, a climactic purpose; it promises as much as the opening of a fairy tale. The sack, it claims, "contains gold coin weighing a hundred and sixty pounds four ounces," and should be given as a reward of gratitude to the unknown Hadleyburg citizen who long ago unwittingly earned it. The sack's donor was once a gambler who was spurred to reform because a man of the town gave him twenty dollars and spoke a sentence that "saved the remnant of my morals." That man, the schemer's note continues—and we have understood from the beginning that all this is a spurious concoction—that man "can be identified by the remark he made to me; I feel persuaded that he will remember it."

This is a story, then, that hangs on a set of words—fictitious, invented words—and as the narrative flies on with increasing complexity, devising painful joke after painful joke, it soon becomes clear that **"The Man That Corrupted Hadleyburg"** is less about gold than it is about language. A sentence that is *almost* "correct"

but contains a vagrant "very," is deemed fraudulent; eventually all versions of the elusive remark fall under a cloud of fraudulence, and threaten the town, and expose its infamous heart. And ultimately even hard gold coin is converted into language, in the form of written checks. It is language itself, even language subjected to comedy, that is revealed as the danger, as a conduit to greed, as an entangler in shame and sin and derision.

Which probably *does* return us to the devil. And why not? Mark Twain, early and late, is always preoccupied with the devil and his precincts: the devil is certainly the hero of ***The Mysterious Stranger*** (a work that is also a product of Vienna), where he is a grand imaginer who appears under the name of Dream, though his dreams are human nightmares, and his poetry destroys. In this view (and who will separate it from Mark Twain's metaphysical laughter?), the devil is a writer, and the corrupter of Hadleyburg a soulless figure who comprehends that words can carry more horror, and spread more evil joy, than any number of coveted treasures in a sack: even in the saving light of ridicule.

* * *

And if we are returned to the devil and his precincts, we are also returned to Vienna. Under the purposefully ambiguous title "Stirring Times in Vienna," Mark Twain published in *Harper's,* in the latter part of 1897, four pieces of journalism reporting on sessions of the parliament of the Hapsburg empire, then known as Austria-Hungary—a political amalgam of nineteen national enclaves that endured for fifty-one years until its dissolution after the First World War. The Austrian parliament, situated in Vienna, and conducted in German (the empire's official language), is, in Mark Twain's rendering, a non-homogeneous Hadleyburg corrupted well past mere greed into the contagion of chaos and contumely. The Hadleyburg townsfolk are uniformly named Richards and Burgess and Goodson and Wilson and Billson; and yet their interests conflict as if they held nothing in common. In the Austrian parliament it is certain that nothing is held in common: the native languages of the members are Polish, Czech, Romanian, Hungarian, Italian, German, etc., and the motley names correspond to their speakers' origins. What is at issue, in December of 1897, is a language dispute. The Bohemians are demanding that Czech replace German as Bohemia's official language; the government (i.e., the majority party) has acceded. But the German-speaking Austrians, who comprise only one-fourth of the empire's entire population, are enraged, and are determined to prevent the government from pursuing all other business—including the ratification of the indispensable *Ausgleich,* the renewable treaty of confederation linking Austria and Hungary—unless and until German is restored in Bohemia.

The analogy with Hadleyburg is not gratuitous. Here again the crux is language. In Hadleyburg there are nineteen worthies complicit in the turmoil of communal shame; in the Austrian parliament there are nineteen states. And just as the nineteen leading citizens of Hadleyburg furiously compete, so do the Austrian parliamentarians: "Broadly speaking, all the nations in the empire hate the government—but they all hate each other too, and with devoted and enthusiastic bitterness; no two of them can combine; the nation that rises must rise alone." And if we can recognize in Hadleyburg the dissolving Austria-Hungary of the 1890's, we can surely recognize the disintegrated components of the former Yugoslavia in the 1990's. Hadleyburg may be emblematic of the imperial parliament in Vienna seventeen years before the outbreak of war in Sarajevo in 1914; even more inescapably, it presages the fin-de-siècle Sarajevo of our own moment.

Yet there is a difference—of reportage—between Mark Twain's Vienna and contemporary Bosnia that turns out to be not quite what we would expect. The facsimile volume presents us with a pair of century-old photographs, one showing the exterior of the parliament, the other a violent interior scene. The parliament buildings appear to stretch over three or four city blocks, with all the majesty of a row of imperial palaces. The interior—"its panelled sweep relieved by fluted columns of distinguished grace and dignity, which glow softly and frostily in the electric light"—offers a mob of unruly screamers, a good number of them clubbing their desks with wooden planks. The photographs are necessarily static and silent, and we might be induced to feel technologically superior in a news-gathering way to a generation that perforce had to do without CNN or Court TV (not omitting the impact of the Army-McCarthy hearings of the 1950's); whereas *we* have television (and the prose of Peter Arnett). Vienna in 1897 had only Mark Twain; and imagination confirms which medium overpowers (or, as we are wont to put it, "outperforms") which. What TV anchor, accompanied by what "brilliant camerawork," can match this introspective portrait of the parliament's Polish president?

> He is a gray-haired, long, slender man, with a colorless long face, which, in repose, suggests a death-mask; but when not in repose is tossed and rippled by a turbulent smile which washes this way and that, and is not easy to keep up with—a pious smile, a beseeching and supplicating smile; and when it is at work the large mouth opens, and the flexible lips crumple, and unfold, and crumple again, and move around in a genial and persuasive and angelic way, and expose large glimpses of teeth; and that interrupts the sacredness of the smile and gives it momentarily a mixed worldly and political and satanic cast.

As for the rest of the assembly, they are "religious men, they are earnest, sincere, devoted, and they hate the Jews."

Mark Twain's dispatches reached New York without tampering. The imperial press was subject to a heavy and capricious censorship; so it is possible that the readers of *Harper's* were more intimately informed of the degradation of an allegedly democratic parliament than the citizens of Austria or of its eighteen coequal provinces. The tactics of the Opposition—i.e., of the Germans who refuse to allow the Czechs their own tongue—begin reasonably enough, in parliamentary fashion, with a heroic one-man filibuster lasting twelve hours. At the speaker's first words, however, decorum instantly and repeatedly gives way to yells, the beating of desks with long boards, and the clamor of threats and name-calling astonishingly gutter-bred. (The members of the assembly include princes, counts, barons, priests, lawyers, judges, physicians, professors, merchants, bankers—and also "that distinguished religious expert, Dr. Lueger, Bürgermeister of Vienna.") A number of these shouted declarations vibrate with a dread familiarity, as if a recording of the sounds of the Vienna of 1938 are somehow being hurled back into that earlier time, forty years before: "The Germans of Austria will neither surrender nor die!" "It's a pity that such a man [one willing to grant language rights to the Czechs] should be a leader of the Germans; he disgraces the German name!" "And *these* shameless creatures are the leaders of the German People's Party!" "You Jew, you!" "I would rather take my hat off to a Jew!" "Jew flunky! Here we have been fighting the Jews for ten years and now you are helping them to power again. How much do you get for it?" "You Judas!" "Schmeel Leeb Kohn! Schmeel Leeb Kohn!"

But let us not misrepresent by overselection. Tainting their opponents with "Jew" may be the most scurrilous offense these princes, counts, barons, priests, judges, etc., can settle on, but it is not the most imaginative. There are also the following: "Brothel-knight!" "East German offal-tub!" "Infamous louse-brat!" "Cowardly blatherskite!"—along with such lesser epithets as "Polish dog," "miserable cur," and *"Die Grossmutter auf dem Misthaufen erzeugt worden"* (which Mark Twain declines to translate from the original).

In short: a parliamentary riot that is soon to turn into street riots. The fourth and last dispatch records the arrival of the militia:

> And now we see what history will be talking of five centuries hence: a uniformed and helmeted battalion of bronzed and stalwart men marching in double file down the floor of the House—a free parliament profaned by an invasion of brute force! . . . They ascended the steps of the tribune, laid their hands upon the inviolable persons of the representatives of a nation, and dragged and tugged and hauled them down the steps and out at the door.

"The memory of it," Mark Twain concludes—and by now all satire is drained away—"will outlast all the thrones that exist today. In the whole history of free parliaments the like of it had been seen but three times before. It takes its imposing place among the world's unforgettable things."

He is both wrong and right. Wrong, because the December 1897 parliamentary upheaval in Vienna is of course entirely forgotten, except by historian-specialists and readers of Mark Twain's least-known prose. And right, because it is an indelible precursor that not merely portends the profoundly unforgettable Viennese mob-events of 1938, but thrusts them into our teeth with all their bitter twentieth-century flavor. Here is no déjà vu, but its prophesying opposite. Or, to say it otherwise: a twenty-year-old rioter enjoying Mark Twain's Vienna easily becomes a sixty-year-old Nazi enjoying *Anschluss* Vienna.

In the immediate wake of the introduction of the militia, the government

> came down with a crash; there was a popular outbreak or two in Vienna; there were three or four days of furious rioting in Prague, followed by the establishing there of martial law; the Jews [who were by and large German-speaking] and Germans were harried and plundered, and their houses destroyed; in other Bohemian towns there was rioting—in some cases the Germans being the rioters, in others the Czechs—and in all cases the Jew had to roast, no matter which side he was on.

* * *

All this was in progress while Europe continued to boil over Dreyfus. Living on top of the fire, so to speak, Mark Twain could hardly overlook the roasting Jews. Consequently, a few months after his parliamentary reports, he published in *Harper's,* in March of 1898, a kind of sequel to "Stirring Times in Vienna"—a meditation entitled "Concerning the Jews." Part polemic, part reprimand, part self-contradictory panegyric, the essay was honorably motivated but ultimately obtuse and harmful. The London *Jewish Chronicle,* for example, commented at the time: "Of all such advocates, we can but say 'Heaven save us from our friends.'" (In the United States in the 1930's, pro-Nazi groups and other antisemites seized on portions of the essay to suggest an all-American signature for the promulgation of hate.)

Mark Twain was not unaware that Sholem Aleichem, the classic Yiddish writer, was affectionately called "the Jewish Mark Twain." This was because Sholem Aleichem, like his American counterpart, was a bittersweet humorist and a transcendent humanist; and also because he reflected his village Jews, sunk in deepest poverty, as intimately and faithfully as Mark Twain recorded the homespun villages of his American South. Both men were better known by their pen names than by their actual names; both stood for liberty of the oppressed; both

were eagerly read by the plain people—the "folk"; and both were nearly unprecedented as popular literary heroes. Sholem Aleichem certainly read Mark Twain (possibly in German translation), but it is hardly likely that Mark Twain read Sholem Aleichem. Even the smallest inkling of Sholem Aleichem's social content would have stood in the way of the central canard of "Concerning the Jews." And to contradict that canard, and to determine the real and typical condition of the shtetl-bound mass of European Jews, Mark Twain had only to look over his shoulder at those Jewish populations nearest to hand in Austro-Hungarian Galicia. Instead he looked to the old hostile myths.

To be sure, "Concerning the Jews" is remembered (perhaps mainly by those who have never read it) as charmingly philosemitic. A single witty—and famous—sentence supports that view: "All that I care to know is that a man is a human being—that is enough for me; he can't be any worse." And we can believe Mark Twain—we *do* believe him—when he avers that he makes "no uncourteous reference" to Jews in his books "because the disposition is lacking." Up to a point the disposition *is* lacking; there is plenty of evidence for it. A curious science-fiction sketch called **"From the 'London Times' of 1904"**—written about the same time as "Concerning the Jews," and striking for its "invention" of the "telectrophonoscope," or television—turns out to be a lampoon of "French Justice" as exemplified in the punishment of the innocent Dreyfus; and if a savage satire can be felt to be delectable, this one is.

The disposition is lacking in other, less political, directions. Jewish charitableness, Jewish generosity, Jewish responsibility are all acknowledged—for the moment. The facts, Mark Twain declares,

> are all on the credit side of the proposition that the Jew is a good and orderly citizen. Summed up, they certify that he is quiet, peaceable, industrious, unaddicted to high crime and brutal dispositions; that his family life is commendable; that he is not a burden upon public charities; that he is not a beggar; that in benevolence he is above the reach of competition. These are the very quintessentials of good citizenship.

And all this is followed by another accolade: the Jew is honest. The proof of it is that the "basis of successful business is honesty; a business cannot thrive where the parties to it cannot trust each other." Who will not affirm this generality? Now add to the assertion of Jewish honesty this quip about the "Jewish brain," from a letter to an American friend, written from Vienna in 1897: "The difference between the brain of the average Christian and that of the average Jew . . . is about the difference between a tadpole's and an Archbishop's." We may laugh at this, but let liberal laughter be on its guard: the Jew, the essay continues, "has a reputation for various small forms of cheating . . . and for arranging cunning contracts which leave him an exit but lock the other man in, and for smart evasions which find him safe and comfortable just within the strict letter of the law, when court and jury know very well that he has violated the spirit of it." From none of this does Mark Twain dissent. So much for his honest Jewish businessman. And so much for praise of the "Jewish brain," which takes us straightway to "cunning contracts" and "smart evasions" and the old, old supersessionist proposition that Judaism attends to the "letter," and not to the "spirit."

Still, the overriding engine of this essay is situated in a much larger proposition. "In all countries," Mark Twain tells us, "from the dawn of history, the Jew has been persistently and implacably hated, and with frequency persecuted." From the dawn of history? And if so, why? Not because the Jew has been millennially blamed for the Crucifixion; "the reasons for it are older than that event," and reside entirely in the Jew's putative economic prowess; theology doesn't apply; at least the Gospels and Pauline and Augustinian traditions don't apply. Skip the Crucifixion, then; penetrate even more deeply behind the veil, into those still earlier mists of pre-history, and let the fault land on Joseph in Egypt—Joseph the provider, "who took a nation's money all away, to the last penny." *There* is your model for "the Jew"! "I am convinced," Mark Twain insists, "that the persecution of the Jew is not due in any large degree to religious prejudice." And here is his judgment of the root of the matter:

> No, the Jew is a money-getter; and in getting his money he is a very serious obstruction to less capable neighbors who are on the same quest. . . . In estimating worldly values the Jew is not shallow, but deep. With precocious wisdom he found out in the morning of time that some men worship rank, some worship heroes, some worship power, some worship God, and that over these ideals they dispute and cannot unite—but that they all worship money; so he made it the end and aim of his life to get it. He was at it in Egypt thirty-six centuries ago; he was at it in Rome . . . ; he has been at it ever since. The cost to him has been heavy; his success has made the whole human race his enemy—but it has paid, for it has brought him envy, and that is the only thing which men will sell both soul and body for.

Reading this, who can help thinking that all of it could go down quite nicely in the Austrian parliament of late 1897, not to mention the Viennese street? There is enough irony here to make even the devil weep. The truth is that Mark Twain was writing of Jews as "money-getters" at a time when the mass emigration of poor Jews by the hundreds of thousands had already begun to cram the steerage compartments of transoceanic ships—Jews in flight from economic hopelessness; and

when the meanest penury was the lot of most Jews; and when Jewish letters and Jewish lore and Jewish wit took "poor" to be synonymous with "Jew." And here comes Mark Twain, announcing that the Jew's "commercial importance is extravagantly out of proportion to the smallness of his bulk." He might have taken in the anguished testimony of Sholem Aleichem's Jews; or the deprivations of Galician Jews down the road, so to speak, from Vienna; or the travail of Russian Jews penned into the Pale of Settlement. Or, in his native land, he might have taken in the real status of all those small storekeepers whose names he notes on their shop-signs (Edelstein, Blumenthal, Rosenzweig), while observing that "commercial importance" means railroads, banks, mining, insurance, steel, shipping, real estate, etc., etc.—industries where he would have been hard put to find a single Jew.

As it happens, he took in almost none of it; and, though eschewing theology, let himself be taken in by an ancient theological canard: the legacy, via the Judas legend, of the Jew's affinity for money—the myth of the Rich Jew, the Jew Usurer. The very use of the generic phrase "the Jew" suggests stigma. Mythology, it develops, is the heart and muscle of Mark Twain's reputedly "philosemitic" essay—the old myths trotted out for an airing in the American idiom. He said he lacked the disposition for slander. It would be wrong to dismiss this statement; but perhaps it would be fairer to suppose that he lacked the disposition for disciplined caution. He knew nothing of Jewish literary or jurisprudential civilization, or of the oceanic intellectual traditions of Jewish biblical commentary; he approached the Joseph tale with the crudity of a belligerent village atheist, and employed it to defame on economic grounds exactly as the charge of deicide defamed on theological grounds.

Yet he was surely capable of renouncing a canard when someone helped him to prise out the truth. The Jew, he had written, "is charged with an unpatriotic disinclination to stand by the flag as a soldier." "You feed on a country," he accused, "but you don't like to fight for it." Nevertheless there is appended, at the end of this essay, a remarkable Postscript: "The Jew as Soldier," wherein instance after historical instance of Jewish "fidelity" and "gallant soldiership" is cited—in the American Revolution, the War of 1812, the Mexican War, and especially the Civil War. It is not the admission of canard that is remarkable, but rather the principle drawn from it: "It is not allowable to endorse wandering maxims upon supposition." That, overall, and despite its contrary motivation, is a precise characterization of "Concerning the Jews"—the endorsement of wandering maxims upon supposition. Only compare George Eliot's "The Modern Hep Hep"—a chapter in her *Impressions of Theophrastus Such,* published just twenty years before Mark Twain's wandering maxims—to see what a generalized essay concerning the Jews, engaging Mark Twain's own questions, might attain to.

* * *

Mark Twain's twenty months of residence in Vienna were among his most prolific. The fifteen short works collected in the 1900 edition of *The Man That Corrupted Hadleyburg and Other Stories and Essays* are a fraction of his output during this period; but they reflect the entire arsenal of his art: the occasionally reckless polemic, the derisive irony, the intelligent laughter, the verbal stilettoes, the blunt country humor, the fervent despair, the hidden jeer, the relishing of palaver and tall tale, the impatient worldliness, the brilliant forays of language—sometimes for purposes of search-and-destroy, sometimes for a show of pure amazement, sometimes for plain delight in the glory of human oddness; most often for story-telling's fragile might. Nothing is too trivial, nothing too weighty. And frequently the trivial and the weighty are enmeshed, as in Hadleyburg, when the recitation of a handful of words touches on depths of deceit. Or as in a lightly turned sketch— **"My Boyhood Dreams"**—that teases such eminences as William Dean Howells and John Hay (U.S. Secretary of State in 1898) with their failure to fulfill their respective childhood ambitions—steamboat mate and auctioneer; never mind that these "ambitions" are wholly of Mark Twain's antic invention. But even so playful an oddment as this begins with a bitter reference to the humiliated Dreyfus.

In fact, aboard Mark Twain's prose you cannot very long rely on the "lightly turned"—whatever sets out with an elfin twitch of the nostrils or a Mona Lisa half-smile is likely to end in prophetic thunder. **"My First Lie, and How I Got Out of It"** starts off with a diaper pin and a twinkle, but its real theme is indifference to injustice—"the silent assertion that there wasn't anything going on in which humane and intelligent people were interested." From slaveholding to Dreyfus is but a paragraph's leap: "From the beginning of the Dreyfus case to the end of it all France . . . lay under the smother of the silent-assertion lie that no wrong was being done to a persecuted and unoffending man." And from Dreyfus how far is it to the "silent National Lie," "whole races and peoples conspir[ing] to propagate gigantic mute lies in the interest of tyrannies and sham"? Beware Mark Twain when his subject looks most severely simple or mild-manneredly innocent: you may speedily find yourself aflame in a fiery furnace of moral indignation.

Sketches, fables, diatribes. Eight months before his death in 1910 he wrote, "I am full of malice, saturated with malignity." More than two decades earlier he had exclaimed to Howells that his was "a pen warmed up in hell." Yet—with relative benignity—the remainder of this volume treats of artists who are ignored while alive and valued only posthumously (**"Is He Living or Is He Dead?"**); of a train companion determined to set right every minor annoyance (**"Travelling with a Reformer"**); and of a celebrated inventor ordered by the Austrian government to teach grade school (**"The Austrian Edison Keeping School Again"**). But that is scarcely the finish of it—there are other exuberances. **"The Private History of the 'Jumping Frog' Story"** not only supplies an ancient Greek version of the joke, but bursts into a spoof of word-for-word translation from the French. "How to Tell a Story" will remind readers of nighttime ghost-scares at summer camp, while **"The Esquimau Maiden's Romance"**—an unrestrained comic lecture on the relative nature of wealth— would hardly pass muster in a contemporary multiculturalist classroom. "About Play-Acting" compares a serious drama in Vienna with the frivolous offerings cut from the New York theater advertisements of Saturday, May 7, 1898; Broadway at this hour (despite spectacular technical advances) is not a whit more substantive or sophisticated. **"At the Appetite Cure,"** with its praise of starvation as the key to health, reflects Mark Twain's own belief in the curative virtues of abstinence from food—a crank piece; but here the jokes are crude and cruel, with a Teutonic edge of near-sadism. All the same, the most stirring—the most startling—real-life narrative in this volume, "My Debut as a Literary Person," concerns starvation: in extremis, at sea, in a small boat, after a shipwreck. Mark Twain defines it in a minor way as a journalistic scoop, but for power, passion, character, and suspense, it belongs among his masterworks.

All these romances—some as slight as skits, and one as rich and urgent as a novel—were set down in Mark Twain's Vienna: a cosmopolis driven by early modernism, saturated in music and theater, populated by gargantuan cultural figures whose influence still shakes the world (Sigmund Freud and Theodor Herzl, to mention only these), ruled by rogues (two of Hitler's idols among them), on occasion ruled by mobs; a society gaudily brilliant, acutely civilized, triumphantly flourishing, and also shameless, brutal. Part heaven, part the devil's precinct. An odd backdrop for a writer reared in Hannibal, Missouri. But in Vienna Mark Twain was close to the peak of what he called his "malignity," and Vienna served him.

Along with Dreyfus in Paris, it gave him a pen warmed up in the local hell.

Note

1. Mark Twain and an avalanche of literature before him employ "man" to represent humankind; and

so will I, without a trace of feminist shame, when the grace of a sentence depends on it.

Laura Skandera-Trombley (essay date June 1997)

SOURCE: Skandera-Trombley, Laura. "Mark Twain's Cross-Dressing Oeuvre." *College Literature* 24, no. 2 (June 1997): 82-96.

[*In the following essay, Skandera-Trombley explores the cultural implications of Twain's use of transvestism in his fiction, demonstrating how his cross-dressing characters and episodes challenge social constructions of gender and race.*]

Mark Twain apparently enjoyed nothing better than writing a rollicking transvestite tale. Beginning with his uncompleted short story **"A Medieval Romance"** (begun in 1868) and continuing in his 1894 novel *Pudd'nhead Wilson,* Twain was irresistibly drawn to loving descriptions and painstaking explorations of the contexts and implications of cross-dressing. He left a myriad of texts that testify to his fascination with transvestism; in addition to the short story and novel mentioned above, cross-dressing can be found in such various works as **"1,002d Arabian Night"** (1883), *Adventures of Huckleberry Finn* (1885), *Personal Recollections of Joan of Arc* (1896), *Following the Equator* (Vol. 2 1897), **"Wapping Alice"** (1898, 1907), **"How Nancy Jackson Married Kate Wilson"** (c. 1902) [also known as **"Feud Story and the Girl who was Ostensibly a Man"**], and **"A Horse's Tale"** (1907).

In his transvestite tales Twain was identifying and challenging social constructions of gender, distribution of power within a patriarchal society, and socially determined racial categories. An evolution of what Marjorie Garber terms "transvestite effects" can be traced in Twain's transvestite tales from his first gender-switch short story where stereotypical gender roles are presented then problematized, to introducing a female "gender-trickster" figure in *Adventures of Huckleberry Finn* who identifies and controls these constructions: to ultimately creating intersections where gender, race, and class identities meet in *Adventures of Huckleberry Finn* and *Pudd'nhead Wilson.*[1]

While I am not the first to discuss Twain's use of cross-dressing (both Susan Gillman and Garber include substantive explorations), what has not been previously explored is the society being reflected in Twain's writings whose culture and history is being portrayed. Indeed, in utilizing the element of cross-dressing in short stories and novels (such as **"A Medieval Romance"** and *Personal Recollections of Joan of Arc),* where gender themes are foremost, Twain may well have been paying tribute to upper-class, European-American female reformers and suffragettes.[2] In addition, in novels where racial themes are paramount, such as *Adventures of Huckleberry Finn* and *Pudd'nhead Wilson,* he was openly recognizing oral and written contributions made by African-American women in the form of slave narratives.

In his first transvestite text, **"Medieval Romance,"** Twain introduced a theme that would resurface in a more developed form in **"1,002d Arabian Night."** In both stories, the sex of the heroine necessitates cross-dressing in order for inheritance and dynastic structures to remain intact. Yet, in inventing the transvestite heroine, Twain was consciously subverting these systems. While the patriarchal order superficially remains intact at the end of these stories, a sexual revolution has been effected by transvestites who transform the monarchy and sultanate into matriarchies. What takes place here is that the figure of the transvestite restructures the existing society.

In **"Medieval Romance,"** the main character Conrad has been raised as a male by her father, who is determined that the throne will belong to his side of the family, not his brother Ulrich's. When Conrad is twenty-eight years old, her father relates the story of her birth and the reasons for her male gender. Appalled, Conrad remonstrates, "Oh, my father! Is it for this my life hath been a lie? Was it that I might cheat my unoffending cousin of her rights? Spare me, father, spare your child!" (*The Complete Short Stories of Mark Twain* 56).

With Conrad, Twain introduced his first gender-trickster transvestite character, although Conrad does not realize she is tricking anyone until her father informs her that her identity has been a deception in order to win the monarchy. However, despite her father's attempts to fool his brother, by the end of the tale Conrad and her father are out-tricked by Ulrich's daughter Constance. Constance has been seduced by one of her Uncle's henchmen, and she has given birth out of wedlock. It is decided that she must stand trial. Conrad, speaking from the throne, informs Constance that she must name the father of her child. Constance, enraged because Conrad has earlier rejected her advances, names Conrad. Conrad and her father, overcome by the accusation, both swoon. Apparently this plot twist complicated the story to such an extent that after this revelation Twain broke off the narrative and printed a disclaimer in the *Buffalo Express* explaining, "I have got my hero (or heroine) into such a particularly close place that I do not see how I am ever going to get him (or her) out of it again, and therefore I will wash my hands of the whole business" (*The Complete Short Stories of Mark Twain* 56). Twain's language, "hero (or heroine)" and "him (or her)," is a good example of what Garber means by the transvestite's causing a "failure of definitional distinction."

Twain's next depiction of transvestism would come eight years after **"A Medieval Romance,"** in the 1876 portion of *Adventures of Huckleberry Finn,* a novel where all of the main characters (Huckleberry, Jim, and Tom) don female dress at different junctures. The two scenes of cross-dressing contained in the first section of the manuscript (chapters 1-18) are of particular interest here. Early in the novel, there occurs an odd incident which Huckleberry Finn matter of factly recounts: a body had been found in the river. This in itself is not particularly unusual; what is noteworthy about this drowning is the victim's apparel:

> Well, about this time [Pap] was found in the river drowned, about twelve mile above town, so people said. . . . They judged it was him, anyway. . . . They said he was floating on his back in the water. They took him and buried him on the bank. But I warn't comfortable long, because I happen to think of something. I knowed mighty well that a drownded man don't float on his back, but on his face. So I knowed then, that this warn't pap, but a woman dressed up in a man's clothes.
>
> (15)[3]

If Huck is correct (and he is regarding Pap), then the reader must contend with the possibility of a female cross-dresser who may have met with foul play. Without any other immediate reference, the aside is easily overlooked when Huck continues his story. Yet this mention, while brief, is crucial and contains two questions begging to be asked: is the drowned woman simply a southern transvestite, or could Twain have been testing his reader's knowledge of African-American antebellum history? There does exist an historical explanation for the identity of the drowning victim: she may have been an African-American woman fleeing North to escape enslavement who in her flight had either accidently drowned or been murdered.

If we pursue the possibility that the drowned woman might have been African-American, this incident would signal the beginning of Twain's conflating gender identification with racial categories.[4] Indeed in this quick aside, Twain seems to be developing a paradigm where gender and race meet. Garber explains that,

> the apparently spontaneous or unexpected or supplementary presence of a transvestite figure in a text . . . that does not seem, thematically, to be primarily concerned with gender difference or blurred gender indicates a category crisis elsewhere, an irresolvable conflict or epistemological crux that destabilizes comfortable binarity, and displaces the resulting discomfort onto a figure that already inhabits, indeed incarnates, the margin.
>
> (17)

Huck's inability to determine the sex of the dead person, and the historical possibilities for explaining his/her presence, certainly indicate a "category crisis elsewhere"—indeed, the "irresolvable conflict" within *Adventures of Huckleberry Finn* is that of slavery.

A connection can be made between this episode and African-American women's slave narratives where cross-dressing was a familiar component. Tales of escape from the South were well known, and hundreds of formerly enslaved African-Americans told their stories on the anti-slavery lecture circuit in the Northeast. According to Henry Louis Gates, Jr., "over one hundred [African-Americans] wrote book-length 'slave narratives,' before the end of the Civil War" (ix). Between the years of 1703 and 1944, these accounts were so numerous it has been estimated that "six thousand and six ex-slaves had narrated the stories of their captivity, through interviews, essays, and books" (*The Classic Slave Narratives* ix).

Among the published narratives were two that received a great deal of attention. William and Ellen Craft's *Running a Thousand Miles for Freedom,* published in London in 1860, is by any measure a remarkable story. Ellen Craft, who was fair-skinned, disguised herself as a European-American southern planter, and her husband assumed the role of her/his slave. Travelling together, they managed to escape to the North and later fled to England. By the time William Still's *The Underground Rail Road* was published in 1883, the Crafts were so renowned that in addition to telling the story of their escape, Still included an account of their post-slavery life (Freedman xv).

Another slave narrative featuring a cross-dressed woman was published in 1861 by Harriet Jacobs under the pseudonym Linda Brent. Gates calls Jacob's *Incidents in the Life of a Slave Girl* "the major black woman's autobiography of the mid-nineteenth century" (*The Classic Slave Narratives* xvi). Could Twain have known of Harriet Jacobs? It seems almost impossible that he would not. Contained within his personal library were histories of slavery by Charles Ball and Still as well as Lydia Maria Child's *Anti-Slavery Catechism* (Gribben 43, 141, 666).[5] In addition, after making her escape from the South in 1849, Jacobs moved to Rochester where she joined abolitionists and began working in an anti-slavery reading room and office located above Frederick Douglass's newspaper, *The North Star* (Yellin xvi). The Langdons were well acquainted with Douglass; Jervis Langdon served as a conductor on the Underground Railroad and had aided Douglass during his escape from slavery (*Mark Twain's Letters. 1867-68* 2: 244). In subsequent years, Douglass was often a guest in the Langdon home. Twain met and spoke with Douglass in December 1869 and later wrote a letter to President Garfield endorsing Douglass for a federal job (*Mark Twain's Letters. 1869* 3: 428). It seems logical that considering the Langdons's times to the Underground Railroad and abolitionist societies and both the Langdons and Twain's personal relationships with Douglass, that they knew of Jacobs's *Incidents.*

This initial transvestite allusion in *Adventures of Huckleberry Finn,* read in isolation from other scenes of transvestism, quickly becomes buried as Huck races along in his narrative. Buried, that is, until the next incident of cross-dressing. Huck, attempting to "find out what was going on," clumsily disguises himself as a girl and inquires at the dwelling of Mrs. Judith Loftus to see if she has any news about the search for him and Jim (47). Loftus informs Huck that she thinks Jim is still in the area—over on Jackson Island. She then proceeds to tell Huck, in precise terms, her husband's plan for the evening. A frightened Huckleberry takes up needle and thread and, after watching him fumble, Mrs. Loftus asks him to throw and catch. Sharp-eyed Mrs. Loftus soon suspects that Huck is not a girl, and after she observes him awkwardly trying to thread a needle, she cleverly devises a series of tests to prove her suspicions: she has Huck throw a lump of lead at a rat and then drops a piece of lead in his skirted lap to see how he catches it—Huck gives scripted "masculine" responses to each of the tests, meaning that his throw is accurate and he clamps his legs together instead of widening them.

After the threading, throwing, and catching is completed, Mrs. Loftus's suspicions have been proven correct: Huck is indeed a boy. Loftus then asks Huckleberry to tell her the real reason he is there: "You just tell me your secret, and trust me. I'll keep it; and what's more, I'll help you. So'll my old man, if you want him to" (52). Mrs. Loftus asks Huck another series of questions to determine if he is from the country or the city and concludes that at least he has not lied to her about his country origin. After his perceptive hostess completes her questions, she then allows Huck to choose his new fake name, George Peters, and cautions him to remember it: "Don't forget and tell me it's Elexander before you go, and then get out by saying it's George-Elexander when I catch you" (53). Before she allows Huck to take his leave, Loftus says "Now trot along to your uncle, Sarah Mary Williams George Elexander Peters [here Loftus verbally acknowledges that Huck's gender identity is still a fabrication], and if you get into trouble you send word to Mrs. Judith Loftus, which is me, and I'll do what I can to get you out of it" (53).

Myra Jehlen poses two important questions in her discussion of the Loftus episode in her essay "Gender": "What is the role in all this of the feminine disguise"; and "Why and to what effect does Huck pass through the crisis of rejecting his born identity dressed as a girl?" (267) What Twain may have been doing in having Huck don female garb is to assist him in gaining insight into Jim's dilemma. Before Huck can understand

Jim's plight, he must experience what it means to be powerless. Twain cannot make Huck African-American, but he can make him a girl (granted Huck isn't exactly a privileged member of the Southern elite, although compared to enslaved African-Americans and women he certainly enjoys more personal freedoms).

Dressed as a girl, Huck, under the guidance of Loftus, learns that being female means, among other things, restricted movement and a required lack of intellectual and physical prowess. What is particularly fascinating about Loftus is that, unlike Twain's preceding and subsequent gender-trickster characters, she reveals her methodology for tricking (thus giving her secrets to and, in conjunction, sharing her power with Huck). In other words, working within Gates's definition of the trickster and signifying language, Loftus, a straight-dressed gender-trickster, is explaining the art of signifying to the transvestite Huck (*Figures in Black* 236-41). The gender-tricksters who appear in Twain's other works act out their roles, either male or female—cross-dressed or not—but never openly discuss and deconstruct the act as Loftus does.

When Loftus tells Huck that missing rats is what girls do, she is giving him a lesson on gender roles and expectations. Loftus is teaching Huck how the game is played, and once the rules are understood by Huck, the implication is not only that he can play but that he can win. Who was once powerless is now empowered. As Mrs. Loftus informs him, "You do a girl tolerable poor, but you might fool men, maybe" (53).

If there are any fools here, Twain seems to be saying, they are those who do not realize that such women as Mrs. Loftus are gender-tricksters who can manipulate and thus subvert socially prescribed gender roles. Huck learns from Loftus the powerlessness associated with female gender; Jim will instruct him about the powerlessness inherent in slavery. Huck, and by implication the reader, will eventually realize that racial hatred is, like gender, a sociocultural construct, not a biological certitude.

There is a close connection between Huck's willingness to cross gender lines and his later act of questioning and rejecting racial categories. These two discourses, race and gender, contain overlapping margins whose intersections surface in the figure of the transvestite. Throughout the novel, Huckleberry (as does Jim) adopts and abandons different male and female disguises as well as rejecting activities considered purely male or female. At the end of the novel, Twain has Jim and Tom share Huck's experience of cross-dressing when the two don Aunt Sally's clothes and flee. With such constancy of cross-dressing it may be possible to reinterpret Huck's flight as a response to the death of the father leading to a quest for contact with the feminine.

During the summer of 1883 when Twain was completing work on *Adventures of Huckleberry Finn,* he was also writing **"1,002d Arabian Night"** (*Mark Twain's Satires and Burlesques* 88). While it is true, as Gillman recognizes, that Twain creates "a hero-heroine pair whose behavior reverses stereotypical masculine and feminine characteristics—but always the sexes are distinguished in terms of traditional traits," unlike **"A Medieval Romance,"** Twain completes the narrative and introduces as the narrator of the tale a third female gender-trickster protagonist (108).

Scherezade, attempting to delay her execution by King Shahriyar, tells him tale "Number One Thousand and Two." Her story concerns two babies whose genders are switched at birth. She chronicles the infants' lives and how they eventually marry and have twins. When the cross-dressed pair show their son and daughter to their celebrating subjects, the people wonderingly comment: "To think that the father, and not the mother, should be the mother of the babes! Now of a truth are all things possible with God . . ." (*Mark Twain's Satires and Burlesques* 91; 132). The pair's unconsciousness of possessing each others' supposed "correct" gender is similar to Conrad's apparent unawareness of being raised male in **"Medieval Romance."**

Scherezade keeps extending her story (and her literal deadline), and the King finally dies. It is important to recognize that while Scherezade acts out the part of the acquiescent and submissive female (each time the king interrupts her narrative she meekly replies "I hear and obey"), by the conclusion she has managed to manipulate her prescribed feminine role until she ultimately triumphs in the misogynist King's demise (*Mark Twain's Satires and Burlesques* 93).

The intersections of gender and race manifested in cross-dressing introduced in *Adventures of Huckleberry Finn* have their fullest rendering nine years later in *Pudd'nhead Wilson,* where various uses of cross-dressing traceable in Twain's earlier works merge in and become inextricable from the narrative. When the reader is first introduced to the world of Dawson's Landing, everything appears to be in order and everyone is carefully controlled: women are firmly deposited in their "sphere," African-Americans know their "place," and the upper class treats the lower strata of society with benign neglect. However, upon closer examination, none of this reflects the reality of the town and its population. As the narrative proceeds, little is as it initially appears to be and all is marked by the figure of the cross-dresser.

Garber argues that category crises "can and do mark displacements from the axis of class as well as from race onto the axis of gender" (17). It is exactly these crises/intersections that form the narrative of *Pudd'head Wilson.* The person upon whom the plot hinges, namely Valet de Chambre, is descended from the recently deceased Colonel Cecil Burleigh Essex, a member of the F.F.V. (First Families of Virginia). Roxana, far from trying to hide her liaison, is outspoken regarding her illicit connection with the upper class: "He was de highest quality in dis whole town—Ol Virginny stock, Fust Famblies, he was" (43). Even before Roxana switches babies, Twain calls her own racial identity into question: "To all intents and purposes Roxy was as white as anybody, but the one-sixteenth of her which was black out-voted the other fifteen" (8). Twain also provides the "percentage" of African-American blood in her son: "Her child was thirty-one parts white, and he, too, was a slave, and by a fiction of law and custom a negro" (9).[6] In addition, Roxana does not remain in her "place," rather at age thirty-five when she is freed she leaves Dawson's Landing to work on a river boat and carefully invests her money so that she may enjoy a worry-free retirement—only to later lose her savings in a bank failure.

Frederick Anderson notes that the way Twain explored what he terms "multiple identity" can be observed in a summary of the roles taken by Chambre and Roxana. Anderson first describes Chambre's instances of cross-dressing: "There are, in sequence, that of a white man with a beard, a young white woman, an old white woman (whose clothes Tom borrows from his Negro mother), a young Negro woman wearing a veil, and finally 'a disguise proper for a tramp'" (294-95).[7] In adopting these various disguises, Anderson contends, Chambre makes "multiple interchanges of sex, race, and social position" even though he must simultaneously maintain "the role of a respectable member of the family of the town's leading citizen, and a corrupt and dissolute gambler in St. Louis. When he learns of his Negro heritage he must assume the further role of a Negro passing as white" (295). Chambre's blurring of social classes, racial categories, and gender roles is indicative of an epistemological crisis in the novel that Twain would deliberately leave unresolved.

Of course, Roxana also acts out a transvestite role, necessitated by her escape from enslavement in the deep South. As Anderson points out, Roxana must "disguise herself further by blackening her face in order to make her skin color conform to her Negro speech" (295). When the history of this cross-dressing duo is traced it becomes evident that Chambre's male power, position in society, and racial superiority decrease each time he assumes female garb, while Roxana's transvestism has the inverse effect. When Roxana enters her son's room during a rainy night in St. Louis, Chambre sees what he thinks is a man's back. The unknown man proceeds to turn around and a frightened Chambre tries to order him away, but he is silenced—for the first time in the text. In the course of their conversation, Roxana deduces that Chambre is lying about the bill for her capture, hatches a plan for Chambre to buy back her freedom, and makes him walk with her to the wharf while she keeps a knife ready to plunge into him at the slightest provocation. The Roxana in this scene is quite a departure from the helpless young mother who, earlier in the narrative, contemplated suicide as her only recourse. Like Huck, she has had a lesson in power—and uses it to her advantage.

Much of the material Twain uses in *Pudd'nhead Wilson* can be found in the slavery narratives of Roxana's real-life counterparts, Ellen Craft and Harriet Jacobs. Just two pages into the Craft's narrative, they challenge the existence of a definable black and white binary: "slavery in America is not at all confined to persons of any particular complexion; there are a very large number of slaves as white as any one . . ." (2-3). This strategy is echoed by Twain when he reveals Roxana and Chambre's blood "percentages" at the beginning of chapter two.

But it is in Jacobs's *Incidents* that the most parallels can be made. Like Roxana, the unmarried Jacobs enters into a sexual liaison with an upper-class European-American male. While both suffer feelings of guilt, it is less for themselves than for the legacy they have brought upon their children. As Jacobs explains, "I will not try to screen myself behind the plea of compulsion from a master; for it was not so. Neither can I plead ignorance or thoughtlessness . . . I knew what I did, and I did it with deliberate calculation" (xxx). Both Jacobs and Roxana have bills posted for their capture, both cross-dress, and both must darken their faces with charcoal in order to pass as African-American.

Gillman recognizes that Chambre and Roxana, in darkening their faces and cross-dressing, "conflate" gender and racial categories. According to Gillman, this combining, "explicitly pursued by Twain after *Pudd'nhead Wilson* . . . comes through partially even here: if 'male' and 'female' are as readily interchanged as 'black' and 'white,' then gender difference may prove to be as culturally constituted" (79). To echo Twain, such distinctions would eventually be recognized as "a fiction of law and custom." Yet, the question that Twain poses in *Pudd'nhead Wilson* and tries in part to answer is: what does one do with this fiction, and how does it fit into preconceived narrative structures? While acknowledging the possibility of conflation, Gillman cautions that if a pattern of association is established between the two categories, "we must ourselves be careful . . . not to blur distinctions" (102). But this is exactly what Twain is trying to do and what Garber identifies: "*Pudd'nhead Wilson* is in fact an exemplary instance of the category crisis, the slippage from one borderline to another, in this case race to gender, or gender to race, marked by the appearance of the transvestite" (289).

This "slippage" of borderlines, how to conceive of this blurring of distinctions and how to understand these intersections, is not restricted to nineteenth-century prose but is also clearly a contemporary issue. Twain did not wait until after *Pudd'nhead Wilson* to explore the social and cultural constitutions of race and gender; actually he began this investigation in his earliest tale of gender switching, and his examination continued into the last years of his life.[8] Gillman is correct in that both gender and racial differences were highly important topics to Twain; however, Twain's investigations of gender constructs using the figure of the transvestite preceded his focus on race. In creating cross-dressing characters Chambre and Roxana, Twain shatters such binaries as what it means to be African-American and European-American, master and slave, and male and female. By the end of the story when Tom is sold down the river, former ways of knowing, have by necessity, been abandoned, and an epistemological crisis looms as no new systems have been constructed to replace the old.

By the end of the story, this intersection of race and gender as evidenced by the figure of the transvestite has so disrupted the world that was Dawson's Landing that there will be no hope of ever restoring it. Within *Pudd'nhead Wilson* there are several related category crises: the first is, again, slavery; the second is reconstruction (it is worth taking into account that Twain wrote *Pudd'nhead Wilson* thirty-two years after emancipation in the aftermath of the failure of Reconstruction), and the third is the difficulty in trying to narrate the reality of the African-American female experience.

In Twain's writing after *Pudd'nhead Wilson*, cross-dressing was a frequent occurrence. Twain's historical transvestite novel, *Personal Recollections of Joan of Arc*, features a young woman whose objective is transgressing defined social boundaries. Joan's transvestism results in some of the most injurious accusations leveled against her at her trial. Among the sixty-six articles with which she is charged are "discard[ing] the decencies and proprieties of her sex" and "irreverently assuming the dress of a man and the vocation of a soldier" (377). When Joan makes her first appearance in court, she approaches the bench in male apparel: "A wide collar of this same black stuff lay in radiating folds upon her shoulders and breast; the sleeves of her doublet were full, down to the elbows, and tight thence to her manacled wrists; below the doublet, tight black hose down to the chains on her ankles" (352).

When Joan is asked by the court whether she would remove her male attire if she were allowed communion, Joan replies: "When one receives the sacrament, the manner of his dress is a small thing and of no value in the eyes of Our Lord" (378). After this response, the court charges Joan with being "stubborn" (379). In conjunction with her transvestism, she is castigated for performing a traditional male role in choosing combat and "deserting the industries proper to her sex" (379). Joan finally loses patience with the court's attempts to "re-sex" her and responds: "Peace! Without the permission of God I will not lay it off [her male clothing] though you cut off my head" (380).

In two incomplete short stories written within one year of *Personal Recollections of Joan of Arc* Twain continues his experiments with gender sans transvestism. In **"John Brown and Mary Taylor,"** no cross-dressing occurs, although there is a crossing-over of gender characteristics. John Brown's distinguishing traits are shyness and passivity, and he is described as "good, gentle, bashful, timid" (*Mark Twain's Short Stories* 381). Mary Taylor, on the other hand, is an active, thoughtful, problem- solver and leader of a band of women.

The story commences with Brown, a fussily dressed Presbyterian Sunday-school superintendent, driving his carriage to Mary Taylor's home to propose marriage. Four miles into his journey, a gust of wind flips off his straw boater and it flies into a creek. Unwilling to present himself to his intended less than completely outfitted, Brown strips and wades into the stream. When he emerges from the water, he discovers that his buggy has disappeared. He chases and catches his horse and dresses himself from the upper body down—but before he can don his pants he spies four women approaching him and he quickly covers himself with his new white, embroidered, linen lap-robe. Coming down the lane are Mary, her mother, and two elderly friends. Mary asks John to drive the aged sisters home and then return. The highly embarrassed Brown, who has remained silent throughout the exchange with the women except to say he is unwell, is relieved upon hearing Mary's plan but he quickly becomes alarmed when she reaches out her hand for the lap-robe. At that point, Twain ends the story and then mischievously adds that it is "the reader's privilege to determine for himself how the thing came out" (387).

In **"Hellfire Hotchkiss,"** like in **"1,002d Arabian Night,"** Twain presents a second female-male couple with switched genders (although neither cross-dress). Rachel, nicknamed "Hellfire," is a fearless heroine who possesses superior athletic ability and rescues a frightened, weeping Oscar "Thug" Carpenter from drowning. In a scene reminiscent of the drowned woman episode in *Adventures of Huckleberry Finn,* Rachel casts aside her bonnet and shawl and leaps into the icy Mississippi with a whiskey flask tucked inside her "bosom" (*Mark Twain's Satires and Burlesques* 189). Hellfire, though, unlike the unfortunate drowned woman, does not succumb to the currents of the river. Instead, after arriving at the emergency scene astride her "great black horse" she swims to the ice floe, makes Thug strap on a life preserver, and pulls him to shore.

Despite initial approbation from the townspeople who witnessed her selfless heroics, Hellfire is later informed by her Aunt Betsy that gossips are maligning her "masculine" ways. After agreeing to cease riding astraddle and going hunting, boating and skating with male companions, Rachel laments: "Oh, everything seems to be made wrong, nothing seems to [be] the way it ought to be" (*Mark Twain's Satires and Burlesques* 199). Here is a marked tonal shift to Twain's later gender-switch stories. Instead of the humor and eventual success of the gender-trickster in **"1,002d Arabian Night,"** in **"Hellfire Hotchkiss"** there is a sense of society closing in and crushing those who tempt to transgress rigid gender bifurcations.

In 1904 Twain completed a short story involving a couple with exchanged genders, namely the extraordinary **"The $30,000 Bequest"** (*Mark Twain Collected Tales* 597-626). Twain's prior gender-switch tales, **"John Brown and Mary Taylor"** and **"Hellfire Hotchkiss"** practically serve as drafts of this later, completed piece. **"The $30,000 Bequest"** features two main characters: "Saladin Foster" nicknamed "Sally" and "Electra Foster" nicknamed "Aleck." Sally is a devoted husband and father who daydreams about spending a thirty thousand dollar bequest to be left to him by a distant male relative on the occasion of his death. Aleck is a loving wife and mother as well as a talented money manager and investor.

The story consists of the two fantasizing about investing and spending their future bequest until Aleck has managed to parlay the initial thirty thousand dollars into an imaginary three hundred million. All is lost, though, in the imaginary Wall Street crash and both Sally and Aleck are plunged into despair. After their fantasy bankruptcy, the story ends with the pair discovering that the relative left no estate at his death and the town was forced to pay for his burial. The discovery that there will be no forthcoming money shatters the make-believe world the two have constructed together and the tale concludes with their deaths.

The remainder of Twain's transvestite writings, *Following the Equator,* **"Wapping Alice,"** **"How Nancy Jackson Married Kate Wilson,"** and **"A Horse's Tale"** all contain cross-dressing themes and subject matter traceable to earlier works. Twain's difficulties with **"Wapping Alice"** (also never completed), especially in his wavering in deciding whether **"Wapping Alice"** is male or female, is reminiscent of his inability to complete the narrative in **"A Medieval Romance."** *Following the Equator* returns to the twin issues of race and gender, and Twain again treads upon familiar ground when he describes his young Singhalese man-servant in ways that denote him as belonging to an indeterminate world. Gillman observes that in describing the young man, Twain draws a connection between race and sex: "a world between: between black and white, masculine and feminine" (99). Such indeterminacy has already been expressed most poignantly by a bitter Tom Driscoll when he replies to Roxana: "Bofe of us is imitation white—dat's what we is—en pow'full good imitation, too—Yah-yah-yah!—we don't 'mount to noth'n as imitation niggers" (35).

"How Nancy Jackson Married Kate Wilson" bears certain similarities to **"A Medieval Romance"** and the Loftus scene in *Adventures of Huckleberry Finn*. This story contains two gender-tricksters who act against each other. Nancy Jackson has been involved in a murder and is forced by Thomas Furlong, the witness, to don male dress, move away from home, and forever after be known as Robert Finlay. After securing Nancy's promise to do as he tells her, Furlong, in a take-off of the Loftus scene, tells Nancy to put on the clothes of a lynched African-American man and to burn her dress: "I'll trim your head and make a young fellow of you. Every day you'll practice, and I'll help you; and by and by when you're letter perfect and can walk and act like a male person and the lynch-fever has blown over, I'll take you out of this region some night and see you safe over the border and on your way" (**"How Nancy Jackson Married Kate Wilson"** 103).

While Furlong is giving lessons on gender-tricking to Nancy, Kate Wilson is falling in love with a young male stranger who will soon desert her. Panicked because she is pregnant and abandoned by the young man, Kate decides to make her father's new hired hand, "Robert Finlay," fall in love with her. She asks Robert to kiss her and is furious when he does not respond. Kate then informs her parents that Robert is the father of her unborn child and they are forced to wed. As in **"Medieval Romance,"** the cross-dressed female trickster is ultimately outfoxed by the female tricking within her feminine gender.

Twain's last transvestite tale, **"A Horse's Tale,"** written during the fall of 1905, owes much to Twain's youngest daughter, Jean Clemens, and to *Personal Recollections of Joan of Arc.*[9] The heroine of the story, nine-year-old Cathy Allison, is sent to live with her uncle, General Allison, after the death of her parents in Europe. Cathy travels to the western territory from Rouen, France (the site of Joan's trial and execution), and immediately becomes the fort's darling. She is made an officer and routinely inspects her soldiers and returns salutes while dressed in medieval military garb similar to the description of Joan's clothes.

After all this exchanging of clothing, it seems fair to ask if Twain himself ever transgressed into cross-dressing. Quite often so it appears. An avid participant in charades and family drama productions, Twain would readily outfit himself to meet the demands of the mo-

ment. Sandra Gilbert and Susan Gubar assert that "for the most part . . . men of letters tended to wear clothes that emphasized some version of masculinity, as if to suggest that the right garments reflect the right relationship not only between the sexes but between anatomy and destiny" (327). This was not the case with Twain. Perhaps in part due to his wife and her family's influence or perhaps because of his own evolving views on race and gender, Twain proved to be willing to explore what other authors feared. Indeed his life might be viewed as a series of categorical crises: impoverished/wealthy, Confederate/Yankee, westerner/easterner, humorous short story writer/serious novelist and social commentator. Twain's personal involvement in cross-dressing quite possibly reflects his willingness to engage the issue fictionally, and his apparent eagerness to don female dress may have allowed him to escape (albeit briefly) and thereby challenge stifling constructions of masculinity. In his life and his writing. Twain extravagantly proved Garber's thesis that "transvestism is a space of possibility structuring and confounding culture."

The most touching artifact of Twain's transvestism is a photograph taken circa 1890 of the author and his eldest daughter, Susy. In the picture the two are posing on the porch of a rustic cabin holding hands high above their heads. Susy is dressed as a princess with a cape, and her father is wearing a woman's dress over rolled-up long underwear with a bonnet on his head and a hot water bottle hanging from his neck. Looking as though he was photographed in the midst of a merry jig, Twain, trickster himself, never stopped dancing between the accepted and the taboo.

Notes

1. In coining the term "gender-trickster," I am indebted to Henry Louis Gates, Jr.'s discussion of African-American trickster figures and signifying language in *Figures in Black* 236-41. Also useful is Lawrence Levine's chapter on signifying language in *Black Cultures and Black Consciousness* (New York: Oxford UP, 1978) 103, 121-23.

   By gender-trickster, I mean several different categories: characters who successfully cross-dress are gender-tricksters, while those characters whose attempts to cross-dress fail (as when Huckleberry dons a dress) are not. Gender-tricksters need not necessarily be cross-dressed. These are characters who either recognize gender as a construction and openly identify it as such (Judith Loftus is the best example), or characters who are clearly manipulating stereotypical gender characteristics without identifying they are doing so Kate Jackson is such an example).

   Marjorie Garber divides her discussion of cross-dressing into two sections entitled "Transvestite Logic" and "Transvestite Effects." According to

Garber, "transvestite logic" occurs when "transvestism creates culture," and "transvestite effects" when "culture creates transvestites." Garber argues that "one of the most consistent and effective functions of the transvestite in culture is to indicate the place of . . . 'category crisis,' disrupting and calling attention to cultural, social, or aesthetic dissonances. . . ." This "category crisis" indicates a "failure of definitional distinction"; in other words, "a borderline that becomes permeable, that permits of border crossing from one . . . category to another": such as male/female, master/slave, black/white, and at various points between the binaries. Therefore, the figure of the cross-dresser becomes a sign for "development [and] progress" (16). The crux of Garber's argument is that "transvestism is a space of possibility structuring and confounding culture" (17).

2. For a detailed history of the Langdon family's political and social activism, including acts of public cross-dressing, see chapters 4 and 5 in Laura Skandera-Trombley's *Mark Twain in the Company of Women* (Philadelphia: U of Pennsylvania P, 1994).

3. Albert Bigelow Paine records how as a young boy Twain, accompanied by several friends, found the body of a drowned slave in a swamp, *Mark Twain: A Biography* (New York: Harper, 1912) 64.

4. Gillman argues that "conflating categories of gender identification with racial categories" first takes place in *Pudd'nhead Wilson* and would be continued in *Following the Equator* (79). I contend that Twain's combining of gender and race first began with this hint in *Adventures of Huckleberry Finn* and would be pursued in the above two works.

5. The three works as listed in Gribben: Charles Ball, *Slavery in the United States: A Narrative of the Life and Adventures of Charles Ball, a Black Man, Who Lived Forty Years in Maryland, South Carolina and Georgia, as a Slave* (1837) 43; Lydia Maria Child, *Anti-Slavery Catechism* (Newburyport, 1836) 141. [Bound as a volume with W. E. Channing's *Letter on Slavery*, along with five other pamphlets.]; William Still, *The Underground Rail Road: A Record of Facts, Authentic Narratives, Letters, &c., Narrating the Hardships, Hair-breadth escapes, and Death Struggles of the Slaves in Their Efforts for Freedom, by Themselves and Others, or Witnessed by the Author* (1883) 666.

Sholom S. Kahn, in a recent *Mark Twain Circular* article, "Mark Twain's 'Original Jacobs's: A Probable Explanation," contends that the title of chapter fifty in *Life on the Mississippi,* "The Original Jacobs," is attributable to Linda Brent's work: "I

want to propose that in the title he gave to Chapter 50 of *LOM*, Clemens was alluding to Jacobs's *Incidents in the Life of a Slave Girl Written by Herself . . .*" (8 Jan-Mar 1994): 4-6. In addition, Kahn reasons that it is likely that Twain had Brent's narrative in mind when he composed "A True Story" (4).

6. The conception and formulation of race is still a problematic issue in American law. Michael Omi and Howard Winant, in a chapter entitled "Racial Formation," in *Racial Formation in the United States* (New York: Routledge, 1994) include the following example of how the law classifies and quantifies racial identity:

> In 1982-83. Susie Guillory Phipps unsuccessfully sued the Louisiana Bureau of Vital Records to change her racial classification from black to white. The descendant of an 18th-century white planter and a black slave, Phipps was designated 'black' on her birth certificate in accordance with a 1970 state law which declared anyone with at least 1/32nd 'Negro blood' to be black. In the end, Phipps lost. The court upheld the state's right to classify and quantify racial identity. . . . Phipps's problematic racial identity, and her effort to resolve it through state action, is in many ways a parable of America's unsolved racial dilemma. It illustrates the difficulties of defining race and assigning individuals or groups to racial categories. It shows how the racial legacies of the past—slavery and bigotry—continue to shape the present.
>
> (53)

7. I agree with Anderson; nonetheless it should be noted that what Anderson terms as examples of "multiple identity" are those places in the text where the transvestite forces various displacements of the kind Garber identifies.

8. Gillman argues that while Twain "unequivocally condemned racial stereotypes . . . his writing circles more hesitantly around the whole problem of gender difference, sometimes affirming, sometimes denying that such a clear-cut system of difference does in fact exist. In short, Twain shows himself to be more aware of the invidiousness of racial than sexual stereotypes" (102).

9. In April 1905, *Harper's Weekly* published a short story by Jean Clemens, "A Word for the Horses," describing the mistreatment of horses by riders using checkreins and martingales. Twain was apparently encouraged by Jean to write a short story exposing Spanish cruelties to bulls and horses used in bullfighting. Twain's "A Horse's Tale" was first published in *Harper's Magazine* in August and September of 1906 and again in 1907 in book form [Everett Emerson, *The Authentic Mark*

Twain: A Literary Biography of Samuel L. Clemens (Philadelphia: U of Pennsylvania P, 1984) 260-61.]

Works Cited

Anderson, Frederick. "Mark Twain and the Writing of Pudd'nhead Wilson." *Pudd'nhead Wilson and Those Extraordinary Twins.* Ed. Sidney Berger. New York: Norton, 1980.

Craft, William and Ellen Craft. *Running a Thousand Miles for Freedom.* New York: Arno, 1969.

Freedman, Florence. Introduction. *Running a Thousand Miles for Freedom.* New York: Arno, 1969.

Garber, Marjorie. *Vested Interests: Cross-Dressing and Cultural Anxiety.* New York: Routledge, 1992.

Gates, Henry Louis, Jr., ed. *Classic Slave Narratives.* New York: Penguin. 1987.

———. *Figures in Black: Words, Signs, and the "Racial" Self.* New York: Oxford UP, 1987.

Gilbert, Sandra, and Susan Gubar. *No Man's Land: The Place of the Woman Writer in the Twentieth Century.* Vol 2: *Sexchanges.* New Haven: Yale UP, 1989.

Gillman, Susan. *Dark Twins: Imposture and Identity in Mark Twain's America.* Chicago: U of Chicago P, 1989.

Gribben, Alan. *Mark Twain's Library: A Reconstruction.* 2 vols. Boston: G. K. Hall, 1980.

Jacobs, Harriet. *Incidents in the Life of a Slave Girl.* Ed. Jean Fagan Yellin. Cambridge: Harvard UP, 1987.

Jehlen, Myra. "Gender." *Critical Terms for Literary Study.* Ed. Frank Lentricchia and Thomas McLaughlin. Chicago: U of Chicago P, 1990.

Twain, Mark. *Adventures of Huckleberry Finn.* Ed. Sculley Bradley. New York: Norton, 1977.

———. "How Nancy Jackson Married Kate Wilson." Ed. Robert Sattelmeyer. *The Missouri Review* 10 (1987): 97-112.

———. *Mark Twain Collected Tales, Sketches, Speeches, and Essays 1891-1910.* New York: Library of America, n.d.

———. *Mark Twain's Letters. 1867-1868.* Ed. Harriet Smith and Richard Bucci. Vol. 2. Berkeley: U of California P, 1990.

———. *Mark Twain's Letters. 1869.* Ed. Victor Fischer and Michael Frank. Vol. 3. Berkeley: U of California P, 1993.

———. *Mark Twain's Satires and Burlesques.* Ed. Franklin R. Rogers. Berkeley: U of California P, 1967.

———. *Mark Twain's Short Stories.* Ed. Justin Kaplan. New York: New American Library, 1985.

———. *Personal Recollections of Joan of Arc.* San Francisco: Ignatius, 1989.

———. *Pudd'nhead Wilson and Those Extraordinary Twins.* Ed. Sidney E. Berger. New York: Norton, 1980.

———. *The Signet Classic Book of Mark Twain's Short Stories.* Ed. Justin Kaplan. New York: Penguin, 1985.

Tom Quirk (essay date 1997)

SOURCE: Quirk, Tom. "The Middle Years, 1874-1890: Literary Respectability and Social Responsibility." In *Mark Twain: A Study of the Short Fiction,* pp. 56-85. New York: Twayne Publishers, 1997.

[*In the following essay, Quirk provides an overview of Twain's life and career during the height of his celebrity, detailing the circumstances surrounding the composition of his stories written between 1876 and 1890.*]

Roughing It was published in February 1872. For the next two years, Clemens's time was hectically but profitably divided between traveling, writing, lecturing, and acting the part of businessman. An authorized English edition of *The Innocents Abroad* was published in 1872, and the jointly authored novel *The Gilded Age* in 1873. A play based on a character from that novel, *Colonel Sellers,* opened in 1874 and proved to be a longstanding success and, eventually, one of the most prosperous children of Twain's imagination. By this time, he had also begun writing *Tom Sawyer* and had planned a book on England and the English. His "Self-Pasting Scrap-Book" was patented in June 1873 and generated a good deal of money for the next several years, though, from Twain's point of view, not enough. He became a director of the American Publishing Company the same year.

What is more, during this period, Twain proved himself to be a most clubbable fellow—he was made an honorary member of the London literary clubs the Whitefriars and, later, the Temple Club; he also became a member of the Lotos Club in New York City. During a visit to England, he met, among other notables, Wilkie Collins, Robert Browning, Herbert Spencer, George MacDonald, and Anthony Trollope; and Twain found that he had to spend extra time preparing after-dinner speeches for one occasion or another. All the instruments that measure success seemed to agree—Mark Twain had arrived.

But Twain was always ambivalent about his fame. He was pleased, and even a bit surprised, by the attention and approval he received, but he was irritated, too, by the constant interruptions and the several demands placed on his time and his good nature. At this time, he was trying to settle into a comfortable and secure domestic life. He bought a lot in the Nook Farm area of Hartford, Connecticut, in 1873 and made arrangements for the construction of a house there. When the Clemenses moved in a year and a half later, the house was still not finished. But that was mere annoyance compared with the happy additions and the sad subtractions in his life—his daughter Olivia Susan (Susy) Clemens was born in March 1872, and his daughter Clara two years later; but his 18-month-old son Langdon died of diphtheria on June 2, 1872, and Clemens unfairly blamed himself for the boy's death.

The unsettled and busy life that Clemens and his wife, Olivia, were leading must have made their stays in Elmira, New York, all the more agreeable, even necessary. Sometimes they stayed in the Langdon house downtown and sometimes with Olivia's adopted sister Susan Crane and her husband Theodore at Quarry Farm, high on a hill overlooking the town in the Chemung Valley. In 1874, when Susan had an octagonal study built for Clemens on the premises, the refuge was complete, and Twain was to do some of his best work there. The Cranes and the Clemenses got along splendidly, and summering at Quarry Farm became something of a habit for years afterward. But there must have been some uneasiness, too, and there were probably many opportunities for Twain to explain his native point of view to a family whose training and background were so different from his own.

One of those differences was sectional. The Langdon family had been active abolitionists; Twain's father-in-law, Jervis Langdon, had helped found the antislavery church in Elmira and had done important work for the underground railroad in the area. Clemens's family, by contrast, had at one time or another owned slaves, but Sam seemed to believe that close acquaintance with blacks during his childhood spoke in his favor. Specifically, Clemens had more than once claimed that because he had lived among and had known blacks in his native Missouri, he was better acquainted with their customs and desires.[1] Evidently, Susan Crane was unconvinced by Clemens's authoritative pronouncements on his understanding of racial matters. In any event, she urged her brother-in-law more than once to have their cook, "Auntie" Mary Ann Cord, tell him her story. And more than once Clemens politely demurred. However, one summer evening in 1874, when the Clemenses and Cranes were sitting on the porch of the farmhouse, Samuel Clemens casually asked Auntie Cord about her history and her seemingly inexhaustible good humor. After some hesitation, she agreed to tell her story. The literary result of this exchange was one of Twain's finest sketches, **"A True Story, Repeated Word For Word As I Heard It,"** published in the *Atlantic Monthly* the

following November. A more immediate result, in Clemens, must have been not only a sudden awareness of his own ignorance of African-American experience but the recognition that he had been tricked into a new understanding by Susan Crane. In other words, Clemens, like his literary persona in tales he had written before, must have known that he had been set up.

In substance, the sketch he published was indeed a true story. Mary Ann Cord (in the tale, she is called Aunt Rachel to give her separation from her children a certain biblical significance) was in fact born in Maryland and raised in Virginia, and she was separated from her family when she was sold at auction to a man from North Carolina. Her favorite son was named Henry, he did manage to escape to freedom when he as about 13 years old, and he did become a barber in Elmira. More important, during the war, Henry did join the Union troops (though perhaps not as a soldier) and kept alive what must have been a desperate hope that he might find his mother somewhere in the South. Finally, against all odds, the two were reunited in rather dramatic fashion.[2]

The story Aunt Rachel tells, then, is autobiographical and therefore personal to her; but it is representative, too. As Philip Foner long ago observed, Twain managed to compress in this brief story much about the humanity of blacks, their liberating role in the Civil War, and their postbellum attempts to find their families, as well as to suggest the barbarity of slavery alongside an unvanquished dignity in the slaves who survived it.[3] Despite the pathos of Aunt Rachel's story, it is not tragic, however; for every Mary Cord who lived to see at least one of her children again, there were a hundred mothers who did not. That Aunt Rachel knows full well that she is one of the lucky ones only adds to her dignity. Her concluding remarks to "Misto C—" suggest none of the qualities she so obviously possesses—love and forgiveness, defiance and patient suffering, courage, nobility, and pride. Instead, her remarks affirm her prayerful gratitude: "De Lord God ob heaven be praise', I got my own ag'in! Oh, no, Misto C—, *I* hain't had no trouble. An' no *joy!*" (*CTS* I [*Mark Twain: Collected Tales, Sketches, Speeches and Essays: 1852-1890*], 582).

When John W. DeForest, the novelist and former Union captain, read **"A True Story"** in the *Atlantic,* he freely confessed to William Dean Howells that the story brought tears to his eyes. The story retains its affective power even today, but the critical emphasis upon Aunt Rachel's story and the studied authenticity of her dialect has tended to obscure other, though quite different, affecting and artistic qualities in the tale. Twain's subtitle, "Repeated Word For Word As I Heard It," was likely inserted in part to call attention to the vividness of dialect he had worked hard to achieve and in part to forewarn readers that the story was not just another comic production. However, the subtitle is misleading in several ways. Although the story Aunt Rachel tells is substantially "true" in most of its details, it has been shaped to achieve a double purpose—first, to dramatize Mary Cord's dignified humanity, and second, to make "Misto C—" not merely foolish but culpable.

After hearing Mary Cord's story, Twain told it to John Hay and was encouraged to write it up. As with so many of Twain's oral performances, the story was probably altered with each subsequent telling, and when he came to write the piece, it likely received still other improvements. From a letter he wrote to Howells, we do know that Twain knew he was working unfamiliar territory and changed the sequence of the telling: "I enclose also 'A True Story' which has no humor in it. You can pay as lightly as you choose for that, if you want it, for it is rather out of my line. I have not altered the old colored woman's story except to begin it at the beginning, instead of the middle, as she did—& traveled both ways" (*MTHL* [*Mark Twain—Howells Letters*] I, 22). Somewhat to Twain's surprise, though Howells rejected the comparatively slight piece that accompanied it, **"Some Learned Fables for Good Old Boys and Girls,"** he accepted **"A True Story"** and paid Twain well for it.

Twain had adopted the mode of the frame tale for this story, but he made the form serve serious purposes. In violation of nearly all the rules he would outline in "How to Tell a Story" (1895), he deliberately avoided the aimlessness that is so amusing in the jumping frog and old ram tales. Moreover, although Aunt Rachel is earnest, she shares very little else with Twain's vernacular narrators. She does not speak in a monotone, she does not ramble, and she is not self-absorbed in the telling—if anything, she is rather canny in the way she involves Misto C— in the narration. And Clemens's own persona in the story is clearly altered to enhance Rachel's dignity and to emphasize his own unfeeling stupidity.

By appearing as "Misto C—" (an only slightly disguised version of Mr. Clemens) instead of Mark Twain, the author has removed the armor of his literary persona in order to absorb more completely the guilt and humiliation that properly belong to him. Moreover, the author does not sponsor the good character of his vernacular narrator, as he had done in the *Roughing It* stories. Instead, he is manifestly wrong about Aunt Rachel, or rather his appreciation of her is altogether misplaced and self-deceived: "She was a cheerful, hearty soul, and it was no more trouble for her to laugh than it is for a bird to sing. She was under fire, now, as usual when the day is done. That is to say, she was being chaffed without mercy, and was enjoying it" (*CTS* I, 578). To reread the opening paragraph after having read the story is to see clearly and feel strongly the sting of a basically well-meaning but clearly self-satisfied bigotry. In the end, by giving the last words to Aunt Rachel, the author invites us to imagine more fully the shame that Misto C— has brought upon himself by the unwanted recognition of the cook's dignity and of his own insufficiency.

"A True Story" is rightly regarded as a vernacular tour de force and rivals even the most powerful speeches Jim delivers in *Huckleberry Finn*. But the tale is remarkable, too, for the stage directions Twain gave to the piece, which were likely a matter of invention rather than recollection. The story begins with Aunt Rachel "sitting respectfully below our level," when Misto C— blunders into asking her, "Aunt Rachel, how is it that you've lived sixty years and never had any trouble." Rachel becomes serious and scrutinizes him. She asks, "without even a smile in her voice," "Misto C—, is you in 'arnest?'" The sudden seriousness sobers Clemens's manner, and she has given him an opportunity to get out from under the onus of his question. Misto C— falters but nervously gives her the entering wedge to continue her story: "Why, I thought—that is, I meant— why, you *can't* have had any trouble. I've never heard you sigh, and never seen your eye when there was n't a laugh in it" (*CTS* I, 578).

Twain had often implicated himself in his humorous tales and thus made himself vulnerable to the laughter he provoked. But this was a serious story, told without the defenses of an established persona. Through the dramatic management of the piece, he made sure that Aunt Rachel's story would embody her natural dignity and humanity, but for Twain, the story also served as self-accusation, even indictment. Within only a few hundred words, Twain moves the cook from below his level (spatially, socially, and morally) to considerably above it. As Rachel continues her story, she gradually rises and "now she towered above us, black against the stars" (*CTS* I, 579).

More to the point, Rachel's story, though it casts its eye backward to her condition as a slave in the antebellum South and brings the narration forward to the reunion with her son just after the war, is delivered with a disturbing presentational immediacy. Rachel compares the stand where she and her family were auctioned off to the porch where Misto C— and, by implication, the Clemenses and Cranes, too, are sitting. And she not only tells but vividly performs her tale. The narration is punctuated with "so" to indicate accompanying physical gestures. Rachel holds the little Henry "clost up to my breas' so"; before the Union officers, she "drops a kurtchy, so, an' I up an' tole 'em 'bout my Henry, dey a-listenin' to my troubles jist de same as if I was white folks"; she reenacts her fierce anger, "my soul *alive* but I was hot! My eye was jist a-blazin'! I jist straightened myself up, so,—jist as I is now, plum to de ceilin'"; and she charges the black soldiers who have invaded her kitchen, "Well, I jist march' on dem niggers,—so, lookin' like a gen'l,—an' dey jist cave away befo' me" (*CTS* I, 579-82).

Clearly, Aunt Rachel is not a woman to be trifled with, and if Misto C— was at first confounded by her unanticipated earnestness, we imagine him now surprised by, perhaps even fearful of, her fierce dignity. The presumably jolly Aunt Rachel now presses her advantage with a shrewd seriousness. It seems unlikely that Mary Ann Cord, a black servant who had known Twain only a few months before she told him her story, should have assumed the physical familiarity she does in the concluding paragraph. Instead, the stage directions were probably Twain's invention and designed to bring her words home with unmistakable force. At any rate, she acts out the recognition of her son in ways that would make anyone squirm:

> I was a-stoopin' down by de stove,—jist so, same as if yo' foot was de stove,—an' I'd opened de stove do' wid my right han'—so, pushin' it back, jist as I pushes yo' foot . . . I see a black face come aroun' under mine, an' de eyes a-lookin' up into mine, jist as I's a-lookin' up clost under yo face now; an' I just stopped *right dah,* an' never budged! just gazed, an' gazed, so. . . . an' I grab his lef' han' an' shove back his sleeve,—jist so, as I's doin' to you,—an' den I goes for his forehead an' push de hair back, so.
>
> (*CTS* I, 582)

To convey something of the power of this scene, one need only recall a more recent anecdote. When John F. Kennedy was running for president, he arranged for a meeting with Jackie Robinson, hoping to obtain his political support and, as a consequence, help secure the black vote. Robinson refused his support for a simple reason—during their lengthy meeting, Kennedy never once looked Robinson in the eye. Aunt Rachel makes Misto C— look her in the eye, and her gaze fixes his guilt and his shame with unmistakable clarity and power.

Twain's rendering of this "true story" surely exceeded whatever Susan Crane had in mind when she urged him to hear Mary Cord's tale. For if Aunt Rachel's story is both personal and severely representative (of both the past and the present), Misto C— is representative, too, not merely of the antebellum South but of a continuing and pervasive white guilt. If one understands the story in this way, one wonders whether the Union veteran Deforest's tears were shed for Aunt Rachel's sake alone or for his own lingering shame as well. Somewhat more certain is the fact that when Twain harnessed the devices of his humor to his capacities as a serious moralist, he was accepting a social responsibility as the fee simple for his gifts as a storyteller.

"A True Story" appeared in the November 1874 issue of the *Atlantic Monthly*. For the first time, Twain had broken into that prestigious Boston-based periodical, and as Justin Kaplan rightly observes, the story's publication represented Twain's "'literary' literary debut."[4] The *Atlantic* meant literature and literary respectability. Twain could identify with Aunt Rachel's situation to the extent that he knew laughter might disguise solemnity and a sense of wounded pride and that perpetual good humor did not accurately register one's true depth of feeling. At any rate, Twain was surely gratified to be counted among the *Atlantic* authors who gathered at a dinner in Boston that December, and he intended to extend the association, for he had already begun to write "Old Times on the Mississippi," which would appear in the *Atlantic* in seven installments beginning in January 1875.

When Howells reviewed **Mark Twain's Sketches, New and Old** (1875), he identified **"A True Story"** as the best piece in the collection (perfect in the "rugged truth" it conveyed), but he lamented that most of the notices of the story saw it as yet another humorous sketch. Howells firmly corrected this misapprehension, but more generally, he also detected in the volume as a whole "a growing sense of seriousness of meaning in the apparently unmoralized drolling, which must result from the humorist's second thought of political and social absurdities."[5] This observation was no doubt gratifying to Twain, and he apparently associated Howells's perceptiveness with the readers of the magazine he edited. In a letter to Howells dated December 8, 1874, Twain noted his responsive attraction to the *Atlantic* audience: "It isn't the Atlantic audience that distresses me; for *it* is the only audience that I sit down before in perfect serenity (for the simple reason that it don't require a 'humorist' to paint himself stripèd & stand on his head every fifteen minutes)" (*MTHL* I, 49).

This remark is all the more poignant when one remembers that not long after that letter, Twain wrote the first of his three domestic farces about the McWilliams family, each story picturing a man going through just these sorts of antics. **"Experience of the McWilliamses with Membranous Croup"** was first published in *Sketches, New and Old*. Twain wrote two other McWilliams sketches a few years later—**"Mrs. McWilliams and the Lightning"** was published in the *Atlantic Monthly* for September 1880, and **"The McWilliamses and the Burglar Alarm"** appeared in a Christmas supplement to *Harper's Monthly Magazine* in 1882. All three stories are built upon the same dramatic situation: Mortimer McWilliams, a New York gentleman, falls into conversation with Twain, and sooner or later, the subject turns to the narration of a recent domestic episode. Mrs. McWilliams is a fearful woman—fearful that their children may come down with the croup, that lightning will enter the bedroom and strike them dead, or that the house will be invaded by burglars. Mr. McWilliams is an accommodating husband who cannot reason with his wife; he cannot convince her that their daughter should not chew a pine stick, that Mrs. McWilliams needn't hide in the closet during a thunderstorm, or that a burglar alarm is not a wise investment.

Slight in themselves, the stories seem somehow to replicate and comment upon the Clemens's own domestic situation, though critics divide over the significance of the sketches. Some see the pieces as proof of Twain's submission to a bourgeois, genteel culture and of his emasculation at the hands of Olivia. Others find the tales a sly form of revenge for daily household concessions to a largely irrational, or at least fussy, domestic routine. Howells, on the other hand, thought the stories were representative, "a bit of *genre* romance which must be read like an abuse of confidence to every husband and father."[6] In any event, the McWilliams stories prefigure Thurber's more accomplished, but also more aggressive, comic pictures of the battle between the sexes. Mrs. McWilliams may be a fretful woman, and in the eyes of her husband an irrational one, but Mr. McWilliams is a buffoon. His conversations with "Mr. Twain" serve as both mild complaint and parodic confession.

In **"Mrs. McWilliams and the Lightning,"** Mortimer announces that "fear of lightning is one of the most distressing infirmities a human being can be afflicted with" and that this fear is "mostly confined to women." He prepares us for his domestic tale of woe by adding that a woman's "fright is something pitiful to see" (*CTS* I, 753). In point of fact, however, we do not see Mrs. McWilliams at all; when the booming starts (presumably from lightning, though it turns out to be cannon fire), she hides in the boot closet and stays there. What we do see instead is Mr. McWilliams making ridiculous accommodations to her worry. In a series of negatives, she advises him from the closet in the customary precautions against lightning—don't stay in the bed; don't light a match; don't stand in front of the fireplace or the window; don't wear wool or turn on the water. And in a series of prescriptions she attempts to secure his well-being against the lightning—do shut up the cat; do stand on a chair in the middle of the room; put the legs of the chair in glass tumblers; put on your fireman's helmet and your saber and spurs; and ring the dinner bell with all your might. The ringing brings several men in the neighborhood, who throw open the shutters and see Mr. McWilliams in nightshirt and helmet standing on the chair ringing his bell. Two of the men die laughing.

Because McWilliams is such a preposterous sight, it is difficult to see how this tale functions as a piece of revenge upon Twain's wife. Because McWilliams's behavior and dress are so far from being buttoned up and proper, it is difficult to imagine how the picture sug-

gests submission to Victorian mores. Howells was surely right. Twain gives us a privileged glimpse into the absurd circus of domestic life, and his "abuse of confidence" of all husbands and fathers who, of their own free will, have been similarly compromised consists in his so thoroughly painting the husband as the clown.

The growing sense of moral "seriousness" Howells discerned in Twain's fiction does not apply to the McWilliams sketches, but it does to a tale he wrote in January 1876 and published in the *Atlantic Monthly* the following June. **"The Facts Concerning the Recent Carnival of Crime in Connecticut"** was, from the beginning, designed to make a serious point. Twain prepared the story for presentation to fellow members of the Monday Evening Club, a group of some 20 notable citizens of Hartford. His previous contributions to this discussion group were relatively proper productions, but with this story, Twain meant to examine "an exasperating metaphysical question . . . in the disguise of a literary extravaganza."[7] The question itself had to do with the nature and function of conscience, and the metaphysical quality of the piece derived in large part from Twain's recent reading of W. E. H. Lecky's *History of European Morals from Augustine to Charlemagne* (1869).

Lecky's book would exert a lifelong, though somewhat contradictory, influence upon Twain, who wrestled with and commented upon the book's argument in the margins of his copy. Lecky had divided the history of morals into two opposing camps—the intuitionists and the utilitarians. He advocated the intuitionist view that one's sense of good and evil is innate and harshly criticized the utilitarian position that denied an innate moral sense and argued instead that one's feelings and actions depend on the degree to which they contribute to individual happiness. Twain was deeply ambivalent about Lecky's argument. On the whole, Twain leaned toward the utilitarian view, increasingly so in his later years, but seemed to agree with Lecky's view of conscience.

Howard Baetzhold observes that **"A Carnival of Crime"** "parallels Lecky's discussion almost exactly." Baetzhold nicely summarizes Lecky's position:

> Conscience is more often a source of pain than of pleasure, and if happiness is actually the sole end of life, then one should learn to disregard the proddings of conscience. If a man forms an association of ideas that inflicts more pain than it prevents, or prevents more pleasure than it affords, the reasonable course would be to dissolve that association or destroy the habit. . . . Therefore, a man who possessed such a temperament would be happier if he were to "quench that conscientious feeling, which . . . prevents him from pursuing the course that would be most conducive to his tranquility."[8]

Twain's wry and antic story of a man who would kill (or "quench") his conscience was largely founded on Lecky's sardonic extension of the utilitarian argument, and the author's reading of the tale was duly appreciated by the Monday Evening Club. Joseph Twichell recorded in his journal the same night he heard the story that the piece was "serious in its intent though vastly funny and splendidly, brilliantly read." A few years later, Howells paid Twain a greater compliment in the pages of the *Century Magazine,* writing that the story "ought to have won popular recognition of the ethical intelligence underlying his humor. . . . Hawthorne or Bunyan might have been proud to imagine that powerful allegory."[9]

The story is the work of a passionate and acute ethical intelligence, of course, but one should not overrate its philosophical heft. As a philosopher, Twain would have made a good third baseman; as a metaphysician, a first-rate pastry chef. When Twain identified the metaphysical question of conscience as "exasperating," he was registering his own annoyance with a nagging sense of guilt that had dogged him all his life—for he was temperamentally disposed to feel remorse and, sometimes, to claim responsibility for events he could not possibly have controlled or prevented. When Twain confessed that the question was disguised as a "literary extravaganza," he was reaffirming a humorist's customary allegiance to hyperbole and incongruity, however grotesque a turn the tale might take, not so much to make light of a serious matter as to make its painful gravity endurable.

The **"Carnival of Crime"** begins and ends in calm and blessed joy. For this reason, it is unlikely that this tale represents, as some critics have claimed, either a rebellion against an oppressive superego or an exorcism of an inherited Puritan past. The story opens with the narrator lighting a cigar, feeling "blithe, almost jocund" (*CTS* I, 644). Ever since the narrator has become immune to his Aunt Mary's nagging, particularly about his smoking, "the one alloy that was able to mar my enjoyment of my aunt's society was gone" and her visits have become a "tranquil satisfaction" (*CTS* I, 644). Conscience in the form of external influence, symbolized by the aunt, has already been defeated before the story ever begins, but the narrator's lies to tramps and budding authors still trouble him a bit. Unlike Aunt Mary, the mossy and ill-formed dwarf who appears, as if summoned by the casual claim that Twain is willing to right any wrong committed against his worst enemy, is an internal agent whose perverse business is to torture the narrator for no other purpose than the satisfaction of it.

Through a series of cagey maneuvers, the narrator manages to kill this figure, this "dim suggestion of a burlesque upon me, a caricature of me in little" (*CTS* I,

645). The dwarf is, of course, the narrator's conscience, and the death of the little man brings "Bliss, unalloyed bliss" (*CTS* I, 660), though his contentment is rather different from the earlier tranquil satisfaction. The difference between these two states of happiness has little to do with any profound distinction Twain was trying to make between an intuitionist's or a utilitarian's view of conscience. This brassy dwarf does not appear as a recognizable moral sense in any of the manifold shapes it might take—a Quaker inner light, a Calvinistic reminder of innate depravity, a Poesque imp of the perverse, or a transcendentally rational categorical imperative. Instead, the dwarf is a nuisance and a trial.

The conscience, Twain seems to be saying, checks our basest impulses by making us agonize and worry but not by mending our flawed human nature, and the toll it takes is worn on the face and experienced in the vitals. The narrator observes that once he had destroyed his conscience, he was free to indulge in his grotesque and whimsical carnival of crime. Since that day, he has been on a delicious rampage. "I killed thirty-eight persons during the first two weeks. . . . I burned a dwelling that interrupted my view. I swindled a widow and some orphans out of their last cow. . . . I have also committed scores of crimes of various kinds, and have enjoyed my work exceedingly, whereas it would have formerly broken my heart and turned my hair gray, I have no doubt" (*CTS* I, 660).

Although the social consequences of loosing a man without a conscience upon the world are both funny and disturbing, Twain betrays little interest in determining the ontological nature of conscience or its spiritual function. The middle part of the story is an interrogation of the repulsive figure, but if the story poses a metaphysical question, the answer remains a surly and grotesque mystery. The narrator is "suffering" to ask his conscience some questions, and he does: Having at last appeared before me, how long will you be visible to me? "Always!" Why can't a conscience punish a man just once for an offense and then let him alone? "Well, *we* like it; that suffices." Do your continual tortures indicate an "honest intent" to improve me? We are "disinterested agents," and we torture you because it is business. "It is our trade." Is there any way to appease the "malignant invention" that goes by the name of conscience? "Well, none that I propose to tell *you,* my son" (*CTS* I, 652-54). The relation between the narrator and his conscience is identified as one between a slave and a master, and the dwarf's proud mastery is as cryptic, dismissive, and tyrannically cruel as he pleases it to be.

"The Facts Concerning the Recent Carnival of Crime in Connecticut" is not really a metaphysical inquiry at all. And as autobiographical as the story sometimes is, it is not solely expressive of Twain's feelings of restraint and regret. Most of the narrator's concerns have to do with comparative judgments. He accepts the information that Robinson and Smith's consciences are taller and more comely than the hideous dwarf that represents the narrator's conscience, and he is willing to believe that his Aunt Mary's conscience "lives in the open air altogether, because no door is large enough to admit her" (*CTS* I, 657). But he is gratified to know that Hugh Thompson's conscience is a small, misshapen figure who sleeps in a cigar box and is absolutely delighted to find out that the conscience of a publisher who once cheated him was put on exhibit under a powerful microscope, though the curious still could not see him.

In other words, the narrator is primarily motivated by a local sense of self-esteem; he measures himself against his neighbors and relatives. His place within the great chain of consciences is a middling one, with a few below him and several above him. The real tyranny of conscience, however, is that he will forever be equally reminded of past sins alongside courteous lies and forgivable misjudgments, for a conscience seems to have no sense of proportion. "Every sentence was an accusation, and every accusation a truth," he recalls. "Every clause was freighted with sarcasm and derision, every slow-dropping word burned like vitriol" (*CTS* I, 648). Nothing so exasperates the narrator, however, as the awful prospect that the dwarf will continually remind him of himself. The dwarf's pertinacity makes the narrator indignant because it is an "exaggeration of conduct which I myself had sometimes been guilty of in my intercourse with familiar friends" (*CTS* I, 645). His language was "hardly an exaggeration of some that I have uttered in my day." And most disconcerting of all, the dwarf's ready accusations are, and henceforth will ever be, "delivered in a tone of voice and with an exasperating drawl that had the seeming of a deliberate travesty of my style" (*CTS* I, 646).

Here in germ is the basis for Twain's later philosophizing in such pieces as "Corn Pone Opinions" (1901) and *What Is Man?* (1906). In "Corn Pone Opinions," for example, he locates the universal impulse to conform in the "inborn requirement of Self-Approval" (*CTS* II [*Mark Twain: Collected Tales, Sketches, Speeches, and Essays, 1891-1910*], 508), but the source of one's self-esteem always comes from the outside, from the approval of other people. However, it would be a mistake to view the **"Carnival of Crime"** as a prolegomenon to the fiction belonging to Twain's darker and more cynical period. The story might more accurately be described as an apologia for the humorist as citizen and moralist. As we have already seen, Clemens often had Twain play the fool and absorb the first wave of laughter and contempt in order to win over his readers and thereby more forcibly laugh the sin, if not the sinner, out of court. This tendency in his short fiction may or may not dramatize his own self-loathing, but it surely

figures as one of his redeeming and most effective comic strategies.

When he delivered this piece before the Monday Evening Club, Twain deliberately engaged in a form of self-mockery and self-accusation that included a satire of the very drawl that club members were hearing as he read the tale. He intentionally made himself foolish and vulnerable in this story, but the dwarf wields the same weapons that the humorist keeps in his arsenal—burlesque, satire, exaggeration, and caricature. The dwarf of conscience merely holds up the altered and grotesque image of the man and makes his shortcomings comically obvious, but the grotesqueness is not of the dwarf's making. Moreover, although the dwarf is invisible to everyone but the narrator, his being and conduct are implicated in the social order. Insofar as the narrator's conscience works in concert with other consciences to harass their victims, and because Twain's conscience has become misshapen according to his own diminished conduct in a world of living men and women, this comedy of conscience is rooted in a social community. As a citizen, Samuel Clemens accepted his part in that community and took a vital, if sometimes haphazard and eccentric, interest in the laws, policies, and attitudes that regulate the national life. As a humorist, however, he was much like the dwarf, a disinterested agent who merely exaggerates existing transgressions and absurdities in order to make us see them more clearly and feel them more completely.

Twain's ethical intelligence underlying the humor on display in this story and others is neither self-righteous nor condescending. Nor does it respect class or condition. Samuel Clemens might hobnob with Hartford's elite, he might even pick up the tab, but the source of his humor, and his morality too, was distinctly plebeian. Enclosed within his Hartford circle, the humorist as moralist had no choice but to bore from within, to appear at once as scapegrace and scapegoat, but not as martyr. Before Howells dramatized his notion of "moral complicity" in his novels *The Minister's Charge* (1887) and *A Hazard of New Fortunes* (1890), Twain had expressed in the coordinated strategies of his humor a willingness to play the fool and to serve as the compromised accomplice to a nation's transgressions and folly. He freely acknowledged his guilty place in the social order, even though the social order had fixed him as a mere humorist. But he was proud, too, and that pride was most eloquent in his sly insistence that like Aunt Rachel, despite appearances, he was not simply jolly but serious too, not exceptional but representative. Publicly, Twain was willing to play the part of an ass, for virtue's sake; privately, he might console himself with the pert observation of a dwarf—"I am not an ass; I am only the saddle of an ass" (*CTS* I, 654).

For the next few years, Twain was preoccupied with a number of projects. He began **"Huck Finn's Autobiog-**

raphy" in the summer of 1876 and would work on it intermittently for the next seven years; he collaborated with Bret Harte on the play *Ah Sin* (1877) and began work on *A Tramp Abroad* (1880) and *The Prince and the Pauper* (1882). Although Twain wrote a few short stories during this period, they are notable more for the patent absurdity of their conception than for the merit of their execution. **"The Canvasser's Tale"** was published in the *Atlantic Monthly* for December 1876. It tells of a man who encourages his uncle in the European custom of collecting *"objets de vertu."* The uncle successively collects cowbells, brickbats, primeval tools, Aztec inscriptions, and stuffed whales but fails each time to corner the market. At last he determines to acquire a complete set of echoes and squanders the family fortune as a result.

Twain and Charles Dudley Warner had named their times "the gilded age," but this satire of material acquisitiveness is better described by Thorstein Veblen's phrase in *The Theory of the Leisure Class* (1899)—"conspicuous consumption." The theme of **"The Canvasser's Tale"** was a potent one at any rate. In *The Portrait of a Lady,* Henry James achieved in his Europeanized American and fastidious collector, Gilbert Osmond, a disturbing picture of cold and egoistical cruelty; and in *McTeague,* Frank Norris's depiction of the misers Trina and Zerkow suggests an erotic and fearful obsession, even madness. But Twain's treatment of the subject is genial and ordinary. The "sad-eyed" nephew who must pay for his uncle's indiscretions has become just another canvasser trying to sell intangible trifles.

Two years later, Twain concocted a romantic tale he called **"The Loves of Alonzo Fitz Clarence and Rosannah Ethelton"** and this time made the lovers themselves intangibles. Alonzo Fitz Clarence, on the telephone with his aunt, hears in the background a young woman singing "In the Sweet By-and-By" and falls in love with the voice. A telephonic courtship of some duration follows, and the romance is complicated by the deceitful intervention of Sidney Algernon Burley, the vile suitor for Rosannah's hand. Burley's plot is spoiled, and the couple is married over the telephone—Rosannah in Hawaii and Alonzo in New York. A few weeks after the marriage, the couple is brought together for the first time. The tale is overlong, and the essential joke of the story is repeated throughout. Clearly, Twain enjoyed the story more than his readers ever will, though a generation familiar with the encouragement of telephone companies to "reach out and touch someone" and with the resources of Internet romance, computer dating, and 900 numbers may be more responsive to the story's comedy than I am.

Twain was both fascinated by and skeptical of improvements, technological and other. In 1879, he installed a telephone in his home, but he also wrote **"A Telephonic Conversation,"** a brief domestic farce about hearing only one side of a conversation. Years later, in *A Connecticut Yankee in King Arthur's Court* (1889), he would import all manner of technological improvements (bicycles, telephones, newspapers, soap, and gunpowder) to Camelot and derive a lot of comedy from the incongruities. But Hank Morgan imported democratic reforms as well, and those sorts of improvements and their unlooked-for consequences were predicted in another story Twain wrote in 1879, **"The Great Revolution in Pitcairn."** In that tale, an American named Butterworth, a visitor to the tranquil and primitive British colony of Pitcairn, sows the seeds of discontent in the community, and before long the total population of 90 citizens has divided into factions. But division is merely the preliminary to his cry for "unification" and independence. Butterworth becomes emperor, randomly passes out titles of nobility, and establishes an army and a navy. Soon a community that had previously had no currency at all is saddled with taxes and a national debt. The people revolt. They hoist the British flag and reject political independence, preferring the mild yoke of colonial indifference to the urgent and debilitating reforms of social improvement and political autonomy.

In 1880, Twain published three short stories. **"Edward Mills and George Benton: A Tale"** was published in the *Atlantic Monthly* for August 1880. **"The Man Who Put Up at Gadsby's"** and **"Jim Baker's Blue Jay Yarn"** first appeared in *A Tramp Abroad* (1880). The first two stories extended themes Twain had explored before, but the blue jay yarn signaled a return to the frontier qualities and the creative verve that had made the jumping frog tale a miniature classic.

"Edward Mills and George Benton" is another good little boy/bad little boy story, though in this instance Twain followed the lives of his characters beyond boyhood into maturity and eventually to the grave. Edward and George are distant cousins who are brought up as foster brothers by a childless couple, the Brants. The boys' upbringing in godly virtue may be summarized by the advice the Brants repeatedly give: "Be pure, honest, sober, industrious, and considerate of others, and success in life is assured" (*CTS* I, 747). Edward lives out this creed with pious devotion; George, however, resists it to the last. The doting couple, and eventually the community at large, leave Edward unassisted in his virtue because godliness seems to be his "natural bent" (*CTS* I, 748). George receives special consideration and dispensation his whole life; he gets more candy and swimming and berrying than his brother, and when the Brants die, George receives their estate because he "needs" it, whereas Edward can rely upon "bountiful Providence" to provide for him.

Providence seems to have a perverse sense of humor, however. The woman who loves Edward throws him over so that she might "reform" poor George. Edward marries another woman, and George abuses his wife and child. Edward is a dutiful husband and business-man; George is a tippler and a gambler. Edward honors his foster parents' wish that he take care of his brother and enters into a business partnership with him, but George's gambling ruins the enterprise. Edward becomes a social disgrace, but George is taken out of the gutter by members of a temperance organization and given a good situation. George backslides continually, and each time, he is rescued with hand-wringing popular acclaim. He is sent to prison for forgery, but the Prisoner's Friend Society obtains a pardon for him and a job with a good salary. Meantime Edward has steadfastly earned his way in the world and has become a cashier in a bank. When he refuses to reveal the combination to the safe, burglars kill him. The chief criminal, it turns out, is George. Edward Mills's family is left penniless; George is sentenced to be hanged. Widows, orphans, and "tearful young girls" plea for a reprieve, but "for once" the governor will not yield. George is executed. Mourners place flowers by his headstone, which reads, "He has fought the good fight." Edward's unkempt grave bears this epitaph: "Be pure, honest, sober, industrious, considerate, and you will never—." People puzzle over the incomplete inscription and pity Edward's widow. She receives no pension or aid, but "a lot of appreciative people . . . have collected forty-two thousand dollars—and built a Memorial Church with it" (*CTS* I, 752).

"**Edward Mills and George Benton**" registers unmistakably Twain's disgust with sentimental reformers who lavish money and attention on the profligate and unworthy while the modest and virtuous must fend for themselves. He had already written the episode about Judge Thatcher's failed attempts to reform Pap in chapter 5 of *Huckleberry Finn* and was once again ridiculing a misplaced sympathy that served no social purpose other than to advertise the reformer's self-satisfied Christian charity. Clearly, Twain was looking back to a simpler form of justice and retribution he had seen in Ned Blakely and had dramatized in "**A Trial.**" He expressed the same desire for simplicity and his impatience with complicated bureaucratic process in "**The Man Who Put Up at Gadsby's.**" In that tale, Twain recalls a conversation he had one wintry night in Washington with his "odd friend" Riley. They are interrupted by Mr. Lykins, who has traveled from California in order to secure the San Francisco postmastership. Lykins wants Riley to help him push the appointment through Congress right away, for as Lykins says, "I ain't the talking kind, I'm the *doing* kind" (*TA* [*A Tramp Abroad*], 264). Riley is amused by the man's spunk and decides to tell him the story of a man from Tennessee who, in 1834, came up to Washington to collect on a minor claim against the government.

This Tennessee man also wanted to conduct business promptly and get back home, but perceiving that there would be some delay, he put up at local hotel, Gadsby's. In a matter of months, he had sold all he owned for the sake of that small claim; 30 years later, the man is still in Washington and still anxious to settle and get back to Tennessee. Lykins fails to perceive the relevance of this tale and finds it rather long and pointless to be told on a snowy street corner. Riley slyly brings the sum and substance of his little parable home: "O, there isn't any particular point to it. Only, if you are not in *too* much of a hurry to rush off to San Francisco with that post-office appointment, Mr. Lykins, I'd advise you to '*put up at Gadsby's*' for a spell, and take it easy" (*TA*, 270-71). Lykins never gets Riley's parable, but then, he never gets the post office appointment either.

"**The Man Who Put Up at Gadsby's**" bears a resemblance in theme and tone to "**The Facts in the Case of the Great Beef Contract**" and "**The Facts in the Great Landslide Case**"; indeed, an earlier version of the sketch was written about the same time as those stories, in 1868, and published in the *Territorial Enterprise*. Twain rewrote and expanded this piece and interpolated it into *A Tramp Abroad*, a book about his travels in Switzerland, Germany, and Italy. In the context of that book, the immediate appropriateness of the sketch is the narrator's amused observation of Swiss fishermen lining the banks of a lake in front of his hotel. After waiting a good while to see a fish caught, the narrator concludes "that the man who proposes to tarry till he sees somebody hook one of those well-fed and experienced fishes will find it wisdom to 'put up at Gadsby's' and take it easy'" (*TA*, 271). However, this reworked story participates in the same sort of emotional state that seems to have prompted the creation of another tale interpolated into *A Tramp Abroad* and widely regarded as one of Twain's finest stories, "**Jim Baker's Blue Jay Yarn.**"

In order to fully appreciate both stories, we must back up a bit. Riley is a cagey storyteller, but Twain regards his friend as a bit "odd," and Lykins is too self-absorbed and obtuse to see the point of the story at all. As a storyteller, Riley is profoundly misunderstood, but then Twain himself had been in a similar position when he delivered his notorious "Whittier Birthday Speech" on December 17, 1877. Howells had arranged for Clemens to make an after-dinner speech on the occasion of John Greenleaf Whittier's 70th birthday, in the presence of Boston's literary elite. This speech, about Twain trying out the virtue of his nom de plume on a lonely California miner, was an amusing and gracious way of affirming the humorist's pleasure, and his right, to be in the presence of New England's literary worthies.

The miner is unimpressed by Twain's credentials, for he is the fourth literary fellow to visit the miner in 24 hours. The night before, three men on their way to

Yosemite and claiming to be Emerson, Longfellow, and Oliver Wendell Holmes had imposed upon the man's hospitality. Emerson was a "seedy little bit of a chap," the miner recalled, Longfellow was built like a "prize-fighter," and Holmes was "fat as a balloon." The men had been drinking and were disposed to quote (or misquote) lines of verse. They ate the miner's food, drank his whiskey, and in the end, stole his boots. The miner confesses that he "ain't suited to a littery atmosphere" and means to move away from there. Twain assures the man that those three intruders were imposters; the miner eyes him and replies, "Ah—imposters, were they?—are *you?*" (*CTS* I, 699). The comedy of this exquisite little speech, as Twain and Howells somewhat inaccurately remembered it, was largely lost on the dinner guests, who remained quizzically and courteously silent.[10]

Howells thought the speech a "hideous mistake," a "fatality," an offense that might eventually be repaired but carrying with it a shame that could not be outlived. Critical newspaper notices seemed to confirm Howells's perception. Twain was humiliated by the event and, at Howells's urging, wrote notes of apology to Longfellow, Emerson, and Holmes, protesting the innocence of his intent and at the same time describing himself as a heedless "savage." No mossy dwarf of conscience could have shamed Twain as much that unfortunate occasion. On December 23, Twain wrote to Howells, "My sense of disgrace does not abate. It grows. I see that it is going to add itself to my list of permanencies—a list of humiliations that extends back to when I was seven years old, & which keep on persecuting me regardless of my repentancies" (*MTHL* I, 212). Twain even offered to withdraw his story of the telephone romance between Alonzo Fitz Clarence and Rosannah Ethelton, scheduled for publication in the *Atlantic Monthly,* and concluded that it "will be best that I retire from before the public at present." In fact, Twain did retire from the scene. Though he had planned the trip beforehand, when he took his family to Germany the next April, the journey had the quality of guilty escape.

Quite apart from any exaggerated sense of impropriety, however, the "Whittier Birthday Speech" must have contributed to Twain's sense of confusion about literary respectability and his proper audience. Since the publication of **"A True Story,"** he had published 16 pieces in the prestigious *Atlantic Monthly.* In 1876, he had also written *[Date 1601] Conversation, As It Was by the Social Fireside, in the Time of the Tudors* in the form of a letter to his friend and Hartford pastor, Joseph Twichell. Twain knew well enough that this ribald story of profanity and flatulence in Queen Elizabeth's court was vulgar; in his "Autobiography," he recalled that he put into the mouths of these august figures "grossnesses not to be found outside Rabelais."[11] Twain never sought to publish *1601 [Conversation, As It Was by the Social Fireside, in the Time of the Tudors*], but it was read and circulated privately, and he knew that the piece was a hit among respectable New England gentlemen.

The next year, again indulging the coarser side of his fancy, Twain wrote up a little tale that Twichell had told him when they traveled to Bermuda. This piece was meant for publication but would not see print until five years later. Twain had published in the *Atlantic* "Some Rambling Notes of an Idle Excursion" in a four-part series beginning in October 1877, but Howells had advised that Twain exclude **"The Invalid's Story"** from this contribution because it was indelicate. Later, Howells recommended that he remove it from *A Tramp Abroad.* Twain continued to like the piece, however, and he included it in his collection **The Stolen White Elephant, Etc.** (1882). It is true that this tale of a man accompanying what he takes to be a casket containing a dead friend (actually, due to a mix-up at the train station, he is tending a crate of guns) is crude. The crate has been placed beside a carton of Limburger cheese, and the narrator and the baggage man mistake the ripeness of the cheese for the putrefaction of his friend. Twain gets some good scatological fun out of the mistake, and the tale is notable for the vigorous slang of the baggage man.

The mountain of genteel respectability had not come to Mark Twain, so Mark Twain had gone to the mountain. He had tried to adjust to life in New England and to the requirements of his literary fame, but he seemed to be getting mixed signals. He may well have had a rather contradictory sense of what would play in the parlor for mixed company, as opposed to in the smoking room. He knew that a reader's expectations in Virginia City differed from those in Hartford or Boston, but the difference was hard to define. He knew as well that his popularity seemed to rest on his western point of view, while his reputation as a serious writer depended on other, and presumably higher, considerations. That a Connecticut pastor who had an earthy sense of humor might tell him a story unsuitable for the *Atlantic* was surely perplexing. Henry Nash Smith admirably summarizes the author's predicament: "The confusion of tastes and attitudes in nineteenth-century American culture made it impossible for Mark Twain to arrive at a workable idea of his vocation. If he hoped to be accepted as a serious writer, he was apparently obliged to conform to the priestly role of the man of letters. If he devoted himself to humor he must be content with the humble function of providing comic relief from higher concerns. The program of the Whittier dinner was virtually a pageant translating his problem into quasi-dramatic terms."[12]

The failure of the Whittier speech only exacerbated Twain's sense of confusion and frustration. He may have rightly concluded that if a man wants his due from a coterie of Boston Brahmins, he may as well "'put up at Gadsby's' and take it easy." But it was difficult for a proud and self-conscious man to take it easy. His performance that December night seemed to haunt him with uncertainty; many years later, in 1906, he inspected the speech once again and concluded that it "hasn't a defect in it. . . . It is smart; it is saturated with humor. There isn't a suggestion of coarseness or vulgarity in it anywhere." But a few days later, he reversed himself: "I find it gross, coarse . . . I didn't like any part of it, from the beginning to the end." A few days after that unequivocal judgment, he reversed his opinion yet again.[13]

Whether we locate this confusion of taste and attitude in nineteenth-century culture or in Twain himself hardly matters, but as we will see in the final chapter, the literary persona that in the early days had allowed him to speak with an original and authentic voice had itself become the problem, not the solution. Quite apart from the vocational difficulty Twain faced, Clemens's dignity had been compromised, or so he thought, and he indulged in a muted form of revenge when he came to write **"Jim Baker's Blue Jay Yarn."**

Twain prepares the reader of *A Tramp Abroad* for the blue jay yarn with marvelous grace and facility. He recalls that he had been reading deeply in German legends and fairy tales, and when he got lost in the Neckar forest outside of Heidelburg, he "fell into a train of dreamy thought about animals which talk" and other "legendary stuff" (*TA*, 31). Through vagrant thoughts and imaginings, he adopts the "right mood to enjoy the supernatural" (*TA*, 32), and at that moment, a raven appears and seems to be inspecting him. Twain's meditative mood suddenly turns to humiliation and anger: "I felt something of the same sense of humiliation and injury which one feels when he finds that a human stranger has been clandestinely inspecting him in his privacy and mentally commenting upon him" (*TA*, 32). Soon, another raven joins in the scrutiny, and the narrator becomes more and more embarrassed. They seem to rain insults down on him—"What a hat!" "O, pull down your vest!"—and that sort of thing "hurts you and humiliates you, and there is no getting around it with fine reasoning and pretty arguments" (*TA*, 35).

The ostensible purpose of these introductory paragraphs is to serve as a transition into the blue jay story. Twain's experience in the forest reminds him that animals do indeed talk and that the only man he ever knew who could understand them was Jim Baker. This bridging device is simple and effective. However, in the course of those few pages, Twain has also recapitulated the sort of shame he felt in the aftermath of the Whittier birthday speech.

Unlike the roles he had his persona sometimes play, the Mark Twain who is insulted and humiliated here is truly innocent. He has committed no crimes, domestic or civil; he has made no thoughtless blunders. Instead, his embarrassment is the result of being too minutely inspected, as though by naturalists who have discovered a new kind of bug. He has merely wandered into alien territory and been found to be a curiosity by a few pesky ravens who ridicule his hat and vest and ask, "Well, what do *you* want here?" (*TA*, 32).

The story that follows is one of Twain's finest tall tales, and Walter Blair rightly describes it, with *Huckleberry Finn*, as the author's "other masterpiece."[14] The story is remarkable, at any rate, for the apparent ease with which Twain returned to the idiom and a freedom of view he had practiced 15 years earlier, and the story is in fact among those he had heard Jim Gillis tell in Calaveras County. Like Simon Wheeler and Jim Blaine and other of Twain's vernacular narrators, Jim Baker is a "simple-hearted" fellow, but he is neither abstracted nor tipsy, and he does not speak in a monotone. Instead, he knows blue jays, and he has passionate convictions about them: "whatever a blue-jay feels, he can put into language. And no mere commonplace language, either, but rattling, out-and-out book-talk—and bristling with metaphor, too—just bristling!" (*TA*, 36). Cats use good grammar, it is true, but they are excitable creatures and in a fight use grammar that would give a person "lockjaw." When blue jays use bad grammar, they are ashamed of themselves. Cats can swear, of course, but not like a blue jay. A jay can swear and scold and laugh and cry and gossip and reason and plan. What is more, a blue jay has a sense of humor: "a jay knows when he is an ass just as well as you do—maybe better. If a jay ain't human, he better take in his sign, that's all" (*TA*, 37).

This brag on behalf of blue jays requires some proof, and Jim Baker immediately begins to tell "a true fact" about some blue jays. The story is simple enough: A blue jay finds a hole in the roof of an abandoned cabin next to the miner's. He tries to fill up the hole with acorns and gets mighty mad in the process. A fellow jay comes along to see what all the cussing is about, and then another, and another. A last the mystery is discovered, and every jay in the neighborhood falls to laughing over the fact that the first jay had tried to fill up a whole house with acorns. But the manner of Jim Baker's telling is a masterful blend of awe and insistent conviction.

That animals can talk is not to be doubted; that is the incontrovertible premise of the beast fable. Baker's story is as eloquent as a jay's, and just bristling with metaphor: When the blue jay spies the hole, he shuts one eye and peers into it "like a 'possum looking down a jug," he gives a "wink or two" with his wings, his smile fades away "like breath off'n a razor," he works so hard at filling the hole that he is "sweating like an ice-pitcher," and so many blue jays come around to see what the trouble is that "the whole region 'peared to have a blue flush about it" (*TA*, 38-41). As Howells observed of Twain, as a writer, he was a slave to the concrete detail. These metaphors are not merely bristling, they are a brilliant fusion of minute observation and fantastic conception, and their accuracy lends an air of credibility to the absurd tale he tells.

In only a few pages, Twain gives us the luxurious feeling of relaxed recollection, but the tale itself is neither aimless nor wandering and is remarkable for its compactness. The yarn is meant to corroborate Baker's steadfast beliefs about animals in general, and blue jays in particular. Blue jays can reason, he insists, and Baker's jay does just that. After scrutinizing the hole, the jay arrives at a syllogism: "It looks like a hole, it's located like a hole,—blamed if I don't believe it *is* a hole" (*TA*, 38). Blue jays can ponder and plan: "must be a mighty long hole; however, I ain't got no time to fool around here, I got to 'tend to business; I reckon it's all right—chance it, anyway." A blue jay can curse: "Then he began to get mad . . . his feelings got the upper hand of him presently, and he broke loose and cussed himself black in the face" (*TA*, 39). We know that a blue jay can gossip because it isn't long before every bird in the United States knows of that first jay's struggle with that hole. Perhaps most important, blue jays have a sense of humor, and each one takes a turn looking into the cabin floor strewn with acorns and nearly suffocates with laughter.

There are elements in the blue jay yarn that are reminiscent of the Whittier speech and the humiliation Twain felt afterward. In what amounts to a prologue to the tale, Twain records his undeserved feelings of injury occasioned by scoffing ravens, and we are left to imagine the embarrassment the blue jay feels at the hands of his fellow creatures. There are other parallels as well. Both take place near a lonely miner's cabin in California; both, though in rather different ways, dramatize the comedy of misjudgment and of being imposed upon; and both make telling references to visiting a natural wonder of the West. In the birthday speech, the three impostors are on their way to Yosemite and stop at the miner's cabin along the way. In the blue jay yarn, another visitor from the East stops by to see the legendary hole. Every bird in the country could see the point of the story of the jay and the hole "except an owl that come from Nova Scotia to visit the Yo Semite, and he took this thing in on his way back. He said he couldn't see anything funny in it. But then he was a good deal disappointed about Yo Semite, too" (*TA*, 42). A humorless owl from the East, equally unresponsive to the natural grandeur of Yosemite and local folklore and humor, is far more pathetic than an overeager jay who tries to fill a bottomless hole with acorns.

Comedians are perpetually vulnerable to those who will not or cannot see the point of their good-natured, if ex-

cessive, humor, but they typically have a ready rejoinder—"To hell with them if they can't take a joke." Twain managed to get something of that quality into his blue jay yarn, but it would be a mistake to see the story exclusively as disguised but bitter remonstrance. After all, at about the same time that he wrote this story, he confessed in a letter to Howells that he was having difficulty managing the satire he meant to get into *A Tramp Abroad*: "Of course a man can't write successful satire except he be in a calm judicial good-humor . . . in truth I don't ever seem to be in a good enough humor with ANYthing to *satirize* it" (*MTHL* I, 248-49). **"Jim Baker's Blue Jay Yarn"** is not exactly satire, but the story does show that the author was in good enough humor with the subject of the tale to draw upon his richest resources as a humorist.

And the story is masterful. In a brief space, Twain manages to move his beast fable from a mood of evocative enchantment to firm and eager conviction to full-fledged tall-tale humor. From the opening description of the German forest as possessing a certain twilight melancholy, one is led to expect something on the order of "Rip Van Winkle" or "The Legend of Sleepy Hollow." But Twain effortlessly shifts his scene and his tone from the comic Gothicism of an Irving to the straightforward and insistent claims of a lonely California miner. The question for Jim Baker is not whether under the magical influence of a forest reverie one might almost believe that animals can talk—"Animals talk to each other, of course. There can be no question about that" (*TA*, 36). Instead, the question is which sort of animal is the best talker, and this is the sort of question that may be resolved according to accepted rational criteria. Which animal is never at a loss for words? has the largest vocabulary? can take profanity to a new level of expression? uses the best grammar? has the most fluent delivery? The blue jay, of course. What is more, a blue jay has a full range of concerns and is subject to vacillations of thought and feeling that make his gifts not merely articulate but eloquent. However frustrated Twain might have been with writing *A Tramp Abroad*, he must have taken an exquisite pleasure in writing this story, and the reader who fails to respond to the infectious joy of the blue jay yarn ought to pass up Yosemite as well.

In addition to **"The Man Who Put Up at Gadsby's"** and **"Jim Baker's Blue Jay Yarn,"** Twain originally intended to include in *A Tramp Abroad* **"The Stolen White Elephant,"** but he changed his mind, and it appeared as the title story in a collection of sketches published in 1882. Twain was always tempted by burlesque, and this was one of the reasons he could never quite shake the reputation of funny fellow. This rollicking treatment of the incompetence of detectives was inspired by a recent and unusual kidnapping. The body of a wealthy New York merchant was stolen from a cemetery vault, and the robbers demanded $50,000 ransom. Newspapers avidly covered the case, reporting in sensational detail the failed efforts of police and detectives to recover the body.

The humor of Twain's tale, told by a Siamese gentleman, is largely topical and, though it retains much of its hilarity, seems somewhat dated now. The idea that the gift of a white elephant, bound from Siam to England as a means of "propitiating an enemy" (*CTS* I, 804), should be lost in Jersey City is amusing enough. So are the ridiculous efforts of Inspector Blunt and his crew of detectives to locate the beast. Perhaps of most lasting interest is Twain's shrewd understanding of the nature of public reputation. Blunt is a thinly disguised version of Alan Pinkerton, who established his national detective agency in 1850 and promoted its reputation through several detective novels based on the work of his operatives. Blunt is unflappable despite the comic misadventures of his investigators. He knows that incompetence is no obstacle to greatness; one may be famous for being famous. He tells his client, the desperate Siamese gentleman, "As to the newspapers, we *must* keep in with them. Fame, reputation, constant public mention—these are the detective's bread and butter. . . . We must constantly show the public what we are doing, or they will believe we are doing nothing" (*CTS* I, 812). Due to Blunt's expensive strategies to retrieve the elephant, the Siamese gentleman loses his reputation and his fortune, but his continuing admiration for Blunt amounts to a form of idolatry. Since Twain himself had only recently decided to retire from the public eye for a while, this story of self-promotion has a certain poignancy about it.

Another story, **"The Professor's Yarn,"** was also meant for *A Tramp Abroad* but was removed and would eventually appear in chapter 36 of *Life on the Mississippi* (1883). An early version of Karl Ritter's revenge story, usually reprinted as **"A Dying Man's Confession,"** was probably composed at about the same time and may have been intended for inclusion in *A Tramp Abroad* as well; it would appear as chapters 31 and 32 of *Life on the Mississippi*. However, as Horst H. Kruse has shown, the Ritter story was so altered to fit into the narrative plan of the Mississippi book that to take the Ritter tale as a freestanding short story may be unwise.[15] **"The Burning Brand"** was certainly prepared for *Life on the Mississippi*, though it may have been written solely for the purpose of padding the book in order to meet the requirements of an agreement Twain had with his publisher; it appeared as chapter 52 of the volume.

None of these stories merit special commentary, nor does the story **"A Curious Experience,"** which Twain published in the November 1881 issue of *Century Magazine*. It should be pointed out, however, that all of them deal, in greater or lesser degree, with mistaken identity.

When one recalls that Twain's longer works during this period—*A Tramp Abroad, Life on the Mississippi, The Prince and the Pauper,* and, of course, *Huckleberry Finn*—also often deal in masquerade, deception, and misplaced sympathy, it becomes clear that mistaken identity was a preoccupation with Samuel Clemens, a.k.a. Mark Twain. As Everett Emerson has persuasively argued, Clemens wanted above all else to be "authentic," even if his authenticity appeared in the person of his nom de plume. However, at this time, the literary persona seemed to be fracturing; at least it seems to play no vital role in the short fiction that appeared below his name. During this period, there is often a distancing of the Twain persona who begins the tale from the story to be told. Sometimes, as in **"A Dying Man's Confession"** or in **"The Professor's Yarn,"** the tale is told by a casual acquaintance, who may recur to an experience several decades old. Sometimes the stories, such as **"A Curious Experience"** or **"The Burning Brand,"** are twice-told tales, more or less faithful accounts derived from earlier documents or published materials, and leave little room for the author's exuberant improvisations. In either case, Mark Twain as literary persona is not much of a player in the fiction, nor a vital part of the dramatic scene of its telling.

He had more than compensated for any loss of imaginative power invested in his literary persona, however, by cultivating in his longer works the art of ventriloquism. In *A Connecticut Yankee in King Arthur's Court* (1889), Mark Twain plays only a small role, preparing the stage for Hank Morgan's weird adventures in time travel. And in *Adventures of Huckleberry Finn* (1885), a novel the author had been working on since 1876, Twain is obliterated altogether. Evidently the author felt that his young hero required no testimonials from him about Huck's simple heart and no apologies for his untutored gifts as a storyteller. Huck simply declares in the opening paragraph that "Mr. Mark Twain" told some "stretchers" in *Tom Sawyer* and then launches into the narrative without further delay.

When Clemens decided to allow Huck Finn to tell his own story, Mark Twain humbly retreated into the background. For any number of reasons, Twain's identification with Huck was a strong one. Although Twain had little in common with this unwashed and illiterate boy, the author obviously envied Huck's innocent freedom and admired his self-sufficiency. He knew that Huck had a story to tell and that only Huck could tell it. When the novel was at last completed, however, Clemens made sure that his readers knew unmistakably that it was Mark Twain, not Huckleberry Finn, who wrote this novel—he inserted a heliotype of the Karl Gerhardt bust of himself as a frontispiece and provided both a "Notice" and an "Explanatory" by "The Author" that called attention to Twain as a deliberate artist and as the creator of the work. Mark Twain wished to preside over this novel without being particularly implicated in it; this is not a criticism (part of the genius of the novel derives from the author's invisibility), but it does say something about what Everett Emerson calls "the disappearance of Mark Twain."[16]

Eight years elapsed between the appearance of the three relatively uninspired stories in *Life on the Mississippi* and the publication of the story **"Luck"** in the August 1891 issue of *Harper's Magazine.* But we should not leave this period in Twain's career without mentioning a piece that, while not strictly speaking a work of fiction, benefited from his craft as a storyteller at the same time that it seemed to reinvent his literary persona. In May 1885, Robert Underwood Johnson, an editor for *Century Magazine,* requested that Twain contribute a piece to his "Battles and Leaders of the Civil War" series. The result was **"The Private History of a Campaign That Failed,"** published in the *Century* the following December. Though this autobiographical reminiscence looks back to a period before Samuel Clemens adopted his nom de plume, it is signed "Mark Twain." There is even some reason to suppose that Clemens thought of his "war-paper" as a short story, for he later included it in his collection of short fiction, *Merry Tales* (1892).

Whether one considers it autobiography or fiction, **"The Private History of a Campaign That Failed"** is an exquisite piece of writing. Moreover, there are several departures from perpendicular fact (whether these are the result of a faulty memory, minor wish fulfillment, or conscious dramatic invention does not matter), and the whole bears the unmistakable impress of a shaping creative intelligence. This piece has a discernible resemblance to the recently published *Huckleberry Finn* in several different ways: Twain's record of his adventures in 1861 in the outfit of Confederate irregulars known as the Marion Rangers is spoken from the point of view of a social pariah, a deserter. Perhaps he and the countless other deserters like him who set out to do something but did not "ought not to be allowed much space among better people," but there must be some value to an account that may "explain the process by which they didn't do anything" (*CTS* I, 863).

That process is largely a mixture of moral and political confusion coupled with a boyish inclination to play the part of warriors only when it is convenient and appeals to their fancy. The action of the piece, as John Gerber observed, "is precisely the pattern which recurs repeatedly in *Huckleberry Finn.* . . . Huck gets into a series of scrapes of increasing complexity and annoyance until finally when matters reach a climax he can't stand any longer, he 'lights out.'"[17] Most of these soldiers conform to military observances only when they don't interfere with swimming, smoking, or fishing; and they are full of Tom Sawyeresque romantic pretension; one

fellow goes so far as to change his name from the ordinary Peterson Dunlap to the majestic "Pierre d'Unlap."

They move in and around Marion County, retreating mostly, and face no greater danger to their "holiday" than an encounter with a few dogs. Much of **"The Private History"** is sheer burlesque, but Twain introduced an episode that was surely an invention but gave his story a moral center. The soldiers are nervous from hearing rumors that enemy troops are in the vicinity, and one night, a stranger rides close to their encampment in a barn. They fire upon the man, only to discover that he is unarmed and not in uniform. They watch him gasp out his dying breath. For Twain, at least, their campaign was "spoiled." The author's expressed feelings of guilt and remorse are vivid, but because in all likelihood there was no stranger and no killing, they are a powerful fiction posing as an autobiographical fact: "The thought of him got to preying upon me every night: I could not get rid of it. I could not drive it away, the taking of that unoffending life seemed such a wanton thing. And it seemed an epitome of war" (*CTS* I, 880).

The feeling of moral revulsion Twain describes here is precisely the sort he had dramatized several times in Huck Finn—in his witnessing the Boggs shooting, or the death of his friend Buck Grangerford, even the tarring of the king and the duke. In the character of Huckleberry Finn, Twain had created a boy who had "a sound heart and a deformed conscience," as he said. In **"The Private History,"** Twain presented himself as the possessor of that heart and that conscience. As Huck had done so many times in the novel, Twain displays no overt contempt for a cruel and wicked world but criticizes himself for his failure to understand and function in that world: "My campaign was spoiled. It seemed to me that I was not rightly equipped for this awful business; that war was intended for men, and I for a child's nurse. I resolved to retire from this avocation of sham soldiership while I could save some remnant of my self-respect" (*CTS* I, 880). In this "war-paper," Twain was rewriting his own life according to the experience of another Missouri boy, Huck Finn, who did not seem to fit in.

Part of Twain's motive for writing **"The Private History of a Campaign That Failed,"** however, had to do with criticisms made about his recent association with Ulysses S. Grant. Twain's newly formed publishing house had an agreement to publish the *Personal Memoirs of U. S. Grant.* In **"The Private Campaign,"** Twain says that his outfit came within a few hours of encountering Grant at a time "when he was as unknown as I was myself" (*CTS* I, 882), but this was another fiction. Twain and Grant actually came within a few weeks of meeting each other, but no closer. By 1885, both men were not at all unknown, of course, and in a curious way, Twain is asserting his right to share with Grant a nation's esteem. Grant was a soldier, and his reputation rested upon his demonstrated military heroism. Twain was a humorist, but he wanted to be known as Howells knew him, as one with "an indignant sense of right and wrong" and an "ardent hate of meanness and injustice."[18] His war-paper was an attempt to justify himself on individual moral grounds at the same time that it recorded his avoidance of military duty.

After his brief experience as a soldier, Clemens, like Huck Finn, lighted out for the territory; it was in Nevada that Samuel Clemens became Mark Twain. By reinventing his own history in 1885 and presenting himself as someone who, in 1861, went West to avoid any further contamination of his virtue and to preserve his self-respect instead of to improve his own opportunities, Twain was reaffirming his identity as a serious writer who also happened to be funny. By defining his moral nature in terms that better applied to Huck Finn than Sam Clemens, and by locating this dramatic representation of himself at a point in his life just before he became a professional writer, Twain was somehow coloring the whole of his whole literary career.

After publishing **"The Private History,"** Twain turned to other projects. He was overseeing his publishing house; he was also attempting to continue the adventures of Huck Finn and Tom Sawyer in another novel, but that project stalled. Twain the short fiction writer would return soon enough, however, and when he did, there would often be a sombreness, even a bitterness, in his fables that no one would mistake for the antics of a mere humorist. But there would be imaginative vitality, too, and, despite recurring creative faltering and hesitation, genuine literary achievement. That is the subject of the final chapter.

Notes

1. For example, in 1877, when John Lewis, a black servant for the Cranes, performed a remarkable feat of heroism by stopping a runaway cart with Olivia's sister-in-law aboard, Clemens's reaction was telling. He interceded in what was largely a family matter and claimed that because he had grown up among blacks and therefore knew what they would most appreciate, he would advise the family on the proper way to reward Lewis. See Arthur G. Pettit, *Mark Twain and the South* (Lexington: University of Kentucky Press, 1974), 96.

2. Twain may have altered the details of the recognition scene between Rachel and her son. In "A True Story," Aunt Rachel uses a phrase she had picked up from her mother: "I wa'nt bawn in de mash to be fool' by trash! I's one o' de ole Blue Hen's Chickens, I is!" The expression appropri-

ately emphasizes Aunt Rachel's pride and her righteous indignation and is distinctive enough to confirm Henry's suspicions that she is his mother. However, the story, as it was told among Mary Cord's descendants, notes that Henry recognized his mother by the ring he had given her when he was a child. See Herbert A. Wisbey Jr., "The True Story of Auntie Cord," *Mark Twain Society Bulletin* 4, no. 2 (June 1981): 1, 3-5.

3. Philip Foner, *Mark Twain: Social Critic* (New York: International Publishers, 1958), 204.

4. Kaplan, introduction to *Mark Twain's Short Stories,* xii.

5. Howells, *My Mark Twain,* 121.

6. Howells, *My Mark Twain,* 122.

7. Quoted in Gladys Bellamy, *Mark Twain as a Literary Artist* (Norman: University of Oklahoma Press, 1950), 135.

8. Howard Baetzhold, *Mark Twain and John Bull: The British Connection* (Bloomington: Indiana University Press, 1970), 57-58.

9. Howells, *My Mark Twain,* 141.

10. For a discussion of this speech and its cultural significance for Twain, Howells, and others, see Harold K. Bush Jr., "The Mythic Struggle between East and West: Mark Twain's Speech at Whittier's 70th Birthday Celebration and W. D. Howells' *A Chance Acquaintance,*" *American Literary Realism* 27, no. 2 (Winter 1995): 53-73.

11. Mark Twain, *The Autobiography of Mark Twain,* ed. Charles Neider (New York: Harper & Row, 1959), 293.

12. Smith, *Mark Twain: The Development of a Writer,* 110.

13. Quoted in Smith, *Mark Twain: The Development of a Writer,* 112.

14. Walter Blair, "Mark Twain's Other Masterpiece: 'Jim Baker's Blue-Jay Yarn,'" *Studies in American Humor* 1, no. 3 (January 1975): 132-47.

15. See Horst H. Kruse, *Mark Twain and "Life on the Mississippi"* (Amherst: University of Massachusetts Press, 1981), 22-30.

16. See Everett Emerson, *The Authentic Mark Twain: A Literary Biography* (Philadelphia: University of Pennsylvania Press, 1984), 100-126.

17. John Gerber, "Mark Twain's 'Private Campaign,'" *Civil War History* 1 (March 1955): 37-60.

18. Howells, *My Mark Twain,* 141.

Selected Bibliography

Primary Works

Collected Tales, Sketches, Speeches, & Essays, 1853-1890. Edited by Louis J. Budd. New York: Library of America, 1992.

Collected Tales, Sketches, Speeches, & Essays, 1891-1910. Edited by Louis J. Budd. New York: Library of America, 1992.

[Date, 1601] Conversation As It Was by the Social Fireside in the Time of the Tudors. Privately published, 1880.

Early Tales & Sketches, 1851—1864. Edited by Edgar Marquess Branch and Robert H. Hirst. Berkeley and Los Angeles: University of California Press, 1979.

Early Tales & Sketches, 1864-1865. Edited by Edgar Marquess Branch and Robert H. Hirst. Berkeley and Los Angeles: University of California Press, 1981.

How to Tell a Story and Other Essays. New York: Harper, 1897.

Life on the Mississippi. Boston: James R. Osgood, 1883. "A Dying Man's Confession," "The Professor's Yarn," "A Burning Brand."

Mark Twain's Own Autobiography: The Chapters from the North American Review. Edited by Michael J. Kiskis. Madison: University of Wisconsin Press, 1990.

Mark Twain's Sketches. New York: American News, 1874. "Map of Paris," "The Facts in the Case of the Great Beef Contract."

Mark Twain's Sketches, New and Old. Hartford: American Publishing, 1875. "My Watch," "Experience of the McWilliamses with Membranous Croup," "Some Learned Fables for Good Old Boys and Girls," "A Curious Dream," "A Ghost Story," "How I Edited an Agricultural Paper Once," "Political Economy," "Journalism in Tennessee," "Story of the Good Little Boy Who Did Not Prosper," "A Visit to Niagara," "A Medieval Romance," "A True Story," "Legend of the Capitoline Venus," "Science *vs.* Luck," "Cannibalism in the Cars," "A Mysterious Visit."

Merry Tales. New York: Charles L. Webster, 1892. "The Private History of a Campaign That Failed," "Luck," "The Invalid's Story," "Mrs. McWilliams and the Lightning."

The Mysterious Stranger and Other Stories. New York: Harper & Brothers, 1922. "My Platonic Sweetheart," "The McWilliamses and the Burglar Alarm," "A Fable," "Hunting the Deceitful Turkey."

Punch, Brothers, Punch! and Other Sketches. New York: Slote, Woodman, 1878. "Punch, Brothers, Punch!" "An Encounter with an Interviewer," "The Loves of Alonzo Fitz Clarence and Rosannah Ethelton," "The Canvasser's Tale."

Roughing It. Hartford: American Publishing, 1972. "The Facts in the Great Landslide Case," "Buck Fanshaw's Funeral," "Captain Ned Blakely," "Jim Blaine and His Grandfather's Old Ram," "Dick Baker and His Cat," "A Letter from Horace Greeley."

The Stolen White Elephant, Etc. Boston: James R. Osgood, 1882. "The Stolen White Elephant," "The Great Revolution in Pitcairn," "A Curious Experience," "Mrs. McWilliams and the Lightning."

The $30,000 Bequest and Other Stories. New York: Harper & Brothers, 1906. "The $30,000 Bequest," "Was It Heaven? Or Hell?" "Edward Mills and George Benton: A Tale," "The Five Boons of Life," "The Californian's Tale."

A Tramp Abroad. Hartford: American Publishing, 1880. "Jim Baker's Blue-Jay Yarn," "The Man Who Put Up at Gadsby's."

A True Story and the Recent Carnival of Crime. Boston: James R. Osgood, 1877. "Facts concerning the Recent Carnival of Crime in Connecticut."

Secondary Works

Baetzhold, Howard G. *Mark Twain and John Bull: The British Connection.* Bloomington: Indiana University Press, 1970.

Bellamy, Gladys. *Mark Twain as a Literary Artist.* Norman: University of Oklahoma Press, 1950.

Foner, Philip. *Mark Twain, Social Critic.* New York: International Publishers, 1958.

Howells, William Dean. *My Mark Twain: Reminiscences and Criticisms.* New York: Harper and Brothers, 1910.

Pettit, Arthur G. *Mark Twain and the South.* Lexington: University of Kentucky Press, 1973.

Smith, Henry Nash. *Mark Twain: The Development of a Writer.* Cambridge: Harvard University Press, 1962.

Peter Messent (essay date summer 1998)

SOURCE: Messent, Peter. "Carnival in Mark Twain's 'Stirring Times in Austria' and 'The Man That Corrupted Hadleyburg.'" *Studies in Short Fiction* 35, no. 3 (summer 1998): 217-32.

[*In the following essay, Messent analyzes the relation between "The Man That Corrupted Hadleyburg" and "Stirring Times in Austria" in terms of Mikhail Bakhtin's concept of carnival, comparing the social and political dimensions of the public meeting at the center of both works.*]

The publication of the 29 volume *The Oxford Mark Twain* in 1996 provided, both for the writers and critics involved in the project, and for its readers, an unusual opportunity for an overview and reassessment of the work Twain published during his lifetime. Essays like that written by Toni Morrison on *Adventures of Huckleberry Finn,* where she speaks eloquently of her responses to different "encounters" with the novel, focusing in particular on what she has come to see as "the silences that pervade it . . . entrances, crevices, gaps, seductive invitations flashing the possibility of meaning. Unarticulated eddies that encourage diving into the novel's undertow" (Morrison xxxi, xxxiii, xxxvi), promise to become the critical lens through which a new generation of readers approach the text.

Another result of the project, however, has been to remind us of the original context in which some of Twain's best-known short fictions appeared. So Cynthia Ozick, in her introduction to the 1900 collection, *The Man that Corrupted Hadleyburg and Other Stories and Essays,* draws revealing comparisons between the title story and the little-known essay, "Stirring Times in Austria," which appears later in the same volume. I use Ozick's essay, and also Bruce Michelson's analysis of **"The Man That Corrupted Hadleyburg"** in his fine recent book, *Mark Twain on the Loose,*[1] as twin points of departure for my own critical work here.

It is not, though, merely the connections between the lead story and the later essay about Austrian politics that emerge when re-reading Twain's *Hadleyburg* [*The Man that Corrupted Hadleyburg and Other Stories and Essays*] book. However casual Twain and his publishers might have been in pulling together the stories and essays written between 1893 and 1900 that make up the collection (Jeffrey Rubin-Dorsky dismisses all but three of them as "periodical literature, written for the moment and for money" [1]) a set of recurring concerns do bring it some unity, however loose that may be. Most noticeable are the references to the Dreyfus Case scattered through the book. Twain makes direct reference to this case on four different occasions (144-46, 170, 270, and 388-89). Moreover, he wrote **"The Man That Corrupted Hadleyburg"** in 1898 in Vienna, the same year Zola published *J'accuse,* and Ozick astutely draws connections between Twain's story and this wider historical context when she writes that:

> the notion of a society—even one in microcosm, like Hadleyburg—sliding deeper and deeper (and individual by individual) into ethical perversion and contamination was not far from a portrait of Europe undergoing the contagion of its great communal lie. The commanding theme of **"The Man That Corrupted Hadleyburg"** *is* contagion; and also the smugness that arises out of self-righteousness, however rooted in lie it may be.
>
> (xxxv)

Ozick's reference to the "communal lie" directly echoes the idea of the "colossal National Lie" (180) that Twain analyzes in "My First Lie, And How I Got Out Of It,"

another essay in the *Hadleyburg* book. Communal hypocrisy, ethical perversion, the Dreyfus Case, failures of systems of justice, and anti-Semitism, provide a cluster of related themes that draws together much of the material in the collection.[2]

There are, too, other repeated themes that both further unify the book and connect it to the other work Twain was producing in the period. The subjects of mistaken and twinned identities, and of personal dislocation and alienation, obsessed Twain throughout his career, and especially in its final stages. In *Hadleyburg,* the comic potential inherent in the former pairing is exploited, to varying degree, in two pieces: "My Debut as a Literary Person" and "My Boyhood Dreams." In the first, Twain has a contribution on the shipwreck of the *Hornet* (a story fully reprised in this essay) accepted by an important New York magazine, but his dreams of literary glory are dashed by the publication of his nom de plume not as "MARK TWAIN" but as "'Mike Swain' or 'MacSwain,' I do not remember which" (85). In **"My Boyhood Dreams,"** the gap between dreamed and actual career becomes comic source, as Twain plays off the figures of friends like Howells, Hay, and Cable, reporting on their supposed "dream-failure[s]" (389). Thus he claims that Cable, for instance, once dreamt of being a "ring-master in the circus" but has ended up instead "Nothing but a theologian and novelist" (393).

Sketches like **"My Boyhood Dreams"** may be slight, but Twain's improvisations on themes of career reversal, the relationship between identity and career, and between dream and reality, will take more thematic weight, and more somber resonance, in his other later writing. And though the Mark Twain/MacSwain confusion is a passing reference, the additional comment that the name Mark Twain "had some currency on the Pacific coast" keys into another repeated theme in the book: that of exchange, currency, and the existence—or lack of it—of some kind of firm gold standard (here, the authorial identity). This takes us from the "gold coin" (4) that turns out to be "virgin lead" (67) in **"The Man That Corrupted Hadleyburg"** to the metaphoric analogy between fraudulent gold and false language running throughout the story, with early description of the "golden remark . . . worth forty thousand dollars, cash" (20) followed by later reference to the "magic document [the stranger's letter], each of whose words stood for an ingot of gold" (41).[3] The question of relative values (and currencies) later features as the central theme of **"The Esquimau Maiden's Romance,"** a comic story in which ethnocentric assumptions are undermined in the representation of cultural difference and alterity that occurs (Kruse). The defamiliarizing disjunctions represented in this story, and undermining of any firm value base, relates in turn to the epistemological uncertainty that always shadows Twain's writing. Mary's remark in **"The Man That Corrupted Hadley-**

burg" that "the foundations of things seem to be crumbling from under us" (28) could act as a motto for much of the work he produced, and especially in his later years.

The theme of dislocation and alienation, too, is increasingly prominent in this period, and is often linked to that of self-division.[4] In **"Is He Living or Is He Dead?,"** Twain narrates how a (fictional) François Millet fakes his own death, with the help of artist friends, and takes on a new identity; and how his works then rise phenomenally in price. This might be read biographically both in terms of some buried desire on the author's part to shuck off the burdens of his invented public persona, or as a fictional exploration at a time of some financial anxiety of the question of the "value" of that persona as measured both in personal and professional terms. The view given of Theophile Magnan (the renamed Millet), who now appears "alone in the world, . . . always looks sad and dreamy, and doesn't talk with anybody" (182), and who, despite his financial rewards, goes (it seems) ungreeted even by his previously "doting" and "inseparable" friend (184), speaks of anxieties about identity and estrangement that are repeated, in different ways, over and over in Twain's late fiction.

I am arguing, then, that the writings put together in the *Hadleyburg* collection are not quite the rag-bag of disparate materials we might expect, especially given the speed with which Twain was churning out books at this time (15 between 1889 and 1900; 12 from 1902 to 1909 [Rubin-Dorsky 1, 2]). The correlative of this is to suggest that we might gain critically by looking more closely at Twain's short stories and essays in the full context of the book in which they first appeared. Rather than extending my analysis of the other stories and essays in *Hadleyburg,* however, I narrow focus to set the one short story **"The Man That Corrupted Hadleyburg"** against the political essay "Stirring Times in Austria" (on a series of dramatic events in the Austrian parliament in late 1897). In doing this, I extend Cynthia Ozick's initial exploration of the complementary nature of these texts, where she writes of the Austrian parliament, as Twain represents it, as "a non-homogeneous Hadleyburg corrupted well past greed into the contagion of chaos and contumely." The trace of the word "Hapsburg" in "Hadleyburg" helps to reinforce the analogy made here.

If the Hadleyburg townspeople, unlike the Hapsburg parliament with its 19 national groupings, are apparently from the same ethnic background, Ozick notes that "their interests [too] conflict as if they held nothing in common" (xxxix).[5] For her, the crux of both pieces lies in the issue of language. In "Stirring Times in Austria," Twain explains how ratification of the *Ausgleich,* the treaty that formally links the Austro-Hungarian Empire, has been jeopardized by the deal Count Bedani,

leader of the government, has made with the Czechs, "making the Czech tongue the official language in Bohemia in place of the German." The German-speaking minority, "incensed" (292) by this move, obstructs government business—in particular that of the *Ausgleich*—until the status of their own language should once more be restored. Ozick compares the 19 states in the Austrian parliament to the 19 worthies in Hadleyburg, and sees the way both the parliamentarians and leading citizens "furiously compete" as analogous: "we can recognize in Hadleyburg the dissolving Austria-Hungary of the 1890's" (xl).

Ozick's critical work here is extremely valuable, but it is noticeable that she does not quite pin down her point about the comparative use of the language theme in the two texts. Also, she remains curiously blind to what I see as their main point of comparison—the way in which description of the sessions of the Austrian parliament structurally mirrors the representation of the Hadleyburg town meeting. Prompted by the use of Bakhtinian terms in Bruce Michelson's analysis of **"The Man That Corrupted Hadleyburg"** (though he nowhere uses the Soviet theorist's name), I use Bakhtin as a lens through which the *public meetings* at the center of both texts can be analyzed. The conclusions I reach concerning social and political hierarchies and the way they work, and the view of human nature presented, will come as no surprise to those familiar with Twain's late work. They serve, though, to further illustrate the close relationship between these two "Austrian" texts.[6]

Bakhtin's notion of *carnivalization* provides an ideal model to apply to **"The Man That Corrupted Hadleyburg."** It can also be applied to "Stirring Times in Austria," even if its relevance here is less immediately obvious. Bakhtin's consistent interest is in the way language serves as a site of conflict, registering the power relations in any particular culture, as one "social speech type" (that is, the voice of a particular professional, regional, ethnic, age-related, or other social or political group) is set against another in a multilayered whole.[7] He sees centripetal impulses within any given socio-political world as in dynamic tension with centrifugal ones. The centripetal is the unhealthy urge toward the closed system—the establishing of a single officially-recognized language—and toward "cultural centralization" (Bakhtin, *Dialogic* 271), while the centrifugal "endlessly develop[s] new forms which parody, criticize and generally undermine the pretensions of the ambitions toward a unitary language" (Murray 119). In his favoring of the centrifugal, Bakhtin asserts his commitment to social diversity and change rather than to the hierarchical. For a culture is not, for him, something fixed, rigid and ordered. He emphasizes rather its multilanguaged aspects, assigning qualities of health and vitality to those ongoing forces of disunification and decentralization that the authorities and ruling classes of any society would try to deny.

"Carnivalization" is a key term for Bakhtin and one directly related to the centripetal-centrifugal axis. For it is the model of carnival festivity "transposed into the language of literature," life turned upside down as conventional hierarchical barriers are removed (Bakhtin, *Problems* 122). Bakhtin's preference for "low" languages over "high" is evident in the emphasis in carnival on the comic overturning of official systems of life and thought by an unofficial folk culture, and the energies with which the latter is associated. Carnival is a time of masquerade, as masks and false identities are assumed that blur the boundaries between high and low and decenter authoritative systems and structures. And carnival is associated with public space (and especially the public square) where normal hierarchies are suspended as the festival runs its course and where all types of people can meet and mingle freely and easily together. Carnivalization primarily means laughter, a laughter "directed toward something higher—toward a shift of authorities and truths." What results is the relativizing of "all structure and order, of all authority and all (hierarchical) position" (Bakhtin, *Problems* 127, 124). In communal performance, the very essence of carnival, the language and structure of officialdom (law, prohibition and restriction) are overturned on behalf of the vital and indecorous folk-energies there allowed release.

The version of carnival that takes place in "Stirring Times in Austria" is a distorted one, with the idea of folk energy[8] and the laughter that accompanies it present only in corrupt form. The language and structure of officialdom are subject to contest and potential overthrow, with energies loosed that are normally harnessed, but such action takes place primarily in a limited arena, and any sense of a life-affirming folk culture ("the folk as an untamable, rebellious, and regenerative force that will destroy the status quo") is absent.[9] Such an absence, and the way the essay portrays the relationship between authority and social diversity, points (despite the difference in setting between the Vienna represented here and the small American town of Hadleyburg) both to the intertextual connections traversing Twain's work, whatever its generic form, and to the bleak view of human behavior, and the way social hierarchies function, that underlies it.

The parliamentary meetings described in "Stirring Times in Austria" differ from the town meeting in **"The Man That Corrupted Hadleyburg,"** but the centrality of these public assemblies in both texts is highly significant. The parliament in "Stirring Times" ["Stirring Times in Austria"] is not the carnival area (the public square) where all types of people can mingle freely together, but it is, to an extent, a microcosmic version of the pluralistic Austro-Hungarian whole, with a membership representing "peoples who speak eleven languages" (292), and coming "from all the walks of life and from all the grades of society" (316). Moreover the sense of the multi-layered communal whole indicated here—something we might expect in a representative body—is reinforced in the way Twain carefully structures his essay to draw links between what occurs within and outside the parliament. Thus the essay starts with a striking metaphor of diffuse electrical energy in which this connection is immediately made: "The atmosphere is brimful of political electricity. All conversation is political; every man is a battery, with brushes overworn, and gives out blue sparks . . ." (284). Despite public confusion about the real nature of the political situation,[10] energies within the parliament have their counterpart on the streets outside. "Stirring Times" both starts and finishes with larger public restlessness, the final references to "a popular outbreak or two in Vienna" and rioting elsewhere (340) a direct result of the parliamentary turbulence described at the essay's core.

Parliamentary events, then, are linked to the release of energies in the larger community in the essay. And within the parliament, elements of the carnivalesque are clearly apparent. As governmental authority is challenged, so events in parliament take on (sporadically) a masquerade quality with formal debate drowned in the "general exuberance" (320) bursting forth. Dr. Lecher does finally get a hearing for his 12-hour speech, holding up the attempt quickly to push through the *Augsleich,* but he commences in "pantomime," his voice drowned out by the "wild and frantic and deafening clamor" (299-300) from the house floor. At another point in the proceedings Lecher and Wolf (another key member of the opposition) "spoke at the same time, and mingled their speeches with the other noises, and nobody heard either of them" (308). All types of wild energies are loosed as language (reasoned or otherwise) is drowned out, first by "explosions of yells" (299), later by the "slam-banging" of desk-boards (305), and then by a form of music, as Wolf "struck the idea of beating out a *tune* with his board" (308). This festive overturning of officialdom, as normal parliamentary business is disrupted, is paralleled in the next sitting of the house when "ceaseless din and uproar, . . . shouting, stamping and desk-banging" (320) are followed by the bursting forth of personal insults, first singly, and then in the form of communal song:

> in their rapture [the Christian Socialists] flung biting epithets with wasteful liberality at specially detested members of the Opposition; among others this one at Schönerer: *"Bordell in der Krugerstrasse!"* Then they added these words, which they whooped, howled, and also even sang, in a deep-voiced chorus: *"Schmul Leeb*

Kohn! Schmul Leeb Kohn! Schmul Leeb Kohn!" and made it splendidly audible above the banging of desk-boards and the rest of the roaring cyclone of fiendish noises.

(325)

The unruly nature of these parliamentary events have a carnival element about them, but, as I have indicated, the urge toward heterogeneity and the celebration of communality that Bakhtin associates with that term are denied here. Laughter is present (see 325) but far outweighed by forms of irony and abuse. Any antithesis between authority systems and a festive and pluralistic community is interrogated by the fact that the government is associated both with an extra-legal exercise of power (the President "persistently ignoring the Rules of the House in the interest of the government side" [320]) but also with the centrifugal impulse, since the very fact of "*dis*union" has kept this [Austro-Hungarian] empire together (285). And not just the opposition but the government benches too share in the carnival nature of the events taking place, in the latter's own use of "pure noise" (308) to short-circuit the legislative process. Most crucially, given Bakhtin's celebrations of linguistic diversity and social difference, it is the government that, as a means of retaining its authority, works toward linguistic pluralism (allowing Czech as the official language in Bohemia) while the opposition fights for linguistic purity: "that the country's public business should be conducted in one common tongue, and that tongue a world language—which German is" (293). The fact that the boundaries are so blurred in this (microcosmic) parliamentary context between the imposition of authority and a carnivalistic sense of release, and between the acceptance of heterogeneity and the demand for a unitary official language system, completely undermines any note of celebration concerning the positive expression of diversity, the regenerative nature of the communal performance, and the fulfilling release of folk energies, we might otherwise (from a Bahktinian perspective) hope to expect.

Indeed it is the more sinister and pessimistic notes that sound in this essay that remain most strongly with the reader. For if the dark carnival Twain describes, with energy loosed to no positive end, may be no more than accurate reportage of events, the ambition for German as a potential "world language" and the racial intolerance loosed within the parliament, are, from a later historical perspective, chilling. As Ozick says:

the parliamentary upheaval [Twain describes] is an indelible precursor that not merely portends the profoundly unforgettable Viennese mob-events of 1938, but thrusts them into our teeth with all their bitter twentieth-century flavor. Here is no déjà-vu, but its

prophesying opposite. Or, to say it otherwise: a twenty-year-old rioter enjoying Mark Twain's Vienna easily becomes a sixty-year-old Nazi enjoying *Anschluss* Vienna.

(Ozick, "Introduction" xlii-xliii)[11]

Carnival is swiftly ended in the parliament with the sudden introduction (on the government's command) of "an invasion of brute force . . . a uniformed and helmeted battalion of bronzed and stalwart men marching in double file down the floor of the House" (339), and this is soon followed both by the collapse of the government and by public riot. The mix of racist and anti-Semitic abuse within parliament ("'You Jew, you! . . .' 'East-German offal tub!'" [321, 325]) is thus transformed into open violence on the streets. This is no open expression of a Bakhtinian "folk energy," though, but its corrupt, narrowly nationalistic, and anti-humanistic underside (the uses to which Hitler would put the celebration of "the folk" come quickly to mind). For Twain reports that, in the outbreaks that take place (in Vienna, Prague and elsewhere), "in some cases the Germans [were] the rioters, in others the Czechs—and in all cases the Jew had to roast, no matter which side he was on" (340). Twain's figure of speech provides another example of that prophesying opposite of déjà vu to which Ozick refers, as images of the festivity, entertainment and laughter associated with carnival are entirely obliterated in the anti-Semitism, racial hatred, and destructive mob violence then released.

The events that Twain describes in "Stirring Times in Austria" are nonfictional and occur in a turbulent European political setting. Nonetheless, the central sequence in his essay (completed on 9 December 1897 [Dolmetsch 72]) significantly foreshadows the portrayal of the town meeting in his short story, **"The Man That Corrupted Hadleyburg,"** written in Vienna late in the following year.[12] The essay also bears certain comparison with the short story in their different depictions of the way in which a particular community functions, and in what we can construct of the notion of folk energy from each such representation.

Carl Dolmetsch briefly alludes to the similarity between the two texts when he compares the technique used in the climactic sequence of **"Hadleyburg"** to that in the main section of "Stirring Times":

Depicting the same atmosphere of "delightful pandemonium," the scene is theatrically staged, with the chair attempting to keep order while raucous taunts and insults are exchanged and speaker after speaker is jeered or shouted down by a "storm," a "cyclone," or a "tornado" of voices, the same imagery he had used in "Stirring Times."

(Dolmetsch 234)

There is more to it than this, though. Both texts have public meetings at their center. In "Stirring Times" this takes a representative form, with a certain separation between parliamentary members, crowded viewing galleries inside the House, and general public outside. Whereas in the small town of Hadleyburg (called, like St. Petersburg in *The Adventures of Tom Sawyer*, "town" and "village" variously) the whole community pack into the Town Hall, its numbers boosted by a variety of "strangers," including "a strong force of special correspondents who had come from everywhere" (38) and even a representative from Barnum's (66). However, the form and progression of both meetings are similar, as, in "Hadleyburg" too, ordered process gives way to pandemonium and reasoned discussion to "all manner of cries . . . scattered through the din" (53-54). Again, individual speech is replaced first by *Many Voices* (58) acting as communal chorus, and then by outbreaks of musical festivity. Such festivity, as the local worthies are mocked, takes the shape both of parodic hymn, "a massed and measured and musical deep volume of sound (with a daringly close resemblance to a well known church chant)" (59), and travesty of light opera:

"Hooray! hooray! it's a symbolical day!"

Somebody wailed in, and began to sing this rhyme (leaving out "it's") to the lovely "Mikado" tune of "When a man's afraid of a beautiful maid"; the audience joined in, with joy [adding further lines to that first] . . . Then the happy house started in at the beginning and sang the four lines through twice, with immense swing and dash. . . .

(55-56)

If the transition from speech to uproar to song is the similar in both texts,[13] the version of carnival represented in "Hadleyburg" is a fuller and more positive one, as Bruce Michelson suggests in describing how, here:

a too-settled social order gives way to folklife, to a springtime of human society in which collective talk and humor flow free, overcoming repression, inhibition and decorum. It is a springtime with power and identity residing nowhere and everywhere.

(Michelson 182)

In the town meeting, the established social order is turned upside down. The discredited and "best-hated" (9) man in the community, Rev. Mr. Burgess, is given authority as chairman, and the chief citizens of the community are made fun of, as their greed and hypocrisy is exposed. During the meeting "the monolithically serious" life of this firmly hierarchical community is undermined by the typical form of carnival laughter, where "ridicule [is] fused with rejoicing" (Bakhtin, *Problems* 125, 127). "The pandemonium of delight" that follows banker Pinkerton's humiliation was, we are told, "of a sort to make the judicious weep. Those whose withers were unwrung laughed till the tears ran down" (53). Laughter becomes king here (as it never fully is in "Stirring Times") and the jester who shares its crown is

Jack Halliday, the town's "loafing, good-natured, no-account, irreverent" (22) who helps instigate the festival that the meeting becomes.[14] As the town-hall becomes the meeting place for the variety of social types that make up the community, as the exchange of gifts (associated with carnival abundance [Bakhtin, *Problems* 125])—first the gold sack, then the large checks—occurs, and as the "nineteen principal citizens and their wives" (21) are reduced from beaming self-congratulation to public humiliation while indecorous folk energies find expressive release, all the conditions of carnival literature appear successfully complete.

If my use of Bakhtin is more explicit, the analysis I propose here has much in common with Michelson's. But my main interest is not (as his is) in the nature of the gap between the dissolve of individual identity, with its celebration of a foundational version of folk life where all subjects merge in a healthy communal whole, and a countering awareness of the way selfhood is defined both by the nature of external events and by social and psychological circumstance. I am more concerned with the representation of social diversity that Twain gives us here. For if in my reading of "Stirring Times in Austria" I noted how any opposition (in the way parliament functioned) between centralizing and decentralizing impulses were blurred, so—and to an extent analogously—the portrayal of social hierarchy in "Hadleyburg" is less clear cut than it at first seems. Both this fact, and the narrative closure that occurs, undercut the impact of that celebration of communal energy in the town hall meeting. The conclusions I reach here do not significantly differ from those of prior critics, but my focus on the issues of class and authority that are engaged, and the ironic attitude toward folk culture I identify, help both to twin this text thematically with Twain's Vienna essay, and to place it in the context of other texts by Twain—and particularly *Huckleberry Finn*—that can be read from a similar thematic perspective.[15]

Carnival depends on the upsetting of established hierarchies, and, at first view, this is exactly what happens in "The Man That Corrupted Hadleyburg," with 18 of its 19 principle citizens exposed as "liars and thieves" (64) by a stranger who had once received "deep offence" (63) while passing through the town. The only name we have for this stranger is "Howard L. Stephenson," signed to a letter (supposedly from a quite other "stranger") written to put the plan of revenge in action. At the public meeting, as exposure occurs, these 18 "Symbols of Incorruptibility" (54) become the object of complete public ridicule, as the remainder of the community loose their voices in exuberant mockery of them. Thus, to quote Bakhtin, "the *joyful relativity* of all structure and order, of all authority and all (hierarchical) position" occurs as the "high" town authorities (the first three men exposed are the Deacon, Lawyer and Banker) are brought low, and "mass actions . . . and . . . the outspoken carnivalistic word" are given their day (Bakhtin, *Problems* 124, 123).

The social reversal that takes place here is compromised, however, by the position of the main protagonists in the narrative, Mary and Edward Richards. Edward is, we have to assume, one of the 19 principal citizens of Hadleyburg. He gets one of Stephenson's letters, and it is he who is left unexposed, his (nineteenth) letter claiming the gold unread by Burgess, due to an old debt he owes to Edwards. For the latter once warned Burgess, on the occasion of his unspecified disgrace, of the town's plans to "ride him on a rail" (11). The fact that the "town" as a whole is early identified with a violent act against an innocent man warns us not to take the opposition between "the authorities" and "the folk" too seriously here. And if the town is socially heterogeneous (the tanner, we are told, cannot get recognition as one of the 19), any clear gap between high and low is interrogated by the Richardses role.

For Edward Richards is the cashier at the bank. An old man who is neither rich nor successful, his working life consists of being "always at the grind, grind, grind, on a salary—another man's slave" (6). What he is doing here among the "aristocracy" (65) is never explained. The town meeting expresses its respect, honor, and love for Richards: ironically as he tries to interrupt it to confess his own greed and guilt. Jack Halliday validates that judgment, in a resonant metaphor, as the "hall-marked truth" (57). And if, to recall Michelson, power and identity come in the story to reside nowhere and everywhere as folk-life erupts at the meeting, then we might take the Richardses very name as signaling their membership of the general mass rather than the aristocracy. I am thinking here of his similarity of name to Henry Edwards in *The Great Dark,* and Michelson's description of the Edwardses as a couple who do "not exist, not as real folk nor even in some respect as characters, for they are . . . presented as middle-class American everybodies and nobodies . . . nonpeople" (Michelson 218). If this description itself calls the definition of "real folk" into question, that does not seem inappropriate once we return to **"Hadleyburg."** Here it might be argued that in the use of the Richardses, "the town's representative consciousness" (Briden 131), Twain deconstructs the opposition he appears to construct between classes, and between town authorities and folk-life, to suggest a lack of essential difference in kind between them.[16] In "Concerning the Jews," he famously wrote: "I think I have no color prejudices nor caste prejudices nor creed prejudices. All that I care to know is that a man is a human being—that is enough for me; he can't be any worse" (254). This statement might be applied, I would suggest, (with the possible exceptions of Sam Halliday and the dead Barclay Goodson) to the community of Hadleyburg. Class dif-

ference and social status matter very little if to be a man is to be a human being, and to be a human being is to be a self-interested hypocrite. Any positive conception of folk-life collapses with this equation.

Even Sam Halliday, unbound by the social constraints of others in the town, is by no means an entirely positive folk figure. The mocking laughter associated most strongly with him, then shared by others, brings, as I shall argue, no sense of communal renewal. Moreover, despite his position on the fringes of the community, he does not see entirely clearly. This text is one in which human behavior remains largely impenetrable and the "free familiar contact" of carnival is never entirely achieved (Bakhtin, *Problems* 123). The story has a striking early image of Halliday carrying "a cigar-box round [like] a camera and [saying], "Ready!—now look pleasant, please," but the Howellsian idea of realist transparency does not work here. Halliday is puzzled by the changing expressions of the 19 couples' faces at various stages following the receipt of Stephenson's letters, "and didn't know what to make of it" (37). "Stephenson" himself, the manipulator of events, is taken in by the apparent innocence of Richards. Burgess does not know Richards, the warmth of his feelings based on partial ignorance; for Richards in fact has proof that Burgess is innocent of his supposed crime, and "could have saved him" (10) from his disgrace had he chosen to do so. And Richards does not know Burgess, seeing the latter's concealment of his letter as an act of vengeance and not of gratitude. Finally, at the end of the narrative, the townsfolk know Burgess little better than at the beginning, his "impassioned" denial of the motives attributed to him by Richards in the latter's death-bed confession falling "on deaf ears" (83). In a community where the thoughts and motives of others are rarely transparent, the full expression and free familiarity of carnival is never properly achieved, neither in the town meeting nor in the subsequent behavior of the town's inhabitants.

Indeed any celebration of the folk spirit seems well and truly quashed by the narrative's end. If Bakhtin, in his celebration of Carnival, tends to underestimate the fact that such festivity only *temporarily* upsets established hierarchies, Twain does not. As the town meeting concludes, "Dr." Harkness buys the sack of bogus coins and uses them to ensure his election to the Legislature. In doing so, he "reviv[es] the recent vast laugh" (77), but directs it away from himself to the single person of his political opponent, Pinkerton. The festivity that has occurred is finally ended, then, with the public energies that have been released channeled to selfish and power-oriented ends: for we are told that what is at stake here in the election are the "two or three fortunes" to be made in the routing of a new railway (70). That the election itself is contested by two of the discredited 18 suggests that nothing fundamentally has changed in the town, despite the humiliation that has occurred, and that social hierarchies have been immediately restored.

The claim that a change in moral sensibility results from the carnival that has occurred (Scharnhorst, among many others, sees the story as "Twain's parable of the Fortunate Fall" [64]) also seems highly dubious. For the final line of the story—"[Hadleyburg] is an honest town once more, and the man will have to rise early that catches it napping again" (83)—might rather be seen as, in James D. Wilson's words, "fraught with irony." As he explains:

> The first clause is patently absurd, for Hadleyburg was never an honest town; furthermore, the syntax suggests a restoration, not a transformation—a return to pride in a deceptive, misconceived self-concept. The second clause . . . implies not that Hadleyburg has changed morally but that it is simply cleverer, less naive—no one will catch "it napping again."
>
> (Wilson 212)[17]

The final focus on the town as a collective whole, moreover, undermines the sense of conflict between "the folk" and the "aristocracy" that gives the scene of the town meeting its energy and power. Such a stress on community may seem logical if we read the story as illustrating how folk values have helped to reform the whole town. But if we take the more ironic option sketched above, the very notion of a life-giving folk energy is placed under erasure, as *all* town members are represented as a collective, and unimproved, social and moral unit.

The structural movement of "Stirring Times in Austria" is from populace to parliamentary meeting, and thence back to public riot and racial hatred, with the events that take place in the centrally-placed representative forum containing strong elements of the carnivalesque. In **"Hadleyburg,"** the carnival structure is even more pronounced and the idea of communal renewal appears to carry much more positive resonance. But the folk laughter released in **"Hadleyburg"** turns out, under close analysis, to lack transformative power. Indeed the very difference between folk-values and those of the authorities they would upset is subject to question. The essay and the story in the **Hadleyburg** volume can then (despite obvious difference in genre, location and subject matter) be read as twinned texts, both of which hinge on public meetings and their loosing of (types of) carnival. If the one text ends with everything back in its ordered social place, and the other with the possibility of political revolution, neither conclusion has much of a positive ring. The attitude toward democratic values and folk energies is ambivalent even in Twain's earliest works, but by this stage in his writing career it has darkened very considerably. "About Play-Acting," another essay in the **Hadleyburg** collection, glosses a play

Twain had recently seen and admired in Vienna (*The Master of Palmyra*). He writes here of the figure of Death appearing on stage, and how "always its coming made the fussy human pack seem infinitely pitiful and shabby and hardly worth the attention of either saving or damning" (239). Such a judgment, I would suggest, could be applied with equal justice in both "Stirring Times in Austria" and **"The Man That Corrupted Hadleyburg."**

Notes

1. See especially 175-88.

2. Ozick's critical analysis of Twain's "Concerning the Jews," another piece in the *Hadleyburg* volume, is sharply relevant here in its discussion of the problematic nature of Twain's attitudes toward Jewishness. See "A Tale" 10-14.

3. See Ozick, "Introduction" xxxviii-xxxix.

4. For discussion of the brief narrative of "treacherous self-divisions" in *Following the Equator* (1897), concerning the "young American boy raised . . . in the Sandwich Islands, whose cross-cultural background erupts in delirium," and a fascinating analysis of it in terms of the function of Hawaii in Twain's career as "a kind of imperial unconscious of national identity," see Kaplan 237-48. The quotations used here are on 238.

5. As Ozick's words here suggest, her distinction between a "homogenous" Hadleyburg and a "non-homogenous" Austria-Hungary does not entirely hold.

6. Twain lived in Vienna from September 1897 to May 1899 and wrote both his essay and short story during this time. Carl Dolmetsch's *"Our Famous Guest": Mark Twain in Vienna* is an invaluable resource on this period of Twain's life.

7. I am here radically condensing Bakhtin's complex arguments, and, in particular, the importance he gives to novel form, for him (because of the "multiplicity of social voices" it represents) the one literary form in "living contact with unfinished, still evolving contemporary reality (the open-ended present)." See *Dialogic Imagination,* 264 and 7. The quotation in the main text is from 262. For a fuller analysis of Bakhtin's theories, and their application to *Adventures of Huckleberry Finn,* see Messent, *New Readings* 204-42. I borrow from that text in my explication here.

8. A term that relates closely to Bakhtin's "folk-carnival life." What Bakhtin says about the decline of carnival life (and the cutting off of carnival forms from their "folk base") is relevant to the argument that follows. See *Problems* 130-31. For a short but pertinent discussion of carnival in a contemporary literary context, see McHale 171-75.

9. See Katerina Clark and Michael Holquist (310). They are commenting here on the way Bakhtin "consistently idealizes the folk" in his work. The status quo (the Badeni regime) is, as I will describe, finally upset in "Stirring Times" but to no positive end.

10. Due to repressive mechanisms employed by the political authorities, and especially the censorship of the public press (287-92). See also Ozick, Introduction li.

11. Jeffrey Rubin-Dorsky's incisive account of the shift in tone of the essay from "Marx Brothers movie" to "Lenny Bruce nightmare" (10) is also relevant to my discussion.

12. Dolmetsch writes that it was completed in October (232). James D. Wilson says December (199).

13. Bruce Michelson also notes the relationship between writing and oral discourse in "The Man That Corrupted Hadleyburg." While "written words prove part of Hadleyburg's crisis," Michelson sees the "*oral* discourse of talk and song" linked to a "dream of primordial freedom—from social conformity, from culture-founded ideas, and from selfhood as a modern construct." See Michelson 183.

14. Though see Michelson (182) on Halliday and the "tide of namelessness" that comes to take over the text.

15. I cannot develop this argument here, but would direct the reader to my *New Readings of the American Novel* and *Mark Twain* (86-109), where the status of carnival and folk energies in *Huckleberry Finn* are discussed

16. Susan K. Harris sees the Richardses as "aliens to the town," sharing the harshly realistic views Barclay Goodson (a "psychological outsider") has of the town. This view does not hold water, since it is clear at the town meeting that other members of the community, too, see through the chief citizens' facades. See Harris 483, 474.

17. Wilson sees the final focus on the Richardses as illustrating the larger message that "humans do not make moral choices at all but behave as they must according to nature, conditioning, and circumstance" (211). Earl F. Briden places the story in the context of Twain's other writings of the time to argue strongly that "'Hadleyburg' thematizes the inoperability of the fortunate-fall doctrine in a world far gone in depravity." He presents the Richardses as initially motivated (after the town meeting) by public opinion, and shows how, at the narrative's end, "the pair obviously can learn no abiding lesson from their sin because they lose their reason." See Briden 128, 131.

Works Cited

Bakhtin, M. M. *The Dialogic Imagination: Four Essays.* Trans. Caryl Emerson and Michael Holquist. Austin: U of Texas P, 1981.

———. *Problems of Dostoevsky's Poetics.* Trans. Caryl Emerson. Manchester: Manchester UP, 1984

Briden, Earl F. "Twainian Pedagogy and the No-Account Lessons of 'Hadleyburg.'" *Studies in Short Fiction* 28 (1991): 125-34.

Clark, Katerina, and Michael Holquist. *Mikhail Bakhtin.* Cambridge, Massachusetts: Harvard UP, 1984

Dolmetsch, Carl. *"Our Famous Guest": Mark Twain in Vienna.* Athens: U of Georgia P, 1992

Harris, Susan K. "'Hadleyburg': Mark Twain's Dual Attack on Banal Theology and Banal Literature." *American Literary Realism* 16 (1983): 240-52. Rpt. Sloane 469-88.

Kaplan, Amy. "Imperial Triangles: Mark Twain's Foreign Affairs." *Modern Fiction Studies* 43 (1997): 237-48

Kruse, Horst H. "Mark Twain and the Other: A Contextual Reading of 'The Esquimau Maiden's Romance.'" Elmira Conference on *The State of Mark Twain Studies.* Elmira College. Elmira, New York. August 1997.

McHale, Brian. *Postmodernist Fiction.* New York: Methuen, 1987.

Messent, Peter. *Mark Twain.* Basingstoke: Macmillan, 1997

———. *New Readings of the American Novel: Narrative Theory and Its Application.* Basingstoke: Macmillan, 1990.

Michelson, Bruce. *Mark Twain on the Loose: A Comic Writer and the American Self.* Amherst: U of Massachusetts P, 1995.

Morrison, Toni. Introduction. *Adventures of Huckleberry Finn.* [1885]. By Mark Twain. The Oxford Mark Twain. Series ed. Shelley Fisher Fishkin. New York: Oxford UP, 1996. xxxi-xli.

Murray, David. "Dialogics: Joseph Conrad, *Heart of Darkness.*" *Literary Theory at Work: Three Texts.* Ed. Douglas Tallack. London: Batsford, 1987.

Ozick, Cynthia. Introduction. Twain xxxi-xlix.

———. "A Tale of Two Scholars." *Commentary.* August 1995: 10-14.

Rubin-Dorsky, Jeffrey. Afterword. Twain 1-11.

Scharnhorst, Gary. "Paradise Revisited: Twain's 'The Man That Corrupted Hadleyburg.'" *Studies in Short Fiction* 18 (1981): 59-64.

Sloane, David E. E., ed. *Mark Twain's Humor: Critical Essays*. New York: Garland, 1993.

Twain, Mark. *"The Man That Corrupted Hadleyburg" and Other Stories and Essays*. The Oxford Mark Twain. Series ed. Shelley Fisher Fishkin. New York: Oxford UP, 1996.

Wilson, James D. *A Reader's Guide to the Short Stories of Mark Twain*. Boston: Hall, 1987.

Horst H. Kruse (essay date October 1998)

SOURCE: Kruse, Horst H. "Mark Twain and the Other: 'The Esquimau Maiden's Romance' in Context." *Essays in Arts and Sciences* 27 (October 1998): 71-82.

[*In the following essay, Kruse demonstrates Twain's use of "otherness" and "translation" in "The Esquimau Maiden's Romance" by focusing on his reading and writing habits.*]

Because Mark Twain's work as a whole has richness and diversity, it always responds to new critical approaches. The most recent of concepts in cultural studies, the concept of alterity (of "otherness" or of "the other"), serves as a case in point. Along with the concomitant concept of "translation" (which results from the perception of "otherness"), it would seem to open up new perspectives on some of Mark Twain's basic concerns and at the same time to testify to the perennial relevance and significance of what he wrote.

In setting up the premises of my investigation and introducing my key terms I shall give a brief survey of how the notion of "otherness" and the perception of "the other" pervade much of what Mark Twain wrote. I shall then proceed to demonstrate the author's deliberate use of "otherness" and "translation" by looking at **"The Esquimau Maiden's Romance"** and by contextualizing the story with regard to Mark Twain's reading and writing.

In a recent essay entitled "On Translatability: Variables of Interpretation" Wolfgang Iser asks the following question: "Why has translatability been elevated to a key-concept in the encounter between cultures and in interaction between intracultural levels? Is it more than a metaphor for cultural exchange, and if so, to what extent can one assess the range covered by such a concept?" And he goes on to provide the following explanation:

> Nowadays, it is not only languages that have to be translated. In a rapidly shrinking world, many different cultures have come into close contact with one another, calling for a mutual understanding not only in terms of one's own culture, but also in terms of the one encoun-

tered. The more alien the latter, the more a kind of translation is bound to occur, as the specific nature of the culture encountered can be grasped only when projected onto what is familiar. In this respect a foreign culture is not simply subsumed under one's own frame of reference; instead, the very frame is subjected to alterations in order to accommodate what does not fit. Such a transposition runs counter to the idea of one culture being superior to another, and hence translatability emerges as a counter-concept to cultural hegemony.[1]

It can be argued—in order to apply what has been quoted to a reading of Mark Twain—that what Iser claims to be a phenomenon of our own times, the coming into close contact with one another of many different cultures, was not at all uncommon in the melting-pot situation of 19th-century America. Of course, Mark Twain in particular, through his extended travels, had in his own person and in his role as an American encountered many different cultures and learned about and actually experienced their "otherness." It can be argued, furthermore, that in writing about such encounters and in exploiting—as he was wont to do in all of his travel books—"otherness," he was of course constantly faced with the problem of "translatability." It would seem, in fact, that the experience of "otherness" and the theme of what in his own terminology he would call a "contrast of civilizations"[2] existed in his work from the very beginning, interculturally or cross-culturally (i.e. between different cultures) as well as intraculturally (i.e. between different stages or levels or sections of the same culture). First, there is the encounter of the regional and the sectional "other" in such works as **"The Dandy Frightening the Squatter," "Jim Smiley and His Jumping Frog"** and *Roughing It*; next, there is the discovery of the national and the ethnic "other" in *The Innocents Abroad* and *A Tramp Abroad*; then, the discovery of the racial "other" in *Adventures of Huckleberry Finn*; and finally, the discovery of sectional or national differences in combination with the contrast of different periods or epochs in both *Life on the Mississippi* and *A Connecticut Yankee in King Arthur's Court*. It can be observed that in the course of this development Mark Twain became increasingly aware of "translatability." By the end of the 1880s (and certainly when he came to write **"The Esquimau Maiden's Romance"** in 1893) he had long since ceased to advance or overtly to maintain the stances (interculturally speaking) of hegemony or dominance and (intra-culturally speaking) of hierarchy which had informed whole sections of *The Innocents Abroad* as well as, for instance, certain rash and somewhat notorious judgments regarding the American Indian and the Frenchman. Being averse to ideas of cultural hegemony and cultural hierarchy in his encounters with the "other" of necessity implies, in Iser's equation, the discovery of "translatability," because (as Iser has it) "translatability emerges as a counter-concept to cultural hegemony" just as much as it is "a counter-concept to the otherwise prevailing idea of cultural hierarchy" (299).

How does such translation—such translatability—function in Mark Twain's writings? How, and to what extent, are traditional frames of reference subjected to alterations in order to accommodate what does not fit? I shall deal with these questions by examining a series of uniquely related items and incidents which can be seen to reflect stages in the author's growing awareness of "otherness" and its potential as a literary topic: first, Mark Twain's discovery of and response to *The Citizen of the World,* a series of essays or letters by Oliver Goldsmith; then, his reading of and response to a book entitled *Memoirs of Hans Hendrik, the Arctic Traveller*; and finally, his writing of **"The Esquimau Maiden's Romance"** in 1893.

Like Jonathan Swift's *Gulliver's Travels, The Citizen of the World* by Oliver Goldsmith was an early favorite of Mark Twain's. Along with Swift's classic, it may have helped to nurture his interest in the *voyage imaginaire,* a genre that readily lent itself to exploitation for purposes of social and moral criticism and to adaptation in a great many utopian novels in 19th-century American literature, including, of course, *A Connecticut Yankee in King Arthur's Court.* In terms of the concept of "otherness" Goldsmith's text reverses the more traditional mode as exemplified by Swift. In *The Citizen of the World* it is not the native with his familiar frame of reference who invades the realm of the "other" and then translates what he perceives for the native reader, but rather the "other" with his alien frame of reference who translates the familiar into "otherness," as it were, supposedly for an alien audience, but actually once again for the native reader. Mark Twain must have been drawn by the effectiveness of this procedure. Having the familiar culture penetrated by something "other" for the purpose of comical and serious "defamiliarization" proved a ready means of subjecting the traditional frame to alterations and preventing the dominance of one frame over another. In 1870-1871 he deliberately revived Goldsmith's Chinese traveler Lien Chi Altangi as Ah Song Hi in a series of seven letters written for the New York *Galaxy.*[3] Using for these letters the title **"Goldsmith's Friend Abroad Again"** is as much of an intertextual reference of his to one particular English (or rather Irish) author as the name of Ah Song Hi is a reference to Bret Harte, an American writer. Just a few months earlier Harte had created his own Chinese character, Ah Sin, the deceitful euchre player of "Plain Language from Truthful James" as published in the San Francisco-based *Overland Monthly* on the other side of the continent.[4] What we observe here is a constant crossing of boundaries between various cultures and sections as well as between different moral constitutions. Turning the innocent and gullible and thoroughly noble Ah Song Hi, a victim of California villainy and cruelty,

into an outright lover of the American nation and its ideals merely adds to such confusion and effectively contributes to the fact that "otherness" becomes relative. In the account itself and in the mind of the reader the respective frames of reference interpenetrate, with each frame being (in Iser's phrase) "subjected to alterations in order to accommodate what does not fit" (299).

We have to bear in mind such interpenetration of standards and such activity of translation when we actually look at **"The Esquimau Maiden's Romance"** from the point of view of alterity. But it is important to note that unlike Goldsmith's Chinese, who by means of careful circumstantiation drawn from the rich tradition of the *lettres chinoises* is made to represent the standards and convictions of Far Eastern culture as they actually exist, Mark Twain's counterpart is only a mere pseudo-Chinese. Although through his national origin he does pose as what (vis-à-vis America) I would like to call the "conspicuously other," he is, in fact, a mere fabrication conceived and devised to bring common sense and the principles of liberty and equality to bear on the cultural prejudices of 19th-century America.

It is in this respect now that the *Memoirs of Hans Hendrik, the Arctic Traveller,* as written by himself in his native language and published in an English translation in London in 1878, differs significantly. And Mark Twain duly notes on the second flyleaf that he finds this volume to be "A very valuable book—& unique."(*)[5] Such positive evaluation is easy to understand. Hendrik had been in the service of the arctic explorers Kane, Hayes, Hall, and Nares from 1853 to 1876. Mark Twain from his childhood had shared the general interest in the search for the Northwest passage and the quest for the North Pole, endeavors which to the 19th century resemble what space travel is to the twentieth. More importantly, Hendrik's report appealed to him as a reader who always professed an interest in histories and memoirs, in biography and autobiography, in letters and in factual reports rather than in fiction. But there is also evidence that it was the problem of "otherness"—even before anything else—that appealed to him when he read the book.

Like Goldsmith's *The Citizen of the World,* Hans Hendrik's memoir presented Mark Twain with a "conspicuously other" person and once again a "conspicuously other" person in direct contact with Western civilization. Unlike Lien Chi Altangi or the persona of Ah Song Hi that Mark Twain had derived from him, however, Hendrik himself was a real person. Accordingly, his adventures and his encounters of "otherness" aboard American ships and eventually in the United States itself were also real rather than imaginary. Mark Twain's marginalia and underlinings that stem from his reading of the book in Munich in January of 1879—in a setting, that is, that may have heightened his sensitivity to experiences of "the other"—testify to his fascination with cultural differences, with encounters of "otherness," and with the resulting need for translation. Mere linguistic translation with its specific difficulties, as we shall see, turns out to be indicative (here as elsewhere) of the more important problems of intracultural and cross-cultural translation on an abstract level between phenomena that are "conspicuously other."

The elaborate process of rendering the work in English hints at such complexity. Hendrik's account was first translated from the Inuk language by Dr. Henry Rink, director of the Royal Greenland Board of Trade, then subsequently edited by Dr. George Stephens, Fellow of the Society of Antiquaries, Professor at the University of Copenhagen and a renowned authority on the popular antiquities of Iceland. Despite the work of two academic mediators between the Inuk culture and Western civilization, the resulting text still remains full of parenthetical notes and explanations and occasional failures to understand the original at all. The linguistic problem in its trans-linguistic implications is epitomized, as it were, in the text itself in the tragic fate of one Umarsuak, an Eskimo who serves on the expedition. His last recorded words are, "That is the only awkward thing, to understand neither Danish nor English" (38). After that he disappears in the darkness, never to be found again: "Although we still kept up a faint hope of his return," Hendrik writes, "he was quite lost, and his memory left a deep impression upon me, he being the only friend whom I loved like my brother." So both Umarsuak and he himself, as well as of course the expedition as a whole, are victims of the failure of "translatability." Mark Twain responds with a marginal "Poor devil" (*), a notation that would seem to refer to the dismal end of Umarsuak as much as to the cause of it and to the person who felt the loss and so demonstrate his empathetic awareness of the problem of alterity.

Other responses concern the problem of "translatability" between the Inuk world of the text and Mark Twain's world as that of a perceptive but remote reader. A simple and laconic question-and-answer conversation between Hendrik and some native strangers about hare-hunting with a gun, a weapon the others have never seen, strikes him as odd. In a marginal note he calls it "Ollendorfian" (*)(24), obviously because of—as he had put it in *Roughing It*—"interminable repetitions of questions which have never occurred and are never likely to occur in any conversation among human beings."⁶ But they did occur, as the authentic transcription in the text tells him, albeit in a different culture, and they now invite him to alter his frame of reference, as it were.

In a parallel way, Mark Twain is struck by the names of Hendrik's brothers—Simion, Joel and Nathaniel. He responds by writing "Only observe these names!" (*)(22),

simply because he had been unaware of the work of Moravian missionaries among the Inuk population. If he did reflect on the naming, he would have recognized a blatant instance of cultural dominance and—given his general dislike of Christian missionaries that goes back to observing the effect of their work among the natives of the Sandwich Islands—would have disapproved of the custom.

Another instance of an encounter of "otherness" that caught Mark Twain's attention occurs within the world of the text itself in a long conversation between Hendrik and a comrade about the custom of flogging aboard an American man-of-war. Hendrik finds the practice detestable and incomprehensible. Though he must have been aware that his services had been invaluable in furthering America's Arctic enterprises, he actually considers working for the English in the future. The impact of such an account on the culturally conditioned frame of reference of an American reader in particular does not differ much from the impact of what Mark Twain wrote in **"Goldsmith's Friend Abroad Again."** Still, there is a difference between what is actually a pseudo-confrontation of alien cultures in Mark Twain's early piece and what is a real confrontation of alien cultures in Hendrik's memoir.

This difference can best be demonstrated in terms of the necessity of purely linguistic translation of what is "other" in the alien culture into one's own language. Mark Twain, in **"Goldsmith's Friend Abroad Again,"** has his Ah Song Hi translate the term "photographer" as "a kind of artist who makes likenesses of people with a machine."⁷ He also has him explain "police court lawyer" by adding a parenthesis: "termed, in the higher circles of society, a 'shyster'" (468). Although the latter translation is in the interest of social criticism, a deliberate attempt to be funny would seem to impair or even defeat that very purpose. Hendrik in his account is similarly faced with the necessity of translating into his own vocabulary some of the phenomena that he observes during his stay in the United States. But his attempt to appropriate the alien world is wholly authentic and without any self-conscious or deliberate humor whatsoever. The American President for him is the "Chief of America," a railroad is "a steamer on wheels" (only the translator into English of his account feels the need to explain that this is his term for "railroad train"). One recalls, of course, the fact that the Eskimo language has long served linguists to demonstrate the incompatibility of different vocabularies and the untranslatability of certain terms, notably those that denote different kinds of snow and different stages of ice. Henrik's account in its English translation furnishes many examples that would be useful to the specialist and at the same time demonstrate that linguistic translation is, in fact, just a special case of solving problems of "otherness."

What takes us from Hans Hendrik's memoir directly to Mark Twain's **"The Esquimau Maiden's Romance"** is the description of an incident that occurred a few days before Hendrik's return from the United States to Upernivik on Greenland. Together with a friend he was paying a visit to an American who had traveled in the polar regions:

> Towards evening he said: "Anything ye should wish to demand, any amount of money, I will give you." My comrade and I, after having deliberated, replied, that we should like to have some cigars. Of course, I also liked money, but could not use it now, as it could not be bartered in other countries. . . .
>
> (80-81)

My claim that the *Memoirs of Hans Hendrik* can be considered to be a significant source for **"The Esquimau Maiden's Romance"** draws upon the recurrence of this very motif of the arbitrary valuation of money in both works, and also, of course, on the recurrence of the Eskimo background and the deliberate use of "otherness" and "translation" in the juxtaposition of Inuk culture and American culture. I see myself supported in my claim by Alan Gribben, who finds that it was from Hendrik that Mark Twain "probably obtained the facts about Eskimo hunting techniques. . . ."[8] My further claim that *The Citizen of the World* may also have contributed to the conception of the story is based on general similarities as well as on the common knowledge that the Irish author was indeed a perennial favorite of Mark Twain's. *The Citizen of the World* in particular constituted one of his "*beau ideals* of fine writing."[9] More specifically, however, my argument for this work as a source is based on the fact that the inhuman method of "trial by water" that furnishes the climax in Mark Twain's story is also alluded to by Goldsmith. In his Letter 69 he ridicules the English fear of mad dogs. "Their manner of knowing whether a dog be mad or no," his Chinese visitor writes, "somewhat resembles the ancient Gothic custom of trying witches. The old woman suspected was tied hand and foot and thrown into the water. If she swam then she was instantly carried off to be burnt for a witch, if she sunk, then indeed she was acquitted of the charge, but drown'd in the experiment."[10]

I am not primarily interested, however, in these earlier texts as sources whose transformations demand to be studied, but rather as foils that can help us perceive Mark Twain's own handling of the theme of "otherness" in this particular case. And I am not interested in subverting existing negative evaluations of **"The Esquimau Maiden's Romance"** either. In fact, while the texts that I have considered do alert us to the importance of alterity in Mark Twain's story, they also enable us to see that from the arsenal of available techniques he perhaps could have chosen better—and by better I

mean: more effective—means to dramatize "otherness." **"The Esquimau Maiden's Romance"** remains poor fiction, as Emerson and Geismar have asserted[11]; and Mark Twain obviously wrote it for money. Baldanza, Wilson, and others have found it to be a parody of the sentimental love story.[12] According to Geismar it is also "a parody of the impact of wealth upon a primitive society" (199).

Once we start looking at the 1893 story from the point of view of "otherness" and "translation," however, the parodic love story becomes a mere vehicle. Instead, our interest focuses on the juxtaposition of the cultural "otherness" of the world of Mark Twain, the American narrator, and that of Lasca, the Eskimo maiden. Total incompatibility of the views and the standards of the representatives of either culture creates humor, of course, but it also demonstrates what happens in an encounter with the "conspicuously other" when no translation takes place. It is true that Mark Twain, the narrator-persona, appears to be "the representative of the dominant culture" (as Wilson has it), and that in the story Inuk culture is wholly subsumed under the frame of that culture, as it were. But it is also true that Mark Twain the narrator is not at all to be identified with Mark Twain the author and that therefore the dominant culture does not provide a reliable frame of reference. Such a valid frame of reference is given implicitly rather than explicitly, and it will emerge only in an adequate reading of the text.

At the opening of the story the narrator has already spent a whole week observing the 20-year-old Lasca. He describes her as "a beautiful creature," immediately adding, however, that he is speaking "from the Esquimau point of view."[13] He has followed her in all of her activities, such as fishing, sealing, digging blubber from a whale and hunting a bear, but always, out of disdain and cowardice, keeping a safe distance. The frame adequately prepares and sets the tone for the story itself, which consists of Lasca's account of her short life in singular Eskimo luxury, living in a "great mansion of frozen snow-blocks . . . seven feet high and three or four times as long as any of the others," with "luxurious appointments . . . quite beyond the common," "bedded far deeper in furs than is usual" (119) and provided with two "slop-tubs . . . in the parlor, and two in the rest of the house" (120). The narrator quickly learns how to applaud her and goad her on with false compliments and equivocal comparisons with life in the United States. In doing so, he manages to sketch out what wealth consists of in his own country. Calling her rich father a "polar Vanderbilt" (124) epitomizes such procedure, and the fact that his wealth consists of "*twenty-two fish-hooks*—not bone, but foreign—*made out of real iron*" turns out to be the source of tragedy on two counts. For one thing, such immense wealth corrupts the tribe, everybody becomes avaricious; all now want the foreign type of hook that symbolizes corruption and also cultural dominance over a primitive society. For another instance, one of the hooks disappears in Lasca's hair when her father proudly displays his treasure before her suitor, but the suitor is accused of having stolen it. He is subjected to the infamous method of "trial by water" as detailed above, found guilty and set on an iceberg to drift south to perish. "Trial by water" is also referred to as a foreign (and obviously Christian) invention by which the "poor, ignorant savages" (132) of Lasca's tribe come under alien cultural hegemony. Such indictment alone helps to undercut the narrator's stance of superiority, and his initial failure to participate or to share in the activities of the tribe is now shown to be indicative of his arrogance and his smugness. In the story Mark Twain the narrator sets out to judge and to decry the standards of Eskimo primitivism and seems to be subsuming the culture of the "conspicuously other" under his own frame of reference. But Mark Twain the writer is at work throughout to show that what is true of the corrupting power of wealth with the Eskimo is also true of the corrupting power of wealth in the United States itself. The foreign origin of the iron fishhooks and the custom of "trial by water" are an accusation of still prevalent Colonialism that refuses to translate the "otherness" of primitivism and continues to exert cultural hegemony.

Mark Twain drives home such lesson by yet another seemingly humorous instance that concerns the prejudice against soap as a foreign import: "Yes—but that was only at first; nobody would eat it. [. . .] It was just a prejudice. The first time soap came here from the foreigners, nobody liked it, but as soon as it got to be fashionable everybody liked it, and now everybody has it that can afford it" (122). The outright and spun-out humor of the scene should not deceive us about the fact that the attempt of the narrator and the dominant society to exploit and to capitalize on—rather than to abolish—the widely differing standards of civilization and primitivism, their own failure to translate "otherness," constitutes the serious theme of the story. Soap, as one recalls, had already served the author in chapter 16 of *A Connecticut Yankee in King Arthur's Court* to denote civilization and to help Hank Morgan in his attempt to colonize a native population and exert cultural dominance. But the strategy had failed, as Mark Twain had been forced to admit when bringing his story to an as yet ambiguous conclusion. **"The Esquimau Maiden's Romance"** now avoids such ambiguity: Mark Twain the author plainly denounces all exploitation on the part of Mark Twain the narrator. The perspective of "otherness" enables us to see this and to read the story as a deliberate and timeless plea against cultural dominance and for exploring and achieving "translatability." In the overall view of the author's development **"The Esquimau Maiden's Romance"** thus becomes an important signpost, somewhat imperfect, but nonetheless in-

teresting, on the road from *A Connecticut Yankee in King Arthur's Court* to the overtly anti-imperialist writings of Mark Twain's later years.[14] In fact, what at first appears to be a major blemish of the story—the result, perhaps, of its hasty composition—namely using for the arrogant representative of the dominant culture the very name of Mark Twain, could well signal, deliberately or inadvertently, the author's recognition of his partisanship with, and his silent participation in, colonialist measures. It may even mark the very point at which he was making the transition from an imperialist to an anti-imperialist position that had to wait until the turn of the century to become the dominant stance of his satires.

Notes

1. "On Translatability: Variables of Interpretation" in: *Anglistentag 1994 Graz: Proceedings,* ed. by Wolfgang Riehle and Hugo Keiper (Tübingen: Niemeyer, 1995), 299. Subsequent references to this and other sources in the notes are in the text; pages are not provided for succeeding quotations on the same page.

2. About *A Connecticut Yankee in King Arthur's Court* Mark Twain wrote Mrs. Fairbanks, "The story isn't a satire peculiarly, it is more especially a *contrast.*" (SLC to MF, Hartford Nov. 16/86, *Mark Twain to Mrs. Fairbanks,* ed. Dixon Wecter [San Marino, California: Huntington Library, 1949], 257.)

3. They were published in October and November 1870 and in January 1871.

4. The poem appeared in the September 1870 issue, early enough for Mark Twain to have read it before writing his series of letters.

5. *Memoirs of Hans Hendrik, the Arctic Traveller, Serving under Kane, Hayes, Hall and Nares, 1853-1876,* written by himself, translated from the Eskimo language by Dr. Henry Rink, Director of the Royal Greenland Board of Trade, ed. by Prof. Dr. George Stephens, F. S. A., London: Trübner & Co., 1878. Mark Twain's copy of the book is in the Yale Collection of American Literature, Morse Collection, Beinecke Library, Yale University. Subsequent references given parenthetically in the text. Mark Twain's previously unpublished words quoted here are ©1997 by Edward J. Willi and Manufacturers Hanover Trust Company as Trustees of the Mark Twain Foundation, which reserves all reproduction and dramatization rights in every medium. Quotation is made with the permission of the U of California P and Robert H. Hirst, Editor of the Mark Twain Project. Each quotation is identified by an asterisk (*).

6. Mark Twain, *Roughing It,* ed. by Harriet Elinor Smith and Edgar Marquess Branch (Berkeley: U of California P, 1993), 197. (The Works of Mark Twain 2)

7. "Goldsmith's Friend Abroad Again" in: Mark Twain, *Collected Tales, Sketches, Speeches, & Essays 1852-1890* (New York: Library of America, 1992), 463-4.

8. *Mark Twain's Library: A Reconstruction* (Boston: Hall, 1980), I, 307.

9. Mark Twain to Orion Clemens, St. Louis, 18 March 1861, *Mark Twain's Letters, Volume I, 1853-1866,* ed. by Edgar Marquess Branch, Michael B. Frank, Kenneth M. Sanderson (Berkeley: U of California P, 1988), 117.

10. *The Citizen of the World, Collected Works of Oliver Goldsmith,* ed. by Arthur Friedman (Oxford: OUP, 1966), II, 287.

11. Everett Emerson, *The Authentic Mark Twain: A Literary Biography of Samuel L. Clemens* (Philadelphia: U of Pennsylvania P, 1984), 189; Emerson says: "[The narrator] and the author seem unable to decide whether the story is sentimental or satiric." Since the context here suggests satire, Mark Twain is guilty of having failed to make this sufficiently clear.—Maxwell Geismar, *Mark Twain: An American Prophet* (Boston: Houghton Mifflin, 1970), p. 199.

12. Frank Baldanza, *Mark Twain: An Introduction and Interpretation* (New York: Barnes & Noble, 1961), p. 100; James D. Wilson, *A Reader's Guide to the Short Stories of Mark Twain* (Boston: Hall, 1987), pp. 72-73.

13. "The Esquimau Maiden's Romance" in: *Mark Twain, Collected Tales, Sketches, Speeches, & Essays 1891-1910* (New York: Library of America, 1992), 118.

14. On the continuity of Mark Twain's anti-imperialist thinking see John Carlos Rowe, "How the Boss Played the Game: Twain's Critique of Imperialism in *A Connecticut Yankee in King Arthur's Court,*" in: Forrest G. Robinson, ed., *The Cambridge Companion to Mark Twain* (Cambridge: CUP, 1995), 175-192.

Gary Sloan (essay date winter 2000)

SOURCE: Sloan, Gary. "Twain's 'The Man That Corrupted Hadleyburg.'" *Explicator* 58, no. 2 (winter 2000): 83-5.

[In the following essay, Sloan explains the thematic significance of Stephenson's ignorance of Richards's guilt in "The Man That Corrupted Hadleyburg."]

In a compelling analysis, tainted only by one curious omission, Earl Briden reads Mark Twain's short story **"The Man That Corrupted Hadleyburg"** as an ironic parable on the Fortunate Fall, with the character Howard L. Stephenson, the titular "Man," as a guise for Satan in his conventional role as temper and master of guile. Henry Rule had already laid some of the groundwork by adducing copious textual evidence of the Stephenson-Satan nexus; Stanley Brodwin, Mary Rucker, Gerald Marshall, Susan Harris, and others had adumbrated the ironic dimension.

Hadleyburg's fall from grace, the scandalous disclosure that its vaunted honesty is all pretense, fails, Briden shows, to precipitate any collective moral redemption. The fall is fortunate only in a crass, mercenary sense. In Briden's words, "[T]he town learns only a 'commercial' lesson from its experience: it adds cleverness, prudence, a cagey circumspection to its 'virtues,' and thus reveals a superego still infantile in its concern to sidestep apprehension and enable the community to hold on to its new good name" (133). In their moral enslavement to the communal mind, the Richardses are representative. Edward Richards's deathbed confession that he is no better than the other Nineteeners is prompted by fear of exposure, not moral transformation (131-32). Unexplained by Briden and the others is the thematic import of Stephenson-Satan's lasting ignorance of Richards's guilt.[1] Unaware that Mr. Burgess has suppressed Richard's self-incriminating note, Satan (as Stephenson will hereinafter be called) gives Richards forty thousand dollars, the proceeds from the sale of the gilded lead. In a note to Richards, Satan explains the gift:

> "I am a disappointed man. Your honesty is beyond the reach of temptation. I had a different idea about it, but I wronged you in that, and I beg pardon, and do it sincerely. I honor you—and that is sincere too. This town is not worthy to kiss the hem of your garment. Dear sir, I made a square bet with myself that there were nineteen debauchable men in your self-righteous community. I have lost. Take the whole pot, you are entitled to it."

> (Twain, *Short Stories* [*The Complete Short Stories*] 386)

After the note, Satan vanishes from the story. Since Satan is conventionally the Prince of Lies, one might at first suspect that the note is sardonic and the intent malevolent. Perhaps Satan knows Richards is guilty and aims to prick his conscience. Were that Satan's design, it is speedily balked: "Within twenty-four hours after the Richardses had received their checks their consciences were quieting down, discouraged; the old couple were learning to reconcile themselves to the sin which they had committed" (387). True, the Richardses are soon sucked into a maelstrom of inward torment—not, however, from penitent conscience, but from fear of being "found out" (387). Twain drops no narrative hints that Satan's note might be disingenuous. Throughout the story, the narrator candidly delineates characters' motives, thoughts, and intentions. All textual evidence points to a reliable narrator. Twain, then, must have wanted Satan to be duped, to think Richards is honest and upright. Why? Just for the frivolous irony of depicting the Archdeceiver deceived? Irony of a deeper sort may be afoot.

Twain had a lifelong empathy for Satan, with whom he came to identify. He was on the side of the devil and knew it. He thought that Christians unfairly stigmatized and suppressed Satan, not letting him tell his story. Twain considered Lucifer-Satan morally superior to Jehovah and Jesus Christ.[2] As Twain grew older, he became thoroughly disillusioned with the "damned human race." For himself, he abandoned all hope of any secular salvation predicated on belief in human goodness. His brooding anguish as intermitted only when he was writing.[3]

In **"The Man That Corrupted Hadleyburg,"** Twain may have hit on a way to save himself vicariously. He could do so by saving his alter ego, Satan, and at the same time, he would right a long-standing wrong to the fallen cherub. To be eligible for redemption, Satan must believe in the little lump of goodness that leavens the whole loaf; he must believe that unalloyed virtue is not all a dream. In short, the Prince of Lies must be lied to. Hence, Twain grants Satan the illusion that Richards is a paragon of virtue. To safeguard the illusion, Twain must remove Satan from the story before Richards makes his public confession. Viewed in this way, the story might be subtitled: "The Corrupt Town that Saved Satan."

Notes

1. Rejecting Rule's and Clinton Burhans's argument that Stephenson is an ironic savior figure, Brodwin comments: "[T]he many complex ironies in the story suggest another interpretation. Satan-Stephenson, as in the traditional Christian view, wins only to lose, since at the end he is duped into thinking Richards was in fact incorruptible" (209). Brodwin does not suggest any authorial motive for the duping.

2. In his autobiography, Twain wrote: "I have always felt friendly toward Satan. Of course that is ancestral; it must be in the blood, for I could not have originated it." He also says his mother did not think Satan was "treated fairly" because Christians never prayed for his salvation as they did for that of other sinners (Twain, *Autobiography* 16, 26). In a letter to his publisher, Twain went so far as to sign himself "Satan" (*Essays* 333). In Twain's "That Day in Eden" (*Essays*), Satan tenderly and sincerely commiserates with Adam and Eve. Brodwin, who explores Twain's complex lit-

erary uses of the Satan figure, discusses Twain's estimation of Satan vis-à-vis Jehovah and Jesus.

3. Maxwell Geismar notes that as Twain's gloom deepened, "[H]e found his opiate and his salvation and his resurrection in the creative act itself" (145).

Works Cited

Briden, Earl F. "Twainian Pedagogy and the No-Account Lessons of 'Hadleyburg.'" *Studies in Short Fiction* 28 (1991): 125-34.

Brodwin, Stanley. "Mark Twain's Masks of Satan: The Final Phase." *American Literature* 45 (1973): 206-27.

Burhans, Clinton S., Jr. "The Sober Affirmation of Mark Twain's Hadleyburg." *American Literature* 34 (1962): 375-84.

Geismar, Maxwell. *Mark Twain: an American Prophet.* Abr. ed. New York: McGraw, 1970.

Harris, Susan K. "'Hadleyburg': Mark Twain's Dual Attack on Banal Theology and Banal Literature." *American Literary Realism* 16 (1983): 240-52.

Marshall, W. Gerald. "Mark Twain's 'The Man That Corrupted Hadleyburg' and the Myth of Baucis and Philemon." *Mark Twain Journal* 20.2 (1979): 4-7.

Rucker, Mary E. "Moralism and Determinism in 'The Man That Corrupted Hadleyburg.'" *Studies in Short Fiction* 14 (1977): 49-54.

Rule, Henry B. "The Role of Satan in 'The Man That Corrupted Hadleyburg.'" *Studies in Short Fiction* 6 (1969): 619-29.

Twain, Mark. *The Complete Short Stories.* Ed. Charles Neider. Garden City: Doubleday, 1957.

———. *The Autobiography.* Ed. Charles Neider. New York: Harper, 1959.

———. *The Complete Essays.* Ed. Charles Neider. Garden City: Doubleday, 1963.

Roy Blount, Jr. (essay date 2001)

SOURCE: Blount, Roy, Jr. Foreword to *A Murder, a Mystery, and a Marriage,* by Mark Twain, pp. 9-17. New York: W. W. Norton & Company, 2001.

[*In the following essay, Blount describes the historical and cultural significance of* A Murder, a Mystery, and a Marriage *within the context of Twain's career and politics.*]

In 1876, when he was forty and the nation a century old, Mark Twain concocted a project, in conjunction with the *Atlantic Monthly,* that came to nothing until 2001. There's a story in that.

"Very often, of course," Mark Twain writes in "How to Tell a Story," "the rambling and disjointed humorous story finishes with a nub, point, snapper, or whatever you like to call it. Then the listener must be alert, for in many cases the teller will divert attention from that nub by dropping it in a carefully casual and indifferent way, with the pretense that he does not know it is a nub. Artemus Ward used that trick a good deal; then when the belated audience presently caught the joke he would look up with innocent surprise, as if wondering what they had found to laugh at."

Twain far more than Ward was a master of such deadpan trickery. Once at a gala banquet, Twain delivered a toast to Ulysses S. Grant that seemed to be a long drawn-out insult. Then he paused "for a sort of shuddering silence" (as he wrote exultantly to his wife, Livy); and then he delivered the snapper. Grant cracked up. "The audience *saw* that for once in his life he had been knocked out of his iron serenity," Twain wrote Livy. "The house came down with a crash."

Another time Twain came onstage and just stood there, expressionless, as if he weren't even aware that he was the speaker. He realized that he could hold people silent on the edge of their seats for just about as long as he wanted to without uttering a word. "An audience captured in that way," he wrote home, "*belongs* to the speaker, body and soul."

But that's not the only silent verdict an audience can render. A few days before the not-yet-notorious presidential election of 1876, Twain's enduringly clueless older brother, Orion Clemens—who had moved just outside slave-state Missouri and declared himself an abolitionist Republican back in the 1850s, when it was unpopular thereabouts—suddenly went over to the other party, and was given a chance to speak at a Democratic rally. "He wrote me jubilantly," Twain wrote later to his friend William Dean Howells, "of what a ten-strike he was going to make with that speech. All right—but think of his innocent and pathetic candor in writing me something like this, a week later: 'I was more diffident than I had expected to be, and this was increased by the silence with which I was received when I came forward, so I seemed unable to get the fire into my speech which I had calculated upon, and presently they began to get up and go out, and in a few minutes they all rose up and went away.' How *could* a man uncover such a sore as that and show it to another? Not a word of *complaint*, you see—only a patient, sad surprise."

Twain, too, could be sadly surprised at a rostrum. In 1877 he mortified Howells and himself by his insufficiently reverential attempt to pull the venerable legs of Henry Wadsworth Longfellow, Oliver Wendell Holmes, and Ralph Waldo Emerson—the honored guests at a banquet sponsored by the *Atlantic*. After Howells rose to assure the gathering that here was a humorist who was never offensive, Twain proceeded to spin a long straight-faced western yarn in which Longfellow, Holmes, and Emerson *seemed* to appear as ruffians . . . then came the pause . . . then the snapper . . . and then . . . none of the honorees laughed. (Emerson was not listening in any case.) The audience sat, said Howells, in "silence, weighing many tons to the square inch, which deepened from moment to moment."

But we're getting ahead of our story. When Twain came up with the project that is just now coming to partial fruition, it was around the Ides of March, 1876. He proposed to Howells, who was then editor of the *Atlantic*, that they round up "a good and godly gang" of authors—including the preeminent Boston Brahmins James Russell Lowell and Holmes, the recently lionized mining-camp local colorist (from Albany, New York) Bret Harte, and the young Henry James—who would each write a story based on one "skeleton" plot devised by Twain. The stories would appear serially in the *Atlantic*, the nation's foremost bastion of literary standards. Throughout the rest of that year, Twain kept urging Howells to get this unlikely project off the ground. Howells sent out feelers. (Though evidently not to anyone so august as Holmes or Lowell. When Howells had taken Twain to meet Lowell two years before, that worthy had not been impressed, except that something about Twain's nose lent fuel to Lowell's belief that all humanity was descended from the Jews.) "The difficulty" about the stories, as Howells put it, was "to get people to write them."

During that very period, history was holding its breath. Two projects of enormously greater importance than Twain's "skeleton novelette" were in abeyance. Rutherford B. Hayes and Samuel Tilden were pitted in a presidential race whose muddled outcome would have to be resolved by deal making in and out of the House of Representatives. And Twain himself got stuck halfway through *The Adventures of Huckleberry Finn*—lost interest, said he might burn the manuscript.

Two great, and not unrelated, turning points in American history and culture. The result of the 1876 election would be seen as a betrayal of the verdict of the Civil War. As it turned out, Tilden won the popular vote—thanks in good measure to intimidation of southern blacks, who would have voted Republican—and Hayes won the electoral vote by a 185-184 margin—if you counted results in three states that were contested and weren't ever going to be recounted impartially. An Electoral Commission was formed, which voted for Hayes, strictly along party lines. Tilden's Democrats in the House mounted a filibuster. So Hayes's Republicans agreed to pull out of the South the Federal troops that had been enforcing Reconstruction. The party of Lincoln thus relinquished its commitment to advancing the rights and opportunities of African Americans, who had been emancipated but were still far from being included in common American advantages. That 1876 election has often been cited in regard to our most recent, chad-splitting presidential imbroglio, whose outcome has led to apprehension or anticipation that affirmative action, a fruit of the civil rights movement, will be abandoned as a federal goal. If Reconstruction had worked as planned, we wouldn't have *needed* a civil rights movement a hundred years after the war.

And what if Twain had neglected to finish his masterpiece? That novel—in which a poor, good-natured white boy from a slave state comes to respect and assist a runaway slave, in defiance of all the dictates of antebellum society—would blend standard English and New World vernacular, black and white, into the template of American narrative. All modern American literature, Ernest Hemingway would say in 1935, began with that book.

If we could come up with a skeleton plot for the quintessential American writer's career, wouldn't it call for him to realize the momentousness of 1876? Twain was himself a refugee from a slave state and indeed the Confederate Army. His earliest storytelling influence was a slave named Uncle Daniel, who would weave a ghostly web and then *jump out* at the black and white children gathered around him. Twain's first contribution to the *Atlantic,* published in 1874, was a poignant tale in the form of an ex-slave's monologue, **"A True Story."** The *Atlantic,* though culturally conservative and independent of party affiliation, had firmly supported the abolitionist Republican position before and during the war. Now both Reconstruction and the Great American Novel were hanging in the balance. And yet, judging from the letters back and forth between Twain and Howells at the time, what was weighing most heavily on Twain's mind was *A Murder, a Mystery, and a Marriage,* the skeletal project that never went beyond the story you are about to read.

He got coy about showing his odd fiction to Howells—whether he ever did, and exactly what became of the manuscript over the next seventy years or so, is unclear. In 1945 two men who had bought the manuscript from an auction house printed up sixteen copies in hopes of establishing copyright, but the Twain estate sued to prevent publication, and a court decided in 1949 that the work could not be published. In 2000, the Buffalo and Erie County Public Library acquired the rights to publish the work. This links the story in another way to the separate halves of *Huckleberry Finn.* In 1885, the year the novel was finally published (he hadn't returned to writing it until 1879 or 1880), the Young Men's Association Library in Buffalo, New York, which later became the Buffalo and Erie County Public Library, asked Twain to donate the manuscript to its collection. Twain, who had lived briefly in Buffalo some fifteen years before, replied that as far as he knew the first half had been destroyed by the printer, but he sent the second half on. One hundred and five years later, the first half was discovered, in an attic in of all places Hollywood, California. Researchers on the staff of the Mark Twain

Papers in the Bancroft Library at the University of California then dug up an 1887 letter in which Twain said he had found the first half after all and was forwarding it to the Young Men's Association Library. The curator there meant to get the first half bound, but he didn't get around to it. When he died, the manuscript was left in a trunk, which his widow conveyed to Hollywood in the 1920s when she moved there to be close to her daughter. So now the two halves of the handwritten *Huckleberry Finn* are together in Buffalo, and they are joined by one of the distractions that kept the writing of them apart.

Over the years *A Murder, a Mystery, and a Marriage* has been ignored almost entirely by the myriad scholars who have scrutinized every other scrap of Twain's writing voluminously. *Mark Twain A to Z,* a reliable and comprehensive book of reference, confuses it with an earlier, unfinished piece.

Now, the story seems more interesting. Does it reflect in any way Twain's deepest concerns? What made him want to share it with such a disparate band of writers? (Particularly, *Henry James*?) Why did Twain give one of its meanest characters, David Gray, the name of a sweet-natured friend of his? What was he *thinking*? And what were Mark Twain's politics, anyway?

An afterword to the story will fill in the history of Twain's project and attempt to answer the questions that it raises, including what mugwumpery meant to Twain and what his mark may have been on another great American novel, whose plot has to do with determining and influencing the leanings of a dangling or disconnected character named, as it happens, Chad.

But here, with illustrations by Peter de Sève, is *A Murder, a Mystery, and a Marriage* by Mark Twain, published for the first time in book form.

Michael Tritt (essay date fall 2003)

SOURCE: Tritt, Michael. "Twain's 'The Man That Corrupted Hadleyburg' and Stowe's *Oldtown Folks*." *Explicator* 62, no. 1 (fall 2003): 19-21.

[*In the following essay, Tritt examines the import of two allusions to Harriet Beecher Stowe's* Oldtown Folks *in* "The Man That Corrupted Hadleyburg."]

When he describes Jack Halliday as "the typical 'Sam Lawson' of the town" in **"The Man that Corrupted Hadleyburg,"** Mark Twain artfully invokes not only the character of Sam Lawson from Harriet Beecher Stowe's *Oldtown Folks* but also the community of Oldtown (Twain 29). To date, critics have given only the slightest attention to the reference to Lawson and no attention at all to the communal resonance.[1] Yet Stowe's dewy-eyed portrayal of Lawson and of village life is layered within—and significantly contributes to—Twain's cynical view of the individual and of the society portrayed in his story.

Stowe's novel, published in 1869, traces the fortunes of three orphans who find refuge in Oldtown, a small village in postrevolutionary New England. There, they experience what one of the characters describes as "the simplest, purest, and least objectionable state of society that the world ever saw" (Stowe 120). Notably, it is a community thoroughly imbued with integrity: "the one thing that was held above all things sacred and inviolate in a child's education in those old Puritan days was to form habits of truth" (Stowe 38).

Twain's village, initially characterized as quaint, neighborly, and, above all, honest, appears to resemble Oldtown. The narrator describes Hadleyburg as a "[. . .] most honest and upright town [. . . which] began to teach the principles of honest dealing to its babies in the cradle, and made the like teachings the staple of their culture" (Twain 11). Yet, as the story develops, the corruptibility of the villagers is revealed, as is their un-Christian lack of charity. Early in the story, Mary Richards suggests that the inhabitants "cared not a rap for strangers" (Twain 12) and that the town was "narrow, self-righteous and stingy" (Twain 17). Twain pointedly evokes the issue of charity at home—and abroad—when he depicts Mary Richards reading the *Missionary Herald* as the stranger arrives with the sack of gold. Stowe makes specific mention of the popularity of the *Herald* among the New England folk as well; by contrast, however, it is entirely in keeping with the charitable nature (at home and abroad) of that community characterized by its "ethic of care" and its "extended network of friendship and kin [. . .]" (Stowe, xxxii).

Such striking echoes and yet ironic contrasts between the communities are easy to enumerate. In Oldtown, so honest are the inhabitants that "[. . .] one could go to sleep at all hours of the day or night with the house door wide open, without bolt or bar, yet without apprehension of any to molest or make afraid" (Stowe 902). The Richards do not lock the door of their house either, yet when gold is introduced into their home, Mary "flew to [the door] all in a tremble and locked it, then pulled down the window shades and stood frightened, worried and wondering if there was anything else she could do toward making herself and the money more safe" (Twain 13-14). In Oldtown, the "fundamental principle of life in those days" was a "grand contempt for personal happiness when weighed with things greater and more valuable [. . .]" (Stowe 313); in Hadleyburg, self-interest seems to obliterate just about everything else as, one by one, the nineteeners succumb to dreams of personal advancement. Stowe's New England village is a simple, neighborly place, with its meetinghouse, schoolhouse, tavern, and town store. Inhabitants typically spend a "leisure moment in discussing politics or

theology from the top of codfish or mackerel barrels, while their wives and daughters were shopping among the dress goods and ribbons [. . .]" (Stowe 88). Such neighborly chitchat, and even the dialogue between husband and wife, effectively end in Hadleyburg with the temptation of gold: the streets were "empty and desolate," "lifelong habit[s]" were "dead and gone and forgotten, [. . .] nobody talked now, nobody read, nobody visited—the whole village sat at home, sighing, worrying, silent [. . .]" (Twain 77-78).

Twain's allusion to Sam Lawson forces a specific comparison with Jack Haliday. Yet the similarity is limited to each being considered "the village do-nothing" in his respective community. The kindness of the first and the meanness of the second are consistent with the tenor of the villages in which they live. Although Halliday is described as "[. . .] the loafing, good-natured, no-account, irreverent fisherman, hunter, boy's friend, stray-dog's friend [. . .]" (Twain 29), there is no such good nature evident. Rather, he takes great pleasure in the misery of his fellows. This is manifest in his comments, for example, which "grew daily more and more sparklingly disagreeable [. . .]" (Twain 25), and in his derisive behavior, as he "laugh[s] at the town, individually and en masse" (Twain 31). Lawson, on the other hand, is compassionate and humble to a fault. A comment he makes to the narrator reveals his nature: "There's all sorts of folks that go to make up a world, and Lord massy, we mustn't be hard on nobody; can't spect everybody to be right all around" (Stowe 1157). Not only does Lawson believe that "money ain't everything in this world," but he is "ready to come down at any moment to do any of the odd turns which sickness in a family makes necessary [. . .]" (Stowe 917).

Although **"The Man that Corrupted Hadleyburg"** has been described as "self-indulgent, crowded with incident and anecdotal digression [. . .]" (Seelye 151), the allusion to Sam Lawson, and by extension to the New England community in *Oldtown Folks,* integrally connected to the author's ironic and scathing portrayal of small-town America, belies such criticism. At the same time, it illustrates the extent to which "every syllable, every word, every utterance set to paper reflects amalgamation and repetition of countless types, stereotypes and precedents" (Plotel and Charney xv).

Note

1. Henry Nash Smith, for example, despite a most stimulating discussion of the tale, pretty much dismisses Halliday: "But Mark Twain has so little interest in Halliday that he forgets the vernacular precedents in his own work invoking as a model a character in Mrs. Stowe's *Oldtown Folks* who is portrayed from the patronizing viewpoint of local-color writing" (184). Most other readers have described Halliday as an innocent and/or representative of an earlier untarnished type. He is described as "the pagan Huck Finn character of the story"

(Geismar): as "the author's satiric voice, a grown-up Huck Finn" (Brodwin): and as "a kind of 'natural' man or grown up Huck Finn" (Rule): and as "someone summoning up in the reader's mind allusions [to kindliness] especially useful to his purpose" (Covici 193). Helen Nebeker exceptionally does more justice to Halliday's unsavory nature when she briefly describes him as "not generous and joyous but mean and petty" (636).

Works Cited

Brodwin, Stanley. "Mark Twain's Masks of Satan: The Final Phase." *American Literature* 34 (November 1962): 375-84.

Covici, Pascal. *Mark Twain's Humor: The Image of the World.* Dallas: Southern Methodist U, 1962.

Nebeker, Helen E. "The Great Corrupter or Satan Rehabilitated." *Studies in Short Fiction* 8 (1971): 635-46.

Plotel, Jeannine, and Hanna Charney, ed. "Introduction." *Intertextuality: New Perspectives in Criticism.* Vol. 2. New York: New York Literary Forum, 1986. xv.

Rule, Henry B. "The Role of Satan in 'The Man That Corrupted Hadleyburg.'" *Studies in Short Fiction* 6 (1969): 619-29.

Seelye, John. "On Mark Twain and 'The Man That Corrupted Hadleyburg.'" *The American Short Story.* Vol. 2. New York: Dell Publishing, 1980. 151-60

Smith, Henry Nash. *Mark Twain: The Development of a Writer.* New York: Atheneum, 1972.

Stowe, Harriet Beecher. *Three Novels: Uncle Tom's Cabin, The Minister's Wooing, & Oldtown Folks.* New York: The Library of America, 1982.

Twain, Mark. *"The Man that Corrupted Hadleyburg" and Other Essays and Stories.* Harper & Brothers, 1900.

FURTHER READING

Criticism

Blount, Roy, Jr. Afterword to *A Murder, a Mystery, and a Marriage,* by Mark Twain, pp. 67-105. New York: W. W. Norton & Company, 2001.

Chronicles the composition process of "A Murder, a Mystery, and a Marriage," detailing its literary sources, cultural influences, and historical effects on Twain's subsequent career.

Delaney, Paul. "The Genteel Savage: A Western Link in the Development of Mark Twain's Transcendent Figure." *Mark Twain Journal* 21, no. 3 (spring 1983): 29-31.

Discusses Twain's fragmentary story "Huck Finn and Tom Sawyer among the Indians."

Messent, Peter B. *The Short Works of Mark Twain: A Critical Study.* Philadelphia: University of Pennsylvania Press, 2001, 280 p.

Book-length study on Twain's short fiction.

Raveendran, P. P. "Focalizing Narration: Reflections on a Mark Twain Story." *Indian Journal of American Studies* 22, no. 1 (winter 1992): 81-3.

Centers on the role of the narrator in "A Dog's Tale."

Additional coverage of Twain's life and career is contained in the following sources published by Thomson Gale: *American Writers; American Writers: The Classics,* **Vol. 1;** *Authors and Artists for Young Adults,* **Vol. 20;** *Beacham's Encyclopedia of Popular Fiction: Biography & Resources,* **Vol. 3;** *Beacham's Guide to Literature for Young Adults,* **Vols. 2, 3, 11, 14;** *Children's Literature Review,* **Vols. 58, 60, 66;** *Concise Dictionary of American Literary Biography: 1865-1917; Contemporary Authors,* **Vols. 104, 135;** *Dictionary of Literary Biography,* **Vols. 11, 12, 23, 64, 74, 186, 189;** *DISCovering Authors; DISCovering Authors: British Edition; DISCovering Authors: Canadian Edition; DISCovering Authors Modules: Most-studied Authors* **and** *Novelists; DISCovering Authors 3.0; Exploring Novels; Exploring Short Stories; Junior DISCovering Authors; Literary Movements for Students,* **Vol. 1;** *Literature and Its Times,* **Vol. 2;** *Literature Resource Center; Major Authors and Illustrators for Children and Young Adults,* **Eds. 1, 2;** *Modern American Literature,* **Ed. 5;** *Nonfiction Classics for Students,* **Vol. 4;** *Novels for Students,* **Vols. 1, 6, 20;** *Reference Guide to American Literature,* **Ed. 4;** *Reference Guide to Short Fiction,* **Ed. 2;** *St. James Guide to Fantasy Writers; St. James Guide to Science Fiction Writers,* **Ed. 4;** *St. James Guide to Young Adult Writers; Short Stories for Students,* **Vols. 1, 7, 16, 21;** *Short Story Criticism,* **Vols. 6, 26, 34;** *Something About the Author,* **Vol. 100;** *Supernatural Fiction Writers; Twayne's United States Authors; Twentieth-Century Literary Criticism,* **Vols. 6, 12, 19, 36, 48, 59, 161;** *World Literature Criticism; Writers for Children; Writers for Young Adults;* **and** *Yesterday's Authors of Books for Children,* **Vol. 2.**

Giovanni Verga
1840-1922

Italian short story writer, novelist, and playwright.

The following entry provides an overview of Verga's short fiction. For further information on his life and short fiction career, see *SSC,* Volume 21.

INTRODUCTION

Regarded as a major figure in the evolution of Western literature, Verga was the leading proponent of *verismo,* a literary movement bridging the realism of Gustave Flaubert and the naturalism of Émile Zola. Best known as the author of the short story "Cavalleria rusticana," Verga wrote highly detailed tales about the beauty and tragedy of nineteenth-century Sicilian peasant life, using a distinct style characterized by plain language, colloquial dialogue, and indirect narration or *style indirect libre,* which minimizes the need for authorial intrusion to develop character or plot. Verga's mastery of stylistic simplicity and concrete description has also ranked his short fiction among the most moving stories ever written. Before his death, Verga was relatively unknown beyond the borders of his native Italy, which continues to celebrate him as a national treasure, but modern critics have acknowledged both his anticipation of several modernist narrative techniques and his considerable influence upon the post-World War II Neorealist movement.

BIOGRAPHICAL INFORMATION

The son of land-owning patricians, Verga was born in 1840 on the eastern coast of Sicily in Vizzini, Catania, where many of his most famous stories are set. At a young age, he freely circulated among the local peasants and fishermen, watching them at work and play, while he voraciously read literature. Although Verga studied law at the University of Catania for some time, he indulged his literary interests at the provincial school of Don Antonio Abate, a noted humanist. As a student Verga aspired to write historical, patriotic novels in the manner of Victor Hugo and Alexandre Dumas, whose style he mastered in his first published novel, *I Carbonari della montagna* (1861).

During the late 1860s, Verga tried to further his literary career by frequently traveling for extended periods of time to the cosmopolitan cities of Florence and Milan

in northern Italy, which had politically, economically, and culturally dominated southern Italy since the nation's unification in 1861. In 1869 Verga settled in Milan where he wrote fashionable romances about the sophisticated mores and tastes of Milanese high society, most notably *Eva* (1873) and *Eros* (1875), but these novels proved unsuccessful. Verga increasingly felt alienated among the northern bourgeoisie and became disillusioned with the ideals of Italian nationalism. Therefore, he dramatically shifted his literary focus away from romanticism and metropolitan culture toward realism and rural life, producing the short story "Nedda" (1874), which many critics view as his first successful effort to articulate his *verismo* style.

In 1879 Verga returned to Catania and moved into his boyhood home at Vizzini, where he drew inspiration for the writings upon which his reputation rests. During the 1880s Verga published his best-known works, including the novels *I Malavoglia* (1881; *The House by the Medlar Tree*) and *Maestro-don Gesualdo* (1888), the short story collections *Vita dei campi* (1880; *Cavelleria Rusticana and Other Stories*) and *Novelle rusticane* (1882; *Little Novels of Sicily*), and the play *Cavalleria rusticana* (1884), a dramatic revision of his own short story which Pietro Mascagni adapted as the libretto for his popular opera of the same name. After these triumphs, Verga wrote little else through the turn of the century and then lapsed into literary silence before he died in 1922.

MAJOR WORKS OF SHORT FICTION

Verga's finest short stories appear in the collections *Cavalleria Rusticana* and *Little Novels of Sicily,* both of which D. H. Lawrence first translated into English in the 1920s, after Verga's death. These stories exemplify *verismo,* a literary style marked by simple language, descriptive accuracy, and idiomatic dialogue and narration that strives for objective representation of everyday life. To this end, Verga's tales are typically structured by using direct and indirect speech patterns in order to develop the characters and to advance the plot with as little authorial interference as possible. In addition, communal values and other background information are often conveyed by means of a chorus, a common device in classical epic literature. Set in the villages on the arid plains of Catania, most of Verga's short fiction sympathetically details the poverty, hardships, and miseries of Sicilian laborers who struggle daily to escape the ancient customs and rigid moral codes defining their lives, yet often fail, because of their own passion, pride, or ambition.

Themes of love, infidelity, and honor recur throughout *Cavalleria Rusticana,* and several stories concern the tragic results of sexual indiscretion. In the collection's title story, the bored, flirtatious wife of a rich, arrogant man entices her young former lover to stray from his virtuous fiancée, who faithfully waits for his return. "La Lupa" ("The She-Wolf") focuses on the insatiable carnal desire of the title character, a femme fatale who possesses magical, nearly primal powers of seduction which no man, including the village priest, can resist— except young Nanni, her daughter's husband. The tale concludes ambiguously as Nanni contemplates whether to yield to the seductress or murder her. Infidelity plays a major role in "Fantasticheria" ("Caprice"), in which a Milanese society matron impulsively accompanies her Sicilian lover for a month's visit to his native village. Initially, she declares the town picturesque, but after two days she grows bored and leaves him, revealing the pettiness and apathy of her bourgeois mentality. "Jeli il pastore" ("Ieli") traces the vicissitudes in the life of an ingenuous shepherd, who gladly marries a childhood friend after she sullies her reputation by "carrying on" with another of his friends, although the shepherd can-

not believe it ever happened. When he finally witnesses his wife's continuing infidelity with his friend at a sheep-shearing festival, the shepherd cuts her lover's throat with a pair of shears. Like many of Verga's protagonists, the shepherd's candor is both a virtue and a curse. Taking its title from the nickname of its protagonist, "Rosso Malpelo" recounts the tragic circumstances of a sullen redheaded orphan who completely identifies with the cruelty directed at him by the villagers after they willfully fail to rescue his father from a collapsing mine. While later working at the mine, Rosso looks after a new mineworker, a lame boy whom he cruelly belittles and beats but also helps with his work and poignantly meets his needs, until the boy dies. In his own harsh way, Rosso encourages the boy to face the miseries of living and to embrace the mercies of dying.

The stories in *Little Novels of Sicily* demonstrate further refinement of Verga's narrative simplicity and emotional intensity, rendering the morals of these tales concretely but indirectly. For example, the impoverished protagonist of "La roba" ("Property") works his way to a life of wealth and prosperity at the expense of his family, his peace of mind, and his soul; while the peasant narrator of "I galantuomini" ("The Gentry") quietly reports the shame and humiliation of several upper-class families who fall from privilege into the same poverty and trouble experienced by the peasantry on a daily basis. Other stories in this collection focus on specific hardships of peasant life, including "Malaria," which equates the disease's effects with the peasants' efforts to survive or escape, and "Black Bread," which describes the high costs of both hunger and salvation.

CRITICAL RECEPTION

Although his reputation as one of the most significant writers of modern Europe has slowly evolved since his death, critics in Italy have long hailed Verga as one of their country's greatest authors since Giovanni Boccaccio. Verga's talent for letting dialogue and action tell his stories has earned him universal praise from critics, regardless of their national origins. Dierdre O'Grady has observed that "his images are seen through the eyes of the humble folk, and put forward in their local forms of expression and proverbs."

While some scholars have debated whether Verga developed his *verismo* style independently of others, most have rarely questioned his mastery of the literary technique. Many reviewers have examined the consistent objectivity of his storytelling style as not only his hallmark but also a precursor of such modernist literary devices as interior monologue and stream of consciousness.

Commentators have also noted Verga's achievement as the first Italian writer to precisely represent the nuanced colloquialisms of the idiom spoken by Sicilians; however, others, including Ulrich Weisstein, have pointed out the challenges such accuracy presents to translators. Literary scholars have also studied the archetypal symbolism and the structure of Verga's fiction, while cultural critics have examined the significance of Italian history within the context of his stories. Most critics, especially Massimo Verdicchio, have suggested that Verga's most important legacy lies in the apparent simplicity of his narrative style, which has continued to fascinate professional and ordinary readers alike.

PRINCIPAL WORKS

Short Fiction

Nedda: Bozzetto siciliano 1874
Vita dei campi [*Cavalleria Rusticana and Other Stories*] 1880
Novelle rusticane [*Little Novels of Sicily*] 1882
Per le vie 1883
Vagabondaggio 1887
Under the Shadow of Etna: Sicilian Stories from the Italian of Giovanni Verga 1896
Tutte le novelle 1945
The She-Wolf and Other Stories 1958

Other Major Works

I Carbonari della montagna (novel) 1861
Eva (novel) 1873
Eros (novel) 1875
I Malavoglia [*The House by the Medlar Tree*] (novel) 1881
Cavalleria rusticana (play) 1884
Mastro-don Gesualdo (novel) 1888

CRITICISM

Deirdre O'Grady (essay date 1989)

SOURCE: O'Grady, Deirdre. "The Vicious Circle: Giovanni Verga as Storyteller." In *Italian Storytellers: Essays on Italian Narrative Literature*, edited by Eric Haywood and Cormac Ó Cuilleanáin, pp. 204-28. Dublin: Irish Academic Press, 1989.

[*In the following essay, O'Grady discusses the dominant motifs, narrative strategies, and symbolism of "L'amante di Gramigna," "Rosso Malpelo," and "Cav-* *alleria rusticana," focusing on the stifling conditions of rural Sicilian life, the efforts of some protagonists to break free, and the effects of meeting their destinies.*]

> Quando nel romanzo l'affinità e la coesione di ogni sua parte sarà cosí completa, che il processo della creazione rimarrà un mistero, come lo svolgersi delle passioni umane, e l'armonia delle sue forme sarà cosí perfetta, la sincerità della sua realtà cosí evidente, il suo modo e la sua ragione di essere cosí necessarie, che la mano dell'artista rimarrà assolutamente invisibile, allora avrà l'impronta dell'avvenimento reale, l'opera d'arte sembrerà *essersi fatta da sé,* aver maturato ed esser sorta spontanea come un fatto naturale, senza serbare alcun punto di contatto col suo autore, alcuna macchia del peccato d'origine.
>
> *Rivista minima,* February 1880

Verga addressed these words to Salvatore Farina, editor of the journal in which his short story **"L'amante di Gramigna"** was first published.[1] The passage quoted here is more than just a statement of intention and technique. In the history of Italian storytelling, it marks the abdication of the teller in favour of the tale—one of the many devices adopted by Verga in order to project the vicious circle which traps the Sicilian rustic in a life of hardship and hopelessness, governed by outmoded codes of behaviour and local customs. Such a society offers little physical and emotional outlet. Geographically and intellectually isolated, Verga's protagonists emerge as bestial, ferocious and fatalistic. Their attempts to escape their confines are thwarted by destiny and social pressures. Indeed the vicious circle can be regarded as the dominant motif of Verga's stories.

The present essay will consider life within such a suffocating ambience, the attempts of some protagonists to escape, and the consequences of their struggle with fate. In addition, Verga's narrative techniques and symbolism will be illustrated, drawing on three tales from *Vita dei campi* (1880), and on his last completed novel, *Mastro-don Gesualdo* (1889).

In communicating his vivid impressions of existence in underprivileged areas of Italy, Verga draws on a wealth of resources. His images are seen through the eyes of the humble folk, and put forward in their local forms of expression and proverbs.[2] In addition, Verga provides a variety of visual observations, ranging from sweeping spans of arid landscape to a series of highly coloured pictorial images. In striving to project an enduring impression of essential characteristics, the Sicilian author frequently indulges in exaggeration, leading to the creation of caricatures bordering on the grotesque. The result is often the dissolution of characters as psychological entities.

Although the behaviour patterns of the protagonists are studied with scientific rigour, rather than providing an explicit psychological character analysis, the storyteller sets up a series of perceptions in the reader's mind, and this points indirectly to the emotional turmoil of his creations.[3] A further dimension is added by Verga's subtle identification of his peasants with the heroes of legends and folk-tales, by providing fairy-stories in reverse, devoid of happy endings, and by parodying the world of the chivalric romance.

While Verga was not the first Italian novelist to write about low and rustic life, his way of doing so was highly original. Alessandro Manzoni, in the first quarter of the nineteenth century, had also dealt with the fate of the weakest members of society, at the mercy of the strong.[4] In *I promessi sposi,* the betrothed couple of his title occupy the lowest rung of the social ladder. But the title also contains a reference to the central theme of the novel: that of promise. *I promessi sposi* traces the causes and effects of promises, imposed, freely and hastily made, reviewed and broken. The theme is carried across the full spectrum of social classes, and ranges from the sublime to the trivial—from the philosophy of a religious vow to the social consequences of a flippant bet. As well as this moral and theological theme, there is an allegorical dimension: the rustic protagonists Renzo and Lucia can be seen as symbolizing the active life and the contemplative life, while Renzo's physical journey from Milan to Bergamo may be interpreted as a passage from tyrannical chaos to the ordered freedom of the Venetian republic. Verga's rustics are far removed from all this: they are too passive to make promises; their travels are purely physical, with no moral dimension. Manzoni provides a multi-faceted portrayal of the human will; but Verga, in depicting the plight of the socially deprived, gives life to figures devoid of willpower. Their plight cannot be attributed to the foreign domination of Italy, which is one of Manzoni's principal concerns, but is a direct consequence of the vicious circle in which they exist, and of which they are victims.

In the newspaper *La tribuna* of 2 February 1910, Riccardo Artuffo published an article which came to be regarded as a real scoop,[5] although the editor of Verga's letters, Gino Raya, later relegated it to the status of journalistic fabrication.[6] Artuffo's account of the birth of literary realism in Italy made a good story, and has found its way into most assessments of Verga's approach to narrative.[7] It tells how Verga came across his new style by a fortuitous discovery: "One day, I don't know how, there came into my hands a sort of broadside, a sheet, sufficiently ungrammatical and disconnected, in which a sea-captain concisely related all the vicissitudes through which his sailing-ship had passed. Seaman's language, short, without an unnecessary phrase. It struck me, and I read it again. It was just what I was looking for, without definitely knowing it."

In a letter of 18 February 1911, however, Verga dismissed all this as mere invention. He insisted that his technique was based on a presentation of images and

words as seen through the eyes of his characters, and expressed in their language. The basis of Verga's new approach to literature has been the subject of heated discussion. With the appearance of Raya's edition of Verga's letters, the "caso Verga" took on a new dimension, and critics such as Asor Rosa, Luperini and Masiello suggested that Verga's literary intentions might have derived from an idealistic desire to provide a voice for the rural section of society, rather than from any basic wish for artistic renewal or reform.

Verga's realistic fiction, then, is based on the visual observation of gestures and actions, and expressed in what was intended to be the language of the people.[8] The setting is physically isolated and slightly exotic: the reader is brought face to face with olive-pickers, bandits, soldiers, mine-workers, carriers and fisherfolk, in a setting which stands both geographically and intellectually apart from the Italian mainland.[9] In the hands of the Sicilian author, this setting gives rise to a close-up of local customs, ranging from the details of traditional dress to religious observances and codes of honour. The individual is swallowed up in a colourful extravaganza of ritualistic practices, processions and folk festivals. As G. Cocchiara remarks, "l'uomo, nel caso specifico il contadino siciliano, vive nell'opera del Verga coi suoi usi e coi suoi costumi."[10] The words and actions of Verga's peasant characters communicate and demonstrate the reality of the social circle to which they belong. Man becomes a product of his social setting; individual identity and aspirations are sacrificed; man's innermost needs are subordinated to the will of the group, which in its turn is symbolized by local convention. Deep personal religious feelings yield to the social credo of the "religione della roba", the pursuit of property, while the "religione del caminetto", or cult of the family hearth, creates its own victims. Verga's Sicilian tales portray the futility and frustration of life as a vicious circle: in the words of D. Woolf, "there is something about the world in which we live, [Verga] seems to be saying, that ineluctably thwarts our dreams, irrespective of our merits or defects."[11] At first sight, Verga's fiction seems to constitute a literature of extreme, intensified simplicity, devoid of sophistication in either form or content, with complexity of ambience substituted for complexity of character. An analysis of *Vita dei campi,* on one level, simply demands clarity and directness of critical approach. But I also hope to show that Verga is not merely a creator of popular literature, rooted in peasant life. In seeking to confer a poetic permanence on the deprived, he uses types and conventions of storytelling which had already rendered their heroes immortal.[12]

The collection *Vita dei campi* (1880), which deals with dramatic themes and elemental passions, clearly serves to illustrate life within a "vicious circle". The three stories that I have chosen for analysis also demonstrate, I believe, Verga's ability to adapt different genres to his own purposes. **"L'amante di Gramigna"** tells of a futile attempt to reject the circle and all that goes with it. **"Rosso Malpelo"** depicts frustration transformed into violence, and traces an impossible struggle with fate. **"Cavalleria rusticana",** one of the most celebrated short stories ever written, is a savage tale of jealousy and dishonour.

In telling the story of Peppa, the village girl from Licodia who abandons her well-to-do fiancé in order to follow the bandit Gramigna, Verga provides an objective description of behaviour which seemingly defies logical explanation.[13] In moral and psychological terms, the story may be seen as a refusal to pursue material possessions, and a rejection of the comforts which a prosperous farmer can provide. But as well as being a quest for personal freedom and an outcry against materialism, **"L'amante di Gramigna"** represents a desire for adventure and the unknown. It can be seen as an adventure story with a difference, a fairy-tale in reverse.[14] The story develops at first by way of descriptive narrative and statement. A theme of fantasy is then introduced, and juxtaposed with a shift into brutally expressed dramatic dialogue; the story closes with a return to narrative. This structure spans the adventures of the bandit Gramigna.

Echoes of ritualized folk narrative can be sensed in the threefold repetitions occurring in the episode of the couple's "courtship", which is central to the story. The traditional theme of love is presented in reverse. This courtship, based on mistrust, leads to Peppa becoming Gramigna's servant, subjected to threats of violence.[15] It is conveyed in scenes of terse dialogue, consisting of three interrogatives followed by three imperatives (Mondadori edition, pp. 203-04). The speaker is Gramigna. First he asks: (i) "Che vieni a far qui?" Later he asks: (ii) "Sei pazza, o sei qualche spia?" Finally he asks: (iii) "Vuoi venire con me?" Similarly, the three commands issued by Gramigna chart his growing acceptance of Peppa's presence: (i) "Vattene—Vattene finché t'aiuta Cristo!"; (ii) "Bene, va a prendermi un fiasco d'acqua"; (iii) "Tu resti qui, o t'ammazzo com'è vero Dio." First he orders her to leave, then to serve him, and finally to stay with him. This acceptance of her presence is based on fear rather than trust, but the fear manifests itself in the form of brute force. Attraction is based on violence, and tested by loyalty in the face of threats. A love-story with a difference, then, where the borderline between love and hate, sex and violence is seen in all its startling reality.[16] The tale then concludes with a return to the technique of descriptive narrative used at the opening; there is a stark statement of the fate of Gramigna, his lover and their child.

Verga's juxtaposition of two scales, two planes of storytelling, contributes to his success in creating an atmosphere of fantasy. This fairy-story effect is partly achieved by his exaggeration in presenting his characters; they often remain on the level of caricature, bordering on the grotesque. For example, the hunt for Gramigna, set against the backdrop of the huge plain of Catania, allows for an effect of superhuman vastness and space. The pursuit of this man, "da un capo all'altro della provincia", "di giorno, di notte, a piedi, a cavallo, col telegrafo, senza esser riesciti a mettergli le unghie addosso" (p. 201), coupled with the strength of this individual who dares to pit his energy against the entire province and its inhabitants ("era solo ma valeva per dieci": p. 201), indicates that Gramigna, having become the talking-point of society, has succeeded in travelling and affecting the length and breadth of the countryside.

By contrast, the description of the hill-town of Licodia presents us with a miniature world, peopled by small, lifeless caricatures. Peppa's fiancé, "Candela di sego" ("Tallow Candle"), is a fine young fellow, whose suitability as a prospective husband is based on the fact that he possesses "terre al sole, e una mula baia in stalla" (p. 201). This virile pillar of society carries the standard of St Margaret in procession as though it truly were a pillar. Not only that, but he can provide his bride-to-be with linen in sets of four, earrings reaching to the shoulders, and a ring for every finger. Here too, subtlety is sacrificed for effect, and the emotional turmoil of the protagonists is expressed in terms of exaggerated physical poses and actions. When the blow falls, "Candela di sego" is stunned, and is depicted "a bocca aperta"; Peppa's mother tears at her hair, while Peppa herself, acting as a heroine of fantasy, escapes through the window.

A fairy-story in reverse, then? Far from providing an escape from the adult world, however, this "fairy-story" serves to illustrate the limits and shortcomings of that world. It also shows the impossibility of breaking out of society's vicious circle: the romance between the village girl and the heroic bandit will end in disaster for both. In fact, as each figure in the story follows its own impulses, the simplification and exaggeration employed in projecting these figures leads to the dissolution of the characters as psychological entities, and we are left with elemental struggles between forces which transcend the individual. For instance, the heroine is regarded as a woman possessed by a demon (p. 203), so that her fate becomes part of the struggle between good and evil.

"L'amante di Gramigna", then, can be seen as having implications which go well beyond the conventions of realistic storytelling. The next short story which I have chosen for analysis also presents mythical or legendary dimensions. **"Rosso Malpelo",** the story of a boy working in a sand mine, whose father was buried alive in the mines and who eventually meets his own end underground, deals with themes of labour, heredity and a repressed desire for love, expressed in the terms of a perverted logic. The protagonist, regarded by his fellow mine-workers as unlucky or even cursed, is presented as a larger-than-life figure, and the story develops along the lines of a tragedy of revenge.[17] As we shall see, Verga constructs his story symbolically on three levels of existence, and conveys the message that certain life patterns resemble burial alive. The weak members of society, seen as mere tools in the hands of the strong, are beaten and exploited, being of no more significance than the long-suffering grey donkey in the story.

The opening of **"Rosso Malpelo"** objectively demonstrates the illogical processes of deduction which are at work in the minds of the unfortunate mine-workers. "Malpelo si chiamava cosí perché aveva i capelli rossi ed aveva i capelli rossi perché era un ragazzo malizioso e cattivo, che prometteva di riescir un fior di birbone. Sicché tutti alla cava della rena rossa lo chiamavano Malpelo, e persino sua madre, col sentirgli dir sempre a quel modo aveva quasi dimenticato il suo nome di battesimo" (Mondadori edition, p. 186). The boy is called Malpelo *because* he has red hair, and he has red hair *because* he is nasty and ill-mannered. Therefore everybody at the sand-mine calls him Malpelo, as do ourselves, the readers, because we do not know him by any other name. Malpelo's world appears to be his punishment for having been born, and it is portrayed through a series of contradictions in logic, highlighting the basic social injustices and social prejudices which render normal feelings next to impossible. Never having received a caress from him, his mother gave him none; although his father was a good man, he too was treated as a "bestia da lavoro" and carried a nickname with animal connotations, "Misciu Bestia", meaning both beast and blockhead. In a final reversal of justice, "Bestia" was left to die in the mine, buried alive, while the engineer in charge of the excavations spent an evening at the theatre. But in this world everything is turned upside down; as G. Bàrberi Squarotti remarks, "il mondo di Rosso Malpelo è tale che perfino i rapporti di sangue sono, per lui, stravolti e capovolti."[18] Verga designs the imaginative world of the story on three physical levels, corresponding to three possible forms of existence. First there is the mine, below ground level, where the miners spend the greater part of their lives. Then there is ground level, where farmers and carriers work, and sometimes sing. Finally, beyond all this, there is a fantastic world of justice, invoked by Ranocchio (Malpelo's fellow worker), where children who obey their parents are rewarded.

The battle for survival is conducted at the first, underground, level. Malpelo's father Misciu Bestia, trapped by a collapsing pillar in the mine, struggles against the active force of fate, symbolized by the pillar, which eventually destroys him. Verga states the facts, circumstances and outcome of this struggle: "il pilastro gli si era piegato proprio addosso, e l'aveva sepolto vivo; si poteva persino vedere tuttora che mastro Bestia aveva tentato istintivamente di liberarsi, scavando nella rena e aveva le mani lacerate e le unghie rotte" (p. 193). In recording the evidence, Verga seems to be making the point that even creatures as unfortunate as Malpelo's father are born with an instinct for self-preservation. But the pillar too appears instilled with life, twisting and turning in the struggle for survival as Misciu Bestia strikes desperately against a force stronger than himself.

As the struggle continues, it is played out not so much between the strong and the weak (as is often claimed), but rather between the weak and the weaker, with the survival of the fittest. The protagonists of this continuing nightmare are Malpelo, his workmate Ranocchio ("Frog"), and the grey donkey. Malpelo, treated as an animal, behaves like one. With Verga's usual technique, Malpelo's psychological state and feelings are not analyzed directly, but expressed indirectly through physical actions: he tyrannizes his young victim Ranocchio, and torments insects and animals. He claims that his mistreatment of Ranocchio is designed to make Ranocchio stronger, but this is really a cry of powerless frustration. Malpelo's philosophy is as follows: the donkey is beaten because it cannot return the blows, whereas if one is strong then one is allowed to win. But Malpelo is confusing strength with violence. For him, violence becomes a logical form of self-expression, as well as a defence against the world which allowed his father to be buried alive. Malpelo's acceptance of violence is a final futile attempt to convince himself of his own strength.

The alternative to Malpelo's existence is not a better existence, but simply non-existence. He does not search for a life above and beyond the confines of the mine. He accepts the permanence of a world played out in an infernal underground labyrinth. Escape from the vicious circle of existence, for Rosso Malpelo, does not involve a rejection of life below ground, but rather a permanent acceptance of that life. As Bàrberi Squarotti observes, "il Verga sottolinea molto efficacemente il carattere d'immortalità, che ha assunto, con la sua misteriosa sparizione nel cuore della terra."[19] Malpelo disappears from view—"se ne andò: né più si seppe nulla di lui." From a nightmare existence, he enters the world of legend and local myth. By the end of the tale, he has taken on the characteristics of a bogey-man in a children's story, liable to reappear at any time, "coi capelli rossi, e gli occhiacci grigi" (p. 199).

Up to this point, as well as looking at the legendary dimensions of Verga's stories, I have focussed attention mainly on the protagonists' reactions to the social pressures which surround them, resulting in a desire to escape from the vicious circle. Both Peppa and Malpelo are frustrated characters who reject the social group into which they were born. In the third story which I have chosen, **"Cavalleria rusticana"**, we are given a close-up of life within the confines of the circle.

A tale of love, jealousy, betrayal and revenge, **"Cavalleria rusticana"** traces a pattern of deception and dishonour in a small community. The story, based on fact, was originally included as an episode in Verga's novel *I Malavoglia* (1881), but eliminated during revision and later developed into an independent work. In 1883 the author re-wrote the tale as a one-act tragedy, which was performed with the great Eleonora Duse in the role of Santa (renamed Santuzza in the dramatized version); Mascagni's opera of the same name had its first performance in 1889.[20] The plot is almost too famous to need summarizing: Turiddu Macca, returning from military service, finds that his beloved Lola is about to marry another man, Alfio, a prosperous carter. Turiddu pays court instead to Lola's young neighbour Santa; but when Santa realizes that Turiddu is still seeing Lola, she is overcome by jealousy and tells Alfio about the affair; the two men fight, and Turiddu is killed.

In the short story version of **"Cavalleria rusticana"**, a central function of the plot is the projection of word-pictures, pictorial poses, and still images. Here, as never before, Verga chooses to show us events as they happen, allowing Sicilian costume and local colour to lend an air of brightness to the whole. The first striking visual detail is the uniform of the *bersaglieri* (the famous Italian infantry corps), which attracts attention from all quarters. Turiddu Macca wears his regimental hat with its red tassle, which will assume a fatalistic symbolic significance: "ogni domenica si pavoneggiava in piazza coll'uniforme da bersagliere e il berretto rosso, che sembrava quello della buona ventura" (Mondadori edition, p. 139). The girls could hardly take their eyes off him—"le ragazze se lo rubavano cogli occhi"—as they coyly went to mass, their noses tucked in their mantillas. The local boys buzzed around him like flies. He also smoked a pipe decorated with a carving of the King on horseback, and when he wanted to strike a match on his trouser seat, he raised his leg as though he were about to kick someone—"come se desse una pedata." On hearing of Lola's engagement to Alfio, the financially comfortable local carter, Turiddu lets off steam by singing all the disdainful songs that he knows, under her window. By presenting all of this in a fast-moving sequence of visual images, Verga places his reader in the position of one who observes, watches with interest, even spies on his next-door neighbour. This painter of word-pictures pays particular attention to details of the characters' faces, eyes and headdress. In fact, the physical impression conveyed by their headgear assumes a crucial significance. It is the visual manifestation of personality, in Verga's world of pictorial images—for, in keeping with the author's objective technique of storytelling, mentioned at the beginning of this essay, the

reader is not allowed to penetrate directly into the minds of the characters; instead, their appearance, dress and gestures speak for them. Turiddu's tassle and uniform attract attention. When Lola is embarrassed, she adjusts the ends of her headscarf. The young girls bury their noses in their mantillas. Alfio, Lola's husband, is described as the kind of carter who wears his cap on the side of his head, over one ear (p. 142), and his cap is down over his eyes as he walks to the final duel (p. 144). As the plot develops, the reader is allowed a closer view of the central group in the story. Such opportunity for observation allows the reader to eavesdrop and spy on the protagonists as they betray each other.

Verga's letter of 18 February 1911, as we have seen, emphasized that his narrative technique was based on images seen through the eyes of his characters, and expressed in their language. We have looked at the importance of visual images in **"Cavalleria rusticana"**; it is also worth noting that the four passages of conversation in the story have the function of dramatic dialogue, illustrating events already mentioned in the narrative. D. Woolf considers that the most outstanding feature of the story is the fact that these dialogues are structurally superfluous.[21] But this fact underlines their crucial contribution to Verga's achievement here as a realistic storyteller. The four structurally superfluous conversations prove, beyond question, the writer's adherence to his own plan and statement of technique, as expressed in the letter about **"L'amante di Gramigna"** quoted at the beginning of the present essay. They are prime examples of the withdrawal of the storyteller, and the emergence of the characters speaking their own distinctive language. The four conversations, which I do not propose to analyze at this stage, are between Turiddu and Lola on the latter's return from a pilgrimage (appropriately to Our Lady of Peril); between Turiddu and Santa (a well-described flirtatious encounter); between Santa and Alfio, as Santa takes revenge for Turiddu's continuing liaison with Lola; and finally between Turiddu and Alfio, when the two men fight to the death. We sense the vicious circle of social observation which controls the protagonists' lives. Santa and Lola silently spy on Turiddu, and on each other. "Lola che ascoltava ogni sera, nascosta dietro il vaso di basilico, e si faceva pallida e rossa . . ."; "Turiddu tornò a salutarla cosí spesso che Santa se ne avvide e gli batté la finestra sul muso" (p. 142). Silent observation is transformed into an undercurrent of sarcastic gossip on the part of the neighbours, who function as the chorus in the story. There are five references to their participation in this drama of nudges and whispers: "Che non ha nulla da fare Turiddu della gnà Nunzia—dicevano i vicini—che passa le notti a cantare come una passera solitaria?" (p. 139); "Che direbbero in paese se mi vedessero con voi?" (p. 140); "la figliuola gli aprí la finestra, e stava a chiacchierare con lui ogni sera, che tutto il vicinato non parlava d'altro" (p. 141); "i vicini se lo mostravano con un sorriso" (p. 142); "gli amici avevano lasciato la salsiccia zitti zitti, e accompagnarono Turiddu sino a casa" (p. 143).

In this fast-moving game of intrigue, the tragedy is played out through a series of images associated with sight and the eyes. This line of imagery constitutes a unifying force in the story, drawing together the themes of love, guilt, revenge and betrayal. In the duel, Alfio, with his cap drawn over his eyes, first blinds Turiddu with a handful of dust and then stabs him to death. The image of blindness is associated with jealousy; it denotes a lack of perception, insight and enlightenment. But throughout the story, eyesight has been a constant theme. We have already noted that the girls on their way to Mass, seeing Turiddu in his rifleman's uniform, "se lo rubavano cogli occhi." And when Turiddu first meets Lola coming back from her pilgrimage, his salutation to her is "Beato chi vi vede." She in turn reveals both guilt and embarrassment: "Che direbbero in paese se mi vedessero con voi?" Later, the impersonal narrator records Lola's ostentatious display of the jewellery that her husband has given her. Turiddu's flirting conversation with Santa has eyes expressing both observation and action: "vi mangerei cogli occhi". Again, Alfio's threat, when Santa tells him about his wife's infidelity, relates to Santa's eyes—"se non avete visto bene, non vi lascerò gli occhi per piangere"—while Santa's reply picks up the image and throws it back at him: "non ho pianto nemmeno quando ho visto con questi occhi Turiddu della gnà Nunzia entrare di notte in casa di vostra moglie."[22] Afterwards, the way that Alfio eyes Turiddu in the tavern indicates that the final clash is inevitable: "soltanto dal modo in cui gli piantò gli occhi addosso, Turiddu comprese che era venuto per quell'affare." Alfio explains that he has come because he has not seen Turiddu for some time. During the duel, Turiddu talks about the image of his mother's face, which floats continually before his eyes; whereupon Alfio invites him to open those eyes wide. The fatal stabbing follows Alfio's blinding of his adversary: sight yields to darkness and finally to blood. Turiddu's tragic fate is the result of his seeing Lola and being seen with her. In fact Verga is providing a rustic version of Dante's *contrappasso,* whereby the sinner is deprived of the sense through which he has transgressed. The outcome is an intensely visual one: the image of the *bersagliere* in the opening passage, complete with the red tassel which is so attractive to both Lola and Santa, yields to the final image of the young man covered in his own blood.

The foregoing analysis has shown that while **"Cavalleria rusticana"** is a story of elemental savagery, the storytelling techniques used by its author are sophisticated and poetic. Of course **"Cavalleria rusticana"** is a realistic, even brutal, account of life constrained by a vicious circle of social pressures, but it is also a story which draws on rhythms and archetypes which go beyond its immediate setting. For example, one may note the rhythmic way in which the verb "tornare" recurs at key points in the plot. It appears when Turiddu meets Lola returning from her pilgrimage: "Finalmente s'imbatté in Lola che tornava dal *viaggio* alla Madonna del Pericolo" (p. 139). Turiddu emphasizes that himself has just returned from military service: "la volontà di Dio fu che dovevo tornare da tanto lontano per trovare ste belle notizie, gnà Lola!" Alfio learns of his wife's infidelity on his return to the village: "Compare Alfio tornò colle sue mule, cariche di soldoni" (p. 142). And finally, Turiddu hints to his mother that he will never come home again: "Mamma—le disse Turiddu—vi rammentate quando sono andato soldato, che credevate non avessi a tornar piú?" (p. 143).

"Cavalleria rusticana" can be seen, then, not only as a story about dangerous liaisons and the defence of property and honour, but also as a story about sight and blindness, departures and returns. And I believe that a further level of interpretation can be suggested by considering the title. The words **"Cavalleria rusticana"** announce a work which will be concerned with codes of honour and methods of avenging dishonour. It is thus based on chivalric romance, which tells of the adventures of legendary heroes in love, war and religion. But Verga offers us a polarized model of the chivalric world, expressed in an unsophisticated local code rather than in medieval legal complexities, set against a rustic rather than a courtly background, and in a world of primitive Catholicism rather than amid the campaigns of militant Christendom. Despite these differences, however, **"Cavalleria rusticana"** contains the same basic constituents as the tales of Tristan and Isolde, Lancelot and Guinevere, Paolo and Francesca. Like those medieval stories, it is built around the convention of marriage as a social and commercial transaction. Like them, it tells of cloak-and-dagger intrigue, deception, betrayal and revenge. In both chivalric and rustic society, we witness fatal deceptions and delusions. In each case, the husband in the story is seen as industrious, generous and just. Honour is always defended. **"Cavalleria rusticana"** presents the traditional elements in a distorted form. Turiddu returns, not from the Crusades, but from military service (which had been made compulsory in Italy in the 1860s). His shining armour is only the uniform of the *bersaglieri,* but he struts around as proudly as a knight, his heraldic trappings consisting of "una pipa col re a cavallo". His lady had given him a handkerchief as a love-token on his departure, but now she is to marry a wealthy man who owns four mules: a feudal lord rather than a wandering knight. Turiddu departs from the code of the perfect courtly lover when he seeks consolation with Santa, after singing not a medieval love-lyric, but all the disdainful songs he knows, under Lola's window; but Santa in turn acts out the role of the crafty dwarf in the story of Tristan and Isolde, when she reports everything to the wronged husband. The two gentlemen finally confront each other in a duel which could be interpreted as a parody of such confrontations in chivalric romance.

Turiddu's moral transgressions are of two kinds, the second of which would disqualify him as a hero of courtly romance. Not only does he violate the sanctity of marriage, but he is a disloyal lover, switching his affections from Lola to Santa and back to Lola again. In the duel, he defends himself not with a sword but with a forbidden weapon: his flick-knife, which he had hidden in the straw when he went away on military service. Thus Verga fuses the two worlds of rustic society and courtly love—as Chaucer had done for comic effect five centuries earlier in "The Nonnes Preestes Tale".[23] Lola's and Santa's courtyards, which provide the settings for amorous conversation, take the place of the balcony in chivalric romance. In the dialogue between Santa and Turiddu, the courtly and rustic levels come together when Verga's peasants use images of fabulous wealth in talking about their impossible attachments. Turiddu explains that he is no longer laying siege to Lola: "La gnà Lola ha sposato un re di corona ora" (p. 141). Santa picks up the image: "Io non sposerò un re di corona, come la gnà Lola, ma la mia dote ce l'ho anch'io, quando il Signore mi manderà qualcheduno" (*ibid.*). Turiddu insists on his extravagant love for Santa: "Vorrei essere il figlio di Vittorio Emanuele per sposarti" (p. 142).

In the three stories under discussion, then, Verga has used many imaginative resources of storytelling to describe the vicious circle which encloses his characters, and to highlight attitudes to property, industry and especially marriage.[24] He does this not just by realistic description, but by a creative manipulation of the reader's perceptions, and the use of different measures of description. We have seen how two geographical scales are adopted to evoke the bandit's adventures in **"L'amante di Gramigna"**; **"Rosso Malpelo"** offers a vision of existence on three levels; while **"Cavalleria rusticana"** presents a cumulative picture of life in a village community through the characters' movements and the reader's observations and impressions. There are also marked differences in focus. Gramigna's world is a remote one, appealing to the imagination. The sufferings of Rosso Malpelo, on the other hand, are pictured in close-up. Life in Vizzini (the original setting for **"Cavalleria rusticana"**) assumes the proportions and texture of small-town provincial life. By varying his narrative approaches, and by combining elements of both exaggeration and precise observation, Verga succeeds in drawing larger-than-life figures, indelibly impressed on the reader's mind.

One may infer that his interests in these three stories from *Vita dei campi* are both literary and social. His

aim was not merely to projecct images of life, but also to provoke reactions to a series of intolerable situations—to expose the social tragedy of the vicious circle.

With the creation of the figure of Gesualdo Motta, protagonist of the novel *Mastro-don Gesualdo,* Verga turns his attention to the conscious efforts of a wealthy man to break out of the circle into which he was born. This novel traces the fate of the self-made man, who builds his house and his destiny with his own hands. Gesualdo is a craftsman builder, intelligent, industrious and above all ambitious. He understands the coexistence of two overlapping social circles in Sicily, and he is determined to buy his way into the decadent aristocracy. As V. Masiello observes, the novel presents two worlds: "Da una parte il mondo fatiscente e decrepito della vecchia aristocrazia spiantata . . . Di fronte a questo mondo in sfacelo, il mondo, altrettanto cinico e brutale, dei *parvenus,* dei nuovi ricchi, che alla ricchezza sono ascesi attraverso l'improbo travaglio quotidiano, e quella ricchezza, che è costato sudori e fatiche, tenacemente e spietatamente difendono."[25]

Having risen above his own circle, Gesualdo plans a marriage alliance with the local nobility, the house of Trao, and dreams of founding a new dynasty. But here his grip on reality has paradoxically changed into self-deception. We are still caught in a vicious circle: Verga is describing the tragedy of materialism, which can be just as grim as the tragedy of poverty that he has already illustrated at the other end of the social scale. In the words of Giovanni Cecchetti, "the utter isolation born of greed, of ambition, and of the consequent inability to understand one another is the tragic theme of the novel."[26]

By marrying the silent and long-suffering Bianca Trao, Gesualdo Motta (now known as Mastro-don Gesualdo) has in theory forged a social link with the upper class. In practice, however, he has reneged on the social values of his own circle, and is effectively rejected by both groups.

The social links which he attempts to create are symbolized in the story by objects and poetic images. As already argued in the case of the three short stories, Verga's art in *Mastro-don Gesualdo* embraces both realistic and romantic themes, as well as a historical dimension. The symbolic objects most frequently associated with Mastro-don Gesualdo's social climbing are the ladders described as tools in the hands of the Motta family (Oscar Mondadori edition, p. 9), and the bridge constructed by Mastro-don Gesualdo and his co-workers (p. 76). The collapse of this bridge gives rise to different symbolic readings. It can be seen as signifying the evaporation of the protagonist's hopes, the failure of his marriage, and Bianca's failure to provide him with the heirs needed for the establishment of a new social order. It can also be interpreted as conveying Mastro-don Gesualdo's failure to bridge the two social circles. Then again, the broken bridge may symbolize the breakdown of relations with family, friends and his loyal servant Diodata who, ironically, has borne him two sons. Verga proves that while it may not be socially possible to bridge two different circles, it is artistically possible to do so. The merging of the figures of Bianca and her daughter Isabella constitutes one of the poetic highlights of the novel, as well as providing continuity between the earlier and later sections. The novel deals with identity, with being and becoming, with individuality and isolation. Isabella is not the daughter of the *nouveau-riche* Mastro-don Gesualdo; her dowry is provided by her father, the "baronello" Niní Rubiera, and it serves, together with Mastro-don Gesualdo's generous contributions, to support her husband's dissipated existence. Gesualdo Motta's failure to transfer from one social circle to another is contained in his two conflicting titles, "Mastro" and "Don". The combination of two classes, the artisan and the aristocratic, within one protagonist makes this man into one of Verga's most powerful tragic figures, caught between the contradictory social attitudes of two groups, and trapped in the vicious circle of social identity, which allows no man to escape his past.

In portraying figures such as Gramigna, Peppa, Malpelo, Turiddu, Lola and Gesualdo Motta, Verga creates universal fictional types, often containing echoes of earlier ages of storytelling, and carrying the reader back to the folk-tales and fairy-stories of childhood. The love of a "good girl" for a bandit is as illogical, and as compelling, as the tale of Beauty and the Beast. Rosso Malpelo is no Cinderella, but his situation is reminiscent of hers. Like Cinderella (or Snow White), he has lost the parent who represented love and kindness, and is left with a mother who lacks affection, and a sister who takes no interest in his well-being. Mastro-don Gesualdo, like a classic woodcutter's son, woos and wins a Princess. He exchanges his commonplace clothes and manners for sophisticated attire, and the right to die in a palace in Palermo.

Children reading fairy-stories probably do not ask the "inevitable" social questions: why a character is good or evil, or how love could overcome social and cultural differences. The truth of the stories lies in their psychological symbolism, not in social realism. It seems irrelevant to ask, in "The Sleeping Beauty", whether the wicked fairy was excluded from the christening because she was evil, or became evil because she was excluded. How exactly could love transform the ugliness of the Frog Prince? The classic fairy stories do not provide logical answers; theirs is a world of magic, where a fairy godmother can change everything with the wave of a wand. In drawing on these fictional archetypes, Verga cannot provide impossible solutions, but only the

harsh logic of a deprived and inhuman society. Rosso Malpelo has no fairy godmother. Gesualdo and his Bianca do not live happily ever after.

Verga's stories make a powerful appeal to the social consciousness of his reading public. This is not, however, a simple call for social reform, but a twofold appeal which contains somewhat contradictory messages. On the one hand there is a cry for the improvement of the quality of life for the deprived, who reside eternally within their vicious circle, like the damned in Dante. On the other hand there is a sharp warning to ignore the temptation to venture beyond the limits of one's own social circle.

Both Peppa and Rosso Malpelo have failed to escape to a better existence. Mastro Gesualdo Motta has become Don Gesualdo Motta, but at a terrible price. In this second, and last complete, novel of the projected cycle of *I vinti* ("The Vanquished"), Verga seems to underline the pessimistic conclusion that "il mondo è negozio." The poor can afford little or nothing. The wealthy may buy what they please, but each purchase must be paid for in bitter experience. The vicious circle remains unbroken.

Notes

1. This letter provides an excellent introduction to the work of Verga's maturity. D. Woolf (*The Art of Verga: A Study in Objectivity* (Sydney, 1977), pp. 115-16) argues that Verga conveys here the germ of an idea, rather than a fully-fledged theory, since there is no attempt to show how his future writing will differ from previous fiction.

2. Similar changes had been taking place in France, where there had been a steady development of realistic fiction since the days of Stendhal and Balzac. In particular, the treatment of Corsican traditions in Mérimée's *Colomba* (1840), and the presentation of the world of gypsies in the same author's *Carmen* (1846), had demonstrated the possibilities of regional literature and explored the effects of environment on the individual.

3. D. Woolf (*op. cit.*, pp. 96-103) draws a distinction between intellectual and emotional understanding in Verga's short stories, corresponding to two different degrees of objectivity.

4. For a comparative study of Manzoni and Verga, see F. Lanza, "Manzoni e Verga", in the (forthcoming) *Atti del convegno internazionale su Manzoni e l'Europa* (Viterbo, 1985)

5. See A. Alexander, *Giovanni Verga* (London, 1972), pp. 78-79.

6. G. Verga, *Lettere a Dina*, ed. G. Raya (Rome, 1962): letter of 18 February 1911.

7. D. H. Lawrence quotes the story in his preface to a collection of Verga's stories which he had translated: *Cavalleria Rusticana and Other Stories* (New York, 1928). B. Croce, in an article entitled "Dalle memorie di un critico" (*Critica,* 20 January 1916), stated that he had heard the story from Verga himself. L. Russo quotes Artuffo's article with the comment: "preziosa questa testimonianza diretta dello scrittore." (*G. Verga,* 5th ed. (Bari, 1955), p. 65).

8. A detailed study of Verga's language may be found in the following: T. De Mauro, *Storia linguistica dell'Italia unita* (Bari, 1963), *passim*; G. Devoto, "I piani del racconto", *Boll. Centro di studi filologici e linguistici siciliani* 2 (1954), 272-791; G. Ragonese, *Interpretazione del Verga* (Rome, 1977), pp. 184-287; G. Raya, *La lingua del Verga* (Florence, 1962); L. Spitzer, "L'originalità della narrazione nei *Malavoglia*", *Belfagor* 1 (1956), 37-53. For an assessment of the literary significance of Verga's prose the following should be consulted: M. Fubini, *Critica e poesia* (Bari, 1956), pp. 370-78; G. Devoto, *Profilo della storia linguistica italiana* (Florence, 1953), pp. 154-58; N. Sapegno, "La poetica dei veristi", quoted in G. Viti, *Verga verista* (Florence, 1970), pp. 281-83. One should take note of Petronio's opinion that Verga's language is completely artificial: see G. Petronio, *Dall'illuminismo al verismo* (Palermo, 1962), pp. 264-65; *id., L'attività letteraria in Italia* (Palermo, 1964); A. Navarria, *Lettura di poesia nell'opera di Giovanni Verga* (Florence, 1962); A. Navarria, *G. Verga* (Rome, 1964).

9. "La Sicilia già geograficamente fa mondo a sé in quanto isola; e in quanto fa mondo a sé l'isola. Sicilia può apparire allo sguardo contemplante come una realtà detemporalizzata" (S. Campailla, *Anatomie verghiane* (Bologna, 1978), pp. 110-11).

10. G. Cocchiara, *Popolo e letteratura in Italia* (Turin, 1959), pp. 456-62 (p. 456).

11. D. Woolf, *op. cit.,* p. 111.

12. The opening of the present essay referred to links between Verga's storytelling and the traditions of legend, fairy-story and chivalric romance. These will be examined later in the essay. But L. Russo sees a link with classical tragedy and its modern revivals. In relation to the theme of incest in "La lupa", he points out that Verga is following in the footsteps of the Greek poets and Alfieri: "Ormai sappiamo che questo è il suo ufficio nuovo: cogliere nei primitivi gli stessi drammi, che una letteratura dotta ha fino allora rappresentato in personaggi illustri" (L. Russo, *Giovanni Verga,* 4th edition (Bari, 1955), p. 122).

13. The figure of Gramigna is, however, based on fact. See L. Capuana, "La Sicilia nei canti popo-lari e nella novellistica contemporanea", in *Isola del sole,* ed. N. Giannota (Catania, 1893); A. Navarria, *op. cit.,* pp. 89-93.

14. The story was first published with the title "L'amante di Raja" in *Rivista minima* (Milan, February 1880), which was edited by S. Farina. It was reprinted with the present title, and with a shortened version of Verga's letter to Farina, in *Vita dei campi* (Milan, 1880). A third version is to be found in the 1897 version of the collection. The three versions of the tale reveal significant divergences of both presentation and narrative detail. My references are to the standard text of "L'amante di Gramigna", established by L. and V. Perroni (Milan, Mondadori, 1942). For a comparison of versions see A. Navarria, "'L'amante di Raja' e 'L'amante di Gramigna'", *Belfagor* (March 1951).

15. "Gramigna's treatment of Peppa and her acquiescence are further evidence that her interest is not in Gramigna himself but in his strength" (D. Woolf, *op. cit.,* p. 5). I am more willing to believe that Peppa's true desire is to break the vicious circle of rural customs and convention dominated by the "religione della roba". Her only hope rests upon a man whose very strength represents a threat to the social group.

16. See G. Marzot, "L'arte del Verga", *Estr. Annuario R. Ist. Fogazzaro* 5930 (1930), 35-37.

17. For a concise analysis of the structure and scene sequence of "Rosso Malpelo", see S. Campailla, *op. cit.,* pp. 157-219. The three most significant contributions to appear in the last decade are, in my opinion: R. Luperini, *Saggio su "Rosso Malpelo": Verga e le strutture narrative del realismo* (Padua, 1976); G. Baldi, "Ideologia e tecnica narrativa in 'Rosso Malpelo'", *Lettere italiane* 4 (1973), which also appears in his *L'artificio della regressione* (Naples, 1980); and G. Bàrberi Squarotti's chapter "Il filosofo nella cava", in his *Giovanni Verga: le finzioni dietro il verismo* (Palermo, 1982), pp. 91-148.

18. G. Bàrberi Squarotti, *op. cit.,* p. 97.

19. *Ibid.,* p. 134.

20. For an account of the events surrounding the adaptation of Verga's drama for the operatic stage, see A. Alexander, *op. cit.,* pp. 137-80.

21. D. Woolf, *op. cit.,* p. 11.

22. "Santa sa benissimo di condannare a morte Turiddu: la sua è una testimonianza di un testimone oculare, che giura, quindi, sull'assoluta verità di quanto dice" (G. Bàrberi Squarotti, *op. cit.,* p. 84).

23. In the *Canterbury Tales.* Such comic mixtures have had a long history. To quote a further ex-

ample, rustic and courtly elements had been fused by F. Romani in his libretto for Donizetti's opera *L'elisir d'amore* (1832).

24. Peppa flees from an unwanted marriage. Lola pursues social advancement through marriage. The short story "Pane nero", in the collection *Novelle rusticane,* could almost be called an illustrated guide to marriage in a rustic society. The novel *I Malavoglia* shows preparations for a marriage which does not take place.

25. V. Masiello, *Verga tra ideologia e realtà* (Bari, 1970) pp. 96-98.

26. G. Cecchetti, *Giovanni Verga* (Boston, 1978), p. 139.

Ulrich Weisstein (essay date 1989)

SOURCE: Weisstein, Ulrich. "Giovanni Verga's 'Cavalleria Rusticana': A Translator's Nightmare?" In *Comparative Literature East and West: Traditions and Trends,* edited by Cornelia N. Moore and Raymond A. Moody, pp. 91-106. Honolulu: College of Languages, Linguistics and Literature, University of Hawaii and the East-West Center, 1989.

[*In the following essay, Weisstein scrutinizes a number of adaptations and translations of "Cavalleria rusticana," analyzing their effect on the story's subsequent critical reception in Italy and abroad.*]

> "We have read the *Cavalleria rusticana*: a veritable blood-pudding of passion. It is not at all good, only in some odd way, comical, as the portentous tragic Italian is always comical."[1]
>
> D. H. Lawrence

The present undertaking, which focuses on a quartet of translations into English of Giovanni Verga's striking novella, forms part of a larger project, tentatively entitled "The Medium is the Message: Giovanni Verga's 'Cavalleria rusticana' as a Subject for Comparative Literature and the Comparative Arts," that is designed to encompass the whole range of transformations—translations, adaptations, and transpositions—which this small-scale masterpiece of Italian literature has undergone in the course of its history. The trajectory extends from the publication of the story itself in 1880, by way of the author's own stage version (written for Eleonora Duse) which premiered in 1884,[2] and Pietro Mascagni's one-act opera of 1890,[3] to D. H. Lawrence's 1928 English translation, and beyond.

Having been kept alive in consequence of this triple metamorphosis, **"Cavalleria rusticana"** could have (and certainly should have) become a canonical work, included in all standard anthologies of modern literature; unfortunately, that is not the case. For, in inverse proportion to its intrinsic merit, the opera, often performed in tandem with Ruggiero Leoncavallo's *Pagliacci* has taken much of the wind out of the novella's sails—to the point where many falsely assume, as did Lawrence,[4] that Verga himself was responsible for the libretto. In actual fact, the linguistically flat and dramaturgically flawed operatic text was written, without the author's knowledge—much less his consent—by G. Targioni-Tozzetti and G. Menasci, who came to Mascagni's rescue when the latter, who wanted to enter a competition launched by the Milan music publisher Sonzogno, was left in the lurch by professional writers. Oddly enough, and much to his own surprise, Mascagni triumphed over the other competitors, more than seventy in all, and was on his way to a successful, though in hindsight not overly distinguished, career as head of the *verismo* School that swept the musical stages of Europe in the final decade of the nineteenth century.

What I shall seek to demonstrate in the more comprehensive study of which this essay constitutes a large and fairly self-contained segment, is the fact that in this instance, as in many similar ones, the further one moves away from the original medium, the greater the loss from an artistic point of view and the less forceful the message. However, redeeming features may surface, from time to time, in the other media in which it finds itself ensconced. More precisely, the translations of **"Cavalleria rusticana"** which I shall scrutinize in the following pages are, almost across the board and in numerous ways still to be detailed, patently inferior to the model, not only because the resources available in the target language are inadequate but also, and specifically in D. H. Lawrence's case, because the translator's linguistic competence left much to be desired. Thus, it comes to pass that, while creative treason is knowingly committed on occasion, unknowingly perpetrated betrayal (in the form of blunders, slip-ups and stylistic infelicities) carries the day. The fear of falling into such traps engenders, even in the most conscientious renditioners, a translatorial nightmare which is hard to shake off and which must be held ultimately responsible for the work's failure to reach out beyond it's innate linguistic borders.

Whether explicitly or implicitly, creative treason is also bound to occur in the transfer of a work from one medium, and/or genre, to another. Thus, in adapting his novella for the stage, Verga knew full well that he was making concessions to popular taste and to the conventions of late nineteenth-century melodrama; and, for good measure, he added artistically superfluous folkloristic trappings. And Mascagni, ever his true self in hankering after theatrical effect, shamelessly exploited not only the music of Bizet's *Carmen* and Verdi's *Otello* but added a hefty dose of overblown musical rhetoric.

Verga himself never doubted that the novella, which manifests an uncompromising "will to style," was superior to the drama of his own making, a view which was shared by his finest critical exponent, Luigi Russo, although not, for example, by Benedetto Croce.[5]

Before engaging in the task of comparatively assessing a foursome of English versions of **"Cavalleria rusticana,"** I must briefly touch upon the prehistory of that novella. As is so often the case with fiction of the veristic kind, of which this is an outstanding example, Verga's novella harks back to a *fait divers* ("historical anecdote") or series of events said to have taken place fifteen years prior to its creation. The sensational happenings which lie at its heart were summarized in the appendix of a memoir written almost a hundred years after the fact by Verga's longtime friend Giuseppe Paterno. I will reproduce it here in full because the account, never before translated into English, is hard to come by even in the original Italian. It runs as follows:

> This, one of Giovanni Verga's best novellas, is based on an actual story that occurred in Vizzini in the year 1865. Its protagonists were: Turridu; Lucia, his mother; Santuzza, an orphan; "Uncle" Cosimo, an old bachelor and Lucia's assistant in her wine shop; Alfio, a *mafioso* and head of the Vizzini carters; and Lola, an eighteen-year old, beautiful and star-eyed girl, the daughter of a rich man.
>
> This is what happened: Turridu, the twenty-year-old son of Lucia, the owner of a wine shop on the *piazetta* Santa Teresa in Vizzini, was engaged to marry Lola after his return from military service which, at that time, lasted between three and four years. Assigned to the Bersaglieri corps, he departed for Palermo.
>
> In the beginning, the two young people corresponded regularly, but less frequently so after a few months, so that it seemed that Turridu had forgotten Lola, his first love. Lola's parents realized that it would be useless to wait for Turridu, for with the passing years young maidens turn into spinsters. So they decided to give their daughter a husband, in view of the fact that Alfio, a mature and handsome man of forty-two, owner of a horse-and-buggy as well as a stable, and a house with garden and bower, had persistently courted Lola. The marriage was arranged, and the wedding celebrated, in the presence of the parents and their friends and neighbors, with music, dance, and song.
>
> The first years of marriage passed quietly and happily; but unfortunately no child was born to the pair. After four long years, Turridu was discharged from the army and returned home to embrace his old mother who, during his absence, had enjoyed the precious company of the beautiful fifteen-year-old orphan Santuzza, who was helping her like a true daughter while "Uncle" Cosimo assisted her in the wine shop. *Mamma* Lucia had raised Santuzza in every way at her convenience and, in her heart, had prepared a new spouse for Turridu since Lola had married Alfio. The affectionate mother had even prepared a layette for their baby; for she had shrewdly guessed that Turridu and Santuzza were having an affair and hoped that after the imminent Easter holidays their marriage could be sealed.
>
> In the few months that had elapsed since Turridu's return, his first love, never forgotten, had reawakened, and he had entered into the heart of the witch Lola, who enticed him with all the arts at the disposal of an evil woman, deceiving Alfio, who, unaware of her adultery, was busy with his work as a carter hauling wine barrels and foodstuffs from Vizzini to Francofonte, Militello, and Gramichele, spending lots of money to adorn his beautiful Lola with rings, as if she were the queen of the land.
>
> Lucia's fervent attempts to dissuade her son from his wild plans did not succeed, nor did Santuzza's reproofs and admonitions. Finally, racked with jealousy, the latter told Alfio to keep Lola in check. At this warning, Alfio swore vengeance and told Santuzza he would teach her a lesson if she had not told him the truth. Duly forewarned, he verified the facts, and on Easter eve, in Lucia's shop, when Turridu offered him a glass of wine, he replied: "Your wine poisons my blood," threw the glass at his rival's feet, approached him in order to embrace him and kiss him with a small bite on the ear as a sign of his challenge. The challenge was accepted, and on Easter morning, in a rustic duel on the floor of the tannery, Turridu was killed, drowning in his own blood.[6]

It would be interesting to show in detail how Verga used the facts reported in this or some other account,[7] which features he retained, eliminated, or modified, what new elements he added, and how he reassembled the mosaic pieces into his novella. It would be equally interesting to show, with reference to the text of the stage adaptation, for example, how, in the theatrical version, Verga restored certain facts reported in his source, such as Lucia being a prosperous wine seller rather than an impoverished widow, and Santa-Santuzza an orphan rather than the daughter of a wealthy farmer. Both inquiries would, however, far exceed the limits of this paper.

As for the genesis of Verga's novella, it should be noted that, according to Francesco de Roberto, whose article "Stato civile della *Cavalleria rusticana*" is richly illustrated with photographs depicting the pertinent Sicilian localities, the most salient moment of the action, the bite on the ear that signifies the so-called *fida* ("challenge"), was, to use a Goethean term, the *Ur-Erlebnis,* the primitive core around which the narrative crystallized. Nor should we forget that what became an autonomous work fending for itself was originally meant for inclusion in Verga's first major novel, *I Malavoglia.*[8] When Verga decided to remove it from that context, he published it separately in the Sunday supplement of the newspaper *Fanfulla* on March 10, 1880. The evidence, scrutinized by Giovanni Cecchetti and Paolo Marchi among others,[9] shows that this early version of **"Cavalleria rusticana"** is fairly close to but not fully identical with the standard version found in the volume **Vita dei Campi,**[10] which has formed the sole basis for all subsequent editions and translations, from which it differs in several ways.

There are some minor discrepancies in punctuation and in the use of grammatical forms, for example, as well as in the choice of certain words (*giubba* instead of *farsetto*), phrases ("non fanno farina" in lieu of "non ne affastellano sarmenti"), and entire sentences ("Turridu morse leggermente il lobo dell'orecchio del carretiere" instead of the slightly more refined "Turridu strinse fra i denti l'orecchio del carretiere"). By far the most striking and, in my opinion, subtly calculated emendation concerns the dying Turridu's words at the end of the story. In the *Fanfulla della domenica* version, our protagonist cries "Ah! la mia povera vecchia!" but in the standard text he simply exclaims "Ah! mamma mia!" It could be argued that this change is for the better; for while the first exclamation, consistent with the sentiment expressed throughout the final episode (which offers "la mia vecchierella" and "la mia vecchia" as well), is too predictable and perhaps too much in character to serve as an effective punch line, the latter, at once more banal and more succinct, underscores, in its pointed reference to Santa's repartee at the end of her second conversation with Turridu, the existential irony of the situation.

Let us turn to the novella itself and to its four English offspring.[11] To translate a narrative like **"Cavalleria rusticana"** successfully demands that the translator convey not only the text's literal, metaphorical, and symbolic meaning, but its stylistic *and* linguistic peculiarities as well; for, with regard to language, Verga's story exists on three different levels which occasionally intermesh: 1) the rarely used Sicilian dialect (some would regard it as a separate language); 2) the pervasive presence of lexical and syntactic Sicilianisms, and 3) the solid underpinning provided by standard literary Italian. If he has an ear attuned to linguistic nuances, the translator will quickly realize that he must find a way of reproducing or recreating the interplay between the second and third levels. (For purists like Luigi Russo and several modern editors of Verga's prose, this cohabitation was a clear sign of artistic immaturity and, hence, a constant source of irritation.[12])

In **"Cavalleria rusticana,"** the actual use of Sicilian parlance is limited to a single proverb ("facemo cuntu ca chioppi e scampau, e la nostra amicizia finiu," meaning, roughly, "let's forget about the past") which the jilted lover Turridu hurls at Lola, terminating their first conversation. What is the translator to do in this instance, given the fact that even Italian editors feel compelled to resort to commentary and/or literal translation? He will want to follow suit, as does the reliable Cecchetti ("Let's pretend it rained, then cleared up, and our friendship is over," footnoted "a Sicilian saying that means 'Let's forget completely about everything connected with the past'"). D. H. Lawrence, on the other hand, by italicizing and thereby estranging the passage, alerts the reader to its special status. For the rest,

Lawrence does the author, and his audience, a disservice by refashioning parts of the dialogue in the patois of his native Nottinghamshire. For example, Turridu's words (or, rather, his thoughts) "Voglio fargliela sotto gli occhi a quella cagnaccia" appear as "I'll show that bitch summat, afore I've done," a passage Cecchetti renders straightforwardly as "I'll get even with her right under her eyes, the dirty bitch."

As for the lexical and syntactic "idiotisms" which abound in the novella to the point where, cumulatively, they constitute its dominant stylistic feature, all are fully documented in the apparatus of various scholarly editions. In Gino Tellini's edition of Verga's work, for example, **"Cavalleria rusticana"** is supported by thirty-nine explanatory footnotes.[13] Luigi Russo, among others, even goes to the trouble of showing how, in the lexical sphere, Verga often wavered between Sicilianisms and Tuscanisms and to what extent his grammatical quirks are reflections of an oral style that is characteristic of the "folk." Thus, while the label *babbo,* which is attached to Santa's father, is common in Florence, *massaro,* the term used to fixate the civic status of Lola's father, has a distinctly Southern ring, and *-ste,* the short form for *queste* used throughout the novella, is used colloquially in both the North and the South.

On the syntactical side, the postpositional repetition of certain words or phrases—"quanto ci siete voi che la gna Lola non è degno di portarvi le scarpe, non è degna" and "Per voi tirerei su tutta la casa, tirerei," for instance—is a particularly effective means of conveying a sense of orality. What are translators (those highly vulnerable amphibious creatures) to make of this stylistic *mélange,* and how are they to convey across the linguistic chasm that separates languages the anomalies caused by the seemingly random interweaving of pure dialect, "stylized" dialect and standard literary Italian? If it is hard for readers from Torino, Venice, or Milan to cope with this problem, how much harder must it be for translators and their public. A solution like the one which Eric Bentley preferred in his early translations of Bertolt Brecht's dramas—that of using the standard language throughout, with only minor deviations—will hardly suffice.

Let us test the waters by scrutinizing the four versions of the phrase cited at the beginning of the previous paragraph, "la gna Lola non è degno di portarvi le scarpe, non è degno." None of the translators offers a literal rendition but, as usual, Cecchetti's apt formulation ("Lola doesn't deserve to carry your shoes, she doesn't"), in its outright colloquialism, comes closest to echoing the spirit as well as the letter of the original, while that of the pseudonymous "Alma Strettel" ("For Mistress Lola isn't worthy to wear your shoes, that she isn't") is marred by a lexical error ("wear" for "carry") and suffers from the rhythmically disturbing use of the emphatic "that" after the comma. Lawrence's "Lola's not fit to bring you your shoes, she is not" brings no improvement, for, in addition to scorning the colloquial ellipsis "isn't" in the second instance, it employs "bring" instead of "carry," and labors under the redundancy "you your." Alexander's version ("Lola is nothing, she is not even fit to clean your shoes"), finally, is altogether out of the running and deserves to be castigated not only by the Beckmessers among the critical *Merker*, who will find it offensive on at least three counts: firstly, for the awkward syntactical parallelism "Lola . . . she"; secondly, for the substitution of "clean" for "carry" ("tie your shoes" might have done the trick); and thirdly, for dropping the repetition.

In order to underscore my second point, I would like to examine a sentence which, as Russo has pointed out, demonstrates how Verga intermingles the Sicilian and Tuscan tongues in **"Cavalleria rusticana."** The sentence, "La vigilia di Pasqua avevano sul desco un piatto di salsiccia," elicits the following comment from Russo: "That *Salsiccio* is most fortunate, (reflecting) the singular-plural preferred in the Sicilian tongue. (A Tuscan would have seen 'un piatto di salsicci'.) But the *desco* sounds a bit too Tuscan and learned to me and has no Verghian ring to it."[14]

Here, to judge by our fourfold sampling, the translators have thrown in the towel. Thus, even though Italian by birth and sensitive to regional usage, Cecchetti simply repeats Lawrence's bland "They had a dish of sausages on the table" (which, in turn, goes back to Alma Strettel's translation), and Alexander ("They had a plateful of sausages on the table") follows suit. They all sweep the linguistic problem under the rug. In fact, a comparative study of their translations makes it clear that in this case there are simply too many hurdles placed in the path of a perfect translation.

Taken by themselves, simple mistakes or oversights in the rendition of terms, technical or otherwise, may be innocuous; but they can have a devastating cumulative effect, to the point of subverting the overall meaning. In the English versions of **"Cavalleria rusticana,"** we come across various instances of such lexical perversion. Alma Strettel, for instance, takes the word *ballatoio* ("terrace" or "balcony") to mean "dancing floor," on the assumption that it is derived from *ballo* ("dance" or "Ball"). Less offensive but more than mildly annoying is the practice, fairly common among modern translators, of retaining a word in its original form and explaining it in a footnote, presumably because they regard it as untranslatable or wish to stress the Otherness of the setting. Thus Alma Strettel keeps, but comments on, *mantellina* ("cape" or "small cloak"), Lawrence and Cecchetti explicate the meaning of *ballatoio*, and Cecchetti, for reasons of his own, leaves Turridu's "Ah! mamma mia!" in the original Italian.

While these terms are certainly familiar to Verga's compatriots, some Italian editors have found it necessary to provide a brief semantic analysis of designations like *gna, massaro,* and *compare,* labels and forms of address which serve as indicators of the socio-economic standing of the persons to whom they are attached. The same applies to place names such as Licodia, Francofonte, and Canziria, which will sound just as strange and distant to most Italians as they do to Londoners and New Yorkers.

Both semantically and grammatically, Lawrence was greatly handicapped by his "little Italian and less Sicilian." Due to his patent linguistic shortcomings, he totally missed, among other things, the point made by Alfio in his final words to the dying Turridu: "Ora tua madre lascerà stare le galline" ("Now your mother will leave the chickens alone"). Turning the intended meaning upside down, he wrote: "And now your mother can mind her fowls." And in the phrase "il berretto rosso, che sembrava quello della buona ventura," which occurs in the opening paragraph of the story, he loses sight of the qualifying *dello,* making the fortune teller himself take the place of his cap in the analogy. More significantly, as far as the psychological tone of the narrative is concerned, he misunderstands or misrepresents Turridu's pointed and poignant reference to the far-off place where he was stationed and where "si perdeva persino il nome del nostro paese" ("where even the name of our town was lost," as Cecchetti puts it). Writing "I'd almost forgotten even the name of where I came from," Lawrence changes the perspective; for what Verga meant to say, unquestionably, was not that Lola's lover had forgotten her and the whole affair but that, being so far away, he himself had been lost sight of.

More far-reaching yet easily defined are translatorial choices which affect what one might call the atmosphere of Verga's novella, i.e., the emotional and psychological aura in which the characters are bathed and which cements their personal and social relationship. Lawrence, in particular, shows a startling lack of sensitivity with regard to these more or less intangible but essential values. Perhaps the most striking illustration of this lack of *Fingerspitzengefühl* ("tact") is his rendition of the sentence with which, speaking euphemistically, Alfio invites Turridu to the duel: "Se domattina volete venire nei ficchidindia della Canziria, potremo parlare di quell'affare, compare," which Cecchetti, skipping the concluding form of address, renders "If you want to come to the cactuses of Canziria tomorrow, we can talk about that business."

Throughout **"Cavalleria rusticana,"** *compare* is used noncommittally in polite intercourse: Lola and Alfio greeting Turridu (perhaps with some condescension), and Santa addressing Alfio. Alma Strettel, in whose rendition *compare* usually appears as "Master" (an expression that sounds quaint to the ears of a late twentieth-century reader, who would probably associate it with British upper middle-class schoolboys) here deviates from her own norm by using "comrade," while Alexander simply italicizes Verga's term. Lawrence, who drops the label in all other instances, here, oddly enough, feels called upon to use a word with strongly contemptuous overtones. In his painfully contorted translation, the sentence reads: "Shall you come to the cactus grove at Canziria to-morrow morning, and we can talk about that bit of business of ours, boy?" By doing so, he conveys a sense of moral superiority on Alfio's part that is distinctly absent from the original, where the two rivals, about to engage in what one may well regard as a tribal ritual, appear as equals. Precisely for that reason, Alma Strettel's "comrade," though somewhat ironic, comes much closer to hitting the mark.

One particularly illuminating example of how translators, regardless of their linguistic skills, are bound to succeed in communicating a weighty *double entendre* due to a semantic kinship between the source and target languages relates to a cluster of diminutives which Verga employs to pinpoint important sentimental and socio-economic aspects of his novella. On the affective side, Turridu, having been jilted by Lola and feeling down in the mouth, is described, early on, as a *poveraccio*—rendered "poor fellow," "poor man," "poor chap," and "poor devil" respectively by Alma Strettel, Lawrence, Alexander, and Cecchetti—but his use of the epithet in regard to his mother also indicates their state of impoverishment and the fact that, in contrast to Santa and Lola, he neither comes from nor will marry into a prosperous family.

Gna Nunzia is, in her own words, not only a *vecchierella* ("poor old woman" [Lawrence, Alexander, and Cecchetti] and "my old woman" [Alexander]) but, quite distinctly, a *poveretta* ("poor mother" [Alma Strettel], "poor old mother" [Lawrence], "mother" [Alexander], and, most propitiously, "poor woman" [Cecchetti]) who, in order to survive during her son's long absence, had to sell her most precious possessions, the bay mule and the small piece (*pezzetto*) of land used for cultivating grapes. To be poor, then, in the world depicted in this narrative, means not only to be an object of pity but also to have a low socio-economic status.

What adds spice and esthetic significance in this case is the realignment of the diminutives which Verga, going back to the historical anecdote, decided to use when preparing his adaptation for the stage. In the drama, these belittling and/or prettifying suffixes are no longer assigned to Turridu and his mother, whose affluence now makes her appear as a veritable pillar of village society, but to Santa (re-)transformed into the pregnant orphan Santuzza. As the Italian scholar Vann Bosco-

Malvica has demonstrated in an essay specifically concerned with such *altérés*, the relocation of the diminutives is a telling sign of "la participation affective de l'auteur à un personnage du drame dont il a changé l'importance et le caractère."[15] Artistically, this change of emphasis is harmful in so far as sentiment turns into sentimentality and takes on a maudlin and, at least in Mascagni's opera, a pathetic, if not downright pathological, cast.[16]

In an astonishing variety of ways, translatorial fidelity can be tested with regard to realms other than the linguistic one which, rightly or wrongly, tends to dominate most scholarly analyses of the *traducteur*'s martyrial acts of faith. In the English versions of **"Cavalleria rusticana,"** for example, the observant reader is bound to notice certain inconsistencies on what may be called the micro- or macro-structural levels. To begin with the former: as an author, Giovanni Verga had a special way of paragraphing his text by segmenting narrative matter into units that are not separated in accordance with units of setting or action but manifest a programmatic preference for bracketing contrasting phenomena. In doing so, he creates a shock effect that is felt not so much in the first reading as in the subsequent perusals of the novella.

In all Italian versions of **"Cavalleria rusticana,"** including the original text published in *Fanfulla della domenica*, the first paragraph, here given in Cecchetti's translation, looks as follows:

> When Turridu Macca, Nunzia's son, came back from the service, he used to strut in the square on Sundays in his *bersagliere*'s uniform with the red cap that looked like the one worn by the fortune teller who sets up a bench with a cage of canaries. The girls, on the way to Mass, their noses in their mantillas, eyed him longingly, and the urchins buzzed around him like flies. He had also brought a pipe with a carving of the king on horseback that seemed alive, and he lit his matches on the rear of his pants, lifting his leg as if giving a kick. But in spite of all this, *massaro* Angelo's daughter, Lola, had not shown herself at Mass or on her balcony because she had become engaged to a certain man from Licodia, a cart driver who had four mules in his stable. As soon as Turridu found out, damn it! he was going to tear that Licodian's guts from his belly, he was! But he did nothing of the kind and vented his rage by singing all the scornful songs he knew under the girl's window.

The actions and events which Verga telescopes into a single paragraph—Turridu's return from military service, his braggadocio, the townspeople's behavior, the explanation for Lola's absence, and finally Turridu's rather violent reaction to the news that Lola is about to be married—could easily have been divided into a number of distinct segments. What, in a "realistic" account, might have required four or five pages of elaborate description and psychological analysis, is here, thanks to the author's art of concision, imbibed from his great model, Guy de Maupassant, and the sparing use of characteristic detail crammed into a single paragraph occupying less than twenty lines on the page.

None of the four translators of the novella whose efforts we are scrutinizing seems to have found this authorial *tour de force* to his or her liking; for none of them has stuck to Verga's guns. Thus, while Cecchetti divides the paragraph into two halves of approximately equal length (from "Turridu Macca" to "kick," and from "But in spite of all this" to "window"), Alma Strettel and Lawrence, adding a *fermata* after "stable," opt for a tripartite scheme, and Alexander, breaking after "canaries" as well, a quadripartite one.

In the case of a similarly sutured paragraph—"Turridu went back to greet her so often that Santa noticed it and slammed the window in his face. The neighbors pointed out the bersagliere with a smile or a nod when he passed. Lola's husband was making his round of the fairs with his mules"—there are no traitors, perhaps because the translators realized that three one-sentence paragraphs in a row would look odd. But in this instance, the usually alert Cecchetti "nods" when he attaches Lola's final words in the preceding dialogue ("If you want to greet me, you know where I live") to the auctorial narrative which follows it, thereby disrupting the carefully calculated rhythmic alternation of narration and dialogue which is a hallmark of Verga's style.

On a more modest scale, the test of "beautiful fidelity" can be applied to the handling of two ellipses in the text of **"Cavalleria rusticana."** As the evidence shows, one of these, marking a significant gap or *Leerstelle*—to use a term associated with Wolfgang Iser's version of reader response theory—has been uniformly retained, whereas the other was just as uniformly ignored. The translators' adherence to the model manifests itself with regard to the proverb "Le volpe quando all'uva non ci poté arrivare . . ." ("when the fox couldn't reach the grapes . . .") whose conclusion Santa aborts and which the quick-witted Turridu completes capriciously: "Disse: come sei bella, *racinedda* mia" ("he said: how beautiful you are, my sweet little grape!"), turning the situation to his own advantage.

The second use of ellipsis, following Lola's remarks "lasciate mi raggiungere le mie compagne. Che direbbero il paese se mi vedessero con voi . . ." ("let me catch up with my friends. What would they say in town if they saw me with you?"), seems to have been overlooked because it is much less conspicuous, although perhaps no less important; for it seems to be the author's way of indicating that her answer, perfectly reasonable within the context as a reflection of the prevailing social norms, is decidedly inconclusive in so far as Lola, newly attracted to the youth, would much rather continue the conversation.

One of the most challenging tasks awaiting the translator as "structuralist" is that of charting and conveying whatever patterns the author of the original text may have established, whether in the form of central images or the repetitive use of key words or phrases. To ignore such constellations, whether out of indifference or in the presumed knowledge that it would be hard, if not impossible, to retain them in the target language, is tantamount to ignoring authorial intentions and thus to subverting, in certain instances, the inherent sense of a passage or even the entire piece. In a narrative as succinct as **"Cavalleria rusticana,"** where such constellations abound, they are obviously significant and must be re-created.

Verga uses simple but "loaded" repetitions which can be divided into two different but related groups: one occurs within a given dialogue where a key word or phrase is bounced back and forth between two speakers like a ball; the other is usually re-introduced toward the end of a narrative section, and prods the reader to measure the distance between two points. **"Cavalleria rusticana"** offers two striking examples of the former kind, one in a quick-fire exchange between Santa and Turridu, and the other in the less animated but extremely poignant conversation between Lola and her ex-fiancé. In the first instance, the pivotal verb is *mangiare* ("to eat"), and in the second *salutare* ("to greet").

As one Italian critic has noted, the metaphorical use of *mangiare,* endemic throughout the novella, is eloquent proof that Verga sought to keep his figures down to earth while concurrently investing their speech with symbolic strength. In the bantering exchange between Turridu and Santa, application is made when, the girl having rebuffed her impetuous suitor's advances ("Ohé! quelle mani, compare Turridu!" ["Hey! watch those hands, Turridu!"]), the following battle of wits ensues:

TURRIDU:

Avete paura che vi mangi?

SANTA:

Paura non ho, ne de voi ne del vostro Dio.

TURRIDU:

Eh! vostra madre era di Licodia, lo sappiamo. Avete il sangue risosso. Uh! che vi mangerei cogli occhi!

SANTA:

Mangiatemi pure cogli occhi, che bricciole non ne faremo . . .

. . . . .

(TURRIDU:

Are you afraid I'll eat you?

SANTA:

I'm not afraid of you or your God.

TURRIDU:

> Eh! your mother was from Licodia, we know that you've got fighting blood! Uh! I'd eat you with my eyes!

SANTA:

> Go ahead and eat me with your eyes, and we won't leave any crumbs!)

The eating here is done figuratively with the eyes rather than, literally, with the mouth—with obvious implications. In any case, our four translators had no difficulty being consistent on both levels; for in both Italian and English, as in most Western languages for that matter, the cannibalistic implications of kissing and loving signify male possessiveness.

The verb which dominates the other interchange is more subtly shaded, and at least two of the four translators failed to see, or at least express, the inherent sexual innuendo. Here is the text of the passage I have in mind:

> Lola che ascoltava ogni sera, nascosta dietro il vaso di basilico, e si faceva pallida e rossa, un giorno chiamò Turridu.
>
> "E così, compare Turridu, gli amici vecchi non si salutano più?"
>
> "Ma, sospirò il giovinetto, beato chi può salutarvi."
>
> "Si avete intenzione di salutarmi, lo sapete dove sto di casa" rispose Lola.
>
> Turridu torno a salutarla così spesso che Santa se ne avvide e gli batte la finestra sul muso.
> . . . . .
> (Lola, who listened every evening, hidden behind a pot of sweet basil, and turned pale and red, one day called Turridu.
>
> "And so, Turridu, old friends don't greet each other any more?"
>
> "Well . . ." sighed the young man, "it's a lucky person who can greet you!"
>
> "If you want to greet me, you know where I live," answered Lola.
>
> Turridu went back to greet her so often that Santa noticed it and slammed the window in his face.)

Surely, the reader is given to understand that Lola, to use an expression introduced by Santa when she broaches the matter to Alfio, the carter, is inviting Turridu to "adorn his house for him." This is confirmed by the narrator's ironic stance ("Turridu tornò a salutarla così spesso") as well as by subsequent events.

Further improving his record of accuracy, Cecchetti gets the message and safely conveys it by using "greet" consistently throughout the passage. Alma Strettel does not lag far behind but slightly mars her record by using the circumlocution "if you have any intentions of bringing me your greetings." Lawrence, missing the point,

substitutes "speak" for "greet," while Alexander, settling on the sequence "know . . . say hello . . . see . . . see" upsets the apple cart. (He could have exploited, instead, the Biblical sense of "knowing.")

The second kind of repetition, bracketing, is exemplified by the recurrent use of an idiomatic expression denoting anger and shame. The first time Verga brings the phrase into play, he does so in order to characterize Lola's socially correct behavior in her first encounter with the newly discharged Turridu: "Finalmente Turridu imbattè in Lola, che tornava dal *viaggio* alla Madonna del Pericolo, e al vederlo non si fece ni bianca ni rossa" ("He finally ran into Lola, who was returning from a pilgrimage to Our Lady of Peril, and, seeing him, she turned neither white nor red, as if it were none of her business"). The telling phrase resurfaces when Lola, hiding behind the pot of basil, turns both pale and red (*pallida e rossa*). The distance between two points in the narrative measured here is that between a girl formally promised to a man other than the one she loves but outwardly in full control of her feelings, and a married woman unable to suppress her continued emotional *engagement*.

How have the four translators coped with this, by all appearances, simple problem? Fairly well, on the whole, in so far as three of them—Alma Strettel, Cecchetti, and Alexander—retain the nuance implied by the progression from *bianco* to *pallido,* the one invoking the proverbial maiden color and maiden blush, and the other denoting the anguish and wrath of a woman chastened by marriage. True to form, Lawrence botches the matter; for his Lola, rather than turning red and white/pale, never "turn(s) a hair" and goes "hot and cold by turns."

Let us round out the survey by glancing at three additional cases of bunching in **"Cavalleria rusticana"** and their equivalents in the four English-language versions. A small grouping of terms that is more than a mere *quantité négligeable* pertains to Sicily's flourishing oenoculture. I have mentioned the relevant passage in connection with the proverb that is left hanging, with the expected word *uva* ("grape") being replaced by *racinedda* ("little raisin" or "sweet little grape"). But this is not the only time that grapes are mentioned, as Lola later tells her reinstated lover, who seeks to dissuade her from going to confession, that she has dreamt of black grapes, an evil omen, and must therefore do penance: "Domenica voglio andare a confessarmi, che stanotte ho sognato dell'uva nera." We thus get the sequence *uva, racinedda, uva nera,* which propels us from the grape, Lola, whom the fox, Turridu, cannot obtain, to the sweet Santa, whom he takes to be easier prey, and the self-fulfilling prophecy of a nightmare.

It is easy to see why this would be a real crux for the translator. To begin with the well informed and usually reliable Cecchetti, in his version we have "grapes," followed by "sweet little grapes," and then by the ominous "black grapes," which are duly footnoted, as they are in two of the other renditions. Not quite sure what to make of the slightly awkward *racinedda,* Alma Strettel moves from "grapes" to "little cluster" and on to "black grapes," while Alexander has "grapes," "sweet little thing," and "black grapes" respectively. The test of translatorial strength thus comes clearly with the term of endearment applied to Santa. All's not well with the above solutions, and one cannot help but admiring Lawrence for his bold choice of "little gooseberry," on the grounds that, by introducing this vulgar designation for the female breast, the English author, although roughening the discourse, succeeds in conveying the sexual overtones.

Still another frequently mentioned item on the list of familiar things which collectively make up the world in which Verga's characters live (and with which the narrator, in truly veristic fashion, seeks to identify as closely as possible) is the *berretto* ("cap"), which, so the Italian editors tell us, is worn in the country side, unlike the *cappello* ("hat"), which is worn by city dwellers. In **"Cavalleria rusticana,"** two kinds of *berretto* are featured: the red "fez" of the *bersagliere* Turridu, which becomes an object of universal admiration; and the ordinary white one worn by the carter Alfio.[17] Proud man that he is, the latter initially wears it over his ears, but at the end, on the way to the duelling place, he pulls it over his eyes, so as to blot out the world and, presumably, hide his shame. Thus, the reader must cope with the sequence *berretto rosso, berretto, berretto sull' orecchio,* and *berretto sugli occhi,* introduced in that order.

Regardless of whether the translators render *berretto* with "cap" (Alma Strettel and Cecchetti), "fez cap" (Lawrence) or "red cap" (Alexander), nothing will prevent them from being literal in the first two instances, while in the fourth, that of the *berretto* worn *sugli occhi,* it is more or less a matter of phrasing. The crucial link in the chain, linguistically speaking, is the cap worn *sull' orecchio*; for here the literal translation preferred by three members of our quartet—"cap on the ear" (Alma Strettel), "cap over the ear" (Lawrence) and "caps right over their ears" (Alexander)—will not strike the anglophone reader as familiar and will make sense only in context. Only Cecchetti's rendition ("chip on their shoulders") does justice to the idiomatic phrase, albeit at the price of breaking the mold, which seems worth paying in this instance.

The most comprehensive and pervasive pattern by far is that which relates to the act of seeing. It offers relatively few problems to the translator of **"Cavalleria rusticana"** in so far as its word field is, for all practical purposes, limited to the verb *vedere* ("to see") and the pertinent sense organ, *occhio* ("eye"), which, used for weeping (*piangere*) as well as viewing, functions in a variety of ways. It not only serves to confirm the patent truth of external reality ("ho visto co miei occhi") but also as a channel for desire ("ti mangerei cogli occhi"). On the opposite pole of the semantic spectrum, the obverse condition, that of blindness, prevails, signaling the muting of the world, either literally or figuratively.

Verga makes especially cogent use of this web in the concluding portion of the novella, where he describes the duel between Alfio and Turridu, preceded by their common walk. Turridu opens the conversation by telling his rival that he has decided to fight it out, rather than let himself be killed as the guilty party he is, because he has *seen* his mother feed the chickens ("Ho visto la mia vecchia che si era alzata per vedermi partire, col pretesto di governare il pollaio"). He continues to see her in his mind's eye as he opens the duel by stabbing Alfio, emblematically, in the groin: "Ora che ho visto la mia vecchia nel pollaio, mi pare di averla sempre dinanzi agli occhi" ("Now that I've seen my old mother in the chicken coop, she seems to be always before my eyes"). Alfio responds, first by asking him, sarcastically, to *open his eyes* ("Apriteli bene, gli occhi!") and then by blinding him with a handful of dust he has gathered from the ground ("Acchiappò rapidamente una manata di polvere e la gettò negli occhi dell'avversario"). In so doing, he inflicts upon Turridu the very punishment which, earlier, he had threatened to mete out to Santa and her entire family should she have falsely accused his wife ("Se non avete visto bene, non vi lascierò gli occhi per piangere, a voi e a tutto il vostro parentado"). As we can see, this is an exceptionally rich pattern, but one that, fortunately, even the least able of translators is unlikely to distort beyond recognition.

I have reached the end of my journey. What this comparative study of four English versions of **"Cavalleria rusticana,"** although by no means complete, has shown, with the help of a large number of illustrations meant to characterize the various levels of discourse with which the translator has to cope, is that in spite of the many pitfalls, whether lexical, grammatical, syntactic, semantic or structural, the original can, after all, be satisfactorily rendered, as is the case with Cecchetti's translation. While Alma Strettel's rendition strikes one, at least in hindsight, as being rather coy and slightly prettifying, Alexander's version sins by its inconsistency, which at times borders on capriciousness, while Lawrence's attempt, marred by many lapses and some overly bold deviations from the original, strikes one as being more of a recreation than a translation in the ordinary sense. None of these texts are complete disasters, however; and the real translatorial nightmare they might have engendered begins only when the transfer is not merely from language to language, as is here the case, but from one genre or medium (novella to drama, and drama to opera) to another. It is there that, a veritable Doppelgänger, the Mephistophelean *traditore* steps out of the shadow of the well-intentioned but easily side-tracked *traduttore*.

Notes

1. D. H. Lawrence, *Letters,* ed. J. T. Bolton and A. Robertson, vol. 3 (Cambridge: Cambridge UP, 1984) 53.

2. On Verga, the playwright, see especially Anna Barsotti, *Verga drammaturgo: Tra commedia borghese e teatro verista siciliano* (Florence: La Nuova Italia, 1974), and Siro Ferrone, *Il teatro di Verga* (Rome: Bulzoni, 1974). Eric Bentley's translation of the dramatized *Cavalleria rusticana* first appeared in the first volume of the series *From the Modern Repertory* (Garden City, N. Y.: Doubleday, Anchor Books, 1954).

3. Especially useful information about the genesis of Mascagni's opera is found in the volume *Cinquantenario della "Cavalleria rusticana" di Pietro Mascagni MDCCCXC-MCMXL: Le lettere ai librettisti durante la creazione del capolavoro (inedite),* ed. Carlo Ravasio (Milan: Edizioni d'Arte Emilio Bestetti, 1940), which reproduces the letters the composer wrote while he was working on the piece. A rather detailed account of the latter's genesis, as well as of the circumstances surrounding the dramatic adaptation made for the Duse, is given by Alfred Alexander, *Giovanni Verga: A Great Writer and His Work* (London: Grant & Cutler, 1972) chapters 6 and 7. Chapter 8, entitled "*Cavalleria* litigata," deals with the legal action taken by Verga against Mascagni in order to secure some of the profits from the successful and widespread performances of the opera.

4. "Everybody knows, of course, that Verga made a dramatised version of 'Cavalleria rusticana,' and that this dramatized version is the libretto of the ever-popular little opera of the same name. So that Mascagni's rather feeble music has gone to immortalise a man like Verga, whose only *popular* claim to fame is that he wrote the aforesaid libretto. But that is fame's fault, not Verga's." From Lawrence's introduction to the volume *Cavalleria rusticana* (London, 1923), reprinted in his *Selected Literary Criticism,* ed. Anthony Beal (New York: The Viking Press, 1956) 291.

5. In his article "Stato civile della. 'Cavalleria rusticana,'" which is primarily concerned with Verga's own dramatization of his novella, F. De Roberto states emphatically: "il Verga preferiva e preferisce di gran lunga la novella al dramma" (*La Lettura* [Milan], January 1921: 10).

6. Translated from Giuseppe Paterno, *Giovanni Verga: Scrittore, Romanziere, Novelliere* (Catania: Tipografia Etna, 1974) 37-39.

7. A parallel story is adduced by Vanna Bosco-Malvica in her essay "La Fonction de quelques *altérés* dans 'Cavalleria rusticana' di Giovanni Verga," *Revue des Etudes Italiennes* 23 (1977): 63.

8. The matter is discussed by V. Perroni in an essay entitled "Sulla genesi de *I Malavoglia*" in the journal *Le Ragioni critiche* Oct.-Dec. 1972: 471-526, especially pp. 483 and 514, as well as in "Storia de *I Malavoglia,*" *Nuova Antologia* 75 (1948): 105-131.

9. Following the success of the drama, the volume was renamed *Cavalleria rusticana,* the title under which it has been reprinted ever since.

10. After having perused Gian Paolo Marchi's *Concordanze Verghiane: Cinque Studi con un appendice di scritti rari* (Verona: Fiorini, 1970), which contains a chapter entitled "Per una storia del testo," as well as the chapter "Il testo di *Vita dei Campi* e le correzioni verghiane" of Giovanni Cecchetti's book *Il Verga maggiore: Sette studi* (Florence: La Nuova Italia, 1968), I managed to obtain a copy of the original text through the Indiana University Interlibrary Loan Office.

11. They are, in order of appearance: 1) Alma Strettel, trans., "*Cavalleria rusticana*" *and Other Tales of Sicilian Peasant Life* (London: T. Fisher Unwin, 1903) 7-22; 2) D. H. Lawrence, trans., "*Cavalleria rusticana*" *and Other Stories* (London: Cape, 1928); 3) Giovanni Cecchetti, trans., "*The She-Wolf*" *and Other Stories* (Berkeley: Univ. of California Press, 1962), 10-18; 4) Albert Alexander, *Giovanni Verga: A Great Writer and His World* (London: Grant & Cutler, 1972) 100-106. Lawrence's version has been discussed by Cecchetti, in an essay entitled "Verga and D. H. Lawrence's Translations," *Comparative Literature* 9 (1957): 333-344), and by G. M. Hyde in the chapter "Lawrence and Verga: The Short Stories" of his book *D. H. Lawrence and the Art of Translation* (London: Macmillan, 1981) 36-59.

12. Luigi Russo (*Giovanni Verga,* 4th ed. [Bari: Laterza, 1947] 146) speaks of the "fraseggiare dialettale che il Verga non riesce ancora a tradurre nella sua originalissima lingua," and of his "crudezze dialettali" (378); and in his edition of Verga's *Opere* (Milan/Naples: Ricciardi, 1955) 118, he castigates the author for his inability, in these novellas, to rise to the level of the ideal Platonic language which transcends the inferior dialectal sphere.

13. Giovanni Verga, *Le Novelle,* ed. Gino Tellini (Rome: Salerno, 1980) 113, 122.

14. "Quel salsiccio è felicissimo, singolare-plurale preferito nella lingua di Sicilia. (Un toscano

avrebbe visto un piatto di salsicci.) Ma quel desco mi suona troppo toscano e dotto, e poco verghiano" (Russo 389).

15. Bosco-Malvica 68.

16. In "Una traduzione tedesca del dramma *Cavalleria rusticana*," *Rivista di Letterature moderne e comparate* 28 (1975): 7, Raffaela Bertazzoli quotes (in German) from a letter in which Verga admonishes a German stage director to avoid excessive pathos at all costs.

17. For a more detailed explanation, see Verga, *Le Novelle*, ed. Gino Tellini 119.

Massimo Verdicchio (essay date autumn 1993)

SOURCE: Verdicchio, Massimo. "Theory and Practice in 'L'amante di Gramigna.'" *Quaderni d'italianistica* 14, no. 2 (autumn 1993): 261-76.

[*In the following essay, Verdicchio examines both the prefatory letter to, and the narrative technique of, "L'amante di Gramigna" in order to re-evaluate their relevance for understanding the aesthetics of Verga's verismo.*]

The importance of the "abbozzo di racconto," as Verga calls the short story **"L'amante di Gramigna,"** for an understanding of his poetics and brand of *verismo* would not seem to be in question.[1] Verga himself stresses the theoretical importance of his tale by accompanying it with a letter to the editor in which he explains the objectives of the new art form, "nuova arte" (Verga 233). The letter, which has since been published as the theoretical preface to the story, spells out in the first paragraph Verga's idea of *verismo* and his claims to a conception of literature as a document of the drama of human passions.

> Caro Farina, eccoti non un racconto, ma l'abbozzo di un racconto. Esso almeno avrà il merito di esser brevissimo, e di essere storico—un documento umano, come dicono oggi—interessante forse per te, e per tutti coloro che studiano nel gran libro del cuore.
>
> (Verga 230-31)

It comes as somewhat a surprise, therefore, to note that most critics in discussing questions of *verismo* and Verga's poetics always disregard the story and look elsewhere for works more representative of Verga's method. Giacomo Debenedetti, for instance, after discussing the letter to Farina turns to the story **"Rosso Malpelo,"** also from *Vita dei campi,* to contrast Verga's theory of *verismo* with its literary practice (413 ff.). When **"L'amante di Gramigna"** is read as the literary exemplification of a theory of *verismo,* as in a recent study

by Giorgio Bàrberi Squarotti, the result is a naturalistic, literal reading that does not go much beyond paraphrase. Bàrberi Squarotti believes that Verga's *verismo* amounts to a shift from a literary or metaphorical mode of representation to a naturalistic and literal one: "lo scrittore si defila, scompare dalla scena, dichiara l'abbandono della letteratura come la positiva esemplificazione di un discorso che *è* il fatto, senza bisogno che il lettore debba . . . cercarlo nell'inevitabile metaforicità della scrittura letteraria" (Squarotti 15). The summary is in order because one is dealing not so much with literature, which would require interpretation, as with real life documents that only need summing up.

The theoretical relevance of the letter has been similarly reduced. Verga's remarks, when they are taken seriously, are generally deemed to be applicable only in part to the short stories but not to the later and more mature novels.[2] The major objection to the letter comes, once again, from Debenedetti who speaks of serious shortcomings in Verga's theoretical pronouncements, "(di) quel suo modo corto e un po' confuso, tutto insieme semplicistico e inceppato, di parlare per idee generali" (383). For Debenedetti, there is great discrepancy between the vague theoretical generalization stated in the letter and the short story. "Ma questi enunciati sono più tardivi, rimangono abbastanza generici, non collimano rigorosamente con la pratica, con l'operare del Verga artista" (384). Verga is the artist of *verismo,* not its theorist (the honour goes to Capuana) mainly because he has no reflex knowledge of his artistry and falls easily prey to generalizations:

> perché nel Verga, personalmente, la consapevolezza della propria arte non riesce mai a dichiararsi del tutto, e in ogni caso è aliena dal pronunciarsi in modo esplicito. Quando il Verga vuol parlare in generale, casca nel generico o per lo meno in una involontaria ambiguità . . . con le effettive opere d'arte. *Il Verga sa fare, non sa dire quello che fa.*"
>
> (17, italics mine)

Between the theory and the literary practice there is a qualitative difference because the artist not only is not a theorist but not even his best critic, and is quite incapable of describing what he otherwise excels at.

Verga and his *verismo* have not fared much better in more recent criticism. In his important work on self-conscious narrative in Italian fiction, which claims to break away from traditional critical practice, Gregory Lucente chooses nonetheless **"Rosso Malpelo"** as exemplary of Verga's narrative style and brand of *verismo,* "because the novella was of distinctive import both for *Vita dei campi* and for the overall development of Verga's realist oeuvre" (69). The reasons for Lucente's choice do not stem entirely from theoretical considerations based on the novella but are dictated by tradition since, as he writes in a note, critics from Russo to Luperini have always looked to **"Rosso Malpelo"** as the story that most exemplifies Verga's brand of *verismo*:

> Since Luigi Russo first described the story as "il racconto più organico" . . . of *Vita dei campi* . . . many other writers have characterized the novella as Verga's most unified, most important, or simply as his best. The importance of the story is further indicated by Romano Luperini's dedication of an entire monograph to it, *Verga e le strutture narrative del realismo: Saggio su Rosso Malpelo...* .
>
> (Lucente 348)

Luperini, in fact, considers this novella exemplary of the "stylistic and linguistic revolution" that marks a radical departure from Verga's early works, and even **"Nedda,"** toward a poetics of *verismo*.

> La rottura tra **"Nedda"** e **"Rosso Malpelo"** non sta nella tematica esistenziale dell'esclusione, che è comune ai due racconti, ma *nella rivoluzione stilistica e linguistica che divide quella da questo e che presuppone un cambiamento radicale nella visione del mondo verghiana. . . . Il fatto è che tra* **"Nedda"** *e* **"Rosso Malpelo"** *c' è stata la scelta dell'impersonalità, l'adesione al verismo.*
>
> (Luperini 43, my italics)

According to Luperini, Verga's radical shift in poetics ("rovesciamento di poetica" 44), admirably exemplified in **"Rosso Malpelo,"** consists in a new impersonality whereby the author no longer intervenes to defend his characters, as in **"Nedda,"** but leaves it to the narrating voice: "le motivazioni del carattere del protagonista sono date dalla voce narrante e lo scrittore si guarda bene dall'intervenire a ristabilire la 'sua' verità" (45). The same occurs in *I Malavoglia* where Verga's judgement is similarly expressed by a chorus of characters: "nei *Malavoglia* la stessa scena sarebbe stata rappresentata proprio dal punto di vista delle 'comari'" (45). In my analysis I shall argue just the opposite since the chorus of characters stands for the mystification that Verga is denouncing.

These critics' choice of novella to exemplify Verga's *verismo* is both acceptable and suspect. It is acceptable because, after all, as one of the novellas from *Vita dei Campi,* **"Rosso Malpelo"** is just as valid as any novella to demonstrate Verga's narrative method. It is suspect since the privileging of **"Rosso Malpelo"** is made, as Lucente emphasizes, on traditional grounds that the story is a complete and unified narrative. The risk inherent in this choice is that the novella becomes the recipient not so much of Verga's *verismo* as of our traditional ways of reading Verga. Our reading of the novella, as Luperini's comments demonstrate, tend to focus on the substance and meaning of the novella rather than on its process and dynamics, as Verga inti-

mates. They focus on the "what" rather than the "how." The advantage in examining **"L'amante di Gramigna"** for an understanding of Verga's poetics does not lie just in the fact that the story exemplifies for its author his new narrative method but because it is a "bozzetto di storia," the sketch of a story. Its brief and bare outline makes it possible to determine quickly and accurately the modalities of Verga's new impersonal narrative which can be read in other stories and novels. This is the objective of my paper which will examine first Verga's letter to Farina and then the story in order to reassess their relevance for an understanding of Verga's poetics of *verismo*.

THE THEORY

In the letter to Farina, Verga writes that the prose sketch is not only brief but historical ("storico"). What Verga means is clarified by the phrase "un documento umano" by which he does not mean a factual account or an historical document. While the human document has its referent necessarily in historical fact, the source Verga alludes to is the great book of the heart ("nel gran libro del cuore"). Verga's appeal to Farina is not simply to an editor who may find his views interesting ("interessante forse per te"), but is made to a fellow writer who can understand what he means.

Verga has in mind an experience which is first of all *literary* and common to every writer who has read in "the great book of the heart" and knows the heart of man and his passions. Another name for this book is "literature" and, in this case, Italian literature, which since Dante's *Vita Nuova,* if not earlier, has always dealt with the predicament of human passions.

> Il misterioso processo per cui le passioni si annodano, si intrecciano, maturano, si svolgono nel loro cammino sotterraneo, nei loro andirivieni che spesso sembrano contraddittori.
>
> (232)

Literature, from time immemorial, has always strived to understand and portray the mysterious process of human passions, how they are born, nurtured and develop. In connection with the subject of Love, which is the central passion of **"L'amante di Gramigna,"** we could mention the love poetry of Guinizelli, Cavalcanti and Dante, to mention only a few examples from one period. The list, clearly, is endless and would include most literary works. Verga, in other words, wants to say that his objective is not different from that of his literary predecessors. The difference is in *how* he chooses to deal with this eternal subject and *how* he represents the mysterious workings of human passion.

> Io te lo ripeterò così come l'ho raccolto pei viottoli dei campi, press'a poco colle medesime parole semplici e pittoresche della narrazione popolare.
>
> (232)

He intends to portray this process not from the omniscient point of view of an author but from the limited perspective of a bystander who, having heard the story at secondhand, recounts it in his own words, in the simple and picturesque language of country folk. Verga wants to give the reader a sense of immediacy, of being a participant in the action of the story, rather than being mediated by the words of explanation and commentary of the author ("faccia a faccia col fatto nudo e schietto, senza stare a cercarlo fra le linee del libro, attraverso la lente dello scrittore" [232]).

Verga does not mean, however, that the reader as observer will be confronted with the events proper, as is so often thought, but with *how* others recount these events and what they say about them. The result is a mediated immediacy which does not allow events to be experienced directly as they are but always presents them distorted through others. The reader never quite experiences the historical event, which becomes secondary, only the mysterious process that moves the human heart and its passions. This process becomes the "true" event of the story and the one Verga's *verismo* aims to imitate and portray.

The narrated events, nonetheless, are still under the control of the writer. Verga reminds Farina that his approach to narrative is not very different from that of the many great works of literature, or "monumenti gloriosi." The difference, once again, is in the emphasis that Verga chooses to place on the narrative.

> Noi rifacciamo il processo artistico al quale dobbiamo tanti monumenti gloriosi, con metodo diverso, più minuzioso e più intimo. Sacrifichiamo volentieri l'effetto dei fatti verso la catastrofe resa meno impreveduta, meno drammatica forse, ma non meno fatale.
>
> (232)

Verga shifts his emphasis from the effects to the causes to focus on the mysterious process of the unfolding of passions and events. This critical stand is meant to be somewhat polemical toward the type of melodramatic literature popular at the time and in which the stress, instead, is on the surprising and dramatic finale. Like all those who take an interest in the study of the human heart, Verga focuses on the process which brings about the character's tragic demise, on the "legame oscuro tra cause ed effetti" (232). The tragic ending does not need elaboration since it is just as predictable as it is inevitable. By describing this process, Verga fulfills his role and duty as writer which is to teach the reader a lesson in the science of the human spirit ("la scienza del cuore umano" [233]). Once again, Verga's objectives are not very different from what other writers have set themselves. Dante's *Commedia* is one example that comes to mind.

Verga has been unjustly accused of looking forward to a future without literature, when "i fatti diversi," that is chronicles of everyday facts and occurrences, will take its place. Croce, for example, declared: "Queste idee sono chiaramente erronee" (Croce 19). Verga, however, meant something quite different.

> Si arriverà mai a tal perfezionamento nello studio delle passioni, che diventerà inutile il proseguire in cotesto studio dell'uomo interiore? La scienza del cuore umano, che sarà il frutto della nuova arte, svilupperà talmente e così generalmente tutte le virtù dell'immaginazione, che nell'avvenire i soli romanzi che si scriveranno saranno *i fatti diversi*?
>
> (233)

These declarations accompanied by question marks are more rhetorical than intended. The full realization of a science of the human heart does not rest solely with the author or with the new writers but with the reader. Only when readers will learn to read and understand the human heart as writers can, will literature become obsolete. The fact that Verga is asking the question implies that he is not very optimistic that it may occur any time soon. The answer to the question posed by Verga, therefore, is "no," and as added proof we could mention our own limited understanding of Verga's works as records of the human heart.

The last section of the letter is, perhaps, the most problematic. Here Verga raises the issue of the impersonality of the work of art and looks forward to a work of literature where the hand of the writer will be invisible and the work will seem to have sprung up naturally by itself without the help of the writer.

> la mano dell'artista rimarrà assolutamente invisibile, allora [il romanzo] avrà l'impronta dell'avvenimento reale, l'opera d'arte sembrerà *essersi fatta da sé*, aver maturato ed esser sorta spontanea, come un fatto naturale, senza serbare alcun punto di contatto col suo autore, alcuna macchia del peccato d'origine.
>
> (233)

The passage has given rise to all sorts of speculation most of it negative because Verga's claim has seemed preposterous and outright false. Bàrberi Squarotti, for instance, regards the claim as a strategy to shirk from his authorial responsibilities, as a way of hiding from the reader (or the critic?) who will not be able to blame or criticize the author who, supposedly, is only representing facts:

> e la strategia dello scrittore . . . diviene allora davvero decisiva e arbitraria, nel momento in cui appare e rifiuta di dichiararsi complice degli eventi narrati e dei personaggi rappresentati, cioè si nasconde per dare a credere di non esserci più e il lettore non può quindi prendersela più con lui, che non c'è, ed è insensato prendersela con i fatti contenuti nella narrazione, dal momento che sono perfettamente "reali."
>
> (20)

The hypothesis justifies the subtitle of Bàrberi Squarotti's book, *Le finzioni dietro il verismo,* fictions which the critic aims to demystify and denounce. In my view, however, we are not dealing with any subtle stratagem to deceive or neutralize readers or critics. In any case, this would be an almost impossible task with critics like Bàrberi Squarotti. Rather, Verga's claim is based on a conception of the work of art which sees "coesione" between the "mysterious" process of the passions represented and the creative process which represents it. Since for Verga the two processes coincide, the claim of impersonality is not only understandable but inevitable. The first part of the quotation, which I omitted earlier, is as follows:

> Quando nel romanzo l'affinità e la coesione di ogni sua parte sarà così completa, *che il processo della creazione rimarrà un mistero, come lo svolgersi delle passioni umane,* e l'armonia delle sue forme sarà così perfetta, la sincerità della sua realtà così evidente, il suo modo e la sua ragione di essere così necessari... .

> (233, italics mine)

The effect of placing the reader "face to face" with the event is made possible by a mode of representation where by the mysterious process represented coincides with the writing process. The reader/observer can easily ignore the fact that he is reading a novella or a novel because the language of the work is one and the same with the characters' language of passion. As our analysis of **"L'amante di Gramigna"** will show, the mystery of human passions represented by Verga is the result of a process which, in origin, is independent of the characters and events narrated, as well as of the writing process which represents it and exemplifies it. Verga's objective to place readers in a situation where they are listening to someone recounting or experiencing an event, has to be taken more seriously than it is usually. For Verga it is not simply a literary device but an essential aspect of his poetics which closely concerns the representation of the mysterious process of human passions. Failure to understand this point has led critics like Bàrberi Squarotti to believe that the "original sin" meant by Verga is literature which the author would gladly exchange for some type of automatic writing.

> Il *"peccato d'origine"* è, evidentemente, la *letteratura:* dal romanzo moderno dovrà essere del tutto cancellata a favore del fatto così com'è, e il "mistero" della scrittura presso che automatica potrà così pareggiare il conto con il mistero delle passioni umane.

> (Squarotti 14-15)

The "original sin" consists in the fact that the work of art is, after all, a work of fiction and, as such, liable to be misunderstood and taken to be what it is not, namely, a fiction. In other words, it is liable to be misrepresented and not taken as a representation of true events. This is the risk of any literary work when it is taken to be nothing more than a work of fiction. Hence the notion of "original sin" which condemns fiction to always being fiction even when it makes the effort of portraying the "real" ("i fatti diversi"). For Verga's *verismo,* therefore, it is not so much literature which is an impediment to understanding as much as the readers' understanding which, despite the author's intentions, will always regard his works as fiction rather than as fictious equivalents of "real" life situations. As I indicated earlier, this is the greatest barrier to the evolution of literature from fiction to "i fatti diversi" envisaged, if not hoped for, by Verga.

To sum up the theoretical "sense" of Verga's letter to Farina, we could say that Verga's new kind of writing seeks to represent the historical reality of human events with the stylistic efficacy that would give readers the illusion of having been there and having heard it for the first time. However, he is not interested in representing facts, history or reality, but in drawing the readers' attention to the mysterious and baffling logic of human passions which inexorably and inevitably leads men to tragedy. This process and the process of writing are one and the same. Verga will not tell readers what happens in the story in so many words; rather, he confronts them with events and lets them make up their own minds. In so doing he achieves that objectivity and impersonality associated with *verismo* that allows readers to be observers of "real" events rather than readers of a story about the event. Verga's aim is *not,* as Bàrberi Squarotti suggests, to negate literature in favour of some kind of automatic writing or even to shirk from his responsibilities as a writer. The aim of his "new art" is to remind readers that what is being represented is not a product of the author's imagination (although the story and its characters are his invention) but something completely independent of his will and fiction. This is the theory that Verga's sketches for Farina and which we should find translated in narrative form in **"L'amante di Gramigna."**

THE STORY

The title of the story is itself telling because the name of the outlaw "Gramigna" already alludes to that "mysterious" process of human passions that Verga refers to in the letter and which constitutes the focus of the novella.[3] The name "Gramigna" literally means "mala pianta" (weed, evil plant) and has all the connotations of evil: "un brigante, certo *Gramigna,* se non erro, un nome maledetto come l'erba che lo porta" (Verga 233). In the story, Gramigna functions as an evil weed destroying everything in his path. He creates fear and terror in the countryside and threatens to destroy the local harvest because the landowners and the farmers are too afraid to work in the fields.

Per giunta si approssimava il tempo delle messi, tutta la raccolta dell'annata in man di Dio, ché i proprietari non s'arrischiavano a uscir del paese pel timore di Gramigna.

(234)

Compare Finu, for example, a young and wealthy landowner is afraid that Gramigna might set fire to his harvest:

nel tornare ogni sera dalla campagna, lasciava la mula all'uscio della Peppa, e veniva a dirle che i seminati erano un incanto, se Gramigna non vi appiccava fuoco.

(235, italics mine)

Most important, Gramigna destroys Compare Finu's future marriage to Peppa which was to be celebrated soon after the harvest.

Compare Finu not only owned many lands ("aveva terre al sole e una mula baia nella stalla"), but was young, strong and handsome, "un giovanotto grande e bello come il sole" (235). He is the best catch in town. "Le comari . . . avevano invidiato a Peppa il seminato prosperoso, la mula baia, e il bel giovanotto che portava lo stendardo di Santa Margherita senza piegar le reni" (236). He is everything a woman might wish for in a husband but Peppa decides, mysteriously, to break off her promised marriage to him and to run off to live with Gramigna. "Ma Peppa un bel giorno gli disse:—La vostra mula lasciatela stare, perché non voglio maritarmi—" (235).

This is the central concern of the story: Why Peppa leaves the man to whom she is betrothed to seek out a bandit she has never even seen? How could Peppa, "una delle più belle ragazze di Licodia" (234), degenerate to the point of becoming, at the end of the story, "lo strofinacciolo della caserma" (239), a servant to the soldiers who had captured Gramigna? These are the questions that any bystander would ask when hearing the story "faccia a faccia col fatto nudo e schietto," or as they hear it related from a passer-by on a country road, or as they read it in a newspaper as one of the many "fatti diversi." Verga's concern in narrating the story of Peppa and Gramigna is to answer these questions by providing the readers with an insight into the mysterious process of human passions and to provide them with an understanding ("scienza") of the human heart.

Peppa's infatuation with Gramigna is explained gradually and indirectly. Although she has never set eyes on him, the talk she "hears" about his prowess and accomplishments makes her believe he was a "real" man and she gradually falls in love with that image.

Che è, che non è, Peppa s'era scaldata la testa per Gramigna, senza conoscerlo neppure. Quello sì che era un uomo!—Che ne sai?—Dove l'hai visto?—Nulla.

(235, my italics)

The more Peppa hears stories about Gramigna's accomplishments the more she becomes infatuated with him and the more she desires him.

Però ella seguitava a dire che non lo conosceva neanche di vista quel cristiano; ma invece pensava sempre a lui, lo vedeva in sogno, la notte, e alla mattina si levava colle labbra arse, assetata anch'essa, come lui.

(236)

Her mother's attempts to prevent her from hearing more about him and to dissuade her from her blind passion fail.

Allora la vecchia la chiuse in casa, perché non sentisse più parlare di Gramigna, e tappò tutte le fessure dell'uscio con immagini di santi. Peppa ascoltava quello che dicevano nella strada, dietro le immagini benedette, e si faceva pallida e rossa, come se il diavolo le soffiasse tutto l'inferno nella faccia.

(236, italics mine)

The origin of Peppa's passion for Gramigna is in the stories she hears about him related by passers-by and by those around her. These stories prey on the young woman's imagination by creating an idealized image of Gramigna as a "real man" in whom she blindly believes and comes to desire.

It is clear from the story that the people who talk about Gramigna and his heroics have never seen him. What they know and relate is what they have "heard" from someone else. In other words, what Peppa "hears" about Gramigna, as well as what we readers know and read about him, is what people in the countryside have heard and, in their turn, have repeated to others. These stories, therefore, do not narrate real events but are the grossly exaggerated tales that people spin about people and events they know nothing about, which is why they invent them. The fact that Gramigna is still on the loose and not much else is known about him is sufficient to stimulate people's imaginations to invent and exaggerate details about a Gramigna with superhuman qualities. These fictions transform Gramigna from a petty bandit and a fugitive from justice into a larger-than-life hero, feared, admired and loved. The following description, which readers usually read as a true account of actual events, is in fact the exaggerated account of what people invent about Gramigna and which Peppa and the reader "hear."

Carabinieri, soldati, e militi a cavallo, lo inseguivano da due mesi, senza esser riusciti a mettergli le unghie addosso: era solo, ma valeva per dieci, e la mala pianta minacciava di moltiplicarsi. . . . Il prefetto fece chiamare tutti quei signori della questura, dei carabinieri, dei compagni d'armi, e subito in moto pattuglie, squadriglie, vedette per ogni fossato, e dietro ogni muricciolo: se lo cacciavano dinanzi come una mala bestia per tutta una provincia, di giorno di notte, a piedi, a cavallo, col telegrafo. Gramigna sgusciava loro di mano, o rispondeva a schioppettate, se gli camminavano un po' troppo sulle calcagna. *Nelle campagne, nei villaggi, per le fattorie, sotto le frasche delle osterie, nei luoghi di ritrovo, non si parlava altro che di lui, di Gramigna, di quella caccia accanita, di quella fuga disperata.* I cavalli dei carabinieri cascavano stanchi morti; i compagni d'armi si buttavano rifiniti per terra, in tutte le stalle; le pattuglie dormivano all'impiedi: *egli solo, Gramigna, non era stanco mai, non dormiva mai, combatteva sempre, s'arrampicava sui precipizi, strisciava fra le messi, correva carponi nel folto dei fichidindia, sgattajolava come un lupo nel letto asciutto dei torrenti.* Per duecento miglia all'intorno, correva la leggenda delle sue gesta, del suo coraggio, della sua forza, di quella lotta disperata, lui solo contro mille, stanco affamato, arso dalla sete, nella pianura immensa, arsa, sotto il sole di giugno.

(234, italics mine)

This account of Gramigna does not correspond to real events but reproduces only the exaggerated version fabricated by people's fears, ignorance and vivid imaginations. This fiction takes the place of reality and becomes for those who create it and keep it alive the only reality. This is the "reality" Peppa falls in love with and the fiction that Verga claims is independent of the author who represents it, and rightly so.

The exaggerated tales that transform Gramigna into a hero inflame Peppa's imagination and arouse her passion. As a young and impressionable girl, perhaps betrothed to someone she does not love, she readily believes them *as if* they were *real*. In her mind, the prospect of being married to the wealthiest and most handsome man in town—Verga purposedly exaggerates the physical attributes and material wealth of Compare Finu—is not as exciting and thrilling as a life with a man who risks his life everyday in combat against hundreds of soldiers and whose adventurous life is in her eyes a welcome relief from the humdrum existence in which she lives and will live as Compare Finu's wife. It comes as no surprise, therefore, that Gramigna appears to her as more of a man and more of an object of desire than the man she is soon to wed.

Verga explains Gramigna's transformation from unknown criminal to hero as the terror, or evil, of fame: "il terrore della sua fama." Verga wants to allude not only to the fear that Gramigna instills in those who spread rumors about his "deeds," but also to the destruction he causes in his wake such as the break up of Peppa's engagement to Compare Finu and her eventual tragic end. The two, in fact, are but aspects of the same process since the terror that Gramigna creates in others is the result of the stories people relate about him.

To appreciate what is really going on in this short but complete sketch, we must distinguish between what Verga tells us of Gramigna, the character, from Grami-

gna, the terror that fame has created. The distinction entails a differentiation between Verga the author and Verga the observer, from whose point of view the story is partly told, and who poses as any bystander who hears the story of Gramigna and Peppa "pei viottoli dei campi." While the presence of the author marks the inevitable "peccato d'origine" of which Verga speaks in the letter to Farina, it is also the necessary presence which allows the reader to differentiate fact from fiction, which usually are identical in a naturalistic story, and determine the cause of Peppa's afflictions and the mysterious workings of the human heart.

The presence of Verga the writer undermines what is being stated by Verga the observer and denounces the discrepancy between the "real" Gramigna from the larger-than-life hero that fame has created. At the beginning of the tale, Verga goes out of his way to emphasize that Gramigna was virtually an unknown, "*un* brigante, *certo* Gramigna, *se non erro*" (233, italics mine). Verga wants to dispel any doubt the reader may have that Gramigna is the great bandit people are making him out to be. This is also confirmed by the episode where Peppa meets up with the bandit for the first time. We see him, then, for what he really is, a ruthless, unfeeling and despicable man who takes advantage of Peppa's infatuation to serve his own selfish ends (237).

The key insight the reader gains from an awareness of the discrepancy between the two Gramignas is what Verga calls the "terror of fame." He describes the mysterious process whereby an unknown outlaw becomes, in the people's imagination, a feared bandit capable of standing up alone against a thousand men. By virtue of this process, the initial story of Gramigna, a lone and unknown bandit, "grows" and multiplies ("era solo, ma valeva per dieci") like weeds in the mouths of those who spread stories about him. Likewise, the number of soldiers sent after him multiplies, and this only increases his prowess as he is always able to elude them and defend himself against hundreds. Similarly, talk of Gramigna multiplies everywhere ("non si parlava d'altro che di lui"). He becomes the talk of the town and people constantly speak, or invent stories, about him. This process escalates to the point that the rumours attribute to him almost supernatural powers. He is always fighting and he is never tired, whereas those in pursuit are made to seem inept and fatigued. He becomes the legendary hero ("la leggenda delle sue gesta"), strong and courageous, and always successful.

Gramigna's power is the power of "gramigna," of "mala pianta," or, which is the same, the power of fame since, as I indicated earlier, "fama" and "mala pianta" are words for the same thing. The story is based on and develops from this pun until it has distorted the characters' sense of reality and destroyed all that is good in its path. The process describes the "semplice fatto umano" that for Verga explains the "misterioso processo" that stirs human passions. This is the process whereby the hyperbolic and exaggerated language of hearsay excites the imaginations and passions of a young woman and (mis)leads her into believing in the reality of a fiction that eventually destroys her. For the nature of this mysterious process is such that no one and nothing can stop it once it has been set in motion. Even the confrontation with the *real* Gramigna is unable to open Peppa's eyes. Even long after his capture, and the humiliations she suffers for him, Peppa remains faithful to the image of the man she loves despite the fact that from the moment she meets him everything contradicts it.

The mysterious unfolding of human passions and the fictitious language of hearsay, which triggers it, are not only mirror images of the same process but they are also at one with the creative process. This identity between the language of hearsay, the language of passion and the language of the story justifies Verga's claim of objectivity. The key term common to all these processes, which in the story is differently rendered as "gramigna," "mala pianta," "fama," is language, *figural or metaphorical language,* as the initial pun suggests: the language of passion in Peppa's case, the language of fear for the townspeople, and the descriptive language of the story which imitates their exaggerated tales. In each case we are dealing with a process that only apparently is within the control of the speaker. This is clearly the case with the language of fame which easily moves beyond the meaning intended by the speakers transforming and distorting the reality which they believe they are describing.

> Nelle campagne, nei villaggi, per le fattorie, sotto le frasche delle osterie, nei luoghi di ritrovo, *non si parlava d'altro che di lui,* di gramigna, di quella caccia accanita, di quella fuga disperata.
>
> (234, italics mine)

It is a language that does not state things as they are but distorts the reality of things making them appear different or, as in Peppa's case, more appealing than they are. The language of fame or hearsay is not rooted in reality but takes the real as its starting point inventing its story as it goes independently of the original meaning which it distorts and does violence to. For, as it is clear from the story and its title name "mala pianta," this language is ultimately destructive. When this language is allowed to take the place of the real and is believed to be real, as in Peppa's case, it blinds the character to a reality from which she becomes increasingly severed and precipitates her toward her inevitable tragic fate. What in the story is called the terror of fame is really the terror of language.

Similarly, the exaggerated tales of the townspeople about Gramigna's extraordinary feats, which are symptomatic of their fears and their ignorance of what is re-

ally going on, multiply as their tales become more terrifying and threatening. The terror of their tales generates more tales to account for or dispel those fears, and so on. In both cases, the real threat is not Gramigna but this language, these tales, which people invent and which now come back to haunt them. And in both cases the process is destructive. At the level of textual representation, the figural or tropological equivalent to this process is the trope of personification. Gramigna, as I indicated, is a pun, a play on words, to personify evil, or better, the destructive process of evil, as exemplified by the destructive growth of weeds which, growing rampant in a field destroy all vegetation. Gramigna, as the personification of this evil, can be said to allegorize the proliferation of figural language from the initial pun to ever more terrifying and threatening transformations, distorting and doing violence to our own sense of reality. As in the story of Frankenstein, the man-created monster that goes out of control until it destroys everything in its path including its creator, in Verga the monster "Gramigna" is this figural language which creates havoc amongst the characters which feed it and nourish it until it has destroyed the very people that keep it alive. Peppa is not the only victim. Besides her and Compare Finu, Peppa's mother dies heartbroken for the shame her daughter has brought on her house and family. The reader is also another victim. Reading this tale as just a simple tale of a woman who falls in love with a bandit, the reader's sense of what is really going on is distorted and violated. But, then, this is one of the objectives Verga's *verismo* hoped to achieve.

The same can be said of the author. Verga has no more control over this language than the townspeople or Peppa. In representing the simple and picturesque words of popular narrative, "press'a poco colle medesime parole semplici e pittoresche della narrazione popolare" (232), Verga is equally caught within this process as the others are and can only represent it as it unravels. The inevitability of this process, to which even the author must abide, ensures, the impersonality and objectivity that Verga claimed in the letter to Farina. From this perspective, one can easily see how Verga can state that the work of art will seem to have been made by itself ("essersi fatta da sé") and to have arisen spontaneously "as a natural fact."

The difference between Verga and his characters lies precisely in the awareness of the constitutive figural nature of this process. Verga calls it "il peccato d'origine," the original sin which, in theory, discriminates between the literary event of the story from everyday events, the "fatti diversi." At the narrative level, however, it is exemplified as an awareness of the constitutive fictional or narratological nature of the process which enables the reader to become aware of the mystification inherent in the process. Through this process, the reader can gain an insight into the depth and complexity of the human heart, of the mysterious process of human passions that inevitably lead man to catastrophe. Verga imitates the arbitrary and mysterious process that drives men and women to their fate and denounces its inherent fictitious and figural nature by calling attention to it and paving the way towards a deeper and greater understanding of the human psyche and its passions.

Our analysis of **"L'amante di Gramigna"** proves that there is no discrepancy between the story and Verga's letter to Farina, between the theory and the narrative practice. The prose sketch stands as the "perfect" narrative equivalent to the theoretical statement. It illustrates in a narrative, or allegorical mode, what the author had already stated theoretically. Contrary to traditional opinion, Verga can be said to be very much the theorist of his own brand of *verismo* and to possess a very clear understanding of his work. It could not be otherwise. It would be impossible for a writer of Verga's stature not to possess a theoretical understanding of his own literary constructs. We could go one step further and say that Verga is a theorist of *verismo* because he is a great writer of the genre, or at least of his own genre of *verismo*. Capuana may be a better theorist of *verismo*, as Debenedetti claims, but since he is not reputed to be as great a writer as Verga, his understanding of *verismo* is bound to be theoretical and abstract making it highly doubtful that he would be capable of probing the depths of Verga's prose.

It goes without saying that what has been said of **"L'amante di Gramigna"** applies not only to Verga's other stories but also to **"Rosso Malpelo."** All of them can be said to be allegories of Verga's theory of *verismo* expounded in the letter to Farina. It would not be difficult to show, for example, that, like Peppa's, Rosso's tragic fate is the result of the misnomer "malpelo" and follows the same destructive path as Gramigna's "mala pianta." The townfolks' arbitrary and initially innocent naming of Rosso as "malpelo" condemns the boy to an image of himself he feels he must live up to, regardless of his true nature, until the process (generated by the name and the reputation) brings about his demise. Rosso, like Peppa, is a victim of people's "hearsay" about him and, like Peppa, he is caught in a process he cannot control but can only resign himself to and accept.

A similar process is at work in the novels and clearly in *I Malavoglia* where the main characters have equally been branded with a misnomer that can't wait to be fulfilled. Although they are a hard-working family, they are known as "I malavoglia," as lazy and indolent. The mysterious process of man's passions resurfaces in the Malavoglia family's desire to improve their lot, to have a better and more prosperous future, "la vaga bramosia dell'ignoto, l'accorgersi che non si sta bene, o che si potrebbe stare meglio" (Verga 177). Once this desire is acted upon and translated into reality, by purchasing the rotten lupines, a process similar to the one described in **"L'amante di Gramigna"** is set into motion with no hope of arresting it until the entire family goes to ruin and the name "malavoglia" becomes a fit description of at least one of their members.

In the introduction to his novel, Verga alludes to this process as "fiumana." The term describes not only the mysterious process in which the main characters of *I Malavoglia* are caught but also the fatal journey of humanity that Verga, with full irony, calls man's progress:

> Il cammino fatale, incessante, spesso faticoso e febbrile che segue l'umanità per raggiungere la conquista del progresso. ...
>
> (Verga, *Opere* 178)

This process is "grandioso" only when viewed from a distance ("da lontano"). On closer analysis what may seem a virtuous undertaking is only a vehicle for vice and points to the corruption that underlies these grandiose results:

> le irrequietudini, le avidità, l'egoismo, tutte le passioni, tutti i vizi . . . tutte le debolezze . . . tutte le contraddizioni.
>
> (Verga, *Opere* 178)

Like Gramigna's "mala pianta," the "fiumana" of progress ("Dalla ricerca del benessere materiale alle più elevate ambizioni") sweeps away everyone without discrimination including those who at first sight may appear to be the makers of history. From *I Malavoglia* to *Mastro don Gesualdo,* to the *Duchessa di Leyra,* to the *Onorevole Scipione* to *L'Uomo di Lusso,* all the main characters of these novels are losers, "vinti." Like Peppa, they are all swept away by their desires and drowned, "altrettanti vinti che la corrente ha deposti sulla riva, dopo averli travolti e annegati, ciascuno colle stimmate del suo peccato, che avrebbero dovuto essere lo sfolgorare della sua virtù" (Verga, *Opere* 178).

In **"L'amante di Gramigna,"** and in other stories of *Vita dei Campi,* Verga deals with human passions, namely, love, fear, respect, honor. In the novels he takes up other and more grandiose passions like the desire for well-being, ambition, greed. In all these cases the process in which the characters are caught is the same. Whether the desire is for a "real" man or, simply, for a more comfortable living, these characters are caught in a process in which only apparently are they protagonists who have control over their actions. Whether the process is called "gramigna," "malpelo" or "fiumana," these characters are caught in a mechanism which sweeps them away on the shore of their inevitable catastrophe. In all cases we are confronted with a process which is linguistic in essence since the "mysterious" process of human passions that Verga represents is not separate from the language that triggers it, sustains it and, finally, sweeps these characters away. To have portrayed this link between language and passion is what is revolutionary in Verga's *verismo* and stands as his great contribution to the science of the human heart.

Although **"Rosso Malpelo,"** or any of his works could be used to explain Verga's poetics, in principle, it is clear from the way they have been read, traditionally, that it has not been equally possible to determine the relevant narrative structures that single them out. This is because, as Verga well knew, only an "abbozzo di storia," without the trimmings and trappings of a unified and complete narrative, can expose the essential and vital mechanism that underlies it and makes it work. For this reason, **"L'amante di Gramigna"** should rightly be considered paradigmatic not only of *Vita dei Campi* but of Verga's writing in general, as Verga had intended.

As for Verga who is equally caught within this process, all he can do is stand back and portray this "mysterious" process objectively and dispassionately, without judging it.

> Chi osserva questo spettacolo non ha il diritto di giudicarlo . . . è già molto se riesce a trarsi un istante fuori del campo della lotta per studiarla senza passione, e rendere la scena nettamente, coi colori adatti, tale da dare la rappresentazione della realtà com'è stata, o come avrebbe dovuto essere
>
> (Verga, *Opere* 179, my italics)

Whether we call this process "irony" or "verismo," as traditional criticism has it, so be it, but we should not let a definition of *verismo,* as we traditionally understand it, dictate the way we read Verga. The dangers of "hearsay," even in the field of literary criticism, are clearly too dire for us to choose to ignore its warnings.

Notes

1. The short story was initially published as "L'Amante di Raja" in the February 1880 issue of *Rivista minima di scienze, lettere ed arti.* In the same year it was included in the collection of stories *Vita dei campi.*

2. This attitude is also echoed by Cecchetti who believes, however, that the letter can point to many common characteristics of Verga's prose (Cecchetti 32 ff.).

3. The importance of the name is evident in Verga's decision to change the bandit's name from Raja to Gramigna.

Works Cited

Bàrberi Squarotti, Giorgio. *Giovanni Verga. Le finzioni dietro il verismo.* Palermo: S.F. Flaccovio, 1982.

Cecchetti, Giovanni. *Il Verga maggiore. Sette studi.* Firenze: La Nuova Italia, 1968.

Croce, Benedetto. *La letteratura della Nuova Italia.* Vol. 3. Bari: Laterza, 1956.

Debenedetti, Giacomo. *Verga e il Naturalismo.* Milano: Garzanti, 1976.

Lucente, Gregory. *Beautiful Fables. Self-consciousness in Italian Narrative from Manzoni to Calvino.* Baltimore and London: The Johns Hopkins UP, 1986.

Luperini, Romano. *Verga e le strutture narrative del realismo. Saggio su "Rosso Malpelo."* Padova: Liviana Editrice, 1976.

Verga, Giovanni. *Le Novelle di Giovanni Verga.* Ed. Gino Tellini. 2 vols. Roma: Salerno, 1970.

———. *Opere.* Milano, Napoli: Ricciardi, 1961.

Daniela Bini (essay date spring 1999)

SOURCE: Bini, Daniela. "*Cavalleria Rusticana* from Verga and Mascagni to Zeffirelli." *Forum Italicum* 33, no. 1 (spring 1999): 95-106.

[*In the following essay, Bini explores the contradictions in the Sicilian male's perception of woman, tracing its cultural significance in the contexts of "Cavalleria rusticana" and several dramatic adaptations of the story.*]

In his essay "Pirandello e la Sicilia," Leonardo Sciascia undertakes a very delicate operation: that of analyzing the Sicilian male's complex attitude toward sexuality. A very delicate operation, indeed, since he is at the same time subject and object of his analysis. Starting with the Sicilian's ancient feeling of historical insecurity and therefore with his obsessive sense of possession, his excessive attachment to "la roba" (I am purposely using the masculine pronoun, since in his analysis the subject is male and the object is female), Sciascia writes: "degradata da persona ad oggetto di piacere (e s'intende, d'onore) la donna, il siciliano ha una particolare morale sessuale e un particolare comportamento erotico: la morale del possesso esclusivo e un comportamento che, riconoscendo nella donna una vita soltanto istintiva, tende a soddisfarne i sensi per ridurre il margine di apprensione, di insicurezza relativamente alle sue azioni." A primate type of behavior, Sciascia calls it, and he continues with an intriguing examination of such behavior that "si compone di elementi puramente vitali, primitivi o comunque appartenenti a civiltà ormai lontane [. . .] e di elementi dottrinali di estrazione cristiana che si configurano in una specie di stilnovismo patologico [. . .] Questi due elementi, l'elemento vitale e l'elemento cristiano, agiscono anch'essi dialetticamente, nel duplice e inverso movimento dell'esaltazione e della disgregazione." Sciascia considers this attitude toward sexuality a religious one, and concludes that the vital, pagan element of Sicilian sexuality "si rovescia, non diremo nella sessuofobia cristiana, ma indubbiamente in una concezione della donna che attinge alla dottrina cristiana e cattolica" (Sciascia 1058, 1059).

It is precisely this "conception of woman feeding out of Christianity and Catholicism" that I would like to explore in relation to **"Cavalleria rusticana,"** Verga's short story, and even more in his one act play, in Mascagni's opera and finally in Zeffirelli's spectacular production of it. The "stilnovismo patologico" that Sciascia so cleverly diagnosed, I would like to argue, not only reveals the male's own feelings toward sex, but also and more interestingly, his contradictory perception of woman. It is not by chance that Sciascia chose the word "stilnovismo" to define this attitude. The term takes us back in time to an angel woman, considered as the trait-d'union between man and god, whose outer beauty was nothing but the reflection of divine beauty, and whose task, therefore, was teaching man the true object of love. It takes us to Beatrice whose spiritual love leads us to paradise. It is the cult of a feminine figure appropriated from Catholicism, that of the Virgin Mary, and it is this feminine figure that the Sicilian male (and not only the Sicilian) worships and seeks in his mother and wife. Woman, however, is also eroticism, passion, sexuality. Yet within this "pathological" conception this earthly aspect cannot coexist with the other, the spiritual; thus the dichotomic perception that Sicilians have of woman: on the one hand, they place on the altar the image of the Virgin Mother who conceives without man, lives in function of the son, and triumphs through her spirit of abnegation and self-sacrifice. On the other hand, they fear the erotic woman, Verga's She-wolf, the whore, the witch, whose sexuality cannot be resisted because it is superhuman.[1] Within this "pathological stilnovismo" the figures of husband and father are cancelled, better yet, they do not exist. The Mother figure lives in a close (and obsessive) relationship with her son—he is, in fact, the purpose, and the reason of her existence, her identity being that of mother, thus determined and given to her by her son. The function of the erotic woman, instead, is that of satisfying her sexual desires and of enslaving the male. Whereas the Virgin Mother receives her power directly from God, the erotic woman receives it from the forces of hell. Both, therefore, possess superhuman qualities against which any struggle is to no avail.

From short story to play, from opera libretto to film, from Verga to Zeffirelli, **"Cavalleria rusticana"** develops and progressively displays the dichotomy erotic woman/virgin mother, so ingrained in the Sicilian psyche and culture. Verga wrote the short story in 1880 and the play in 1883-84. In 1889 Mascagni set to music the libretto by Targioni-Tozzetti and Menasci, which

followed the play almost verbatim. He composed the music in a hurry, completing it in only four months since he needed to meet the May deadline for the Sonzogno competition.[2] The greatest changes took place in the play which undoubtedly lost some of the Sicilian flavor. Writing for the stage, Verga had to adapt his story to the dramatic needs. The libretto of the opera remains faithful to the play with some minor, yet relevant changes. Zeffirelli's film of the opera develops the opposition between the two female roles, sanctioning the centrality of the mother figure.

Gna' Nunzia (Turiddu's mother) of the short story and the play becomes Mamma Lucia in the opera as the role of the mother acquires more and more significance. Lola, Alfio's wife, represents the erotic woman. Before going in the army, Turiddu and Lola were in love, and he had left with the hope she would wait for his return. Lola, however, decided to marry Compar Alfio "che aveva quattro muli di Sortino in stalla" and on Sunday "si metteva sul ballatoio colle mani sul ventre per far vedere tutti i grossi anelli d'oro che le aveva regalati suo marito," thus revealing the materialistic traits of the mercenary woman (Verga, *Le novelle* 198, 200). Between Lola and Mamma Lucia stands Santa—she had a rich father in the short story, but lost him in the play—who is neither a mother figure, nor an erotic one. She is therefore a misfit, and as such is doomed to failure. Santa is used by Turiddu to make Lola jealous and bring her back to him. Her role grows progressively from story to play—Verga hoped that Eleonora Duse would play it—and from play to opera with a main addition. Santa has lost her honor, having given in to Turiddu's sexual demands and promises of marriage. From Santa in the story, where she has her dignity and a social status, she becomes Santuzza in the play and opera, having lost even her only feminine dowry—virginity.[3] It is precisely Santuzza's larger role that underlines the opposition between the two main female figures. She cannot compete with either, hence her tragedy.

Zeffirelli begins his film with a scene that is neither in Verga's play nor in Targioni-Tozzetti-Menasci's libretto.[4] As dawn approaches, Turiddu rises from Lola's bed, kisses her and leaves her house, while Santuzza, hidden behind a bush, witnesses his departure. The scene is accompanied by the intense cords of the Prelude and is followed by the words of the "Siciliana," the Sicilian sensual love song that Turiddu/Placido Domingo sings as he leaves on his horse. It stirs the viewers' emotions plunging them right from the start in the midst of this intense drama of passions. If Turiddu can defy the strict honor code of his town, if he is ready to risk his life for a night of love with Lola, the woman married to the rich "carrettiere" Alfio, her erotic power must come from the realm of the supernatural. Likewise if Lola can defy the social code, that is even stricter for a woman and a wife than for a man, her erotic drive must be immense. Woman's eroticism comes from the underworld, from the forces of hell; it has the strength of the Etna erupting from the womb of the earth burning fields and meadows. It is the power of "La lupa," against whom there is no escape, not even in the church.[5] In Zeffirelli's production the church appears right after this first scene where the tragedy is already foreshadowed in the encounter between Turiddu and Alfio at dawn, as they return to their respective homes. No words are exchanged; only an intense gaze in which passion, jealousy, betrayal, rage are all mingled together. Santuzza, distraught by the discovery of Turiddu's betrayal, enters the church and her gaze stops in front of the statue of the Mater Dolorosa. As the music reaches its dramatic climax, the camera lingers on the image of the Madonna, thus foregrounding the contrast between mother and erotic woman. The mother figure takes the stage again immediately after as singing women walk across golden fields of wheat, carrying enormous amphoras with water for their men. The idyllic scene takes place in a solar landscape, ideal space for the nursing mother, source of life. Accompanied by children she sings her hymn to life. A representation of the sacred family closes this choral event as a mother, father and son reunite, embrace and enter their humble home.

In the play the power of the erotic woman appears in the first scene, when Santuzza goes to gna' Nunzia to ask about Turiddu. When she finally confesses to her that Turiddu is seeing Lola at night, she uses words that confirm the demonic power of the erotic woman and man's impotence before her. Placing the emphasis on Lola's eyes ("me lo rubava con gli occhi, quella scomunicata!"—that call immediately to mind the black eyes, "occhi neri come il carbone", "occhi da satanasso" of La lupa (*Le novelle* 209, 206)), Santuzza accuses Lola of "temptation," calls her "malafemmina" and attributes to her the power of a witch. "Quella malafemmina diventò gelosa a morte; e si mise in testa di rubarmelo. Mi cambiò Turiddu di qua a qua" (Verga, *Opere* 805). In this duel between women, Turiddu has no part whatever, and no power. But the forces at fight are not even. Lola is a witch, her power of magic wins over Santuzza's human love. Later in the story, when Turiddu is arguing with Santuzza, the sound of Lola's voice singing from afar, just like the song of the mermaid, is enough to light up his face and fill his body with passion, making him oblivious to the argument, to Santuzza and the whole world. Lola is singing "Fior di giaggiolo," a Tuscan stornello that Turiddu had probably taught her in one of their nights of love. Later on, as Lola together with a crowd of town people exits the church after the Easter Mass and in spite of Santuzza's curse against him ("A te la mala Pasqua!"), he is once again mesmerized by Lola's power, and cannot help flirting with her and offering her a glass of wine. But more on that later.

In the short story as well as in the play Turiddu's mother is called Gna' Nunzia, but in the opera her role as mother is underlined by the name change. She becomes Mamma Lucia, mother of the whole town. In the first scene another major change occurs. As Santuzza comes to her tavern to ask for Turiddu, she reveals her sin and Turiddu's betrayal to gna' Nunzia in a scene that is a true confession. The play dilutes the intensity of the dramatic action by interjecting the comments of a few other characters who come by and ask Nunzia questions. Moreover in the play Nunzia is more controlled and less moved by Santa's pain. Instead, she seems more concerned about her son's fate and her own ("O poveretta me! Cosa mi vieni a dire! . . . Non può essere; ti sbagli"). As Santuzza begs her "Non mi scacciate anche dalla porta, gnà Nunzia, se volete fare come il Signore misericordioso che andate a pregare in chiesa. Lasciatemi qui, vi dico! Lasciate che parli con lui quest'ultima volta, per l'anima dei vostri morti!" gnà Nunzia exclaims, leaving for church: O Signore, pensateci voi!"(Verga, *Opere,* 805-806) In the opera, Gaillard Corsi had already noted, gnà Nunzia, who is by now Mamma Lucia, has a more affectionate relationship with Santuzza, and "becomes vicariously Santa's mother, as well." (Mamma Lucia's words are slightly changed, but enough to show that she cares about Santa, that she wishes to share her pain. "Poveretta me" becomes "Miseri noi" and she no longer doubts the truth of Santa's revelation. Mamma Lucia's affection gives courage to Santa who begs her "Andate o mamma, ad implorare Iddio, e pregate per me." The general prayer of the play has now become an appeal for a personal prayer, for maternal help. But the most dramatic change, in line with this interpretation, lies in the mother's last exclamation "Aiutatela voi, Santa Maria!" Not only is Mamma Lucia asking for divine help for Santa, but the divine to whom she appeals is no longer the Lord, as in the play. It is the mother of all mothers, the Virgin Mary. Mamma Lucia is taking upon herself the role of mother, and her identification with the Madonna is underlined by Santa's refusal to enter her home, similar to her refusal to enter the church. "Io son dannata" she exclaims in the opera, and her damned soul cannot enter either place of cult. Mamma Lucia's identification with the figure of the Virgin Mother is also underscored by the absence of a husband and of a father for Turiddu. Neither is ever mentioned; he does not exist; he might never have existed.

It is in Zeffirelli's production that the mother figure becomes central. And for this purpose the director exploits to its maximum an element that Verga had added to the play: the time setting. Whereas the story in the novella is set on Easter Eve with only the duel happening at dawn the following morning, the events in the play and the opera take place on Easter Sunday, the day of Christ's Resurrection that the town celebrates with a lavishly baroque procession. (In the short story, in fact,

Verga gives this detail in an offhanded manner, toward the end of the story and does not exploit it in any way). Zeffirelli, enamoured with the Baroque and rich scenery, went to Sicily to shoot this scene, and the procession not only occupies the center of the opera, but it takes over and dominates the plot. Unfolding before the viewer it lasts six minutes and interestingly enough the central piece in it it is not the statue of Christ, who appears several times in a reclining position, looking prostrated by the pain, but that of the Mater Dolorosa who offstages the protagonist of the event. It is here, in this procession that the power of the erotic woman's antagonist is displayed in all her strength. To the reclining battered body of Christ, the erect, majestic figure of the Virgin Mary, standing in grief, serves as counterpoint. Rather than her son's resurrection, it is her pain that is celebrated. Rather than as mother of the Savior, she is worshiped as *Mater Dolorosa,* symbol of the maternal suffering before the death of her son. She is the mother facing her final tragedy: the loss of her identity, the end of her being. She is the Black Madonna in mourning, foreshadowing the final tragedy of our story, the death of another of her sons. The camera returns to her over and over, and then frames Mamma Lucia in church and in her bedroom kneeling before the altar of the Mother of Christ in a prayer that will not be answered. And it cannot be answered because Turiddu has betrayed the town religion, the honor code which is stricter than that of God and contemplates no forgiveness; only revenge and retribution.

In the piazza of the town in front of the church where the Easter Mass has just been celebrated, another rite is going to take place, a rite that also contemplates a communion, the sharing of wine, a kiss, and a final sacrifice. It is the last act of a rite of honor—the retribution of a betrayal, the most serious crime according to the honor code. As the piazza fills again with town people exiting the church, Turiddu calls everybody for some wine. He is paying for it and wants everyone to take part in his communion. Whereas in the play the action at this point centered on an exchange between Lola and Turiddu—she is provoking him with allusions to his feminine conquests while in the army and he accuses women of being fickle and easily forgetful of past loves—the stage in the opera is charged with an intense, Dionysiac hymn to wine. The scintillating drink is compared to the smile of a lover that can instill joy in the hearts. The sincerity of wine is praised together with its ability to turn pain into joy. It is the wine of Dionysus, not the blood of Christ, but of a pagan cult which is, however, imbued with Catholic elements. The sincerity provoked by wine draws Turiddu close to Lola, but also to Alfio who suddenly appears during this pagan celebration. Turiddu hands him a glass, too, probably aware of the consequences of his action, and perhaps willingly offering himself to the deserved punishment. Alfio refuses the wine; the two men under-stand each other without words, they hug, and Turiddu bites Alfio on the ear, thus sealing their pact in blood.

Before going to his death, Turiddu performs his final rite: a prayer to his mother not for himself, since he does not deserve it, but for Santa. His famous aria—certainly the climax of the opera—begins with the invocation to the mother. Once again there are a few and slight changes from play to opera, but they are very relevant to the centrality of the mother figure. In the play, Turiddu begs his mother to "embrace" him as she did when he left for the army; in the opera he asks for her blessing, thus underlining the religious connotation of maternity. Moreover in the latter he begs her to pray to God on his behalf and entrusts her with the life of Santa. This last element, already present in the play, was there understated: "Se mai . . . alla Santa, che non ha nessuno al mondo, pensateci voi, madre." In the opera, underscored by the repetition of the refrain and the highly dramatic chords that accompany his words, Turiddu begs: "Se io non tornassi . . . Voi dovrete fare da madre a Santa," and he repeats the sentence in the imperative mood just before running out of the house "Fate da madre a Santa!".

The sanctification of the mother figure and the identification of Mamma Lucia with the Virgin Mary are realized in Zeffirelli's skillful filming of the last scene. As Turiddu runs inside to bid his mother farewell, the place looks more like the stable that received the birth of Christ than a tavern. A donkey, a goat and a sheep are standing in a corner next to a hay stack as Mamma Lucia approaches to feed them. Turiddu sings his moving last aria kneeling before her with devotion as she sits higher like a Madonna in throne, reproducing one of the hundreds icons of Madonna and child. Mamma Lucia knows her son's fate, just as Mary knew that of hers, and does not try to stop him. She also knows that death is what awaits him—a just retribution for his crime. If the Easter procession with the *Mater Dolorosa* and the deposed body of Christ will be followed by the stupendous icon of Pietà, there will be no Pietà for Mamma Lucia, no resurrection for Turiddu. She will remain alone on stage as the scream "hanno ammazzato Compare Turiddu!" pierces our ears.

It might seem odd that such a central character has no major aria in the entire opera. Mamma Lucia does not sing any aria, as all other characters do. Yet if we think of what she represents, her silence might become less strange. She embodies the model of abnegation, self effacement, and sacrifice; she only exists in function of her son who determines her very essence. She has no identity, no voice of her own. Yet she is the fulcrum, the life giver to the entire plot. Carlo Parmentola had already remarked Mamma Lucia's central position in the opera "anche in senso fisico perché la sua casa-osteria costituisce il centro di aggregazione profano del paese" (186). It is a center, I might add, that is placed right in front of the religious one, the church, in an obvious counterpoint. On the one hand the Madonna with her dead and resurrected son, on the other, Mamma Lucia with hers who will not rise from death. Two *matres dolorosae* representing two religions, the catholic and the Sicilian, both contemplating the sacrifice of the son.

Giovanni Verga, we should note, had already hinted at the central role of the mother figure even in his brief novella. While Turiddu and Alfio walk to the place of their duel, the former admits to the latter his guilt and his acceptance of the consequences, his readiness to die. Nevertheless Turiddu tells Alfio that he will fight with all his strength to remain alive, because of his mother. "Come è vero Iddio so che ho torto e mi lascerei ammazzare. Ma prima di venire ho visto la mia vecchia che si era alzata per vedermi partire, col pretesto di governare il pollaio, quasi il cuore le parlasse, e quant'è vero Iddio vi ammazzerò come un cane per non far piangere la mia vecchierella." Later on while fighting, to Alfio's exclamation "Ah! compare Turiddu! avete proprio intenzione d' ammazzarmi!" he replies "Si, ve l'ho detto; ora che ho visto la mia vecchia nel pollaio, mi pare di averla sempre dinanzi agli occhi." (**Le novelle** I, 204, 205). Yet at the end of the duel with blood gurgling out of his slashed throat, "non poté profferire nemmeno: 'Ah! mamma mia!'" Turiddu knows that his death would also be that of his mother. In the play and opera the lines were changed and Mamma Lucia was replaced by Santa, for the sake of the drama. The role of Santa having grown with her personal tragedy—her poverty, lack of family and dishonor—it was necessary that Turiddu thought of her in his last moments. Entrusting Santa to his mother and begging her to be a mother to Santa, he is helping Mamma Lucia to survive, continuing a role without which she would cease to exist.

Forty years later another Sicilian play was set to music by an Italian composer. Just as the more famous *Cavalleria rusticana,* Pirandello's play *La favola del figlio cambiato,* was first conceived and written as a short story ("Il figlio cambiato"). The composer who set it to music was Gian Francesco Malipiero and the opera, which premiered in Germany in January 1934 and two months later in Rome, in spite of Pirandello's alliance to Fascism, was boycotted and then forbidden. It was perceived as a mocking of the state and of political leaders. For our discourse, instead, Pirandello's story is yet another proof of the strength of the Sicilian conception of woman. Although the dichotomy erotic woman/ mother is a constant theme in Pirandello's entire literary production (short stories, novels and plays), this short piece, which was set to music and also reworked in the his final myth, *I giganti della montagna,* is a constant companion of his production and can be taken as emblematic of such a conception.

In a letter, written on April 30, 1930, Pirandello recounts to Marta Abba the legend from which he had taken his story.

> All over southern Italy there is the popular belief that in winter, windy and moonless nights, witches called "the Women" fly around and enter houses through chimneys and attics. They take away babies from their poor sleeping mothers, or braid the babies' hair in such a way that it cannot be undone; and woe to those who touch it with a comb or try to cut it; the child will die. Or they brush the babies' eyelids with their fingers, and the next morning the babies wake up cross-eyed; or they exchange babies: they take away a beautiful child and leave an ugly one in his place.
>
> (*Lettere,* 429-30)

This folktale exemplifies the conception that has been discussed and *La favola del figlio cambiato* well explains it. The feminine gender is divided in two opposite types: there are the Mothers (*le Madri*)—in the play no one has a name, "creature di Dio" whose identity consists in their dependence on their creations; and there are the Women (*le Donne*), "figlie dell'inferno," witches of the wind, "streghe della notte," "gatte" always in heat, constantly copulating and never satisfied (*Maschere nude* II, 1231). They take revenge for their sterility, just punishment for their sexual appetite— eroticism and maternity cannot coexist—by using their witchcraft against *le Madri* and their children. At the beginning of Pirandello's play a beautiful child (a boy, of course), "bello come Gesù," is stolen from his mother by *le Donne* and taken to a far a way land where he lives as the son of a king. Separated from his mother, however, the child grows weak and falls ill. Only after the final reunion with his mother his health is restored.[6] Once again the father figure is absent; the only positive relationship is that of mother and child. The mother's antagonist is the figure of the Donna, the erotic woman, who is punished for her sexual life with her inability to conceive and procreate. In the Southern psyche the two can never coexist. As Sciascia had said, this conception is ingrained in man's fear of sexuality, which is seen as sinful and manifests itself in his attributing to the erotic female witchcraft, powers aimed at excusing the male from his sexual drive. The culprit of his sexual sins is the witch whose power cannot be defeated except through exorcism or death.

Since good must prevail before the public of the opera, both works, *Cavalleria rusticana* and *La favola del figlio cambiato,* end with the triumph of the mother figure. Although Mamma Lucia will remain without her son—a son, though, who had deserved and almost chosen death—she will continue to perform her maternal role with Santa; perhaps even with the child of her child, if, as some critics of the play read it, she had become pregnant. Thus one could imagine a future scenario very similar to Pirandello's play *La vita che ti diedi* (a mother living next to his dead son's woman waiting for the birth of the child she is carrying). And here again the father figure is absent so that the maternal role could be performed and dominate the stage. If music, as Nietzsche wrote, expresses the Dionysian principle, the shapeless, the unexplainable, the mystery in us, and words manifest the rational, logical attempt, or the Apollonian need to make sense and give order to chaos, in opera we could see those two principles exemplified by the music and by the libretto, and certainly, it is the former that often takes over and overrides the latter. Within the frame of the two operas discussed above, these two principles at battle can also be represented in the two opposite figures of the erotic and the maternal, in so far as the second is the attempt to sublimate the first, to create order and form—the procreation of a human being—out of chaos—the irrational, impetuous sexual drive. In the Sicilian world of Verga and Pirandello it is the Apollonian that must prevail at all costs, but it does prevail through a forced act of the will, and only because the Dionysian antagonist is truly the stronger.[7]

Notes

1. Sciascia makes the connection erotic woman-witch more explicit in his "La strega e il capitano," a story he wrote using historical sources from the early 17th century. Such a conception of woman was by no means confined to Sicily or the south. The dreadful trail of Caterina Medici that ended with her torture and death at the stake, took place in the duchy of Milan. In narrating the atrocious trial, Sciascia examines the word "diabolical" used by the prosecutors to describe Caterina ("carnosa ma di ciera diabolica") and interprets it as sensual and sexual (Sciascia 232). The main reason why this woman was persecuted and prosecuted was her power of temptation, that made sexually dependent on her even important and respectable people, specifically the senator Luigi Melzi.

2. For a complete accounting of the events surrounding the Sonzogno competition see Pietro Mascagni's *Epistolario*.

3. The commodification of women in *Cavalleria rusticana* is even more apparent in the short story than in the play and opera. Santa's father is described as "ricco come un maiale" (Verga, *Novelle* 200) and Santa mentions her dowry. Moreover, the depiction of Lola's golden rings on her fingers placed on her abdomen underscores her quality as property, as commodity. She is the possession of her husband who has paid for her, and owns and controls even her reproductive system—her womb. Alonge had already commented on the changes in Santa from story to play, underlined by that of the name, in his "Le valenze operistiche del teatro di Giovanni Verga" (60).

4. Zeffirelli probably took it from *Mala Pasqua,* an opera by Stanislao Gastaldon, whose libretto was also a remake of *Cavalleria rusticana* by G. D. Bartocci-Fontana. The opera was completed for the Sonzogno prize together with the other 72, and was placed last. Mascagni's *Cavalleria* won first prize. For further information about the subject, see Jone Gaillard Corsi, 57-68.

5. It is unfortunate that Giacomo Puccini did not write the music for Verga's *La lupa,* as he had agreed to do. The composer had too many doubts about the length of the dialogues. Even more than *Cavalleria rusticana,* the play *La lupa* had lost all its power that was achieved through the brevity and graphic quality of its descriptions. For more information on *La lupa,* see Gaillard Corsi, 69-76.

6. For further information on Pirandello's treatment of this theme, see Bini, especially 129-134.

7. Giacomo De Benedetti gives an interesting interpretation of these two principles in the opera of Wagner who, in his view, succeeds better than any other composer in using the orchestra to express the unconscious. On the other hand, he argues, the characters of our [Italian] melodrama are "more fraternal than symbolic: very strong, easily recognizable because they are similar to us [. . .] but they do not allude to the obscure that exists inside of us," as those created by Wagner do (131).

Works Cited

Alonge, Roberto. "Le valenze operistiche del teatro di Giovanni Verga" in Piero and Nandi Ostali, eds. *Cavalleria rusticana 1890-1990. Cento Anni di un Capolavoro.* Milan: Casa Musicale Sonzogno di P. Ostali, 1990: 57-63.

Bini, Daniela. *Pirandello and His Muse: The Plays for Marta Abba.* Gainsville: University Press of Florida, 1998).

Corsi, Jone Gaillard. *Il libretto d'autore 1860-1930.* West Lafayette: Bordighera, 1997.

De Benedetti, Giacomo. *Verga e il Naturalismo.* Milan: Garzanti, 1976.

Mascagni, Pietro. *Epistolario.* Ed. by M. Morini, R. Iovino and A. Paloscia. Libreria Musicale Italiana, 1996.

Permentola, Carlo. "La Giovane Scuola [1977]" in Piero and Nandi Ostali, eds. *Cavalleria rusticana 1890-1990. Cento Anni di un Capolavoro.* Milan: Casa Musicale Sonzogno di P. Ostali, 1990.

Sciascia, Leonardo. *Opere 1984-1989.* Milan: Bompiani, 1991.

Verga, Giovanni. *Le novelle* 2 vols. Milan: Garzanti, 1980.

———. *Opere*. Milan: Mursia, 1988.

Zeffirelli, Franco. Film of *Cavalleria rusticana* at La Scala, Milan, the ICET film studios, UNITEL/ARIES, 1982.

Piero Garofalo (essay date January 2002)

SOURCE: Garofalo, Piero. "Once Upon a Time . . . Narrative Strategies in Verga's 'Jeli il pastore' and 'Rosso Malpelo.'" *MLN* 117, no. 1 (January 2002): 84-105.

[*In the following essay, Garofalo explicates the formal limitations of the discursive practices of verismo exhibited in "Jeli il pastore" and "Rosso Malpelo," focusing on the mythical and folkloric allusions that inform the characters, temporal structures, and style of both stories.*]

> Cesare Pavese che molti si ostinano a considerare un testardo narratore realista, specializzato in campagne e periferie americano-piemontesi, ci scopre in questi *Dialoghi* un nuovo aspetto del suo temperamento. Non c'è scrittore autentico, il quale non abbia i suoi quarti di luna, il suo capriccio, la musa nascosta, che a un tratto lo inducono a farsi eremita. [. . .] Ha smesso per un momento di credere che il suo totem e tabù, i suoi selvaggi, gli spiriti della vegetazione, l'assassinio rituale, la sfera mitica e il culto dei morti, fossero inutili bizzarrie e ha voluto cercare in essi il segreto di qualcosa che tutti ricordano [. . .].[1]

Through *Dialoghi con Leucò,* Pavese responds to the critical reception of his literary texts by both challenging the authorial construct and celebrating the mythical-poetic. These dialogues explicate a discursive strategy that was always already present in his so-called realist narratives. Giovanni Verga's most acclaimed literary texts have endured a similar reductive reading that also obfuscates the heterogeneity of his poetics. Mythical language characterizes much of Verga's early narrative production—*Una peccatrice, Eva,* and *Eros* are evincive of this tendency. This articulation is a discursive strategy, which is also present in his later works.

In order to discern these non-realist articulations it is first necessary to dismantle the veristic façade that obstructs an analysis of this type. I do not propose to expose the fictions lying beneath the philosophical premises of *verismo*;[2] rather, I seek to explicate the formal limitations of this literary referent. By raising the realist veil enshrouding Verga's texts, I emphasize other cultural formations central to his poetics.

The sophism of realist art is that the reality the writer purports to present, via the object of the narration, also conveys assent on the morals the authorial persona de-sires to suggest—it naturalizes a social construct. Realism deputes the demonstration to the so-called facts, thereby relieving the authorial voice of all contingent accountability. The realist discourse then becomes all the more compelling as the reader's potential to challenge the performative construct is limited before events and characters that are inscribed in a seemingly objective reality. In this sense, the realist discourse naturalizes both itself and its object.

In a letter to Luigi Capuana dated 19 February 1881, Verga asserts the primacy of the text over the writer and the subsequent necessity of suppressing the authorial persona:

> Che cos'è non il tuo nome, né il mio, ma quel del Manzoni, o di Zola, in faccia ai *Promessi Sposi* e all'*Assommoir*? L'opera d'arte non val più dell'autore? se è riescita ben inteso. Parmi che si deve arrivare a sopprimere il nome dell'artista dal piedistallo della sua opera, quando questa vive da sé; sai la mia vecchia fissazione di una ideale opera d'arte tanto perfetta da avere in sé stessa tutto il suo organismo.[3]

Forma dat esse rei. This mask of fidelity to fact serves to conceal the parenthetic and demonstrative intent of the author by naturalizing the ideological. While falling short of proclaiming the death of the author, Verga's mimetic strategy is one of displacement, to use Northrop Frye's term, that produces a tension between form and content.[4] The distancing of the authorial voice from the text defers accountability while establishing a textual space for participation in the social order. As Giorgio Bàrberi Squarotti argues, the reader is also implicated in this discursive strategy:

> La maschera della fedeltà al fatto vale a coprire l'intento parenetico e dimostrativo, che è poi una forma di collaborazione all'ordine della società com'è: non che essere una forma di letteratura di tipo "progressivo" ovvero rivoluzionario, il romanzo realista e verista propone una fruizione di sé come lezione sui mali inevitabili che comporta ogni attentato alla norma. Ha in sé, in ultima analisi, l'esigenza di ottenere dal lettore la liberazione dall'impulso a mutare qualcosa nell'ordine sociale, indicandogli tutta la sequenza dei mali che inevitabilmente ne deriva.[5]

In mimetic representations, the aesthetic and the ideological are complementary referents in the formation of power relations. *Verismo* displaces the performative role of the author and establishes a textual site that locates its authority within its own performance. Thus, *verismo*'s negotiation, which at first glance appears to empower the reader, in practice delineates the epistemic boundaries of interpretation.

This discussion does nothing to challenge Verga's literary designation as a Verist writer; rather, it reiterates that reality, as a textual construct, cannot be universalized. For the modern reader, the advent of relativism eliminates the possibility of an objective knowledge of realities independent of referents. Relativism does not negate the mimetic aspects of a writer's prose; however, it does challenge the premises that underlie and undermine that particular discursive strategy.

I propose that even Verga's Verist poetics negotiate a discursive strategy imbued with the language of myth and folklore. My investigation focuses on **"Jeli il pastore"** and **"Rosso Malpelo,"** two stories that occupy a liminal position in the development of Verga's experimental narrative.[6] In particular, I examine three distinct textual aspects of these stories: the *dramatis personae,* the temporal structure, and the style. While this is not a study in poetic mythologies, some preliminary critical references will clarify my methodology in regards to the relation between myths and folk tales.

Fundamental, in this respect, are Carl Gustav Jung's theories on archetypes because they provide a compelling literary model for approaching narrative tropes. Jung distinguishes archetypes as universal forms in the collective unconscious:

> In addition to our immediate consciousness, which is of a thoroughly personal nature and which we believe to be the only empirical psyche, there exists a second psychic system of a collective, universal nature which is identical in all individuals. This collective unconscious does not develop individually but is inherited. It consists of pre-existent forms, the archetypes, which can only become conscious secondarily and which give definite form to certain psychic contents.[7]

Jung provides a theoretical framework for conceptualizing archetypes as literary manifestations of a collective unconscious. Vladimir Propp arrived at similar conclusions in his seminal study on the morphology of the folk tale.[8] The aim of his investigation was to expose the common pattern governing narrative propositions derived from a corpus of close to two hundred Russian folk tales, in which the constant elements had to be abstracted from the variable, specific events and characters constituting the individual stories. He labeled the constant element a "function," and it represented "an act of a character, defined from the point of view of its significance for the course of the action."[9] Propp argued that the functions remained constant even when the identity of the agent changed. In other words, the *dramatis personae* of folk tales are literary representations of archetypes. Their names may change, but they remain the same.

In addition, Jung and Propp converge independently on another aspect of interest to the present analysis. The latter concludes that, "the study of attributes makes possible a scientific interpretation of the tale. From a historical point of view, this signifies that the fairy tale in its morphological bases represents a *myth.*"[10] Jung

discerns a similar rapport: "Tribal lore is concerned with archetypes [. . .] they have been changed into conscious formulae taught according to tradition. [. . .] Another well-known expression of the archetypes is myth and fairytale."[11] He proceeds to develop this intuition more concretely: "The product of the collective unconscious resembles the type of structures to be met with in myth and fairytale so much so that we must regard them as related."[12] Lévi-Strauss further solidifies this complementary relationship between myth and folk tale:

> [L]'esperienza etnologica attuale ci induce invece a pensare che, al contario, mito e favola sfruttino una sostanza comune, ma ognuno alla sua maniera. La loro relazione non è di anteriore a posteriore, di primitivo a derivato, ma è piuttosto una relazione di complementarità. Le fiabe sono miti in miniatura, in cui le stesse opposizioni sono riportate in scala ridotta, ed è questo in primo luogo che le rende difficili da studiare.[13]

Lévi-Strauss's literary anthropological analysis implies that the discriminatory divide between the two narratives is permeable. These conclusions suggest that while folk tales, fairy tales, myths, and legends designate distinct narrative representations, they share generic discursive strategies. I would argue that *verismo* assimilates these discursive strategies into its poetics thereby challenging its capacity to negotiate a mimetic representation. As a system, Verism presents elements that connote specific mythical significations.[14] However, in the present context, my use of these narrative categories is not culturally specific and respects their taxonomic slippage.

"Jeli il pastore"

With these preliminary considerations aside, let us turn our attention to Verga's texts. **"Jeli il pastore"** traces the life of a young herder from his idyllic solitary youth to his entrance into the social order. The homonymous protagonist shares traits characteristic of the Child God/*puer* archetype.[15] Jeli tends to his horses in isolation, removed from the constraints and regulations of society. For Jung, the word "child" suggests something evolving toward independence, destined to free itself from its origins. In fact, abandonment emerges as a necessary condition for the creation of the Child God. The *puer* possesses a superior consciousness, which marginalizes his social position; solitude expresses the conflict between the Child and his environment.[16] Paradoxically, even though the *puer* possesses powers superior to those surrounding him, he is in constant peril of erasure, due to the fact that although he is divine, he is also a child.

In so far as the content of archetypes is expressed through metaphors, Jeli's textual identification with the Child God emerges as a recurring motif. From Jeli's introduction into the narrative, he is presented as a mythical figure, born and raised amongst the animals: "—Vedete Jeli il pastore? è stato sempre solo pei campi come se l'avessero figliato le sue cavalle [. . .]" (**"JP"** [**"Jeli il pastore"**], 138-39). He is also referred to as a divine gift: "«Era piovuto dal cielo, e la terra l'aveva raccolto» come dice il proverbio; era proprio di quelli che non hanno né casa né parenti" ("JP," 139). Just as the archetype of the Child God must be abandoned in order to develop, Jeli also endures this ritualistic passage: both his parents expire.[17]

Jeli's textual representation emphasizes his singularity and his naturalized relation to the environment. His knowledge is presented as almost primordial: "conosceva come spira il vento quando porta il temporale, e di che colore sia il nuvolo quando sta per nevicare. Ogni cosa aveva il suo aspetto e il suo significato [. . .]" ("JP," 140). Even in his social relations, Jeli privileges nature over society. He possesses an intimate rapport with the animals and communicates with them with greater facility than with humans. His inability to articulate his thoughts and the ease with which he converses with the horses are symptomatic of this tendency. For example, while driving the herd to the fair, Jeli carries on a conversation with the horses rather than with his assistant: "E senza curarsi che Alfio il ragazzo, non rispondeva nulla [. . .]. Così [Jeli] andava parlando all'uno e all'altro dei puledri" ("JP," 152). Even after he enters the social order Jeli remains incapable of acclimating himself to verbal communication, a failure that contributes to the *dénouement*:

> —Non andare! disse egli a Mara, come don Alfonso la chiamava perché venisse a ballare cogli altri. Non andare, Mara!
>
> —Perché?
>
> —Non voglio che tu vada. Non andare!
>
> —Lo senti che mi chiamano.
>
> Egli non profferiva più alcuna parola intelligibile, mentre stava curvo sulle pecore che tosava.
>
> ("JP," 171)

Jeli's inarticulate exposition is limited to imperatives and degenerates into a maundering that adumbrates the final shearing of the *capretto* Don Alfonso.

The story opens in an idyllic, pastoral setting in which Jeli lives contentedly. He is the indisputable ruler of this bucolic kingdom. The iterative use of *bello* in the diegetic description of Tebidi's seasons [Illegible Text] the indeterminate memory with melancholy:

> Ah! le *belle* scappate pei campi mietuti, colle criniere al vento! i *bei* giorni d'aprile, quando il vento accavallava ad onde l'erba verde, e le cavalle nitrivano nei pascoli; i *bei* meriggi d'estate, in cui la campagna, bianchiccia, taceva, sotto il cielo fosco, e i grilli scoppi-

ettavano fra le zolle, come se le stoppie si incendiassero! il *bel* cielo d'inverno attraverso i rami nudi del mandorlo, che rabbrividivano al rovajo, e il viottolo che suonava gelato sotto lo zoccolo dei cavalli, e le allodole che trillavano in alto, al caldo, nell'azzurro! le *belle* sere di estate che salivano adagio adagio come la nebbia [. . .].

> ("JP," 137-38, emphasis mine)

This romantic longing for a life in harmony with nature's cycle is not a projection of Jeli's desires, but rather it is that of the narrative voice's: "Jeli, lui, non pativa di quella malinconia [. . .]" ("JP," 138). His physical surroundings as well as his human environment are trait-connoting metaphors. As long as Jeli remains within the confines of this Arcadia, he wants for nothing and no one: "Insomma, purché ci avesse la sua sacca ad armacollo, non aveva bisogno di nessuno al mondo [. . .]" ("JP," 138). The preludial pastoral sequence is a metaphor for the boy's innocence; once Jeli leaves this symbolic space for that of social reality, he ceases to function as an archetype. In addition, when he enters society, the wondrous skills he possesses lose all symbolic and economic value. In a Bakhtinian inversion of hierarchies, his signifiers now signify with a *différance*. The traits that marked him as adept in the wilds mark him as inept in society. Similarly, the stability and plenitude of Jeli's subject-position cannot be inscribed into the symbolic order that he has entered. In fact, it is the inability to form a determinate subjectivity that results in Jeli's concluding expulsion from the social order.

The narrative hinges on the typically romantic clash between the myths of natural innocence and social corruption that characterize the human condition. This conflict is one of binary oppositions. The mythological form produces within itself an *enantiodromia*, a conversion into its opposite. In the narrative, this process occurs when Jeli attempts to integrate himself into society. He loses his privileged position and is forced to occupy the lowest rung on the social ladder: "non l'avevano voluto nemmeno per guardare i porci [. . .]" ("JP," 158). In the story's deterministic conclusion, the synthesis of the narrative tensions induces Jeli's self-extinguishing eruption.

Another *dramatis persona,* the childhood friend Mara, is the catalyst for Jeli's socialization. Even though they had not seen each other for several years, Jeli's first acknowledgment of his solitude occurs when he returns to Tebidi and discovers that Mara's family is moving to Marineo:

> Massaro Agrippino e sua moglie si erano avviati colla carretta, Mara correva loro dietro tutta allegra, portando il paniere coi piccioni. Jeli volle accompagnarla sino al ponticello, e quando Mara stava per scomparire nella vallata la chiamò:—Mara! oh! Mara!

—Che vuoi? disse Mara.

Egli non lo sapeva che voleva.—O tu, cosa farai qui tutto solo? gli domandò allora la ragazza.

—Io resto coi puledri.

Mara se ne andò saltellando, e lui rimase lì fermo, finché poté udire il rumore della carretta che rimbalzava sui sassi.

                                                    ("**JP**," 149-50)

While Mara moves on with her life, Jeli's thoughts are filled with images of her. The text appropriates a discursive strategy similar to that of the folk tale in which physical separation represents psychological distance. Mara's absence constitutes a new awareness in Jeli's socialization: "Mara, come se ne fu andata a Marineo in mezzo alla gente nuova, e alle faccende della vendemmia, si scordò di lui; ma Jeli ci pensava sempre a lei, perché non aveva altro da fare, nelle lunghe giornate che passava a guardare la coda delle sue bestie" ("**JP**," 150). The narrative voice subsumes Mara's departure to mitigate the textual contradiction between Jeli's earlier existence when "c'era sempre che vedere e che ascoltare in tutte le ore del giorno" ("**JP**," 140) and his current state of *ennui*. He cannot continue to live as he has and remain satisfied. Desire and lack have entered into his consciousness.

Mara's representation evinces the traits characteristic of the Anima archetype. According to Jung, the Anima is the female that lives within each male: "She intensifies, exaggerates, falsifies and mythologizes all emotional relations with his work and with other people."[18] The relationship between Jeli and Mara is represented as one of conflicts. Their interests, needs, and desires are completely non-complementary, as is neatly summed up in the observation: "Infatti Mara non era fatta a far la pecoraia [. . .]" ("**JP**," 166). While Mara is the object of Jeli's desire, she is able to resist his interpellation because they lack mutual recognition. Her infringement as other into his self-contained environment, disrupts/corrupts his natural state. This misogynistic representation accentuates the mythologizing tendency of the narrative by inserting the text into the archetypal literary tradition of foundational narratives—specifically, that of edenic expulsions.

This aesthetic performance organizes the temporal structure of the text, which presents a complex relationship between chronological time and psychological time. Myths are located outside of time, *in illo tempore,* to adopt Mircea Eliade's felicitous phrase, and so is Jeli's world.[19] The text disregards the effective sequence of temporal periods and concentrates almost exclusively on events that have a strong emotional charge. The opening pastoral description situates the narrative in an idyllic framework in which the passage of time lacks precise chronological referents. Concomitant to the pre-

sentation of this atemporal dimension is the rapid, elliptical movement of time in the description of Jeli and Mara's friendship. The first sentence of each paragraph, for six consecutive paragraphs, represents an indefinite temporal leap: "Ma da quel giorno in poi [. . .]. Al tempo dei fichidindia poi [. . .]. Durante l'inverno [. . .]. Col marzo tornarono [. . .]. Così passarono tutta l'estate [. . .]. In quel tempo [. . .]" ("**JP**," 144; 145; 145; 145; 146; 146). The temporal references are all indeterminate. The flowing of time is not anchored in the calendar, but in the flow of the seasons, an ethnological time of the eternal return juxtaposed to the linear narrative.

The repetition of events produced by negotiating interchanges between narrative present, analepsis (the narrative excursion into past textual events), and prolepsis (the narrative excursion into future textual events) temporally organizes the text. Thus, the discrepancy between what the Russian Formalists referred to as the *fabula* (or story), the temporal-causal sequence of narrated events, and the *sjuzet* (or plot), the way in which these events are textually manipulated, is constantly brought into play. Mara's presentation in the narrative illustrates this technique. She is introduced in a conversation between Jeli and Don Alfonso, another childhood friend, after which the history of her character is given. The flashback is now the new temporal reference for narrative progression. Time is effectively disjointed; analepsis becomes prolepsis.

The same textual mechanism is set in motion with the prolepsis of the fair followed by the expanded narrative development of the event:

Egli [Jeli] rivide soltanto la ragazza [Mara] il dì della festa di San Giovanni, come andò alla fiera coi puledri da vendere: una festa che gli si mutò tutta in veleno, e gli fece cascare il pan di bocca per un accidente toccato ad uno dei puledri del padrone, Dio ne scampi. Il giorno della fiera il fattore aspettava [. . .].

                                                    ("**JP**," 150)

In all these instances the narrative manipulates not only chronological sequences but also *durée*. Prolepsis induces acceleration in the narrative, while analepsis actuates deceleration. The result is a double reading of the text in which the significant events are repeatedly embedded in the *fabula* thereby replicating the chronological moment.

Prolepsis acts not only as an anticipatory element, but also as a mythical one in the text. This is evident in the episode describing Mara's affair with Don Alfonso and Jeli's unwillingness to believe such a betrayal possible. The narrator's declaration that "Fu da quel momento che lo chiamarono per soprannome *Corna d'oro*, e il soprannome gli rimase, a lui e tutti i suoi, anche dopo che ei si lavò le corna nel sangue" (**"JP,"** 169) is not just foreshadowing, but prophetic in tone. The propensity of prolepsis is to extend time beyond the confines of history into the temporal sphere of legends. In fact, when Jeli kills Don Alfonso, his violence is portrayed not as the result of assimilation of a social construct, but as *nature naturée*: "—Come!—diceva—Non dovevo ucciderlo nemmeno? . . . Se mi aveva preso la Mara! . . ." (**"JP,"** 172). Jeli is incapable of articulating his sentiments and can express them only through action.[20] Rather than being representative of a Sicilian vendetta, Jeli's reaction to Mara's adultery is narrated as the *de facto* response of human nature. The concluding suspension points situate both the reader and the narrative voice in a subordinate position with respect to the text and demarcate a textual space for them to reflect upon what has been omitted. The reader is textually coerced into assuming the narrative voice's point of view and is therefore complicit in accepting the text's ideological implications.

A stylistic analysis of the text reinforces these observations. The use of free indirect discourse enhances the polyvocality of the text by bringing into play numerous speakers and attitudes. The polyphonic elements increase through both chorality and the integration of intersecting discourses (other texts and proverbs). The strategic use of adages or colloquial expressions evokes an eternal past, an oral tradition through which knowledge is disseminated from generation to generation, comprising the base of present day myths and folk tales. This textual assimilation of popular aphorisms contributes toward the reader's impression that the narrative is an orally transmitted text.

Verga's attention to and appropriation of these oral traditions during the composition of **Vita dei campi** and *I Malavoglia* is amply documented. Several letters to Luigi Capuana attest to his sustained interest in further examining these materials. In a correspondence dated 17 May 1878, Verga requests assistance in identifying suitable texts: "Potresti indicarmi una raccolta di *Proverbi* e *Modi di dire* siciliani?"[21] Subsequently, on 10 April 1879, he reiterates this desire:

> Fammi il piacere di mandarmi per suo mezzo [Mazzoni], se tu non verrai presto, tutte quelle raccolte di proverbi e modi di dire siciliani che hai e che ti rimanderò, «in ottimo stato di riparazioni locative», fra un paio di settimane, se pure non verrai a rilevarle tu stesso.[22]

Ten days later he writes again to Capuana:

> [T]i rimando il tuo Pitré ancora vergine, giacché del Pitré ne avevo anch'io una copia, colla medesima copertina color pietronciana e non ci avevo trovato gran cosa. Ciò che vado cercando con desiderio è la raccolta dei proverbi del Rapisarda, stampata in Catania, e introvabile.[23]

Verga's familiarity with Giuseppe Pitré's research and his interest in Santo Rapisarda's text during this period is evident in the composition of **"Jeli il pastore."** The Verist concern Verga expressed in distancing the authorial voice from the text produces a deliberately ambiguous appropriation of popular expressions that suggest either approval/identification or derision/hostility. The slippage between direct discourse, indirect discourse, and free indirect discourse, to which this folkloric voice is central, obfuscates the distance between the narrative voice's position and that of the characters, thereby producing an ambivalent tension.

The narrator situates himself at the extradiegetic level, in accordance with the tenets of *verismo,* distancing himself from the narration and impressing upon the reader his unquestionable reliability. The text constructs an atmosphere of indisputable reality, which mirrors that of folk tales and myths, in which the impersonal narrator reinforces the eternal quality implicit in these cultural forms thereby sustaining a specific field of power. In addition, the text reconstructs the social structure by verbally evoking the imaginary participation of the reader thus concealing the structure in its very form of presentation to produce what Pierre Bourdieu refers to as the *effet de croyance* [belief effect].[24]

"Rosso Malpelo"

Similar challenges to narrative realism can also be discerned in **"Rosso Malpelo,"** a story that relates how a child mineworker is transformed into a popular legend. The homonymous protagonist is defined by his name, which ascribes to a popular tradition whereby a certain behavior is a natural result of a person's appearance (and vice versa)—in this case, the association between obstinate meanness and red hair:

> Malpelo si chiamava così perché aveva i capelli rossi; ed aveva i capelli rossi perché era un ragazzo malizioso e cattivo, che prometteva di riescire un fior di birbone. Sicché tutti alla cava della rena rossa lo chiamavano Malpelo; e persino sua madre col sentirgli dir sempre a quel modo aveva quasi dimenticato il suo nome di battesimo.
>
> (**"RM"** [**"Rosso Malpelo"**], 173)

The incipit provides an *a priori* assertive argumentation that organizes the narrative. As Carlo Muscetta notes, this physiognomic identification is derived from folklore: "Il titolo è tratto dall'aforisma "russu malu pilu", ove l'ellissi del verbo vuole sancire la verità di una legge di natura (chi è rosso è cattivo)."[25] Gregory Lucente argues that this color imagery inscribes a chthonian mark on the body: "In terms of popular belief, his red hair is the color of Judas' and, through Judas, the sign of Cain."[26] The opening predication expresses this tautology through the iterative usage of subordinating conjunctions ("perché [. . .] perché [. . .] sicché") that are more expletory than explicatory. This essentialist substantiation by which the body serves as an index to order and to explain the subject is both explicit and supra-temporal. Consequently, the frequent presence of such physiognomic associations in the text produces a rational, authoritative, and static impression. Hence, the metonymic/metaphoric relation between external appearance and character-traits becomes a tautological certainty.[27] In addition, the erasure of his proper name from communal memory—not once is it mentioned—symbolically marginalizes Malpelo to an extra-baptismal state. This deterministic effacement of identity adumbrates the narrative's concluding imagery of Malpelo's "unbaptized" spirit wandering through the limbo of subterranean passage-ways for eternity.

Color imagery does not just mark Rosso Malpelo as excluded from the integrated community; it also establishes his identity-forming relation with the red-sand pit.[28] Not only is his hair red, but he is always covered in red dust: "Era sempre cencioso e lordo di rena rossa, ché la sorella s'era fatta sposa, e aveva altro pel capo: nondimeno era conosciuto come la bettonica per tutto Monserrato e la Carvana, tanto che la cava dove lavorava la chiamavano 'la cava di Malpelo', e cotesto al padrone gli seccava assai" (**"RM,"** 173-74). His metonymic relationship to the quarry is not one of ownership, but instead is one of identity.[29] Regardless of the owner's annoyance, Malpelo's presence is not disruptive to the capitalist order.

Despite these superficial differences, Rosso Malpelo, like Jeli, shares a similar textual representation to that of the *puer divinus* archetype. He appears as a mythical figure, metaphorically born of beasts. His father is more animal than man, "lo chiamavano mastro Misciu Bestia, ed era l'asino da basto di tutta la cava" (**"RM,"** 174), and Malpelo too lacks basic anthropomorphic qualities: "non aveva più nulla di umano [. . .]" (**"RM,"** 176). Like Jeli, Malpelo has also been abandoned, as all Child gods must be.[30] His contact with other humans is limited; he prefers the company of animals: "Il cane gli voleva bene, perché i cani non guardano altro che la mano la quale dà loro il pane" (**"RM,"** 177). Significantly, the only human relationship that he is able to develop is with Ranocchio, a name that suggests something less than human-connoting traits. Of course, the bonding between a social-outcast protagonist and an animal is typical of folk tales.

Rosso Malpelo's appearance distinguishes him as unique, different, and to be feared; it reveals to the world his chthonic origins, which are both diabolical and divine.[31] He is described as being of the worst sort, as if possessed by the devil: "sembrava ci avesse messo la coda il diavolo" (**"RM,"** 179), "Malpelo avea il diavolo dalla sua" (**"RM,"** 176), and "sembrava che stesse ad ascoltare qualche cosa che il suo diavolo gli sus-

surava negli orecchi" (**"RM,"** 176). The textual comparison between the legendary tale of the lost miner's wandering ghost and the fantastic story of Malpelo's own disappearance into the darkness underscores his autochthonous nature: "Prese gli arnesi di suo padre, il piccone, la zappa, la lanterna, il sacco col pane, e il fiasco del vino, e se ne andò: né più si seppe nulla di lui" (**"RM,"** 189). The narrative concludes by enacting a new narrative, relegated to oral tradition, in which Rosso Malpelo becomes a legend to be spoken of in hushed voices by the children of the quarry: "Così si persero persin le ossa di Malpelo, e i ragazzi della cava abbassano la voce quando parlano di lui nel sotterraneo, ché hanno paura di vederselo comparire dinanzi, coi capelli rossi e gli occhiacci grigi" (**"RM,"** 189). The syntactic shift to the present tense is also a temporal shift to an indeterminate *hic et nunc*. Rather than achieving linear closure, the intratextual conclusion returns the cyclical narrative to the introduction: "Malpelo si chiamava così perché aveva i capelli rossi; ed aveva i capelli rossi perché era un ragazzo malizioso e cattivo [. . .]" (**"RM,"** 173). A myth of eternal return is textually reenacted through the hybridization of literary strategies.

The central image of the quarry is reminiscent of another archetype, that of the Mother. Jung associates these qualities with this ambiguous figure:

> [M]aternal solicitude and sympathy [. . .]. The place of magic transformation and rebirth, together with the underworld and its inhabitants are presided over by the mother [. . .] the mother archetype may connote anything secret, hidden, dark, the abyss, the world of the dead, anything that devours, seduces and poisons, that is terrifying and inescapable like fate.[32]

These conflicting manifestations of the archetype find their textual correspondence in the representation of the mine shaft. While Ranocchio fears the cave, Malpelo embraces it. In his depiction, the red-sand pit assumes the traits characteristic of an entrance to the chthonic realm. It is the legendary locus in which spirits dwell:

> Ei [Malpelo] narrava [. . .] come degli uomini ce n'erano rimasti tanti, o schiacciati, o smarriti nel buio, e che camminano da anni e camminano ancora, senza poter scorgere lo spiraglio del pozzo pel quale sono entrati, e senza poter udire le strida disperate dei figli, i quali li cercano inutilmente.
>
> (**"RM,"** 181-82)

Malpelo is intimately associated with the labyrinthine mine. As a child his father led him by hand through this maternal maze; it is his home and his family. However, the pit is also a cruel mistress who nurtures and destroys—both womb and tomb. In this sense, as the Mother archetype, the quarry is a symbolic representation of the *vagina dentata*.

In Book VII of Plato's *Republic,* Socrates evokes the image of a cave in which people sit facing a wall. The cave is a negative symbol; it is a parable of ignorance. Plato's allegory examines the projection of fictions in the educational process. Socrates argues that it is necessary first to distance oneself from the images in order to perceive their phenomenological condition and then to reexamine them with this new knowledge. Rosso Malpelo performs this operation and opts for the life of the quarry. He is in constant tension between the chthonic lure, which both terrifies and fascinates him, and the world of the living, in which he finds no space for himself:

> Almeno sottoterra, nella cava della rena, brutto e cencioso e sbracato com'era, non lo beffavano più, e sembrava fatto apposta per quel mestiere persin nel colore dei capelli, e in quegli occhiacci di gatto che ammiccavano se vedevano il sole. Così ci sono degli asini che lavorano nelle cave per anni ed anni senza uscirne mai più, ed in quei sotterranei, dove il pozzo di ingresso è verticale, ci si calan colle funi, e ci restano finché vivono. Sono asini vecchi, è vero, comprati dodici o tredici lire, quando stanno per portarli alla Plaja, a strangolarli; ma pel lavoro che hanno da fare laggiù sono ancora buoni; e Malpelo, certo, non valeva di più, e se veniva fuori dalla cava il sabato sera, era perché aveva anche le mani per aiutarsi colla fune, e doveva andare a portare a sua madre la paga della settimana.

> (**"RM,"** 180-81)

The red-sand pit is a wasteland, a pack animal's graveyard in which Malpelo feels most at home. The textual identification between the protagonist and the quarry suggests that the physical landscape is also a psychological one—a standard romantic motif. A specific monetary value is affixed to the boy and reiterates his bestial representation. The donkeys used in the mine are working on borrowed time, and so, it would appear, is Rosso Malpelo.[33] He has no need to leave the pit but does so only because he can and because he needs to provide for his mother.

While Malpelo does engage in a poetic rumination on life outside the mine, he is resigned to his fate: "Ma quello era stato il mestiere di suo padre, e in quel mestiere era nato lui" (**"RM,"** 181). The relationship established amongst the protagonist, his biological mother, and his archetypal mother is both affective and economic: the cave is his comfort and his mother's means of subsistence. Instead of a loving family's embrace, Malpelo's emotive protensions are for the mine itself, which envelops him completely:

> Ei [Malpelo] narrava che era stato sempre là, da bambino, e aveva sempre visto quel buco nero, che si sprofondava sotterra, dove il padre soleva condurlo per mano. Allora stendeva le braccia a destra e a sinistra, e descriveva come l'intricato laberinto delle gallerie si stendesse sotto i loro piedi dappertutto, di qua e di là [. . .].

> (**"RM,"** 181)

He recognizes himself in this infernal labyrinth and takes comfort in its unsettling immensity. In fact, even when Malpelo imagines other types of existences, his fantasies are framed by similar desires for solitude and limitless space:

> Certamente egli avrebbe preferito di fare il manovale, come Ranocchio, e lavorare cantando sui ponti, in alto, in mezzo all'azzurro del cielo, col sole sulla schiena—o il carrettiere, come compare Gaspare che veniva a prendersi la rena della cava, dondolandosi sonnacchioso sulle stanghe, colla pipa in bocca, e andava tutto il giorno per le belle strade di campagna—o meglio ancora avrebbe voluto fare il contadino che passa la vita fra i campi, in mezzo al verde, sotto i folti carrubbi, e il mare turchino là in fondo, e il canto degli uccelli sulla testa.

> (**"RM,"** 181)

Malpelo's concerns are not limited to his physical environment, which is a manifestation of his desire for the other, but extend to forms of social interaction and the power relations therein. He does not fantasize social integration, but instead he seeks even greater social isolation. His ultimate dream to be a farmer reflects his desire to achieve complete social and economic autarchy.

In his conversations with Ranocchio, Malpelo's behavior is similar to Plato's philosopher: his pedagogical approach attempts to reconcile the two worlds that he inhabits. In the end, however, he opts for the mine and what it represents to him. As Bàrberi Squarotti observes, the *puer* rejects Christianity's eschatological vision in favor of a *quasi*-Aenean descent into the abyss: "L'ultima discesa nella cava di Malpelo è, appunto, una cosciente discesa agli inferi a ritrovare il padre e il suo mondo di minatori sepolti, là dove sono i 'buoni' come mastro Misciu, e non in cielo, come dice a Ranocchio che gli espone le idee religiose avute dalla madre [. . .]."[34] Malpelo overturns society's theological hierarchy in a sort of Bakhtinian carnival in which a subversive strategy of reversal and inversion challenges the organization of the hegemonic culture. However, Malpelo's resistance to the social order is rooted in neither emancipatory politics nor Christian *caritas.* He expounds to Ranocchio a philosophy of power relations predicated on the premise of impunity: "L'asino va picchiato, perché non può picchiar lui; e s'ei potesse picchiare, ci pesterebbe sotto i piedi e ci strapperebbe la carne a morsi" (**"RM,"** 178). According to his logic, society regulates itself by means of a literal *argumentum ad baculum* that falls nothing short of anthropophagy. Of course, Malpelo's iterative textual identification with the asses of the quarry, especially il *grigio,* delimitates his spatial as well as his economic status in the social order.

In **"Jeli il pastore"** many temporal transitions are lacking; nevertheless, the reader can still perceive an underlying diachronic sequence. In **"Rosso Malpelo,"** the syntactic treatment of time is carried even further: the narrative privileges simultaneity over progression and continuity. The text is organized around the homodiegetic analepsis of mastro Misciu's death, which impels the narrative by establishing a father-son motif that privileges psychological development at the expense of chronological progression. Bàrberi Squarotti argues that this discursive strategy does not abide by the poetics of *verismo*:

> Il fatto è che questa (ma anche altre novelle verghiana) non è tanto la fedele stesura di una vicenda, condotta secondo i criteri veristi, quanto piuttosto un esempio, una dimostrazione, nella quale le coerenze temporali e l'assoluta verosimiglianza non contano certamente più del messaggio che viene affidato al personaggio che è protagonista, all'ambiente, al 'coro' che racconta la vicenda.[35]

The choral voice, which is both singular and plural, underscores the tensions in a displacement strategy that defers mimetic representations. The frailty of the *fabula* is due to the scarcity of concrete, sequential actions, which is reflected linguistically in the privileged usage of the imperfect, the tense of the indefinite, at the expense of the present perfect. The paucity of autonomous narrative sequences confers an indeterminate temporal organization on the narrative. This discursive strategy challenges *verismo*'s poetics by expunging history from the story in favor of an ahistorical tension that defies mimetic representation.

It is not possible to determine the actual *durée* of the narrative. The transitions between episodes are distinguished by generic chronological incipit: "Tutt'a un tratto [. . .]. Ma una volta [. . .]. Due o tre giorni dopo [. . .]. In quel tempo [. . .]. Da lì a poco [. . .]. Verso quell'epoca [. . .]. Una volta [. . .]" ("**RM**," 175; 182; 182; 183; 186; 188; 188).[36] These indeterminate *in illo tempore* markers situate the *fabula* beyond the limits of mimetic poetics and inside the ahistorical realm of the fairy tale. This temporal distancing produces hermeneutic gaps that make the narrative's concluding syntactic shift to the present tense all the more unsettling and fantastic.

The same narrative strategy observed in "**Jeli il pastore**" is implemented to similar effect in "**Rosso Malpelo**": an accelerated prolepsis followed by a decelerated analepsis. This technique is particularly evident in the scene relating the father's death: "Insomma lo tenevano [Malpelo] addirittura per carità e perché mastro Misciu, suo padre, era morto nella cava. Era morto così [. . .]" ("**RM**," 174). Mastro Misciu's demise, in turn, serves as the catalyst for the prolepsis alluding to Malpelo's own fate: "—Va' là, che tu non ci morrai nel tuo letto, come tuo padre. Invece nemmen suo padre ci morì nel suo letto, tuttoché fosse una buona bestia" ("**RM**," 174). The refrain is repeated toward the end of

the story by the escaped convict in conversation with Rosso Malpelo: "tu ci andrai [in prigione] e ci lascerai le ossa. Invece le ossa le lasciò nella cava, Malpelo, come suo padre, ma in modo diverso" ("**RM**," 188). This iterative prolepsis prefigures the cyclical nature of the inter- and intra-generational relationships. While underscoring the presence of an extradiegetic authorial voice, the repetition also accentuates the artifice of the narrative positing it outside of history.[37]

Significantly, the verbal tenses shift to the present only at the end of the narrative. The present tense distances the representation of Malpelo into a legendary past, while simultaneously emphasizing his supra-temporal survival in the memories of the living. All that remains of Malpelo are the legend and the myth:

> Prese gli arnesi di suo padre, il piccone, la zappa, la lanterna, il sacco col pane, e il fiasco del vino, e se ne andò: né più si seppe nulla di lui.
>
> Così si persero persin le ossa di Malpelo, e i ragazzi della cava abbassano la voce quando parlano di lui nel sotterraneo, ché hanno paura di vederselo comparire dinanzi, coi capelli rossi e gli occhiacci grigi.
>
> ("**RM**," 189)

With the tools of the father and the last supper, he departs on his solitary sacrificial journey and is enveloped by the earth. There is a certain romantic Titanism in Malpelo's implicit acceptance of his exclusionary status as societal scapegoat. His decision not to revolt maintains the social order, but he does not endorse it: "Quando lo mandarono per quella esplorazione si risovvenne del minatore, il quale si era smarrito, da anni ed anni, e cammina e cammina ancora al buio gridando aiuto, senza che nessuno possa udirlo; ma non disse nulla. Del resto a che sarebbe giovato?" ("**RM**," 189). The concluding rhetorical question is not entirely extradiegetic; it also constitutes Malpelo's definitive *anagnorisis* immediately preceding the *peripeteia* of his dissolution. The repetition of the lost miner's tale and its internal verbal iterations are stylistic traces that articulate both an oral and a cyclical narrative. The story has come full circle in Malpelo's acquiescence to fulfill his nominal *moira*.

Giacomo Debenedetti laments the presence of the concluding line of the story, which he deems unnecessary.[38] Indeed, the semantic relationship between signifiers and signifieds is overdetermined because it is the nexus of negotiation between conflicting discursive strategies. Malpelo's story is not a simple *tranche de vie*. In the end, the narrative abandons the historical past for the present, which is the tense of the eternal now that sustains Malpelo's representation. However, this temporal shift also transforms the boy from narrative subject to pure text—from Rosso Malpelo to "**Rosso Malpelo**." The concluding image of an errant specter reinforces this reading by echoing the story's introductory description of Malpelo. This intratextual iteration suggests a cyclical narrative that is not bound by temporal conventions.

The polyphonic semantic density discerned in **"Jeli il pastore"** is even more pronounced in **"Rosso Malpelo."** We have already observed that the mine shaft assumes symbolic significance as the entrance to the chthonic domain and have argued that this representation establishes textual intersections with diverse cultural traditions including Plato's *Republic.* Another scene that enhances the polysemous resonance of the text is the callous extradiegetic reference to *Hamlet* at the death of mastro Misciu. The operations manager of the quarry was called from the theater to view the disaster, but returned to his box seat when he realized there was nothing to be done: "L'ingegnere se ne tornò a veder seppellire Ofelia [. . .]" (**"RM,"** 176). The narrative voice's ironic allusion aside, mastro Misciu's living interment and Ophelia's theatrical one establish a parallelism between the two texts in terms of death and spiritual unrest. The ghost of Hamlet *père* wanders the battlements of Elsinore in search of his son, and the ghost of Malpelo roams the galleries of the quarry in search of his father. Although Malpelo is unable to slay his Claudius, he too must come to terms with his past and confront existential dilemmas. *La rena* that killed mastro Misciu is also *l'arena* in which Malpelo faces himself. By agreeing to explore the untested passageway—a dangerous assignment that all the other workers refuse out of fear and common sense—Malpelo tacitly chooses not to be.

PROVISIONAL CONCLUSIONS

In this textual analysis of the short stories **"Jeli il pastore"** and **"Rosso Malpelo,"** *verismo* emerges as an involucrum that glosses the hermeneutic gaps in Verga's narratives. Underlying this superficial aesthetic are complex discursive strategies that articulate myth and folklore or, as Pavese described them, "inutili bizzarrie" within Verga's poetics.

Verismo integrates the morphology of the text with the ethnographic observations of the narrative voice. Myths and folklore are hyperstructural; they form a metalanguage in which structure operates at all textual levels. Mimetic strategies obfuscate these properties thereby instilling a tension typical of historical or romantic narratives. In folk tales and myths, vocabulary is presented as *nature naturée.*[39] It is a semiotic code with its own laws that in turn organize the representation of both the real and the mythical. *Verismo* plays on this linguistic code by purporting to describe reality via a mythical structure. As such, *verismo* negotiates a new narrative representation that is at once a new folk legend in the present. As Giacomo Debenedetti observed: "Verga non è epico, come taluno può dire, è leggendario [. . .]."[40]

The narrative's dependence on archetypal representations emerges in the examination of the relationship between the *dramatis personae* and the archetypes of the collective unconscious: characters based not on their singularity, but on their universality as social types. The temporal structure is based not on a linear chronology, but on an interior, subjective chronometer without fixed physical orientations. This textual strategy recreates the atemporal and indeterminate tension of the folk tales: the past, the present, and the future. In addition, the literary style is based not on mimetic foundations, but on oral traditions. The linguistic register reinforces the reliability of the narrator, who, as an invisible, unidentifiable chorus, underscores the atemporal aspects of the text.

Having posited the premise that Verga's poetics diverge from mimetic representation, one might still attribute the formal elaboration of his texts to realism. However, as I have argued, these texts vacillate between contextualized historical specificity and metahistorical ambiguity. Instead of producing meaning within a social reality, the texts suggest atemporal, mythical readings decontextualized from social reality. Textually the social context is variable while the fixed figures are permanent and, as such, subject to creative manipulation. The narrative structures express an evasion, which in its circularity obfuscates the need to challenge realism. Ultimately, the texts naturalize a fiction in a metahistorical context in order to justify a specific social-historical condition. Thus, the context emerges as a pretext for the narrative experimentation of the *scriptor* as *auctor*—a strategy that achieves its most felicitous expression in *I Malavoglia.*

Notes

1. Cesare Pavese, presentation, *Dialoghi con Leucò,* by Cesare Pavese (Torino: Einaudi, 1965) 201. Pavese wrote this presentation for the jacket cover of the first edition (1947).

2. "Il 'verismo' com'è attuato nella particolare impersonalità dei *Malavoglia,* non è 'realismo', affatto: la referenzialità sociologica è il pretesto, o lo strato di base, per un'operazione linguistica e letteraria che, la si chiami simbolismo o decadentismo, comunque proietta Verga al di là del suo tempo e della sua scuola." Gian-Paolo Biasin, "Come si fa lo stufato" in *Studi di Italianistica in onore di Giovanni Cecchetti,* eds. Paolo Cherchi and Michelangelo Picone (Longo; Ravenna, 1982) 263. Biasin's conclusion is significant because the stylistic techniques employed in *Vita dei campi* provide the impetus for the narrative procedures enacted in *I Malavoglia.* Cf. Giorgio Bàrberi Squarotti, *Giovanni Verga: le finzioni dietro il verismo* (Palermo: S. F. Flaccovio, 1982); Giacomo Debenedetti, *Verga e il naturalismo* (Milano: Gar-

zanti, 1991); and Tullio Pagano, *Experimental Fictions: From Emile Zola's Naturalism to Giovanni Verga's Verism* (Madison and Teaneck: Fairleigh Dickinson UP; London; Cranbury, NJ: Associated U Presses, 1999).

3. Giovanni Verga, *Lettere a Luigi Capuana,* Gino Raya ed. (Firenze: Le Monnier, 1975) 158-59.

4. See Northrop Frye, *Fables of Identity: Studies in Poetic Mythology* (New York: Harcourt, Brace & World, 1963) 36.

5. Bàrberi Squarotti 29.

6. "Rosso Malpelo" was published in serial form in the Roman newspaper *Il Fanfulla* on 2 and 4 August 1878. A preliminary version of "Jeli il pastore" appeared in *La fronda* on 29 February 1880. The first edition of *Vita dei campi* was published in Milan by Treves in late August 1880. For an analysis of the "Rosso Malpelo" variants, see Carla Riccardi, "Il problema filologico di 'Vita dei campi'," *Studi di filologia italiana,* XXXV (1977): 301-36; and Romano Luperini, *Verga e le strutture narrative del realismo. Saggio su 'Rosso Malpelo'* (Padova: Liviana, 1976) 20-40. All textual references to these stories are from Giovanni Verga, *Tutte le novelle,* Carla Riccardi ed. (Milano: Mondadori, 1979) and shall be hereafter referred to and cited in the body of the text in this manner: "Jeli il pastore" as JP and "Rosso Malpelo" as RM. Riccardi, with minor editorial corrections, follows the 1880 edition of *Vita dei campi.*

7. Carl Gustav Jung, *The Archetype and the Collective Unconscious* (Princeton: Princeton UP, 1990) 43.

8. Vladimir Propp, *Morphology of the Folktale,* Louis A. Wagner ed., trans. Laurence Scott (Austin: U of Texas P, 1988).

9. Propp 21.

10. Propp 90.

11. C. G. Jung 5.

12. C. G. Jung 155.

13. Claude Lévi-Strauss, "La struttura e la forma. Riflessioni su un'opera di Vladimir Ja. Propp" in Vladimir Ja. Propp, *Morfologia della fiaba,* Gian Luigi Bravo ed. (Torino: Einaudi, 1972) 183. Cf. Claude Lévi-Strauss, *Antropologie structurale* (Paris: Plon, 1955), chapters 9 and 14; Max Lüthi, *The European Folktale: Form and Nature* (Bloomington: Indiana UP, 1986) 81-133; and Max Lüthi, *The Fairytale as Art Form and Portrait of Man* (Bloomington: Indiana UP, 1984) 40-75.

14. Cf. Roland Barthes, *Mythologies,* trans. Annette Lavers (New York: The Noonday Press, 1991) 109-59.

15. See C. G. Jung, 151-81. Cf. James Hillman et al., eds., *Puer Papers* (Irving, TX: Spring Publications, Inc., 1979); and Marie-Louise von Franz, *Puer aeternus* (Santa Monica: Sigo Press, 1981).

16. "This loneliness expresses the conflict between the bearer or symbol of higher consciousness and his surroundings. The conquerors of darkness go far back into primeval times, and, together with many other legends, prove that there once existed a state of original psychic distress, namely unconsciousness." C. G. Jung 169.

17. Jeli's textual representation conflates the archetypes of the *puer divinus,* the *puer aeternus,* and the myth of the wild child. Regarding the myth of the wild child, cf. Claude Lévi-Strauss, *The Elementary Structures of Kinship* (Boston: Beacon Press, 1969) 3-12 and 84-98.

18. C. G. Jung 70.

19. See Eliade's discussion of archetypes and repetition in Mircea Eliade, *The Myth of the Eternal Return* (New York: Pantheon Books, 1954) 21.

20. Lüthi identifies this tendency to project character psychology through external action rather than through internal development as typical of folk tales. See *The European Folktale,* 11-23.

21. Verga, *Lettere a Luigi Capuana,* 93.

22. Verga, *Lettere a Luigi Capuana,* 121.

23. Verga, *Lettere a Luigi Capuana,* 122. Verga is referring to Santo Rapisarda's *Raccolta di proverbi sciliani ridotti in canzoni di l'Abbati Santu Rapisarda,* published in Catania in 4 volumes in 1824, 1827, 1828, and 1842 respectively. Subsequently, the text was reissued in a single expanded volume (Catania: Giannotta, 1881). The Pitré edition that Verga references is most likely Giuseppe Pitré, *Proverbi siciliani, raccolti e confrontati con quelli degli altri dialetti da Giuseppe Pitré, con discorso preliminare, glossario,* 4 vols. (Palermo: Pedone Lauriel, 1880). Cf. Ferruccio Cecco, "Contributo allo studio dei proverbi nei *Malavoglia*" in *Studi di letteratura italiana offerti a Dante Isella* (Napoli: Bibliopolis, 1983) 371-90.

24. Pierre Bourdieu, *Les règles de l'art. Genèse et structure du champ littéraire* (Paris: Éditions du Seuil, 1992) 455-58.

25. Carlo Muscetta (lecture notes taken by C. Sciré), in Romano Luperini, *Verga* (Roma-Bari: Laterza, 1988) 41. Cf. Paolo Mantegazza's physiognomic

study in which he observes: "Red hair, although rare, is disliked by nearly all because it is an almost monstrous type" in *Physiognomy and Expression* (London: Walter Scott, 1892) 62.

26. Gregory Lucente, *Beautiful Fables: Self-consciousness in Italian Narrative from Manzoni to Calvino* (Baltimore and London: The Johns Hopkins UP, 1986) 83.

27. In narrative fiction external appearance has frequently implied character-connoting traits, however, in the nineteenth century, this organizational topos acquired a pseudo-scientific status through the Swiss philosopher and theologian Johann Caspar Lavater (1741-1801). His theory of physiognomy (*Physiognomische Fragmente, zur Beförderung der Menschenkenntniß und Menschenliebe*, 4 vols. Leipzig and Winterthur: Weidmann, Reich, and Steiner, 1775-78) heavily influenced European writers. The first Italian translation of Lavater's opus appeared in 1803—subsequent redactions followed in 1819, 1827, and 1863. On Lavater's influence on nineteenth-century literature see Graeme Tyler, *Physiognomy in the European Novel: Faces and Fortunes* (Princeton: Princeton UP, 1982).

28. The privileging of pure colors, in this instance red, is characteristic of folk tales. See Lüthi, *The European Folktale*, 27-8.

29. Verga's usage of the referent "cava" conflates the meanings of quarry, pit, cave, and mine.

30. Malpelo's mother remarries and moves away as does his sister. All that remains of mastro Misciu after his death are his tools of the trade, which for Malpelo are nothing less than folkloric *Zaubergaben*.

31. Bàrberi Squarotti argues for a Christological reading of Malpelo's abuse: "Figura del *Christus patiens*, Rosso Malpelo, che prende le botte anche quando non è colpevole e rifiuta di discolparsi perché sa che sarebbe inutile, in quanto egli è per nascita e natura colui che prende su di sé le colpe di tutti [. . .]" (97).

32. C. G. Jung 82.

33. The color-coding of Rosso Malpelo's "occhiacci grigi" (RM, 189) in the story's conclusion neatly reinforces the textual identification between the boy and the gray donkey known as "il *grigio.*"

34. Bàrberi Squarotti 108.

35. Bàrberi Squarotti 102.

36. Luperini identifies these temporal expressions as marking the narrative sequences of the fabula. *Verga e le strutture narrative del realismo,* 55.

37. Luperini argues that the use of repetition reinforces the mythologizing traits in the story: "Ma in *Rosso Malpelo* la tecnica della ripresa ha anche un significato originale: facendo ricorso, nei momenti cruciali del racconto (all'inizio e alla fine), a un artificio tipico della poesia epica popolare, lo scrittore accentua la tendenza alla mitizzazione: lo stile della leggenda accresce la valenza metastorica della vicenda di Rosso allontanandola ancora di più dalla bruciante esperienza storica e sociale da cui pure nasce." *Verga e le strutture narrative del realismo,* 58.

38. Debenedetti 414.

39. Cf. Vladimir Propp, *Theory and History of Folklore* (Minneapolis: University of Minnesota Press, 1984) 188.

40. Debenedetti 426. Regarding the formation of new legends, see Lüthi, *The European Folktale,* 83.

James Wood (essay date 10 March 2003)

SOURCE: Wood, James. "The Unwinding Stair: Can Literature Be Simple?" *New Republic* 228, no. 4599 (10 March 2003): 25-30.

[*In the following excerpt, Wood analyzes the aesthetics and the technique of literary simplicity within the context of "Rosso Malpelo," explaining their effects on readers.*]

I.

Here are four sentences: "And it still seemed that there was some most important thing which he did not have, of which he once vaguely dreamed, and in the present he was stirred by the same hope for the future that he had had in childhood." "He began to play, himself not knowing what it was, but it came out plaintive and moving, and tears flowed down his cheeks . . . 'Ah, ah!' he said, as the tears crawled down his cheeks and splashed on his green frock-coat." "What was certain was that his own mother had never known him to embrace her, so she had never done the same to him either." "Ivan Ilyich's life was most ordinary, therefore most terrible."

The first is from Chekhov's story "The Bishop," and the second from "Rothschild's Fiddle." The terrifying line about how "what was certain was that his own mother had never known him to embrace her, so she had never done the same to him either" is from Giovanni Verga's great story **"Rosso Malpelo,"** and the last sentence, of course, is from Tolstoy's novella *The Death of Ivan Ilyich.* When we hear these lines, we hear the sound of simplicity: the direct access to deep emotion; the clarity of phrasing; the willingness to use vernacular and conversational language and repetition rather than obviously literary constructions; the sense that literary artifice has been pushed out of the way by the coarse elbow of metaphysics. There is a fearlessness in this writing, which in turn is fearful, a simplicity which in turn is complex.

We know that simplicity has always been an aesthetic ideal, because of the abundant testimony to it in ancient and modern literature; and we know that it is rarely achieved because of the abundant complexity with which it is idealized. Plato has Socrates, in the *Republic,* warn against such gratuities as Attic pastries and Corinthian girlfriends. These superfluities are likely to distract the soldier and to make him sick, he says, just as unnecessary embellishment in songs and in lyric odes gives rise to licentiousness. Simplicity, temperance, is all. Such notions are similarly found in the ancient treatises on rhetoric, such as Quintilian's.

In modern literature, however, simplicity is always elegiac. It is that which has been mysteriously lost, and which cannot be re-found. Simplicity is often honored in the breach, as in Yeats's little poem "The Fascination of What's Difficult," which complains about complexity:

> The fascination of what's difficult
> Has dried the sap out of my veins,
> and rent
> Spontaneous joy and natural content
> Out of my heart.

Many literary cultures seem to have their own favored examples of lost simplicity and fallen naturalness. Molière is sometimes invoked by the French, and Pushkin has long represented a founding simplicity for Russian writers. Gogol suggested that Pushkin was able to serve art for art's sake because, in some way, he had no complex anxiety about what art was: by contrast, "we can no longer serve art for art's sake," wrote Gogol, "without having first comprehended its highest purpose and without determining what it is given to us for. We cannot repeat Pushkin." The Czechs revere Jaroslav Hašek's easiness; Bohumil Hrabal marveled that Hašek's novel, *The Good Soldier Švejk,* was "written as though he tossed it off with his left hand, after a hangover, it's pure joy in writing." And Cervantes has functioned this way for writers as different as Flaubert, Dostoevsky, and Kundera.

All these writer-founders are idealized as somehow simple, at one with nature, almost premodern; they are envied because they are seen as unencumbered by artifice. Schiller's famous essay "On Naïve and Sentimental Poetry" is both the greatest example of this modern nostalgia and the most sharply self-aware and dialectical commentary on it. Schiller sees modern poets as writers who have lost an antique simplicity, one of whose components was a direct concord with nature. Modern writers, says Schiller, in their relationship to the ancients, are like sick people lusting after health. Goethe, he says, is rare and remarkable, because although he is a modern poet—and therefore a "sick" one—he still retains an extraordinary premodern simplicity and directness.

The "sickest" modern writer (in Schillerian terms) is Flaubert, and it is hardly surprising to find him groaning that Rabelais, Cervantes, and Molière had it easy because they were so simple. "They are great," he wrote to Louise Colet in 1853, "because they have no techniques." Those three writers "achieve their effects, regardless of Art." Of course, every reader of Cervantes knows that there is abundant "technique" in *Don Quixote,* and that Cervantes mobilizes all kinds of techniques that are premodern only because they had not yet been identified as techniques. They seem simple because they do not seem self-conscious. But for Flaubert this absence of artistic self-consciousness meant that these writers were mere beasts of instinct. He felt that he could not be free as they were. "One achieves style," he wrote, "only by atrocious labor, a fanatic and dedicated stubbornness."

Flaubert was not only a sick modern, but one who infected everyone who came after him. He does indeed represent a watershed. After Flaubert, style in fiction will always be a problem, always a trapped decision, because it is an overwhelmingly aesthetic one. Even simplicity, after Flaubert, is no longer innocent, but is a simplicity that has become weary of congestion. (Think of Hemingway's intensely self-conscious and artful simplicity.) Nothing is more nostalgic for aesthetic innocence than Flaubert's story "A Simple Heart," in which he tried to prove that he could use his aestheticism to achieve a fable-like purity. And the moderns know it too: both Robbe-Grillet and Sarraute, those exponents of the *nouveau roman,* used to say that without doubt Flaubert was their "precursor."

* * *

Both this story and Verga's great and terrifying tale **"Rosso Malpelo"** seem almost cruel. Certainly, both writers belonged to societies that, by late nineteenth-century bourgeois standards, really were cruel. Giovanni Verga was born in Sicily in 1840. At the end of the nineteenth century, Sicily was probably the poorest place in Europe. Verga was a patrician, born into a landowning family in Catania. At school, a patriotic teacher inspired him to write fiery and romantic works, and his early novels, the so-called *romanzi giovenili,* were popular and sentimental, influenced by the most vivid storytellers of the day—Dumas, Hugo, Scott. But around 1880, partly influenced by Luigi Capuana, Verga began to experiment with a new kind of writing, a style that came to be called *verismo*. This is sometimes said to be the Italian counterpart of French naturalism, and Verga had indeed read Zola; but although Verga and Chekhov never knew of each other's existence, the Sicilian sounds more like the Russian than like the Frenchman.

Verga took as his new subjects shepherds and illiterate fishermen. The style of narration is as if written by a peasant—more exactly, as if written by the village community. Scholars of Verga call this "narration by the village chorus." The stories and the novels that he wrote in the 1880s abound with non sequiturs, proverbial sayings, and pieces of nonsensical folk wisdom, sometimes spoken by his characters and sometimes woven invisibly into the narration. "Some people carry their conscience on their backs, so they can't see it." "Saint Joseph shaved himself first and then the others." "Uncle Crocifisso was in just the right mood to discuss that business, which never seemed to end, because, as they say, 'long things turn into snakes.'" "Marriages and bishops are made in heaven."

Since these stories are narrated as if by a member of the community, they themselves at first glance seem to be without much mercy for their protagonists. But of course these stories are not cruel. Both Chekhov and Verga are masters of the anti-sentimental principle; they know that the more brutally they deprive their characters of obvious sympathy, the more we long to apply it covertly. Verga knowingly uses the cruelty of his Sicilian world to provoke the reader's sympathy.

The best example of this method in Verga's work is **"Rosso Malpelo."** This story is about a little boy who works in the mines under Mount Etna. Rosso's father was also a miner, and he died in a terrible accident underground. Ever since, Rosso has been a problem—a vicious, pathetic, feral child, shunned by the rest of the community. His name, Malpelo, literally means "evil-haired"; he is so nicknamed because he has red hair, and the community has the usual folk-suspicion of people with red hair. This is how the story begins: "He was called Malpelo because he had red hair, and he had red hair because he was a mischievous rascal who promised to turn out a real knave. So everyone at the sand mine called him Malpelo, and even his mother, hearing him always referred to in that way, had almost forgotten the name he was christened with."

Evil because he had red hair, red hair because he was evil: the story begins with a non sequitur, an illogicality, a circularity. And the story is founded on this non sequitur, because we rapidly gather that the community, which is in effect telling this tale, has no interest in knowing Rosso Malpelo. He is too difficult to deal with.

He has been cast out. For the community, to know him is to blame him. Verga takes to an even greater pitch of extremity Chekhov's principle of denying or frustrating access; in some amazing way Verga's story is founded on the impossibility of knowing Rosso Malpelo. Verga writes that the miners beat Malpelo "even when he was not to blame, on the grounds that if Malpelo was not responsible, he was quite capable of having done it." And Malpelo accepts this regime of the vicious non sequitur. When he is beaten for a crime he did not commit, he never denies it, but merely shrugs and says: "What's the use? I'm Malpelo."

Certainly, Malpelo is nasty. He is (as we would say) an abused abuser. His father died in the mine, smothered by sand, and his mother shrinks from her son. The narrator adds that "his own mother had never known him to embrace her, so that she had never done the same to him either," a terrifying line, given out with all of Verga's usual brusque simplicity. But this is also the very principle of the story's narration, which effectively insists on the unembraceability of Malpelo, so that the reader desires to embrace him instead. The only thing that Malpelo understands is force. He beats the poor mule that works underground, muttering, "That'll kill you off more quickly." In some way Malpelo wants to be dead, and wants everyone else to be dead, too. Like his father, he emits a guttural groan, "Ah, ah!" as he works at the sand, the exclamation sounding like a death cry. When a new boy arrives at the mine, Malpelo takes him under his wing and begins to tutor him in the ways of cruelty. He tells him: "The mule gets beaten because it can't fight back, and if it could, it would trample us under its feet and steal the food out of our mouths." When the mule eventually dies, Malpelo comments: "It would have been better for him if he'd never been born at all."

The new boy at the mine is cruelly nicknamed The Frog, because he once fell off some scaffolding and dislocated his leg: "When he was carrying his basket of sand on his back, the poor wretch would hop along as if he was dancing the tarantella, and all the mineworkers laughed at him and called him The Frog." As elsewhere in his work, Verga here flourishes a cruelty, told entirely from within the terms and the values of the mine community, but prompts us to defy the cruel laughter of the men—and therefore the laughter of Verga's own narration—with that epithet, "poor wretch." And Verga means us to do likewise with Malpelo. Malpelo is a poor wretch too, even if no one will acknowledge it.

In the story's most awful series of scenes, The Frog, whose health is poor, is taken ill. Malpelo considers The Frog a sissy, and boasts of his own strength. He tries to force some health into The Frog by hitting him, but he hits him so hard that The Frog begins to cough blood. Malpelo is alarmed: "He swore that he could not have done him any great harm by hitting him as he did, and just to prove it he beat himself severely about the chest and the back with a large stone."

But The Frog is seriously ill, and he is taken to his bed, where he wheezes for breath, and begins to wither away. Malpelo visits the boy, and sits staring at him, "with those huge eyes of his bulging out of his forehead, as though he was going to paint his portrait." Malpelo is bewildered by the boy's failing health, and thinks that he is being self-indulgent. He cannot understand why The Frog's mother is weeping so much, and asks The Frog why his mother is making such a fuss, "when for two months he had been earning less than it cost to feed him." After all, Malpelo's mother has never once embraced him. "But The Frog paid no attention to him, and simply seemed intent on lying there in bed."

I remember first reading that last sentence, and then slowly, almost frightenedly returning to it, and reading it once again: "But the Frog paid no attention to him, and simply seemed intent on lying there in bed." Of course, this makes it sound as if The Frog is choosing to luxuriate in bed, as if he had a choice, when in fact he is dying. He is not indolent, he is chained by his fate to his bed. The sentence is presented as third-person narration by Verga, but it must represent the thought of Malpelo, to whom The Frog's bedriddenness seems a perplexing luxury. And in this bleak story death is a kind of luxury, since it is a relief from work, from life. The Frog dies, and a little later Malpelo gets lost in one of the labyrinthine mine shafts that stretch under the volcano, and he is "never heard of again." It would indeed have been better if he had never been born at all.

As in Chekhov, Verga's use of this narration-as-if-by-the-community is extraordinarily subtle, because readers, faced with such pitiless judgment, tend to work against the narration, against the community, in order to extract the pathos we require. Verga uses a style of writing in which the writer appeals to something consensual that everyone knows. Roland Barthes used to call this the "reference code," and it is common in eighteenth- and nineteenth-century fiction. Tolstoy habitually uses it with great simplicity and force. In *The Death of Ivan Ilyich,* he describes a group of men who are discussing the recent news of Ivan's death. Tolstoy remarks that, "as is usual in such cases," each man was thinking that he was glad that it was Ivan Ilyich who was dead and not him. In such an instance, we are encouraged to agree with Tolstoy about this universal fact of life.

But Verga uses the "reference code" to effect almost the opposite reaction, almost disagreement, because the familiar truths and the universal facts with which we are asked to concur are so cruel, and so brutally stated, that

the reader is forced to rise up against them. The most blatant example in **"Rosso Malpelo"** might be the passage where Verga describes how Rosso lovingly looked after the shoes of his dead father: "He carefully hung the shoes on the same nail where he kept his pallet, as though they were the Pope's slippers, and on Sundays he would take them down, polish them and try them on. Then he would place them on the floor, one beside the other, and stare at them for hours on end with his elbows on his knees and his chin resting in the palms of his hands, and it was anybody's guess what ideas were running through that calculating little head of his." Of course, we are being prompted by the story to resist this cruelty; we strongly suspect that although Rosso may be a monster, he is looking at the shoes and simply grieving for his father.

In both Verga and Chekhov, then, simplicity is achieved by using complex literary techniques to break through literary complexity. You might say that literature is used against itself. Of course, simplicity will always be complex in literature, because literary effects are always complex. But literary results are not always complex. The great artists of complexity, such as James and Mann and Proust, are always giving us a great deal—of themselves, of their intellects, of their prose, of their gathered data. But one way of looking at the simplicity of Chekhov and Verga is to note how much they subtract, how little they give us, how often they invite us to fill their bareness with our own feeling.

Note how, for instance, in both stories, characters are described in terms of the simplest exclamations: the tearful grunts of appreciation given by the Jew in "Rothschild's Fiddle": "Ah, ah!" And the similar groans— "Ah, ah!"—that both Rosso and his father give when they are digging away at the sand. Eliot once wrote an essay about the difference between Dryden's version of *Antony and Cleopatra* and Shakespeare's. He was interested in the death of Charmian, and in the way each poet treated her last two lines. Both poets had similar verse, except that Shakespeare had added to the couplet two extra words: "Ah, soldier!" Eliot said that he could not quite identify why this was great, but that he knew that in this addition lay the secret of great literature. I think, after reading Chekhov and Verga, we know that secret. "Ah, soldier"; "Ah," "Oh"—just two vowels. It is the very sigh of simplicity.

George Guida (essay date summer 2003)

SOURCE: Guida, George. "Giovanni Verga and the Roots of Italian America." *Italian Americana* 21, no. 2 (summer 2003): 150-63.

[*In the following essay, Guida details multiple aspects of southern Italian peasant life represented in Verga's*

*short fiction, describing the social, political, and eco-
nomic customs and folk values of the region and their
translation by Italian immigrants to America.*]

Even though he was not himself a peasant, Giovanni
Verga sought to interpret the world of the peasants in
their own terms. Born in 1840, in Catania, Sicily, to an
aristocratic family, Verga at age twenty-five published
his first novel and moved to Florence, and then, eight
years later, to Milan. During the 1870s, he published
autobiographical novels of upper-class romantic intrigue, all of which reflect the influence of French realism, but none of which stands as a literary achievement
of any great merit.

Only in the mid 1870s did Verga turn his attention to
the subject of his later masterpieces, the way of life of
southern Italian, particularly Sicilian, peasants. That
way of life inspired two great novels, *I Malavoglia*
(1881) and *Maestro Don Gesualdo* (1889); and two superb collections of short stories, **Vita dei Campi** (1880)
and **Novelle Rusticane** (1883) (the collections originally translated into English by D. H. Lawrence).

Verga's Sicilians live the lives of most late nineteenth
century *contadini*, the peasants of the Mezzogiorno.
Their condition, often their survival, depended upon the
year's harvest. Poverty, custom and a rigid moral code
set the tone of their lives. These strictures fueled passions and unexpected violence that disrupted a seemingly idyllic existence (Cecchetti, "Introduction" xii).
Simply to maintain their humble place in society, peasants had constantly to check their desires, since one af-
front to the honor of a woman or family, one protest to
his landlord, could spell a peasant's end. This condition
is the lens through which Verga's Sicilian tales project
the peasants' lives.

The types of people who inhabit Verga's tales—day laborers, small landowners, shepherds, and other economically marginal figures—accounted for up to two-
thirds of the population of many Sicilian towns
(Gabaccia 6). As Verga presents them, these peasants
are proud people accustomed to misery, seeking whatever joy they can find in their difficult lives. The author
captures the details and values of their traditional world,
in a dignified rendition of their own language and
thought patterns. The sum of his themes and techniques
came to be known as *verismo*. *Verismo*, which means
literally "realism," does not correspond to the
nineteenth-century literary realism of English and
American authors. Italian *veristi*, among whom Verga
was preeminent, explored the conflicts between man's
(often humble, futile) life and his ambitions. In this
way, their work stands midway between what American
critics would call realism and naturalism.

Verga's tales portray both the economic predicament of
Southern peasants and their resulting sense of impotence to change their situation: a situation that fosters a
typically Sicilian, tragic view of life (Toschi 14). Since
the peasant life that Verga depicts has largely vanished
in the *Mezzogiorno,* his literary recreation is as near an
experience of actual nineteenth-century peasant existence, and of the future emigrants' consciousness, as we
have.

In general, Verga's stories convey a strong sense of
campanilismo—the peasants' limitation and attachment
to their town and its environs—and their suspicion of
outsiders. They convey also, at every turn, the effects of
poverty. Verga's third-person narrators speak as villagers, as if they are reminding readers, not necessarily informing them, of the village personae and local places
they describe. Yet, they speak with knowledge beyond
the limits of the villagers' consciousness. This balance
between identification and distance from subject lends
Verga's voice a journalistic objectivity that renders the
tragedy of his tales even more shocking and powerful.
Witness the opening lines of a tale upon which Leoncavallo based his classic opera, **"Cavalleria Rusticana"** (1880): "When Turiddu Macca, Nunzia's son,
came back from the service, he used to strut in the
square on Sundays in his *bersagliere* uniform with the
red cap that looked like the one worn by the fortune-
teller who sets up a bench with a cage of canaries"
(10). For the townspeople, with whom the narrator
shares certain knowledge (of a particular kind of fortu-
neteller, for instance), Turiddu, an impoverished former
soldier, is both an object of admiration and resentment.
The mixed feelings that he inspires within the community ultimately seal his doom.

Like Turiddu, the protagonists of Verga's other Sicilian
tales contend with the various hardships that forced so
many peasants to emigrate. All three characters in
"Black Bread" (1882), Santo, Lucia (Santo's sister),
and Nena (Santo's wife), work like dogs in order to eat.
Lucia resents their lot, even as she accepts it; and at
various points, she expresses the sort of class resentment common among the *contadini* (Mangione and
Morreale 48-53). From her point of view, we understand the interplay of economic and social life. "That
crook of a field watchman had done himself a favor by
marrying off his daughter [Nena] without a dowry, and
now it was up to Santo to support her. Since Nena had
been with him, Santo saw that he didn't have enough
bread for both of them and they would have to snatch it
by the sweat of their brow from the land . . ." (Verga
172). For her part, Lucia realizes too late that the only
way to have saved her dying mother would have been
to accede to the unwanted romantic advances and dowry
of an older *galantuomo* (or gentleman), a member of
the landowning upper class. In this world, the wish for
marriage, like the wish for salvation, comes at a heavy
price.

As common in the Mezzogiorno as class conflict and
suppression of desire was illness: illness arising from

the peasants' very livelihood, the land. Following the Risorgimento, a new crop of landlords set about clearing large tracts of Southern forests, in order to maximize their profits from agriculture. Deforestation led to soil erosion, which turned areas of formerly hospitable valleys into marshes, breeding grounds for malaria-carrying insects (Nelli 20). Peasants often walked miles each day through these marshes, from their hill towns to the fields they worked. Many contracted malaria.

Verga allows us to feel the ravages of the disease as the peasants felt them, in his 1881 tale **"Malaria."** The narrator of the tale expresses the connection between peasant labor in the post-Risorgimento South and illness, in a single metaphor. **"Malaria,"** he remarks, "gets into your bones with the bread you eat" (Verga 118). He goes on to describe the effects of the disease from the peasant perspective. Malaria "snatches up the villagers in the deserted streets and nails them in front of the door of their houses plasterless from the sun, and they shake with fever under their overcoats and under all the bed blankets piled upon their shoulders" (118). Verga changes the tone of his narrative voice here from folkloric ("snatches up the villagers") and Christian ("nails them in front of the door") to documentary ("they shake with fever"). For him, malaria is a mythical, as well as a literal, plague. It precipitates the peasants' flight from a homeland that is also, metaphorically, ancient Egypt; as it is a cause of emigration rooted in socio-historical conditions. Day in and day out, the peasants endure malaria at work and play, escaping it only when they leave, because as "Wife-killer" (a character whose several wives all die of the disease) reasons, "for those people there just isn't malaria!" (127). Unless and until, like many real *contadini* of the period, Verga's peasants overcome their fatalism and emigrate, they simply assume the risks and accept the frequently fatal consequences as a fact of life.

"Freedom" (1882), prefiguring *Il Gattopardo*, recounts yet another peasant hardship, disappointment with the Risorgimento. The story begins, "They hung the tricolor kerchief [the flag of united Italy] from the campanile, sounded the alarm with the bells, and began to shout in the square: 'Hail to freedom!'" (206). It ends, "The charcoal man, while they were handcuffing him again, stammered: 'Where are you taking me? To jail? Why? I didn't even get a foot of land. And they had said there was freedom! . . .'" (216). The freedom Garibaldi's liberators promised evolves into a new form of imprisonment of the peasants, at the hands of the civil authorities that the Garibaldini helped to establish. From the 1860s through the 1880s, disastrous agricultural practices, along with an onerous system of taxation, plunged the peasants even deeper into *La Miseria*. Corrupt landowners and ruthless overseers went unchecked by a distant government whose policies reflected its own susceptibility to corruption. As land grew less productive through mismanagement, taxes rose until they were the highest in Europe (Nelli 23), and inequitable to boot. Cows, usually owned by wealthy landlords, were not taxable commodities; mules, usually owned by *contadini* (and used by Verga as symbols of peasant suffering and survival) were (Mangione and Morreale 63). The peasants, though no longer serfs, were now slaves to capital.

It may be difficult for us to imagine how the peasants of the Mezzogiorno survived the wrath of all the forces—social, natural, political, economic—arrayed against them. Verga's characters show us how. In **"Property"** (1882), they survive through ceaseless work and *furberia* (cleverness, cunning) (Gambino, *Blood* 134). The protagonist of **"Property,"** Mazzarò, embodies *furberia*. His name itself echoes both the Sicilian *massaro,* one given to "diligent application" of himself (Gabaccia 6), and the Italian *amazzare,* "to kill," suggesting all at once Mazzarò's all-consuming diligence, his social and spiritual suicide, and his symbolic killing off of masters. "He had gotten together all that property himself, with his hands and with his mind, by not sleeping at night, by catching fever from anxiety or from malaria, by toiling from morning till night, and going around in the sun and in the rain, by wearing out his boots and his mules . . ." (Verga 143-44). Mazzarò has not achieved the ends of property according to peasant values—the preservation of family and folkways—but he has mastered the means.

Although he has "no children, nor grandchildren, nor other relatives" (144) and no peace of mind, Mazzarò understands full well that "[p]roperty doesn't belong to those who have it, but to those who know how to get it'" (144). He understands too what the proprietor must do to maintain property. "After he had gotten his property, he certainly didn't send word that he was coming to supervise the harvest or the vintage, and when and how, but turned up unexpectedly, on foot or on a mule, without watchmen, with a piece of bread in his pocket; and he slept near his sheaves, his eyes open, and his shotgun between his legs" (144-45). This final image of Mazzarò crystallizes Verga's depiction of his *furberia,* and his accumulation of property. Mazzarò overcomes economic oppression through a relentless effort that deprives him of family and spiritual comfort. "So, when they told him that the time had come to leave his property and think of his soul, he staggered out into the courtyard like a madman" (147). The peasant is, and in reality frequently was, forced to choose between his livelihood on one hand, and his family and traditional values on the other.

In other tales, Verga portrays, with both sympathy and scorn, the values and folkways that sustain peasants and, later, emigrants from the Mezzogiorno. In **"Cavalleria Rusticana,"** a young man, Turiddu, dies in the name of honor, at the hands of his true love's husband, Alfio. Forbidden to marry the beautiful Santa for lack of money, Turiddu becomes her lover. Alfio finds out and must defend his honor. The Southern Italian code of honor compelled the offended to respond quickly and decisively to whatever person has sullied his or his family's character. Adherents to this code, the *contadini*, held marriage as the fullest expression of family integrity and any challenge to an established marriage as the ultimate offense (Alba 33). A husband's honor, and his family's honor, depended upon his wife's (and his other female relatives') loyalty and to shame (Rando 24). Anything less than restoration of honor would endanger the peasant's own economic and social status and that of his family, since family honor, its interplay with social status and property, formed the basis of useful social ties (Gabaccia IV, 9, 220). Turiddu recognizes Alfio's masculine obligation to defend his family's honor and agrees to a dual in which Alfio kills him. Alfio is triumphant. "'That's for making a cuckold of me in my own house'" (18), he declares. Turiddu is, on the other hand, tragic, his death grotesque. "For a while Turiddu staggered here and there among the cactuses and then fell like a log. Blood gurgled up and foamed in his throat, and he couldn't even gasp: *Ah, mamma mia!" (18)*. He begins the tale as a popinjay marching in uniform through the town square, an object of admiration as well as resentment; and ends up like dog in the dust, an object of scorn, dead young, in service of the Mezzogiorno code of honor.

As much as they lived by this code of honor, the Southern Italian peasants lived by a complex system of superstitions and religious beliefs. In **"Rosso Malpelo"** and **"War Between Saints"** (1880) Verga renders important aspects of Southern pagan superstition and saint-worship. Many Sicilians, peasant and otherwise, believed that redheads had evil dispositions (Cecchetti, *Giovanni* 65), a belief which determines the fate of the story's protagonist, Malpelo (literally, "evil hair"). Superstitions like this one were common among the peasants, products of age-old uncertainty and vulnerability. Over the centuries, the *contadini's* Biblical vicissitudes led them to speculate that warring saints and demons dictated their destinies (Gambino, *Blood* 213-14), that free will, if it existed at all, was a relatively weak force. In this spirit, they testified to the endurance of *Magna Graecia*.

From the outset of his story, superstition binds Malpelo. "He was called Malpelo because he had red hair; and he had red hair because he was a mean and bad boy, who promised to turn into a first-rate scoundrel. So everybody at the red-sand quarry called him Malpelo, and even his mother, having always heard that name, had almost forgotten his real one" (Verga 65). Verga makes clear that, like superstition itself, Malpelo's hair and name are self-fulfilling prophecies. Onto the young boy, Verga projects peasant fatalism.

Verga's narrator speaks with the voice of superstitious peasants, in his condemnation of the unfortunate lad. "[H]e would go and huddle in a corner," the narrator reveals, "his basket between his legs, to nibble his piece of dark bread, as *animals like him do*" (emphasis added) (Verga 66). Here, Verga compares Malpelo to a beast, valued for what he can do and not for who he is. No one cares for Malpelo, because of his red hair (Selig 35), a trait upon which the peasant consciousness of the narrative seizes as a means of explaining the boy's otherwise inexplicable malignancy; and because no one cares for him, he is sent to work on a dangerous project in the same quarry that killed his father. No "man with a family wanted to take a chance, nor would he let his own flesh and blood run such a risk for all the gold in the world. But as for Malpelo, he didn't even have anyone who would want to take all the gold in the world for his hide, if it was really worth that much: so they thought of him" (85). Malpelo does not protest this or any other mistreatment. "'What for?'" he asks, resigned, "I'm Malpelo'" (73). In the absolute, article-less manner of the Italian language, "Malpelo" is adjective as noun, defining identity as well as quality. (To say, for example, "I am a Southerner," one would say, "*Sono meridionale,*" not "*Sono un meridionale.*")

If the peasants believed that supernatural forces controlled their destinies, then for them no force was greater than their patron saints. In the *Mezzogiorno,* the peasant called upon his patron saint to bless the land, and he believed the saint's benediction would have a material, often immediate, effect (De Rosa 5). His interaction with his saint, as with God and the Holy Family, was personal, familiar (Gambino, *Blood* 221). Verga plumbs the depth of this belief in **"War Between Saints."** The narrator of the story recounts the battle for processional rights through a small town, between the devotees of Saint Rocco and those of Saint Paschal. Depending upon where they reside, the peasants pray to one or the other, for rain and immunity to cholera. To supplicate according to custom—a custom that survives to this day in Italy and Little Italies throughout the world (Orsi, "Religious" 330)—they march icons of the saints through town in ritual procession.

> In fact, they did carry Saint Paschal in procession, to the east and to the west, and they held him high on the hill to bless the fields, one sultry, cloudy day in May— one of those days when the farmers tear their hair in front of their burnt fields, and the wheatears bend down just as if they were dying.
>
> (Verga 103)

Nino, one of these afflicted farmers, who lives in the rival district of Saint Rocco, blames his rivals' saint for his problems. "'Damned Saint Paschal!' he shouts, "spitting in the air running through the wheat field like a madman. 'You've ruined me, Saint Paschal, you thief! All you've left me is a sickle to cut my throat with!'" (103)

Later, Nino heaps abuse on his own patron, who, as he sees it, has done equally little to improve his condition. "'Ah, Saint Rocco, you thief!' Nino began to lament. 'I didn't expect this from you! . . .' Ah, Saint Rocco!' said he. "This is a dirtier trick than Saint Paschal played on us!'" (106). His reliance, anger, imprecation of his own saint reflect the nature of the Southern *contadino* saint worship, which could often end in outright icono-clasm and deposition of the patron in favor of another (Salamone-Marino 172-74).

Verga presents this peasant approach to worship as both charming and senseless. In his stories, Saints mean much to peasants, but do not materially change their lives. At the close of **"War Between Saints,"** the two main characters, Nino and Saridda, recovering together from cholera, continue to argue the relative power their patron saints, neither of whom has done anything to al-leviate either drought or illness.

> "And you? Do you think it was Saint Rocco who kept you alive?"
>
> "Why don't you stop it!" broke in Saridda.
>
> "Or we'll need another cholera to make peace!"
>
> (Verga 107)

In Saridda's irony we hear Verga's. It is irony, however, which, while it satirizes the peasants' reliance on saints to deliver them, stops short of discounting saint wor-ship entirely. The *feste* surrounding it was, after all, one of the joys of peasant life.

Certainly, peasant life could, in many ways, be joyous and beautiful, but its hardships appear to us now less than nostalgia-inspiring. Yet, a longing for peasant life in the *Mezzogiorno* marks a great deal of Italian Ameri-can narrative. That longing is often nostalgia for *bell'Italia,* the beautiful land itself. I have heard Italians remark, *"C'e il mare, c'e il sole. Che cos'altro ci vuole?"* ("We have the sea and the sun. What else do we need?"). Verga's **"Ieli"** (1880) illustrates this senti-ment, a deep feeling for the land, not only as soil, but also as landscape, idealized site of innocence and sim-plicity.

Ieli, a poor shepherd boy, and Don Alfonso, the young son of a wealthy landowner, share days together in the pastures.

> Ah, the wonderful chases over the mown fields, manes in the wind! the beautiful days of April, when the wind piled up the green grass into waves and the mares neighed in the pastures! the beautiful summer after-

noons, when the whitish countryside lay silent under the hazy sky, and the grasshoppers crackled among the clods, as if the stubble were catching fire! the beautiful winter sky through the naked branches of the almond tree that shivered in the north wind, and the path that sounded frozen under the horses' hoofs, and the sky-larks that sang high up in the warmth, in the blue! the beautiful summer evenings that came up very slowly, like fog, the good smell of the hay in which you sank your elbows, and the melancholy humming of the evening insects, and those two notes of Ieli's pipe, al-ways the same—ee-oo! ee-oo! ee-oo!

> (20)

The narrative reminiscence foreshadows the loss of in-nocence and simplicity of which Ieli's life becomes a symbol; an innocence and simplicity that Don Alfonso and, later, immigrants from Italy, convinced themselves they had had and lost; an imaginary, timeless life (Boelhower, *Immigrant* 103-08), which was in reality the existence of a people held in poverty and ignorance by immemorial custom (Mangione and Morreale 51); a life at least as miserable as it was innocent and simple.

Portions of **"Ieli,"** like portions of many Italian Ameri-can narratives, are pastoral reconstructions of Mezzo-giorno life. Classical pastoral locates simplicity and in-nocence in the shepherd, presenting his life as (Christ-like) ideal. In the pastoral tale, the shepherd suffers and savors simple pleasures for the entire community (Marinelli 6). (The Italian title of the story has been translated as "Ieli the Shepherd.") Verga's pastoral, like those of Theocritus and the Italian American immigrant autobiographers, begins with an experienced adult look-ing back on an innocent childhood (10). As he grows older, Don Alfonso learns to read—which causes Ieli to look "at the book and at him suspiciously" (Verga 26). Don Alfonso then assumes his position in the rigid caste system (Covello 75) of the Mezzogiorno, the position of *galantuomo*. The *galantuomini* (gentlemen) were well-to-do men, landowners associated, usually by blood, with baronial estates. They recognized each oth-er's cultural and class superiority, and forced the lower social classes to do the same (97). After he has taken his rightful position and left Ieli behind in the fields, Don Alfonso has an affair with Mara, the woman who, in part because Don Alfonso ruins her reputation, agrees to marry Ieli.

Class distinction and Mara's attraction to Alfonso ulti-mately corrupt and destroy Ieli. Though slow, Ieli slowly comes to recognize his wife's adultery with Al-fonso and to feel a shame and anger about it that he cannot fully comprehend. During an argument, a shep-herd boy tells Ieli what everyone else in the town al-ready knows, that Don Alfonso "has taken your wife" (Verga 60). Labeled a "cuckold," the strongest of all in-sults in Southern Italy (Alba 34), even the gentle, un-suspecting Ieli must react. "Even when he thought of

Don Alfonso, he couldn't believe that such a dirty trick was possible; he still could see him at Tebedi [the pasture lands], with his kind eyes and his smiling little mouth coming to bring sweets and white bread, so long ago—such a dirty trick! And since he hadn't seen him any more, for he was a poor shepherd who stayed in the country the whole year round, he always remembered him that way" (Verga 62). His wife's and Alfonso's corruption raise Ieli's consciousness of his limitation as peasant and his disgrace as cuckold, poisoning his contentment.

At a "picnic in the country at shearing time" (63), in the company of both Mara and Don Alfonso, Ieli is at first able to overcome incipient feelings of shame and anger, and enjoy the pastoral scene. From his point of view, so close to the natural world, we hear, "It was a beautiful, warm day in the golden fields with the flowering hedges and the long green rows of vines. The sheep were gamboling and bleating with pleasure at feeling themselves freed from all that wool, and in the kitchen the women were making a big fire to cook all the things that the owner had brought for dinner" (63). Still, amid the simple gaiety of the country outing—one of the peasants' few escapes from ceaseless labor and suffering (qtd. in Salamone-Marino 123), Ieli is reminded of his class inferiority and his disgrace. "Meanwhile, the rich men who were waiting had gone into the shade under the carob trees, and were having someone play the tambourines and bagpipes, and those who wanted to, danced with the women of the farm" (Verga 63).

In this pastoral setting, Don Alfonso's and Mara's corruption infects Ieli, and he finally succumbs. "Ieli, while he was shearing the sheep, felt something gnaw inside him, without knowing why, like a thorn, a driven nail, a pair of fine shears that worked around inside him bit by bit, worse than poison" (63). When, over Ieli's objections, Mara goes off to dance with Alfonso, Ieli slits Alfonso's throat with his shears, transforming from innocent to murderer and symbol of growing peasant discontent with the ongoing inequities of post-Risorgimento Italy.

To understand fully Verga's use of symbolism and other narrative elements, we need to recognize the prevalence, in nineteenth-century Mezzogiorno life, of the folktale, the timeless peasant narrative form and means of transmitting cultural and moral customs and lessons (Covello 266-68). Writing in 1960, Mario Pei recognized the lingering power of myth and legend in Southern Italian society. "Even today," wrote Pei, "the miraculous exploits of mythological and legendary heroes continue to be recounted by *cantastorie,* those often illiterate bards who wander from village to village" (Preface ix). In order to understand the Southern Italian peasant consciousness of cyclical time and attachment

to elemental, pre-industrial life, as well as the influence of creeping capitalism upon that consciousness (Propp 17), we must recognize this living tradition.

Verga often layers the realistic detail of his short stories over folkoric narrative structures. He employs this strategy most strikingly in **"Story of the Saint Joseph Donkey"** (1881). The story is an elaboration of a traditional Italian folktale form, the animal fable or animal tale, a brief narrative of a particular animal's adventures (Calvino xx; Dégh 68). The Saint Joseph Donkey of the title is the tale's principal character, his life and death a metaphor for peasant hardship. Verga's choice of a donkey as protagonist suits the theme of peasant hardship especially well, since the peasants he depicts typically work like donkeys, the humblest, most docile, and most encumbered of the Mezzogiorno's domesticated beasts (Pacifici 11). The donkey, a creature common in Italian folklore from the time and influence of storytellers like Aesop, symbolizes a number of proverbial, and in many cases, real Southern peasant values and traits: humility, obstinacy, patience, simplicity (Cooper, *Illustrated* 16). Ubiquitous in folktales of the Italian South, the donkey as protagonist made stories of their own troubles tolerable to the the peasants' ears (Mangione and Morreale 35). **"Story of the Saint Joseph Donkey"** is then a sophisticated folktale, an authentic expression of peasant consciousness.

Like the Saint Joseph Donkey, as the least productive donkeys of the Mezzogiorno were known, peasants, regardless of their labors, were little valued, treated as nothing by the upper classes and government of their society, rendered mute in their resistance to authority by their inability to speak anything but a local dialect, by the power of feudal custom, and by brute force, (Viscusi, "Narrative" 80-82).[1] Adding insult to injury, a nobleman might sarcastically call a peasant *"Santu"* ("Saint"), poking fun as his saintly poverty (Covello 79). What Verga gives us then is a triple analogy—symbolic, serious, sarcastic—of donkey, peasant, saint. His story recounts the life and death of one particular Saint Joseph Donkey. The Donkey, like the peasants, is treated as a commodity: an object valued for the work he can perform, an^{2}d devalued to nothingness as he is able to perform less and less work. The Donkey's breeder spends an entire day haggling his price with the Donkey's first owner, Neli.

> "It's a beautiful colt," said the owner, "and he's worth more than thirty-five *lire*. Don't pay attention to that black and white coat like a magpie's . . . In all honesty, I don't know where the colt got that magpie coat. But his build's good, believe me! You don't judge men by their faces. Look what a chest he's got! And those legs like pillars! Look how he holds his ears! When you have a donkey who keeps his ears that straight, you can put him to a cart or to a plow, just as you like, and make him carry four *tumoli* of buckwheat better

than a mule, I swear by the holy day that's today! Feel this tail; you and your whole family could hang on it!"

(Verga 149)

The breeder denies the Donkey's individuality, his "magpie coat" and its association with saintliness, to take full economic advantage of him, to have his whole family, in an economic sense, hang on the donkey's tail. In Verga's Mezzogiorno, you don't judge donkeys by their coats or "men by their faces." The analogy becomes clear: the breeder in his prevarication, the landowners in their control, the Donkey in his sturdiness and compliance, the peasants in their nothingness.

The analogy gains in clarity and force as the plot progresses. With each episode the Donkey becomes more of an individual, more human. As events unfold, we frequently see, hear, and feel them from the Donkey's perspective. "Meanwhile, [the Donkey] kept tripping along behind Neli, trying to bite his jacket for fun, as if he knew it was the jacket of his new owner, and as if he didn't care that he was forever leaving the stable where he had been warm beside his mother, where he had rubbed his muzzle on the edge of the manger, or had butted and capered with the ram, and had teased the pig in its little corner" (155). As the "colt" (156) and his labor change hands, he is gradually broken in both body and spirit.

> Eventually, he became so tired that he didn't even feel like biting into the pile of straw . . . Then he let his muzzle and his ears droop, like a full-grown donkey, his eyes lifeless, as if he were tired of looking at that vast white countryside which . . . seemed made only to let you die of thirst and to make you trot around on the sheaves. In the evening, he went back to the village with his saddlebags full, and the owner's boy kept pricking him in the withers, as they went along the path's hedges which seemed alive with the chirping of the titmice and the fragrance of catmint and rosemary, and the donkey would have liked to take a bite, if they hadn't made him trot all the time so that the blood went down to his legs and they had to take him to the farrier; but his owner didn't care at all, because the harvest had been good, and the colt had made his thirty-two and a half *lire*.
>
> (156)

Like a peasant child made to work in the fields, the immature Donkey is prematurely exploited and downtrodden.

Verga compares the Donkey explicitly to a human being in the episode at the farrier's, in which the Donkey "tried to break loose from the twisted rope which squeezed his lip, his eyes wild from the pain as if he were human" (157). Like the peasants, the Donkey falls further and further into misery. The narrator remarks, "And yet there are so many Christians who are no better off" than animals, the donkey and other beasts who

"shielded themselves by huddling close together" under "stars that were shining like swords," beasts whose "harness sores shuddered and quivered in the cold as if they could speak" (162). The comparison is culturally apt as well as explicit, since, in Mezzogiorno society of the era, men and their beasts often worked, rested, and celebrated side by side (Manoukian 17).

At story's end, the personified Donkey has suffered nearly to death. It is only then that he is given some comfort by "a poor widow, in a hut more broken down than the lime kiln itself, where the stars went through the roof like swords" (Verga 162). This old peasant woman lives under the same conditions as the Donkey, "as if she were in the open" (162); and she sees fit, despite her poverty, to care for him. The "poor Saint Joseph donkey was better off during his last days, since the widow kept him like a treasure, thanks to the money he had cost her, and at night she went to find straw and hay for him, and kept him in the hut beside her bed, where he gave off heat like a little fire; and in this world one hand washes the other" (163). Here, the widow gives care based on affection, but at least as much on economic interdependence: the dual motivation of relations among members of the peasant family. Although, for example, children were, naturally, loved by their parents and siblings, they also were expected to work with the rest of the family as soon as they were able (Alba 32). Fathers, in return, were expected to earn the lion's share of family bread; and mothers, if and when they were not working in the fields, were expected to keep household order (Gambino, *Blood* 128-182).

When the Donkey "knelt down just like the real Saint Joseph donkey in front of the Christ Child, and he didn't want to get up any more" (Verga 164), the widow and her own fever-stricken son are left without their only means of earning bread, the donkey, the one-time conveyance of the Christian world's savior. By this point in the narrative, the Donkey's treatment in death seems no worse than his treatment in life. A passerby tells the widow, "'I'm buying only the wood, because here's all the donkey's worth . . .' And he kicked the carcass, which sounded like a broken drum" (164). The folkloric Donkey suffers and dies, the way centuries of Southern folk did, most often bound in thankless, hopeless, and endless servitude to their landowning masters, or, at best, to their own tiny pieces of land.

Yet, to this land that both sustained them and sapped their strength, peasants remained true. Life there, like the familiar folktale, was the only story they knew: not necessarily a happy one, but one from which they could draw discernable themes and learn practical lessons. While it is true that many ultimately left, driven by economic crisis and the desire to improve their condition, they did so reluctantly (Nelli 31). Their village and its surroundings, every hovel, stone, and meadow, contained all they knew of history and life (Alba 28). Their attachment to their *paesi*, as oysters to rock, was a spiritual one, and at a distance, they conceived of those *paesi* as pastorals to which they would happily, must even, return.

Prior to the 1880s, Southern Italian migration meant, in most cases, movement within the Italian peninsula. And most of the landless laborers who migrated, as was later the case with emigrants to America, were men. These men were typically *giornalieri,* day laborers. Ninety per cent of all male peasants belonged to this group (Mack Smith 149). These men moved from place to place, in pursuit of work, living away from their families most of the time (Alba 79).

Such movement for economic survival finds expression in the Sicilian version of a folktale like those that influenced Verga, entitled "Out in the World." It begins, "There was a widow with two daughters and a son named Peppi, who was at a loss to earn his bread. While mother and daughters were spinning one day, Peppi said, 'Listen, Mother; with your leave, I am going out into the world'" (Calvino 616). Peppi represents the young, unmarried men who made up seventy-five per cent of emigrants from Mezzogiorno towns (Archdeacon 139; Douglass 101). Once out in the world, he works at first for room and board, and seeks money only in order to return to his family. He pleads with the landowner for whom he labors, "Carnival is coming, and you couldn't give me a little money just this one time so I could go and celebrate with my mother and sisters?" (Calvino 617). The landowner refuses to remunerate labor, a problem for Peppi, but an absolute barrier to upward mobility for late nineteenth-century peasants caught between feudalism and capitalism (Douglass 35-36; Mack Smith 148-57; Nelli 22-23), victims of the Mezzogiorno's near exclusion from the emerging international capitalist economy (Alba 38). While the Southern landowners themselves generally did not have enough capital to transform their *latifondia* from subsistence to market operations (Mack Smith 151), the landless Southern peasant could not even imagine such operations.

The solution for Peppi is a sly, "tough" (Calvino 618), anthropomorphic ox, a symbol of peasant *furberia,* cleverness, and perseverence. The ox instructs Peppi to ask the master, who hates the ox, to give him to Peppi in place of money, which the master does. One day, Peppi hears a proclamation: "Whoever feels up to plowing fifty acres of land in one day's time will receive the King's daughter in marriage; or, in the event he's already married, two piles of Gold.. But whoever tries and fails, dies." (618). Peppi and the ox succeed in plowing fifty acres of land in a single day. The king is reluctant to marry his noble daughter to "that ugly peasant" (619), so he asks Peppi, "'What do you want, two

piles of gold coins?'" To which Peppi replies, "'I'm a bachelor, Majesty. What would I do with gold pieces? I've come for my wife'" (619). Once the king agrees, Peppi endears himself by slaughtering the ox, as the ox instructs him, for the wedding feast. Peppi kills off the symbol of his servitude, whose magical hoof causes his matrimonial bedchamber to grow "full of flowers and fruit out of season" (620). Peppi himself, a peasant at heart, is himself out of season as a noble living in a castle.

Peppi's solution to poverty is characteristic of the folktale, with its pre-capitalistic sensibility (Propp 17). It is a solution that relies still on the graces of the *galantuomini,* the nobility. Such a solution was an unlikely one for the real peasants of the Mezzogiorno; and for Peppi it is only temporary. After his wedding, his sisters and brothers-in-law conspire to rob him of his money, by exploiting his trust. They learn the secret of his fertility from his wife, wager him that they know it, and when they win the wager, literally send him packing, "set out dressed as a peasant and carrying his knapsack" (Calvino 621).

Only Peppi's initiative and his curiosity restore him to his fortune and wife. He goes off in quest of the Sun, through a series of fantastic feats comes to speak with it, and bargains with it to set at an unusual hour, so that he can win back his possessions from his in-laws, as they had done from him. Upon winning this second wager, Peppi initially refuses his reward, announcing to the court, "'I intend to show you the heart of a peasant'—as they still called him . . . 'I have no desire for the property of others, but only for my own'" (622). When the king hears this, he "insisted on embracing [Peppi] and, removing his crown, placed it on Peppi's head . . . So goes the story of Peppi, who started out as a starving cowherd and ended up the wealthiest and happiest of kings" (622). Peppi renounces property gained through trickery, and ultimately gains it through humility and abstention, enacting the values and virtues practical only in the Italy of a folktale. A more realistic portrayal of values, but still not representative of reality, is Mazzarò's obsessive acquisition of property in Verga's **"Property."** Of course, Mazzarò's degree of success would have been nearly as rare for a peasant as Peppi's crown.

"Out in the World," then, inculcates the peasant virtues of hard work, humility, initiative, perseverance, but it does not offer a realistic solution to peasant problems. That solution could exist only outside of the society in which such tales were widely told. It would be left to the peasants who took part in the great emigration of the late nineteenth and early twentieth centuries; who, although they did not share Peppi's means, shared his values and virtues.

The actual peasants who became the great emigration were not of the lowest economic class. They were those peasants who feared falling into the abyss of poverty, *spinti,* driven, or, literally, pushed, to improve their lot. As one American official of the era stated, "One of the complaints of the present day of the Italian officials is that the very best young blood of the Italian plebes is going out of the country. They recognize that fact. It is the man with the initiative who leaves" (McLaughlin qtd in Nelli 33). In danger of being driven over the brink of indigence by a rash of economic disasters—the unfair redistribution of lands and the dissolution of feudal ties, combined with the effects of extended drought, pervasive phylloxera, overproduction of agricultural products (especially wine and wheat), burdensome taxes, and the restrictive agricultural trade policies of the Italian government—nearly twenty million Italians, full of hope for a brighter economic future, emigrated (from 1861 to 1940) from an Italy that in 1901 contained a population of only thirty-three million (Sori 19). Most of these, young men alone, planned to return and buy pieces of their native soil. Most of the immigrants to the United States, ninety percent of whom came from the Mezzogiorno (Nelli 32), had never ventured beyond their villages; when they arrived in America, they found themselves alone or with just a few people who spoke their language; and they were, most often, illiterate.

As the immigrants who remained in the New World—approximately half of those who came (Archdeacon 137-140)—would discover, literacy in English, at least a degree of literacy, was tantamount to success in America. Understandably, the trope of literacy is central to Italian immigrant autobiography. To understand why the autobiographers held literacy out as a symbol of success in early twentieth-century America, one needs to understand that in the United States, then as now, productivity depended upon oral and written communication. Such was not necessarily the case in Italy, where in 1901, the illiteracy rate was 70 per cent in Campania, 69.5 per cent in Apulia, 75.4 per cent in Basilicata, 78.7 per cent in Calabria, and 70.9 per cent in Sicily (Covello 246).

A problem for the Italian immigrants, the "birds of passage"—so-called by Americans, most of whom did not believe they could assimilate (Alba 40)—were the vast and many differences between the two societies of which they would take part: Post-Risorgimento Italy and Gilded Age/Progressive Era America. The peasants came from a rural, feudal, rigidly stratified society governed by unwritten, traditional laws of community and local allegiances. They arrived in an increasingly urban, capitalistic, mobile society governed, at least in theory, by official legislation. In his 1995 novel, *Astoria,* Rob-

ert Viscusi crystallizes their dilemma: "A whole nation walked out of the middle ages, slept in the ocean, and awakened in New York in the twentieth century" (22).

While contradicting the Italian government's official encouragement of emigration during the period in question, "Gli emigranti," by Emilio Salgari (1863-1911), a newspaper account of the immigrants' passage to America, provides a telling Italian perspective on the peasants' disjuncture.

> Many times you have heard talk of those poor peasants who, without means of earning their bread in their own little *paesi,* go to seek their fortune in distant America, and perhaps you have seen many of them depart, crowding onto train cars, carrying their few rags, their last bit of wealth.
>
> Those wretches, before reaching America, must cross an immense ocean, the Atlantic, and travel twenty-five days, sometimes thirty, aboardship.
>
> We present to you now a scene of emigration. Look at all those peasants, who have abandoned our beautiful Italy, gathered together in the hold of a ship. With them are their women and children.
>
> It's dinnertime. All crowd around the cooks and the sailors to receive their bowls of soup. But the ocean is not calm, and the ship, tossed by the waves, bounces around wildly, jostling everyone.
>
> The bowls overturn, children fall to the floor, losing their soup, others cling to their mommies' skirts and howl with fright, or they are helped by their older brothers and sisters, while the parents run back and forth, everywhere, for fear of going without dinner.
>
> At sea, these are veryday occurences, scenes played out over and over again, which try the patience and the hunger of those poor peasants.
>
> But finally, the ocean crossed, the coastline of America is in sight, they debark onto those distant shores. But how many disillusionments often await them there, and how many return to their fatherland poorer than they left! (translation mine)
>
> (Savana and Straniero 341)

Given the trauma of the their experience, we can easily understand how Italy, the familiar, must have returned, again and again, as an ideal society to those who remained in the Italian colonies of America.

Notes

1. Robert Viscusi, in "Narrative and Nothing," illuminates the peasants' experience of nothingness, its role in understanding the society Verga portrays, and its impact on immigrant and later Italian American authors.

   The *cafoni* [peasants], unlike the authorities, do not need to be divided among themselves in order to be rendered harmless. Their separation is of a different kind. They are removed from the drama of power by three layers of Nothing. And even these are precise. At the top, under the guards and dogs, there is that Nothing closest to the rich and powerful. Let us call this The Nothing of the Deaf: in *Fontamara* [Ignazio Silone's twentieth-century novel of peasant life], the rich systematically misinterpret what the *cafoni* say, insisting that every request for help is an act of transgression, and the treating a desperate plea for water as if it were an act of revolutionary terrorism. At the bottom, just above the *cafoni,* there is the Nothing of those who cannot represent themselves. Let us call the The Nothing of the Mute: the *cafoni* do not know what to say even when they say it. They arrive at the festival carrying the wrong flag, their clothes are laughable, their accent is sidesplittingly awkward. After all, they *cannot,* actually cannot, speak the language of the nation, but only the local tongue belonging to their narrow little crevasse in the primeval hills—what is called a dialect but has in practice the effect of a visible stigma. They speak with a wordlist and a *cantilena* that mark them out as simply not worth listening to, mark them out no less vividly than a bright red tattoo across the mouth.

Then there is the middle Nothing. It stands for that which cannot even attempt to speak or to hear. This is The Nothing of the Dead: it represents that which ought to be there but is not. It represents those who have so totally failed to claim a right to existence that they have either died or emigrated, or both . . ." (81).

Works Cited

Archdeacon, Thomas J. *Becoming American: An Ethnic History.* New York: The Free Press, 1983.

Boelhower, William. *Immigrant Autobiography in the United States.* Verona: Essedue Edizioni, 1982.

Calvino, Italo. *Italian Folktales.* 1956. Trans. George Martin. New York: Pantheon Books, 1981.

Cecchetti, Giovanni. *Giovanni Verga.* Boston: Twayne Publishers, 1978.

Cooper, J. C. *An Illustrated Encyclopaedia of Traditional Symbols.* London: Thames and Hudson, 1978.

Covello, Leonard. *The Social Background of the Italo-American School Child.* Leiden: E. J. Brill, 1967.

Dégh, Linda. "Folk Narrative." *Folklore and Folklife: An Introduction.* Ed. Richard M. Dorson. Chicago: U of Chicago P, 1972. 53-83.

De Rosa, Gabriele. *Chiesa e religione popolare nel Mezzogiorno.* Roma-Bari: Laterza, 1978.

Douglass, William A. *Emigration in a South Italian Town.* New Brunswick, N. J.: Rutgers UP, 1984.

Gabaccia, Donna R. *From Sicily to Elizabeth Street: Housing and Social Change among Italian Immigrants, 1880-1930.* Albany: SUNY P, 1984.

Gambino, Richard. *Blood of My Blood.* New York: Anchor Books, 1975.

Mack Smith, Denis. *Italy: A Modern History.* Ann Arbor: U of Michigan P, 1959.

Mangione, Jerre and Ben Morreale. *La Storia: Five Centuries of the Italian American Experience.* New York: HarperCollins, 1992.

Manoukian, Agopik. "La Famiglia dei contadini." *La Famiglia italiana dall'Ottocento a oggi.* Ed. Piero Melograni, with Lucetta Scaraffia. Roma-Bari: Laterza, 1988. 3-60.

Marinelli, Peter. *Pastoral.* The Critical Idiom Series. 15. London: Methuen and Co., 1971.

Nelli, Humbert. *From Immigrants to Ethnics: The Italian Americans.* New York: Oxford UP, 1983.

Orsi, Robert. "The Religious Boundaries of an Inbetween People: Street *Feste* and the Problem of the Dark-Skinned Other in Italian Harlem, 1920-1990." *American Quarterly* 44.3(1992): 313-47.

Pacifici, Sergio. "The Tragic World of Verga's Primitives." *From Verismo to Experimentalism: Essays on the Modern Italian Novel.* Ed. Sergio Pacifici. Bloomington: Indiana UP, 1969. 4-38.

Pei, Mario. Preface. *The Golden Carnation and Other Stories Told in Italy.* Frances Toor. New York: Lothrop, Lee and Shepard Co., 1960. vii-x.

Propp, Vladimir. *Theory and History of Folklore.* Trans. Adriadna Y. Martin and Richard P. Martin and several others. Ed. Anatoly Lieberman. Minneapolis: U of Minneapolis P, 1984.

Rando, Flavia. "'My Mother Was a Strong Woman': Respect, Shame, and the Feminine Body in the Sculpture of Nancy Azara and Antonette Rosato." *Voices in Italian Americana* 7.2 (1996): 21-34.

Salomone-Marino, Salvatore. *Customs and Habits of the Sicilian Peasant.* 1897. Trans. and Ed. Rosalie N. Norris, from *Costumi e usanze di contadini di Sicilia.* Ed. Aurelio Rigoli. 1968. Rutherford, NJ: Fairleigh Dickinson UP, 1981.

Savana, A. V. and M. L. Straniero, eds. *Canti dell'emigrazione.* Milan: Garzanti Editore, 1976.

Sori, Ercole. *L'Emigrazione italiana dall'Unità alla Seconda Guerra Mondiale.* Bologna: Il Mulino, 1979.

Toschi, Paolo. *Invito al folklore italiano: Le Regioni e le feste.* Roma: Editrice Stadium, 1963.

Verga, Giovanni. *Maestro Don Gesualdo.* 1889. New York: Greenwood Press, 1976.

———. *I Malavoglia.* 1881. New York: Schoenhofs Foreign Books, 1991.

———. *Tutte le novelle.* New York: Schoenhofs Foreign Books, 1950.

———. *The She-Wolf [La Lupa] and Other Stories.* Trans. Giovanni Cecchetti. Berkeley: U of California P, 1973.

Viscusi, Robert. *Astoria.* Toronto: Guernica Editions, 1995.

———. "Narrative and Nothing: The Enterprise of Italian American Writing." *Perspectives* 6-7 (Spring/ Autumn 1994): 77-99.

Martin Greenberg (essay date 2006)

SOURCE: Greenberg, Martin. "Giovanni Verga's Verismo." *New Criterion* 22, no. 9 (May 2004): 18-24.

[*In the following essay, which originally appeared in the* New Criterion *in May 2004 and was revised for its publication here, Greenberg provides an overview of Verga's short fiction, observing its relevance to the development of the short story genre.*]

> . . . il vero
> dell' aspra sorte e del depresso loco
> che natura ci die.
>
> —*La Ginestra,* Leopardi

Italy, a late united nation, lagged too in producing a modern narrative literature. That had to wait till the 20th century. She did nevertheless produce two outstanding if very different novelists in the 19th century: Alessandro Manzoni, whose *I Promessi Sposi* (*The Betrothed*), written in the 1820s, is a vivid, discursively narrated work of romantic historism; and writing toward the end of the century Giovanni Verga, the chief figure of Italian *verismo* and one of the great European realists, though little recognized outside his own country. D. H.Lawrence, who admired both writers and translated three of the latter's books, asked—complained— back in the 1920s: "Who stills reads them, even (outside the classroom) in Italy?" You can ask the same question today. In 1947 Visconti made a movie, *La Terra Trema,* out of Verga's *I Malavoglia* (known in English as *The House by the Medlar Tree*), filming it in the very Sicilian fishing village, Aci-Trezza, that is the setting of the novel. Yet the postwar fascination with Italy and the neo-realist Italian movies and novels, for which the realist Verga was an inspiration, didn't make him better known abroad; he remains an obscure figure. This has its good side. Because reading Verga is to experience

the pleasurable shock of unfamiliar great writing. The big names of 19th century prose narrative came preceded by a marching band of reference, allusion, criticism; you seemed to know them before you knew them. But Verga, about whom one has known little or nothing, is news—news for those to whom the great works of 19th century realism aren't just literary history.

Giovanni Verga was born in 1840 into a landowning family in the city of Catania, on the east coast of Sicily, almost in the shadow of Etna. He began to write early. In 1865 he departed for the mainland, first to Florence and then Milan. A young provincial, he was entranced by metropolitan excitements: high society, love affairs, art, journalism, literature. Fashionable life—fashionable sexual life—provided much of the matter of his early efforts as a novelist, which tended toward the insipid. But he hadn't shaken the dust of his native island from his feet. Sicily began to intrude itself into his work. This was a time in which the young writers of Italy, where the old rhetorical traditions were still strong, were responding excitedly to the new ideas of French realism and naturalism, exemplified by Flaubert, the Goncourts and Zola. Especially the latter's example moved Verga (but Verga's realism is not at all Zolaesque). And at the end of the 1870s one of literature's many miracles occurred. A hitherto mediocre writer abandoned a shallow subject matter and a traditional style to write a series of vivid, violent short stories and two novels about the abysmally poor, primitive Sicilian life in the midst of which he had grown up.

If Verga's realism took its lead from France, that doesn't mean he was a country cousin trailing after "the literary smarties in Paris" (Lawrence). Verga sounded his own note. Sounded is the right word for a language that strives to be his characters' own speech. With his laconic narrative art he anticipated a later time; with his peasant stories he recalled as early a time as Boccaccio's. The 19th century on the whole was long-winded and slow-paced (with notable exceptions like Stendhal), achieving its masterpieces by a fullness, often fatness, of exposition. That is one way. Verga's was the way of brevity, an abruptness aiming at absolute impersonality. Of course absolute impersonality is impossible. But a repudiation of the self-delighting fine writing of the Italian rhetorical tradition—that was possible.

Italy before her unification in 1860 was a backward country with a supercivilized past. Her upper classes looked northwards beyond the Alps in emulation of the civilization of Northern Europe. And following the Risorgimento she modernized quickly—that is, the Italian North did. What independence and unification revealed was that the South, the glorious South of ancient times, was stuck fast in semi-feudal sloth and squalor. Among the educated classes two main ways of looking at the South emerged, which are the subject of an excellent study, *The View from Vesuvius: Italian Culture and the Southern Question,* by Nelson Moe. One way saw the Italian South as fascinatingly picturesque, full of the romantic charm of a remote part of the world left behind by time. The other, realistic way, of which Professor Moe makes out two branches, saw it as almost another country, primitive, nasty, miserable, Naples or even Rome being where Africa began. This Italian South cried out for modernization. But another kind of realism saw its age-old primitivism as a more authentic, more vital, unbourgeois-corrupted life. The great Italophile Stendhal praised Italy as a place where greed and generosity, tenderness and violence, passionate love and passionate hatred were still freely expressed; he jeered at his fellow Frenchmen whose civilization had left them as their sole remaining passion the one for "money, which gave them the means to strut about importantly." In Italy itself he distinguished between the civilized North and the region south of the Tiber where "you'll find the energy and exuberance of savages." This "question" of the South was a matter of lively discussion in the intellectual circles of Milan in which Verga moved.

He dealt with the question in an early story, **"Fantasticheria,"** (translated by D. H. Lawrence as **"Caprice"**). It is addressed to a Milanese society lady by the Sicilian narrator who had been her lover-guide on a trip to the island. Her caprice was, when seeing from their railroad car the fishing village of Aci-Trezza, framed like a picture in the train window, to say, How pretty it looks, how nice it would be to spend a month down there. So down they went with her mountain of luggage. In two days' time she was bored to death and left. Close up, Aci-Trezza lost all its picturesque charm. Her lover too couldn't have pleased her much, for with gentle mercilessness he holds up to her her bourgeois blindness to the humanity of the Sicilian poor, her triviality of mind and occupations.

"Fantasticheria" is less interesting as a story than as an introduction to his remarkable first collection of stories, *Vita dei Campi (Life in the Fields),* published in 1880. Among these **"The She-Wolf," "Ieli [the Herd Boy]"** and **"Rosso Malpelo,"** all works taut with Verga's narrative intensity, stand out. Two of these three stories end with dire retribution for sexual violation. The brilliantly told **"She-Wolf"** has a strong classical suggestion in its fateful movement. The She-Wolf is called so by the village women because, a a kind of maenad with her "arrogant breasts," coal-black eyes and red lips, always roaming about, she has devoured "all their sons and husbands" and even the village priest, insatiably. A returned soldier, handsome Nanni, sets her afire. Day after day working under the fiery sun she follows after him in the fields, mowing hay and gathering sheaves, never falling behind. "What is it?" he would ask. "What do you want, Pina?" One evening she tells

him. "You, I want you, beautiful as the sun, sweet as honey." "'And I want that young virgin of a daughter of yours,'" Nanni answers, laughing." Her direct, unembarrassed avowal has the innocence and also dangerousness of nature. Nanni's response, equally unembarrassed, refuses nature; he lives by the human laws of the land, its first law being family.

With his innocent laugh, Nanni is on the way to being destroyed. The She-Wolf forces her daughter to marry him, gives him her house, keeps only a corner for herself. He laughs again, at her black eyes fixed in a devouring stare on him—but now he crosses himself as well. One blazing afternoon she wakes Nanni dozing on the threshing floor. "Go away, go away!" he cries, sobbing, "No decent woman goes roaming around between noon and vespers." Again she comes, and again, and again. Nanni's protests cease.

"Vile mother!" her daughter says and goes to the Sergeant. "It's the temptation of hell," sobs Nanni, "lock me up, kill me!" He offers masses, licks the pavement in front of the church, swears he'll kill her if she comes to the threshing floor again. "Kill me," she answers, "I can't live without you." The conclusion is breath-taking:

> When he saw her in the distance, in the green wheat fields, Nanni stopped hoeing in the vineyard and went to pull his axe out of the elm tree. The She-Wolf saw him advancing toward her, pale and wild-eyed, the axe blade glittering in the sun, but she didn't fall back one step, didn't lower her gaze, kept on coming, her hands full of red poppies, devouring him with her black eyes.

> "Oh, damn your soul," stammers Nanni.

The story's few pages, which cover a lot of barely indicated time, don't produce an effect of speed but rather of deliberateness, inexorability. Everything is seen—heard—from close up, there is no narrative remove. Verga's realism, as with all the great realists, is often touched with poetry. With **"The She-Wolf"** it is the result of narrative conception; in later works, sometimes of literary style. This poetic quality allows freer admittance to the shadow of the Fatal Woman visible behind the She-Wolf: Eve, Clytemnestra, Vittoria Corombona, La Belle Dame Sans Merci. In a nearer time you find something of her in the killer female Mildred in *Of Human Bondage* and in the southern "bitch" of Lillian Hellman's *The Little Foxes.* But the theme no longer has its old power. Marriage having lost its sacramental character, its destruction by a modern *femme fatale* (if such a creature still exists) is no longer tragic. Helpless subjection in modern love (the word "thralldom" no longer suits) suggests not the uncanny but obsession.

Though a tragedy, **"The She-Wolf"** arouses no emotions of pity and fear. Its spare, dispassionate style excludes all feelings except that of the overwhelming power of sexual passion. The fatal woman's power is sexual, but each exercises her power according to her nature. Eve is a foolish woman and draws Adam into her folly; Clytemnestra is a revenger; Vittoria a devil; the Belle Dame a seductive sprite from a sinister faeryland. For Nanni the She-Wolf's power is from Hell. But the writer suggests nothing of the kind. Carnal desire in her is so absolute as to transcend itself and reach a height that death can neither frighten nor defeat. The story would have confirmed Stendhal in his conviction of an Italy of uncorrupted feeling.

The tragic carnal of **"The She-Wolf"** changes to the tragic pastoral of **"Ieli [the Herdboy]."** **"Ieli"** is told less dispassionately because of Verga's fondness for his endearing youth, who lives out in the fields with the horses he tends with loving care, a child so innocent, so good, as to seem the very incarnation of Christian meekness. Thanks to his friend Don Alfonso, a gentleman's son, and Mara, a farmer's child whom Ieli adores, his hard childhood is made happy by their companionship in the outdoors. But the novella darkens as it moves through the vicissitudes of Ieli's growing up to culminate in catastrophe. Mara, palmed off as a wife on the guileless,/still-adoring shepherd (as he now is) because her reputation has been lost for "carrying on" with Don Alfonso, continues to carry on. When Ieli sees Mara walk into his arms to dance at a sheep-shearing feast, the truth overwhelms him. With a single stroke he cuts Don Alfonso's throat, as he had cut two kids' throats a minute ago for the feast. Brought before the judge, Ieli says, "What! How shouldn't I have killed him. He'd taken Mara!" His innocence is as pure as the She-Wolf's carnality.

"Tragedy seems to be the cathartic element [in Verga] which is necessary whenever human values must be saved," writes Giovanni Cecchetti in his introduction to his Verga translation (***The She-Wolf and Other Stories***). This is so. Both stories defend marriage and lawfulness. But at the same time they go farther, do more. The She-Wolf attains to a height of sexual sublimity that is beyond all judgment, as Ieli's goodness rises above all moral (though not legal) condemnation of his deed of murder.

There is no pity in these two stories. The She-Wolf and Ieli must be what they tragically, simply, are. The third story, **"Rosso Malpelo,"** lacks pity too, any tragic feeling, but breathes an intense pitifulness. You would think pitifulness a less profound emotion than any kind of tragical feeling. Yet the infinite sadness of **"Rosso Malpelo"** is just as harrowing as the tragic sexual force of the **"The She-Wolf,"** if not more so. Its unpurged desolation is like an abyss. The boy whose nickname gives the story its title is called Malpelo ("evil-haired") because he has red hair, and he has red hair because he's wicked and malicious—"an ugly thing, a surly, sullen

brat whom everybody avoided, that you gave a kick to when he got too close." The "you" speaking here are the Sicilian villagers whose men go down into an underground quarry to dig sand (as Malpelo and other children do too). It is their voices, a harsh village chorus—in which Malpelo's own voice has a part—that constitutes the story; the boy's voice too because he has accepted into himself the village's view of him. "Knowing he was *malpelo,* he tried to live up to that name"; if anything went wrong he was to blame, and even if he wasn't he was, because it was just the kind of thing a *malpelo* would do. The only affection ever shown him was by his father, who was called the Jackass and half shut out from the village by contempt, as his son is completely shut out by revulsion and fear. The father, working overtime, dies under a sand fall he should never have exposed himself to, just like a jackass. The people hardly bestir themselves to rescue him. The boy howls with terror and grief, digging the sand like a madman to find his buried parent. The miners have to drag him away by his hair.

The story is very simply told, as James Wood writes, with the simpleness of an older, unself-conscious time. But also as he writes, it is not simple. It has a doubleness. There is the surface text, the words of the village chorus, which is betrayed by the undertext. This duplicity is apparently ambiguous. For Prof. Moe says that Malpelo is wholly "committed to the . . . violence and oppression in which he lives. There is little that is charming or pleasant about him"; and Wood, among other, more sympathetic words, says he is "a vicious, pathetic, feral child. . . . Certainly he is nasty." I read it differently.

Cruelly treated, the boy is cruel in turn—certainly. But because Verga gives the language of the story over to the villagers, it's the latter's judgment we hear. When the text uses the third person, it isn't the authorial third person but the third person of "free, indirect discourse," what German aestheticians were the first to identify as *erlebte Rede:* the thoughts, sentiments, intentions, etc., etc., of the characters—here the village collectivity—given in their own words, which "frees" them from their creator's control to say just how *they* understand things. And their understanding of the filthy, ragged, skulking Malpelo is pitiless. What has lack of *charm* and *pleasantness* got to do with Malpelo's terrible story or his seeming *feral*? He's not the savage one, the people of the village are.

Yes, the boy beats the poor stumbling pit donkey mercilessly, saying, "This way you'll die sooner!" But we come to understand these words better at the end of the story.

"He certainly felt a strange pleassure in remembering the ill treatment . . . they had made his father bear, and the way they had let him die." Is it a *strange pleasure* for a son to remember with hatred the neighbors' indifference to his father's fate?

"Out of refined cruelty he seemed to have made himself the protector of a poor little [new] boy," a hobbling cripple whom the miners call the Frog. When Frog whines under a heavy load, Malpelo scolds and hits him—it is his hard way of encouraging him to be brave and strong. "Beat the donkey with all your might, as he would beat you if he could," is the kind of advice Malpelo gives Frog. But he also helps Frog with work too hard for him, buys the sickly boy wine and hot soup, carries him on his back, visits him when he is dying. This is what the surface text, the communal voice, calls *refined cruelty.*

After Gray the donkey died, Malpelo and Frog had gone to look at the carcass—a kind of memorial visit. "See those ribs of Gray? Now he doesn't suffer any more. . . . No more! No more! . . . But it would have been better for him if he had never been born." Here Malpelo echoes a sentiment you find expressed from Sophocles to Auden. Behind his beating the donkey lurked some kind of thought: he was hastening the kindness of death. "If [Malpelo himself] was beaten, it didn't matter . . . to him, for when he would become like Gray or like Frog, he wouldn't feel anything any more."

Of no account in the village, he is the one sent to explore the mine's perilous winding passages. One day, as he knew must happen, as had happened to others, he doesn't return. In Rosso Malpelo's world, where man has little love for his neighbor, the surly, sullen brat who loved his father and was kind to Frog, had struggled without help, in ignorance, in the only way he knew, to show human generosity and love.

The communal chorus Verga had discovered as the narrative form for **"Rosso Malpelo"** he carried over to his novel *The House by the Medlar Tree* (*I Malavoglia*) on a greatly enlarged scale. It has a cast of fifty characters, the natives of the poor fishing village of the already mentioned Aci-Trezza. All are individuals with names (and nicknames), have individual voices that shout and whisper, hold forth and denounce, murmur and mutter, wail and weep and laugh—a medley that rises and falls like the sound of the sea at their door. Within this vocal world the novel tells the story of the fall of one family, the Malavoglia, overwhelmed by misfortune after misfortune, honorable, well-intentioned people (in contradiction to the "ill will" of their name). Behind Verga's deadpan, you detect a looking back with the Malavoglia family to an older, nobler time, as Leopardi looked back in disaffection with modern progress.

Italians count *The House by the Medlar Tree* Verga's masterpiece. It is strikingly original in its language and structure. The best translation of it that I know is by Raymond Rosenthal (who translated Primo Levi's *Periodic Table* brilliantly). Yet his English fails, it seems to me, can't help failing, to catch the choral character of *I Malavoglia.* In the Italian the village chorus is literally a chorus, rhythmical, musical—so Rosenthal and the Italian critics describe it. But how can English syllables catch that Mediterranean music, flavored with dialect and resounding on almost every page, Sancho Panza-like, with proverbs that are almost impossible to bring over in any true-sounding form? In English what you hear is a confusion of names and voices. However, you can catch a sense of gaiety in the village volubility, and a rough humor.

The pathetic story of the Malavoglia, in English, teeters on the edge of sentimentality. Lawrence wrote that the novel "is rather overdone on the pitiful side. . . . Just knock off about twenty per cent of the tragedy . . . and see what a great book remains." What you would knock off first of all is the young Malavoglia daughter's going wrong in the big city. But even if you knocked off more than twenty per cent, that would still leave Master 'Ntoni, the patriarchal head of the family, at the center of the novel; and he is a bit of a Mr. Peggotty. In Verga's own language, so Italian critics claim, he is able to avoid sentimentality; which is likely since language is so determinative with him. But I lack enough Italian to hear, and therefore feel, and therefore know the novel in its vital vocal texture, so I'll stop my discussion of it here.

Verga followed *The House by the Medlar Tree* with his other notable piece of long fiction, the very different *Mastro-Don Gesualdo.* No "choral novel," it tells its story in a more or less familiar 19th century style. And it is different too in its whole feeling. The Malavoglia have the heroism of endurance in the face of misfortune, loss and poverty. Their ethic of family and work dignifies them in their losing struggle against commercial modernity, even as it renders their efforts more and more futile. In *Mastro-Don Gesualdo,* Verga shifts his attention to the highborn and lowborn of a rural town. Hardly a soul among them, among the gentry especially, has anything the least bit fine or brave about him—or her: what horrors the women are. All is greed, motive- and money-calculation, vanity and envy and fear. This is Verga's *verismo* for fair.

Don Gesualdo has climbed up from ragged, hod-carrying poverty to be the richest man in the region. He is a better person than his townsmen—when his greed to own and own with no thought of material comfort or any other kind of largeness, relaxes for a moment and allows him to show some humanity towards others and towards himself. But he is undone by marrying into the aristocracy. Of course they despise him. He dies sick and unregarded in the wing of the palazzo of a polite, ice-cold Palermo Duke who had married his daughter or rather his money.

Why should the novel's story—a mastro (a skilled worker, Gesualdo had been a mason) among the dons—move so heavily, even drearily? Did Verga write the novel out of his head—unlike his peasant stories which come from a deeper source—because he had undertaken a Zolaesque project (never completed) to treat each class of Sicilian society in a separate work? *Mastro-Don Gesualdo* has vivid descriptions of the stark and stony mountain landscape of Sicily, lashed by a terrible sun; and also of the green, luxuriant countryside where the Dons take refuge from the cholera. But Don Gesualdo is less successful as a character than he should be. Seen intermittently as a master bossing working peasants, he has animation; but as a Don defeated by his ailing aristocratic wife longing hopelessly for her young lover, and by the sneering gentry, he lacks vitality in his defeat. It is the writer's defeat.

Before he wrote *Mastro-Don Gesualdo,* Verga had published another collection of stories, the **Novelle Rusticane** (Country Tales), or **Little Novels of Sicily** in Lawrence's translation. These are different from his earlier stories, having, most of them, less dramatic tension and less violence. The narrative voice is easy-going, rather resigned. He looks with complete, unsentimental understanding into his peasants' lives and the changeless injustice to which they must submit. These novelle confirm Verga's place, I believe, in the front rank of short story writers.

One story, not about peasants as it happens, but about poor, desperate gentry, begins so:

> They know how to read and write—that's the trouble. The white frost of dark winter dawns and the burning dog days of harvest time fall upon them as upon every other poor devil, since they're made of flesh and blood like their fellow man, and since they've got to go out and watch to see that their fellow man doesn't rob them of his time and his day's pay. But if you have anything to do with them, they hook you by . . . the beak of that pen of theirs, and then you'll never get your name out of their ugly books ever again.

There is no lack of narrative vitality here, perhaps because he is writing about gentry fallen into poverty and trouble so that their class brutality has been humbled enough for him to pity them: Don Giovannino sold up for debt, hiding his face for shame; Don Marco whose fields are obliterated by lava pouring down from Etna; Don Piddu sold up too, but worse, finding his doweryless daughter in the arms of the stable boy. He is counselled by his confessor "to offer his anguish to God." This provokes the narrator to violate his rule of impersonality by concluding the story, most unusually, with a comment of his own. "But what the priest should really have said to Don Piddu" was:

> You see, your honor, when the same trouble falls on other poor folks they keep quiet, because they are poor, and can't read and write, and can't let out what they feel without getting sent to the galleys.

Many of the stories are not stories in the usual sense. If you knew nothing more about **"The Gentry," "Malaria," "Property"** and **"Liberty"** than their titles you'd think them accounts of social conditions. As in a certain way they are, non-dramatic narratives vivid in their detail, fuller in their recounting than his earlier work, with a conclusion that tells you that to be a Sicilian peasant, even a rich one, was a piece or very bad luck.

"Property" begins with a long, echoing, periodic sentence beautifully translated by Lawrence, far more resonant than Verga's usually restrained writing:

> The traveller passing along by the Lake of Lentini . . . and by the burnt up stubble fields of the Plain of Catania, and the evergreen orange trees of Francoforte, and the gray cork trees of Resecone, and the deserted pasture lands of Passanetto and of Passinatello, if ever he asked, to while away the tedium of the long dusty road, under the sky heavy with heat, in the hour when the litter bells ring sadly in the immense campagna, and the mules let their heads and tails hang helpless, and the litter driver sings his melancholy song so as not to be overcome by the malaria-sleep, "All this land, whose is it?"—he would get for answer, "Mazzarò's."

And Mazzarò's are the farmstead as big as a village, the endless vineyards, the olive grove thick as a woods, the herds of oxen coming home at evening, the flocks of sheep. The earth itself seemed Mazzarò's, a paltry-looking fellow, once a poor peasant whose backside his boss of a Baron used to kick regularly. By cunning, tireless work and hardly pausing to eat even the crusts his miserliness allows himself, he amasses a huge amount of property, including all the Baron's. When old and ailing and reminded to forget property and think about his soul, Mazzarò staggers out into the courtyard and kills his ducks and turkeys—if he must die, they'll die too, a curse on all of you.

He never married, marriage costs money. He dies utterly alone amid his property reaching to the horizon, furious, all his consolation of possession gone. Peasant (and provincial bourgeois) avarice are a familiar subject in 19th century literature (Balzac, de Maupassant). Mazzarò's avarice is distinctively Italian, and as absolute in its way as the She-Wolf's passion is in its way.

Some of these novelle seem perfect of their kind to me. I single out **"The Orphans,"** a masterpiece of the art of narrative plainness and immediacy. The inconsolable Meno has just lost his second wife, a treasure, whose like he'd never find again, who wouldn't let him call the doctor for her, who got up the day before she died to see to the foal just weaned, who didn't wash herself so as not to dirty water, who took care of him like a servant, who loved his little girl by his first wife because she was her niece, and whose dowry he'd have to give back because they'd had no children—was there every anybody so unfortunate? The women surrounding him try to reassure him but he can't be reassured, they offer him a bite which he can't eat but eats, they are already scheming to find him a third wife.

Verga's stories don't sound the note of social militancy that Zola's do. Politically, he was a liberal. But in his heart he was a Christian, in his resignation, in his wisdom about human suffering.

Even my paraphrase of **"The Orphans"** above exhibits the transparency of his prose. His realism is the clear-window kind; we hear directly the harshness of life of a beset humanity, and their endurance. Behind the impersonal voice, silently, lie tenderness and humor. This is different from Flaubert, whose story is only seen through the highly worked medium of his beautiful prose (beautiful except for the bad poetry of his surprisingly inept similes):

> . . . Emma easily persuaded herself that the marvellous passion of love, which hitherto had hovered up above her like a great, rosy-plumaged bird in the splendor of poetic skies, was something she at last possessed.—And now it was hard for her to believe that the quiet life she was leading was the happiness she had dreamed of.

Flaubert lends Emma his words; the peasants lend Verga theirs. Two kinds of realism, one using all the care of art, the other (apparently) artless.

Neighbor Meno, while never ceasing to lament the loss of his wife, answers the women's plea to go and do something for Widow Angela's sick ass, her only support in the world. But the ass is beyond help. Standing around the dead creature, they urge Cousin Alfia on

him, who, unlike his dead wife's sister, is not too young and won't fill the house with girl children, God help us, and also has a bit of land.

> Cousin Alfia saw it was time for her to put in too, with a long face, and she began praising the dead woman again. She had arranged her in the coffin with her own hands, and put a handkerchief of fine linen on her face. Because she had plenty of linen and white things, though she said it herself. Then Neighbor Meno, touched, turned to Widow Angela, who never moved, no more than if she was made of stone, and said, "Well now, what are you waiting for, why don't you have the ass skinned? At least get money for the hide."

FURTHER READING

Criticism

Pagano, Tullio. "Zola and Verga beyond Naturalism." In *Experimental Fictions: From Emile Zola's Naturalism to Giovanni Verga's Verism,* pp. 149-62. Madison, N.J.: Fairleigh Dickinson University Press, 1999.
> Delineates Verga's struggle in his later works with the relationship between reality and simulation, tracing literary modernism's debt to the techniques and subject matter of *verismo* and naturalism.

Pedroni, Peter N. "The Dramatization of Giovanni Verga's Narrative." *Canadian Journal of Italian Studies* n.s. 14, nos. 42-43 (1991): 35-41.
> Contrasts the literary achievements of Verga's theater with those of his fiction.

Sansone, Matteo. "Verga, Puccini and *La Lupa.*" *Italian Studies* 44 (1989): 63-76.
> Chronicles the narrative difficulties of adapting "The She-Wolf" as a drama and a libretto.

Additional coverage of Verga's life and career is contained in the following sources published by Thomson Gale: *Contemporary Authors,* Vols. 104, 123; *Contemporary Authors New Revision Series,* Vol. 101; *Encyclopedia of World Literature in the 20th Century,* Ed. 3; *European Writers,* Vol. 7; *Literature Resource Center; Reference Guide to Short Fiction,* Ed. 2; *Reference Guide to World Literature,* Eds. 2, 3; *Short Story Criticism,* Vol. 21; *Twentieth-Century Literary Criticism,* Vol. 3; and *World Literature and Its Times,* Vol. 7.

How to Use This Index

The main references

> **Calvino, Italo**
> 1923-1985 .... **CLC 5, 8, 11, 22, 33, 39,**
> **73; SSC 3, 48**

list all author entries in the following Gale Literary Criticism series:

AAL = *Asian American Literature*
BG = *The Beat Generation: A Gale Critical Companion*
BLC = *Black Literature Criticism*
BLCS = *Black Literature Criticism Supplement*
CLC = *Contemporary Literary Criticism*
CLR = *Children's Literature Review*
CMLC = *Classical and Medieval Literature Criticism*
DC = *Drama Criticism*
HLC = *Hispanic Literature Criticism*
HLCS = *Hispanic Literature Criticism Supplement*
HR = *Harlem Renaissance: A Gale Critical Companion*
LC = *Literature Criticism from 1400 to 1800*
NCLC = *Nineteenth-Century Literature Criticism*
NNAL = *Native North American Literature*
PC = *Poetry Criticism*
SSC = *Short Story Criticism*
TCLC = *Twentieth-Century Literary Criticism*
WLC = *World Literature Criticism, 1500 to the Present*
WLCS = *World Literature Criticism Supplement*

The cross-references

> See also CA 85-88, 116; CANR 23, 61;
> DAM NOV; DLB 196; EW 13; MTCW 1, 2;
> RGSF 2; RGWL 2; SFW 4; SSFS 12

list all author entries in the following Gale biographical and literary sources:

AAYA = *Authors & Artists for Young Adults*
AFAW = *African American Writers*
AFW = *African Writers*
AITN = *Authors in the News*
AMW = *American Writers*
AMWR = *American Writers Retrospective Supplement*
AMWS = *American Writers Supplement*
ANW = *American Nature Writers*
AW = *Ancient Writers*
BEST = *Bestsellers*
BPFB = *Beacham's Encyclopedia of Popular Fiction: Biography and Resources*
BRW = *British Writers*
BRWS = *British Writers Supplement*
BW = *Black Writers*
BYA = *Beacham's Guide to Literature for Young Adults*
CA = *Contemporary Authors*
CAAS = *Contemporary Authors Autobiography Series*
CABS = *Contemporary Authors Bibliographical Series*
CAD = *Contemporary American Dramatists*
CANR = *Contemporary Authors New Revision Series*
CAP = *Contemporary Authors Permanent Series*
CBD = *Contemporary British Dramatists*
CCA = *Contemporary Canadian Authors*
CD = *Contemporary Dramatists*
CDALB = *Concise Dictionary of American Literary Biography*
CDALBS = *Concise Dictionary of American Literary Biography Supplement*
CDBLB = *Concise Dictionary of British Literary Biography*

CMW = *St. James Guide to Crime & Mystery Writers*
CN = *Contemporary Novelists*
CP = *Contemporary Poets*
CPW = *Contemporary Popular Writers*
CSW = *Contemporary Southern Writers*
CWD = *Contemporary Women Dramatists*
CWP = *Contemporary Women Poets*
CWRI = *St. James Guide to Children's Writers*
CWW = *Contemporary World Writers*
DA = *DISCovering Authors*
DA3 = *DISCovering Authors 3.0*
DAB = *DISCovering Authors: British Edition*
DAC = *DISCovering Authors: Canadian Edition*
DAM = *DISCovering Authors: Modules*
    DRAM: *Dramatists Module;* **MST:** *Most-studied Authors Module;*
    MULT: *Multicultural Authors Module;* **NOV:** *Novelists Module;*
    POET: *Poets Module;* **POP:** *Popular Fiction and Genre Authors Module*
DFS = *Drama for Students*
DLB = *Dictionary of Literary Biography*
DLBD = *Dictionary of Literary Biography Documentary Series*
DLBY = *Dictionary of Literary Biography Yearbook*
DNFS = *Literature of Developing Nations for Students*
EFS = *Epics for Students*
EXPN = *Exploring Novels*
EXPP = *Exploring Poetry*
EXPS = *Exploring Short Stories*
EW = *European Writers*
FANT = *St. James Guide to Fantasy Writers*
FW = *Feminist Writers*
GFL = *Guide to French Literature,* Beginnings to 1789, 1798 to the Present
GLL = *Gay and Lesbian Literature*
HGG = *St. James Guide to Horror, Ghost & Gothic Writers*
HW = *Hispanic Writers*
IDFW = *International Dictionary of Films and Filmmakers: Writers and Production Artists*
IDTP = *International Dictionary of Theatre: Playwrights*
LAIT = *Literature and Its Times*
LAW = *Latin American Writers*
JRDA = *Junior DISCovering Authors*
MAICYA = *Major Authors and Illustrators for Children and Young Adults*
MAICYAS = *Major Authors and Illustrators for Children and Young Adults Supplement*
MAWW = *Modern American Women Writers*
MJW = *Modern Japanese Writers*
MTCW = *Major 20th-Century Writers*
NCFS = *Nonfiction Classics for Students*
NFS = *Novels for Students*
PAB = *Poets: American and British*
PFS = *Poetry for Students*
RGAL = *Reference Guide to American Literature*
RGEL = *Reference Guide to English Literature*
RGSF = *Reference Guide to Short Fiction*
RGWL = *Reference Guide to World Literature*
RHW = *Twentieth-Century Romance and Historical Writers*
SAAS = *Something about the Author Autobiography Series*
SATA = *Something about the Author*
SFW = *St. James Guide to Science Fiction Writers*
SSFS = *Short Stories for Students*
TCWW = *Twentieth-Century Western Writers*
WLIT = *World Literature and Its Times*
WP = *World Poets*
YABC = *Yesterday's Authors of Books for Children*
YAW = *St. James Guide to Young Adult Writers*

Literary Criticism Series
Cumulative Author Index

Africa, Ben
See Bosman, Herman Charles

Afton, Effie
See Harper, Frances Ellen Watkins

Agapida, Fray Antonio
See Irving, Washington

Agee, James (Rufus) 1909-1955 ...... **TCLC 1, 19**
See also AAYA 44; AITN 1; AMW; CA 108; 148; CANR 131; CDALB 1941-1968; DAM NOV; DLB 2, 26, 152; DLBY 1989; EWL 3; LAIT 3; LATS 1:2; MAL 5; MTCW 2; MTFW 2005; NFS 22; RGAL 4; TUS

Aghill, Gordon
See Silverberg, Robert

Agnon, S(hmuel) Y(osef Halevi) 1888-1970 .... **CLC 4, 8, 14; SSC 30; TCLC 151**
See also CA 17-18; 25-28R; CANR 60, 102; CAP 2; EWL 3; MTCW 1, 2; RGSF 2; RGWL 2, 3; WLIT 6

Agrippa von Nettesheim, Henry Cornelius 1486-1535 .... **LC 27**

Aguilera Malta, Demetrio 1909-1981 .... **HLCS 1**
See also CA 111; 124; CANR 87; DAM MULT, NOV; DLB 145; EWL 3; HW 1; RGWL 3

Agustini, Delmira 1886-1914 .... **HLCS 1**
See also CA 166; DLB 290; HW 1, 2; LAW

Aherne, Owen
See Cassill, R(onald) V(erlin)

Ai 1947- .... **CLC 4, 14, 69**
See also CA 85-88; CAAS 13; CANR 70; DLB 120; PFS 16

Aickman, Robert (Fordyce) 1914-1981 .... **CLC 57**
See also CA 5-8R; CANR 3, 72, 100; DLB 261; HGG; SUFW 1, 2

Aidoo, (Christina) Ama Ata 1942- .... **BLCS; CLC 177**
See also AFW; BW 1; CA 101; CANR 62, 144; CD 5, 6; CDWLB 3; CN 6, 7; CWD; CWP; DLB 117; DNFS 1, 2; EWL 3; FW; WLIT 2

Aiken, Conrad (Potter) 1889-1973 .... **CLC 1, 3, 5, 10, 52; PC 26; SSC 9**
See also AMW; CA 5-8R; 45-48; CANR 4, 60; CDALB 1929-1941; CN 1; CP 1; DAM NOV, POET; DLB 9, 45, 102; EWL 3; EXPS; HGG; MAL 5; MTCW 1, 2; MTFW 2005; RGAL 4; RGSF 2; SATA 3, 30; SSFS 8; TUS

Aiken, Joan (Delano) 1924-2004 ...... **CLC 35**
See also AAYA 1, 25; CA 9-12R, 182; 223; CAAE 182; CANR 4, 23, 34, 64, 121; CLR 1, 19, 90; DLB 161; FANT; HGG; JRDA; MAICYA 1, 2; MTCW 1; RHW; SAAS 1; SATA 2, 30, 73; SATA-Essay 109; SATA-Obit 152; SUFW 2; WYA; YAW

Ainsworth, William Harrison 1805-1882 .... **NCLC 13**
See also DLB 21; HGG; RGEL 2; SATA 24; SUFW 1

Aitmatov, Chingiz (Torekulovich) 1928- .... **CLC 71**
See Aytmatov, Chingiz
See also CA 103; CANR 38; CWW 2; DLB 302; MTCW 1; RGSF 2; SATA 56

Akers, Floyd
See Baum, L(yman) Frank

Akhmadulina, Bella Akhatovna 1937- .... **CLC 53; PC 43**
See also CA 65-68; CWP; CWW 2; DAM POET; EWL 3

Akhmatova, Anna 1888-1966 ..... **CLC 11, 25, 64, 126; PC 2, 55**
See also CA 19-20; 25-28R; CANR 35; CAP 1; DA3; DAM POET; DLB 295; EW 10; EWL 3; FL 1:5; MTCW 1, 2; PFS 18; RGWL 2, 3

Aksakov, Sergei Timofeyvich 1791-1859 .... **NCLC 2**
See also DLB 198

Aksenov, Vasilii (Pavlovich)
See Aksyonov, Vassily (Pavlovich)
See also CWW 2

Aksenov, Vassily
See Aksyonov, Vassily (Pavlovich)

Akst, Daniel 1956- .... **CLC 109**
See also CA 161; CANR 110

Aksyonov, Vassily (Pavlovich) 1932- .... **CLC 22, 37, 101**
See Aksenov, Vasilii (Pavlovich)
See also CA 53-56; CANR 12, 48, 77; DLB 302; EWL 3

Akutagawa Ryunosuke 1892-1927 ... **SSC 44; TCLC 16**
See also CA 117; 154; DLB 180; EWL 3; MJW; RGSF 2; RGWL 2, 3

Alabaster, William 1568-1640 .... **LC 90**
See also DLB 132; RGEL 2

Alain 1868-1951 .... **TCLC 41**
See also CA 163; EWL 3; GFL 1789 to the Present

Alain de Lille c. 1116-c. 1203 .... **CMLC 53**
See also DLB 208

Alain-Fournier .... **TCLC 6**
See Fournier, Henri-Alban
See also DLB 65; EWL 3; GFL 1789 to the Present; RGWL 2, 3

Al-Amin, Jamil Abdullah 1943- .... **BLC 1**
See also BW 1, 3; CA 112; 125; CANR 82; DAM MULT

Alanus de Insluis
See Alain de Lille

Alarcon, Pedro Antonio de 1833-1891 .... **NCLC 1; SSC 64**

Alas (y Urena), Leopoldo (Enrique Garcia) 1852-1901 .... **TCLC 29**
See also CA 113; 131; HW 1; RGSF 2

Albee, Edward (Franklin) (III) 1928- .. **CLC 1, 2, 3, 5, 9, 11, 13, 25, 53, 86, 113; DC 11; WLC**
See also AAYA 51; AITN 1; AMW; CA 5-8R; CABS 3; CAD; CANR 8, 54, 74, 124; CD 5, 6; CDALB 1941-1968; DA; DA3; DAB; DAC; DAM DRAM, MST; DFS 2, 3, 8, 10, 13, 14; DLB 7, 266; EWL 3; INT CANR-8; LAIT 4; LMFS 2; MAL 5; MTCW 1, 2; MTFW 2005; RGAL 4; TUS

Alberti (Merello), Rafael
See Alberti, Rafael
See also CWW 2

Alberti, Rafael 1902-1999 .... **CLC 7**
See Alberti (Merello), Rafael
See also CA 85-88; 185; CANR 81; DLB 108; EWL 3; HW 2; RGWL 2, 3

Albert the Great 1193(?)-1280 ...... **CMLC 16**
See also DLB 115

Alcaeus c. 620B.C.- .... **CMLC 65**
See also DLB 176

Alcala-Galiano, Juan Valera y
See Valera y Alcala-Galiano, Juan

Alcayaga, Lucila Godoy
See Godoy Alcayaga, Lucila

Alciato, Andrea 1492-1550 .... **LC 116**

Alcott, Amos Bronson 1799-1888 .... **NCLC 1**
See also DLB 1, 223

Alcott, Louisa May 1832-1888 . **NCLC 6, 58, 83; SSC 27; WLC**
See also AAYA 20; AMWS 1; BPFB 1; BYA 2; CDALB 1865-1917; CLR 1, 38; DA; DA3; DAB; DAC; DAM MST, NOV; DLB 1, 42, 79, 223, 239, 242; DLBD 14; FL 1:2; FW; JRDA; LAIT 2; MAICYA 1, 2; NFS 12; RGAL 4; SATA 100; TUS; WCH; WYA; YABC 1; YAW

Alcuin c. 730-804 .... **CMLC 69**
See also DLB 148

Aldanov, M. A.
See Aldanov, Mark (Alexandrovich)

Aldanov, Mark (Alexandrovich) 1886-1957 .... **TCLC 23**
See also CA 118; 181; DLB 317

Aldington, Richard 1892-1962 .... **CLC 49**
See also CA 85-88; CANR 45; DLB 20, 36, 100, 149; LMFS 2; RGEL 2

Aldiss, Brian W(ilson) 1925- . **CLC 5, 14, 40; SSC 36**
See also AAYA 42; CA 5-8R, 190; CAAE 190; CAAS 2; CANR 5, 28, 64, 121; CN 1, 2, 3, 4, 5, 6, 7; DAM NOV; DLB 14, 261, 271; MTCW 1, 2; MTFW 2005; SATA 34; SCFW 1, 2; SFW 4

Aldrich, Bess Streeter 1881-1954 .... **TCLC 125**
See also CLR 70; TCWW 2

Alegria, Claribel
See Alegria, Claribel (Joy)
See also CWW 2; DLB 145, 283

Alegria, Claribel (Joy) 1924- .... **CLC 75; HLCS 1; PC 26**
See Alegria, Claribel
See also CA 131; CAAS 15; CANR 66, 94, 134; DAM MULT; EWL 3; HW 1; MTCW 2; MTFW 2005; PFS 21

Alegria, Fernando 1918- .... **CLC 57**
See also CA 9-12R; CANR 5, 32, 72; EWL 3; HW 1, 2

Aleichem, Sholom .... **SSC 33; TCLC 1, 35**
See Rabinovitch, Sholem
See also TWA

Aleixandre, Vicente 1898-1984 .... **HLCS 1; TCLC 113**
See also CANR 81; DLB 108; EWL 3; HW 2; MTCW 1, 2; RGWL 2, 3

Aleman, Mateo 1547-1615(?) .... **LC 81**

Alencar, Jose de 1829-1877 .... **NCLC 157**
See also DLB 307; LAW; WLIT 1

Alencon, Marguerite d'
See de Navarre, Marguerite

Alepoudelis, Odysseus
See Elytis, Odysseus
See also CWW 2

Aleshkovsky, Joseph 1929-
See Aleshkovsky, Yuz
See also CA 121; 128

Aleshkovsky, Yuz .... **CLC 44**
See Aleshkovsky, Joseph
See also DLB 317

Alexander, Lloyd (Chudley) 1924- ... **CLC 35**
See also AAYA 1, 27; BPFB 1; BYA 5, 6, 7, 9, 10, 11; CA 1-4R; CANR 1, 24, 38, 55, 113; CLR 1, 5, 48; CWRI 5; DLB 52; FANT; JRDA; MAICYA 1, 2; MAICYAS 1; MTCW 1; SAAS 19; SATA 3, 49, 81, 129, 135; SUFW; TUS; WYA; YAW

Alexander, Meena 1951- .... **CLC 121**
See also CA 115; CANR 38, 70, 146; CP 7; CWP; FW

Alexander, Samuel 1859-1938 .... **TCLC 77**

Alexeyev, Constantin (Sergeivich)
See Stanislavsky, Konstantin (Sergeivich)

Alexie, Sherman (Joseph, Jr.)
1966- .... **CLC 96, 154; NNAL; PC 53**
See also AAYA 28; BYA 15; CA 138;
CANR 65, 95, 133; CN 7; DA3; DAM
MULT; DLB 175, 206, 278; LATS 1:2;
MTCW 2; MTFW 2005; NFS 17; SSFS
18

al-Farabi 870(?)-950 .... **CMLC 58**
See also DLB 115

Alfau, Felipe 1902-1999 .... **CLC 66**
See also CA 137

Alfieri, Vittorio 1749-1803 .... **NCLC 101**
See also EW 4; RGWL 2, 3; WLIT 7

Alfonso X 1221-1284 .... **CMLC 78**

Alfred, Jean Gaston
See Ponge, Francis

Alger, Horatio, Jr. 1832-1899 .... **NCLC 8, 83**
See also CLR 87; DLB 42; LAIT 2; RGAL
4; SATA 16; TUS

Al-Ghazali, Muhammad ibn Muhammad
1058-1111 .... **CMLC 50**
See also DLB 115

Algren, Nelson 1909-1981 ..... **CLC 4, 10, 33;
SSC 33**
See also AMWS 9; BPFB 1; CA 13-16R;
103; CANR 20, 61; CDALB 1941-1968;
CN 1, 2; DLB 9; DLBY 1981, 1982,
2000; EWL 3; MAL 5; MTCW 1, 2;
MTFW 2005; RGAL 4; RGSF 2

**al-Hariri, al-Qasim ibn 'Ali Abu
Muhammad al-Basri**
1054-1122 .... **CMLC 63**
See also RGWL 3

Ali, Ahmed 1908-1998 .... **CLC 69**
See also CA 25-28R; CANR 15, 34; CN 1,
2, 3, 4, 5; EWL 3

Ali, Tariq 1943- .... **CLC 173**
See also CA 25-28R; CANR 10, 99

Alighieri, Dante
See Dante
See also WLIT 7

al-Kindi, Abu Yusuf Ya'qub ibn Ishaq c.
801-c. 873 .... **CMLC 80**

Allan, John B.
See Westlake, Donald E(dwin)

Allan, Sidney
See Hartmann, Sadakichi

Allan, Sydney
See Hartmann, Sadakichi

Allard, Janet .... **CLC 59**

Allen, Edward 1948- .... **CLC 59**

Allen, Fred 1894-1956 .... **TCLC 87**

Allen, Paula Gunn 1939- .... **CLC 84, 202;
NNAL**
See also AMWS 4; CA 112; 143; CANR
63, 130; CWP; DA3; DAM MULT; DLB
175; FW; MTCW 2; MTFW 2005; RGAL
4; TCWW 2

Allen, Roland
See Ayckbourn, Alan

Allen, Sarah A.
See Hopkins, Pauline Elizabeth

Allen, Sidney H.
See Hartmann, Sadakichi

Allen, Woody 1935- .... **CLC 16, 52, 195**
See also AAYA 10, 51; AMWS 15; CA 33-
36R; CANR 27, 38, 63, 128; DAM POP;
DLB 44; MTCW 1; SSFS 21

Allende, Isabel 1942- ... **CLC 39, 57, 97, 170;
HLC 1; SSC 65; WLCS**
See also AAYA 18; CA 125; 130; CANR
51, 74, 129; CDWLB 3; CLR 99; CWW
2; DA3; DAM MULT, NOV; DLB 145;
DNFS 1; EWL 3; FL 1:5; FW; HW 1, 2;
INT CA-130; LAIT 5; LAWS 1; LMFS 2;
MTCW 1, 2; MTFW 2005; NCFS 1; NFS
6, 18; RGSF 2; RGWL 3; SATA 163;
SSFS 11, 16; WLIT 1

Alleyn, Ellen
See Rossetti, Christina

Alleyne, Carla D. .... **CLC 65**

Allingham, Margery (Louise)
1904-1966 .... **CLC 19**
See also CA 5-8R; 25-28R; CANR 4, 58;
CMW 4; DLB 77; MSW; MTCW 1, 2

Allingham, William 1824-1889 ...... **NCLC 25**
See also DLB 35; RGEL 2

Allison, Dorothy E. 1949- .... **CLC 78, 153**
See also AAYA 53; CA 140; CANR 66, 107;
CN 7; CSW; DA3; FW; MTCW 2; MTFW
2005; NFS 11; RGAL 4

Alloula, Malek .... **CLC 65**

Allston, Washington 1779-1843 .... **NCLC 2**
See also DLB 1, 235

Almedingen, E. M. .... **CLC 12**
See Almedingen, Martha Edith von
See also SATA 3

Almedingen, Martha Edith von 1898-1971
See Almedingen, E. M.
See also CA 1-4R; CANR 1

Almodovar, Pedro 1949(?)- .... **CLC 114;
HLCS 1**
See also CA 133; CANR 72; HW 2

Almqvist, Carl Jonas Love
1793-1866 .... **NCLC 42**

**al-Mutanabbi, Ahmad ibn al-Husayn Abu
al-Tayyib al-Jufi al-Kindi**
915-965 .... **CMLC 66**
See Mutanabbi, Al-
See also RGWL 3

Alonso, Damaso 1898-1990 .... **CLC 14**
See also CA 110; 131; 130; CANR 72; DLB
108; EWL 3; HW 1, 2

Alov
See Gogol, Nikolai (Vasilyevich)

al'Sadaawi, Nawal
See El Saadawi, Nawal
See also FW

Al Siddik
See Rolfe, Frederick (William Serafino Aus-
tin Lewis Mary)
See also GLL 1; RGEL 2

Alta 1942- .... **CLC 19**
See also CA 57-60

Alter, Robert B(ernard) 1935- .... **CLC 34**
See also CA 49-52; CANR 1, 47, 100

Alther, Lisa 1944- .... **CLC 7, 41**
See also BPFB 1; CA 65-68; CAAS 30;
CANR 12, 30, 51; CN 4, 5, 6, 7; CSW;
GLL 2; MTCW 1

Althusser, L.
See Althusser, Louis

Althusser, Louis 1918-1990 .... **CLC 106**
See also CA 131; 132; CANR 102; DLB
242

Altman, Robert 1925- .... **CLC 16, 116**
See also CA 73-76; CANR 43

Alurista .... **HLCS 1; PC 34**
See Urista (Heredia), Alberto (Baltazar)
See also CA 45-48R; DLB 82; LLW

Alvarez, A(lfred) 1929- .... **CLC 5, 13**
See also CA 1-4R; CANR 3, 33, 63, 101,
134; CN 3, 4, 5, 6; CP 1, 2, 3, 4, 5, 6, 7;
DLB 14, 40; MTFW 2005

Alvarez, Alejandro Rodriguez 1903-1965
See Casona, Alejandro
See also CA 131; 93-96; HW 1

Alvarez, Julia 1950- .... **CLC 93; HLCS 1**
See also AAYA 25; AMWS 7; CA 147;
CANR 69, 101, 133; DA3; DLB 282;
LATS 1:2; LLW; MTCW 2; MTFW 2005;
NFS 5, 9; SATA 129; WLIT 1

Alvaro, Corrado 1896-1956 .... **TCLC 60**
See also CA 163; DLB 264; EWL 3

Amado, Jorge 1912-2001 ... **CLC 13, 40, 106;
HLC 1**
See also CA 77-80; 201; CANR 35, 74, 135;
CWW 2; DAM MULT, NOV; DLB 113,
307; EWL 3; HW 2; LAW; LAWS 1;
MTCW 1, 2; MTFW 2005; RGWL 2, 3;
TWA; WLIT 1

Ambler, Eric 1909-1998 .... **CLC 4, 6, 9**
See also BRWS 4; CA 9-12R; 171; CANR
7, 38, 74; CMW 4; CN 1, 2, 3, 4, 5, 6;
DLB 77; MSW; MTCW 1, 2; TEA

Ambrose, Stephen E(dward)
1936-2002 .... **CLC 145**
See also AAYA 44; CA 1-4R; 209; CANR
3, 43, 57, 83, 105; MTFW 2005; NCFS 2;
SATA 40, 138

Amichai, Yehuda 1924-2000 .. **CLC 9, 22, 57,
116; PC 38**
See also CA 85-88; 189; CANR 46, 60, 99,
132; CWW 2; EWL 3; MTCW 1, 2;
MTFW 2005; WLIT 6

Amichai, Yehudah
See Amichai, Yehuda

Amiel, Henri Frederic 1821-1881 .... **NCLC 4**
See also DLB 217

Amis, Kingsley (William)
1922-1995 ...... **CLC 1, 2, 3, 5, 8, 13, 40,
44, 129**
See also AITN 2; BPFB 1; BRWS 2; CA
9-12R; 150; CANR 8, 28, 54; CDBLB
1945-1960; CN 1, 2, 3, 4, 5, 6; CP 1, 2,
3, 4; DA; DA3; DAB; DAC; DAM MST,
NOV; DLB 15, 27, 100, 139; DLBY 1996;
EWL 3; HGG; INT CANR-8; MTCW 1,
2; MTFW 2005; RGEL 2; RGSF 2; SFW
4

Amis, Martin (Louis) 1949- .... **CLC 4, 9, 38,
62, 101, 213**
See also BEST 90:3; BRWS 4; CA 65-68;
CANR 8, 27, 54, 73, 95, 132; CN 5, 6, 7;
DA3; DLB 14, 194; EWL 3; INT CANR-
27; MTCW 2; MTFW 2005

Ammianus Marcellinus c. 330-c.
395 .... **CMLC 60**
See also AW 2; DLB 211

Ammons, A(rchie) R(andolph)
1926-2001 ...... **CLC 2, 3, 5, 8, 9, 25, 57,
108; PC 16**
See also AITN 1; AMWS 7; CA 9-12R;
193; CANR 6, 36, 51, 73, 107; CP 1, 2,
3, 4, 5, 6, 7; CSW; DAM POET; DLB 5,
165; EWL 3; MAL 5; MTCW 1, 2; PFS
19; RGAL 4; TCLE 1:1

Amo, Tauraatua i
See Adams, Henry (Brooks)

Amory, Thomas 1691(?)-1788 .... **LC 48**
See also DLB 39

Anand, Mulk Raj 1905-2004 ...... **CLC 23, 93**
See also CA 65-68; 231; CANR 32, 64; CN
1, 2, 3, 4, 5, 6, 7; DAM NOV; EWL 3;
MTCW 1, 2; MTFW 2005; RGSF 2

Anatol
See Schnitzler, Arthur

Anaximander c. 611B.C.-c.
546B.C. .... **CMLC 22**

Anaya, Rudolfo A(lfonso) 1937- ...... **CLC 23,
148; HLC 1**
See also AAYA 20; BYA 13; CA 45-48;
CAAS 4; CANR 1, 32, 51, 124; CN 4, 5,
6, 7; DAM MULT, NOV; DLB 82, 206,
278; HW 1; LAIT 4; LLW; MAL 5;
MTCW 1, 2; MTFW 2005; NFS 12;
RGAL 4; RGSF 2; TCWW 2; WLIT 1

Andersen, Hans Christian
1805-1875 .... **NCLC 7, 79; SSC 6, 56;
WLC**
See also AAYA 57; CLR 6; DA; DA3;
DAB; DAC; DAM MST, POP; EW 6;
MAICYA 1, 2; RGSF 2; RGWL 2, 3;
SATA 100; TWA; WCH; YABC 1

Anderson, C. Farley
See Mencken, H(enry) L(ouis); Nathan, George Jean

Anderson, Jessica (Margaret) Queale
1916- .... **CLC 37**
See also CA 9-12R; CANR 4, 62; CN 4, 5, 6, 7

Anderson, Jon (Victor) 1940- .... **CLC 9**
See also CA 25-28R; CANR 20; CP 1, 3, 4; DAM POET

Anderson, Lindsay (Gordon)
1923-1994 .... **CLC 20**
See also CA 125; 128; 146; CANR 77

Anderson, Maxwell 1888-1959 .... **TCLC 2, 144**
See also CA 105; 152; DAM DRAM; DFS 16, 20; DLB 7, 228; MAL 5; MTCW 2; MTFW 2005; RGAL 4

Anderson, Poul (William)
1926-2001 .... **CLC 15**
See also AAYA 5, 34; BPFB 1; BYA 6, 8, 9; CA 1-4R, 181; 199; CAAE 181; CAAS 2; CANR 2, 15, 34, 64, 110; CLR 58; DLB 8; FANT; INT CANR-15; MTCW 1, 2; MTFW 2005; SATA 90; SATA-Brief 39; SATA-Essay 106; SCFW 1, 2; SFW 4; SUFW 1, 2

Anderson, Robert (Woodruff)
1917- .... **CLC 23**
See also AITN 1; CA 21-24R; CANR 32; CD 6; DAM DRAM; DLB 7; LAIT 5

Anderson, Roberta Joan
See Mitchell, Joni

Anderson, Sherwood 1876-1941 .. **SSC 1, 46; TCLC 1, 10, 24, 123; WLC**
See also AAYA 30; AMW; AMWC 2; BPFB 1; CA 104; 121; CANR 61; CDALB 1917-1929; DA; DA3; DAC; DAM MST, NOV; DLB 4, 9, 86; DLBD 1; EWL 3; EXPS; GLL 2; MAL 5; MTCW 1, 2; MTFW 2005; NFS 4; RGAL 4; RGSF 2; SSFS 4, 10, 11; TUS

Andier, Pierre
See Desnos, Robert

Andouard
See Giraudoux, Jean(-Hippolyte)

Andrade, Carlos Drummond de ..... **CLC 18**
See Drummond de Andrade, Carlos
See also EWL 3; RGWL 2, 3

Andrade, Mario de .... **TCLC 43**
See de Andrade, Mario
See also DLB 307; EWL 3; LAW; RGWL 2, 3; WLIT 1

Andreae, Johann V(alentin)
1586-1654 .... **LC 32**
See also DLB 164

Andreas Capellanus fl. c. 1185- .... **CMLC 45**
See also DLB 208

Andreas-Salome, Lou 1861-1937 ... **TCLC 56**
See also CA 178; DLB 66

Andreev, Leonid
See Andreyev, Leonid (Nikolaevich)
See also DLB 295; EWL 3

Andress, Lesley
See Sanders, Lawrence

Andrewes, Lancelot 1555-1626 .... **LC 5**
See also DLB 151, 172

Andrews, Cicily Fairfield
See West, Rebecca

Andrews, Elton V.
See Pohl, Frederik

Andreyev, Leonid (Nikolaevich)
1871-1919 .... **TCLC 3**
See Andreev, Leonid
See also CA 104; 185

Andric, Ivo 1892-1975 .... **CLC 8; SSC 36; TCLC 135**
See also CA 81-84; 57-60; CANR 43, 60; CDWLB 4; DLB 147; EW 11; EWL 3; MTCW 1; RGSF 2; RGWL 2, 3

Androvar
See Prado (Calvo), Pedro

Angela of Foligno 1248(?)-1309 .... **CMLC 76**

Angelique, Pierre
See Bataille, Georges

Angell, Roger 1920- .... **CLC 26**
See also CA 57-60; CANR 13, 44, 70, 144; DLB 171, 185

Angelou, Maya 1928- ... **BLC 1; CLC 12, 35, 64, 77, 155; PC 32; WLCS**
See also AAYA 7, 20; AMWS 4; BPFB 1; BW 2, 3; BYA 2; CA 65-68; CANR 19, 42, 65, 111, 133; CDALBS; CLR 53; CP 4, 5, 6, 7; CPW; CSW; CWP; DA; DA3; DAB; DAC; DAM MST, MULT, POET, POP; DLB 38; EWL 3; EXPN; EXPP; FL 1:5; LAIT 4; MAICYA 2; MAICYAS 1; MAL 5; MAWW; MTCW 1, 2; MTFW 2005; NCFS 2; NFS 2; PFS 2, 3; RGAL 4; SATA 49, 136; TCLE 1:1; WYA; YAW

Angouleme, Marguerite d'
See de Navarre, Marguerite

Anna Comnena 1083-1153 .... **CMLC 25**

Annensky, Innokentii Fedorovich
See Annensky, Innokenty (Fyodorovich)
See also DLB 295

Annensky, Innokenty (Fyodorovich)
1856-1909 .... **TCLC 14**
See also CA 110; 155; EWL 3

Annunzio, Gabriele d'
See D'Annunzio, Gabriele

Anodos
See Coleridge, Mary E(lizabeth)

Anon, Charles Robert
See Pessoa, Fernando (Antonio Nogueira)

Anouilh, Jean (Marie Lucien Pierre)
1910-1987 . **CLC 1, 3, 8, 13, 40, 50; DC 8, 21**
See also AAYA 67; CA 17-20R; 123; CANR 32; DAM DRAM; DFS 9, 10, 19; DLB 321; EW 13; EWL 3; GFL 1789 to the Present; MTCW 1, 2; MTFW 2005; RGWL 2, 3; TWA

Anselm of Canterbury
1033(?)-1109 .... **CMLC 67**
See also DLB 115

Anthony, Florence
See Ai

Anthony, John
See Ciardi, John (Anthony)

Anthony, Peter
See Shaffer, Anthony (Joshua); Shaffer, Peter (Levin)

Anthony, Piers 1934- .... **CLC 35**
See also AAYA 11, 48; BYA 7; CA 200; CAAE 200; CANR 28, 56, 73, 102, 133; CPW; DAM POP; DLB 8; FANT; MAICYA 2; MAICYAS 1; MTCW 1, 2; MTFW 2005; SAAS 22; SATA 84, 129; SATA-Essay 129; SFW 4; SUFW 1, 2; YAW

Anthony, Susan B(rownell)
1820-1906 .... **TCLC 84**
See also CA 211; FW

Antiphon c. 480B.C.-c. 411B.C. .... **CMLC 55**

Antoine, Marc
See Proust, (Valentin-Louis-George-Eugene) Marcel

Antoninus, Brother
See Everson, William (Oliver)
See also CP 1

Antonioni, Michelangelo 1912- .... **CLC 20, 144**
See also CA 73-76; CANR 45, 77

Antschel, Paul 1920-1970
See Celan, Paul
See also CA 85-88; CANR 33, 61; MTCW 1; PFS 21

Anwar, Chairil 1922-1949 .... **TCLC 22**
See Chairil Anwar
See also CA 121; 219; RGWL 3

Anzaldua, Gloria (Evanjelina)
1942-2004 .... **CLC 200; HLCS 1**
See also CA 175; 227; CSW; CWP; DLB 122; FW; LLW; RGAL 4; SATA-Obit 154

Apess, William 1798-1839(?) .... **NCLC 73; NNAL**
See also DAM MULT; DLB 175, 243

Apollinaire, Guillaume 1880-1918 .... **PC 7; TCLC 3, 8, 51**
See Kostrowitzki, Wilhelm Apollinaris de
See also CA 152; DAM POET; DLB 258, 321; EW 9; EWL 3; GFL 1789 to the Present; MTCW 2; RGWL 2, 3; TWA; WP

Apollonius of Rhodes
See Apollonius Rhodius
See also AW 1; RGWL 2, 3

Apollonius Rhodius c. 300B.C.-c. 220B.C. .... **CMLC 28**
See Apollonius of Rhodes
See also DLB 176

Appelfeld, Aharon 1932- ... **CLC 23, 47; SSC 42**
See also CA 112; 133; CANR 86; CWW 2; DLB 299; EWL 3; RGSF 2; WLIT 6

Apple, Max (Isaac) 1941- .... **CLC 9, 33; SSC 50**
See also CA 81-84; CANR 19, 54; DLB 130

Appleman, Philip (Dean) 1926- .... **CLC 51**
See also CA 13-16R; CAAS 18; CANR 6, 29, 56

Appleton, Lawrence
See Lovecraft, H(oward) P(hillips)

Apteryx
See Eliot, T(homas) S(tearns)

Apuleius, (Lucius Madaurensis)
125(?)-175(?) .... **CMLC 1**
See also AW 2; CDWLB 1; DLB 211; RGWL 2, 3; SUFW

Aquin, Hubert 1929-1977 .... **CLC 15**
See also CA 105; DLB 53; EWL 3

Aquinas, Thomas 1224(?)-1274 ..... **CMLC 33**
See also DLB 115; EW 1; TWA

Aragon, Louis 1897-1982 .... **CLC 3, 22; TCLC 123**
See also CA 69-72; 108; CANR 28, 71; DAM NOV, POET; DLB 72, 258; EW 11; EWL 3; GFL 1789 to the Present; GLL 2; LMFS 2; MTCW 1, 2; RGWL 2, 3

Arany, Janos 1817-1882 .... **NCLC 34**

Aranyos, Kakay 1847-1910
See Mikszath, Kalman

Aratus of Soli c. 315B.C.-c. 240B.C. .... **CMLC 64**
See also DLB 176

Arbuthnot, John 1667-1735 .... **LC 1**
See also DLB 101

Archer, Herbert Winslow
See Mencken, H(enry) L(ouis)

Archer, Jeffrey (Howard) 1940- .... **CLC 28**
See also AAYA 16; BEST 89:3; BPFB 1; CA 77-80; CANR 22, 52, 95, 136; CPW; DA3; DAM POP; INT CANR-22; MTFW 2005

Archer, Jules 1915- .... **CLC 12**
See also CA 9-12R; CANR 6, 69; SAAS 5; SATA 4, 85

Archer, Lee
See Ellison, Harlan (Jay)

Archilochus c. 7th cent. B.C.- .... **CMLC 44**
See also DLB 176

Arden, John 1930- .... **CLC 6, 13, 15**
  See also BRWS 2; CA 13-16R; CAAS 4;
  CANR 31, 65, 67, 124; CBD; CD 5, 6;
  DAM DRAM; DFS 9; DLB 13, 245;
  EWL 3; MTCW 1

Arenas, Reinaldo 1943-1990 .. **CLC 41; HLC 1**
  See also CA 124; 128; 133; CANR 73, 106;
  DAM MULT; DLB 145; EWL 3; GLL 2;
  HW 1; LAW; LAWS 1; MTCW 2; MTFW
  2005; RGSF 2; RGWL 3; WLIT 1

Arendt, Hannah 1906-1975 .... **CLC 66, 98**
  See also CA 17-20R; 61-64; CANR 26, 60;
  DLB 242; MTCW 1, 2

Aretino, Pietro 1492-1556 .... **LC 12**
  See also RGWL 2, 3

Arghezi, Tudor .... **CLC 80**
  See Theodorescu, Ion N.
  See also CA 167; CDWLB 4; DLB 220;
  EWL 3

Arguedas, Jose Maria 1911-1969 .... **CLC 10, 18; HLCS 1; TCLC 147**
  See also CA 89-92; CANR 73; DLB 113;
  EWL 3; HW 1; LAW; RGWL 2, 3; WLIT 1

Argueta, Manlio 1936- .... **CLC 31**
  See also CA 131; CANR 73; CWW 2; DLB
  145; EWL 3; HW 1; RGWL 3

Arias, Ron(ald Francis) 1941- .... **HLC 1**
  See also CA 131; CANR 81, 136; DAM
  MULT; DLB 82; HW 1, 2; MTCW 2;
  MTFW 2005

Ariosto, Lodovico
  See Ariosto, Ludovico
  See also WLIT 7

Ariosto, Ludovico 1474-1533 ... **LC 6, 87; PC 42**
  See Ariosto, Lodovico
  See also EW 2; RGWL 2, 3

Aristides
  See Epstein, Joseph

Aristophanes 450B.C.-385B.C. .... **CMLC 4, 51; DC 2; WLCS**
  See also AW 1; CDWLB 1; DA; DA3;
  DAB; DAC; DAM DRAM, MST; DFS
  10; DLB 176; LMFS 1; RGWL 2, 3; TWA

Aristotle 384B.C.-322B.C. .... **CMLC 31; WLCS**
  See also AW 1; CDWLB 1; DA; DA3;
  DAB; DAC; DAM MST; DLB 176;
  RGWL 2, 3; TWA

Arlt, Roberto (Godofredo Christophersen)
  1900-1942 .... **HLC 1; TCLC 29**
  See also CA 123; 131; CANR 67; DAM
  MULT; DLB 305; EWL 3; HW 1, 2;
  IDTP; LAW

Armah, Ayi Kwei 1939- . **BLC 1; CLC 5, 33, 136**
  See also AFW; BRWS 10; BW 1; CA 61-
  64; CANR 21, 64; CDWLB 3; CN 1, 2,
  3, 4, 5, 6, 7; DAM MULT, POET; DLB
  117; EWL 3; MTCW 1; WLIT 2

Armatrading, Joan 1950- .... **CLC 17**
  See also CA 114; 186

Armitage, Frank
  See Carpenter, John (Howard)

Armstrong, Jeannette (C.) 1948- .... **NNAL**
  See also CA 149; CCA 1; CN 6, 7; DAC;
  SATA 102

Arnette, Robert
  See Silverberg, Robert

Arnim, Achim von (Ludwig Joachim von Arnim) 1781-1831 .. **NCLC 5, 159; SSC 29**
  See also DLB 90

Arnim, Bettina von 1785-1859 ...... **NCLC 38, 123**
  See also DLB 90; RGWL 2, 3

Arnold, Matthew 1822-1888 ..... **NCLC 6, 29, 89, 126; PC 5; WLC**
  See also BRW 5; CDBLB 1832-1890; DA;
  DAB; DAC; DAM MST, POET; DLB 32,
  57; EXPP; PAB; PFS 2; TEA; WP

Arnold, Thomas 1795-1842 .... **NCLC 18**
  See also DLB 55

Arnow, Harriette (Louisa) Simpson
  1908-1986 .... **CLC 2, 7, 18**
  See also BPFB 1; CA 9-12R; 118; CANR
  14; CN 2, 3, 4; DLB 6; FW; MTCW 1, 2;
  RHW; SATA 42; SATA-Obit 47

Arouet, Francois-Marie
  See Voltaire

Arp, Hans
  See Arp, Jean

Arp, Jean 1887-1966 .... **CLC 5; TCLC 115**
  See also CA 81-84; 25-28R; CANR 42, 77;
  EW 10

Arrabal
  See Arrabal, Fernando

Arrabal (Teran), Fernando
  See Arrabal, Fernando
  See also CWW 2

Arrabal, Fernando 1932- ... **CLC 2, 9, 18, 58**
  See Arrabal (Teran), Fernando
  See also CA 9-12R; CANR 15; DLB 321;
  EWL 3; LMFS 2

Arreola, Juan Jose 1918-2001 .... **CLC 147; HLC 1; SSC 38**
  See also CA 113; 131; 200; CANR 81;
  CWW 2; DAM MULT; DLB 113; DNFS
  2; EWL 3; HW 1, 2; LAW; RGSF 2

Arrian c. 89(?)-c. 155(?) .... **CMLC 43**
  See also DLB 176

Arrick, Fran .... **CLC 30**
  See Gaberman, Judie Angell
  See also BYA 6

Arrley, Richard
  See Delany, Samuel R(ay), Jr.

Artaud, Antonin (Marie Joseph)
  1896-1948 .... **DC 14; TCLC 3, 36**
  See also CA 104; 149; DA3; DAM DRAM;
  DFS 22; DLB 258, 321; EW 11; EWL 3;
  GFL 1789 to the Present; MTCW 2;
  MTFW 2005; RGWL 2, 3

Arthur, Ruth M(abel) 1905-1979 ..... **CLC 12**
  See also CA 9-12R; 85-88; CANR 4; CWRI
  5; SATA 7, 26

Artsybashev, Mikhail (Petrovich)
  1878-1927 .... **TCLC 31**
  See also CA 170; DLB 295

Arundel, Honor (Morfydd)
  1919-1973 .... **CLC 17**
  See also CA 21-22; 41-44R; CAP 2; CLR
  35; CWRI 5; SATA 4; SATA-Obit 24

Arzner, Dorothy 1900-1979 .... **CLC 98**

Asch, Sholem 1880-1957 .... **TCLC 3**
  See also CA 105; EWL 3; GLL 2

Ascham, Roger 1516(?)-1568 .... **LC 101**
  See also DLB 236

Ash, Shalom
  See Asch, Sholem

Ashbery, John (Lawrence) 1927- .. **CLC 2, 3, 4, 6, 9, 13, 15, 25, 41, 77, 125; PC 26**
  See Berry, Jonas
  See also AMWS 3; CA 5-8R; CANR 9, 37,
  66, 102, 132; CP 1, 2, 3, 4, 5, 6, 7; DA3;
  DAM POET; DLB 5, 165; DLBY 1981;
  EWL 3; INT CANR-9; MAL 5; MTCW
  1, 2; MTFW 2005; PAB; PFS 11; RGAL
  4; TCLE 1:1; WP

Ashdown, Clifford
  See Freeman, R(ichard) Austin

Ashe, Gordon
  See Creasey, John

Ashton-Warner, Sylvia (Constance)
  1908-1984 .... **CLC 19**
  See also CA 69-72; 112; CANR 29; CN 1,
  2, 3; MTCW 1, 2

Asimov, Isaac 1920-1992 ..... **CLC 1, 3, 9, 19, 26, 76, 92**
  See also AAYA 13; BEST 90:2; BPFB 1;
  BYA 4, 6, 7, 9; CA 1-4R; 137; CANR 2,
  19, 36, 60, 125; CLR 12, 79; CMW 4;
  CN 1, 2, 3, 4, 5; CPW; DA3; DAM POP;
  DLB 8; DLBY 1992; INT CANR-19;
  JRDA; LAIT 5; LMFS 2; MAICYA 1, 2;
  MAL 5; MTCW 1, 2; MTFW 2005;
  RGAL 4; SATA 1, 26, 74; SCFW 1, 2;
  SFW 4; SSFS 17; TUS; YAW

Askew, Anne 1521(?)-1546 .... **LC 81**
  See also DLB 136

Assis, Joaquim Maria Machado de
  See Machado de Assis, Joaquim Maria

Astell, Mary 1666-1731 .... **LC 68**
  See also DLB 252; FW

Astley, Thea (Beatrice May)
  1925-2004 .... **CLC 41**
  See also CA 65-68; 229; CANR 11, 43, 78;
  CN 1, 2, 3, 4, 5, 6, 7; DLB 289; EWL 3

Astley, William 1855-1911
  See Warung, Price

Aston, James
  See White, T(erence) H(anbury)

Asturias, Miguel Angel 1899-1974 .... **CLC 3, 8, 13; HLC 1**
  See also CA 25-28; 49-52; CANR 32; CAP
  2; CDWLB 3; DA3; DAM MULT, NOV;
  DLB 113, 290; EWL 3; HW 1; LAW;
  LMFS 2; MTCW 1, 2; RGWL 2, 3; WLIT 1

Atares, Carlos Saura
  See Saura (Atares), Carlos

Athanasius c. 295-c. 373 .... **CMLC 48**

Atheling, William
  See Pound, Ezra (Weston Loomis)

Atheling, William, Jr.
  See Blish, James (Benjamin)

Atherton, Gertrude (Franklin Horn)
  1857-1948 .... **TCLC 2**
  See also CA 104; 155; DLB 9, 78, 186;
  HGG; RGAL 4; SUFW 1; TCWW 1, 2

Atherton, Lucius
  See Masters, Edgar Lee

Atkins, Jack
  See Harris, Mark

Atkinson, Kate 1951- .... **CLC 99**
  See also CA 166; CANR 101; DLB 267

Attaway, William (Alexander)
  1911-1986 .... **BLC 1; CLC 92**
  See also BW 2, 3; CA 143; CANR 82;
  DAM MULT; DLB 76; MAL 5

Atticus
  See Fleming, Ian (Lancaster); Wilson,
  (Thomas) Woodrow

Atwood, Margaret (Eleanor) 1939- ... **CLC 2, 3, 4, 8, 13, 15, 25, 44, 84, 135; PC 8; SSC 2, 46; WLC**
  See also AAYA 12, 47; AMWS 13; BEST
  89:2; BPFB 1; CA 49-52; CANR 3, 24,
  33, 59, 95, 133; CN 2, 3, 4, 5, 6, 7; CP 1,
  2, 3, 4, 5, 6, 7; CPW; CWP; DA; DA3;
  DAB; DAC; DAM MST, NOV, POET;
  DLB 53, 251; EWL 3; EXPN; FL 1:5;
  FW; GL 2; INT CANR-24; LAIT 5;
  MTCW 1, 2; MTFW 2005; NFS 4, 12,
  13, 14, 19; PFS 7; RGSF 2; SATA 50;
  SSFS 3, 13; TCLE 1:1; TWA; WWE 1;
  YAW

Aubigny, Pierre d'
  See Mencken, H(enry) L(ouis)

Aubin, Penelope 1685-1731(?) .... **LC 9**
  See also DLB 39

EXPS; LAIT 5; MAL 5; MTCW 1, 2;
MTFW 2005; NCFS 4; NFS 4; RGAL 4;
RGSF 2; SATA 9; SATA-Obit 54; SSFS
2, 18; TUS

Baldwin, William c. 1515-1563 .... **LC 113**
See also DLB 132

Bale, John 1495-1563 .... **LC 62**
See also DLB 132; RGEL 2; TEA

Ball, Hugo 1886-1927 .... **TCLC 104**

Ballard, J(ames) G(raham) 1930- . **CLC 3, 6,
14, 36, 137; SSC 1, 53**
See also AAYA 3, 52; BRWS 5; CA 5-8R;
CANR 15, 39, 65, 107, 133; CN 1, 2, 3,
4, 5, 6, 7; DA3; DAM NOV, POP; DLB
14, 207, 261, 319; EWL 3; HGG; MTCW
1, 2; MTFW 2005; NFS 8; RGEL 2;
RGSF 2; SATA 93; SCFW 1, 2; SFW 4

Balmont, Konstantin (Dmitriyevich)
1867-1943 .... **TCLC 11**
See also CA 109; 155; DLB 295; EWL 3

Baltausis, Vincas 1847-1910
See Mikszath, Kalman

Balzac, Honore de 1799-1850 ... **NCLC 5, 35,
53, 153; SSC 5, 59; WLC**
See also DA; DA3; DAB; DAC; DAM
MST, NOV; DLB 119; EW 5; GFL 1789
to the Present; LMFS 1; RGSF 2; RGWL
2, 3; SSFS 10; SUFW; TWA

Bambara, Toni Cade 1939-1995 .... **BLC 1;
CLC 19, 88; SSC 35; TCLC 116;
WLCS**
See also AAYA 5, 49; AFAW 2; AMWS 11;
BW 2, 3; BYA 12, 14; CA 29-32R; 150;
CANR 24, 49, 81; CDALBS; DA; DA3;
DAC; DAM MST, MULT; DLB 38, 218;
EXPS; MAL 5; MTCW 1, 2; MTFW
2005; RGAL 4; RGSF 2; SATA 112; SSFS
4, 7, 12, 21

Bamdad, A.
See Shamlu, Ahmad

Bamdad, Alef
See Shamlu, Ahmad

Banat, D. R.
See Bradbury, Ray (Douglas)

Bancroft, Laura
See Baum, L(yman) Frank

Banim, John 1798-1842 .... **NCLC 13**
See also DLB 116, 158, 159; RGEL 2

Banim, Michael 1796-1874 .... **NCLC 13**
See also DLB 158, 159

Banjo, The
See Paterson, A(ndrew) B(arton)

Banks, Iain
See Banks, Iain M(enzies)
See also BRWS 11

Banks, Iain M(enzies) 1954- .... **CLC 34**
See Banks, Iain
See also CA 123; 128; CANR 61, 106; DLB
194, 261; EWL 3; HGG; INT CA-128;
MTFW 2005; SFW 4

Banks, Lynne Reid .... **CLC 23**
See Reid Banks, Lynne
See also AAYA 6; BYA 7; CLR 86; CN 4,
5, 6

Banks, Russell (Earl) 1940- .... **CLC 37, 72,
187; SSC 42**
See also AAYA 45; AMWS 5; CA 65-68;
CAAS 15; CANR 19, 52, 73, 118; CN 4,
5, 6, 7; DLB 130, 278; MAL 5;
MTCW 2; MTFW 2005; NFS 13

Banville, John 1945- .... **CLC 46, 118**
See also CA 117; 128; CANR 104; CN 4,
5, 6, 7; DLB 14, 271; INT CA-128

Banville, Theodore (Faullain) de
1832-1891 .... **NCLC 9**
See also DLB 217; GFL 1789 to the Present

Baraka, Amiri 1934- .... **BLC 1; CLC 1, 2, 3,
5, 10, 14, 33, 115, 213; DC 6; PC 4;
WLCS**
See Jones, LeRoi
See also AAYA 63; AFAW 1, 2; AMWS 2;
BW 2, 3; CA 21-24R; CABS 3; CAD;
CANR 27, 38, 61, 133; CD 3, 5, 6;
CDALB 1941-1968; CP 4, 5, 6, 7; CPW;
DA; DA3; DAC; DAM MST, MULT,
POET, POP; DFS 3, 11, 16; DLB 5, 7,
16, 38; DLBD 8; EWL 3; MAL 5; MTCW
1, 2; MTFW 2005; PFS 9; RGAL 4;
TCLE 1:1; TUS; WP

Baratynsky, Evgenii Abramovich
1800-1844 .... **NCLC 103**
See also DLB 205

Barbauld, Anna Laetitia
1743-1825 .... **NCLC 50**
See also DLB 107, 109, 142, 158; RGEL 2

Barbellion, W. N. P. .... **TCLC 24**
See Cummings, Bruce F(rederick)

Barber, Benjamin R. 1939- .... **CLC 141**
See also CA 29-32R; CANR 12, 32, 64, 119

Barbera, Jack (Vincent) 1945- .... **CLC 44**
See also CA 110; CANR 45

Barbey d'Aurevilly, Jules-Amedee
1808-1889 .... **NCLC 1; SSC 17**
See also DLB 119; GFL 1789 to the Present

Barbour, John c. 1316-1395 .... **CMLC 33**
See also DLB 146

Barbusse, Henri 1873-1935 .... **TCLC 5**
See also CA 105; 154; DLB 65; EWL 3;
RGWL 2, 3

Barclay, Alexander c. 1475-1552 .... **LC 109**
See also DLB 132

Barclay, Bill
See Moorcock, Michael (John)

Barclay, William Ewert
See Moorcock, Michael (John)

Barea, Arturo 1897-1957 .... **TCLC 14**
See also CA 111; 201

Barfoot, Joan 1946- .... **CLC 18**
See also CA 105; CANR 141

Barham, Richard Harris
1788-1845 .... **NCLC 77**
See also DLB 159

Baring, Maurice 1874-1945 .... **TCLC 8**
See also CA 105; 168; DLB 34; HGG

Baring-Gould, Sabine 1834-1924 ... **TCLC 88**
See also DLB 156, 190

Barker, Clive 1952- .... **CLC 52, 205; SSC 53**
See also AAYA 10, 54; BEST 90:3; BPFB
1; CA 121; 129; CANR 71, 111, 133;
CPW; DA3; DAM POP; DLB 261; HGG;
INT CA-129; MTCW 1, 2; MTFW 2005;
SUFW 2

Barker, George Granville
1913-1991 .... **CLC 8, 48**
See also CA 9-12R; 135; CANR 7, 38; CP
1, 2, 3, 4; DAM POET; DLB 20; EWL 3;
MTCW 1

Barker, Harley Granville
See Granville-Barker, Harley
See also DLB 10

Barker, Howard 1946- .... **CLC 37**
See also CA 102; CBD; CD 5, 6; DLB 13,
233

Barker, Jane 1652-1732 .... **LC 42, 82**
See also DLB 39, 131

Barker, Pat(ricia) 1943- ...... **CLC 32, 94, 146**
See also BRWS 4; CA 117; 122; CANR 50,
101; CN 6, 7; DLB 271; INT CA-122

Barlach, Ernst (Heinrich)
1870-1938 .... **TCLC 84**
See also CA 178; DLB 56, 118; EWL 3

Barlow, Joel 1754-1812 .... **NCLC 23**
See also AMWS 2; DLB 37; RGAL 4

Barnard, Mary (Ethel) 1909- .... **CLC 48**
See also CA 21-22; CAP 2; CP 1

Barnes, Djuna 1892-1982 .... **CLC 3, 4, 8, 11,
29, 127; SSC 3**
See Steptoe, Lydia
See also AMWS 3; CA 9-12R; 107; CAD;
CANR 16, 55; CN 1, 2, 3; CWD; DLB 4,
9, 45; EWL 3; GLL 1; MAL 5; MTCW 1,
2; MTFW 2005; RGAL 4; TCLE 1:1;
TUS

Barnes, Jim 1933- .... **NNAL**
See also CA 108; 175; CAAE 175; CAAS
28; DLB 175

Barnes, Julian (Patrick) 1946- . **CLC 42, 141**
See also BRWS 4; CA 102; CANR 19, 54,
115, 137; CN 4, 5, 6, 7; DAB; DLB 194;
DLBY 1993; EWL 3; MTCW 2; MTFW
2005

Barnes, Peter 1931-2004 .... **CLC 5, 56**
See also CA 65-68; 230; CAAS 12; CANR
33, 34, 64, 113; CBD; CD 5, 6; DFS 6;
DLB 13, 233; MTCW 1

Barnes, William 1801-1886 .... **NCLC 75**
See also DLB 32

Baroja (y Nessi), Pio 1872-1956 .... **HLC 1;
TCLC 8**
See also CA 104; EW 9

Baron, David
See Pinter, Harold

Baron Corvo
See Rolfe, Frederick (William Serafino Austin Lewis Mary)

Barondess, Sue K(aufman)
1926-1977 .... **CLC 8**
See Kaufman, Sue
See also CA 1-4R; 69-72; CANR 1

Baron de Teive
See Pessoa, Fernando (Antonio Nogueira)

Baroness Von S.
See Zangwill, Israel

Barres, (Auguste-)Maurice
1862-1923 .... **TCLC 47**
See also CA 164; DLB 123; GFL 1789 to
the Present

Barreto, Afonso Henrique de Lima
See Lima Barreto, Afonso Henrique de

Barrett, Andrea 1954- .... **CLC 150**
See also CA 156; CANR 92; CN 7

Barrett, Michele .... **CLC 65**

Barrett, (Roger) Syd 1946- .... **CLC 35**

Barrett, William (Christopher)
1913-1992 .... **CLC 27**
See also CA 13-16R; 139; CANR 11, 67;
INT CANR-11

Barrett Browning, Elizabeth
1806-1861 ... **NCLC 1, 16, 61, 66; PC 6,
62; WLC**
See also AAYA 63; BRW 4; CDBLB 1832-
1890; DA; DA3; DAB; DAC; DAM MST,
POET; DLB 32, 199; EXPP; FL 1:2; PAB;
PFS 2, 16, 23; TEA; WLIT 4; WP

Barrie, J(ames) M(atthew)
1860-1937 .... **TCLC 2, 164**
See also BRWS 3; BYA 4, 5; CA 104; 136;
CANR 77; CDBLB 1890-1914; CLR 16;
CWRI 5; DA3; DAB; DAM DRAM; DFS
7; DLB 10, 141, 156; EWL 3; FANT;
MAICYA 1, 2; MTCW 2; MTFW 2005;
SATA 100; SUFW; WCH; WLIT 4; YABC
1

Barrington, Michael
See Moorcock, Michael (John)

Barrol, Grady
See Bograd, Larry

Barry, Mike
See Malzberg, Barry N(athaniel)

Barry, Philip 1896-1949 .... **TCLC 11**
See also CA 109; 199; DFS 9; DLB 7, 228;
MAL 5; RGAL 4

Bart, Andre Schwarz
See Schwarz-Bart, Andre

Belcheva, Elisaveta Lyubomirova
1893-1991 .... **CLC 10**
  See Bagryana, Elisaveta

Beldone, Phil "Cheech"
  See Ellison, Harlan (Jay)

Beleno
  See Azuela, Mariano

Belinski, Vissarion Grigoryevich
1811-1848 .... **NCLC 5**
  See also DLB 198

Belitt, Ben 1911- .... **CLC 22**
  See also CA 13-16R; CAAS 4; CANR 7,
  77; CP 1, 2, 3, 4; DLB 5

Belknap, Jeremy 1744-1798 .... **LC 115**
  See also DLB 30, 37

Bell, Gertrude (Margaret Lowthian)
1868-1926 .... **TCLC 67**
  See also CA 167; CANR 110; DLB 174

Bell, J. Freeman
  See Zangwill, Israel

Bell, James Madison 1826-1902 .... **BLC 1;**
  TCLC 43
  See also BW 1; CA 122; 124; DAM MULT;
  DLB 50

Bell, Madison Smartt 1957- ...... **CLC 41, 102**
  See also AMWS 10; BPFB 1; CA 111, 183;
  CAAE 183; CANR 28, 54, 73, 134; CN
  5, 6, 7; CSW; DLB 218, 278; MTCW 2;
  MTFW 2005

Bell, Marvin (Hartley) 1937- .... **CLC 8, 31**
  See also CA 21-24R; CAAS 14; CANR 59,
  102; CP 1, 2, 3, 4, 5, 6, 7; DAM POET;
  DLB 5; MAL 5; MTCW 1

Bell, W. L. D.
  See Mencken, H(enry) L(ouis)

Bellamy, Atwood C.
  See Mencken, H(enry) L(ouis)

Bellamy, Edward 1850-1898 ..... **NCLC 4, 86,**
  147
  See also DLB 12; NFS 15; RGAL 4; SFW
  4

Belli, Gioconda 1948- .... **HLCS 1**
  See also CA 152; CANR 143; CWW 2;
  DLB 290; EWL 3; RGWL 3

Bellin, Edward J.
  See Kuttner, Henry

Bello, Andres 1781-1865 .... **NCLC 131**
  See also LAW

**Belloc, (Joseph) Hilaire (Pierre Sebastien
Rene Swanton)** 1870-1953 .... **PC 24;**
  TCLC 7, 18
  See also CA 106; 152; CLR 102; CWRI 5;
  DAM POET; DLB 19, 100, 141, 174;
  EWL 3; MTCW 2; MTFW 2005; SATA
  112; WCH; YABC 1

Belloc, Joseph Peter Rene Hilaire
  See Belloc, (Joseph) Hilaire (Pierre Sebastien Rene Swanton)

Belloc, Joseph Pierre Hilaire
  See Belloc, (Joseph) Hilaire (Pierre Sebastien Rene Swanton)

Belloc, M. A.
  See Lowndes, Marie Adelaide (Belloc)

Belloc-Lowndes, Mrs.
  See Lowndes, Marie Adelaide (Belloc)

Bellow, Saul 1915-2005 ...... **CLC 1, 2, 3, 6, 8,
10, 13, 15, 25, 33, 34, 63, 79, 190, 200;
SSC 14; WLC**
  See also AITN 2; AMW; AMWC 2; AMWR
  2; BEST 89:3; BPFB 1; CA 5-8R; 238;
  CABS 1; CANR 29, 53, 95, 132; CDALB
  1941-1968; CN 1, 2, 3, 4, 5, 6, 7; DA;
  DA3; DAB; DAC; DAM MST, NOV,
  POP; DLB 2, 28, 299; DLBD 3; DLBY
  1982; EWL 3; MAL 5; MTCW 1, 2;
  MTFW 2005; NFS 4, 14; RGAL 4; RGSF
  2; SSFS 12; TUS

Belser, Reimond Karel Maria de 1929-
  See Ruyslinck, Ward
  See also CA 152

Bely, Andrey .... **PC 11; TCLC 7**
  See Bugayev, Boris Nikolayevich
  See also DLB 295; EW 9; EWL 3

Belyi, Andrei
  See Bugayev, Boris Nikolayevich
  See also RGWL 2, 3

Bembo, Pietro 1470-1547 .... **LC 79**
  See also RGWL 2, 3

Benary, Margot
  See Benary-Isbert, Margot

Benary-Isbert, Margot 1889-1979 .... **CLC 12**
  See also CA 5-8R; 89-92; CANR 4, 72;
  CLR 12; MAICYA 1, 2; SATA 2; SATA-
  Obit 21

Benavente (y Martinez), Jacinto
1866-1954 .... **DC 26; HLCS 1; TCLC 3**
  See also CA 106; 131; CANR 81; DAM
  DRAM, MULT; EWL 3; GLL 2; HW 1,
  2; MTCW 1, 2

Benchley, Peter 1940- .... **CLC 4, 8**
  See also AAYA 14; AITN 2; BPFB 1; CA
  17-20R; CANR 12, 35, 66, 115; CPW;
  DAM NOV, POP; HGG; MTCW 1, 2;
  MTFW 2005; SATA 3, 89, 164

Benchley, Peter Bradford
  See Benchley, Peter

Benchley, Robert (Charles)
1889-1945 .... **TCLC 1, 55**
  See also CA 105; 153; DLB 11; MAL 5;
  RGAL 4

Benda, Julien 1867-1956 .... **TCLC 60**
  See also CA 120; 154; GFL 1789 to the
  Present

Benedict, Ruth (Fulton)
1887-1948 .... **TCLC 60**
  See also CA 158; DLB 246

Benedikt, Michael 1935- .... **CLC 4, 14**
  See also CA 13-16R; CANR 7; CP 1, 2, 3,
  4, 5, 6, 7; DLB 5

Benet, Juan 1927-1993 .... **CLC 28**
  See also CA 143; EWL 3

Benet, Stephen Vincent 1898-1943 ..... **PC 64;
SSC 10, 86; TCLC 7**
  See also AMWS 11; CA 104; 152; DA3;
  DAM POET; DLB 4, 48, 102, 249, 284;
  DLBY 1997; EWL 3; HGG; MAL 5;
  MTCW 2; MTFW 2005; RGAL 4; RGSF
  2; SUFW; WP; YABC 1

Benet, William Rose 1886-1950 ..... **TCLC 28**
  See also CA 118; 152; DAM POET; DLB
  45; RGAL 4

Benford, Gregory (Albert) 1941- ..... **CLC 52**
  See also BPFB 1; CA 69-72, 175; CAAE
  175; CAAS 27; CANR 12, 24, 49, 95,
  134; CN 7; CSW; DLBY 1982; MTFW
  2005; SCFW 2; SFW 4

Bengtsson, Frans (Gunnar)
1894-1954 .... **TCLC 48**
  See also CA 170; EWL 3

Benjamin, David
  See Slavitt, David R(ytman)

Benjamin, Lois
  See Gould, Lois

Benjamin, Walter 1892-1940 .... **TCLC 39**
  See also CA 164; DLB 242; EW 11; EWL
  3

Ben Jelloun, Tahar 1944-
  See Jelloun, Tahar ben
  See also CA 135; CWW 2; EWL 3; RGWL
  3; WLIT 2

Benn, Gottfried 1886-1956 .. **PC 35; TCLC 3**
  See also CA 106; 153; DLB 56; EWL 3;
  RGWL 2, 3

Bennett, Alan 1934- .... **CLC 45, 77**
  See also BRWS 8; CA 103; CANR 35, 55,
  106; CBD; CD 5, 6; DAB; DAM MST;
  DLB 310; MTCW 1, 2; MTFW 2005

Bennett, (Enoch) Arnold
1867-1931 .... **TCLC 5, 20**
  See also BRW 6; CA 106; 155; CDBLB
  1890-1914; DLB 10, 34, 98, 135; EWL 3;
  MTCW 2

Bennett, Elizabeth
  See Mitchell, Margaret (Munnerlyn)

Bennett, George Harold 1930-
  See Bennett, Hal
  See also BW 1; CA 97-100; CANR 87

Bennett, Gwendolyn B. 1902-1981 .... **HR 1:2**
  See also BW 1; CA 125; DLB 51; WP

Bennett, Hal .... **CLC 5**
  See Bennett, George Harold
  See also DLB 33

Bennett, Jay 1912- .... **CLC 35**
  See also AAYA 10; CA 69-72; CANR 11,
  42, 79; JRDA; SAAS 4; SATA 41, 87;
  SATA-Brief 27; WYA; YAW

Bennett, Louise (Simone) 1919- .... **BLC 1;
CLC 28**
  See also BW 2, 3; CA 151; CDWLB 3; CP
  1, 2, 3, 4, 5, 6, 7; DAM MULT; DLB 117;
  EWL 3

Benson, A. C. 1862-1925 .... **TCLC 123**
  See also DLB 98

Benson, E(dward) F(rederic)
1867-1940 .... **TCLC 27**
  See also CA 114; 157; DLB 135, 153;
  HGG; SUFW 1

Benson, Jackson J. 1930- .... **CLC 34**
  See also CA 25-28R; DLB 111

Benson, Sally 1900-1972 .... **CLC 17**
  See also CA 19-20; 37-40R; CAP 1; SATA
  1, 35; SATA-Obit 27

Benson, Stella 1892-1933 .... **TCLC 17**
  See also CA 117; 154, 155; DLB 36, 162;
  FANT; TEA

Bentham, Jeremy 1748-1832 .... **NCLC 38**
  See also DLB 107, 158, 252

Bentley, E(dmund) C(lerihew)
1875-1956 .... **TCLC 12**
  See also CA 108; 232; DLB 70; MSW

Bentley, Eric (Russell) 1916- .... **CLC 24**
  See also CA 5-8R; CAD; CANR 6, 67;
  CBD; CD 5, 6; INT CANR-6

ben Uzair, Salem
  See Horne, Richard Henry Hengist

Beranger, Pierre Jean de
1780-1857 .... **NCLC 34**

Berdyaev, Nicolas
  See Berdyaev, Nikolai (Aleksandrovich)

Berdyaev, Nikolai (Aleksandrovich)
1874-1948 .... **TCLC 67**
  See also CA 120; 157

Berdyayev, Nikolai (Aleksandrovich)
  See Berdyaev, Nikolai (Aleksandrovich)

Berendt, John (Lawrence) 1939- ...... **CLC 86**
  See also CA 146; CANR 75, 93; DA3;
  MTCW 2; MTFW 2005

Beresford, J(ohn) D(avys)
1873-1947 .... **TCLC 81**
  See also CA 112; 155; DLB 162, 178, 197;
  SFW 4; SUFW 1

Bergelson, David (Rafailovich)
1884-1952 .... **TCLC 81**
  See Bergelson, Dovid
  See also CA 220

Bergelson, Dovid
  See Bergelson, David (Rafailovich)
  See also EWL 3

Berger, Colonel
  See Malraux, (Georges-)Andre

Bitov, Andrei (Georgievich) 1937- ... **CLC 57**
 See also CA 142; DLB 302
Biyidi, Alexandre 1932-
 See Beti, Mongo
 See also BW 1, 3; CA 114; 124; CANR 81;
 DA3; MTCW 1, 2
Bjarme, Brynjolf
 See Ibsen, Henrik (Johan)
Bjoernson, Bjoernstjerne (Martinius)
 1832-1910 .... **TCLC 7, 37**
 See also CA 104
Black, Robert
 See Holdstock, Robert P.
Blackburn, Paul 1926-1971 .... **CLC 9, 43**
 See also BG 1:2; CA 81-84; 33-36R; CANR
 34; CP 1; DLB 16; DLBY 1981
Black Elk 1863-1950 .... **NNAL; TCLC 33**
 See also CA 144; DAM MULT; MTCW 2;
 MTFW 2005; WP
Black Hawk 1767-1838 .... **NNAL**
Black Hobart
 See Sanders, (James) Ed(ward)
Blacklin, Malcolm
 See Chambers, Aidan
Blackmore, R(ichard) D(oddridge)
 1825-1900 .... **TCLC 27**
 See also CA 120; DLB 18; RGEL 2
Blackmur, R(ichard) P(almer)
 1904-1965 .... **CLC 2, 24**
 See also AMWS 2; CA 11-12; 25-28R;
 CANR 71; CAP 1; DLB 63; EWL 3;
 MAL 5
Black Tarantula
 See Acker, Kathy
Blackwood, Algernon (Henry)
 1869-1951 .... **TCLC 5**
 See also CA 105; 150; DLB 153, 156, 178;
 HGG; SUFW 1
Blackwood, Caroline (Maureen)
 1931-1996 .... **CLC 6, 9, 100**
 See also BRWS 9; CA 85-88; 151; CANR
 32, 61, 65; CN 3, 4, 5, 6; DLB 14, 207;
 HGG; MTCW 1
Blade, Alexander
 See Hamilton, Edmond; Silverberg, Robert
Blaga, Lucian 1895-1961 .... **CLC 75**
 See also CA 157; DLB 220; EWL 3
Blair, Eric (Arthur) 1903-1950 .... **TCLC 123**
 See Orwell, George
 See also CA 104; 132; DA; DA3; DAB;
 DAC; DAM MST, NOV; MTCW 1, 2;
 MTFW 2005; SATA 29
Blair, Hugh 1718-1800 .... **NCLC 75**
Blais, Marie-Claire 1939- .... **CLC 2, 4, 6, 13,**
 22
 See also CA 21-24R; CAAS 4; CANR 38,
 75, 93; CWW 2; DAC; DAM MST; DLB
 53; EWL 3; FW; MTCW 1, 2; MTFW
 2005; TWA
Blaise, Clark 1940- .... **CLC 29**
 See also AITN 2; CA 53-56, 231; CAAE
 231; CAAS 3; CANR 5, 66, 106; CN 4,
 5, 6, 7; DLB 53; RGSF 2
Blake, Fairley
 See De Voto, Bernard (Augustine)
Blake, Nicholas
 See Day Lewis, C(ecil)
 See also DLB 77; MSW
Blake, Sterling
 See Benford, Gregory (Albert)
Blake, William 1757-1827 . **NCLC 13, 37, 57,**
 127; PC 12, 63; WLC
 See also AAYA 47; BRW 3; BRWR 1; CD-
 BLB 1789-1832; CLR 52; DA; DA3;
 DAB; DAC; DAM MST, POET; DLB 93,
 163; EXPP; LATS 1:1; LMFS 1; MAI-
 CYA 1, 2; PAB; PFS 2, 12; SATA 30;
 TEA; WCH; WLIT 3; WP

Blanchot, Maurice 1907-2003 .... **CLC 135**
 See also CA 117; 144; 213; CANR 138;
 DLB 72, 296; EWL 3
Blasco Ibanez, Vicente 1867-1928 . **TCLC 12**
 See Ibanez, Vicente Blasco
 See also BPFB 1; CA 110; 131; CANR 81;
 DA3; DAM NOV; EW 8; EWL 3; HW 1,
 2; MTCW 1
Blatty, William Peter 1928- .... **CLC 2**
 See also CA 5-8R; CANR 9, 124; DAM
 POP; HGG
Bleeck, Oliver
 See Thomas, Ross (Elmore)
Blessing, Lee (Knowlton) 1949- .... **CLC 54**
 See also CA 236; CAD; CD 5, 6
Blight, Rose
 See Greer, Germaine
Blish, James (Benjamin) 1921-1975 . **CLC 14**
 See also BPFB 1; CA 1-4R; 57-60; CANR
 3; CN 2; DLB 8; MTCW 1; SATA 66;
 SCFW 1, 2; SFW 4
Bliss, Frederick
 See Card, Orson Scott
Bliss, Reginald
 See Wells, H(erbert) G(eorge)
Blixen, Karen (Christentze Dinesen)
 1885-1962
 See Dinesen, Isak
 See also CA 25-28; CANR 22, 50; CAP 2;
 DA3; DLB 214; LMFS 1; MTCW 1, 2;
 SATA 44; SSFS 20
Bloch, Robert (Albert) 1917-1994 .... **CLC 33**
 See also AAYA 29; CA 5-8R, 179; 146;
 CAAE 179; CAAS 20; CANR 5, 78;
 DA3; DLB 44; HGG; INT CANR-5;
 MTCW 2; SATA 12; SATA-Obit 82; SFW
 4; SUFW 1, 2
Blok, Alexander (Alexandrovich)
 1880-1921 .... **PC 21; TCLC 5**
 See also CA 104; 183; DLB 295; EW 9;
 EWL 3; LMFS 2; RGWL 2, 3
Blom, Jan
 See Breytenbach, Breyten
Bloom, Harold 1930- .... **CLC 24, 103**
 See also CA 13-16R; CANR 39, 75, 92,
 133; DLB 67; EWL 3; MTCW 2; MTFW
 2005; RGAL 4
Bloomfield, Aurelius
 See Bourne, Randolph S(illiman)
Bloomfield, Robert 1766-1823 ..... **NCLC 145**
 See also DLB 93
Blount, Roy (Alton), Jr. 1941- .... **CLC 38**
 See also CA 53-56; CANR 10, 28, 61, 125;
 CSW; INT CANR-28; MTCW 1, 2;
 MTFW 2005
Blowsnake, Sam 1875-(?) .... **NNAL**
Bloy, Leon 1846-1917 .... **TCLC 22**
 See also CA 121; 183; DLB 123; GFL 1789
 to the Present
Blue Cloud, Peter (Aroniawenrate)
 1933- .... **NNAL**
 See also CA 117; CANR 40; DAM MULT
Bluggage, Oranthy
 See Alcott, Louisa May
Blume, Judy (Sussman) 1938- .... **CLC 12, 30**
 See also AAYA 3, 26; BYA 1, 8, 12; CA 29-
 32R; CANR 13, 37, 66, 124; CLR 2, 15,
 69; CPW; DA3; DAM NOV, POP; DLB
 52; JRDA; MAICYA 1, 2; MAICYAS 1;
 MTCW 1, 2; MTFW 2005; SATA 2, 31,
 79, 142; WYA; YAW
Blunden, Edmund (Charles)
 1896-1974 .... **CLC 2, 56; PC 66**
 See also BRW 6; BRWS 11; CA 17-18; 45-
 48; CANR 54; CAP 2; CP 1, 2; DLB 20,
 100, 155; MTCW 1; PAB

Bly, Robert (Elwood) 1926- .... **CLC 1, 2, 5,**
 10, 15, 38, 128; PC 39
 See also AMWS 4; CA 5-8R; CANR 41,
 73, 125; CP 1, 2, 3, 4, 5, 6, 7; DA3; DAM
 POET; DLB 5; EWL 3; MAL 5; MTCW
 1, 2; MTFW 2005; PFS 6, 17; RGAL 4
Boas, Franz 1858-1942 .... **TCLC 56**
 See also CA 115; 181
Bobette
 See Simenon, Georges (Jacques Christian)
Boccaccio, Giovanni 1313-1375 ... **CMLC 13,**
 57; SSC 10, 87
 See also EW 2; RGSF 2; RGWL 2, 3; TWA;
 WLIT 7
Bochco, Steven 1943- .... **CLC 35**
 See also AAYA 11; CA 124; 138
Bode, Sigmund
 See O'Doherty, Brian
Bodel, Jean 1167(?)-1210 .... **CMLC 28**
Bodenheim, Maxwell 1892-1954 .... **TCLC 44**
 See also CA 110; 187; DLB 9, 45; MAL 5;
 RGAL 4
Bodenheimer, Maxwell
 See Bodenheim, Maxwell
Bodker, Cecil 1927-
 See Bodker, Cecil
Bodker, Cecil 1927- .... **CLC 21**
 See also CA 73-76; CANR 13, 44, 111;
 CLR 23; MAICYA 1, 2; SATA 14, 133
Boell, Heinrich (Theodor)
 1917-1985 ..... **CLC 2, 3, 6, 9, 11, 15, 27,**
 32, 72; SSC 23; WLC
 See Boll, Heinrich (Theodor)
 See also CA 21-24R; 116; CANR 24; DA;
 DA3; DAB; DAC; DAM MST, NOV;
 DLB 69; DLBY 1985; MTCW 1, 2;
 MTFW 2005; SSFS 20; TWA
Boerne, Alfred
 See Doeblin, Alfred
Boethius c. 480-c. 524 .... **CMLC 15**
 See also DLB 115; RGWL 2, 3
Boff, Leonardo (Genezio Darci)
 1938- .... **CLC 70; HLC 1**
 See also CA 150; DAM MULT; HW 2
Bogan, Louise 1897-1970 .... **CLC 4, 39, 46,**
 93; PC 12
 See also AMWS 3; CA 73-76; 25-28R;
 CANR 33, 82; CP 1; DAM POET; DLB
 45, 169; EWL 3; MAL 5; MAWW;
 MTCW 1, 2; PFS 21; RGAL 4
Bogarde, Dirk
 See Van Den Bogarde, Derek Jules Gaspard
 Ulric Niven
 See also DLB 14
Bogosian, Eric 1953- .... **CLC 45, 141**
 See also CA 138; CAD; CANR 102; CD 5,
 6
Bograd, Larry 1953- .... **CLC 35**
 See also CA 93-96; CANR 57; SAAS 21;
 SATA 33, 89; WYA
Boiardo, Matteo Maria 1441-1494 .... **LC 6**
Boileau-Despreaux, Nicolas 1636-1711 . **LC 3**
 See also DLB 268; EW 3; GFL Beginnings
 to 1789; RGWL 2, 3
Boissard, Maurice
 See Leautaud, Paul
Bojer, Johan 1872-1959 .... **TCLC 64**
 See also CA 189; EWL 3
Bok, Edward W(illiam)
 1863-1930 .... **TCLC 101**
 See also CA 217; DLB 91; DLBD 16
Boker, George Henry 1823-1890 . **NCLC 125**
 See also RGAL 4
Boland, Eavan (Aisling) 1944- .. **CLC 40, 67,**
 113; PC 58
 See also BRWS 5; CA 143, 207; CAAE
 207; CANR 61; CP 1, 7; CWP; DAM
 POET; DLB 40; FW; MTCW 2; MTFW
 2005; PFS 12, 22

Braddon, Mary Elizabeth
1837-1915 .... **TCLC 111**
See also BRWS 8; CA 108; 179; CMW 4;
DLB 18, 70, 156; HGG

Bradfield, Scott (Michael) 1955- .... **SSC 65**
See also CA 147; CANR 90; HGG; SUFW
2

Bradford, Gamaliel 1863-1932 .... **TCLC 36**
See also CA 160; DLB 17

Bradford, William 1590-1657 .... **LC 64**
See also DLB 24, 30; RGAL 4

Bradley, David (Henry), Jr. 1950- .... **BLC 1;
CLC 23, 118**
See also BW 1, 3; CA 104; CANR 26, 81;
CN 4, 5, 6, 7; DAM MULT; DLB 33

Bradley, John Ed(mund, Jr.) 1958- . **CLC 55**
See also CA 139; CANR 99; CN 6, 7; CSW

Bradley, Marion Zimmer
1930-1999 .... **CLC 30**
See Chapman, Lee; Dexter, John; Gardner,
Miriam; Ives, Morgan; Rivers, Elfrida
See also AAYA 40; BPFB 1; CA 57-60; 185;
CAAS 10; CANR 7, 31, 51, 75, 107;
CPW; DA3; DAM POP; DLB 8; FANT;
FW; MTCW 1, 2; MTFW 2005; SATA 90,
139; SATA-Obit 116; SFW 4; SUFW 2;
YAW

Bradshaw, John 1933- .... **CLC 70**
See also CA 138; CANR 61

Bradstreet, Anne 1612(?)-1672 ...... **LC 4, 30;
PC 10**
See also AMWS 1; CDALB 1640-1865;
DA; DA3; DAC; DAM MST, POET; DLB
24; EXPP; FW; PFS 6; RGAL 4; TUS;
WP

Brady, Joan 1939- .... **CLC 86**
See also CA 141

Bragg, Melvyn 1939- .... **CLC 10**
See also BEST 89:3; CA 57-60; CANR 10,
48, 89; CN 1, 2, 3, 4, 5, 6, 7; DLB 14,
271; RHW

Brahe, Tycho 1546-1601 .... **LC 45**
See also DLB 300

Braine, John (Gerard) 1922-1986 . **CLC 1, 3,
41**
See also CA 1-4R; 120; CANR 1, 33; CD-
BLB 1945-1960; CN 1, 2, 3, 4; DLB 15;
DLBY 1986; EWL 3; MTCW 1

Braithwaite, William Stanley (Beaumont)
1878-1962 .... **BLC 1; HR 1:2; PC 52**
See also BW 1; CA 125; DAM MULT; DLB
50, 54; MAL 5

Bramah, Ernest 1868-1942 .... **TCLC 72**
See also CA 156; CMW 4; DLB 70; FANT

Brammer, Billy Lee
See Brammer, William

Brammer, William 1929-1978 .... **CLC 31**
See also CA 235; 77-80

Brancati, Vitaliano 1907-1954 .... **TCLC 12**
See also CA 109; DLB 264; EWL 3

Brancato, Robin F(idler) 1936- .... **CLC 35**
See also AAYA 9, 68; BYA 6; CA 69-72;
CANR 11, 45; CLR 32; JRDA; MAICYA
2; MAICYAS 1; SAAS 9; SATA 97;
WYA; YAW

Brand, Dionne 1953- .... **CLC 192**
See also BW 2; CA 143; CANR 143; CWP

Brand, Max
See Faust, Frederick (Schiller)
See also BPFB 1; TCWW 1, 2

Brand, Millen 1906-1980 .... **CLC 7**
See also CA 21-24R; 97-100; CANR 72

Branden, Barbara .... **CLC 44**
See also CA 148

Brandes, Georg (Morris Cohen)
1842-1927 .... **TCLC 10**
See also CA 105; 189; DLB 300

Brandys, Kazimierz 1916-2000 .... **CLC 62**
See also CA 239; EWL 3

Branley, Franklyn M(ansfield)
1915-2002 .... **CLC 21**
See also CA 33-36R; 207; CANR 14, 39;
CLR 13; MAICYA 1, 2; SAAS 16; SATA
4, 68, 136

Brant, Beth (E.) 1941- .... **NNAL**
See also CA 144; FW

Brant, Sebastian 1457-1521 .... **LC 112**
See also DLB 179; RGWL 2, 3

Brathwaite, Edward Kamau
1930- .... **BLCS; CLC 11; PC 56**
See also BW 2, 3; CA 25-28R; CANR 11,
26, 47, 107; CDWLB 3; CP 1, 2, 3, 4, 5,
6, 7; DAM POET; DLB 125; EWL 3

Brathwaite, Kamau
See Brathwaite, Edward Kamau

Brautigan, Richard (Gary)
1935-1984 .... **CLC 1, 3, 5, 9, 12, 34, 42;
TCLC 133**
See also BPFB 1; CA 53-56; 113; CANR
34; CN 1, 2, 3; CP 1, 2, 3, 4; DA3; DAM
NOV; DLB 2, 5, 206; DLBY 1980, 1984;
FANT; MAL 5; MTCW 1; RGAL 4;
SATA 56

Brave Bird, Mary .... **NNAL**
See Crow Dog, Mary (Ellen)

Braverman, Kate 1950- .... **CLC 67**
See also CA 89-92; CANR 141

Brecht, (Eugen) Bertolt (Friedrich)
1898-1956 ..... **DC 3; TCLC 1, 6, 13, 35,
169; WLC**
See also CA 104; 133; CANR 62; CDWLB
2; DA; DA3; DAB; DAC; DAM DRAM,
MST; DFS 4, 5, 9; DLB 56, 124; EW 11;
EWL 3; IDTP; MTCW 1, 2; MTFW 2005;
RGWL 2, 3; TWA

Brecht, Eugen Berthold Friedrich
See Brecht, (Eugen) Bertolt (Friedrich)

Bremer, Fredrika 1801-1865 .... **NCLC 11**
See also DLB 254

Brennan, Christopher John
1870-1932 .... **TCLC 17**
See also CA 117; 188; DLB 230; EWL 3

Brennan, Maeve 1917-1993 ... **CLC 5; TCLC
124**
See also CA 81-84; CANR 72, 100

Brenner, Jozef 1887-1919
See Csath, Geza
See also CA 240

Brent, Linda
See Jacobs, Harriet A(nn)

Brentano, Clemens (Maria)
1778-1842 .... **NCLC 1**
See also DLB 90; RGWL 2, 3

Brent of Bin Bin
See Franklin, (Stella Maria Sarah) Miles
(Lampe)

Brenton, Howard 1942- .... **CLC 31**
See also CA 69-72; CANR 33, 67; CBD;
CD 5, 6; DLB 13; MTCW 1

Breslin, James 1930-
See Breslin, Jimmy
See also CA 73-76; CANR 31, 75, 139;
DAM NOV; MTCW 1, 2; MTFW 2005

Breslin, Jimmy .... **CLC 4, 43**
See Breslin, James
See also AITN 1; DLB 185; MTCW 2

Bresson, Robert 1901(?)-1999 .... **CLC 16**
See also CA 110; 187; CANR 49

Breton, Andre 1896-1966 .. **CLC 2, 9, 15, 54;
PC 15**
See also CA 19-20; 25-28R; CANR 40, 60;
CAP 2; DLB 65, 258; EW 11; EWL 3;
GFL 1789 to the Present; LMFS 2;
MTCW 1, 2; MTFW 2005; RGWL 2, 3;
TWA; WP

Breytenbach, Breyten 1939(?)- .. **CLC 23, 37,
126**
See also CA 113; 129; CANR 61, 122;
CWW 2; DAM POET; DLB 225; EWL 3

Bridgers, Sue Ellen 1942- .... **CLC 26**
See also AAYA 8, 49; BYA 7, 8; CA 65-68;
CANR 11, 36; CLR 18; DLB 52; JRDA;
MAICYA 1, 2; SAAS 1; SATA 22, 90;
SATA-Essay 109; WYA; YAW

Bridges, Robert (Seymour)
1844-1930 .... **PC 28; TCLC 1**
See also BRW 6; CA 104; 152; CDBLB
1890-1914; DAM POET; DLB 19, 98

Bridie, James .... **TCLC 3**
See Mavor, Osborne Henry
See also DLB 10; EWL 3

Brin, David 1950- .... **CLC 34**
See also AAYA 21; CA 102; CANR 24, 70,
125, 127; INT CANR-24; SATA 65;
SCFW 2; SFW 4

Brink, Andre (Philippus) 1935- . **CLC 18, 36,
106**
See also AFW; BRWS 6; CA 104; CANR
39, 62, 109, 133; CN 4, 5, 6, 7; DLB 225;
EWL 3; INT CA-103; LATS 1:2; MTCW
1, 2; MTFW 2005; WLIT 2

Brinsmead, H. F(ay)
See Brinsmead, H(esba) F(ay)

Brinsmead, H. F.
See Brinsmead, H(esba) F(ay)

Brinsmead, H(esba) F(ay) 1922- ...... **CLC 21**
See also CA 21-24R; CANR 10; CLR 47;
CWRI 5; MAICYA 1, 2; SAAS 5; SATA
18, 78

Brittain, Vera (Mary) 1893(?)-1970 . **CLC 23**
See also BRWS 10; CA 13-16; 25-28R;
CANR 58; CAP 1; DLB 191; FW; MTCW
1, 2

Broch, Hermann 1886-1951 .... **TCLC 20**
See also CA 117; 211; CDWLB 2; DLB 85,
124; EW 10; EWL 3; RGWL 2, 3

Brock, Rose
See Hansen, Joseph
See also GLL 1

Brod, Max 1884-1968 .... **TCLC 115**
See also CA 5-8R; 25-28R; CANR 7; DLB
81; EWL 3

Brodkey, Harold (Roy) 1930-1996 .. **CLC 56;
TCLC 123**
See also CA 111; 151; CANR 71; CN 4, 5,
6; DLB 130

Brodsky, Iosif Alexandrovich 1940-1996
See Brodsky, Joseph
See also AITN 1; CA 41-44R; 151; CANR
37, 106; DA3; DAM POET; MTCW 1, 2;
MTFW 2005; RGWL 2, 3

Brodsky, Joseph . **CLC 4, 6, 13, 36, 100; PC
9**
See Brodsky, Iosif Alexandrovich
See also AMWS 8; CWW 2; DLB 285;
EWL 3; MTCW 1

Brodsky, Michael (Mark) 1948- .... **CLC 19**
See also CA 102; CANR 18, 41, 58; DLB
244

Brodzki, Bella ed. .... **CLC 65**

Brome, Richard 1590(?)-1652 .... **LC 61**
See also BRWS 10; DLB 58

Bromell, Henry 1947- .... **CLC 5**
See also CA 53-56; CANR 9, 115, 116

Bromfield, Louis (Brucker)
1896-1956 .... **TCLC 11**
See also CA 107; 155; DLB 4, 9, 86; RGAL
4; RHW

Broner, E(sther) M(asserman)
1930- .... **CLC 19**
See also CA 17-20R; CANR 8, 25, 72; CN
4, 5, 6; DLB 28

Bronk, William (M.) 1918-1999 .... **CLC 10**
See also CA 89-92; 177; CANR 23; CP 3,
4, 5, 6, 7; DLB 165

Bronstein, Lev Davidovich
See Trotsky, Leon

Bronte, Anne 1820-1849 ..... **NCLC 4, 71, 102**
See also BRW 5; BRWR 1; DA3; DLB 21,
199; TEA

Bronte, (Patrick) Branwell
1817-1848 .... **NCLC 109**

Bronte, Charlotte 1816-1855 ...... **NCLC 3, 8, 33, 58, 105, 155; WLC**
See also AAYA 17; BRW 5; BRWC 2;
BRWR 1; BYA 2; CDBLB 1832-1890;
DA; DA3; DAB; DAC; DAM MST, NOV;
DLB 21, 159, 199; EXPN; FL 1:2; GL 2;
LAIT 2; NFS 4; TEA; WLIT 4

Bronte, Emily (Jane) 1818-1848 ... **NCLC 16, 35; PC 8; WLC**
See also AAYA 17; BPFB 1; BRW 5;
BRWC 1; BRWR 1; BYA 3; CDBLB
1832-1890; DA; DA3; DAB; DAC; DAM
MST, NOV, POET; DLB 21, 32, 199;
EXPN; FL 1:2; GL 2; LAIT 1; TEA;
WLIT 3

Brontes
See Bronte, Anne; Bronte, Charlotte; Bronte,
Emily (Jane)

Brooke, Frances 1724-1789 .... **LC 6, 48**
See also DLB 39, 99

Brooke, Henry 1703(?)-1783 .... **LC 1**
See also DLB 39

Brooke, Rupert (Chawner)
1887-1915 ..... **PC 24; TCLC 2, 7; WLC**
See also BRWS 3; CA 104; 132; CANR 61;
CDBLB 1914-1945; DA; DAB; DAC;
DAM MST, POET; DLB 19, 216; EXPP;
GLL 2; MTCW 1, 2; MTFW 2005; PFS
7; TEA

Brooke-Haven, P.
See Wodehouse, P(elham) G(renville)

Brooke-Rose, Christine 1926(?)- ..... **CLC 40, 184**
See also BRWS 4; CA 13-16R; CANR 58,
118; CN 1, 2, 3, 4, 5, 6, 7; DLB 14, 231;
EWL 3; SFW 4

Brookner, Anita 1928- .. **CLC 32, 34, 51, 136**
See also BRWS 4; CA 114; 120; CANR 37,
56, 87, 130; CN 4, 5, 6, 7; CPW; DA3;
DAB; DAM POP; DLB 194; DLBY 1987;
EWL 3; MTCW 1, 2; MTFW 2005; TEA

Brooks, Cleanth 1906-1994 . **CLC 24, 86, 110**
See also AMWS 14; CA 17-20R; 145;
CANR 33, 35; CSW; DLB 63; DLBY
1994; EWL 3; INT CANR-35; MAL 5;
MTCW 1, 2; MTFW 2005

Brooks, George
See Baum, L(yman) Frank

Brooks, Gwendolyn (Elizabeth)
1917-2000 ... **BLC 1; CLC 1, 2, 4, 5, 15, 49, 125; PC 7; WLC**
See also AAYA 20; AFAW 1, 2; AITN 1;
AMWS 3; BW 2, 3; CA 1-4R; 190; CANR
1, 27, 52, 75, 132; CDALB 1941-1968;
CLR 27; CP 1, 2, 3, 4, 5, 6, 7; CWP; DA;
DA3; DAC; DAM MST, MULT, POET;
DLB 5, 76, 165; EWL 3; EXPP; FL 1:5;
MAL 5; MAWW; MTCW 1, 2; MTFW
2005; PFS 1, 2, 4, 6; RGAL 4; SATA 6;
SATA-Obit 123; TUS; WP

Brooks, Mel .... **CLC 12**
See Kaminsky, Melvin
See also AAYA 13, 48; DLB 26

Brooks, Peter (Preston) 1938- .... **CLC 34**
See also CA 45-48; CANR 1, 107

Brooks, Van Wyck 1886-1963 .... **CLC 29**
See also AMW; CA 1-4R; CANR 6; DLB
45, 63, 103; MAL 5; TUS

Brophy, Brigid (Antonia)
1929-1995 .... **CLC 6, 11, 29, 105**
See also CA 5-8R; 149; CAAS 4; CANR
25, 53; CBD; CN 1, 2, 3, 4, 5, 6; CWD;
DA3; DLB 14, 271; EWL 3; MTCW 1, 2

Brosman, Catharine Savage 1934- ..... **CLC 9**
See also CA 61-64; CANR 21, 46

Brossard, Nicole 1943- .... **CLC 115, 169**
See also CA 122; CAAS 16; CANR 140;
CCA 1; CWP; CWW 2; DLB 53; EWL 3;
FW; GLL 2; RGWL 3

Brother Antoninus
See Everson, William (Oliver)

The Brothers Quay
See Quay, Stephen; Quay, Timothy

Broughton, T(homas) Alan 1936- ..... **CLC 19**
See also CA 45-48; CANR 2, 23, 48, 111

Broumas, Olga 1949- .... **CLC 10, 73**
See also CA 85-88; CANR 20, 69, 110; CP
7; CWP; GLL 2

Broun, Heywood 1888-1939 .... **TCLC 104**
See also DLB 29, 171

Brown, Alan 1950- .... **CLC 99**
See also CA 156

Brown, Charles Brockden
1771-1810 .... **NCLC 22, 74, 122**
See also AMWS 1; CDALB 1640-1865;
DLB 37, 59, 73; FW; GL 2; HGG; LMFS
1; RGAL 4; TUS

Brown, Christy 1932-1981 .... **CLC 63**
See also BYA 13; CA 105; 104; CANR 72;
DLB 14

Brown, Claude 1937-2002 ... **BLC 1; CLC 30**
See also AAYA 7; BW 1, 3; CA 73-76; 205;
CANR 81; DAM MULT

Brown, Dan 1964- .... **CLC 209**
See also AAYA 55; CA 217; MTFW 2005

Brown, Dee (Alexander)
1908-2002 .... **CLC 18, 47**
See also AAYA 30; CA 13-16R; 212; CAAS
6; CANR 11, 45, 60; CPW; CSW; DA3;
DAM POP; DLBY 1980; LAIT 2; MTCW
1, 2; MTFW 2005; NCFS 5; SATA 5, 110;
SATA-Obit 141; TCWW 1, 2

Brown, George
See Wertmueller, Lina

Brown, George Douglas
1869-1902 .... **TCLC 28**
See Douglas, George
See also CA 162

Brown, George Mackay 1921-1996 ... **CLC 5, 48, 100**
See also BRWS 6; CA 21-24R; 151; CAAS
6; CANR 12, 37, 67; CN 1, 2, 3, 4, 5, 6;
CP 1, 2, 3, 4; DLB 14, 27, 139, 271;
MTCW 1; RGSF 2; SATA 35

Brown, (William) Larry 1951-2004 . **CLC 73**
See also CA 130; 134; 233; CANR 117,
145; CSW; DLB 234; INT CA-134

Brown, Moses
See Barrett, William (Christopher)

Brown, Rita Mae 1944- .... **CLC 18, 43, 79**
See also BPFB 1; CA 45-48; CANR 2, 11,
35, 62, 95, 138; CN 5, 6, 7; CPW; CSW;
DA3; DAM NOV, POP; FW; INT CANR-
11; MAL 5; MTCW 1, 2; MTFW 2005;
NFS 9; RGAL 4; TUS

Brown, Roderick (Langmere) Haig-
See Haig-Brown, Roderick (Langmere)

Brown, Rosellen 1939- .... **CLC 32, 170**
See also CA 77-80; CAAS 10; CANR 14,
44, 98; CN 6, 7

Brown, Sterling Allen 1901-1989 ...... **BLC 1; CLC 1, 23, 59; HR 1:2; PC 55**
See also AFAW 1, 2; BW 1, 3; CA 85-88;
127; CANR 26; CP 3, 4; DA3; DAM
MULT, POET; DLB 48, 51, 63; MAL 5;
MTCW 1, 2; MTFW 2005; RGAL 4; WP

Brown, Will
See Ainsworth, William Harrison

Brown, William Hill 1765-1793 .... **LC 93**
See also DLB 37

Brown, William Wells 1815-1884 ...... **BLC 1; DC 1; NCLC 2, 89**
See also DAM MULT; DLB 3, 50, 183,
248; RGAL 4

Browne, (Clyde) Jackson 1948(?)- ... **CLC 21**
See also CA 120

Browne, Sir Thomas 1605-1682 .... **LC 111**
See also BRW 2; DLB 151

Browning, Robert 1812-1889 . **NCLC 19, 79; PC 2, 61; WLCS**
See also BRW 4; BRWC 2; BRWR 2; CD-
BLB 1832-1890; CLR 97; DA; DA3;
DAB; DAC; DAM MST, POET; DLB 32,
163; EXPP; LATS 1:1; PAB; PFS 1, 15;
RGEL 2; TEA; WLIT 4; WP; YABC 1

Browning, Tod 1882-1962 .... **CLC 16**
See also CA 141; 117

Brownmiller, Susan 1935- .... **CLC 159**
See also CA 103; CANR 35, 75, 137; DAM
NOV; FW; MTCW 1, 2; MTFW 2005

Brownson, Orestes Augustus
1803-1876 .... **NCLC 50**
See also DLB 1, 59, 73, 243

Bruccoli, Matthew J(oseph) 1931- ... **CLC 34**
See also CA 9-12R; CANR 7, 87; DLB 103

Bruce, Lenny .... **CLC 21**
See Schneider, Leonard Alfred

Bruchac, Joseph III 1942- .... **NNAL**
See also AAYA 19; CA 33-36R; CANR 13,
47, 75, 94, 137; CLR 46; CWRI 5; DAM
MULT; JRDA; MAICYA 2; MAICYAS 1;
MTCW 2; MTFW 2005; SATA 42, 89,
131

Bruin, John
See Brutus, Dennis

Brulard, Henri
See Stendhal

Brulls, Christian
See Simenon, Georges (Jacques Christian)

Brunetto Latini c. 1220-1294 .... **CMLC 73**

Brunner, John (Kilian Houston)
1934-1995 .... **CLC 8, 10**
See also CA 1-4R; 149; CAAS 8; CANR 2,
37; CPW; DAM POP; DLB 261; MTCW
1, 2; SCFW 1, 2; SFW 4

Bruno, Giordano 1548-1600 .... **LC 27**
See also RGWL 2, 3

Brutus, Dennis 1924- ... **BLC 1; CLC 43; PC 24**
See also AFW; BW 2, 3; CA 49-52; CAAS
14; CANR 2, 27, 42, 81; CDWLB 3; CP
1, 2, 3, 4, 5, 6, 7; DAM MULT, POET;
DLB 117, 225; EWL 3

Bryan, C(ourtlandt) D(ixon) B(arnes)
1936- .... **CLC 29**
See also CA 73-76; CANR 13, 68; DLB
185; INT CANR-13

Bryan, Michael
See Moore, Brian
See also CCA 1

Bryan, William Jennings
1860-1925 .... **TCLC 99**
See also DLB 303

Bryant, William Cullen 1794-1878 . **NCLC 6, 46; PC 20**
See also AMWS 1; CDALB 1640-1865;
DA; DAB; DAC; DAM MST, POET;
DLB 3, 43, 59, 189, 250; EXPP; PAB;
RGAL 4; TUS

Bryusov, Valery Yakovlevich
1873-1924 .... **TCLC 10**
See also CA 107; 155; EWL 3; SFW 4

Clutha, Janet Paterson Frame 1924-2004
See Frame, Janet
See also CA 1-4R; 224; CANR 2, 36, 76, 135; MTCW 1, 2; SATA 119

Clyne, Terence
See Blatty, William Peter

Cobalt, Martin
See Mayne, William (James Carter)

Cobb, Irvin S(hrewsbury)
1876-1944 .... **TCLC 77**
See also CA 175; DLB 11, 25, 86

Cobbett, William 1763-1835 .... **NCLC 49**
See also DLB 43, 107, 158; RGEL 2

Coburn, D(onald) L(ee) 1938- .... **CLC 10**
See also CA 89-92

Cocteau, Jean (Maurice Eugene Clement)
1889-1963 ...... **CLC 1, 8, 15, 16, 43; DC 17; TCLC 119; WLC**
See also CA 25-28; CANR 40; CAP 2; DA; DA3; DAB; DAC; DAM DRAM, MST, NOV; DLB 65, 258, 321; EW 10; EWL 3; GFL 1789 to the Present; MTCW 1, 2; RGWL 2, 3; TWA

Codrescu, Andrei 1946- .... **CLC 46, 121**
See also CA 33-36R; CAAS 19; CANR 13, 34, 53, 76, 125; CN 7; DA3; DAM POET; MAL 5; MTCW 2; MTFW 2005

Coe, Max
See Bourne, Randolph S(illiman)

Coe, Tucker
See Westlake, Donald E(dwin)

Coen, Ethan 1958- .... **CLC 108**
See also AAYA 54; CA 126; CANR 85

Coen, Joel 1955- .... **CLC 108**
See also AAYA 54; CA 126; CANR 119

The Coen Brothers
See Coen, Ethan; Coen, Joel

Coetzee, J(ohn) M(axwell) 1940- ..... **CLC 23, 33, 66, 117, 161, 162**
See also AAYA 37; AFW; BRWS 6; CA 77-80; CANR 41, 54, 74, 114, 133; CN 4, 5, 6, 7; DA3; DAM NOV; DLB 225; EWL 3; LMFS 2; MTCW 1, 2; MTFW 2005; NFS 21; WLIT 2; WWE 1

Coffey, Brian
See Koontz, Dean R.

Coffin, Robert P(eter) Tristram
1892-1955 .... **TCLC 95**
See also CA 123; 169; DLB 45

Cohan, George M(ichael)
1878-1942 .... **TCLC 60**
See also CA 157; DLB 249; RGAL 4

Cohen, Arthur A(llen) 1928-1986 ...... **CLC 7, 31**
See also CA 1-4R; 120; CANR 1, 17, 42; DLB 28

Cohen, Leonard (Norman) 1934- ...... **CLC 3, 38**
See also CA 21-24R; CANR 14, 69; CN 1, 2, 3, 4, 5, 6; CP 1, 2, 3, 4, 5, 6, 7; DAC; DAM MST; DLB 53; EWL 3; MTCW 1

Cohen, Matt(hew) 1942-1999 .... **CLC 19**
See also CA 61-64; 187; CAAS 18; CANR 40; CN 1, 2, 3, 4, 5, 6; DAC; DLB 53

Cohen-Solal, Annie 1948- .... **CLC 50**
See also CA 239

Colegate, Isabel 1931- .... **CLC 36**
See also CA 17-20R; CANR 8, 22, 74; CN 4, 5, 6, 7; DLB 14, 231; INT CANR-22; MTCW 1

Coleman, Emmett
See Reed, Ishmael (Scott)

Coleridge, Hartley 1796-1849 .... **NCLC 90**
See also DLB 96

Coleridge, M. E.
See Coleridge, Mary E(lizabeth)

Coleridge, Mary E(lizabeth)
1861-1907 .... **TCLC 73**
See also CA 116; 166; DLB 19, 98

Coleridge, Samuel Taylor
1772-1834 ...... **NCLC 9, 54, 99, 111; PC 11, 39, 67; WLC**
See also AAYA 66; BRW 4; BRWR 2; BYA 4; CDBLB 1789-1832; DA; DA3; DAB; DAC; DAM MST, POET; DLB 93, 107; EXPP; LATS 1:1; LMFS 1; PAB; PFS 4, 5; RGEL 2; TEA; WLIT 3; WP

Coleridge, Sara 1802-1852 .... **NCLC 31**
See also DLB 199

Coles, Don 1928- .... **CLC 46**
See also CA 115; CANR 38; CP 7

Coles, Robert (Martin) 1929- .... **CLC 108**
See also CA 45-48; CANR 3, 32, 66, 70, 135; INT CANR-32; SATA 23

Colette, (Sidonie-Gabrielle)
1873-1954 .... **SSC 10; TCLC 1, 5, 16**
See Willy, Colette
See also CA 104; 131; DA3; DAM NOV; DLB 65; EW 9; EWL 3; GFL 1789 to the Present; MTCW 1, 2; MTFW 2005; RGWL 2, 3; TWA

Collett, (Jacobine) Camilla (Wergeland)
1813-1895 .... **NCLC 22**

Collier, Christopher 1930- .... **CLC 30**
See also AAYA 13; BYA 2; CA 33-36R; CANR 13, 33, 102; JRDA; MAICYA 1, 2; SATA 16, 70; WYA; YAW 1

Collier, James Lincoln 1928- .... **CLC 30**
See also AAYA 13; BYA 2; CA 9-12R; CANR 4, 33, 60, 102; CLR 3; DAM POP; JRDA; MAICYA 1, 2; SAAS 21; SATA 8, 70; WYA; YAW 1

Collier, Jeremy 1650-1726 .... **LC 6**

Collier, John 1901-1980 . **SSC 19; TCLC 127**
See also CA 65-68; 97-100; CANR 10; CN 1, 2; DLB 77, 255; FANT; SUFW 1

Collier, Mary 1690-1762 .... **LC 86**
See also DLB 95

Collingwood, R(obin) G(eorge)
1889(?)-1943 .... **TCLC 67**
See also CA 117; 155; DLB 262

Collins, Billy 1941- .... **PC 68**
See also AAYA 64; CA 151; CANR 92; MTFW 2005; PFS 18

Collins, Hunt
See Hunter, Evan

Collins, Linda 1931- .... **CLC 44**
See also CA 125

Collins, Tom
See Furphy, Joseph
See also RGEL 2

Collins, (William) Wilkie
1824-1889 .... **NCLC 1, 18, 93**
See also BRWS 6; CDBLB 1832-1890; CMW 4; DLB 18, 70, 159; GL 2; MSW; RGEL 2; RGSF 2; SUFW 1; WLIT 4

Collins, William 1721-1759 .... **LC 4, 40**
See also BRW 3; DAM POET; DLB 109; RGEL 2

Collodi, Carlo .... **NCLC 54**
See Lorenzini, Carlo
See also CLR 5; WCH; WLIT 7

Colman, George
See Glassco, John

Colman, George, the Elder
1732-1794 .... **LC 98**
See also RGEL 2

Colonna, Vittoria 1492-1547 .... **LC 71**
See also RGWL 2, 3

Colt, Winchester Remington
See Hubbard, L(afayette) Ron(ald)

Colter, Cyrus J. 1910-2002 .... **CLC 58**
See also BW 1; CA 65-68; 205; CANR 10, 66; CN 2, 3, 4, 5, 6; DLB 33

Colton, James
See Hansen, Joseph
See also GLL 1

Colum, Padraic 1881-1972 .... **CLC 28**
See also BYA 4; CA 73-76; 33-36R; CANR 35; CLR 36; CP 1; CWRI 5; DLB 19; MAICYA 1, 2; MTCW 1; RGEL 2; SATA 15; WCH

Colvin, James
See Moorcock, Michael (John)

Colwin, Laurie (E.) 1944-1992 .... **CLC 5, 13, 23, 84**
See also CA 89-92; 139; CANR 20, 46; DLB 218; DLBY 1980; MTCW 1

Comfort, Alex(ander) 1920-2000 .... **CLC 7**
See also CA 1-4R; 190; CANR 1, 45; CN 1, 2, 3, 4; CP 1, 2, 3, 4, 5, 6, 7; DAM POP; MTCW 2

Comfort, Montgomery
See Campbell, (John) Ramsey

Compton-Burnett, I(vy)
1892(?)-1969 .... **CLC 1, 3, 10, 15, 34**
See also BRW 7; CA 1-4R; 25-28R; CANR 4; DAM NOV; DLB 36; EWL 3; MTCW 1, 2; RGEL 2

Comstock, Anthony 1844-1915 ...... **TCLC 13**
See also CA 110; 169

Comte, Auguste 1798-1857 .... **NCLC 54**

Conan Doyle, Arthur
See Doyle, Sir Arthur Conan
See also BPFB 1; BYA 4, 5, 11

Conde (Abellan), Carmen
1901-1996 .... **HLCS 1**
See also CA 177; CWW 2; DLB 108; EWL 3; HW 2

Conde, Maryse 1937- ..... **BLCS; CLC 52, 92**
See also BW 2, 3; CA 110; 190; CAAE 190; CANR 30, 53, 76; CWW 2; DAM MULT; EWL 3; MTCW 1; MTFW 2005

Condillac, Etienne Bonnot de
1714-1780 .... **LC 26**
See also DLB 313

Condon, Richard (Thomas)
1915-1996 .... **CLC 4, 6, 8, 10, 45, 100**
See also BEST 90:3; BPFB 1; CA 1-4R; 151; CAAS 1; CANR 2, 23; CMW 4; CN 1, 2, 3, 4, 5, 6; DAM NOV; INT CANR-23; MAL 5; MTCW 1, 2

Condorcet .... **LC 104**
See Condorcet, marquis de Marie-Jean-Antoine-Nicolas Caritat
See also GFL Beginnings to 1789

Condorcet, marquis de
Marie-Jean-Antoine-Nicolas Caritat
1743-1794
See Condorcet
See also DLB 313

Confucius 551B.C.-479B.C. .... **CMLC 19, 65; WLCS**
See also DA; DA3; DAB; DAC; DAM MST

Congreve, William 1670-1729 ... **DC 2; LC 5, 21; WLC**
See also BRW 2; CDBLB 1660-1789; DA; DAB; DAC; DAM DRAM, MST, POET; DFS 15; DLB 39, 84; RGEL 2; WLIT 3

Conley, Robert J(ackson) 1940- .... **NNAL**
See also CA 41-44R; CANR 15, 34, 45, 96; DAM MULT; TCWW 2

Connell, Evan S(helby), Jr. 1924- . **CLC 4, 6, 45**
See also AAYA 7; AMWS 14; CA 1-4R; CAAS 2; CANR 2, 39, 76, 97, 140; CN 1, 2, 3, 4, 5, 6; DAM NOV; DLB 2; DLBY 1981; MAL 5; MTCW 1, 2; MTFW 2005

Connelly, Marc(us Cook) 1890-1980 . **CLC 7**
See also CA 85-88; 102; CAD; CANR 30; DFS 12; DLB 7; DLBY 1980; MAL 5; RGAL 4; SATA-Obit 25

Connor, Ralph .... **TCLC 31**
See Gordon, Charles William
See also DLB 92; TCWW 1, 2

Dembry, R. Emmet
See Murfree, Mary Noailles

Demby, William 1922- .... **BLC 1; CLC 53**
See also BW 1, 3; CA 81-84; CANR 81;
DAM MULT; DLB 33

de Menton, Francisco
See Chin, Frank (Chew, Jr.)

Demetrius of Phalerum c.
307B.C.- .... **CMLC 34**

Demijohn, Thom
See Disch, Thomas M(ichael)

De Mille, James 1833-1880 .... **NCLC 123**
See also DLB 99, 251

Deming, Richard 1915-1983
See Queen, Ellery
See also CA 9-12R; CANR 3, 94; SATA 24

Democritus c. 460B.C.-c. 370B.C. . **CMLC 47**

de Montaigne, Michel (Eyquem)
See Montaigne, Michel (Eyquem) de

de Montherlant, Henry (Milon)
See Montherlant, Henry (Milon) de

Demosthenes 384B.C.-322B.C. ...... **CMLC 13**
See also AW 1; DLB 176; RGWL 2, 3

de Musset, (Louis Charles) Alfred
See Musset, (Louis Charles) Alfred de

de Natale, Francine
See Malzberg, Barry N(athaniel)

de Navarre, Marguerite 1492-1549 ... **LC 61; SSC 85**
See Marguerite d'Angouleme; Marguerite
de Navarre

Denby, Edwin (Orr) 1903-1983 .... **CLC 48**
See also CA 138; 110; CP 1

de Nerval, Gerard
See Nerval, Gerard de

Denham, John 1615-1669 .... **LC 73**
See also DLB 58, 126; RGEL 2

Denis, Julio
See Cortazar, Julio

Denmark, Harrison
See Zelazny, Roger (Joseph)

Dennis, John 1658-1734 .... **LC 11**
See also DLB 101; RGEL 2

Dennis, Nigel (Forbes) 1912-1989 ...... **CLC 8**
See also CA 25-28R; 129; CN 1, 2, 3, 4;
DLB 13, 15, 233; EWL 3; MTCW 1

Dent, Lester 1904-1959 .... **TCLC 72**
See also CA 112; 161; CMW 4; DLB 306;
SFW 4

De Palma, Brian (Russell) 1940- ...... **CLC 20**
See also CA 109

De Quincey, Thomas 1785-1859 ..... **NCLC 4, 87**
See also BRW 4; CDBLB 1789-1832; DLB
110, 144; RGEL 2

Deren, Eleanora 1908(?)-1961
See Deren, Maya
See also CA 192; 111

Deren, Maya .... **CLC 16, 102**
See Deren, Eleanora

Derleth, August (William)
1909-1971 .... **CLC 31**
See also BPFB 1; BYA 9, 10; CA 1-4R; 29-
32R; CANR 4; CMW 4; CN 1; DLB 9;
DLBD 17; HGG; SATA 5; SUFW 1

Der Nister 1884-1950 .... **TCLC 56**
See Nister, Der

de Routisie, Albert
See Aragon, Louis

Derrida, Jacques 1930-2004 .... **CLC 24, 87**
See also CA 124; 127; 232; CANR 76, 98,
133; DLB 242; EWL 3; LMFS 2; MTCW
2; TWA

Derry Down Derry
See Lear, Edward

Dersonnes, Jacques
See Simenon, Georges (Jacques Christian)

Der Stricker c. 1190-c. 1250 .... **CMLC 75**
See also DLB 138

Desai, Anita 1937- .... **CLC 19, 37, 97, 175**
See also BRWS 5; CA 81-84; CANR 33,
53, 95, 133; CN 1, 2, 3, 4, 5, 6, 7; CWRI
5; DA3; DAB; DAM NOV; DLB 271;
DNFS 2; EWL 3; FW; MTCW 1, 2;
MTFW 2005; SATA 63, 126

Desai, Kiran 1971- .... **CLC 119**
See also BYA 16; CA 171; CANR 127

de Saint-Luc, Jean
See Glassco, John

de Saint Roman, Arnaud
See Aragon, Louis

Desbordes-Valmore, Marceline
1786-1859 .... **NCLC 97**
See also DLB 217

Descartes, Rene 1596-1650 .... **LC 20, 35**
See also DLB 268; EW 3; GFL Beginnings
to 1789

Deschamps, Eustache 1340(?)-1404 .. **LC 103**
See also DLB 208

De Sica, Vittorio 1901(?)-1974 .... **CLC 20**
See also CA 117

Desnos, Robert 1900-1945 .... **TCLC 22**
See also CA 121; 151; CANR 107; DLB
258; EWL 3; LMFS 2

Destouches, Louis-Ferdinand
1894-1961 .... **CLC 9, 15**
See Celine, Louis-Ferdinand
See also CA 85-88; CANR 28; MTCW 1

de Tolignac, Gaston
See Griffith, D(avid Lewelyn) W(ark)

Deutsch, Babette 1895-1982 .... **CLC 18**
See also BYA 3; CA 1-4R; 108; CANR 4,
79; CP 1, 2, 3; DLB 45; SATA 1; SATA-
Obit 33

Devenant, William 1606-1649 .... **LC 13**

Devkota, Laxmiprasad 1909-1959 . **TCLC 23**
See also CA 123

De Voto, Bernard (Augustine)
1897-1955 .... **TCLC 29**
See also CA 113; 160; DLB 9, 256; MAL
5; TCWW 1, 2

De Vries, Peter 1910-1993 ..... **CLC 1, 2, 3, 7, 10, 28, 46**
See also CA 17-20R; 142; CANR 41; CN
1, 2, 3, 4, 5; DAM NOV; DLB 6; DLBY
1982; MAL 5; MTCW 1, 2; MTFW 2005

Dewey, John 1859-1952 .... **TCLC 95**
See also CA 114; 170; CANR 144; DLB
246, 270; RGAL 4

Dexter, John
See Bradley, Marion Zimmer
See also GLL 1

Dexter, Martin
See Faust, Frederick (Schiller)

Dexter, Pete 1943- .... **CLC 34, 55**
See also BEST 89:2; CA 127; 131; CANR
129; CPW; DAM POP; INT CA-131;
MAL 5; MTCW 1; MTFW 2005

Diamano, Silmang
See Senghor, Leopold Sedar

Diamond, Neil 1941- .... **CLC 30**
See also CA 108

Diaz del Castillo, Bernal c.
1496-1584 .... **HLCS 1; LC 31**
See also DLB 318; LAW

di Bassetto, Corno
See Shaw, George Bernard

Dick, Philip K(indred) 1928-1982 ... **CLC 10, 30, 72; SSC 57**
See also AAYA 24; BPFB 1; BYA 11; CA
49-52; 106; CANR 2, 16, 132; CN 2, 3;
CPW; DA3; DAM NOV, POP; DLB 8;
MTCW 1, 2; MTFW 2005; NFS 5; SCFW
1, 2; SFW 4

Dickens, Charles (John Huffam)
1812-1870 .... **NCLC 3, 8, 18, 26, 37, 50, 86, 105, 113, 161; SSC 17, 49; WLC**
See also AAYA 23; BRW 5; BRWC 1, 2;
BYA 1, 2, 3, 13, 14; CDBLB 1832-1890;
CLR 95; CMW 4; DA; DA3; DAB; DAC;
DAM MST, NOV; DLB 21, 55, 70, 159,
166; EXPN; GL 2; HGG; JRDA; LAIT 1,
2; LATS 1:1; LMFS 1; MAICYA 1, 2;
NFS 4, 5, 10, 14, 20; RGEL 2; RGSF 2;
SATA 15; SUFW 1; TEA; WCH; WLIT
4; WYA

Dickey, James (Lafayette)
1923-1997 .... **CLC 1, 2, 4, 7, 10, 15, 47, 109; PC 40; TCLC 151**
See also AAYA 50; AITN 1, 2; AMWS 4;
BPFB 1; CA 9-12R; 156; CABS 2; CANR
10, 48, 61, 105; CDALB 1968-1988; CP
1, 2, 3, 4; CPW; CSW; DA3; DAM NOV,
POET, POP; DLB 5, 193; DLBD 7;
DLBY 1982, 1993, 1996, 1997, 1998;
EWL 3; INT CANR-10; MAL 5; MTCW
1, 2; NFS 9; PFS 6, 11; RGAL 4; TUS

Dickey, William 1928-1994 .... **CLC 3, 28**
See also CA 9-12R; 145; CANR 24, 79; CP
1, 2, 3, 4; DLB 5

Dickinson, Charles 1951- .... **CLC 49**
See also CA 128; CANR 141

Dickinson, Emily (Elizabeth)
1830-1886 ... **NCLC 21, 77; PC 1; WLC**
See also AAYA 22; AMW; AMWR 1;
CDALB 1865-1917; DA; DA3; DAB;
DAC; DAM MST, POET; DLB 1, 243;
EXPP; FL 1:3; MAWW; PAB; PFS 1, 2,
3, 4, 5, 6, 8, 10, 11, 13, 16; RGAL 4;
SATA 29; TUS; WP; WYA

Dickinson, Mrs. Herbert Ward
See Phelps, Elizabeth Stuart

Dickinson, Peter (Malcolm de Brissac)
1927- .... **CLC 12, 35**
See also AAYA 9, 49; BYA 5; CA 41-44R;
CANR 31, 58, 88, 134; CLR 29; CMW 4;
DLB 87, 161, 276; JRDA; MAICYA 1, 2;
SATA 5, 62, 95, 150; SFW 4; WYA; YAW

Dickson, Carr
See Carr, John Dickson

Dickson, Carter
See Carr, John Dickson

Diderot, Denis 1713-1784 .... **LC 26**
See also DLB 313; EW 4; GFL Beginnings
to 1789; LMFS 1; RGWL 2, 3

Didion, Joan 1934- . **CLC 1, 3, 8, 14, 32, 129**
See also AITN 1; AMWS 4; CA 5-8R;
CANR 14, 52, 76, 125; CDALB 1968-
1988; CN 2, 3, 4, 5, 6, 7; DA3; DAM
NOV; DLB 2, 173, 185; DLBY 1981,
1986; EWL 3; MAL 5; MAWW; MTCW
1, 2; MTFW 2005; NFS 3; RGAL 4;
TCLE 1:1; TCWW 2; TUS

di Donato, Pietro 1911-1992 .... **TCLC 159**
See also CA 101; 136; DLB 9

Dietrich, Robert
See Hunt, E(verette) Howard, (Jr.)

Difusa, Pati
See Almodovar, Pedro

Dillard, Annie 1945- ...... **CLC 9, 60, 115, 216**
See also AAYA 6, 43; AMWS 6; ANW; CA
49-52; CANR 3, 43, 62, 90, 125; DA3;
DAM NOV; DLB 275, 278; DLBY 1980;
LAIT 4, 5; MAL 5; MTCW 1, 2; MTFW
2005; NCFS 1; RGAL 4; SATA 10, 140;
TCLE 1:1; TUS

Dillard, R(ichard) H(enry) W(ilde)
1937- .... **CLC 5**
See also CA 21-24R; CAAS 7; CANR 10;
CP 2, 3, 4, 5, 6, 7; CSW; DLB 5, 244

Dillon, Eilis 1920-1994 .... **CLC 17**
See also CA 9-12R; 182; 147; CAAE 182;
CAAS 3; CANR 4, 38, 78; CLR 26; MAI-
CYA 1, 2; MAICYAS 1; SATA 2, 74;
SATA-Essay 105; SATA-Obit 83; YAW

Douglass, Frederick 1817(?)-1895 ..... **BLC 1;**
    NCLC 7, 55, 141; WLC
    See also AAYA 48; AFAW 1, 2; AMWC 1;
    AMWS 3; CDALB 1640-1865; DA; DA3;
    DAC; DAM MST, MULT; DLB 1, 43, 50,
    79, 243; FW; LAIT 2; NCFS 2; RGAL 4;
    SATA 29

Dourado, (Waldomiro Freitas) Autran
    1926- .... **CLC 23, 60**
    See also CA 25-28R, 179; CANR 34, 81;
    DLB 145, 307; HW 2

Dourado, Waldomiro Freitas Autran
    See Dourado, (Waldomiro Freitas) Autran

Dove, Rita (Frances) 1952- . **BLCS; CLC 50,**
    81; PC 6
    See also AAYA 46; AMWS 4; BW 2; CA
    109; CAAS 19; CANR 27, 42, 68, 76, 97,
    132; CDALBS; CP 7; CSW; CWP; DA3;
    DAM MULT, POET; DLB 120; EWL 3;
    EXPP; MAL 5; MTCW 2; MTFW 2005;
    PFS 1, 15; RGAL 4

Doveglion
    See Villa, Jose Garcia

Dowell, Coleman 1925-1985 .... **CLC 60**
    See also CA 25-28R; 117; CANR 10; DLB
    130; GLL 2

Dowson, Ernest (Christopher)
    1867-1900 .... **TCLC 4**
    See also CA 105; 150; DLB 19, 135; RGEL
    2

Doyle, A. Conan
    See Doyle, Sir Arthur Conan

Doyle, Sir Arthur Conan
    1859-1930 . **SSC 12, 83; TCLC 7; WLC**
    See Conan Doyle, Arthur
    See also AAYA 14; BRWS 2; CA 104; 122;
    CANR 131; CDBLB 1890-1914; CMW
    4; DA; DA3; DAB; DAC; DAM MST,
    NOV; DLB 18, 70, 156, 178; EXPS;
    HGG; LAIT 2; MSW; MTCW 1, 2;
    MTFW 2005; RGEL 2; RGSF; RHW;
    SATA 24; SCFW 1, 2; SFW 4; SSFS 2;
    TEA; WCH; WLIT 4; WYA; YAW

Doyle, Conan
    See Doyle, Sir Arthur Conan

Doyle, John
    See Graves, Robert (von Ranke)

Doyle, Roddy 1958- .... **CLC 81, 178**
    See also AAYA 14; BRWS 5; CA 143;
    CANR 73, 128; CN 6, 7; DA3; DLB 194;
    MTCW 2; MTFW 2005

Doyle, Sir A. Conan
    See Doyle, Sir Arthur Conan

Dr. A
    See Asimov, Isaac; Silverstein, Alvin; Sil-
    verstein, Virginia B(arbara Opshelor)

Drabble, Margaret 1939- ...... **CLC 2, 3, 5, 8,**
    10, 22, 53, 129
    See also BRWS 4; CA 13-16R; CANR 18,
    35, 63, 112, 131; CDBLB 1960 to Present;
    CN 1, 2, 3, 4, 5, 6, 7; CPW; DA3; DAB;
    DAC; DAM MST, NOV, POP; DLB 14,
    155, 231; EWL 3; FW; MTCW 1, 2;
    MTFW 2005; RGEL 2; SATA 48; TEA

Drakulic, Slavenka 1949- .... **CLC 173**
    See also CA 144; CANR 92

Drakulic-Ilic, Slavenka
    See Drakulic, Slavenka

Drapier, M. B.
    See Swift, Jonathan

Drayham, James
    See Mencken, H(enry) L(ouis)

Drayton, Michael 1563-1631 .... **LC 8**
    See also DAM POET; DLB 121; RGEL 2

Dreadstone, Carl
    See Campbell, (John) Ramsey

Dreiser, Theodore (Herman Albert)
    1871-1945 .... **SSC 30; TCLC 10, 18, 35,**
    83; WLC
    See also AMW; AMWC 2; AMWR 2; BYA
    15, 16; CA 106; 132; CDALB 1865-1917;
    DA; DA3; DAC; DAM MST, NOV; DLB
    9, 12, 102, 137; DLBD 1; EWL 3; LAIT
    2; LMFS 1; MAL 5; MTCW 1, 2; MTFW
    2005; NFS 8, 17; RGAL 4; TUS

Drexler, Rosalyn 1926- .... **CLC 2, 6**
    See also CA 81-84; CAD; CANR 68, 124;
    CD 5, 6; CWD; MAL 5

Dreyer, Carl Theodor 1889-1968 ...... **CLC 16**
    See also CA 116

Drieu la Rochelle, Pierre(-Eugene)
    1893-1945 .... **TCLC 21**
    See also CA 117; DLB 72; EWL 3; GFL
    1789 to the Present

Drinkwater, John 1882-1937 .... **TCLC 57**
    See also CA 109; 149; DLB 10, 19, 149;
    RGEL 2

Drop Shot
    See Cable, George Washington

Droste-Hulshoff, Annette Freiin von
    1797-1848 .... **NCLC 3, 133**
    See also CDWLB 2; DLB 133; RGSF 2;
    RGWL 2, 3

Drummond, Walter
    See Silverberg, Robert

Drummond, William Henry
    1854-1907 .... **TCLC 25**
    See also CA 160; DLB 92

Drummond de Andrade, Carlos
    1902-1987 .... **CLC 18; TCLC 139**
    See Andrade, Carlos Drummond de
    See also CA 132; 123; DLB 307; LAW

Drummond of Hawthornden, William
    1585-1649 .... **LC 83**
    See also DLB 121, 213; RGEL 2

Drury, Allen (Stuart) 1918-1998 .... **CLC 37**
    See also CA 57-60; 170; CANR 18, 52; CN
    1, 2, 3, 4, 5, 6; INT CANR-18

Druse, Eleanor
    See King, Stephen

Dryden, John 1631-1700 ..... **DC 3; LC 3, 21,**
    115; PC 25; WLC
    See also BRW 2; CDBLB 1660-1789; DA;
    DAB; DAC; DAM DRAM, MST, POET;
    DLB 80, 101, 131; EXPP; IDTP; LMFS
    1; RGEL 2; TEA; WLIT 3

du Bellay, Joachim 1524-1560 .... **LC 92**
    See also GFL Beginnings to 1789; RGWL
    2, 3

Duberman, Martin (Bauml) 1930- ..... **CLC 8**
    See also CA 1-4R; CAD; CANR 2, 63, 137;
    CD 5, 6

Dubie, Norman (Evans) 1945- .... **CLC 36**
    See also CA 69-72; CANR 12, 115; CP 3,
    4, 5, 6, 7; DLB 120; PFS 12

Du Bois, W(illiam) E(dward) B(urghardt)
    1868-1963 ..... **BLC 1; CLC 1, 2, 13, 64,**
    96; HR 1:2; TCLC 169; WLC
    See also AAYA 40; AFAW 1, 2; AMWC 1;
    AMWS 2; BW 1, 3; CA 85-88; CANR
    34, 82, 132; CDALB 1865-1917; DA;
    DA3; DAC; DAM MST, MULT, NOV;
    DLB 47, 50, 91, 246, 284; EWL 3; EXPP;
    LAIT 2; LMFS 2; MAL 5; MTCW 1, 2;
    MTFW 2005; NCFS 1; PFS 13; RGAL 4;
    SATA 42

Dubus, Andre 1936-1999 ..... **CLC 13, 36, 97;**
    SSC 15
    See also AMWS 7; CA 21-24R; 177; CANR
    17; CN 5, 6; CSW; DLB 130; INT CANR-
    17; RGAL 4; SSFS 10; TCLE 1:1

Duca Minimo
    See D'Annunzio, Gabriele

Ducharme, Rejean 1941- .... **CLC 74**
    See also CA 165; DLB 60

du Chatelet, Emilie 1706-1749 .... **LC 96**
    See Chatelet, Gabrielle-Emilie Du

Duchen, Claire .... **CLC 65**

Duclos, Charles Pinot- 1704-1772 .... **LC 1**
    See also GFL Beginnings to 1789

Dudek, Louis 1918-2001 .... **CLC 11, 19**
    See also CA 45-48; 215; CAAS 14; CANR
    1; CP 1, 2, 3, 4, 5, 6, 7; DLB 88

Duerrenmatt, Friedrich 1921-1990 ... **CLC 1,**
    4, 8, 11, 15, 43, 102
    See Durrenmatt, Friedrich
    See also CA 17-20R; CANR 33; CMW 4;
    DAM DRAM; DLB 69, 124; MTCW 1, 2

Duffy, Bruce 1953(?)- .... **CLC 50**
    See also CA 172

Duffy, Maureen (Patricia) 1933- ...... **CLC 37**
    See also CA 25-28R; CANR 33, 68; CBD;
    CN 1, 2, 3, 4, 5, 6, 7; CP 7; CWD; CWP;
    DFS 15; DLB 14, 310; FW; MTCW 1

Du Fu
    See Tu Fu
    See also RGWL 2, 3

Dugan, Alan 1923-2003 .... **CLC 2, 6**
    See also CA 81-84; 220; CANR 119; CP 1,
    2, 3, 4, 5, 6, 7; DLB 5; MAL 5; PFS 10

du Gard, Roger Martin
    See Martin du Gard, Roger

Duhamel, Georges 1884-1966 .... **CLC 8**
    See also CA 81-84; 25-28R; CANR 35;
    DLB 65; EWL 3; GFL 1789 to the
    Present; MTCW 1

Dujardin, Edouard (Emile Louis)
    1861-1949 .... **TCLC 13**
    See also CA 109; DLB 123

Duke, Raoul
    See Thompson, Hunter S(tockton)

Dulles, John Foster 1888-1959 .... **TCLC 72**
    See also CA 115; 149

Dumas, Alexandre (pere)
    1802-1870 .... **NCLC 11, 71; WLC**
    See also AAYA 22; BYA 3; DA; DA3;
    DAB; DAC; DAM MST, NOV; DLB 119,
    192; EW 6; GFL 1789 to the Present;
    LAIT 1, 2; NFS 14, 19; RGWL 2, 3;
    SATA 18; TWA; WCH

Dumas, Alexandre (fils) 1824-1895 ...... **DC 1;**
    NCLC 9
    See also DLB 192; GFL 1789 to the Present;
    RGWL 2, 3

Dumas, Claudine
    See Malzberg, Barry N(athaniel)

Dumas, Henry L. 1934-1968 .... **CLC 6, 62**
    See also BW 1; CA 85-88; DLB 41; RGAL
    4

du Maurier, Daphne 1907-1989 .. **CLC 6, 11,**
    59; SSC 18
    See also AAYA 37; BPFB 1; BRWS 3; CA
    5-8R; 128; CANR 6, 55; CMW 4; CN 1,
    2, 3, 4; CPW; DA3; DAB; DAC; DAM
    MST, POP; DLB 191; GL 2; HGG; LAIT
    3; MSW; MTCW 1, 2; NFS 12; RGEL 2;
    RGSF 2; RHW; SATA 27; SATA-Obit 60;
    SSFS 14, 16; TEA

Du Maurier, George 1834-1896 ..... **NCLC 86**
    See also DLB 153, 178; RGEL 2

Dunbar, Paul Laurence 1872-1906 ... **BLC 1;**
    PC 5; SSC 8; TCLC 2, 12; WLC
    See also AFAW 1, 2; AMWS 2; BW 1, 3;
    CA 104; 124; CANR 79; CDALB 1865-
    1917; DA; DA3; DAC; DAM MST,
    MULT, POET; DLB 50, 54, 78; EXPP;
    MAL 5; RGAL 4; SATA 34

Dunbar, William 1460(?)-1520(?) .... **LC 20;**
    PC 67
    See also BRWS 8; DLB 132, 146; RGEL 2

Dunbar-Nelson, Alice .... **HR 1:2**
    See Nelson, Alice Ruth Moore Dunbar

Duncan, Dora Angela
    See Duncan, Isadora

Enchi, Fumiko (Ueda) 1905-1986 ..... **CLC 31**
See Enchi Fumiko
See also CA 129; 121; FW; MJW

Enchi Fumiko
See Enchi, Fumiko (Ueda)
See also DLB 182; EWL 3

Ende, Michael (Andreas Helmuth)
1929-1995 .... **CLC 31**
See also BYA 5; CA 118; 124; 149; CANR
36, 110; CLR 138; DLB 75; MAICYA 1,
2; MAICYAS 1; SATA 61, 130; SATA-
Brief 42; SATA-Obit 86

Endo, Shusaku 1923-1996 ..... **CLC 7, 14, 19,
54, 99; SSC 48; TCLC 152**
See Endo Shusaku
See also CA 29-32R; 153; CANR 21, 54,
131; DA3; DAM NOV; MTCW 1, 2;
MTFW 2005; RGSF 2; RGWL 2, 3

Endo Shusaku
See Endo, Shusaku
See also CWW 2; DLB 182; EWL 3

Engel, Marian 1933-1985 .... **CLC 36; TCLC
137**
See also CA 25-28R; CANR 12; CN 2, 3;
DLB 53; FW; INT CANR-12

Engelhardt, Frederick
See Hubbard, L(afayette) Ron(ald)

Engels, Friedrich 1820-1895 .. **NCLC 85, 114**
See also DLB 129; LATS 1:1

Enright, D(ennis) J(oseph)
1920-2002 .... **CLC 4, 8, 31**
See also CA 1-4R; 211; CANR 1, 42, 83;
CN 1, 2; CP 1, 2, 3, 4, 5, 6, 7; DLB 27;
EWL 3; SATA 25; SATA-Obit 140

Ensler, Eve 1953- .... **CLC 212**
See also CA 172; CANR 126

Enzensberger, Hans Magnus
1929- .... **CLC 43; PC 28**
See also CA 116; 119; CANR 103; CWW
2; EWL 3

Ephron, Nora 1941- .... **CLC 17, 31**
See also AAYA 35; AITN 2; CA 65-68;
CANR 12, 39, 83; DFS 22

Epicurus 341B.C.-270B.C. .... **CMLC 21**
See also DLB 176

Epsilon
See Betjeman, John

Epstein, Daniel Mark 1948- .... **CLC 7**
See also CA 49-52; CANR 2, 53, 90

Epstein, Jacob 1956- .... **CLC 19**
See also CA 114

Epstein, Jean 1897-1953 .... **TCLC 92**

Epstein, Joseph 1937- .... **CLC 39, 204**
See also AMWS 14; CA 112; 119; CANR
50, 65, 117

Epstein, Leslie 1938- .... **CLC 27**
See also AMWS 12; CA 73-76, 215; CAAE
215; CAAS 12; CANR 23, 69; DLB 299

Equiano, Olaudah 1745(?)-1797 . **BLC 2; LC
16**
See also AFAW 1, 2; CDWLB 3; DAM
MULT; DLB 37, 50; WLIT 2

Erasmus, Desiderius 1469(?)-1536 ..... **LC 16,
93**
See also DLB 136; EW 2; LMFS 1; RGWL
2, 3; TWA

Erdman, Paul E(mil) 1932- .... **CLC 25**
See also AITN 1; CA 61-64; CANR 13, 43,
84

Erdrich, (Karen) Louise 1954- .. **CLC 39, 54,
120, 176; NNAL; PC 52**
See also AAYA 10, 47; AMWS 4; BEST
89:1; BPFB 1; CA 114; CANR 41, 62,
118, 138; CDALBS; CN 5, 6, 7; CP 7;
CPW; CWP; DA3; DAM MULT, NOV,
POP; DLB 152, 175, 206; EWL 3; EXPP;

FL 1:5; LAIT 5; LATS 1:2; MAL 5;
MTCW 1, 2; MTFW 2005; NFS 5; PFS
14; RGAL 4; SATA 94, 141; SSFS 14;
TCWW 2

Erenburg, Ilya (Grigoryevich)
See Ehrenburg, Ilya (Grigoryevich)

Erickson, Stephen Michael 1950-
See Erickson, Steve
See also CA 129; SFW 4

Erickson, Steve .... **CLC 64**
See Erickson, Stephen Michael
See also CANR 60, 68, 136; MTFW 2005;
SUFW 2

Erickson, Walter
See Fast, Howard (Melvin)

Ericson, Walter
See Fast, Howard (Melvin)

Eriksson, Buntel
See Bergman, (Ernst) Ingmar

Eriugena, John Scottus c.
810-877 .... **CMLC 65**
See also DLB 115

Ernaux, Annie 1940- .... **CLC 88, 184**
See also CA 147; CANR 93; MTFW 2005;
NCFS 3, 5

Erskine, John 1879-1951 .... **TCLC 84**
See also CA 112; 159; DLB 9, 102; FANT

Eschenbach, Wolfram von
See Wolfram von Eschenbach
See also RGWL 3

Eseki, Bruno
See Mphahlele, Ezekiel

Esenin, Sergei (Alexandrovich)
1895-1925 .... **TCLC 4**
See Yesenin, Sergey
See also CA 104; RGWL 2, 3

Eshleman, Clayton 1935- .... **CLC 7**
See also CA 33-36R, 212; CAAE 212;
CAAS 6; CANR 93; CP 1, 2, 3, 4, 5, 6,
7; DLB 5

Espriella, Don Manuel Alvarez
See Southey, Robert

Espriu, Salvador 1913-1985 .... **CLC 9**
See also CA 154; 115; DLB 134; EWL 3

Espronceda, Jose de 1808-1842 ..... **NCLC 39**

Esquivel, Laura 1951(?)- ... **CLC 141; HLCS
1**
See also AAYA 29; CA 143; CANR 68, 113;
DA3; DNFS 2; LAIT 3; LMFS 2; MTCW
2; MTFW 2005; NFS 5; WLIT 1

Esse, James
See Stephens, James

Esterbrook, Tom
See Hubbard, L(afayette) Ron(ald)

Estleman, Loren D. 1952- .... **CLC 48**
See also AAYA 27; CA 85-88; CANR 27,
74, 139; CMW 4; CPW; DA3; DAM
NOV, POP; DLB 226; INT CANR-27;
MTCW 1, 2; MTFW 2005; TCWW 1, 2

Etherege, Sir George 1636-1692 . **DC 23; LC
78**
See also BRW 2; DAM DRAM; DLB 80;
PAB; RGEL 2

Euclid 306B.C.-283B.C. .... **CMLC 25**

Eugenides, Jeffrey 1960(?)- .... **CLC 81, 212**
See also AAYA 51; CA 144; CANR 120;
MTFW 2005

Euripides c. 484B.C.-406B.C. .... **CMLC 23,
51; DC 4; WLCS**
See also AW 1; CDWLB 1; DA; DA3;
DAB; DAC; DAM DRAM, MST; DFS 1,
4, 6; DLB 176; LAIT 1; LMFS 1; RGWL
2, 3

Evan, Evin
See Faust, Frederick (Schiller)

Evans, Caradoc 1878-1945 ... **SSC 43; TCLC
85**
See also DLB 162

Evans, Evan
See Faust, Frederick (Schiller)

Evans, Marian
See Eliot, George

Evans, Mary Ann
See Eliot, George
See also NFS 20

Evarts, Esther
See Benson, Sally

Everett, Percival
See Everett, Percival L.
See also CSW

Everett, Percival L. 1956- .... **CLC 57**
See Everett, Percival
See also BW 2; CA 129; CANR 94, 134;
CN 7; MTFW 2005

Everson, R(onald) G(ilmour)
1903-1992 .... **CLC 27**
See also CA 17-20R; CP 1, 2, 3, 4; DLB 88

Everson, William (Oliver)
1912-1994 .... **CLC 1, 5, 14**
See Antoninus, Brother
See also BG 1:2; CA 9-12R; 145; CANR
20; CP 2, 3, 4; DLB 5, 16, 212; MTCW 1

Evtushenko, Evgenii Aleksandrovich
See Yevtushenko, Yevgeny (Alexandrovich)
See also CWW 2; RGWL 2, 3

Ewart, Gavin (Buchanan)
1916-1995 .... **CLC 13, 46**
See also BRWS 7; CA 89-92; 150; CANR
17, 46; CP 1, 2, 3, 4; DLB 40; MTCW 1

Ewers, Hanns Heinz 1871-1943 ..... **TCLC 12**
See also CA 109; 149

Ewing, Frederick R.
See Sturgeon, Theodore (Hamilton)

Exley, Frederick (Earl) 1929-1992 .... **CLC 6,
11**
See also AITN 2; BPFB 1; CA 81-84; 138;
CANR 117; DLB 143; DLBY 1981

Eynhardt, Guillermo
See Quiroga, Horacio (Sylvestre)

Ezekiel, Nissim (Moses) 1924-2004 .. **CLC 61**
See also CA 61-64; 223; CP 1, 2, 3, 4, 5, 6,
7; EWL 3

Ezekiel, Tish O'Dowd 1943- .... **CLC 34**
See also CA 129

Fadeev, Aleksandr Aleksandrovich
See Bulgya, Alexander Alexandrovich
See also DLB 272

Fadeev, Alexandr Alexandrovich
See Bulgya, Alexander Alexandrovich
See also EWL 3

Fadeyev, A.
See Bulgya, Alexander Alexandrovich

Fadeyev, Alexander .... **TCLC 53**
See Bulgya, Alexander Alexandrovich

Fagen, Donald 1948- .... **CLC 26**

Fainzilberg, Ilya Arnoldovich 1897-1937
See Ilf, Ilya
See also CA 120; 165

Fair, Ronald L. 1932- .... **CLC 18**
See also BW 1; CA 69-72; CANR 25; DLB
33

Fairbairn, Roger
See Carr, John Dickson

Fairbairns, Zoe (Ann) 1948- .... **CLC 32**
See also CA 103; CANR 21, 85; CN 4, 5,
6, 7

Fairfield, Flora
See Alcott, Louisa May

Fairman, Paul W. 1916-1977
See Queen, Ellery
See also CA 114; SFW 4

Falco, Gian
See Papini, Giovanni

Falconer, James
See Kirkup, James

French, Albert 1943- .... **CLC 86**
See also BW 3; CA 167
French, Antonia
See Kureishi, Hanif
French, Marilyn 1929- .. **CLC 10, 18, 60, 177**
See also BPFB 1; CA 69-72; CANR 3, 31, 134; CN 5, 6, 7; CPW; DAM DRAM, NOV, POP; FL 1:5; FW; INT CANR-31; MTCW 1, 2; MTFW 2005
French, Paul
See Asimov, Isaac
Freneau, Philip Morin 1752-1832 .. **NCLC 1, 111**
See also AMWS 2; DLB 37, 43; RGAL 4
Freud, Sigmund 1856-1939 .... **TCLC 52**
See also CA 115; 133; CANR 69; DLB 296; EW 8; EWL 3; LATS 1:1; MTCW 1, 2; MTFW 2005; NCFS 3; TWA
Freytag, Gustav 1816-1895 .... **NCLC 109**
See also DLB 129
Friedan, Betty (Naomi) 1921- .... **CLC 74**
See also CA 65-68; CANR 18, 45, 74; DLB 246; FW; MTCW 1, 2; MTFW 2005; NCFS 5
Friedlander, Saul 1932- .... **CLC 90**
See also CA 117; 130; CANR 72
Friedman, B(ernard) H(arper)
1926- .... **CLC 7**
See also CA 1-4R; CANR 3, 48
Friedman, Bruce Jay 1930- ...... **CLC 3, 5, 56**
See also CA 9-12R; CAD; CANR 25, 52, 101; CD 5, 6; CN 1, 2, 3, 4, 5, 6, 7; DLB 2, 28, 244; INT CANR-25; MAL 5; SSFS 18
Friel, Brian 1929- .... **CLC 5, 42, 59, 115; DC 8; SSC 76**
See also BRWS 5; CA 21-24R; CANR 33, 69, 131; CBD; CD 5, 6; DFS 11; DLB 13, 319; EWL 3; MTCW 1; RGEL 2; TEA
Friis-Baastad, Babbis Ellinor
1921-1970 .... **CLC 12**
See also CA 17-20R; 134; SATA 7
Frisch, Max (Rudolf) 1911-1991 ... **CLC 3, 9, 14, 18, 32, 44; TCLC 121**
See also CA 85-88; 134; CANR 32, 74; CD-WLB 2; DAM DRAM, NOV; DLB 69, 124; EW 13; EWL 3; MTCW 1, 2; MTFW 2005; RGWL 2, 3
Fromentin, Eugene (Samuel Auguste)
1820-1876 .... **NCLC 10, 125**
See also DLB 123; GFL 1789 to the Present
Frost, Frederick
See Faust, Frederick (Schiller)
Frost, Robert (Lee) 1874-1963 .. **CLC 1, 3, 4, 9, 10, 13, 15, 26, 34, 44; PC 1, 39; WLC**
See also AAYA 21; AMW; AMWR 1; CA 89-92; CANR 33; CDALB 1917-1929; CLR 67; DA; DA3; DAB; DAC; DAM MST, POET; DLB 54, 284; DLBD 7; EWL 3; EXPP; MAL 5; MTCW 1, 2; MTFW 2005; PAB; PFS 1, 2, 3, 4, 5, 6, 7, 10, 13; RGAL 4; SATA 14; TUS; WP; WYA
Froude, James Anthony
1818-1894 .... **NCLC 43**
See also DLB 18, 57, 144
Froy, Herald
See Waterhouse, Keith (Spencer)
Fry, Christopher 1907-2005 ... **CLC 2, 10, 14**
See also BRWS 3; CA 17-20R; 240; CAAS 23; CANR 9, 30, 74, 132; CBD; CD 5, 6; CP 1, 2, 3, 4, 5, 6, 7; DAM DRAM; DLB 13; EWL 3; MTCW 1, 2; MTFW 2005; RGEL 2; SATA 66; TEA
Frye, (Herman) Northrop
1912-1991 .... **CLC 24, 70; TCLC 165**
See also CA 5-8R; 133; CANR 8, 37; DLB 67, 68, 246; EWL 3; MTCW 1, 2; MTFW 2005; RGAL 4; TWA

Fuchs, Daniel 1909-1993 .... **CLC 8, 22**
See also CA 81-84; 142; CAAS 5; CANR 40; CN 1, 2, 3, 4, 5; DLB 9, 26, 28; DLBY 1993; MAL 5
Fuchs, Daniel 1934- .... **CLC 34**
See also CA 37-40R; CANR 14, 48
Fuentes, Carlos 1928- .. **CLC 3, 8, 10, 13, 22, 41, 60, 113; HLC 1; SSC 24; WLC**
See also AAYA 4, 45; AITN 2; BPFB 1; CA 69-72; CANR 10, 32, 68, 104, 138; CDWLB 3; CWW 2; DA; DA3; DAB; DAC; DAM MST, MULT, NOV; DLB 113; DNFS 2; EWL 3; HW 1, 2; LAIT 3; LATS 1:2; LAW; LAWS 1; LMFS 2; MTCW 1, 2; MTFW 2005; NFS 8; RGSF 2; RGWL 2, 3; TWA; WLIT 1
Fuentes, Gregorio Lopez y
See Lopez y Fuentes, Gregorio
Fuertes, Gloria 1918-1998 .... **PC 27**
See also CA 178, 180; DLB 108; HW 2; SATA 115
Fugard, (Harold) Athol 1932- . **CLC 5, 9, 14, 25, 40, 80, 211; DC 3**
See also AAYA 17; AFW; CA 85-88; CANR 32, 54, 118; CD 5, 6; DAM DRAM; DFS 3, 6, 10; DLB 225; DNFS 1, 2; EWL 3; LATS 1:2; MTCW 1; MTFW 2005; RGEL 2; WLIT 2
Fugard, Sheila 1932- .... **CLC 48**
See also CA 125
Fujiwara no Teika 1162-1241 .... **CMLC 73**
See also DLB 203
Fukuyama, Francis 1952- .... **CLC 131**
See also CA 140; CANR 72, 125
Fuller, Charles (H.), (Jr.) 1939- .... **BLC 2; CLC 25; DC 1**
See also BW 2; CA 108; 112; CAD; CANR 87; CD 5, 6; DAM DRAM, MULT; DFS 8; DLB 38, 266; EWL 3; INT CA-112; MAL 5; MTCW 1
Fuller, Henry Blake 1857-1929 .... **TCLC 103**
See also CA 108; 177; DLB 12; RGAL 4
Fuller, John (Leopold) 1937- .... **CLC 62**
See also CA 21-24R; CANR 9, 44; CP 1, 2, 3, 4, 5, 6, 7; DLB 40
Fuller, Margaret
See Ossoli, Sarah Margaret (Fuller)
See also AMWS 2; DLB 183, 223, 239; FL 1:3
Fuller, Roy (Broadbent) 1912-1991 ... **CLC 4, 28**
See also BRWS 7; CA 5-8R; 135; CAAS 10; CANR 53, 83; CN 1, 2, 3, 4, 5; CP 1, 2, 3, 4; CWRI 5; DLB 15, 20; EWL 3; RGEL 2; SATA 87
Fuller, Sarah Margaret
See Ossoli, Sarah Margaret (Fuller)
Fuller, Sarah Margaret
See Ossoli, Sarah Margaret (Fuller)
See also DLB 1, 59, 73
Fuller, Thomas 1608-1661 .... **LC 111**
See also DLB 151
Fulton, Alice 1952- .... **CLC 52**
See also CA 116; CANR 57, 88; CP 7; CWP; DLB 193
Furphy, Joseph 1843-1912 .... **TCLC 25**
See Collins, Tom
See also CA 163; DLB 230; EWL 3; RGEL 2
Fuson, Robert H(enderson) 1927- .... **CLC 70**
See also CA 89-92; CANR 103
Fussell, Paul 1924- .... **CLC 74**
See also BEST 90:1; CA 17-20R; CANR 8, 21, 35, 69, 135; INT CANR-21; MTCW 1, 2; MTFW 2005
Futabatei, Shimei 1864-1909 .... **TCLC 44**
See Futabatei Shimei
See also CA 162; MJW

Futabatei Shimei
See Futabatei, Shimei
See also DLB 180; EWL 3
Futrelle, Jacques 1875-1912 .... **TCLC 19**
See also CA 113; 155; CMW 4
Gaboriau, Emile 1835-1873 .... **NCLC 14**
See also CMW 4; MSW
Gadda, Carlo Emilio 1893-1973 ...... **CLC 11; TCLC 144**
See also CA 89-92; DLB 177; EWL 3; WLIT 7
Gaddis, William 1922-1998 ... **CLC 1, 3, 6, 8, 10, 19, 43, 86**
See also AMWS 4; BPFB 1; CA 17-20R; 172; CANR 21, 48; CN 1, 2, 3, 4, 5, 6; DLB 2, 278; EWL 3; MAL 5; MTCW 1, 2; MTFW 2005; RGAL 4
Gaelique, Moruen le
See Jacob, (Cyprien-)Max
Gage, Walter
See Inge, William (Motter)
Gaiman, Neil (Richard) 1960- .... **CLC 195**
See also AAYA 19, 42; CA 133; CANR 81, 129; DLB 261; HGG; MTFW 2005; SATA 85, 146; SFW 4; SUFW 2
Gaines, Ernest J(ames) 1933- .. **BLC 2; CLC 3, 11, 18, 86, 181; SSC 68**
See also AAYA 18; AFAW 1, 2; AITN 1; BPFB 2; BW 2, 3; BYA 6; CA 9-12R; CANR 6, 24, 42, 75, 126; CDALB 1968-1988; CLR 62; CN 1, 2, 3, 4, 5, 6, 7; CSW; DA3; DAM MULT; DLB 2, 33, 152; DLBY 1980; EWL 3; EXPN; LAIT 5; LATS 1:2; MAL 5; MTCW 1, 2; MTFW 2005; NFS 5, 7, 16; RGAL 4; RGSF 2; RHW; SATA 86; SSFS 5; YAW
Gaitskill, Mary (Lawrence) 1954- .... **CLC 69**
See also CA 128; CANR 61; DLB 244; TCLE 1:1
Gaius Suetonius Tranquillus
See Suetonius
Galdos, Benito Perez
See Perez Galdos, Benito
See also EW 7
Gale, Zona 1874-1938 .... **TCLC 7**
See also CA 105; 153; CANR 84; DAM DRAM; DFS 17; DLB 9, 78, 228; RGAL 4
Galeano, Eduardo (Hughes) 1940- . **CLC 72; HLCS 1**
See also CA 29-32R; CANR 13, 32, 100; HW 1
Galiano, Juan Valera y Alcala
See Valera y Alcala-Galiano, Juan
Galilei, Galileo 1564-1642 .... **LC 45**
Gallagher, Tess 1943- .... **CLC 18, 63; PC 9**
See also CA 106; CP 3, 4, 5, 6, 7; CWP; DAM POET; DLB 120, 212, 244; PFS 16
Gallant, Mavis 1922- ..... **CLC 7, 18, 38, 172; SSC 5, 78**
See also CA 69-72; CANR 29, 69, 117; CCA 1; CN 1, 2, 3, 4, 5, 6, 7; DAC; DAM MST; DLB 53; EWL 3; MTCW 1, 2; MTFW 2005; RGEL 2; RGSF 2
Gallant, Roy A(rthur) 1924- .... **CLC 17**
See also CA 5-8R; CANR 4, 29, 54, 117; CLR 30; MAICYA 1, 2; SATA 4, 68, 110
Gallico, Paul (William) 1897-1976 ...... **CLC 2**
See also AITN 1; CA 5-8R; 69-72; CANR 23; CN 1, 2; DLB 9, 171; FANT; MAICYA 1, 2; SATA 13
Gallo, Max Louis 1932- .... **CLC 95**
See also CA 85-88
Gallois, Lucien
See Desnos, Robert
Gallup, Ralph
See Whitemore, Hugh (John)

Gent, Peter 1942- .... **CLC 29**
    See also AITN 1; CA 89-92; DLBY 1982
Gentile, Giovanni 1875-1944 .... **TCLC 96**
    See also CA 119
Gentlewoman in New England, A
    See Bradstreet, Anne
Gentlewoman in Those Parts, A
    See Bradstreet, Anne
Geoffrey of Monmouth c.
    1100-1155 .... **CMLC 44**
    See also DLB 146; TEA
George, Jean
    See George, Jean Craighead
George, Jean Craighead 1919- .... **CLC 35**
    See also AAYA 8; BYA 2, 4; CA 5-8R;
    CANR 25; CLR 1; 80; DLB 52; JRDA;
    MAICYA 1, 2; SATA 2, 68, 124; WYA;
    YAW
George, Stefan (Anton) 1868-1933 . **TCLC 2,**
    14
    See also CA 104; 193; EW 8; EWL 3
Georges, Georges Martin
    See Simenon, Georges (Jacques Christian)
Gerald of Wales c. 1146-c. 1223 ... **CMLC 60**
Gerhardi, William Alexander
    See Gerhardie, William Alexander
Gerhardie, William Alexander
    1895-1977 .... **CLC 5**
    See also CA 25-28R; 73-76; CANR 18; CN
    1, 2; DLB 36; RGEL 2
Gerson, Jean 1363-1429 .... **LC 77**
    See also DLB 208
Gersonides 1288-1344 .... **CMLC 49**
    See also DLB 115
Gerstler, Amy 1956- .... **CLC 70**
    See also CA 146; CANR 99
Gertler, T. .... **CLC 34**
    See also CA 116; 121
Gertsen, Aleksandr Ivanovich
    See Herzen, Aleksandr Ivanovich
Ghalib .... **NCLC 39, 78**
    See Ghalib, Asadullah Khan
Ghalib, Asadullah Khan 1797-1869
    See Ghalib
    See also DAM POET; RGWL 2, 3
Ghelderode, Michel de 1898-1962 ..... **CLC 6,**
    11; DC 15
    See also CA 85-88; CANR 40, 77; DAM
    DRAM; DLB 321; EW 11; EWL 3; TWA
Ghiselin, Brewster 1903-2001 .... **CLC 23**
    See also CA 13-16R; CAAS 10; CANR 13;
    CP 1, 2, 3, 4, 5, 6, 7
Ghose, Aurabinda 1872-1950 .... **TCLC 63**
    See Ghose, Aurobindo
    See also CA 163
Ghose, Aurobindo
    See Ghose, Aurabinda
    See also EWL 3
Ghose, Zulfikar 1935- .... **CLC 42, 200**
    See also CA 65-68; CANR 67; CN 1, 2, 3,
    4, 5, 6, 7; CP 1, 2, 3, 4, 5, 6, 7; EWL 3
Ghosh, Amitav 1956- .... **CLC 44, 153**
    See also CA 147; CANR 80; CN 6, 7;
    WWE 1
Giacosa, Giuseppe 1847-1906 .... **TCLC 7**
    See also CA 104
Gibb, Lee
    See Waterhouse, Keith (Spencer)
Gibbon, Edward 1737-1794 .... **LC 97**
    See also BRW 3; DLB 104; RGEL 2
Gibbon, Lewis Grassic .... **TCLC 4**
    See Mitchell, James Leslie
    See also RGEL 2
Gibbons, Kaye 1960- .... **CLC 50, 88, 145**
    See also AAYA 34; AMWS 10; CA 151;
    CANR 75, 127; CN 7; CSW; DA3; DAM
    POP; DLB 292; MTCW 2; MTFW 2005;
    NFS 3; RGAL 4; SATA 117

Gibran, Kahlil 1883-1931 . **PC 9; TCLC 1, 9**
    See also CA 104; 150; DA3; DAM POET,
    POP; EWL 3; MTCW 2; WLIT 6
Gibran, Khalil
    See Gibran, Kahlil
Gibson, Mel 1956- .... **CLC 215**
Gibson, William 1914- .... **CLC 23**
    See also CA 9-12R; CAD; CANR 9, 42, 75,
    125; CD 5, 6; DA; DAB; DAC; DAM
    DRAM, MST; DFS 2; DLB 7; LAIT 2;
    MAL 5; MTCW 2; MTFW 2005; SATA
    66; YAW
Gibson, William (Ford) 1948- ... **CLC 39, 63,**
    186, 192; SSC 52
    See also AAYA 12, 59; BPFB 2; CA 126;
    133; CANR 52, 90, 106; CN 6, 7; CPW;
    DA3; DAM POP; DLB 251; MTCW 2;
    MTFW 2005; SCFW 2; SFW 4
Gide, Andre (Paul Guillaume)
    1869-1951 ..... **SSC 13; TCLC 5, 12, 36;**
    WLC
    See also CA 104; 124; DA; DA3; DAB;
    DAC; DAM MST, NOV; DLB 65, 321;
    EW 8; EWL 3; GFL 1789 to the Present;
    MTCW 1, 2; MTFW 2005; NFS 21;
    RGSF 2; RGWL 2, 3; TWA
Gifford, Barry (Colby) 1946- .... **CLC 34**
    See also CA 65-68; CANR 9, 30, 40, 90
Gilbert, Frank
    See De Voto, Bernard (Augustine)
Gilbert, W(illiam) S(chwenck)
    1836-1911 .... **TCLC 3**
    See also CA 104; 173; DAM DRAM, POET;
    RGEL 2; SATA 36
Gilbreth, Frank B(unker), Jr.
    1911-2001 .... **CLC 17**
    See also CA 9-12R; SATA 2
Gilchrist, Ellen (Louise) 1935- .. **CLC 34, 48,**
    143; SSC 14, 63
    See also BPFB 2; CA 113; 116; CANR 41,
    61, 104; CN 4, 5, 6, 7; CPW; CSW; DAM
    POP; DLB 130; EWL 3; EXPS; MTCW
    1, 2; MTFW 2005; RGAL 4; RGSF 2;
    SSFS 9
Giles, Molly 1942- .... **CLC 39**
    See also CA 126; CANR 98
Gill, Eric .... **TCLC 85**
    See Gill, (Arthur) Eric (Rowton Peter
    Joseph)
Gill, (Arthur) Eric (Rowton Peter Joseph)
    1882-1940
    See Gill, Eric
    See also CA 120; DLB 98
Gill, Patrick
    See Creasey, John
Gillette, Douglas .... **CLC 70**
Gilliam, Terry (Vance) 1940- .... **CLC 21, 141**
    See Monty Python
    See also AAYA 19, 59; CA 108; 113; CANR
    35; INT CA-113
Gillian, Jerry
    See Gilliam, Terry (Vance)
Gilliatt, Penelope (Ann Douglass)
    1932-1993 .... **CLC 2, 10, 13, 53**
    See also AITN 2; CA 13-16R; 141; CANR
    49; CN 1, 2, 3, 4, 5; DLB 14
Gilligan, Carol 1936- .... **CLC 208**
    See also CA 142; CANR 121; FW
Gilman, Charlotte (Anna) Perkins (Stetson)
    1860-1935 ...... **SSC 13, 62; TCLC 9, 37,**
    117
    See also AMWS 11; BYA 11; CA 106; 150;
    DLB 221; EXPS; FL 1:5; FW; HGG;
    LAIT 2; MAWW; MTCW 2; MTFW
    2005; RGAL 4; RGSF 2; SFW 4; SSFS 1,
    18

Gilmour, David 1946- .... **CLC 35**
Gilpin, William 1724-1804 .... **NCLC 30**
Gilray, J. D.
    See Mencken, H(enry) L(ouis)
Gilroy, Frank D(aniel) 1925- .... **CLC 2**
    See also CA 81-84; CAD; CANR 32, 64,
    86; CD 5, 6; DFS 17; DLB 7
Gilstrap, John 1957(?)- .... **CLC 99**
    See also AAYA 67; CA 160; CANR 101
Ginsberg, Allen 1926-1997 .... **CLC 1, 2, 3, 4,**
    6, 13, 36, 69, 109; PC 4, 47; TCLC
    120; WLC
    See also AAYA 33; AITN 1; AMWC 1;
    AMWS 2; BG 1:2; CA 1-4R; 157; CANR
    2, 41, 63, 95; CDALB 1941-1968; CP 1,
    2, 3, 4, 5, 6; DA; DA3; DAB; DAC; DAM
    MST, POET; DLB 5, 16, 169, 237; EWL
    3; GLL 1; LMFS 2; MAL 5; MTCW 1, 2;
    MTFW 2005; PAB; PFS 5; RGAL 4;
    TUS; WP
Ginzburg, Eugenia .... **CLC 59**
    See Ginzburg, Evgeniia
Ginzburg, Evgeniia 1904-1977
    See Ginzburg, Eugenia
    See also DLB 302
Ginzburg, Natalia 1916-1991 .... **CLC 5, 11,**
    54, 70; SSC 65; TCLC 156
    See also CA 85-88; 135; CANR 33; DFS
    14; DLB 177; EW 13; EWL 3; MTCW 1,
    2; MTFW 2005; RGWL 2, 3
Giono, Jean 1895-1970 .... **CLC 4, 11; TCLC**
    124
    See also CA 45-48; 29-32R; CANR 2, 35;
    DLB 72, 321; EWL 3; GFL 1789 to the
    Present; MTCW 1; RGWL 2, 3
Giovanni, Nikki 1943- ...... **BLC 2; CLC 2, 4,**
    19, 64, 117; PC 19; WLCS
    See also AAYA 22; AITN 1; BW 2, 3; CA
    29-32R; CAAS 6; CANR 18, 41, 60, 91,
    130; CDALBS; CLR 6, 73; CP 2, 3, 4, 5,
    6, 7; CSW; CWP; CWRI 5; DA; DA3;
    DAB; DAC; DAM MST, MULT, POET;
    DLB 5, 41; EWL 3; EXPP; INT CANR-
    18; MAICYA 1, 2; MAL 5; MTCW 1, 2;
    MTFW 2005; PFS 17; RGAL 4; SATA
    24, 107; TUS; YAW
Giovene, Andrea 1904-1998 .... **CLC 7**
    See also CA 85-88
Gippius, Zinaida (Nikolaevna) 1869-1945
    See Hippius, Zinaida (Nikolaevna)
    See also CA 106; 212
Giraudoux, Jean(-Hippolyte)
    1882-1944 .... **TCLC 2, 7**
    See also CA 104; 196; DAM DRAM; DLB
    65, 321; EW 9; EWL 3; GFL 1789 to the
    Present; RGWL 2, 3; TWA
Gironella, Jose Maria (Pous)
    1917-2003 .... **CLC 11**
    See also CA 101; 212; EWL 3; RGWL 2, 3
Gissing, George (Robert)
    1857-1903 .... **SSC 37; TCLC 3, 24, 47**
    See also BRW 5; CA 105; 167; DLB 18,
    135, 184; RGEL 2; TEA
Gitlin, Todd 1943- .... **CLC 201**
    See also CA 29-32R; CANR 25, 50, 88
Giurlani, Aldo
    See Palazzeschi, Aldo
Gladkov, Fedor Vasil'evich
    See Gladkov, Fyodor (Vasilyevich)
    See also DLB 272
Gladkov, Fyodor (Vasilyevich)
    1883-1958 .... **TCLC 27**
    See Gladkov, Fedor Vasil'evich
    See also CA 170; EWL 3
Glancy, Diane 1941- .... **CLC 210; NNAL**
    See also CA 136; 225; CAAE 225; CAAS
    24; CANR 87; DLB 175

Gordone, Charles 1925-1995 .. **CLC 1, 4; DC 8**
See also BW 1, 3; CA 93-96, 180; 150; CAAE 180; CAD; CANR 55; DAM DRAM; DLB 7; INT CA-93-96; MTCW 1

Gore, Catherine 1800-1861 .... **NCLC 65**
See also DLB 116; RGEL 2

Gorenko, Anna Andreevna
See Akhmatova, Anna

Gorky, Maxim .... **SSC 28; TCLC 8; WLC**
See Peshkov, Alexei Maximovich
See also DAB; DFS 9; DLB 295; EW 8; EWL 3; TWA

Goryan, Sirak
See Saroyan, William

Gosse, Edmund (William)
1849-1928 .... **TCLC 28**
See also CA 117; DLB 57, 144, 184; RGEL 2

Gotlieb, Phyllis (Fay Bloom) 1926- .. **CLC 18**
See also CA 13-16R; CANR 7, 135; CN 7; CP 1, 2, 3, 4; DLB 88, 251; SFW 4

Gottesman, S. D.
See Kornbluth, C(yril) M.; Pohl, Frederik

Gottfried von Strassburg fl. c.
1170-1215 .... **CMLC 10**
See also CDWLB 2; DLB 138; EW 1; RGWL 2, 3

Gotthelf, Jeremias 1797-1854 .... **NCLC 117**
See also DLB 133; RGWL 2, 3

Gottschalk, Laura Riding
See Jackson, Laura (Riding)

Gould, Lois 1932(?)-2002 .... **CLC 4, 10**
See also CA 77-80; 208; CANR 29; MTCW 1

Gould, Stephen Jay 1941-2002 .... **CLC 163**
See also AAYA 26; BEST 90:2; CA 77-80; 205; CANR 10, 27, 56, 75, 125; CPW; INT CANR-27; MTCW 1, 2; MTFW 2005

Gourmont, Remy(-Marie-Charles) de
1858-1915 .... **TCLC 17**
See also CA 109; 150; GFL 1789 to the Present; MTCW 2

Gournay, Marie le Jars de
See de Gournay, Marie le Jars

Govier, Katherine 1948- .... **CLC 51**
See also CA 101; CANR 18, 40, 128; CCA 1

Gower, John c. 1330-1408 .... **LC 76; PC 59**
See also BRW 1; DLB 146; RGEL 2

Goyen, (Charles) William
1915-1983 .... **CLC 5, 8, 14, 40**
See also AITN 2; CA 5-8R; 110; CANR 6, 71; CN 1, 2, 3; DLB 2, 218; DLBY 1983; EWL 3; INT CANR-6; MAL 5

Goytisolo, Juan 1931- .... **CLC 5, 10, 23, 133; HLC 1**
See also CA 85-88; CANR 32, 61, 131; CWW 2; DAM MULT; DLB 322; EWL 3; GLL 2; HW 1, 2; MTCW 1, 2; MTFW 2005

Gozzano, Guido 1883-1916 .... **PC 10**
See also CA 154; DLB 114; EWL 3

Gozzi, (Conte) Carlo 1720-1806 .... **NCLC 23**

Grabbe, Christian Dietrich
1801-1836 .... **NCLC 2**
See also DLB 133; RGWL 2, 3

Grace, Patricia Frances 1937- .... **CLC 56**
See also CA 176; CANR 118; CN 4, 5, 6, 7; EWL 3; RGSF 2

Gracian y Morales, Baltasar
1601-1658 .... **LC 15**

Gracq, Julien .... **CLC 11, 48**
See Poirier, Louis
See also CWW 2; DLB 83; GFL 1789 to the Present

Grade, Chaim 1910-1982 .... **CLC 10**
See also CA 93-96; 107; EWL 3

Graduate of Oxford, A
See Ruskin, John

Grafton, Garth
See Duncan, Sara Jeannette

Grafton, Sue 1940- .... **CLC 163**
See also AAYA 11, 49; BEST 90:3; CA 108; CANR 31, 55, 111, 134; CMW 4; CPW; CSW; DA3; DAM POP; DLB 226; FW; MSW; MTFW 2005

Graham, John
See Phillips, David Graham

Graham, Jorie 1950- .... **CLC 48, 118; PC 59**
See also AAYA 67; CA 111; CANR 63, 118; CP 4, 5, 6, 7; CWP; DLB 120; EWL 3; MTFW 2005; PFS 10, 17; TCLE 1:1

Graham, R(obert) B(ontine) Cunninghame
See Cunninghame Graham, Robert (Gallnigad) Bontine
See also DLB 98, 135, 174; RGEL 2; RGSF 2

Graham, Robert
See Haldeman, Joe (William)

Graham, Tom
See Lewis, (Harry) Sinclair

Graham, W(illiam) S(idney)
1918-1986 .... **CLC 29**
See also BRWS 7; CA 73-76; 118; CP 1, 2, 3, 4; DLB 20; RGEL 2

Graham, Winston (Mawdsley)
1910-2003 .... **CLC 23**
See also CA 49-52; 218; CANR 2, 22, 45, 66; CMW 4; CN 1, 2, 3, 4, 5, 6, 7; DLB 77; RHW

Grahame, Kenneth 1859-1932 ...... **TCLC 64, 136**
See also BYA 5; CA 108; 136; CANR 80; CLR 5; CWRI 5; DA3; DAB; DLB 34, 141, 178; FANT; MAICYA 1, 2; MTCW 2; NFS 20; RGEL 2; SATA 100; TEA; WCH; YABC 1

Granger, Darius John
See Marlowe, Stephen

Granin, Daniil 1918- .... **CLC 59**
See also DLB 302

Granovsky, Timofei Nikolaevich
1813-1855 .... **NCLC 75**
See also DLB 198

Grant, Skeeter
See Spiegelman, Art

Granville-Barker, Harley
1877-1946 .... **TCLC 2**
See Barker, Harley Granville
See also CA 104; 204; DAM DRAM; RGEL 2

Granzotto, Gianni
See Granzotto, Giovanni Battista

Granzotto, Giovanni Battista
1914-1985 .... **CLC 70**
See also CA 166

Grass, Guenter (Wilhelm) 1927- ... **CLC 1, 2, 4, 6, 11, 15, 22, 32, 49, 88, 207; WLC**
See Grass, Gunter (Wilhelm)
See also BPFB 2; CA 13-16R; CANR 20, 75, 93, 133; CDWLB 2; DA; DA3; DAB; DAC; DAM MST, NOV; DLB 75, 124; EW 13; EWL 3; MTCW 1, 2; MTFW 2005; RGWL 2, 3; TWA

Grass, Gunter (Wilhelm)
See Grass, Guenter (Wilhelm)
See also CWW 2

Gratton, Thomas
See Hulme, T(homas) E(rnest)

Grau, Shirley Ann 1929- .... **CLC 4, 9, 146; SSC 15**
See also CA 89-92; CANR 22, 69; CN 1, 2, 3, 4, 5, 6, 7; CSW; DLB 2, 218; INT CA-89-92; CANR-22; MTCW 1

Gravel, Fern
See Hall, James Norman

Graver, Elizabeth 1964- .... **CLC 70**
See also CA 135; CANR 71, 129

Graves, Richard Perceval
1895-1985 .... **CLC 44**
See also CA 65-68; CANR 9, 26, 51

Graves, Robert (von Ranke)
1895-1985 .. **CLC 1, 2, 6, 11, 39, 44, 45; PC 6**
See also BPFB 2; BRW 7; BYA 4; CA 5-8R; 117; CANR 5, 36; CDBLB 1914-1945; CN 1, 2, 3; CP 1, 2, 3, 4; DA3; DAB; DAC; DAM MST, POET; DLB 20, 100, 191; DLBD 18; DLBY 1985; EWL 3; LATS 1:1; MTCW 1, 2; MTFW 2005; NCFS 2; NFS 21; RGEL 2; RHW; SATA 45; TEA

Graves, Valerie
See Bradley, Marion Zimmer

Gray, Alasdair (James) 1934- .... **CLC 41**
See also BRWS 9; CA 126; CANR 47, 69, 106, 140; CN 4, 5, 6, 7; DLB 194, 261, 319; HGG; INT CA-126; MTCW 1, 2; MTFW 2005; RGSF 2; SUFW 2

Gray, Amlin 1946- .... **CLC 29**
See also CA 138

Gray, Francine du Plessix 1930- ..... **CLC 22, 153**
See also BEST 90:3; CA 61-64; CAAS 2; CANR 11, 33, 75, 81; DAM NOV; INT CANR-11; MTCW 1, 2; MTFW 2005

Gray, John (Henry) 1866-1934 ...... **TCLC 19**
See also CA 119; 162; RGEL 2

Gray, John Lee
See Jakes, John (William)

Gray, Simon (James Holliday)
1936- .... **CLC 9, 14, 36**
See also AITN 1; CA 21-24R; CAAS 3; CANR 32, 69; CBD; CD 5, 6; CN 1, 2, 3; DLB 13; EWL 3; MTCW 1; RGEL 2

Gray, Spalding 1941-2004 .... **CLC 49, 112; DC 7**
See also AAYA 62; CA 128; 225; CAD; CANR 74, 138; CD 5, 6; CPW; DAM POP; MTCW 2; MTFW 2005

Gray, Thomas 1716-1771 .... **LC 4, 40; PC 2; WLC**
See also BRW 3; CDBLB 1660-1789; DA; DA3; DAB; DAC; DAM MST; DLB 109; EXPP; PAB; PFS 9; RGEL 2; TEA; WP

Grayson, David
See Baker, Ray Stannard

Grayson, Richard (A.) 1951- .... **CLC 38**
See also CA 85-88; 210; CAAE 210; CANR 14, 31, 57; DLB 234

Greeley, Andrew M(oran) 1928- ...... **CLC 28**
See also BPFB 2; CA 5-8R; CAAS 7; CANR 7, 43, 69, 104, 136; CMW 4; CPW; DA3; DAM POP; MTCW 1, 2; MTFW 2005

Green, Anna Katharine
1846-1935 .... **TCLC 63**
See also CA 112; 159; CMW 4; DLB 202, 221; MSW

Green, Brian
See Card, Orson Scott

Green, Hannah
See Greenberg, Joanne (Goldenberg)

Green, Hannah 1927(?)-1996 .... **CLC 3**
See also CA 73-76; CANR 59, 93; NFS 10

Green, Henry .... **CLC 2, 13, 97**
See Yorke, Henry Vincent
See also BRWS 2; CA 175; DLB 15; EWL 3; RGEL 2

Green, Julian .... **CLC 3, 11, 77**
See Green, Julien (Hartridge)
See also EWL 3; GFL 1789 to the Present; MTCW 2

Guillen, Nicolas (Cristobal)
1902-1989 .... **BLC 2; CLC 48, 79; HLC 1; PC 23**
See also BW 2; CA 116; 125; 129; CANR 84; DAM MST, MULT, POET; DLB 283; EWL 3; HW 1; LAW; RGWL 2, 3; WP

Guillen y Alvarez, Jorge
See Guillen, Jorge

Guillevic, (Eugene) 1907-1997 .... **CLC 33**
See also CA 93-96; CWW 2

Guillois
See Desnos, Robert

Guillois, Valentin
See Desnos, Robert

Guimaraes Rosa, Joao 1908-1967 .... **HLCS 2**
See Rosa, Joao Guimaraes
See also CA 175; LAW; RGSF 2; RGWL 2, 3

Guiney, Louise Imogen
1861-1920 .... **TCLC 41**
See also CA 160; DLB 54; RGAL 4

Guinizelli, Guido c. 1230-1276 ...... **CMLC 49**
See Guinizzelli, Guido

Guinizzelli, Guido
See Guinizelli, Guido
See also WLIT 7

Guiraldes, Ricardo (Guillermo)
1886-1927 .... **TCLC 39**
See also CA 131; EWL 3; HW 1; LAW; MTCW 1

Gumilev, Nikolai (Stepanovich)
1886-1921 .... **TCLC 60**
See Gumilyov, Nikolay Stepanovich
See also CA 165; DLB 295

Gumilyov, Nikolay Stepanovich
See Gumilev, Nikolai (Stepanovich)
See also EWL 3

Gump, P. Q.
See Card, Orson Scott

Gunesekera, Romesh 1954- .... **CLC 91**
See also BRWS 10; CA 159; CANR 140; CN 6, 7; DLB 267

Gunn, Bill .... **CLC 5**
See Gunn, William Harrison
See also DLB 38

Gunn, Thom(son William)
1929-2004 . **CLC 3, 6, 18, 32, 81; PC 26**
See also BRWS 4; CA 17-20R; 227; CANR 9, 33, 116; CDBLB 1960 to Present; CP 1, 2, 3, 4, 5, 6, 7; DAM POET; DLB 27; INT CANR-33; MTCW 1; PFS 9; RGEL 2

Gunn, William Harrison 1934(?)-1989
See Gunn, Bill
See also AITN 1; BW 1, 3; CA 13-16R; 128; CANR 12, 25, 76

Gunn Allen, Paula
See Allen, Paula Gunn

Gunnars, Kristjana 1948- .... **CLC 69**
See also CA 113; CCA 1; CP 7; CWP; DLB 60

Gunter, Erich
See Eich, Gunter

Gurdjieff, G(eorgei) I(vanovich)
1877(?)-1949 .... **TCLC 71**
See also CA 157

Gurganus, Allan 1947- .... **CLC 70**
See also BEST 90:1; CA 135; CANR 114; CN 6, 7; CPW; CSW; DAM POP; GLL 1

Gurney, A. R.
See Gurney, A(lbert) R(amsdell), Jr.
See also DLB 266

Gurney, A(lbert) R(amsdell), Jr.
1930- .... **CLC 32, 50, 54**
See Gurney, A. R.
See also AMWS 5; CA 77-80; CAD; CANR 32, 64, 121; CD 5, 6; DAM DRAM; EWL 3

Gurney, Ivor (Bertie) 1890-1937 ... **TCLC 33**
See also BRW 6; CA 167; DLBY 2002; PAB; RGEL 2

Gurney, Peter
See Gurney, A(lbert) R(amsdell), Jr.

Guro, Elena (Genrikhovna)
1877-1913 .... **TCLC 56**
See also DLB 295

Gustafson, James M(oody) 1925- ... **CLC 100**
See also CA 25-28R; CANR 37

Gustafson, Ralph (Barker)
1909-1995 .... **CLC 36**
See also CA 21-24R; CANR 8, 45, 84; CP 1, 2, 3, 4; DLB 88; RGEL 2

Gut, Gom
See Simenon, Georges (Jacques Christian)

Guterson, David 1956- .... **CLC 91**
See also CA 132; CANR 73, 126; CN 7; DLB 292; MTCW 2; MTFW 2005; NFS 13

Guthrie, A(lfred) B(ertram), Jr.
1901-1991 .... **CLC 23**
See also CA 57-60; 134; CANR 24; CN 1, 2, 3; DLB 6, 212; MAL 5; SATA 62; SATA-Obit 67; TCWW 1, 2

Guthrie, Isobel
See Grieve, C(hristopher) M(urray)

Guthrie, Woodrow Wilson 1912-1967
See Guthrie, Woody
See also CA 113; 93-96

Guthrie, Woody .... **CLC 35**
See Guthrie, Woodrow Wilson
See also DLB 303; LAIT 3

Gutierrez Najera, Manuel
1859-1895 .... **HLCS 2; NCLC 133**
See also DLB 290; LAW

Guy, Rosa (Cuthbert) 1925- .... **CLC 26**
See also AAYA 4, 37; BW 2; CA 17-20R; CANR 14, 34, 83; CLR 13; DLB 33; DNFS 1; JRDA; MAICYA 1, 2; SATA 14, 62, 122; YAW

Gwendolyn
See Bennett, (Enoch) Arnold

H. D. .... **CLC 3, 8, 14, 31, 34, 73; PC 5**
See Doolittle, Hilda
See also FL 1:5

H. de V.
See Buchan, John

Haavikko, Paavo Juhani 1931- ... **CLC 18, 34**
See also CA 106; CWW 2; EWL 3

Habbema, Koos
See Heijermans, Herman

Habermas, Juergen 1929- .... **CLC 104**
See also CA 109; CANR 85; DLB 242

Habermas, Jurgen
See Habermas, Juergen

Hacker, Marilyn 1942- ...... **CLC 5, 9, 23, 72, 91; PC 47**
See also CA 77-80; CANR 68, 129; CP 3, 4, 5, 6, 7; CWP; DAM POET; DLB 120, 282; FW; GLL 2; MAL 5; PFS 19

Hadewijch of Antwerp fl. 1250- ... **CMLC 61**
See also RGWL 3

Hadrian 76-138 .... **CMLC 52**

Haeckel, Ernst Heinrich (Philipp August)
1834-1919 .... **TCLC 83**
See also CA 157

Hafiz c. 1326-1389(?) .... **CMLC 34**
See also RGWL 2, 3; WLIT 6

Hagedorn, Jessica T(arahata)
1949- .... **CLC 185**
See also CA 139; CANR 69; CWP; DLB 312; RGAL 4

Haggard, H(enry) Rider
1856-1925 .... **TCLC 11**
See also BRWS 3; BYA 4, 5; CA 108; 148; CANR 112; DLB 70, 156, 174, 178; FANT; LMFS 1; MTCW 2; RGEL 2; RHW; SATA 16; SCFW 1, 2; SFW 4; SUFW 1; WLIT 4

Hagiosy, L.
See Larbaud, Valery (Nicolas)

Hagiwara, Sakutaro 1886-1942 .... **PC 18; TCLC 60**
See Hagiwara Sakutaro
See also CA 154; RGWL 3

Hagiwara Sakutaro
See Hagiwara, Sakutaro
See also EWL 3

Haig, Fenil
See Ford, Ford Madox

Haig-Brown, Roderick (Langmere)
1908-1976 .... **CLC 21**
See also CA 5-8R; 69-72; CANR 4, 38, 83; CLR 31; CWRI 5; DLB 88; MAICYA 1, 2; SATA 12; TCWW 2

Haight, Rip
See Carpenter, John (Howard)

Hailey, Arthur 1920-2004 .... **CLC 5**
See also AITN 2; BEST 90:3; BPFB 2; CA 1-4R; 233; CANR 2, 36, 75; CCA 1; CN 1, 2, 3, 4, 5, 6, 7; CPW; DAM NOV, POP; DLB 88; DLBY 1982; MTCW 1, 2; MTFW 2005

Hailey, Elizabeth Forsythe 1938- ..... **CLC 40**
See also CA 93-96, 188; CAAE 188; CAAS 1; CANR 15, 48; INT CANR-15

Haines, John (Meade) 1924- .... **CLC 58**
See also AMWS 12; CA 17-20R; CANR 13, 34; CP 1, 2, 3, 4; CSW; DLB 5, 212; TCLE 1:1

Hakluyt, Richard 1552-1616 .... **LC 31**
See also DLB 136; RGEL 2

Haldeman, Joe (William) 1943- .... **CLC 61**
See Graham, Robert
See also AAYA 38; CA 53-56, 179; CAAE 179; CAAS 25; CANR 6, 70, 72, 130; DLB 8; INT CANR-6; SCFW 2; SFW 4

Hale, Janet Campbell 1947- .... **NNAL**
See also CA 49-52; CANR 45, 75; DAM MULT; DLB 175; MTCW 2; MTFW 2005

Hale, Sarah Josepha (Buell)
1788-1879 .... **NCLC 75**
See also DLB 1, 42, 73, 243

Halevy, Elie 1870-1937 .... **TCLC 104**

Haley, Alex(ander Murray Palmer)
1921-1992 .... **BLC 2; CLC 8, 12, 76; TCLC 147**
See also AAYA 26; BPFB 2; BW 2, 3; CA 77-80; 136; CANR 61; CDALBS; CPW; CSW; DA; DA3; DAB; DAC; DAM MST, MULT, POP; DLB 38; LAIT 5; MTCW 1, 2; NFS 9

Haliburton, Thomas Chandler
1796-1865 .... **NCLC 15, 149**
See also DLB 11, 99; RGEL 2; RGSF 2

Hall, Donald (Andrew, Jr.) 1928- ...... **CLC 1, 13, 37, 59, 151**
See also AAYA 63; CA 5-8R; CAAS 7; CANR 2, 44, 64, 106, 133; CP 1, 2, 3, 4, 5, 6, 7; DAM POET; DLB 5; MAL 5; MTCW 2; MTFW 2005; RGAL 4; SATA 23, 97

Hall, Frederic Sauser
See Sauser-Hall, Frederic

Hall, James
See Kuttner, Henry

Hall, James Norman 1887-1951 ..... **TCLC 23**
See also CA 123; 173; LAIT 1; RHW 1; SATA 21

Hall, Joseph 1574-1656 .... **LC 91**
See also DLB 121, 151; RGEL 2

Harrison, Elizabeth (Allen) Cavanna
1909-2001
See Cavanna, Betty
See also CA 9-12R; 200; CANR 6, 27, 85, 104, 121; MAICYA 2; SATA 142; YAW

Harrison, Harry (Max) 1925- .... **CLC 42**
See also CA 1-4R; CANR 5, 21, 84; DLB 8; SATA 4; SCFW 2; SFW 4

Harrison, James (Thomas) 1937- ...... **CLC 6, 14, 33, 66, 143; SSC 19**
See Harrison, Jim
See also CA 13-16R; CANR 8, 51, 79, 142; DLBY 1982; INT CANR-8

Harrison, Jim
See Harrison, James (Thomas)
See also AMWS 8; CN 5, 6; CP 1, 2, 3, 4, 5, 6, 7; RGAL 4; TCWW 2; TUS

Harrison, Kathryn 1961- .... **CLC 70, 151**
See also CA 144; CANR 68, 122

Harrison, Tony 1937- .... **CLC 43, 129**
See also BRWS 5; CA 65-68; CANR 44, 98; CBD; CD 5, 6; CP 2, 3, 4, 5, 6, 7; DLB 40, 245; MTCW 1; RGEL 2

Harriss, Will(ard Irvin) 1922- .... **CLC 34**
See also CA 111

Hart, Ellis
See Ellison, Harlan (Jay)

Hart, Josephine 1942(?)- .... **CLC 70**
See also CA 138; CANR 70; CPW; DAM POP

Hart, Moss 1904-1961 .... **CLC 66**
See also CA 109; 89-92; CANR 84; DAM DRAM; DFS 1; DLB 7, 266; RGAL 4

Harte, (Francis) Bret(t)
1836(?)-1902 ... **SSC 8, 59; TCLC 1, 25; WLC**
See also AMWS 2; CA 104; 140; CANR 80; CDALB 1865-1917; DA; DA3; DAC; DAM MST; DLB 12, 64, 74, 79, 186; EXPS; LAIT 2; RGAL 4; RGSF 2; SATA 26; SSFS 3; TUS

Hartley, L(eslie) P(oles) 1895-1972 ... **CLC 2, 22**
See also BRWS 7; CA 45-48; 37-40R; CANR 33; CN 1; DLB 15, 139; EWL 3; HGG; MTCW 1, 2; MTFW 2005; RGEL 2; RGSF 2; SUFW 1

Hartman, Geoffrey H. 1929- .... **CLC 27**
See also CA 117; 125; CANR 79; DLB 67

Hartmann, Sadakichi 1869-1944 ... **TCLC 73**
See also CA 157; DLB 54

Hartmann von Aue c. 1170-c.
1210 .... **CMLC 15**
See also CDWLB 2; DLB 138; RGWL 2, 3

Hartog, Jan de
See de Hartog, Jan

Haruf, Kent 1943- .... **CLC 34**
See also AAYA 44; CA 149; CANR 91, 131

Harvey, Caroline
See Trollope, Joanna

Harvey, Gabriel 1550(?)-1631 .... **LC 88**
See also DLB 167, 213, 281

Harwood, Ronald 1934- .... **CLC 32**
See also CA 1-4R; CANR 4, 55; CBD; CD 5, 6; DAM DRAM, MST; DLB 13

Hasegawa Tatsunosuke
See Futabatei, Shimei

Hasek, Jaroslav (Matej Frantisek)
1883-1923 .... **SSC 69; TCLC 4**
See also CA 104; 129; CDWLB 4; DLB 215; EW 9; EWL 3; MTCW 1, 2; RGSF 2; RGWL 2, 3

Hass, Robert 1941- ... **CLC 18, 39, 99; PC 16**
See also AMWS 6; CA 111; CANR 30, 50, 71; CP 3, 4, 5, 6, 7; DLB 105, 206; EWL 3; MAL 5; MTFW 2005; RGAL 4; SATA 94; TCLE 1:1

Hastings, Hudson
See Kuttner, Henry

Hastings, Selina .... **CLC 44**

Hathorne, John 1641-1717 .... **LC 38**

Hatteras, Amelia
See Mencken, H(enry) L(ouis)

Hatteras, Owen .... **TCLC 18**
See Mencken, H(enry) L(ouis); Nathan, George Jean

Hauptmann, Gerhart (Johann Robert)
1862-1946 .... **SSC 37; TCLC 4**
See also CA 104; 153; CDWLB 2; DAM DRAM; DLB 66, 118; EW 8; EWL 3; RGSF 2; RGWL 2, 3; TWA

Havel, Vaclav 1936- ..... **CLC 25, 58, 65, 123; DC 6**
See also CA 104; CANR 36, 63, 124; CDWLB 4; CWW 2; DA3; DAM DRAM; DFS 10; DLB 232; EWL 3; LMFS 2; MTCW 1, 2; MTFW 2005; RGWL 3

Haviaras, Stratis .... **CLC 33**
See Chaviaras, Strates

Hawes, Stephen 1475(?)-1529(?) .... **LC 17**
See also DLB 132; RGEL 2

Hawkes, John (Clendennin Burne, Jr.)
1925-1998 .. **CLC 1, 2, 3, 4, 7, 9, 14, 15, 27, 49**
See also BPFB 2; CA 1-4R; 167; CANR 2, 47, 64; CN 1, 2, 3, 4, 5, 6; DLB 2, 7, 227; DLBY 1980, 1998; EWL 3; MAL 5; MTCW 1, 2; MTFW 2005; RGAL 4

Hawking, S. W.
See Hawking, Stephen W(illiam)

Hawking, Stephen W(illiam) 1942- . **CLC 63, 105**
See also AAYA 13; BEST 89:1; CA 126; 129; CANR 48, 115; CPW; DA3; MTCW 2; MTFW 2005

Hawkins, Anthony Hope
See Hope, Anthony

Hawthorne, Julian 1846-1934 .... **TCLC 25**
See also CA 165; HGG

Hawthorne, Nathaniel 1804-1864 ... **NCLC 2, 10, 17, 23, 39, 79, 95, 158; SSC 3, 29, 39; WLC**
See also AAYA 18; AMW; AMWC 1; AMWR 1; BPFB 2; BYA 3; CDALB 1640-1865; CLR 103; DA; DA3; DAB; DAC; DAM MST, NOV; DLB 1, 74, 183, 223, 269; EXPN; EXPS; GL 2; HGG; LAIT 1; NFS 1, 20; RGAL 4; RGSF 2; SSFS 1, 7, 11, 15; SUFW 1; TUS; WCH; YABC 2

Hawthorne, Sophia Peabody
1809-1871 .... **NCLC 150**
See also DLB 183, 239

Haxton, Josephine Ayres 1921-
See Douglas, Ellen
See also CA 115; CANR 41, 83

Hayaseca y Eizaguirre, Jorge
See Echegaray (y Eizaguirre), Jose (Maria Waldo)

Hayashi, Fumiko 1904-1951 .... **TCLC 27**
See Hayashi Fumiko
See also CA 161

Hayashi Fumiko
See Hayashi, Fumiko
See also DLB 180; EWL 3

Haycraft, Anna (Margaret) 1932-2005
See Ellis, Alice Thomas
See also CA 122; 237; CANR 90, 141; MTCW 2; MTFW 2005

Hayden, Robert E(arl) 1913-1980 ..... **BLC 2; CLC 5, 9, 14, 37; PC 6**
See also AFAW 1, 2; AMWS 2; BW 1, 3; CA 69-72; 97-100; CABS 2; CANR 24, 75, 82; CDALB 1941-1968; CP 1, 2, 3; DA; DAC; DAM MST, MULT, POET; DLB 5, 76; EWL 3; EXPP; MAL 5; MTCW 1, 2; PFS 1; RGAL 4; SATA 19; SATA-Obit 26; WP

Haydon, Benjamin Robert
1786-1846 .... **NCLC 146**
See also DLB 110

Hayek, F(riedrich) A(ugust von)
1899-1992 .... **TCLC 109**
See also CA 93-96; 137; CANR 20; MTCW 1, 2

Hayford, J(oseph) E(phraim) Casely
See Casely-Hayford, J(oseph) E(phraim)

Hayman, Ronald 1932- .... **CLC 44**
See also CA 25-28R; CANR 18, 50, 88; CD 5, 6; DLB 155

Hayne, Paul Hamilton 1830-1886 . **NCLC 94**
See also DLB 3, 64, 79, 248; RGAL 4

Hays, Mary 1760-1843 .... **NCLC 114**
See also DLB 142, 158; RGEL 2

Haywood, Eliza (Fowler)
1693(?)-1756 .... **LC 1, 44**
See also DLB 39; RGEL 2

Hazlitt, William 1778-1830 ...... **NCLC 29, 82**
See also BRW 4; DLB 110, 158; RGEL 2; TEA

Hazzard, Shirley 1931- .... **CLC 18**
See also CA 9-12R; CANR 4, 70, 127; CN 1, 2, 3, 4, 5, 6, 7; DLB 289; DLBY 1982; MTCW 1

Head, Bessie 1937-1986 ...... **BLC 2; CLC 25, 67; SSC 52**
See also AFW; BW 2, 3; CA 29-32R; 119; CANR 25, 82; CDWLB 3; CN 1, 2, 3, 4; DA3; DAM MULT; DLB 117, 225; EWL 3; EXPS; FL 1:6; FW; MTCW 1, 2; MTFW 2005; RGSF 2; SSFS 5, 13; WLIT 2; WWE 1

Headon, (Nicky) Topper 1956(?)- ..... **CLC 30**

Heaney, Seamus (Justin) 1939- ..... **CLC 5, 7, 14, 25, 37, 74, 91, 171; PC 18; WLCS**
See also AAYA 61; BRWR 1; BRWS 2; CA 85-88; CANR 25, 48, 75, 91, 128; CD-BLB 1960 to Present; CP 1, 2, 3, 4, 5, 6, 7; DA3; DAB; DAM POET; DLB 40; DLBY 1995; EWL 3; EXPP; MTCW 1, 2; MTFW 2005; PAB; PFS 2, 5, 8, 17; RGEL 2; TEA; WLIT 4

Hearn, (Patricio) Lafcadio (Tessima Carlos)
1850-1904 .... **TCLC 9**
See also CA 105; 166; DLB 12, 78, 189; HGG; MAL 5; RGAL 4

Hearne, Samuel 1745-1792 .... **LC 95**
See also DLB 99

Hearne, Vicki 1946-2001 .... **CLC 56**
See also CA 139; 201

Hearon, Shelby 1931- .... **CLC 63**
See also AITN 2; AMWS 8; CA 25-28R; CANR 18, 48, 103, 146; CSW

Heat-Moon, William Least .... **CLC 29**
See Trogdon, William (Lewis)
See also AAYA 9

Hebbel, Friedrich 1813-1863 . **DC 21; NCLC 43**
See also CDWLB 2; DAM DRAM; DLB 129; EW 6; RGWL 2, 3

Hebert, Anne 1916-2000 .... **CLC 4, 13, 29**
See also CA 85-88; 187; CANR 69, 126; CCA 1; CWP; CWW 2; DA3; DAC; DAM MST, POET; DLB 68; EWL 3; GFL 1789 to the Present; MTCW 1, 2; MTFW 2005; PFS 20

Hecht, Anthony (Evan) 1923-2004 .... **CLC 8, 13, 19**
See also AMWS 10; CA 9-12R; 232; CANR 6, 108; CP 1, 2, 3, 4, 5, 6, 7; DAM POET; DLB 5, 169; EWL 3; PFS 6; WP

Hecht, Ben 1894-1964 ..... **CLC 8; TCLC 101**
See also CA 85-88; DFS 9; DLB 7, 9, 25, 26, 28, 86; FANT; IDFW 3, 4; RGAL 4

Hedayat, Sadeq 1903-1951 .... **TCLC 21**
See also CA 120; EWL 3; RGSF 2

Hewes, Cady
  See De Voto, Bernard (Augustine)

Heyen, William 1940- .... **CLC 13, 18**
  See also CA 33-36R; 220; CAAE 220;
  CAAS 9; CANR 98; CP 3, 4, 5, 6, 7; DLB
  5

Heyerdahl, Thor 1914-2002 .... **CLC 26**
  See also CA 5-8R; 207; CANR 5, 22, 66,
  73; LAIT 4; MTCW 1, 2; MTFW 2005;
  SATA 2, 52

Heym, Georg (Theodor Franz Arthur)
  1887-1912 .... **TCLC 9**
  See also CA 106; 181

Heym, Stefan 1913-2001 .... **CLC 41**
  See also CA 9-12R; 203; CANR 4; CWW
  2; DLB 69; EWL 3

Heyse, Paul (Johann Ludwig von)
  1830-1914 .... **TCLC 8**
  See also CA 104; 209; DLB 129

Heyward, (Edwin) DuBose
  1885-1940 .... **HR 1:2; TCLC 59**
  See also CA 108; 157; DLB 7, 9, 45, 249;
  MAL 5; SATA 21

Heywood, John 1497(?)-1580(?) .... **LC 65**
  See also DLB 136; RGEL 2

Heywood, Thomas 1573(?)-1641 .... **LC 111**
  See also DAM DRAM; DLB 62; LMFS 1;
  RGEL 2; TEA

Hibbert, Eleanor Alice Burford
  1906-1993 .... **CLC 7**
  See Holt, Victoria
  See also BEST 90:4; CA 17-20R; 140;
  CANR 9, 28, 59; CMW 4; CPW; DAM
  POP; MTCW 2; MTFW 2005; RHW;
  SATA 2; SATA-Obit 74

Hichens, Robert (Smythe)
  1864-1950 .... **TCLC 64**
  See also CA 162; DLB 153; HGG; RHW;
  SUFW

Higgins, Aidan 1927- .... **SSC 68**
  See also CA 9-12R; CANR 70, 115; CN 1,
  2, 3, 4, 5, 6, 7; DLB 14

Higgins, George V(incent)
  1939-1999 .... **CLC 4, 7, 10, 18**
  See also BPFB 2; CA 77-80; 186; CAAS 5;
  CANR 17, 51, 89, 96; CMW 4; CN 2, 3,
  4, 5, 6; DLB 2; DLBY 1981, 1998; INT
  CANR-17; MSW; MTCW 1

Higginson, Thomas Wentworth
  1823-1911 .... **TCLC 36**
  See also CA 162; DLB 1, 64, 243

Higgonet, Margaret ed. .... **CLC 65**

Highet, Helen
  See MacInnes, Helen (Clark)

Highsmith, (Mary) Patricia
  1921-1995 .... **CLC 2, 4, 14, 42, 102**
  See Morgan, Claire
  See also AAYA 48; BRWS 5; CA 1-4R; 147;
  CANR 1, 20, 48, 62, 108; CMW 4; CN 1,
  2, 3, 4, 5; CPW; DA3; DAM NOV, POP;
  DLB 306; MSW; MTCW 1, 2; MTFW
  2005

Highwater, Jamake (Mamake)
  1942(?)-2001 .... **CLC 12**
  See also AAYA 7; BPFB 2; BYA 4; CA 65-
  68; 199; CAAS 7; CANR 10, 34, 84; CLR
  17; CWRI 5; DLB 52; DLBY 1985;
  JRDA; MAICYA 1, 2; SATA 32, 69;
  SATA-Brief 30

Highway, Tomson 1951- ...... **CLC 92; NNAL**
  See also CA 151; CANR 75; CCA 1; CD 5,
  6; CN 7; DAC; DAM MULT; DFS 2;
  MTCW 2

Hijuelos, Oscar 1951- .... **CLC 65; HLC 1**
  See also AAYA 25; AMWS 8; BEST 90:1;
  CA 123; CANR 50, 75, 125; CPW; DA3;
  DAM MULT, POP; DLB 145; HW 1, 2;
  LLW; MAL 5; MTCW 2; MTFW 2005;
  NFS 17; RGAL 4; WLIT 1

Hikmet, Nazim 1902-1963 .... **CLC 40**
  See Nizami of Ganja
  See also CA 141; 93-96; EWL 3; WLIT 6

Hildegard von Bingen 1098-1179 . **CMLC 20**
  See also DLB 148

Hildesheimer, Wolfgang 1916-1991 .. **CLC 49**
  See also CA 101; 135; DLB 69, 124; EWL
  3

Hill, Geoffrey (William) 1932- ...... **CLC 5, 8,
  18, 45**
  See also BRWS 5; CA 81-84; CANR 21,
  89; CDBLB 1960 to Present; CP 1, 2, 3,
  4, 5, 6, 7; DAM POET; DLB 40; EWL 3;
  MTCW 1; RGEL 2

Hill, George Roy 1921-2002 .... **CLC 26**
  See also CA 110; 122; 213

Hill, John
  See Koontz, Dean R.

Hill, Susan (Elizabeth) 1942- ...... **CLC 4, 113**
  See also CA 33-36R; CANR 29, 69, 129;
  CN 2, 3, 4, 5, 6, 7; DAB; DAM MST,
  NOV; DLB 14, 139; HGG; MTCW 1;
  RHW

Hillard, Asa G. III .... **CLC 70**

Hillerman, Tony 1925- .... **CLC 62, 170**
  See also AAYA 40; BEST 89:1; BPFB 2;
  CA 29-32R; CANR 21, 42, 65, 97, 134;
  CMW 4; CPW; DA3; DAM POP; DLB
  206, 306; MAL 5; MSW; MTCW 2;
  MTFW 2005; RGAL 4; SATA 6; TCWW
  2; YAW

Hillesum, Etty 1914-1943 .... **TCLC 49**
  See also CA 137

Hilliard, Noel (Harvey) 1929-1996 ... **CLC 15**
  See also CA 9-12R; CANR 7, 69; CN 1, 2,
  3, 4, 5, 6

Hillis, Rick 1956- .... **CLC 66**
  See also CA 134

Hilton, James 1900-1954 .... **TCLC 21**
  See also CA 108; 169; DLB 34, 77; FANT;
  SATA 34

Hilton, Walter (?)-1396 .... **CMLC 58**
  See also DLB 146; RGEL 2

Himes, Chester (Bomar) 1909-1984 .. **BLC 2;
  CLC 2, 4, 7, 18, 58, 108; TCLC 139**
  See also AFAW 2; BPFB 2; BW 2; CA 25-
  28R; 114; CANR 22, 89; CMW 4; CN 1,
  2, 3; DAM MULT; DLB 2, 76, 143, 226;
  EWL 3; MAL 5; MSW; MTCW 1, 2;
  MTFW 2005; RGAL 4

Himmelfarb, Gertrude 1922- .... **CLC 202**
  See also CA 49-52; CANR 28, 66, 102

Hinde, Thomas .... **CLC 6, 11**
  See Chitty, Thomas Willes
  See also CN 1, 2, 3, 4, 5, 6; EWL 3

Hine, (William) Daryl 1936- .... **CLC 15**
  See also CA 1-4R; CAAS 15; CANR 1, 20;
  CP 1, 2, 3, 4, 5, 6, 7; DLB 60

Hinkson, Katharine Tynan
  See Tynan, Katharine

Hinojosa(-Smith), Rolando (R.)
  1929- .... **HLC 1**
  See Hinojosa-Smith, Rolando
  See also CA 131; CAAS 16; CANR 62;
  DAM MULT; DLB 82; HW 1, 2; LLW;
  MTCW 2; MTFW 2005; RGAL 4

Hinton, S(usan) E(loise) 1950- .. **CLC 30, 111**
  See also AAYA 2, 33; BPFB 2; BYA 2, 3;
  CA 81-84; CANR 32, 62, 92, 133;
  CDALBS; CLR 3, 23; CPW; DA; DA3;
  DAB; DAC; DAM MST, NOV; JRDA;
  LAIT 5; MAICYA 1, 2; MTCW 1, 2;
  MTFW 2005 !**; NFS 5, 9, 15, 16; SATA
  19, 58, 115, 160; WYA; YAW

Hippius, Zinaida (Nikolaevna) .... **TCLC 9**
  See Gippius, Zinaida (Nikolaevna)
  See also DLB 295; EWL 3

Hiraoka, Kimitake 1925-1970
  See Mishima, Yukio
  See also CA 97-100; 29-32R; DA3; DAM
  DRAM; GLL 1; MTCW 1, 2

Hirsch, E(ric) D(onald), Jr. 1928- .... **CLC 79**
  See also CA 25-28R; CANR 27, 51; DLB
  67; INT CANR-27; MTCW 1

Hirsch, Edward 1950- .... **CLC 31, 50**
  See also CA 104; CANR 20, 42, 102; CP 7;
  DLB 120; PFS 22

Hitchcock, Alfred (Joseph)
  1899-1980 .... **CLC 16**
  See also AAYA 22; CA 159; 97-100; SATA
  27; SATA-Obit 24

Hitchens, Christopher (Eric)
  1949- .... **CLC 157**
  See also CA 152; CANR 89

Hitler, Adolf 1889-1945 .... **TCLC 53**
  See also CA 117; 147

Hoagland, Edward (Morley) 1932- .. **CLC 28**
  See also ANW; CA 1-4R; CANR 2, 31, 57,
  107; CN 1, 2, 3, 4, 5, 6, 7; DLB 6; SATA
  51; TCWW 2

Hoban, Russell (Conwell) 1925- ... **CLC 7, 25**
  See also BPFB 2; CA 5-8R; CANR 23, 37,
  66, 114, 138; CLR 3, 69; CN 4, 5, 6, 7;
  CWRI 5; DAM NOV; DLB 52; FANT;
  MAICYA 1, 2; MTCW 1, 2; MTFW 2005;
  SATA 1, 40, 78, 136; SFW 4; SUFW 2;
  TCLE 1:1

Hobbes, Thomas 1588-1679 .... **LC 36**
  See also DLB 151, 252, 281; RGEL 2

Hobbs, Perry
  See Blackmur, R(ichard) P(almer)

Hobson, Laura Z(ametkin)
  1900-1986 .... **CLC 7, 25**
  See also BPFB 2; CA 17-20R; 118; CANR
  55; CN 1, 2, 3, 4; DLB 28; SATA 52

Hoccleve, Thomas c. 1368-c. 1437 ...... **LC 75**
  See also DLB 146; RGEL 2

Hoch, Edward D(entinger) 1930-
  See Queen, Ellery
  See also CA 29-32R; CANR 11, 27, 51, 97;
  CMW 4; DLB 306; SFW 4

Hochhuth, Rolf 1931- .... **CLC 4, 11, 18**
  See also CA 5-8R; CANR 33, 75, 136;
  CWW 2; DAM DRAM; DLB 124; EWL
  3; MTCW 1, 2; MTFW 2005

Hochman, Sandra 1936- .... **CLC 3, 8**
  See also CA 5-8R; CP 1, 2, 3, 4; DLB 5

Hochwaelder, Fritz 1911-1986 .... **CLC 36**
  See Hochwalder, Fritz
  See also CA 29-32R; 120; CANR 42; DAM
  DRAM; MTCW 1; RGWL 3

Hochwalder, Fritz
  See Hochwaelder, Fritz
  See also EWL 3; RGWL 2

Hocking, Mary (Eunice) 1921- .... **CLC 13**
  See also CA 101; CANR 18, 40

Hodgins, Jack 1938- .... **CLC 23**
  See also CA 93-96; CN 4, 5, 6, 7; DLB 60

Hodgson, William Hope
  1877(?)-1918 .... **TCLC 13**
  See also CA 111; 164; CMW 4; DLB 70,
  153, 156, 178; HGG; MTCW 2; SFW 4;
  SUFW 1

Hoeg, Peter 1957- .... **CLC 95, 156**
  See also CA 151; CANR 75; CMW 4; DA3;
  DLB 214; EWL 3; MTCW 2; MTFW
  2005; NFS 17; RGWL 3; SSFS 18

Hoffman, Alice 1952- .... **CLC 51**
  See also AAYA 37; AMWS 10; CA 77-80;
  CANR 34, 66, 100, 138; CN 4, 5, 6, 7;
  CPW; DAM NOV; DLB 292; MAL 5;
  MTCW 1, 2; MTFW 2005; TCLE 1:1

Hoffman, Daniel (Gerard) 1923- . **CLC 6, 13,
  23**
  See also CA 1-4R; CANR 4, 142; CP 1, 2,
  3, 4, 5, 6, 7; DLB 5; TCLE 1:1

Hougan, Carolyn 1943- .... **CLC 34**
See also CA 139

Household, Geoffrey (Edward West)
1900-1988 .... **CLC 11**
See also CA 77-80; 126; CANR 58; CMW
4; CN 1, 2, 3, 4; DLB 87; SATA 14;
SATA-Obit 59

Housman, A(lfred) E(dward)
1859-1936 .... **PC 2, 43; TCLC 1, 10;
WLCS**
See also AAYA 66; BRW 6; CA 104; 125;
DA; DA3; DAB; DAC; DAM MST,
POET; DLB 19, 284; EWL 3; EXPP;
MTCW 1, 2; MTFW 2005; PAB; PFS 4,
7; RGEL 2; TEA; WP

Housman, Laurence 1865-1959 .... **TCLC 7**
See also CA 106; 155; DLB 10; FANT;
RGEL 2; SATA 25

Houston, Jeanne (Toyo) Wakatsuki
1934- .... **AAL**
See also AAYA 49; CA 103, 232; CAAE
232; CAAS 16; CANR 29, 123; LAIT 4;
SATA 78

Howard, Elizabeth Jane 1923- ..... **CLC 7, 29**
See also BRWS 11; CA 5-8R; CANR 8, 62,
146; CN 1, 2, 3, 4, 5, 6, 7

Howard, Maureen 1930- .... **CLC 5, 14, 46,
151**
See also CA 53-56; CANR 31, 75, 140; CN
4, 5, 6, 7; DLBY 1983; INT CANR-31;
MTCW 1, 2; MTFW 2005

Howard, Richard 1929- .... **CLC 7, 10, 47**
See also AITN 1; CA 85-88; CANR 25, 80;
CP 1, 2, 3, 4, 5, 6, 7; DLB 5; INT CANR-
25; MAL 5

Howard, Robert E(rvin)
1906-1936 .... **TCLC 8**
See also BPFB 2; BYA 5; CA 105; 157;
FANT; SUFW 1; TCWW 1, 2

Howard, Warren F.
See Pohl, Frederik

Howe, Fanny (Quincy) 1940- .... **CLC 47**
See also CA 117, 187; CAAE 187; CAAS
27; CANR 70, 116; CP 7; CWP; SATA-
Brief 52

Howe, Irving 1920-1993 .... **CLC 85**
See also AMWS 6; CA 9-12R; 141; CANR
21, 50; DLB 67; EWL 3; MAL 5; MTCW
1, 2; MTFW 2005

Howe, Julia Ward 1819-1910 .... **TCLC 21**
See also CA 117; 191; DLB 1, 189, 235;
FW

Howe, Susan 1937- .... **CLC 72, 152; PC 54**
See also AMWS 4; CA 160; CP 7; CWP;
DLB 120; FW; RGAL 4

Howe, Tina 1937- .... **CLC 48**
See also CA 109; CAD; CANR 125; CD 5,
6; CWD

Howell, James 1594(?)-1666 .... **LC 13**
See also DLB 151

Howells, W. D.
See Howells, William Dean

Howells, William D.
See Howells, William Dean

Howells, William Dean 1837-1920 ... **SSC 36;
TCLC 7, 17, 41**
See also AMW; CA 104; 134; CDALB
1865-1917; DLB 12, 64, 74, 79, 189;
LMFS 1; MAL 5; MTCW 2; RGAL 4;
TUS

Howes, Barbara 1914-1996 .... **CLC 15**
See also CA 9-12R; 151; CAAS 3; CANR
53; CP 1, 2, 3, 4; SATA 5; TCLE 1:1

Hrabal, Bohumil 1914-1997 ...... **CLC 13, 67;
TCLC 155**
See also CA 106; 156; CAAS 12; CANR
57; CWW 2; DLB 232; EWL 3; RGSF 2

Hrabanus Maurus 776(?)-856 .... **CMLC 78**
See also DLB 148

Hrotsvit of Gandersheim c. 935-c.
1000 .... **CMLC 29**
See also DLB 148

Hsi, Chu 1130-1200 .... **CMLC 42**

Hsun, Lu
See Lu Hsun

Hubbard, L(afayette) Ron(ald)
1911-1986 .... **CLC 43**
See also AAYA 64; CA 77-80; 118; CANR
52; CPW; DA3; DAM POP; FANT;
MTCW 2; MTFW 2005; SFW 4

Huch, Ricarda (Octavia)
1864-1947 .... **TCLC 13**
See Hugo, Richard
See also CA 111; 189; DLB 66; EWL 3

Huddle, David 1942- .... **CLC 49**
See also CA 57-60; CAAS 20; CANR 89;
DLB 130

Hudson, Jeffrey
See Crichton, (John) Michael

Hudson, W(illiam) H(enry)
1841-1922 .... **TCLC 29**
See also CA 115; 190; DLB 98, 153, 174;
RGEL 2; SATA 35

Hueffer, Ford Madox
See Ford, Ford Madox

Hughart, Barry 1934- .... **CLC 39**
See also CA 137; FANT; SFW 4; SUFW 2

Hughes, Colin
See Creasey, John

Hughes, David (John) 1930-2005 ..... **CLC 48**
See also CA 116; 129; 238; CN 4, 5, 6, 7;
DLB 14

Hughes, Edward James
See Hughes, Ted
See also DA3; DAM MST, POET

Hughes, (James Mercer) Langston
1902-1967 ..... **BLC 2; CLC 1, 5, 10, 15,
35, 44, 108; DC 3; HR 1:2; PC 1, 53;
SSC 6; WLC**
See also AAYA 12; AFAW 1, 2; AMWR 1;
AMWS 1; BW 1, 3; CA 1-4R; 25-28R;
CANR 1, 34, 82; CDALB 1929-1941;
CLR 17; DA; DA3; DAB; DAC; DAM
DRAM, MST, MULT, POET; DFS 6, 18;
DLB 4, 7, 48, 51, 86, 228, 315; EWL 3;
EXPP; EXPS; JRDA; LAIT 3; LMFS 2;
MAICYA 1, 2; MAL 5; MTCW 1, 2;
MTFW 2005; NFS 21; PAB; PFS 1, 3, 6,
10, 15; RGAL 4; RGSF 2; SATA 4, 33;
SSFS 4, 7; TUS; WCH; WP; YAW

Hughes, Richard (Arthur Warren)
1900-1976 .... **CLC 1, 11**
See also CA 5-8R; 65-68; CANR 4; CN 1,
2; DAM NOV; DLB 15, 161; EWL 3;
MTCW 1; RGEL 2; SATA 8; SATA-Obit
25

Hughes, Ted 1930-1998 . **CLC 2, 4, 9, 14, 37,
119; PC 7**
See Hughes, Edward James
See also BRWC 2; BRWR 2; BRWS 1; CA
1-4R; 171; CANR 1, 33, 66, 108; CLR 3;
CP 1, 2, 3, 4, 5, 6; DAB; DAC; DLB 40,
161; EWL 3; EXPP; MAICYA 1, 2;
MTCW 1, 2; MTFW 2005; PAB; PFS 4,
19; RGEL 2; SATA 49; SATA-Brief 27;
SATA-Obit 107; TEA; YAW

Hugo, Richard
See Huch, Ricarda (Octavia)
See also MAL 5

Hugo, Richard F(ranklin)
1923-1982 .... **CLC 6, 18, 32; PC 68**
See also AMWS 6; CA 49-52; 108; CANR
3; CP 1, 2, 3; DAM POET; DLB 5, 206;
EWL 3; PFS 17; RGAL 4

Hugo, Victor (Marie) 1802-1885 .... **NCLC 3,
10, 21, 161; PC 17; WLC**
See also AAYA 28; DA; DA3; DAB; DAC;
DAM DRAM, MST, NOV, POET; DLB
119, 192, 217; EFS 2; EW 6; EXPN; GFL

1789 to the Present; LAIT 1, 2; NFS 5,
20; RGWL 2, 3; SATA 47; TWA

Huidobro, Vicente
See Huidobro Fernandez, Vicente Garcia
See also DLB 283; EWL 3; LAW

Huidobro Fernandez, Vicente Garcia
1893-1948 .... **TCLC 31**
See Huidobro, Vicente
See also CA 131; HW 1

Hulme, Keri 1947- .... **CLC 39, 130**
See also CA 125; CANR 69; CN 4, 5, 6, 7;
CP 7; CWP; EWL 3; FW; INT CA-125

Hulme, T(homas) E(rnest)
1883-1917 .... **TCLC 21**
See also BRWS 6; CA 117; 203; DLB 19

Humboldt, Wilhelm von
1767-1835 .... **NCLC 134**
See also DLB 90

Hume, David 1711-1776 .... **LC 7, 56**
See also BRWS 3; DLB 104, 252; LMFS 1;
TEA

Humphrey, William 1924-1997 .... **CLC 45**
See also AMWS 9; CA 77-80; 160; CANR
68; CN 1, 2, 3, 4, 5, 6; CSW; DLB 6, 212,
234, 278; TCWW 1, 2

Humphreys, Emyr Owen 1919- .... **CLC 47**
See also CA 5-8R; CANR 3, 24; CN 1, 2,
3, 4, 5, 6, 7; DLB 15

Humphreys, Josephine 1945- ..... **CLC 34, 57**
See also CA 121; 127; CANR 97; CSW;
DLB 292; INT CA-127

Huneker, James Gibbons
1860-1921 .... **TCLC 65**
See also CA 193; DLB 71; RGAL 4

Hungerford, Hesba Fay
See Brinsmead, H(esba) F(ay)

Hungerford, Pixie
See Brinsmead, H(esba) F(ay)

Hunt, E(verette) Howard, (Jr.)
1918- .... **CLC 3**
See also AITN 1; CA 45-48; CANR 2, 47,
103; CMW 4

Hunt, Francesca
See Holland, Isabelle (Christian)

Hunt, Howard
See Hunt, E(verette) Howard, (Jr.)

Hunt, Kyle
See Creasey, John

Hunt, (James Henry) Leigh
1784-1859 .... **NCLC 1, 70**
See also DAM POET; DLB 96, 110, 144;
RGEL 2; TEA

Hunt, Marsha 1946- .... **CLC 70**
See also BW 2, 3; CA 143; CANR 79

Hunt, Violet 1866(?)-1942 .... **TCLC 53**
See also CA 184; DLB 162, 197

Hunter, E. Waldo
See Sturgeon, Theodore (Hamilton)

Hunter, Evan 1926-2005 .... **CLC 11, 31**
See McBain, Ed
See also AAYA 39; BPFB 2; CA 5-8R; 241;
CANR 5, 38, 62, 97; CMW 4; CN 1, 2, 3,
4, 5, 6, 7; CPW; DAM POP; DLB 306;
DLBY 1982; INT CANR-5; MSW;
MTCW 1; SATA 25; SFW 4

Hunter, Kristin
See Lattany, Kristin (Elaine Eggleston)
Hunter
See also CN 1, 2, 3, 4, 5, 6

Hunter, Mary
See Austin, Mary (Hunter)

Hunter, Mollie 1922- .... **CLC 21**
See McIlwraith, Maureen Mollie Hunter
See also AAYA 13; BYA 6; CANR 37, 78;
CLR 25; DLB 161; JRDA; MAICYA 1,
2; SAAS 7; SATA 54, 106, 139; SATA-
Essay 139; WYA; YAW

Jordan, June (Meyer)
   1936-2002 .. **BLCS; CLC 5, 11, 23, 114; PC 38**
   See also AAYA 2, 66; AFAW 1, 2; BW 2, 3; CA 33-36R; 206; CANR 25, 70, 114; CLR 10; CP 3, 4, 5, 6, 7; CWP; DAM MULT, POET; DLB 38; GLL 2; LAIT 5; MAICYA 1, 2; MTCW 1; SATA 4, 136; YAW

Jordan, Neil (Patrick) 1950- .... **CLC 110**
   See also CA 124; 130; CANR 54; CN 4, 5, 6, 7; GLL 2; INT CA-130

Jordan, Pat(rick M.) 1941- .... **CLC 37**
   See also CA 33-36R; CANR 121

Jorgensen, Ivar
   See Ellison, Harlan (Jay)

Jorgenson, Ivar
   See Silverberg, Robert

Joseph, George Ghevarughese .... **CLC 70**

Josephson, Mary
   See O'Doherty, Brian

Josephus, Flavius c. 37-100 .... **CMLC 13**
   See also AW 2; DLB 176

Josiah Allen's Wife
   See Holley, Marietta

Josipovici, Gabriel (David) 1940- ...... **CLC 6, 43, 153**
   See also CA 37-40R, 224; CAAE 224; CAAS 8; CANR 47, 84; CN 3, 4, 5, 6, 7; DLB 14, 319

Joubert, Joseph 1754-1824 .... **NCLC 9**

Jouve, Pierre Jean 1887-1976 .... **CLC 47**
   See also CA 65-68; DLB 258; EWL 3

Jovine, Francesco 1902-1950 .... **TCLC 79**
   See also DLB 264; EWL 3

Joyce, James (Augustine Aloysius)
   1882-1941 .... **DC 16; PC 22; SSC 3, 26, 44, 64; TCLC 3, 8, 16, 35, 52, 159; WLC**
   See also AAYA 42; BRW 7; BRWC 1; BRWR 1; BYA 11, 13; CA 104; 126; CD-BLB 1914-1945; DA; DA3; DAB; DAC; DAM MST, NOV, POET; DLB 10, 19, 36, 162, 247; EWL 3; EXPN; EXPS; LAIT 3; LMFS 1, 2; MTCW 1, 2; MTFW 2005; NFS 7; RGSF 2; SSFS 1, 19; TEA; WLIT 4

Jozsef, Attila 1905-1937 .... **TCLC 22**
   See also CA 116; 230; CDWLB 4; DLB 215; EWL 3

Juana Ines de la Cruz, Sor
   1651(?)-1695 ...... **HLCS 1; LC 5; PC 24**
   See also DLB 305; FW; LAW; RGWL 2, 3; WLIT 1

Juana Inez de La Cruz, Sor
   See Juana Ines de la Cruz, Sor

Judd, Cyril
   See Kornbluth, C(yril) M.; Pohl, Frederik

Juenger, Ernst 1895-1998 .... **CLC 125**
   See Junger, Ernst
   See also CA 101; 167; CANR 21, 47, 106; DLB 56

Julian of Norwich 1342(?)-1416(?) . **LC 6, 52**
   See also DLB 146; LMFS 1

Julius Caesar 100B.C.-44B.C.
   See Caesar, Julius
   See also CDWLB 1; DLB 211

Junger, Ernst
   See Juenger, Ernst
   See also CDWLB 2; EWL 3; RGWL 2, 3

Junger, Sebastian 1962- .... **CLC 109**
   See also AAYA 28; CA 165; CANR 130; MTFW 2005

Juniper, Alex
   See Hospital, Janette Turner

Junius
   See Luxemburg, Rosa

Junzaburo, Nishiwaki
   See Nishiwaki, Junzaburo
   See also EWL 3

Just, Ward (Swift) 1935- .... **CLC 4, 27**
   See also CA 25-28R; CANR 32, 87; CN 6, 7; INT CANR-32

Justice, Donald (Rodney)
   1925-2004 .... **CLC 6, 19, 102; PC 64**
   See also AMWS 7; CA 5-8R; 230; CANR 26, 54, 74, 121, 122; CP 1, 2, 3, 4, 5, 6, 7; CSW; DAM POET; DLBY 1983; EWL 3; INT CANR-26; MAL 5; MTCW 2; PFS 14; TCLE 1:1

Juvenal c. 60-c. 130 .... **CMLC 8**
   See also AW 2; CDWLB 1; DLB 211; RGWL 2, 3

Juvenis
   See Bourne, Randolph S(illiman)

K., Alice
   See Knapp, Caroline

Kabakov, Sasha .... **CLC 59**

Kabir 1398(?)-1448(?) .... **LC 109; PC 56**
   See also RGWL 2, 3

Kacew, Romain 1914-1980
   See Gary, Romain
   See also CA 108; 102

Kadare, Ismail 1936- .... **CLC 52, 190**
   See also CA 161; EWL 3; RGWL 3

Kadohata, Cynthia (Lynn)
   1956(?)- .... **CLC 59, 122**
   See also CA 140; CANR 124; SATA 155

Kafka, Franz 1883-1924 ... **SSC 5, 29, 35, 60; TCLC 2, 6, 13, 29, 47, 53, 112; WLC**
   See also AAYA 31; BPFB 2; CA 105; 126; CDWLB 2; DA; DA3; DAB; DAC; DAM MST, NOV; DLB 81; EW 9; EWL 3; EXPS; LATS 1:1; LMFS 2; MTCW 1, 2; MTFW 2005; NFS 7; RGSF 2; RGWL 2, 3; SFW 4; SSFS 3, 7, 12; TWA

Kahanovitsch, Pinkhes
   See Der Nister

Kahn, Roger 1927- .... **CLC 30**
   See also CA 25-28R; CANR 44, 69; DLB 171; SATA 37

Kain, Saul
   See Sassoon, Siegfried (Lorraine)

Kaiser, Georg 1878-1945 .... **TCLC 9**
   See also CA 106; 190; CDWLB 2; DLB 124; EWL 3; LMFS 2; RGWL 2, 3

Kaledin, Sergei .... **CLC 59**

Kaletski, Alexander 1946- .... **CLC 39**
   See also CA 118; 143

Kalidasa fl. c. 400-455 .... **CMLC 9; PC 22**
   See also RGWL 2, 3

Kallman, Chester (Simon)
   1921-1975 .... **CLC 2**
   See also CA 45-48; 53-56; CANR 3; CP 1, 2

Kaminsky, Melvin 1926-
   See Brooks, Mel
   See also CA 65-68; CANR 16; DFS 21

Kaminsky, Stuart M(elvin) 1934- ..... **CLC 59**
   See also CA 73-76; CANR 29, 53, 89; CMW 4

Kamo no Chomei 1153(?)-1216 .... **CMLC 66**
   See also DLB 203

Kamo no Nagaakira
   See Kamo no Chomei

Kandinsky, Wassily 1866-1944 .... **TCLC 92**
   See also AAYA 64; CA 118; 155

Kane, Francis
   See Robbins, Harold

Kane, Henry 1918-
   See Queen, Ellery
   See also CA 156; CMW 4

Kane, Paul
   See Simon, Paul (Frederick)

Kanin, Garson 1912-1999 .... **CLC 22**
   See also AITN 1; CA 5-8R; 177; CAD; CANR 7, 78; DLB 7; IDFW 3, 4

Kaniuk, Yoram 1930- .... **CLC 19**
   See also CA 134; DLB 299

Kant, Immanuel 1724-1804 ..... **NCLC 27, 67**
   See also DLB 94

Kantor, MacKinlay 1904-1977 .... **CLC 7**
   See also CA 61-64; 73-76; CANR 60, 63; CN 1, 2; DLB 9, 102; MAL 5; MTCW 2; RHW; TCWW 1, 2

Kanze Motokiyo
   See Zeami

Kaplan, David Michael 1946- .... **CLC 50**
   See also CA 187

Kaplan, James 1951- .... **CLC 59**
   See also CA 135; CANR 121

Karadzic, Vuk Stefanovic
   1787-1864 .... **NCLC 115**
   See also CDWLB 4; DLB 147

Karageorge, Michael
   See Anderson, Poul (William)

Karamzin, Nikolai Mikhailovich
   1766-1826 .... **NCLC 3**
   See also DLB 150; RGSF 2

Karapanou, Margarita 1946- .... **CLC 13**
   See also CA 101

Karinthy, Frigyes 1887-1938 .... **TCLC 47**
   See also CA 170; DLB 215; EWL 3

Karl, Frederick R(obert)
   1927-2004 .... **CLC 34**
   See also CA 5-8R; 226; CANR 3, 44, 143

Karr, Mary 1955- .... **CLC 188**
   See also AMWS 11; CA 151; CANR 100; MTFW 2005; NCFS 5

Kastel, Warren
   See Silverberg, Robert

Kataev, Evgeny Petrovich 1903-1942
   See Petrov, Evgeny
   See also CA 120

Kataphusin
   See Ruskin, John

Katz, Steve 1935- .... **CLC 47**
   See also CA 25-28R; CAAS 14, 64; CANR 12; CN 4, 5, 6, 7; DLBY 1983

Kauffman, Janet 1945- .... **CLC 42**
   See also CA 117; CANR 43, 84; DLB 218; DLBY 1986

Kaufman, Bob (Garnell) 1925-1986 . **CLC 49**
   See also BG 1:3; BW 1; CA 41-44R; 118; CANR 22; CP 1; DLB 16, 41

Kaufman, George S. 1889-1961 ...... **CLC 38; DC 17**
   See also CA 108; 93-96; DAM DRAM; DFS 1, 10; DLB 7; INT CA-108; MTCW 2; MTFW 2005; RGAL 4; TUS

Kaufman, Moises 1964- .... **DC 26**
   See also CA 211; DFS 22; MTFW 2005

Kaufman, Sue .... **CLC 3, 8**
   See Barondess, Sue K(aufman)

Kavafis, Konstantinos Petrou 1863-1933
   See Cavafy, C(onstantine) P(eter)
   See also CA 104

Kavan, Anna 1901-1968 .... **CLC 5, 13, 82**
   See also BRWS 7; CA 5-8R; CANR 6, 57; DLB 255; MTCW 1; RGEL 2; SFW 4

Kavanagh, Dan
   See Barnes, Julian (Patrick)

Kavanagh, Julie 1952- .... **CLC 119**
   See also CA 163

Kavanagh, Patrick (Joseph)
   1904-1967 .... **CLC 22; PC 33**
   See also BRWS 7; CA 123; 25-28R; DLB 15, 20; EWL 3; MTCW 1; RGEL 2

Kawabata, Yasunari 1899-1972 ..... **CLC 2, 5, 9, 18, 107; SSC 17**
See Kawabata Yasunari
See also CA 93-96; 33-36R; CANR 88; DAM MULT; MJW; MTCW 2; MTFW 2005; RGSF 2; RGWL 2, 3

Kawabata Yasunari
See Kawabata, Yasunari
See also DLB 180; EWL 3

Kaye, M(ary) M(argaret)
1908-2004 .... **CLC 28**
See also CA 89-92; 223; CANR 24, 60, 102, 142; MTCW 1, 2; MTFW 2005; RHW; SATA 62; SATA-Obit 152

Kaye, Mollie
See Kaye, M(ary) M(argaret)

Kaye-Smith, Sheila 1887-1956 .... **TCLC 20**
See also CA 118; 203; DLB 36

Kaymor, Patrice Maguilene
See Senghor, Leopold Sedar

Kazakov, Iurii Pavlovich
See Kazakov, Yuri Pavlovich
See also DLB 302

Kazakov, Yuri Pavlovich 1927-1982 . **SSC 43**
See Kazakov, Iurii Pavlovich; Kazakov, Yury
See also CA 5-8R; CANR 36; MTCW 1; RGSF 2

Kazakov, Yury
See Kazakov, Yuri Pavlovich
See also EWL 3

Kazan, Elia 1909-2003 .... **CLC 6, 16, 63**
See also CA 21-24R; 220; CANR 32, 78

Kazantzakis, Nikos 1883(?)-1957 .... **TCLC 2, 5, 33**
See also BPFB 2; CA 105; 132; DA3; EW 9; EWL 3; MTCW 1, 2; MTFW 2005; RGWL 2, 3

Kazin, Alfred 1915-1998 ..... **CLC 34, 38, 119**
See also AMWS 8; CA 1-4R; CAAS 7; CANR 1, 45, 79; DLB 67; EWL 3

Keane, Mary Nesta (Skrine) 1904-1996
See Keane, Molly
See also CA 108; 114; 151; RHW

Keane, Molly .... **CLC 31**
See Keane, Mary Nesta (Skrine)
See also CN 5, 6; INT CA-114; TCLE 1:1

Keates, Jonathan 1946(?)- .... **CLC 34**
See also CA 163; CANR 126

Keaton, Buster 1895-1966 .... **CLC 20**
See also CA 194

Keats, John 1795-1821 ...... **NCLC 8, 73, 121; PC 1; WLC**
See also AAYA 58; BRW 4; BRWR 1; CD-BLB 1789-1832; DA; DA3; DAB; DAC; DAM MST, POET; DLB 96, 110; EXPP; LMFS 1; PAB; PFS 1, 2, 3, 9, 17; RGEL 2; TEA; WLIT 3; WP

Keble, John 1792-1866 .... **NCLC 87**
See also DLB 32, 55; RGEL 2

Keene, Donald 1922- .... **CLC 34**
See also CA 1-4R; CANR 5, 119

Keillor, Garrison .... **CLC 40, 115**
See Keillor, Gary (Edward)
See also AAYA 2, 62; BEST 89:3; BPFB 2; DLBY 1987; EWL 3; SATA 58; TUS

Keillor, Gary (Edward) 1942-
See Keillor, Garrison
See also CA 111; 117; CANR 36, 59, 124; CPW; DA3; DAM POP; MTCW 1, 2; MTFW 2005

Keith, Carlos
See Lewton, Val

Keith, Michael
See Hubbard, L(afayette) Ron(ald)

Keller, Gottfried 1819-1890 .... **NCLC 2; SSC 26**
See also CDWLB 2; DLB 129; EW; RGSF 2; RGWL 2, 3

Keller, Nora Okja 1965- .... **CLC 109**
See also CA 187

Kellerman, Jonathan 1949- .... **CLC 44**
See also AAYA 35; BEST 90:1; CA 106; CANR 29, 51; CMW 4; CPW; DA3; DAM POP; INT CANR-29

Kelley, William Melvin 1937- .... **CLC 22**
See also BW 1; CA 77-80; CANR 27, 83; CN 1, 2, 3, 4, 5, 6, 7; DLB 33; EWL 3

Kellogg, Marjorie 1922-2005 .... **CLC 2**
See also CA 81-84

Kellow, Kathleen
See Hibbert, Eleanor Alice Burford

Kelly, Lauren
See Oates, Joyce Carol

Kelly, M(ilton) T(errence) 1947- ...... **CLC 55**
See also CA 97-100; CAAS 22; CANR 19, 43, 84; CN 6

Kelly, Robert 1935- .... **SSC 50**
See also CA 17-20R; CAAS 19; CANR 47; CP 1, 2, 3, 4, 5, 6, 7; DLB 5, 130, 165

Kelman, James 1946- .... **CLC 58, 86**
See also BRWS 5; CA 148; CANR 85, 130; CN 5, 6, 7; DLB 194, 319; RGSF 2; WLIT 4

Kemal, Yasar
See Kemal, Yashar
See also CWW 2; EWL 3; WLIT 6

Kemal, Yashar 1923(?)- .... **CLC 14, 29**
See also CA 89-92; CANR 44

Kemble, Fanny 1809-1893 .... **NCLC 18**
See also DLB 32

Kemelman, Harry 1908-1996 .... **CLC 2**
See also AITN 1; BPFB 2; CA 9-12R; 155; CANR 6, 71; CMW 4; DLB 28

Kempe, Margery 1373(?)-1440(?) ... **LC 6, 56**
See also DLB 146; FL 1:1; RGEL 2

Kempis, Thomas a 1380-1471 .... **LC 11**

Kendall, Henry 1839-1882 .... **NCLC 12**
See also DLB 230

Keneally, Thomas (Michael) 1935- ... **CLC 5, 8, 10, 14, 19, 27, 43, 117**
See also BRWS 4; CA 85-88; CANR 10, 50, 74, 130; CN 1, 2, 3, 4, 5, 6, 7; CPW; DA3; DAM NOV; DLB 289, 299; EWL 3; MTCW 1, 2; MTFW 2005; NFS 17; RGEL 2; RHW

Kennedy, A(lison) L(ouise) 1965- ... **CLC 188**
See also CA 168, 213; CAAE 213; CANR 108; CD 5, 6; CN 6, 7; DLB 271; RGSF 2

Kennedy, Adrienne (Lita) 1931- .... **BLC 2; CLC 66; DC 5**
See also AFAW 2; BW 2, 3; CA 103; CAAS 20; CABS 3; CAD; CANR 26, 53, 82; CD 5, 6; DAM MULT; DFS 9; DLB 38; FW; MAL 5

Kennedy, John Pendleton
1795-1870 .... **NCLC 2**
See also DLB 3, 248, 254; RGAL 4

Kennedy, Joseph Charles 1929-
See Kennedy, X. J.
See also CA 1-4R, 201; CAAE 201; CANR 4, 30, 40; CWRI 5; MAICYA 2; MAIC-YAS 1; SATA 14, 86, 130; SATA-Essay 130

Kennedy, William (Joseph) 1928- ..... **CLC 6, 28, 34, 53**
See also AAYA 1; AMWS 7; BPFB 2; CA 85-88; CANR 14, 31, 76, 134; CN 4, 5, 6, 7; DA3; DAM NOV; DLB 143; DLBY 1985; EWL 3; INT CANR-31; MAL 5; MTCW 1, 2; MTFW 2005; SATA 57

Kennedy, X. J. .... **CLC 8, 42**
See Kennedy, Joseph Charles
See also AMWS 15; CAAS 9; CLR 27; CP 1, 2, 3, 4, 5, 6, 7; DLB 5; SAAS 22

Kenny, Maurice (Francis) 1929- ..... **CLC 87; NNAL**
See also CA 144; CAAS 22; CANR 143; DAM MULT; DLB 175

Kent, Kelvin
See Kuttner, Henry

Kenton, Maxwell
See Southern, Terry

Kenyon, Jane 1947-1995 .... **PC 57**
See also AAYA 63; AMWS 7; CA 118; 148; CANR 44, 69; CP 7; CWP; DLB 120; PFS 9, 17; RGAL 4

Kenyon, Robert O.
See Kuttner, Henry

Kepler, Johannes 1571-1630 .... **LC 45**

Ker, Jill
See Conway, Jill K(er)

Kerkow, H. C.
See Lewton, Val

Kerouac, Jack 1922-1969 ...... **CLC 1, 2, 3, 5, 14, 29, 61; TCLC 117; WLC**
See Kerouac, Jean-Louis Lebris de
See also AAYA 25; AMWC 1; AMWS 3; BG 1; BPFB 2; CDALB 1941-1968; CP 1; CPW; DLB 2, 16, 237; DLBD 3; DLBY 1995; EWL 3; GLL 1; LATS 1:2; LMFS 2; MAL 5; NFS 8; RGAL 4; TUS; WP

Kerouac, Jean-Louis Lebris de 1922-1969
See Kerouac, Jack
See also AITN 1; CA 5-8R; 25-28R; CANR 26, 54, 95; DA; DA3; DAB; DAC; DAM MST, NOV, POET, POP; MTCW 1, 2; MTFW 2005

Kerr, (Bridget) Jean (Collins)
1923(?)-2003 .... **CLC 22**
See also CA 5-8R; 212; CANR 7; INT CANR-7

Kerr, M. E. .... **CLC 12, 35**
See Meaker, Marijane (Agnes)
See also AAYA 2, 23; BYA 1, 7, 8; CLR 29; SAAS 1; WYA

Kerr, Robert .... **CLC 55**

Kerrigan, (Thomas) Anthony 1918- .. **CLC 4, 6**
See also CA 49-52; CAAS 11; CANR 4

Kerry, Lois
See Duncan, Lois

Kesey, Ken (Elton) 1935-2001 ... **CLC 1, 3, 6, 11, 46, 64, 184; WLC**
See also AAYA 25; BG 1:3; BPFB 2; CA 1-4R; 204; CANR 22, 38, 66, 124; CDALB 1968-1988; CN 1, 2, 3, 4, 5, 6, 7; CPW; DA; DA3; DAB; DAC; DAM MST, NOV, POP; DLB 2, 16, 206; EWL 3; EXPN; LAIT 4; MAL 5; MTCW 1, 2; MTFW 2005; NFS 2; RGAL 4; SATA 66; SATA-Obit 131; TUS; YAW

Kesselring, Joseph (Otto)
1902-1967 .... **CLC 45**
See also CA 150; DAM DRAM, MST; DFS 20

Kessler, Jascha (Frederick) 1929- ...... **CLC 4**
See also CA 17-20R; CANR 8, 48, 111; CP 1

Kettelkamp, Larry (Dale) 1933- .... **CLC 12**
See also CA 29-32R; CANR 16; SAAS 3; SATA 2

Key, Ellen (Karolina Sofia)
1849-1926 .... **TCLC 65**
See also DLB 259

Keyber, Conny
See Fielding, Henry

Keyes, Daniel 1927- .... **CLC 80**
See also AAYA 23; BYA 11; CA 17-20R; 181; CAAE 181; CANR 10, 26, 54, 74; DA; DA3; DAC; DAM MST, NOV; EXPN; LAIT 4; MTCW 2; MTFW 2005; NFS 2; SATA 37; SFW 4

Klinger, Friedrich Maximilian von
1752-1831 .... **NCLC 1**
See also DLB 94
Klingsor the Magician
See Hartmann, Sadakichi
Klopstock, Friedrich Gottlieb
1724-1803 .... **NCLC 11**
See also DLB 97; EW 4; RGWL 2, 3
Kluge, Alexander 1932- .... **SSC 61**
See also CA 81-84; DLB 75
Knapp, Caroline 1959-2002 .... **CLC 99**
See also CA 154; 207
Knebel, Fletcher 1911-1993 .... **CLC 14**
See also AITN 1; CA 1-4R; 140; CAAS 3;
CANR 1, 36; CN 1, 2, 3, 4, 5; SATA 36;
SATA-Obit 75
Knickerbocker, Diedrich
See Irving, Washington
Knight, Etheridge 1931-1991 ... **BLC 2; CLC
40; PC 14**
See also BW 1, 3; CA 21-24R; 133; CANR
23, 82; CP 1, 2, 3, 4; DAM POET; DLB
41; MTCW 2; MTFW 2005; RGAL 4;
TCLE 1:1
Knight, Sarah Kemble 1666-1727 .... **LC 7**
See also DLB 24, 200
Knister, Raymond 1899-1932 .... **TCLC 56**
See also CA 186; DLB 68; RGEL 2
Knowles, John 1926-2001 ... **CLC 1, 4, 10, 26**
See also AAYA 10; AMWS 12; BPFB 2;
BYA 3; CA 17-20R; 203; CANR 40, 74,
76, 132; CDALB 1968-1988; CLR 98; CN
1, 2, 3, 4, 5, 6, 7; DA; DAC; DAM MST,
NOV; DLB 6; EXPN; MTCW 1, 2;
MTFW 2005; NFS 2; RGAL 4; SATA 8,
89; SATA-Obit 134; YAW
Knox, Calvin M.
See Silverberg, Robert
Knox, John c. 1505-1572 .... **LC 37**
See also DLB 132
Knye, Cassandra
See Disch, Thomas M(ichael)
Koch, C(hristopher) J(ohn) 1932- .... **CLC 42**
See also CA 127; CANR 84; CN 3, 4, 5, 6,
7; DLB 289
Koch, Christopher
See Koch, C(hristopher) J(ohn)
Koch, Kenneth (Jay) 1925-2002 .... **CLC 5, 8,
44**
See also AMWS 15; CA 1-4R; 207; CAD;
CANR 6, 36, 57, 97, 131; CD 5, 6; CP 1,
2, 3, 4, 5, 6, 7; DAM POET; DLB 5; INT
CANR-36; MAL 5; MTCW 2; MTFW
2005; PFS 20; SATA 65; WP
Kochanowski, Jan 1530-1584 .... **LC 10**
See also RGWL 2, 3
Kock, Charles Paul de 1794-1871 . **NCLC 16**
Koda Rohan
See Koda Shigeyuki
Koda Rohan
See Koda Shigeyuki
See also DLB 180
Koda Shigeyuki 1867-1947 .... **TCLC 22**
See Koda Rohan
See also CA 121; 183
Koestler, Arthur 1905-1983 ... **CLC 1, 3, 6, 8,
15, 33**
See also BRWS 1; CA 1-4R; 109; CANR 1,
33; CDBLB 1945-1960; CN 1, 2, 3;
DLBY 1983; EWL 3; MTCW 1, 2; MTFW
2005; NFS 19; RGEL 2
Kogawa, Joy Nozomi 1935- ...... **CLC 78, 129**
See also AAYA 47; CA 101; CANR 19, 62,
126; CN 6, 7; CP 1; CWP; DAC; DAM
MST, MULT; FW; MTCW 2; MTFW
2005; NFS 3; SATA 99
Kohout, Pavel 1928- .... **CLC 13**
See also CA 45-48; CANR 3

Koizumi, Yakumo
See Hearn, (Patricio) Lafcadio (Tessima
Carlos)
Kolmar, Gertrud 1894-1943 .... **TCLC 40**
See also CA 167; EWL 3
Komunyakaa, Yusef 1947- .. **BLCS; CLC 86,
94, 207; PC 51**
See also AFAW 2; AMWS 13; CA 147;
CANR 83; CP 7; CSW; DLB 120; EWL
3; PFS 5, 20; RGAL 4
Konrad, George
See Konrad, Gyorgy
Konrad, Gyorgy 1933- .... **CLC 4, 10, 73**
See also CA 85-88; CANR 97; CDWLB 4;
CWW 2; DLB 232; EWL 3
Konwicki, Tadeusz 1926- .... **CLC 8, 28, 54,
117**
See also CA 101; CAAS 9; CANR 39, 59;
CWW 2; DLB 232; EWL 3; IDFW 3;
MTCW 1
Koontz, Dean R. 1945- .... **CLC 78, 206**
See also AAYA 9, 31; BEST 89:3, 90:2; CA
108; CANR 19, 36, 52, 95, 138; CMW 4;
CPW; DA3; DAM NOV, POP; DLB 292;
HGG; MTCW 1; MTFW 2005; SATA 92,
165; SFW 4; SUFW 2; YAW
Koontz, Dean Ray
See Koontz, Dean R.
Koontz, Dean Ray
See Koontz, Dean R.
Kopernik, Mikolaj
See Copernicus, Nicolaus
Kopit, Arthur (Lee) 1937- ...... **CLC 1, 18, 33**
See also AITN 1; CA 81-84; CABS 3;
CAD; CD 5, 6; DAM DRAM; DFS 7, 14;
DLB 7; MAL 5; MTCW 1; RGAL 4
Kopitar, Jernej (Bartholomaus)
1780-1844 .... **NCLC 117**
Kops, Bernard 1926- .... **CLC 4**
See also CA 5-8R; CANR 84; CBD; CN 1,
2, 3, 4, 5, 6, 7; CP 1, 2, 3, 4, 5, 6, 7; DLB
13
Kornbluth, C(yril) M. 1923-1958 .... **TCLC 8**
See also CA 105; 160; DLB 8; SCFW 1, 2;
SFW 4
Korolenko, V. G.
See Korolenko, Vladimir Galaktionovich
Korolenko, Vladimir
See Korolenko, Vladimir Galaktionovich
Korolenko, Vladimir G.
See Korolenko, Vladimir Galaktionovich
Korolenko, Vladimir Galaktionovich
1853-1921 .... **TCLC 22**
See also CA 121; DLB 277
Korzybski, Alfred (Habdank Skarbek)
1879-1950 .... **TCLC 61**
See also CA 123; 160
Kosinski, Jerzy (Nikodem)
1933-1991 .... **CLC 1, 2, 3, 6, 10, 15, 53,
70**
See also AMWS 7; BPFB 2; CA 17-20R;
134; CANR 9, 46; CN 1, 2, 3, 4; DA3;
DAM NOV; DLB 2, 299; DLBY 1982;
EWL 3; HGG; MAL 5; MTCW 1, 2;
MTFW 2005; NFS 12; RGAL 4; TUS
Kostelanetz, Richard (Cory) 1940- .. **CLC 28**
See also CA 13-16R; CAAS 8; CANR 38,
77; CN 4, 5, 6; CP 2, 3, 4, 5, 6, 7
Kostrowitzki, Wilhelm Apollinaris de
1880-1918
See Apollinaire, Guillaume
See also CA 104
Kotlowitz, Robert 1924- .... **CLC 4**
See also CA 33-36R; CANR 36
Kotzebue, August (Friedrich Ferdinand) von
1761-1819 .... **NCLC 25**
See also DLB 94

Kotzwinkle, William 1938- ..... **CLC 5, 14, 35**
See also BPFB 2; CA 45-48; CANR 3, 44,
84, 129; CLR 6; CN 7; DLB 173; FANT;
MAICYA 1, 2; SATA 24, 70, 146; SFW
4; SUFW 2; YAW
Kowna, Stancy
See Szymborska, Wislawa
Kozol, Jonathan 1936- .... **CLC 17**
See also AAYA 46; CA 61-64; CANR 16,
45, 96; MTFW 2005
Kozoll, Michael 1940(?)- .... **CLC 35**
Kramer, Kathryn 19(?)- .... **CLC 34**
Kramer, Larry 1935- .... **CLC 42; DC 8**
See also CA 124; 126; CANR 60, 132;
DAM POP; DLB 249; GLL 1
Krasicki, Ignacy 1735-1801 .... **NCLC 8**
Krasinski, Zygmunt 1812-1859 .... **NCLC 4**
See also RGWL 2, 3
Kraus, Karl 1874-1936 .... **TCLC 5**
See also CA 104; 216; DLB 118; EWL 3
Kreve (Mickevicius), Vincas
1882-1954 .... **TCLC 27**
See also CA 170; DLB 220; EWL 3
Kristeva, Julia 1941- .... **CLC 77, 140**
See also CA 154; CANR 99; DLB 242;
EWL 3; FW; LMFS 2
Kristofferson, Kris 1936- .... **CLC 26**
See also CA 104
Krizanc, John 1956- .... **CLC 57**
See also CA 187
Krleza, Miroslav 1893-1981 .... **CLC 8, 114**
See also CA 97-100; 105; CANR 50; CD-
WLB 4; DLB 147; EW 11; RGWL 2, 3
Kroetsch, Robert (Paul) 1927- .... **CLC 5, 23,
57, 132**
See also CA 17-20R; CANR 8, 38; CCA 1;
CN 2, 3, 4, 5, 6, 7; CP 7; DAC; DAM
POET; DLB 53; MTCW 1
Kroetz, Franz
See Kroetz, Franz Xaver
Kroetz, Franz Xaver 1946- .... **CLC 41**
See also CA 130; CANR 142; CWW 2;
EWL 3
Kroker, Arthur (W.) 1945- .... **CLC 77**
See also CA 161
Kroniuk, Lisa
See Berton, Pierre (Francis de Marigny)
Kropotkin, Peter (Aleksieevich)
1842-1921 .... **TCLC 36**
See Kropotkin, Petr Alekseevich
See also CA 119; 219
Kropotkin, Petr Alekseevich
See Kropotkin, Peter (Aleksieevich)
See also DLB 277
Krotkov, Yuri 1917-1981 .... **CLC 19**
See also CA 102
Krumb
See Crumb, R(obert)
Krumgold, Joseph (Quincy)
1908-1980 .... **CLC 12**
See also BYA 1, 2; CA 9-12R; 101; CANR
7; MAICYA 1, 2; SATA 1, 48; SATA-Obit
23; YAW
Krumwitz
See Crumb, R(obert)
Krutch, Joseph Wood 1893-1970 ..... **CLC 24**
See also ANW; CA 1-4R; 25-28R; CANR
4; DLB 63, 206, 275
Krutzch, Gus
See Eliot, T(homas) S(tearns)
Krylov, Ivan Andreevich
1768(?)-1844 .... **NCLC 1**
See also DLB 150
Kubin, Alfred (Leopold Isidor)
1877-1959 .... **TCLC 23**
See also CA 112; 149; CANR 104; DLB 81

Kubrick, Stanley 1928-1999 .... **CLC 16;**
   TCLC 112
   See also AAYA 30; CA 81-84; 177; CANR
   33; DLB 26
Kumin, Maxine (Winokur) 1925- ..... **CLC 5,**
   13, 28, 164; PC 15
   See also AITN 2; AMWS 4; ANW; CA
   1-4R; CAAS 8; CANR 1, 21, 69, 115,
   140; CP 2, 3, 4, 5, 6, 7; CWP; DA3; DAM
   POET; DLB 5; EWL 3; EXPP; MTCW 1,
   2; MTFW 2005; PAB; PFS 18; SATA 12
Kundera, Milan 1929- . **CLC 4, 9, 19, 32, 68,**
   115, 135; SSC 24
   See also AAYA 2, 62; BPFB 2; CA 85-88;
   CANR 19, 52, 74, 144; CDWLB 4; CWW
   2; DA3; DAM NOV; DLB 232; EW 13;
   EWL 3; MTCW 1, 2; MTFW 2005; NFS
   18; RGSF 2; RGWL 3; SSFS 10
Kunene, Mazisi (Raymond) 1930- ... **CLC 85**
   See also BW 1, 3; CA 125; CANR 81; CP
   1, 7; DLB 117
Kung, Hans .... **CLC 130**
   See Kung, Hans
Kung, Hans 1928-
   See Kung, Hans
   See also CA 53-56; CANR 66, 134; MTCW
   1, 2; MTFW 2005
Kunikida Doppo 1869(?)-1908
   See Doppo, Kunikida
   See also DLB 180; EWL 3
Kunitz, Stanley (Jasspon) 1905- .. **CLC 6, 11,**
   14, 148; PC 19
   See also AMWS 3; CA 41-44R; CANR 26,
   57, 98; CP 1, 2, 3, 4, 5, 6, 7; DA3; DLB
   48; INT CANR-26; MAL 5; MTCW 1, 2;
   MTFW 2005; PFS 11; RGAL 4
Kunze, Reiner 1933- .... **CLC 10**
   See also CA 93-96; CWW 2; DLB 75; EWL
   3
Kuprin, Aleksander Ivanovich
   1870-1938 .... **TCLC 5**
   See Kuprin, Aleksandr Ivanovich; Kuprin,
   Alexandr Ivanovich
   See also CA 104; 182
Kuprin, Aleksandr Ivanovich
   See Kuprin, Aleksander Ivanovich
   See also DLB 295
Kuprin, Alexandr Ivanovich
   See Kuprin, Aleksander Ivanovich
   See also EWL 3
Kureishi, Hanif 1954- .. **CLC 64, 135; DC 26**
   See also BRWS 11; CA 139; CANR 113;
   CBD; CD 5, 6; CN 6, 7; DLB 194, 245;
   GLL 2; IDFW 4; WLIT 4; WWE 1
Kurosawa, Akira 1910-1998 ... **CLC 16, 119**
   See also AAYA 11, 64; CA 101; 170; CANR
   46; DAM MULT
Kushner, Tony 1956- .... **CLC 81, 203; DC 10**
   See also AAYA 61; AMWS 9; CA 144;
   CAD; CANR 74, 130; CD 5, 6; DA3;
   DAM DRAM; DFS 5; DLB 228; EWL 3;
   GLL 1; LAIT 5; MAL 5; MTCW 2;
   MTFW 2005; RGAL 4; SATA 160
Kuttner, Henry 1915-1958 .... **TCLC 10**
   See also CA 107; 157; DLB 8; FANT;
   SCFW 1, 2; SFW 4
Kutty, Madhavi
   See Das, Kamala
Kuzma, Greg 1944- .... **CLC 7**
   See also CA 33-36R; CANR 70
Kuzmin, Mikhail (Alexseevich)
   1872(?)-1936 .... **TCLC 40**
   See also CA 170; DLB 295; EWL 3
Kyd, Thomas 1558-1594 .... **DC 3; LC 22**
   See also BRW 1; DAM DRAM; DFS 21;
   DLB 62; IDTP; LMFS 1; RGEL 2; TEA;
   WLIT 3
Kyprianos, Iossif
   See Samarakis, Antonis

L. S.
   See Stephen, Sir Leslie
Laȝamon
   See Layamon
   See also DLB 146
Labe, Louise 1521-1566 .... **LC 120**
Labrunie, Gerard
   See Nerval, Gerard de
La Bruyere, Jean de 1645-1696 .... **LC 17**
   See also DLB 268; EW 3; GFL Beginnings
   to 1789
Lacan, Jacques (Marie Emile)
   1901-1981 .... **CLC 75**
   See also CA 121; 104; DLB 296; EWL 3;
   TWA
Laclos, Pierre-Ambroise Francois
   1741-1803 .... **NCLC 4, 87**
   See also DLB 313; EW 4; GFL Beginnings
   to 1789; RGWL 2, 3
Lacolere, Francois
   See Aragon, Louis
La Colere, Francois
   See Aragon, Louis
La Deshabilleuse
   See Simenon, Georges (Jacques Christian)
Lady Gregory
   See Gregory, Lady Isabella Augusta (Persse)
Lady of Quality, A
   See Bagnold, Enid
La Fayette, Marie-(Madelaine Pioche de la
   Vergne) 1634-1693 .... **LC 2**
   See Lafayette, Marie-Madeleine
   See also GFL Beginnings to 1789; RGWL
   2, 3
Lafayette, Marie-Madeleine
   See La Fayette, Marie-(Madelaine Pioche
   de la Vergne)
   See also DLB 268
Lafayette, Rene
   See Hubbard, L(afayette) Ron(ald)
La Flesche, Francis 1857(?)-1932 ...... **NNAL**
   See also CA 144; CANR 83; DLB 175
La Fontaine, Jean de 1621-1695 .... **LC 50**
   See also DLB 268; EW 3; GFL Beginnings
   to 1789; MAICYA 1, 2; RGWL 2, 3;
   SATA 18
Laforgue, Jules 1860-1887 . **NCLC 5, 53; PC**
   14; SSC 20
   See also DLB 217; EW 7; GFL 1789 to the
   Present; RGWL 2, 3
Lagerkvist, Paer (Fabian)
   1891-1974 ..... **CLC 7, 10, 13, 54; TCLC**
   144
   See Lagerkvist, Par
   See also CA 85-88; 49-52; DA3; DAM
   DRAM, NOV; MTCW 1, 2; MTFW 2005;
   TWA
Lagerkvist, Par .... **SSC 12**
   See Lagerkvist, Paer (Fabian)
   See also DLB 259; EW 10; EWL 3; RGSF
   2; RGWL 2, 3
Lagerloef, Selma (Ottiliana Lovisa)
   .... **TCLC 4, 36**
   See Lagerlof, Selma (Ottiliana Lovisa)
   See also CA 108; MTCW 2
Lagerlof, Selma (Ottiliana Lovisa)
   1858-1940
   See Lagerloef, Selma (Ottiliana Lovisa)
   See also CA 188; CLR 7; DLB 259; RGWL
   2, 3; SATA 15; SSFS 18
La Guma, (Justin) Alex(ander)
   1925-1985 . **BLCS; CLC 19; TCLC 140**
   See also AFW; BW 1, 3; CA 49-52; 118;
   CANR 25, 81; CDWLB 3; CN 1, 2, 3;
   CP 1; DAM NOV; DLB 117, 225; EWL
   3; MTCW 1, 2; MTFW 2005; WLIT 2;
   WWE 1
Laidlaw, A. K.
   See Grieve, C(hristopher) M(urray)

Lainez, Manuel Mujica
   See Mujica Lainez, Manuel
   See also HW 1
Laing, R(onald) D(avid) 1927-1989 . **CLC 95**
   See also CA 107; 129; CANR 34; MTCW 1
Laishley, Alex
   See Booth, Martin
Lamartine, Alphonse (Marie Louis Prat) de
   1790-1869 .... **NCLC 11; PC 16**
   See also DAM POET; DLB 217; GFL 1789
   to the Present; RGWL 2, 3
Lamb, Charles 1775-1834 ..... **NCLC 10, 113;**
   WLC
   See also BRW 4; CDBLB 1789-1832; DA;
   DAB; DAC; DAM MST; DLB 93, 107,
   163; RGEL 2; SATA 17; TEA
Lamb, Lady Caroline 1785-1828 ... **NCLC 38**
   See also DLB 116
Lamb, Mary Ann 1764-1847 .... **NCLC 125**
   See also DLB 163; SATA 17
Lame Deer 1903(?)-1976 .... **NNAL**
   See also CA 69-72
Lamming, George (William) 1927- ... **BLC 2;**
   CLC 2, 4, 66, 144
   See also BW 2, 3; CA 85-88; CANR 26,
   76; CDWLB 3; CN 1, 2, 3, 4, 5, 6, 7; CP
   1; DAM MULT; DLB 125; EWL 3;
   MTCW 1, 2; MTFW 2005; NFS 15;
   RGEL 2
L'Amour, Louis (Dearborn)
   1908-1988 .... **CLC 25, 55**
   See also AAYA 16; AITN 2; BEST 89:2;
   BPFB 2; CA 1-4R; 125; CANR 3, 25, 40;
   CPW; DA3; DAM NOV, POP; DLB 206;
   DLBY 1980; MTCW 1, 2; MTFW 2005;
   RGAL 4; TCWW 1, 2
Lampedusa, Giuseppe (Tomasi) di
   .... **TCLC 13**
   See Tomasi di Lampedusa, Giuseppe
   See also CA 164; EW 11; MTCW 2; MTFW
   2005; RGWL 2, 3
Lampman, Archibald 1861-1899 ... **NCLC 25**
   See also DLB 92; RGEL 2; TWA
Lancaster, Bruce 1896-1963 .... **CLC 36**
   See also CA 9-10; CANR 70; CAP 1; SATA
   9
Lanchester, John 1962- .... **CLC 99**
   See also CA 194; DLB 267
Landau, Mark Alexandrovich
   See Aldanov, Mark (Alexandrovich)
Landau-Aldanov, Mark Alexandrovich
   See Aldanov, Mark (Alexandrovich)
Landis, Jerry
   See Simon, Paul (Frederick)
Landis, John 1950- .... **CLC 26**
   See also CA 112; 122; CANR 128
Landolfi, Tommaso 1908-1979 .... **CLC 11, 49**
   See also CA 127; 117; DLB 177; EWL 3
Landon, Letitia Elizabeth
   1802-1838 .... **NCLC 15**
   See also DLB 96
Landor, Walter Savage
   1775-1864 .... **NCLC 14**
   See also BRW 4; DLB 93, 107; RGEL 2
Landwirth, Heinz 1927-
   See Lind, Jakov
   See also CA 9-12R; CANR 7
Lane, Patrick 1939- .... **CLC 25**
   See also CA 97-100; CANR 54; CP 3, 4, 5,
   6, 7; DAM POET; DLB 53; INT CA-97-
   100
Lang, Andrew 1844-1912 .... **TCLC 16**
   See also CA 114; 137; CANR 85; CLR 101;
   DLB 98, 141, 184; FANT; MAICYA 1, 2;
   RGEL 2; SATA 16; WCH
Lang, Fritz 1890-1976 .... **CLC 20, 103**
   See also AAYA 65; CA 77-80; 69-72;
   CANR 30

Limonov, Edward 1944- .... **CLC 67**
See Limonov, Eduard
See also CA 137

Lin, Frank
See Atherton, Gertrude (Franklin Horn)

Lin, Yutang 1895-1976 .... **TCLC 149**
See also CA 45-48; 65-68; CANR 2; RGAL 4

Lincoln, Abraham 1809-1865 .... **NCLC 18**
See also LAIT 2

Lind, Jakov .... **CLC 1, 2, 4, 27, 82**
See Landwirth, Heinz
See also CAAS 4; DLB 299; EWL 3

Lindbergh, Anne (Spencer) Morrow
1906-2001 .... **CLC 82**
See also BPFB 2; CA 17-20R; 193; CANR 16, 73; DAM NOV; MTCW 1, 2; MTFW 2005; SATA 33; SATA-Obit 125; TUS

Lindsay, David 1878(?)-1945 .... **TCLC 15**
See also CA 113; 187; DLB 255; FANT; SFW 4; SUFW 1

Lindsay, (Nicholas) Vachel
1879-1931 .... **PC 23; TCLC 17; WLC**
See also AMWS 1; CA 114; 135; CANR 79; CDALB 1865-1917; DA; DA3; DAC; DAM MST, POET; DLB 54; EWL 3; EXPP; MAL 5; RGAL 4; SATA 40; WP

Linke-Poot
See Doeblin, Alfred

Linney, Romulus 1930- .... **CLC 51**
See also CA 1-4R; CAD; CANR 40, 44, 79; CD 5, 6; CSW; RGAL 4

Linton, Eliza Lynn 1822-1898 .... **NCLC 41**
See also DLB 18

Li Po 701-763 .... **CMLC 2; PC 29**
See also PFS 20; WP

Lipsius, Justus 1547-1606 .... **LC 16**

Lipsyte, Robert (Michael) 1938- ...... **CLC 21**
See also AAYA 7, 45; CA 17-20R; CANR 8, 57; CLR 23, 76; DA; DAC; DAM MST, NOV; JRDA; LAIT 5; MAICYA 1, 2; SATA 5, 68, 113, 161; WYA; YAW

Lish, Gordon (Jay) 1934- ... **CLC 45; SSC 18**
See also CA 113; 117; CANR 79; DLB 130; INT CA-117

Lispector, Clarice 1925(?)-1977 .... **CLC 43; HLCS 2; SSC 34**
See also CA 139; 116; CANR 71; CDWLB 3; DLB 113, 307; DNFS 1; EWL 3; FW; HW 2; LAW; RGSF 2; RGWL 2, 3; WLIT 1

Littell, Robert 1935(?)- .... **CLC 42**
See also CA 109; 112; CANR 64, 115; CMW 4

Little, Malcolm 1925-1965
See Malcolm X
See also BW 1, 3; CA 125; 111; CANR 82; DA; DA3; DAB; DAC; DAM MST, MULT; MTCW 1, 2; MTFW 2005

Littlewit, Humphrey Gent.
See Lovecraft, H(oward) P(hillips)

Litwos
See Sienkiewicz, Henryk (Adam Alexander Pius)

Liu, E. 1857-1909 .... **TCLC 15**
See also CA 115; 190

Lively, Penelope 1933- .... **CLC 32, 50**
See also BPFB 2; CA 41-44R; CANR 29, 67, 79, 131; CLR 7; CN 5, 6, 7; CWRI 5; DAM NOV; DLB 14, 161, 207; FANT; JRDA; MAICYA 1, 2; MTCW 1, 2; MTFW 2005; SATA 7, 60, 101, 164; TEA

Lively, Penelope Margaret
See Lively, Penelope

Livesay, Dorothy (Kathleen)
1909-1996 .... **CLC 4, 15, 79**
See also AITN 2; CA 25-28R; CAAS 8; CANR 36, 67; CP 1, 2, 3, 4; DAC; DAM MST, POET; DLB 68; FW; MTCW 1; RGEL 2; TWA

Livy c. 59B.C.-c. 12 .... **CMLC 11**
See also AW 2; CDWLB 1; DLB 211; RGWL 2, 3

Lizardi, Jose Joaquin Fernandez de
1776-1827 .... **NCLC 30**
See also LAW

Llewellyn, Richard
See Llewellyn Lloyd, Richard Dafydd Vivian
See also DLB 15

Llewellyn Lloyd, Richard Dafydd Vivian
1906-1983 .... **CLC 7, 80**
See Llewellyn, Richard
See also CA 53-56; 111; CANR 7, 71; SATA 11; SATA-Obit 37

Llosa, (Jorge) Mario (Pedro) Vargas
See Vargas Llosa, (Jorge) Mario (Pedro)
See also RGWL 3

Llosa, Mario Vargas
See Vargas Llosa, (Jorge) Mario (Pedro)

Lloyd, Manda
See Mander, (Mary) Jane

Lloyd Webber, Andrew 1948-
See Webber, Andrew Lloyd
See also AAYA 1, 38; CA 116; 149; DAM DRAM; SATA 56

Llull, Ramon c. 1235-c. 1316 .... **CMLC 12**

Lobb, Ebenezer
See Upward, Allen

Locke, Alain (Le Roy)
1886-1954 ...... **BLCS; HR 1:3; TCLC 43**
See also AMWS 14; BW 1, 3; CA 106; 124; CANR 79; DLB 51; LMFS 2; MAL 5; RGAL 4

Locke, John 1632-1704 .... **LC 7, 35**
See also DLB 31, 101, 213, 252; RGEL 2; WLIT 3

Locke-Elliott, Sumner
See Elliott, Sumner Locke

Lockhart, John Gibson 1794-1854 .. **NCLC 6**
See also DLB 110, 116, 144

Lockridge, Ross (Franklin), Jr.
1914-1948 .... **TCLC 111**
See also CA 108; 145; CANR 79; DLB 143; DLBY 1980; MAL 5; RGAL 4; RHW

Lockwood, Robert
See Johnson, Robert

Lodge, David (John) 1935- .... **CLC 36, 141**
See also BEST 90:1; BRWS 4; CA 17-20R; CANR 19, 53, 92, 139; CN 1, 2, 3, 4, 5, 6, 7; CPW; DAM POP; DLB 14, 194; EWL 3; INT CANR-19; MTCW 1, 2; MTFW 2005

Lodge, Thomas 1558-1625 .... **LC 41**
See also DLB 172; RGEL 2

Loewinsohn, Ron(ald William)
1937- .... **CLC 52**
See also CA 25-28R; CANR 71; CP 1, 2, 3, 4

Logan, Jake
See Smith, Martin Cruz

Logan, John (Burton) 1923-1987 .... **CLC 5**
See also CA 77-80; 124; CANR 45; CP 1, 2, 3, 4; DLB 5

Lo Kuan-chung 1330(?)-1400(?) .... **LC 12**

Lombard, Nap
See Johnson, Pamela Hansford

Lombard, Peter 1100(?)-1160(?) ... **CMLC 72**

London, Jack 1876-1916 .. **SSC 4, 49; TCLC 9, 15, 39; WLC**
See London, John Griffith
See also AAYA 13; AITN 2; AMW; BPFB 2; BYA 4, 13; CDALB 1865-1917; DLB

8, 12, 78, 212; EWL 3; EXPS; LAIT 3; MAL 5; NFS 8; RGAL 4; RGSF 2; SATA 18; SFW 4; SSFS 7; TCWW 1, 2; TUS; WYA; YAW

London, John Griffith 1876-1916
See London, Jack
See also CA 110; 119; CANR 73; DA; DA3; DAB; DAC; DAM MST, NOV; JRDA; MAICYA 1, 2; MTCW 1, 2; MTFW 2005; NFS 19

Long, Emmett
See Leonard, Elmore (John, Jr.)

Longbaugh, Harry
See Goldman, William (W.)

Longfellow, Henry Wadsworth
1807-1882 .... **NCLC 2, 45, 101, 103; PC 30; WLCS**
See also AMW; AMWR 2; CDALB 1640-1865; CLR 99; DA; DA3; DAB; DAC; DAM MST, POET; DLB 1, 59, 235; EXPP; PAB; PFS 2, 7, 17; RGAL 4; SATA 19; TUS; WP

Longinus c. 1st cent. - .... **CMLC 27**
See also AW 2; DLB 176

Longley, Michael 1939- .... **CLC 29**
See also BRWS 8; CA 102; CP 1, 2, 3, 4, 5, 6, 7; DLB 40

Longstreet, Augustus Baldwin
1790-1870 .... **NCLC 159**
See also DLB 3, 11, 74, 248; RGAL 4

Longus fl. c. 2nd cent. - .... **CMLC 7**

Longway, A. Hugh
See Lang, Andrew

Lonnbohm, Armas Eino Leopold 1878-1926
See Leino, Eino
See also CA 123

Lonnrot, Elias 1802-1884 .... **NCLC 53**
See also EFS 1

Lonsdale, Roger ed. .... **CLC 65**

Lopate, Phillip 1943- .... **CLC 29**
See also CA 97-100; CANR 88; DLBY 1980; INT CA-97-100

Lopez, Barry (Holstun) 1945- .... **CLC 70**
See also AAYA 9, 63; ANW; CA 65-68; CANR 7, 23, 47, 68, 92; DLB 256, 275; INT CANR-7, -23; MTCW 1; RGAL 4; SATA 67

Lopez de Mendoza, Inigo
See Santillana, Inigo Lopez de Mendoza, Marques de

Lopez Portillo (y Pacheco), Jose
1920-2004 .... **CLC 46**
See also CA 129; 224; HW 1

Lopez y Fuentes, Gregorio
1897(?)-1966 .... **CLC 32**
See also CA 131; EWL 3; HW 1

Lorca, Federico Garcia
See Garcia Lorca, Federico
See also DFS 4; EW 11; PFS 20; RGWL 2, 3; WP

Lord, Audre
See Lorde, Audre (Geraldine)
See also EWL 3

Lord, Bette Bao 1938- .... **AAL; CLC 23**
See also BEST 90:3; BPFB 2; CA 107; CANR 41, 79; INT CA-107; SATA 58

Lord Auch
See Bataille, Georges

Lord Brooke
See Greville, Fulke

Lord Byron
See Byron, George Gordon (Noel)

Lorde, Audre (Geraldine)
1934-1992 .... **BLC 2; CLC 18, 71; PC 12; TCLC 173**
See Domini, Rey; Lord, Audre
See also AFAW 1, 2; BW 1, 3; CA 25-28R; 142; CANR 16, 26, 46, 82; CP 2, 3, 4; DA3; DAM MULT, POET; DLB 41; FW; MAL 5; MTCW 1, 2; MTFW 2005; PFS 16; RGAL 4

Marley, Bob .... **CLC 17**
See Marley, Robert Nesta

Marley, Robert Nesta 1945-1981
See Marley, Bob
See also CA 107; 103

Marlowe, Christopher 1564-1593 . **DC 1; LC 22, 47, 117; PC 57; WLC**
See also BRW 1; BRWR 1; CDBLB Before 1660; DA; DA3; DAB; DAC; DAM DRAM, MST; DFS 1, 5, 13, 21; DLB 62; EXPP; LMFS 1; PFS 22; RGEL 2; TEA; WLIT 3

Marlowe, Stephen 1928- .... **CLC 70**
See Queen, Ellery
See also CA 13-16R; CANR 6, 55; CMW 4; SFW 4

Marmion, Shakerley 1603-1639 .... **LC 89**
See also DLB 58; RGEL 2

Marmontel, Jean-Francois 1723-1799 .. **LC 2**
See also DLB 314

Maron, Monika 1941- .... **CLC 165**
See also CA 201

Marquand, John P(hillips)
1893-1960 .... **CLC 2, 10**
See also AMW; BPFB 2; CA 85-88; CANR 73; CMW 4; DLB 9, 102; EWL 3; MAL 5; MTCW 2; RGAL 4

Marques, Rene 1919-1979 .. **CLC 96; HLC 2**
See also CA 97-100; 85-88; CANR 78; DAM MULT; DLB 305; EWL 3; HW 1, 2; LAW; RGSF 2

Marquez, Gabriel (Jose) Garcia
See Garcia Marquez, Gabriel (Jose)

Marquis, Don(ald Robert Perry)
1878-1937 .... **TCLC 7**
See also CA 104; 166; DLB 11, 25; MAL 5; RGAL 4

Marquis de Sade
See Sade, Donatien Alphonse Francois

Marric, J. J.
See Creasey, John
See also MSW

Marryat, Frederick 1792-1848 .... **NCLC 3**
See also DLB 21, 163; RGEL 2; WCH

Marsden, James
See Creasey, John

Marsh, Edward 1872-1953 .... **TCLC 99**

Marsh, (Edith) Ngaio 1895-1982 .. **CLC 7, 53**
See also CA 9-12R; CANR 6, 58; CMW 4; CN 1, 2, 3; CPW; DAM POP; DLB 77; MSW; MTCW 1, 2; RGEL 2; TEA

Marshall, Allen
See Westlake, Donald E(dwin)

Marshall, Garry 1934- .... **CLC 17**
See also AAYA 3; CA 111; SATA 60

Marshall, Paule 1929- .. **BLC 3; CLC 27, 72; SSC 3**
See also AFAW 1, 2; AMWS 11; BPFB 2; BW 2, 3; CA 77-80; CANR 25, 73, 129; CN 1, 2, 3, 4, 5, 6, 7; DA3; DAM MULT; DLB 33, 157, 227; EWL 3; LATS 1:2; MAL 5; MTCW 1, 2; MTFW 2005; RGAL 4; SSFS 15

Marshallik
See Zangwill, Israel

Marsten, Richard
See Hunter, Evan

Marston, John 1576-1634 .... **LC 33**
See also BRW 2; DAM DRAM; DLB 58, 172; RGEL 2

Martel, Yann 1963- .... **CLC 192**
See also AAYA 67; CA 146; CANR 114; MTFW 2005

Martens, Adolphe-Adhemar
See Ghelderode, Michel de

Martha, Henry
See Harris, Mark

Marti, Jose
See Marti (y Perez), Jose (Julian)
See also DLB 290

Marti (y Perez), Jose (Julian)
1853-1895 .... **HLC 2; NCLC 63**
See Marti, Jose
See also DAM MULT; HW 2; LAW; RGWL 2, 3; WLIT 1

Martial c. 40-c. 104 .... **CMLC 35; PC 10**
See also AW 2; CDWLB 1; DLB 211; RGWL 2, 3

Martin, Ken
See Hubbard, L(afayette) Ron(ald)

Martin, Richard
See Creasey, John

Martin, Steve 1945- .... **CLC 30**
See also AAYA 53; CA 97-100; CANR 30, 100, 140; DFS 19; MTCW 1; MTFW 2005

Martin, Valerie 1948- .... **CLC 89**
See also BEST 90:2; CA 85-88; CANR 49, 89

Martin, Violet Florence 1862-1915 .. **SSC 56; TCLC 51**

Martin, Webber
See Silverberg, Robert

Martindale, Patrick Victor
See White, Patrick (Victor Martindale)

Martin du Gard, Roger
1881-1958 .... **TCLC 24**
See also CA 118; CANR 94; DLB 65; EWL 3; GFL 1789 to the Present; RGWL 2, 3

Martineau, Harriet 1802-1876 ...... **NCLC 26, 137**
See also DLB 21, 55, 159, 163, 166, 190; FW; RGEL 2; YABC 2

Martines, Julia
See O'Faolain, Julia

Martinez, Enrique Gonzalez
See Gonzalez Martinez, Enrique

Martinez, Jacinto Benavente y
See Benavente (y Martinez), Jacinto

Martinez de la Rosa, Francisco de Paula
1787-1862 .... **NCLC 102**
See also TWA

Martinez Ruiz, Jose 1873-1967
See Azorin; Ruiz, Jose Martinez
See also CA 93-96; HW 1

Martinez Sierra, Gregorio
1881-1947 .... **TCLC 6**
See also CA 115; EWL 3

Martinez Sierra, Maria (de la O'LeJarraga)
1874-1974 .... **TCLC 6**
See also CA 115; EWL 3

Martinsen, Martin
See Follett, Ken(neth Martin)

Martinson, Harry (Edmund)
1904-1978 .... **CLC 14**
See also CA 77-80; CANR 34, 130; DLB 259; EWL 3

Martyn, Edward 1859-1923 .... **TCLC 131**
See also CA 179; DLB 10; RGEL 2

Marut, Ret
See Traven, B.

Marut, Robert
See Traven, B.

Marvell, Andrew 1621-1678 .... **LC 4, 43; PC 10; WLC**
See also BRW 2; BRWR 2; CDBLB 1660-1789; DA; DAB; DAC; DAM MST, POET; DLB 131; EXPP; PFS 5; RGEL 2; TEA; WP

Marx, Karl (Heinrich)
1818-1883 .... **NCLC 17, 114**
See also DLB 129; LATS 1:1; TWA

Masaoka, Shiki -1902 .... **TCLC 18**
See Masaoka, Tsunenori
See also RGWL 3

Masaoka, Tsunenori 1867-1902
See Masaoka, Shiki
See also CA 117; 191; TWA

Masefield, John (Edward)
1878-1967 .... **CLC 11, 47**
See also CA 19-20; 25-28R; CANR 33; CAP 2; CDBLB 1890-1914; DAM POET; DLB 10, 19, 153, 160; EWL 3; EXPP; FANT; MTCW 1, 2; PFS 5; RGEL 2; SATA 19

Maso, Carole (?)- .... **CLC 44**
See also CA 170; CN 7; GLL 2; RGAL 4

Mason, Bobbie Ann 1940- ... **CLC 28, 43, 82, 154; SSC 4**
See also AAYA 5, 42; AMWS 8; BPFB 2; CA 53-56; CANR 11, 31, 58, 83, 125; CDALBS; CN 5, 6, 7; CSW; DA3; DLB 173; DLBY 1987; EWL 3; EXPS; INT CANR-31; MAL 5; MTCW 1, 2; MTFW 2005; NFS 4; RGAL 4; RGSF 2; SSFS 3, 8, 20; TCLE 1:2; YAW

Mason, Ernst
See Pohl, Frederik

Mason, Hunni B.
See Sternheim, (William Adolf) Carl

Mason, Lee W.
See Malzberg, Barry N(athaniel)

Mason, Nick 1945- .... **CLC 35**

Mason, Tally
See Derleth, August (William)

Mass, Anna .... **CLC 59**

Mass, William
See Gibson, William

Massinger, Philip 1583-1640 .... **LC 70**
See also BRWS 11; DLB 58; RGEL 2

Master Lao
See Lao Tzu

Masters, Edgar Lee 1868-1950 ...... **PC 1, 36; TCLC 2, 25; WLCS**
See also AMWS 1; CA 104; 133; CDALB 1865-1917; DA; DAC; DAM MST, POET; DLB 54; EWL 3; EXPP; MAL 5; MTCW 1, 2; MTFW 2005; RGAL 4; TUS; WP

Masters, Hilary 1928- .... **CLC 48**
See also CA 25-28R; 217; CAAE 217; CANR 13, 47, 97; CN 6, 7; DLB 244

Mastrosimone, William 1947- .... **CLC 36**
See also CA 186; CAD; CD 5, 6

Mathe, Albert
See Camus, Albert

Mather, Cotton 1663-1728 .... **LC 38**
See also AMWS 2; CDALB 1640-1865; DLB 24, 30, 140; RGAL 4; TUS

Mather, Increase 1639-1723 .... **LC 38**
See also DLB 24

Matheson, Richard (Burton) 1926- .. **CLC 37**
See also AAYA 31; CA 97-100; CANR 88, 99; DLB 8, 44; HGG; INT CA-97-100; SCFW 1, 2; SFW 4; SUFW 2

Mathews, Harry (Burchell) 1930- ..... **CLC 6, 52**
See also CA 21-24R; CAAS 6; CANR 18, 40, 98; CN 5, 6, 7

Mathews, John Joseph 1894-1979 .. **CLC 84; NNAL**
See also CA 19-20; 142; CANR 45; CAP 2; DAM MULT; DLB 175; TCWW 1, 2

Mathias, Roland (Glyn) 1915- .... **CLC 45**
See also CA 97-100; CANR 19, 41; CP 1, 2, 3, 4, 5, 6, 7; DLB 27

Matsuo Basho 1644(?)-1694 ...... **LC 62; PC 3**
See Basho, Matsuo
See also DAM POET; PFS 2, 7, 18

Mattheson, Rodney
See Creasey, John

Matthews, (James) Brander
1852-1929 .... **TCLC 95**
See also CA 181; DLB 71, 78; DLBD 13

Matthews, Greg 1949- .... CLC 45
  See also CA 135
Matthews, William (Procter III)
  1942-1997 .... CLC 40
  See also AMWS 9; CA 29-32R; 162; CAAS
  18; CANR 12, 57; CP 2, 3, 4; DLB 5
Matthias, John (Edward) 1941- .... CLC 9
  See also CA 33-36R; CANR 56; CP 4, 5, 6,
  7
Matthiessen, F(rancis) O(tto)
  1902-1950 .... TCLC 100
  See also CA 185; DLB 63; MAL 5
Matthiessen, Peter 1927- ... CLC 5, 7, 11, 32,
  64
  See also AAYA 6, 40; AMWS 5; ANW;
  BEST 90:4; BPFB 2; CA 9-12R; CANR
  21, 50, 73, 100, 138; CN 1, 2, 3, 4, 5, 6,
  7; DA3; DAM NOV; DLB 6, 173, 275;
  MAL 5; MTCW 1, 2; MTFW 2005; SATA
  27
Maturin, Charles Robert
  1780(?)-1824 .... NCLC 6
  See also BRWS 8; DLB 178; GL 3; HGG;
  LMFS 1; RGEL 2; SUFW
Matute (Ausejo), Ana Maria 1925- .. CLC 11
  See also CA 89-92; CANR 129; CWW 2;
  DLB 322; EWL 3; MTCW 1; RGSF 2
Maugham, W. S.
  See Maugham, W(illiam) Somerset
Maugham, W(illiam) Somerset
  1874-1965 .. CLC 1, 11, 15, 67, 93; SSC
  8; WLC
  See also AAYA 55; BPFB 2; BRW 6; CA
  5-8R; 25-28R; CANR 40, 127; CDBLB
  1914-1945; CMW 4; DA; DA3; DAB;
  DAC; DAM DRAM, MST, NOV; DFS
  22; DLB 10, 36, 77, 100, 162, 195; EWL
  3; LAIT 3; MTCW 1, 2; MTFW 2005;
  RGEL 2; RGSF 2; SATA 54; SSFS 17
Maugham, William Somerset
  See Maugham, W(illiam) Somerset
Maupassant, (Henri Rene Albert) Guy de
  1850-1893 . NCLC 1, 42, 83; SSC 1, 64;
  WLC
  See also BYA 14; DA; DA3; DAB; DAC;
  DAM MST; DLB 123; EW 7; EXPS; GFL
  1789 to the Present; LAIT 2; LMFS 1;
  RGSF 2; RGWL 2, 3; SSFS 4, 21; SUFW;
  TWA
Maupin, Armistead (Jones, Jr.)
  1944- .... CLC 95
  See also CA 125; 130; CANR 58, 101;
  CPW; DA3; DAM POP; DLB 278; GLL
  1; INT CA-130; MTCW 2; MTFW 2005
Maurhut, Richard
  See Traven, B.
Mauriac, Claude 1914-1996 .... CLC 9
  See also CA 89-92; 152; CWW 2; DLB 83;
  EWL 3; GFL 1789 to the Present
Mauriac, Francois (Charles)
  1885-1970 .... CLC 4, 9, 56; SSC 24
  See also CA 25-28; CAP 2; DLB 65; EW
  10; EWL 3; GFL 1789 to the Present;
  MTCW 1, 2; MTFW 2005; RGWL 2, 3;
  TWA
Mavor, Osborne Henry 1888-1951
  See Bridie, James
  See also CA 104
Maxwell, William (Keepers, Jr.)
  1908-2000 .... CLC 19
  See also AMWS 8; CA 93-96; 189; CANR
  54, 95; CN 1, 2, 3, 4, 5, 6, 7; DLB 218,
  278; DLBY 1980; INT CA-93-96; SATA-
  Obit 128
May, Elaine 1932- .... CLC 16
  See also CA 124; 142; CAD; CWD; DLB
  44

Mayakovski, Vladimir (Vladimirovich)
  1893-1930 .... TCLC 4, 18
  See also Maiakovskii, Vladimir; Mayakovsky,
  Vladimir
  See also CA 104; 158; EWL 3; MTCW 2;
  MTFW 2005; SFW 4; TWA
Mayakovsky, Vladimir
  See Mayakovski, Vladimir (Vladimirovich)
  See also EW 11; WP
Mayhew, Henry 1812-1887 .... NCLC 31
  See also DLB 18, 55, 190
Mayle, Peter 1939(?)- .... CLC 89
  See also CA 139; CANR 64, 109
Maynard, Joyce 1953- .... CLC 23
  See also CA 111; 129; CANR 64
Mayne, William (James Carter)
  1928- .... CLC 12
  See also AAYA 20; CA 9-12R; CANR 37,
  80, 100; CLR 25; FANT; JRDA; MAI-
  CYA 1, 2; MAICYAS 1; SAAS 11; SATA
  6, 68, 122; SUFW 2; YAW
Mayo, Jim
  See L'Amour, Louis (Dearborn)
Maysles, Albert 1926- .... CLC 16
  See also CA 29-32R
Maysles, David 1932-1987 .... CLC 16
  See also CA 191
Mazer, Norma Fox 1931- .... CLC 26
  See also AAYA 5, 36; BYA 1, 8; CA 69-72;
  CANR 12, 32, 66, 129; CLR 23; JRDA;
  MAICYA 1, 2; SAAS 1; SATA 24, 67,
  105; WYA; YAW
Mazzini, Guiseppe 1805-1872 .... NCLC 34
McAlmon, Robert (Menzies)
  1895-1956 .... TCLC 97
  See also CA 107; 168; DLB 4, 45; DLBD
  15; GLL 1
McAuley, James Phillip 1917-1976 .. CLC 45
  See also CA 97-100; CP 1, 2; DLB 260;
  RGEL 2
McBain, Ed
  See Hunter, Evan
  See also MSW
McBrien, William (Augustine)
  1930- .... CLC 44
  See also CA 107; CANR 90
McCabe, Patrick 1955- .... CLC 133
  See also BRWS 9; CA 130; CANR 50, 90;
  CN 6, 7; DLB 194
McCaffrey, Anne 1926- .... CLC 17
  See also AAYA 6, 34; AITN 2; BEST 89:2;
  BPFB 2; BYA 5; CA 25-28R, 227; CAAE
  227; CANR 15, 35, 55, 96; CLR 49;
  CPW; DA3; DAM NOV, POP; DLB 8;
  JRDA; MAICYA 1, 2; MTCW 1, 2;
  MTFW 2005; SAAS 11; SATA 8, 70, 116,
  152; SATA-Essay 152; SFW 4; SUFW 2;
  WYA; YAW
McCaffrey, Anne Inez
  See McCaffrey, Anne
McCall, Nathan 1955(?)- .... CLC 86
  See also AAYA 59; BW 3; CA 146; CANR
  88
McCann, Arthur
  See Campbell, John W(ood, Jr.)
McCann, Edson
  See Pohl, Frederik
McCarthy, Charles, Jr. 1933-
  See McCarthy, Cormac
  See also CANR 42, 69, 101; CPW; CSW;
  DA3; DAM POP; MTCW 2; MTFW 2005
McCarthy, Cormac ...... CLC 4, 57, 101, 204
  See McCarthy, Charles, Jr.
  See also AAYA 41; AMWS 8; BPFB 2; CA
  13-16R; CANR 10; CN 6, 7; DLB 6, 143,
  256; EWL 3; LATS 1:2; MAL 5; TCLE
  1:2; TCWW 2

McCarthy, Mary (Therese)
  1912-1989 .. CLC 1, 3, 5, 14, 24, 39, 59;
  SSC 24
  See also AMW; BPFB 2; CA 5-8R; 129;
  CANR 16, 50, 64; CN 1, 2, 3, 4; DA3;
  DLB 2; DLBY 1981; EWL 3; FW; INT
  CANR-16; MAL 5; MAWW; MTCW 1,
  2; MTFW 2005; RGAL 4; TUS
McCartney, (James) Paul 1942- . CLC 12, 35
  See also CA 146; CANR 111
McCauley, Stephen (D.) 1955- .... CLC 50
  See also CA 141
McClaren, Peter .... CLC 70
McClure, Michael (Thomas) 1932- ... CLC 6,
  10
  See also BG 1:3; CA 21-24R; CAD; CANR
  17, 46, 77, 131; CD 5, 6; CP 1, 2, 3, 4, 5,
  6, 7; DLB 16; WP
McCorkle, Jill (Collins) 1958- .... CLC 51
  See also CA 121; CANR 113; CSW; DLB
  234; DLBY 1987
McCourt, Frank 1930- .... CLC 109
  See also AAYA 61; AMWS 12; CA 157;
  CANR 97, 138; MTFW 2005; NCFS 1
McCourt, James 1941- .... CLC 5
  See also CA 57-60; CANR 98
McCourt, Malachy 1931- .... CLC 119
  See also SATA 126
McCoy, Horace (Stanley)
  1897-1955 .... TCLC 28
  See also AMWS 13; CA 108; 155; CMW 4;
  DLB 9
McCrae, John 1872-1918 .... TCLC 12
  See also CA 109; DLB 92; PFS 5
McCreigh, James
  See Pohl, Frederik
McCullers, (Lula) Carson (Smith)
  1917-1967 .... CLC 1, 4, 10, 12, 48, 100;
  SSC 9, 24; TCLC 155; WLC
  See also AAYA 21; AMW; AMWC 2; BPFB
  2; CA 5-8R; 25-28R; CABS 1, 3; CANR
  18, 132; CDALB 1941-1968; DA; DA3;
  DAB; DAC; DAM MST, NOV; DFS 5,
  18; DLB 2, 7, 173, 228; EWL 3; EXPS;
  FW; GLL 1; LAIT 3, 4; MAL 5; MAWW;
  MTCW 1, 2; MTFW 2005; NFS 6, 13;
  RGAL 4; RGSF 2; SATA 27; SSFS 5;
  TUS; YAW
McCulloch, John Tyler
  See Burroughs, Edgar Rice
McCullough, Colleen 1937- ...... CLC 27, 107
  See also AAYA 36; BPFB 2; CA 81-84;
  CANR 17, 46, 67, 98, 139; CPW; DA3;
  DAM NOV, POP; MTCW 1, 2; MTFW
  2005; RHW
McCunn, Ruthanne Lum 1946- .... AAL
  See also CA 119; CANR 43, 96; DLB 312;
  LAIT 2; SATA 63
McDermott, Alice 1953- .... CLC 90
  See also CA 109; CANR 40, 90, 126; CN
  7; DLB 292; MTFW 2005
McElroy, Joseph (Prince) 1930- ... CLC 5, 47
  See also CA 17-20R; CN 3, 4, 5, 6, 7
McEwan, Ian (Russell) 1948- ... CLC 13, 66,
  169
  See also BEST 90:4; BRWS 4; CA 61-64;
  CANR 14, 41, 69, 87, 132; CN 3, 4, 5, 6,
  7; DAM NOV; DLB 14, 194, 319; HGG;
  MTCW 1, 2; MTFW 2005; RGSF 2;
  SUFW 2; TEA
McFadden, David 1940- .... CLC 48
  See also CA 104; CP 1, 2, 3, 4, 5, 6, 7; DLB
  60; INT CA-104
McFarland, Dennis 1950- .... CLC 65
  See also CA 165; CANR 110
McGahern, John 1934- ... CLC 5, 9, 48, 156;
  SSC 17
  See also CA 17-20R; CANR 29, 68, 113;
  CN 1, 2, 3, 4, 5, 6, 7; DLB 14, 231, 319;
  MTCW 1

Merezhkovsky, Dmitry Sergeyevich
1865-1941 .... **TCLC 29**
See Merezhkovsky, Dmitrii Sergeevich;
Merezhkovsky, Dmitry Sergeyevich
See also CA 169

Merimee, Prosper 1803-1870 ... **NCLC 6, 65;
SSC 7, 77**
See also DLB 119, 192; EW 6; EXPS; GFL
1789 to the Present; RGSF 2; RGWL 2,
3; SSFS 8; SUFW

Merkin, Daphne 1954- .... **CLC 44**
See also CA 123

Merleau-Ponty, Maurice
1908-1961 .... **TCLC 156**
See also CA 114; 89-92; DLB 296; GFL
1789 to the Present

Merlin, Arthur
See Blish, James (Benjamin)

Mernissi, Fatima 1940- .... **CLC 171**
See also CA 152; FW

Merrill, James (Ingram) 1926-1995 .. **CLC 2,
3, 6, 8, 13, 18, 34, 91; PC 28; TCLC
173**
See also AMWS 3; CA 13-16R; 147; CANR
10, 49, 63, 108; CP 1, 2, 3, 4; DA3; DAM
POET; DLB 5, 165; DLBY 1985; EWL 3;
INT CANR-10; MAL 5; MTCW 1, 2;
MTFW 2005; PAB; PFS 23; RGAL 4

Merriman, Alex
See Silverberg, Robert

Merriman, Brian 1747-1805 .... **NCLC 70**

Merritt, E. B.
See Waddington, Miriam

Merton, Thomas (James)
1915-1968 . **CLC 1, 3, 11, 34, 83; PC 10**
See also AAYA 61; AMWS 8; CA 5-8R;
25-28R; CANR 22, 53, 111, 131; DA3;
DLB 48; DLBY 1981; MAL 5; MTCW 1,
2; MTFW 2005

Merwin, W(illiam) S(tanley) 1927- ... **CLC 1,
2, 3, 5, 8, 13, 18, 45, 88; PC 45**
See also AMWS 3; CA 13-16R; CANR 15,
51, 112, 140; CP 1, 2, 3, 4, 5, 6, 7; DA3;
DAM POET; DLB 5, 169; EWL 3; INT
CANR-15; MAL 5; MTCW 1, 2; MTFW
2005; PAB; PFS 5, 15; RGAL 4

Metastasio, Pietro 1698-1782 .... **LC 115**
See also RGWL 2, 3

Metcalf, John 1938- .... **CLC 37; SSC 43**
See also CA 113; CN 4, 5, 6, 7; DLB 60;
RGSF 2; TWA

Metcalf, Suzanne
See Baum, L(yman) Frank

Mew, Charlotte (Mary) 1870-1928 .. **TCLC 8**
See also CA 105; 189; DLB 19, 135; RGEL
2

Mewshaw, Michael 1943- .... **CLC 9**
See also CA 53-56; CANR 7, 47; DLBY
1980

Meyer, Conrad Ferdinand
1825-1898 .... **NCLC 81; SSC 30**
See also DLB 129; EW; RGWL 2, 3

Meyer, Gustav 1868-1932
See Meyrink, Gustav
See also CA 117; 190

Meyer, June
See Jordan, June (Meyer)

Meyer, Lynn
See Slavitt, David R(ytman)

Meyers, Jeffrey 1939- .... **CLC 39**
See also CA 73-76, 186; CAAE 186; CANR
54, 102; DLB 111

**Meynell, Alice (Christina Gertrude
Thompson)** 1847-1922 .... **TCLC 6**
See also CA 104; 177; DLB 19, 98; RGEL
2

Meyrink, Gustav .... **TCLC 21**
See Meyer, Gustav
See also DLB 81; EWL 3

Michaels, Leonard 1933-2003 ..... **CLC 6, 25;
SSC 16**
See also CA 61-64; 216; CANR 21, 62, 119;
CN 3, 45, 6, 7; DLB 130; MTCW 1;
TCLE 1:2

Michaux, Henri 1899-1984 .... **CLC 8, 19**
See also CA 85-88; 114; DLB 258; EWL 3;
GFL 1789 to the Present; RGWL 2, 3

Micheaux, Oscar (Devereaux)
1884-1951 .... **TCLC 76**
See also BW 3; CA 174; DLB 50; TCWW
2

Michelangelo 1475-1564 .... **LC 12**
See also AAYA 43

Michelet, Jules 1798-1874 .... **NCLC 31**
See also EW 5; GFL 1789 to the Present

Michels, Robert 1876-1936 .... **TCLC 88**
See also CA 212

Michener, James A(lbert)
1907(?)-1997 .. **CLC 1, 5, 11, 29, 60, 109**
See also AAYA 27; AITN 1; BEST 90:1;
BPFB 2; CA 5-8R; 161; CANR 21, 45,
68; CN 1, 2, 3, 4, 5, 6; CPW; DA3; DAM
NOV, POP; DLB 6; MAL 5; MTCW 1, 2;
MTFW 2005; RHW; TCWW 1, 2

Mickiewicz, Adam 1798-1855 . **NCLC 3, 101;
PC 38**
See also EW 5; RGWL 2, 3

Middleton, (John) Christopher
1926- .... **CLC 13**
See also CA 13-16R; CANR 29, 54, 117;
CP 1, 2, 3, 4, 5, 6, 7; DLB 40

Middleton, Richard (Barham)
1882-1911 .... **TCLC 56**
See also CA 187; DLB 156; HGG

Middleton, Stanley 1919- .... **CLC 7, 38**
See also CA 25-28R; CAAS 23; CANR 21,
46, 81; CN 1, 2, 3, 4, 5, 6, 7; DLB 14

Middleton, Thomas 1580-1627 ...... **DC 5; LC
33**
See also BRW 2; DAM DRAM, MST; DFS
18, 22; DLB 58; RGEL 2

Migueis, Jose Rodrigues 1901-1980 . **CLC 10**
See also DLB 287

Mikszath, Kalman 1847-1910 .... **TCLC 31**
See also CA 170

Miles, Jack .... **CLC 100**
See also CA 200

Miles, John Russiano
See Miles, Jack

Miles, Josephine (Louise)
1911-1985 .... **CLC 1, 2, 14, 34, 39**
See also CA 1-4R; 116; CANR 2, 55; CP 1,
2, 3, 4; DAM POET; DLB 48; MAL 5;
TCLE 1:2

Militant
See Sandburg, Carl (August)

Mill, Harriet (Hardy) Taylor
1807-1858 .... **NCLC 102**
See also FW

Mill, John Stuart 1806-1873 .... **NCLC 11, 58**
See also CDBLB 1832-1890; DLB 55, 190,
262; FW 1; RGEL 2; TEA

Millar, Kenneth 1915-1983 .... **CLC 14**
See Macdonald, Ross
See also CA 9-12R; 110; CANR 16, 63,
107; CMW 4; CPW; DA3; DAM POP;
DLB 2, 226; DLBD 6; DLBY 1983;
MTCW 1, 2; MTFW 2005

Millay, E. Vincent
See Millay, Edna St. Vincent

Millay, Edna St. Vincent 1892-1950 ..... **PC 6,
61; TCLC 4, 49, 169; WLCS**
See Boyd, Nancy
See also AMW; CA 104; 130; CDALB
1917-1929; DA; DA3; DAB; DAC; DAM
MST, POET; DLB 45, 249; EWL 3;
EXPP; FL 1:6; MAL 5; MAWW; MTCW
1, 2; MTFW 2005; PAB; PFS 3, 17;
RGAL 4; TUS; WP

Miller, Arthur 1915-2005 ..... **CLC 1, 2, 6, 10,
15, 26, 47, 78, 179; DC 1; WLC**
See also AAYA 15; AITN 1; AMW; AMWC
1; CA 1-4R; 236; CABS 3; CAD; CANR
2, 30, 54, 76, 132; CD 5, 6; CDALB
1941-1968; DA; DA3; DAB; DAC; DAM
DRAM, MST; DFS 1, 3, 8; DLB 7, 266;
EWL 3; LAIT 1, 4; LATS 1:2; MAL 5;
MTCW 1, 2; MTFW 2005; RGAL 4;
TUS; WYAS 1

Miller, Henry (Valentine)
1891-1980 .... **CLC 1, 2, 4, 9, 14, 43, 84;
WLC**
See also AMW; BPFB 2; CA 9-12R; 97-
100; CANR 33, 64; CDALB 1929-1941;
CN 1, 2; DA; DA3; DAB; DAC; DAM
MST, NOV; DLB 4, 9; DLBY 1980; EWL
3; MAL 5; MTCW 1, 2; MTFW 2005;
RGAL 4; TUS

Miller, Hugh 1802-1856 .... **NCLC 143**
See also DLB 190

Miller, Jason 1939(?)-2001 .... **CLC 2**
See also AITN 1; CA 73-76; 197; CAD;
CANR 130; DFS 12; DLB 7

Miller, Sue 1943- .... **CLC 44**
See also AMWS 12; BEST 90:3; CA 139;
CANR 59, 91, 128; DA3; DAM POP;
DLB 143

Miller, Walter M(ichael, Jr.)
1923-1996 .... **CLC 4, 30**
See also BPFB 2; CA 85-88; CANR 108;
DLB 8; SCFW 1, 2; SFW 4

Millett, Kate 1934- .... **CLC 67**
See also AITN 1; CA 73-76; CANR 32, 53,
76, 110; DA3; DLB 246; FW; GLL 1;
MTCW 1, 2; MTFW 2005

Millhauser, Steven (Lewis) 1943- .... **CLC 21,
54, 109; SSC 57**
See also CA 110; 111; CANR 63, 114, 133;
CN 6, 7; DA3; DLB 2; FANT; INT CA-
111; MAL 5; MTCW 2; MTFW 2005

Millin, Sarah Gertrude 1889-1968 ... **CLC 49**
See also CA 102; 93-96; DLB 225; EWL 3

Milne, A(lan) A(lexander)
1882-1956 .... **TCLC 6, 88**
See also BRWS 5; CA 104; 133; CLR 1,
26; CMW 4; CWRI 5; DA3; DAB; DAC;
DAM MST; DLB 10, 77, 100, 160; FANT;
MAICYA 1, 2; MTCW 1, 2; MTFW 2005;
RGEL 2; SATA 100; WCH; YABC 1

Milner, Ron(ald) 1938-2004 ..... **BLC 3; CLC
56**
See also AITN 1; BW 1; CA 73-76; 230;
CAD; CANR 24, 81; CD 5, 6; DAM
MULT; DLB 38; MAL 5; MTCW 1

Milnes, Richard Monckton
1809-1885 .... **NCLC 61**
See also DLB 32, 184

Milosz, Czeslaw 1911-2004 .... **CLC 5, 11, 22,
31, 56, 82; PC 8; WLCS**
See also AAYA 62; CA 81-84; 230; CANR
23, 51, 91, 126; CDWLB 4; CWW 2;
DA3; DAM MST, POET; DLB 215; EW
13; EWL 3; MTCW 1, 2; MTFW 2005;
PFS 16; RGWL 2, 3

Milton, John 1608-1674 ..... **LC 9, 43, 92; PC
19, 29; WLC**
See also AAYA 65; BRW 2; BRWR 2; CD-
BLB 1660-1789; DA; DA3; DAB; DAC;
DAM MST, POET; DLB 131, 151, 281;
EFS 1; EXPP; LAIT 1; PAB; PFS 3, 17;
RGEL 2; TEA; WLIT 3; WP

Min, Anchee 1957- .... **CLC 86**
See also CA 146; CANR 94, 137; MTFW
2005

Minehaha, Cornelius
See Wedekind, (Benjamin) Frank(lin)

Miner, Valerie 1947- .... **CLC 40**
See also CA 97-100; CANR 59; FW; GLL
2

Minimo, Duca
See D'Annunzio, Gabriele

Minot, Susan (Anderson) 1956- ...... **CLC 44, 159**
See also AMWS 6; CA 134; CANR 118; CN 6, 7

Minus, Ed 1938- .... **CLC 39**
See also CA 185

Mirabai 1498(?)-1550(?) .... **PC 48**

Miranda, Javier
See Bioy Casares, Adolfo
See also CWW 2

Mirbeau, Octave 1848-1917 .... **TCLC 55**
See also CA 216; DLB 123, 192; GFL 1789 to the Present

Mirikitani, Janice 1942- .... **AAL**
See also CA 211; DLB 312; RGAL 4

Mirk, John (?)-c. 1414 .... **LC 105**
See also DLB 146

Miro (Ferrer), Gabriel (Francisco Victor)
1879-1930 .... **TCLC 5**
See also CA 104; 185; DLB 322; EWL 3

Misharin, Alexandr .... **CLC 59**

Mishima, Yukio ... **CLC 2, 4, 6, 9, 27; DC 1; SSC 4; TCLC 161**
See Hiraoka, Kimitake
See also AAYA 50; BPFB 2; GLL 1; MJW; RGSF 2; RGWL 2, 3; SSFS 5, 12

Mistral, Frederic 1830-1914 .... **TCLC 51**
See also CA 122; 213; GFL 1789 to the Present

Mistral, Gabriela
See Godoy Alcayaga, Lucila
See also DLB 283; DNFS 1; EWL 3; LAW; RGWL 2, 3; WP

Mistry, Rohinton 1952- ... **CLC 71, 196; SSC 73**
See also BRWS 10; CA 141; CANR 86, 114; CCA 1; CN 6, 7; DAC; SSFS 6

Mitchell, Clyde
See Ellison, Harlan (Jay)

Mitchell, Emerson Blackhorse Barney
1945- .... **NNAL**
See also CA 45-48

Mitchell, James Leslie 1901-1935
See Gibbon, Lewis Grassic
See also CA 104; 188; DLB 15

Mitchell, Joni 1943- .... **CLC 12**
See also CA 112; CCA 1

Mitchell, Joseph (Quincy)
1908-1996 .... **CLC 98**
See also CA 77-80; 152; CANR 69; CN 1, 2, 3, 4, 5, 6; CSW; DLB 185; DLBY 1996

Mitchell, Margaret (Munnerlyn)
1900-1949 .... **TCLC 11, 170**
See also AAYA 23; BPFB 2; BYA 1; CA 109; 125; CANR 55, 94; CDALBS; DA3; DAM NOV, POP; DLB 9; LAIT 2; MAL 5; MTCW 1, 2; MTFW 2005; NFS 9; RGAL 4; RHW; TUS; WYAS 1; YAW

Mitchell, Peggy
See Mitchell, Margaret (Munnerlyn)

Mitchell, S(ilas) Weir 1829-1914 .... **TCLC 36**
See also CA 165; DLB 202; RGAL 4

Mitchell, W(illiam) O(rmond)
1914-1998 .... **CLC 25**
See also CA 77-80; 165; CANR 15, 43; CN 1, 2, 3, 4, 5, 6; DAC; DAM MST; DLB 88; TCLE 1:2

Mitchell, William (Lendrum)
1879-1936 .... **TCLC 81**
See also CA 213

Mitford, Mary Russell 1787-1855 ... **NCLC 4**
See also DLB 110, 116; RGEL 2

Mitford, Nancy 1904-1973 .... **CLC 44**
See also BRWS 10; CA 9-12R; CN 1; DLB 191; RGEL 2

Miyamoto, (Chujo) Yuriko
1899-1951 .... **TCLC 37**
See Miyamoto Yuriko
See also CA 170, 174

Miyamoto Yuriko
See Miyamoto, (Chujo) Yuriko
See also DLB 180

Miyazawa, Kenji 1896-1933 .... **TCLC 76**
See Miyazawa Kenji
See also CA 157; RGWL 3

Miyazawa Kenji
See Miyazawa, Kenji
See also EWL 3

Mizoguchi, Kenji 1898-1956 .... **TCLC 72**
See also CA 167

Mo, Timothy (Peter) 1950- .... **CLC 46, 134**
See also CA 117; CANR 128; CN 5, 6, 7; DLB 194; MTCW 1; WLIT 4; WWE 1

Modarressi, Taghi (M.) 1931-1997 ... **CLC 44**
See also CA 121; 134; INT CA-134

Modiano, Patrick (Jean) 1945- .... **CLC 18**
See also CA 85-88; CANR 17, 40, 115; CWW 2; DLB 83, 299; EWL 3

Mofolo, Thomas (Mokopu)
1875(?)-1948 .... **BLC 3; TCLC 22**
See also AFW; CA 121; 153; CANR 83; DAM MULT; DLB 225; EWL 3; MTCW 2; MTFW 2005; WLIT 2

Mohr, Nicholasa 1938- .... **CLC 12; HLC 2**
See also AAYA 8, 46; CA 49-52; CANR 1, 32, 64; CLR 22; DAM MULT; DLB 145; HW 1; JRDA; LAIT 5; LLW; MAICYA 2; MAICYAS 1; RGAL 4; SAAS 8; SATA 8, 97; SATA-Essay 113; WYA; YAW

Moi, Toril 1953- .... **CLC 172**
See also CA 154; CANR 102; FW

Mojtabai, A(nn) G(race) 1938- ..... **CLC 5, 9, 15, 29**
See also CA 85-88; CANR 88

Moliere 1622-1673 ..... **DC 13; LC 10, 28, 64; WLC**
See also DA; DA3; DAB; DAC; DAM DRAM, MST; DFS 13, 18, 20; DLB 268; EW 3; GFL Beginnings to 1789; LATS 1:1; RGWL 2, 3; TWA

Molin, Charles
See Mayne, William (James Carter)

Molnar, Ferenc 1878-1952 .... **TCLC 20**
See also CA 109; 153; CANR 83; CDWLB 4; DAM DRAM; DLB 215; EWL 3; RGWL 2, 3

Momaday, N(avarre) Scott 1934- .... **CLC 2, 19, 85, 95, 160; NNAL; PC 25; WLCS**
See also AAYA 11, 64; AMWS 4; ANW; BPFB 2; BYA 12; CA 25-28R; CANR 14, 34, 68, 134; CDALBS; CN 2, 3, 4, 5, 6, 7; CPW; DA; DA3; DAB; DAC; DAM MST, MULT, NOV, POP; DLB 143, 175, 256; EWL 3; EXPP; INT CANR-14; LAIT 4; LATS 1:2; MAL 5; MTCW 1, 2; MTFW 2005; NFS 10; PFS 2, 11; RGAL 4; SATA 48; SATA-Brief 30; TCWW 1, 2; WP; YAW

Monette, Paul 1945-1995 .... **CLC 82**
See also AMWS 10; CA 139; 147; CN 6; GLL 1

Monroe, Harriet 1860-1936 .... **TCLC 12**
See also CA 109; 204; DLB 54, 91

Monroe, Lyle
See Heinlein, Robert A(nson)

Montagu, Elizabeth 1720-1800 .... **NCLC 7, 117**
See also FW

Montagu, Mary (Pierrepont) Wortley
1689-1762 .... **LC 9, 57; PC 16**
See also DLB 95, 101; FL 1:1; RGEL 2

Montagu, W. H.
See Coleridge, Samuel Taylor

Montague, John (Patrick) 1929- ..... **CLC 13, 46**
See also CA 9-12R; CANR 9, 69, 121; CP 1, 2, 3, 4, 5, 6, 7; DLB 40; EWL 3; MTCW 1; PFS 12; RGEL 2; TCLE 1:2

Montaigne, Michel (Eyquem) de
1533-1592 .... **LC 8, 105; WLC**
See also DA; DAB; DAC; DAM MST; EW 2; GFL Beginnings to 1789; LMFS 1; RGWL 2, 3; TWA

Montale, Eugenio 1896-1981 ... **CLC 7, 9, 18; PC 13**
See also CA 17-20R; 104; CANR 30; DLB 114; EW 11; EWL 3; MTCW 1; PFS 22; RGWL 2, 3; TWA; WLIT 7

Montesquieu, Charles-Louis de Secondat
1689-1755 .... **LC 7, 69**
See also DLB 314; EW 3; GFL Beginnings to 1789; TWA

Montessori, Maria 1870-1952 ...... **TCLC 103**
See also CA 115; 147

Montgomery, (Robert) Bruce 1921(?)-1978
See Crispin, Edmund
See also CA 179; 104; CMW 4

Montgomery, L(ucy) M(aud)
1874-1942 .... **TCLC 51, 140**
See also AAYA 12; BYA 1; CA 108; 137; CLR 8, 91; DA3; DAC; DAM MST; DLB 92; DLBD 14; JRDA; MAICYA 1, 2; MTCW 2; MTFW 2005; RGEL 2; SATA 100; TWA; WCH; WYA; YABC 1

Montgomery, Marion H., Jr. 1925- .... **CLC 7**
See also AITN 1; CA 1-4R; CANR 3, 48; CSW; DLB 6

Montgomery, Max
See Davenport, Guy (Mattison, Jr.)

Montherlant, Henry (Milon) de
1896-1972 .... **CLC 8, 19**
See also CA 85-88; 37-40R; DAM DRAM; DLB 72, 321; EW 11; EWL 3; GFL 1789 to the Present; MTCW 1

Monty Python
See Chapman, Graham; Cleese, John (Marwood); Gilliam, Terry (Vance); Idle, Eric; Jones, Terence Graham Parry; Palin, Michael (Edward)
See also AAYA 7

Moodie, Susanna (Strickland)
1803-1885 .... **NCLC 14, 113**
See also DLB 99

Moody, Hiram (F. III) 1961-
See Moody, Rick
See also CA 138; CANR 64, 112; MTFW 2005

Moody, Minerva
See Alcott, Louisa May

Moody, Rick .... **CLC 147**
See Moody, Hiram (F. III)

Moody, William Vaughan
1869-1910 .... **TCLC 105**
See also CA 110; 178; DLB 7, 54; MAL 5; RGAL 4

Mooney, Edward 1951-
See Mooney, Ted
See also CA 130

Mooney, Ted .... **CLC 25**
See Mooney, Edward

Moorcock, Michael (John) 1939- ...... **CLC 5, 27, 58**
See Bradbury, Edward P.
See also AAYA 26; CA 45-48; CAAS 5; CANR 2, 17, 38, 64, 122; CN 5, 6, 7; DLB 14, 231, 261, 319; FANT; MTCW 1, 2; MTFW 2005; SATA 93; SCFW 1, 2; SFW 4; SUFW 1, 2

Moore, Brian 1921-1999 ... **CLC 1, 3, 5, 7, 8, 19, 32, 90**
See Bryan, Michael
See also BRWS 9; CA 1-4R; 174; CANR 1, 25, 42, 63; CCA 1; CN 1, 2, 3, 4, 5, 6;

Niven, Laurence Van Cott 1938-
See Niven, Larry
See also CA 21-24R, 207; CAAE 207; CAAS 12; CANR 14, 44, 66, 113; CPW; DAM POP; MTCW 1, 2; SATA 95; SFW 4

Nixon, Agnes Eckhardt 1927- .... **CLC 21**
See also CA 110

Nizan, Paul 1905-1940 .... **TCLC 40**
See also CA 161; DLB 72; EWL 3; GFL 1789 to the Present

Nkosi, Lewis 1936- .... **BLC 3; CLC 45**
See also BW 1, 3; CA 65-68; CANR 27, 81; CBD; CD 5, 6; DAM MULT; DLB 157, 225; WWE 1

Nodier, (Jean) Charles (Emmanuel)
1780-1844 .... **NCLC 19**
See also DLB 119; GFL 1789 to the Present

Noguchi, Yone 1875-1947 .... **TCLC 80**

Nolan, Christopher 1965- .... **CLC 58**
See also CA 111; CANR 88

Noon, Jeff 1957- .... **CLC 91**
See also CA 148; CANR 83; DLB 267; SFW 4

Norden, Charles
See Durrell, Lawrence (George)

Nordhoff, Charles Bernard
1887-1947 .... **TCLC 23**
See also CA 108; 211; DLB 9; LAIT 1; RHW 1; SATA 23

Norfolk, Lawrence 1963- .... **CLC 76**
See also CA 144; CANR 85; CN 6, 7; DLB 267

Norman, Marsha (Williams) 1947- . **CLC 28, 186; DC 8**
See also CA 105; CABS 3; CAD; CANR 41, 131; CD 5, 6; CSW; CWD; DAM DRAM; DFS 2; DLB 266; DLBY 1984; FW; MAL 5

Normyx
See Douglas, (George) Norman

Norris, (Benjamin) Frank(lin, Jr.)
1870-1902 .... **SSC 28; TCLC 24, 155**
See also AAYA 57; AMW; AMWC 2; BPFB 2; CA 110; 160; CDALB 1865-1917; DLB 12, 71, 186; LMFS 2; NFS 12; RGAL 4; TCWW 1, 2; TUS

Norris, Leslie 1921- .... **CLC 14**
See also CA 11-12; CANR 14, 117; CAP 1; CP 1, 2, 3, 4, 5, 6, 7; DLB 27, 256

North, Andrew
See Norton, Andre

North, Anthony
See Koontz, Dean R.

North, Captain George
See Stevenson, Robert Louis (Balfour)

North, Captain George
See Stevenson, Robert Louis (Balfour)

North, Milou
See Erdrich, (Karen) Louise

Northrup, B. A.
See Hubbard, L(afayette) Ron(ald)

North Staffs
See Hulme, T(homas) E(rnest)

Northup, Solomon 1808-1863 ...... **NCLC 105**

Norton, Alice Mary
See Norton, Andre
See also MAICYA 1; SATA 1, 43

Norton, Andre 1912-2005 .... **CLC 12**
See Norton, Alice Mary
See also AAYA 14; BPFB 2; BYA 4, 10, 12; CA 1-4R; 237; CANR 68; CLR 50; DLB 8, 52; JRDA; MAICYA 2; MTCW 1; SATA 91; SUFW 1, 2; YAW

Norton, Caroline 1808-1877 .... **NCLC 47**
See also DLB 21, 159, 199

Norway, Nevil Shute 1899-1960
See Shute, Nevil
See also CA 102; 93-96; CANR 85; MTCW 2

Norwid, Cyprian Kamil
1821-1883 .... **NCLC 17**
See also RGWL 3

Nosille, Nabrah
See Ellison, Harlan (Jay)

Nossack, Hans Erich 1901-1978 .... **CLC 6**
See also CA 93-96; 85-88; DLB 69; EWL 3

Nostradamus 1503-1566 .... **LC 27**

Nosu, Chuji
See Ozu, Yasujiro

Notenburg, Eleanora (Genrikhovna) von
See Guro, Elena (Genrikhovna)

Nova, Craig 1945- .... **CLC 7, 31**
See also CA 45-48; CANR 2, 53, 127

Novak, Joseph
See Kosinski, Jerzy (Nikodem)

Novalis 1772-1801 .... **NCLC 13**
See also CDWLB 2; DLB 90; EW 5; RGWL 2, 3

Novick, Peter 1934- .... **CLC 164**
See also CA 188

Novis, Emile
See Weil, Simone (Adolphine)

Nowlan, Alden (Albert) 1933-1983 ... **CLC 15**
See also CA 9-12R; CANR 5; CP 1, 2, 3; DAC; DAM MST; DLB 53; PFS 12

Noyes, Alfred 1880-1958 ...... **PC 27; TCLC 7**
See also CA 104; 188; DLB 20; EXPP; FANT; PFS 4; RGEL 2

Nugent, Richard Bruce
1906(?)-1987 .... **HR 1:3**
See also BW 1; CA 125; DLB 51; GLL 2

Nunn, Kem .... **CLC 34**
See also CA 159

Nussbaum, Martha Craven 1947- .. **CLC 203**
See also CA 134; CANR 102

Nwapa, Flora (Nwanzuruaha)
1931-1993 .... **BLCS; CLC 133**
See also BW 2; CA 143; CANR 83; CD-WLB 3; CWRI 5; DLB 125; EWL 3; WLIT 2

Nye, Robert 1939- .... **CLC 13, 42**
See also BRWS 10; CA 33-36R; CANR 29, 67, 107; CN 1, 2, 3, 4, 5, 6, 7; CP 1, 2, 3, 4, 5, 6, 7; CWRI 5; DAM NOV; DLB 14, 271; FANT; HGG; MTCW 1; RHW; SATA 6

Nyro, Laura 1947-1997 .... **CLC 17**
See also CA 194

Oates, Joyce Carol 1938- .. **CLC 1, 2, 3, 6, 9, 11, 15, 19, 33, 52, 108, 134; SSC 6, 70; WLC**
See also AAYA 15, 52; AITN 1; AMWS 2; BEST 89:2; BPFB 2; BYA 11; CA 5-8R; CANR 25, 45, 74, 113, 129; CDALB 1968-1988; CN 1, 2, 3, 4, 5, 6, 7; CP 7; CPW; CWP; DA; DA3; DAB; DAC; DAM MST, NOV, POP; DLB 2, 5, 130; DLBY 1981; EWL 3; EXPS; FL 1:6; FW; GL 3; HGG; INT CANR-25; LAIT 4; MAL 5; MAWW; MTCW 1, 2; MTFW 2005; NFS 8; RGAL 4; RGSF 2; SATA 159; SSFS 1, 8, 17; SUFW 2; TUS

O'Brian, E. G.
See Clarke, Arthur C(harles)

O'Brian, Patrick 1914-2000 .... **CLC 152**
See also AAYA 55; CA 144; 187; CANR 74; CPW; MTCW 2; MTFW 2005; RHW

O'Brien, Darcy 1939-1998 .... **CLC 11**
See also CA 21-24R; 167; CANR 8, 59

O'Brien, Edna 1932- ..... **CLC 3, 5, 8, 13, 36, 65, 116; SSC 10, 77**
See also CA 1-4R; CANR 6, 41, 65, 102; CDBLB 1960 to Present; CN 1, 2, 3, 4, 5, 6, 7; DA3; DAM NOV; DLB 14, 231, 319; EWL 3; FW; MTCW 1, 2; MTFW 2005; RGSF 2; WLIT 4

O'Brien, Fitz-James 1828-1862 ..... **NCLC 21**
See also DLB 74; RGAL 4; SUFW

O'Brien, Flann .... **CLC 1, 4, 5, 7, 10, 47**
See O Nuallain, Brian
See also BRWS 2; DLB 231; EWL 3; RGEL 2

O'Brien, Richard 1942- .... **CLC 17**
See also CA 124

O'Brien, (William) Tim(othy) 1946- . **CLC 7, 19, 40, 103, 211; SSC 74**
See also AAYA 16; AMWS 5; CA 85-88; CANR 40, 58, 133; CDALBS; CN 5, 6, 7; CPW; DA3; DAM POP; DLB 152; DLBD 9; DLBY 1980; LATS 1:2; MAL 5; MTCW 2; MTFW 2005; RGAL 4; SSFS 5, 15; TCLE 1:2

Obstfelder, Sigbjoern 1866-1900 .... **TCLC 23**
See also CA 123

O'Casey, Sean 1880-1964 .... **CLC 1, 5, 9, 11, 15, 88; DC 12; WLCS**
See also BRW 7; CA 89-92; CANR 62; CBD; CDBLB 1914-1945; DA3; DAB; DAC; DAM DRAM, MST; DFS 19; DLB 10; EWL 3; MTCW 1, 2; MTFW 2005; RGEL 2; TEA; WLIT 4

O'Cathasaigh, Sean
See O'Casey, Sean

Occom, Samson 1723-1792 .... **LC 60; NNAL**
See also DLB 175

Ochs, Phil(ip David) 1940-1976 .... **CLC 17**
See also CA 185; 65-68

O'Connor, Edwin (Greene)
1918-1968 .... **CLC 14**
See also CA 93-96; 25-28R; MAL 5

O'Connor, (Mary) Flannery
1925-1964 .... **CLC 1, 2, 3, 6, 10, 13, 15, 21, 66, 104; SSC 1, 23, 61, 82; TCLC 132; WLC**
See also AAYA 7; AMW; AMWR 2; BPFB 3; BYA 16; CA 1-4R; CANR 3, 41; CDALB 1941-1968; DA; DA3; DAB; DAC; DAM MST, NOV; DLB 2, 152; DLBD 12; DLBY 1980; EWL 3; EXPS; LAIT 5; MAL 5; MAWW; MTCW 1, 2; MTFW 2005; NFS 3, 21; RGAL 4; RGSF 2; SSFS 2, 7, 10, 19; TUS

O'Connor, Frank .... **CLC 23; SSC 5**
See O'Donovan, Michael Francis
See also DLB 162; EWL 3; RGSF 2; SSFS 5

O'Dell, Scott 1898-1989 .... **CLC 30**
See also AAYA 3, 44; BPFB 3; BYA 1, 2, 3, 5; CA 61-64; 129; CANR 12, 30, 112; CLR 1, 16; DLB 52; JRDA; MAICYA 1, 2; SATA 12, 60, 134; WYA; YAW

Odets, Clifford 1906-1963 ..... **CLC 2, 28, 98; DC 6**
See also AMWS 2; CA 85-88; CAD; CANR 62; DAM DRAM; DFS 3, 17, 20; DLB 7, 26; EWL 3; MAL 5; MTCW 1, 2; MTFW 2005; RGAL 4; TUS

O'Doherty, Brian 1928- .... **CLC 76**
See also CA 105; CANR 108

O'Donnell, K. M.
See Malzberg, Barry N(athaniel)

O'Donnell, Lawrence
See Kuttner, Henry

O'Donovan, Michael Francis
1903-1966 .... **CLC 14**
See O'Connor, Frank
See also CA 93-96; CANR 84

Oe, Kenzaburo 1935- .. **CLC 10, 36, 86, 187; SSC 20**
See Oe Kenzaburo
See also CA 97-100; CANR 36, 50, 74, 126; DA3; DAM NOV; DLB 182; DLBY 1994; LATS 1:2; MJW; MTCW 1, 2; MTFW 2005; RGSF 2; RGWL 2, 3

Oe Kenzaburo
See Oe, Kenzaburo
See also CWW 2; EWL 3

O'Faolain, Julia 1932- .... **CLC 6, 19, 47, 108**
See also CA 81-84; CAAS 2; CANR 12, 61; CN 2, 3, 4, 5, 6, 7; DLB 14, 231, 319; FW; MTCW 1; RHW

O'Faolain, Sean 1900-1991 ...... **CLC 1, 7, 14, 32, 70; SSC 13; TCLC 143**
See also CA 61-64; 134; CANR 12, 66; CN 1, 2, 3, 4; DLB 15, 162; MTCW 1, 2; MTFW 2005; RGEL 2; RGSF 2

O'Flaherty, Liam 1896-1984 .... **CLC 5, 34; SSC 6**
See also CA 101; 113; CANR 35; CN 1, 2, 3; DLB 36, 162; DLBY 1984; MTCW 1, 2; MTFW 2005; RGEL 2; RGSF 2; SSFS 5, 20

Ogai
See Mori Ogai
See also MJW

Ogilvy, Gavin
See Barrie, J(ames) M(atthew)

O'Grady, Standish (James) 1846-1928 .... **TCLC 5**
See also CA 104; 157

O'Grady, Timothy 1951- .... **CLC 59**
See also CA 138

O'Hara, Frank 1926-1966 .... **CLC 2, 5, 13, 78; PC 45**
See also CA 9-12R; 25-28R; CANR 33; DA3; DAM POET; DLB 5, 16, 193; EWL 3; MAL 5; MTCW 1, 2; MTFW 2005; PFS 8, 12; RGAL 4; WP

O'Hara, John (Henry) 1905-1970 . **CLC 1, 2, 3, 6, 11, 42; SSC 15**
See also AMW; BPFB 3; CA 5-8R; 25-28R; CANR 31, 60; CDALB 1929-1941; DAM NOV; DLB 9, 86; DLBD 2; EWL 3; MAL 5; MTCW 1, 2; MTFW 2005; NFS 11; RGAL 4; RGSF 2

O Hehir, Diana 1922- .... **CLC 41**
See also CA 93-96

Ohiyesa
See Eastman, Charles A(lexander)

Okada, John 1923-1971 .... **AAL**
See also BYA 14; CA 212; DLB 312

Okigbo, Christopher (Ifenayichukwu) 1932-1967 .. **BLC 3; CLC 25, 84; PC 7; TCLC 171**
See also AFW; BW 1, 3; CA 77-80; CANR 74; CDWLB 3; DAM MULT, POET; DLB 125; EWL 3; MTCW 1, 2; MTFW 2005; RGEL 2

Okri, Ben 1959- .... **CLC 87**
See also AFW; BRWS 5; BW 2, 3; CA 130; 138; CANR 65, 128; CN 5, 6, 7; DLB 157, 231, 319; EWL 3; INT CA-138; MTCW 2; MTFW 2005; RGSF 2; SSFS 20; WLIT 2; WWE 1

Olds, Sharon 1942- .. **CLC 32, 39, 85; PC 22**
See also AMWS 10; CA 101; CANR 18, 41, 66, 98, 135; CP 7; CPW; CWP; DAM POET; DLB 120; MAL 5; MTCW 2; MTFW 2005; PFS 17

Oldstyle, Jonathan
See Irving, Washington

Olesha, Iurii
See Olesha, Yuri (Karlovich)
See also RGWL 2

Olesha, Iurii Karlovich
See Olesha, Yuri (Karlovich)
See also DLB 272

Olesha, Yuri (Karlovich) 1899-1960 . **CLC 8; SSC 69; TCLC 136**
See Olesha, Iurii; Olesha, Iurii Karlovich; Olesha, Yury Karlovich
See also CA 85-88; EW 11; RGWL 3

Olesha, Yury Karlovich
See Olesha, Yuri (Karlovich)
See also EWL 3

Oliphant, Mrs.
See Oliphant, Margaret (Oliphant Wilson)
See also SUFW

Oliphant, Laurence 1829(?)-1888 .. **NCLC 47**
See also DLB 18, 166

Oliphant, Margaret (Oliphant Wilson) 1828-1897 .... **NCLC 11, 61; SSC 25**
See Oliphant, Mrs.
See also BRWS 10; DLB 18, 159, 190; HGG; RGEL 2; RGSF 2

Oliver, Mary 1935- .... **CLC 19, 34, 98**
See also AMWS 7; CA 21-24R; CANR 9, 43, 84, 92, 138; CP 4, 5, 6, 7; CWP; DLB 5, 193; EWL 3; MTFW 2005; PFS 15

Olivier, Laurence (Kerr) 1907-1989 . **CLC 20**
See also CA 111; 150; 129

Olsen, Tillie 1912- ... **CLC 4, 13, 114; SSC 11**
See also AAYA 51; AMWS 13; BYA 11; CA 1-4R; CANR 1, 43, 74, 132; CDALBS; CN 2, 3, 4, 5, 6, 7; DA; DA3; DAB; DAC; DAM MST; DLB 28, 206; DLBY 1980; EWL 3; EXPS; FW; MAL 5; MTCW 1, 2; MTFW 2005; RGAL 4; RGSF 2; SSFS 1; TCLE 1:2; TCWW 2; TUS

Olson, Charles (John) 1910-1970 .. **CLC 1, 2, 5, 6, 9, 11, 29; PC 19**
See also AMWS 2; CA 13-16; 25-28R; CABS 2; CANR 35, 61; CAP 1; CP 1; DAM POET; DLB 5, 16, 193; EWL 3; MAL 5; MTCW 1, 2; RGAL 4; WP

Olson, Toby 1937- .... **CLC 28**
See also CA 65-68; CANR 9, 31, 84; CP 3, 4, 5, 6, 7

Olyesha, Yuri
See Olesha, Yuri (Karlovich)

Olympiodorus of Thebes c. 375-c. 430 .... **CMLC 59**

Omar Khayyam
See Khayyam, Omar
See also RGWL 2, 3

Ondaatje, (Philip) Michael 1943- .... **CLC 14, 29, 51, 76, 180; PC 28**
See also AAYA 66; CA 77-80; CANR 42, 74, 109, 133; CN 5, 6, 7; CP 1, 2, 3, 4, 5, 6, 7; DA3; DAB; DAC; DAM MST; DLB 60; EWL 3; LATS 1:2; LMFS 2; MTCW 2; MTFW 2005; PFS 8, 19; TCLE 1:2; TWA; WWE 1

Oneal, Elizabeth 1934-
See Oneal, Zibby
See also CA 106; CANR 28, 84; MAICYA 1, 2; SATA 30, 82; YAW

Oneal, Zibby .... **CLC 30**
See Oneal, Elizabeth
See also AAYA 5, 41; BYA 13; CLR 13; JRDA; WYA

O'Neill, Eugene (Gladstone) 1888-1953 ... **DC 20; TCLC 1, 6, 27, 49; WLC**
See also AAYA 54; AITN 1; AMW; AMWC 1; CA 110; 132; CAD; CANR 131; CDALB 1929-1941; DA; DA3; DAB; DAC; DAM DRAM, MST; DFS 2, 4, 5, 6, 9, 11, 12, 16, 20; DLB 7; EWL 3; LAIT 3; LMFS 2; MAL 5; MTCW 1, 2; MTFW 2005; RGAL 4; TUS

Onetti, Juan Carlos 1909-1994 ... **CLC 7, 10; HLCS 2; SSC 23; TCLC 131**
See also CA 85-88; 145; CANR 32, 63; CDWLB 3; CWW 2; DAM MULT, NOV; DLB 113; EWL 3; HW 1, 2; LAW; MTCW 1, 2; MTFW 2005; RGSF 2

O Nuallain, Brian 1911-1966
See O'Brien, Flann
See also CA 21-22; 25-28R; CAP 2; DLB 231; FANT; TEA

Ophuls, Max 1902-1957 .... **TCLC 79**
See also CA 113

Opie, Amelia 1769-1853 .... **NCLC 65**
See also DLB 116, 159; RGEL 2

Oppen, George 1908-1984 ..... **CLC 7, 13, 34; PC 35; TCLC 107**
See also CA 13-16R; 113; CANR 8, 82; CP 1, 2, 3; DLB 5, 165

Oppenheim, E(dward) Phillips 1866-1946 .... **TCLC 45**
See also CA 111; 202; CMW 4; DLB 70

Opuls, Max
See Ophuls, Max

Orage, A(lfred) R(ichard) 1873-1934 .... **TCLC 157**
See also CA 122

Origen c. 185-c. 254 .... **CMLC 19**

Orlovitz, Gil 1918-1973 .... **CLC 22**
See also CA 77-80; 45-48; CN 1; CP 1, 2; DLB 2, 5

O'Rourke, P(atrick) J(ake) 1947- .. **CLC 209**
See also CA 77-80; CANR 13, 41, 67, 111; CPW; DAM POP; DLB 185

Orris
See Ingelow, Jean

Ortega y Gasset, Jose 1883-1955 ...... **HLC 2; TCLC 9**
See also CA 106; 130; DAM MULT; EW 9; EWL 3; HW 1, 2; MTCW 1, 2; MTFW 2005

Ortese, Anna Maria 1914-1998 .... **CLC 89**
See also DLB 177; EWL 3

Ortiz, Simon J(oseph) 1941- ... **CLC 45, 208; NNAL; PC 17**
See also AMWS 4; CA 134; CANR 69, 118; CP 3, 4, 5, 6, 7; DAM MULT, POET; DLB 120, 175, 256; EXPP; MAL 5; PFS 4, 16; RGAL 4; TCWW 2

Orton, Joe ...... **CLC 4, 13, 43; DC 3; TCLC 157**
See Orton, John Kingsley
See also BRWS 5; CBD; CDBLB 1960 to Present; DFS 3, 6; DLB 13, 310; GLL 1; RGEL 2; TEA; WLIT 4

Orton, John Kingsley 1933-1967
See Orton, Joe
See also CA 85-88; CANR 35, 66; DAM DRAM; MTCW 1, 2; MTFW 2005

Orwell, George ...... **SSC 68; TCLC 2, 6, 15, 31, 51, 128, 129; WLC**
See Blair, Eric (Arthur)
See also BPFB 3; BRW 7; BYA 5; CDBLB 1945-1960; CLR 68; DAB; DLB 15, 98, 195, 255; EWL 3; EXPN; LAIT 4, 5; LATS 1:1; NFS 3, 7; RGEL 2; SCFW 1, 2; SFW 4; SSFS 4; TEA; WLIT 4; YAW

Osborne, David
See Silverberg, Robert

Osborne, George
See Silverberg, Robert

Osborne, John (James) 1929-1994 .... **CLC 1, 2, 5, 11, 45; TCLC 153; WLC**
See also BRWS 1; CA 13-16R; 147; CANR 21, 56; CBD; CDBLB 1945-1960; DA; DAB; DAC; DAM DRAM, MST; DFS 4, 19; DLB 13; EWL 3; MTCW 1, 2; MTFW 2005; RGEL 2

Osborne, Lawrence 1958- .... **CLC 50**
See also CA 189

Osbourne, Lloyd 1868-1947 .... **TCLC 93**

Osgood, Frances Sargent 1811-1850 .... **NCLC 141**
See also DLB 250

Oshima, Nagisa 1932- .... **CLC 20**
See also CA 116; 121; CANR 78

Oskison, John Milton
1874-1947 .... **NNAL; TCLC 35**
See also CA 144; CANR 84; DAM MULT;
DLB 175

Ossian c. 3rd cent. - .... **CMLC 28**
See Macpherson, James

Ossoli, Sarah Margaret (Fuller)
1810-1850 .... **NCLC 5, 50**
See Fuller, Margaret; Fuller, Sarah Margaret
See also CDALB 1640-1865; FW; LMFS 1;
SATA 25

Ostriker, Alicia (Suskin) 1937- .... **CLC 132**
See also CA 25-28R; CAAS 24; CANR 10,
30, 62, 99; CWP; DLB 120; EXPP; PFS
19

Ostrovsky, Aleksandr Nikolaevich
See Ostrovsky, Alexander
See also DLB 277

Ostrovsky, Alexander 1823-1886 .. **NCLC 30,
57**
See Ostrovsky, Aleksandr Nikolaevich

Otero, Blas de 1916-1979 .... **CLC 11**
See also CA 89-92; DLB 134; EWL 3

O'Trigger, Sir Lucius
See Horne, Richard Henry Hengist

Otto, Rudolf 1869-1937 .... **TCLC 85**

Otto, Whitney 1955- .... **CLC 70**
See also CA 140; CANR 120

Otway, Thomas 1652-1685 ... **DC 24; LC 106**
See also DAM DRAM; DLB 80; RGEL 2

Ouida .... **TCLC 43**
See De la Ramee, Marie Louise (Ouida)
See also DLB 18, 156; RGEL 2

Ouologuem, Yambo 1940- .... **CLC 146**
See also CA 111; 176

Ousmane, Sembene 1923- ... **BLC 3; CLC 66**
See Sembene, Ousmane
See also BW 1, 3; CA 117; 125; CANR 81;
CWW 2; MTCW 1

Ovid 43B.C.-17 .... **CMLC 7; PC 2**
See also AW 2; CDWLB 1; DA3; DAM
POET; DLB 211; PFS 22; RGWL 2, 3;
WP

Owen, Hugh
See Faust, Frederick (Schiller)

Owen, Wilfred (Edward Salter)
1893-1918 ... **PC 19; TCLC 5, 27; WLC**
See also BRW 6; CA 104; 141; CDBLB
1914-1945; DA; DAB; DAC; DAM MST,
POET; DLB 20; EWL 3; EXPP; MTCW
2; MTFW 2005; PFS 10; RGEL 2; WLIT
4

Owens, Louis (Dean) 1948-2002 .... **NNAL**
See also CA 137, 179; 207; CAAE 179;
CAAS 24; CANR 71

Owens, Rochelle 1936- .... **CLC 8**
See also CA 17-20R; CAAS 2; CAD;
CANR 39; CD 5, 6; CP 1, 2, 3, 4, 5, 6, 7;
CWD; CWP

Oz, Amos 1939- ...... **CLC 5, 8, 11, 27, 33, 54;
SSC 66**
See also CA 53-56; CANR 27, 47, 65, 113,
138; CWW 2; DAM NOV; EWL 3;
MTCW 1, 2; MTFW 2005; RGSF 2;
RGWL 3; WLIT 6

Ozick, Cynthia 1928- .... **CLC 3, 7, 28, 62,
155; SSC 15, 60**
See also AMWS 5; BEST 90:1; CA 17-20R;
CANR 23, 58, 116; CN 3, 4, 5, 6, 7;
CPW; DA3; DAM NOV, POP; DLB 28,
152, 299; DLBY 1982; EWL 3; EXPS;
INT CANR-23; MAL 5; MTCW 1, 2;
MTFW 2005; RGAL 4; RGSF 2; SSFS 3,
12

Ozu, Yasujiro 1903-1963 .... **CLC 16**
See also CA 112

Pabst, G. W. 1885-1967 .... **TCLC 127**

Pacheco, C.
See Pessoa, Fernando (Antonio Nogueira)

Pacheco, Jose Emilio 1939- .... **HLC 2**
See also CA 111; 131; CANR 65; CWW 2;
DAM MULT; DLB 290; EWL 3; HW 1,
2; RGSF 2

Pa Chin .... **CLC 18**
See Li Fei-kan
See also EWL 3

Pack, Robert 1929- .... **CLC 13**
See also CA 1-4R; CANR 3, 44, 82; CP 1,
2, 3, 4, 5, 6, 7; DLB 5; SATA 118

Padgett, Lewis
See Kuttner, Henry

Padilla (Lorenzo), Heberto
1932-2000 .... **CLC 38**
See also AITN 1; CA 123; 131; 189; CWW
2; EWL 3; HW 1

Page, James Patrick 1944-
See Page, Jimmy
See also CA 204

Page, Jimmy 1944- .... **CLC 12**
See Page, James Patrick

Page, Louise 1955- .... **CLC 40**
See also CA 140; CANR 76; CBD; CD 5,
6; CWD; DLB 233

Page, P(atricia) K(athleen) 1916- ...... **CLC 7,
18; PC 12**
See Cape, Judith
See also CA 53-56; CANR 4, 22, 65; CP 1,
2, 3, 4, 5, 6, 7; DAC; DAM MST; DLB
68; MTCW 1; RGEL 2

Page, Stanton
See Fuller, Henry Blake

Page, Stanton
See Fuller, Henry Blake

Page, Thomas Nelson 1853-1922 .... **SSC 23**
See also CA 118; 177; DLB 12, 78; DLBD
13; RGAL 4

Pagels, Elaine Hiesey 1943- .... **CLC 104**
See also CA 45-48; CANR 2, 24, 51; FW;
NCFS 4

Paget, Violet 1856-1935
See Lee, Vernon
See also CA 104; 166; GLL 1; HGG

Paget-Lowe, Henry
See Lovecraft, H(oward) P(hillips)

Paglia, Camille (Anna) 1947- .... **CLC 68**
See also CA 140; CANR 72, 139; CPW;
FW; GLL 2; MTCW 2; MTFW 2005

Paige, Richard
See Koontz, Dean R.

Paine, Thomas 1737-1809 .... **NCLC 62**
See also AMWS 1; CDALB 1640-1865;
DLB 31, 43, 73, 158; LAIT 1; RGAL 4;
RGEL 2; TUS

Pakenham, Antonia
See Fraser, Antonia (Pakenham)

Palamas, Costis
See Palamas, Kostes

Palamas, Kostes 1859-1943 .... **TCLC 5**
See Palamas, Kostis
See also CA 105; 190; RGWL 2, 3

Palamas, Kostis
See Palamas, Kostes
See also EWL 3

Palazzeschi, Aldo 1885-1974 .... **CLC 11**
See also CA 89-92; 53-56; DLB 114, 264;
EWL 3

Pales Matos, Luis 1898-1959 .... **HLCS 2**
See Pales Matos, Luis
See also DLB 290; HW 1; LAW

Paley, Grace 1922- .. **CLC 4, 6, 37, 140; SSC
8**
See also AMWS 6; CA 25-28R; CANR 13,
46, 74, 118; CN 2, 3, 4, 5, 6, 7; CPW;
DA3; DAM POP; DLB 28, 218; EWL 3;
EXPS; FW; INT CANR-13; MAL 5;
MAWW; MTCW 1, 2; MTFW 2005;
RGAL 4; RGSF 2; SSFS 3, 20

Palin, Michael (Edward) 1943- .... **CLC 21**
See Monty Python
See also CA 107; CANR 35, 109; SATA 67

Palliser, Charles 1947- .... **CLC 65**
See also CA 136; CANR 76; CN 5, 6, 7

Palma, Ricardo 1833-1919 .... **TCLC 29**
See also CA 168; LAW

Pamuk, Orhan 1952- .... **CLC 185**
See also CA 142; CANR 75, 127; CWW 2;
WLIT 6

Pancake, Breece Dexter 1952-1979
See Pancake, Breece D'J
See also CA 123; 109

Pancake, Breece D'J .... **CLC 29; SSC 61**
See Pancake, Breece Dexter
See also DLB 130

Panchenko, Nikolai .... **CLC 59**

Pankhurst, Emmeline (Goulden)
1858-1928 .... **TCLC 100**
See also CA 116; FW

Panko, Rudy
See Gogol, Nikolai (Vasilyevich)

Papadiamantis, Alexandros
1851-1911 .... **TCLC 29**
See also CA 168; EWL 3

Papadiamantopoulos, Johannes 1856-1910
See Moreas, Jean
See also CA 117

Papini, Giovanni 1881-1956 .... **TCLC 22**
See also CA 121; 180; DLB 264

Paracelsus 1493-1541 .... **LC 14**
See also DLB 179

Parasol, Peter
See Stevens, Wallace

Pardo Bazan, Emilia 1851-1921 .... **SSC 30**
See also EWL 3; FW; RGSF 2; RGWL 2, 3

Pareto, Vilfredo 1848-1923 .... **TCLC 69**
See also CA 175

Paretsky, Sara 1947- .... **CLC 135**
See also AAYA 30; BEST 90:3; CA 125;
129; CANR 59, 95; CMW 4; CPW; DA3;
DAM POP; DLB 306; INT CA-129;
MSW; RGAL 4

Parfenie, Maria
See Codrescu, Andrei

Parini, Jay (Lee) 1948- .... **CLC 54, 133**
See also CA 97-100, 229; CAAE 229;
CAAS 16; CANR 32, 87

Park, Jordan
See Kornbluth, C(yril) M.; Pohl, Frederik

Park, Robert E(zra) 1864-1944 ..... **TCLC 73**
See also CA 122; 165

Parker, Bert
See Ellison, Harlan (Jay)

Parker, Dorothy (Rothschild)
1893-1967 . **CLC 15, 68; PC 28; SSC 2;
TCLC 143**
See also AMWS 9; CA 19-20; 25-28R; CAP
2; DA3; DAM POET; DLB 11, 45, 86;
EXPP; FW; MAL 5; MAWW; MTCW 1,
2; MTFW 2005; PFS 18; RGAL 4; RGSF
2; TUS

Parker, Robert B(rown) 1932- .... **CLC 27**
See also AAYA 28; BEST 89:4; BPFB 3;
CA 49-52; CANR 1, 26, 52, 89, 128;
CMW 4; CPW; DAM NOV, POP; DLB
306; INT CANR-26; MSW; MTCW 1;
MTFW 2005

Parkin, Frank 1940- .... **CLC 43**
See also CA 147

Parkman, Francis, Jr. 1823-1893 .. **NCLC 12**
See also AMWS 2; DLB 1, 30, 183, 186,
235; RGAL 4

Parks, Gordon (Alexander Buchanan)
1912- .... **BLC 3; CLC 1, 16**
See also AAYA 36; AITN 2; BW 2, 3; CA
41-44R; CANR 26, 66, 145; DA3; DAM
MULT; DLB 33; MTCW 2; MTFW 2005;
SATA 8, 108

Ryder, Jonathan
　　See Ludlum, Robert

Ryga, George 1932-1987 .... **CLC 14**
　　See also CA 101; 124; CANR 43, 90; CCA
　　1; DAC; DAM MST; DLB 60

S. H.
　　See Hartmann, Sadakichi

S. S.
　　See Sassoon, Siegfried (Lorraine)

Sa'adawi, al- Nawal
　　See El Saadawi, Nawal
　　See also AFW; EWL 3

Saadawi, Nawal El
　　See El Saadawi, Nawal
　　See also WLIT 2

Saba, Umberto 1883-1957 .... **TCLC 33**
　　See also CA 144; CANR 79; DLB 114;
　　EWL 3; RGWL 2, 3

Sabatini, Rafael 1875-1950 .... **TCLC 47**
　　See also BPFB 3; CA 162; RHW

Sabato, Ernesto (R.) 1911- .... **CLC 10, 23;**
　　HLC 2
　　See also CA 97-100; CANR 32, 65; CD-
　　WLB 3; CWW 2; DAM MULT; DLB 145;
　　EWL 3; HW 1, 2; LAW; MTCW 1, 2;
　　MTFW 2005

Sa-Carneiro, Mario de 1890-1916 . **TCLC 83**
　　See also DLB 287; EWL 3

Sacastru, Martin
　　See Bioy Casares, Adolfo
　　See also CWW 2

Sacher-Masoch, Leopold von
　　1836(?)-1895 .... **NCLC 31**

Sachs, Hans 1494-1576 .... **LC 95**
　　See also CDWLB 2; DLB 179; RGWL 2, 3

Sachs, Marilyn 1927- .... **CLC 35**
　　See also AAYA 2; BYA 6; CA 17-20R;
　　CANR 13, 47; CLR 2; JRDA; MAICYA
　　1, 2; SAAS 2; SATA 3, 68, 164; SATA-
　　Essay 110; WYA; YAW

Sachs, Marilyn Stickle
　　See Sachs, Marilyn

Sachs, Nelly 1891-1970 .... **CLC 14, 98**
　　See also CA 17-18; 25-28R; CANR 87;
　　CAP 2; EWL 3; MTCW 2; MTFW 2005;
　　PFS 20; RGWL 2, 3

Sackler, Howard (Oliver)
　　1929-1982 .... **CLC 14**
　　See also CA 61-64; 108; CAD; CANR 30;
　　DFS 15; DLB 7

Sacks, Oliver (Wolf) 1933- .... **CLC 67, 202**
　　See also CA 53-56; CANR 28, 50, 76;
　　CPW; DA3; INT CANR-28; MTCW 1, 2;
　　MTFW 2005

Sackville, Thomas 1536-1608 .... **LC 98**
　　See also DAM DRAM; DLB 62, 132;
　　RGEL 2

Sadakichi
　　See Hartmann, Sadakichi

Sa'dawi, Nawal al-
　　See El Saadawi, Nawal
　　See also CWW 2

Sade, Donatien Alphonse Francois
　　1740-1814 .... **NCLC 3, 47**
　　See also DLB 314; EW 4; GFL Beginnings
　　to 1789; RGWL 2, 3

Sade, Marquis de
　　See Sade, Donatien Alphonse Francois

Sadoff, Ira 1945- .... **CLC 9**
　　See also CA 53-56; CANR 5, 21, 109; DLB
　　120

Saetone
　　See Camus, Albert

Safire, William 1929- .... **CLC 10**
　　See also CA 17-20R; CANR 31, 54, 91

Sagan, Carl (Edward) 1934-1996 .... **CLC 30,**
　　112
　　See also AAYA 2, 62; CA 25-28R; 155;
　　CANR 11, 36, 74; CPW; DA3; MTCW 1,
　　2; MTFW 2005; SATA 58; SATA-Obit 94

Sagan, Francoise .... **CLC 3, 6, 9, 17, 36**
　　See Quoirez, Francoise
　　See also CWW 2; DLB 83; EWL 3; GFL
　　1789 to the Present; MTCW 2

Sahgal, Nayantara (Pandit) 1927- .... **CLC 41**
　　See also CA 9-12R; CANR 11, 88; CN 1,
　　2, 3, 4, 5, 6, 7

Said, Edward W. 1935-2003 .... **CLC 123**
　　See also CA 21-24R; 220; CANR 45, 74,
　　107, 131; DLB 67; MTCW 2; MTFW
　　2005

Saint, H(arry) F. 1941- .... **CLC 50**
　　See also CA 127

St. Aubin de Teran, Lisa 1953-
　　See Teran, Lisa St. Aubin de
　　See also CA 118; 126; CN 6, 7; INT CA-
　　126

Saint Birgitta of Sweden c.
　　1303-1373 .... **CMLC 24**

Sainte-Beuve, Charles Augustin
　　1804-1869 .... **NCLC 5**
　　See also DLB 217; EW 6; GFL 1789 to the
　　Present

Saint-Exupery, Antoine (Jean Baptiste
　　Marie Roger) de 1900-1944 .... **TCLC 2,**
　　56, 169; WLC
　　See also AAYA 63; BPFB 3; BYA 3; CA
　　108; 132; CLR 10; DA3; DAM NOV;
　　DLB 72; EW 12; EWL 3; GFL 1789 to
　　the Present; LAIT 3; MAICYA 1, 2;
　　MTCW 1, 2; MTFW 2005; RGWL 2, 3;
　　SATA 20; TWA

St. John, David
　　See Hunt, E(verette) Howard, (Jr.)

St. John, J. Hector
　　See Crevecoeur, Michel Guillaume Jean de

Saint-John Perse
　　See Leger, (Marie-Rene Auguste) Alexis
　　Saint-Leger
　　See also EW 10; EWL 3; GFL 1789 to the
　　Present; RGWL 2

Saintsbury, George (Edward Bateman)
　　1845-1933 .... **TCLC 31**
　　See also CA 160; DLB 57, 149

Sait Faik .... **TCLC 23**
　　See Abasiyanik, Sait Faik

Saki .... **SSC 12; TCLC 3**
　　See Munro, H(ector) H(ugh)
　　See also BRWS 6; BYA 11; LAIT 2; RGEL
　　2; SSFS 1; SUFW

Sala, George Augustus 1828-1895 . **NCLC 46**

Saladin 1138-1193 .... **CMLC 38**

Salama, Hannu 1936- .... **CLC 18**
　　See also EWL 3

Salamanca, J(ack) R(ichard) 1922- .. **CLC 4,**
　　15
　　See also CA 25-28R, 193; CAAE 193

Salas, Floyd Francis 1931- .... **HLC 2**
　　See also CA 119; CAAS 27; CANR 44, 75,
　　93; DAM MULT; DLB 82; HW 1, 2;
　　MTCW 2; MTFW 2005

Sale, J. Kirkpatrick
　　See Sale, Kirkpatrick

Sale, Kirkpatrick 1937- .... **CLC 68**
　　See also CA 13-16R; CANR 10

Salinas, Luis Omar 1937- ... **CLC 90; HLC 2**
　　See also AMWS 13; CA 131; CANR 81;
　　DAM MULT; DLB 82; HW 1, 2

Salinas (y Serrano), Pedro
　　1891(?)-1951 .... **TCLC 17**
　　See also CA 117; DLB 134; EWL 3

Salinger, J(erome) D(avid) 1919- .. **CLC 1, 3,**
　　8, 12, 55, 56, 138; SSC 2, 28, 65; WLC
　　See also AAYA 2, 36; AMW; AMWC 1;
　　BPFB 3; CA 5-8R; CANR 39, 129;
　　CDALB 1941-1968; CLR 18; CN 1, 2, 3,
　　4, 5, 6, 7; CPW 1; DA; DA3; DAB; DAC;
　　DAM MST, NOV, POP; DLB 2, 102, 173;
　　EWL 3; EXPN; LAIT 4; MAICYA 1, 2;
　　MAL 5; MTCW 1, 2; MTFW 2005; NFS
　　1; RGAL 4; RGSF 2; SATA 67; SSFS 17;
　　TUS; WYA; YAW

Salisbury, John
　　See Caute, (John) David

Sallust c. 86B.C.-35B.C. .... **CMLC 68**
　　See also AW 2; CDWLB 1; DLB 211;
　　RGWL 2, 3

Salter, James 1925- .. **CLC 7, 52, 59; SSC 58**
　　See also AMWS 9; CA 73-76; CANR 107;
　　DLB 130

Saltus, Edgar (Everton) 1855-1921 . **TCLC 8**
　　See also CA 105; DLB 202; RGAL 4

Saltykov, Mikhail Evgrafovich
　　1826-1889 .... **NCLC 16**
　　See also DLB 238:

Saltykov-Shchedrin, N.
　　See Saltykov, Mikhail Evgrafovich

Samarakis, Andonis
　　See Samarakis, Antonis
　　See also EWL 3

Samarakis, Antonis 1919-2003 .... **CLC 5**
　　See Samarakis, Andonis
　　See also CA 25-28R; 224; CAAS 16; CANR
　　36

Sanchez, Florencio 1875-1910 .... **TCLC 37**
　　See also CA 153; DLB 305; EWL 3; HW 1;
　　LAW

Sanchez, Luis Rafael 1936- .... **CLC 23**
　　See also CA 128; DLB 305; EWL 3; HW 1;
　　WLIT 1

Sanchez, Sonia 1934- .... **BLC 3; CLC 5, 116,**
　　215; PC 9
　　See also BW 2, 3; CA 33-36R; CANR 24,
　　49, 74, 115; CLR 18; CP 2, 3, 4, 5, 6, 7;
　　CSW; CWP; DA3; DAM MULT; DLB 41;
　　DLBD 8; EWL 3; MAICYA 1, 2; MAL 5;
　　MTCW 1, 2; MTFW 2005; SATA 22, 136;
　　WP

Sancho, Ignatius 1729-1780 .... **LC 84**

Sand, George 1804-1876 ..... **NCLC 2, 42, 57;**
　　WLC
　　See also DA; DA3; DAB; DAC; DAM
　　MST, NOV; DLB 119, 192; EW 6; FL 1:3;
　　FW; GFL 1789 to the Present; RGWL 2,
　　3; TWA

Sandburg, Carl (August) 1878-1967 . **CLC 1,**
　　4, 10, 15, 35; PC 2, 41; WLC
　　See also AAYA 24; AMW; BYA 1, 3; CA
　　5-8R; 25-28R; CANR 35; CDALB 1865-
　　1917; CLR 67; DA; DA3; DAB; DAC;
　　DAM MST, POET; DLB 17, 54, 284;
　　EWL 3; EXPP; LAIT 2; MAICYA 1, 2;
　　MAL 5; MTCW 1, 2; MTFW 2005; PAB;
　　PFS 3, 6, 12; RGAL 4; SATA 8; TUS;
　　WCH; WP; WYA

Sandburg, Charles
　　See Sandburg, Carl (August)

Sandburg, Charles A.
　　See Sandburg, Carl (August)

Sanders, (James) Ed(ward) 1939- .... **CLC 53**
　　See Sanders, Edward
　　See also BG 1:3; CA 13-16R; CAAS 21;
　　CANR 13, 44, 78; CP 1, 2, 3, 4, 5, 6, 7;
　　DAM POET; DLB 16, 244

Sanders, Edward
　　See Sanders, (James) Ed(ward)
　　See also DLB 244

Sanders, Lawrence 1920-1998 .... **CLC 41**
　　See also BEST 89:4; BPFB 3; CA 81-84;
　　165; CANR 33, 62; CMW 4; CPW; DA3;
　　DAM POP; MTCW 1

Szirtes, George 1948- .... **CLC 46; PC 51**
See also CA 109; CANR 27, 61, 117; CP 4, 5, 6, 7

Szymborska, Wislawa 1923- ... **CLC 99, 190; PC 44**
See also CA 154; CANR 91, 133; CDWLB 4; CWP; CWW 2; DA3; DLB 232; DLBY 1996; EWL 3; MTCW 2; MTFW 2005; PFS 15; RGWL 3

T. O., Nik
See Annensky, Innokenty (Fyodorovich)

Tabori, George 1914- .... **CLC 19**
See also CA 49-52; CANR 4, 69; CBD; CD 5, 6; DLB 245

Tacitus c. 55-c. 117 .... **CMLC 56**
See also AW 2; CDWLB 1; DLB 211; RGWL 2, 3

Tagore, Rabindranath 1861-1941 .... **PC 8; SSC 48; TCLC 3, 53**
See also CA 104; 120; DA3; DAM DRAM, POET; EWL 3; MTCW 1, 2; MTFW 2005; PFS 18; RGEL 2; RGSF 2; RGWL 2, 3; TWA

Taine, Hippolyte Adolphe
1828-1893 .... **NCLC 15**
See also EW 7; GFL 1789 to the Present

Talayesva, Don C. 1890-(?) .... **NNAL**

Talese, Gay 1932- .... **CLC 37**
See also AITN 1; CA 1-4R; CANR 9, 58, 137; DLB 185; INT CANR-9; MTCW 1, 2; MTFW 2005

Tallent, Elizabeth (Ann) 1954- .... **CLC 45**
See also CA 117; CANR 72; DLB 130

Tallmountain, Mary 1918-1997 .... **NNAL**
See also CA 146; 161; DLB 193

Tally, Ted 1952- .... **CLC 42**
See also CA 120; 124; CAD; CANR 125; CD 5, 6; INT CA-124

Talvik, Heiti 1904-1947 .... **TCLC 87**
See also EWL 3

Tamayo y Baus, Manuel
1829-1898 .... **NCLC 1**

Tammsaare, A(nton) H(ansen)
1878-1940 .... **TCLC 27**
See also CA 164; CDWLB 4; DLB 220; EWL 3

Tam'si, Tchicaya U
See Tchicaya, Gerald Felix

Tan, Amy (Ruth) 1952- . **AAL; CLC 59, 120, 151**
See also AAYA 9, 48; AMWS 10; BEST 89:3; BPFB 3; CA 136; CANR 54, 105, 132; CDALBS; CN 6, 7; CPW 1; DA3; DAM MULT, NOV, POP; DLB 173, 312; EXPN; FL 1:6; FW; LAIT 3, 5; MAL 5; MTCW 2; MTFW 2005; NFS 1, 13, 16; RGAL 4; SATA 75; SSFS 9; YAW

Tandem, Felix
See Spitteler, Carl (Friedrich Georg)

Tanizaki, Jun'ichiro 1886-1965 ... **CLC 8, 14, 28; SSC 21**
See Tanizaki Jun'ichiro
See also CA 93-96; 25-28R; MJW; MTCW 2; MTFW 2005; RGSF 2; RGWL 2

Tanizaki Jun'ichiro
See Tanizaki, Jun'ichiro
See also DLB 180; EWL 3

Tannen, Deborah F(rances) 1945- .. **CLC 206**
See also CA 118; CANR 95

Tanner, William
See Amis, Kingsley (William)

Tao Lao
See Storni, Alfonsina

Tapahonso, Luci 1953- .... **NNAL; PC 65**
See also CA 145; CANR 72, 127; DLB 175

Tarantino, Quentin (Jerome)
1963- .... **CLC 125**
See also AAYA 58; CA 171; CANR 125

Tarassoff, Lev
See Troyat, Henri

Tarbell, Ida M(inerva) 1857-1944 . **TCLC 40**
See also CA 122; 181; DLB 47

Tarkington, (Newton) Booth
1869-1946 .... **TCLC 9**
See also BPFB 3; BYA 3; CA 110; 143; CWRI 5; DLB 9, 102; MAL 5; MTCW 2; RGAL 4; SATA 17

Tarkovskii, Andrei Arsen'evich
See Tarkovsky, Andrei (Arsenyevich)

Tarkovsky, Andrei (Arsenyevich)
1932-1986 .... **CLC 75**
See also CA 127

Tartt, Donna 1964(?)- .... **CLC 76**
See also AAYA 56; CA 142; CANR 135; MTFW 2005

Tasso, Torquato 1544-1595 .... **LC 5, 94**
See also EFS 2; EW 2; RGWL 2, 3; WLIT 7

Tate, (John Orley) Allen 1899-1979 .. **CLC 2, 4, 6, 9, 11, 14, 24; PC 50**
See also AMW; CA 5-8R; 85-88; CANR 32; 108; CN 1, 2; CP 1, 2; DLB 4, 45, 63; DLBD 17; EWL 3; MAL 5; MTCW 1, 2; MTFW 2005; RGAL 4; RHW

Tate, Ellalice
See Hibbert, Eleanor Alice Burford

Tate, James (Vincent) 1943- ..... **CLC 2, 6, 25**
See also CA 21-24R; CANR 29, 57, 114; CP 1, 2, 3, 4, 5, 6, 7; DLB 5, 169; EWL 3; PFS 10, 15; RGAL 4; WP

Tate, Nahum 1652(?)-1715 .... **LC 109**
See also DLB 80; RGEL 2

Tauler, Johannes c. 1300-1361 ...... **CMLC 37**
See also DLB 179; LMFS 1

Tavel, Ronald 1940- .... **CLC 6**
See also CA 21-24R; CAD; CANR 33; CD 5, 6

Taviani, Paolo 1931- .... **CLC 70**
See also CA 153

Taylor, Bayard 1825-1878 .... **NCLC 89**
See also DLB 3, 189, 250, 254; RGAL 4

Taylor, C(ecil) P(hilip) 1929-1981 .... **CLC 27**
See also CA 25-28R; 105; CANR 47; CBD

Taylor, Edward 1642(?)-1729 . **LC 11; PC 63**
See also AMW; DA; DAB; DAC; DAM MST, POET; DLB 24; EXPP; RGAL 4; TUS

Taylor, Eleanor Ross 1920- .... **CLC 5**
See also CA 81-84; CANR 70

Taylor, Elizabeth 1912-1975 ..... **CLC 2, 4, 29**
See also CA 13-16R; CANR 9, 70; CN 1, 2; DLB 139; MTCW 1; RGEL 2; SATA 13

Taylor, Frederick Winslow
1856-1915 .... **TCLC 76**
See also CA 188

Taylor, Henry (Splawn) 1942- .... **CLC 44**
See also CA 33-36R; CAAS 7; CANR 31; CP 7; DLB 5; PFS 10

Taylor, Kamala (Purnaiya) 1924-2004
See Markandaya, Kamala
See also CA 77-80; 227; MTFW 2005; NFS 13

Taylor, Mildred D(elois) 1943- .... **CLC 21**
See also AAYA 10, 47; BW 1; BYA 3, 8; CA 85-88; CANR 25, 115; CLR 9, 59, 90; CSW; DLB 52; JRDA; LAIT 3; MAICYA 1, 2; MTFW 2005; SAAS 5; SATA 135; WYA; YAW

Taylor, Peter (Hillsman) 1917-1994 .. **CLC 1, 4, 18, 37, 44, 50, 71; SSC 10, 84**
See also AMWS 5; BPFB 3; CA 13-16R; 147; CANR 9, 50; CN 1, 2, 3, 4, 5; CSW; DLB 218, 278; DLBY 1981, 1994; EWL 3; EXPS; INT CANR-9; MAL 5; MTCW 1, 2; MTFW 2005; RGSF 2; SSFS 9; TUS

Taylor, Robert Lewis 1912-1998 .... **CLC 14**
See also CA 1-4R; 170; CANR 3, 64; CN 1, 2; SATA 10; TCWW 1, 2

Tchekhov, Anton
See Chekhov, Anton (Pavlovich)

Tchicaya, Gerald Felix 1931-1988 .. **CLC 101**
See Tchicaya U Tam'si
See also CA 129; 125; CANR 81

Tchicaya U Tam'si
See Tchicaya, Gerald Felix
See also EWL 3

Teasdale, Sara 1884-1933 .... **PC 31; TCLC 4**
See also CA 104; 163; DLB 45; GLL 1; PFS 14; RGAL 4; SATA 32; TUS

Tecumseh 1768-1813 .... **NNAL**
See also DAM MULT

Tegner, Esaias 1782-1846 .... **NCLC 2**

Teilhard de Chardin, (Marie Joseph) Pierre
1881-1955 .... **TCLC 9**
See also CA 105; 210; GFL 1789 to the Present

Temple, Ann
See Mortimer, Penelope (Ruth)

Tennant, Emma (Christina) 1937- .. **CLC 13, 52**
See also BRWS 9; CA 65-68; CAAS 9; CANR 10, 38, 59, 88; CN 3, 4, 5, 6, 7; DLB 14; EWL 3; SFW 4

Tenneshaw, S. M.
See Silverberg, Robert

Tenney, Tabitha Gilman
1762-1837 .... **NCLC 122**
See also DLB 37, 200

Tennyson, Alfred 1809-1892 ... **NCLC 30, 65, 115; PC 6; WLC**
See also AAYA 50; BRW 4; CDBLB 1832-1890; DA; DA3; DAB; DAC; DAM MST, POET; DLB 32; EXPP; PAB; PFS 1, 2, 4, 11, 15, 19; RGEL 2; TEA; WLIT 4; WP

Teran, Lisa St. Aubin de .... **CLC 36**
See St. Aubin de Teran, Lisa

Terence c. 184B.C.-c. 159B.C. ...... **CMLC 14; DC 7**
See also AW 1; CDWLB 1; DLB 211; RGWL 2, 3; TWA

Teresa de Jesus, St. 1515-1582 .... **LC 18**

Teresa of Avila, St.
See Teresa de Jesus, St.

Terkel, Louis 1912-
See Terkel, Studs
See also CA 57-60; CANR 18, 45, 67, 132; DA3; MTCW 1, 2; MTFW 2005

Terkel, Studs .... **CLC 38**
See Terkel, Louis
See also AAYA 32; AITN 1; MTCW 2; TUS

Terry, C. V.
See Slaughter, Frank G(ill)

Terry, Megan 1932- .... **CLC 19; DC 13**
See also CA 77-80; CABS 3; CAD; CANR 43; CD 5, 6; CWD; DFS 18; DLB 7, 249; GLL 2

Tertullian c. 155-c. 245 .... **CMLC 29**

Tertz, Abram
See Sinyavsky, Andrei (Donatevich)
See also RGSF 2

Tesich, Steve 1943(?)-1996 .... **CLC 40, 69**
See also CA 105; 152; CAD; DLBY 1983

Tesla, Nikola 1856-1943 .... **TCLC 88**

Teternikov, Fyodor Kuzmich 1863-1927
See Sologub, Fyodor
See also CA 104

Tevis, Walter 1928-1984 .... **CLC 42**
See also CA 113; SFW 4

Tey, Josephine .... **TCLC 14**
See Mackintosh, Elizabeth
See also DLB 77; MSW

Ustinov, Peter (Alexander)
1921-2004 .... **CLC 1**
See also AITN 1; CA 13-16R; 225; CANR
25, 51; CBD; CD 5, 6; DLB 13; MTCW
2

U Tam'si, Gerald Felix Tchicaya
See Tchicaya, Gerald Felix

U Tam'si, Tchicaya
See Tchicaya, Gerald Felix

Vachss, Andrew (Henry) 1942- .... **CLC 106**
See also CA 118, 214; CAAE 214; CANR
44, 95; CMW 4

Vachss, Andrew H.
See Vachss, Andrew (Henry)

Vaculik, Ludvik 1926- .... **CLC 7**
See also CA 53-56; CANR 72; CWW 2;
DLB 232; EWL 3

Vaihinger, Hans 1852-1933 .... **TCLC 71**
See also CA 116; 166

Valdez, Luis (Miguel) 1940- ..... **CLC 84; DC
10; HLC 2**
See also CA 101; CAD; CANR 32, 81; CD
5, 6; DAM MULT; DFS 5; DLB 122;
EWL 3; HW 1; LAIT 4; LLW

Valenzuela, Luisa 1938- .... **CLC 31, 104;
HLCS 2; SSC 14, 82**
See also CA 101; CANR 32, 65, 123; CD-
WLB 3; CWW 2; DAM MULT; DLB 113;
EWL 3; FW; HW 1, 2; LAW; RGSF 2;
RGWL 3

Valera y Alcala-Galiano, Juan
1824-1905 .... **TCLC 10**
See also CA 106

Valerius Maximus fl. 20- .... **CMLC 64**
See also DLB 211

Valery, (Ambroise) Paul (Toussaint Jules)
1871-1945 .... **PC 9; TCLC 4, 15**
See also CA 104; 122; DA3; DAM POET;
DLB 258; EW 8; EWL 3; GFL 1789 to
the Present; MTCW 1, 2; MTFW 2005;
RGWL 2, 3; TWA

Valle-Inclan, Ramon (Maria) del
1866-1936 .... **HLC 2; TCLC 5**
See del Valle-Inclan, Ramon (Maria)
See also CA 106; 153; CANR 80; DAM
MULT; DLB 134; EW 8; EWL 3; HW 2;
RGSF 2; RGWL 2, 3

Vallejo, Antonio Buero
See Buero Vallejo, Antonio

Vallejo, Cesar (Abraham)
1892-1938 .... **HLC 2; TCLC 3, 56**
See also CA 105; 153; DAM MULT; DLB
290; EWL 3; HW 1; LAW; RGWL 2, 3

Valles, Jules 1832-1885 .... **NCLC 71**
See also DLB 123; GFL 1789 to the Present

Vallette, Marguerite Eymery
1860-1953 .... **TCLC 67**
See Rachilde
See also CA 182; DLB 123, 192

Valle Y Pena, Ramon del
See Valle-Inclan, Ramon (Maria) del

Van Ash, Cay 1918-1994 .... **CLC 34**
See also CA 220

Vanbrugh, Sir John 1664-1726 .... **LC 21**
See also BRW 2; DAM DRAM; DLB 80;
IDTP; RGEL 2

Van Campen, Karl
See Campbell, John W(ood, Jr.)

Vance, Gerald
See Silverberg, Robert

Vance, Jack .... **CLC 35**
See Vance, John Holbrook
See also DLB 8; FANT; SCFW 1, 2; SFW
4; SUFW 1, 2

Vance, John Holbrook 1916-
See Queen, Ellery; Vance, Jack
See also CA 29-32R; CANR 17, 65; CMW
4; MTCW 1

**Van Den Bogarde, Derek Jules Gaspard
Ulric Niven** 1921-1999 .... **CLC 14**
See Bogarde, Dirk
See also CA 77-80; 179

Vandenburgh, Jane .... **CLC 59**
See also CA 168

Vanderhaeghe, Guy 1951- .... **CLC 41**
See also BPFB 3; CA 113; CANR 72, 145;
CN 7

van der Post, Laurens (Jan)
1906-1996 .... **CLC 5**
See also AFW; CA 5-8R; 155; CANR 35;
CN 1, 2, 3, 4, 5, 6; DLB 204; RGEL 2

van de Wetering, Janwillem 1931- ... **CLC 47**
See also CA 49-52; CANR 4, 62, 90; CMW
4

Van Dine, S. S. .... **TCLC 23**
See Wright, Willard Huntington
See also DLB 306; MSW

Van Doren, Carl (Clinton)
1885-1950 .... **TCLC 18**
See also CA 111; 168

Van Doren, Mark 1894-1972 .... **CLC 6, 10**
See also CA 1-4R; 37-40R; CANR 3; CN
1; CP 1; DLB 45, 284; MAL 5; MTCW
1, 2; RGAL 4

Van Druten, John (William)
1901-1957 .... **TCLC 2**
See also CA 104; 161; DLB 10; MAL 5;
RGAL 4

Van Duyn, Mona (Jane) 1921-2004 .. **CLC 3,
7, 63, 116**
See also CA 9-12R; 234; CANR 7, 38, 60,
116; CP 1, 2, 3, 4, 5, 6, 7; CWP; DAM
POET; DLB 5; MAL 5; MTFW 2005;
PFS 20

Van Dyne, Edith
See Baum, L(yman) Frank

van Itallie, Jean-Claude 1936- .... **CLC 3**
See also CA 45-48; CAAS 2; CAD; CANR
1, 48; CD 5, 6; DLB 7

Van Loot, Cornelius Obenchain
See Roberts, Kenneth (Lewis)

van Ostaijen, Paul 1896-1928 .... **TCLC 33**
See also CA 163

Van Peebles, Melvin 1932- .... **CLC 2, 20**
See also BW 2, 3; CA 85-88; CANR 27,
67, 82; DAM MULT

van Schendel, Arthur(-Francois-Emile)
1874-1946 .... **TCLC 56**
See also EWL 3

Vansittart, Peter 1920- .... **CLC 42**
See also CA 1-4R; CANR 3, 49, 90; CN 4,
5, 6, 7; RHW

Van Vechten, Carl 1880-1964 ... **CLC 33; HR
1:3**
See also AMWS 2; CA 183; 89-92; DLB 4,
9, 51; RGAL 4

van Vogt, A(lfred) E(lton) 1912-2000 . **CLC 1**
See also BPFB 3; BYA 13, 14; CA 21-24R;
190; CANR 28; DLB 8, 251; SATA 14;
SATA-Obit 124; SCFW 1, 2; SFW 4

Vara, Madeleine
See Jackson, Laura (Riding)

Varda, Agnes 1928- .... **CLC 16**
See also CA 116; 122

Vargas Llosa, (Jorge) Mario (Pedro)
1936- .... **CLC 3, 6, 9, 10, 15, 31, 42, 85,
181; HLC 2**
See Llosa, (Jorge) Mario (Pedro) Vargas
See also BPFB 3; CA 73-76; CANR 18, 32,
42, 67, 116, 140; CDWLB 3; CWW 2;
DA; DA3; DAB; DAC; DAM MST,
MULT, NOV; DLB 145; DNFS 2; EWL
3; HW 1, 2; LAIT 5; LATS 1:2; LAW;
LAWS 1; MTCW 1, 2; MTFW 2005;
RGWL 2; SSFS 14; TWA; WLIT 1

Varnhagen von Ense, Rahel
1771-1833 .... **NCLC 130**
See also DLB 90

Vasari, Giorgio 1511-1574 .... **LC 114**

Vasiliu, George
See Bacovia, George

Vasiliu, Gheorghe
See Bacovia, George
See also CA 123; 189

Vassa, Gustavus
See Equiano, Olaudah

Vassilikos, Vassilis 1933- .... **CLC 4, 8**
See also CA 81-84; CANR 75; EWL 3

Vaughan, Henry 1621-1695 .... **LC 27**
See also BRW 2; DLB 131; PAB; RGEL 2

Vaughn, Stephanie .... **CLC 62**

Vazov, Ivan (Minchov) 1850-1921 . **TCLC 25**
See also CA 121; 167; CDWLB 4; DLB
147

Veblen, Thorstein B(unde)
1857-1929 .... **TCLC 31**
See also AMWS 1; CA 115; 165; DLB 246;
MAL 5

Vega, Lope de 1562-1635 ... **HLCS 2; LC 23,
119**
See also EW 2; RGWL 2, 3

Vendler, Helen (Hennessy) 1933- ... **CLC 138**
See also CA 41-44R; CANR 25, 72, 136;
MTCW 1, 2; MTFW 2005

Venison, Alfred
See Pound, Ezra (Weston Loomis)

Ventsel, Elena Sergeevna 1907-2002
See Grekova, I.
See also CA 154

Verdi, Marie de
See Mencken, H(enry) L(ouis)

Verdu, Matilde
See Cela, Camilo Jose

Verga, Giovanni (Carmelo)
1840-1922 .... **SSC 21, 87; TCLC 3**
See also CA 104; 123; CANR 101; EW 7;
EWL 3; RGSF 2; RGWL 2, 3; WLIT 7

Vergil 70B.C.-19B.C. ..... **CMLC 9, 40; PC 12;
WLCS**
See Virgil
See also AW 2; DA; DA3; DAB; DAC;
DAM MST, POET; EFS 1; LMFS 1

Vergil, Polydore c. 1470-1555 .... **LC 108**
See also DLB 132

Verhaeren, Emile (Adolphe Gustave)
1855-1916 .... **TCLC 12**
See also CA 109; EWL 3; GFL 1789 to the
Present

Verlaine, Paul (Marie) 1844-1896 .. **NCLC 2,
51; PC 2, 32**
See also DAM POET; DLB 217; EW 7;
GFL 1789 to the Present; LMFS 2; RGWL
2, 3; TWA

Verne, Jules (Gabriel) 1828-1905 ... **TCLC 6,
52**
See also AAYA 16; BYA 4; CA 110; 131;
CLR 88; DA3; DLB 123; GFL 1789 to
the Present; JRDA; LAIT 2; LMFS 2;
MAICYA 1, 2; MTFW 2005; RGWL 2, 3;
SATA 21; SCFW 1, 2; SFW 4; TWA;
WCH

Verus, Marcus Annius
See Aurelius, Marcus

Very, Jones 1813-1880 .... **NCLC 9**
See also DLB 1, 243; RGAL 4

Vesaas, Tarjei 1897-1970 .... **CLC 48**
See also CA 190; 29-32R; DLB 297; EW
11; EWL 3; RGWL 3

Vialis, Gaston
See Simenon, Georges (Jacques Christian)

Vian, Boris 1920-1959(?) .... **TCLC 9**
See also CA 106; 164; CANR 111; DLB
72, 321; EWL 3; GFL 1789 to the Present;
MTCW 2; RGWL 2, 3

Wajda, Andrzej 1926- .... **CLC 16**
  See also CA 102
Wakefield, Dan 1932- .... **CLC 7**
  See also CA 21-24R, 211; CAAE 211;
  CAAS 7; CN 4, 5, 6, 7
Wakefield, Herbert Russell
  1888-1965 .... **TCLC 120**
  See also CA 5-8R; CANR 77; HGG; SUFW
Wakoski, Diane 1937- ...... **CLC 2, 4, 7, 9, 11,
  40; PC 15**
  See also CA 13-16R, 216; CAAE 216;
  CAAS 1; CANR 9, 60, 106; CP 1, 2, 3, 4,
  5, 6, 7; CWP; DAM POET; DLB 5; INT
  CANR-9; MAL 5; MTCW 2; MTFW
  2005
Wakoski-Sherbell, Diane
  See Wakoski, Diane
Walcott, Derek (Alton) 1930- ... **BLC 3; CLC
  2, 4, 9, 14, 25, 42, 67, 76, 160; DC 7;
  PC 46**
  See also BW 2; CA 89-92; CANR 26, 47,
  75, 80, 130; CBD; CD 5, 6; CDWLB 3;
  CP 1, 2, 3, 4, 5, 6, 7; DA3; DAB; DAC;
  DAM MST, MULT, POET; DLB 117;
  DLBY 1981; DNFS 1; EFS 1; EWL 3;
  LMFS 2; MTCW 1, 2; MTFW 2005; PFS
  6; RGEL 2; TWA; WWE 1
Waldman, Anne (Lesley) 1945- .... **CLC 7**
  See also BG 1:3; CA 37-40R; CAAS 17;
  CANR 34, 69, 116; CP 1, 2, 3, 4, 5, 6, 7;
  CWP; DLB 16
Waldo, E. Hunter
  See Sturgeon, Theodore (Hamilton)
Waldo, Edward Hamilton
  See Sturgeon, Theodore (Hamilton)
Walker, Alice (Malsenior) 1944- .... **BLC 3;
  CLC 5, 6, 9, 19, 27, 46, 58, 103, 167;
  PC 30; SSC 5; WLCS**
  See also AAYA 3, 33; AFAW 1, 2; AMWS
  3; BEST 89:4; BPFB 3; BW 2, 3; CA 37-
  40R; CANR 9, 27, 49, 66, 82, 131;
  CDALB 1968-1988; CN 4, 5, 6, 7; CPW;
  CSW; DA; DA3; DAB; DAC; DAM MST,
  MULT, NOV, POET, POP; DLB 6, 33,
  143; EWL 3; EXPN; EXPS; FL 1:6; FW;
  INT CANR-27; LAIT 3; MAL 5; MAWW;
  MTCW 1, 2; MTFW 2005; NFS 5; RGAL
  4; RGSF 2; SATA 31; SSFS 2, 11; TUS;
  YAW
Walker, David Harry 1911-1992 ...... **CLC 14**
  See also CA 1-4R; 137; CANR 1; CN 1, 2;
  CWRI 5; SATA 8; SATA-Obit 71
Walker, Edward Joseph 1934-2004
  See Walker, Ted
  See also CA 21-24R; 226; CANR 12, 28,
  53
Walker, George F(rederick) 1947- .. **CLC 44,
  61**
  See also CA 103; CANR 21, 43, 59; CD 5,
  6; DAB; DAC; DAM MST; DLB 60
Walker, Joseph A. 1935-2003 .... **CLC 19**
  See also BW 1, 3; CA 89-92; CAD; CANR
  26, 143; CD 5, 6; DAM DRAM, MST;
  DFS 12; DLB 38
Walker, Margaret (Abigail)
  1915-1998 .... **BLC; CLC 1, 6; PC 20;
  TCLC 129**
  See also AFAW 1, 2; BW 2, 3; CA 73-76;
  172; CANR 26, 54, 76, 136; CN 1, 2, 3,
  4, 5, 6; CP 1, 2, 3, 4; CSW; DAM MULT;
  DLB 76, 152; EXPP; FW; MAL 5;
  MTCW 1, 2; MTFW 2005; RGAL 4;
  RHW
Walker, Ted .... **CLC 13**
  See Walker, Edward Joseph
  See also CP 1, 2, 3, 4, 5, 6, 7; DLB 40
Wallace, David Foster 1962- ... **CLC 50, 114;
  SSC 68**
  See also AAYA 50; AMWS 10; CA 132;
  CANR 59, 133; CN 7; DA3; MTCW 2;
  MTFW 2005

Wallace, Dexter
  See Masters, Edgar Lee
Wallace, (Richard Horatio) Edgar
  1875-1932 .... **TCLC 57**
  See also CA 115; 218; CMW 4; DLB 70;
  MSW; RGEL 2
Wallace, Irving 1916-1990 .... **CLC 7, 13**
  See also AITN 1; BPFB 3; CA 1-4R; 132;
  CAAS 1; CANR 1, 27; CPW; DAM NOV,
  POP; INT CANR-27; MTCW 1, 2
Wallant, Edward Lewis 1926-1962 ... **CLC 5,
  10**
  See also CA 1-4R; CANR 22; DLB 2, 28,
  143, 299; EWL 3; MAL 5; MTCW 1, 2;
  RGAL 4
Wallas, Graham 1858-1932 .... **TCLC 91**
Waller, Edmund 1606-1687 .... **LC 86**
  See also BRW 2; DAM POET; DLB 126;
  PAB; RGEL 2
Walley, Byron
  See Card, Orson Scott
Walpole, Horace 1717-1797 .... **LC 2, 49**
  See also BRW 3; DLB 39, 104, 213; GL 3;
  HGG; LMFS 1; RGEL 2; SUFW 1; TEA
Walpole, Hugh (Seymour)
  1884-1941 .... **TCLC 5**
  See also CA 104; 165; DLB 34; HGG;
  MTCW 2; RGEL 2; RHW
Walrond, Eric (Derwent) 1898-1966 . **HR 1:3**
  See also BW 1; CA 125; DLB 51
Walser, Martin 1927- .... **CLC 27, 183**
  See also CA 57-60; CANR 8, 46, 145;
  CWW 2; DLB 75, 124; EWL 3
Walser, Robert 1878-1956 ..... **SSC 20; TCLC
  18**
  See also CA 118; 165; CANR 100; DLB
  66; EWL 3
Walsh, Gillian Paton
  See Paton Walsh, Gillian
Walsh, Jill Paton .... **CLC 35**
  See Paton Walsh, Gillian
  See also CLR 2, 65; WYA
Walter, Villiam Christian
  See Andersen, Hans Christian
Walters, Anna L(ee) 1946- .... **NNAL**
  See also CA 73-76
Walther von der Vogelweide c.
  1170-1228 .... **CMLC 56**
Walton, Izaak 1593-1683 .... **LC 72**
  See also BRW 2; CDBLB Before 1660;
  DLB 151, 213; RGEL 2
Wambaugh, Joseph (Aloysius), Jr.
  1937- .... **CLC 3, 18**
  See also AITN 1; BEST 89:3; BPFB 3; CA
  33-36R; CANR 42, 65, 115; CMW 4;
  CPW 1; DA3; DAM NOV, POP; DLB 6;
  DLBY 1983; MSW; MTCW 1, 2
Wang Wei 699(?)-761(?) .... **PC 18**
  See also TWA
Warburton, William 1698-1779 .... **LC 97**
  See also DLB 104
Ward, Arthur Henry Sarsfield 1883-1959
  See Rohmer, Sax
  See also CA 108; 173; CMW 4; HGG
Ward, Douglas Turner 1930- .... **CLC 19**
  See also BW 1; CA 81-84; CAD; CANR
  27; CD 5, 6; DLB 7, 38
Ward, E. D.
  See Lucas, E(dward) V(errall)
Ward, Mrs. Humphry 1851-1920
  See Ward, Mary Augusta
  See also RGEL 2
Ward, Mary Augusta 1851-1920 ... **TCLC 55**
  See Ward, Mrs. Humphry
  See also DLB 18
Ward, Nathaniel 1578(?)-1652 .... **LC 114**
  See also DLB 24
Ward, Peter
  See Faust, Frederick (Schiller)

Warhol, Andy 1928(?)-1987 .... **CLC 20**
  See also AAYA 12; BEST 89:4; CA 89-92;
  121; CANR 34
Warner, Francis (Robert le Plastrier)
  1937- .... **CLC 14**
  See also CA 53-56; CANR 11; CP 1, 2, 3, 4
Warner, Marina 1946- .... **CLC 59**
  See also CA 65-68; CANR 21, 55, 118; CN
  5, 6, 7; DLB 194; MTFW 2005
Warner, Rex (Ernest) 1905-1986 ...... **CLC 45**
  See also CA 89-92; 119; CN 1, 2, 3, 4; CP
  1, 2, 3, 4; DLB 15; RGEL 2; RHW
Warner, Susan (Bogert)
  1819-1885 .... **NCLC 31, 146**
  See also DLB 3, 42, 239, 250, 254
Warner, Sylvia (Constance) Ashton
  See Ashton-Warner, Sylvia (Constance)
Warner, Sylvia Townsend
  1893-1978 .. **CLC 7, 19; SSC 23; TCLC
  131**
  See also BRWS 7; CA 61-64; 77-80; CANR
  16, 60, 104; CN 1, 2; DLB 34, 139; EWL
  3; FANT; FW; MTCW 1, 2; RGEL 2;
  RGSF 2; RHW
Warren, Mercy Otis 1728-1814 ..... **NCLC 13**
  See also DLB 31, 200; RGAL 4; TUS
Warren, Robert Penn 1905-1989 .. **CLC 1, 4,
  6, 8, 10, 13, 18, 39, 53, 59; PC 37; SSC
  4, 58; WLC**
  See also AITN 1; AMW; AMWC 2; BPFB
  3; BYA 1; CA 13-16R; 129; CANR 10,
  47; CDALB 1968-1988; CN 1, 2, 3, 4;
  CP 1, 2, 3, 4; DA; DA3; DAB; DAC;
  DAM MST, NOV, POET; DLB 2, 48, 152,
  320; DLBY 1980, 1989; EWL 3; INT
  CANR-10; MAL 5; MTCW 1, 2; MTFW
  2005; NFS 13; RGAL 4; RGSF 2; RHW;
  SATA 46; SATA-Obit 63; SSFS 8; TUS
Warrigal, Jack
  See Furphy, Joseph
Warshofsky, Isaac
  See Singer, Isaac Bashevis
Warton, Joseph 1722-1800 .... **NCLC 118**
  See also DLB 104, 109; RGEL 2
Warton, Thomas 1728-1790 .... **LC 15, 82**
  See also DAM POET; DLB 104, 109;
  RGEL 2
Waruk, Kona
  See Harris, (Theodore) Wilson
Warung, Price .... **TCLC 45**
  See Astley, William
  See also DLB 230; RGEL 2
Warwick, Jarvis
  See Garner, Hugh
  See also CCA 1
Washington, Alex
  See Harris, Mark
Washington, Booker T(aliaferro)
  1856-1915 .... **BLC 3; TCLC 10**
  See also BW 1; CA 114; 125; DA3; DAM
  MULT; LAIT 2; RGAL 4; SATA 28
Washington, George 1732-1799 .... **LC 25**
  See also DLB 31
Wassermann, (Karl) Jakob
  1873-1934 .... **TCLC 6**
  See also CA 104; 163; DLB 66; EWL 3
Wasserstein, Wendy 1950-2006 . **CLC 32, 59,
  90, 183; DC 4**
  See also AMWS 15; CA 121; 129; CABS
  3; CAD; CANR 53, 75, 128; CD 5, 6;
  CWD; DA3; DAM DRAM; DFS 5, 17;
  DLB 228; EWL 3; FW; INT CA-129;
  MAL 5; MTCW 2; MTFW 2005; SATA
  94
Waterhouse, Keith (Spencer) 1929- . **CLC 47**
  See also CA 5-8R; CANR 38, 67, 109;
  CBD; CD 6; CN 1, 2, 3, 4, 5, 6, 7; DLB
  13, 15; MTCW 1, 2; MTFW 2005

Waters, Frank (Joseph) 1902-1995 .. CLC 88
   See also CA 5-8R; 149; CAAS 13; CANR
   3, 18, 63, 121; DLB 212; DLBY 1986;
   RGAL 4; TCWW 1, 2
Waters, Mary C. .... CLC 70
Waters, Roger 1944- .... CLC 35
Watkins, Frances Ellen
   See Harper, Frances Ellen Watkins
Watkins, Gerrold
   See Malzberg, Barry N(athaniel)
Watkins, Gloria Jean 1952(?)- .... CLC 94
   See also BW 2; CA 143; CANR 87, 126;
   DLB 246; MTCW 2; MTFW 2005; SATA
   115
Watkins, Paul 1964- .... CLC 55
   See also CA 132; CANR 62, 98
Watkins, Vernon Phillips
   1906-1967 .... CLC 43
   See also CA 9-10; 25-28R; CAP 1; DLB
   20; EWL 3; RGEL 2
Watson, Irving S.
   See Mencken, H(enry) L(ouis)
Watson, John H.
   See Farmer, Philip Jose
Watson, Richard F.
   See Silverberg, Robert
Watts, Ephraim
   See Horne, Richard Henry Hengist
Watts, Isaac 1674-1748 .... LC 98
   See also DLB 95; RGEL 2; SATA 52
Waugh, Auberon (Alexander)
   1939-2001 .... CLC 7
   See also CA 45-48; 192; CANR 6, 22, 92;
   CN 1, 2, 3; DLB 14, 194
Waugh, Evelyn (Arthur St. John)
   1903-1966 .. CLC 1, 3, 8, 13, 19, 27, 44,
   107; SSC 41; WLC
   See also BPFB 3; BRW 7; CA 85-88; 25-
   28R; CANR 22; CDBLB 1914-1945; DA;
   DA3; DAB; DAC; DAM MST, NOV,
   POP; DLB 15, 162, 195; EWL 3; MTCW
   1, 2; MTFW 2005; NFS 13, 17; RGEL 2;
   RGSF 2; TEA; WLIT 4
Waugh, Harriet 1944- .... CLC 6
   See also CA 85-88; CANR 22
Ways, C. R.
   See Blount, Roy (Alton), Jr.
Waystaff, Simon
   See Swift, Jonathan
Webb, Beatrice (Martha Potter)
   1858-1943 .... TCLC 22
   See also CA 117; 162; DLB 190; FW
Webb, Charles (Richard) 1939- .... CLC 7
   See also CA 25-28R; CANR 114
Webb, Frank J. .... NCLC 143
   See also DLB 50
Webb, James H(enry), Jr. 1946- ...... CLC 22
   See also CA 81-84
Webb, Mary Gladys (Meredith)
   1881-1927 .... TCLC 24
   See also CA 182; 123; DLB 34; FW
Webb, Mrs. Sidney
   See Webb, Beatrice (Martha Potter)
Webb, Phyllis 1927- .... CLC 18
   See also CA 104; CANR 23; CCA 1; CP 1,
   2, 3, 4, 5, 6, 7; CWP; DLB 53
Webb, Sidney (James) 1859-1947 .. TCLC 22
   See also CA 117; 163; DLB 190
Webber, Andrew Lloyd .... CLC 21
   See Lloyd Webber, Andrew
   See also DFS 7
Weber, Lenora Mattingly
   1895-1971 .... CLC 12
   See also CA 19-20; 29-32R; CAP 1; SATA
   2; SATA-Obit 26
Weber, Max 1864-1920 .... TCLC 69
   See also CA 109; 189; DLB 296

Webster, John 1580(?)-1634(?) ...... DC 2; LC
   33, 84; WLC
   See also BRW 2; CDBLB Before 1660; DA;
   DAB; DAC; DAM DRAM, MST; DFS
   17, 19; DLB 58; IDTP; RGEL 2; WLIT 3
Webster, Noah 1758-1843 .... NCLC 30
   See also DLB 1, 37, 42, 43, 73, 243
Wedekind, (Benjamin) Frank(lin)
   1864-1918 .... TCLC 7
   See also CA 104; 153; CANR 121, 122;
   CDWLB 2; DAM DRAM; DLB 118; EW
   8; EWL 3; LMFS 2; RGWL 2, 3
Wehr, Demaris .... CLC 65
Weidman, Jerome 1913-1998 .... CLC 7
   See also AITN 2; CA 1-4R; 171; CAD;
   CANR 1; CD 1, 2, 3, 4, 5; DLB 28
Weil, Simone (Adolphine)
   1909-1943 .... TCLC 23
   See also CA 117; 159; EW 12; EWL 3; FW;
   GFL 1789 to the Present; MTCW 2
Weininger, Otto 1880-1903 .... TCLC 84
Weinstein, Nathan
   See West, Nathanael
Weinstein, Nathan von Wallenstein
   See West, Nathanael
Weir, Peter (Lindsay) 1944- .... CLC 20
   See also CA 113; 123
Weiss, Peter (Ulrich) 1916-1982 .. CLC 3, 15,
   51; TCLC 152
   See also CA 45-48; 106; CANR 3; DAM
   DRAM; DFS 3; DLB 69, 124; EWL 3;
   RGWL 2, 3
Weiss, Theodore (Russell)
   1916-2003 .... CLC 3, 8, 14
   See also CA 9-12R; 189; 216; CAAE 189;
   CAAS 2; CANR 46, 94; CP 1, 2, 3, 4, 5,
   6, 7; DLB 5; TCLE 1:2
Welch, (Maurice) Denton
   1915-1948 .... TCLC 22
   See also BRWS 8, 9; CA 121; 148; RGEL
   2
Welch, James (Phillip) 1940-2003 ..... CLC 6,
   14, 52; NNAL; PC 62
   See also CA 85-88; 219; CANR 42, 66, 107;
   CN 5, 6, 7; CP 2, 3, 4, 5, 6, 7; CPW;
   DAM MULT, POP; DLB 175, 256; LATS
   1:1; RGAL 4; TCWW 1, 2
Weldon, Fay 1931- . CLC 6, 9, 11, 19, 36, 59,
   122
   See also BRWS 4; CA 21-24R; CANR 16,
   46, 63, 97, 137; CDBLB 1960 to Present;
   CN 3, 4, 5, 6, 7; CPW; DAM POP; DLB
   14, 194, 319; EWL 3; FW; HGG; INT
   CANR-16; MTCW 1, 2; MTFW 2005;
   RGEL 2; RGSF 2
Wellek, Rene 1903-1995 .... CLC 28
   See also CA 5-8R; 150; CAAS 7; CANR 8;
   DLB 63; EWL 3; INT CANR-8
Weller, Michael 1942- .... CLC 10, 53
   See also CA 85-88; CAD; CD 5, 6
Weller, Paul 1958- .... CLC 26
Wellershoff, Dieter 1925- .... CLC 46
   See also CA 89-92; CANR 16, 37
Welles, (George) Orson 1915-1985 .. CLC 20,
   80
   See also AAYA 40; CA 93-96; 117
Wellman, John McDowell 1945-
   See Wellman, Mac
   See also CA 166; CD 5
Wellman, Mac .... CLC 65
   See Wellman, John McDowell; Wellman,
   John McDowell
   See also CAD; CD 6; RGAL 4
Wellman, Manly Wade 1903-1986 ... CLC 49
   See also CA 1-4R; 118; CANR 6, 16, 44;
   FANT; SATA 6; SATA-Obit 47; SFW 4;
   SUFW
Wells, Carolyn 1869(?)-1942 .... TCLC 35
   See also CA 113; 185; CMW 4; DLB 11

Wells, H(erbert) G(eorge) 1866-1946 . SSC 6,
   70; TCLC 6, 12, 19, 133; WLC
   See also AAYA 18; BPFB 3; BRW 6; CA
   110; 121; CDBLB 1914-1945; CLR 64;
   DA; DA3; DAB; DAC; DAM MST, NOV;
   DLB 34, 70, 156, 178; EWL 3; EXPS;
   HGG; LAIT 3; LMFS 2; MTCW 1, 2;
   MTFW 2005; NFS 17, 20; RGEL 2;
   RGSF 2; SATA 20; SCFW 1, 2; SFW 4;
   SSFS 3; SUFW; TEA; WCH; WLIT 4;
   YAW
Wells, Rosemary 1943- .... CLC 12
   See also AAYA 13; BYA 7, 8; CA 85-88;
   CANR 48, 120; CLR 16, 69; CWRI 5;
   MAICYA 1, 2; SAAS 1; SATA 18, 69,
   114, 156; YAW
Wells-Barnett, Ida B(ell)
   1862-1931 .... TCLC 125
   See also CA 182; DLB 23, 221
Welsh, Irvine 1958- .... CLC 144
   See also CA 173; CANR 146; CN 7; DLB
   271
Welty, Eudora (Alice) 1909-2001 .. CLC 1, 2,
   5, 14, 22, 33, 105; SSC 1, 27, 51; WLC
   See also AAYA 48; AMW; AMWR 1; BPFB
   3; CA 9-12R; 199; CABS 1; CANR 32,
   65, 128; CDALB 1941-1968; CN 1, 2, 3,
   4, 5, 6, 7; CSW; DA; DA3; DAB; DAC;
   DAM MST, NOV; DLB 2, 102, 143;
   DLBD 12; DLBY 1987, 2001; EWL 3;
   EXPS; HGG; LAIT 3; MAL 5; MAWW;
   MTCW 1, 2; MTFW 2005; NFS 13, 15;
   RGAL 4; RGSF 2; RHW; SSFS 2, 10;
   TUS
Wen I-to 1899-1946 .... TCLC 28
   See also EWL 3
Wentworth, Robert
   See Hamilton, Edmond
Werfel, Franz (Viktor) 1890-1945 ... TCLC 8
   See also CA 104; 161; DLB 81, 124; EWL
   3; RGWL 2, 3
Wergeland, Henrik Arnold
   1808-1845 .... NCLC 5
Wersba, Barbara 1932- .... CLC 30
   See also AAYA 2, 30; BYA 6, 12, 13; CA
   29-32R; 182; CAAE 182; CANR 16, 38;
   CLR 3, 78; DLB 52; JRDA; MAICYA 1,
   2; SAAS 2; SATA 1, 58; SATA-Essay 103;
   WYA; YAW
Wertmueller, Lina 1928- .... CLC 16
   See also CA 97-100; CANR 39, 78
Wescott, Glenway 1901-1987 .. CLC 13; SSC
   35
   See also CA 13-16R; 121; CANR 23, 70;
   CN 1, 2, 3, 4; DLB 4, 9, 102; MAL 5;
   RGAL 4
Wesker, Arnold 1932- .... CLC 3, 5, 42
   See also CA 1-4R; CAAS 7; CANR 1, 33;
   CBD; CD 5, 6; CDBLB 1960 to Present;
   DAB; DAM DRAM; DLB 13, 310, 319;
   EWL 3; MTCW 1; RGEL 2; TEA
Wesley, John 1703-1791 .... LC 88
   See also DLB 104
Wesley, Richard (Errol) 1945- .... CLC 7
   See also BW 1; CA 57-60; CAD; CANR
   27; CD 5, 6; DLB 38
Wessel, Johan Herman 1742-1785 .... LC 7
   See also DLB 300
West, Anthony (Panther)
   1914-1987 .... CLC 50
   See also CA 45-48; 124; CANR 3, 19; CN
   1, 2, 3, 4; DLB 15
West, C. P.
   See Wodehouse, P(elham) G(renville)
West, Cornel (Ronald) 1953- .... BLCS; CLC
   134
   See also CA 144; CANR 91; DLB 246
West, Delno C(loyde), Jr. 1936- .... CLC 70
   See also CA 57-60

Literary Criticism Series
Cumulative Topic Index

This index lists all topic entries in Gale's *Children's Literature Review* (CLR), *Classical and Medieval Literature Criticism* (CMLC), *Contemporary Literary Criticism* (CLC), *Drama Criticism* (DC), *Literature Criticism from 1400 to 1800* (LC), *Nineteenth-Century Literature Criticism* (NCLC), *Short Story Criticism* (SSC), and *Twentieth-Century Literary Criticism* (TCLC). The index also lists topic entries in the Gale Critical Companion Collection, which includes the following publications: *The Beat Generation* (BG), and *Harlem Renaissance* (HR).

SSC Cumulative Nationality Index

Nationality Index

SSC-87 Title Index

ISBN 0-7876-8884-3

90000